Columbia Literary History of the United States

Columbia Literary History of the United States

Emory Elliott, General Editor

Associate Editors: Martha Banta, Terence Martin, David Minter, Marjorie Perloff, Daniel B. Shea

Advisory Editors: Houston A. Baker, Nina Baym, Sacvan Bercovitch, Louis D. Rubin, Jr.

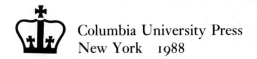
Columbia University Press
New York   1988

The Press gratefully acknowledges the substantial contribution of
the Andrew W. Mellon Foundation toward the costs of planning
and writing the manuscript of this volume.

Costs of publication of the *Columbia Literary History of the United
States* were borne in part by gifts made in memory of Charles G.
Proffitt, longtime director of the Press, who was architect of the
reference book publishing program that built on the success of *The
Columbia Encyclopedia*.

Library of Congress Cataloging-in-Publication Data

Columbia literary history of the United States.

   Includes index.
   1. American literature—History and criticism.
2. United States—Intellectual life.   I. Elliott,
Emory, 1942–   .   II. Banta, Martha.   III. Baker,
Houston A.
PS92.C64   1987   810'.9   87-14672
ISBN 0-231-05812-8 (alk. paper)

Columbia University Press
New York   Guildford, Surrey
Copyright © 1988 Columbia University Press
All rights reserved

Printed in the United States of America

Clothbound editions of Columbia University Press books are
Smyth-sewn and printed on permanent and durable acid-free paper.

Book design by Ken Venezio

Contents

Preface   *xi*

General Introduction   *xv*

Note on the Text   *xxv*

Acknowledgments   *xxvii*

Part One Beginnings to 1810
Associate Editor, Daniel B. Shea

I.   A Key into the Languages of America   *3*

  The Native Voice   *5*

  The Literature of Discovery and Exploration   *16*

  English Literature at the American Moment   *24*

  The Puritan Vision of the New World   *33*

II.   The Prose and Poetry of Colonial America   *45*

  History and Chronicle   *47*

  Sermons and Theological Writings   *56*

  Biography and Autobiography   *67*

  The Poetry of Colonial America   *83*

III.   America in Transition   *99*

  From Cotton Mather to Benjamin Franklin   *101*

Jonathan Edwards, Charles Chauncy, and the Great Awakening   *113*

Thomas Jefferson and the Writing of the South   *127*

IV.   The Literature of the New Republic   *137*

The American Revolution as a Literary Event   *139*

Poetry in the Early Republic   *156*

Charles Brockden Brown and Early American Fiction   *168*

Toward a National Literature   *187*

Part Two 1810–1865
Associate Editor, Terence Martin

I.   The Age in Perspective   *205*

Idealism and Independence   *207*

II.   Cultural Diversity and Literary Forms   *227*

Washington Irving and the Knickerbocker Group   *229*

James Fenimore Cooper and the Writers of the Frontier   *240*

Edgar Allan Poe and the Writers of the Old South   *262*

William Cullen Bryant and the Fireside Poets   *278*

The Rise of the Woman Author   *289*

Forms of Regional Humor   *306*

A New Nation's Drama   *324*

III.   Intellectual Movements and Social Change   *343*

Social Discourse and Nonfictional Prose   *345*

The Transcendentalists   *364*

IV.   The American Renaissance   *379*

Ralph Waldo Emerson   *381*

Henry David Thoreau   *399*

Nathaniel Hawthorne   *413*

Herman Melville *429*

Walt Whitman *448*

Part Three 1865–1910
Associate Editor, Martha Banta

I. Signs of the Times *465*

Literature and Culture *467*

Culture and Consciousness *482*

II. Genre Deliberations *499*

Realism and Regionalism *501*

Naturalism and the Languages of Determinism *525*

III. Literary Diversities *547*

Literature for the Populace *549*

Immigrants and Other Americans *568*

Women Writers and the New Woman *589*

IV. Major Voices *607*

Emily Dickinson *609*

Mark Twain *627*

Henry Adams *645*

Henry James *668*

Part Four 1910–1945
Associate Editor, David Minter

I. Contexts and Backgrounds *693*

The Emergence of Modernism *695*

Intellectual Life and Public Discourse *715*

Literary Scenes and Literary Movements *733*

II.   Regionalism, Ethnicity, and Gender: Comparative
      Literary Cultures *759*

      Regionalism: A Diminished Thing *761*

      Afro-American Literature *785*

      Mexican American Literature *800*

      Asian American Literature *811*

      Women Writers Between the Wars *822*

III. Fiction *843*

      The Diversity of American Fiction *845*

      Ernest Hemingway, F. Scott Fitzgerald, and
      Gertrude Stein *873*

      William Faulkner *887*

IV.   Poetry and Criticism *911*

      The Diversity of American Poetry *913*

      Robert Frost *937*

      Ezra Pound and T. S. Eliot *947*

      William Carlos Williams and Wallace Stevens *972*

      Literary Criticism *993*

Part Five 1945 to the Present
Associate Editor, Marjorie Perloff

I.   The Postwar Era *1021*

      Culture, Power, and Society *1023*

      The New Philosophy *1045*

      Literature as Radical Statement *1060*

II.   Forms and Genres *1077*

      Poetry *1079*

      Twentieth-Century Drama *1101*

Neorealist Fiction   *1126*

Self-Reflexive Fiction   *1142*

III. The Present   *1159*

The Fictions of the Present   *1161*

The   Avant-Garde   and   Experimental
Writing   *1178*

Notes on Contributors   *1201*

Index   *1211*

Preface

In the Preface to the last collaborative effort of this kind, the *Literary History of the United States* (1948), Robert E. Spiller and his co-editors declared that "each generation should produce at least one literary history of the United States, for each generation must define the past in its own terms." Earlier, just after World War I, the editors of the *Cambridge History of American Literature* had made much the same point. In fact, however, the 1948 literary history has stood for nearly forty years, leading its editors to observe in the 1974 edition that their work had belied their "original pronouncement that 'each generation must define the past in its own terms.'"

Among the many questions that readers will ask upon opening this new volume is why the prophecy of 1948 failed and why the present work appears now. Adequate answers to these questions require an understanding of the social, political, and intellectual history of the last four decades, as well as a grasp of the new critical approaches to our national literature that have emerged in that time. Events such as the Cold War, the war in Vietnam and the protests against it, the civil rights movement, the women's movement, and the struggles of various minority groups to achieve equity in American society have reformed the way many Americans view their nation and thereby their national literature and culture. The very pressures, conflicts, and cultural reevaluations in American political and intellectual life that created an atmosphere unconducive to a "redefinition of our literary past" during the 1960s and 1970s have, in part, generated exciting new critical perspectives and literary expressions that are represented in this book.

This work does not, however, constitute a new consensus about the history of the literature of the United States. For many reasons, some discussed in our General Introduction, concurrence remains impossible at this time. There is today no unifying vision of a national identity like that shared by many scholars at the closings of the two world wars. We have therefore sought to represent the variety of viewpoints that enliven current scholarship. While the individual essays demonstrate considerable variations in approach, tone, and style, all of the writers have undertaken their assignments as teachers of history and literature seeking to share their perspectives and knowledge with students, fellow scholars, and general readers.

Our work is organized into five parts, reaching from Native American cave narratives to the present. Each part has been fashioned under the supervision of an associate editor and begins with at least one general essay that introduces the period. Although period divisions are often marked by significant historical events, such as the end of the Civil War, these markers represent organizational convenience and do not imply watersheds in literary developments. As the introductory essays suggest, many movements and careers exceed period boundaries. Within each part, essays examine genres, particular schools, and special social, political, and historical developments.

During the last twenty years the rediscovery of numerous authors has significantly broadened the scope of the study of American writing. The present literary history aims to discuss as many of these figures as possible and to contribute to the current effort to reconstruct the history of the literature of the United States in ways that do not exclude certain writers because of biases involving gender, race, or ethnic and cultural background. Another competing desire, however, is to examine more fully those writers whose works, in the views of the editors, deserve broader study. The very composition of a literary history involves choices by a small group of individuals regarding what can and cannot possibly be included and how much space and attention to devote to each author and subject. These decisions—such as whether or not to devote a chapter to Robert Frost, William Faulkner, Edith Wharton, or Frederick Douglass, or whether to have chapters on individual writers at all—are difficult and finally depend upon the judgments of the editors. Such judgments are based upon principles that must be acknowledged as intellectually "elitist," just as are notions of what constitutes "art" and "literature," for they are founded upon the idea that a group of professional scholars may decide that some acts of expression are more worthy of attention than others. Such selections are determined, to a degree, by attitudes and assumptions that are acquired consciously through education and unconsciously through complex processes of cultural transmission. It is because opinions differ among critics and change over time that each generation must write its own history. Many writers included here might have been discussed at much greater length, but the aim of providing readers with a compact reference tool made this impossible. The treatments could not be exhaustive, but they attempt to establish an overview from which readers may move to other sources.

Many of the reviewers of the 1948 *Literary History* called it a "monument." The metaphorical dimension of this word has special relevance, for the construction of a literary history may be thought of in terms of architecture and building. The work is commissioned by a client who engages editors to design the basic structure and gather experts to complete assigned tasks. The editors and the publisher cooperate to construct a book that will satisfy artistic and financial considerations and be acceptable to scholars and readers. The vast majority of the people who actually use the construct will judge it less by the criteria of its makers than by its usefulness and general appearance. Of a literary history, people demand that it have informative and interesting essays on the writers and works most likely to be inquired about or worthy of a reader's curiosity and attention, sensible chapter divisions, readable type, and a good index, and that it be durable and physically convenient to use.

The *Literary History of the United States* of 1948 reflects the culture that produced a style that many critics of architecture have labeled "modern": streamlined, uniform, and confident in its aim of useful service. By contrast, the present project is modestly postmodern: it acknowledges diversity, complexity, and contradiction by making them structural principles, and it forgoes closure as well as consensus. Designed to be explored like a library or an art gallery, this book is composed of corridors to be entered through many portals intended to give the reader the paradoxical experience of seeing both the harmony and the discontinuity of materials.

In the General Introduction we try to provide a main entryway with descriptions of the floor plans and the various exhibits. In the general essays at the beginning of each part, authors lead readers into each historical period. Because of limitations of space, each essay must also serve not so much as a summary of information on the topic but primarily as another portal into specific works, authors, and movements. Given the sheer size of the subject and our desire to make this book widely available, we can only hope to provide a contemporary *introduction* to the literary history of the United States.

General Introduction

The literary history of this nation began when the first human living in what has since become the United States used language creatively. Presumably, that moment occurred many centuries ago when one of the members of the numerous Native American tribes formulated a poetic expression or told a story. As the opening essay of this volume suggests, the earliest recorded evidence of written expression in North America exists in the Southwest, where American Indians carved and painted narratives on the walls of caves. When the first explorers from the north and south of Europe advanced upon the New World, they brought with them their own literatures and languages. While at first they tried to preserve their ties to their homelands and to transport their literary cultures, the time and distance separating them from home and the clash of competing verbal worlds in the Americas forever altered the languages and literatures of the immigrant as well as of the native populations. The complexity in the literature, as well as the diversity of the people, of the United States testifies to the clashes and commingling of many cultures.

The *Columbia Literary History of the United States* is an examination of the emergence of a national literature, the particular nature of that literature, the extraliterary factors that have been significant in its formation, and the practice of the literary arts in various forms by writers and speakers. Even this fairly detailed definition cannot express the complexity of the subject. Many aspects of this project are the result of significant developments in the theories of history and criticism that have affected the writing of literary history today. In order to appreciate the special characteristics of this volume, it is necessary to have a sense of the fundamental transformations in literary criticism that have occurred on the theoretical level over the last twenty-five years.

During the 1950s and the early 1960s, most historians and literary scholars continued to base their accounts of the past upon a philosophical foundation that may most simply be described as realist and positivist. That is,
they believed that the facts of the past were ascertainable through research,
were verifiable, and could thereby be proven true or false. Once established, facts could be used to create an accurate account of actual events,
their causes, and their meanings. Similarly, literary historians believed that
works of literature could be examined in the context of these valid accounts
of history and that relationships between the literary text and historical
contexts could be detected, analyzed, and employed to help to explain the
meaning of a text. An understanding of this meaning could then be used to
support interpretations of the intentions and values of the author, even aspects of the history and culture in which the work was composed.

In contrast to, and sometimes in conflict with, such historical critics were
those more interested in the inherent aesthetic qualities of texts. For these
formalist critics, primarily the "New Critics" of the 1940s and 1950s, an
interpretation of a text should be based upon an analysis of the internal
technical elements of the work itself. A well-trained critic, sensitive to the
nuances of language, could discover the meaning of a work by delicate explication of the structure, imagery, allusions, symbolism, style, and themes.
The main debate among literary scholars, therefore, was between the historical scholars who argued that a detailed reconstruction of the context was
a necessary preparation for an informed reading of a text, and the formalist
critics who held that such background was not only not necessary but might
even distract readers from an immediate response to the text itself—a pleasure always heightened by the fullest knowledge of the forms and structures
of language. Of course, there were many scholars and teachers who applied
these approaches in a less restricted manner than a brief summary can suggest, but on the whole, students of literature trained during those decades
usually found themsleves forced to choose between these two competing
views.

Beginning primarily in France and Germany in the mid-1960s and quickly
spreading to the United States, a series of major theoretical challenges to
the established methods of both these schools of criticism emerged. The
philosophers whose work enabled the new developments in the writing of
history and criticism challenged the validity of a number of categories of
thought used in discussions of ethics, aesthetics, and epistemology. Their
philosophical revisions led some literary theorists and historiographers, especially those employing the methods of "structuralism" and "deconstruction," to question the idea of a fixed relation between mind and material

reality, and thus the very nature of knowledge, especially as it pertains to literary texts, history, meaning, and truth. Some theorists have argued that the limits of human knowledge require us to accept a radical relativism beyond the individual perceiver. Two people might agree that the Mississippi River exists in reality, but each knows only the Mississippi colored, shaped, and shaded by individual experience, reading, and imagination. There are as many real Mississippis as there are minds to contemplate the Mississippi.

Similarly, the old records, diaries, letters, newspapers, official firsthand documents, or statistical figures examined by the historian are no longer thought of as reflecting "the" past; rather, there is no past except what can be construed from these documents as they are filtered through the perceptions and special interests of the historian who is using them. Thus, the historian is not a truthteller but a storyteller, who succeeds in convincing readers that a certain rendition of the past is "true" not by facts but by persuasive rhetoric and narrative skill. A nation's official history is ultimately no more than a story about which there is widespread agreement. A people's account of their "history" is apt to be different from another people's image of that "history." For each, the account is "true."

Having proposed the complete theoretical relativism of the meaning of historical and literary texts, some theorists argue further that all histories, texts, and readings of them are "interested" in the sense that ideological and cultural beliefs control them. The producer of a text has ideological assumptions; so does the reader. From this theoretical standpoint, every reading of a text (whether that "text" is a historical event or a work of literature) is just another form of misreading. Thus, in the creation and reading of texts, language and politics are always going to be intertwined. (For more detailed discussions of these issues, see the essays on criticism and on the new philosophy in Parts Four and Five of this volume.)

For traditional scholars and teachers of history and literature, and especially for "literary historians" in the years since 1948, these theories have raised fundamental questions: Is historical criticism possible, and is there such a thing as literary history? While at first it did seem that the new theories were discouraging to criticism and especially destructive to historical interpretations of literature and society, the effect has actually been quite enlivening. For, after serious consideration of these matters, other thinkers have proposed a more pragmatic resolution to these paralyzing dilemmas: we must admit our limitations but also recognize the human psychological need and continuing desire to understand human nature, experience, and works of the creative imagination. People will not stop reading and interpreting what they read simply because they cannot be sure of the true meaning of the past or a literary text. The function of the literary historian and critic can still be to provide interpretations that may enrich a person's understanding of a text and appreciation of a work of art. To be honest and most useful, however, this rendering of possible meanings should be presented in the context of a self-conscious awareness on the part of the critic and reader of the tentative nature of all human assertions, pronouncements, and conclusions, thus permitting multiple readings, whether complementary or competing.

For literary historians and historical critics, this position means that the scholar has the responsibility of providing an admittedly personal, yet informed and persuasive, account of the historical material deemed relevant to a particular work as well as a useful reading of the text in relation to the history. It is no longer necessary or desirable for the critic to argue that one reading is truer than any other, for the aim of historical criticism is to provide the reader with an interesting and feasible approach to a text, informed by a relevant interpretation of historical material. Once the skeptical arguments had cut the tie between the text and "reality," between the "meaning" and "truth," and had exposed the rhetorical and political nature of all writing about human experience, "fictional" or "historical," many critics and historians felt a great relief at no longer having to "prove" their readings to be the only true and correct ones. Criticism has been freed to be more daring and speculative so that some critics have begun to rival the creative artists themselves with interpretive essays that are quite original in style and perspective. No longer required to sound authoritative and magisterial, the voice of the individual critic can be more distinctive and personal.

Perhaps the critics who have gained the most from this revolution of critical consciousness have been those interested in writers overlooked in the past and not previously accepted into the standard canon. Such scholars have discovered that the new questioning of established "truths" opened up new areas for research. Advocates of writers who had long been dismissed as "minor," especially female, minority, popular, and regional authors, have convinced colleagues and publishers to reexamine and republish many such figures. This process has led to the reevaluation of many authors and the creation of a new body of criticism on these writers, especially from social and political perspectives. Universities and colleges have also seen the establishment of many courses on women writers, on the literatures of ethnic and minority groups, and on popular writing. These courses are broadening the definition of literature for a new generation of readers. At the same time, standard interpretations of well-established writers are being challenged and revised.

As a result of these developments, the *Columbia Literary History of the United States* proceeds from assumptions about the nature of literature, history, and criticism that are fundamentally different from those that formed the foundation for previous works of this kind. In external respects, of course, this volume has the appearance of a traditional literary history, but in many instances the essays challenge established concepts. In view of the changes in theory and method, even the meanings of terms of the title are different from those of earlier literary histories of the United States. It is important, therefore, that we be quite precise about defining these terms at the outset.

First, what do we mean by "United States," and how do the words "Literary History of the United States" in the title signify something different from "A History of American Literature"? To place the stress upon the United States is to acknowledge that for many people in the world the term "American" is not synonymous with "United States" but refers to all of the countries on the North American continent. By the use of the term "United States," however, we do not wish to exclude the pre-Columbian and colonial writing that preceded 1776. A related problem is that of language: because English is the dominant language in the United States today, should non-English writings be excluded from this study? The answers to these questions involve matters of judgment about which there is much debate. For the sake of clarity and consistency in this volume, we have concluded that by the "literature of the United States" we mean all written and oral literary works produced in that part of the world that has become the United States of America.

No less complex and important a matter is what we mean by "literary." The editors of the 1948 *Literary History of the United States* defined the term as pertaining to works of "excellent expression." In the last forty years, the practice of criticism has called the usefulness of such a definition into question by asking whether the prerogative to determine what is literary is that of the author, the critic, or the readers, and how such a seemingly arbitrary decision can be made at all. At the moment, critics are too divided on these issues to concur in a single definition of literary art, and the definition of "literature" has expanded to include various forms of expression, such as the diary, the journal, scientific writing, journalism, autobiography, and even film. For this volume, decisions about what texts are treated as "literary" have been largely the responsibility of each contributor in consultation with the editors. These choices will always be open to debate.

Finally, there is the term "history." From the theoretical viewpoint discussed earlier, this term refers to a conception of past events formulated by historians who use documents, records, statistics, and other indicators of those events to construct an interpretive account of the past that readers and others may accept as "true." For the "literary historian," there is a double challenge: not only to present a persuasive story of the past but also to explicate texts, generate interpretations, and instill understanding and appreciation of the aesthetic qualities of works of art in relation to "history." Because of the wide variety of critical methods in use today, there are considerable variations in the ways different critics respond to these challenges. Some scholar-critics write with a confidence that shows little evidence of the theoretical upheaval of recent years, while others proceed with obvious tentativeness and uncertainty. Again, because there is no consensus on these matters, each contribution to this volume represents the individual critic's own solution to these tensions between the tasks of the historian and those of the literary critic.

As a result of this many-angled vision, some essays in the volume are more concerned with history while others focus more closely upon matters of style, language, and technique. Because the same literary figure may appear in more than one essay, however, it often occurs that a writer is discussed within different frameworks and through different critical approaches. The reader of this literary history should consult the index to see the different places in which a particular writer is treated and should recognize that relationships among the various essays are important.

For example, the specific contributions on Herman Melville and Ralph Waldo Emerson might best be read in conjunction with the piece that opens Part Two, "Idealism and Independence," and with the essay "The Transcendentalists." That combination would place their writings in relation to two accounts of the philosophical ideas current in the period. A reader interested in Melville and social issues, however, should also read the essay "Social Discourse and Nonfictional Prose" in order to see Melville's works in relation to the political writings of the abolition and women's rights movements. Similarly, someone interested in Mark Twain might want to study the essays "Realism and Regionalism" and "Literature for the Populace" in Part Three. Also, since Twain's career as a humorist really begins before 1865, that reader would probably find it useful to consult the essay "Forms of Regional Humor" in Part Two.

Further examination of the index will reveal that many figures are examined in relation to more than one cultural or historical context. While special essays on writers by gender, region, race, and ethnic heritage ensure that certain figures do appear, the more general pieces on genres and movements also contain discussions of some of the same writers in different contexts. Accordingly, writers like Kate Chopin and Edith Wharton are examined in the essays on realism and regionalism as well as in pieces on women writers. The number of times that a writer is cross-referenced in the index is one indication of the breadth of influence and appeal that author had had in our literary history. Reading selectively, a person may also trace the development of religious and philosophical thought and expression from New England Puritanism, through the debates of the Great Awakening and the Enlightenment, the reasonings of Jefferson and the Constitution, to the upheavals of romanticism, modernism, and postmodernism. Similarly, selective study of the essays devoted to particular genres will provide a survey of the developments of poetry, drama, criticism, and the novel over time. The index is a guide to such continuous as well as multiple treatments. In important ways, then, the reader of this work will always be involved in an act of creating his or her own interpretations of the literary history of the United States by combining related essays.

In contrast to the 1948 volume, we have made no attempt to tell a "single, unified story" with a "coherent narrative" by making changes in the essays. That is, the editors have not revised the beginnings and endings of essays to create the appearance of one continuous narrative. No longer is it possible, or desirable, to formulate an image of continuity when diversity of literary materials and a wide variety of critical voices are, in fact, the distinctive features of national literature. The research and criticism of the last thirty years has revealed that the history of the literature of the United States is not one story but many different stories. American Indian writers did not fall silent when Europeans arrived; they continued to produce literatures themselves, and they began to influence the new Americans, from Roger Williams and John Eliot to Henry Thoreau to Gary Snyder. Blacks did not wait until after the end of slavery to create a literary culture. The first black writers of fiction and poetry emerged during the eighteenth century, and other early forms of expression, such as songs and slave narratives, demonstrate highly conscious literary skill. Similarly, Anne Bradstreet and Emily Dickinson were not the only women writers before the twentieth century; there have been many important women writers since the seventeenth century, some of whom even dominated the literary scene during certain periods. Contrary to previous assumptions, Asian American, Hispanic, and Jewish-American writers have been producing literature in their native and adoptive languages since the nineteenth century. Finally, the writers of New England have not been the only "American" writers, as many anthologies and histories would have us believe. Authors in other parts of the United States are and have always been writers of the national literature and have contributed substantially to the literary heritage.

While we have sought to be inclusive and to represent the complexity of our literary history, we have also tried to provide some guiding principles and to suggest certain continuities. These conceptions and connections are different, however, from those that have unified previous histories and anthologies. Our emphasis is upon the varied voices within the one nation. For example, rather than provide only one beginning to this narrative, which invariably creates the impression that the culture originated in a common experience and has developed along a single "mainstream," this work has four parallel departure points in order to stress that from the very start there has always been diversity. The cultures of the Native Americans, the Anglicans in England, the explorers of the Southwest, and the Puritans in New England were markedly different and competing fiercely in seventeenth-century America. Yet each played a formative role in the creation of our literary culture.

A glance at the table of contents of this volume indicates immediately that such clashes among different heritages and values has, in fact, characterized every period of our literary history. The New England Fireside Poets, the early fictionists and humorists of the mid-Atlantic and the frontier, and their contemporaries in the South seem to have lived and written in worlds apart, as the uprooted and frustrated Edgar Allan Poe discovered. In antebellum Massachusetts, the high-minded, male-dominated transcendentalists expounded social idealism and utopianism, but they soared away from the practical concerns of political writers like Frederick Douglass and Lydia Maria Child. At the same time, Hawthorne and Melville felt themselves in competition with a host of women novelists such as Harriet Beecher Stowe whose very popularity doomed them to later obscurity; only recently has Stowe's place as a major and influential writer begun to be recognized.

Some of the combinations of essays in each part are designed to reflect the social and political tensions that are so frequently represented in the literature. For example, Part Three juxtaposes the official literary line of the essay "Literature and Culture" with the diversity exemplified in the essay "Literature for the Populace," while the intellectual life of the established writers of the period expressed in the essay "Culture and Consciousness" is amplified through the essays "Immigrants and Other Americans" and "Women Writers and the New Woman." Throughout the volume, the struggles between those who controlled the literary establishment and those who opposed it or sought to enter it have been viewed as energizing and creative forces in the literature.

The composition of a literary history today necessarily involves a fundamental tension. On the one hand, there is the attempt to unify and to provide coherence and organization to our literary heritage. Because this work is a history and its authors are inclined to provide a sense of order to events, it belongs, in many ways, to a convergent or centripetal mode of discourse. On the other hand, because it also involves creative acts of critical interpretation, the work contains efforts to challenge existing orders, efforts that sustain its centrifugal impulses and divergent modes of thinking. Within the literary history itself, these two modes of thought and expression are constantly engaged in what the Russian theorist Mikhail Bakhtin called a "dialogic opposition."

In describing the difference between history and the novel, Bakhtin said that histories tend to be centripetal and concern themselves "with strata of legal codes etc., in order to create a series of moments in which the interaction of these forces can be seen in their simultaneity as well as their continuity," whereas the novel dramatizes the gaps that exist between what is told and the telling of it. He also proposed that history, the Bible, and the epic share a presumption of authority, "a claim to absolute language," which he saw as "absolutely foreign to the novel's joyous awareness of the inadequacies of its own language."

Certainly, the *Columbia Literary History of the United States* is not a novel. But it is also not an authoritative proclamation. While the distinction of its publisher and its imposing title may suggest authority, its editors and contributors know that perspectives and interpretations of every topic treated here do exist. Many elements of the work honestly express an awareness that gaps occur between past events and present accounts, or between literary texts and interpretations. At the same time, this recognition is also part of the sense of excitement in today's scholarship in which new theories and new discoveries are enlarging the possibilities for reading, research, and criticism. A goal of this volume is to intersect the lines of tension between the centralizing and unifying forces of our society and those decentralizing powers of individual creative and critical imaginations. Taken together, the contributions in this book reveal the strains and contradictions, as well as the cohesive and stabilizing elements, of the national culture in which literature and literary histories participate and, in turn, express.

Note on the Text

The prodigious volume of scholarship on American literature and history that has accumulated in recent years has made the inclusion of even a selective bibliography impractical. The limited space available for the essays would have to have been severely restricted, and still many valuable studies could not have been listed. Contributors refer to a few essential sources directly in their essays, but they have avoided footnotes and other scholarly apparatus for the sake of clarity and economy. For additional studies on particular topics, readers are encouraged to consult some of the excellent reference works readily available. Three especially useful works are the separate bibliography volume of the *Literary History of the United States*, eds. Robert E. Spiller et al. (New York, 1974); the volumes of annotated bibliographies published annually since 1963 by Duke University Press, *American Literary Scholarship* (Durham, N.C.); and the annual bibliography issue of *PMLA*. Where they are known, years marking the life-span of every author mentioned appear with the author's name in the index.

Acknowledgments

In addition to the editors and authors, many others contributed to this work. The people at Columbia University Press involved in this project have been most cheerful and helpful. In the early stages, William P. Germano, former editor in chief of the Press, provided intelligent, thoughtful, and enthusiastic guidance; he was assisted by Peggy Seip. In the later phase, William F. Bernhardt provided expert editing. Several scholars not formally involved in the project contributed valuable advice and suggestions: Louis J. Budd, Edwin H. Cady, Edward H. Davidson, Richard Ellmann, Deborah Esch, Charles Feidelson, Jr., Henry Lewis Gates, Daniel Hoffman, Annette Kolodny, Paul Lauter, David Levin, Amy Ling, Valerie Smith, and David Van Leer. The book also benefited from the comments of the faculty and fellows of the Salzburg Seminar 242, June, 1985. Providing administrative and research assistance were Carolyn Denard, Susan Mizruchi, Susan Powlaski, Sandy Qualls, Helen Wright, Jocelyn Taylor, Anna Marie Reynolds, and Sally Wolff. The prime mover of the project was the President and Director of the Press, John D. Moore; he has been a wise and supportive colleague from inception through production. It has also been a special pleasure to have the guidance and encouragement of Willard Thorp, co-editor of the 1948 *Literary History of the United States*.

Acknowledgment is made to the following publishers and individuals for permission to reprint copyrighted material; to New Directions and Faber and Faber for "In a Station of the Metro" and "Liu Ch'e" from Ezra Pound's *Personae* (copyright 1926 by Ezra Pound; reprinted by permission of New Directions Publishing Corporation) and from *Collected Shorter Poems* by Ezra Pound (reprinted by permission of Faber and Faber Ltd.); to Harvard University Press for poems by Emily Dickinson (reprinted by permission of the publishers and the Trustees of Amherst College from *The Poems of Emily Dickinson*, edited by Thomas H. Johnson, Cambridge, Mass.: The Belknap

Press of Harvard University Press, copyright 1951, © 1955, 1979, 1983 by
the President and Fellows of Harvard College); to New Directions and Car-
canet Press Ltd. for "The Red Wheelbarrow" and "This Is Just to Say" by
William Carlos Williams, from William Carlos Williams, *Collected Poems*,
Volume I: 1909–1939 (copyright 1938 by New Directions Publishing Corporation); to Henry Holt and Company and Jonathan Cape Ltd. for "The
Road Not Taken" and "Mowing" by Robert Frost (copyright 1916, 1934,
© 1969 by Holt, Rinehart and Winston, Inc.; copyright 1944, © 1962 by
Robert Frost; reprinted from *The Poetry of Robert Frost*, edited by Edward
Connery Lathem, by permission of Henry Holt and Company, Inc.); to
Charles Bernstein for "Air Shaft," © Charles Bernstein, 1983 (from *Resis-
tance*, Windsor, VT: Awede Press, 1983); and to Sally Goodman for the
poem "My anarchy as I grow old" by Paul Goodman.

Part One

Beginnings to 1810

I. A Key into the Languages of America

The Native Voice

Write vt 1 a (1): to draw or form by or as by scoring or incising a surface

Webster's Seventh
New Collegiate Dictionary

Imagine: somewhere in the prehistoric distance a man holds up in his hand a crude instrument—a brand, perhaps, or something like a daub or a broom bearing pigment—and fixes the wonderful image in his mind's eye to a wall or rock. In that instant is accomplished really and symbolically the advent of art. That man, apart from his remarkable creation, is all but impossible to recall, and yet he is there in our human parentage, deep in our racial memory. In our modern, sophisticated terms, he is primitive and preliterate, and in the long reach of time he is utterly without distinction, except: he draws. And his contribution to posterity is inestimable; he makes a profound difference in our lives who succeed him by millennia. For all the stories of all the world proceed from the moment in which he makes his mark. All literatures issue from his hand.

Language and literature involve sacred matter. Among sacred places in America, places of deepest mystery and ancient origin, there is one that comes to my mind again and again. At Barrier Canyon, Utah, there are some twenty sites upon which are preserved prehistoric rock art. One of these, known as the Great Gallery, is particularly arresting. Among arched alcoves and long ledges of rock is a wide sandstone wall on which are drawn large, tapering anthropomorphic forms, colored in dark red pigment. There on the geologic picture plane is a procession of gods approaching inexorably from the earth. They are informed with irresistible power; they are beyond our understanding, masks of infinite possibility. We do not know what they mean, but we know that we are involved in their meaning. They persist through time in the imagination, and we cannot doubt that they are invested with the very essence of language, the language of story and myth and primal song. They are two thousand years old, more or less, and they remark as closely as anything can the origin of American literature.

The native voice in American literature is indispensable. There is no true literary history of the United States without it, and yet it has not been clearly delineated in our scholarship. The reasons for this neglect are perhaps not far to find. The subject is formidable; the body of songs, prayers, spells, charms, omens, riddles, and stories in Native American oral tradition, though constantly and considerably diminished from the time of European contact, is large, so large as to discourage investigation. The tradition has evolved over a very long and unrecorded period of time in numerous remote and complex languages, and it reflects a social and cultural diversity that is redoubtable. Research facilities are inadequate, by and large, and experts in the field are few. Notwithstanding, the need is real and apparent.

Ancestors of modern American Indians were at the top of North America as early as 25,000 years ago. They were hunters whose survival was predicated upon the principle of mobility. Their dispersal upon the continent was rapid. In the hard environment of the far north there remains little evidence of their occupation, but they knew how to make fire and tools, and they lived as we do in the element of language.

American literature begins with the first human perception of the American landscape expressed and preserved in language. "Literature" we take commonly to comprehend more than writing. Writing, if we understand that word to mean visible constructions within a framework of alphabets, is not more than six or seven thousand years old, we are told. Language, and in it the formulation of that cultural record that is literature, is immeasurably older. Oral tradition is the foundation of literature.

A comparison of the written and oral traditions is of course a matter of the greatest complexity. Those who make this comparison are irrevocably committed to the written tradition. Writing defines the very terms of our existence. We cannot know what it is to exist within an oral tradition, or we cannot know entirely. But we can know more than we do, and it behooves us to learn as much as we can, if for no other reason than to gain possession of invaluable resources that are rightfully ours, to discover, that is, a great and legitimate part of our literary heritage.

Writing engenders in us certain attitudes toward language. It encourages us to take words for granted. Writing has enabled us to store vast quantities of words indefinitely. This is advantageous on the one hand but dangerous on the other. The result is that we have developed a kind of false security where language is concerned. There has come about a deterioration of our sensitivity to language. And we have become in proportion insensitive to silence.

But in the oral tradition one stands in a different relation to language. Words are rare and therefore dear. They are jealously preserved in the ear and in the mind. Words are spoken with great care, and they are heard. They matter, and they must not be taken for granted; they must be taken seriously, and they must be remembered.

With respect to the oral tradition of the American Indian, these attitudes are reflected in the character of the songs and stories themselves. Perhaps the most distinctive and important aspect of that tradition is the way in which it reveals the singer's and the storyteller's respect for and belief in language.

At the heart of the American Indian oral tradition is a deep and unconditional belief in the efficacy of language. Words are intrinsically powerful. They are magical. By means of words can one bring about physical change in the universe. By means of words can one quiet a raging weather, bring forth the harvest, ward off evil, rid the body of sickness and pain, subdue an enemy, capture the heart of a lover, live in the proper way, and venture beyond death. Indeed there is nothing more powerful. When a person ventures to speak, when he utters a prayer or tells a story, he is dealing with forces that are supernatural and irresistible. He assumes great risks and responsibilities. He is clear and deliberate in his mind and in his speech; he will be taken at his word. Even so, he knows that he stands the chance of speaking indirectly or inappropriately, or of being mistaken by his hearers, or of not being heard at all. To be careless in the presence of words, on the inside of language, is to violate a fundamental morality.

But one does not necessarily speak in order to be heard. It is sometimes enough that one places one's voice on the silence, for that in itself is a whole and appropriate expression of the spirit. In the Native American oral tradition expression, rather than communication, is often first in importance. In the Yeibichai of the Navajo, for example, the singers chant in the strange and urgent language of the mountain spirits, a language that is unintelligible to us mortals. Although meaningless in the ordinary sense of the word, the chant is nonetheless deeply moving and powerful beyond question.

In this sense, silence too is powerful. It is the dimension in which ordinary and extraordinary events take their proper places. In the Indian world a word is spoken or a song is sung, not against, but within the silence. In the telling of a story there are silences in which words are anticipated or held on to, heard to echo in the still depths of the imagination. In the oral tradition silence is the sanctuary of sound. Words are wholly alive in the hold of silence; there they are sacred.

Properly speaking, then, language is sacred. It will not suffice to say that the verbal and the sacred are related; they are indivisible. Consider this ritual formula from the Navajo:

> Reared within the Mountains!
> Lord of the Mountains!
> Young Man!
> Chieftain!
> I have made your sacrifice.
> I have prepared a smoke for you.
> My feet restore for me.
> My legs restore for me.
> My body restore for me.
> My mind restore for me.
> My voice thou restore for.
> Restore all for me in beauty.
> Make beautiful all that is before me.
> Make beautiful all that is behind me.
> It is done in beauty.
> It is done in beauty.
> It is done in beauty.
> It is done in beauty.

This has the formality of prayer and the measure of poetry. It is immediately and essentially religious in its tone and statement. That is to say, the attitude that informs it is holy. In such a formulaic context as this, where the words are precisely fitted into the context of religious ceremony, the oral tradition achieves a remarkable stability, an authority not unlike that of Scripture. It is significant that in this rich, ceremonial song the singer should end upon the notion of beauty, of beauty in the physical world, of man in the immediate presence and full awareness of that beauty. And it is significant, indeed necessary, that this whole and aesthetic and spiritual sense should be expressed in language. Man has always tried to represent and even to re-create the world in words. The singer affirms that he has a whole and irrevocable investment in the world. His words are profoundly simple and direct. He acknowledges the sacred reality of his being in the world, and to that reality he makes his prayer as an offering, a pledge of his integral involvement, commitment, and belief. He aspires to the restoration of his body, mind, and soul, which in his cultural and religious frame of reference is preeminently an aesthetic consideration, a perception of well-ordered being and beauty, a design of which he is the human center. And the efficacy of his prayer is realized even as he makes it; it is done in beauty.

Often the words are returned upon themselves in a notable and meaningful way. They transcend their merely symbolic value and become one with the idea they express. They are not then intermediate but primary; they are at once the names of things and the things named.

> You have no right to trouble me,
> Depart, I am becoming stronger;
> You are now departing from me,
> You who would devour me;
> I am becoming stronger, stronger.
> Mighty medicine is now within me,
> You cannot now subdue me—
> I am becoming stronger,
> I am stronger, stronger, stronger.

This magic formula from the Iroquois, like the Navajo prayer above, accomplishes its purpose in itself. The strength of which the singer stands in need is imparted in the very utterance of his words. The singer not only acknowledges and affirms his strength; indeed he brings it about, he creates it of his own breath; it is done in belief.

The power and beauty of words are sometimes inherent in apparently the most benign and understated utterance, as in this Crow charm, meant to bring sleep upon an enemy:

At night when we lie down, listening to the wind rustling through the bleached trees, we know not how we get to sleep but we fall asleep, don't we?

or this Chippewa love song:

> A loon I thought it was,
> But it was my love's splashing oar.
> To Sault Ste. Marie he has departed,
> My love has gone on before me,
> Never again can I see him.
> A loon I thought it was,
> But it was my love's splashing oar.

Among the most succinct and potent of American Indian verbal formulas are the warrior songs.

> Let us see, is this real,
> Let us see, is this real,
> Let us see, is this real,
> This life I am living?
> Ye gods, who dwell everywhere,
> Let us see, is this real,
> This life I am living.

This song from the Pawnee is an epitome of the warrior ideal. The singer means to place even his life on the line; if the life he lives is not perfectly real, so seems the consequent meaning, then he had better know it, that he might make a right resolution. It is a moral necessity that he put the matter to the test. There is a quiet irony in this, a rhetorical force that is so closely controlled as to be almost subliminal. The whole formula underscores the quality of life, yet the attitude toward life itself is uncompromisingly rational, the pose nearly indifferent, nearly haughty. Or this, from the Sioux:

soldiers
you fled
even the eagle dies

In this song we have one of the most concentrated and beautiful examples of American Indian oral tradition that I know. It is a nearly perfect formula; there is only the mysterious equation of soldiers and flight on the one hand, and the eagle and death on the other. Yet it is a profound equation in which the eternal elements of life and death and fear are defined in terms of freedom and courage and nobility. One might well brood upon the death of eagles; I have looked at these words on the page a long time, and I have heard them grow up in the silence again and again. They do not fade or fail. This Sioux formula embodies in seven words the essence of literature, I believe. It is significant that the song was transcribed; that is, it was not composed in writing, but it is preserved on the printed page, it exists now in written form. What was lost or gained in the process of translation and transcription? This we cannot know, but it is perhaps enough to know that the song, as we have it, is alive and powerful and beautiful and that it is eminently worthy of being preserved for its own sake. It is literature of the highest order.

In order to understand the nature of the American Indian oral tradition and its place in American literature, we must first understand something about the storyteller and his art. Stories, as such, constitute but one of many constructions within the oral tradition; it is the one, however, that is no doubt most widely recognized as literature. It will be helpful to consider several general propositions, as follows.

Stories are composed of words and of such implications as the storyteller places upon the words. The choice of words, their arrangement, and their effect are by and large determined by the storyteller. The storyteller exercises close control over the storytelling experience.

There are different kinds of stories. The basic story is one that centers upon an event. In American Indian oral tradition stories range from origin myths through trickster and hero tales to prophecy. With the exception of epic matter and certain creation myths, they are generally short. Concentration is a principle of their structure. Stories are formed. The form of the story is particular and perceptible.

Stories are true. They are true to our common experience, actual or imagined; they are statements that concern the human condition. To the extent that the human condition involves moral considerations, stories have moral implications. Beyond that, stories are true in that they are established squarely upon belief. In the oral tradition stories are told not merely to entertain or to instruct; they are told to be believed. Stories are not subject to the imposition of such questions as true or false, fact or fiction. Stories are realities lived and believed. In this sense they are indisputably true.

The storyteller is he who tells the story. To say this is to say that the storyteller is preeminently *entitled* to tell the story. He is original and creative. He creates the storytelling experience and himself and his audience in the process. He exists in the person of the storyteller for the sake of telling the story. When he is otherwise occupied, he is someone other than the storyteller. His telling of the story is a unique performance. The storyteller creates himself in the sense that the mask he wears for the sake of telling the story is of his own making, and it is never the same. He creates his listener in the sense that he determines the listener's existence within, and in relation to, the story, and it is never the same. The storyteller says in effect: "On this occasion I am, for I imagine that I am; and on this occasion you are, for I imagine that you are. And this imagining is the burden of the story, and indeed it is the story."

I have lived with the Kiowa story of the arrowmaker all my life. I have literally no memory that is older than that of hearing my father tell it to me when I was a small child. Such things take precedence in the mind. I set the story down in writing for the first time, and I have expressed my thoughts concerning it. I have told the story many times to many people in many parts of the world, and I believe that I have not yet found out its whole meaning.

If an arrow is well made, it will have tooth marks upon it. That is how you know. The Kiowas made fine arrows and straightened them in their teeth. Then they drew them to the bow to see that they were straight. Once there was a man and his wife. They were alone at night in their tipi. By the light of a fire the man was making arrows. After a while he caught sight of something. There was a small opening in the tipi where two hides had been sewn together. Someone was there on the outside, looking in. The man went on with his work, but he said to his wife: "Someone is standing outside. Do not be afraid. Let us talk easily, as of ordinary things." He took up an arrow and straightened it in his teeth; then, as it was right for him to do, he drew it to the bow and took aim, first in this direction and then in that. And all the while he was talking, as if to his wife. But this is how he spoke: "I know that you are there on the outside, for I can feel your eyes upon me. If you are a Kiowa, you will understand what I am saying, and you will speak your name." But there was no answer, and the man went on in the same way, pointing the arrow all around. At last his aim fell upon the place where his enemy stood, and he let go of the string. The arrow went straight to the enemy's heart.

Consider that until very recently the story of the arrowmaker has been the private possession of a few, a tenuous link in that most ancient chain of language that we call the oral tradition; tenuous because the tradition itself appears to be so; for as many times as the story has been told, it was always but one generation removed from extinction. That is to say, it has been neither more nor less durable than the human voice, and neither more nor less concerned to express the meaning of the human condition.

The story of the arrowmaker is a remarkable act of the imagination, a realization of words and meanings that is altogether simple and direct, yet nonetheless rare and profound, and it illustrates more clearly than anything else in my own experience something of the essential character of the imagination—and in particular of that personification that in this instance emerges from it: the man made of words.

It is important that the story of the arrowmaker returns in a special way upon itself. It is about language, after all, and it is therefore part and parcel of its own subject. Virtually there is no difference between the telling and that which is told. The point of the story lies, not so much in what the arrowmaker does, but in what he says—and indeed *that* he says it. The principal fact is that he speaks, and in so doing he places his very life in the balance. It is this aspect of the story that interests me most, for it is here that the language becomes most conscious of itself; here we are very close to the origin and object of literature; our sense of the verbal dimension is very keen, and we are aware of something in the nature of language that is at once perilous and compelling. "If you are a Kiowa, you will understand what I am saying, and you will speak your name." Everything is ventured in this simple declaration, which is also a question and a plea. Precisely at this moment is the arrowmaker realized completely, and his reality consists in language. Implicit in his simple speech is all of his definition and all of his destiny, and by implication all of ours. He ventures to speak because he must; language is the repository of his whole knowledge and experience, and it represents the only chance he has for survival. Instinctively and with great care he deals in the most honest and basic way with words. "Let us talk easily, as of ordinary things," he says. And of the ominous unknown he asks only the utterance of a name, only the most nominal sign that he is understood, that a word or a syllable is returned to him on the sheer edge of meaning. But there is no answer, and the arrowmaker knows at once what he has not known before: that his enemy is, and is present, and that he, the arrowmaker, has gained a crucial advantage over him. Make no mistake, the words of the arrowmaker reveal his peril clearly. The presence outside is decidedly an enemy; twice the storyteller tells us so. The venture is complete and irrevocable, and it ends in the restoration of order and well-being. The story is meaningful. It is so because it is in the nature of language that it proceeds to the formulation of meaning. Moreover, the story of the arrowmaker, especially, centers upon this procession of words toward meaning. It seems in fact to turn upon the very idea that language involves the elements of risk and responsibility; and in this it seeks to confirm itself. In a word, it seems to say, everything is a risk. That may well be true, and it may also be that the whole of literature rests upon that truth.

The story of the arrowmaker is supremely metaphorical; indeed it is acutely and incisively a story about story; it is both an example and a definition of literature. It is complex, and yet it is clear; it seems to give more and more of itself in time. Clear it is, and yet there is a kind of resistance in it, as in a riddle; it is the richer for that. It is a kind of prism.

The arrowmaker is preeminently the man made of words. He has consummate being in language; it is the world of his origin and of his posterity, and there is no other. But it is a world of definite reality and of infinite possibility. I have come to believe that there is a sense in which the arrowmaker has a quality of being that is more viable than that of other men in general, and as nearly a perfect right to be. We can imagine him, as he imagines himself, whole and vital, going on into the unknown darkness and beyond.

And yet the story has it that he is cautious and alone, and we are given to understand that his peril is great and immediate, and that he confronts it in the only way he can. I have no doubt that this is true. Language determines the arrowmaker, and his story determines our literary experience. A word, then, on an essential irony that marks the story and gives peculiar substance to the man made of words. The storyteller is nameless and unlettered. We know very little about him, except that in the story is his presence and his mask. And that is enough. He tells of his life in language, and of the risk involved. It occurs to us that he is one with the arrowmaker, and that he has survived, by word of mouth, beyond other men. For the arrowmaker, language does indeed represent the only chance for survival. It is appropriate that he survives in our time and that he has survived over a period of untold generations.

On the one hand, the native voice in American literature has gone largely unheard; on the other hand, it is and always has been pervasive. Even those writers, among them some of the major figures in our literary history, who have known next to nothing about the American Indian oral tradition have consistently acknowledged that tradition and perpetuated it. That tradition is so deeply rooted in the landscape of the New World that it cannot be denied. And it is so distinguished an expression that we cannot afford to lose it.

One of the most important developments in our literary history has been the emergence of the native voice in modern and contemporary letters. Certain works that one might think of as transitional, or as bridging the gap between American Indian oral tradition and contemporary literature, are highly important. John G. Neihardt's *Black Elk Speaks* (1932), for example, has been and remains a standard introduction to American Indian oral tradition. An indispensable element here is the voice of Neihardt himself, who was a poet and could see clearly into the lyrical heart of Black Elk's speech and preserve it in its true spirit.

As with all literary productions, so close in the foreground, it is difficult to draw critical conclusions. There is a considerable group of American Indian poets whose published work constitutes an important corpus in American literature. There are relatively few novelists. Perhaps the disparity is due to the fact that poetry bears a closer relationship to forms of oral tradition than does the novel. Notwithstanding, several contemporary novelists have made their mark, and others will emerge to the level of public acclaim in the next few years.

> The air is full.
> Bewildered bees are a lost constellation.
> Through compound eyes
> They see me again and again.
> Multiplied
> divided
> in the confusion of a hundred earths
> and rising moons.

This is from a poem entitled "Bees in Transit: Osage County," by the Chickasaw poet Linda Hogan. These lines seem the true reflection of oral tradition, notwithstanding a kind of scientific orientation in "constellation" and "compound eyes." In its central character the poem is not unlike this Chippewa formula from the oral tradition:

As my eyes
search the prairie
I feel the summer
in the spring

The work of Simon Ortiz, an Acoma poet, is consistently strong and clear. He evokes the modern world, often the darkest face of it, in ancient and lovely rhythms, the inexorable and organic rhythms of the Pueblo world. Strong and clear also is the poetry of Joy Harjo, a Creek woman. In virtually all of her work she brings her heritage to bear upon her intense involvement as a woman in the contemporary world. In the process she gives us to know something about the feminine power of the Indian world.

Among contemporary American Indian novelists, James Welch is especially deserving of attention. His first novel, *Winter in the Blood* (1974), has become a classic story of Indian reservation life. He has written two other novels, *The Death of Jim Loney* (1979) and *Fool's Crow* (1986), both of which are notable. Louise Erdrich has written two novels that evoke life on the Northern Plains: *Love Medicine* (1984) and *The Beet Queen* (1985). Leslie Silko's *Ceremony* (1977) is a skillful treatment of the contemporary Pueblo world. The Chippewa writer Gerald Vizenor is at once a brilliant and evasive trickster figure. His *Darkness in Saint Louis Bearheart* (1978) has become an underground classic. He is perhaps the supreme ironist among American Indian writers of the twentieth century.

There is an interesting dichotomy here. We have side by side on our library shelves anthologies of American Indian songs and stories from the oral tradition and books by contemporary American Indian poets and novelists. We must understand that the dichotomy is more apparent than real, that the one expression informs the other and that the voice is the same. The continuity is unbroken. It extends from prehistoric times to the present, and it is the very integrity of American literature.

N. Scott Momaday

The Literature of Discovery and Exploration

If, as Edmundo O'Gorman has argued, America had to be invented after its discovery—since the closed space of European thought had no room for new worlds—it was in the writings of those Europeans who first visited America that this invention began. In a language the roughness of which caught the strain of their hard traveling by land or sea or river, such writers handed over to their homeland audiences fresh news of doings beyond the horizon. From such sources, piecemeal and fugitive as they were, the Old World slowly composed its American imagery. The first classics of American literature were written for, if not always in, Europe.

And most were written not in English but in Spanish and French. Christopher Columbus himself left no single major text, but in the documents collected in such a volume as J. M. Cohen's *The Four Voyages of Christopher Columbus* (1969), one senses the deepening gloom with which he recorded the loss of what he had so lately found. When he declaims about the "vast plains, groves, and very fruitful fields" seen in 1492, the burst of wonder cannot hold; too soon come the doubts of the second voyage, the pain of the third, the near insanity of the last. Having asserted early in his American career that "the farther one goes, the more one learns," Columbus was to verify that profoundly modern principle with a richness of moral learning he might have wished to avoid. "Such is my fate," he lamented to the Spanish Crown in a letter sent from Jamaica in 1503, "that the twenty years of service through which I have passed with so much toil and danger, have profited me nothing." The man who had found Spain a New World owned at this point not even a house for himself in Spain. In his writings we first detect the voice of the American exile, the unhoused wanderer left with little but open space and the pain of enduring it. This, too, was part of what the Genoan discovered.

The lands he found were quickly appropriated by men more fortunate than he. Among the conquistadores, Hernán Cortés was especially vocal. His five surviving letters to Charles V (written 1519–26) show his high ideal—to rectify Spanish abuse of the natives—too quickly foundering in the bloody conquest; his rich catalogue of Aztec wonders too soon gives way to the dirty business of imperial administration. But here, too, is a kind of irony of circumstance, a syncopation of bright image and dark story, which like that in Columbus gives to the prose of Cortés an incidental literary tension. In the prose of another man of Cortés's generation, Álvar Núñez Cabeza de Vaca, such ironies achieved their first artful maturity. Núñez's *Relación* (1542) of the abortive Narváez expedition to Florida, which began with four hundred men in 1528 and ended in 1536 when Núñez and three others at last entered Mexico overland, catches far better than the other Spanish documents of the South—from the foray of Ponce de León in 1513 to those of Hernando de Soto in 1539–42 or Francisco de Coronado in 1540–42—the inner deflection of the strange landscapes there. A tale of spiritual struggle, great loss, and final victory, his book is full of understatement and mystery at once, and is told with an eye for detail and latent meaning very rare in its age. Like the Indian captives of a later period, Núñez surrendered piece after piece of his European identity as he fought to survive, keeping only the essential, intangible elements. His book, he said, was all that one who came back "naked" from America could offer his King, more a testament than a trove of exotic images.

Even before Núñez had landed in Florida, other powers were probing the upper reaches of the continent and finding the same great emptiness and the same irony there. The Genoan John Cabot and his son Sebastian had searched the North very early, at first for England, but with no immediate results and a small verbal consequence. Giovanni da Verrazano of Florence coasted for the French Crown in 1524 from the Carolinas north in search of a sea passage; ten years later came the first of three voyages of Jacques Cartier, through whose attraction to the shadowy reports of the Cabots the French for the first time were brought into the heart of America. Although Cartier left important records, they were so neglected in France at the time that the first narrative was printed some twenty years after the fact, in the third volume of the *Delle Navigationi et Viaggi* (1556) of Giovanni Battista Ramusio; from this Italian text John Florio produced an English one in 1580, and it was from Florio's English that the account eventually was retranslated, as late as 1598, into French. It was not just in their matter that so many early American texts were fugitive.

By the 1570s, this was changing, and even failures in the New World were likely to attract quick and wide notice in Europe. Thus the French Fort Caroline, established in the Carolinas in 1562 as a Huguenot refuge and wiped out by the irate Spaniards in 1565, had barely ceased to be before several sizable narratives appeared. And by that time, too, the hitherto rather sluggish English had begun to inquire more actively into the New World. Florio's Cartier suggests as much; so does the fact that the Caroline narrative of Jean Ribaut, *The Whole and True Discovery of Terra Florida* (1563), first was circulated in manuscript in England, where its Protestant author had found temporary refuge, and soon was translated and published there. Almost immediately, it set the English Queen herself thinking about the possibility of an American destiny.

Until quite late in the sixteenth century, it was more through such foreign examples than any native tradition of exploration that the English learned of the New World. In the 1570s and 1580s, as rivalries heated up in Europe, as English piratical activity in Spanish America began, and as English mariners started exploring the North American coast from Florida to beyond Baffin Island, there emerged the first elements of an Anglo-American library, from which ultimately American literature itself was to spring. Once finally aroused, English interest did not subside; but as the tentative forays of the late 1500s gave way to the permanent settlements at Jamestown (1607), Plymouth (1620), Boston (1630), Charleston (1670), and Philadelphia (1682), the early rush of English delight in the "newe founde world"—and of terror before its perplexities—became a tightening and dulling possession. A language of the settled land—usually American in origin and mood—began then to replace the exotic images by which the earlier European rovers had sought to codify their passages to and in the West.

In the years from 1576 to 1583, when Martin Frobisher and Humfry Gilbert bore English exploration northward, the bleak world they encountered made the accounts of their baffled attempts suitably grim. Thus, the narratives written by a trio of Frobisher's men who flourished briefly in the 1570s and 1580s—Christopher Hall, Dionise Settle, and Thomas Ellis—are rich in irony and blind fumbling, with sharp cold northern settings, the "vehement rigor" of which (to quote Ellis) brings the high ends of the enterprise to the dead level of reality. First printed separately—Richard Hakluyt later collected them in the *Principal Navigations* (1598–1600)—each centers on the theme of Frobisher's rebuke by a New World he too easily thought to subdue. In Gilbert's case, the presumptions were more nearly tragic; Edward Hayes caught in his narrative, also in Hakluyt, the withering force of the northern weather, but he caught too Gilbert's moral profile:

for Gilbert was obsessed with rumors about his incompetence, preferring "the wind of a vaine report to the weight of his own life," and thus found ill luck, and showed bad skill, at sea. Sticking with desperate extremity aboard his pinnace through a fierce storm, he is last shown by Hayes—as if in a trance—seated on the rear deck, with Thomas More's *Utopia* (1516) in his hand, reciting from it the death-defying sentiments of Hythlodaye: "giving foorth signes of joy, the Generall sitting abaft with a booke in his hand, cried unto us in the *Hind* (so oft as we did approch within hearing) We are as neere to heaven by sea as by land." He was a man, as Hayes said, "between extremities," a man whose fate it was to act out his tragedy "on ground imagined good."

Thus ran on—and out—the English dream of the North. The southern reports were more sanguine at first. Sir Walter Raleigh, Gilbert's half-brother, went with the latter on his abortive first voyage but had enough of his own short luck left in 1583 to miss the fatal one. Redirecting the dead Gilbert's schemes to more temperate regions, he dispatched the otherwise obscure Philip Amadas and Arthur Barlowe on the first of the Roanoke voyages in 1584. While off the Outer Banks, one of the two reported in an account printed by Hakluyt, they "smelt so sweet, and so strong a smel" even before they saw the mainland that they expected a "delicate garden" rather than a wilderness. They took possession for Elizabeth I, hastily explored the shore, treated with—and treated well—the natives, then rushed home with their goodly news. But the idyll could not hold. Richard Grenville, planting a colony in 1585, ruined the peace with the Indians, and his ruination was to haunt John White, who accompanied Grenville in 1585 and succeeded him in 1587.

Having collaborated in 1585 with the naturalist Thomas Harriot, the second edition of whose Roanoke text *A Brief and True Report . . . of Virginia* (1590) he illustrated, White had caught in his drawings the brief poise of better hopes. All too soon, for him and the English, the hopeful images were replaced by news of desperate action. When White's relief expedition of 1588 was delayed until 1590, and at last he found no survivors amid the ruins of Roanoke, the sweetness sensed by Amadas and Barlowe in 1584 had yielded to tragedy on the island. In what was the first English attempt at plantation, everything seemed to go wrong, and White, the man whose wondering vision had caught his nation's Western excitement, became—in the letters and reports Hakluyt printed—the unlikely chronicler of England's blasted expectations. The sense of America in his last utterance, the account of the 1590 voyage that Hakluyt urged him to write, hardly bolstered the bold projects of which Hakluyt himself was master: ". . . wee founde five Chests,'" he wrote, "that had bene carefully hidden of the Planters, and of the same chests three were my owne, and about the place many of my things spoyled and broken, and my bookes torne from the covers, the frames of some of my pictures and Mappes rotten and spoyled with rayne, and my armour almost eaten through with rust."

And yet Hakluyt, and the English, persisted. Across the century's end, English mariners—Raleigh, John Hawkins, Francis Drake, and Thomas Cavendish—were circumnavigating the globe and preparing, as it turned out, for the renewed settlement of Raleigh's (and White's) Virginia in 1607. The circumnavigators found their place in Hakluyt's *Principal Navigations;* there, too, in what amounted to the first anthology of American writings in English, Hakluyt gave to the scattered New World reports of the previous century a new order and force. Barred by circumstance from fulfilling his real wish—a voyage to America himself—the preacher Hakluyt was England's western chaplain, delivering the sermon of empire (as in his *Discourse of Western Planting* of 1584) and expending in the process much of his spirit. "What restlesse nights, what painefull dayes, what heat, what cold" he had endured in tracing out the literary fortunes of the English overseas—so he himself proclaimed in 1598, appropriating the actions he chronicled as the image for his editorial labors. And yet what masses of material he had left too for his literary heir, Samuel Purchas, in whose *Hakluytus Posthumus; or, Purchas His Pilgrimes* (1625) the English found yet another record of their worldly doings. The American imagery in this collection, as in Hakluyt's own, was an imagery of action, of heroic striving; but both collections were large enough to contain the ironic or the tragic as well.

With the first permanent English settlement at Jamestown in 1607, the heroic mood was harder to maintain. The writers who saw—as George Percy said in his *Discourse on the Plantation* (written 1607)—the "faire meddowes and goodly tall Trees" of the new land, and were "almost ravished at the first sight thereof," stayed on to endure the "miserable distress" of near starvation, and for them—if not for the Hakluyts and Purchases—such suffering inevitably tempered the initial enthusiasm. Some of the sufferers, to be sure, managed to bolster the imperial vision of those who had stayed home; William Strachey, although he had been wrecked in the Bermudas, thus wrote of the disaster and the subsequent debacle at Jamestown, in his "A True Reportory of the Wracke, and Redemption of Sir Thomas Gates" (printed in Purchas), with a blithe denial of any darker themes. As the man who later drew up for Virginia the *Lawes, Divine, Morall, and Martiall* (1610), Strachey failed to see that the challenge to Gates's authority in the Bermudas (or in Virginia)—an American theme that went back as far as Cortés and Núñez and was to find its place in *The Tempest*, which took Strachey as a source—had both more interest and more truth. Percy in this way as others was the more typical Virginia writer, and in his *A Trewe Relacyon* (written c. 1622–25) he caught the brutal exchanges between Englishman and Indian with dire art. This was the tone of a tentatively native voice: it was not order but disorder that marked the American accent, less imagery than narrative that mattered.

The voice is to be heard, too, in the narratives of Captain John Smith, who, although he spent less than half as much time in Virginia as Percy, knew a similar extremity and never ceased complaining of it. The common suffering he knew well, too; but it was his own that galvanized his prose, from *A True Relation* (1608) to *A Map of Virginia* (1612) and *The Generall Historie of Virginia, New-England, and the Summer Isles* (1624). What sets him apart from the other early Virginians—indeed, from most other early American writers—is the intensity of his vision of the New World as peculiarly his own domain, the space in which his identity is to be forged and defended. Hence he represents the new contingency of American writing in general, its intimate engagement with geography. In him we may perceive for the first time that felt mixture of self and world, personality and place, which has made the role of space in American art as much an affair of the spirit as of topography pure and simple. The sheer energy of his prose, which reaches out fearlessly to engage the world, reflects the degree to which he made such an identification himself; and the pain of his exile, most sensible in the 1624 book, suggests how much he had conflated his own story and that of England's America by that time. So brief a resident in Virginia, he had so intensely the imagination of an inhabitant that we would do well to call him still our first American author.

In Virginia and the other colonies that followed, a shift in social needs forced a shift in writing; soon it was the imaginative task of the artist to help hold the land, not just to see it, name it, or record its initial marvels. There are few "sweet smells" in such later writings, even though—as in *New Englands Prospect* (1634) by William Wood, *New England's Rarities* (1672) by John Josselyn, *Leah and Rachel* (1656) by John Hammond, *A Character of the Province of Maryland* (1666) by George Alsop, *A Further Account of the Province of Pennsylvania* (1685) by William Penn, or *A New Voyage to Carolina* (1709) by John Lawson—the idea of discovery remains a strong originating point in them, and as late as William Carlos Williams and F. Scott Fitzgerald that same mood still could generate new lyrical raptures. When we look back from such a modern revival of the mood to the first words of the historian William Bradford on New England, in *Mourts Relation* (1622), we find a similarly sensuous language, a thorough engagement with the tangible; Bradford is a man for whom the "fine small gale" as the voyage opens matters intensely. By comparison Bradford's *Of Plimmoth Plantation* (written 1630–50) seems burdened by a weight of intangibilities; it was this shift to matters less visible, to the intricacies of colonial administration, that marked the coming onto the increasingly familiar land of a literature that theretofore had stayed largely at its edge, where it was lavish of imagery but frugal in its use of narration.

The English order along the seventeenth-century coast was, to be sure, a thin decoration on a vast terrain. But it was the French, not the English, who probed it before 1700. Already by the year of Plymouth's founding, Etienne Brulé had been perhaps as far as the head of Lake Superior, while Jean Nicolet had reached by 1634 almost to the upper Mississippi. Their master, Samuel de Champlain, had probed New York before the Dutch settled there and had coasted New England even earlier than John Smith. From all these ventures, it was Champlain who matured the best literary fruits, especially in his *Voyages* (1613), his *Voyages et Découvertes* (1619)—here Brulé's incredible story is outlined—and his largest and final work, *Les Voyages de la Nouvelle France* (1632). Always frustrated in his search for a Northwest Passage but never wholly daunted, Champlain indefatigably pursued the chimera because France had so much to gain by its discovery. Yet his faith often led him astray, as when Nicolas de Vignau admitted inventing his story of the Passage—told to Champlain in France, it had motivated an expensive new voyage—merely to secure passage back to Canada for himself. A historian of such unending disappointments, Champlain added much to Europe's sense of America's vastness and its capacity for engulfing human dreams.

By 1700, the English had secured the shore from Maine to South Carolina—including New Netherland, the literary traditions of which, as evidenced in *Vertoogh van Nieu-Neder-land* (1650) and *Beschryvinge van Nieuw Nederlant* (1655) by Adriaen van der Donck, gradually faded into those of the English—and the French were preparing to found their second American empire. Médard Chouart and Pierre Esprit Radisson, the latter an uproariously comical explorer of the English language in his "Auxoticiat Voyage into the Great and Filthy Lake of the Hurons" (in his *Voyages*, 1669), had pressed farther into the upper lakes at mid-century. The southward thrust was carried by Louis Jolliet and Jacques Marquette; the latter's *Journal* (1681) tells well the tale of their tough expedition down the Mississippi. But it was René Robert Cavelier, sieur de La Salle, who knew both the river and its toughness best. Aside from the mass of letters and court memorials he left behind at his murder, there are good accounts by Louis Hennepin in his *Description de la Louisiane* (1688), and by Henri de Tonti in his two *Mémoires*, covering the periods 1678–83 and 1687–91, respectively, both of which remained in manuscript at his death. Most moving, though, is the version by La Salle's aide, Henri Joutel, in his *Journal* (1713); here the frustrated final search for the "fatal river," as Joutel calls it, leads the French leader to a mean death, ambushed by his followers, his body dragged into the bushes afterward so that "the ravenous Wild Beasts" might consume his flesh.

Almost two centuries after Columbus first landed on New World soil, great hopes and the direst of ends were thus still oddly threaded together. That, in a sense, was the deepest of discoveries; that was the moral terrain whose strange contours still awaited exploration. But from this point on the exploration would be largely an American venture, and the verbal effects of that exploration, while at times they included the native exoticism of a William Bartram, were registered more and more in the products of an increasingly domestic imagination. Schooled in space, that imagination would return to space again and again in the classic texts of American literary art. No longer was American literature a European creation.

Wayne Franklin

English Literature at the American Moment

It is only an apparent paradox that the literature treating the new American experience in the New World was profoundly indebted to an English literary heritage. Writers, like the rest of us, can only perceive and accommodate the new through forms at least partly familiar, though the best of them succeed in making the familiar strange. Accordingly, literary historians now recognize that early American literature is as much a product of continuities as an indigenous creation.

These continuities result of course from a common culture and national experience. Both English and colonial education centered on the Latin language, the philosophy, history, and literature of Greece and Rome, Ciceronian and Ramist rhetoric, and oratorical performances of the kind exemplified in John Milton's *Prolusions*. In addition, both English people and colonists shared the experience—and myth—of the English Reformation, marking England as an elect nation: the Virgin Queen as the great deliverer of Protestant England from Spain and Bloody Mary; the providential miracles of the Armada and Guy Fawkes Day; and the apocalyptic events (however interpreted) of Civil War, Regicide, and rule by the Puritan Saints. They also shared the great literary embodiments of that myth—John Foxe's *Book of Martyrs* (1563, 1570), William Shakespeare's history plays, Edmund Spenser's *Faerie Queene* (1590, 1596), John Milton's *Paradise Lost* (1667), John Bunyan's *Pilgrim's Progress* (1678, 1684)—as well as its foundation text, the vernacular Bible, especially the widely circulated Geneva version (1560) with its extensive Calvinist annotations. Moreover, the Reformation caveat to apply everything in Scripture to the self and the concern of Protestant typology to assimilate contemporary events and even individual lives to the providential scheme of recapitulations and fulfillments throughout history provided common exegetical terms for interpreting historical experience on both shores. George Herbert, the most honored and influential religious lyric poet in England, explicitly proclaimed an English-American continuity in enacting the Reformation myth: "Religion stands on tip-toe in our land,/Readie to pass to the *American* strand"—lines that created licensing difficulties for his poetic volume *The Temple* (1633).

English people responded imaginatively to, and participated in, the American experience in a variety of ways: as courtier-adventurers (like Sir Walter Raleigh, who promoted the first colony on Roanoke Island); as temporary settlers and administrators; and as speculators who bought shares in the merchant companies financing trading ventures and settlement. The English poet and inveterate traveler George Sandys is a case in point: he was resident treasurer of Virginia from 1621 to 1625, and his celebrated translation of Ovid's *Metamorphoses* (1626) was the first English poetry of any significance written in America. His dedication to King Charles describes that translation, with its massive commentary synthesizing classical, medieval, and Renaissance interpretations of Ovidian myth, as "Sprung from the Stocke of the ancient Romanes; but bred in the New-World, of the rudenesse whereof it cannot but participate"—pointing thereby to the challenge of joining a classical literary heritage to New World experience. Also, Richard Hakluyt's epic compendium, *Principall Navigations, Voyages, Traffiques, and Discoveries of the English Nation* (1598–1600)—a potpourri of adventures, marvels, and realistic detail from almost a century of English mariners' narratives, travelers' tall tales, promotional tracts, geographical descriptions, and ships' logs—provided a model for the heroic accounts of American exploration and settlement by Captain John Smith, William Bradford, Thomas Morton, and others.

It is hardly surprising, then, that this common heritage supplied the mythic frames through which Englishmen, explorers, and colonists viewed nature and life in the New World. One such myth, Arcadia—part golden age, part country pastoral—contrasts tranquil and unspoiled natural beauty, rural simplicity, and contentment with the corruption, ambition, and weighty responsibilities of court and city life. The Arcadian ethos informs numerous English pastoral poems, dramas, and romances, though often (as in Sir Philip Sidney's *Arcadia* [1590, 1593] and Spenser's *Faerie Queene*, Book VI) it shows itself very vulnerable to the onslaught of evil. The idea of America as Arcadia lies behind Prospero's island in *The Tempest* (1611)—though Caliban is hardly a noble savage, and, ironically, Miranda refers not to natives but to shipwrecked Europeans in her exclamation "O brave new world, that has such people in it." In America, Thomas Morton's *New English Canaan* (1637) projected an Arcadian antitype of the biblical promised land, replete with goodness, joy, and ease.

More pervasive in seventeenth-century literature is the contrary myth— that humankind and the entire natural world were blighted by the Fall and will degenerate steadily until the end of time. In such terms John Donne's "Anatomie of the World" (1611) analyzes "The Frailty and the Decay of this Whole World," and Milton's *Paradise Lost* portrays the world throughout all history "To good malignant, to bad men benign,/ Under her own weight groaning" (*PL* 12.537–39). Puritan Englishmen invoked this myth to explain the collapse and defeat of their cause after the victories of the Civil War, as did American Puritans to account for the many calamities that plagued the first American settlements. William Bradford explained the licentiousness of Morton's Merrymount in such terms, defending the destruction of that settlement; and the preachers of jeremiads could read such "declension" as provoking God's stern care for his people. On both shores the signs of the world's decline counted as evidence that the millennium was at hand.

English literary tradition also supplied the constituent elements for a myth of America as nature restored or transformed by grace. From Protestant emblematics, developed through such emblem books as Geoffrey Whitney's *Choice of Emblems* (1586), Joachim Camerarius's *Centuries* (1605), and Henry Peacham's *Minerva Britanna* (1612), and such emblematic poems as Henry Vaughan's "The Palm Tree," "The Bird," "The Timber," "The Rain-bow," "The Water-fall" (1650–55), came terms for interpreting the creatures of the natural world as symbols of divine things. Half a century later the American poet Edward Taylor also interpreted nature as emblem in several poems, and Jonathan Edwards in the mid-eighteenth century wedded the emblem tradition to typology in his elaborate treatment of instituted natural types in *Images or Shadows of Divine Things*.

Another component is descriptive poetry informed by biblical myth. English country-house poems such as Ben Jonson's "To Penshurst" (1616) and Andrew Marvell's "Upon Appleton House" (1652?) present those estates as quasi-Edenic places, though in them (as in Milton's reformed masque, *Comus* [1634]) the restoration of nature takes place only within the bounds of the noble, virtuous, and religious household. However, Andrew Marvell's lyric "Bermudas" (1652?) celebrates the American settlement of the title in much more sweeping (though still somewhat paradoxical) terms, as an Edenic or millennial place nurturing pristine gospel religion:

He lands us on a grassy Stage;
Safe from the Storms, and Prelat's rage.
He gave us this eternal Spring,
Which here enamells every thing;
And sends the Fowl's to us in care,
On daily Visits through the Air.

　　　　. . . .

He makes the Figs our mouths to meet;
And throws the Melons at our feet.
But Apples plants of such a price,
No Tree could ever bear them twice.
With Cedars, chosen by his hand,
From *Lebanon*, he stores the Land.

This myth informed countless sermons calling upon the colonists to realize the divine mission of America as a new Eden, new Israel, new Canaan, or new Jerusalem, raised up by God in the wilderness.

The myth of America as nature restored was also supported by the English utopian tradition—from Thomas More's *Utopia* (1516) to Francis Bacon's *New Atlantis* (1626, 1643) to James Harrington's *Oceana* (1656). No concept is more pervasive within Puritanism than the idea of the Holy Community, whether conceived as the chosen nation, the national church, the gathered churches of saints, or the family; the utopian disposition to embody that concept in laws and institutions is alike manifested in the *Holy Commonwealth* (1659) by the English Presbyterian Richard Baxter, in *The Christian Commonwealth* (1659) by the millenarian missionary to the Indians John Eliot, and in continual American efforts to establish select, perfectable communities—from the Plymouth of the Mayflower Compact to Brook Farm. It underlies as well the conception of the American Constitution as an ideal political instrument for a good society.

English literary tradition also provided many of the genres and modes through which the American experience could be registered and articulated. New Englanders had scant use for some kinds of sixteenth- and seventeenth-century literature—Ovidian amatory verse, Elizabethan and Jacobean drama, masques, Caroline and Cavalier lyrics. Their largest debts, not surprisingly, were to several prose forms fostered by the English Reformation, chief among them the sermon. The English pulpit provided a full spectrum of sermonic kinds and also of competing stylistic models: the witty word-by-word explications characteristic of Lancelot Andrewes; the colloquial sermons of Richard Sibbes or Thomas Adams, eloquent in their use of biblical metaphor; the Presbyterian scholastic model with its intricate Ramist divisions and constant scriptural quotation; and (the major model for the colonists) the "doctrines and uses" sermon in an undecorated "plain style," recommended by William Perkins in his very influential manual on preaching, *The Arte of Prophesying* (1607).

Several related prose kinds were also popular on both sides of the Atlantic: manuals of theology such as William Ames's *Marrow of Sacred Divinity* (1623, 1638); "Cases of Conscience," dealing with moral issues as they are affected by particular circumstances; works of spiritual direction and consolation such as William Perkins's *Golden Chaine* (1591), analyzing the signs, emotions, and feelings pertaining to the various stages of the spiritual life—election, calling, justification, adoption, sanctification, glorification. Also, colonists as well as Englishmen participated in the outpouring of controversial and polemical tracts provoked by the English Civil War, on such issues as church government, the duties of the Christian magistrate, Christian Liberty, toleration, the locus of political power and sovereignty, predestination versus free will, and more.

As poets and prose writers, the American Puritans were heirs to a Protestant biblical poetics, which identified supreme examples of and models for all kinds of literature and poetic language in the Bible, on grounds of art as well as truth. This poetics was formulated in Guillaume Salluste Du Bartas's *Uranie* (1564), and most fully exemplified in his massive, unfinished epic on the seven days of creation and the seven ages of biblical history, *Les Semaines* (1578, 1584), translated and often reissued by Joshua Sylvester as *The Divine Weekes and Workes* (1605, 1608). Sir Philip Sidney assimilated this biblical poetics to the amalgam of Platonic, Horatian, Aristotelian, and Ciceronian principles in his *Defense of Poesy* (1595); and it was elaborated in George Wither's *Preparation to the Psalter* (1619), George Herbert's "Jordan" poems, and Milton's *Reason of Church Government* (1642, Preface, Book 2). It gave rise to well over three hundred verse paraphrases of the Psalms in the period from the Sternhold-Hopkins Old Version (1562) to the *Bay Psalm Book* (1640)—used, respectively, for congregational singing in England and America. It also prompted major and minor poets alike to compose poetic versions of the Psalms or other parts of Scripture, and led directly to the flowering of English religious lyric poetry with large debts to the Psalms—from Barnabe Barnes in the sixteenth century to Donne, Herbert, and Vaughan in the seventeenth, including finally Edward Taylor in America.

The first important American poets called directly upon biblical poetics and Bartesian example for their ambitious long poems of epic scope. Anne Bradstreet readily acknowledged Du Bartas's hexaemeron, with its mix of science, natural history, philosophy, and biblical history, as the primary model for her *Quaternion*—four poems of four books each on "The Humours," "The Ages of Man," "The Seasons," and the "Four Monarchies" (1650). Bradstreet's elegy and epitaph on Sir Philip Sidney (long after his death), and her verse epistle in praise of Du Bartas in 1641, clearly indicate her sense of herself as their direct (if unworthy) poetic heir. Michael Wigglesworth's apocalyptic *Day of Doom* (1662) is in thematic terms a completion of Du Bartas's unfinished *Seconde Semaine* and Bradstreet's unfinished "Four Monarchies."

For poetry and prose in the public manner, Protestant biblical poetics offered a heroic myth of providential history to which contemporary events could be assimilated through Protestant typology. During the decades of Puritan controversy, civil war, and interregnum, the terms of this heroic myth were developed in numerous English sermons, tracts, and poems, Milton's prominent among them: an elect nation battling the forces of Antichrist in apocalyptic struggle; the imminent rule of the saints; the judgments of God visited upon the reprobate—or upon the backsliding elect—through military defeats and other calamities. Colonial poets employed the same myth: Bradstreet's "Dialogue between Old England and New" at the outbreak of Civil War (1642) concludes with an ecstatic call to England to crush the Church's foes with "the sword of God and Gideon"; Wigglesworth's epic *Day of Doom* and his poetic jeremiad *God's Controversy with New England* (1662) interpret the Restoration and especially the Great Drought in New England in 1662 as auguries of Apocalypse and Judgment. Of course the finest flowering of this poetics is Milton's *Paradise Lost*, with its sweeping vision of cosmic history (within which contemporary events take their place) and its profound exploration of human sin, loss, and grace through all time.

For the several rapidly developing genres of poetry and prose that explore and analyze the self—meditation, journals, diaries, autobiography, biography, lyric poetry—Protestant poetics supplied paradigms from biblical story or theological scheme to interpret life experiences. Paradigms were provided by the Exodus narrative, the Pauline metaphors of Christian pilgrimage or Christian warfare, the Christian life as a "progress of the soul" according to the stages defined by Hebrews 8 (or William Perkins), the conversion experience as recounted by Paul or Augustine's *Confessions*, and the Psalms (read as an account of David's sins and repentance). Self-analysis was encouraged by the Protestant imperative to apply Scripture to the self, and by the Protestant emphasis upon the individual Christian as antitype or postfiguration of the Old (or New) Testament types—an Israelite wandering in the wilderness, a David in his griefs and groans of repentance, a Jonah or Jeremiah calling backsliders to repentance and conversion, a saint engaging in the Lord's apocalyptic battles. It was also furthered by pre-scriptions and practices outlined in seventeenth-century manuals of Protes-tant meditation—Joseph Hall's influential *Arte of Divine Meditation* (1606), and later treatises by Isaac Ambrose (1659) and Edmund Calamy (1680).

Occasional or extemporal meditations were short, essaylike reflections on the creatures, or on events of the daily round, or on the special divine providences in one's own life: Hall's own *Occasionall Meditations* (1630) has titles such as "Upon the Crowing of a Cocke," "Upon the Beginning of a Sicknesse," and "Upon the Tolling of a Passing-Bell." Familiar examples of English poems in this kind include Donne's "Hymne to God My God, in My Sickness," on an illness in 1623 expected to be terminal; Donne's "Hymne to Christ, at the Authors Last Going into Germany," on the dangers antic-ipated in a sea journey in 1619; and Vaughan's several meditations on the creatures, among them, "Cock-Crowing," "The Lampe," "The Showre." American examples include Anne Bradstreet's "Occasional Meditations"—with such titles as "For Deliverance from a Fever," "Upon My son Samuel His Going for England, Nov. 6, 1657," "Upon the Burning of Our House"—as well as her wide-ranging "Contemplations" on the creatures. Of the same kind are Edward Taylor's "When Let by Rain," "Upon Wedlock, and Death of Children," and "Upon the Sweeping Flood Aug: 13:14. 1683."

Deliberate meditations, the second major kind, were carefully structured exercises recommended as preparation for the sacrament, or as sabbath ex-ercises elaborating upon the sermon, or as a regular daily duty of watchful-ness and repentance. The several varieties normally begin from a scriptural text or the state of the soul or some providential occurrence, then develop a logical analysis according to the method of a sermon, and then stir up the affections by close application to the self. Meditations upon the soul—its sinfulness, conversion, the evidences of election—are illustrated in several of William Perkins's tracts, and also in several of Donne's agonized "Holy Sonnets." Meditations on experience—God's providences, afflictions, and graces—are raised to high art in Donne's *Devotions upon Emergent Occasions* (1624), a prose analysis of the course of his illness as a sequence of provi-dential occurrences affording him spiritual instruction and grace. The method of Heavenly Meditation—an analysis of earthly things as foretastes and si-militudes of heavenly joys—is illustrated by Joseph Hall, Richard Sibbes, and especially by Richard Baxter in *The Saints Everlasting Rest* (1650); this perspective (but with heaven's joys seen as present to us now) also informs Thomas Traherne's magnificent prose *Centuries of Meditation* and many of his poems. Christopher Sutton, Arthur Hildersam, and Richard Sibbes provide English examples of preparatory meditation for the sacrament—the kind to which Edward Taylor relates his prose *Treatise Concerning the Lord's Supper* (1694, published 1966) and also his two numbered sequences of devotional poems. Taylor's poetic sequences also follow Herbert's *The Temple* and Vaughan's *Silex Scintillans* (1650, 1655) in presenting a Protestant paradigm of spiritual growth—a progress of the soul.

Autobiography, spiritual and secular, also came into its own in the seventeenth century on both sides of the Atlantic, stimulated in part by Renaissance military journals, ships' logs, travel diaries, and commercial accounts, which led readily enough to more comprehensive journals of significant spiritual and secular events, such as John Winthrop's *Journal* of the Massachusetts Bay Colony from 1630 to 1649. But the self-conscious, analytic, psychologically probing "spiritual" autobiography was especially indebted to the Puritan practice of keeping a careful, daily record of everything that might have spiritual significance. Sixteenth- and seventeenth-century English spiritual diaries by Richard Rogers, Samuel Ward, Richard Norwood, Arthur Wilson, William Waller, and George Fox, and New England journals and memoirs by Thomas Shepard, Michael Wigglesworth, Samuel Sewall, and Cotton Mather stand very close indeed to the full-fledged spiritual autobiography, as an extended, sequential narrative interpreting one's own life. Thomas Shepard provides an early American example (1646, published 1972), but Bunyan's *Grace Abounding to the Chief of Sinners* (1666) is much more impressive and influential: it is a startlingly vivid, almost Kafkaesque portrayal of Bunyan's helplessness before the forces, divine and satanic, acting upon him and in him, of biblical metaphors made literal in his own experience, and of biblical typology continually enacted in his life.

In biography also, both in England and in America, historical facts were interpreted according to various paradigms. One of these—the subject as ethical type, a noteworthy example of virtue and vice—was provided by Plutarch's *Parallel Lives* (translated by Thomas North in 1579) and exemplified in Thomas Fuller's *The Holy State; the Profane State* (1642, 1648). Another was the saint's life, hagiography, informing the stories of persecution, witness, torture, and death in Foxe's *Book of Martyrs*, and most impressively, Izaak Walton's *Life of John Donne* (1640), portraying the poet as a latter-day St. Augustine. These paradigms fuse in Cotton Mather's biographies of New England worthies in the *Magnalia Christi Americana* (1702); for example, Governor John Winthrop is a parallel for Plutarch's great men and he is also (in typological terms) a New England Moses and Nehemiah. By an epic proposition echoing Herbert's *Church-Militant*, Mather at once claims epic status for his collection of lives and identifies it as a sequel to Foxe's

Book of Martyrs: "I WRITE the *Wonders* of the CHRISTIAN RELIGION, flying from the Depravations of *Europe,* to the *American Strand.*"

From the perspective of Restoration England with its new aesthetic precepts and genres (bawdy comedy, heroic drama, neoclassical satire, graceful lyrics, secular and realistic biography and autobiography, diaries of social manners), literature in the colonies must seem somewhat belated. But from a longer perspective, American literature assimilated and transformed its English heritage. If Edward Taylor found himself unable to use the conventions of biblical poetics for his religious lyric with the directness and skill of a Herbert, he nevertheless made that poetics a counterpoint to his own deliberately homely style, releasing a new vein of creativity. Milton was as central to American as to English writers of the eighteenth and nineteenth centuries: the American epic *Moby-Dick* owes as much to *Paradise Lost* as Wordsworth's *Prelude* does, and Americans could respond (as Englishmen sometimes could not) to Milton as rebel, polemicist, and Puritan. And while Bunyan's *Pilgrim's Progress* was popular with the new middle-class reading public in England, nurtured on the Bible and often nonconformist, it was even more popular in New England, where it could usually be found in even the most meager personal library. By 1830 there were some 50 editions of *Pilgrim's Progress* published in America, and more than 85 editions of Bunyan's works overall.

In the American colonial period the themes, the genres, and the biblical poetics promoted by the Reformation were nourished by the culture in ways no longer true in England. But they were not simply replicated when transplanted to the New World. Instead they suffered a sea change into something new and strange.

Barbara Kiefer Lewalski

The Puritan Vision of
the New World

Looking back in the autumn of 1692, the bicentennial of Columbus's transatlantic passage, to the "antiquities" of colonial New England, Cotton Mather recognized that those "twin migrations" were the key to a great design. To begin with, the voyage of 1492 was one of three shaping events of the modern age, all of which occurred in rapid succession at the turn of the sixteenth century: the "resurrection of literature," which had been made possible by the invention of the printing press (1456) and which in turn made the Bible accessible for the first time to the entire community of believers; the discovery of America, which opened a New World, hitherto shrouded in "heathen darkness," to the light of the Gospel; and the Protestant Reformation, which signaled the dawn of a new era "after the long night of Catholic persecution." And in turn all three beginnings—textual, geographical, and spiritual—pointed forward to something grander still: the imminent renovation of all things in "a new heavens and a new earth." A new beginning, then, and a newly urgent sense of an ending; and intermediate between these, at once linking them in time and confirming the overall design, like an apocalyptic play-within-a-play, was the story of New England. That, too, had its providential beginnings, culminating in 1630 when the fleet under the *Arbella* set sail for Massachusetts Bay. Mather describes the journey in language appropriate to its momentous spiritual-geographical-textual significance: "The *Church* of our Lord Jesus Christ, well compared unto a *Ship*, is now *victoriously* sailing round the Globe . . . [carrying] some thousands of *Reformers* into . . . an *American Desart*, on purpose that . . . He might there, *To* them first, and then *By* them, give a *Specimen* of many Good Things, which He would have His Churches elsewhere aspire and arise unto. . . . *Geography* must now find work for a *Christiano-graphy* in . . . the HISTORY OF A NEW-ENGLISH ISRAEL . . . to anticipate the state of the *New Jerusalem*."

By the 1690s all this was cultural commonplace. Mather's recognition is a summing up of local tradition, the re-cognition of a long-nurtured view of the colony's origin and mission. One reason for its persistence was the power of the vision itself. Another reason was that on some basic level it told the truth: not only the truth as rhetoric, the growth of New England as the Puritans perceived it, but historical truth, as the events bore out their perception, and specifically the three events of which Mather spoke. Of these, the invention of the printing press, along with the "resurrection of literature," is most obviously an example of the connection between rhetoric and fact. "Gutenberg's galaxy," as Marshall McLuhan termed it, marks a decisive turning point in Western culture. It has particular relevance to the New England Puritans because of their extraordinary reliance on texts. They were not only, like all Puritans, a self-declared people of the Book. They were a community that invented its identity *ex verbo*, by the word, and continued to assert that identity through the seventeenth century, expanding, modifying, and revising it in a procession of sermons, exhortations, and declarations, histories and hagiographies, covenants and controversies, statements and restatements of purpose—a stream of rhetorical self-definition unequaled by any other community of its kind (and proportionately, perhaps of any kind). The legacy of the Puritan vision, as the first-begotten corporate offspring of the printing press, was a rationale, a technique, and (in the material sense of the word) a *process* whereby a community could constitute itself by publication, declare itself a nation by verbal fiat, define its past, present, and future by proclamation, and justify its definition in histories like Mather's *Magnalia Christi Americana* (1693–1702) that in one form or another translated geography into Christiano-graphy.

The Puritan vision was also the offspring of the two other germinal events to which Mather referred: the discovery of America and the growth of Protestantism. It was an unlikely mixed marriage at the start. The discovery of America was preeminently a secular venture, a process of exploration and appropriation empowered by what scholars have come to call the forces of modernization: capitalist enterprise, state nationalism, the expansion of Western European forms of society and culture throughout the world. So considered, "America" meant the triumph of European imperialism. It was an act of naming that doubly certified the invaders' control of the continent: it meant control by brute power (land-grabbing, enslavement, genocide), and control by metaphor and trope. "America" denoted far more than the

Italian entrepreneur Amerigo Vespucci whose falsified sightings, once published, claimed the *terra incognita* for the Spanish throne. "America" entitled a carnival of European fantasies. It meant the fabled land of gold, the enchanted Isles of the West, springs of eternal youth, and "lubberlands" of ease and plenty. It verified theories of "natural man" and "the state of nature." It promised opportunities for realizing utopia, for unlimited riches and mass conversions, for the return to pastoral arcadia, for implementing schemes for moral and social perfection. Columbus thought that this new continent, providentially set between the cultured West and ancient East, had been the actual site of Eden. Later explorers and settlers, translating the myths of biblical geography into the landmarks of Renaissance geo-mythology, spoke of America as a second Eden, inhabited by pagan primitives (or perhaps the ten lost Hebrew tribes) awaiting the advent of civilization.

History and rhetoric: conquest by arms and conquest by the word—the "discovery of America" is the modern instance par excellence of how these two kinds of violence are entwined; how metaphor becomes fact, and fact, metaphor; how the realms of power and myth can be reciprocally sustaining; and how that reciprocity can encompass widely disparate outlooks. The same thing may be said about the rise of Protestantism, though from a wholly different perspective. Protestantism was from its origins a spiritual movement. It began as a protest against the worldliness of the Roman Catholic church—against the Catholic emphasis on temporal authority (as in the papacy), geographic locale (the Holy Roman Empire), and mercenary practices, from the selling of indulgences to political alliances. Above all, the early Reformers claimed, Christianity demanded an unmediated relation between the believer and Christ, the one true Mediator—which was to say, between the believer on the one hand, and on the other hand Christ as he manifested himself (through grace) in the believer's soul, and as he was manifest for all to see in the Bible (both the Old Testament, prophetically, and the New). *Sola fides* and *sola scriptura*, the primacy of personal faith and the supreme authority of Scripture: upon these twin principles Protestantism was established. But once established it, too, like every other venture in transcending human limitations, found itself entangled in the webs of history and rhetoric.

For in spite of their emphasis on the individual, the Protestants identified themselves, collectively, as a church or association of churches. And through their emphasis on the Bible, they identified themselves temporally, as part of the gradual progress of God's people, from the chosen Israelites to the New Christian Israel to the "latter-day" Israel that would usher in the millennium. The main text for that divine plan, the Book of Revelation, spoke in figures or types of an "elect nation" that in the "last days" would defeat "Antichrist," and so prepare the way for the Second Coming. That in any case was Martin Luther's view of Reformation history. For a time he identified Germany as the elect nation, and although he later abandoned that particular hope, he and the other founding Reformers retained the basic tenets of his historiography. Protestantism, they declared, was the true church; Catholicism, the Antichrist; and the conflict between these, the central action of this final period of time, attended by all the long-awaited "signs and wonders" (political and natural as well as ecclesiastical) of the apocalypse.

After its initial spiritual protest, then, Protestantism returned to history with a vengeance. But it was a special kind of history, sacred as distinct from secular. It was the story not of mankind but of God's "peculiar people," the covenanted saints who constituted the real subject of the unfolding drama of redemption. Basically, that is, Protestant rhetoric retained its traditional Christian roots—remained grounded in the belief that Christ's kingdom was not of this world—and so could break free, if necessary, of any local specificity. Still, the rhetoric of elect nationhood remained an intrinsic if not essential element of European Protestantism, and in the late sixteenth century it became entwined with the chauvinism of Elizabethan England.

By 1630 there were (broadly speaking) three groups of English Puritans. The largest, most eclectic group adopted the national or federal covenant as the basis for revolution and the establishment of a commonwealth under Oliver Cromwell (1649–60). The smallest of the three groups, the Separatists, took the opposite course. They purified their faith to the point where they refused allegiance to any institutional authority, including that of the English Protestant church, whether Anglican or Presbyterian. Instead, they hoped to join the progress of the "universal invisible church" in small congregations, modeled after the first Christian communities. Some remained in England, others fled persecution to Amsterdam, and then, in the case of the Plymouth Pilgrims, to the New World. The Massachusetts Bay immigrants of 1630 sought a "middle way" between these extremes. In doing so, they meant not to compromise but to perfect. They set out to combine what seemed to them in each case a partial gesture at reformation, in church and in state. Accordingly, they proclaimed their "purified church-state" a model for all Christendom. They were congregationalists in a "federal" or "national" covenant; a community of "visible saints" gathered for a venture in history; de facto Separatists who insisted not only on their vital connection to English Protestantism but (through this) on their central role in the worldwide struggle against Antichrist.

The Puritan immigrants do not seem to have had a distinct vision of the New World itself. Their focus was on the Reformation already under way: New England was to be a "model of Christian charity" for Protestants abroad, "a city set upon a hill" as a beacon to Europe. These phrases come from John Winthrop's justly famous lay sermon aboard the *Arbella* (1630), and when he added that "the eyes of all people are upon us" he was thinking mainly of the peoples of England, Germany, Holland, and other Protestant countries. The same may be said of virtually all other first-generation attempts at corporate self-definition: in promotional tracts (Edward Winslow), apologias for the church-state (Richard Mather), and evangelical treatises (John Norton), in sermons on "preparation" and conversion (Thomas Shepard, Thomas Hooker, John Eliot), in exegesis of scriptural prophecy (John Cotton, Ephraim Huit, Thomas Parker), in histories, "prognostics," and poetry (Edward Johnson, Thomas Aspinwall, Anne Bradstreet), and in polemics against sectarians at home (Anne Hutchinson, Roger Williams) and opponents abroad. In all cases, the Puritan vision was transatlantic, rather than American; it tended toward the universalist aspect of the immigrants' ambiguously universal-national outlook. By placing New England at the apex of history, the colonists were admitting their dependency on the Old World. So it was that after the failure of the English Puritan Commonwealth—and with it the waning of apocalyptic fervor throughout Protestant Europe—they found themselves trapped in an embarrassing paradox. They had declared themselves the advance guard of the Reformation, committed themselves to a worldwide mission, and invested their credentials of authority in scriptural prophecy. In 1660 the vision was intact, the community prospering, and their authority still dominant; but with Charles II now on the throne history seemed to have betrayed them. They were a beacon unheeded by the world, a city on a hill that no one noticed, or noticed only to scorn. In Perry Miller's words, they "were left alone with America."

Not entirely alone, however; for the rhetoric they carried with them offered a ready means of compensation. It allowed them by scriptural precedent and prophecy to *consecrate* their "outcast," "exiled," "wilderness condition." If they could not compel the Old World to yield to their vision, they could interpret the New in their own image. Having been left alone with America, the second- and third-generation Puritans felt free to incorporate Renaissance geo-mythology, as it suited their purposes, into their own vision. Explicitly and implicitly, they adapted the European images of

America (land of gold, second paradise, utopia, "primitivism" as moral regeneration) to fit the Protestant view of progress. And having thus taken possession of the rhetoric of America, they proceeded one crucial step further. Recasting the relational aspect of their vision, from a transatlantic to a transcontinental direction, they situated the Protestant apocalypse—or what amounted to the same thing, the Protestant road to the apocalypse—in the New World.

We can hardly overestimate the importance of that astonishing westward leap of the imagination. It was an achievement comparable in its way to the two great rhetorical shifts on which it built: the Hebrews' redefinition (by verbal fiat) of Canaan—territory, name, "antiquities," and all—as *their* country; and the imperialism of the *figura* or type, whereby the Church Fathers declared that the Old Testament, the story of Israel in its entirety, from Adam through Abraham and David to the Messiah, heir of David, really belonged to Christ. Upon these foundations the Puritans built the rhetorical structures that once and for all resolved the paradox of vanguard isolation. Confronted with the uncertain meaning of their locale, they discovered the New World in Scripture—not literally (like Columbus) as the lost Eden, but figurally (in the manner of the Church Fathers discovering Noah in Moses and both in Jesus) as the second paradise foreseen by all the prophets. New Canaan was not a metaphor for them, as it was for other colonists. It was the continent before them, reserved from eternity for the latter-day elect nation that would be gathered, as choice grain from the chaff of Europe/Babylon/Egypt, so that God might "*To* them first, and then *By* them, give a *Specimen* of many Good Things" to come. In short, forced back by history upon the resources of rhetoric, the second- and third-generation New Englanders united geography, textuality, and the spirit in what amounted to a new symbology, centered on the vision of America.

The decisive decades in this development were the 1660s and 1670s, when a series of crises threatened to put an end to the enterprise: the restoration of Charles, an apparent decline of religion among the immigrants' children, and the Indian nations' alliance to reclaim their land. The literary result of these "Wars of the Lord" (as the Puritans termed all these events) was the first native flowering of New England mythology, through the first English-language genre developed in the New World, the American Puritan jeremiad. The immigrants had imported that jeremiad as an immemorial mode of lament over the corrupt ways of the world. They transformed it for their own purposes into a vehicle of social continuity. Here as nowhere else, the clergy explained, God's afflictions were like a "refining fire," intended to purify and strengthen, or like the punishment meted out by a loving father, the token of His special care. "God's controversy with New England," wrote the poet Michael Wigglesworth in 1662, *ensured* the colony's success. In the words of the Reverend Arthur Dimmesdale in *The Scarlet Letter*, it signaled "a high and glorious destiny for this newly chosen people of the Lord."

Dimmesdale is an immigrant minister, of course, here delivering the election-day sermon of 1649. This was not inaccurate on Hawthorne's part: there were ample first-generation foreshadowings of the American Puritan jeremiad; but as a distinctive genre the American jeremiad was essentially a ritual of continuity through generational rededication. It required a set of *local* precedents, a pride of tribal heroes to whom the community could look back in reverence, and from whom, therefore, it could inherit its mission. The immigrants had imported the rhetoric; their children and grandchildren supplied the antiquities needed to make the rhetoric American. They enshrined their forebears in scriptural tropes and types, re-cognized them as giants of a golden age, like Virgil's legendary Trojans entering upon the future site of Rome. Winthrop could compare himself to Moses only by implication. The next generations could entitle him the New England Moses—or, as Cotton Mather did, "the American Nehemiah" (after the prophet who "rebuilt the walls of Jerusalem")—and John Cotton the American Abraham, Joshua, and John the Divine combined. These and other immigrant leaders they canonized as founding fathers, translated their Atlantic crossing as the Great Migration, antitype of the Hebrew exodus, and consecrated their church-state as a venture that, *because* it fulfilled Old World prophecy, was wholly an event of this New World. It led by promise from New England *then* to New England as it *would be*, when the *"American Desart"* would flower into the *"Theopolis Americana."* It was an errand into America, by the American Israel, for America first and then the world.

The Puritans made three lasting contributions to the American way. First, they invested America with a mythology of its own. Other colonists and explorers brought utopian dreams to the New World, but in doing so they claimed the land (New Spain, New France, Nova Scotia) as European Christians, by virtue of the superiority of Christian European culture. They justified their invasion of America through European concepts of progress. The Puritans denied the very fact of invasion by interpreting the newness of the New World as progress and then identifying *themselves* as the people peculiarly destined to bring that interpretation to life. "Other peoples," John Cotton pointed out in 1630, "have their land by providence; we have it by promise." The next generation of New Englanders drew out the full import of his distinction. They were not claiming America by conquest, they explained; they were reclaiming what by promise belonged to them, as the

Israelites had once reclaimed Canaan, or (in spiritual terms) as the church had reclaimed the name of Israel. By that literal-prophetic act the Puritans raised America into the realm of *figura*. It was *"pulchèrrima inter mulieres,* the youngest and loveliest of Christ's brides"—the last, best hope of mankind, whether mankind knew it or not.

That vision of the New World was the harvest of the Renaissance rhetoric of discovery. It marked the Puritans' first contribution to American identity; and the second was inextricably bound up with it. I refer to the corporate ideal through which they resolved the ambiguities of their national-universalist venture. For as their opponents were quick to point out, this self-proclaimed Protestant Israel was unprecedented either in secular or in sacred history. On the one hand, the Puritans' national covenant differed in its Protestant emphasis (personal, voluntarist, and spiritual) from the nationalism of any other community, past or present. On the other hand, New England's Protestantism differed in its tribal, worldly emphasis (its insistence on locale, local origins, and territorial errand) from any other Christian community. The first generation tried to solve the problem through a rhetorical balancing act: "visible saints," "nonseparating congregationalism," "church-state." The second and third generations extended these ambiguities into a new, federal model of community. For as Cotton Mather might have put it, the concept of national election was heaven-sent for the Massachusetts Bay colonists. They were a community in search of an identity commensurate with their New World mission, and when they adopted the federal covenant as their "peculiar" social bond, the concept of elect nation became incarnate in the first wholly Protestant contribution to modern nationalism, the American Israel.

Thus it was that the colony came to signify a "Way," an "errand *into* the [indefinite American] wilderness." "New England" denoted a people that was neither merely national nor purely religious, but that nonetheless combined both these terms in a voluntary contract that merged the principles of *sola fides* and *sola scriptura,* the inward spiritual road to salvation and the communal road in time and space to the millennium. To recognize the meaning of New England, as Samuel Danforth explained in his great election-day address of 1670, was to re-cognize the colony in terms of its cause and end, in relation to its New World antiquities and to the New World Jerusalem, of which those antiquities were a specimen. Inevitably, this was to realize (through an inward sight of sin) "how far we have fallen" and at the same time to realize (through prophetic insight) "how far we must rise to make ourselves worthy of our errand." And that double sense of shortcoming implied its own remedy: an *act* both personal and public, through which the inward turning to the spirit issued in a social commitment to progress.

Danforth's *Brief Recognition of New England's Errand into the Wilderness* is characteristic in this regard. It echoes and is echoed in turn by a long procession of exhortations—among others, those of John Higginson (1663), William Stoughton (1669), Uriah Oakes (1673), Increase Mather (1674), William Adams (1679), Samuel Torrey (1683), John Whiting (1686), and James Allen (1689). These addresses constitute a triumph of the colonial Puritan imagination, and to some extent they persisted in their own right, as a literary genre, through intertextual connections from one ritual occasion to the next—on fast and thanksgiving days, days of humiliation, election days, and days of covenant-renewal. But above all they persisted for functional reasons, as an organic expression of the community. They were the *cultural* issue of a venture dedicated to the proposition that prophecy is history antedated, and history, postdated prophecy. They represented a community in crisis and therefore using crisis as a strategy of social revitalization; a plantation in peril and therefore drawing strength from adversity, transition, and flux; a company-in-covenant deprived by history of their identity and therefore using their self-declared newness to create a vision of America that re-cognized history at large (including that of the Old World) as hinging on their failure or success.

The legacy of this ritual mode may be traced through virtually every major event in the culture, from the Great Awakening through the Revolution and the westward movement to the Civil War, and from that "Armageddon of the Republic" to the Cold War and the Star Wars of *our* latter days. At every point, the rituals of generational rededication build on the distance between fact and promise; at every point they interpret that distance in terms of "errand" or its various equivalents ("manifest destiny," "continuing revolution," "new frontiers"); and at every point the errand is defined as the special obligation of the "Israel of our time," federally covenanted as "the nation of futurity" to be "the heir of the ages" and "the haven for God's outcasts and exiles"—"a new breed of humans called an American," destined "to begin the world over again" and "to build a land here that will be for all mankind a shining city on a hill."

These phrases come from a variety of Americans, as distant in time from each other, and as different in mind and imagination, as John Adams, Herman Melville, and Ronald Reagan. My purpose in running their words together is not to blur the differences, but, on the contrary, to highlight the disparate uses to which the Puritan vision lent itself. In particular, I want to call attention in this regard to our literary tradition: the internalized, adversarial, visionary "America" that inspired Emerson and his heirs; "the only true America," as Thoreau called it, which our major authors have recurrently drawn upon (or withdrawn into) as an alternative to the dominant American Way. That alternative America is the third aspect I referred to of the Puritan legacy, and it has its roots in the last phase of the New England Puritan vision. By 1693, when Cotton Mather started on his *Magnalia Christi Americana*, the church-state was defunct, and in his view New England had tragically abandoned its calling. The *Magnalia* self-consciously affirms the vision *in spite of* social continuities; it re-cognizes the entire errand, from its antiquities in the Great Migration to its fulfillment in the millennium, *as rhetoric.* "I write the wonders of the Christian religion, flying from the depravations of Europe to the American strand": with this double allusion to what he considered the main epics of classical and of Reformation history, Virgil's *Aeneid*, the myth of Rome's founding, and John Foxe's *Book of Martyrs*, the founding myth of England's national election, Mather began his would-be greater New World epic; and then he added, a little later in the General Introduction: "But whether *New-England* may *Live* any where else or no, it must *Live* in our *History!*"

This poignant-defiant transvaluation of fact into trope may be seen as the logical end of the Puritan vision. The second-generation colonists had turned to rhetoric to compensate for the betrayal of Europe. Mather took their strategy one step further: he transformed the rhetoric into compensation for the betrayal of history. For him, too, "New England" was a conjunction of geography, Scripture, and the spirit; he too created his symbology out of the rhetoric of discovery, the authority of the word, and the primacy of personal faith. But his aim in all this was not to clothe local history in myth. It was to preserve the myth from the course of history. This was the aim, too, of many of his later works as well as the works of other Old Guard visionaries—for example, Joshua Scottow (1694), Nicholas Noyes (1698), and Joseph Morgan (1715)—all of which might have been titled, like Samuel Sewall's tract of 1697, *Phaenomena quaedam Apocalyptica; or, A Description of the New Heavens as It Makes to Those Who Stand Upon the New Earth.* This anachronistic procession of cloud-capped Americas, passing largely unheeded into Yankee New England, would seem to be an apt *finale* to the apocalyptic play-within-a-play of "the history of New English Israel." "Elect nation," "New World," "*the* wilderness," "New Canaan," "latter-day Israel"—all the foundations of the New England Way were figures of speech. Conceived in rhetoric, they sprang to life for a season—a nation born *ex verbo* in a day—and then returned in due time to the realm of rhetoric.

There is a satisfying sense of closure in this view, and a certain poetic justice as well. But it happens to be historically inaccurate. The fact is that the Puritan vision survived the demise of the church-state. Like Hawthorne's anachronistic Grey Champion, it returned as an agent of social cohesion at every stage of cultural transition—including, ironically, the transition from Puritan colony to Yankee province. The fact is, too, that New England retained its mythic status as the origin of American identity (long after the region had lost its national importance), just as the telos it claimed to prefigure remained in one form or another (and quintessentially in scriptural form) inherent in the American dream. And the fact is, finally, that the strategy of Mather's *Magnalia*, his determination to make "history" of *his* Theopolis Americana—to bring interpretation to "life," whether it lived historically anywhere else or not—became a ritual mode of our literary tradition. Intrinsic to this process of ritual re-cognition, from the Romantic period onward, was the spiritual use of geography as *American* nature, the geographic specificity of consciousness as *American* self-realization, and the sustained use of Scripture as pre-text of *America*'s promise. That symbology our classic writers never disavowed. However universalist their outlook, however fixed they were on transcendence and the self, they invested the meaning of those concepts in the same federal vision. In their optative moods, they spoke as unacknowledged representatives of America. In their despairing moods they interpreted the betrayal of the vision as the betrayal of all human aspirations—inverted millennium into doomsday, and mankind's best hope into its *last*.

Looking back now to the antiquities of "New England"—re-cognizing these through the interpretative modes of our time (our suspicion of language, our disagreements about the meaning of the dream, and our tendency to replace Puritan providence with a metaphysics of material causation)—it seems clear that in part the vision persisted because it facilitated the development of a new way of life, the nascent capitalist modes that Christopher Hill has shown to have been dominant in seventeenth-century English Puritanism, and that applied *in extremis* to the society established by the Massachusetts Bay Company, Incorporated. The literary legacy is more problematic. The New World vision that the Puritans bequeathed became in our major writers variously a symbolic battleground, an ideal to which they could aspire *because* it could never be realized in fact, and an alternative *cultural* authority through which they could denounce (or even renounce) the United States. But here, too, rhetoric and history are inextricable. The vision of New England was the child of Protestantism, Renaissance exploration, and the printing press. But "America," as the single most potent cultural symbol of the modern world, and also (in its various re-cognizable forms) as the symbolic center of our literary tradition, was the discovery of Puritan New England.

Sacvan Bercovitch

II. The Prose and Poetry of Colonial America

History and Chronicle

The writing and rewriting of history are continuing human activities, since how a writer thinks about the past is largely determined by his needs and those of his contemporaries. For this reason, among others, the reading of historical accounts by early Americans provides great insight into the past—both the events that the historian thinks of himself as describing and the attitudes and values of the historian, who is himself a historical figure. The historical moment of the writer is thus quite as important as the times he ventures to describe. Americans are blessed by having a large number of historical works from the seventeenth and eighteenth centuries. At least a few of them, such as those by William Bradford and Cotton Mather, can be set alongside the writings of America's greatest historians, such as Francis Parkman.

Captain John Smith lived for two and a half years at Jamestown, the first permanent English colony in America, and he contributed heavily to the colony's survival. After returning to England in 1609 as a result of being incapacitated by injury, he continued his interest in America by writing, while he eagerly sought to return, and in 1614 he explored the New England coast. Of Smith's nine works, the best known is *The Generall Historie of Virginia, New-England, and the Summer Isles* (Bermuda), which appeared in 1624. Its original appearance was as a handsome 260-page folio, with four folding maps, commendatory verses, several pictures of Indians, and an engraving of that famous event, Pocahontas's rescue of Smith when he was about to be slain by Powhatan's men. (Smith's story of the rescue is given less than a sentence in the *Historie*.)

Smith's *Historie* is a compilation of rewritten versions of several of his earlier works and the writings of others. Book II is derived from Smith's valuable "Description of Virginia," published in 1612 as part of *A Map of*

Virginia, and Book VI is an updated version of Smith's *Description of New England* (1616), based on his 1614 exploration. In Books III and IV, on Virginia, Smith acted as a historian as well as an editor. What Smith wrote was heavily colored by events of 1622, when Indians attacked and killed 350 colonists. Smith wanted his readers to know that he had a clear record of being able to cope with the Native Americans and that he had understanding, even respect, for them. To him they were strong, agile, hardy; they knew their land, knew what places were "most frequented with deer, beasts, fish, fowl, roots, and berries." He had tried to explain "how those strange miracles of misery [the massacre] might have beene prevented, . . . but few would believe me till now too deerly they have paid for it."

Smith had another role to play, that of propagandist for colonization of both Virginia and New England. His words had results, for both the Pilgrims of Plymouth and the Puritans of Massachusetts Bay knew his *Description of New England*. Smith himself reports that the Pilgrims declined his services because they judged "my books and my maps . . . much better cheap than myself." Smith saw the New World as a place to get ahead. "I am not so simple [as] to think," he wrote, "that ever any other motive than wealth will ever erect there a commonwealth."

Smith's writings provide vivid pictures of Europeans trying to make a place for themselves in a land far from home. But his most compelling pictures are of himself. Recent scholarship has done much to vindicate his accounts of his life after many years during which his reputation suffered from the aspersions of Henry Adams and others because he told stories of Hungarian adventures and being rescued by Pocahontas. In Smith's pages one meets the prototype of the American hero. Burdened by being almost anonymously named, this son of a Lincolnshire yeoman farmer made a place for himself in the American imagination by his own stories of himself. Individualist, dreamer, but a practical person too, Smith thought of himself when he urged his readers to imitate the "brave spirits that advanced themselves from poor soldiers to great captains, their posterity to great lords, and their king to be one of the great potentates on earth, and the fruits of their labors his greatest glory, power and renown."

Smith's egotism contrasts sharply with the attitude of the author of the one widely acknowledged masterpiece of seventeenth-century American literature written in English. *Of Plimmoth Plantation* is the masterful account by William Bradford of the separatist colony, the second permanent English settlement in America after Jamestown. Governor of Plymouth and so a maker as well as a writer of history, he had been since 1606 a member of the religious group that had founded the colony. He described the history of his group as one of constant struggle with the Devil and judged the best instrument in the struggle to be the church, a gathering of "the Lords free people, joyned . . . [by a covenant of the Lord] into a church estate, in the fellowship of the gospell, to walke in all his wayes, made known, or to be made known unto them, according to their best endeavours, whatsoever it should cost them, the Lord assisting them."

Bradford composed his history at two different times. He began in 1630, a decade after he and his fellows had arrived on the Massachusetts coast, a place Bradford repeatedly called "this wilderness." His occasion may have been the arrival, not very far to the north, of the much larger group under John Winthrop. This first part of his story takes Bradford only to the moment when the settlers "begane to erect the first house for commone use to receive them and their goods." He makes the achievement the result of heroic faith and of the triumph of God's providence. His audience, the children of the colony's founders, should know with "what difficulties their fathers wrastled in going through these things in their first beginnings."

Just before 1646, when Bradford began the second book, striking signs suggested that the colony was losing its identity. Wickedness had broken forth, even a case of bestiality; Elder William Brewster, one of the colony's spiritual leaders, had died; and many members of the Plymouth church had moved fifty miles away to Nauset on the outer part of Cape Cod. Bradford now wrote the story of the years after 1620 as an effort to determine what had gone wrong. It was not the Devil but the double-dealing of the agents and London financiers that the Pilgrims then had to deal with. In contrast to the deceitfulness that he sees everywhere, Bradford writes with simplicity and clarity, never overly confident of his own ability to understand exactly what has happened. In his modest third-person history, his own achievements—those of the man he refers to as "the Governor"—pass unnoticed.

In a memorable episode Bradford describes the nearby settlement at Mount Wollaston, later called Merrymount. There Thomas Morton "became lord of misrule, and maintained (as it were) a schoole of Athisme." The depths of the Merrymounters' depravity were shown by the setting up of a maypole, "as if they had anew revived & celebrated the feasts of the Roman Goddes Flora, or the beastly practieses of the madd Bacchinalians." Morton himself supplied a countering account of the colony in his 1637 publication *New English Canaan*. He found the Indians "more full of humanity" than the nearby Christians. The contrast between Bradford's and Morton's accounts has engaged many American writers, notably Nathaniel Hawthorne in "The Maypole of Merrymount." (Hawthorne did not read Bradford's own account, since that history was not published until 1856, but he had access to other works for which Bradford's manuscript served as a source.)

Bradford did not end his history; he simply stopped writing because, apparently, he could not find meaning any longer in the history he was setting forth. He could not see God's hand at work. His is finally not a success story but one of disillusionment; Bradford could only call up nostalgia for comfort. He could read the words he had written in 1630: "May not & ought not the children of these fathers [the colony's founders] rightly say: *Our fathers were Englishmen which came over this great ocean, and were ready to perish in this wilderness; but they cried unto the Lord; and he heard their voyce, and looked on their adversitie.*" A wise, thoughtful, pious man, Bradford was profoundly engaged in his task of writing the history of his own time. Since he was governor, his work is authoritative, and since he cared deeply about Plymouth, he was an ideal historian.

Unfortunately, the Massachusetts Bay Colony did not have a historian of the excellence of Bradford, but its leading governor, John Winthrop, kept a highly valuable journal that he called a "History of N. England." A mine of information, it quite lacks the integrity of Bradford's history, since Winthrop did not write retrospectively. The journal begins with a day-by-day account of the sea voyage to America, but thereafter Winthrop usually focused on three or four events each month. During twelve of the nineteen years he kept the journal (1630–49), Winthrop served as governor. He was simply too busy to write a reflective history.

Like Bradford, Winthrop refers to himself in the third person, for he intended his manuscript to be read as a record of the colony's history, an official history of his governorship and magistrateship. Indeed, it has been suggested that he took as a model the historical books of the Old Testament, such as Exodus and Judges. Like them, Winthrop's story was intended to be an account of God's chosen people, of backsliding and God's wrath in the promised land. In a matter-of-fact style, Winthrop never tired of recording human depravity and of the necessity of punishing those who had broken God's laws.

Winthrop's journal, like Bradford's history, was not published till long after his death. At the end of Winthrop's life, another Massachusetts man was writing *A History of New-England*, and this work, the first full-scale history of New England, appeared in 1654. Best known by its running title, *Wonder-working Providence of Sions Saviour in New-England*, it was published as one of the defenses of the "New England Way"—the close cooperation of church and state—being mounted in the 1640s and early 1650s in response to criticisms from English presbyterians and others. (Nathaniel Ward's *The Simple Cobler of Aggawam* [1647] is another aspect of the defense.) Since Edward Johnson envisioned the events of Massachusetts history as part of God's grand providential design, his reading of history thus constitutes his response. To him New England is "the place where the Lord will create a new Heaven, and a new Earth," the fulfillment of scriptural prophecy. In short, Johnson mythicizes New England's history. His account constantly echoes the Bible to show the parallels between the experience of the American Puritans and that of the Old Testament Israelites. "As the Lord surrounded his chosen Israel with dangers deepe to make his miraculous deliverance famous throughout, and to the end of the World, so here behold the Lord Christ, having egged a small handful of his people forth in a forlorne Wildernesse, stripping them naked from all humane helps."

The writing of history continued to be a major New England preoccupation. Several books are accounts of the colonists' conflicts with the Indians, such as Increase Mather's *A Brief History of the Warr with the Indians* (1676) and his *A Relation of the Troubles Which Have Hapned in New-England, by Reason of the Indians There* (1677), and William Hubbard's popular *Narrative of the Troubles with the Indians* (1677). Here the Indian wars are presented as battles between Christianity and the Devil. The Indian leader Philip resembles "a Salvage and wild Beast."

The most ambitious history written in early New England is Cotton Mather's gigantic *Magnalia Christi Americana* (1702). (A literal translation would be *The Great American Works of Christ*.) Mather had laid plans for the book as early as 1693, and it included seventeen of his earlier publications. This great work of a Boston clergyman whose grandfathers had been founders of the colony is complex in its intentions and a worthy precursor of *Moby-Dick* in its style. Its contents provide almost an encyclopedia of early New England.

Mather had three distinct purposes in composing his big book. He wished to glorify New England's achievements, denounce backsliders of the second and third New England generations, and demonstrate New England's fidelity to Old England. He unified the book by his style, an elevated one, often witty and heavily spiced with quotations in the learned tongues. Mather's book deals with everything, or nearly everything, that had happened in New England, though most readers do not find it easy to uncover what they might be looking for. There are a great many biographies, notable ones of William Bradford, John Winthrop, and Sir William Phips, a recent governor. One book is devoted to Harvard, another to the results of the synods that had determined church policy. One entire book is given over to miracles, providences, sea deliverances, wonders of the invisible world, and an account of the missionary work among the Indians.

For many years Cotton Mather was the whipping boy of Puritanism, and the *Magnalia* because of its size has been ridiculed as a suitable indication of the egotism of the author of over 450 separate publications. Recently Mather has been treated with much greater respect, and his *Magnalia* is now recognized as a work of serious importance. It is an epic, after the model of Virgil. At the end of the Puritan era, the Boston clergyman created a monument to his region's past, to the place he called "this remote and vast wilderness." If the New England he knew in quotidian existence did not meet his need, he would create one that did, imaginatively. He declared in his General Introduction, "But whether *New-England* may *Live* any where else or no, it must *Live* in our *History!*"

The controlling notion of the biographies in the *Magnalia* is the analogy of New England's leaders and those of the Old Testament, as well as those of ancient history and mythology. Winthrop is a Moses, a Nehemiah. Of William Phips, Mather writes, "So *obscure* was the *original* of that memorable person, whose *actions* I am going to relate, that I must, in a way of Writing, like that of *Plutarch*, prepare my Reader for the intended Relation, by first searching the Archives of Antiquity for a *Parallel*." He decorated his biographies with extended plays on his subjects' names. Samuel Whiting had so suffered in England as the victim of "ecclesiastical sharks" that "this Whiting" was driven "over the Atlantic sea unto the American strand." Urian Oakes's name is the occasion for a digression on oak trees and druids that ends with a picture of Harvard College as "a rendezvous of Happy Druids."

Mather also addressed his book to English readers whom he would persuade that New England's religion was mainstream Christianity—this at a time when the Massachusetts Bay Colony was trying to maintain some continuing political independence. Mather describes the Puritans of New England as "PROTESTANTS that highly honoured and affected The Church of ENGLAND, and humbly Petition to be a Part of it; But by the Mistake of a few powerful *Brethren*, driven to seek a place for the Exercise of the *Protestant Religion*, according to the Light of their consciences, in the Desarts of *America*." One can imagine both of Mather's grandfathers protesting this reduction of the meaning of their exile.

There was to be no wholly worthy successor to Mather among New England historians of the eighteenth century, though two men may be mentioned honorably. Another Boston minister, Thomas Prince, published *A Chronological History of New England in the Form of Annals*, the first part of which appeared in 1726. Its objectivity and its spare annalistic method are in sharp contrast to what one finds in the *Magnalia*. The last royal governor of the Massachusetts Bay, Thomas Hutchinson, published an ambitious and still valuable *History of the Colony* in three volumes beginning in 1764. Like Prince's, this work of Hutchinson is far more objective than the histories of Bradford, Johnson, or Mather, but it lacks the sense of the historical moment, of the historian himself being an actor on the stage of history, provided by the earlier works.

Few historians to the south of New England wrote works as highly regarded as the ones so far considered. Cadwallader Colden carefully documented the Iroquois in his *History of the Five Indian Nations* (1727), a work intended to show how useful the Indians could be in defending New York against French expansionism. John Lawson's *A New Voyage to Carolina* (1709) is a promotion tract that stresses the pleasures of life in the Sun Belt. It offers valuable descriptions of flora and fauna and a sympathetic description of the Indians, who were, according to Lawson, both healthier and happier in the days before the coming of the Europeans. *A True and Historical Narrative of the Colony of Georgia* (1741), by Patrick Tailfer and others, provides information about the colony but is chiefly a brilliant satirical attack on its founder, James Oglethorpe.

Virginia fared far better than its neighbors. In addition to Captain John Smith, that colony had two highly skilled writers of history, Robert Beverley and William Byrd II. Beverley's *The History and Present State of Virginia* (1705) is such a complex and subtle work that its virtues have only recently been recognized. Its epic contours, its complex and original style, its tragic recognition of the destruction of the Indians, its picture of the possibility of pastoral harmony—all add richness to Beverley's report of Virginia's settlement, original inhabitants, natural history, and lost opportunities. To Beverley, the New World is not a wilderness but a garden.

Beverley's "preface" declares, "I am an *Indian*, and don't pretend to be exact in my Language: But I hope the Plainness of my Dress, will give him [the reader] the kinder Impressions of my Honesty, which is what I pretend to." This attention-getting declaration suggests one of Beverley's major concerns in his book, the possibility of freedom in America, a possibility that Beverley identified with the Indians, whose happiness and innocence he associates with "their simple State of Nature." He thus links the attractions of the New World with its original inhabitants. This insight beautifully informs his whole book and makes it one of the major achievements of early American prose. To the Indians, "God is the giver of all good things, but they flow naturally and promiscuously from him; . . . they are showr'd down upon all Men indifferently without distinction; . . . God does not trouble himself, with the impertinent affairs of Men, nor is concern'd at what they do: but leaves them to make the most of their Free Will, and to secure as many as they can, of the good things that flow from him."

William Byrd of Westover was a historian of a different sort from the others discussed here, as the title of his work suggests: *The History of the Dividing Line betwixt Virginia and North Carolina, Run in the Year of Our Lord 1728.* Byrd himself had been one of the leaders of the surveying party, and his account—or rather accounts, for he also wrote *The Secret History of the Line*—was not published in his lifetime though clearly it is a careful work of art that Byrd prepared for publication. Significantly, it was published first in 1841 by William Ruffin, an advocate of Southern nationalism. Ruffin was to argue that there was an absolute bond between "the institution of negro slavery" and "the social and political existence of the south." Publication of Byrd's *History* was intended to demonstrate that the concept of "the south" was not new.

Since Byrd's world was one in which hierarchy and order, not freedom, were fundamental, the subject of his history is properly the making of a dividing line. His witty, urbane, ironic account tells how a portion of America was converted from a state of nature into real estate by means of a survey that made possible the legal ownership of property. The line divided the structured society of Virginia, with landed gentry such as Byrd at the top, from the "Lubberland" of North Carolina, whose inhabitants live disgustingly close to the state of nature. Byrd's own self-portrait is that of an intelligent, cultivated, learned gentleman whose superiority permits him to be tolerant. As an American who had lived in London for nearly twenty years, Byrd wanted to put the best face on his appearance in his native habitat.

Byrd's picture of the Indians of Virginia is much less sympathetic than Beverley's. He found their notion of an afterlife "a little gross and sensual, like Mahomet's Paradise. But how can it be otherwise in a people that are contented with nature as they find it?" He despised the Indians, who "chose to continue in their stupid idleness and to suffer all the inconveniences of dirt, cold, and want rather than disturb their heads with care or defile their hands with labor." His plan to reclaim them from barbarity was to advocate intermarriage.

Americans of the seventeenth and eighteenth centuries were busy with the difficult tasks of daily living far from centers of civilization. Yet a number of them, people of talent, were seriously dedicated to thinking about the historical significance of America. They judged the creation of a new society, the task in which they themselves were engaged, to be of the greatest historical importance, regardless of whether they admired or disliked the place where the new society was being created or the original inhabitants of this place. Such men as William Bradford, Cotton Mather, and Robert Beverley wrote with high seriousness about the America that was ours before we were the land's.

Everett Emerson

Sermons and Theological Writings

In the seventeenth century the sermon was an astonishingly popular form of literature. Between 1639 and 1729, 40 percent of all books published in America were sermons. Early sermonic "best-sellers" in England and America included *The Practice of Piety* by Lewis Bayley, which had seen twenty-five editions by 1630; *The Sincere Convert* by Thomas Shepard, issued twenty-two times between 1640 and 1692; and *The Poor Doubting Christian* of Thomas Hooker, printed seventeen times between 1629 and 1700. In the years of America's first colonization, the sermon was clearly in its heyday.

This emphasis on preaching was particularly characteristic of the Puritans. Since Puritanism was essentially a devotional movement intended to return the English church to a biblically sanctioned purity in its forms of worship, the central emphasis was on the Word—as recorded in Scripture and interpreted by preaching. The Bible was seen as the ultimate source of Truth, but the minister was "God's messenger," the "conduit" by means of which scriptural truth was channeled to the people, or, in another popular image, the "breasts" from which believers drew the milk of saving truth. The sermon was the chief means of grace, the *sine qua non* of the Puritan's religious life.

Perhaps the main reason for the form's vitality in Puritan circles was that the art of preaching was governed by the rule of clarity. As early as December 9, 1621, a layman at Plymouth Colony, Robert Cushman, urged that "to paint out the Gospell in plaine and flat English, amongst a company of plaine English-men (as we are) is the best and most profitable teaching." The clergy were in full agreement; even a man like Thomas Hooker, who had spent fourteen years at Cambridge, always made an effort "to accommodate myself (though it may be somewhat rudely) to the capacity of the meanest." Increase Mather said his father Richard Mather's exemplary "way of preaching was plain, aiming to shoot his Arrowes not over people's heads, but into their Hearts and Consciences." Preaching in this clear, "plain" manner in England made the most powerful preachers eminently understandable to the large groups of people who flocked to hear them. Their influence—social and political as well as religious—became so great that the government and the church hierarchy felt a need to silence numbers of them, forcing many to flee to "the American strand," where John Eliot was frequently moved to rejoice, "O blessed be God, that we have Christ so much and so well preached in poor New England."

But if this emphasis on clarity and directness had also amounted to dullness, the Puritan sermon could never have remained so popular. In fact, Puritan homiletics encouraged not only plainness but also invention. At the hands of an imaginative preacher who lived close to the daily experiences of his people's lives, the Puritan sermon had the potential for truly artistic achievement. By using a variety of "similitudes"—metaphors, extended similes, parallel constructions, analogies—the best of the preachers imbued the abstractions of theology and redemption theory with sensory reality, relying especially on reference to the daily chores of housekeeping and farming, the trades, travel, family ties, even bodily functions and sexual relations. These uses of the imagery of common experience were enhanced by borrowing literary and rhetorical tools from other forms of literature. Such resources as the "character," imagined dialogues, dramatic scenes, and even the adoption of a persona by the speaker often gave sermons the quality of drama or fictional narrative. Occasional aphorisms, puns, and slang helped keep the attention of the audience. Attentiveness was further encouraged by the ministers' occasionally instructing their congregations in the biblical typology of the good hearer, urging emulation of good listeners like Cornelius, Jonah, Samuel, and David. Preacher and listener alike needed to remember, as John Preston put it, that "Every sermon which is heard sets us nearer Heaven or Hell." The skillful use of these literary tools, enriched by typological exegesis that encouraged discovery of parallels not only between the Old and New Testaments but, by the seventeenth century, between biblical and contemporary experience, gave sermons a decided vitality.

Homiletic theory also prescribed a standard four-part organizational pattern. Each sermon began with the reading and explication of a biblical text. Then followed the statement of a "Doctrine," in effect a thesis statement, succeeded in turn by the "Reasons" and finally the "Uses" or "Applications." This pattern was based on the period's understanding of faculty psychology, which held that the mind or understanding must be persuaded before the "heart"—the will and emotions—could be reached. The first three portions of the sermon, therefore, all address primarily the rational understanding of the listener, while the final section, the Uses, demands a response of some kind from the will and affections. This intentional wedding of rhetorical and psychological theory made the sermon genre adaptable, on occasion, to secular as well as religious purposes. It also allowed for different emphases by different preachers, the intellectually inclined John Cotton, for instance, relishing textual exegesis while Hooker, in contrast, was famous for his Applications. Yet both evinced a lively awareness of the Bible's figurative language and its appeal to the intuitive and emotional capacities of their audiences.

Three kinds of guides served to instruct preachers in their creation of sermons. The most important were model sermons embedded in Scripture by such exemplary types of the powerful preacher as Jesus, David, Isaiah, Luke, Paul, and John the Baptist. A second set of models were those remembered teachers and colleagues who had not emigrated but whose preaching in England had been part of the formative experience of many in the first generation of New Englanders—men like William Perkins, Laurence Chaderton, Richard Sibbes, John Preston, John Dod, and John Rogers. Finally, several "textbooks" were available to the ministers, who were first exposed to some of them in college. Such texts were as ancient as Augustine, who had advocated plain speaking, as had another authority, John Calvin, who stressed the pastoral role, the comforting, nurturing side of the minister's approach to his listeners' needs. More recent English manuals included William Perkins's *The Arte of Prophesying* (1592 in Latin; 1607 in English) and *Of the Calling of the Ministerie* (1605), *The Faithfull Shepheard* (1607) by Richard Bernard, and a section of *The Marrow of Sacred Divinity* (1638) by William Ames. William Chappell's *The Preacher*, first published in Latin as *Methodus Concionandi* (1648), emphasized the need for logicality, showing how to apply to preaching the system of the very influential French logician of the previous century, Peter Ramus. Sermons on preaching also began to accumulate, including John Preston's *A Patterne of Wholesome Words* (1658), the third book of Thomas Hooker's *The Application of Redemption* (1656), Charles Chauncy's *Gods Mercie, Showed to His People* (1655), and, much later, the *Manuductio ad Ministerium* (1726) of Cotton Mather.

The same English spiritual and educational traditions that would so strongly influence the first century of life in New England contributed, even earlier, to the establishment of colonial society in the South. Scattered Puritan communities there, like the prominent one at Annapolis, were part of a broader mixture of religious points of view. Although almost no Southern colonial sermons from before the 1690s have survived, sermons were an important part of life in the seventeenth-century South. The very first colonial sermon published, in fact, was from Virginia. Alexander Whitaker, Cambridge-raised and -educated, sailed to Virginia in 1611. His *Good Newes from Virginia* (1613), actually a generic hybrid, originated as a sermon stressing the providential dealings of God with the Virginia colonists. In midcourse, however, the published version turns into a promotional tract urging the Virginia Company's financial support of the colony, and ends by praising Virginia's geography, flora, fauna, and natural resources.

Much later in the century Deuel Pead, an Anglican who later preached before the English King and Parliament, delivered a sermon at Jamestown in 1686, which has also survived. Though other scattered sermons exist by such voices as the Presbyterian Francis Makemie, the Anglican Thomas Bray, and the Quaker-turned-Anglican George Keith, the emergence of a significant body of sermon literature in the South was an eighteenth-century phenomenon, marked especially by the appearance of the collected sermons of James Blair, published in five volumes in 1722.

In New England, however, seventeenth-century sermons have survived in great abundance. There could be no better demonstration of the centrality of the sermon from the very beginning than the migratory experience of the first group of Massachusetts Bay colonists in 1630. The departure of the *Arbella* from the port of Southampton was marked by the preaching of the famous sermon, "God's Promise to His Plantations," by the revered John Cotton; her arrival in colonial Boston was immediately preceded by the preaching of the even more famous sermon, "A Modell of Christian Charity," by John Winthrop. Cotton, who was staying behind, reminded his listeners as they set out for a "land of promise" to remember their duty to God, who would remain their "Landlord," wherever they might reside. Winthrop admonished the people to ground their new lives on the "bond of love." Such love is expressed in a double covenant, one binding believer with believer, a church covenant among the colonists themselves, the other a covenant with God, a promise of fidelity to the Lord who had been so generous to them, "especially in these extraordinary times and occasions." Winthrop closes with his much-quoted admonition to "Consider that wee shall be as a Citty upon a Hill, the eies of all people are uppon us." For Winthrop, as for Cotton, secular history was serving a sacred cause in the Puritans' settlement of New England. In sounding the covenant motif, they were echoing a strain in English sermons like Hooker's Dedham sermon of

c. 1629, "The Faithful Covenanter" (published 1644), a strain that would be repeated many times in New England sermons like those in *The Gospel-Covenant* (1646) by Peter Bulkeley and various versions of Cotton's *Treatise of the Covenant of Grace* (1659). Covenant fidelity was the fundamental condition for New England's fulfillment of its divine destiny.

The primary subject and purpose of sermons by the earliest colonial ministers, once they were safely established in New England, was redemption. Their understanding of the *ordo salutis*, the "stages of grace," was an elaboration of the schema propounded by Calvin. Though some English Puritans who never emigrated were well known for their description of the stages of grace, it was the New Englanders who acquired particular notice for their detailed narrations of the saint's progress. William Chappell, concluding the first English-language edition of *The Preacher* (1656) with a topical list of exemplary sermonic works, listed under the heading "On True Conversion" eight works by the three most prolific ministers in New England: Thomas Shepard's *The Sound Believer* (1645) and *The Sincere Convert* (1646), John Cotton's *The Way of Life* (1641), and Thomas Hooker's *The Soules Preparation* (1632), *The Soules Humiliation* (1637), *The Soules Vocation* (1637), *The Soules Implantation* (1637), and *The Soules Exaltation* (1638), a series that Hooker revised and enlarged in New England as *The Application of Redemption* in two volumes (1656). What makes such sermons particularly impressive even today is the success with which they capture the reader's imagination. In following the hopeful soul through the successive stages of contrition, humiliation, vocation, justification, adoption, sanctification, and glorification, the ministers gave their "pilgrim's progress" an almost tangible reality, describing what was necessarily an invisible, spiritual experience as a real-life adventure story, an arduous progression over the rough terrain of temptation and self-doubt, through valleys of consternation and humiliation, across rivers of destruction. Hooker, for instance, drew on the experience of his Cambridge and Hartford congregations, living as they did on major rivers, to describe a moment early in the soul's journey, comparing the soul to "a poore travelling man" who "comes to the Ferry; he cryes to the other side; Have over, have over. . . . So, Christ is in heaven, but we are here on earth (as it were) on the other side of the river; the ordinances of God are but as so many Boats to carry us, and to land us at Heaven where our hopes are; and our hearts should be."

In the hands of the most skillful ministers, the soul's lifelong laborious journey became a kind of folktale, or saga, with the earnest listener who sat on the meetinghouse bench imaginatively playing the heroic role in the story. It was not a brief experience, but the occupation of a lifetime—in Cotton's words, "the way of life." The spiritual life as a pilgrimage is a biblical notion; Hebrews 11, for instance, recalls Abel, Abraham, Sarah, Isaac, Joseph, Moses, and other figures sojourning in "the land of promise." Well before John Bunyan, therefore, Puritan preachers were narrating their own version of the religious myth that *The Pilgrim's Progress* (1678) rendered permanent for all readers. This allegorical tenor of thought was, of course, grounded in the sensory world and thus was entirely apropos to a generation of "pilgrims" who knew not only the allegorical poetry of Edmund Spenser but also the actual dangers and challenges of a sea-crossing and a wilderness settlement. Once established, the allegorical imaginative mode remained important in America, appearing variously in later periods in *The History of the Kingdom of Basaruah* (1715) by Joseph Morgan, a Calvinist allegory depicting the fall of man, and in still later assorted manifestations in the works of Nathaniel Hawthorne, Emily Dickinson, T. S. Eliot, and many others.

Though the first generation is typically remembered for the words and deeds of such ministers as Cotton, Hooker, Shepard, Bulkeley, John Davenport, John Norton, and Richard Mather, another who deserves mention for his special use of the sermonic tradition is John Eliot. More than any other of his generation, Eliot enacted the principle expressed in nearly all the pre-migration departure literature that a major reason for colonization was to bring the gospel to the Native North Americans. This "apostle to the Indians" not only preached to them but also translated the Bible into Algonquian, the first complete Bible published in the colonies (New Testament, 1661; Old Testament, 1663). Though there is disagreement among scholars on both the motivation and the efficacy of the work of the Indian missionaries, Eliot's Bible, with his later *Indian Grammar Begun* (1666) and *Indian Primer* (1669), had genuine religious and linguistic value, while also unfortunately presuming to "civilize," even anglicize the Native Americans. Similarly important works were produced by Roger Williams (*A Key into the Language of America* [1643]) and Daniel Gookin, the humanitarian layman whose writings on the Native Americans, published long after his death (*Historical Collection of the Indians in New England* [1792] and *An Historical Account of the Doings and Sufferings of the Christian Indians* [1836]), are among the most important contemporary documents on their subject from any period.

Despite the heavy emphasis on sermons, first-generation New Englanders spent a great deal of effort on other kinds of writing as well, especially in refining the applications of their theology to fit the practical demands of colonial life. Three issues in particular had notable literary results: (1) the rise of dissident opinions, of which the earliest and most important was antinomianism, (2) the defense of congregational church polity, and (3) the question of toleration.

Numerous documents were produced during and following the period of the antinomian controversy (1636–38) ranging in form from personal letters to trial records. Though the controversy involved several issues, including the relationship between justification and sanctification, faith and works, and the role of women in the church, Cotton's Boston colleague John Wilson claimed the controversy was chiefly about the antinomians' "slightynge of Gods faythfull Ministers and contemninge and crying downe them as Nobodies." Thomas Weld put it more colorfully, saying the ministers had "dung cast on their faces." In a sermon-oriented, minister-revering culture like that in Massachusetts Bay, a perceived attack on "God's messengers" by radical spiritists inspired by Mrs. Anne Hutchinson, who affirmed "an immediate revelation" "by the voice of [God's] own spirit to my soul," questioned the need for ministers in the work of salvation. At her examination she cautioned the General Court as well, prophesying that "if you go on in this course . . . you will bring a curse upon you and your posterity, and the mouth of the Lord hath spoken it." Social order was further threatened when John Wheelwright preached a fast-day sermon implicitly charging the General Court with being unredeemed, while forthrightly acknowledging that his sermon would "cause a combustion in the Church and common wealth." This seditious sermon earned its author and his supporters banishment from the colony, a fate soon shared by Mrs. Hutchinson despite her quick-witted and spirited self-defense.

Other sectarian issues surfaced in the 1640s and 1650s, producing numerous works of controversy. Published volleys from radicals like Samuel Gorton, John Clarke, and William Pynchon were parried by establishment answers from Edward Winslow, Thomas Cobbett, and John Norton. Ultimately, minor official accommodations were made here and there in church practice and civil law in response to the vocal radicals, contributing to the evolution of the political and social as well as the literary shape of seventeenth-century New England.

News of the controversies—especially the antinomian—stirred up concern among many clergy in England about political, doctrinal, and ecclesiastical developments in New England. A major literary occupation of ministers in the 1640s, as a result, was producing treatises justifying "the New England Way" of church polity to the brethren in England. Whereas most of the published sermons by first-generation ministers had not been explicitly intended for the press by their authors but had been published, usually in London, from auditors' notes or from unrevised manuscripts, these controversial works were written to be published. The key texts by the New Englanders included Richard Mather's *Church-Government and Church-Covenant Discussed* (1643), Davenport's *Answer of the Elders . . . unto Nine Positions* (1643), Cotton's *The Keyes of the Kingdom of Heaven* (1644) and *The Way of the Churches of Christ in New-England* (1645), Hooker's *A Survey of the Summe of Church Discipline* (1648), and Norton's *Responsio ad totam quaestionum syllogen* (1648).

Though there was widespread agreement among New Englanders on church polity, the matter of toleration proved a more knotty issue. In 1647 Nathaniel Ward published *The Simple Cobler of Aggawam*, a work whose very lively but quirkish style owed literary debts to models in both Sir Thomas Browne and the Marprelate Tracts of 1588–90. Ward told the tolerationists where to get off: "all Familists, Antinomians, Anabaptists, and other Enthusiasts shall have free Liberty to keepe away from us." The colony generally agreed, viewing toleration of outspoken radicals, whether spiritists, separatists, Baptists, Quakers, or radical millenarians, as a sure route to disruption of the community's peace as well as the order of the church. The banished Roger Williams, however, residing in his Rhode Island sanctuary, wrote two major statements in favor of toleration: *The Bloudy Tenent of Persecution, for Cause of Conscience* (1644) and *The Bloody Tenent Yet More Bloody* (1652), the latter an answer to John Cotton's *The Bloudy Tenent, Washed and Made White in the Bloud of the Lamb* (1647). History eventually vindicated Williams's radical position on toleration, though the course of events ran equally rapidly against Williams's radicalism as a Seeker advocating a stringent exclusionism in church membership. By the close of the century, America was still a long way from democracy.

In the later decades of the century, sermons remained central to the community's experience, now more frequently voicing communal concerns as well as the traditional stress on personal salvation. This tendency was encouraged by the increasing frequency with which local or colonial governments declared public days of humiliation, fasting, thanksgiving, or election. The "occasional" sermons that were always preached on such days reflect an increasing concern for the collective spiritual health of New England, which the colonists had always viewed as the place where God's Kingdom could be most perfectly established, where scriptural prophecy and history would at last be harmonized. As the great founders began to die off around mid-century, to be replaced by men often not quite their equal in zeal or eloquence, a note of concern emerged in the sermons—a fear that God might, after all, be finding New England unworthy. This frame of mind was expressed both in the form of generational conflict and in the belief that the present outward signs of God's displeasure—dissension, worldliness among the young, drought, Indian war—were merely indications of God's loving attention, to be followed surely by the full rewards of continued fidelity. The form ideally suited to the expression of this dual vision was the jeremiad, a sermon form that served both to admonish and to encourage.

The second generation's tendency to accuse itself of declension is epitomized in a comment by William Stoughton in *New Englands True Interest* (1670): "We want many seasonings which our Fathers had, we are poor raw things; we want those eminent Conversions, those Schools of Experience, those Opportunities and Advantages of gaining knowledge, etc. which they had." As late as 1685 Increase Mather was still asserting that "the present Generation in New-England is lamentably degenerate" (*A Discourse Concerning the Danger of Apostacy*). Though the writers of these jeremiads tended to exaggerate their lack of merit, the process of public agonizing served to produce a rhetoric and a myth that once again interpreted New England's experience in the larger view of God's plan for his people.

The pure jeremiad had largely fallen into disuse in the early years of New England settlement because the conditions provoking its use—unhappiness with either the government's or the people's own waywardness, or both—were temporarily perceived as having been left behind in the "Babylon" from which the new "Israelites" had escaped to their land of Canaan. A land of milk and honey was not fertile soil for jeremiads. Jeremiads preached in New England before mid-century, like Thomas Shepard's *Wine for Gospel Wantons* of 1645, were just as apt to lament "the sad estate of the Lords people in England" as that of New Englanders. Samuel Danforth's *Brief Recognition of New England's Errand into the Wilderness* (1671), however, is typical of the second-generation jeremiad in that it attacks a present danger in New England by: (1) citing a scriptural example of normal conditions, (2) listing a series of condemnations of the community's waywardness and infidelity, (3) reminding the people of God's promises, and finally (4) assuring the listeners that God's blessings will soon return abundantly. The jeremiad always announces a major gap between actual and ideal conditions. In the 1670s, especially, preachers often prophesied as their fathers had done in England in the 1620s and 1630s (see Hooker's 1626 *The Churches Deliverances* [published 1638] or his 1631 *The Danger of Desertion* [published 1641]) pointing to signs of God's departure. Citing a popular image from

Revelation, Stoughton warned that "God threatens to *remove the Candlestick.*" Sermons of Thomas Shepard, Jr., Urian Oakes, Samuel Hooker, Jonathan Mitchel, and others, usually surviving as single, occasional publications, reinforce the notion of merited affliction. But, as Increase Mather said in his 1674 *The Day of Trouble Is Near*, "Though troubles come, why should we be dismayed thereat? . . . for a glorious issue and happy deliverance out of all these troubles, shall certainly arise to the Church in due time: Jer. 30: 7, 'It is even the time of Jacob's trouble, but he shall be saved out of it.' " The scriptural types of the present difficulties in New England thus inevitably point to the ultimate return to the full love and favor of God. This millennialist strain, stemming from the influential sermons of Joseph Mede in England in the 1620s and, in New England's first generation, sermons especially of John Cotton (notably his *Briefe Exposition on the Whole Book of Canticles* [1642]), preserved even in "the day of trouble" a heightened expectation of New England's importance in God's plan for his people.

Other changes were also at work in the later part of the century, which one historian describes as a time of "shattered synthesis." In the Connecticut Valley, Edward Taylor and Solomon Stoddard sharply disagreed on the administration of the sacrament of communion, with Taylor traditionally limiting the sacrament to converted members while Stoddard was using it as a *means* of conversion. Even in Boston, where in the 1670s Increase Mather was leading the chorus denigrating the present generation, Samuel Willard, the new minister of the Old South Church, whose *The Only Sure Way to Prevent Threatned Calamity* (1682) defends the need for jeremiads, soon began to preach in a more positive tone, emphasizing—as Taylor would do in his *Christographia* sermons in 1701–3—Christ's role as loving Son of God and redeemer of men's sins. Willard's magnum opus, *A Compleat Body of Divinity* (1726), a collection of 250 sermons on the Shorter Catechism of the Westminster Assembly, stresses the Pauline doctrine of assurance, which since the 1640s had become somewhat overshadowed by the people's contentions and self-accusations. *A Compleat Body* has been called "the declaration of independence of Willard's own risen generation," culminating the strain he had preached in earlier sermons with such telling titles as *The Duty of a People That Have Renewed Their Covenant* (1680) and *The Child's Portion; or, The Unseen Glory* (1681).

The tendency to see the New World as the stage for the enactment of divine plans encouraged a tendency to read experience symbolically. This inclination is fully reflected in one of the period's most interesting nonsermonic prose works, Increase Mather's *An Essay for the Recording of Illustrious*

Providences (1684). By concentrating on actual case histories of "sea-deliverances," "things preternatural," "apparitions," "earthquakes," etc., in New England, Mather draws out the allegorical/symbolic evidence of God's continuing concern for his people there. This work affirmed the seventeenth-century Puritans' reading of their covenant relationship with a God who is actively involved in their lives while also, as we see in retrospect, foreshadowing a later tendency of American writers to render experience symbolically.

A very different work, which argued even more directly for New England's special role in the fulfillment of prophecy, was the *Phaenomena quaedam Apocalyptica* (1697) by Judge Samuel Sewall. Here Sewall, relying on evidence from both biblical typology and contemporary history, while putting a new emphasis on the symbolic significance of America's natural beauties, reasserts the traditional belief in a coming millennium. Important in quite another way is Sewall's *The Selling of Joseph* (1700), the first antislavery tract published in America. Sewall employs sermonic techniques, including liberal quotation from Scripture, in his impassioned humanitarian plea. He was roundly criticized by certain contemporaries, however, including Cotton Mather and especially a Boston merchant, John Saffin, whose *Brief and Candid Answer to . . . The Selling of Joseph* (1701) met with broader public acceptance. Though Sewall's antislavery efforts were unsuccessful, his landmark essay had an influence on later, more successful attempts, including especially those of the Quakers in New Jersey and Pennsylvania where Anthony Benezet and John Woolman, among others, were powerful early voices for the abolitionist cause.

At the close of the seventeenth century, the old ways were being challenged in a time of increasing secularization and materialism, but the sermons and other writings of the first two or three generations had established a "language of Canaan" expressing perceptions of worldly as well as spiritual experience that would retain a strong influence on American writing for decades, even centuries more, as the early popular sermon rhetoric and symbology was repeatedly adapted to the changing needs and conditions of the evolving culture.

Sargent Bush, Jr.

Biography and Autobiography

The genres of biography and autobiography during the colonial period embrace all writing about the self-as-subject; each document exhibits the perspective of an author treating a separate subject, even when the subject is a persona of the self, while reflecting dominant ideological concerns that governed the writing of all kinds of personal narratives. It is important to understand that each biographer of the colonial period was less interested in fidelity to factual detail than in the more didactic emphasis of establishing his account in a religious or spiritual tradition. Although some life-writing was achieved in the Southern colonies, as the studies of Richard Beale Davis have shown, and while the *Secret Diary of William Byrd of Westover, 1709–1712* (1941) may be regarded as eminently representative of autobiography in early eighteenth-century America, the overwhelming literary output of Puritan New England during the seventeenth and eighteenth centuries, with its cohesive, didactic, and spiritual purpose, must form the core of any discussion about literary production during those formative years.

New England's spiritual and literary unity is the result of Puritan tribalism, as Cecelia Tichi has shown in her studies of the "Lord's Remembrancers," those historians and biographers who saw in the lives of New England's leaders spiritual parallels to biblical leaders. Similarly, the colonial historians paralleled early New England biographers by writing the life of a tribal group that was, like the individual's experience, guided by divine providence and expressed as a journey of Christian wayfarers from the earthly city of Babylon to the eternal and holy city upon a hill, Jerusalem. Literary precedents for this fusion of biographical and historical horizons include Plutarch's *Lives* and the Bible, and in their own time Puritan life-writers could turn to the example of John Bunyan, who spiritualized his own autobiographical account in *Grace Abounding* (1666). It is little wonder that at the end of the colonial era, the essayist Ralph Waldo Emerson would declare that "there is properly no history; only biography," and that Thomas Carlyle, whose English Calvinist background resembled Emerson's, would also assert that "history is the essence of innumerable biographies." For the colonial writer, biography and autobiography were specific genres in which a spiritual record of God's protective providence might be recorded for the reassurance of his contemporary saints and for the edification of posterity.

In colonial New England, biographical writing is best represented by Cotton Mather's *Magnalia Christi Americana* (1702), and the autobiography was wrought masterfully in Benjamin Franklin's *Autobiography*. Though Franklin's work is one of the best-known autobiographies produced in America, it is incomplete; the narrative concludes in 1759, while Franklin lived from 1706 to 1790. Its achievement lies more in its representative value as an image of the rising American than in its accurate portrayal of Franklin's life. Though written and circulated in various forms much earlier, Franklin's masterpiece was not available in English until 1818, not fully published until 1868, and has only recently been edited authoritatively, by J. A. Leo Lemay and Paul M. Zall (1981). As a secular example of the "spiritual" autobiography, it extends the tradition established by the Puritans and records for contemporary readers the achievements of a "sanctified" individual whose exemplary life would become a model for the "new man" in America, thus providing an appropriate response to Hector St. John de Crèvecoeur's intense question, "What is this American, this new man?" rhetorically asked in his *Letters from an American Farmer* (1782). Less heralded but equally important forms of autobiographical writing include the Indian captivity narratives and the *Personal Narrative* (1765) of Jonathan Edwards, which is a superb example of spiritual autobiography, as are some accounts of imported black slaves and indentured servants, whose perceptions of the colonial experience provide an excellent counterpoint to the assurances of divine guidance that pervade Puritan biographies and autobiographies. Mary Rowlandson and John Williams dominate the popular Indian captivity narrative literature, while Elizabeth Ashbridge relates not only her indentured immigration to America but also her conversion to the Quaker persuasion in *Some Account of the Fore-Part of the Life of Elizabeth Ashbridge . . . Wrote by Herself* (1774).

The slave narratives frequently provide vivid accounts of human suffering and hardship, while religiously motivated personal narratives such as Edwards's account or Thomas Shepard's *Autobiography* (first published 1832) describe more particularly the struggles of these writers to find a pattern of divine grace in their past experience. In one of the slave narratives, both Indian captivity and black slavery are ingeniously combined. In 1760, Briton Hammon wrote his autobiographical *A Narrative of the Uncommon Sufferings, and Surprizing Deliverance of Briton Hammon, a Negro Man . . . How He Was Cast Away in the Capes of Florida; the Horrid Cruelty and Inhuman Barbarity of the Indians in Murdering the Whole Ship's Crew, and the Manner of His Being Confined Four Years and Seven Months in a Close Dungeon, and the Remarkable Manner in Which He Met with His Good Old Master in London, and Returned to New-England, a Passenger, in the Same Ship.* All the essential elements of spiritual autobiography are here: the first-person account of a deliverance from earthly peril by divine providence; the journey motif, suggesting a circular migration governed by God, who moves the action forward toward a predetermined end known only to him; and the essential, innate depravity of mankind, except for those saintly few who are especially designated to carry forward the course of divine history. Slave narratives sometimes combined elements of the Puritan spiritual accounts to give the reader another parallel to the biblical Israelites, those persecuted wayfarers who could only look forward to a better life in the next world. Ironically, in Hammon's case deliverance means reenslavement; his "liberation" comes when he is reunited with his original master.

For all the Puritan life-writers, the experience of eminent figures became the most prominent means of articulating New England's place in providential history. Both biography and autobiography were governed by this overriding concern, and the objectives of the historians as well as the biographers remained constant: to prove that New England and her people stood in a particular relation to God. Cotton Mather's conviction that history should be the biography of saints derived from a commonly shared belief that scriptural history itself worked in this manner, and that the Bible was a compilation of achievements among God's chosen people, so that their story was best told through biographical and autobiographical narratives. For Mather, the models of Scripture and classical literature sufficiently justified this method of composing contemporary biography. In the pagan writers of Greece and Rome he found analogies to the providentially guided writers of biblical history. In the *Magnalia Christi Americana* itself, Mather stated clearly the relationship between classical and Christian examples, particularly in *Pietas in Patriam, the Life of His Excellency Sir William Phips* (1697), first published separately but reprinted in the *Magnalia* in 1702. Mather wrote: "So *obscure* was the *original* of that memorable person, whose *actions* I am going to relate, that I must, in a way of writing, like that of *Plutarch,* prepare my reader for the intended relation, by first searching the *archives* of antiquity for a *parallel*." Those "archives" of antiquity included the Old Testament, Greek and Roman mythology, and a number of figures from ancient and classical history. Cotton Mather's work was extensive; but he spoke for all Puritan historians, biographers, and autobiographers when he showed how the genres composed by these writers were inextricably bound to each other. All narrative accounts were a means of understanding the divine will acted out in human time, and historical writing was thus filled with biographical and autobiographical narratives, exemplary accounts of eminent lives that would thus become sources for comprehending God's teleological plan for New England.

Not only did the Puritan writers regard the history of New England to be evidence of God's continuing providence as a leader for his New Chosen; they also attempted to use scriptural parallels metaphorically to establish specific correspondences between Old Israel and New England. It was the calling or duty of the Puritan saint to establish a life and a society of lives that could make a progressive advance in the eternal struggle between the good and evil forces that governed the universe, and if contemporary events could be identified by reading ancient and biblical narratives to discover biographical parallels, it could also be asserted that New England was moving forward toward a preordained end, known only to God. In this context, the New World, and New England in particular, were repeated historical episodes in the larger framework of the History of Redemption. The Puritan writer's foremost objective was to show that New England was under the continuous guidance of providence, and the purpose of the parallels with pagan figures, or the analogies they drew between contemporary leaders and Old Testament leaders (both William Bradford and John Winthrop were called "Moses" in their life-accounts in Mather's *Magnalia*), was primarily illustrative. Cotton Mather, for example, did not regard Greek or Roman history to have been guided by providence, from which both old Israel and New England had received direction. Mather's adaptation of Plutarch's reading of history by way of biographical accounts of the lives of prominent individuals and special events was, moreover, not unique; but a sense of biographical composition as an important aspect in the process of historical redemption gave the life-writers of seventeenth-century New England a specific role in shaping the inspired accounts of God's revealed historical purpose.

Similarly, American biographical writing originated in primitive attempts to cite the example of a person's life, usually that of a hero admired by the

Puritan tribe, as an *exemplum* for didactic and instructive purposes, a use that the Judeo-Christian tradition has found most convenient in its development of the lives of biblical heroes and saints who faithfully followed the commandments of God or who imitated the life of Christ. This kind of *hagiography*, or the use of biographical and autobiographical writing to reinforce a tradition of belief that existed prior to the subject's life and informed the actual composition of the narrative, was a commonplace in colonial America, where the entire enterprise of expansion was conceived as an extensive analogy to the movement of the Israelites from Egypt (England), across the wilderness (the Atlantic Ocean), into the promised land (the New Canaan). Thus the "New English Israel" was led on its spiritual "errand into the wilderness" by such leaders as John Winthrop, John Cotton, and William Bradford, whose own *Of Plimmoth Plantation* (composed 1630–51) contains an extensive "Life of William Brewster" as the entry for *Anno.* 1643. Similarly, the numerous lives contained in Mather's exhaustive *Magnalia Christi Americana* would have a lasting influence on the composition of biography and autobiography in colonial America. Mather was careful to articulate a methodology for his own life-writing in a doctrinal statement that is representative of much colonial biography and autobiography. In *Parentator* (1724), the life of his father, Increase, Cotton Mather stated: "I know not how the *Pen* of an *Historian* can better be Employ'd than in *Reporting* the *Vertuous* tempers and Actions of Men that have therein *shown forth the Vertues of our Blessed Redeemer*, and been the *Epistles* of Christ unto the Rest of Mankind."

This didactic approach to the recording of a life quickly found a place in Puritan New England, so that life-writing became the examination of a saint's life, in which the formulaic accounts tended to emphasize the process of conversion at an early stage in the life of the subject. The earliest examples of this process, as we know from Patricia Caldwell's study, *The Puritan Conversion Narrative* (1983), are the autobiographical confessions of faith given in the Massachusetts Bay Colony's first decades as a qualification for church membership and transcribed by such pastors as Thomas Shepard and Michael Wigglesworth. Thus the sanctified life which followed and the good works that pervaded the later portions of the narrative would have a clear foundation in the spiritual experience of conversion and transformation. These formulas govern Increase Mather's biography of *his* father, founder of the Mather dynasty and patriarch of the Massachusetts Bay Colony: *The Life and Death of That Reverend Man of God, Mr. Richard Mather* (1670). The habit of mind that led Increase Mather to compose his own *Autobiography* (first published in 1962) is represented in Cotton Mather's statement of purpose quoted here, and this principle governed the uniformly crafted sixty-odd lives that appear in his own *Magnalia Christi Americana.*

Not all of New England's life-writing conforms to this paradigm. In his *Apologia* (published 1964), Robert Keayne used the occasion of his *Last Will and Testament* in 1653 to construct an anguished defense of himself against charges of usury and excessive profit-taking. But these complex beliefs governed the composition of many diaries and journals, conceived with the intention of discovering patterns in the events of one's life which would provide some indication that one had been elected for salvation. Moreover, in the writing of a chronicle of one's life-experience, the diarist would find some clues as to the final outcome of his earthly trial. Although subjective thoughts were poured into the pages of diaries and journals, a sound theological practice governed this kind of autobiographical writing. All human activity was considered to be directed by God through providence, and, following the Calvinist idea of predestination and election, the Puritans shared the common view that some were fortunate members of God's elect or chosen, but that they were forever uncertain of their actual roles in this grand design. Even so, it was also felt that God would provide signs along the way to indicate those whom he had elected to save and those who were not filled with grace. These signs were usually manifested in everyday life, and "special providences" or particular examples of God's unusual concern for the individual needs of his saints were considered excellent indications of the subject's election for salvation. Thus for the individual, *diaries* chronicled progress toward salvation, and these personal accounts paralleled historical writings on God's chosen New English Israel.

This early, purely functional approach to the Puritan diary gradually underwent sophistication and refinement, so that by the mid-seventeenth century, diaries and some types of journals were part of the larger literature of self-examination, as Daniel Shea has shown in his *Spiritual Autobiography in Early America* (1968). The result was a literary and theological art form among New England Puritans that surpassed their efforts at biography, most of which had resulted in eulogizing hagiography. Despite the fragmentary nature of diaries like Michael Wigglesworth's, which covers only the years 1653 to 1657, they suggest forcibly the writer's experience of the doctrine he professes, as when Wigglesworth complains, "My goodness (if any there be) is like the morning dew that is dried up." This is no less true of Edward Taylor's "Spiritual Relation" or Anne Bradstreet's "To My Dear Children," two important autobiographical testimonies by the two major colonial American poets, who reverse the formula of the diaries by compressing their spiritual expression into utterances of a single occasion. Probably the most prominent examples are the Puritan diaries of Cotton Mather and Samuel Sewall, or the *Journal* of the Quaker John Woolman; and Southern writers are represented by William Byrd's "secret diaries" for 1709–12 and 1739–41, as well as his *London Diary* (published 1958) for 1717–21.

These longer diaries are expansive, comprehensive for the years they purport to cover, and sufficiently full of examples to allow the modern reader an opportunity to assess each author as a richly, if not fully developed, personality. In more public journals like John Winthrop's account of his early years in office as governor of the Massachusetts Bay Colony, or in more deliberately didactic historical narratives like William Bradford's *Of Plimmoth Plantation* (not published until 1856), the focus is less on the individual than it is on the community of *gathered individuals*, whose special purpose overshadows the entire narrative composition. Samuel Sewall was able to make his diary a compelling image of both his secular and his sacred experience, and his narrative is endowed with the unique qualities of his anguished personality. Sewall had been a judge at the Salem witchcraft trials in 1692, a role that he later regretted and an event whose cruel actions he repented publicly. His *Diary* (1673–1729; first published 1878–82) carries an account of this transformation, including his courageous act in asking his pastor to read a public apology for his participation at Salem.

Because of their consistent focus on God's interactions with the personal life of his elected saint, the diary accounts of Sewall and Mather differ greatly from the record kept by William Byrd II, a Virginia planter and entrepreneur and a very privileged young man who was given an English education in London schools, where he was essentially trained in earthly matters rather than spiritual exercises. Byrd's *Diary* is thus more worldly than contemporary Puritan accounts, and it represents the most highly cultivated metropolitan social groups of his day. For example, while the Puritans in England castigated the drama and theater as evil and profane, Byrd knew in London the Restoration playwrights William Wycherley and William Congreve. Thus his account is more a literal record of daily experience than it is a document designed to exemplify the sanctified or providentially guided life of a saint. We are told of his daily habits, repeatedly, and how "I did my dance," a form of physical, not spiritual, exercise. Though he occasionally uses the metaphorical constructions of New England's journey-like "errand into the wilderness," and though he once wrote that "we are very happy in our Canaans if we could but forget the onions and fleshpots of Egypt," Byrd is a Southern Anglican, essentially concerned with commercial trade with Britain, and his beloved Westover was a neoclassical earthly paradise, a pastoral plantation that in no way resembles the Garden of Eden sought by the Puritans. Byrd's conceptual framework for the *Diary* is a long way from the "howling wilderness" in which the New England Puritans found themselves abandoned by all except God. Rather, Byrd's wilderness is a positive recapitulation of the gardens of the Golden Age of Greece and Rome, establishing Byrd as a citizen of the earthly rather than the heavenly kingdom. The title itself suggests Byrd's preoccupation with his own world rather than an expression of communal values: *The Secret Diary of William Byrd of Westover*. Other Southern diaries include those of the tobacco-planter Colonel Landon Carter for the years 1752–78 (published 1965) and the *Diary of a Journey to England and Scotland, 1753–1755* (published 1967) by Samuel Davies, the Virginia preacher and poet. However, the Byrd diary stands out as the best available example of life-writing in the Southern colonies.

Diary writing and the keeping of journals gradually became shaped into the self-conscious patterns of life-narrative in which one would select and edit the events of his life in order to tell a story from a particular, and often biased, point of view. During the eighteenth century, in America and in England, life-writing was much more an expression of human personality, even in its relation to God, than it was a recording of divine intervention in human affairs. The publication of the Earl of Shaftesbury's *Characteristicks of Men, Manners, Opinions, Times* (1711) suggests a preoccupation with personality types, and in the art of biographical and autobiographical composition, sophisticated forms evolved that were concerned with the subject's human personality, even when the subject was oneself and the writing required a distancing from the subject or persona. In the seventeenth century and especially in Puritan New England, there was always a tension between the author's attempt to render a figure representative of the values and attitudes of the culture and his disclosure of more human and natural perspectives. For example, in Thomas Shepard's *Autobiography* (edited and published by Michael McGiffert as *God's Plot: The Autobiography of Thomas Shepard* [1973]) there is a human personality in focus as well as a pervasive concern with the spiritual frame of reference in which the personality develops. Shepard's account is narrative, rather than a chronicle like Byrd's *Diary*, and because of the shift toward life-reckoning rather than life-chronicling it provides an excellent example of the shaped life-narrative with a theocentric focus. Though the Shepard *Autobiography* is a fine example of personality development, it also contains a record of the providential guidance of an early New England community in its encounter with Indian antagonists, so that the personality is often subordinated to the spiritual power pervading its experience. Similarly, Mather's *Diary*, first published as a separate document in 1911–12, resulted from the author's reshaping of multiple diaries into a self-consciously self-styled autobiographical image. Sometimes the fine line between life-chronicling and life-reckoning blurs. When Cotton Mather wished to present his wayward son, Increase, with a more coherently edifying autobiographical personality than that contained in his diaries, he simply transposed many of his original diary entries while fashioning new summations for his autobiography, *Paterna* (published 1976).

Early personal narratives and journals, including the *Journal of John Woolman* (1774) and the *Personal Narrative* of Jonathan Edwards, adopted a confessional mode that attracted the reader into the subject's interior self, inviting a private and personal glimpse at the most intimate moments of conversion and psychological development. Woolman, a Quaker who lived in New Jersey, incorporates incidents that intersect interestingly with slave narratives, as he was once clerk in a law firm that handled transactions among slave owners and was routinely asked to prepare bills of sale for human property. In a moving section of the narrative, he relates how these duties anguished his soul and how, after reflection and prayer, he relinquished his post as assistant to a lawyer rather than prepare another indenture for servitude or slave transaction. Like Herman Melville's Bartleby, Woolman would quietly "prefer not to," and he clearly shows the internal process by which he reasoned his change of vocation. These sections of the Woolman journal are important because they show the immediate and human drama of the slave trade in ways that would not appear in print for another fifty years, when abolitionists began to write sympathetically of the injustices perpetrated by human slavery in the United States. Woolman writes movingly and inspirationally in his account of this conversion, part of a much larger frame of reference, the gradual opening of his soul to communications from God that come through human experience. His life-story exhibits a directness, sincerity, and honesty or simplicity also found in another eighteenth-century confessional narrative, the *Personal Narrative* of Jonathan Edwards. The Edwards account is more formulaic and ritualistic than Woolman's confession; Edwards also recalls the moment of conversion, but he is careful to link every significant natural experience with appropriate passages from Scripture, suggesting that revelation was finally a mixture of the understanding made available to man through God's word and the direct impressions made on the senses by the natural environment. Edwards like Woolman *sensed* the natural world around him; that is, he reached an understanding of the divine through his perception of the natural, and his narrative is a record of these experiences linked to a central perception of God as revealed in Scripture. Unpublished in his own life-time, Edwards's narrative could not have the impact of his spiritual por-traits of converts touched by the Great Awakening, in *A Faithful Narrative of the Surprising Work of God* (1737), or his *Life of David Brainerd* (1749), the presentation of a saintly but melancholy Indian missionary, often reprinted in the decades to follow.

Autobiographical accounts echoing Edwards and Woolman which are special variants of the providential history theme are the slave narratives and the Indian captivity narratives. The most popular and influential cap-tivity narratives were those of Mary Rowlandson, *The Soveraignty and Good-ness of God . . .* (1682), and the Reverend John Williams of Deerfield, *The Redeemed Captive, Returning unto Zion* (1707). Each account establishes the parallel between the Egyptian captivity of the Israelites and the experience of New England communities in Indian captivity; in each, also, the notion that God's providential guidance brought the survivors back to the civilized and Christian course of history provides a structural model that reflects the wanderings of ancient Israel prior to entry into Canaan. Neither account is unique; there were literally hundreds of Indian captivity narratives in co-lonial New England, and the genre continued to be popular down into the late nineteenth century, with the publication of such fantasy-tales as *Nathan Todd; or, The Fate of the Sioux Captive* (1860). The captivity narratives of Rowlandson and Williams, by contrast, are popular accounts precisely be-cause they are credible and detailed, and thus provided readers with a spir-itual framework within which they could comprehend the harsh reality of the frontier experience.

As formal expressions of autobiographical writing in early America, the captivity narratives constitute a generic subgroup in which the reader not only finds the predictable sense of God's providential guidance in the safe delivery of his elected saints from the pagan Indians but is also witness to the autobiographer's immersion in a Native American culture quite foreign to his own. This curious mixture of Puritan religious perspective and an-thropological investigation results in a document that is at once a theological account of providence acting in specific human events and a stimulating intrusion into the culture of the original inhabitants of North America. Thus the captivity narrative, as an example of autobiographical writing, is less spiritually didactic than the biographies in Cotton Mather's *Magnalia*, and the resulting accounts are not always the severe condemnations of heathen Indians often found in the Puritan histories, like Increase Mather's *A Rela-tion of the Troubles Which Have Hapned in New-England, by Reason of the Indians There* (1677). In Mary Rowlandson's narrative, for example, the expression "captivity narrative" is not entirely accurate, as her account presents a succession of "removes," or a progression of withdrawals from her civilized, Christian existence into a close association with the Indian experience. The literal narrative suggests an immediate and personal account of trial and deliverance and it develops a predetermined episode of providential guidance and movement. Rowlandson was held a relatively brief period—eleven weeks—and she wrote her account soon after her return, so that the narrative is intimate rather than abstract and theological, and her account provides the modern reader a very human perspective on the captivity experience. The "voice" through which she narrates seems to answer those many questions about primitive Indian culture that the reader is curious to ask: what were the rituals of eating? in what way did marriage function within the tribal community? how was survival possible under the extreme conditions presented by captivity in the New World, where survival was already a challenge?

John Williams's captivity narrative covers a much longer period—two years—and is more historically abstract, its title providing the reader with a general frame of reference for understanding its purpose and design. Like the larger-than-life heroes of the mythological American West, or the invincible crime fighters of modern television serials, John Williams presents his experience in the persona of a contemporary saint who is redeemed from the beginning of the narrative. On the literal level, there are many significant differences between the Rowlandson and Williams narratives; for example, Rowlandson is not carried off into Canada and her narrative therefore focuses more on the everyday experience of her life with the Indians, while Williams continuously perceives his deliverance as part of the larger linear drama of divine predestination and salvation. Rowlandson's "removals" took place during King Philip's War in 1676; Williams's story is part of the larger context of the French and Indian Wars, thus obviously introducing a more complex cast of characters than the shorter Rowlandson piece. *The Redeemed Captive* also differs from Rowlandson's account because it is focused on the minister's confrontation with Catholicism. Thus Roman Catholicism is added to Indian paganism as an opposing force for the persecuted Puritan pilgrims. For Williams, the dramatic experience of imminent terror is transformed into a larger-than-life account of the eternal contest between good and evil, in this case, the Protestant and Catholic churches in North America.

Captivity narratives inevitably were structured as journeys, and indeed the journey provides the metaphorical framework for these two narratives. However, in Williams's account, the journey is carried out by actors in a larger divine drama, while in Rowlandson's saga the perspective is that of a spiritual heroine who develops a social and cultural perspective as well as the view of a Christian wayfarer. Williams provides more of a continuous movement toward a preordained end, not unlike the biographies and histories in this regard; Rowlandson uses the dramatic structure of a captivity narrative so that she may illustrate the divine drama, yet she also attains insights into Indian culture. The Indians for Williams are opponents who contend for the soul of the wayfaring captive in his journey from earth to heaven, but the Catholic French are also enemies who must be resisted or overcome. Williams is clearly assured of salvation and deliverance, so that his narrative reflects more the process of a metaphorical journey than it relates the intimate details of a potentially dangerous and terminal episode. Mary Rowlandson, by contrast, seems less concerned with the outcome, and while her general design is didactic, intended to teach the value of faith and commitment to God's plan for his chosen people, it is a narrative more filled with suspense and human drama.

Other individual life-accounts provided, as did Mary Rowlandson's, a window into particular kinds of human experience and an intimate sense of another culture than that of the Protestant or Puritan audience. Examples of this type of autobiographical writing are the slave narratives, all clear forerunners of *The Life and Times of Frederick Douglass* (1845), a nineteenth-century account of the transformed life of a liberated former slave, whose life-experience closely parallels those earlier accounts of Puritans whose conversions gave their lives a "before" and "after" structure. The best-known and most powerful of the early slave narratives include the aforementioned *A Narrative of the Uncommon Sufferings, and Surprizing Deliverance of Briton Hammon, a Negro Man* (1760); John Marrant, *A Narrative of the Lord's Wonderful Dealings with John Marrant, a Black, Now Going to Preach the Gospel in Nova Scotia, Born in New York, in North America* (1785); Venture Smith, *A Narrative of the Life and Adventures of Venture, a Native of Africa* (1798); and the masterpiece of early slave narratives, Olaudah Equiano's *The Interesting Narrative of the Life of Olaudah Equiano, or Gustavus Vassa, the African, Written by Himself* (1789). The slave narratives, like the Indian captivity narratives, contain formulaic accounts of brutality and deliverance, and the pervasive metaphor for all life-writing of this kind was the teleological journey, that purposeful trek from birth to death that is punctuated by episodes and digressions. However, it is ultimately redeemed spiritually and artistically by the guidance of providence and the earthly agents of God.

The language of the Equiano narrative is erudite and polished, obviously the work of an educated, even learned writer. Like many of the Puritan narratives it resembles, it commences with an apology, which contains many apostrophes to God, but which in this instance reveals much about the personality of its author. Very self-conscious about thrusting his life-story onto a reading public, Equiano argues that "it is not a little hazardous in a private and obscure individual, and a stranger, too, thus to solicit the indulgent attention of the public, especially when I own I offer here the history of neither a saint, a hero, nor a tyrant." This modesty pervades the narrative, but Equiano, like Phillis Wheatley in her poetry, ascribes the good things of his life to the operations of divine providence. "I might say that my sufferings were great; but when I compare my lot with that of most of my countrymen, I regard myself, as a particular favorite of heaven, and acknowledge the mercies of providence in every occurrence of my life." Objectively regarding the literary importance of his own life-story, Equiano concludes that "I am not so foolishly vain as to expect from it either immortality or literary reputation. If it affords any satisfaction to my numerous friends, at whose request it has been written, or in the smallest degree promotes the interests of humanity, the ends for which it was undertaken will be fully attained, and every wish of my heart gratified." What follows is a detailed description of a life in Africa, from which Equiano was abducted into slavery in America, together with an account of that abduction and its consequences.

While the Equiano narrative is obviously a very early example of slave narrative, it is closely paralleled by the gripping account of Elizabeth Ashbridge in *Some Account of the Fore-Part of the Life of Elizabeth Ashbridge*. This story of an indentured servant-girl details the agonies suffered by those immigrating to America during the eighteenth century, through a cruel system of indentured servitude almost as barbaric as the slave trade. Moreover, Ashbridge converts to Quakerism, and the double focus of the narrative makes it exemplary among immigration tales and conversion experiences. Elizabeth Ashbridge exhibits neither the spiritual assurances of the Puritan life-writers, nor does her account possess the stylistic formality of Equiano's narrative. The simplicity of her chronicle obviously reflects the simplicity of her experience and the pathetic consequences of her vulnerable posture in the colonial world, as time and time again she is victimized, only to rise again out of the nadir of her experience to encounter, repeatedly, the "real world." It is a fascinating account, the life of a young girl whose idealistic migration to America is a *Bildungsroman* of youthful growth and mature experience, and whose relation of that experience leaves the reader stirred by the very innocence of her numerous encounters with the betraying, unscrupulous, even malicious external world. "Now those to whom I had been instrumental to preserve life proved treacherous to me," she writes, disillusioned that after revealing a potential mutiny, she is nevertheless sold into indentured servitude by the ship's captain. "I was a stranger in a strange land," she writes.

Modern literary histories of America do not contain much information about Equiano and Elizabeth Ashbridge, even though their accounts represent the experience of ancestors of a numerical majority of United States citizens today. And only in recent anthologies of American literature have students been treated to snippets of *The Journal of Madame Knight*, a modestly popular autobiographical work in its day. Though Sarah Kemble Knight was a schoolteacher who may have taught Cotton Mather and Benjamin Franklin in her Boston school, she is noted for the record she made of a harsh overland journey from Boston to New Haven and back in the years 1704 and 1705. Through this first-person narrative we are given a close look at travel experience in colonial America, as this was a very hazardous journey through hostile Indian territory (the Deerfield Massacre and John Williams's captivity occurred in February 1704) and a traveler would not undertake such a dangerous journey casually in the early eighteenth century. Madame Knight's account is an entertaining narrative, filled with examples and illuminating details, chronicling her journey in a literal rather than spiritually metaphorical or didactic style.

It is clear that most life-writers of early America, and the historians of the early American experience, had a specific purpose when they put pen to paper, and that neither slave narratives, immigration experiences, nor difficult overland journeys of women travelers were sufficient to compete with the saints' lives produced by the New England Puritan writers during the seventeenth and early eighteenth centuries. But as the literary tastes of colonial America became increasingly secular, tales of worldly success like Franklin's *Autobiography* gained popularity and evolved as representatives of popular attitudes and values. Even here, the form remained consistent with the saint's life that had for so long captured the imagination of the colonial reading public. Several examples will illustrate this point.

While topographical studies such as *The Travels of William Bartram* (1791) were published because they provided pseudoscientific information about the natural territories being settled during the first two centuries of colonial expansion, human and dramatic accounts like those of Equiano and Ashbridge provided not only a social perspective narrated by a member of a minority group whose experience was firsthand but also a well-articulated example of the providential deliverance. Nevertheless, because the colonial settler sought the comfort that could be provided only by the sanction of group consciousness and tribal values, and because the American Revolution caused an immediate need for heroes who would be recognizable to the people of the new nation, Equiano and Ashbridge languished in obscurity while Parson Mason Weems, that astonishing raconteur, filled school and library shelves with a secular collection of saints' lives. Weems's biographies of George Washington (1800) and Benjamin Franklin (1815) contain much apocryphal information, like the story of George Washington and the cherry tree, a fictional device invented by Weems to adorn the character of this unassailable founding father, a man who owned slaves like Equiano. The hagiography of the late eighteenth and early nineteenth centuries was beginning to provide the new nation with a galaxy of heroes like Franklin, Jefferson, and Washington, associating these grand figures with classical heroes from antiquity. The United States was, after all, a neoclassical "republic," no longer a band of nomadic Israelites seeking the Promised Land. Not only did Thomas Jefferson author the famous *Notes on the State of Virginia* (1781); he also contributed to the numerous early national autobiographies, writing his own in 1821. America was in an optimistic mood, surging with expansion and potential, and she was in no frame of mind to sympathize with the sufferings of slaves and indentured servants when there were new heroes to emulate, new visions of the future promise of Manifest Destiny to embrace, and new frontiers to conquer just to the west of the Ohio River, a prospect captured in John Filson's fictional autobiography of Daniel Boone, in *The Discovery, Settlement, and Present State of Kentucke* (1784).

For the time, the autobiographies of Benjamin Franklin and Thomas Jefferson would provide the kind of life-writing that the new nation craved. Franklin's *Autobiography* resembles the personal narrative of Puritan writers in superficial ways, but Franklin's didactic purpose was to embrace, in a single life-chronicle, the values and attitudes of the people of these United States, embodying America in his own persona, like Walt Whitman's comprehensive "self." To achieve this ambitious goal, Franklin becomes not one persona but several, and the story of his evolution from youth to adult maturity is told as though he and America were growing up together, each learning from the other the moral lessons necessary to success in the richly endowed setting of the New World. In the context of the various pressures of early nationalism, the emergence of the new nation and the desperate need to identify America as somehow different from Mother England, and in view of the broad, secular vision embraced by Franklin's *Autobiography*, it is little wonder that the intensely personal accounts of Woolman, Edwards, Equiano, and Ashbridge would not be as widely received as Weems's chronicles of secular saints. But taken together, this valuable collection of early American biography and autobiography makes available distinct pictures of individual experience while providing a composite portrait of those early settlers who in their various idioms articulated their versions of personal experience and national purpose.

Mason I. Lowance, Jr.

The Poetry of Colonial America

The poetry of colonial America exhibits a rich variety in type and manner, a variety deriving in part from early and late influences: early influences include the Bible and the classics as well as the writings of Guillaume Du Bartas, Edmund Spenser, Sir Philip Sidney, Michael Drayton, Joshua Sylvester, Francis Quarles, George Herbert, and John Milton; late influences include the writings of Samuel Butler, John Dryden, and Alexander Pope. Sometimes, in both early and late colonial verse, these models are followed somewhat slavishly by the colonial poet, but not always; and whatever differences emerge are fascinating to consider. Often, too, the colonial poet, especially in New England, tends to subordinate art and artist to utilitarian design and communal identity, but sometimes a curious tension arises between cultural theological restraint and personal emotion. This tension is least evident in colonial public verse, which includes, as we shall see, translations of biblical and classical texts, elegies, satires, hortatory long narrative poems often tinged with the tradition of the jeremiad, and nature poetry. The tension between cultural limits and personal emotion most frequently emerges in colonial private verse, which includes personal poems of meditation, often incorporating emblem tradition.

At the forefront of popular public verse in the Puritan colonies was *The Whole Book of Psalms* (1640), commonly known as *The Bay Psalm Book*, which went through many editions and was revised in 1651 by Henry Dunster and Richard Lyon. A cooperative undertaking by such people as John Cutter, John Eliot, Richard Mather, Thomas Welde, and John Wilson, the first edition of *The Bay Psalm Book* represented an attempt to improve upon the Sternhold-Hopkins psalter popular among the Puritans while they resided in England. This revisionary attempt included the aim of translating literally the Hebrew text of the Psalms and of rendering this translation in English meter; accordingly, the Preface of *The Bay Psalm Book* announces,

If therefore the verses are not always so smooth and elegant as some may desire or expect; let them consider that God's Altar needs not our polishings: *Ex. 20.* for we have respected rather a plain translation, than to smooth our verses with the sweetness of any paraphrase. . . .

This undertaking resulted in verses with wrenched syntax and dissonant verbal combinations. The famous Twenty-third Psalm, for instance, begins:

The Lord to me a shepherd is,
  want therefore shall not I.
He in the folds of tender grass,
  doth cause me down to lie.

Nevertheless, musically and metrically *The Bay Psalm Book* is simpler and easier to sing than is the Henry Ainsworth psalter used by the Pilgrims and occasionally echoed in the Puritan Psalter.

Just as the translation of the Psalms was a major undertaking, so was the translation by George Sandys of a classical text, Ovid's *Metamorphoses* (1626), of which he had already translated five books before leaving England. Like the Puritans of the Northern colonies, Sandys in Virginia believed that the myths recorded in classical works revealed truth obliquely and that these myths could be readily reconciled to the truths of Scripture. Maintaining that poetry, even pagan verse, conducts divine truth to human minds, Sandys tried to make his translation of *Metamorphoses* reflect features of Ovid's rhetoric so that Sandys's English version, still well regarded today, would not interfere with the transmission of the underlying truths of the myths in Ovid's poem. In his aim for this fidelity in translation Sandys in effect did for a classical text what Richard Mather and others did for the biblical text of the Psalms.

Besides translation, another prevalent mode of public poetry in colonial America was the elegy. During the English Renaissance the term *elegy* referred to an occasional poem concerned either with death or, if it were more aligned to classical models, with a gravely reflective subject usually expressed in lines of dactylic hexameter alternating with lines of dactylic pentameter. In seventeenth-century English poetics the classical authority for the elegaic tradition was augmented by allusions to such scriptural models as the Psalms and the Lamentations of Jeremiah. Like their English originals, no more and no less, New England's elegies are didactic and communal in emphasis and exhibit a fascination with acrostics, poems in which the first or final letters of each line collectively spell the name of the deceased.

Such facts perplex efforts to detect any indigenous features of New England funeral elegies, which were printed on broadsides, attached to the hearse, and thrown into the grave, and which were not deliberately preserved before the appearance of Nathaniel Morton's *New Englands Memoriall* (1669). However, several of these elegies, particularly during the post-1660 period, highlight features of the genre (as practiced prior to the restoration of King Charles II in England) that emphasize a turning within upon the isolated colonial community as a whole, as a collective self, in which ministers represent the soul (reason and will) ideally guiding the New Israelites' society, or corporation (*corpus/body*). The practice of depicting society as a collective self evincing faculties equivalent to those of the human self does not occur in extant seventeenth-century English elegies. In a number of post-Restoration New England funeral elegies on ministers, however, the consoling communal frame (history and tradition) of the English variety of the genre collapses in upon itself (even as the Puritan saint was instructed to assail himself) to indict an intrinsically vulnerable and unstable collective identity.

This pattern is evident in Urian Oakes's *An Elegie upon . . . Thomas Shepard* (1677), an outstanding example of the Puritan funeral elegy. Oakes develops and finely tunes imagery depicting the deceased as the soul and the laity as the body of a communal collective self. Moreover, identifying with Shepard's role, Oakes presents himself as a soul-principle trying to resuscitate the communal body, the "lifeless Corporation" of Shepard's laity. Oakes's elegy fails to proffer any sense of consolation similar to that of contemporary English funeral elegies; his poem provides only unanswered questions:

> What! must we with our God, and Glory part?
> Lord is thy treaty with New-England come
> Thus to an end? And is War in thy Heart?

These questions replace the consolation provided by nature, society, and art in English elegies; and they direct the poem's audience to contemplate its communal failure to achieve an ideal collective self.

In other words, the late-century elegy finally emphasizes, not the deceased minister, but a text of self, where there exists, as it were, an internal elegy to be read within each person. For the dead need no such memorials; they are presumably among the living in heaven, whereas the bereaved, typically explains Samuel Torrey in "Upon the Death of Mr. William Tompson" (1666), have not been "By Death deliverd from [the] liveing grave" and are "the lively portrature of Death, a walking tomb, a living sepulcher." Similarly, a remarkable and somewhat cryptic untitled epitaph (1666) written by Benjamin Tompson again on the death of William Tompson, his father, transfers the burden of its message away from itself (as an imagistically ingenious text) to its audience: ministers who are implicitly instructed to read the hidden text in their own hearts concerning how well they have discharged their duty in instructing each of their parishioners in reading his or her elegiac text of self. Like other post-1660 examples, Tompson's elegy (one of more than twenty he wrote) eschews prideful selfhood as a lasting memorial; in its need to be completed in the self of each member of its audience, it is, as it were, consumed or funerated.

Puritan elegists would later speak in a more individual voice and would focus more often on women and children, but the dead seriousness of the genre, early or late, provoked irreverent satire. Antagonist Thomas Morton, for example, embedded in his attack on the Puritans in *New English Canaan* (1637) a mock elegy on an unsaintly camp follower:

Shee was too good for earth, too bad for heaven.
Why then for hell the match is somewhat even.

Morton's mock elegy is hardly Puritan in sentiment, nor were several seventeenth-century satirical ballads deriding the New Israelites. However, that some Puritans were not bereft of a satirical impulse is evident in occasional humorous verse, with practical lessons, in New England almanacs; in the prose and poetry in *The Simple Cobler of Aggawam in America* (1647), where Nathaniel Ward focuses on religious and political problems during the reign of Charles I; in several poems in *A Key into the Language of America* (1643), where Roger Williams reflects on the ways English civilization mirrors Native American barbarity; in the epic *New Englands Crisis* (1676), where Benjamin Tompson stresses the social ills underlying English attitudes toward Native Americans that led to King Philip's war; in occasional verse by Sarah Kemble Knight, who emphasizes such social problems as drunkenness; and in poetry by Boston merchant Joseph Green, who wittily criticized prominent figures of his day, the hymns of Mather Byles, and the religious frenzy of the Great Awakening, a time of rapid religious conversions in the colonies.

The Puritans did not particularly nurture satire, whereas in the Southern colonies it publicly flourished, especially in late seventeenth- and early eighteenth-century newspapers. Southern colonial satire is more secular than the relatively scarce Northern variety. Southern colonial elegies, too, rarely allude to the Bible and, infrequently grim, they often are mocking or ironic in attitude.

Southern colonial satiric verse manifests a considerable resemblance to its English sources. Much of it is derivative. Nevertheless, from the wit of these satiric works emerges a voice that might have helped early Southerners to deal with annoyances, inconveniences, and problems of colonial life. This voice, it might be plausibly argued, anticipates the quality of mind that would be evident in the leading national figures of the South during the Revolutionary years.

Southern colonists such as William Byrd II, who under the pseudonym "Mr. Burrard" published several poems in a miscellany, wrote short panegyric and satiric verse typical of the period. These latter works, often stressing unusual human characteristics or physical features, Byrd circulated among his friends and correspondents. Among the best of public satires produced in the colonial South are *The Sot-Weed Factor* (1708), *Sotweed Redivivus* (1730), and "The History of Colonel Nathaniel Bacon's Rebellion in Virginia" (in *The Maryland Muse* [1730]) by Ebenezer Cook (or Cooke). Set in Maryland, *The Sot-Weed Factor* (which apparently saw two revised editions) lampoons the naïveté of settlers who arrive in the New World with expectations nurtured by advertisement literature and promotional tracts written about early colonial America. Cook's work might in fact be a satire on satires on such tracts, for the narrator of the poem might be an Old World criminal and is certainly the subject of Cook's ridicule. The narrator of *The Sot-Weed Factor* learns quickly that America is hardly Edenic and America's economic resources hardly abundant or easy to obtain. Cook's satirical poem is replete with sexual nuance, misogynous portraits of women, references to New World animals distressing in the extreme, and the depiction of Maryland's barely civilized inhabitants as dangerous animal-like predators.

Cook's *The Sot-Weed Factor* is a long narrative poem, a generally less satiric variety of which was also popular in the South. But the distinctly nonsatiric long narrative poem especially thrived in the Northern colonies during the late seventeenth and early eighteenth centuries. Many of these long narrative poems are second- or third-generation jeremiads—that is, reprimands and forecasts of divine retribution upon New England for departing (like fallen Israel) from the divine mission articulated by first-generation Puritan ministers. William Bradford, for example, not only wrote a famous prose history of the Pilgrims but also composed at least seven poems that parallel his transformation of *Of Plimmoth Plantation* from a public record to a private journal and document his personal sense of the failure of the Pilgrim mission. This movement toward private concerns is completed in his last known poem, "Epitaphium Meum" (c. 1657), in which Bradford meditates on his own sorrowful life and disappointment.

Most of these jeremiads by Bradford and others leave no room for humor, satiric or otherwise, but Benjamin Tompson's *New Englands Crisis* is at once a hortatory and a mock-heroic epic giving an account of the war between the colonists and Native Americans led by the Wampanoag chief, King Philip. Humor also appears in *Gods Determinations Touching His Elect* (c. 1685, published 1939) by Edward Taylor, who also wrote a long narrative poem on the history of Christianity and various miscellaneous poems, including elegies as well as paraphrases of the Psalms. An especially ambitious undertaking, *Gods Determinations* is a long sequence of doctrinal poems written in a variety of verse forms. It exhibits the possible influence of morality plays, Theocritan song contests, Ignatian meditative practices, and homiletic tradition. Apparently directed at halfway members of his church (that is, people who were baptized but not yet admitted to the Lord's Supper), *Gods Determinations* domesticates transcendent truths in terms of the mundane present, emphasizes experience over dogma, and concludes with an image of the saints as church members on their way to heaven. *Gods Determinations* demonstrates Taylor's humor, his capacity for conveying dramatic effects (particularly in his characterization of Satan), his relish for paradox, and his ability to organize and unify a long work; but it is not so successful as the best poems of his *Preparatory Meditations* (1682–1725, published 1939, 1960).

The most popular long narrative poems in colonial New England were by Michael Wigglesworth. "God's Controversy with New England" (1662), warning the Puritans not to fall away from their mission, and *Meat Out of the Eater* (1670), arguing that affections experienced by sinners can be turned by God into heavenly profit, were both much read. But by far the most popular of Wigglesworth's writings was *The Day of Doom* (1662), the first edition (1,800 copies) of which was completely sold in the first year of its publication and ten editions of which appeared by 1777. Based on a dream Wigglesworth had in 1653 and written while he was unable to preach regularly in Malden because of a lingering illness, *The Day of Doom* was memorized by generations of Puritan children. Replete with biblical allusions and written in ballad meter, the nearly nine hundred lines of *The Day of Doom* present a harrowing account of judgment day, the onset of which (in the opening stanzas of the poem) is very sudden:

> For at midnight brake forth a Light,
>   which turned the night to day,
> And speedily an hideous cry
>   did all the world dismay.

Wigglesworth's readers doubtless recalled the frequent occasions when they had been told in sermons that one's life on earth is equivalent to sleep-walking in darkness, unless one is suddenly awakened by the burning light of divine grace. The scene of the ultimate midnight conflagration in *The Day of Doom* makes this metaphorical notion literal by suggesting that on the last day the entire world will undergo an experience similar to conversion, when even reprobates will see (as if their "carnal reason" were awakened and transformed into "right reason") and will ache in their hearts (as if their heart, or will, were graciously "turned"); but it is now too late for them to be contrite ("they see't with tears") and to benefit from this new awareness and feeling: "Their galled hearts with pois'ned darts but now too late repenting."

Any feeling of security in his audience was also disturbed by Wigglesworth's use of words and images that had a well-established context in his time but that in *The Day of Doom* evince a fresh nuance—a little surprise of new insight nudging the reader away from his or her complacent conventional recognition of these words. The poet also demonstrates how a false sense of security can be generated by language, especially when, unchecked by grace, it produces damningly self-serving arguments derived from postlapsarian modes of thought by "carnal reason." In *The Day of Doom* Christ does not refute by means of the methods of "fallen" human reason; Christ simply affirms, even as in the poem the elect affirm through their silent assent. Finally, a false sense of security is undercut in the poem by Wigglesworth's depiction of life on earth as so unattractive that by implication the reader wonders how much worse must be one's existence in hell.

If for Wigglesworth life on earth was unattractive, for several other colonial poets, both north and south, the world of nature seemed fetching. These poets, not at all interested in transforming their works into jeremiads, particularly paid homage to the wonder and beauty of nature in the New World. *New Englands Prospect* (1634), a tract by William Wood promoting settlement in the Northern colonies, contains poems consisting of catalogues of plants and animals that convey a fascination with the variety of nature in New England. Similarly, *A Character of the Province of Mary-Land* (1666), a seriocomic tract by George Alsop promoting settlement in a Southern colony, contains poems imaging Maryland as an "Emblem of Tranquility" and as a virgin land waiting for fertilization. In his almanac of 1647, Samuel Danforth modeled some poems after Virgil's example to celebrate the cycle of the seasons, the beauty of the New England wilderness, and the pleasures of everyday life in the midst of nature in the New World.

Even Samuel Sewall, who was very busy as a successful merchant and later as a judge, found time to write more than fifty poems, one of which concerns the beauty of some springs at Plymouth Beach.

Not streams but a storm at sea captured the imagination of another New England merchant and contemporary of Sewall, Richard Steere, who wrote a Nativity poem—unusual for New England—who in "Earth's Felicities, Heaven's Allowance" saw nature as a temptation to be managed through moderation, and who in "Sea-Storm nigh the Coast" marveled over how "Liquid Mountains on the Cliffs were hurld/ As to a Chaos they would shake the World." In Maryland the foremost colonial poet of nature, Richard Lewis, also wrote a vivid poem on a thunderstorm; but he is best known for his images of nature in the oddly titled "Food for Criticks" (1731), which describes the idyllic scenery along the Severn River in Maryland, and in "A Journey from Patapsco in Maryland to Annapolis" (1730), which marks the progress of an April day from dawn to night, notes many natural phenomena (for example, a hummingbird who, "as he moves his ever-flutt'ring Wings/ Ten thousand Colours he around him flings"), and allegorically applies the journey to his life ("Thus far *my Life* does with the *Day* agree,/ Oh! may its coming Stages from Storms be free").

Storms figure not only in poetry by Lewis in Maryland and Steere in Connecticut but also in verse by Samuel Davies, a Virginian who wrote *Miscellaneous Poems, Chiefly on Divine Subjects* (1752). Davies, however, principally focused on straightforward (in contrast to Edward Taylor's highly metaphorical) meditations, which in the period following the Great Awakening provided Southern Anglicans and Presbyterians with sacred poetry. If nature fascinated such Southern poets as Davies and Lewis and such Northern poets as Steere, it also apparently made an impression on residents of the middle colonies, especially William Livingston. Livingston's *Philosophic Solitude* (1747), a long poem abounding in classical and biblical allusions, celebrates "the pleasure of rural life,/ From noise remote, and ignorant of strife"; it contrasts in vivid images the beauty of serene woodland delights with the confusion, crowds, and pretenses of city life.

Long poems focusing on nature as well as on humanity were written a century earlier by Anne Bradstreet. Born in England and educated by her father in classical literature, Bradstreet immigrated in 1630 to New England, where she wrote poetry in the sparse intervals of freedom from the demands of raising eight children in the frontier settlement of Ipswich. During her first twenty years in New England Bradstreet composed long poems designed for a public audience, especially for her father and her husband. These works include "The Four Elements," "The Four Humors of Man,"

"The Four Ages of Man," "The Four Seasons," "The Four Monarchies," and a few shorter works. These poems demonstrate Bradstreet's wide Renaissance knowledge, but despite occasional flashes of inspiration they tend to be pedestrian and pedantic.

Whether Bradstreet ever intended these long poems to reach an audience wider than her relatives is uncertain. Nevertheless, at least one relative, her brother-in-law John Woodbridge, thought so well of her poetic achievement that he had the poems published in England as *The Tenth Muse Lately Sprung Up in America* (1650). The appearance of this edition surprised Bradstreet, who recorded her reaction in "The Author to Her Book"; in this verse Bradstreet uses metaphors drawn from motherhood to express her discontent with what she calls the "ill-form'd offspring of my feeble brain," stolen from her side by well-meaning friends and exposed, in rags, to the world:

At thy return my blushing was not small,
My rambling brat (in print) should mother call.

Displeased with what she saw in *The Tenth Muse*, Bradstreet immediately began to revise this edition of her work. But more important, her newly achieved self-consciousness over her verse led her to rethink her role as poet. The awkward rhymed couplets of the somewhat labored quarternions in *The Tenth Muse* gave way in Bradstreet's later poetry to experimentation in versification, poetic organization, imagery, and theme. Abandoning the public voice of the quarternions, Bradstreet now evinced more personal modes of expression in elegies on deceased relatives, love poems to her husband, verse on her illnesses, and several other works, including her best poem, "Contemplations." Some of these poems remained in manuscript, but many were printed in the posthumous *Several Poems* (1678). The more private voice of these later poems in effect manifested Bradstreet's personal search for appropriate poetic forms and techniques.

If this more private voice is interesting to note in its conscious management of Bradstreet's later verse, even more fascinating is the observation of its unconscious effects on this poetry. For instance, in "Upon the Burning of Our House, July 10th, 1666" Bradstreet begins by recalling in detail many of the prized material possessions lost in the fire. For more than thirty lines she lovingly revisualizes these lost objects, when suddenly she halts her reminiscence as if she had a last-minute realization that the momentum of the poem's abiding sentiment threatens to take her in an unacceptable direction: that is, toward anger at God for her loss. This momentum is stopped by the short, choked line "Adieu, Adieu; All's vanity." Here she resorts to formulaic cant to change the direction of her implicitly rebellious thoughts in the poem, and this moment is then followed by several questions designed to resist the earlier thrust of her thoughts in the poem, questions in which Bradstreet unconsciously reveals how hard it is for her to give up her material possessions and to dissipate her sense of anger over their loss. Similarly, in "Upon My Son Samuel His Goeing to England, Novem. 6, 1657" Bradstreet begins by remarking the extent to which she will praise God if her son returns to her safe and sound after his transatlantic voyage. This sentiment informs the first sixteen lines of the poem, and then suddenly the poet halts the momentum of these lines with the abbreviated, tense, "If otherwise I goe to Rest,/ Thy Will bee done, for that is best," followed by two concluding lines indicating her insistence on being persuaded to accept God's will. The possible loss of her son is a reality Bradstreet must entertain, but it is not a reality she can treat as forthrightly as she can his safe return. Again she resorts to formulaic submission—"Thy Will bee done, for that is best"—and the reader again senses the poet's unconscious revelation of how hard it will be for her to give up her son to God and to dissipate her anger at the deity for such a loss.

The word *vanity* in the poem on her burned house actually sounds a thematic concern prevalent in many of Bradstreet's poems. She apparently sensed within herself a somewhat rebellious disposition toward a number of features in her world, a rebelliousness she tended to think of as a manifestation of pride or vanity. Time and again her poetry reflects her personal search for humility, the virtue opposed to vanity. Even in her brief autobiography she stresses the tug of war in herself between pride and humility:

About 16, the Lord layd his hand sore upon me and smott mee with the small pox. When I was in my affliction, I besought the Lord, and confessed my Pride and Vanity and he was entreated of me, and again restored me. But I rendered not to him according to the benefitt received.

After a short time I changed my condition and was marryed, and came into this Country, where I found a new world and new manners, at which my heart rose. But after I was convinced it was the way of God, I submitted to it and joined the church at Boston.

In fact, Bradstreet seems to have been a very outspoken person, a quality that she liked in herself but that she worried about carrying to vain excess both in her life and in her verse. It is a mistake to see her as someone subdued or to see her poetry as work deflated by the pressure of an androcentric Puritan culture. She readily puts males in their place in "The Prologue" to *The Tenth Muse*, a book published by males; in this poem she vigorously (albeit without vanity) advocates women's ability to create, to use "Female wits." And in a long poem (1643) on Queen Elizabeth in the same collection she presents the queen as an excellent example of women's abilities: "She hath wip'd off th' aspersion of her Sex,/ That women wisdome lack." It is this forthright, feeling person we especially meet in the late poetry, where she is more personally engaged in her quest for poetic form and technique.

In one poem especially, the late "Contemplations," Bradstreet's personal voice is particularly noteworthy. This poem of thirty-three stanzas exhibits several unifying patterns of imagery, including seasonal metaphors, the diurnal cycle, a balanced contrast and comparison of earth and heaven, and mutually reinforcing biblical and classical allusions. In the poem Bradstreet begins by contemplating the Book of Nature, which (especially in its autumn-leaved trees) is so resplendent that it seems like a medieval illuminated manuscript. Nature's cycles in this poem, in contrast to some nineteenth-century Romantic works to which Bradstreet's poem is sometimes compared, provide no consolation for the human mind. The poet in fact feels as if she were indicted by nature and consequently is struck dumb by the songs of the grasshoppers and the crickets, songs (in her opinion) better than her own. At this point (stanza 10) the poet turns to Bible history in order to put the Book of Nature into perspective; then she can continue her artistic meditation beyond the muteness caused in her by God's artistry in nature. Fortified with the memory provided by the biblical account of the Fall and of the loss of the prelapsarian "vertical" mode of divine worship, the poet may now (stanza 21) turn again to the Book of Nature and there discern not the vertical trees but the "horizontal" flowing river as a postlapsarian emblem of the stream of time as well as of each life as a rivulet contributing to this flow of time. Identifying with the postlapsarian horizontal rivulet in "Contemplations," Bradstreet now keeps her poetic self "down to earth," or humble, whereas her initial encounter with nature in the poem, before the leveling memory of biblical history, struck her mute because her early perspective was based on a doomed, prideful "looking up" at the vertical trees for a glimpse of the sun (God) beyond the trees. In "Contemplations" Bradstreet made use of public conventional emblems and well-known biblical stories, but she did not write a public poem; instead, she reshaped the public features of her materials into a very personal, original meditation on the conflict within herself between pride and humility.

Private meditational poetry designed for no audience other than God and the poet was apparently prevalent in early colonial New England. Not many of these private works have survived to our time. Exceptions include, among others, a single religious acrostic by Mary English, who was a victim of the Salem witchcraft trials, and the poetry of Philip Pain, about whom we know very little. Pain wrote at least sixty-four six-line verse meditations on death that were printed posthumously in *Daily Meditations* (1668). Although these poems are essentially Puritan in their sentiment, they do not in an instance or two conform to the most conservative beliefs of New England Congregationalism and thereby remind us that Puritanism was a polymorphous culture. Pain's meditations reflect the influence of the English poets Francis Quarles and George Herbert, particularly in their tendency toward an emblematic mode of presentation.

Emblems in verse—that is, epigrammatic observations on a picture depicting an idea—appealed to Puritan poets, especially in private poems similar to "Contemplations," in which Bradstreet speaks of a flowing river as "Emblem true, of what I count the best." Public Puritan poetry too could be instructively emblematic, as is evident in the brief poems ending each chapter of *A Key into the Language of America* by Roger Williams, who was concerned with the tragic consequences of colonial settlers' behavior and their influence on Native Americans. Rich in paradox, word play, and sometimes satire, these emblematic poems complete the theme of the chapters they conclude in Williams's book by explicating a symbolic picture suggested by the chapter.

Just how ingenious a Puritan poet could be in the creation of emblems is evident in the private meditations of Edward Taylor. Far from demonstrating derivativeness or the exhaustion of the emblem tradition, Taylor's poems often reveal a startling capacity to generate innovative emblems. In "Meditation 1.8," for example, the poet interrelates macrocosm and microcosm through a series of parallel emblems: the picture of the poet looking into a starry sky at night, which becomes the picture of a downed birdlike soul in a cagelike body, which becomes the picture of a starving creature unable to reach the crumblike stars at the "bottom" of the barrel-like heavens, which becomes the picture of a potential saint being nourished by an overflow from God's bowels in the inverted crystal (that is, of Christ) meal bowl (and bowel) of the starry heavens. And in "Meditation 2.3" Taylor uses his own face as an emblem; it is described in detail as if it were a natural terrain characterized by topography, climate, flora, and fauna.

This liveliness of the emblem tradition is only one feature of the abundant artistic creativity evident in Taylor's verse, which is commonly recognized as the most outstanding literary achievement of colonial America. It is surprising that only one elegy (in a pamphlet, 1713[?]) and two stanzas of a poem (in Cotton Mather's *Right Thoughts in Sad Hours* [1689]) were published by Taylor during his lifetime, and it is fortunate that his poetry survived in manuscript until it was presented to the public in 1937.

Born in Sketchley, Leicestershire, Taylor received a nonconformist education that was completed, after his arrival in Massachusetts Bay in 1668, at Harvard College. Shortly after his graduation from Harvard in 1671, he accepted a call to Westfield, a Massachusetts frontier town where he served as minister and physician for more than fifty years. Taylor possessed a remarkable library of nearly two hundred books, including a copy of Bradstreet's *The Tenth Muse,* and he also copied extensive passages from borrowed books.

Taylor's current literary reputation derives from our high regard for his *Preparatory Meditations,* more than two hundred private poems he wrote in two series and in apparent conjunction with certain of his sermons. Exhibiting the meditational traditions of the sixteenth and seventeenth centuries, these devotional poems were written in preparation for Taylor's administration of the Lord's Supper, although evidence indicates that several of these works were occasional poems and that he revised and recast a number of the poems at later times. Several of them can be grouped into clusters; for example, in the Second Series, "Meditation 1" to "Meditation 30" concern biblical typology and "Meditation 115" to "Meditation 133" concern the allegory of Canticles.

Besides meditational traditions and biblical typology and allegory, these poems also reflect the verbal ingenuity of seventeenth-century English "metaphysical" poetry; but they are by no means merely derivative. Among their idiosyncratic features departing from the example of the "metaphysical" poets is a deliberately executed decorum of imperfection: the poet's limiting of himself to ineffectual amplification when he speaks of God and to well-managed *meiosis* (rhetorical self-diminishment) when describing himself or postlapsarian humanity. Second, Taylor's poems also reveal his adherence, in contrast to George Herbert (whom, like Pain, Taylor sometimes echoes), to an exclusionist typological system—a conservative sense of the parallels between the Old Testament and the New Testament that are essentially completed with Christ and so do not centrally include the saint, who at best is a peripheral participant in the typological scheme. Third, with an ambivalence characteristic of his Puritan culture, Taylor departs from the example of the "metaphysical" poets by precariously balancing the assertion of poetic self and the abrogation of this assertion, so that the poet is curiously within and outside his poem at the same time. Taylor manages the tension between cultural, theological restraint and personal emotion by creating (through a pyrotechnical use of verbal nuance) a liminal space between despair and presumption; appropriately he tends to conclude his meditations uncertainly in the subjunctive mode, in petition rather than in resolution. Often Taylor's poems manifest a verbal ingenuity designed to attract the attention of God to the underlying potentiality of the childlike poet's "Lisp of Non-sense" so that God will transform the postlapsarian lisp through grace and make the poet an adopted child capable of singing God's praise in genuinely adroit poetry.

Taylor's fascination with language, especially with rich imagery and subtleties of nuance and argument, has disturbed some critics, who have related these poems to Anglican sources and alleged Roman Catholic influences. In spite of the fact that this alleged association with Roman Catholicism and the supportive (if unlikely) notion that Taylor enjoined his heirs never to publish his verse have properly declined in recent scholarship, critics still tend to approach the sacramental features (especially the transubstantiating metaphors) of Taylor's poetry as if they stand apart from the mainstream of Puritan orthodoxy. This attitude will recede still further as critics approach a more clarified perception of (*a*) the Puritan high regard for the capacity of imagery and symbol (as instanced in the emblems of nature) to define and perhaps bridge the gap between visible creation and its creator, (*b*) Puritan Eucharistic piety and liturgical sacramentality utilizing graphic symbolization, and (*c*) the pluralism of colonial Puritanism generally.

Initial interest in *Preparatory Meditations* emphasized theme, theology, intellectual heritage (sources), and aesthetic theory. These concerns continue to be of interest, although Taylor's exuberant and pyrotechnical imagery has still eluded precise critical categorization and understanding. Generally this imagery in Taylor's verse is thought to reflect a baroque and free-associative manner, but this notion is rebutted by the example of meditations in which Taylor manages an intricate artistic integrity, a developmental consistency of imagery, and a logical pattern of transition based on aesthetics, theology, and science. In "Meditation 2.10," for example, Taylor easily blends together biblical typology and seventeenth-century scientific data on comets to demonstrate the harmony between the will of God and the phenomena of the world. In "Meditation 2.26" Taylor's abundant references to specific herbs are not gratuitous or random, but contribute to an underlying pattern informed by a thrice reiterated tripartite progression from purgation, through improving health, to regeneration. Similarly, the apparently random shifting from image to image in "Mediation 2.25" actually evinces an underlying unity derived from the traditions of biblical exegesis typical of the poet's time. Again in "Meditation 1.39" the proliferation of Taylor's imagery seems baroque and free-associative, but actually it suggests a sequential narrative plot: that the sick poet needs Christ the physician to cure him, then Christ the advocate to plead his case for the transgressions committed by the poet's animal passions during his illness, and then Christ the blacksmith to forge (through the crucifixion) "Nails made of heavenly Steel, more Choice than gold/ Drove home, Well Clencht," to pen and secure once and for all the animal passions of the poet's body. Often in *Preparatory Meditations* these transitions involving aesthetics, theology, and science are elliptical and elusive as a result of the personal associations (biographical, social, doctrinal) in Taylor's poetry and, as well, the modern reader's unfamiliarity with commonplace facts of Puritan daily life, belief, and knowledge that the poet takes for granted.

The tradition of meditative verse, so aesthetically elevated in Taylor's poetry, reaches a peculiar end in the example of Roger Wolcott, governor of Connecticut (1750–53, 1755), who wrote the first book of verse published in that colony. Wolcott's *Poetical Meditations* (1725) reveals the transformation of Puritan imagery and poetric forms from modes of private religious expression to modes of purely political expression. The six formulaic meditations in *Poetical Meditations* were designed by Wolcott to predispose the reader favorably to "A Brief Account of the Agency of the Honourable John Winthrop," a long poem in the book that covertly argues in Winthrop's voice for the author's position in a controversy over land owned by Wolcott but claimed by the family of John Mason. Serving merely as a vehicle for Wolcott's defense of his political self-interest in *Poetical Meditations*, the Puritan religious and literary heritage of the meditative poem, epitomized by Taylor's example, clearly had declined. And even when politics was not the central issue, some eighteenth-century colonial verse tends, as in the instance of some verse by Jane Colman Turell and *Poems on Several Occasions* (1744) by Mather Byles, to de-emphasize religious concerns per se and, instead, to strive for a religious sublime—the use of sublime natural scenes to appeal to the reader's imagination, where ideally theology and art fuse. As the eighteenth century lengthened, the Puritan religious literary heritage in verse evolved into an Augustan-influenced, aesthetically self-conscious, and politically motivated poetry concerned with the emergence of America as a new, independent nation.

William J. Scheick

III. America in Transition

From Cotton Mather to Benjamin Franklin

Cotton Mather: Puritan bigot, hunter of witches. Benjamin Franklin: Enlightenment sage, friend of mankind. These caricatures persist in the popular imagination of the American past, although often discredited. Yet they reduce to the comforting familiarity of folklore two disturbingly complex and elusive personalities. And posed as antitheses they ignore several respects in which Franklin brought forward Mather's Puritanism into the more secular Age of the Democratic Revolution.

In the Boston where Franklin spent his first sixteen years, Mather was a conspicuous presence. Grandson of two revered founders of New England —the English Puritan ministers Richard Mather and John Cotton—and son of the famed minister Increase Mather, he preached at the celebrated North Church some forty-five years. In the same period he also counseled or challenged a succession of governors, sought to christianize the Indians of New England, helped oversee the policies of Harvard College, raised fifteen children (of whom thirteen died in his lifetime), and, as the chief labor of his controversial but fruitful career, published some 388 works.

That Mather still figures as the archetypal Puritan is ironic. For he was the product and the apologist of a New England that many Puritans felt had betrayed the first settlers' hope of building New Jerusalem in America. The year before his birth—to summarize briefly this much-debated story of betrayal and decline—a synod met in Boston to solve the problem of dwindling church membership. It adopted the Halfway Covenant, which extended baptism for the first time to children of persons who had not undergone religious conversion. This change was often cited later as having opened a way for the more drastic innovations in worship introduced by the elderly iconoclast Solomon Stoddard and by Benjamin Colman, the young minister of the Brattle church. The Puritans' lives suffered many other disruptions. Boston's commercial growth transformed manners and morals, bringing a new splendor in housing and dress, and a proliferation of taverns, horse races, and brothels; the Salem witchcraft trials weakened trust in the ministry and in public officials; from abroad came the new rationalistic philosophies associated with the Enlightenment. But what finally put the founders' hopes beyond realization was the revocation by the English Crown, in 1691, of the Massachusetts charter, which had entitled the first generation to elect their own governor and virtually to bar non-Puritans from their communities. The new charter empowered the king to appoint the governor, and enfranchised all Christians except Catholics. This charter meant that New England was no longer a Wilderness Zion for the Puritans to consecrate to God, but a royal possession to be disposed as the king pleased.

Mather felt deeply drawn to the differing worlds of both the old charter and the new. Elements of each appear in his views on religion, science, economics, and politics, indeed in most facets of his career save his prose style. His life, like those of his forebears, centered on the fervent religious experiences he recorded in his lengthy diaries and in his autobiography, *Paterna* (unpublished until 1976). Continually he examined himself for signs of grace—that inner transformation wrought by the Holy Ghost, signifying salvation—ever fearful he had misperceived the true state of his soul and was merely a well-behaved hypocrite. Unceasing prayer, meditation, and fasting gave him a sense of nearness to the realm of spiritual beings, evident in such works as *Memorable Providences* (1689) and *The Wonders of the Invisible World* (1693). He felt privy to communications about the future sent from heaven ("Particular Faiths") and in about his thirtieth year even experienced a visit from a fully visible angel who spoke with him. He confronted devils as well, and believed that on one occasion he physically prevented them from binding a young girl with invisible chains.

And like most Puritans, Mather was also wary lest such direct dealings with the supernatural lead him into antinomianism. He clung to the Word as revealed in the Bible and institutionalized in the church. How intently he did so is witnessed by his stupendously long, never-published "Biblia Americana" (The American Bible), in which he attempted to interpret all of Scripture in the light of all the knowledge of his time. Reading the Old Testament typologically, as a prophecy of the New, he also undertook in *Psalterium Americanum* (An American Psalter, 1718) to present the Book of Psalms as a shadowing forth of the Second Coming of Christ. And in *Ratio*

Disciplinae (The System of Discipline, 1726) he explained and defended in detail the principles of Congregationalism, the New England Puritans' unique form of church organization.

These elements of Mather's religious life all evince his kinship with the world of the old charter. But other features show his simultaneous allegiance to that early, moderate stage of the Enlightenment, focused in London, whose heroes were Bacon, Newton, and Locke. He found the thinking of Christian rationalists appealing, although aware that it undermined the doctrine of the Trinity or even conduced to atheism. Enthusiasm for the so-called physicotheologians, who found in recent scientific discoveries evidence of divine purpose, pervades his *The Christian Philosopher* (1721). Here he described a universe that is but a "mighty *Engine*" designed by an ingenious Newtonian God, an intricate and perfect mechanism in whose operation Christ the Savior plays little part. Like many others in the eighteenth century, he also considered respect for the diversity of Christianity a mark of Enlightenment. He preached at the ordination of a Baptist minister, boasted a religious unity with "our beloved *Friends*" the Quakers (who to earlier Puritans seemed scarcely less reprehensible than Catholics), and proclaimed that "*Liberty of Conscience* is the Native Right of Mankind." In his ecumenical *Malachi* (Messenger of God, 1717) and elsewhere he devalued questions of church organization to inessentials, although the first generation of Puritans had proudly considered their Congregational form distinctive. Instead he set forth a "*Reasonable Religion*" suitable for cosmopolitan Christians of whatever denomination, contained in only three principles on which they all could agree: "*Fearing* of God, and in *Prizing* of His CHRIST, and in *Doing of Good* unto Men."

As the third principle suggests, Mather also gave greater importance than did the earlier Puritans to the social utility of religion. He relished the humanitarian ideas of the early Enlightenment, especially those of the German Pietists. "The grand Intention of my Life is," he declared in 1713, "*to Do Good.*" Each day he entered in his diary a "G.D." or "Good Devised," setting for himself the accomplishment that day of some specific act of good, for instance procuring clothing for an aged man in want. His influential *Bonifacius* (1710), popularly known as *Essays to Do Good*, appeared in over fifteen later editions. Addressing himself to ministers, physicians, rich men, and similar social groups, he advised them on Doing Good as he conceived it, that is, on how to spread the Reformation, reduce vice, and relieve the distressed and needy.

The worlds of the old and of the new charters mingled also in Mather's practice of science. Even in his youth the Copernican system and the materialist philosophy of Descartes were beginning to take hold in New England. Through his wide reading and voluminous correspondence he kept abreast of these and other revolutionary ideas that transformed the picture of the universe. He wrote on geology, botany, astronomy, and a half-dozen other sciences, notably in *The Christian Philosopher* and in "Curiosa Americana," a series of eighty-two scientific dispatches composed between 1712 and 1724 and sent to the London Royal Society, for which that prestigious scientific group elected him a Fellow. But he did his most effective and original work in medicine. To him and to the Boston physician Zabdiel Boylston belongs credit for having introduced smallpox inoculation into America. His lengthy *Angel of Bethesda* (unpublished until 1972), containing prescriptions for the treatment of many illnesses, was the only comprehensive medical work of the colonial period. And by encouraging the scientific work of others, such as the Boston mathematician Isaac Greenwood, he also stimulated the advancement of colonial American science.

Just the same, Mather's scientific thinking remained tied to a belief in invisible beings and occult forces. His speculations on meteorology, however in some ways advanced, took in the question of whether the devil can use lightning for his own purpose. Having spoken with an angel, he also balked at accepting wholly the eighteenth-century picture of a mechanical cosmos. Rather he pondered all his life the workings of what he called the "Nishmath Chajim" (The Breath of Life), a vitalistic universal force that might account not only for such phenomena as human reproduction but also for the means by which ghosts contact the living. Moreover, he understood scientific investigation largely as an attempt to explain what nature offered. He had virtually no interest in the active questioning of nature under conditions defined by the investigator, which was of the essence of the experimental method and the new science.

Mather respected the earlier Puritans' distinctive literary culture, which he knew intimately. His rich history of New England, *Magnalia Christi Americana* (The Great Works of Christ in America, 1702), contains a small anthology of New England verse by Benjamin Tompson and others, and praises the poems of Anne Bradstreet as "a Monument for her Memory beyond the Stateliest *Marbles*." Other works by Mather have verse by Michael Wigglesworth and one of the two known publications before the twentieth century of poetry by Edward Taylor. He himself wrote several lengthy versions of the traditional New England elegy. Yet in forming his own prose he cut himself off from the earlier Puritan ideal of a plain style. To be sure, when he wrote with urgency and counted on being understood he could write bare unfigured prose. And when addressing overseas intellectuals, men he imagined to be of refined tastes, he could attempt something of the intimacy, wit, and elegance of the *Spectator*, to which he once thought of contributing. But he wrote *Magnalia* and some other major works in a showy baroque agglomerate he called the "Massy" style, marked by long complex sentences behung with classical quotations, obscure allusions, biblical citations, and learned trivia. (His taste for this style seems to have been psychologically determined, the outpour of gorgeous speech probably serving to reassure him against a recurrent stutter that first afflicted him in childhood.)

In his economic views, Mather again attempted to adapt the older Puritanism of the founders to the changed order. He continued to preach the doctrine of the Calling, according to which every Christian has been suited by God to some occupation and is obliged to follow it industriously. "The most of your *Time* is to be Spent in your *Work*," he wrote in *Honesta Parsimonia* (Honorable Thrift, 1721). "The *Time* you Spend in *Recreations*, must be no more than will *Whet* you and *Fit* you for your Work." As Boston growingly prospered he reasserted the Puritans' high ethical standards and spirit of community. In works like *Lex Mercatoria* (Commercial Law, 1705) and *Theopolis Americana* (The American City of God, 1710) he attacked the adulteration of goods, denounced *caveat emptor* as an unchristian principle, and condemned the economic "*Sharks*, that are all for themselves, and that would gladly make *Minims* & *Morsels* of all mankind."

Yet Mather was himself attracted to the opulence and urbanity that accompanied Boston's commercial growth. He took to wearing a large wig, although earlier Puritans had abominated the practice. And while he partly shared his forebears' deep regard for social hierarchy, he devoted the longest of the many biographies in *Magnalia* to Sir William Phips, an upwardly mobile hotheaded adventurer who got rich quick. Phips was the first governor under the new charter, but as drawn in *Magnalia* he contrasts startlingly with such worthies as governors William Bradford and John Winthrop. His life is the story of a gunsmith's son who became apprenticed to a carpenter, learned to read and write only as a young adult, and had a prophetic dream of owning "a *Fair Brick-House* in the *Green-Lane* of *North-Boston*." His dream materialized, for with "Enterprizing *Genius*" he discovered a sunken treasure ship in Hispaniola, from the booty of which he received more than £11,000—about seven times what Mather earned in salary during his whole life. Phips's two-part cry when he at last fished up a lump of silver from the deep bespeaks the worlds first of the old charter then of the new: *"Thanks be to God!"* he exclaims, *"We are made."* Mather's biography of Phips depicts not so much The New England Governor as it does The Self-Made Man.

In his political views Mather similarly shared the first settlers' profoundly historical imagination, with its sense of divine errand, but he also understood that British imperial policy had assigned present New England a more passive role. In *Magnalia* he lent the Puritan past epic stature, as both inspiration and warning to the present. He composed a gallery of ideal portraits of earlier Puritan ministers, magistrates, and governors, aiming to hold up their lives—rich in study, devotion, and a sense of historic mission—to the present generation of New Englanders so as to halt the "visible *shrink*" from the founders' grandeur. Realistically, however, he also understood that the new charter made the conception of an isolated City Upon a Hill obsolete. As he knew and preached, New England's future welfare concerned no longer antagonizing the Crown with shows of its specialness and independence. "It is no Little Blessing of God, that we are a part of the *English Nation*," he wrote in 1700. "Our Dependence on, and Relation to, that brave *Nation*, that man deserves not the Name of an *English man*, who despises it." So while *Magnalia* portrays the Fathers as a chosen people, it also insists on their loyalty to the English church. And while the book glorifies the Puritan past, present New England appears there not as Christian Israel in America but as what it had been forced to be, an ecumenical place open to Congregationalists, Presbyterians, Episcopalians, and Baptists alike.

Cotton Mather illustrates more fully than anyone else in his time the most pregnant religious, scientific, and social issues in the culture that produced Benjamin Franklin. And on many of these issues, as Mather can be seen as the step from the first Puritan settlers to Franklin, so Franklin can be seen as the step from Mather to the American Romantic writers and to us.

The lives of the two men often ran parallel or touched. Like Mather's, Franklin's ancestors were English Dissenters, his mother's family having immigrated to New England in 1635. His father, Josiah, a soap and candle maker, was an active member of the Boston South Church, in which Franklin himself grew up. In fact, as a boy Franklin was designed by his father for the ministry. He heard Increase Mather preach, and very likely also Cotton, who gave several sermons at the South Church as a guest minister. In adolescence Franklin visited Cotton Mather in his study, and enjoyed and remembered his "pleasant and instructive Conversation." Later in life he stayed in contact with Mather's son Samuel and with Mather's nephew, the poet and wit Mather Byles.

Yet Franklin was very much a product of the world of the new charter. Born into the Boston of the royal governor Joseph Dudley (a professed Anglican), of the new un-Puritan sensibility disinclined to melancholy, the new cosmopolitanism that offered an alternative to the old exclusivism, the new language of the rights of Englishmen and the balance of trade that was replacing the Puritan idiom of divine covenants and of the Calling, Franklin epitomized that younger generation against whom ministers like Mather often preached for having fallen away from their fathers. Indeed, he wrote his first published essay in the guise of the widowed "Silence Dogood," whose name twits Mather's many well-known efforts to Do Good and attempts to keep silent.

The satirical pseudonym helps explain Franklin's flight in adolescence to Philadelphia, for in that city's fluid and diverse society the secular, egalitarian values of the Enlightenment flourished. Although he never joined those eighteenth-century radicals who scoffed at Christianity as blind superstition, he was scornful of sects, suspicious of ministers, and in Puritan terms no longer able to feel the content of religion. To him and to many in the Revolutionary generation, Mather's quasi-mystical regime of prayer and fasting, his converse with devils and angels, could only have seemed deplorable and even unintelligible. Institutionally he simply abandoned his native Congregationalism, reserving Sunday not for churchgoing but for study. Nevertheless he held to a belief in a deity, of whose nature his opinions often changed. In his youthful "Dissertation on Liberty and Necessity, Pleasure and Pain" (1725) he grudgingly postulated an Aristotelian Cause: "1. There is said to be a *First Mover*, who is called GOD." Three years later, however, his "Articles of Belief and Acts of Religion" (1728) speaks, polytheistically, of several gods. And in old age he drifted toward more conventional Christian views, even proposing at the Constitutional Convention that the members join in prayer (the motion was defeated). Understandably, John Adams, who considered Franklin an outright atheist, remarked, "The Catholics thought him almost a Catholic. The Church of England claimed him as one of them. The Presbyterians thought him half a Presbyterian, and the Friends believed him a wet Quaker." But however many religious postures Franklin adopted, they all took in rationalistic notions, left out the drama of Fall and Redemption, and made little room for Christ, whose divinity he doubted.

In never undergoing conversion, Franklin missed the central experience of Puritanism. Yet as a young man he preserved in secular form something resembling the Puritan hope of regeneration. While Mather and the earlier Puritans believed that only supernatural grace could purge the self of evil, young Franklin believed he could make himself good. For grace he substituted what he described in his *Autobiography* as "the bold and arduous Project of arriving at moral Perfection." He proposed expanding this naturalistic version of divine grace into a treatise on the Art of Virtue, and founding his own "Sect" for initiates in his thirteen-week regime. In his "arduous Project" the fervent Puritan hope for self-transformation has become the American passion for self-improvement.

Franklin also retained but enlarged the side of Mather's religion devoted to philanthropy. Good Works, and not prayer or meditation, he considered the only service in human power of a God too great to need human praise. "The noblest question in the world," he wrote in *Poor Richard* (1737), "is *What Good may I do in it?*" Here Mather's impress is clear-cut. As a boy Franklin found in his father's small library *Essays to Do Good*, which he read receptively: the book "gave me such a turn of thinking, as to have an influence on my conduct through life," he wrote later, "and if I have been . . . a useful citizen, the public owes the advantage of it to that book." The "G.D.s" of Mather's diaries may also resound in the famous schedule Franklin drew up as a Philadelphia printer, whereby he began each day asking "What Good shall I do this Day?" and concluded each evening asking "What Good have I done to day?" Franklin's association for young tradesmen and mechanics, the Junto, also recalls the mutual benefit societies of young people that Mather founded in Boston.

But here, too, what Franklin carried forward from Mather he also detached from its basis in Puritan religion. For Mather, Doing Good meant glorifying God, not only by relieving the distressed but also by universalizing the Reformation; and one could not Do Good without have been regenerated, for only those who had grace could know what goodness is. Franklin considered God beyond human aid or praise and aimed at serving him by helping man: Doing Good meant becoming a "useful citizen." In this sense he did legendarily much good, assisting the public as politician and diplomat for nearly fifty years, and becoming a founder of such institutions as the Pennsylvania Hospital, the school that became the University of Pennsylvania, the first subscription library in America, and the Pennsylvania Society for the Abolition of Slavery. His understanding of benevolence was also shaped by eighteenth-century ideas of Progress. He often conceived the good as the New and Improved. Devoted to enhancing human comfort, he devised better ways of lighting, cleaning, and heating the city. For such popular inventions as the Franklin stove he refused to take out a patent.

As Mather had done in Boston, Franklin encouraged scientific activity in Philadelphia, home of many creditable amateur and professional scientists. He promoted the botanist John Bartram and the physician Benjamin Rush (later noted for his work on yellow fever and on psychiatry); popularized science through his almanacs; and drew up a plan for an intercolonial scientific group that eventually issued in the American Philosophical Society, of which he became the first president. And he too—despite an often-expressed distrust of reason—wrote and speculated on many different scientific topics. Yet unlike Mather he addressed them apart from religious considerations. He disdained occult and supernatural explanations and sharply separated the realms of matter and spirit. Where Mather wrote of a neoplatonic "Nishmath Chajim," Franklin used for the first time, in an electrical sense, such terms as "plus," "minus," "positive," "negative," and "battery." Where Mather pondered whether lightning tended toward churches, Franklin became the first person to assert that the identity of lightning and electricity could be proved experimentally—illustrating his own characterization of his epoch as "the Age of Experiments." His *Experiments and Observations on Electricity, Made at Philadelphia* (1751) went through five English editions in his lifetime. With his practical genius and the stimulus of his utilitarian age, he converted many of his theoretical investigations to practical uses, as in his widely installed lightning rods.

While Franklin advanced the scientific interests of Mather and the Puritans, he in most ways departed from their literary culture. In his seventh Dogood essay, written at sixteen, he mocked as "wretchedly Dull and Ridiculous" the hallowed tradition of New England funeral elegies. He kept from his prose the Puritans' typological symbolism and copious biblical references, and used few classical allusions either, for like others in eighteenth-century America he came to think the teaching of Latin and Greek outmoded and impractical. He tuned his style rather to the taste of a new reading public that desired not sermons and volumes of theology but newspapers and pamphlets. The paper in which his Dogood essays appeared, the *New England Courant* (1721–26)—the first American periodical with literary pretensions—was inspired by the new journalism of Joseph Addison and Richard Steele. Young Franklin himself took the *Spectator* for his model, publishing his early essays under such pen names as Anthony Afterwit and Celia Single, in such forms as letters-to-the-editor and lay sermons, on such subjects as apparel and bachelorhood, and with the overall aim of correcting in a lighthearted way the follies of the time. The "Speech of Miss Polly

Baker" (1747) and some of his later essays also contain a vein of ribaldry common in eighteenth-century America and England but unthinkable in the Boston of the Puritan fathers.

Aware of the vast new powers of the press to affect a large public, Franklin made it his stylistic creed that "one cannot be too clear." For the sake of clarity he shunned both the colloquial and the grand, neologisms as well as archaisms. In doing so, he might be said to look back past Mather to the earlier Puritans' ideal of a plain style. As he once wrote, "I love economy exceedingly." Typically, the compactness of the statement reaches far: his love of economy embraced household management, where he could be stingy; philanthropy, where by producing large good through small means he often achieved a moral elegance; science, where he tested fundamental principles of nature by such homely apparatus as a kite and key; and especially prose style, where abhorring cant and wordiness he ever seized the gist of the subject and made every word serve its expression.

Like Mather, Franklin approved of capitalist striving, but without seeking to christianize the marketplace or to preserve class and hereditary distinctions. Indeed, to many in the eighteenth century Franklin came to symbolize how the concept of Privilege had given way to the concept of Merit. Schooled in the grasping and expansive economic life of Philadelphia, he spoke for the aspirations of many poor and middle-class people in Europe and America. How compellingly he did so can be measured by the fact that in the last quarter of the century his *The Way to Wealth* (1757) went through ten reprintings in Italian translation alone. (It has also appeared in French, German, Dutch, Swedish, Greek, Chinese, Hungarian, Russian, Welsh, Gaelic, and Catalan, among other languages.) Consisting of about a hundred Poor Richard maxims reeled off by an elderly speaker named Father Abraham, the essay resembles a sermon. Yet Father Abraham does not try to justify wealth in religious terms. He preaches simply Industry and Frugality, that is, how to get money and how to keep it. In his often cynical view, moreover, economic well-being can depend on inverting religious values. Cautioning his audience against trusting others too much, he observes, "*In the Affairs of this World, Men are saved, not by Faith, but by the Want of it.*" Franklin never confused prosperity with transcendence.

Franklin's fullest exposition of economic individualism and social mobility is of course his *Autobiography*, written between 1771 and 1790. Here he shows how he was able to escape his "low Beginning" and in effect retire at age forty-two by acquiring habits of, and a reputation for, industry, temperance, and probity. "I was seen at no Places of idle Diversion," he writes, "I never went out a-fishing or shooting; a Book, indeed, sometimes debauch'd me from my Work; but that was seldom, snug, and gave no Scandal." The restrictions owe something to the Puritans' doctrine of the Calling, but detached from their tragic consciousness of the past and respect for social hierarchy. On these matters the *Autobiography* reverses the Puritan ethos. It praises not copying one's family but surpassing it, not deferring to one's elders but outfoxing them, trusting and assigning authority not to others and to God but to oneself. Despite some expressions of gratitude to Providence, the book retains just half the exclamation of Mather's Sir William Phips, omitting his *"Thanks be to God!"* but reechoing with satisfaction his *"We are made."* It remains the classic statement of the American dream of material success.

Franklin retained still less of the Puritans' expectations for the New World. Mather, to recall, swayed between the old-charter ideal of America as the seat of the millennial New Jerusalem and the diminished new-charter hope that, as an ecumenical outpost of imperial Britain, New England might assist in spreading the Reformation. Franklin disregarded both possibilities and instead foresaw a mighty continental empire stretching west, devoted to advancing secular happiness. An important source of his view was his large firsthand experience of America (far broader geographically than that of any New Englander before him), including his involvement in Pennsylvania politics, business dealings in the Southern colonies, and investments in Western land, as well as his part in writing the Declaration of Independence, his role as American Minister Plenipotentiary to France, and his attendance at the convention that devised the Constitution of the United States. Another source was his prescience as a demographer. In "Observations Concerning the Increase of Mankind" (1751) he predicted that owing to early marriage the population of America must double every twenty-five years. This certainty of rapid increase also went into forming and confirming his expansionist vision of a numerous and prosperous people manifesting their destiny westward.

Not that Franklin's concept of America replaced that of Mather or of the earlier Puritans, which stayed alive in such later New England writers as Timothy Dwight. Indeed, it has stayed alive. For despite ceaseless celebration of The American Dream, Americans have often been divided by their allegiance to one of Two American Dreams. The antagonism appears, for instance, in the "Baker Farm" chapter of *Walden* (1854), where the Franklinian America of an Irish immigrant—in which a working man can put steak on the table and send his children to college—is belittled by Thoreau's Puritan sense of America as a place of spiritual self-realization. The conflict emerged again in the 1960s when hardhats and hippies clashed on Wall

Street. The time from the first Puritans and Mather to the Revolutionary generation and Franklin thus not only covers the complex transition from Puritan piety, idealism, and provincialism to the more secular, utilitarian, and cosmopolitan values of the American Enlightenment. It also marks the establishment of two enduring visions of America that have often competed for authority.

Kenneth Silverman

Jonathan Edwards, Charles Chauncy, and the Great Awakening

Of the plenitude of "religious" writers who filled the American literary landscape in the years between the twilight of Puritanism and the emergence of the ideological struggles of the Revolution, only Jonathan Edwards has held his place in the American literary canon. His chief critic and opponent, Charles Chauncy, has recently enjoyed a full-dress biography, but his writings have seldom been republished, certainly never in their entirety. Samuel Johnson, who before his reversion to Episcopacy had served as one of Edwards's Yale tutors, was honored—perhaps as an act of filial piety by Columbia University, of which he was (when it was still King's College) the first president—with a four-volume edition of his writings more than fifty years ago, and has ever since been regarded as America's "first philosopher."

Edwards, meanwhile, has been the subject of a plethora of biographies and special studies. Yale University Press promises us, perhaps within our lifetimes, a "complete" edition of all of Edwards's writings, published and unpublished. And something of Edwards—most commonly the highly unrepresentative sermon *Sinners in the Hands of an Angry God* (1741)—finds its way into nearly every anthology of literature concerned with the period. Edwards has, indeed, come to be recognized as perhaps the finest mind ever to emerge in America and, by some, as among our supreme architects of prose. Yet it might be asked whether Edwards would loom so large among his contemporaries, even whether his creativity would have been so immense, had it not been for his participation in, commentaries on, and obsession with the issues raised by one of the salient episodes in all American history: the Great Awakening.

Between 1739 and 1742 nearly the whole of the American colonies experienced religious "revivals" that dwarfed, in numbers and in intensity, nearly anything that had gone before. A "great and general awakening" it was called at the time, and for two centuries and more the "Great Awakening" has been acknowledged as a special moment in American religious history. Lesser revivals persisted throughout the decade and, indeed, well into the 1750s, when the Awakening was carried into Virginia; and, as late as 1763, students of the giants of the Great Awakening—such as Samuel Buell, whose ordination sermon had been preached by Jonathan Edwards— were enjoying new "refreshings" on Long Island. It could be said, indeed, that America experienced continuing revivals, the hiatus of the Revolutionary years excepted (if these years were in fact an exception), to the turn of the century, which witnessed both a "Second Great Awakening" in the churches of New England and the massive camp-meetings of the trans-Allegheny West.

Yet it is largely since World War II that the Great Awakening has come to be viewed as a significant "watershed" in our intellectual, social, and even political history. Perry Miller's *Jonathan Edwards* (1949) argued that the revival, at least as understood through the mind of Edwards, marked America's leap into "modernity." As early as 1937, to be sure, H. Richard Niebuhr, in *The Kingdom of God in America*, laid the groundwork for a view of the Awakening that made it, and the millenarian expectations it aroused, the fountainhead of American national self-consciousness, to, through, and even beyond the Revolution. As that insight has been expanded on, however, the question has been raised whether the Great Awakening either represented or brought forth *anything* new or unique as a contribution to American culture—whether it was not, for instance, simply a continuation of the spiritual revivals that, for a half-century or more, had occurred among a variety of dissenter groups, of those outside the prevailing orthodoxy, the fanatical "Rogerenes" of New England among them.

The hypothesis of a relationship between the visions of the Awakening and the actualities of the Revolution has been challenged, indeed assailed, and the view that evangelical revivalism represented a meaningful counter-thrust, in the eighteenth century and afterwards, to the Rationalism V. L. Parrington celebrated has been elaborately questioned and debated. Even those who allow that the Awakening brought *some* shift in colonial religious attitudes disagree as to whether its legacy was a new individualism, accompanied by a growing anticlericalism, or whether it brought into being a new commitment to community, accompanied by a resurgence of the status of the ministry. Was it indeed America's "leap into modernity," leaving behind forever the semischolasticism of the world of Puritanism, or was it simply the dying gasp of that outmoded religious culture, a mere interlude, even an aberrant one, in America's triumphant march toward a Jeffersonian Enlightenment?

While these debates will surely persist, there can be little doubt that the Awakening marked a special moment in the history and development of American literary theory and practice. A culture increasingly given to imitation of Joseph Addison's style as an essayist, and, in the pulpit, to the serene prose of Archbishop Tillotson, was suddenly and rudely challenged by a "preacher newly come from *England*," George Whitefield, the "grand itinerant," who, starting in Georgia and South Carolina, moved northward through Pennsylvania to New England, preaching a new gospel to multitudes, and preaching in a manner that struck colonial Americans as wholly novel. The establishment, wherever he preached, was outraged, not so much by Whitefield's doctrinal assertion that "Archbishop Tillotson knew no more of Christianity than Mahomet" as by the "noble negligence" of Whitefield's manner of preaching (to quote Josiah Smith, a Harvard graduate whose celebration of Whitefield's triumphs in Charleston was frequently reprinted in the North): a negligence soothing and seraphic and yet capable of discharging the "artillery of heaven," a combination that aroused and attracted thousands previously indifferent to the American churches and their preachers.

Until the arrival of Whitefield, eighteenth-century American literature seemed destined to be defined by the increasing importance of the written word: history, biography, almanacs, even magazines, looked to replace the sermon as (to use Kenneth Murdock's phrase, applied to seventeenth-century New England) the "staple literary diet" of the American public. Benjamin Franklin in Philadelphia (and, along with his brother, earlier in Boston), Mather Byles briefly in Boston, and, in 1752, just as the Awakening was deemed over, William Livingston in New York devoted their energies to magazine publication: Addisonian essays, versification modeled on Alexander Pope, political argument, which soon expanded into pamphlet form. "The press," complained one of Livingston's critics, had come to be "what the pulpit was in times of Popery"—as though preaching was relevant, much less central, only a long time ago and far, far away.

One can in fact probably date the new dispensation as beginning at least a half-decade before Whitefield's arrival: with Edwards's sermons entitled

Justification by Faith Alone (1734), the instrument, he believed, of the "Valley" revivals of 1735, or from the sermons in which Theodorus Frelinghuysen and Gilbert Tennent justified their practice of excluding the unregenerate from the Lord's Supper—ecclesiastical innovations among the Dutch Reformed and Presbyterians of New Jersey and Pennsylvania that perhaps inspired their own modest "revivals" of the mid-1730s. Yet the 1740s stand out most clearly as *the* decade in which American literary practice became unquestionably defined by the sermon—the *spoken* word—and, often more intensely than with the doctrinal debates that accompanied the Awakening, by differences of opinion over the theory and practice of preaching.

There were, of course, doctrines at issue in the Awakening; or, more accurately perhaps, the particular doctrine that Edwards in 1735 had recalled as "the principle hinge of Protestantism," but that was, or became, a neo-Calvinism centered on what Whitefield defined in the title of one of his more celebrated discourses, *The Nature and the Necessity of Our New Birth* (1737). Just as Edwards in the mid-1730s had defended the "evangelical scheme" in terms of its success in producing religious *experiences*, so too did the notion of unconditional (and abrupt) regeneration become in Whitefield's preaching and that of the Awakening generally an *experiential* doctrine: "the Belief and Expectation of a certain happy *Moment*," according to one of Whitefield's critics, "when, by the *sole* and *specifick* Work of the *Holy Spirit*, you shall at once (as 'twere by Magic Charm) be matamorphosed [*sic*]." According to the revivalists, experience was *all*: Scripture itself had to be grasped, "not merely in a doctrinal Way, but by an Experimental Acquaintance." Not quite new matter, this was, as proclaimed in a new manner, and as defended in terms of its efficacy in bringing on the "New Birth," the new dispensation of the Awakening.

Still, at the height of the revival ecstasy, manner took precedence over matter in both the sermons of the revivalists and the jibes of their opponents. Charles Chauncy, soon to emerge as *the* critic of the Awakening, was able, in 1740, to preach on something doctrinally akin to Whitefield's insistence on the necessity of the "New Birth," but as for Whitefield's *manner*, Chauncy defended a more "rational" mode of discourse and allowed that "eloquence"—of the Whitefieldian sort—could well be "a gift less valuable than others." Whereas Whitefield's apologists—partisans of the more emotional religion of the Awakening—proclaimed that his chief virtue lay, not in his defense of received doctrine, but in his talents "in moving the affections." Though one can detect, as early as Joseph Morgan's *History of the Kingdom of Basaruah* (1715), a sense that the old divinity had left pious Americans with a sense of spiritual emptiness, with the Awakening it became clear it was the old homiletics, above all, that had proven "stale and unsavory" to American "palates."

The novelty of Whitefield's preaching was underscored by his indifference to parish boundaries. He "itinerated," even intruded on churches to which he had not been invited. This soon became a common practice, particularly among the "New Side" Presbyterians of New Jersey and Pennsylvania who, at first trained to move into "vacant" parishes, began to travel wherever they felt called upon to go. Gilbert Tennent and Samuel Finley both toured New England, the latter forcibly removed from Connecticut as a herald of sedition. Undoubtedly the most notorious of the itinerants was James Davenport, grandson of the founder of New Haven colony, whose aberrant ways led to his being proclaimed insane by the Massachusetts authorities. His *Confession and Retractations* (1744), one of the most personally moving utterances to come out of the revival, repudiates a number of his excesses, but not itinerancy itself. Indeed, in a less dramatic way, scores of ministers occupied, by invitation, the pulpits of others. It may well be that it was simply by hearing new voices that many were moved out of what Edwards called their "complacency": "old soldiers," he once called them, "deaf to the roaring of heaven's cannon" as it sounded, week after week, so much the same. Indeed, Edwards's famous *Sinners*, though probably preached first at Northampton, there produced no reports of any special congregational response; its renowned impact occurred only when he carried the same message to Enfield.

The doctrinal target of the itinerants, indeed of the Awakening preachers generally, was "Arminianism"—the notion, *contra* Calvin, that man can earn his own salvation—first charged against the growing Church of England, but suspected, by the mid-1730s, to have corrupted "dissenter" pulpits and congregations as well. In this respect, one might date the onset of the Awakening from the shock and scandal of the reversion to Episcopacy, in 1722, of the Rector of Yale, along with several tutors and graduates. Ironically, however, the spokesmen of the Church of England were not so much participants in the debates of the Awakening as its beneficiaries. Divisions among the "dissenters" caused scores to flee to the Church of England for "safety," or, as Samuel Johnson happily reported, for "refuge" from the "raging enthusiasm" of the day. Quietly, however, Anglicans began during the Awakening to codify their homiletic differences from all dissenters, as they had their criticisms of the disorder and illegitimacy of other colonial churches (as in Samuel Johnson's condescending *Three Letters to Dissenters* [1733, 1734, 1737]). Like Richard Hooker long before them, colonial Anglicans in the Carolinas or in New England (the Virginia Church remained relatively unscathed until Samuel Davies carried the revival out of Pennsylvania) preferred the sacramental and liturgical, the altar to the pulpit, the Book of Common Prayer to the sermon, all in terms, again according to Johnson, of the comfort provided by tradition to those whose gifts were not those of the preacher. To the colonial Anglican, with the possible exception of Virginia's Commissary Blair, Whitefield was not one of the brethren—indeed he was taken to be a "Methodist." (Which he most surely was not; he had broken with the Wesleys over their adoption of what he took to be notions of "free will"; "the constant Tenour of my preaching in *America*," Whitefield insisted, "has been *Calvinistical.*") Anglicans ridiculed Whitefield's preaching and its impact: he would "have produced the same Effects," complained Commissary Garden of Charleston in the first Episcopal blast at Whitefield, "whether he had acted his Part in the pulpit or on the Stage." But for the most part the contributions of Anglicanism to the literature of the Awakening were primarily cautiously reasoned ecclesiastical tracts or statistic-filled and self-congratulatory letters to the Bishop of London.

However central to the Awakening the preached word, one cannot dismiss—indeed one should celebrate—the lengthier and more philosophical works prepared directly for the press during the Awakening. Edwards's *Some Thoughts Concerning the Present Revival of Religion in New England* (1742) and Chauncy's *Seasonable Thoughts on the State of Religion in New-England* (1743) stand, not merely as the major *opera* of the Awakening itself—one its major defense, the second its most sustained critique—but as classics of the American mind. Perry Miller rightly detected that in this combat the leaders of New England's "two armies" shifted their focus from the nature of God to the nature of man. One might also note, however, that the interchange in many respects—certainly for Edwards—marked the end of the high "sermonic" phase of the Awakening. Thereafter Edwards increasingly set himself to the composition of the treatises—each of them to be sure in some way related to the issues of the Awakening—on which his enduring intellectual reputation chiefly rests: the *Treatise Concerning Religious Affections* (1746); the paradigmatic *Life and Diary of David Brainerd* (1749), an imaginative effort to sustain the doctrines of the *Religious Affections* that proved to be the most continuingly popular of Edwards's writings; and, of course, the *Freedom of the Will* (1754), *The Great Christian Doctrine of Original Sin Defended* (1758), and the two posthumously published dissertations *The Nature of True Virtue* and *Concerning the End for Which God Created the World* (1765). Only one later sermon of Edwards remains central to his reputation—the celebrated *Farewell Sermon* of 1750 (the model, one suspects, at least in fantasy, for all who have spent a lifetime confronting an unreachable audience). Yet in the same year Edwards also composed a preface to Joseph Bellamy's *True Religion Delineated*, an effort, after a decade of controversy, to clarify and set aright the doctrinal implications of the Awakening.

Chauncy, for his part, continued to pour forth sermons and lectures, but it is noteworthy that he never stooped, or dared, to reply to any of Edwards's later treatises. He did do battle against the idea of an Anglican Bishop for the colonies—a favorite subject of threatened "rational" clergymen in the two decades before the Revolution. But it was not until nearly three decades after the Awakening that Chauncy produced a sustained volume, as distinguished from a tract, arguing against Episcopacy itself. Just shortly before his death in 1787, Chauncy published three comparatively immense treatises, together constituting his theological *summa*, embodying the Universalism toward which he had been quietly and privately tending: ". . . all intelligent moral beings . . . going on, while they suitably employ and improve their original faculties, from one degree of attainment to another; and, hereupon, from one degree of happiness to another, without end." The *Elementa Philosophica* (1752) of Samuel Johnson also focused on an increase in human happiness, rather than on the glory of God. (Though in his later years Johnson, like his British namesake, began to reclaim something of a sense of man's original sin.) Dependent though he was on Berkeleian idealism, Johnson produced what was probably, as has been alleged, the first "original" philosophic treatise in America, and certainly the first systematic one.

Whatever one may think of these later monuments of religious prose, one still cannot escape the fact that it was the sermonizing of the Awakening, and the assumptions thereby imbued as to the proper role of the ministry, that wrought perhaps the most radical transformation in American intellectual life: popularizing and democratizing the relationship between speaker and audience, demanding a fervor of the intellectual (and an "experimental religion" of the Christian) that remained a part of the American grain at least as late as the Civil War. In this regard, probably the most influential utterance of the entire eighteenth century was the sermon preached by Gilbert Tennent, spokesman of the "New Side" Presbyterians, on March 8, 1740, *The Dangers of an Unconverted Ministry*. Considered "one of the most severely abusive sermons that was ever penned," Tennent's "Nottingham Sermon" was an attack on the Scotch-trained "Old Side" Presbyterian ministry for, among other things, culpable greed ("their Eyes, with *Judas*, fixed upon the Bag") as well as for "moral formalism." It was also, if only by example, the literary manifesto of the Awakening. Tennent's language, as Isaac Backus, subsequently the leader of New England's Baptists, was to say, was "short and cutting, like Luther's formerly." To the revival mind, doctrine and delivery were inseparable, as their critics acknowledged when they complained of the incessant attacks of Tennent and his colleagues on the "dry Formalists of this Generation."

Tennent's Nottingham sermon is, in its rhetorical potency, probably unmatched by anything else that has been left us by the spokesmen of the Presbyterian revival: Samuel Finley, whose *Christ Triumphing and Satan Raging* (1741) predicted the coming of the Kingdom of God once the enemies of the revival were defeated; Jonathan Dickinson (one of the few Yale-educated leaders of the middle colony revival), whose *A Display of God's Special Grace* (1742) was phrased in the form of a dialogue and, like Edwards's writings of the same year, was as concerned by the antinomianism emerging among the awakened as by its formalist and Arminian opposition; and Samuel Davies, who, though educated at the "Log College" (created by the Tennents to provide a native education for American Presbyterians), was undoubtedly the most learned of the Awakeners, other than perhaps Edwards himself. Davies's sermon style, somewhat more "florid" than that of his elders, was carried over into his *Miscellaneous Poems, Chiefly on Divine Subjects* (1752), characterized as his poems are by the rhetorical cadences and sensuosity of the hymns of Isaac Watts and Philip Doddridge, Davies's classical learning, his interest in such proto-romantic poetry as Edward Young's *Night Thoughts*, and, perhaps most notably, by his fascination with the concept of the "sublime."

Yet for all their invocation of the Reformers, or of certain of their Puritan forebears, the revivalists brought something new to American literary theory and practice. In the minds of some, their contribution was an "anti-intellectualism" that endured through two more centuries of American experience, although it was not "learning" per se they assailed (indeed, the Awakening brought at least three new colleges into being) as "learning without piety." Jonathan Edwards, himself ordinarily (for obvious reasons) exempted from the charge of "anti-intellectualism," perhaps most eloquently stated the objection to the "rational" clergy's emphasis on a clergyman's "learning."

When there is light in a minister, consisting in human learning, great speculative knowledge, and the wisdom of the world, without a spiritual warmth and ardor in his heart, and a holy zeal in his ministrations, his light is like the light of an *ignis fatuus*, and some kinds of putrifying carcasses that shine in the dark, though they are of a stinking savour.

Not only did Edwards thereby anticipate John Randolph's celebrated thrust at Henry Clay; he, and the Awakening generally, restored and revivified that "oratorical" mode that F. O. Matthiessen once defined as central to the literature of the American Renaissance: to Emerson, Melville, and Whitman.

The critics of the Awakening brought nothing so new to the American literary scene. For the most part they were content to revile the Awakening and the Awakeners as madmen and fomenters of disorder and to do so, at least at the outset, in angry and discordant diatribes of their own. The most noteworthy of their utterances was, among the Presbyterians, John Thomson's *The Government of the Church of Christ* (1741), at once the most coherent and the most scurrilous of attacks on the "censoriousness" of the Awakeners and their practice of "itinerating" and intruding on established parishes. Increasingly, however, critics of the revival made explicit the rational view of religion that, in the early days of the Awakening, had been assailed as "formalism." "The Holy Spirit converts and sanctifies men," proclaimed William Hart of Connecticut in a 1742 sermon, *The Nature of Regeneration*, "and improves them in holiness, by opening their Understanding, and leading them to a just and *rational* View and Belief in the great Truths contained in the Scriptures."

So rational a view of religious experience—cumulative and not sudden, derived from man's learning and not the immediate work of the Holy Spirit— of course called for a more "instructional" style of preaching. Although the partisans of reason acknowledged that the "passions" might on occasion be useful, no sermon was to raise hearers "to such a height as really to unfit" them for "the exercise of their *reasonable* powers." Over time younger rational ministers began to indulge in such rhetorical flourishes as suggested they were the cultural equals of any Anglican, but this occurred only as the dangers—even the memory—of revival enthusiasm had waned. The archetypal antirevival sermon, in doctrine, argument, and style, was that delivered, shortly after the Harvard Commencement of 1742, by Charles Chauncy. His *Enthusiasm Describ'd and Caution'd Against* at once revealed him as the leader of the antirevival forces and provided them, through his use of John Locke's treatment of "enthusiasm" in *An Essay Concerning Human Understanding*, intellectual rather than merely *ad hominem* or ecclesiastical and political arguments against the revival. "Keep close to the Scripture," Chauncy warned, and "Make use of the Reason and the Understanding." A measured discourse, almost a lecture rather than a sermon, his work set the tone for many of Chauncy's contemporaries and, perhaps more significantly, for a later generation who, as in Lemuel Briant's *The Absurdity of Depreciating Moral Virtue* (1749), began to promote more thoughtfully that measured defense of "reason" and morality that would culminate, intellectually and rhetorically, in William Ellery Channing's *Moral Argument against Calvinism* (1820).

By the end of the 1740s, even well before, the attention of Edwards and others had turned from promoting or defending the Awakening to decrying its "excesses." The charge of "antinomianism" leveled against the revival (especially in New England, where the passage of a century had not dimmed the memory of the troublesome Anne Hutchinson) came also to be taken up by the defenders of the revival. Although Edwards's sermon at Yale, *The Distinguishing Marks of a Work of the Spirit* (1741), was a nearly uncompromising defense of the revival (perhaps inspiring David Brainerd, then a student, to the indiscretions that led to his expulsion), his *Thoughts on the Revival*, published a year later, began the questioning of "false affections" that found fuller expression in the sermons Edwards was then delivering and later converted into his *Treatise Concerning Religious Affections*. Though Edwards, by the end of the decade, despaired of another Awakening until a "new generation" came "on the stage," he hoped, through refinement of doctrine, psychology, and historical vision, to make certain that the "errors" of the Awakening would never again be replicated.

Yet even as Edwards turned to near-solitary composition of his treatises, the earlier sermonic ideal lived on, in hundreds of utterances, it is beginning to be discovered, that survive only in manuscript form. Of Edwards's own students, Jonathan Parsons, we know, preached much the same matter, and in the same manner, right into the Revolution; he was one of the few New Englanders, other than Edwards, to have his sermons collected and published. Another disciple, Joseph Bellamy, was acknowledged, in the years after Edwards's death, to be "the most eloquent man in America." It was said (and this troubled Bellamy himself) that he could do anything he "pleased with an audience." His sermon *The Millennium* (1758, the year of Edwards's death) revived and made public the historical vision Edwards first disclosed in his unpublished (at the time) sermons entitled *The History of the Work of Redemption* (1774) and in his almost desperate effort, in *An Humble Attempt to Promote Explicit Agreement and Visible Union of God's People* . . . (1747), to promote the Kingdom of God, not through the preached word, but through ecclesiastical innovation. Bellamy's sermon also restored, as central to pulpit discourse, a vision of the Church Militant, battling to bring the Kingdom of God to earth, that had been for the moment transmuted in the "patriotic" sermons of many Awakening veterans during the French and Indian Wars.

On the other side, among the next generation there was Jonathan Mayhew, a younger critic of the Awakening (he had suffered through it while a student at Harvard) who in 1748 openly described his sermons as "lectures" and, during his foreshortened life, served as "tutor," for the most part, to the Boston young, urging them, as an aspect of "Christian Sobriety," to take "the part of an ingenuous inquirer after truth," hearkening to those ("some men are superior to others") with "the knowledge of some things which they would not have known without their assistance." Portions of his sermons were more "eloquent" than any of Chauncy's: "We ought not to be so fond of a rational religion, as to suppose that it consists in cold dry speculation, without having any concern for the affections." But Mayhew, far more than Chauncy, elaborated on, and made explicit, the intellectual elitism that from the outset had been an undercurrent of the attack on religious enthusiasm and the dangers of arousing an unwashed multitude.

Memories both of the Awakening experience and of its issues long lingered in the mind of pre-Revolutionary America. Isaac Backus invoked the example of Whitefield's preaching and defended him, well into the years of the Revolution, against Chauncy's criticisms of enthusiasm and itinerancy. Yet for Backus, as for other evangelicals, Whitefield did not prove to be particularly quotable. One of the anomalies of the literature of the Awakening is that Whitefield's sermons, as they now appear on the printed page, themselves seem somewhat "stale and lifeless." Here and there—especially at those moments when he chooses to dramatize dialogues between earth and heaven—one can glimpse some of the sources of his oratorical power. But even when the sermons are read aloud, whereby one can capture something of his sonorousness and the power of his assonance (the actor David Garrick was moved simply by Whitefield's pronunciation of the word "Mesopotamia"!), one must accept, almost on faith, the reputation he garnered through thirty years of visitation to the colonies. (On his death in 1770, Phillis Wheatley, the African-born Boston poet, and Philip Freneau and Hugh Henry Brackenridge, in their original version of "The Rising Glory of America," were inspired to apostrophize Whitefield as both emblem and engineer of a new America.) Quite possibly Whitefield's contribution to the sermon style of the colonies derived from his not being heir to the Puritan literary tradition, and his ability, therefore, to hasten the already emerging departure from the classic Puritan sermon, with its lingering dependence on William Perkins's notion of the sermon's proper fourfold division.

The transition would undoubtedly have occurred in any case, insofar as Edwards's own thinking, confirmed by Locke, led to an abandonment of the "faculty psychology" on which the old division of reason, doctrine, and uses had been based. Edwards, viewing the personality as an organic whole, could no longer address each of the "faculties" in turn. Assuming that the will could not but be moved as the understanding perceived, Edwards argued, in his *Treatise Concerning Religious Affections*, that spiritual knowledge differed from a mere notional or speculative understanding, and consisted "in a sense of the heart" that could not but express itself in holy practice: "Godliness in the heart has as direct a relation to practice, as a fountain has to a stream, or as the luminous nature of the sun has to beams sent forth, or as life has to breathing." The *Religious Affections*, as a series of sermons and even as expanded into a lengthier treatise, displays certain of Edwards's progressive modifications of his sermon style in ways that only a systematic survey of his entire *corpus* would otherwise demonstrate. He insists on a chastening of metaphoric language (which, he allows, had led to some of the "vain imaginings" of those who merely *thought* they had been overwhelmed with true affection); he inverts, in effect, the role of Scripture and reason, establishing his argument with the latter, making it more compelling with the language of the former:

Lest I mention a great many things, and places of Scripture, that the world will judge but frivolous reasons for the proof of what I drive at, [I] . . . bring 'em in so that the force of the reasons will naturally and unavoidably be brought to the mind of the reader.

Assonance, alliteration, repetition, progressive and rhythmic expansion of clauses—even in his nonsermonic writings—attest that Edwards always, like his Puritan forebears, attempted to address the ear as well as the eye. Indeed, in his careful use of commonly understood "simile," he was, if only in this respect, the most "Puritan" of the Puritans: a consummate practitioner of the "plain style."

Many of Edwards's rhetorical strategies can be discerned in earlier sermons, as in *Justification by Faith Alone*, where Edwards converts some of the more "obscure" and metaphoric language of Scripture into a Newtonian simile that makes the "covenant" between God and man gravitational rather than contractual. They culminate, of course, in the last two dissertations, most notably in his vision (toward the close of *Concerning the End for Which God Created the World*) of the Church Triumphant as atoms gravitationally ascending back toward the godhead, and in his celebration of light (a reminder that Milton, along with Locke and Newton, impinged profoundly on Edwards), a hymn that concludes with almost perfunctory citation of Scripture. (*Concerning the End*, with its characterization of a Deity aesthetically determined to emanate his grace among his creatures, ought to be read in conjunction with the recently republished [1971] *Treatise on Grace*, wherein Edwards describes, in some of his most evocative prose, how the divine outpouring flows into the human personality.)

From Newton, one assumes, Edwards also derived the meaning of one of the central words in his vocabulary, "consent": in his *Images or Shadows of Divine Things* (published 1948), a series of notebook entries never designed for publication but revealing throughout Edwards's attempts to read "nature" as, like Scripture, God's metaphor or similitude, perhaps the central image is this:

79. The whole material universe is preserved by gravity or attraction, or the mutual tendency of all bodies to each other. . . . This is a type of love or charity in the spiritual world.

Nor was Edwards, one surmises, using the word "type" idly, as mere image or emblem. It was, as in its scriptural usage, both harbinger and promise, in this case of that "amiable . . . union" in society he defined, in *An Humble Attempt*, as presaging the Kingdom of God on earth. The same aesthetic vision, further refined, controls his definition—ultimately phrased as "consent to Being in General"—in *The Nature of True Virtue:*

The reason, or at least one reason why God has made this kind of mutual consent and agreement of things beautiful and grateful to those intelligent Beings that perceive it, probably is, that there is in it some image of the true, original beauty which has been spoken of; consisting in Being's consent to Being, or the union of minds or spiritual Beings in a mutual propensity and affection of heart. . . . because therein is some image of the consent of mind, of the different members of a society or system of intelligent Beings, sweetly united in a benevolent agreement of heart.

The "rationalist" critics of the Awakening had little to say of beauty, and nothing whatever, of course, of "sweet mutual consents." Chauncy once opined he hoped *Paradise Lost* might be translated into prose, and his social and political vision was contractually Lockean to the core. But another, though quite contrasting, aesthetic vision can be discerned in the words of Edwards's one-time tutor, the Churchman Samuel Johnson. At first suspicious of the "new philosophy" as threatening to all revealed religion, Johnson by 1730 was a correspondent of Bishop George Berkeley and soon became an ardent adherent and disciple. (It is questionable whether Edwards, for all the similarities between his "idealism" and Berkeley's, ever read the latter.) In his sermons, however, Johnson refrained from denying Locke's differentiation between "primary" and "secondary" qualities and continued to treat the created world as real, not as a congeries of perceptions. In his unpublished dialogue (written probably no earlier than 1763) "Raphael; or,

The Genius of English America: A Rhapsody," Johnson moved directly from a vision of nature to a prophecy of a future—"the business allotted to me is to be the guardian or genius of New England"—as structured, and ordered, as that he conceived the polity and society of Britain to be. It was to his parishioners, however, that Johnson most vividly portrayed the created world as the analogue, even the emblem, of matters more social and spiritual:

And as all the beauty and usefulness of the natural world thus depends upon giving and receiving, so it is from hence that all the harmony and happiness of the moral world does in like manner entirely derive; all depends upon a perpetual exchange of mutual good offices. Thus the parents must nourish and educate the children, and the children must return duty and obedience to the parents. The magistrate must protect and govern the subjects, and they must return honor and submission to the magistrate. The pastor must instruct and guide the flock, and they must yield reverence and submission to him. The master must be just and kind to the servant, and the servant must be obedient and faithful to the master. The knowing must instruct the ignorant, and they must be obsequious to their instructors.

Somewhere between these two visions—that of Edwards's *Humble Attempt*, the hope and promise of a new community, and Johnson's "Raphael," a panegyric to semifeudal order, lay the view, too often implied by Chauncy, that social classes owe little or nothing to each other. One need not judge among them—though posterity has presumably not erred in singling out Edwards as *the* creative mind of the age—in order to acknowledge that these three intelligences, each abetted by myriad colleagues, helped set the agenda, in the years between the Awakening and the Revolution, for our endless debate over the nature of the American character and society.

Alan Heimert

Thomas Jefferson and the Writing of the South

The earliest memory Thomas Jefferson had was of being carried on a silk pillow by a slave. Monticello, the fabulous plantation mansion he himself designed, was built on his "little mountain" near Charlottesville, Virginia, by slave labor. He was brought to his grave on the slope below Monticello in a slave-built coffin. Yet while Jefferson was an integral member of the plantation patriciate and never even imagined the possibility of altering his social status as a slave master, he publicly opposed the institution of slavery all his life.

A long life, it was paradoxically dedicated to one great end: freedom of the mind. In accordance with his own instructions, the legend on the monument above his grave memorializes the three accomplishments Jefferson deemed most exemplary of this dedication: his authorship of the Declaration of Independence (1776) and of the Virginia Statute for Religious Freedom (enacted 1786) and his fathering of the University of Virginia (chartered by the General Assembly in 1819). In these achievements Jefferson bequeathed to the new republic the conception that the individual mind is sovereign over both state and church, owing its ultimate allegiance only to the republic of letters, a "great fraternity spreading over the whole earth" (see Jefferson's letter to John Hollins in 1809). This cosmopolitan realm of letters and learning, having originated in the secularization of the university in the aftermath of the Middle Ages, was both the source and the context of the great critique of nature and God, man and society, that marks the inception of modernity. In a sense the establishment of the University of Virginia at Charlottesville simply represented an expansion of the republic of letters as it had been symbolized for fifty years by nearby Monticello, at once the seat of a dominion of land and slaves and a microcosmic representation of the universal order of letters and learning. That the legend Jefferson himself devised for his tomb now seems ironic is not because Jefferson himself was aware of any irony in being both a slave master and a man of letters. Following the tendency of his native culture to associate mind and letters with the figure of the plantation master, he made Monticello the prime symbol in America of the plantation as a literary and intellectual domain, a climactic expression of the equation in the Southern planting society—especially in the Virginia version of this society—of land, slaves, and mind.

The equation is clearly present in the careers of William Fitzhugh, Robert Carter, and Robert Beverley. Lawyer and member of the House of Burgesses, Fitzhugh, a tobacco planter, acquired a large estate in Stafford County, Virginia, where he forecast the future of the South by introducing slavery on a large scale. A noted authority on law, Fitzhugh carried on a correspondence that because of its personal and detailed quality has, like the letters of William Byrd II, been accorded a marked place in colonial literature. Called "King Carter" because of his wealth and influence unmatched in Virginia, Robert Carter possessed a library of legal, religious, and historical works substantial enough to give the family home at Cortoman a literary and intellectual aura. The relation between letters and the plantation, however, was more completely, if more austerely, expressed by the second Robert Beverley, a native Virginian, who left Jamestown and public life in 1706 to take up his residence for the last eighteen years of his life at Beverley Park in King and Queen County, Virginia. Here Beverley, a widower, lived plainly and self-sufficiently. While he directed his slaves and indentured servants in the cultivation of grapes, hoping he could redeem his land from its depletion by the excessive cultivation of tobacco, he enjoyed the pleasures of what was for the time and place a large library. In the classic colonial work for which he is remembered, *The History and Present State of Virginia* (first edition, 1705; second edition, 1722), Beverley refers to the "plainness" of his dress but employs a carefully crafted simplicity and precision of style and diction that belies the implicit apology for his lack of sophistication. The effectiveness of Beverley's strategy derived from a major phenomenon of the secularizing process in postmedieval culture, the attraction to the Greco-Roman pastoral. In the light of Beverley's literary education, the pastoral motif is predictable and we can ascribe to it no element of originality; but in his very adherence to the Virgilian tradition of the man of letters as moral authority, Beverley presents his image in a new guise, the man of letters as Virginia plantation master. In this semblance the author on a remote plantation on the southern seaboard of the British colonial settlement in America becomes a figure of literary authority, who, it is suggested, presides over a symbolic extension of the cosmopolitan realm of letters.

The pre-Jeffersonian image of the man of letters in the Southern colonies was not, to be sure, exclusively embodied in the figure of the planter. The role was incarnated in someone like James Reid. Reid, who may have come to the colonies as an indentured tutor, composed a few moralistic essays for the *Virginia Gazette* in 1768–69. In 1769 he also wrote *The Religion of the Bible and the Religion of King William County Compared* (not published until 1967), a lengthy prose satire in which Reid plays on the notion that the typical young Virginia gentleman is not an "esquire" but an "Ass-queer," who "drinks, fights, bullies, curses, swears, games." The man of letters was more significantly represented by a medical doctor, Dr. Alexander Hamilton. Founder of the Tuesday Club in Annapolis, Hamilton was a leading physician in his city. His travel narrative, *Itinerarium* (not published until 1907), an account of Hamilton's horseback journey in the Northern colonies, is among the best colonial records of domestic travel. The Southern ecclesiastic also represented the man of letters, as, for example, in the instance of the Reverend Hugh Jones, whose *The Present State of Virginia* (1724) is different from Beverley's book in that it praises Virginia life as a faithful replication of life in England. A more considerable example of the clergyman as man of letters is offered in the instance of the Reverend William Stith, author of *The First Discovery and Settlement of Virginia* (1747). In his research into the rights of colonials as citizens of England, Stith anticipates the debate about liberty in the Revolutionary era. In addition to writers like Jones and Stith, the Southern colonies also knew the printer as man of letters, notably in William Parks. Founder of the *Virginia Gazette* in Williamsburg in 1736 (after having established the *Maryland Gazette*, the first newspaper in the Southern colonies, in 1727), Parks did not rival Benjamin Franklin in genius but he did rival him in his understanding of the medium of print and his devotion to it. His importance was not unrecognized by his contemporaries. The first known poem he printed, twenty years before he began the *Virginia Gazette*, was in part a tribute to Parks himself. The author of this poem was John Markland, who seems to have been a lawyer who had been schooled at Cambridge University.

But neither the figure of the clergyman nor the printer as man of letters counted for as much in the Southern as in the Northern colonies. From its representation by Beverley—a self-conscious colonial who worked his ground with a combination of indentured and slave labor, who to an extent rebelled against a colonial identity and had intimations of being radically different from the master of the English estate—the Southern man of letters evolved into its representation by Jefferson, slave master and rebel against the authority of king and church.

Meanwhile, the representation of the colonial author by Beverley's younger contemporary, William Byrd II, provided a logical transition to the Jeffersonian image. By the 1730s, when William Byrd II had replaced the house his migrant father built at Westover with a far more elegant structure—one appropriate to the seat of a dominion that would eventually encompass over 179,000 acres in Virginia and North Carolina—the connection between chattel slavery and the Virginia plantation economy had become virtually complete. Seeking the hand of Mary Smith in London in 1718, Byrd informed her father that he possessed "about 43000 acres of land and 220 Negroes at work upon it," observing that some of his land was "let out to tenants" but that the usual method in Virginia "is to seat our slaves" on the land and "send the fruit of their labour" to England. Yet even though, after the last and longest of his sojourns in England (1715–26), Byrd established himself with his slaves at Westover, compiled one of the largest libraries in the colonies (3,600 volumes, of which a notable number were in the realm of belles lettres), and wrote *The History of the Dividing Line* and other works for which he is now known (including an addition to his notorious diaries in secret code), he can hardly be said to have affixed a firm seal on the relationship land and slavery would bear to mind by Jefferson's time. Always the man of letters as colonial gentleman—he would remain an unpublished author until 1841, a century after his death—Byrd accepted slavery as an expediency. He participated in its expansion in America with no grasp of the underlying rationale of his action and, although fearful at moments that the increase in the number of slaves might result in a rebellion, no appreciable sense of its political, social, or moral consequences.

Why chattel slavery became the dominant labor system in most of the Southern colonies in the eighteenth century is not altogether clear. The obvious reason seems to have been the accelerating need for laborers to work a constantly expanding extent of cultivated land; by the second decade of the eighteenth century planters had committed themselves to the slave system, their commitment becoming more absolute as they formed the practice of converting land and chattels into cash when crop or market failed. But economic expediency was not the only reason why slavery became a fixed institution in the Southern colonies. Planters developed a fateful political stake in slavery. As Edmund Morgan (in *American Slavery, American Freedom: The Ordeal of Colonial Virginia* [1975]) has convincingly suggested, slavery answered to the need to stem the prospective insurgency of a class of free white poor that was growing apace as laborers bound for a limited term of service were released from their indentured status. Pursuing this expediency, though without altogether realizing they were doing so, those in power in the largest, most populous, and wealthiest Southern colony established a society that found a rational solution not only to the most vexatious economic problem in the Old World, that is, the poverty of the masses, but to the political problem of the influence of mobs. The compatibility of rational mind and slavery was summed up with simplistic yet penetrating clarity by an English traveler who said in 1805 that Virginians "can profess an unbounded love of liberty and of democracy in consequence of the mass of the people, who in other countries might become mobs, being there nearly altogether composed of their own Negro slaves."

The nature and meaning of this complex, ironic, ultimately tragic historical situation can be studied in George Washington of Mount Vernon and other Virginia planters and men of letters who were active proponents of the Revolution: the diarist and pamphleteer Landon Carter of Sabine Hall; the author of the prototype of the Declaration of Independence, the Virginia Bill of Rights, George Mason of Gunston Hall; the orator and pamphleteer Richard Henry Lee of Chantilly; the political philosopher, later fourth President, James Madison of Montpelier; the dramatist Robert Munford of Richland; and the poet St. George Tucker of Matoax. It can be studied too in the career of Patrick Henry. The "organ of the great body of the people," as one admirer called him, Henry was a backcountry lawyer who occupied a somewhat anomalous position among the plantation men of letters. But the power of his eloquence made him the preeminent example of the man of letters as orator in an age when the spoken word was a vital literary genre and frequently of crucial influence. Another important exemplar of the art of oratory in the Southern colonies, Richard Henry Lee, had a more finished style but was less effective in the Continental Congress than Henry, who foreshadowed the omnipresent influence of the orator on the common citizenry of the South.

But the historical situation of the South in the Revolutionary age received its most revealing expression not in the discourse of public assembly but in a work that its author did not intend for public distribution, Jefferson's *Notes on the State of Virginia* (privately printed, 1785; publicly printed, 1787). The underlying subject of this book, though not by purposeful design, is the intricate connection between slavery and the rational ethos. Structured as a series of replies to queries propounded by François Marbois, secretary of the French legation in Philadelphia, *Notes on Virginia*—which established

Jefferson as the archetypal Southern man of letters—was the product of hard work during a period of anxious leisure; for it was written mostly in 1781–82, the dark time when, having retired from the governorship and under investigation because of military reverses in Virginia, Jefferson had taken refuge at his Poplar Hill plantation. Nearing forty, he had acquired a command of knowledge comparable in its width and diversity to that of Voltaire in history and of Franklin in science. *Notes on Virginia,* to be sure, places Jefferson in the company of the great minds of his century. A deeply personal document, it exhibits the mind of a man of letters under pressures generated by an involved endeavor to represent both the cosmopolitan republic of letters and his own provincial society—a society that was on the one hand a slave order and on the other a revolutionary order that had rejected slavery to a king in the name of the sovereignty of the self and the freedom and equality of all selves.

Out of the complex tensions of *Notes on Virginia,* the most important book written by a Southerner before the Civil War, a tangled drama of historical representation emerges. Embracing not only Virginia and the other Southern states but the whole nation, this drama derives from the enmeshment of Americans in the determinative motif of modern history, which may be described as the human mind's transference into itself, by its own act of willing, not only God and nature, man and society, but mind itself. Yet, unlike the Declaration of Independence, *Notes on Virginia* distinctly implies doubt both in the mind's capacity to incorporate existence and in the validity of the mind's own conception of itself as the instrument of reason.

The doubt of mind's capacity haunts especially the chapters on law, religion, and manners in *Notes on Virginia.* It is nowhere so graphically indicated as it is in the discussion of manners (the eighteenth chapter), in which Jefferson indicates his apocalyptic fear that even if the Virginians are capable of freeing themselves from enslavement to both king and church, they may not be capable of freeing themselves from bondage to their own slaves. Portraying the "whole commerce between master and slave" as "a perpetual exercise of the most boisterous passions, the most unremitting despotism" on the part of the masters and "degrading submissions" on the part of the slaves, Jefferson—within one highly concentrated paragraph that is the whole of his response to Marbois's query about "customs and manners" in Virginia—makes the most eloquent, desperate, and frightening appeal on behalf of "total emancipation" to be found in the American literature of slavery. Unless emancipation occurs he sees an end to the acceptance of their condition by the enslaved and the "extirpation" of the moral monsters who are their masters, this being accomplished either by the oppressed themselves or by "supernatural interference." In the era of the South's fierce defense of slavery after his death, Jefferson was anathematized as a traitor to his own community. In view of the evidence about the actuality of plantation life at Mount Vernon, Sabine Hall, Montpelier, or Monticello, Jefferson undoubtedly did misrepresent the observable fact of the everyday relationship of slaves and their masters; yet it would seem that, in doing so, he was assuming the license of a poet or a novelist to represent the inner truth of his own historical time and place through a symbolic fiction. Justifying the reading of fiction, Jefferson had once advised young Robert Skipwith (in a letter dated August 3, 1771), "Considering history as a moral exercise, her lessons would be too infrequent if confined to real life." In a moment of Faulknerian intensity in *Notes on Virginia*, Jefferson would seem to have been transported into a dark fiction of the plantation, in which he not only sees himself and his peers sunk in rage and indolence but envisions their children corrupted, possibly beyond redemption, by "odious peculiarities" of character resulting from imitating their parents in the daily exercise of tyranny. In the inward reaches of Jefferson's imagination rational discrimination between "real life" and fiction fades; in fact, it virtually vanishes when Jefferson—ignoring his conviction that scientific evidence proves the inferiority of Africans—refers to the "statesman" who is guilty of "permitting one half the citizens . . . to trample on the rights of the other," and in effect acknowledges his African slaves (though he would never do so again) as his fellow citizens.

Yet a year before Jefferson began *Notes on Virginia*, while he was still in the governor's office, the Virginia General Assembly—assuming a pragmatic connection between republican liberty and slavery—enacted legislation awarding soldiers engaged in the struggle for liberty against the Crown three hundred acres and a slave. Dramatizing the profound tension between liberty and slavery in Jefferson's world, *Notes on Virginia* defines a crisis in the relationship of land, slaves, and mind that would become pervasive in the Southern states.

Not the least significance of Jefferson's denunciation of the life of the plantation society is that it destroyed the image Robert Beverley and William Byrd had suggested and that Jefferson had fostered, and continued always to foster at Monticello, of the plantation as the homeland of the mind in the New World. One of the inarticulate ironies in *Notes on Virginia* is Jefferson's essential repression of his nightmarish vision of the plantation society by presenting in the immediately succeeding chapter ("Manufactures") an apposite apocalypse, a vision of Virginia (and the new nation) as a world of self-subsistent husbandmen, each rooted on his own freehold, where he harbors the "peculiar deposit of substantial and genuine virtue" that God bestows on independent tillers of the soil. But while Jefferson in the guise of the pastoral poet could create the fiction of the dominion of the autonomous farmer, he could not conceive of the yeoman as a man of letters. The life of mind and letters in the planting states was vested in the image of the plantation, and Jefferson continued to envision Monticello in this image throughout his life. Transmitted to the South of William Gilmore Simms and Edgar Allan Poe, the image of the literary plantation was realized at Woodlands, Simms's noted South Carolina home; and symbolically, in an ironic, correlative sense, in Poe's depiction of Roderick Usher's melancholy dominion.

Becoming active defenders of slavery, the post-Jeffersonian generation of writers developed extremists like George Fitzhugh, who condemned Jefferson for failing to make slavery the necessary basis of freedom, and thus becoming an "architect of ruin." But while those who argued for what Southerners called their "peculiar institution" as a "positive good" were intolerant of antislavery sentiment and hardly believed with Jefferson in the "free right to the unbounded exercise of freedom and opinion," they faithfully imitated him in refusing to admit the irony of the historical situation of the South. They fulfilled what Jefferson had anticipated: the closure of the mind of the South in the apologetics and politics of the Lost Cause. But in his sense of enhancing the moral exercise of history, in his momentary fictional revelation of the inner ironic truth of the history of the world the slaveholders had made, and in his act of repressing his terrible vision in a counterfiction of the world of autonomous small farmers, Jefferson also anticipated a major shift in the perspective of the postbellum Southern writer. The shift is first fully evident in Mark Twain, who, as Allen Tate, following W. B. Yeats, observed (in "A Southern Mode of the Imagination" [1965]), transformed the Southern quarrel with others into a quarrel within the self. In *Adventures of Huckleberry Finn* (1885) and *Pudd'nhead Wilson* (1894) Mark Twain brings both the dominion of the slaveholders and that of the small farmers and villagers under the scrutiny of a singular comic-pathetic-tragic backward vision of the antebellum South he had experienced. Another generation would elapse before Southern writers, notably William Faulkner and Robert Penn Warren, would deliberately confront the paradoxical history of the South. Choosing Jefferson as the name of the seat of Yoknapatawpha, his mythical county in northern Mississippi, Faulkner—preeminently in *Absalom, Absalom!*, *Go Down, Moses*, and *The Hamlet*—joined the moral exercise of history and the fictional representation of Southern history in a microcosmic vision of modern history. Explicitly stating what

Faulkner believed implicitly, that "history is the big myth we live, and in our living, constantly remake," Warren—most patently in his "Tale in Verse and Voices," *Brother to Dragons* (first version, 1953; new version, 1979), a dramatic poem in which the ghost of Jefferson is the leading actor—discovered that the most consequential literary aspect of the Jeffersonian heritage is the irony of Jefferson's suppression of the irony of history. In his act of suppression, Warren suggests, Jefferson forecast the quintessential anxiety about freedom, slavery, and the identity of the writer—of the literary mind—that marks modern literature.

Lewis P. Simpson

IV. The Literature of the New Republic

The American Revolution
as a Literary Event

The central literary manifestation of the American Revolution is generally conceived to be the body of polemical prose that, extending over the decades from the end of the French and Indian Wars in 1763 to the adoption of the Constitution in 1789, laboriously hammered out the concepts and the language by which the American nation and its polity came to be construed. That body of writing is a massive one, occupying thousands of columns of print in the newspapers of the period and hundreds of separately published pamphlets. It was as if the tracts and treatises of religious controversy that form the dominant literary activity of the seventeenth and early eighteenth centuries in America had undergone a secular transformation by which the quest for salvation was translated into the pursuit of liberty. But though the polemicists of the Revolutionary era turned their attention from the next world to this one, they retained something of their predecessors' millennial vision and preoccupation with values larger and more lasting than the interests immediately at risk in a specific political controversy. From the very outset of the debate in the 1760s, the most thoughtful of the pamphlets and newspaper essays reached beyond the legalistic refinement of the distinctions between internal and external taxation or between actual and virtual representation in Parliament to engage the great questions: the source and scope of political authority, the basis and extent of individual rights, and, beyond all, the enigmas of human nature, from which spring both the necessity of government and the possibility of limiting its actions.

But only a small portion of the writings that were generated by the two and a half decades of political debate is distinguished by both that breadth of interest and a commensurate literary strength. Most of them, like Daniel Dulany's *Considerations on the Propriety of Imposing Taxes in the British Colonies* (1765), Richard Bland's *Inquiry into the Rights of the British Colonies* (1766), or James Wilson's *Considerations on the . . . Authority of the British Parliament* (1774), were written by lawyers for lawyers; they are highly respectable arguments, fascinating to the intellectual historian for their adaptation of the rhetoric and opinions of eighteenth-century English political radicalism to American circumstances, but devoid of appeal to the imagination or emotions. Even the pamphlets of James Otis, whose brilliant political career was to darken in madness and whose life was to be ended by a lightning bolt, only occasionally reward the reader with departures from the decorum of the correct legal brief, as when, in *The Rights of the British Colonies* (1764), his demonstration of the injustice of taxation without representation becomes for a moment an impassioned denunciation of black slavery, or when, in *A Vindication of the British Colonies* (1765), his closing plea for moderation immoderately projects the "shambles of blood and confusion" that an independent America would become.

Otis's fear of the consequences of independence was shared by most responsible writers of the 1760s, among them John Dickinson, whose *Letters from a Farmer in Pennsylvania*, first published serially in newspapers in 1767–68 and then as a pamphlet in 1768, was the most influential political work written in America before the war began in 1775. But the traditional emphasis on Dickinson's caution and restraint in the *Letters* is misplaced, evidently deriving from his notorious opposition to independence in 1776 and not from any relative timidity in 1768. The subdued tone of the *Letters* is an element in the rhetorical strategy of the work, appropriate to the modest and unassuming pose of lawyer Dickinson's farmer persona and useful as a cover for implications that border on the inflammatory. Thus in the very letter in which the Pennsylvania Farmer observes that the "cause of *liberty* is a cause of too much dignity to be sullied by turbulence and tumult," he also notes in passing that if "at length it becomes UNDOUBTED that an inveterate resolution is formed to annihilate the liberties of the governed, the *English* history affords frequent examples of resistance by force." Written chiefly in response to the Townshend Acts of 1767, which imposed duties on a variety of imported goods, Dickinson's *Letters* moves beyond the issue of taxation to become a lesson in the moral requirements of freedom, urging Americans to attain the "prudence, justice, modesty, bravery, humanity and magnanimity" that will allow them to triumph over the "ambitious, artful men" who govern Great Britain. They are to emulate the ancient Spartans, who marched into battle "not to the sound of trumpets, but to the sound of flutes." If the *Letters* sounds less like the blare of a trumpet than the low tones of a flute, the summons is nonetheless to battle.

By the 1770s, the writings concerned with the controversy between the colonies and Great Britain took on a far more strident note. The violence of incidents like the Boston Massacre of 1770 and the burning of the customs schooner *Gaspee* in 1772 found a rhetorical equivalent in sermons and orations that waved the bloody shirt of atrocity. A little more than a month before the outbreak of fighting at Concord and Lexington, Joseph Warren was inviting those who heard and later read *An Oration Delivered March Sixth* (1775) to imagine the plight of the children whose fathers were slain in the Boston Massacre: "Take heed, ye orphan babes, lest, while your streaming eyes are fixed upon the ghastly corpse, your feet slide on the stones bespattered with your father's brains!" Contemplating the prospect of renewed oppression as British troops once more occupy Boston, Warren wonders if the "only way to safety is through fields of blood," a portentous speculation from a man who, three months later, was to fall at Bunker Hill.

Contributing to the change in the tone of the pamphlets of the 1770s was the appearance of writers who had little in common with men like Otis and Dickinson, successful lawyers and established leaders of their communities. The most colorful of the newcomers was John Allen, a Baptist minister who, dismissed by his church in England, came to America sometime before December 3, 1772, when he delivered *An Oration, upon the Beauties of Liberty* (1773) as the Thanksgiving Day Address at the Second Baptist Church in Boston. Allen, who had been imprisoned for debt in England, was eloquent on his subject, achieving a crude vigor and scriptural rhythmicity that most lawyers would disdain and, as the immense popularity of his pamphlet testifies, reaching an audience that few of them could attract. A very different but equally unprecedented voice was that of Charles Lee, a Rousseau-reading soldier of fortune who came to America in late 1773 armed with a letter of introduction from Benjamin Franklin and intent upon establishing himself as a military authority in the colonies. Responding to *A Friendly Address* (1774) by the Reverend Thomas Chandler, which warned rebellious Americans against opposing the combined might of the Royal Army and its Loyalist allies, Lee's *Strictures on a Pamphlet* (1774) invoked the mock-epic tradition of eighteenth-century satire as it pictured his ecclesiastical adversary at the head of his forces, "an inquisitorial frown upon his brow, his bands and canonicals floating to the air." Like Allen's *Oration*, Lee's *Strictures* was to become one of the six most widely circulated pamphlets published before the Declaration of Independence.

Chandler's pamphlet, on the other hand, is evidence of still another new element in the political writings of the early 1770s, the sharply increased activity of able and persistent supporters of the Crown and its measures. In the previous decade, the argument had been chiefly between American writers and English ones, but with the increasingly divisive character of the controversy in the 1770s as armed resistance began to be openly considered, the debate became more and more internalized. Like Chandler, a number of those who recommended submission to Great Britain were Anglican clergymen. In Virginia, Jonathan Boucher preached with loaded pistols at hand "On Civil Liberty, Passive Obedience, and Nonresistance," a sermon intended for publication when it was delivered in 1775, but not finding its way into print until 1797, when it was issued in London together with twelve companion pieces. In New York, Samuel Seabury, rector of St. Peter's Church in New Rochelle, wrote a series of four pamphlet letters under the name of the Westchester Farmer in late 1774 and early 1775 for James Rivington's Tory press, so effective in their denunciation of Congress and its nonimportation decrees that they provoked two answering pamphlets, *A Full Vindication of the Measures of Congress* (1774) and *The Farmer Refuted* (1775), from Alexander Hamilton. Another of the many newcomers to the controversy, Hamilton responded to Seabury's Hobbesian argument for the necessity of rigorous government by making a fervent appeal to the "sacred rights of mankind," which "are not to be rummaged for among old parchments or musty records. They are written, as with a sunbeam, in the whole volume of human nature, by the hand of divinity itself, and can never be erased or obscured by mortal power."

The young Hamilton's rejection of constitutional and historical arguments in favor of a direct appeal to the needs and claims of human nature points to a sharp change that was occurring in the polemical writing of Revolutionary America. The last major example of the older legalistic mode of defining American rights and justifying resistance to Great Britain is a series of twelve essays that John Adams contributed to the *Boston Gazette* in the early months of 1775 in reply to seventeen letters by Daniel Leonard then being printed in the *Massachusetts Gazette* under the pen name "Massachusettensis." To Leonard's charge that the Whigs by their demagogic exaggeration of trivial grievances were moving Massachusetts to the verge of catastrophe, Adams, writing as "Novanglus," responded first by contending that the oppressive acts of Great Britain were neither petty nor isolated incidents but the consequence of a long-standing conspiracy between the British government and its American agents to subjugate the colony, and then by accumulating a mass of common law and statutory precedents to prove that Americans owed allegiance only to the person of the British monarch, not to his government or to Parliament. The Novanglus essays represent the furthest development of an argument that Adams and his fellow Whig lawyers had been refining for ten years, but even he must have realized that the volleys of musket fire at Lexington only two days after the last of the essays appeared made the whole effort an irrelevance. All such arguments had become, as the greatest of the Revolutionary pamphlets, Thomas Paine's *Common Sense*, was shortly to observe, "like the almanacs of the last year."

It was under the vastly changed circumstances of armed conflict, then, that *Common Sense* appeared and made its tremendous impression. The pamphlet was first published in Philadelphia in early January 1776 and was quickly reprinted throughout the colonies and in Europe, attaining a sale of more than 100,000 copies within a few months. Surely a large measure of the appeal of the pamphlet can be attributed to the fact that its author was a newcomer to America and its quarrel with Great Britain. Paine had arrived in Philadelphia from England late in 1774. Like John Allen, he left behind him a past he would prefer to forget; like Charles Lee, he came equipped with Franklin's endorsement and, with it, access to the Whig circles at the center of the rising storm; and like Hamilton, if not so precociously, he had arrived at the conviction that the rights of man were not matters of law and custom but were divinely implanted in human nature itself.

Thus prepared, Paine could dismiss all previous arguments and move directly to the task at hand, the effort to bring American attitudes into consonance with American realities. Asserting that reconciliation "is *now* a fallacious dream," he urges acceptance of the independence from Great Britain that warfare, by then spreading from Virginia to Canada, was fast establishing as a fact. Without the local allegiances that still made a New Englander regard a Carolinian as an exotic, Paine could take the newly popular word *continental* seriously and exhort his readers to think and act as Americans, a people with obligations both to their posterity in the future and to all mankind in the present, for whom the new nation furnishes both example and asylum. It is difficult to imagine any of Paine's predecessors in the pamphlet wars that preceded the Revolution achieving as he does an Adamic vision that in its superb confidence looks forward to Walt Whitman: "We have it in our power to begin the world over again." Possessed of the skills of a journalist rather than those of a gentleman-lawyer, gifted with an acute ear for cadence and echo, and animated by an immediate sympathy for the experience of common people, Paine is, with the exception of Thomas Jefferson in the Declaration of Independence, the one political writer of the Revolution whose language still lives in the national mind.

Just as *Common Sense* prepared the ground for the acceptance of American independence as a goal, the sixteen essays that Paine published from time to time throughout the war under the title of *The Crisis* were written to sustain the will to achieve it. When he brought the series to a close on April 19, 1783, the eighth anniversary of Concord and Lexington, he could hope that he had not only rendered service to the country but "likewise added something to the reputation of literature by freely and disinterestedly employing it in the great cause of mankind and showing that there may be genius without prostitution." And then, with a gesture that again seems to anticipate Whitman, he bids his audience farewell, assuring them that his part in their ordeal will remain a source of pride to him, "whatever country I may hereafter be in." It is as if he were some vagrant spirit that had fulfilled its mission in the New World and was now passing on to other tasks in other places. There were indeed other tasks, among them the writing of those two primary documents of the revolutionary era of Europe, *The Rights of Man* (1791–92) and *The Age of Reason* (1794–96), but by then Paine had become *persona non grata* in the United States, vilified as a Jacobin and an atheist. Even so, he returned to America in 1802 after years of vicissitude in Europe. It was fitting that ten years after his death in poverty and disgrace in New Rochelle, William Cobbett had his bones removed to England.

If Paine's reputation in America was to subside almost as quickly as it had flared, his central belief in the sanctity of the rights of man was perpetuated in American political life by Thomas Jefferson in the Declaration of Independence (1776), the necessarily final statement in the long debate over the right relationship of America and Great Britain. Jefferson's first contribution to that debate had been *A Summary View of the Rights of British America* (1774), a pamphlet that differs from other advanced formulations of the Whig position only in the nobility of its language and its occasional unhistorical appeal to rights that derive from nature or from nature's God rather than from civil law. Although *A Summary View* was the credential that won Jefferson the assignment of drafting the Declaration, it in no way forecast the structural simplicity and inevitability that give the latter document its enduring strength.

Grounded on the three terms of its controlling syllogism, the Declaration moves from its opening proclamation of the people's right to overthrow a destructive government, through its accumulated evidence of the destructive nature of British rule in America, to its concluding declaration of the independence of the colonies from that rule. There is no pretense at originality in Jefferson's argument; indeed, as he later observed, he intended the document "to be an expression of the American mind," a distillation and announcement of the assumptions and attitudes on which the decade of debate and the year of combat had produced widespread agreement. When the Continental Congress struck from Jefferson's draft its two most stirring passages—one of which caps the list of crimes attributed to George III by charging him with responsibility for the slave trade, and the other of which accuses the British people of waging fratricidal warfare against Americans—it made the Declaration a more accurate reflection of the opinions of his countrymen, many of whom did not share his deep sense of the atrocity of slavery or his unconcern for wounding the feelings of whatever friends America might still have among the British people. And if the deletions diminished the emotional intensity of the Declaration, they enhanced its dominant tone of restrained reasonableness, its maintenance of a calm and dignified logic in the face of outrage and unreason.

None of the revisions on which the Congress insisted changed the essential character of the Declaration. In its assertion of the Lockean doctrines of natural rights and the consent of the governed as the only basis of legitimate rule, it became the most radical, as well as the most fundamental, of the national documents, subjecting all future American governments to its own stern tests of justice and right. To the world at large, it marked the opening of the age of revolution, taking its place as the first of the great manifestos of human rights that the next two centuries would call forth.

The poise and assurance of the Declaration of Independence stand in sharp contrast to the varying tone and welling uncertainties of *Notes on the State of Virginia* (1785), Jefferson's one book. For all its celebration of the size and fertility of American nature, *Notes on Virginia* returns again and again to a mood of anxiety, as its author contemplates the fragility of democratic institutions and the transience of the impulse that supports them. The values of the Revolution must be secured now, he urges, while the liberal and humane temper still reigns in America, for sadly "the spirit of the times may alter, will alter. Our rulers will become corrupt, our people careless."

To many Americans in the 1780s, the threat posed by the future to the goals of the Revolution resided not in the tyranny that Jefferson feared but in a collapse into anarchy. The ineffectuality of the national government under the Articles of Confederation, adopted in 1781, led the Continental Congress in early 1787 to call a convention to revise the Articles. The Constitution proposed by that convention in September 1787 for ratification by the states was to account for the final phase of the polemical writing of the Revolutionary era and the creation of the only American contribution to the classic political literature of the world, *The Federalist*.

By and large, however, the pamphlets and newspaper essays that were occasioned by the debate over ratification of the Constitution in late 1787 and early 1788 do not form a distinguished body of writing. The opponents of the proposal shared Jefferson's distrust of concentrated power and his preference for civil liberties over governmental efficiency, but no one who possessed his intellectual ability or eloquence entered the battle. Instead the cause was left in the hands of such lesser spirits as Elbridge Gerry of Massachusetts and Melancthon Smith of New York, who saw in the absence of a bill of rights and the failure to prohibit such potential instruments of oppression as a standing army a betrayal of the Revolution. Even the most popular of the opposition pamphlets, *Letters from the Federal Farmer* (1787–88) by Richard Henry Lee of Virginia, though it seeks to speak "the language of 1774" as it condemns the Constitution as "a transfer of power from the many to the few," lacks force and point. Nor did most of the defenders of the proposal do better. Some, like Noah Webster in *An Examination into the Leading Principles of the Federal Constitution* (1787), sought to overpower their opposition with a rhetoric that looks forward to the windiest heights of nineteenth-century oratory. Others, like that veteran of the pamphlet wars John Dickinson in *The Letters of Fabius* (1788), contented themselves with the bland reiteration of familiar truths about the need to relinquish a degree of individual freedom in the interests of an orderly society. Apart from *The Federalist*, only John Jay's *Address to the People of the State of New-York* (1788) brought to the argument a steady vigor, clarity, and reasonableness, advocating adoption of the Constitution as a means of safeguarding the aims of the Revolution by demonstrating to the world that republican forms are not inconsistent with domestic peace and security.

But Jay is better remembered as the least of the three authors of *The Federalist* than for his own fine pamphlet, a small indication of the prestige that the collective work has acquired. *The Federalist* originated as a series of seventy-seven letters that appeared in New York newspapers from October 27, 1787, to April 4, 1788. A first volume of the essays was published in March 1788, and a second in May, reprinting the remainder of the series and adding a concluding eight essays to bring the total to eighty-five. The prime mover of the project was Alexander Hamilton, who initiated the scheme, designed the general plan of the essays, and enlisted the aid of Jay and James Madison in their composition. Although the series was published over the pen name "Publius," students of *The Federalist* are in general agreement that five of the essays are the work of Jay, twenty-four are Madison's, fifty-one are Hamilton's, and three are the joint productions of Madison and Hamilton; the authorship of two of the essays remains in dispute. The reader who is aware of these attributions may believe that he can distinguish the styles and stances of the three writers, but the very existence of controversy over the disputed letters suggests that such distinctions are marginal, if not imaginary. The voice of Publius is a consistent one, devoid of personality and admirably appropriate to his public identity and concerns.

Although *The Federalist* is probably not what Jefferson called it in a letter to Madison in late 1788, "the best commentary on the principles of government, which ever was written," it is surely one of the most attractive to the general reader. Because it originated not as a treatise in political science but as a campaign document and was written not by philosophers and academicians but by practical men, it ballasts its recitations of history and theory with appeals to one's own experience of popular government, invoking a world of jarring pressure groups, of widespread but wrongheaded impulses, of demagogues and elitists, all ultimately modulated by the surprising if intermittently manifested sanity and justice of the majority. For most readers, then, the value of *The Federalist* lies less in its lucid explication of federalism, the separation of powers, or the distinction between direct and representative democracy than in this realistic apprehension of the necessity of designing a government that will withstand, as Hamilton puts it, "a common portion of the vicissitudes and calamities which have fallen to the lot of other nations."

Despite its realism, *The Federalist* shares with the other political writings certain severe limitations as a representation of the era of the American Revolution. The political pamphlets and newspaper essays of the period tend to persuade the modern reader that the Revolution was an intellectual event, "an affair of the mind" in Bernard Bailyn's phrase, rather than an experience that aroused the emotions, engaged the imagination, and, for tens of thousands of people, tormented the body. The texture and dimensions of that experience are best apprehended not in the exposition and argument of the political writings but in the images of anger, exultation, confusion, and suffering that were generated by other sectors of literary activity in the period.

The Revolution proved to be a remarkably strong stimulus to imaginative writing in America. It was responsible for both the first substantial body of secular poetry and the first extensive activity in the drama. And though the first unalloyed examples of prose fiction were not to appear until after the war, the Revolutionary era gave rise to a variety of experiments in imaginative prose, most of them unprecedented in colonial literature. No high art was to emerge from the Revolution, but the very circumstances that worked against such a possibility—the urgency of the occasions that prompted the literature and the requirement that it move its readers immediately and forcefully—encouraged American writers to go beyond the safely derivative and conventional limits that previously had circumscribed most of their efforts and to achieve a new intensity and range.

Given the century and the circumstances, it is not surprising that the dominant form of the imaginative literature associated with the Revolution is verse satire. Satiric verse had served as an auxiliary in the pamphlet skirmishing of the 1760s and early 1770s, but it did not achieve major expression until after the outbreak of the war. The best known example, *M'Fingal* by John Trumbull, made its first appearance in the month in which *Common Sense* was published, January 1776, though it was then only half the length it was to have when it was reissued in 1782. The fifteen hundred couplets of the completed poem tell the story of a turbulent New England town meeting in which the Tory squire M'Fingal comes to blows with the local supporters of the Whig side of the controversy. In the catastrophe, M'Fingal is tarred and feathered, a fate that does not prevent him from attaining the prophetic vision of the outcome of the Revolution that ends the poem. Heavy though Trumbull's debts to the eighteenth-century British satirists Samuel Butler and Charles Churchill are, his poem is more than a clever imitation, for it succeeds in adapting its imported mode to its native materials. Even the steady parodic reference to James Macpherson's *Ossian* works surprisingly well in establishing the mock-epic tone of this raucous and often funny poem. But there is a strange coolness to *M'Fingal*, for it thrusts us into a world of comic violence in which there is no heroism and no suffering. The poem is finally a parody of political conflict itself; it suggests that revolutions are full of sound and fury but signify very little.

The other satiric verse of the war is not so genial or detached. In that of the passionately anti-British Philip Freneau, the issues of the Revolution gather a dark seriousness, as in "American Independent," or inspire a savage bitterness, as in "On the Fall of General Earl Cornwallis," a poem written, so the opening lines warn us, in "rage." Freneau's thirty or so Revolutionary satires are weapons, quickly and often crudely fashioned and clearly intended to wound. If they are bludgeons, the poems of the Loyalist Jonathan Odell, like Freneau a Princeton graduate, are rapiers. Forced to take refuge in occupied New York City, Odell served the British forces there as chaplain, surgeon, secret agent, and, most memorably, as satirist. In such poems as *The Congratulation* (1779) and *The American Times* (1780), Odell proved himself to be the most skillful satirist of the Revolution, able at his best to maintain in his fury the precision of an Alexander Pope.

Beyond satire, the poetry of the period ranges from formal celebratory poems like Phillis Wheatley's "To His Excellency General Washington" (1775) to rollicking doggerel like "Yankee Doodle," in all its infinite variety of verses. Some of the miscellaneous verse retains its capacity to amuse, as does Francis Hopkinson's comic narrative "The Battle of the Kegs" (1778), or to move, as does the anonymous ballad "Nathan Hale," with its haunting repetitions. But the only verse of the period that truly outlives its age is the work of Freneau in those few poems in which he succeeded in transmuting his anger into art. The largest example of that accomplishment is *The British Prison-Ship* (1781), a long narrative in heroic couplets that tells the story of Freneau's own confinement on board the prison ship *Scorpion* and the hospital ship *Hunter* in New York harbor. In it the nightmarish imagery of atrocity and ordeal takes its place within a controlled passage from bright hope through pain and despair to hatred and grim resolve. At the opposite end of the scale of size is the justly admired little poem "To the Memory of the Brave Americans (1781), which in its simplicity and restrained pathos foreshadows the Civil War elegies of Herman Melville.

No such distinction belongs to the handful of plays, Whig or Tory, that were inspired by the approach and outbreak of the Revolution, but in their energy and diversity they offer an inviting and accessible window on the era. First into the field was Mercy Otis Warren, sister of James Otis and sister-in-law of Joseph Warren, with *The Adulateur* (1773), a neoclassical tragedy *à clef* in which a transparently veiled version of the Boston Massacre forms the central incident. In *The Group* (1775), corrected for the press by John Adams and printed on the day before the battle of Lexington, Warren descends from the lofty manner of her first play to exhibit the treachery and selfishness of the Tory place-seekers and profiteers who infest the government of Massachusetts. Abandoning blank verse for prose, *The Motley Assembly* (1779) rather mildly rebukes the practice of admitting Tories to the social circles of wartime Boston. Often attributed to Warren but almost certainly by another hand, probably both male and military, is *The Blockheads* (1776), a bawdy and scatological prose farce depicting the plight of the British and their Tory allies under Washington's siege of Boston and apparently written in answer to General John Burgoyne's *The Blockade* (1776), the text of which no longer survives.

By far the most eloquent of the verse-plays of the period are two heroic dramas by Hugh Henry Brackenridge, Freneau's classmate and collaborator at Princeton. *The Battle of Bunkers-Hill* (1776) and *The Death of General Montgomery* (1777), both written for performance by the students at the academy where Brackenridge was then teaching, demonstrate an impressive facility in the dramatic use of blank verse, achieving, most apparently in the second play, both dignity and naturalness. Otherwise the plays are notable for the virulence of the author's hatred for the British, still more vehemently expressed in the sermons that he later preached as a chaplain in the army, and (in *The Battle of Bunkers-Hill*) for the most extraordinary stage direction in American dramatic literature: "Enter Gardiner, with seven hundred men."

But even with such severe demands on the resources of the theater, Brackenridge's plays seem models of stagecraft by comparison with *The Fall of British Tyranny*, a chronicle play usually ascribed to one John Leacock and published in Philadelphia in 1776. With a cast of characters numbering more than forty, the play shuttles between the Old World and the New, providing inside glimpses of the deliberations of the British ministry and thumbnail sketches of war scenes in Massachusetts, Virginia, and Canada. At the opposite extreme is Robert Munford's tightly constructed comedy *The Patriots*, not published until 1798 but evidently written shortly after July 1776. Displaying a thorough acquaintance with the eighteenth-century comic tradition, Munford neatly exposes the hypocrisy of those who hide their ambition beneath a mask of patriotism. It is a crisp and charming work, perhaps the only play of the Revolution that still merits performance.

The surviving Tory comedies show less finesse. *The Battle of Brooklyn*, an anonymous farce published in New York in 1776, is a rowdy libel on the American military leadership in which Israel Putnam is a clownish cattle thief and George Washington pays for the favors of a maidservant. *The Blockheads; or, Fortunate Contractor* (1782) is a ballad opera and masque that warns America against the dangers of its alliance with France. Simpler and more effective is *A Cure for the Spleen* (1775) by Jonathan Sewall, "a conversation on the times, over a friendly tank and pipe" in a New England tavern. The easy country speech of Sewall's characters makes the case for cooperation with Great Britain more persuasively than does any Tory pamphlet of the day.

In its village setting, Sewall's little dialogue looks forward to the most trenchant of the dramatic writings of the Revolutionary period, "Landscapes" by St. John de Crèvecoeur, apparently written in 1778 for publication as a pamphlet but left in manuscript at his death. The work consists of six scenes of a typical day in the life of a Hudson Valley community under the control of a Committee of Public Safety. With an irony that is unprecedented in his other writings, Crèvecoeur lays bare this little world of committeemen and militia captains, darkly rendering the American village as the spawning ground of a revolution that has inverted the moral structure of society.

Just as Crèvecoeur's single experiment in dramatic form is the most compelling of the plays of the period, so his Revolutionary sketches overshadow the imaginative prose of other writers. There are some ingenious rivals, such as Francis Hopkinson's *A Pretty Story* (1774), an allegorical review of the history of the quarrel between the colonies and Great Britain, or Benjamin Franklin's hoaxes, most notably "An Edict by the King of Prussia" (1773) with its clever transformation of England's claims over the American colonies into Prussia's over England, and "The Sale of the Hessians" (1777), a Swiftian condemnation of the use of human beings as cannon fodder. But Crèvecoeur's sketches, simply vignettes and anecdotes of the disruption of American life by civil war, are among the very few works of the period that treat the events of the Revolution not as subjects in themselves but as instances of universal experience.

Like "Landscapes," Crèvecoeur's Revolutionary sketches were among those writings in English that he did not incorporate in his famous *Letters from an American Farmer* (1782). Written shortly before he left his Pine Hill, New York, farm in early 1779 to return to his native France, the Revolutionary pieces had to wait until 1925 for their first publication, when, as the most significant element of the volume titled *Sketches of Eighteenth-Century America*, their bitter pathos came in startling contrast to the supposed naïve optimism of the author of the *Letters*. Alone among the major writings of the Revolution, they denounce not one side or the other but the war itself as they depict the consequences of Whig persecution and Tory terrorism. Rejecting all political rhetoric as false, they inspect the lives of ordinary people amid the misery and degradation of violence. Here even the victimizers are victims, as when a veteran Tory guerrilla leader at the very moment of tomahawking a young mother is swept by a sudden recognition of the horror that he has become. For no other writer of the period did the war become so overwhelmingly a matter of consciousness and conscience, perhaps because none had the imagination and the art that such a realization required.

Of all the genres of the literature of the Revolution, the richest and most appealing—as well as the simplest and least assuming—is the personal narrative. Written by authors who range from Old World aristocrats to Yankee farmers' sons, the accounts of individual experience in the turmoil of the Revolution rival the political pamphlets in mass and provide the essential corrective to their abstract representation of the conflict. Like Crèvecoeur's sketches, the personal narratives convey a sense of the Revolution as something lived through, though they render it not in poignant images of extreme emotion and intense awareness but as the ground of daily experience, the controlling circumstance over months or years of a lifetime. If many of the hundreds of narratives that have survived from the period are little more than soldiers' journals, barely literate and important chiefly for the historical evidence they provide, the best of them take a place in that long line of distinguished autobiographical writings that forms one of the chief strengths of American literature.

Just as the political pamphlets have antecedents in earlier religious argumentation, the Revolutionary narratives descend from older accounts of providential deliverances from danger by land or sea, most obviously the narratives of Indian captivity. Indeed, a few of the Revolutionary writings, like *The Narrative of the Perils and Sufferings . . . of John Slover* (1783)—told by the illiterate Slover to Hugh Henry Brackenridge and first printed in Freneau's *Freeman's Journal*—are full-fledged examples of Indian captivity narratives, complete with lurid descriptions of savage cruelty and miraculous escapes. More commonly, however, the patterns of Indian captivity are adapted to the circumstances of capture and imprisonment by the British, as in *A Narrative of Colonel Ethan Allen's Captivity* (1779), where the hero of Ticonderoga fends off the persecutions of his captors with the bluster and bravado of a frontiersman.

In the Revolutionary captivity narratives, the prison ships of New York harbor loom, as in Freneau's poem, as the most terrible manifestations of British oppression, floating death camps where young Americans died by the thousands. The dozen or so narratives by survivors are best represented by *Recollections of the Jersey Prison-Ship* (1829) by Thomas Dring with its somber portrayal of the putrid atmosphere, the swarming vermin, and the appalling night sounds of the ship, and *The Old Jersey Captive* (1833) by Thomas Andros, who steadily refers his experience to the hand of Providence and interprets it by the grimmest of Calvinist teachings: for Andros, the *Jersey* becomes a type of the world at large, that "great prisonhouse of guilty, sorrowful, and dying men." The popularity of the Revolutionary captivity narratives suggests that for their first readers they had some special significance, not in Andros's terms as allegories of sin and salvation, but more simply and immediately as enacting in their sequence of imprisonment and release the national passage from subjection and violence to independence and peace.

If the other Revolutionary narratives of personal experience lack the cohesiveness and symbolic resonance of the accounts of captivity, the best of them have a range and variety that are attractive in themselves. None of the soldiers' narratives covers more ground than *A Military Journal during the American Revolutionary War* (1823) by James Thacher, who, fresh from his medical studies, joined Washington's army at Cambridge and served with it throughout the war, not resigning his commission until January 1783. Praised by John Adams as "the most natural, simple, and faithful narration of facts that I have seen," Thacher's book is memorable less for its grand scenes, such as the siege of Yorktown, than for its details of camp life, from the duels of young officers to the floggings and hangings by which military discipline was enforced. For all his particularity, however, Thacher himself remains a faceless young man, a faithful reporter but little more. No such diffidence inhibits Alexander Graydon, whose *Memoirs of a Life* (1811) is pervaded by his arrogant personality. The son of the widowed keeper of a fashionable Philadelphia boardinghouse, Graydon secures an appointment as captain in a battalion of the Pennsylvania line and joins Washington's forces in their unsuccessful effort in the summer and fall of 1776 to prevent New York City from falling into the hands of the British. Shocked by the low breeding of the officers of the New England units and unmoved by the Declaration of Independence, he is at last captured at the surrender of Fort Washington in November. After eight months of captivity in New York, where he is comfortably paroled while his men sicken and starve, he returns to Pennsylvania, marries, and sits out the remainder of the war. Insufferable though Graydon himself must have been, he is a spirited and sophisticated writer whose gentleman's-eye view of the Revolution is engagingly unorthodox.

A still different perspective is offered by the narratives of European participants in the Revolution, the most attractive of which is the *Journal* of Baroness von Riedesel, originally published in Berlin in 1800 and first translated into English in 1827. The wife of the commander of the German troops in Burgoyne's army, this young noblewoman with her three young daughters joined her husband in Canada in 1776 and accompanied him on his southward march. Enduring the terror and confusion of the defeat at Saratoga in October 1777, she shared her husband's long captivity, not returning to Europe until 1783. Throughout the narrative, her unconscious courage and quiet sense of responsibility are much in evidence, as are her alert eye and excellent judgment. In every way, she is the antithesis of Graydon, displaying a nobility of character that has nothing to do with her social rank.

But the two personal narratives that best represent the form are both by native writers. *Narrative of the Adventures of an American Navy Officer* (1806) by Nathaniel Fanning is an extraordinarily lively account of the war at sea. After being captured on board a privateer, Fanning is exchanged and sent to France, where he enlists as a midshipman in the leaking sixty-year-old *Bon Homme Richard* under the command of John Paul Jones, survives the hellish battle with the *Serapis* and the kicks and cuffs that Jones deals his officers, and goes on to command his own vessels in Jones-like attacks upon British shipping. It is a fine book, rough and ready in its style but always vivid and convincing. Invaluable for its extended portrait of Jones and its depiction of the stratagems and butchery of naval combat in the eighteenth century, Fanning's *Narrative* also offers a running account of a young Connecticut Yankee's explorations in the alien world of Europe, where he is awakened by the clatter of wooden shoes on the pavements, puzzled by the Catholic use of holy water and Latin, and shocked by the behavior of the women, who are, he finds, "rather loose in the handle."

Still more novelistic is *A Narrative of the Adventures, Dangers and Sufferings of a Revolutionary Soldier* (1830) by Joseph Plumb Martin. Written while Martin was in his sixties, the book constitutes a remarkable act of imaginative recovery as Martin returns himself and his reader to the time when he, a fifteen-year-old Connecticut farm boy, badgered his grandfather into permitting him to join the militia. Full of adolescent high spirits and unaware of half the risks that he runs, he survives the retreat from Long Island and Manhattan in 1776, though the British were at times so close "that I could see the buttons on their clothes." In early 1777 he enlists for the duration of the war in the Continental Army, serves in the defense of Philadelphia later that year, winters at Valley Forge, sees action in the battle of Monmouth in 1778, and fights in the front lines at Yorktown in 1781, all the time growing to manhood. There are no heroics in Martin's *Narrative*, no glorifications of war. The real enemies are the weather, sometimes "cold enough to cut a man in two," and the Continental Congress, which lets its troops go for months without pay and allows them to starve in the midst of a plentiful but indifferent country. "I often found," he wryly observes, "that those times not only tried men's souls, but their bodies too." Throughout the account of his eight years of service with its unfaded recollection of the misery of hunger and exhaustion there runs a bright thread of the humor that would later be called American: "As the old woman said [to] her husband, when she baked him instead of his clothes, to kill the vermin, 'You must grin and bear it,' " advice that forms the central theme of this truthful, brave, and oddly cheerful book.

If personal narratives like Martin's are not art, they furnish the materials of art, as James Fenimore Cooper, who read Graydon and Fanning, knew. It is not an accident that the most poignant and humane rendering of the Revolution in all literature, Melville's *Israel Potter* (1855), is drawn directly from three autobiographical narratives: Ethan Allen's, Nathaniel Fanning's, and the *Life and Remarkable Adventures of Israel R. Potter* (1824), another of these simple and unpretentious accounts in which the American Revolution still lives as an experience, and not as an event merely.

Thomas Philbrick

Poetry in the Early Republic

Ears accustomed to the quest for symbolic beauty in the lyrics of Edgar Allan Poe and Ralph Waldo Emerson, or to the commanding egoisms of Walt Whitman and Emily Dickinson, have found precious little in the poetry of the American Revolutionary era that is indigenously American, few images that are evocative rather than didactic, and even fewer lines that are poetry rather than verse. The recurrent charge against the dominant poets of the time—Philip Freneau, John Trumbull, Joel Barlow, Timothy Dwight, and David Humphreys—was made as early as 1818 by William Cullen Bryant:

It was their highest ambition to attain a certain lofty, measured, declamatory manner—an artificial elevation of style from which it is impossible to rise or descend without abruptness and violence, and which allows just as much play and freedom to the faculties of the writer as a pair of stilts allows the body. The imagination is confined to one trodden circle, doomed to the chains of a perpetual mannerism, and condemned to tinkle the same eternal tune with its fetters. Their versification, though not equally exceptionable in all, is formed upon the same stately model of balanced and wearisome regularity.

Bryant's aversion has been unknowingly shared by later poets; none of these five once acclaimed writers has influenced the poets we now deem most important in American literature—except through fleeting distaste. Aside from a few of Freneau's shortest pieces and Barlow's "The Hasty Pudding" (1793), which are still anthologized for students, the poems of the era have kept no place in our living literary culture. Only an occasional specialist in literary history ever reads the better long poems of the era (Trumbull's *M'Fingal* [1776, 1782], Barlow's *The Vision of Columbus* [1787], Dwight's *Greenfield Hill* [1794]). Once the imitation of British forms and diction ceased being regarded as sophisticated practice, the era's verse seemed as dated as the cultural crises to which much of it was addressed.

No one, however, who associates the word "poetry" with a highly crafted lyric expression of individual feeling is likely to understand, let alone appreciate, the purposes and achievements of these writers. Except for John Trumbull, all of them attended college expecting to enter the ministry or the law. At New Haven and at Princeton, they were educated in Ciceronian oratory, the odes of Horace, the rhetorics of Kames, Blair, and Ward, and the sacred authority of the Christian word. Valuing the Moderns as highly as the Ancients, they steeped themselves in Dryden and Pope, Milton and Thomson, Gray and Collins. Their first poems were public declamations that modified the form of a Ciceronian oration (exordium, narratio, proof-disproof, peroration, etc.) in order to persuade academic audiences of the sure glory of their culture's future. Five years before warfare even began, Trumbull, Freneau, and Dwight were adapting blank verse and heroic couplet to the ends of communal persuasion, thereby investing poetry with a ministry of secular political prophecy, itself laden with millennial and apocalyptic terms. But by the time of Constitutional ratification, all five poets had become embroiled in prominent public careers as diplomats, editors, journalists, judges, ministers, educators, or some changing combination thereof. The writing of poetry necessarily became subordinate to these other vocations, not only because poetry was profitless, but because the poet and the man were publicly committed to a much larger cause than either: the spread of universal republicanism as it was variously understood.

To continue to group four of these poets (Trumbull, Dwight, Humphreys, and Barlow) under the familiar term "The Connecticut Wits" will only prolong misunderstanding by clinging to a distorting, parochial label. The collaborative mock epic titled *The Anarchiad* (1786–87), which gave rise to the term, was hardly representative of their willed optimism and high public ambitions. "Wits" in the modern sense they never intended to be; nor did they believe, with Alexander Pope, that "True Wit is Nature to advantage dress'd/ What oft was thought, but ne'er so well expressed." Their aim was rather to use the old verse forms, the old diction, in order to convince an outsetting people of the truths of new thought, and thereby to supersede the British tradition through imitating it.

Although all four poets had Connecticut origins and Yale College in common, none of them was local in his career, provincial in his values, or narrowly national in his loyalties. After 1788, Joel Barlow's formative attachments were to Paris and Washington, and his intellectual associations were with English radicals, French revolutionaries, and Virginia Republicans.

Even Timothy Dwight, whose life and writings seem intensely of Connecticut, ended his only local poem, *Greenfield Hill*, with a lengthy assurance that the agrarian competencies of the Connecticut way of life can and should become a model for New World republicanism. So divisive and turbulent an era bred centrifugal forces, drawing Joel Barlow toward Deistic utopianism, Dwight toward New Light Congregationalists and the Federalist party, and John Trumbull toward ridicule of alegal activists of all persuasions.

Any promptings these poets might have felt to write what we now call a "pre-romantic lyric" were thus, by 1775, decidedly secondary to the need to give public testimony to whatever values they hoped their fledgling culture might embrace. For many years after completing "The Beauties of Santa Cruz" (1776), Philip Freneau was to place his pen in the service of the Revolution, rather than to adapt politics to the service of poetry. All the longer poems of Dwight, Barlow, and Humphreys are secular sermons addressed to a people in need of a described present, a mapped future, and specific instruction on matters ranging from farming practices, military protocol, Indian policy, and family governance, up to the divine plan for a progressive republic that absorbed their grandest hopes and anxieties.

To advance their civic mission, the poets combined Scottish Common-Sense epistemology and a particular idea of the fancy into a poetic aesthetic that the following generation was to overturn. Truth was considered to exist beyond the perceiving mind; reality was already present in the objects, institutions, and spiritual forces of the external world. It was a poet's duty to combine images that denoted general aspects of reality into a reliable guide to the whole. A poet was not to re-create the world through his unique imagination; he was to describe or evoke it through a diction of generic categories. Poetic invention, Timothy Dwight argued, is "nothing but compounding the ideas which the mind has derived from observation, so as to form new images or pictures out of these materials." Phillis Wheatley's "On Imagination" (1773) condones Newtonian ways of knowing: the poet's "mental optics" should "Measure the skies, and range the realms above./ There in one view we grasp the mighty whole,/ Or with new worlds amaze th'unbounded Soul." Although the poet's special faculty was usually called the fancy, the fancy's purpose was to retrieve images consistent with a universal Reason, itself still dependent, for many, on the scriptural word. Hence Richard Alsop's 2,300-line poem *The Charms of Fancy* (1788) holds out the fancy as man's "magic mirror . . . whose magic pow'r can raise/ Th'events of past, and deeds of future days." Even Freneau's familiar tribute to "The Power of Fancy" (1770) is "pre-romantic" only in a most restrictive sense.

The fancy may be a "Wakeful, vagrant, restless thing,/ Ever wandering on the wing," but its office is to roam through worlds physical and spiritual in order to integrate "endless images of things," all of which are "Thoughts on reason's scale combin'd/ Ideas of the Almighty mind."

Such a poetics, accepted by a generation that revered Pope and Milton, encouraged the young American poet of the 1770s to invoke his new culture into being through the conventional diction and forms of British poetry. David Humphreys's vision of America's westering future, in his once popular "A Poem Addressed to the Armies of the United States of America" (1780), provides a fair sample of the texture of such verse:

> With all that's ours, together let us rise,
> Seek brighter plains and more indulgent skies;
> Where fair Ohio rolls his amber tide,
> And nature blossoms in her virgin pride;
> Where all that beauty's hand can form to please
> Shall crown the toils of war with rural ease.
> The shady coverts and the sunny hills,
> The gentle lapse of ever-murm'ring rills,
> The soft repose amid the noon-tide bow'rs,
> The evening walk among the blushing flow'rs,
> The fragrant groves that yield a sweet perfume,
> And vernal glories in perpetual bloom,
> Await you there; and heav'n shall bless the toil,
> Your own the produce, as your own the soil.

Here, even in a passage of the middle rather than sublime style, are the "artificial elevation" and "balanced and wearisome regularity" of which Bryant was to complain. Every noun has its adjective; the march of iambs rarely varies. The nativist claim of the final couplet is compromised by Humphreys's diction, which suggests a Miltonic garden of literate leisure, rather than Ohio fields cleared by toiling farmers. Studied practice at such approvable prosody enabled Humphreys to write his "addresses" at the rate of fifty lines a day, and Joel Barlow to write 2,400 lines of *The Vision of Columbus* in a month. But such predictability also suggests an urgency of cultural need that Bryant was to overlook. To Humphreys, poetry was a form of persuasion written to further a divine cultural promise. His lines served to reassure prospective settlers that, thanks to New World ownership of land, familiar images of pastoral bliss were to be permanently regained.

The crisis of America's self-definition led patriotic poets to cherish one particular poetic subgenre—an oratorical prophecy, between 200 and 600 lines in length, written in heroic couplets or (less frequently) blank verse, a form that has been variously called the prospect poem, the vision poem, or the rising glory poem. The better-known examples are: Trumbull's "Prospect of the Future Glory of America" (1770), Freneau and Brackenridge's "The Rising Glory of America" (1771), Dwight's "America; or, A Poem on the Settlement of the British Colonies" (1772?), Barlow's "The Prospect of Peace" (1778), and Humphreys's "A Poem on the Happiness of America" (1786). Less known and less elaborate variants include Paul Allen's "Poem on the Happiness of America" (1781), Samuel Low's "Peace" (1783), Phillis Wheatley's "Liberty and Peace" (1784), Joseph Brown Ladd's "Prospect of America" (1785), John Blair Linn's "The Blessings of America" (1791), Benjamin Prime's "Columbia's Glory" (1791), and the first of them, Alexander Martin's "America" (1769). The prototype of the genre was surely the archangel Michael's prophecy in the last two books of *Paradise Lost* (1674), as shortened and secularized in the British "landscape poems," especially the much-admired conclusion of Pope's "Windsor Forest" (1713). But, in American hands, the future vision seen from a high hill repeatedly outgrew its placement at the climax of a narrative. The vision became the very subject for a poetic oration, whether delivered or not.

The uncertainties of the Revolution led the prospect poet to adapt predictable poetic conventions to volatile views of the future. Midst a dark grove, atop a swelling mount, or deep in gloomy cell, a seraph or muse appears to the poet, assuring him that the American pursuit of happiness will eventually be rewarded. Speaking with an authority both secular and spiritual, the newly inspired poet then ranges backward and forward in history, ascribing the American Revolution to the progressive protestant spirit of the forefathers, showing how the *translatio studii* has brought the forces of empire to the New World, and ending with a prospect in which various forms of republicanism, peace, and empire spread from the United States of America across the western hemisphere, and often over the globe. Farm and manufactory, church spire and marketplace, Science and Art, Freedom and Law, all spread across the wilderness in somehow complementary fashion. Sometimes the America yet-to-be is described as the beginning of the Millennium, sometimes it is merely described through millennial language, and less often through imagery of the golden age. Whatever variety of republican empire is anticipated, however, its future is said to be secure as long as its believers will act upon their faith.

However one may judge the artistic quality of these prospect poems, their importance as an articulation of the American republic's earliest self-image is hard to overestimate. In these poems we find progressive and protective assumptions that were to be crucial to the Monroe Doctrine, Manifest Destiny, the Homestead Act, and the imperialism of the 1890s. By accepting contrary aspects of cultural growth as parts of one evolutionary law, these poems served, not only to define the American future in long-familiar ways, but to release the energies necessary to build it. Unlike the British landscape poems of Sir John Denham, Alexander Pope, and John Dyer, which had meditated upon a pastoral civilization visible to the on-looker, the American prospect poem was relentlessly futuristic. In its most extreme form, it projected an entire culture upon a void.

The open-endedness of the prospect poem enabled it to be conveniently adaptable in length. Francis Scott Key's "The Star Spangled Banner" (1814), with its thumping anapestic couplets, its rhetorical exclamations ("O say, can you see"), and its assurances of victory, peace, and freedom descending in the dawn upon our "heav'n rescued land," is a shortened variant of the prospect poem, much like Dwight's "Columbia, Columbia, to Glory Arise" (1783). While providing glimpses of America's embattled glory, both poems owed their fame to the melodies of British drinking songs. They thus provide telling examples of the era's need to pour new wine into old skins.

More commonly, however, the prospect poem was expanded rather than compressed. Trumbull's *M'Fingal*, Dwight's *The Conquest of Canaan* (1785), Barlow's *The Vision of Columbus*, Dwight's *Greenfield Hill*, Freneau's unfinished *The Rising Empire* (1790), and Alsop's *The Charms of Fancy* all culminate in extractable prospect visions. The form of Barlow's *The Columbiad* (1807), his recasting of *The Vision of Columbus*, is best regarded not as an epic narrative but as a gigantic expansion of the rising glory orations with which his versifying began. Straining to discern the republic's future, the prospect poets confronted problems of later generations. They strove to reconcile universal Reason with the authority of Scripture; they attacked the slavery of nether regions; they insisted upon woman's subordinate divinity as the domestic keeper of man's morality. Although *The Columbiad* promptly became a safe target for ridicule, few of its few readers have ever noticed that its last book predicts the Panama Canal, submarines, airplanes, the United Nations, and a universal language, all the while warning the reader that international commerce might finally be man's only deterrent to global war.

Such an accumulative rhetoric, suited for celebratory occasions, encouraged the suppression of the poet's doubts. Because the achieving of the Republic proved to be both long and perilous, however, the fears of the public poet had to surface in separate visions of apocalyptic darkness. Accordingly, public orations of unqualified hope were followed by closet orations of nearly unqualified despair. Trumbull's "Prospect of the Future Glory of America" (1770) gave way to his little-known "An Elegy on the Times"

(1774); in the later poem, the British closing of the port of Boston provoked Trumbull to nightmarish glimpses of the dead gods of the Old World, all frowning in molten gold upon Columbian Freedom and submerging the new land in a whelming flood of oppression. Timothy Dwight's first hope for America had been that Joshua's conquest of the old Canaan might provide a biblical type and an epic prefigurement for George Washington's founding of the new. Only three years after *The Conquest of Canaan* was published, however, Dwight warned that the true westward course of empire might prove to be the reign of Satanic Infidelity upon the American strand ("The Triumph of Infidelity" [1788]). Freneau's youthful anticipation of "a new Jerusalem," "another Canaan," yielded to a prospect of all America resembling the hellish hold of a British prison ship; republicans should now know, Freneau insisted, that Old World tyrants "Aim to extend their empire o'er the ball,/ Subject, destroy, absorb and conquer all." Even Colonel David Humphreys, the most guardedly conventional of optimists, predicted in "A Poem on the Death of General Washington" (1800), and in his revised "Poem on the Future Glory of America" (1804), that lengthy days of darkness must follow the death of the nation's father, especially because America had recently displayed such cowardice in the face of Algerine captors.

Despite final reassurances that the night is darkest before the dawn, these poems suggest that the very openness of prospect verse was drawing poets toward images of surety or infidelity, order or anarchy, millennium or apocalypse, Eden or hell. As the diverse forms of villainy embodied in Lord Cornwallis, Charles Chauncy, Daniel Shays, Voltaire, Paine, Burke, Hamilton, and Jefferson replace one another in the sequence of prophetic poems, we must conclude that the brightness of republican hope summoned up the blackest of conspiracy fears. These two kinds of prophecy, opposite in conclusion, are ultimately one in their imaginative extremity, as well as in form. Because there was not yet an America against which to validate a prophecy, these poems project hopes and fears upon an unformed polity and a vacant landscape. Regarded as separated halves of one composite vision, this doubled genre reflects an outlook far more complex than the naïve confidence often associated with the era. When David Humphreys, echoing a phrase used by Homer, Virgil, and Milton, asserts "Thrice happy we, the sons of Freedom fair," he lays claim to generational heroism by literary analogy, a strategy that, in the military context of 1780, smacks of whistling in the dark.

The self-divided vision of the era is most apparent in the verse of Joel Barlow, whose commitment to republican theory reflects a belief that ideas have men, rather than men having ideas. The only heroic trait Barlow's Columbus displays is his unfailing ability to make the proper republican response, alternately euphoric at the seraph's revelations of libertarian progress, or despairing at the seraph's revelations of aristocratic and priestly subversion. If Dwight's angry gloom over the triumph of infidelity in America now seems paranoid owing to its scarcity of evidence, so does the shrill fear Barlow expresses in "The Conspiracy of Kings" (1792). Not until Barlow wrote his last poem, "Advice to a Raven in Russia" (1812), was the apocalyptic variant of the rising glory poem to be grounded in historical reality. This forceful, bitter poem, written in Poland during the French retreat from Moscow, magnifies Napoleon into a symbol of all the military and monarchical forces Barlow had long detested, while acknowledging that these forces are in fact devastating the civilized world. Vistas of the soldiers' frozen corpses, their open eyes accusing God, enable Barlow to invest the bird-of-prey motif (the raven is advised to fly south for warmer meat) with the epic grandeur that had long eluded him. In so nihilistic and global a vision, the genre of the rising glory poem, as practiced by "The Connecticut Wits," has its unexpected end.

Unlike Hopkins, Dwight, or Barlow, Philip Freneau cultivated, in his patriotic verses, a workmanlike simplicity of diction that long caused him to be regarded as the plain-dealing republican bard who had fought the Revolution through newspaper verse. Because of Freneau's compromises with the loftier universalities of the literary heritage, Dwight, Humphreys, Trumbull, and Barlow all ignored him. Francis Hopkinson, gentleman, and Philip Freneau, workingman, even referred to one another, respectively, as "scapegrace" and "Francis Fiddlesticks." But even if Freneau's war poems are callously dismissed as propaganda, there are other Philip Freneaus who deserve consideration: the familiar poet of graceful short meditations on mortality ("The Wild Honeysuckle" [1786]), on the imagined afterlife ("The Indian Burying Ground" [1788]), on popular contempt for poetry ("To an Author" [1788]), and on aging ("On Observing a Large Red-streak Apple" [1822]); the poet who conveys Caribbean sensual delights and their cost in political guilt ("The Beauties of Santa Cruz" [1779], "Written at Port Royal" [1788]); and the sea poet who emblemizes a world of directionless chaos ("The Argonaut" [1788], "The Hurricane" [1785]).

The longer poems of Freneau's later years constitute an ever-varying debate upon the premise of America's rising glory. "A Picture of the Times" (1782), "A Warning to America" (1792), "The Millennium: To a Ranting Field Orator" (1797), and "Reflections . . . on the Gradual Progress of Nations from Democratical States to Despotic Empires" (1815) express an increasing skepticism about the viability of Freedom. Concerned lest Americans forever pursue the phantom shade of happiness, Freneau will abandon neither his hopes for progress nor the facts that contradict them. His political meditations gain an honest dignity, just as his poems on mortality have a saving humor. In variety of subject and complexity of attitude, Freneau's verse—taken as a whole—has a range unequaled by any American contemporary.

Even if a poem is conceived to be a timeless aesthetic artifact, the poetic achievement of the era might not be as negligible as Bryant believed. The urgency of the republican mission, together with its long verse apologies, promptly obscured the possibility that the best-crafted poems of the era are mock epics and burlesques, rather than epics and panegyrics. John Trumbull's *The Progress of Dulness* (1772, 1773) and *M'Fingal* (1775, 1782) are adroit comic narratives that skewer both the common "characters" of the day (the fop, the flirt, the John Bull Tory) and cherished props of the emerging republic (a classical education, the Standing Order of the Congregational Church, the Sons of Liberty). No practitioner of the octosyllabic couplet, including Samuel Butler or Jonathan Swift, has ever been more deft at following a seemingly unintended off rhyme with a complementary exact rhyme. In the following four lines, Tom Brainless concludes his "rare adventure" of graduating from Yale College:

> Our hero's wit and learning now may
> Be prov'd by token of *Diploma*
> Of that Diploma, which with speed
> He learns to construe—and to read.

At a time when Dwight, Barlow, Nathaniel Tucker, Richard Snowden, and others were worrying about the properly convincing way of elevating Revolutionary patriots to Homeric stature, Trumbull showed that Toryism could be more memorably quelled by burlesquing the single combat and the epic simile:

> The deadly spade discharg'd a blow
> Tremendous on his rear below:
> His bent knee fail'd, and void of strength,
> Stretch'd on the ground his manly length;
> Like antient oak o'erturn'd he lay,
> Or tow'rs to tempests fall'n a prey,
> And more things else—but all men know 'em
> If slightly vers'd in Epic Poem.

Throughout his brief, precocious career as a poet (1770–82), Trumbull was aware of literary effects in ways none of his contemporaries could approach.

He understood that playful recall of English artists (Hogarth, Swift, Macpherson, Churchill) worked better than dogged imitation. He recognized that a mixture of tone was ultimately more persuasive than unyielding seriousness or bludgeoning satire. Above all, he never forgot the merit of poetic brevity, the proper moment to stop.

At writing short comic verse, American poets were to prove equally adept, perhaps because they were, at least for the moment, not so intent upon climbing Parnassus. The opening number of *The Anarchiad* (1786–87), with its stunning political variation upon lines of *The Dunciad* ("Thy Constitution, Chaos, is restor'd;/ Law sinks before thy uncreating word"), shows how effectively Federalist fear of anarchy could be expressed through an appeal to the British mock-epic tradition. Freneau might well have envied Hopkinson his "Battle of the Kegs" (1778), a durable "oral" ballad that mocks the oafishness of redcoats who futilely assail rebels believed to be floating along, each in his unsinkable, separate barrel. The brevity, nostalgia, and sexual puns of "The Hasty Pudding" have allowed Barlow always to keep a limited readership.

In addition to these familiar titles, there are many short comic poems that deserve to be known: Trumbull's "Epithalamion" and "The Owl and the Sparrow"; Joseph Brown Ladd's "Epitaph on an Old Horse" and "What Is Happiness?"; Royall Tyler's "Anacreontic to Flip" and "Ode Composed for the Fourth of July"; St. George Tucker's "The Cynic" and "The Discontented Student"; Lemuel Hopkins's caustic exposures of medical and ministerial pretense, "Epitaph on a Patient Killed by a Cancer Quack" and "The Hypocrite's Hope." Passages of Rowland Rugeley's *The Story of Aeneas and Dido Burlesqued* (1774) capture a spirit of mock-epic ribaldry that recalls Henry Fielding. A whole era's reverence for *Paradise Lost* is scurrilously upended in Royall Tyler's "The Origin of Evil." Published anonymously for good reason, Tyler's quatrains inform us that Eve actually took a willing Fall after sucking the liquid fruit of Adam's tree.

Insofar as we now know, black American poetry had its beginnings in the late eighteenth century, not in the poems of Phillis Wheatley, but in Lucy Terry's negligible "Bars Fight, August 28, 1746" and in Jupiter Hammon's "An Evening Thought. Salvation by Christ" (1760). Whereas Wheatley affirms Christianity through heroic couplets and consciously poetic diction, Hammon fits plain English to hymn meters, creating poems probably intended as slave songs. Although the Christian orthodoxy and personal loyalty of both poets were doubtless necessary for publication, their reassuring deference seems to have been unfeigned. Only occasionally does either poet allow a controlled hint of resentment. Hammon's "The Kind Master and the Dutiful Servant," written during the Revolutionary War, reminds wealthy, worried slave owners that, as true Christian servants, we should all "see the dangers of the day/ And fly unto our king." Wheatley's familiar couplet ("Remember, Christians, Negroes, black as Cain,/ May be refin'd, and join th'angelic train") may concede the spiritual darkness of the Negro, but it clearly warns whites that salvation holds forth an eternity of raceless equality.

Space permits only the most superficial categorizing of other poets: the Loyalist versifiers Jacob Bailey, Jonathan Odell, and Joseph Stansbury; virtually unread Southern poets such as Thomas Burke, Andrew Burnaby, William Duke, John Johnston, and William Munford; long biblical or churchly poems by Thomas Brockway, Elijah Fitch, Charles Crawford, Chauncey Lee, Thomas Odiorne, and Elhanan Winchester; domestic and undomestic poems by Elizabeth Fergusson, Sarah Morton, Judith Murray, Susanna Rowson, and Mercy Otis Warren; other mid-Atlantic and New England poets such as William Cliffton, Nathaniel Evans, Thomas Godfrey, Benjamin Prime, George Richards, and John Searson. These listings take no account of anonymous newspaper verse, hymn texts, broadsides, or whatever is recoverable of folk song tradition. Amidst so immense an amount of verse, there will surely prove to be poems salvageable for other than antiquarian interest.

In the late twentieth century, when poetry has lost any public function, while poems are valued for their complexity and originality, nearly all American verse of the Revolutionary era seems a desert where no art can bloom. Unless poetry should again become a medium for public persuasion, or comic verse become an acknowledged tradition, this judgment is not likely to change. Poets like Dwight, Barlow, and Freneau, trained in poetic and oratorical imitation, were not likely ever to have striven for an individual poetic medium or a distinctive voice. Even if they ever did so, the onset of the Revolution brought their public responsibilities to the fore. A clear sign of the stifling effect of assumed republican obligations is that the era's most subtly crafted long poem, John Trumbull's *The Progress of Dulness*, was completed in 1773 by a playful skeptic who still thought of himself as a poet, rather than the lawyer, judge, and loyal Federalist he was to be.

The price that the Revolution exacted upon the era's poetry is ultimately measurable in shattered lives. Benjamin Church II, grandson of the Puritan hero of King Philip's War, anticipated a good life of public service and private domesticity in his admired poem "The Choice" (1757). By 1765, however, Church abandoned his apolitical posture by publishing an anti-imperial satire, "The Times," thereby professing an allegiance he later compromised by writing unsigned editorials against, as well as for, revolutionary agitation. Court-martialed by General Washington, Church was encouraged to embark for the West Indies; no trace of his ship has ever been found. Poets who remained did not necessarily fare better. Ann Eliza Bleecker wrote two compelling posthumous poems, "Written in the Retreat from Burgoyne" and "On Reading Dryden's Virgil" (1777?), in which she attacks American readers for their continuing concern for the dead heroes of epic poetry while New York's towers are burning and women fair as Creusa fall under the knife of yelling savages. The ready, smug conclusion that offers itself about such poems is that the Revolution brought forth the writer's best verse. Before we thus safely consign Mrs. Bleecker to literary history, however, we should recall that she was to die in 1783 of "an irremediable melancholy" following the deaths of her mother, sister, and cousins, the capture of her husband by Loyalists, the pillaging of her estate by Indian mercenaries, and the deaths of two children after flights from the war zone. In the face of such wasted promise, critical condescension toward the era's limited poetic achievement seems a scholar's luxury.

John McWilliams

Charles Brockden Brown and Early American Fiction

Henri Petter, in an inclusive account of the fiction that appeared during the period 1790–1800, the decade when Charles Brockden Brown's most important writing was published, has listed as one of its virtues that it makes Brown's novels look good by comparison. Certainly, American writing during the Federal period and for some time after is often dreary stuff, most particularly when compared with British literature of the same era. And yet, as readers in Great Britain attested, Brockden Brown's fiction held its own against foreign competitors, and there are those who feel that his novels may be read even today without apology. But even if Brown's work does not need to be placed in context to shine, doing so reveals the extent to which he shares with his contemporaries—and they with each other—a number of formal and thematic characteristics. Petter's survey bears this out at considerable length; here, however, we must limit ourselves to a handful of notable and representative writings by Brown's contemporaries and, likewise, to his most important works.

For purposes of convenience (which dictates definition) we will be limiting ourselves also to authors who were either born in North America or who died there, an arbitrary distinction admittedly, particularly during the period in question, when writers in the United States looked to the Old World for models. Authors on both sides of the Atlantic yielded to the didactic impulse of the age: sentiment and sensibility, comic, tragic, and triumphant heroics, rape and marriage, are all well-worn transatlantic tropes and themes, employed chiefly in the service of moral instruction. Likewise familiar to both countries are the epistolary, picaresque, and adventure modes of fiction, while the Gothic novel in America is definably identified with the emergence of Brockden Brown, in whose hands it took new direction.

In order to explain that American difference and departure, we shall also be paying attention to recently established genre categories, for example, the Jacobin/Anti-Jacobin fiction inspired by the example of William Godwin and other radical writers in Great Britain, early instances of the novel of ideas though often called "novels of purpose"—a confusing label, given the general didacticism of the time. Specifics of landscape description—whether regional, geopolitical, or proto-romantic—are also important to any discussion of Brockden Brown and his contemporaries. But, once again, our emphasis will be on the milieu from which Brown's fiction appeared, the context without which no text is complete.

Finally, having begun this introductory note by citing the encyclopedic work of Henri Petter, we end by evoking the pyrotechnics of Leslie Fiedler, whose work—especially *Love and Death in the American Novel* (1960)—has shed a lurid but enlightening glare on the whole of our national fiction. Fiedler has inspired a generation of critics to read established greats like Herman Melville and Nathaniel Hawthorne with new insight and has reinforced the importance of marginal figures like Brown by demonstrating how stereotypical characters and formulaic plots can be transformed by genius into startling configurations. Following the efforts of scholars like Harry Warfel to revive Brown's reputation, Fiedler's epochal study transformed our sense of Brown's novels and directed subsequent discussion for the past quarter century.

More recently, feminist critics like Cathy Davidson and Jane Tompkins have aroused by redefinition our interest in the sentimental tradition: giving new direction to Fiedler's psychosexual emphasis, they have revealed a hidden empire of cultural politics, sociosexual tensions still relevant to modern concerns. Davidson, in particular, has concentrated on reader response, historically considered, instead of merely exercising critical insightfulness in the service of an aroused feminist sensibility, and the present essay shares her concern with the cultural context of early American fiction. But the larger debt remains with Fiedler, who by opening the canon of American literature to include—and celebrate—works of popular culture made all subsequent revisions and redefinitions possible.

The Power of Sympathy (1789) by William Hill Brown enjoys the arbitrary distinction of being the first American novel, a chronological triumph that testifies to the influence in this country of Samuel Richardson's *Clarissa Harlowe* (1747–48). Richardson's dominance, along with the infectious example of Laurence Sterne, determined that the bulk of early American fiction would be didactic in purpose, sentimental in tone, and sensational in materials, but did not guarantee an equivalent level of genius. Consequently, the bulk of early American fiction remains aesthetically unavailable to modern sensibilities, barriers of taste further strengthened by a relatively low level of authorial talent. Recent attempts to revise the American canon make it no longer possible to scorn the sentimental mode, which has been shown to reflect with savage accuracy the helplessness of women in republican America, but even revisionist critics continue to stress the continuing importance of the picaresque and adventure modes. A minority fiction that followed the models provided by Tobias Smollett and Daniel Defoe, these American ventures are markedly inferior to their originals, but redeem themselves by qualities of humor and physical movement. Despite aesthetic clumsiness, they remain closer to modern tastes than does the sentimental novel.

That sentiment and morality are not inimical to the production of great literature in America is shown by *Uncle Tom's Cabin* (1851–52), a mighty exception that proves the rule, for Harriet Beecher Stowe's novel sustains its didactic weight by means of rapid-paced action and melodramatic situations, as well as by comic high-jinks and verbal humor. The first two of these alleviating qualities are shared by *Charlotte Temple* (1791), the author of which was the British-born Susanna Rowson, and which was first published in America in 1794 as *Charlotte: A Tale of Truth*. Both Stowe and Rowson also demonstrate in their works that sentiment need not always be identified with specious emotion, for they manage even now to arouse in their readers pity for the oppressed and anger against oppressors. Rowson's novel shares many of the unfortunate characteristics of early American fiction, and like modern writers who seek wide readership, she did not perplex her audience with complex characterization or puzzle it with difficult philosophical issues. Yet *Charlotte Temple* is a powerful work of art that illuminates unrelentingly the injustices suffered by victims of social inequity, her Charlotte like Stowe's Uncle Tom a figure who appeals to the basic humanity in us all.

Before settling permanently in the United States in 1793 (she had spent a decade in this country during the Revolutionary era as the child of a British naval officer), Susanna (Haswell) Rowson had become a professional actress as well as author, her husband having turned to the theater after his hardware business failed. Rowson remained active on the American stage until 1797, when she took up teaching and editing as well as writing in order to support her family. In *Charlotte*, Rowson successfully blended the histrionic and pedagogic modes, mitigating her moral burden with melodrama. Rowson's novel also has the admirable virtue of brevity. These qualities, along with the stimulating pathos derived from the sufferings of a beautiful young woman who has been seduced and abandoned, recommended it to a popular audience for more than a century.

Like Rowson herself, *Charlotte* begins in Great Britain, then moves to North America, and the heroine's tragic destiny is transacted in New York City during the Revolution. The migration of author, book, and heroine warrants our consideration of Rowson's novel as American literature, but what is troublesome chiefly in that regard is the lack of any obvious connection between action and setting. Charlotte's seducer and betrayer (the role is divided between two men) are officers in the service of the King, and since the heroine suffers in hands similar to those holding Manhattan captive, something by way of allegory might have been derived from her story had she been an American, but she is not. It is possible to read her story as an early version of *les misères de l'immigrée*, save that Charlotte's suffering is the fault of her fellow Britons. Most important, we receive few particulars, save for place names, of the American landscape.

Carrying Charlotte to New York seems a device used chiefly to get her out of the care and supervision of her parents—not that she might be the more easily seduced but so that, having been abandoned, she might suffer uninterruptedly. Still, it must be said that eighteenth-century British authors of sentimental fiction were also unspecific about setting, which figures fleetingly, like the bits of scenery detected over the shoulder of a subject in a period portrait. Detailed descriptions of landscape are associated with Romantic literature, and in fiction with the Gothic novel, while *Charlotte* is in the Golgothic mode, in which all roads converge as the Via Crucis, and all places are reduced to stations of the Cross. The suffering woman or female Christ is a figure common to the sentimental novel in Great Britain and the United States, her anguish demonstrating that the consequences attending a moral transgression can be transfiguring, a sad version of the fortunate fall.

Charlotte suffers because she allows herself to be seduced (under the impression she was about to be married), and much of the movement in the novel is staged against a series of increasingly shabby living accommodations, a Hogarthian setting for her symbolic decline. "Charlotte" contains verbal echoes of "harlot," subliminal wordplay that spells out the terms of her tragedy, much as "Temple" connotes the sacred space that has been violated, while still holding out hope that sufficient pain will resanctify it. Forgiveness in these kinds of fictions most generally, like the arrival of help, comes too late. Equally uniform in much sentimental fiction is the requirement that the ultimate scene of transfiguring suffering be given an urban setting: raised in a rural region of England, Charlotte ends her humiliating descent in the snowy streets of New York.

Rural felicity and urban suffering provide a thematic axis also in William Hill Brown's *The Power of Sympathy*, a book that by its chronological precedence set down the terms for *Charlotte* and other American examples of sentimental fiction. Despite the publisher's attempts to promote Brown's novel by appealing both to his customers' patriotism and their prurience, the "First American Novel" did not sell. Shaped as an epistolary novel (*Charlotte*, remarkably, is not), Brown's book alternated matters of seduction with less seductive matters, and many of the "letters" are boringly discursive, unconvincingly opposing the horrors of illicit sex with the pleasures of virtue. Notably, seducers and their victims operate mostly within the purlieus of Boston, while the spokespersons of virtue send out letters from "Belleview," a pastoral asylum whose inhabitants, when not writing moral epistles and praising the beauties of Sterne, read aloud to one another from *The Vision of Columbus* and *The Conquest of Canaan*. It would be difficult to imagine a more perfect expression of provincial smugness, a moral trunk nailed shut with the assurance that all within was "founded on fact."

Rowson too claimed that *Charlotte* was "A Tale of Truth," a compromise with the received Puritan aversion for fiction and a bid for journalistic sensationalism. No historic basis for Rowson's claim has been found, but Brown demonstrably based his novel on a tragic scandal well known to at least his Boston readers. By means of a footnote, moreover, he included specific reference to a second tragedy of considerable notoriety, which became the precedent for *The Coquette* (1797) by Hannah Foster, a novel that, unlike Brown's, was kept in print well into the next century. Both forgotten footnote and popular epistolary novel were inspired by the story of Elizabeth Whitman ("Eliza Wharton" in Foster's book), a resident of Hartford, Connecticut, who died under mysterious and suspicious circumstances in the suburbs of Boston, retribution resulting from her reputation as a flirt. Unlike Brown, Foster managed to fashion a believable story, evoking sympathy for her fated heroine that carries even today.

Sentimental novels of the early republic have a distinctly antiaphrodisiacal quality, a terminal emphasis on the awful consequences of seduction that has its equivalent in cautionary children's tales of the same period: like the story of Little Red Riding Hood, they are designed to keep young women away from the wolf's door. Like those tales also, they strike the modern reader as unduly restrictive, putting forth a version of sexual politics intended to reinforce conventional pieties while demonstrating how stifling

convention was to women in the young republic. The world of the sentimental novel is in all ways closed, like the homes inhabited by its intended
readers, a hermetic continuum from which contemporary concerns are excluded, a parlor environment shut off from the sphere of masculine matters—save for the strategies of seduction. For politics other than sexual, as
for specifics of the American landscape beyond the headings of letters in
epistolary novels, we must turn elsewhere.

We must, that is, leave the sentimental mode and take up stories of picaresque adventure, departing the aegis of Richardson and Sterne for that of
Defoe and Smollett, evinced in *The Algerine Captive* (1797) by Royall Tyler
and *Modern Chivalry* (1792–1815) by Hugh Henry Brackenridge. Though
both authors shared with sentimental novelists the didactic impulse of the
day, the demands of satire as a genre (and travel as a device) privileged
Tyler and Brackenridge to exercise their male prerogatives, rights that also
required them to deal with the uniqueness of American experience, geopo-
litically considered. William Spengemann has defined the fiction that resulted as more typically "American" than the sentimental novel, and certainly the muse of adventure would animate most of the nineteenth-century
writers who now dominate the canon. But in the late eighteenth century,
adventure was distinctly a minority mode, with results so uneven as to
challenge the sentimental novel in matters of authorial clumsiness. Being an
"American" male in the 1790s, as today, involved a number of strategic
uncertainties, political and social disjunctions that caused, in the works of
both Tyler and Brackenridge, structural problems that are counterparts to
the flaws distinguishing the sentimental mode. If novels by Brown, Rowson, and Foster seem too closed and morally tidy for modern tastes, they
are at least very clear in promoting their moral concerns, while the more
open structures devised by Tyler and Brackenridge evince ideological confusion. As a comparison of *Moby-Dick* and *Uncle Tom's Cabin* testifies, the
novel of adventure intended as a vehicle of ideas can deal with matters that
seldom occur in sentimental novels of moral purpose, but the comparison
also suggests that adventure fiction laden with ideas often founders in its
own unintelligibility.

Like their published works, the public careers of Scottish immigrant Hugh
Henry Brackenridge and New England native Royall Tyler present a series
of contrasts and correspondences in which the latter prevail. Having graduated from Princeton, Brackenridge served as a chaplain in the Continental
Army during the Revolution, and then, in order to support his writing
ambitions, abandoned the ministry for law, migrating across the Alleghen-

ies to Pittsburgh. Though Brackenridge was at first an advocate of Western interests against the entrenched Eastern establishment, his republicanism was shaken by the Whiskey Rebellion of 1794, and though he continued to write, working on *Modern Chivalry* until he died, he devoted more and more time to the practice of law, and in 1799 was appointed a justice of the Pennsylvania Supreme Court.

Tyler, who graduated from Harvard in 1776, also fought on the side of rebellion, but in 1787 helped put down the revolt of New England farmers captained by Daniel Shays: as a Federalist, Tyler seems not to have shared Brackenridge's initial sympathies for insurrectionist grievances. Like his fellow writer, however, he followed the frontier—in his case to Vermont—and in 1807 became Chief Justice of the State Supreme Court. Where Brackenridge's politics were made more conversative by his frontier experiences, Tyler's years in Vermont seem to have mellowed his Federalist outlines considerably. Yet both men at the start shared the elitism of the early Republic, and in their writings put forth the officer-veterans of the Revolution as containing the best hope for American leadership, Tyler by means of Captain Manly in his play *The Contrast* (1787) and Brackenridge with Captain Farrago in *Modern Chivalry*.

Like Tyler in his stage comedy, Brackenridge deals in satiric contrasts, playing off the republican idealism of Farrago against the overreaching aspirations of his Irish manservant, Teague O'Regan. Though the division suggests Don Quixote and Sancho Panza, the Hudibrastic influence is such that one could hardly say of Farrago and O'Regan what Samuel Taylor Coleridge said of Cervantes's pairing, that each man is one half of an ideal whole. They seem instead to stand for divided and unreconcilable directions. Yet Brackenridge did hit upon a characteristic American dichotomy, for much as the setting of his novel is divided between Philadelphia and regions west of the Alleghenies—geopolitical zones reflecting sectional differences, while mirroring and magnifying the urban/rural division in the sentimental novel—so the aristocratic idealism of Farrago is identified with the East, O'Regan's ill-formed democratic aspirations with the West. This dualism suggests that Brackenridge's republican pluralism stopped short of pure democracy, and that his comic, blundering Irishman is an immigrant who introduces an ethnic as well as a geopolitical tension. Moreover, as Brackenridge's optimism for the future of the American republic began to wane, the satire in *Modern Chivalry* became increasingly brutal. The novel does not end but (like William Bradford's *Of Plimmoth Plantation* and Ezra Pound's *Cantos*) simply stops, death terminating the process by which the

"Rising Glory" envisioned by the author in 1770 had become by 1816 a blinding Pittsburgh smoke.

The geopolitical division in Tyler's *Algerine Captive*, as in Rowson's *Charlotte* is not continental but transatlantic, and though the author begins his novel by having satiric fun at the expense of his hero—a fledgling physician ill-prepared for either his profession or the world by a rigid education in ancient languages—the quixotic element does not dominate. Picaresque satire, moreover, gives way to adventure in the second volume, as the narrator-hero, Updike Underhill, sets sail for the Old World and is taken captive by Algerian pirates. Serving as doctor on an American slave ship, Underhill finds suddenly he is a slave himself, but though his Algerian sufferings substantiate his earlier satire on slavery in America, the connection is more tacit than otherwise. Algerian piracy (and American captives) were serious problems for the United States in 1797, but instead of aiming a Federalist broadside at the Algerians, Underhill bends into a cipher in his attempts to render a favorable account of Islam and Muslims. Slavery may be a cruel and dehumanizing institution, Islam a religion dark in superstition, but like an early victim of the Stockholm syndrome, Underhill puts his captors in a kindly light. Still, where Brackenridge's novel trails off into silence, Tyler ends his with a jeremiad against foreign entanglements, sentiments clearly in line with Federalist policy in 1797.

The disintegration of form in *Modern Chivalry* is explained by Brackenridge's political disillusionment, but the ambiguities in Tyler's novel seem to stem from authorial uncertainty, all the more puzzling given the neat satiric (and transatlantic) arrangement in *The Contrast*. Still, both Brackenridge and Tyler anticipate subsequent geopolitical divisions in the American novel, and pose much broader, complex, and nationalistic contrasts than can be found in the simple country/city divisions of their sentimental counterparts. The same may be observed of *The Emigrants* (1793) by Gilbert Imlay, first published in England but not in America until 1964. Imlay's novel has not shared the canonical stature of American works already discussed—though Alexander Cowie devoted several admiring pages to it in *The Rise of the American Novel* (1951)—and the book's contemporary reputation was undoubtedly hurt by that of the author, who was chiefly known then (as now) as the man who seduced and then abandoned Mary Wollstonecraft. Yet Imlay's novel is a unique accomplishment, blending the fiction of sentiment and purpose (ideas) with the literature of travel and adventure, a hybrid interesting despite its instant demise, in important ways prognostic of Brockden Brown's equally complex and ideological works.

As in the novels of Rowson and Brackenridge, geography in *The Emigrants* reflects the career of its author. Born in New Jersey, Imlay served as an officer in the Revolution, then headed for Kentucky, where he became involved in real-estate speculation. Lawsuits resulted from conflicting land claims (not unusual at the time), forcing Imlay to return east, and by 1786 he had apparently left the United States. He appears next in England as the editor of a *Topographical Description of the Western Territory of North America* (1792), a physiocratic anthology of pamphlets extolling Kentucky's virtues, including Imlay's series of imaginary "letters" praising same. His talent for epistolary fiction had its chief flowering in *The Emigrants*, Imlay's most elaborate expression of optimism concerning the pastoral promise of life in the Ohio Valley.

While in England Imlay met a number of radicals, including Mary Wollstonecraft, resulting in the famous affair that began in Paris in 1793, and that took added passion and meaning from the French Revolution, a Jacobin bond that did not however survive the Reign of Terror and the birth of a daughter, in 1794. Imlay, like other Americans in Paris, took commercial advantage from the situation, nor was he averse to forming libidinous liaisons as well as business connections, the both offensive to his idealistic lover. We do not have Imlay's side of the story, but Wollstonecraft's was published as her posthumous *Memoirs* (1798) by William Godwin, who had married her after Imlay's departure, and who saw to it that the American's name would be forever associated with political radicalism and sexual philandering.

Because Imlay's brief creative efflorescence is linked to his relationship with Wollstonecraft, *The Emigrants* has been attributed to her, though both chronology and style suggest otherwise. But Imlay's novel, like Mary's writing, is distinctly in the radical vein and is definably of a type with a number of novels published in England during the reform period inspired by revolutionary events in America and France. Styled "Jacobin" by conservative opponents, these early novels of ideas include Wollstonecraft's *Mary; a Fiction* (1787), Robert Bage's popular *Hermsprong* (1796), as well as Godwin's influential *Caleb Williams* (1794). Moreover, Imlay's novel stresses one of Wollstonecraft's favorite themes—the unjustness of contemporary divorce laws—and has as its heroine a "new woman" (c. 1793), the daughter of English emigrant parents and of Wollstonecraft's *Vindication of the Rights of Woman* (1790). The action is set in America, with a transmontane emphasis, commencing in Philadelphia, then crossing the mountains to Pittsburgh, before traveling down the Ohio to Louisville, with a concluding and climactic excursion to the unsettled regions along the Illinois River. The geography is similar to that in *Modern Chivalry*, but with a much more radical coloration, and Imlay promotes an erotic Western landscape that verifies Annette Kolodny's thesis concerning the frontier as an erogenous zone.

In his *Topographical Description*, Imlay proposed that officer-veterans of the Revolution would provide ideal settlers for Kentucky, bringing into that already legendary territory of wildness the necessary Eastern elements of law and order. In this, Imlay is in harmony with Brackenridge, and the hero of *The Emigrants* is likewise an American officer-veteran, chivalrously inclined. Moreover, like Royall Tyler in *The Contrast*, Imlay frames a dichotomy between decadent European manners and those produced by a regenerative American atmosphere. But Imlay includes the Eastern seaboard as Europeanized terrain, and where Brackenridge tends to see the Ohio Valley as an asylum of Yahooism, Imlay portrays it as a sanctuary of moral regeneration. Moreover, he puts forth the Western landscape in such priapic language as to broaden in several dimensions the polite urban/pastoral division in *The Power of Sympathy*, while giving a far more positive treatment to the immigrant/erotic experience found in Rowson's *Charlotte*. Published the year following the appearance in England of that novel, *The Emigrants* can be read as a response: the officer-lover, the Anglo-American crossing, the encounter with the New World, all are transformed by Imlay into a prose version of Watteau's *Embarkation for Cythera*, a radical repudiation of Rowson's middle-class morality. Ironically, the tragic consequences of Imlay's subsequent affair with Wollstonecraft acted to substantiate Rowson's cautionary tale, nor was the lesson lost on Charles Brockden Brown.

An epistolary novel, *The Emigrants* has a plot of considerable complexity, intermixing the sentimental formulaics of impeded love with the materials of travel and adventure—including an episode of Indian captivity, one of the first in American fiction. But it is perhaps most interesting for the basic situation, in which Europeans find new freedom and ideas by means of a transforming passage into the Ohio Valley. Imlay's is finally a utopian novel, for the American officer and his British bride settle down in "Bellefont," a community on the banks of the Ohio that is ordered according to true (that is, Godwinian) notions of political and social justice. Imlay thereby not only anticipates the use of the frontier as a literary territory but initiates a long-lived if minor American genre, producing an eroticized equivalent to Crèvecoeur's *Letters from an American Farmer* (1782).

Still, activities on the American literary frontier thenceforth would seldom involve (voluntary) erotic couplings, and our national fiction has been

primarily antiutopian, anti-Jacobin, along lines established by Brackenridge
and Tyler, and immigration as a literary experience likewise continues to
verify Rowson's tragic version. These subsequent directions are typical also
of novels by Charles Brockden Brown, and are given added darkness by his
use of materials from the Gothic novel. Critics have long acknowledged
Brown's precedence to Hawthorne and Melville, resulting in his accepted
place at the head of the American romantic tradition. But in terms of his
own generation of writers, if *The Emigrants* can be seen as repudiating *Charlotte*, then Brown's novels, drawing on Imlay's models, may be regarded as
a refutation of the Jacobin mode, the three writers providing a dialectic
series that is valid beyond the possibilities of actual influence.

Charles Brockden Brown is a novelistic hybrid whose works are derived
from or sympathetic to themes and situations found in the writings of his
contemporaries, both in America and abroad, yet he eventually transcended
the perimeters of the late eighteenth-century novel. He commenced his literary career an advocate of the ideas of Godwin and Wollstonecraft: at an
early point Brown planned a novel blending the sentimental morality of
Clarissa with the political radicalism of *Caleb Williams;* he wrote a philosophical dialogue, *Alcuin* (1798), that echoed Wollstonecraft's defense of woman's rights; and he contemplated a play based on Bage's *Hermsprong*. But by
the time he entered the major phase of his work, Brown had mixed feelings
about radical idealism, and increasingly found the Gothic romance more
congenial than the Jacobin novel to his darkening view of human possibilities. By the turn of the century Brown's transformation was complete, his
Jacobinism having reverted to Jacobean blackness.

Charles Brockden Brown was born in 1771 into a Quaker family of Philadelphia, an inheritance mingling religion with business in ways often successful to its practitioners but irritating to neighbors and fellow citizens.
His father, Elijah, entertained radical political sympathies, read Godwin
and other Jacobin authors, but like his fellow Quakers did not actively support the Revolution. The senior Brown's business suffered as a result, so
that his son grew up in an environment in which Christian and political
idealism produced ambivalent values and financial insecurity was a constant
fact, though hardly a stabilizing factor. He was on the threshold of adolescence when the war ended, and was already something of a prodigy, with
an active fantasy life that sustained his earliest fiction. His secondary education, in the Friends Latin School, lasted from his eleventh to his fifteenth
year, and was of that sort satirized by Royall Tyler as unsuited for useful
pursuits. Like a literary quixote, moreover, Brown received his primary

education from works of romantic fiction, so that though his father had him instructed in law, young Brown elected to make a livelihood through his writing. It was an ambition testifying to the impracticality of his education.

As the example of the older generation of American writers demonstrates, earning a living by authorship alone was not possible in the early republic. And yet Brown did *try*, setting the model for our first successful man of letters, Washington Irving, by editing magazines chiefly of his own composition and cultivating the society of other young authors, like the playwright William Dunlap and the poet-preacher John Blair Linn—whose sister, Elizabeth, Brown married. He anticipated also another later man of letters, Edgar Allan Poe, by displaying an artistic "temperament," psychological instability that found expression in the gothicism of his fiction. Brown's literary career lasted about a decade—from 1792 to 1802—a period bracketed by the adoption of the Constitution and the political disarray caused by the triumph of the Jeffersonian Republicans over the Federalists. Brown continued to write until his early death from tuberculosis, in 1810, supporting his family by running a store, but his last works were historical in nature and commercial in aim. They were also Federalist in politics.

Like his temperament, Brown's career seems a preview of Poe's, his tragic history a chart of the fate of an artist in a materialistic, middle-class culture. But his fiction was less a romantic gesture of rebellion than a heightened if parabolic reflection of the political temper of his age, mirroring darkly the uncertainty of a nation split from within by party division and threatened from without by affairs in France—a sister republic gone mad with post-revolutionary frenzy. By 1798 the Jacobin virus had spread to the United States, where it took the reactionary form of the Alien and Sedition Acts—a result of Federalist anti-Republican paranoia. If we realize that Brown's important novels appeared between 1798 and 1800, then the peculiar and often self-contradictory directions that his fiction took can be better understood—if not perfectly comprehended. As we have seen, Brown's older contemporaries wrote novels in which geopolitical division provided convenient moral watersheds, and though Brown was much more conscious than they of landscape as an aesthetic fact, his fiction expresses divisions not easily accommodated to the lay of the land. They reflect rather a mixture of political anxiety and psychological abnormality, the result of historical conditions and personal qualities that account for both the power and the perplexities of his designs.

The difficulty of comprehending Brown's meanings is increased by the confusion concerning the composition and publication of his novels. Thus *Arthur Mervyn* (1799, 1800) was apparently commenced (or at least conceived) while Brown was still under the influence of William Godwin, but was not published until after the appearance of *Wieland* (1798), a definably anti-Jacobin novel. Moreover, it was published in two parts, the last of which takes off in a contrary direction to the first. And yet, as with *Modern Chivalry*, the contradictions in Brown's most Godwinian novel are a key to his changing political ideas: the hero begins as a Rousseauistic innocent but ends with a much more realistic—that is, materialistic—view of the world. *Arthur Mervyn* is doubly a *Bildungsroman*, a projection of the author's own intellectual and political growth that couples the fall of an American Adam with his rise on the social scale.

Arthur's Adamic origins are associated with the rural landscape, his eventual rise with Philadelphia, a city presented as a cesspool of corruption, symbolized by the outbreak of yellow fever during Arthur's second period of residence there. Critics have not been slow to see this pestilence as a counterpart to the gold fever that animates the hero's Philadelphia patron, Welbeck, throughout the novel. Arthur's rural idealism sustains him during most of the action, and he resolves to marry the daughter of a farmer who has befriended him during one of his periodic retreats into the country, thereby fulfilling Brown's original plan for the novel, a Jacobin contrast between country virtue and city vice. But during the course of the second part of the story, Arthur's character perceptibly changes, and he ends by giving up his bucolic Eliza for Achsa Fielding, an older woman of Jewish antecedents and considerable wealth, apparently having decided that the simple joys of the country are no competition for the sophisticated pleasures of the city. This resolution not only belies the neat divisions of sentimental fiction, reversing the traditional moral dichotomy, but also seems to confound the ideological implications imposed on the rural/urban division by Jacobin writers like Imlay.

Since this final twist to the plot asserts values that the burden of the action would seem to deny, and since modern readers tend to share Enlightenment preferences for country over city life—at least so far as ethical values are concerned—the contrast between the "two" Arthur Mervyns has led a number of critics to suspect that Brown is being ironic, that the "first" Arthur is not the innocent he claims to be. He is instead a fictionalized Ben Franklin, that worldly Philadelphian who understood the value of appearances to commercial advancement, and his final decision is a cynical betrayal of his early idealism, which we as readers should reject. Such an interpretation would seem to be sustained by information gathered by one of Arthur's urban benefactors from persons who knew him as a child. But information provided by those who knew Charles Brockden Brown, especially his friend and biographer, William Dunlap, suggests that his slapdash method of composition could not have allowed for a sustained experiment in unreliable narration. Rather, the change between the first and second parts of *Arthur Mervyn* seems to reflect a shift in Brown's attitude toward his materials, for if he was the first American novelist of ideas, he was never hesitant about changing his mind. As Warner Berthoff has shown, Brown's literary method was one of improvised conjecture, a way of searching not finding, for he used his fiction to work out the implications of sequential moral dilemmas, not with a particular solution in mind, but rather with a love of pure ethical inquiry for its own sake. Typically, Arthur does not end his story by marrying Achsa, but merely tells us he intends to do so.

Such an inconclusive conclusion is an extreme instance of Brown's indeterminacy, but it does provide a gloss to the whole, and explains why he has been held in high regard by modern critics, who see in his novels the kind of ambiguities in which Hawthorne (who acknowledged Brown's influence) and Melville would deal. But where the ambiguity of those greater (if no more admirable) novelists is a self-conscious contrivance, a carefully articulated series of opposed possibilities, Brown's method is improvisatory, a dialectical progression that never comes to a pat conclusion or poses an obvious balance of alternatives. It is here that Brown differs from not only his posterity but his peers, whether the pointed morality of Rowson and Foster, the political purposefulness of Imlay, or the incoherent because indecisive plots of Brackenridge and Tyler.

The implication of Arthur Mervyn's transformation for Brown's intellectual progress is better understood by placing it in the context of his two coterminous novels. In *Wieland* (1798), the author's anti-Jacobinism is clearer, and in the titular hero-villain of *Ormond* (1799), Godwinian idealism takes perverse and sinister shape, twisting the Jacobin emphasis on pure reason to evil ends. Both novels were apparently influenced by "exposures" published in the 1790s of the Bavarian Illuminati—a secret society associated with Freemasonry and with the extremes of the French Revolution. Such revelations found a receptive audience in America among the Federalists, who in 1798 were suffering from political paranoia inspired by events in France and the rise of Jeffersonian Republicanism.

Twin products of this francophobia were Jedidiah Morse's "exposé" of the purported activities of the Illuminati in America, published in 1798, and the Alien and Sedition Acts, forced through Congress that same year by Federalists. The year 1798 also saw the publication of Godwin's *Memoirs* of Mary Wollstonecraft, which coupled Imlay's betrayal of both her love and her political idealism with the extremist stage of the French Revolution that resulted in the Reign of Terror. The impact of these revelations is most clearly evinced in *Ormond*, which demonstrates how Jacobin theories, in the wrong hands, can become instruments of an evil far greater than the social abuses they were intended to correct. But in *Wieland* we can detect subtle shifts of ideological emphasis that should be placed between the two parts of *Arthur Mervyn* as preludic to *Ormond*.

Regarded as the premier instance of the Gothic novel in America, *Wieland* is certainly a psychological tale of terror, but much as the European Gothic mode was a reaction to the eighteenth-century emphasis on neo-classical balance and reason, so Brown's romance contains a critique of Enlightenment idealism. Though all the characters are virtuous and well-meaning, their rational motives are often confounded by ambiguous circumstances, so that they undertake actions that result in tragic events. Even the title of the book casts a double image, referring to both Wieland senior and his son, to whom the father, though dead, has passed on a weird inheritance. A religious fanatic who suffered from morbid feelings of superstitious guilt, the father died from spontaneous combustion, as if eaten up by the internal fury of self-hatred. At the start of the novel, Wieland's son and daughter lead lives far different from his own: in place of his mad Calvinism, they follow the precepts of the Enlightenment, and the temple built by Wieland to his terrible Judeo-Christian God has been converted to a pastoral retreat. There the young people gather to read and play music, activities in harmony with those pursued by the enlightened folk in William Hill Brown's republican haven, "Belleview," and in Imlay's Jacobin utopia, "Bellefont."

But the Wieland asylum has an inheritance of insanity, symbolized by a dark ravine below the temple, whence comes Carwin, a strange and moody young man, whereupon things start to go awry in the family's orderly, rational world. Mysterious and prophetic voices are heard, threatening dire events and giving warnings of alarm, and Theodore Wieland—who despite his love of reason has inherited his father's superstitious disposition—is driven to madness. "Obeying" the voices, he kills his wife and children, and threatens his sister, Clara, the epistolator of the tale. Carwin appears at this critical moment and saves her life, and in so doing reveals that he is a ventriloquist: the source of the ominous warnings, he has bedeviled the family to death and disarray, and all, Carwin claims, for reasonable ends.

Though influence is unlikely, in *Wieland* we find curious parallels with *The Power of Sympathy*, from the epistolary form to the destruction of a family by inherited propensities (resulting, in the earlier novel, in incest and suicide), suggesting a Calvinist reading. Unlike William Hill Brown, however, Brockden Brown provides no party of virtue and right reason, but leaves his narrator-heroine seated amidst the ruins of her life. Moreover, *Wieland* has a subterranean political dimension, revealed in a fragmentary "Memoirs of Carwin," which suggests that the troublemaker was a member of the Illuminati. This is hardly the main thrust of *Wieland*, which is clearly psychological in emphasis, demonstrating how madness can dwell under the surface of a reasonable world, but it does link Carwin's destructive behavior to Federalist paranoia, thereby informing the novel with a larger insanity.

It is in *Ormond*, once again, that the anti-Jacobin mood of 1798 is most pointedly expressed, by means of a heroine who possesses the virtues of both Richardson's Clarissa and Wollstonecraft's "new woman" and a hero-villain who seems a compound of Godwin and Lovelace. First evinced in the darkly handsome Carwin, toward whom Clara Wieland is perversely drawn, the dangers of sexual attractiveness, coupled with suggestions of preternatural power (that Ormond is a manifestation of Satan is not a far-fetched supposition), result in a complex presence at once threatening and beguiling. Constantia Dudley finds herself pulled irresistibly into an increasingly evil orbit, and though, as in the novels of Rowson and Foster, seduction is the theme, *Ormond* lacks the sustaining middle-class framework of sentimental fiction. Toward the end of the novel, the "narrator" reveals herself to be not an impersonal voice but Sophia Westwynd Courtland, a family friend and virtually an allegorical personification of middle-class values. But this artistic afterthought has little impact on the reader, and even Constantia's powerful sense of virtue seems quaint in Ormond's nihilistically pluralistic world.

Like Carwin, Ormond is one of the double-tongued Illuminati, a mad product of the Enlightenment, but he is much more true to their code (as cracked by Jedidiah Morse). Laying vast plans for establishing a utopian empire in some vague western region, the foreign-born (read "French") Ormond, like Imlay, is unscrupulous in his personal dealings, ruthless behavior "logically" excused by the present corruptions of society. Awaiting the millennium he is about to effect, Ormond leads a life of absolute libertinism, a Jacobin version of Antichrist. At the same time, he is capable of great charm, and his advocacy of conduct dictated by pure reason is expressed in an articulate, witty, and logical form. It is only when Constantia sees the effects of Ormond's "reason" on others that she comprehends his true nature, for his theoretic advocacy of ideal behavior is, in practice, heartlessly cruel, entirely self-seeking, and often purposefully destructive, even to the point of rape and murder.

As with *Wieland*, it is possible to detect the shadow plot of a sentimental novel in *Ormond*, with the hero-villain as transcendent Rakehell and the heroine as the virtuous woman, like Hannah Foster's Eliza, who seeks, futilely, to reform him. But when threatened with rape, Constantia unlike Clarissa Harlowe turns the knife against her oppressor not herself, reversing the sentimental formula, and is left like Clara Wieland among the ruins of her life; nor do the moralizing cluckings of her friend Sophia provide more light than does a single candle in a tomb. Like his contemporaries, Brown was a didactic novelist, but his fiction operates on a more speculative plane, where moral values are seldom absolute, ethics are situational, conclusions indeterminate. Presuming that his readers shared either the conventional morality of Rowson or Imlay's enlightened faith in the efficacy of reason and environment, we can see the uniqueness of Brown's brand of didacticism, which seems aimed at educating his audience away from any easy faith in rational or "moral" behavior. His use of madness and obsession is part of his Gothic machinery, but beyond the melodrama we can see a deeper purpose, a dark shadow cast by the full glare of the Enlightenment, a fictional counterpart to the Reign of Terror.

Such was the quality of Brockden Brown's imagination that nothing he wrote is without some interest, and his last two novels, *Clara Howard* and *Jane Talbot* (1801), though relatively conventional efforts reflecting Brown's increasing conservatism, evince the versatile mind-play found in his best fiction. But it is, finally, with *Edgar Huntly* (1799) that this essay ends, the last of his novels that establishes the peripheries of what would become a distinctly American fiction. In theme, *Edgar Huntly* marks a return to a general critique of Enlightenment optimism, abandoning his anti-Jacobin specifics. But in terms of the future of the American novel, *Edgar Huntly* is an advance over *Wieland* and *Ormond*, for it is in the last of Brown's important works that the landscape takes on a defining, even participatory, role.

In his previous novels, as in the sentimental fiction of his contemporaries, the landscape is so generalized that Charlotte Temple would feel right at home: American place names do not an American place create. But in *Edgar Huntly*, Brown developed a geographic division essential to our national experience, that frontier line used by both Brackenridge and Imlay but to far different ends. In place of Hudibrastic satire and Enlightenment idealism, Brown gave a Gothic darkness to the frontier setting, establishing the tone for much American fiction to follow, as Leslie Fiedler and Edwin Fussell have shown us. *Edgar Huntly* also anticipates the detective story, for it commences on a violent note—a murder has been committed—producing a mystery that the narrator-hero is compelled to solve, rational inquiry that, as in the detective stories by Poe, is the sort of light that only increases the Gothic gloom.

Huntly tells his story through letters to the sister of the murdered man, but, unlike the passive Clara Wieland, he is a highly active participant in the action. Suspecting an immigrant Irish servant, Clithero Edny, of the crime, he starts to track him, and though the Irishman is innocent of the recent death, he believes himself guilty of an earlier murder. Edny leads Huntly into the mountains of western Pennsylvania, where he has taken refuge, driven mad by guilt and fear of detection. Huntly describes himself as a romantic lover of Nature in her wilder forms, but his pursuit of the madman takes him into a zone where his Burkean love of the sublime proves an inadequate guide. At the farthest point, Huntly's wilderness quest carries him into the heart of American darkness, for a Gothic cavern-conduit leads him into the midst of a group of slumbering savages who have taken a young white girl captive. Imlay made an erotic finale from the same frontier situation, but for Brown it provides yet another episode of terror.

Huntly makes his way eventually back to civilization, but stubbornly persists in tracing the complicated history of Clithero, for like Godwin's Caleb Williams he has a dangerous bump of curiosity. Though lacking the political implications of Brown's earlier novels, *Edgar Huntly* is yet another narrative in which rational inquiry brings the hero to the dark threshold of madness and self-destruction. The world of Nature is both a lunatic asylum and a sanctuary for murderous beasts and men, nor does civilization provide a reasonable alternative: domestic matters are characterized by treachery, murder, bereavement. Though anticipating Cooper's frontier, Brown's brutal wilderness contains no noble Mohicans, no chivalric hunters, and rational behavior among civilized men is an unsure moral guide.

Commencing his career with plans to write a novel in which Richardsonian morality was wed to a Rousseauistic sensibility, Brown ended by repudiating the validity of both, and while borrowing the materials of the Jacobin novel, he instilled his plots with such a Jacobean élan as to obliterate all signs of the genre. Looking back over the fiction produced during the 1790s in America, we can see the complex way in which Brown interacted with the moral and political concerns of his fellow authors, for the impact of contemporary events, compounded with the influence of Godwin and the example of Gothic romance, inspired him to write a new kind of novel, in which questions are more important than answers, ideas more vital than lessons. Rowson's *Charlotte Temple* points the way to *Uncle Tom's Cabin,* being a transcendent example of the sentimental novel, while Brown's *Edgar Huntly,* like *Moby-Dick,* is a transcendent Gothic romance, ending in a cipher that solves no codes but rounds all questions with an O.

John Seelye

Toward a National Literature

Revolution and the establishment of an independent republic provided American literature with what is still perhaps its dominant theme—America itself, or its corollary, the state of being American. "What then is the American, this new man?" asks St. John de Crèvecoeur in *Letters from an American Farmer* (1782). His answer is almost reverential. Writing as James, a thriving farmer who works his own land, he pictures the American as one who, freed from "servile dependence, penury and useless labour," acquires a new self-respect and status, sheds Old World "prejudices and manners," and begins to act "upon new principles" and "entertain new ideas." The transformation is virtually a new birth. "Here man is free as he ought to be"; here "men are become men: in Europe they were so many useless plants."

Ironically James is not a citizen of the United States but a British subject. The Revolution is not mentioned until the last of his letters. The freedom he boasts of is that ostensibly guaranteed by English law, the freedom that American Patriots claimed to be upholding. He cannot condone British treatment of the colonies, but, disturbed by the violence of Whig resistance, he remains neutral in the war. His confidence in America is obviously shaken. Already in an earlier letter, shocked by the brutality of slavery in the South, James has at least briefly lapsed into the traditional view of human nature as innately evil. After all, a slave had no chance of becoming, in Crèvecoeur's terms, an American, that is, a "new" human being.

But the celebration of American freedom and prosperity in the early letters has endured and kept the book alive. Crèvecoeur's optimism differs little from that of the rising glory poets, but it sounds more convincing in James's relatively unadorned prose than in their characteristically ostentatious verse. Crèvecoeur deliberately chose to speak as an ordinary farmer without pretensions to learning. He even dramatized the issue of style or language by having a subsidiary character convince James that if he writes about what he knows intimately and uses the language of ordinary speech, his letters will be read: "if they be not elegant, they will smell of the woods." Here was the kernel of a theory of American style.

Peering into America's utopian or millennial future, the nationalistic poets invariably predicted the coming of American Homers, Virgils, and Miltons. They wanted a literature commensurate with the civic eminence of the emerging republic. They conceived of the epic as what it had often been for readers in earlier societies, a monumental poetic embodiment of a nation's ethos and sense of destiny. But, hoping for almost instantaneous greatness in American poetry, they tended not to see the underlying inconsistency between their commitment to freedom and their tendency to accept many of the artificialities of style and form sanctified by the aristocratic taste of the past.

The wise old farmer who offers homely advice on husbandry and morality in Timothy Dwight's *Greenfield Hill* (1794) has some resemblance to James in Crèvecoeur's prose pastoral. But Dwight, as self-conscious pastoral "poet," does most of his own talking, and he is clearly aware that his writing will be read in England and judged by rigorous standards—some would say prejudices. This was a major problem. British critics, who often condescended to American authors as distressingly provincial, had considerable influence on American taste.

By 1800 many Americans were anxious about their literature. The patriotic outpouring in verse was clearly a disappointment, except perhaps to the most ardent nationalists. Drama and prose fiction, long viewed with puritanic suspicion, were only in their infancy in the United States. Samuel Miller, a scholarly New York clergyman, surveying the American literary scene in *A Brief Retrospect of the Eighteenth Century* (1803), observed that "*theological* and *political* works" abounded and had met with success. He also credited Americans with achievements in history, natural science, and other branches of learning. But he stated flatly that American writings "in general" were "less learned, instructive, and elegant" than those in Britain and elsewhere in Europe. Reasons for the poor showing included substandard higher education in the United States, shortages of books and libraries, want of a substantial leisure class, and a relatively low regard for literature. Americans were primarily "*commercial*" in spirit and still tied to Britain by "language, manners, taste." The English books they preferred could easily be imported or cheaply reproduced in America.

A long and complicated debate ensued on the state and prospects of the nation's literature. The optimistic were willing to be patient, foreseeing that conditions and attitudes would gradually change so that a mature literature could develop. Others were discouraged, none more so than the high Federalist congressman, orator, and classical scholar, Fisher Ames of Massachusetts, who maintained in an essay entitled "American Literature" (*The Works of Fisher Ames* [1809]) that it was ridiculous to expect a society so commercialized, with a political system so democratized, to produce a great literature. Some argued that Americans could expect no distinctive literature because they lacked a language of their own. Noah Webster, however, at work on his *American* dictionary, insisted that there was already an authentic American variety of English that should be carefully cultivated and standardized. An argument that was to worry some writers for decades was that the country lacked fit subjects for great literature: everything was too new to be interesting, or too ordinary and dull—the consequence of republicanism.

For a decade or so concern with correct taste, elegance, rules of composition, and linguistic purity dominated the discussion, whatever the positions of the participants. After the War of 1812, however, greater receptivity to the aesthetics of romanticism made possible a more viable literary nationalism. *The North American Review*, founded in Boston in 1815, led the way by stressing originality as the key to literary eminence. The magazine's first editor, William Tudor, complained in the issue of November 1815 that scenic "descriptions" in American poems owed more to "the study of classical poets" than to familiarity with native landscapes. What he was asking for, though not in so many words, was a romantic sensitivity to nature. Rejecting the notion that America was literarily uninteresting, Tudor argued that wilderness settings would enhance epic depictions of the nation's "romantick" past, especially the "century of conflicts" between Britain and France for the New World. He also saw tragic possibilities in the fate awaiting the American "Aborigines." Except that they did not write in verse, James Fenimore Cooper and Francis Parkman were eventually to realize Tudor's vision.

Even more telling was a brief essay in *The North American Review* in 1816, "On Models in Literature," by Edward Tyrell Channing, professor of rhetoric and oratory at Harvard. Genius, he asserted, with its "indignant freedom," is in eternal conflict with "rules for versification, laws of taste, books of practical criticism, and approved standards of language." Nature, not books, and solitude, not society, are what primarily nurture great literature. Channing believed that his doctrine was valid for writers in any society, but it was clearly calculated to stir the imaginations of those living in a nation committed to personal freedom. Even though his essay contains no trace of transcendentalist metaphysics, his aesthetic is substantially that which enabled Ralph Waldo Emerson and Henry David Thoreau, both later his students, to express themselves with a freedom now generally recognized as unquestionably indigenous.

Useful as the controversy undoubtedly was in the long run, it left the work of the two or three generations of writers prior to 1820 in low esteem. Even in the twentieth century scholars have tended to accept the early literary nationalists' severe judgment on their own contemporaries. The history of American literature is now commonly conceived as an evolution toward indigenousness. The approach is a tribute to the perspicacity of Channing and other contributors to *The North American Review*, but until recently it has discouraged close examination of the literature of the early republic, which is so obviously dependent on conventions derived from the Old World.

Healthy as we may find Channing's charge to "genius" to ignore models, the fact remains that the history of literature consists to a large extent of the adaptation, conscious or unconscious, of old forms and styles to new situations and purposes. Certain forms require only minimal alteration in new contexts, but the process of adaptation can also be complicated. Where superficial readings see only imitation, for instance, writers may be parodying the conventions they use, even if unconsciously so. Philip Freneau in his longer war poems, for instance, full of rage against Britain, and sliding back and forth uneasily between seriousness and satire, seems to be trying to do violence to the restraints that that great instrument of British order, the heroic couplet, imposes on him. And a similarly divided consciousness reveals itself in moments when the labored pretentiousness of Charles Brockden Brown's prose seems to mock both itself and his high-minded characters.

Sometimes, moreover, the provincial writer's linguistic exorbitance seems to work in spite of itself. The most astounding verbal artifact of the early republic is probably *Travels through North and South Carolina, Georgia, East & West Florida* (1791) by the Quaker naturalist William Bartram. The book is an unlikely mixture of scientific observation, lyric rapture, and religious meditation. The author is a largely solitary traveler who has left his excess baggage behind and exposed himself, virtually defenseless, to the combined beauty and terror of the wilderness. His ethic is that of the Society of Friends—tolerance, peace, respect for life in all its myriad forms—rather than that of the hunter or Indian-fighter. But his ornate language is the very opposite of plain Quaker speech. It seems to begin with his delight in the sounds and sense of taxonomic Latin—"magnolia grandiflora," for instance, for "the great Laurel Tree," or "Quercus sempervirens" for "Live Oak." Latinate poeticisms and elaborate syntactical sonority are the substance of his style. And as his grandiloquence strains language, so his imagination strains the truth. He has been accused of telling tall tales—the simple Quaker as frontier boaster—of padding his accounts of the abundance of wildlife, or turning a brawl between two crocodiles into an epic battle that literally shakes the earth. But if he is gulling the reader, he seems to be gulling himself as well. For Bartram, creation is miraculous. Trying to convey this perception keeps drawing him into lush hyperbole, the ultimate irony being that there seems to be something unnatural about nature.

The personal experience that Channing's doctrine calls on the writer to be true to was often for early Americans one of cultural disorientation. The literary nationalists were to a degree caught up in the cultural inferiority complex to which they themselves were calling attention. Concerned primarily with poetry, their pride piqued by American failures in the epic, they did not pay much attention to the writing of those of their contemporaries and immediate predecessors who had more modest ambitions. In particular they tended to discount political writing as hopelessly mired in prejudice and passion.

Yet ironically the larger vision that poets sought to project in epic or quasi-epic form was already substantially inscribed in partisan political texts, mostly in prose. A national mythology of sorts had evolved, giving the ethos of republican freedom a substantial figural form. The culture had its sacred symbols, its legendary heroes and antagonists, its recollection of ancestors and origins, and of founders struggling in the wilderness to preserve the ancient truths and commitments that by 1776 had evolved into an American "civil religion."

Through pertinent allusions, pamphleteers and preachers, illustrators and street demonstrators lured into contemporary contexts figures from the Bible, Western literature, classical mythology, and Greek and Roman, as well as Anglo-American, history. Liberty herself and other personified abstractions appeared allegorically in parades, cartoons, and printed texts. Audiences, familiar with the constantly reiterated central images, were geared to respond to the diverse iconography. True, myth might take liberties with the truth—always in the name of Liberty, of course. And rhetoric reduced at times to chauvinistic rant. Yet the figural language, concretizing abstract argument, was often highly persuasive. Eclectic in origin and never compellingly embodied in a single comprehensive text, it was nonetheless a collective American literary creation.

Mythologizing had begun early, particularly in New England, thanks to Puritanism's predilection for typological readings of Scripture and history. The Puritan conception of America as the foreordained site of the completion of the Reformation—later of the onset of the millennium—is tied historically to the extravagant American self-image projected in the literature of the Revolution. John Adams makes the connection strikingly clear in a statement from a preliminary draft of the essay that came to be known as *A Dissertation on the Canon and Feudal Law* (1765): "I always consider the settlement of America . . . as the opening of a grand scene and design in Providence for the illumination of the ignorant and the emancipation of the slavish part of mankind." Here we have in one sentence the mythologized rendering of American history that Joel Barlow was ultimately to versify so extensively as *The Vision of Columbus* (1787). Many of the political tracts, however, less interested in making a "literary" impression, present the myth more powerfully.

What had "peopled America," Adams maintained in his *Dissertation*, was the Reformation and the Renaissance, personified in the Puritans as they struggled against Stuart "tyranny." They recognized that government, whether of church or state, is "a plain, simple, intelligible thing, founded in nature and reason and quite comprehensible by common sense." Well educated, they also knew that the "servile dependencies" of feudalism had had no place in the classical "seats of liberty, the republics of Greece and Rome." Within this large historic schema Adams saw the Stamp Act as a "design" to subvert "the whole system of our fathers." It would strip Americans "of the means of knowledge by loading the press, the colleges, and even an almanack and a newspaper, with restraints and duties." And it would rob the poor to provide new jobs in the imperial service for political placemen, who for Adams equate with feudal dependents.

Patriot rhetoric made much of the image of arbitrary government as a self-generating, ever-expanding, corrupt and corrupting bureaucracy. Years later in a historical analysis that keeps slipping into grotesque satire Barlow was to expand the image to a gargantuan size. His provocative, if näively American, defense in prose of the French Revolution, *Advice to the Privileged Orders in the Several States of Europe* (1792, 1795), pictures major institutions of the *ancien régime*—the judicial system, the standing army, and the funding system—as extensions of feudalism transformed into fantastic "engines" for keeping the masses awed, servile, and impoverished.

The American mythology owed a great deal to the writings of a vocal minority of "true Whigs" or "Commonwealthmen" in Britain, who were widely read in eighteenth-century America. While English liberty was widely

heralded after the Glorious Revolution of 1688–89 as one of the wonders of
the world, true Whigs often viewed that freedom as under siege, constantly
threatened by widespread corruption in government and society. Many
Americans shared this anxiety, particularly after the Stamp Act. Pension-
ers, placemen, and imperial "tools"—customs officers, for instance—seemed
to multiply, as Samuel Adams kept saying, "like the Locusts in Egypt."
Britain was charged with what Silas Downer of Rhode Island colorfully
called a deliberate "design" to "fix" Americans "in the lowest bottom of
slavery."

Alas, poor Liberty! That chaste maid or goddess was being forced out of
Britain by George III and "the ministry." Or had she fled long ago to the
American wilderness and, transformed into a tender shoot, flourished as
the omnipresent Liberty Tree—gathering place for the Patriots who called
themselves her "Sons"? Wherever she was, whatever she was, she was always an endangered species. An anonymous writer in the *Boston Gazette and
Country Journal* (April 18, 1763) remembered how Julius Caesar had undermined the "liberties" of republican Rome by "flattery and intrigues." The
great commander, "employed by the commonwealth to conquer for it," had
"succeeded in his commission," becoming "the benefactor of his country.
But as a reward he took the commonwealth for his pains."

Reflecting divisions and contradictions in American culture, the high public
myth of freedom was not always self-consistent. Thomas Jefferson's version, for instance, differed from John Adams's in part because of historical
differences between Virginia and Massachusetts. The former colony had
obviously not been "peopled" through resistance to Stuart tyranny. With
his own dramatic flair, however, Jefferson in *A Summary View of the Rights
of British America* (1774) linked "our ancestors," who had migrated to Virginia in the seventeenth century, to earlier "Saxon ancestors," who had
migrated from "wilds and woods in the north of Europe," taken possession
of Britain, and there established "that system of laws which has so long
been" its "glory and protection." Many students of history, John Adams
included, doubted that the origins of English liberty truly lay in the German forest of the dark ages. But the image of the Saxons as prefeudal republicans or democrats had considerable appeal in America, perhaps in part
because of its pastoral overtones.

The Liberty Tree itself, derived from old English custom or ritual, was
a striking pastoral image, a visible reminder of a central article of American
political faith, that government should be simple, direct, natural—and commonsensical. Not surprisingly Thomas Paine's *Common Sense* (1776), in a
typically apt and concise figure, explicitly links such a polity with the "first

peopling" of a country—"or of the world." Of the participants in such ventures, he says, "Some convenient tree will afford them a State House, under the branches of which the whole Colony may assemble." Thus American experience was made to seem to reenact the primitive virtuous beginnings of the public life of the human species—in the Lockean state of nature.

In some texts the mythology revealed itself in a blend of metaphors that evoked both the Whig story of the perils of Anglo-American liberty and the Christian story of reformed religion's exodus from the Old World in search of a promised land. Idealized as a domain of liberty created in the wilderness by agrarian virtue and industry, America was also, for many descendants of the Puritans, the land where "every man" sat "under his vine and under his fig tree," an image suggesting both the earlier Canaan and, prophetically, a world at peace in the "last days" (Micah, 4:1–4).

Patriot clergymen tended to make the rhetoric of freedom and the rhetoric of personal and national redemption virtually identical. Sermons formulated as jeremiads exhorted God's people simultaneously to resist parliamentary encroachment and to renew themselves in virtue. Corruption—in biblical terms, enslavement to sin and Satan—in any form, in any situation, loomed as a threat to liberty. Adherence to nonimportation agreements— abstinence from luxuries like tea—became a religious as well as a civic obligation. Stalwart New England Protestants like Nathaniel Niles and Levi Hart warned Americans that to countenance African slavery while complaining of Britain's "conspiracy" to enslave the colonies was to risk remaining spiritually in what Hart called a "more than Egyptian bondage." When war broke out and independence beckoned, some students of Scripture, recalling Israel's clamoring for kings as the abandonment of something like republicanism, equated monarchy with idolatry. About to establish a republic, Americans could now view themselves as reclaiming liberties surrendered not only by Romans to the empire but also by Jews to the kings they had been warned against.

There is very little American writing of any significance between 1765 and 1815 that is not touched by the mythology of freedom. *The Federalist* (1787–88), for instance, celebrated though it is for its realistic political vision, is nonetheless also partially responsible for the mystique that envelops the Constitution. While James Madison recognizes the inevitability of political factions in the tenth number, the papers generally assure readers that the Constitution will spare the nation what Whig ideologues had traditionally warned against—a neglect of the common welfare in frenzies of partisanship and the pursuit of special interests. Temporarily ignoring their sharp political differences, Alexander Hamilton, John Jay, and Madison write not as themselves but as "Publius," a name that, like Latin pseudonyms used by Patriots, evokes the memory of disinterested Roman republican virtue. The mythic overtones persist: Liberty wants only the ratification of the new compact to be permanently enshrined in America. *The Federalist* itself, with its majestic prose and noble structural proportions, figures as a classic temple to the august deity.

Liberty was also a Roman goddess for Mercy Warren, sister of James Otis and author of a *History of the Rise, Progress and Termination of the American Revolution* (1805), one of several histories and biographies written after the war to justify independence and republicanism. The others are *The History of the Rise, Progress, and Establishment of the Independence of the United States of America* (1788) by William Gordon, an English-born Massachusetts preacher, and *The History of the American Revolution* (1789) by David Ramsay of South Carolina, both, like Warren's, large, readable narratives, though mostly compiled from secondary sources. Chief Justice John Marshall's *The Life of George Washington* (1804–7) and William Tudor's *The Life of James Otis of Massachusetts* (1823) are more original as scholarship but heavier in style. Except for Marshall's, the least colorful, all these works substantially mythologize American history, none more so than Warren's. Hers is also at once the most democratic politically and, ironically, the most aristocratic in tone and style. The conflict is related to the fact that for her the Revolution is so much a struggle between republic and empire, reenacting, though in reverse, the civil strife that convulsed Rome under Caesar and his successors. Her sympathies in both cases are with the republic: George III is another Caesar and, like him, a symbol of a virtue lost to corruption. But her strident anti-imperial rhetoric often rings out imperiously or dictatorially. One is not always comfortable being driven into the fray by Warren's commanding prose and then discovering that one is cheering unthinkingly while she verbally demolishes an enemy like Thomas Hutchinson, the hated Tory governor of Massachusetts.

Commitment to the mythology of the republic helped sustain the correspondence between Jefferson and John Adams, which was revived after the intensely partisan years of their presidencies. Flourishing until their deaths in 1826, it became one of the premier literary achievements of the age. And perhaps no one more fully lived the ideal of republican virtue than Adams's wife, Abigail, whom he consistently acknowledged to be his superior as a writer. Her letters to him during the Revolution, eloquent outpourings of support for her husband and the new nation, rely heavily on the basic Puritan, Whig, and Roman components of the mythology. Moreover, Abigail Adams saw clearly that the logic of republican theory demanded the participation of women in the new government. "Do not put such unlimited power into the hands of Husbands," she wrote her own spouse. "Remember, all Men would be tyrants if they could." But John Adams could not take her seriously.

The high public mythology belonged primarily to a white male elite, men of property, status, and education (often lawyers) who were accustomed to being deferred to by their less privileged compatriots. That it was not altogether suited to a republic becoming increasingly democratic after 1800 is suggested by William Wirt of Virginia in his *Sketches of the Life and Character of Patrick Henry* (1817). In spite of certain misgivings, Wirt, a self-made man himself, strongly identifies with his "plebeian" hero. Henry speaks not only for America against British tyranny but also for Virginia's rising western democracy against domination by the Tidewater aristocrats. And Wirt has him speak, as William R. Taylor has shown, with a raw untutored force, his natural or native voice a challenge to the Ciceronian oratorical style of the planter leaders, whose culture leans, perhaps excessively, on Roman patrician ideals.

Wirt's Patrick Henry recalls an even more "obscure and unpolished rustic" who had made his way into American myth. He was Yankee Doodle, the bumpkin who came off the farm or out of the backwoods to lick the redcoats. Initially not much more than a joke, his story originated well before the Revolution in some oddly ambiguous lyrics devised apparently by New Englanders themselves. Seeming to mock their own rusticity, the song, as J. A. Leo Lemay suggests, may well have been a trick to dupe those who presumed to look down on Yankees as provincial—British troops stationed in the colonies, for instance, who relished the song as a satire on the natives.

Came April 19, 1775, and the redcoats or "lobster-backs" marched to the battle of Concord singing "Yankee Doodle," were beaten off by Yankee minutemen, and were forced into retreat. The event acted out the implications of the song, at least as the colonials heard it. From then on it belonged to them, and they taunted the enemy with it throughout the war. The Yankee clown was on his way to becoming a national symbol, the personification of something in the American character that baffled and ultimately defeated Britain—a ragtag simplicity and naturalness masking unexpected shrewdness and practicality. The myth transformed traditional British military formality and spit-and-polish drill work into foppish affectation. A "burlesque of discipline" is what Ethan Allen called what happened at Fort Ticonderoga in May 1775 when the Green Mountain Boys surprised the sleeping British garrison and captured it.

Out of the war came numerous songs and stories celebrating similar triumphs. Many of the songs could be sung to the tune we know as "Yankee Doodle," though they had nothing literally to do with the original story. One such song, Francis Hopkinson's "Battle of the Kegs," facetiously claims victory for the British—in a battle that never took place—while simultaneously attributing to them an enormous fear of rebel trickery. A clever anonymous ballad, "The Dance" (1781), which allegorizes the final campaign of the war as a sequence of "country" and "courtly" dances, both metrically imitates the verse of the folk song and plays on a line from the chorus—"Mind the music and the step." The story has Cornwallis, not altogether successful at dancing in the Southern countryside with Nathaniel Greene and Lafayette, retire to Yorktown, thinking himself more fit for a "courtly ball."

> Yet are red heels and long-lac'd skirts,
>   For stumps and briars meet, sir?
> Or stand they chance with hunting-shirts,
>   Or hardy veteran feet, sir?

But in town the "ever-dancing peer" is humiliated by the dancing of George Washington, who, in spite of his aristocratic Virginia upbringing, turns out symbolically a Yankee: "taught" by "easy nature," he has a "grace which can't by pains be won" or by "Plutus' gold" be "bought, sir."

The same British general had earlier been victimized in "The Cornwalliad, an Heroi-comic Poem" in four cantos, which appeared anonymously in Hugh Henry Brackenridge's *United States Magazine* in 1779. On the surface a conventional eighteenth-century mock epic, "The Cornwalliad" is more fundamentally an American tall tale about British fear of Yankee trickery. At the climax two British armies attack each other, each convinced that it is fighting some of Washington's troops who have defeated a detachment of redcoats and stolen their uniforms.

The Narrative of Colonel Ethan Allen (1779) is a hastily and crudely composed account of that Green Mountain boy's two and one-half years as a prisoner of war in jails and prison ships in America and England. Blatant Patriot propaganda, it is given literary vitality by its unabashed yet knowing innocence. The loquacious Allen was not only a frontiersman and soldier but also a self-taught divinity student and philosopher—later the author of *Reason the Only Oracle of Man* (1784). He boasts how "in a fit of anger" he "twisted off a nail" in his handcuffs "with my teeth," while "at the same time I swaggered over those who abused me." He was also able to "come the Yankee" over his English jailer, that is, play the simpleminded

American, so that a letter he had written, ostensibly to the Continental Congress, would fall into the hands of Lord North. Dressed in a Canadian "fawn-skin jacket" and strutting before residents of Falmouth, England, who came to gawk at American prisoners, he both traded insults with them and talked "moral philosophy and christianity"—a wild American who astoundingly could "understand a syllogism."

Yankee jubilation also echoes through John Trumbull's *M'Fingal* (1782), for all its indebtedness to the English burlesque tradition. Trumbull adroitly interwines allusions to the comic song and story with satire based on the public myth of the conspiracy against Anglo-American Liberty. The action punctures the Tory pretense that the war is a sort of schoolboy rebellion that the stern rod of parental discipline wielded by Britain will quickly quash. In the end M'Fingal's being taught—instead of teaching—a lesson rounds out a narrative that opens with the world turned upside down at Lexington and Concord, where "Yankies, skill'd in martial rule,/First put the British troops to school" and, among other skills, taught them the "true war-dance of Yanky-reels."

During the Revolution, and even later, the two myths, the high and the vernacular, worked side by side without undue tension. As the ever-earnest Manly and the down-to-earth Jonathan in Royall Tyler's *The Contrast*, for instance, Publius and Yankee Doodle teamed up to save American virtue from the seductions of British luxury. And Robert Slender, O.S.M. ("one of the swinish multitude"), Philip Freneau's innocent persona in the overtly Jeffersonian *Letters on Various Interesting and Important Subjects* (1799), had an educated "Latinist" as friend to help him see why he was actually a Democratic-Republican when he thought he was a Federalist. Brackenridge's *Modern Chivalry* (1792–1815), however, with the gentlemanly Captain Farrago and his bog-trotting servant Teague O'Regan locked in unending conflict, foreshadowed the coming reality of social and economic conflict in the United States.

The Yankee proved more adaptable than Publius to the increasingly democratic polity. His myth survived and flourished as a key component in the vernacular comic tradition now known as "native American humor." Racist and sexist biases in that tradition reflected deep tensions in the culture generally. But both the humor and the culture proved to have the potential for expanded tolerance. The high public language meanwhile lost vitality from overuse. Its lofty sounds might still on occasion cast spells over democratic audiences, but on the whole it was only the disenfranchised—especially women and blacks—and their supporters who could wring new meaning out of it.

In a society increasingly committed to free speech and freedom of the press, the cheapening of language in partisan shrillness had long been a theme of political controversy. During the Revolution, Patriot and Tory adversaries had ridiculed each other's arguments as hollow rhetoric or sheer wind. Thus the image of ventosity is implicit throughout Trumbull's travesty of British claims on America, as we hear in the twisted logic and blustering clichés of M'Fingal's orations to the Whigs. And in "The Word of Congress" (1779), an anonymous Tory satire—probably by Jonathan Odell—the entire American rebellion is brilliantly reduced to airy talk or meaningless marks on paper. Congress appears as a hydra-headed monster, making animal-like noises out of many mouths at once. The word of Congress has endless extensions beyond its walls—in petitions, proclamations, speeches, pamphlets, and other propagandistic utterances made by members or their agents. The ambiguity of the word "word" itself clinches the satire. Congress, not being true to its word, in a sense has none. Stamped on the notoriously debased Continental currency, its word is a fraudulent promise to pay.

The war of course did not end vituperative journalism. In "Some Thoughts on Diseases of the Mind," published in the *Pennsylvania Gazette* (1788), Francis Hopkinson proposes, tongue in cheek, that two newspapers be given a monopoly on venting political spleen. His idea is to cure by purgation the "disease" he terms *"Cacoethes maledictionis*, or an insatiable rage for slander and abuse." He takes this to be a malady "peculiar to free governments." So does the aging Brackenridge in *Modern Chivalry*, as he sharply satirizes the tawdry reality of American political culture and challenges the myth of the virtuous republic. Incensed, for instance, at a particularly abusive pro-Federalist paper, he attacks the journal by name in a comic skit that equates it with a man who keeps a caged skunk on his premises and provokes it into emptying its bladder on the passersby. More generally Brackenridge blasts the American political press at large as "abominably gross, and defamatory"—a national "disgrace."

While *Modern Chivalry* mocks the aristocratic pretensions of the high Federalists, it has a greater fear that the gradual democratization of the republic will undermine standards of public behavior and produce a virulent anti-intellectualism. Committed to free speech and a free press, however, Brackenridge has little with which to combat this tendency—except a scathing satire. His appeals for "delicacy" and "good breeding" in political debate largely fall on deaf ears. He argues that what gets printed should be "what [it] would become a gentleman to say in promiscuous society." But implicitly he acknowledges the hopelessness—if not the sterility—of this view.

Once granted, popular rights are going to be used. It is foolish to think otherwise, as the quixotic Farrago does when he maintains that it is enough for "the lowest citizen" to have the right to public office and "not absolutely necessary" for him "to exercise it."

A recent immigrant, Farrago's man Teague expects to rise quickly in the land of opportunity and is particularly drawn to politics. The gift of blarney makes him appealing to the average voter, but his ignorance and unscrupulousness are a threat to the republic. Farrago is one of the educated patrician few who, assuming that they know better than the plebeian multitude what is best for the nation as a whole, expect to govern. But neither Teague nor the electorate pays much attention to the Captain's long discourses on civic responsibility. His undying commitment to the high ideal of the virtuous republic is what makes him thoroughly quixotic. Meanwhile the members of the rising democracy are irrepressible.

Brackenridge voices agreement with Farrago's views but dramatizes their futility in an action that disintegrates over the years into an imitation of a society going mad. At the same time, constantly commenting on his own text, the waggish "author" becomes the protagonist in a secondary story— the writing of his book. He pretends that his only purpose is to offer a model of good prose style, clear and correct but unostentatious. We are asked to believe that what he says is of no importance, that all that matters is the way he says it. Obviously he hopes for readers sophisticated enough to see that he takes himself seriously as both literary stylist and social observer—but not too seriously. But he is altogether ignored—at least this is his story. Nothing he says makes a difference. Successive installments of the book appear (1792, 1793, 1797, 1804, 1805, 1815), and democratic distraction is simply compounded. Still he writes on, a self-conscious Quixote to the end, somehow clinging to the republican ideal.

Meanwhile *Salmagundi*, a burlesque periodical published anonymously in New York (1807–8), borrowing a term recently coined by the English wit Sydney Smith, identified the infant republic as "a pure LOGOCRACY or *government of words*." A "reverence" for " 'the voice of the sovereign people' " has, in *Salmagundi*'s view, turned the United States into a nation of tongue-waggers and scribblers. Newspaper editors, or "SLANG-WHANGERS," lead the people in *"wordy battle"* and *"paper war."* And "a man of superlative ventosity" appropriately presides over the logocracy, that renowned writer, philosopher, and "huge bladder of wind," Thomas Jefferson. With partisan views of its own, *Salmagundi* was obviously a part of the logocracy. Though disgusted with the scurrilousness of American journalism, the magazine, one of whose author/editors was the youthful Washington Irving, could not have existed unless it felt free to ridicule any public figure, even the President.

In *A History of New York* (1809), the first work in belles lettres by an American to catch the public imagination and endure, Irving, writing as the eccentric Diedrich Knickerbocker, presents much the same image of politics in the United States, though often it is thinly disguised as the politics of seventeenth-century New Netherland. The early Irving's burlesque style was in part a youthful pose, a playful rebellion against the quaint gentility of his elders. Ultimately, however, it suggests a distrust of language itself. Obviously a lover of words, he writes as though he has few of his own, his often high-flown prose full of mocking echoes of conventional manners of speaking. Like Knickerbocker, Irving knows "how much my beloved country" owes "to a praise-worthy figure in rhetoric, generally cultivated by your little great men, called hyperbole." In a logocracy more and more words mean less and less.

The iconoclasm of the *History of New York* suggests a society, only nominally the Dutch colony of New Netherland, blinded by the myth of its own greatness. A true patriot of a country that no longer exists and never did amount to much, Knickerbocker aspires filiopietistically to memorialize it with all "the dignity, the grandeur and magnificence of Livy." But the gap between his language and reality keeps exposing him as ridiculous or, when he acknowledges its existence, hopelessly confused.

No such confusion, however, muddles the refreshingly prosaic journals kept by Meriwether Lewis and William Clark on their arduous journey of discovery up the Missouri River, across the northern Rockies, down the Columbia to the Pacific, and back, between 1804 and 1806. For a century the journals were available only in versions drastically condensed and rewritten in the interests of general readability. Not until the publication of *The Original Journals of the Lewis and Clark Expedition*, in eight volumes, edited by Reuben Gold Thwaites in 1904–5, was the language of the explorers themselves revealed. Clark's is crudely simple and direct, Lewis's a shade bookish though often almost as erratic in grammar, syntax, spelling, and punctuation. Yet what both write is remarkably lucid and graphic because so fundamentally factual.

The expedition was freighted with national significance. Conceived and arranged by President Jefferson himself, it was given added urgency, just as it was getting started, by the Louisiana Purchase, which on the instant more than doubled the size of the republic. Lewis and Clark had to function in part as emissaries to the Indians from the great white father in Washington. But that is perhaps the only myth in which they knowingly participate. On the whole they are admirably noncondescending toward Native Americans and their cultures. They do not write as agents or publicists of Manifest Destiny, rather as practical frontiersmen and observers with a job to do. The expedition largely put to rest the dream of a Northwest Passage by water to the Orient. It is not Providence that Lewis and Clark invoke to get them to the Pacific and back but their own resourcefulness, about which they have no need to boast. For all the courage and perseverance they show, they do not make themselves heroes of romance or epic.

Tedious detail so clutters their narrative that readers are advised to explore it initially in a modern abridgment, such as Bernard De Voto's *The Journals of Lewis and Clark* (1953). But the careful recording of what happened and what was observed—pursuant to a direct order from Jefferson— is the explorers' ultimate triumph. It eventuates in an image of the West that is archetypal because totally real and massively a matter of fact—the vastness of the continent, which is its own myth, balanced against the thirty-odd explorers, who include York, a black slave, Sacajawea, the Shoshone wife of a French-Canadian interpreter, and Pompey, her infant son. The wilderness dwarfs but does not overawe these pioneers, who have the patience and discipline to learn from it and survive. Lewis and Clark outrank the others but essentially speak their language, particularly Clark, whose misspellings signalize a rich backcountry vernacular. The company are not eminent for puritanical virtue. They dance, drink whiskey when they can get it, carouse with the Native American women, and contract venereal disease. But they do their job together for the duration of the journey. They are the vanguard of the legions of Americans who, moving westward, were to eliminate or push out of their way most of the bison, the grizzlies, and the Indians, and, with an indefatigable industry and enterprise, ultimately create a modern transcontinental technological society. *The Journals* is their book.

William L. Hedges

Part Two

1810–1865

I. The Age in Perspective

Idealism and Independence

When Emerson finally came to discuss the creed of "The Transcendentalist," he offered a curiously mixed estimate of its scope and power. On the one hand, historically, the person of truly catholic learning would easily recognize that "what is popularly called Transcendentalism among us" is really nothing but "Idealism as it appears in 1842"; as such, Emerson clearly implied, its venerable history assures it a cogency at least the equal of "Materialism," its ancient and agonistic alternative. On the other hand, however, more locally, the transcendentalist was a member of a small and embattled minority, perhaps a vanishing breed. Thus the lecture's conclusion famously turns to (and perhaps *on*) its decidedly popular audience, with an almost shrill plea for the right to continued existence. The metaphors of the penultimate paragraph reduce the contemporary idealists to "some few finer instruments"; and finally the audience is challenged to declare whether it will not "tolerate one or two voices" speaking for a truth otherwise considered imperishable.

The hyperbole is evident, of course, even in the mode of the minimum. Most of the gatherings of Frederic Hedge's so-called Transcendental Club had been cumbersome in their attendance; nor had the lapse of such meetings spelled the end of the movement. Orestes Brownson had defected, but surely *The Dial*, still ably edited by Margaret Fuller, would recruit many worthy replacements. Yet Emerson sounds serious: not only is "Society" in mortal danger, as always, of failing to verify its bearings from its few "superior chronometers," but the party of purity and strictness seems rushing to its rhetorical extinction. Perhaps Emerson's "Transcendentalist" was not indeed a precipitated spiritual essence but only an endangered ideological species—leaving the literary historian to wonder if the ideal interest of that creature had not been, all along, somewhat greater than his real influence.

And yet not all historical witnesses can be made to agree. One who decidedly did not was Nathaniel Hawthorne, that cross-minded and ambivalent observer who was just then (in the summer of '42) coming to live "at the opposite extremity of [Emerson's] village," and whose subsequent reflections (in "The Old Manse" [1846]) create the impression that the place was being overrun with persons who had beheld the "intellectual fire" of transcendentalism as a "beacon burning on a hill-top." In that view Emerson's party appeared as successful as America itself. Possibly Emerson's lecture "The Transcendentalist" had been, after all, only one more "Jeremiad," grimly imagining a worst-case scenario it did not at all predict. So that, if Hawthorne's account were the true one, the question of transcendentalism and American literary history would open up again.

That account is satirical, of course, as hyperbolic in its way as Emerson's own. Yet it too seems serious, as Hawthorne himself had to strive—variously, as it now comes to appear—to unite integrity of self-expression with a decent respect to the popular norm. Nor is it his only such pronouncement. The curious preface to the original version of "Rappaccini's Daughter" (*Democratic Review*, 1844) struggles, with ingenious third-person awkwardness, to justify the "inveterate love of allegory"; but it also provides a much more assured and authoritative evocation of the present writerly context. The hapless (and linguistically transparent) "M. de l'Aubépine" is said to occupy a distinctly "unfortunate position" on the current literary scene: his unmodish, virtually genreless writings fall into the gap separating the "great body of pen-and-ink men who address the intellect and the sympathies of the multitude" from the "Transcendentalists (who, under one name or another, have a share in all the current literature of the world)."

The verdict remains indirect, a reflex of one more of Hawthorne's attempts to place himself in a world he seldom felt congenial and often found bizarre. Yet it seems to acquire conviction from the very fact of its (parenthetical) indirection: unsought-for in itself, the historical condition appeared as the inevitable ground of one's own compulsive explorations. Whatever "Hawthorne" was, his age—*pace* Emerson—was preeminently "transcendental."

Of course it was also in a sense "popular"—increasingly, and to an extent unprecedented in any previous epoch of American letters. And surely it is necessary to notice, in both moral theory and literary practice, that Hawthorne would never prejudicially identify the cause of "the sympathies of the multitude" with Emerson's "Materialism." Yet it is equally significant that Hawthorne specifically contrasts the popular writing of his age to the current "literature" of the world. His position is elitist, no doubt, as it would be at least that, later, with regard to his "damned mob of scribbling women." So that other authority must be invoked by those who understandably seek to enlarge the canon of the "American Renaissance" into the more inclusive domain of "Literary Democracy." Short of that project, however, and prior to it still, there remains the task of explaining the private bewilderments and mutual contradictions of Emerson and Hawthorne, especially those touching the appearance of idealism which marked their common age.

Emerson worried, possibly even *feared*, that transcendentalism was losing the day. Hawthorne perceived, or perhaps only *feared*, that it might be grandly winning. Attitudes, as always, are free. Yet what Hawthorne may have grasped—better, oddly, than Emerson himself—was that the real movement was actually quite large and various, and that it flourished under more than one literary denomination. Its power, Hawthorne seems to have sensed, was the power to subsume: to embrace, to elevate, and to rename (though not precisely to christen) all that seemed worthy in human faith and hope; and thence to liberate ideal wish as spiritual aspiration, national or otherwise. So much so that even certain popular themes, such as the "idea of democracy," might owe more to the logic of idealism than to the miscellaneous productions of the "pen-and-ink men." Or women. So much so that it may yet help us explain how literate America moved, with an acceleration truly remarkable, from the anxious demand for a native tradition of European-style belles lettres to a self-assured revival of spiritual intelligence and cultural autonomy.

Obviously Emerson's "1842" is an accidental date—ironic, even: the moment of present (even latter-day) elaboration and not at all of historic apocalypse. Emerson may not have realized that 1836 would come to be seen as the *annus mirabilis* of the movement, or that his *Nature* (1836) and Sampson Reed's *Observations on the Growth of the Mind* (1826) would be declared, respectively, its New and Old Testaments. But surely he knew that the "light," which is "always the same," had already fallen on quite a few objects of study. Already Brownson's *New Views of Christianity, Society, and the Church* (1836) had looked past the powerful example of William Ellery Channing's "Likeness to God" (1828) to declare that, under the aspect of history, "Unitarianism belongs to the material order." Risking somewhat more by way of propositional analysis, George Ripley's *Discourses on the Philosophy of Religion* (1836) had already assembled men's reasons for believing they share the divine nature, relating them all to the idealist discovery that "the outward universe is to a great extent dependent on our souls for its character and influence." And Bronson Alcott's most radical *Conversations with Children on the Gospels* (1836) had already trusted Plato to guarantee his search, in the "integrity of the young mind," for the "Divine Idea of Man, as Imaged in Jesus."

To name but a few of the bold experiments already on the record. Indeed, the number of self-conscious "Manifestoes" of idealism still appears impressive, even as selected and excerpted in Perry Miller's anthology of *The Transcendentalists* (1960). Many of them are somewhat more than position papers, declarations of spiritual independence, or "groundplans" for further intellectual work. And all speak of a common cultural impoverishment which is at bottom a question of "mental philosophy."

To be sure, none is exclusively "philosophical" by intention or genre. All speak, as they feel, to certain wider, more democratic concerns of religion or society. Yet so too had most of their more urgent models: Plato theorized the love of wisdom as a condition of the blessed life, both individual and social; the Cambridge Platonists were primarily "moralists"; Swedenborg was a typological theologian; Berkeley a Christian Bishop. Not even Kant proved the grand exception: the audience of "The Transcendentalist" would surely know that his "extraordinary profoundness and precision . . . had given vogue to his nomenclature"; but then they would surely also know that what motivated his most technical "critiques" of philosophy was the desire to make room for Protestant "faith." Then too, it readily appears, his own influence was mediated by writers entirely less precise—Carlyle, for example, and the Coleridge of the *Biographia Literaria* (1817) and the *Aids to Reflection* (1825). Indeed, the American editor and sponsor of Coleridge—James Marsh—was identically a Calvinist minister; and his influential "Preliminary Essay" (1829) to the *Aids* made perfectly clear that the use of philosophy could only be to regenerate the national character.

As "religious," therefore, the initial concerns of all Emerson's idealist peers and precursors are fairly enough epitomized in the so-called Miracles Controversy which, between 1833 and 1840, alternately simmered in the religious journals and boiled over into the Boston newspapers, and which provides one necessary context for Emerson's climactic "Divinity School Address" (1838). Were the long-cherished, socially necessary, but increasingly disputed doctrines of Christian redemption founded on the miraculously endorsed teachings of the historic Jesus? Or did they require—also, or more fundamentally, or even exclusively, in the most radical view—a prior authority in the human mind itself? More was at issue, clearly, than the prestige of the Harvard degree in divinity, which clearly emphasized the "historicity" of the Christian problem, or of the scholarly reputation of the

Reverend Andrews Norton, whose three-volume *Genuineness of the Gospels* (1837) would rest its case in the "empirical" order of credible miracles reliably reported. The position was taught everywhere in America's Christian colleges, even in so "retired" a "seminary of learning" as Bowdoin, where Hawthorne and classmate Henry Wadsworth Longfellow learned it from the pages of William Paley's *View of the Evidences of Christianity* (1794). And Ripley and other proponents of the "New Views" saw it as the representative error of the American Mind.

Lurking deep down, of course, was David Hume's notorious rejection of the very idea of miracles, and his virtual "deconstruction" of the crucial opposition—between nature and supernature—on which it appeared to rest. Deeper still, perhaps, though few of the controversialists seem to have recognized the fact, was the accomplished tendency of "Liberal" Christianity to reduce the old "Anselmian" system of sacrifice and atonement to a set of ethical principles, even to Kant's "categorical imperative" itself. So reduced, it could be argued, Christianity scarcely required support from quasi-magical demonstrations of powers far beyond those of mortal men. So considered, it was indeed "as old as creation," though not precisely as certain eighteenth-century Deists had supposed. Demystification was one thing, "Natural Supernaturalism" quite another. They differed, for the moment, as Benjamin Franklin's pragmatic endorsement of certain "common notions" differed from an idealist interpretation of Kant's "categories."

What proved the Sermon on the Mount, therefore, was less its putative distribution as an age-old and worldwide theory of true benevolence than its evident "correspondence" to mental possibility and moral need. Channing knew the argument well enough to compress it into one penultimate paragraph of his otherwise conservative "Dudleian Address" of 1821, "The Evidences of Revealed Religion." Emerson deploys it in a number of his Unitarian sermons, particularly "The Authority of Jesus" (1830) and "Miracles" (1831). All that remained was for Ripley to "popularize" it, first indirectly, in a series of articles on Schleiermacher and other exemplars of German hermeneutics, and then head-on, in the open clash with Norton, the Unitarian "Pope," over whose was *really* "The Latest Form of Infidelity." What proved Christianity "democratically"—to the masses, then and now—was all that could ever prove a "spiritual" teaching to anybody: its power to enact a truth already latent in the mind itself. This was the true empiricism. All the rest, including the miracles, was materialism simply, grounded in John Locke's implicitly mechanical model of knowledge, tediously elaborated in the "associationist" psychology of British Unitarians such as David Hartley and Joseph Priestley, and entirely unredeemed by a variety of Scottish "common-sense" philosophers variously endorsed in the American colleges, including Harvard itself.

So that if the transcendentalists went first and most noticeably to meet a religious challenge—to save American Christianity from the limits of the system with which it was temporarily, disastrously allied—they nevertheless all launched themselves from a position coherent enough to be called philosophical and precise enough to be labeled idealism: they all meant to save the soul with a doctrine of the mind, one more current and yet more venerable than that of latter-day British Empiricism. Nothing was in the mind that was not first in the senses: except The Mind, which was not nothing, and even less a passive receptacle for representations of things that came into it full-formed. Christian love was in the mind. It never *had* been in the senses, whatever Jonathan Edwards may have supposed. It must have been, therefore, "always already" in the mind itself, though less as an innate idea than as an inherent structural possibility. All that was required for virtue was the appropriate occasion. For religion, the perfect manifestation. The soul would recognize its own. To suppose otherwise, as by requiring miracles, was to be false to the entire tradition of Protestant spirituality, surrendering religion itself to what both Hegel and Emerson know to call "the positive." Beyond that lay only the phenomenological impoverishment we now recognize as "the abolition of man." And behind it lay a common response to the "empiricist" emphasis of the philosophy of the American schools, a response representatively expressed in the *Autobiography* of James Freeman Clarke, the transcendentalist minister who happened to sanctify the marriage of Nathaniel and Sophia Peabody: "something in me revolted against all . . . attempts to explain soul out of sense."

That many of these transcendental reformers of empirical religion went on to apply their philosophic Mind to other aspects of social living is evident from all accounts of America's passion for "Reform" in the three decades before the Civil War: the question of education in its relation to labor and leisure, as at Ripley's Brook Farm (1841–47) and Alcott's Fruitlands (1843–44); the plight of "The Laboring Classes" as such, defined by Brownson's essay of 1840; the correlative sociopolitical problem of "The Merchants" as a class, in Theodore Parker's trenchant 1846 "Sermon"; the status and the soul of women, in Margaret Fuller's "Great Lawsuit" (1843) and *Women in the Nineteenth Century* (1845); and ultimately, of course, the great question of "Abolition," which consumed Parker and drew in even such Olympians as Emerson and Thoreau. All of which was perfectly appropriate, if not always absolutely congenial: as the prevailing modes of (neo-Lockean) metaphysics were perceived to have deleterious consequences for all departments of life and thought, so it was only proper that newer insights should be applied with equal scope. Yet these important facts are only part of the complicated story of "Transcendentalism and Reform." For quite aside from the significant contributions of the several members of "the Newness" to the various projects of melioration—including the (largely rhetorical) ones of Emerson himself—there is something "transcendental" about the entire reform movement.

The point is delicate but important. The "New Views" are by no means identical with what social historians have all but literalized as "the Ferment": neither explains the other, in intention or comprehension; nor has any third term, such as "Revivalism" or "Millennialism," shown power to subsume them both. Yet fundamental relation there well may be, as it is hard to avoid the impression that an entire culture is enacting some sort of synthetic *a priori:* as if the idea of "the better" (of Christian aspiration) or indeed of "the Perfect" (of Platonic desire) had been discovered in the mind and released unmediated on the hitherto recalcitrant phenomena of worldly experience; as if some marvelous apocalypse of mind could come true in literal fact. In this guarded and impressionistic sense an entire social episode seems aptly symbolized by an inclusive convocation of 1840 called the "Convention of the Friends of Universal Reform"—the idea of which Emerson only partially captured in the "partialist" satires that lead up to his summary account of "The New England Reformers" (1844). The idea was "practical" rather than "pure"; but then under the circumstances it could scarcely have been otherwise.

Nor did Emerson quite realize, as we began by noticing, that the "light" whose witness he bore might attract, one way or another, even more "literary" votaries than he himself had literal disciples. More is at issue than the miscellaneous attempts at a Transcendentalist belles lettres which *The Dial* managed to sponsor in its brief half-life of 1840–44: the self-and-nature poems of Thoreau and Hedge and Ellery Channing (the younger), the somewhat more spiritual epiphanies of Jones Very, the *ex parte* literary criticism of Margaret Fuller—though even these strengthen the impression of a concerted literary effort as authentic and central as any previous association of American "Wits," wherever gathered together. Surely the mild "idealizations" of Longfellow and of the Fireside Poets bespeak an idealism of *some* sort; particularly in the Quakerish mind of John Greenleaf Whittier, whose deviations from the "categorical" opposition to slavery are almost always into such celebrations of "things near" as Emerson applauds in "The American Scholar" (1837). At issue in all such low-romantic appropriations of the ordinary is less a cultural interest in "local color" than the Spirit's own ability to redeem the conditions of its temporary habitat. Even more revealing is the positive Platonism of William Cullen Bryant, whose moral meditations on "Waterfowl," "Violet," and "Gentian" are not to be separated from his philosophical sense that all of nature exists as "an emanation of the indwelling Life" that is, in fact, "the soul of this great universe" ("A Forest Hymn" [1825]). And most of all, of course, there is the example of Poe.

Always loyal to the South, with whose early nineteenth-century writers he undeniably shares a certain Byronic inspiration, Edgar Allan Poe is yet more powerfully related to the Renaissance of Idealism than any American writer who had the luck to begin a literary career before the publication of Emerson's *Nature*. Yet the problem of his misprision is an old one: Emerson, who explicitly rejected him as "the jingle man," probably meant to discredit him further, in "The Poet" (1844), as but another of those "men of talents who sing"; and Poe, who decimated the writers of *The Dial*, and who never tired of indicting the New England group with "the heresy of the didactic," never realized that he and Emerson were indeed "children of the [same] fire."

Unlike Emerson, Poe was something of an "aesthete." That is to say: where Emerson mystified the True and especially the Good, Poe raised the appetite for Beauty to transcendental primacy; where Emerson vied with Milton, if only in the privacy of his journals (September 17, 1833), for utter love of "moral perfection," Poe strove like none before to establish the reign of "Taste." An odd word, perhaps, yet the transcendental meaning is perfectly clear; and Poe's entire career is intelligible chiefly as a movement toward the twin revelations of *Eureka* (1848) and "The Poetic Principle" (posthumously, 1850): that the universe is satisfactorily apprehended only as a poem and that man's truest intimation of "perennial existence" is that "immortal instinct" for harmonious perfection we call "a sense of the Beautiful." It would go beyond the present state of scholarly certitude to propose that "surely" Poe's aesthetic of taste owes as much to Kant's third *Critique* as Emerson's epistemology and moral theory to his first and second. Nevertheless, it is sufficiently evident that both Emerson and Poe have staked the salvation of man's soul on a similar sense of the metaphysical implications of the *a priori* capacities of his mind. And it may yet be possible to realize that Hawthorne's "Artist of the Beautiful" (1844) recognizes Poe as a more formidable Platonist than Emerson himself, and that the fearsome apocalypse of his "Birth-mark" (1843) implicates an idealist habit of mind common to them both.

Certainly Emerson had missed something in Poe's "Al Aaraaf" (1829), if indeed he read it, not to notice that its peculiar pseudo-Miltonic "world" is a world of the mind, that its angelic "characters" are not persons but faculties and appetites, habits and categories; especially odd, as he did not even have our excuse of needing to read everything "symptomatically." How could he have required the essays of the modern epistemologist-poet Richard Wilbur to suggest that Poe's "Ligeia" (1838) celebrates not German gothicism but the soul's undying will to harmony? And what accomplished reader of the translations of Thomas Taylor could fail to recognize the perfectly "Plotinian" plot of Poe's deathless address "To Helen" (1831)?—as some better Ulysses flees not "to the fatherland" of Ithaca but first to certain "monuments of unageing intellect" and thence to the mind itself: home safe if not quite free. So clear are Poe's ideal loyalties that had accident cast his lot of literary nurture in New England, we can easily imagine Emerson designating him, and not Bronson Alcott, his own more perfect Platonist. Yet (as always) the fact is better as it stands: dismiss "what is popularly called Transcendentalism" as, plausibly enough, the proper form of Concord mental color, and idealism yet appears to break the bounds of local culture. Probably on purpose.

The contributions of Emerson and his *most* notable disciples might seem too familiar to name, except that they are seldom recognized for what they most strenuously attempt to be—contributions to an aesthetic reappropriation of the world under the aspect of idealism; and that, as such, they exist in large part to free the American Mind, including the fledgling Imagination, from its peculiar problem of imitation. An inspirational use of Coleridge's Kant or Thomas Taylor's Plotinus would be one thing: entirely acceptable, as "the light" really *was* "always the same." But a mimetic dependence on the specific conditions of local culture—or worse, a literary debt to writers who imitated those (alien) social habits—would be quite another. "America" might or might not embody "the Ideal," but its experience of literature had to register, in the formula of Emerson's *Nature*, an "original relation to the universe." Somehow it had to express the aboriginal union of Man with Ideas.

The idealist basis of Emerson's thought is clear long before the famous sixth chapter of *Nature*, however that philosophical "move" may have puzzled Francis Bowen, the Harvard mentor who reviewed the work for *The Christian Examiner* (January 1837). The earlier chapters prepare quite strategically—"structurally," if not quite "argumentatively"—for the climactic revelation that the world is "ideal for me so long as I cannot try the evidence of my senses": if ecstatic experience and the several departments of human thought and enterprise all really do imply that man is related to nature as telos and epitome, then how is it surprising when some Berkeley or Kant should proclaim, with great empirical strictness (though in significantly different senses), that the world's being can be confirmed only as a "for me"? In this view, all humanistic thought—footnote to Plato or not—had been nothing but a prelude to this great "Copernical Revolution" in philosophy. The inference waited to be made, whether the Harvard faculty favored subjectivity or not.

This is what it means, nonpedantically, to discover that there are strong imitations of the doctrine of *Nature* in many of Emerson's earlier, more conventional writings—in the 1833 lectures on "Natural Science," for example, and even in the more pious and lyrical affirmations of the 1828 sermon on "Summer": the Rationalist Christian version of the "teleological argument" proved either much more or much less than the perfect design of a Benevolent God. What it really proved was that the mind variously revealed in men's several attempts to deal with the world was all One Mind. The discovery was not so much circular (or skeptical) as it was "categorical" or, quite simply, epistemological as such: the transcendental conditions of mentality are all you know on earth. Yet philosophers such as Fichte and Hegel, if not Kant himself, were not persuaded that the doctrine did not have, somewhere, metaphysical applications. Nor was the Emerson who went on, obscurely, in his chapter on "Spirit," to imagine how the new table of "transcendent" contents might yet appear. And on, in the prime selections of his *Essays: First Series* (1841), to make the interim applications of the One Mind to "History" and "Self-Reliance," "Love" and "Friendship." And on, in the most powerful of the later essays, to defend its autonomy from the erosions of "Experience" (1844), the irony of "The Skeptic" (1846), and the determination of "Fate" (1850).

Yet predictably, the first application was to religion. In the "Divinity School Address" (1838) Emerson first summarized the doctrine of *Nature* and then applied it, "with authority," in a way that endorsed and then transcended the position of Ripley in the "Miracles Controversy"; and in a way that validated, not quite accidentally, the insight which had cut the "Dudleian" knot that once bound him to the Unitarian ministry. In rough paraphrase of Channing, and in clear advance of Ripley, Emerson's journal for 1832 had quietly wondered why, if his own heart taught "the same thing" as Jesus taught, he should not go to his "own heart at first." Now—that he had paid, in *Nature*, his proper philosophic dues—he was perfectly bold to declare that this was exactly what he and everybody else *must* do. Religious Truth was Subjectivity in some high yet clearly Protestant sense:

salvation was not the kind of thing to be got historically, or at any other second hand; either it appeared to the mind or it did not. And the philosophical reason of this was perfectly apparent: the Moral Sentiment was aboriginally and indestructably an "I ought," leaving all the "Thou shalts" in the world in the arena of "the cultic" where, absent the Father, Jesus strives with Moses to create the supreme Anxiety of Influence.

All of which is (or should be) well enough understood: Emerson's habit of thought is as authentically philosophical as that of any writer in his group or generation; his personal problem as profoundly religious, its eventual solution as deeply radical as any we know to recognize in the entire nineteenth century. He well fits, epitomizes even, the cultural pattern or "group life" we (almost) recognize as "the Transcendentalist Minister": intellectually irritated and spiritually balked by the philosophical idiom which lent rational support to the (liberalized) religious inheritance, he appropriated the insights of idealism to restore not an older but an "original" sense of pious aperception; alternately bored and affronted by the ragged evolutions of religious culture, he rediscovered and reaffirmed the categories or structures that made it all possible. But here he stopped. Or, rather, here he consciously decided it was better simply to elaborate himself than to risk one more repetition in the mode of culture. And this is the point at which he—rather than the equally earnest Alcott, Brownson, Ripley, or Parker—rises up from the forum of antebellum ideology to command the attention of those who make anthologies of "literature" and to enlist the allegiance of those who wish to "make it new."

What Emerson seems to have sensed—rightly or wrongly—was that the only way to go *on* was not practically, in the available projects of social reform, or even in the still privileged domain of religion itself, but purely, in some original yet now entirely recognizable version of "the literary." Except in Kant's high "moral" sense, the practical meant the political, where Association demanded first compromise and then conformity. In the secular arena the result could be only one more party, in religion but another cult. Of which enough already, even in America.

The necessary alternative was the way of "The Poet," never really distinct from "the newborn bard of the Holy Ghost" of the revolutionary "Address." That worthy—the *real* transcendentalist after all—would require the self-reliant daring "to write his autobiography in colossal cipher, or into universality"; but never in a merely personal or meanly egotistical way. Rather, an entirely disinterested "representative" would speak "not of his wealth, but of the common wealth" of Ideas expressed in Nature, the "externalization of the soul." Most radically of all, perhaps, he would not concern himself with the forms of "fashion, custom, authority" but only with the Form of Beauty itself, an artist of "the Beautiful" in very fact. As "Imitation cannot go above its model," so not *only* preaching needed to "refuse the good models" for that ideal faith which "makes its own forms" and which can, without Puritanic anxiety, redeem "a whole popedom of forms." As the glowing rhetoric of the famous "Ode" (1846) meant to instruct the too ardent reformer W. H. Channing that "the state" must follow the virtuous individual "how it can," so the relentless logic of Emerson's unfolding doctrine of transcendental literature assured the awaited Poet that he may regard only the "beauty, half seen, which flies before him," and trust that his own thought may be simply "ejaculated, as Logos, or Word."

In this context the "Scholar's" famous farewell to "the courtly muses of Europe" comes to seem one of Emerson's more conservative literary utterances; for the Poet rejects not only *their* formal constructions but in fact *all* the formations of culture and history as such. The conclusion is radical, but the ideal premise permits as much and demands no less. In this context, too, it is possible to see how Emerson's "influence" would touch not only the disciples of his own literary circle but also writers who, like Whitman, were quite innocent of the Unitarian crisis and the Concord tone; and how it may be discerned in writings which are generically unlike anything Emerson ever thought to essay.

The poets of *The Dial* we have already mentioned: including the early Thoreau, they merely translate into verse one or another of Emerson's propositions of idealist theory or moral practice; present at the creation, they enjoy a blessed state of inspiration without anxiety. The plot thickens somewhat with Thoreau's mature works of prose, where a radical criticism of society mixes with natural epiphanies which tend (increasingly) toward "naturalism" itself. Yet the accomplished early works have always been recognized, correctly, as practical realizations of the Emersonian project: a socially unencumbered Self walks westward (to "Wachusett" [1842]), or merely outdoors (into the local "Winter" [1843]), or floats (for a mythic "Week on the Concord and Merrimack" [1849]—without so much as a living brother, in the literary version) amidst a Nature which can activate Ideas enough. Society exists not mimetically but only critically, the rejected point of departure; and the structures of composition, which criticism has yet to describe adequately, are trusted to follow from the overflow of natural experience. *Walden* (1854) only completes the pattern and perfects the (organic) form: its subject is nothing but the metatheme of "Life itself" and its structure is the very archetype of seasonal variation. All freely given and all transcendentally Good. What more could be demanded of life than the acceptance—of literature, than the verbal embodiment?

The crucial case of Idealism as Influence is obviously Whitman—not only because, in most accounts, his example mediates that of Emerson for a long and still vital tradition of "modern" American poetry, but also, and more crucially, because the culture of his mind had been, and the movement of his awakened poetic sentences would become, so unlike Emerson's own. Yet in fact the rare spiritual outcome of a fairly precious epistemological debate in post-Puritan New England could be received by a scrabbling Democratic newspaperman of Brooklyn at no more than the average rate of literary misprision. Even as the *very* New Englandish Edward Everett Hale clearly recognized in his *(Putnam's Monthly)* review of the original (1855) *Leaves of Grass:* somehow "Yankee transcendentalism and New York rowdyism" had managed to "fuse and combine with the most perfect harmony"; evidently an "original perception of nature" could do much to neutralize the most America could accomplish by way of cultural difference. Apparently, that is to say, Mind and Nature were transcendentally the same. And arguably, at least, the function of American literature was to register that truth.

From Whitman's own side, of course, the nexus of Emersonian influence is perfectly easy to detect, as the "It is in me, and shall out" of "The Poet" suffers only dialectical variation to become the "Walt, you understand enough. . . . why don't you let it out then?" of the original (untitled) "Song of Myself"; or as Emerson's "ejaculated" Logos comes literal enough, repaying as if in kind a provocative ocean of natural meaning. The sexual difference, though famous, is easy to overstate: on the one hand, the sexual entendre is already clearly there in Emerson himself; and on the other, Whitman's more explicit sexual references are never clear of metaphor. At issue, always, is the model of perfect *literary* unrepression. The Self is responsible only to Nature. And no one has ever received this Emersonian teaching more purely.

Thus it may be of only minor interest to notice that at least two of Whitman's most accomplished early poems are precise enactments of an idealist epistemology—that the 1855 version of "There Was a Child Went Forth" tells the (compressed) story of "the growth of the poet's mind" with a more than Wordsworthian insistence on the nondifference between the biographical experiences which "became part of that child who went forth every day" and the readerly ones of "him or her that peruses them now"; and that the 1856 form of "Crossing Brooklyn Ferry" widens this local case of the soul's articulation into a pseudo-Platonic (or Hegelian) plot of the emanation of the Real. The significant point is indeed much simpler; namely, that the Emersonian program for a literature of the Self and Nature freed Whitman to create a nationalistic but entirely noncultural epic out of "these states." Other, earlier champions of an American "national literature" might argue, anxiously, that America's unique mixture of races and traditions would hasten to combine in a culture richer and more generative of humane letters than any the world had seen so far. But Whitman, content with himself, and safe in the doctrine of the soul, made astonishing good speed to enunciate what already appeared.

Thus his truly revolutionary and yet not altogether unprecedented "Song of Myself" is indeed an enactment of the prefatory claim that "the United States themselves are essentially the greatest poem"—but only in the sense that their variety stands for the plentitude of the soul's procession into form, and as the ease of their meta-cultural unity inspires a certain organic nonchalance. The poem contains, indeed it is sustained by, an astonishing catalogue of dramatic vignettes, from one-line evocations like that of "The youngster and the redfaced girl [who] turn aside up the bushy hill" (l. 142, 1855) to the full-stanza "fall of Alamo" (ll. 864–89). All this can fairly be regarded as an inspired (but largely neglected) table of contents for realists and naturalists to come, for scores of social novelists and hundreds of short-form students of multiform local color. Yet Whitman personally declines these cultural opportunities. He even calls them into question: shall the idealist poet make a "list of things in the house and skip the house that supports them"? Further, his reckless, accomplished speed suggests an aim utterly simple and philosophical: all this is "the meal pleasantly set" for the "natural hunger" of the mind; these are the forms the soul can take.

What Whitman proves, presumably, is that, as nature's evolving forms are on the side of the soul, so the aching aspiration of Emerson's ideal Poet need never ally himself with the *contemptus mundi* of Edgar Poe. All the two programs have in common, finally, is a refusal to accept the premise that literature must reflect the factitious configurations of the *merely* historical, in any of its local manifestations. This (negative) similarity will appear great or small depending on the premises of the observer. And surely *American* literary historians are not the only ones still trying to decide.

That not all of America's notable antebellum writers shared the idealist program of a literature in despite of culture will be obvious enough. Clearly, that is to say, Hawthorne's verdict on "*all* the current literature" is inspired tendentiousness and not nominal reporting—otherwise, we should all have taken it in long ago. And otherwise, more importantly, the literary history of the American Renaissance and its "long foreground" would be perfectly simple to write. All it would involve, really, is an extension to *all* genres, received or invented, of what is famously asserted of the American preference for pastoral or psychological "romance" over the more social form of the "novel": Americans everywhere accept the Self and Nature as altogether inevitable; "manners" they regard as factitious and dangerous, an imported luxury. Clearly that verdict omits or distorts too much. And yet if Hawthorne's instincts were at all correct, it may be useful to view the competing literary projects, briefly, as embattled dissent from a growing national consensus.

Evidently Washington Irving begs to be considered in just this way. Innocent of Emerson, of course, his *Sketch Book* (1819–20) nevertheless offers itself as a studied alternative to the project of "nature." "Romantic" though in some sense Irving undeniably is, his mind moves not through the primary forms of American scenery, which an author's prefatory "Account of Himself" explicitly considers and rejects; nor even through those scenes of minimum society Whitman would attempt to naturalize. The locus of his measured reflections is, almost everywhere, not American nature but the "storied" places of England; humanized places, that is, where some secondary imagination has already translated nature into culture. And even the famous "American" pieces—"Rip Van Winkle" and "The Legend of Sleepy Hollow"—may exist primarily to confer on the defiantly new American landscape some faint approximation of the Old World's sense of interest by association: henceforth let Hudson and Kaatskill be scenes of somewhat more than the mind's original play.

Most crucially, in this regard, the peculiar faculty at play in Irving's collection can never be regarded as that author's own natal mind. Not only is Rip's enduring archetype ascribed to the posthumous papers of Diedrich Knickerbocker, left over from that hoax in search of a history called "New York"; but the entire performance is ascribed to the minor-romantic fancy of one Geoffrey Crayon. And however credible we find that enabling convention, however consistently maintained or successfully adumbrated, the fact remains that the *Sketch Book* calls attention to itself as a fiction in precisely the way *Walden* and "Song of Myself" do not, insisting instead on a speaker who is (at once) perfectly biographical and yet totally representative. Not "the soul" has caught or made all these literary associations, but some "narrator" hath done these things. Fragments against ruin, they appear to deny in advance the Emersonian myth of "original relation."

Equally (if less pointedly) at odds with the Emersonian convention is a fairly ample body of fiction which really does try to ground itself on the question of American social difference. Much that is discussed, formally, as "historical romance" may fit this material description with equal reason. All that would be required is a willingness to suppose that Hawthorne was not alone in sensing that America's three famous "matters"—the Puritans, the Indians, and the Revolution—constituted not so much available literary themes as necessary historical conditions; and that, for better or worse, certain structures from the past endured to shape the possibilities of present experience. From this perspective, Emersonianism would come to seem more Holgrave-wish than Pyncheon-fact. Or else it might be some great half-truth, the other half of which we have learned to call the "Molineux theme"—the imputation of identity through history.

James Fenimore Cooper must serve as a single (non-Hawthornean) example, though novelists such as William Gilmore Simms, John Pendleton Kennedy, and Catharine Sedgwick seem also to suspect that the American past is somewhat more than a colorful backdrop for the soul's essential drama. Part of Cooper's essential distinction is simply the amount he wrote, the number of episodes he touches and issues he presses, in a career that spans the three decades from Irving's *Sketch Book* to Hawthorne's *Scarlet Letter* and Emerson's *Representative Men*, and includes more than two dozen (mostly) readable fictions of American experience and/or European bias. Sinewed by the (utterly) acute social observations of his *Notions of the Americans* (1828) and structured by the (almost) coherent politics of *The American Democrat* (1838), Cooper's body of novels amply demonstrates not only that the colonial past was as rich in historical forecast as in literary opportunity but also that his own sociopolitical present—a queer mix of "the Jacksonian Persuasion" and "the Political Culture of the American Whigs"—is a more vital subject of interest than one can learn from the generalizations of Emerson's "Politics" or the abstentions of his "Transcendentalist."

Not that Cooper is a "social novelist" in quite the "poor foolish Reality" sense of William Dean Howells: the lure of the pastoral—and indeed of plot-bound excitement and romantic adventure—is far too strong. But the wish to order the American world according to an entirely temporal logic of cause and effect is everywhere keenly present as well. The redundantly famous Leatherstocking series is as much a consideration of racial and cultural conditions of the American frontier, and of the founding conditions of American law and social justice, as it is an evocation of the Adamic myth. And the "Preface" to *Satanstoe* (1845), the undervalued first novel in the Littlepage trilogy, makes clear an historicist motive operating not only there but in most of Cooper's fiction: "Every chronicle of manners has a certain value," and particularly so "when customs are connected with principles, in their origin, development, or end." The antitranscendentalism is evident: "manners" are worth recording because, even in "Nature's Nation," they constitute the very stuff of historical difference; they may seem like costume merely, but then the soul is never permitted to appear undressed.

But of course it is Hawthorne who looms largest as antagonist of Emerson—not only because he began in the same cultural half-world of Irving and Cooper and still managed to invent the curiously unanxious "twice-told" tale to tell the uniquely American (and almost social) story of "the moral argument" for and "against Calvinism"; but also because his later tales, the *Mosses*, so powerfully influenced the major critique of transcendentalism we recognize in Melville's major fiction. That critique stands, along with Hawthorne's "Three American Romances," against the cultural overbearing of *Walden* and "Song of Myself," to guarantee the High Renaissance of the 1850s as a truly dialogic event and not merely a "Shock of Recognition." That story constitutes a literary history in itself, reminding us how much there really is to tell about the intertextual (and interpersonal) career of American letters between any given date and 1865. Yet an outline may appear.

Beginning with the standard American college training in Scottish "associationism," and never losing the conservative sense that "the more historical associations we can like with our locations, the richer will be the daily life that feeds on the past," Hawthorne early produced a number of "moral histories" that easily—though ironically—proved the American locale could become "storied" without benefit of Irvingesque importation. But the sense of Salem and of Merry Mount was not Hawthorne's only concern, as he also wrote a more than equal number of altogether less historical "sketches": adumbrating the inherited epistemology, a localized observer makes quotidian observations and arranges them in the linear pattern of the mind's well-known patterns of association; or else, pressing the limits of that neo-Lockean system, a more obsessive mind is "haunted" by the "gothic" suspicion (of Brockden Brown's *Wieland*) that "ideas exist in our minds that can be accounted for by no established laws." But then, when Freud threatened, reality intruded. For better and for worse, the miscellaneous collection of the *Twice-told Tales* (1837) "opened an intercourse" with first the bustling world of Boston and next the transcendental one of Concord itself. So that, after the (1841) stay at Brook Farm, Hawthorne's tales would have to deal with just that.

That they *mean* to do so is clearly suggested by the whimsical "opposite extremity of our village" strategy of "The Old Manse," written explicitly to introduce the 1846 collection, and also by a plain thematic tendency. Retreating, as it finally does, from the "original" world of Concord's refulgent nature into the altogether fictive world of the "study," it somehow manages to unwrite *Walden* well in advance: the Self and the Seasons give way to some narrators and to an assortment of tales and sketches of transcendental irony. The Germanic "Giant" of "The Celestial Rail-road" (1843) is a light hit; but the jest crawls further in "Earth's Holocaust" (1844), where an ideal observer reasons while the stuff of culture burns; and further still in "The Hall of Fantasy" (1843), where the Christian Advent of Father Miller lapses easily into the mental apocalypse of Emerson himself. Christian history subsumed by the "Prospects" of the mind, what further need of worldliness? Or of real "objects" of art, as some priceless composite of Emerson and Poe learns to transcend all mimetic anxiety as "Artist of The Beautiful" (1844), possessing nothing but his own "spirit" in the (endless) process? Bad news for students of material culture, no doubt; yet the Soul is *not* a butterfly. And fair enough in its own "spiritual" terms, we suppose; unless the rare philosophic skepticism of "The Christmas Banquet" (1844) means to suggest that the human spirit is itself more shadow than substance. Who would not then wish, nostalgically, for the "solid" world once more?

Finally, however, it is to "The Birth-mark" (1843) and "Rappaccini's Daughter" (1844) that Melville testified most powerfully—the latter as its manipulation of the transcendental doctrine of faith and evidence lends moral support to the inspired ravages of *Pierre* (1852) and the more temperate musings of *The Confidence-Man* (1856), and the former as Aylmer's mad symbolic quest seems surely to have validated the full pursuit of Ahab's deeper monomania. In doubt or in madness, the real world always does disappear: not only in its several realms of human culture, eclectically assembled aboard the *Pequod*, from *Typee* (1846) and *Mardi* (1849) and wherever else Melville's real or mental voyages had taken him; but even in its most rare philosophic function as a regulative idea, troubling the "meditations" of post-Cartesian Ishmael, but nihilated utterly by the "last, last crime" of Ahab's final "critique."

What Ahab's fatal career reveals, presumably, is that the transcendental identity of Self and Nature remains a "phantom" always beyond the grasp of the individual mind; and that its too earnest pursuit is an intensely odd, even dangerously self-reflexive activity—as if, in Pip's witty formulation, one were "all on fire to unscrew" the navel of knowledge as we know it. Possibly that one deconstruction truly is unsafe to attempt. Subject and object indeed appear maddeningly fit for one another. But better let the

Reason rest—the more so, perhaps, as other "felicity" clearly is "attainable." The mind grasps "other" but not a perfect self thereby. Hands grasp other hands. And sub-subs have their function, though bound to history and to culture. Put down your Plato. Take up your novel. Or at least your "historical romance."

Except that Melville never could take his own thematic advice. With the possible exception of *Billy Budd*, nothing that follows *Moby-Dick* shows the slightest indication that Melville was prepared to leave off the question of epistemology, which—as sufficient experience has since shown—always ends in an idealism of some sort. Not even the more "domestic" of his inland adventures in short fiction evince a settled resolution to accept the world of ordinary experience as sufficient literary *donnée*. The curious result is that he may appear to win certain local battles against Emerson but also helps to lose the war. Rather like the embattled academic conservative who defers his project of criticism to answer the theorists. Epistemology is a dangerous project, he everywhere implies; but *Walden* and "Song of Myself" are glorious beyond argument. They even appear to create a world of their own.

Thus Hawthorne is left alone, to struggle with the finally unmanageable problem of socializing his own "inveterate love of allegory." *The Scarlet Letter* (1850) insists that Puritan language lies powerfully at the source of the peculiarly American Self. *The House of the Seven Gables* (1851) does all a "romancer" ever could to draw lines of inheritance. *The Blithedale Romance* (1852) actually attempts, though with outrageous narrative indirection, the project of a transcendental tragicomedy of manners. But few have been able to blame Henry James for failing to see the point. And then, finally, after another interval of politics and the lapse of considerable cultural time, *The Marble Faun* (1860) proves only what James and Howells would surely know by instinct: the "International Romance" is an impossible genre, an oxymoronic confusion of thought. Nor could Harriet Beecher Stowe nor whole *mobs* of "scribbling women" quite supply the needed social model. So that, whatever the truth of the case, the Renaissance of American letters seemed to occur no place so really as in the mind itself. And almost by design.

None of this literary plot is quite separable, of course, from that larger setting Perry Miller invoked as the "context of international Romanticism." As Hawthorne's characterization is of "all the current literature" of a world much larger than merely America, so each of the writers noticed here has some plausible precedent or analogue in transatlantic literary practice. Yet the local application of Hawthorne's remark has a special cogency. For if the American Renaissance is not quite the epitome of Romanticism, it certainly seems to be the locus of a literature given over to mental rather than to historical events, to Imperial rather than to social selfhood, to transcendental apperception rather than to worldly experience.

Reasons for this fact—or all-but-realized literary tendency—have never been wanting. Tocqueville found them, proleptically, in the "individualistic" spirit of American religion, and in a virtually definitive desire for "liberty" in the Jeffersonian sense, of liberation from all inherited or legislated constraint. And Hawthorne, from the moment itself, and James, looking backward, offered their impressive lists of literary materials America seemed to lack. Those famous inventories are neither identical nor redundant: the "Preface" to *The Marble Faun* laments the absence of the romancer's materials of "shadow," "antiquity," "mystery," "picturesque and gloomy wrong," whereas James's verdict, in his biography of *Hawthorne* (1879), compares "the coldness, the thinness, the blankness" of the American scene to the "denser, richer, warmer . . . spectacle" of European social life. Taken together, however, they very nearly isolate the available subject: the transcendental self and original, correspondent nature. What wonder, then, if the subject were seized?

The wonder, perhaps, is that the American transcendentalists—local avatars of a worldwide interest in the mystery of human subjectivity—could hold and press their theme so hard as to make it seem first inevitable and next an utter glory, even as certain latter-day Puritans managed to make America itself seem significant, in spite of its noticeable failure to conclude the drama of human history. Doubtless there *were* other themes. And doubtless too these writers felt their option as forced by the fullness of the spirit and not by the poverty of affairs: materialism threatened, in both its popular and academic varieties; the way of salvation was the idealist way. Yet a sense of paradox survives. And with it a sense of special revelation.

Fearing the determination of history and opposing the accumulations of institutional culture—and lacking the genres to express their potent original desire—Poe, Emerson, Thoreau, and Whitman all invent ways of making the topic of idealist epistemology seem not recessive but resplendent; so much so that even their would-be antagonists are drawn into the plot. Leaving a next generation of writers free (but puzzled) to consider the "realistic" possibilities of ordinary life and language, in America as elsewhere.

Michael J. Colacurcio

II. Cultural Diversity and Literary Forms

Washington Irving and the Knickerbocker Group

Washington Irving's earliest work as a writer does not suggest that he would be the one to put the lie to Sydney Smith's disparaging remarks on the state of American artistic endeavor. With no sense of vocation, but recognizing his talent with words, Irving involved himself in several local literary enterprises. Even their general success did not confirm him in the profession of authorship—a rather desperate business for an American in the early nineteenth century. But inclination, financial circumstances, and emotional difficulties finally made him a professional author when he was almost forty years old; from that time on he capitalized on his limited strengths so well that he became, through his stories, essays, histories, and biographies, one of the best-known American writers in the world.

Neither a romantic nor a neoclassical sentimentalist, Irving was a transitional figure who faced his country, his contemporaries, and his craft with both involvement and alienation. We see now that such contradictions are virtually endemic in American literature and that Irving is a critical figure in the development of an American literary consciousness. He was among the first to confront the difficulty of finding a literary identity in a country lacking its own distinct cultural heritage. In his case, it took a long time to become "Washington Irving"; for he passed through other literary personalities and noms de plume until 1824, when (ostensibly giving up his current role as a genial, conservative, antiquarian writer of fiction) he became a man of sober though romantic historical pursuits. While his literary identity and the tone of his writing changed over time, the essential Irving—if there really is one to be discerned—may be seen in certain themes and attitudes common to his early and later work.

The most persistent such attitude is a melancholy awareness of "mutability." This sad sense of the impermanence of all things human colors most of Irving's writing, early and late. Other notable characteristics are a need to give imaginative life to daily reality, a tendency to sentimentalize, and a contrasting humorous appreciation of the insignificance of human affairs. And one should add to these a commercial awareness that kept him writing books that made his publishers happy. (Never for him the dilemma of Herman Melville—the feeling of having to write what he hoped would sell, even as he was moved to write what he knew would not.) Irving came to prominence, at least in part, by correctly gauging his market. Because his work was narrative and descriptive without being seriously analytical, because his aesthetics were not tied to deeply held political or religious convictions, because he did not address metaphysical questions, he could produce work of delightful and moving superficial qualities in response to his readers' interest and out of his own eclectic experience.

Irving was born in New York City in 1783, named after the hero of the new country by his patriotic parents, and grew up in a fixedly religious household whose restrictions were offset by a good library and the cultural activities of his brothers. A desultory student, he never made the most of his schooling; a family-financed tour of Europe in 1804–6 was his substitute for Columbia College. He did, reluctantly, read for the law, particularly with Judge Josiah Hoffman, but he was too busy having intellectual and social fun to devote himself to legal study—even if it was socially important for a gentleman to have a profession. With his brothers William, Peter, and Ebenezer, his friend James Kirke Paulding, and others, he formed a bachelors' club of sorts called "The Nine Worthies of Cockloft Hall" or "The Lads of Kilkenny." The relationships formed in this club may help to explain the series of bachelor identities in Irving's work and perhaps even his own bachelorhood, although the fact that he never married has often been attributed to the effect of Matilda Hoffman's death on his emotional life. Irving fell in love with Judge Hoffman's young daughter when he was twenty-four—and was understandably desolate when she died at the age of seventeen. For many years he longingly remembered an idealized Matilda. The effect of her death on him was certainly powerful, but it should not be exaggerated. In later years he found a number of women attractive, proposed to at least one, and was the object of romantic pursuit. Ultimately, however, he seems to have needed the distance or masculine independence of the single life.

Irving's first published work (1802–3) came in the form of contributions to the *Morning Chronicle*, the newspaper owned by his brother Peter. Signed "Jonathan Oldstyle," these pieces humorously satirized the New York scene, focusing on the theater in particular. The pseudonym does not necessarily certify Irving's supposed preference for all things old or for the traditional over the innovative. Rather, Irving as Oldstyle fashioned a *style*, not positions on matters of great or of little concern. Juxtaposing the occasionally reasonable comment with any number of absurd or ironic ones, that style reduces all to foolishness, including the author's persona. Irving's fun with the game, in other words, seems to be the real object of these "Oldstyle" contributions. When in 1804 Peter Irving became editor of *The Corrector*, which, like the *Morning Chronicle*, supported Aaron Burr, Washington Irving wrote anonymous, sarcastic political articles for it. Now the erstwhile Federalist was writing in behalf of Burrite Republicanism. Irving enjoyed politics and participated even at the ward level. Not tied to party, he was able to attack the silliness he saw everywhere in political activity.

In collaboration with his brother William and their fellow New Yorker Paulding, Irving next wrote *Salmagundi; or, The Whim-Whams and Opinions of Launcelot Langstaff, Esq., and Others* (January 1807–January 1808). The word "salmagundi" signifies a mixed dish of meat, onions, and other ingredients; as it is used in this title, it characterizes the miscellaneous quality of the essays by Will Wizard, Anthony Evergreen, and Launcelot Langstaff, the personas adopted and shared by three young authors who clearly found their inspiration in Joseph Addison and Oliver Goldsmith. While Wizard concentrated on criticism and Evergreen on fashion, Langstaff was free to treat a range of subjects. At one time or another Washington Irving probably assumed each of these personas. Together with his collaborators, he produced twenty numbers before the series was discontinued.

Some of the most interesting political and social play in *Salmagundi* occurs in the several letters supposedly written by a foreign visitor to New York, Mustapha Rub-a-Dub Keli Khan, captain of a Tripolitan slave ship. In the mode of the Goldsmithian "oriental visitor," the ironic naïveté of these letters results in a skewering of national characteristics. And Mustapha's definition of the United States as a "logocracy" (a state ruled by words) anticipates Irving's satirizing the logocratic government of Thomas Jefferson in *A History of New York* (1809).

James Kirke Paulding, the original "Lancelot Langstaff" of *Salmagundi* and Irving's friend for many years, deserves special attention in his own right. Ultimately an important literary and political figure, Paulding first gained prominence with *Salmagundi* and retained it with such strong anti-British satires as *The Diverting History of John Bull and Brother Jonathan* (1812).

Although he was an excellent literary critic, Paulding did his best work as a novelist of the frontier (in *The Dutchman's Fireside* [1831]) and as a humorist in his long-popular play, *The Lion of the West* (1831), which featured a thinly disguised Davy Crockett. Among other accomplishments, his life of George Washington (praised by Edgar Allan Poe) remained standard until Irving's biography of the first president began to appear twenty years later.

Along with Paulding, Fitz-Greene Halleck, Gulian Verplanck, and John Howard Payne, as well as Lydia Maria Child, Bayard Taylor, and others, have been associated with Irving as "Knickerbocker" writers (as have James Fenimore Cooper and William Cullen Bryant). Linked by their common involvement in the New York literary scene, by their frequent association with the *Knickerbocker Magazine* (founded in 1832), and in some cases by the use of humor similar to that of Irving's *History of New York*, these diverse authors are commonly but inappropriately referred to as the "Knicker-bocker School." It is a "School" that owes more than a little of its identity to the adventitious Irving connection.

After *Salmagundi*, Irving continued to develop the role of parochial author with *A History of New York*, supposedly written by another old bachelor. Though he began the *History* (with his brother Peter) as a short parody of a pretentious guidebook, it ultimately explored a more ambitious and thought-provoking subject. The pompous full title of the work *(A History of New York from the Creation of the World to the End of the Dutch Dynasty)* not only hints at the parody of Dutch New York that was to stir the indignation of some contemporary Dutch descendants but suggests Irving's skeptical attack on history and the writing of history. Often Swiftian, the book's ridicule of human activity is given a bumbling charm by Irving's historian, Diedrich Knickerbocker, a man unable to distinguish bad from good, large from small. Like Jonathan Swift, whom one reviewer called "his obvious model," Irving finds that the supposed glories of humanity are actually testaments to pettiness and *in*humanity. And because Knickerbocker's zany intelligence upredictably bounces from subject to subject, confounding the apparently significant with the blatantly trivial, praising the ignoble and dwelling on the ignominious, history becomes an indiscriminate heap of actions and events.

As for the writing of history, it may be no more than the imposition of the historian's personality on evidence of dubious origin. Historical skepticism, then, is the radical position from which Irving operates. But if, in a strict sense, history cannot be written, its empty trappings may still be usefully appropriated. Inflated rhetoric, presumptions of factuality, absurd scholarship, partisan sentiments, and hero worship (the historian's supposed stock in trade) are Knickerbocker's tools; and so well does Irving wield them that Diedrich becomes an unknowingly comic fictionist, his epic history a farce.

That he was making tongue-in-cheek attacks on the contemporary political scene and on certain public figures in 1809 was apparent to some of Irving's readers from the first, though they may not have seen the extent of his specific allusions. Most obvious is the parody of Thomas Jefferson in the person of Wilhelmus Kieft, who ludicrously governs by unsuccessful proclamation, pursues scientific experiments to the point of absurdity, and garbles significant issues in economics and foreign policy. In later editions (particularly that of 1848) Irving modified the political implications and individual portraits to accord with changed times. Throughout its long publishing history Knickerbocker's account of Dutch New York remained a pertinent though increasingly subdued comment on American politics, local and national.

For the next ten years Irving seems to have drifted virtually without purpose. He lobbied in Washington, D.C., for the interests of the Irving family firm, edited the poems of Thomas Campbell, wrote some brief biographies of naval heroes of the War of 1812, and served as aide-de-camp to Governor Daniel Tompkins of New York for a time during that war. For two years he was editor of the *Analectic Magazine;* his primary responsibility was to select reprintable material from British journals—work so onerous to him that he never accepted another editorial post, though several attractive ones were later offered. In 1815, "weary of everything" including himself, he sailed to Liverpool, planning more European travel.

In Liverpool, however, he found his brother Peter unequal to the challenges facing the family import-export business. Despite Irving's long and earnest efforts to keep it solvent, the business went bankrupt in 1818. Compounded by his mother's death during his absence and Peter's own grave illness, this eventuality brought Irving to despair. He escaped from these sorrows by turning again to his pen and writing *The Sketch Book of Geoffrey Crayon, Gent.* (1819–20). With the publication of this book in England and America, Irving gained almost instant international fame. Since that time his popular recognition has rested largely on *The Sketch Book.*

Once again in this volume Irving chose an American bachelor as his persona—the sentimental, melancholy, antiquarian, and anglophilic Geoffrey Crayon. Crayon's predilection for sketching British scenes made this first internationally acclaimed book by an American author distinctly non-American in focus. Written in England, filled with English scenes and quotations from English authors, faithful to British orthography (rather than the "American" spellings advocated by Noah Webster's dictionary), *The Sketch Book* is conservative in attitude and antiquarian in allegiance. Crayon shows his preference for the traditional over the new, for aristocracy over democracy, for the rural over the urban. Using an urbane and gentlemanly style admired by readers well into the twentieth century, he exalts the humble peasantry and praises the paternalism of the British upper classes.

Accordingly, some English reviewers characterized Irving as the best British writer America had yet produced. And despite the proud chorus of praise in this country for his outstanding literary achievement, some Americans, including Richard Henry Dana, Sr., chided what they saw as Irving's uncritical anglophilia. Anglophilic Irving was, but not uncritical. First of all, Geoffrey Crayon is not to be identified with Washington Irving. Second, Crayon's tongue is sometimes in his cheek (as in "The Author's Account of Himself" and the *Salmagundi*-like "Little Britain"), and he even levels mild criticism at the British in "English Writers on America." More important, Crayon's love is for an England that was, not for the country that is. Aristocracy and rural life preserve traditional ways, while cities and merchants do not. Especially in the Christmas sketches, but also in such pieces as "The Angler" and "The Country Church," he exalts a disappearing England. Behind Crayon stands Irving, juxtaposing the Old World and the New, manipulating his own antiquarian interest with artistic perspectives to which he was even more committed.

These English sketches were calculated to appeal to a segment of Irving's audience, as were the sentimental ones: "The Pride of the Village" and "The Widow and Her Son," among others, are in the mode of eighteenth-century sentimentality; bereavement, early death, and loss of love are the stock situations, and the characters are intended to address our common humanity. Many readers in our time find these stories uncomfortably saccharine, suffused with a sentimentalism that seems the common property of persona and author, of Crayon and Irving. And at the heart of such objections, we can see, is the characterization of women. All of the sentimental tales and sketches (some are told to Crayon, in others he is a first-hand observer) focus on a woman. In "The Pride of the Village" it is the lovely, innocent young girl who wastes away· after the young soldier she loves proves unworthy; in "The Widow and Her Son" it is the old mother who bears for years the burden of a disappeared only child, finally to have him return to die in her arms. No brokenhearted young men, no old fathers or widowers suffer as do these women.

The women in these stories doubtless owe something to Irving's ability to project aspects of his experience—his grief at the death of his mother, for example, his devastation at the time of Matilda Hoffman's death. But they also derive from the attitude evident in Crayon's assertion that for men love is an adjunct to their public lives whereas for women it is all. Such women characters render to men a loyal, subservient, and undemanding love, thus fulfilling male assumptions and making a certain kind of story possible. Although their real-life counterparts no doubt existed, these angels in the house are imaginative reductions of women to categories of wish-fulfillment: "The Wife," for example, is predictably soft, delicate, and lovely, yet strong and supportive when such qualities are needed. But the only American wife in the book, as every reader will recall, is a far cry from this stereotype. Perhaps confirming Irving's literal and literary bachelorhood, Dame Van Winkle drives her husband from the house with her constant—and justified—nagging.

Only four of the thirty-three essays and stories in *The Sketch Book* are properly about American subjects; and only two of those—"Rip Van Winkle" and "The Legend of Sleepy Hollow"—were newly written. Each a masterpiece of storytelling, "Rip" and "Sleepy Hollow" are set on a fictional ground in which reality and imagination interpenetrate; although they are based on German sources, they anticipate the work of Hawthorne and Poe and achieve a distinct New World tone and theme. The supposed finding of the stories among the papers of the late Diedrich Knickerbocker connects *The Sketch Book* with the *History of New York;* but this is a saner Knickerbocker, whose tales eschew mad pedantry—although their effect still depends on the reader's ironic vision of the narrator.

The story of Ichabod Crane, Brom Bones, and Katrina Van Tassel is a blend of several narratives: it is at once the eternal triangle story, the tale of the country bumpkin outwitting the city slicker, and a fiction that mocks literary traditions of love, heroism, and ghosts. Building on the regional antipathies between New York and New England, Irving brings his pretentious and pusillanimous Connecticut Yankee into the Hudson River Valley, where he is soundly defeated in the game of love, after which he goes on to some success in the small-claims court. Because Ichabod had dreamed of buying and developing huge tracts of land in Kentucky or some other far western locale, this small-claims accomplishment also makes the tale something of a mock American success story.

Supposedly a "Legend," filled with intimations of a shadowy, wonder-filled Sleepy Hollow, Irving's story contains a hard and consistent core of rationality; all of its supposed mysteries are explained—albeit not admitted. The result is an ironic gothicism that is complemented by the manner of

"Rip Van Winkle." Again, in a tale remembered most widely because of Rip's twenty-year sleep, fiction masquerades as history, a Knickerbockerian stance obviously related to that of *A History of New York*. But here the tone is different: Irving puts the reader between national history and sheer fancy, where the two mix to create a fictional territory of a sort that Hawthorne was later to call a "neutral ground." The result is a deeply American story that, despite the charm of the telling, is not particularly happy. Its depiction of expansion and of cultural as well as political change is founded on a dissatisfaction with American development traceable not simply to the preferences of the narrator but to the social conservatism of Irving. An inevitably changing America is the backdrop for Rip's story, which shows Diedrich Knickerbocker and Geoffrey Crayon in agreement on the preferability of the past to the present—in this case the superiority of the peaceful Dutch backwater under distant royal rule to the growing, disputatious, and democratic village Rip finds on his return.

Like Knickerbocker and his predecessors, Geoffrey Crayon thus embodies traits of the conversative and bachelor Irving. The same is true for Rip, who, single again at the end of the tale, finds an identity in the new nation by serving his village as a link to its past and to the imagination. In the busy, rational America imaged by the transformed Catskill village at the end of "Rip Van Winkle," Washington Irving performed a similar function. Although Irving's role was to change before long, and although his doubts about authorship (evident in such sketches as "The Art of Book Making" and "The Mutability of Literature") were to recur, he would no longer doubt that he was a professional writer.

Irving's next work, popularly called his "English *Sketch Book*" just as *The Alhambra* was to become the "Spanish *Sketch Book*," extends some of the least significant material from the original collection to the point of superficiality. Maria Edgeworth was right about *Bracebridge Hall* (1822) when she said, "The workmanship surpasses the work." Irving's primary effort in this volume is to transform the Christmas sketches in *The Sketch Book* into vignettes that dwell on personalities and events at the county seat of "Squire" Bracebridge during the time of a wedding. The result is disappointing; what was minor in its earlier form becomes a mere exercise in style, leaving *Bracebridge Hall* simple in subject, tone, and execution. Though "The Stout Gentleman" rises above the common level, none of the other interpolated stories has similar merit. Two years later, however, Irving did somewhat better. Despite the fact that it was not received as well, *Tales of a Traveller* has a more beguiling strength than its predecessor—largely but not entirely because of the stories told by the "nervous gentleman" (the same vague narrator who related "The Stout Gentleman"). It is a book of fictional ploys, stories within stories. Particularly noticeable in the tales of the nervous gentleman is a bawdy streak harking back to *A History of New York* and the earlier works but missing from Irving's most recent productions.

Aware that his last two books lacked the creative energy and appeal of *The Sketch Book*, Irving was glad to accept an essentially titular appointment to the American legation in Spain, which would give him, he thought, the opportunity to translate an authoritative scholarly life of Christopher Columbus into English. But the work of translation gave way to the labors of biography. And with *The Life and Voyages of Christopher Columbus* (1828), Irving's career took a distinct turn; although he would still use the techniques of characterization and scene-setting found in his fiction, he was now willing to abandon his self-protective narrative distance and irony. The erstwhile scoffer at history became the historian he had earlier lampooned. *The Conquest of Granada* (1829), *Voyages of the Companions of Columbus* (1831), and *Legends of the Conquest of Spain* (1835) were the results of careful research. But Irving could not remain at ease with the conventional stance of historian; perforce he made the perspective his own. *Granada*, he said, is an "experiment," something "between a history and a romance." Its invented chronicler, Fray Antonio Agapida, is what Diedrich Knickerbocker had become now that for Irving both fiction and history were serious business.

Still, from this period, only *The Alhambra* (1832), a retelling of Spanish folk stories and a volume often compared to *The Sketch Book*, stands out as imaginatively engaging. It shares with that earlier work the desire to escape from the dusty present to live in the sadly vanished glories of the past. Both the original *Alhambra* and its 1850 revision suggest a narrative advance beyond the persona of Geoffrey Crayon. Into the legend-filled Alhambra Irving-the-writer withdraws. He sees—from his own perspective—the problems of the detached dreamer, the artist, the observer he has been. When he leaves, he has solved nothing, has found no new sources of creativity. But he knows himself more clearly—a good basis for a return home.

After seventeen years in Europe, Irving came back to the United States in 1832, famous, honored, and courted. Uneasy about having been away too long to know what his country had become in the interval, intrigued by Andrew Jackson and his western roots, and thinking that the American West with its frontiersmen and Indians might be a rich subject and source for his literary efforts, Irving decided to learn about this new America. During the next few years he traveled extensively, north and south, but most significantly, west—to Oklahoma with Indian commissioner Henry

Ellsworth. From their month-long horseback excursion on the Oklahoma plains Irving fashioned *A Tour on the Prairies* (1835)—the first of his "Western" books. The others, strongly influenced by this encounter with the West, are *Astoria* (1836) and *The Adventures of Captain Bonneville* (1837).

Irving's interest in the frontier was of long standing. As early as 1803, for example, he had made a difficult wilderness trip to Montreal; he had read many books of Western travel; he had written two appreciative essays about Indians for the *Analectic Magazine* while he was its editor, and later revised them for *The Sketch Book;* he knew Cooper's *The Pioneers.* Now, in the 1830s, aware of the powerful symbolism and the political importance of the West, Irving wrote works that served not only his own interests as an author but also the cause of westward expansion and Manifest Destiny.

Though he felt free to embellish incidents and to exaggerate or even invent traits of character in his companions, Irving did adhere closely to his notes, scrupulously taken throughout the trip, so as to produce a reliable record of place and circumstance. Incorporating scraps of folklore and legend, using comparisons with Europe as well as allusions to modern and classical literature, and maintaining a certain genteel distance from the roughness of the frontiersmen, Irving put the American West into a familiar and elevating cultural context. That was his way of dealing with the romantically attractive yet realistically disturbing wildness of the land, of the Indians, and of his own companions. It would also prove an effective technique for exalting the activities celebrated in his next books.

Irving wrote *Astoria; or, Anecdotes of an Enterprise Beyond the Rocky Mountains* at the request of John Jacob Astor. With access to a number of authoritative documents, a genuine interest in the fur trade, and research help from his nephew (and later biographer) Pierre Irving, he produced another accurate though elaborated history—this time of a bold commercial dream that ended in failure. Here, as in the *Adventures of Captain Bonneville,* his picturesque descriptions of nature, his depictions of eccentric characters, and his sympathetic treatment of the Indians create the Irvingesque quality associated with his work of fifteen to twenty years earlier.

The last dozen years of Irving's life were in their own way as significant as any other period. Though he did produce some undistinguished work of various kinds, he also went again to Europe and served notably for four years as President John Tyler's ambassador to Spain during a period of tension in that country. Returning from Spain to settle in at his lovely home, "Sunny-side," on the Hudson River near Tarrytown, New York, he wrote another respectable history, *Mahomet and His Successors* (1850), and then the five-volume *Life of George Washington* (1855–59), with which he struggled greatly, completing it shortly before his death. He considered this biography his masterwork. Despite its obvious competence, however, it is heavy reading, perhaps open to some of the criticisms of historical writing he had made in *A History of New York* so many years before. Irving had long since become an official American voice rather than a satirist of officialdom. Like many aging men, he had found that he had a stake in that quotidian reality and mythic possibility called America.

At the time of his death it was averred that anyone who read English had read Washington Irving. His contemporaries and successors in American literature certainly knew his work: good cases can be made for Irving's importance to a large number of American writers, including Bryant, Longfellow, Whittier, both Danas, Hawthorne, and Bret Harte. Some of them acknowledged the debt. Moreover, the characteristics of his writing in the "Knickerbocker" mode of caricature, satire, and local allusion are apparent not simply in productions of the Knickerbocker "School" but in the work of Cooper, Poe, and Melville, as well. And the clarity and grace of Irving's "Crayon" style impressed most American authors who commented on it—whatever reservations they may have had about his apparent politics. In a different vein, his romantic histories influenced professional historians, among them William Hickling Prescott and Francis Parkman. And of course some of his works have remained sources not only of literary inspiration but of popular culture.

Any judgment of Irving as a writer of minor importance must be qualified by the clear evidence of his influence and the variety of his achievement. Admittedly, his career as a whole shows him as a man of his time rather than for all time—provocatively describing and commenting on (but not probing) his world. Yet in some of his narrators and characters we feel more—the isolation and alienation that is at the heart of much American writing before the Civil War, that may express inescapably contradictory tensions in American culture. The "half-shut eye" in the epigraph to "The Legend of Sleepy Hollow" is an apt figure for Irving's literary career: it was half-shut to unsatisfying reality, half-open to imaginative possibility.

Haskell Springer

James Fenimore Cooper and the Writers of the Frontier

More fully than any of his contemporaries, James Fenimore Cooper recognized and exploited the possibilities of the American frontier for fiction. One way to identify Cooper's unique and original contribution to the development of the frontier novel, and to American fiction generally, is to place him in relation to the two other major frontier writers of his time, Robert Montgomery Bird of Philadelphia, and William Gilmore Simms of Charleston, South Carolina.

Bird was trained as a physician but turned his attention early to letters, and became a successful playwright as well as a novelist. Between 1834 and 1839 he published several works of fiction, one of which continues to command attention as a singularly haunting rendering of American frontier experience. In its stark, violent realism, *Nick of the Woods* (1837)—set in the Kentucky wilderness of the late eighteenth century—contrasts with Cooper's characteristically theatrical settings and formal dramatic situations. The contrast is not accidental. As he explained in one of his prefaces to the novel, Bird wrote *Nick of the Woods*, in part, to correct what he regarded as Cooper's fraudulent rendering of the frontier, particularly the latter's treatment of the Indians.

There is nothing remarkable about the traditional romantic plot of *Nick of the Woods*, or about its conventional hero, Roland Forrester. The novel's interest for the modern reader resides instead in the psychological portrait of one of its secondary characters, an apparently pacifist Quaker named Nathan Slaughter whose public pieties conceal his secret identity as an Indian killer. Before the time setting of the novel, Nathan had been an innocent, trusting settler who welcomed into his frontier home a band of Shawnee Indians, who proceeded brutally to murder his wife and five children and to inflict on him an almost fatal head-wound. To public view, Nathan remains a pacifist after this horrible event, but in the cover of the tangled Kentucky wilderness he takes systematic, brutal revenge on every Indian who crosses his path. Known by the Indians as the Jibbenainosay—the dead man who walks—and by the white settlers as Nick of the Woods, he carves into the chests of his victims the sign of the cross. Though the novel's final developments leading to Nathan's killing of the hated Indian chief Wenonga are predictable, Nathan's interwoven, mysterious presence in earlier portions of the book lifts the narrative above its conventional elements and its tidy, happy ending.

But if *Nick of the Woods* engages the modern imagination with its fascinating view of the psychology of an Indian killer—its dark, interior vision links it to the work of Poe, Hawthorne, and Melville—the novel's bluntly racist attitude toward the Indians reveals the shortsightedness of Bird's historical vision. For Bird, American history had begun with European settlement and its "civilizing" influence upon the New World; unlike Cooper, he was eager to forget the Indians' dispossession as rapidly as possible and was apparently untroubled by the darker implication of American progress.

This contrast shows up most pointedly in comparison between *Nick of the Woods* and Cooper's *The Last of the Mohicans* (1826), because more than any other of Cooper's novels *Mohicans*—set in the Lake George region of colonial New York during the French and Indian Wars—shares Bird's unflinching view of the frontier as the scene of grim, unrelenting, and unpredictable violence. Yet for all their similarity of material and setting, these two works differ profoundly. While the conflict represented in *Nick* draws an all too simple contrast between white "civilization" and red "savagery," *Mohicans* takes account of the force and complication of history, demonstrating that all the contestants in the struggle for possession of North America in the middle of the eighteenth century were overwhelmed by forces beyond their control. The novel characterizes colonial America as a fallen world, in which nature's beauty has been sullied by violence; a previously idyllic pond, for example, has become the bloodied burial site of French soliders caught in an ambush.

The Last of the Mohicans also provides evidence against Bird's charge that Cooper had rendered Indian life falsely. In fact, his portrayal of Indian ritual and beliefs in *Mohicans* and in his other wilderness tales is as authentic as that of any novelist of his generation. He had conscientiously consulted and assimilated the best Indian sources that were available to him—particularly the writings of the missionary John Heckewelder—and had interviewed several of the great Indian chiefs of his time. Cooper's understanding of the Indians is reflected in Leatherstocking's distinction between red and white "gifts," an idea that anticipates modern cultural relativism. It is true, on the other hand, the *Mohicans* employs Cooper's characteristic division between "good" and "bad" Indians (Delawares and Hurons); but this is mitigated by his convincing historical justification for the treachery of his villain, Magua, who has been corrupted by his association with European military forces. Bird, of course, provides no such justification for Wenonga, whose dignity is entirely stripped away.

Another index of the difference between Bird's and Cooper's vision of the frontier is the role of the genteel hero in *Nick of the Woods* and *Mohicans*. Bird's investment in Roland Forrester as the bearer of Western values and ideals is total; Cooper's treatment of Duncan Heyward, on the other hand, characterizes the comparable figure in *Mohicans* as inept and ineffectual—until late in the novel when he begins to learn the ways of the wilderness. But in this environment of terrible and violent change, even Natty Bumppo, whose extraordinary wilderness skills take on mythic status in other of the Leatherstocking tales, is unable to exercise his usual heroic command. In this work, the only character who emerges as an unqualified hero is the great Delaware chief, Uncas (the son of Natty's companion, Chingachgook), whose tragic death confirms the novel's prevailing themes of dispossession and loss. Needless to day, the love shared by Uncas and Colonel Munro's daughter Cora—with its suggestion of a union between the races—would have been unthinkable for Bird.

Unlike Bird, William Gilmore Simms shared Cooper's sense of the tragedy of Indian dispossession; this and several other aspects of Simms's long, varied, and prolific career justify his reputation as Cooper's Southern counterpart. After setting aside a career in the law at an early stage, Simms turned to literature; he produced more than thirty works of fiction, much verse, several volumes of biography, and some useful criticism (in which, for example, he elaborated an important distinction between the romance and the novel). Like Bird's, however, Simms's modern reputation rests upon a single novel, *The Yemassee* (1835), which depicts the early eighteenth-century struggle among the English, the Spanish, and the indigenous Yemassee Indians for possession of colonial South Carolina. As in Cooper's fictional treatment of the French and Indian Wars, here the Indians are represented as a fearsome and proud people who are moved to violence by the threat of displacement. Though Simms was to treat the American Indians again in short fiction and in a late novel (*The Cassique of Kiawah* [1859]), it is clear that this work is the one—comparable to *The Last of the Mohicans* in this way—in which he set about to dramatize the historical moment at which Indian dispossession in his region became inevitable. And while the novel communicates unmistakably Simms's belief in the superiority of European civilization over what he regards as Indian primitivism, his sense of historical loss is also unmistakable.

In *The Yemassee*, the issue of Indian dispossession is embodied centrally in the character Occonestoga, whose betrayal of his people testifies to the corrupting influences of the European colonial presence in America. The scene in which his mother kills him mercifully, to save him from torture at the hands of his tribe, is one of the most powerful in the book; it rivals Cooper's best Indian ritual scenes. And while the wilderness setting of *The Yemassee* lacks the sense of unremitting terror of *Nick of the Woods* or of *The Last of the Mohicans*, the book contains individual scenes of sharply drawn frontier violence whose skillful placement gives them a shocking effect.

Nevertheless, Simms was never as fully at home in the fictive world of the wilderness as was Cooper. (He was more comfortable with the historical materials of the American Revolution, about which he wrote seven novels.) In a work like *Guy Rivers* (1834), for example, characters frequently invoke the Cherokee Nation to the west of the novel's setting in frontier Georgia as a region of adventure and possibility. Yet Simms fails to depict this region with the authenticity of Cooper's wilderness in *Mohicans* or his Western plains in *The Prairie* (1827). One reason for this is his deep commitment to community. Ultimately, Simms's unshakable fidelity to the structured world of Charleston, South Carolina, and to the genteel hero who represents its values—Ralph Colleton of *Guy Rivers* is such a figure—became a fatal burden to his full realization as a frontier novelist. We can see the problem also in *The Yemassee*, where Gabriel Harrison (actually Charles Craven, the governor of the territory, in disguise) dominates the action of that novel to a singular and detrimental effect. By overinvesting in characters like Harrison and Colleton, Simms cut off for himself the possibility of creating the authentic frontier hero that Cooper created in Leatherstocking.

That Cooper's historical vision was more capacious than that of Bird and his rendering of the frontier more authentic than that of Simms is vividly apparent in his first true frontier novel, *The Pioneers* (1823). While Cooper's first two works (*Precaution* [1820]; *The Spy* [1821]) show him struggling successfully to find an audience, this work, as he said in his 1823 preface, was written exclusively to please himself. Set in the world of his remembered childhood in Cooperstown, New York—the settlement community founded by his land-baron father, William Cooper, and to which James himself had been taken in the first year of his life—the novel is poignantly autobiographical and reveals the distinctively personal meanings of frontier experience for Cooper. Indeed, the fact that frontier experience *was* a matter of personal history for him suggests the reasons for his success.

The view of the frontier that Cooper depicts in *The Pioneers* is complex. On the one hand, the richly detailed descriptions of community life and of the surrounding wilderness communicate a strong sense of the pastoral (lines from James Thomson's *The Seasons* provide the epigraph to the opening chapter, and the slow, sure movement of nature's annual cycle gives the novel its structure); that readers have consistently responded to this aspect of *The Pioneers* is witnessed in Cooper's own time by the genre paintings it inspired, and in the twentieth century by D. H. Lawrence's famous appreciation of its lovely pictures. On the other hand, within the frame of these lovely pictures, Cooper characterizes a human world full of potentially destructive change. The community's makeshift architecture, its ugly, unfinished streets, and the settlers' unmindful destruction of natural resources dramatize civilization's intrusion upon the pristine wilderness. Cooper was enough of his father's son to be excited by the process of making a world in the wilderness, and one feels that excitement in this novel and in all of the writer's novels depicting the settlement stage. But *The Pioneers* betrays a good deal of uneasiness about this process; its poignantly rendered scenes of natural destruction give it importance as one of the earliest statements of the modern ecological conscience. Like much of Cooper's later fiction, *The Pioneers* can be read as a warning; its prophetic dimension is emphasized by observing that the passenger pigeons slaughtered by cannon shot in the novel's most powerful scene of this kind were extinct by 1900.

As serious an issue as ecological destruction was for Cooper, however, a still more troubling aspect of change for him was that of social instability, and here too the writer was issuing a warning. In characters of narrow self-interest like Richard Jones and Hiram Doolittle he saw a dark underside of democracy emerging, and in later novels their spiritual descendants threaten the very structure of American communities. But *The Pioneers* contains these forces within its larger pastoral vision; Jones is characterized as comic and somewhat ineffectual, and Doolittle (who stands for a whole class of migratory Americans) moves west as the narrative concludes.

Jones's and Doolittle's power is blunted most immediately, however, by the novel's representative of lawful authority, Judge Marmaduke Temple, surely modeled in some respects after William Cooper. Though Temple is not infallible (he gives in to the excitement of the pigeon-shoot, for example), he nevertheless stands for protection of the environment and for the imposition of order and restraint in the wilderness; in this he would seem to be allied with Natty Bumppo, the aged Leatherstocking, who kills only what he needs. But in fact the Judge and Natty are deeply divided, for Natty's commitment belongs to a world that is rapidly being displaced by everything that Temple represents; his is a world of the past in which the original owners of the land, the Indians, roamed its forests. Leatherstocking's companion, Indian John, is the last representative in these hills of the earlier Indian presence, and John's debasement (shown poignantly by his drunkenness in the tavern scene) and death (a ritual event of large symbolic importance) are sure indications that the wilderness of this novel—like that of William Faulkner's "The Bear"—is doomed. *The Pioneers* thus sets the forces of an emerging civilization starkly against those of nature, but unlike some of Cooper's later novels here the narrative works toward a reconciliation of past and present.

The primary agent of reconciliation is Oliver Effingham, a close companion of Leatherstocking and of Indian John whose grandfather—the original English claimant of the Templeton lands—was made a chief by the Delawares. Thus, the European and Indian past are united in and represented by Oliver, whose marriage to the Judge's daughter Elizabeth tentatively resolves conflict between Templeton's past and future. Cooper invests in this marriage his profound hope that American democracy will follow a course of orderly change, led firmly by a progressive, enlightened gentry. But before this resolution is effected, the novel raises sharply the issue of rightful ownership of the land. Oliver's muted anger toward Judge Temple through much of the narrative reflects his conviction that the Judge is a usurper (only late in the novel does he learn that Temple's actions had protected the Effingham claim from the widespread dispossession of Loyalist families during the Revolution). In the contest between these two figures we may wish to see a conflict between father and son—that is, between Cooper himself and the immensely powerful and autocratic William Cooper. But more significantly, this is a conflict between two parts of Cooper himself: the part committed to and inspired by civilization-building and the march of American progress across the continent, and the part committed to a nostalgic pastoral vision he associated with his own childhood in a frontier community. The first of these visions is inexorably temporal, and the other is essentially timeless. Like *The Pioneers*, the Leatherstocking tales as a whole can be viewed as a working out of the terms of this polarity as its meanings shifted for Cooper through the eighteen years that passed between the first- and last-written of the tales.

That Cooper chose to write an early novel about a conflict over rightful possession of a place drawn after his childhood home is significant, for the biographical facts of this period describe a literal dispossession of the writer's Cooperstown holdings. The years of Cooper's emergence as a novelist have usually been depicted as comfortable; he was, after all, one of the heirs to his father's vast holdings in central New York State and he was an immediate inheritor of $50,000 upon his father's death in 1809. After concluding his active service in the U.S. Navy in 1810, he married in the following year Susan De Lancey, the daughter of a wealthy New York family, and following a brief period in Cooperstown settled into the life of a gentleman farmer in Westchester County.

Cooper's years at his Westchester farm (and intermittently at a rented house in New York City) must have had the appearance of well-being, but in fact this was a period of trouble and uncertainty. The estate William Cooper had left to his heirs was deeply mired in a complex set of legal entailments, and much of it was rapidly lost through mismanagement by James's older brothers, all four of whom died untimely deaths by 1820. Faced with the insistent demands of creditors and having suffered losses from an unsuccessful investment in whaling, Cooper was forced to sell and mortgage properties both in the Cooperstown area and in Westchester County. The elaborate financial manipulations of this period suggest an extended and desperate attempt at solvency. Cooper's circumstances deteriorated so rapidly that in 1823—the publication year of *The Pioneers*—the sheriff of New York inventoried and confiscated (though did not ultimately sell off) the household possessions of the writer's New York City home.

These biographical facts invite us to reconsider the common perception of the origins of Cooper's literary career. The famous story of his wife challenging him to write a better novel than the one he was reading has long given the impression that this beginning was fortuitous. One reason the story has endured is that without it Cooper's emergence as a writer seems difficult to explain. Though he appears to have displayed early a gift for inventive storytelling and had read widely in literature (he studied at a preparatory school in Albany in his youth and attended Yale for two years before being expelled from the university for perpetrating a prank), there is little else in Cooper's experience prior to the 1820s to suggest that he would have undertaken a literary career. Indeed, the Cooper of the years immediately before his marriage is very much a man of action: a common sailor aboard a merchant ship and later a midshipman in the U.S. Navy. Given his social role as a member of the landed gentry whose father had encouraged careers of public service for his children, we might have expected him eventually to have found his vocation in politics or government.

What the emerging biographical facts of these early years suggest is that, while the initial impetus toward authorship may have been fortuitous, Cooper's literary career once undertaken was driven immediately by acute financial need. His first full-length work of fiction—*Precaution*, a novel of manners highly imitative of the kind then in fashion—has all the marks of an attempted best-seller; and his second, *The Spy*, a tale of the Revolution, brilliantly exploits America's emerging feelings of national identity. This is the work that brought Cooper (then thirty-two years old) to the attention and favor of his countrymen and launched his literary career. But it required all of the substantial earnings brought by *The Spy* and the writer's other early successes to prevent his economic ruin. And, indeed, financial difficulty followed him for the rest of his life.

Clearly, we need to revise our persistent view of Cooper as a gentlemen of leisure who turned to literature for amusement. The insistently serious themes of the novels themselves have always invited such a revision, and their most central theme—dispossession—reflects the crisis of his early career. The novelist's resulting sense of threatened class and power informs all of his fiction and helps to explain why his representation of dispossession—including Indian dispossession—is so intensely charged with meaning. Cooper's genius lay in his ability to transform the personal terms of his crisis into larger terms—to give them a transpersonal dimension with national and even mythic implications.

The conflict over possession of the land that lies at the center of *The Pioneers* is not unique in Cooper's fiction. Generally defined and energized by conflict, his novels characteristically turn on a fictional paradigm adapted from Walter Scott's Waverley novels, that of the neutral ground: a region of rapid change contested by at least two warring factions. From this paradigm comes the setting of Cooper's first American novel, *The Spy*. Set in the rocky highlands above New York City during the Revolution, this work dramatizes a world full of confusion and ambiguity. One might almost say that the novel's hero, Harvey Birch (a counterspy for the American forces), is born out of the setting's confusion; that is, *The Spy* requires a character of supreme skill to negotiate its threatening environment and to bring order out of its chaos. Harvey's uncanny abilities in this regard define his heroism and make him a clear prototype for Leatherstocking. Part of the novel's confusion has to do with the Revolution itself, which figures as a central and symbolic event in several of Cooper's early works. Though *The Spy* unequivocally celebrates the American cause of independence, it also shows how noble motive and high purpose can be distorted by the violence and chaos that accompany social rebellion. Alongside heroic figures like Harvey Birch and

George Washington we find the avaricious and murderous Skinners, out-laws who pretend allegiance to the American side but use the war as a pretext for acts of plunder.

We have already noted how the Revolution threatened to dispossess from the Effingham family its Templeton holdings in *The Pioneers*, the novel Cooper published immediately after *The Spy*. In the two works that follow *The Pioneers*, he further explored the issue. *The Pilot* (1824), which dramatizes military conflict between British and American naval forces during the Revolution, may be considered the world's first true nautical novel, even though more than half its action takes place on land. Cooper had not yet fully discovered the potential of the nautical tale, and his unqualified celebration of the freedom of the sea would have to await his second and third works in this subgenre, *The Red Rover* (1827) and *The Water Witch* (1830). (The first of these, with a fully realized Byronic pirate for its central character, is Cooper's most exciting and skillfully rendered tale of the sea; the second treats the running of contraband off the coast of colonial New Jersey and is the novelist's most lyrical rendering of the nautical setting.) Despite its landed quality, however, *The Pilot* has well-rendered and exciting scenes of naval battle and tempest, in which the heroic Tom Coffin performs deeds of extraordinary heroism; this character's skill and simplicity of spirit link him closely to Leatherstocking. But it is in the character of John Paul Jones, who goes in disguise as a common pilot for much of the narrative, that Cooper's attitude toward the Revolutionary struggle is best revealed. Jones's keen eye penetrates with uncanny accuracy the murky atmosphere of the rocky, fog-shrouded English coastline on which the narrative is set, and his probing vision accounts for the Americans' success. Yet Cooper severely qualifies the Pilot's heroism by exposing his turbulent inner life and his overweening ambition. While the novel ultimately endorses the ideals of the Revolution and approves the American destiny, in the figure of Jones it draws into question the motives that generate political rebellion. This ambivalence can be seen to anticipate the political conservatism of Cooper's later years.

Lionel Lincoln (1825) is Cooper's most direct treatment of the American Revolution. He originally saw this work as the beginning of a thirteen-part series treating different aspects of that great struggle, and the novel shows intense concern for capturing historical detail. But *Lionel Lincoln* was a failure both artistically and commercially, and the writer abandoned his plan. Its failure, however, is instructive, for in this work Cooper attempted to combine the elements of the historical and the Gothic novel and for him the mixture did not work. The hero of the tale returns to Boston, the city of his birth, as a British soldier sent by the Crown to stifle rebellion; caught up in a labyrinthine mystery of family origins, he wanders in a state of disorientation through the novel's dark and war-torn landscape. *Lionel Lincoln*'s nightmare vision of Revolutionary Boston takes the conflict and confusion of Scott's neutral ground to an extreme of obscurity.

In a variety of ways, the settings of all Cooper's early works are continuous with that of *The Pioneers*. Whether set on land or sea, in the frontier settlement or in the landscape of war, they dramatize conflict over a contested territory and the confusion of claims that such conflict produces. But it remains true that, among the various subgenres of Cooper's fiction, the settlement novel most clearly opens a view to the writer's inner life. The setting of such works—characteristically a fortified but vulnerable and endangered central structure—objectifies to an unusual degree Cooper's personal sense of threatened boundary. After *The Pioneers*, the author wrote three more settlement novels: *The Wept of Wish-ton-Wish* (1829), *Wyandotté* (1843), and *The Crater* (1847). Considered together with *The Pioneers*, these works virtually span the course of the writer's career, and they describe an ever-darkening treatment of the subject. The Connecticut Valley settlement of *The Wept*, for example, is attacked and destroyed by Narragansett Indians (during the period of King Philip's War) not once but twice during the course of the narrative; and, in *Wyandotté*, the attack on a wilderness settlement in colonial New York State leaves its beautiful valley a wasteland of death and destruction.

This is not to say, however, that the treatment of settlement in these works is uniform. For all the continuous sense of threatened violence in *The Wept of Wish-ton-Wish*, the novel ultimately suggests redemption and regeneration. Its regenerative emphasis is given compelling expression in the scene in which the settlers, following the complete destruction of their fortress by fire, emerge from a deep well-shaft, reborn from the earth, as it were, to begin again. Another factor that qualifies the pervasive violence of this work is the historical setting Cooper chose for it. His settlers in *The Wept* are Puritans, and the novel is in part an examination and condemnation of the Puritan mind. (Many of the plundering figures in the writer's other works are of New England origin; he believed that American Calvinism had bred narrow acquisitiveness and exaggerated self-interest.) Cooper represents Puritanism's greatest excesses of zealotry and cruelty in the character Meek Wolfe, whose name conveys the mixture of piety and rapaciousness that Cooper so detested. At the novel's conclusion, Wolfe insists upon the execution of the Indian chief Conanchet (whose marriage to the settlement's lost member, Ruth Heathcote—the "wept" of the title—realizes the miscegenation that *Mohicans* had only hinted at) because Conanchet refuses to be Christianized. In this event, the novel implicitly makes the case for the integrity of the Indians' culture and, like *Mohicans*, mourns their destruction.

Wyandotté has the same spatial design as *The Wept of Wish-ton-Wish:* a beautiful valley enclosed by wilderness. Captain Hugh Willoughby is able to transform his frontier patent into a thriving agricultural settlement almost overnight by draining a 400-acre beaver pond. One senses in the early portions of the novel the same excitement about world-building that characterizes *The Pioneers*. But this excitement is soon replaced by a pervasive sense of threat to the security of the Hutted Knoll, the fortress that Captain Willoughby has constructed at the center of his valley. As in earlier novels, the Revolutionary War forms a background of historical turbulence; a manipulative land overseer, Joel Strides, attempts to represent Captain Willoughby as a Tory sympathizer, to the end that Willoughby's lands will be confiscated and turned over to Strides himself. In place of *The Wept*'s proud Conanchet, this novel's Indian presence is represented by an outcast, alcoholic member of the Tuscarora tribe (Nick, or Wyandotté) who harbors a fierce resentment against Captain Willoughby for a beating the Captain once inflicted on him; near the novel's conclusion he kills Willoughby. This murder is, however, but a prelude to the wholesale violence that follows: a fullscale attack on the Hutted Knoll by hostile Indians and marauding whites disguised as Indians. In this event of savage ferocity, the defenses of the Hutted Knoll collapse and several of its inhabitants, including the Captain's wife, die. The carnage depicted in this novel is so sweeping that even Edgar Allan Poe found it disproportionate.

In his final novel in this subgenre, Cooper removed the process of settlement from America and dramatized its developments on an imaginary island in the Pacific Ocean. *The Crater*, which may be considered our first true allegorical novel, represents symbolically the course of America's empire—its past, present, and future. Shipwrecked on a barren reef, Mark Woolston witnesses a vast volcanic upheaval that creates a world for him to develop and colonize. Much of the novel is given over to the pleasures of world-building, and its descriptions are rendered in rich and compelling detail. As in *The Wept of Wish-ton-Wish* and *Wyandotté*, the settlement is severely threatened by hostile forces—by natives from neighboring islands and by pirates. But these forces are overcome, and as a society develops out of its rudimentary beginnings the greatest threat to the integrity of the island ultimately comes from within. Mark is displaced from his rightful role as the island's governor, finding himself defeated by irresponsible journalism, political and religious factionalism, social and educational experimentation, and abuses of the majority rule—in short, by everything in American life that by 1847 Cooper had come to hate. When a second volcanic eruption finally sinks the entire world of Crater Island into the sea, Cooper's deeply felt anger toward his native land, and his sense of doom about its future, are unmistakable.

The movement from the cautious optimism of *The Pioneers* to the apocalyptic vision of *The Crater* indicates the essential direction of Cooper's career. We find the same movement that the settlement novels exhibit in the various other subgenres of his work. For example, the strong sense of adventure and possibility of the early nautical tales is replaced in a work like *The Two Admirals* (1842) by a pervasive didacticism, and in late novels of the sea by an increasingly bleak vision of life. *Jack Tier* (1848), published immediately after *The Crater*, is a particularly dark work, in which greed and violence have their way to a considerable and surprising degree; the central character is a vicious murderer who does not hesitate even to sever the hands of a matronly woman as she attempts to cling to a small boat in the open sea.

The novel that follows *Jack Tier* suggests Cooper's answer to his escalating sense of chaos. *The Sea Lions* (1849) mounts an insistent argument for Trinitarianism; its hero, Roswell Gardiner, is a good man who initially resists the entreaties of his fiancée to adopt the formal tenets of the Christian faith, and the novel's action chastens him into belief. This novel reminds us of *The Crater* in its strong allegorical overtones (two ships of the same name pursue treasure and sealskins on parallel journeys toward the Caribbean and Antarctica), as well as in the power of its natural description. (As in *The Crater*, and earlier in *The Prairie*, Cooper has in *The Sea Lions* translated the reports of explorers into dazzling scenery.) But where earlier novels of the sea had given expression to Cooper's themes implicitly through action and setting, here the voice of the narrator intrudes repeatedly. *The Sea Lions* shows how much Cooper had come to feel, in the final decade of his life, the need to impose order on a world he saw spinning out of control. Indeed, the Trinitarianism Cooper espouses in this work (of Quaker origins, he converted to high Episcopalianism late in his life) is itself an expression of the need to bring order out of chaos.

A movement from adventure to didacticism can also be found in the wilderness tales. Almost contemporaneously with *The Sea Lions*, Cooper published an analogous work called *The Oak Openings* (1848). Like its nautical counterpart, it contains beautifully realized scenes of natural description;

the novel is set in the parklike meadows and forests of western Michigan during the War of 1812. While the novel's mixture of natural beauty and the violence of warfare is characteristic of Cooper's earlier wilderness tales, its intense moralizing is not. The writer's moralizing impulse focuses itself on a fearsome Indian leader named Onoah, or Scalping Peter, who is convinced—through the noble suffering and sacrificial death of a missionary—to forgo his savage paganism and convert to Christianity. When we consider the autonomy and integrity of Indian culture as Cooper represented it in earlier wilderness tales, the Christianization of Scalping Peter must come as a sharp disappointment. It can be seen as a reflection of the way in which formal religious belief became a solace for the author in his later years.

The striking difference between Cooper's early and late work is not the result of a gradually evolving movement from a progressive to a conservative perspective. Rather, the shift is abrupt and decisive, and it pivots on the writer's return to America in 1833 from a seven-year sojourn (1826–33) in Europe. Shortly following the publication of *The Last of the Mohicans*, Cooper took his family to Paris. The earlier success of *The Spy*, *The Pioneers*, and *The Pilot* had brought him the enthusiastic favor of his countrymen, and when he sailed for Europe in 1826 he departed as a national hero. In the early years in Europe he extended his reputation, both at home and abroad, through his publication of *The Prairie*. With its evocation of the vast American sublime this novel implicitly celebrates the possibilities of American life, and soon after its publication Cooper made a more overt statement in his *Notions of the Americans* (1828). In this work, Cooper speaks through the genial voice of a traveling bachelor named John Cadwallader, who views America's young, democratic society and its pastoral villages and landscapes with a shrewd but approving eye. In a less direct way Cooper's European novels of the early 1830s—*The Bravo* (1831), *The Heidenmauer* (1832), and *The Headsman* (1833)—promote American interests by exploring the Old World's dark, feudal past, and implicitly contrasting it with America's bright, democratic future.

But Cooper was no chauvinist, and his exacting standards for the development of American democracy were misunderstood by many of his countrymen, especially those in the press, as disaffection. His involvement in European political issues—particularly the so-called Finance Controversy—had been unpopular at home, as had his European novels. Cooper's relations with his native land were thus already strained when he arrived in New York (where he refused a testimonial dinner) in November of 1833, and soon after his return he began to recognize the dramatic changes that the Jacksonian era had brought to American life. He was deeply shocked by these changes, particularly by what he regarded as the downward leveling tendencies of democracy, and from this point forward to the end of his life he waged an insistent argument—in his novels and political writings, in repeated legal actions against the press, and in community disputes—with his countrymen. Later in the 1830s the writer made Cooperstown his primary residence, and Otsego Hall—the family home that Cooper repossessed and renovated in this period—became a citadel from which he defended himself and the threatened gentry he represented against a democracy that had, in his view, strayed fatally from its early republican principles.

In the year following his return to America, Cooper issued his famous *Letter to His Countrymen* (1834), in which he described his victimization at the hands of the press, made an appeal for American independence of mind, and announced his retirement from authorship. He did not stop writing, of course. The years that followed his *Letter* saw the publication of his European travel books (*Sketches of Switzerland* [1836], *Sketches of Switzerland: Part Second* [1836], *Gleanings in Europe* [1837], *Gleanings in Europe: England* [1837], and *Gleanings in Europe: Italy* [1838]); he also published in this period a social and political allegory called *The Monikins* (1835), which satirizes life in England and America by representing both countries as civilizations of monkeys on the Antarctic continent.

Significantly, Cooper's next work of fiction returned him imaginatively to Templeton. The specific purpose of the two-part narrative, *Homeward Bound* and *Home as Found* (1838), was to show how the leveling tendencies of the Jacksonian era had subverted the early promise of the nation as it had been characterized in *The Pioneers*. The first of the two novels uses the shipboard setting of an Atlantic homeward voyage from Europe to establish the central issues and to present some of the representational characters who speak for them: in particular the narrow-minded and provincial Yankee newspaper editor and extreme democrat Steadfast Dodge, the principled Captain Truck, and most important, the Effingham family—descendants of Oliver and Elizabeth of *The Pioneers*. But *Homeward Bound* is not only preparation for its companion work; unable to resist the possibilities for adventure that his beloved nautical setting presented, Cooper interwove into the novel's social and political discourse harrowing escapes from tempest and plunderers.

Nevertheless, Cooper's real focus here is the voyagers' destination. In the Templeton of the present day, the Effinghams are a beleaguered and threatened class. *Home as Found* focuses on its almost literal rendering of an autobiographical incident—the Three-Mile Point controversy—in which the author did legal battle with the people of Cooperstown to recover a piece of lakefront property long used as a public picnic area. But Cooper's targets are much broader; his novel recounts all of the abuses of Jacksonian America as he saw them: a slanderously irresponsible press, urban centers of narrow commercial interests and social life characterized by vicious gossip, the total breakdown of decorum in social relations generally, and most disturbing, rampant materialism. What had been comic in a figure like Hiram Doolittle or Richard Jones now becomes ominously threatening in Aristabulus Bragg, a greedy land agent and lawyer who subscribes to extreme majority rule.

It is a measure of Cooper's shock and anger that this novel is so convoluted; its extraordinarily complicated plot, which discloses only on its final pages that the male hero, Paul Powis, is really an Effingham, replicates the writer's own convoluted response to social displacement. As in *The Pioneers*, the novel's action and issues are resolved in a marriage; but where the marriage of Oliver Effingham and Elizabeth Temple had symbolized prospect and possibility for the American experiment, the marriage of Eve and Paul—two blood cousins of the Effingham clan—suggests a severe closing of ranks and an almost hysterical response to social change. Contemporaneously with *Homeward Bound* Cooper published his second major political and social treatise, *The American Democrat* (1838), and its damaging assessment of his native land showed how far he had come from the earlier idealized conception that informed *Notions of the Americans*.

The literary failure of *Home as Found* tells us much about Cooper's particular strengths and weaknesses as a novelist. In this work the writer was literally too close to home, and his anger is transparent in the book's insistent polemicizing and its tangled plot. It is interesting to observe what happened when Cooper employed the same essential structure and developments as those of *Homeward Bound* and *Home as Found* in a setting removed from Cooperstown (Templeton). Nautical adventure dominates the first volume of the paired *Afloat and Ashore* and *Miles Wallingford* (1844), and the second volume dramatizes the hero's dispossession and recovery of his landed estate (the novel concludes with a consolidating marriage to his childhood sweetheart). Though this two-part narrative is not one of Cooper's stronger works, its relative clarity and its brightness of spirit contrast instructively with the dark convolution of its earlier-written counterpart.

Works like *Home as Found* are of enduring interest as examples of a mid-nineteenth-century conservative response to social change. But Cooper was at his best as a novelist when the political and social issues of his work recede into the background of his narratives, and, more particularly, when these issues find implicit expression in action and setting. This lesson is especially apparent in one interesting and important series written in the 1840s, the Littlepage trilogy. Cooper's purpose here was to trace through American history the events that had led to the antirent controversy of New York State in the 1840s (in which landed families were threatened with dispossession of their estates by long-term tenants). The first novel in the series, *Satanstoe* (1845), is one of Cooper's most compelling works: it narrates through the first-person voice of its appealing hero, Cornelius Littlepage, the events surrounding the Littlepage family's claiming of a patent in the northern wilderness of colonial New York. The novel is filled with richly drawn images of colonial life, including one of the most memorable scenes in all of Cooper's fiction: Cornelius's rescue of his future wife, Anneke Mordaunt, from a terrifying upheaval of ice on the Hudson River. Absent from this work is the intrusive authorial voice the reader hears in several of Cooper's other social novels. In part the historical distance of the setting accounts for this, but more important is the fact that Cooper knew he had two more novels in which to make his overt case against antirentism. The imaginative freedom that this knowledge gave him results in one of the writer's most beautifully crafted works of fiction.

In the second novel in the series, *The Chainbearer* (1845), Cooper follows the fortunes of the Littlepage family into the immediate post-Revolutionary war period. The narrator is Mordaunt Littlepage, the only surviving son of Cornelius and Anneke, who has the responsibility of subdividing two extensive portions of the family's northern patents. In what has now become an area of settlement (the historical period is the same as that of *The Pioneers*), Mordaunt discovers the beginnings of conflict between landed ownership and tenantry. The conflict is dramatized principally by the actions of two symbolic characters: the Chainbearer (Andries Coejemans), whose occupation as a layer of boundary lines represents the establishment of order and the preservation of historical claims, and Thousandacres (Aaron Timberman), a squatter from Vermont who illegally timbers the Littlepage forests with reckless abandon. Jason Newcome, a Yankee land agent who in *Satanstoe* had been a merely comic figure, purchases the lumber from Thousandacres, and in his secret manipulations Cooper anticipates the greatest future threat to the landed gentry. The strength of *The Chainbearer* is the credibility of these representational characters, the way in which Cooper has found in them appropriate symbolic vehicles for his ideas. (Its success in these terms makes it analogous to Cooper's last novel, *The Ways of the*

Hour [1850], which effectively uses the focused setting of a murder trial to explore the excesses and confusion of American social life at mid-century.)

In the final novel of the Littlepage trilogy, *The Redskins* (1846), Cooper brings his historical drama into the present. Ro Littlepage (the second son of Mordaunt) and his nephew Hugh return to America from their travels in the Middle East and discover that the long-developing conflict between owners and renters has erupted into open warfare. Disguising themselves as Indians (the "redskins" of the novel's ironic title), the antirent forces threaten the physical destruction of the Littlepage estate (significantly, real Indians, led by the ancient Susquesus, help the Littlepages defend their holdings). As Cooper looks straight at these vigilante actions of his own time, his anger comes to the surface and the result is a stridently polemical novel almost as confusing as *Home as Found*. The historical charm of *Satanstoe* and the effectively rendered symbolism of *The Chainbearer* give way to pure, frenzied didacticism.

Taken as a whole, however, the Littlepage trilogy must be seen as one of Cooper's most coherent and sustained fictional treatments of American life. It ranks very near the top of the writer's achievement. But, as Cooper himself knew, the works for which he would be best remembered are not the Littlepage novels but the Leatherstocking tales. Unlike the Littlepage trilogy, these tales were not preconceived as a series, and the Leatherstocking hero was not born out of a carefully conceived program for the analysis of American social life. Natty Bumppo's mournful attitude toward the passing of the wilderness gives him a distinctive and important role in *The Pioneers*, but from another point of view he is only one more of Templeton's frontier "characters"; his presence is needed to fill out the broad spectrum of humanity that the writer wishes to present in his first settlement novel. When Cooper took up his Leatherstocking figure again in *The Last of the Mohicans*, returning him to middle age as a tracker and warrior, he was clearly beginning to have a sense of a developing saga and of a legendary American hero. Yet, as we saw earlier, the Leatherstocking of this novel is not at the center of its action. His powers have begun to diminish, and he functions primarily as a guide in both a literal and a symbolic sense—directing his white and red companions along the paths of their polar destinies.

In *The Prairie*, Natty finally emerges as a fully mythic figure; indeed, Cooper virtually apotheosizes him in the scene depicting his death in America's far West. Everything about this third Leatherstocking tale is larger than life; Natty himself first appears in the novel imaged gigantically (through an optical illusion) against the setting sun, and it is clear that Cooper removed his hero from the forests of New York State to the prairie so that he might draw the nation's westward movement in great, broad strokes. But while *The Prairie* turns away from the realism of the first two Leatherstocking tales toward a more mythic and legendary treatment, in other important ways this novel is continuous with *The Pioneers* and *Mohicans*. It can be said to recapitulate and extend the issues of these earlier works. For example, in Dr. Obed Bat we have an extreme case of narrow self-interest of the kind that Cooper criticized in figures like Richard Jones in *The Pioneers*. Bat is a natural scientist with astonishingly bad judgment whose observations of phenomena are totally shaped by his narrow preconceptions. And while *The Pioneers* depicts a frontier settlement in which law is sometimes arbitrary, *The Prairie* describes a Western wilderness in which the only law is the law of the powerful—a point strikingly dramatized by Ishmael Bush's execution of his brother-in-law, Abiram White. In his menacing violence, Bush represents a threat to the American future, and in the novel's vast, barren setting we find an analogous warning: Natty sees this environment as a silent, visual prophecy of what the Eastern forests will become if ecological destruction proceeds without restraint.

Like *Mohicans*, *The Prairie* has its good Indians (the Pawnees) and its bad (the Sioux), and the fundamental point is the same as in the earlier novel: both tribes have been displaced by the encroachments of white civilization, and their violence (most vividly depicted in the raging prairie fire set by the Sioux) is a response to displacement. Finally, the redemptive marriage of *The Pioneers* is recapitulated in the union of Captain Duncan Uncas Middleton and Inez Augustin de Certevallos (who has been kidnapped by Abiram White), and here too Cooper broadens his symbolic meaning. Inez is of Spanish Catholic descent, and Middleton—the grandson of Duncan Heyward and Alice Munro of *Mohicans*—represents an established American family. Cooper thus symbolically joins the Old World of southern Europe out of which America had its beginnings to a new, emerging American identity. This process of reconciliation of past and present is dramatized by the novel's procedures, for *The Prairie* takes explicit account of developments in the two previous Leatherstocking tales—especially through Natty's memories of his life in the Eastern forests. The result is a very strong sense of an ending: with its hero delivered from his humble beginnings as an aged hunter in *The Pioneers* to a mythic death in *The Prairie*, the Leatherstocking saga seemed complete.

Thirteen years after the publication of *The Prairie*, however, Natty Bumppo returned to life in *The Pathfinder* (1840) and *The Deerslayer* (1841). His rebirth owes partly to public demand; Natty had been by far Cooper's most pop-

ular fictional character. Having fallen into the deep disfavor of his readership in the 1830s, the writer must have hoped that his resumption of the
Leatherstocking tales would restore his reputation as the greatest novelist
of his generation. But the quality of these two last-written tales suggests
another, deeper reason. Because Cooper's imagination was primarily and
distinctively visual—he was a kindred spirit of the Hudson River School of
artists—his landscapes are always the surest index of the moral climate of
his works. And we find in these final Leatherstocking novels a virgin wilderness of strong pastoral definition whose landscapes differ significantly
from the threatened forests of *The Pioneers*, the broken and difficult terrain
of *Mohicans*, and the barren plains of *The Prairie*. In part, this difference
reflects the writer's European travels, which had interceded between the
earlier- and later-written tales. As his travel books make clear, Cooper had
absorbed from Europe's parks and gardens a more refined sense of space,
which informs all his late wilderness novels, from *The Pathfinder* to *The Oak
Openings*.

Yet the more fundamental reason for the late tales' altered quality is suggested by the sense of retreat they communicate. In these works, Cooper
seems to turn his back on the troubled present and to seek in the distant
past a simpler and more attractive world (the same can be said of the contemporaneous *Wing-and-Wing* [1842], a romantic sea tale set in the Mediter-
ranean during the Napoleonic Wars). The full significance of this sense of
retreat is best revealed by comparing *The Pathfinder* to the earlier *Mohicans*,
for on the surface these works have much in common. They share the same
general setting—the wilderness of colonial New York during the French
and Indian Wars (the action of *The Pathfinder* is centered on the waters and
southern shore of Lake Ontario, where Cooper had been stationed during
the final stages of his Navy enlistment). Like *Mohicans*, *The Pathfinder* takes
up the Leatherstocking hero's career in his early middle age, and its essential elements of character and plot follow closely those of the earlier novel.
It begins, for example, with the heroine's wilderness journey—disrupted
by a duplicitous Indian guide—to an outpost where her father is stationed.
And both works dramatize vividly a savage, climatic Indian assault on English defenses. Yet, for all its scenes of frontier warfare, *The Pathfinder* does
not communicate the sense of violent historical turbulence that characterizes
Mohicans. In part, this is the result of the novel's pervasively pastoral landscape. But more important is the prominence and mediating effect of its
love theme. Where Natty Bumppo had been in *Mohicans* a stoic figure of
fierce independence, fully suited to the violent world of that novel, here,
for the first time in the Leatherstocking tales, he falls in love.

The love theme of *The Pathfinder* has large significance, for its shows Cooper attempting to reconcile what had by 1840 become for him (and for his culture as well) a polarized vision: on the one hand an Adamic myth of pure wilderness freedom and on the other an ethos of domesticity. *The Pathfinder* is the work in which the novelist experiments with a merging of these visions. Natty confesses to Mabel Dunham (whose father has encouraged her to marry Leatherstocking) that his love for her has replaced his former pleasures of wilderness adventure. His solution is to imagine a life with Mabel in a cabin situated deep in the forest, thus joining imaginatively his dream of forest seclusion to one of happy domesticity. But *The Pathfinder* ultimately shows this to be an impossible dream. Mabel has fallen in love with Natty's young companion, Jasper Western, and recognizing this, Leatherstocking relinquishes her, returning heartbroken to the forest with his Indian companion Chingachgook.

In a retrospective view, we learn that Jasper and Mabel make their married life in New York City where Jasper becomes a successful merchant. Thus the novel sharply divides adventure from domesticity and, implicitly, the nation's Edenic, natural past from its complex, urban future. As the penultimate chapter's Miltonic portrait of the couple suggests, theirs is a (necessarily) fallen world. Natty's return to a celibate life of wilderness adventure can be seen, in this light, as a gesture of acknowledgment on Cooper's part; by denying marriage to his hero, he accepts the impossibility of wedding America's Edenic past to the historical realities of the present. Yet, paradoxically, Leatherstocking's return to the forest also signals the author's increasingly intense imaginative commitment to the past. Finally, Natty Bumppo cannot marry because he is the writer's one permanent link to that valued past and to the privileged world of his own childhood memory with which he associated it.

It is in just this way that *The Pathfinder* prepares for *The Deerslayer*, for in the last-written of the tales Cooper returns literally to the world of his childhood—Lake Otsego and its surrounding wilderness—but in a period long before the writer himself could have known it firsthand. Taking his hero back to his beginnings as an uninitiated youth, he creates a world so isolated in time and space that it is virtually immune to the forces of history. Like previous Leatherstocking tales, this one has its share of bloody combat, and it includes plunderers of the kind we have seen repeatedly in Cooper's other works: the racist and bullying Harry March and the corrupt Thomas Hutter. Yet the power of these characters is contained by the setting itself, which in its isolation and immensity overwhelms them.

Corresponding to the focused centrality of *The Deerslayer*'s setting is its treatment of its hero, Leatherstocking; in this environment he comes to the absolute center of the novel's stage. In each of the previous Leatherstocking tales, he had shared that stage with a conventional hero who represents civilization's values and interests. The class status of this hero diminishes considerably in *The Pathfinder*'s Jasper Western, and in *The Deerslayer* he drops out altogether. Now the reader's singular focus of attention becomes Natty himself—his great courage (dramatized by his refusal to yield to the Hurons' torture) and his extraordinary skill with a rifle. No longer a disappointed lover, as he had been in *The Pathfinder*, Leatherstocking is now beloved—by the beautiful Judith Hutter. He cannot marry Judith, of course, because this novel asserts unequivocally that the forest is his bride; but the fact that he is the object of love confirms his central role in the narrative.

The setting of Natty's exploits in *The Deerslayer* is the same as that of *The Pioneers*, yet at a point in the past (1740) long before the intrusion of Judge Temple and his settlers and at an even farther remove from the beleaguered world of Templeton represented in *Home as Found*. The "home" as Cooper imagines it here is a profoundly better one than that described in *The Pioneers*. In that work, Cooper repossessed in imagination the actual world of his childhood in Cooperstown, depicting not only the charm of that remembered setting but also its more troubling features (social change and ecological destruction). As an autobiographical novel *The Pioneers* has its implicit obligations to historical truth. But *The Deerslayer* restores a world that existed prior to Cooper's personal history and that is transpersonal in nature. It is a world created rather than remembered, a creation, as Lawrence recognized, of wish-fulfillment. By removing Otsego to a point in the past where, in its spatial and temporal remoteness, it lies safely beyond the reach of anyone's palpable possession, Cooper was able to take full imaginative possession of it for himself and for his readers. He thus took back his cherished lake in the only way that, by 1840, was possible for him: by transforming it from Otsego to Glimmerglass.

It is exactly in this transformation of an autobiographical into a mythic element that Cooper's greatest power as a novelist lies. *The Deerslayer* shows vividly how at times his work answers profoundly to nineteenth-century America's deepest sense of itself as nature's nation. This is the yearning myth that Lawrence located in the Leatherstocking tales; in these tales, Cooper worked out the terms of this myth and explored its inherent conflicts more fully than any writer of his generation. But, as we have seen, his modern reputation does not rest on the Leatherstocking tales alone. In fact, we are only now beginning to take the full measure of this writer's prodigious and complex achievement. As we follow the career, we discover not only its thirty-two novels but also major works of social and political criticism, travel books, shorter fiction, and even an authoritative history of the U.S. Navy (1839). And among the novels we find an extraordinary number of initiations: nautical fiction (Melville and Conrad both expressed their indebtedness to Cooper), the international novel, distinctively American forms of the novel of manners and of allegorical fiction, and, of course, the western.

While a canon of this size is necessarily uneven (there is little, for example, to recommend Cooper's drearily overextended story of Columbus's discovery of America, *Mercedes of Castile* [1840]), it in fact includes few outright disasters. That Cooper's fiction is a more finished and coherent body of work than has previously been assumed is supported by modern scholarship; we have learned, for example, that he did, after all, give himself to studied revision of at least some of his works. Yet it remains true that he was no deliberate craftsman of fiction in the way that Hawthorne or Poe were; he lacked their critical sophistication and in fact was little interested in literary criticism as such. Yet what he lacked in sophistication he made up for plentifully in imagination, energy, and an extraordinary gift for storytelling. And, as we have seen, his greatest contribution to American literature is his haunting articulation of an enduring myth of our culture.

H. Daniel Peck

Edgar Allan Poe and the Writers of the Old South

One of the most striking features of Southern literature is the contrast between writing of the late nineteenth and the twentieth century and that of the long preceding era. Before the war between the states, despite a powerful cultural construct informed by mythic significance, only one major national writer, Edgar Allan Poe, emerged from the "Old South." This judgment is not merely a modern one. Antebellum Southern magazinists and publishers continually decried the dearth of Southern literature compared with that of the North, increasingly so as tensions mounted toward 1861. Southern culture, they protested, refused to support a regional literature. Yet they were convinced that the South possessed a "slumbering genius" that needed only to be awakened.

Southern concern for a unique Southern literature has been traced by scholars in the most famous of the magazines of the Old South, the *Southern Literary Messenger*. The significance of the *Messenger* comes partly from its association with Poe, who contributed poems, stories, and hundreds of reviews to its pages and increased its circulation sixfold in his brief period of editorship from 1835 to 1837. As the most enduring of Southern magazines (1834–64), the *Messenger* also reflects the shift away from cultural accommodation with the North. In its early years, it actively sought contributions from Northern writers and maintained a moderating position on Northern and Southern differences and on the issue of slavery. Its pages featured certain insistent themes: the beauty of the Southern landscape; the history of idealism and chivalry in the Southern people; the rightness of Southern institutions. Another major theme appeared early: the need for a professional class of men of letters to awaken the genius of the South. But the magazinists overestimated the desire of Southerners for their own press. Literary magazines in the South died young; books published in the South did not sell.

Over the decade of the 1830s the theme of the rightness of Southern institutions became more persistently linked with a conviction of the wrongness of the North. By 1841 the mild proslavery stance of the *Messenger* had given way to the idea of defending Southern rights and interests. The decade of the 1850s saw repeated complaints about the lack of patronage and payment for professional writers along with exhortations to Southern writers to defend the "identify" of their region.

The career of the *Messenger* replicates in little the germination of separatism in the South, seemingly present from the beginning. The justification of slavery in a class-conscious hierarchical system sanctioned by late medieval and Renaissance visions of world order runs a parallel course with visions of autonomy. As in the North, the idea of the New World was from the first charged with significance in the South: here was the world garden, the golden land of plenty. But whereas the Puritans sought by their "errand" into the wilderness to create an exemplary "City upon a Hill," colonists in the South developed a vaguely medieval culture based on a mythologized glorification of feudal organization. This new culture was led, not by God-fearing divines, but by knights and cavaliers along a more worldly providential plan. The mythos of the separate "southern Country," with the planter class the natural leaders, lay just under the surface during the years of the Revolution and the early republic; from these seeds the figure of the cavalier "Southern gentlemen" grew steadily as a counter to the image of the Northern money-making "Yankee."

Intellectually, the great Southern mythos was informed by permutations of the Great Chain of Being. Economically, the established families were becoming dependent on a single crop requiring a large and cheap labor force; this conjunction solidified a theory of the natural gradation of all existence as a metaphysical justification for slavery and its ultimate benevolence. At first, the "southern Country" was not so unified as the myth suggests (South Carolina and Georgia were especially critical of the new American union under Virginian dominance); but when the North began in the nineteenth century to harass the slaveholding states, the South became more closely knit. After the Missouri Compromise of 1820 effected a balance of slave and free states, the abolitionist movement in the North became more vociferous. As it did, moderate Southern writers fell quiet, and the "literary" defense of the South as a separate culture intensified.

Yet the final exasperated calls for a uniquely Southern literature in the

Messenger and other magazines strike a note of defensiveness. One can feel a frustrated sense of irony over the fact that the progeny of the early Puritans should have developed an art and literature seemingly superior to that of the descendants of noble adventurers and cavaliers with a vigorous literary tradition in England. Perhaps a more notable historical irony is that the one original voice out of the Old South is that of a writer whose "Southernness" is suspect—that of Poe.

Edgar Allan Poe and the historical romancer William Gilmore Simms are the two most important figures of the literature of the Old South. But unlike the works of Simms, whose settings, characters, and themes are centrally Southern, few of Poe's works feature Southern locales and characters, and virtually none has distinctive Southern themes. In his reviews of Southern authors, Poe usually ignored or played down the Southern element. Throughout his career, he fought for an honest, independent criticism and sought to create a literary magazine free of regional bias. In review after review, he strove to be impartial while attacking what he saw as the corrupt relationship among publishers, magazines, and reviewers. He was not totally successful, for he too got caught up in literary warfare and gamesmanship. Poe's driving ambition, partially imbibed from the literary situation of the South, was to become what the Southern literary leaders said they wanted—a genuine professional. But, for Poe, that meant that he could not be merely Southern in his views. Although concerned for a native American literature, Poe saw the proper stage for the professional man of letters as, not the South, nor even America, but the world.

In contrast to Poe, the typical nineteenth-century Southern writer was regional in focus. The important literature of the nineteenth-century South took four basic forms: nature lyrics on the Southern landscape; collections of framed sketches of backwoods character types; episodic novels or linked sketches on the model of the epic historical romance; and romantic-satiric narrations of idyllic plantation life. The major influences in poetry were the eighteenth-century British poets and the first generation of romantic poets, and in fiction the somewhat unlikely combination of Henry Fielding, Sir Walter Scott, and Washington Irving.

In poetry, the Old South was less fortunate than in fiction. Samuel Kettell, in his three-volume *Specimens of American Poetry* (1829), included only one Southern poet, St. George Tucker. Most Southern poets of the period, by common critical assent, are flatly imitative of British models and overly concerned (like Poe) with metrics and sonorous effects. Other than Poe, only two Southern poets are much remembered, Paul Hamilton Hayne and

Henry Timrod, the latter known as "the Poet Laureate of the Confederacy." Much of their work appeared only after the war. Timrod and Hayne both responded to the call for a Southern man of letters, although both were balked by circumstances. When Charleston, South Carolina, was burned by Northern troops, Hayne retreated to the pine barrens near Augusta, Georgia, where he built with his own hands a "shanty" for his family. There he spent the rest of his life trying to earn money by "literary craft" alone. He managed to write a large number of poems celebrating the Southern environment, most of them conventional and sentimental.

Timrod published one volume of poems (1859) but later became discouraged when the efforts of friends to publish a second came to nothing. It was only after his death that another volume appeared (1873), edited by his lifelong friend, Hayne. It is instructive to compare Timrod's early poems on the eve of the war with those in the middle years and after. "Ethnogenesis" (written 1861; published 1873), a poem upon the occasion of the meeting of the first Southern Congress, fuses nature imagery with a visionary evocation of the new republic of the South. "The Cotton Boll" (1861; 1873) asserts the coming of a final victory for the South that will make all the suffering worthwhile. Two years later, in "The Unknown Dead" (1863; 1873), Timrod conjoins the desire to read a storm as the skies' weeping for the martyred Southern patriots with the seeming indifference of "Nature's self." In "Ode Sung on the Occasion of Decorating of the Confederate Dead, at Magnolia Cemetery" (1866; 1873), he writes that even though no marble column marks the spot, the seeds of flowers in the park are garlands of fame to come, for "somewhere, waiting for its birth,/ The shaft is in the stone." Even in the midst of defeat, the Southern mythos endures: the South will rise again when a new Arthur pulls the sword from the stone.

Of the more minor figures, only James Mathewes Legaré and Thomas Holley Chivers need be mentioned. The former is known for one slender volume, *Orta-Undis* (1848). The latter owes what modern reputation he retains to his association with Poe, who called him one of the best and at the same time one of the worst poets in America. Of his volumes published before the war, Chivers's *The Lost Pleiad* (1845) and *The Eonchs of Ruby* (1851) contain works that feature refrains, phrasings, and names similar to those of Poe's "The Raven" (1845) and other poems. Chivers claimed that the works in question were written before "The Raven," but each poet, over the years, was accused of plagiarizing from the other.

The second important literary form, the framed and linked sketches and tales of the frontier settlements, constitutes one of the highwater marks of the literature of the Old South. Not all of the "Old Southwestern humorists" were born in the South. Among those who were, the most interesting are Augustus Baldwin Longstreet, David Crockett, Johnson J. Hooper, Joseph Glover Baldwin, and Henry Clay Lewis. Noteworthy for its focus on the Southern element, Longstreet's *Georgia Scenes* (1835) is the only volume of Old Southwest humor Poe reviewed. Poe remarks that Longstreet is "imbued with a spirit of truest humor" and possesses a "penetrating understanding of *character* in general, and of Southern character in particular." He suggests that the book would make the author's fortune in England and that proper judges in America would see its merit, too—if they would sift its "particular merits from amid the *gaucheries* of a Southern publication."

The other two major forms of the literature of the Old South, the plantation idyll and the historical romance, are closely related in theme, situation, and character types. These works sometimes took the form of linked sketches or letters, sometimes conformed to a main plot line with subplots, sometimes were a mix. Although the works were not unreservedly in favor of Southern institutions, the issues of feudalism and slavery were central, and the separatist sentiment shows a steady development. The sense of a separate "manifest destiny" is hinted at as early as *Letters of the British Spy* (1803) by William Wirt, in which a pattern typical of many a Southern narrative is set. As in the volumes of Old Southwest humor, an outsider visits a Southern locale; here an Englishman writes home from Virginia his impressions of the Southern landscape and of Southern ideals and manners.

In later versions of this form, a central device is a debate between the outsider and the planter aristocrat over Southern institutions. In *The Valley of Shenandoah* (1824), for example, George Tucker presents a Yankee visitor in conflict with a Southern plantation owner fallen in fortune. The two have discussions in which the Southern hero "defends" slavery and the feudal system while admitting gross injustices. Later, the Northerner stabs the Southerner to death in New York in a quarrel over a woman, is eventually exposed as a seducer and scoundrel, and dies a drunkard. Tucker, professor of moral philosophy and economics at the newly established University of Virginia, is one of the more interesting figures of the Old South. It is possible, for example, that he may have had a hand in the anonymous *Letters from Virginia* (1816), which condemns slavery and ridicules the planters. He wrote several economic treatises (in one of which he predicted the death of slavery by 1925 for economic reasons), a biography of Jefferson, lectures on rhetoric and belles lettres, and a satiric romance, *A Voyage to the Moon* (1827), which Poe, as his student at the university, seems to have read.

The long historical romance of the pre-Revolutionary and Revolutionary South, at the center of which is a knightly hero leading his companions to a present glory that implies a more glorious future, reached its height from the 1830s through the 1850s. Sir Walter Scott's *Waverley* novels, beginning in 1814, captured the imagination of the literary South, resonating as they did with the cavalier mythos. The Scott influence extended from John Pendleton Kennedy and William A. Caruthers in the 1830s to Philip Pendleton Cooke, who published several novellas and stories in the *Messenger* from 1848 to 1851, and his brother John Esten Cooke, whose *The Virginia Comedians* (1854) develops a somewhat different mode for the Southern romance. Cooke presents a tension between the old order and a new democratic sensibility, portraying the common man as more innately noble than the planter aristocrat; but he finds republican strength in the merging of the two classes (through, for example, marriage). Similar themes are found in his romance of the great-grandson of Pocahontas, *Henry St. John, Gentleman* (1859).

In the 1830s, John Pendleton Kennedy made use of both the plantation idyll and the cavalier romance in three novels set in the South prior to the nineteenth century. *Swallow Barn* (1832), like his earlier *Red-Book* (1818–19), shows the strong influence of Washington Irving in its linked sketches and humorous tone. A New Yorker visits the plantation of his Virginia cousin and finds that his Northern assumptions about the South are not entirely accurate. The Southern planter agrees that slavery is wrong but maintains that to free the slaves immediately would be to leave them in a deplorable condition. Although there are evocations of the beauty of the landscape and of the historical mythos from Pocahontas on, the book is also satiric in its descriptions of plantation life. Whereas in *Rob of the Bowl* (1838) Kennedy deals satirically with political and religious strife in seventeenth-century Maryland, in *Horse-Shoe Robinson* (1835) he depicts the Tory ascension in South Carolina during the Revolution by means of a series of adventures based on those of an actual partisan. In a review in 1835, Poe remarked that "the novelist has been peculiarly fortunate in the choice of an epoch, a scene and a subject," but he makes no specific Southern reference.

In 1836, Nathaniel Beverly Tucker published two novels partaking of the conventions of the historical romance. *George Balcombe*, while condoning slavery, idealizing the planter aristocracy, and defending states' rights, has as its basic frame and plot a Godwinian mystery involving the recovery of a will. Reviewing the novel in 1837, Poe observes merely that the action covers the territory from Missouri to Virginia before turning his attention to matters of plot and structure. *The Partisan Leader: A Tale of the Future* bears the fictive publication date 1856 and projects the reader to the year 1849, when Martin Van Buren is about to run for a fourth term as president. The South has seceded without armed conflict; but Virginia, caught in the geographic middle, is in danger of being subverted by Northern agents. The polemics are shrill, but the conclusion is elliptical, merely implying the ultimate victory of the partisans, and, of course, in 1836, sounding the alarm.

In the 1830s and 1840s, William Alexander Caruthers published three books in the mode of the plantation idyll and cavalier romance. *The Kentuckian in New York* (1834) is an epistolary fiction in which two South Carolinians and a Kentuckian visiting New York correspond with a Virginian visiting South Carolina. *The Cavaliers of Virginia* (1835) and *The Knights of the Golden Horse-Shoe* (serialized 1841; book publication 1845) are notable for their mythic glorification of Virginia. Whereas *The Kentuckian* incorporates the idea that sectional differences can be resolved, the other two works embody an idea of "manifest destiny" for Virginia. The historical basis of *The Cavaliers*, for example, is Bacon's Rebellion in 1676. Nathaniel Bacon is portrayed as the defender of individual liberty and of the rights of the colony of Virginia against enemies both without and within. *The Knights* is cast as an American quest romance on the theme of the destiny of Virginia to expand westward. Its historical basis is the 1716 expedition of Alexander Spotswood, lieutenant governor of the colony, into the Valley of Virginia and to the Great Lakes. For Caruthers the destiny of American empire would seem to lie with Virginia.

William Gilmore Simms, of Charleston, South Carolina, on the contrary, portrayed his own state as the locus of Southern destiny. In his early days, he was, like Kennedy, pro-unionist; but Simms gradually became vehemently separatist. As a professional writer (with over eighty volumes of poetry, fiction, drama, biography, history, geography, speeches, essays, criticism) whose main theme was the South, he was exactly what the Southern editors had called for. Ironically, he was generally ignored in the South (except by Poe) and thus was dependent on readers in the North, who saw him as "the Southern Cooper." Simms began his career as a novelist with a tale of crime, *Martin Faber* (1833), which Poe found attractive. In 1834–35, Simms published three historical romances, *Guy Rivers*, *The Yemassee*, and *The Partisan*. The last is the first volume of what came to be a seven-volume "epic saga" of the Revolution. Twenty-five years in the making, the saga covers three periods from the seventeenth to the nineteenth century: the "heroic" colonial period; the strife-torn Revolutionary period; and the "border" period of expansion westward and establishment of the new order of the present as the Southern Country.

In marked contrast to the ideas of Simms and the other writers mentioned above, Poe's conception of letters is virtually devoid of regionalist sentiment. Only once in nearly one thousand reviews, articles, columns, and critical notices written over a fifteen-year period does Poe let the issue of Southernness get the better of a purely literary judgment; and the brief flash of Southern temper is revealing—in its very singularity—of Poe's conception of the profession of letters. Moreover, this review of James Russell Lowell's *A Fable for Critics* (1849) is the only instance of Poe's taking any kind of stand on the issue of slavery. (The notorious review of two books defending slavery in the *Messenger* in 1836, upon which some critical interpretations of Poe's *Narrative of Arthur Gordon Pym* have been based, was written not by Poe but in all likelihood by Beverly Tucker.) With this single exception, aside from an occasional comment that something promises better days for Southern letters, Poe does not campaign for a Southern literature. It is American literature on the world stage that is important to him.

Yet the question of Poe's Southernness is one of recurrent critical debate. Among his supposed Southern qualities are a high formalism of prose style, an idealization of women, a scorn for democracy and the idea of progress, and an uneasiness about the age of the machine. In addition, the Southern writer, like Poe, is supposedly preoccupied with death and fatality and addicted to the modes of the Gothic and the grotesque. Such elements, of course, do not bear up as specifically Southern. Many of them can be found in the work of Hawthorne, Melville, and other Northern writers. Moreover, Poe is not consistent in using them. His style is not always formal but frequently colloquial and humorous. His distrust of progress and criticism of abstract system are counterpointed by a fascination with physical science and mathematics. His book-length "philosophical" treatise, *Eureka* (1848), attempts a universal system of cosmology, embodying a concept of "progress" toward godhead, but it begins with the basic proposition that ultimate annihilation is fundamentally inherent in existence.

Whether or not the above qualities constitute Southern themes, or consistent themes in Poe, the point is that as a highly conscious man of letters Poe modifies theme and mode from an almost exclusively aesthetic concern for a particular effect. His portrayal of women, for example, depends on his literary objective. In one work he will use the image of a woman as a Hellenic statue in a window-niche, holding a lamp, symbol of the ideal ("To Helen"). In others, he will picture a woman as cadaverous and feverish ("The Fall of the House of Usher," "Metzengerstein"), as the siren temptress of neurasthenic man ("Ligeia"), or as vapid and absurd ("How to Write a Blackwood Article"). His idealization of women in certain poems and essays ("The Poetic Principle") is counterpointed in fiction by female characters who are subjected to violent physical assault ("The Murders in the

Rue Morgue," "The Black Cat"). In one work, the beauty of nature may be enhanced by the intervention of the human will ("The Domain of Arnheim"); in others, nature is sublimely destructive ("A Descent into the Maelström") or paradoxical (*The Narrative of Arthur Gordon Pym*). As a professional writer, Poe fashions his materials for a literary end in each text.

There are, of course, pervasive and habitual features to Poe's work. An obsession with death and a predisposition to violence, perversity, and madness are among the traits familiar to every reader. Even in his obsession with dark forces, however, Poe exploits the contemporary taste for the Gothic and the grotesque.

Poe began his career as a poet, emulating Byron, Shelley, and Thomas Moore. In his early "nature" lyrics he employs an "indefinitive" imagery and diction rather than the beauties of a Southern landscape; he thereby reaches toward a visionary state of "supernal beauty" evoked by the manipulation of sound and rhythm and, increasingly, by incantatory repetition. His first volume was the slender *Tamerlane and Other Poems* (1827). The longish title poem casts the Mongol conqueror as a prideful and tormented spirit brooding over his worldly ambition and lost love. The tone recalls Byronic world-weariness; the imagery of dreams and distant stars, mist and night, suggests a theme of infinite regress consequent to a dimming of perception. The nine shorter lyrics recur to the same images and themes. In his second volume, *Al Aaraaf, Tamerlane, and Minor Poems* (1829), Poe added to the first collection the title poem and a half-dozen shorter works, one of which stands as an introduction to "Al Aaraaf." The speaker of "Sonnet—to Science" laments the passing of ancient poetic myths before the encroachments of science; but he reembodies their poetic legacy by invoking Diana, the Hamadryad, and the Naiad. Al Aaraaf is a distant star world where "nothing earthly" save the reflected ray of "Beauty's eye" is to be found and where imagination has fled from an earth bereft of poetry; the poem begins with an evocation of "supernal beauty" and ends in the destruction of the star.

Poems, Second Edition (1831) contains extensive revisions of the earlier poems along with a handful of new works, some of which feature an ambivalent self-irony. Otherwise, except for the idealized peace restored to the "weary, way-worn wanderer" of "To Helen," the implicit unrest of the first volume and the explicit apocalyptic vision of "Al Aaraaf" in the second volume have come to dominate the third. "The City in the Sea" presents a double picture of doomed Sodom and Gomorrah either visible under the waters or about to sink into their waiting reflections. "The Sleeper" and "The Valley of Unrest" depict bizarre landscapes in which the human world shades into nightmare. The blighted vision of the earthly poet vainly seeking the otherworldly is intensified in "Israfel": the speaker claims that if he could but change places with the star god "a bolder note" might swell from his "lyre within the sky" and that Israfel "might not sing so wildly well—/ A mortal melody." Themes of ruin and apocalypse intensify in several poems of the early 1840s, one of which, "The Coliseum," retains the idea of poetic transcendence found in "Sonnet—to Science." The speaker claims that the former glory of the Roman coliseum is not entirely past; the poet feels it again and re-creates it in his verse. "Dream-Land" returns to the trembling world of "Al Aaraaf," evoking "bottomless vales" and "Mountains toppling evermore/ Into seas without a shore," seas that in turn surge into limitless "lakes of fire."

In a series of essays and reviews from 1831 to the end of his career, Poe tried to develop a poetics of language as a medium of sensuous sound that embodied the idea of the otherworldly. The earliest of these pieces is the preface to *Poems* (1831), the "Letter to B——," in which Poe distinguishes among the aims of poetry, music, and science and concludes that indefinitiveness is the most poetic of effects. These ideas are refined in a number of reviews and developed in such essays as "The Rationale of Verse" (1848) and "The Poetic Principle" (1850). The paradoxical relation between mundane reality and the otherworldly is likewise explored in Poe's *Marginalia* notes on Tennyson (December 1844) and on the "Power of Words" (March 1846). At the same time that Poe sought a visionary spiritual beauty, of course, he emphasized meticulous craftmanship and minute attention to detail. In his later poems, he transforms the dramatic monologue of "Tamerlane" into brooding scenarios constructed around the central issue of unconscious psychological revelation. In "Ulalume," for example, the speaker is warned not to continue his walk down a cypress lane. He persists, however, and comes to the tomb of his beloved Ulalume. Only by forgetting her existence has he repressed his grief during the past year. Now his anguish erupts, like molten lava flowing down an ice-locked volcano, to never-ending remembrance. Although the final stanza is ambiguous, the poem can be read as a study of the compulsive desire to torture oneself.

Such a theme is more clearly, though still ambiguously, embodied in Poe's most famous poem, "The Raven." Anguished by the death of his beloved Lenore, and increasingly aware that the raven can speak only a single word, the narrator compulsively puts questions the answer to which heightens his pain. In "The Philosophy of Composition" (1845), Poe purports to explain the calculated manner in which he constructed this poem, though it is difficult to tell how serious he is. He reiterates his dictum that a conception of overall effect and precise denouement must precede actual writing. The first consideration, he says, was length: for unity of effect the poem must be brief enough to be read at a single sitting. The effect sought in "The Raven" was a sustained tone of melancholy beauty; and the most "poetical" subject linking melancholy and beauty was clearly the death of a beautiful woman. Among the most significant aspects of "The Philosophy of Composition" is Poe's ability to put his general ideas about poetry in the service of a specific strategy for the revelation of character. The lover-narrator enacts "that species of despair which delights in self-torture." He asks the bird questions that will bring him the "luxury of sorrow, through the anticipated answer 'Nevermore.' " An undercurrent of meaning, suggesting the supernatural but not "overstepping the limits of the real," Poe continues, is designed to heighten the effect, so that the reader feels the scene as does the lover, even while maintaining aesthetic distance from the lover's point of view.

In "The Raven" and its attendant essay, we see the central artistic conception of Poe's more complex prose tales: a unified interior drama of the self with a careful balance of real, psychological, and supernatural elements—all of which yields an undercurrent of suggestion and a precise symbolic meaning, for the reader as distinct from the character. In such famous tales as "The Cask of Amontillado" (1845), "Ligeia" (1838), and "The Fall of the House of Usher" (1839), for example, understanding the character of the narrator is a thematic and formal necessity.

Montresor, the narrator of "Amontillado," sets up two conditions for successful revenge in the opening paragraph of his story: the murderer must make himself known as an avenger, and he must get away with impunity. Yet the ironically named Fortunato never understands why Montresor chains him to the cellar wall and bricks him in. Moreover, the Catholic Montresor is telling the story as his deathbed confession to a priest. He has not escaped with impunity; he has carried his guilt buried in his heart for fifty years. The dramatic irony of the tale, the theme of self-torment, the subtle implications of the situation, and the manipulation of conventions (here especially Gothic) are parallel to the technique of "The Raven" and characteristic of Poe's fiction in general.

"Ligeia" and "Usher" are also structured around careful exploitation of point of view. It cannot be proved textually that "Ligeia" is from first to last a rendering of psychotic mental experience from the internal perspective of the narrator, but the text is resonantly indeterminate in its presentation of two radically different interpretations of the described events, a supernatural story and a psychological story. This indeterminateness extends to compatible Freudian and Jungian readings and reveals Poe as strikingly modernist in his fictional conceptions. "The Fall of the House of Usher" takes point of view one step further. A seemingly objective and peripheral narrator appears to confirm the supernatural or preternatural events centered on Roderick Usher. But this conventionally Gothic tale exists within a structure of realistic and psychological explanations of events; the aura of Gothic mystery is not dissolved but held in tension with the other possible readings. The transformation of the reasonable narrator into the fearful double of Usher is accomplished without sacrificing a sense of supernatural mystery. A tour de force in point of view, "Usher" is a logical development from the strategies of "Ligeia."

At an early point Poe conceived of an interrelated sequence of experiments with generic forms of popular literature. One of the first was called "Eleven Tales of the Arabesque." Although what Poe meant by "arabesque" is not fully clear, one thing is certain: he did not mean by the term to distinguish between so-called serious tales of Gothic mystery as "arabesque" and comic-satiric tales of the "grotesque" when he called his 1840 collection *Tales of the Grotesque and the Arabesque*. "Arabesque" was a term then current from Germanic romantic literature; it indicates a form of "romance" embodying a pervasive irony of intent and structure, including self-reflexive self-parody.

The "Eleven Tales of the Arabesque" included the ostensibly serious Gothic tales, "Metzengerstein," "MS. Found in a Bottle," "The Assignation," "Silence," and possibly "Descent into the Maelström." Among the other tales were such blatantly comic and satiric works as "The Duc de L'Omelette," "A Tale of Jerusalem," "Loss of Breath," and "Bon-Bon." The whole series, Poe explained to a potential publisher in 1833, was a burlesque not only of contemporary styles of tale writing but also of current modes of criticism: for the tales were the products of a literary club, and after each author has read his tale, the other members comment upon it, the whole following a carefully determined sequence. Between 1831 and 1835, Poe wrote a preface for the collection, to be expanded and renamed *Tales of the Folio Club*. It was never published as such, though two sheets survive in manuscript. Especially significant for an adequate understanding of Poe's fictional genre is the probable inclusion of "Ligeia" and "The Fall of the House of Usher" among the Folio Club tales, indicating a highly complex and self-reflexive element of parody in these "serious" imitations of popular Gothic tales in the best-selling magazines, like *Blackwood's*.

The word "arabesque" also best describes Poe's puzzling extended work of fiction, *The Narrative of Arthur Gordon Pym* (1837–38). One of the unifying themes of what seems initially a bewildering narrative of a journey to the end of the world is the experience of the inner mind. A perverse fate, augmented by man's own treachery and perverseness, repeatedly overtakes the characters; a series of plot reversals and ironies progressively reveals that the reality of the world is capable of sudden disintegration. The book was launched in the *Messenger* as a hoax, purporting to be a true account of Mr. Pym's adventure as written by Mr. Poe. In its later book publication the hoax was simultaneously continued and subverted. Pym says in the preface that he intends to give the reading public the true account of what actually happened rather than Poe's fictionalizing of his adventures. In addition to this initial ironic frame, the book concludes with an appendix (presumably the "publisher's") in which we are informed that Pym's recent disappearance has prevented him from telling the final truth about what happened and that Poe, the original editor, had failed to see the significance of the narrative.

More than a straightforward journey to the South Pole, Pym's adventures suggest a journey back in time, a quest for origins and ends. But the narrative breaks off; the ultimate secret is not to be found. As suggestively indeterminate as Poe's famous Gothic tales, *Pym* has been read in radically different ways—as an adventure hoax, an experiment in science fiction, an allegory of the dispersed tribes of Israel or of black and white relations in America. Still other interpretations see Pym's journey as a Freudian retreat into the womb, a metaphysical disappearance into void, or an anticipation of *Eureka* in its suggestion that destructiveness abets the creative cycle of the universe. More recently, the book has been seen as an experiment in metafiction that goes beyond the foregrounding of narrativity in the frames. According to this view, *Pym* is an encoding of the artistic process: it is a fiction about fictionality that yields (in the very writing) the creation of the writing self. Despite the astonishing range of readings, what emerges from all the critical attention is that there is in *Pym* a coherent and symmetrical structure of events that generates a haunting ambiguity. Once regarded as an unfinished or a hastily finished mistake, the arabesque romance of *Arthur Gordon Pym* exemplifies Poe's method of resonant indeterminateness and his affinities both with modernism and with postmodernism.

In all this experimentation in fiction, Poe manipulates conventions even as he parodies the literary formulas of the day. Moreover, he resists the coercive cultural politics of nineteenth-century America. As practical critic, Poe exposed shoddy work and literary theft; as practicing journalist, he stood against literary cliques that promoted inferior regional writing, especially those centered on (but not confined to) Northern periodicals. Poe defended not the cause of Southern letters but the American quest for literary independence. Yet, at the same time that he attacked slavish imitation of European models, he opposed the excesses of literary nationalism. Although he was deeply involved in the literary warfare of his time, his driving force was to establish an eminent magazine of letters freed from petty conflict, social prejudice, and the prevailing moral bias of the age. To achieve this, he had to be free both from Northern and from Southern bias, while simultaneously encompassing both traditions—no easy task, but a necessary one given Poe's concept of the professional man of letters.

It was in the South, of course, that Poe first gained recognition as a professional—the fearless critic of the *Southern Literary Messenger*. As part of his campaign for what he called a national "republic" of letters, he attempted to write unbiased assessments of contemporary American literature. At the same time, he wrote essays on the evils of literary regionalism, on literary cliques, on the economics and ethics of publishing, and on the principles of literary criticism. Poe's effort to shape the *Messenger* into his ideal of a literary magazine, however, quickly evoked Southern opposition and interference with his policies. When he moved North, the pattern repeated itself with two projected ventures, the "Penn Magazine" and "The Stylus." The prospectus for "The Stylus" promised "an absolutely independent criticism" guided "by the purest rules of Art," a criticism "aloof from all personal bias" and steadfastly opposed to "the arrogance of organized *cliques*." Poe's magazine would "endeavor to support the general interests of the republic of letters, without reference to particular regions; regarding the world at large as the true audience of the author." The truth as Poe saw it had its costs: neither the "Penn" nor the "Stylus" attracted enough subscribers to go into operation.

Poe is quite consistent in this antiregionalist stand. In 1845, in response to attacks from Boston papers, he published in the *Broadway Journal* a defense of his poetry taken from a South Carolina paper. Although pleased that "friends in the Southern and Western country" are taking up arms for him and that the South apparently sees no "farther necessity for being ridden to death by New-England," he comments that this defense is really "in the cause of a national as distinguished from a sectional literature." But even a national literature was not quite the desideratum. Earlier in the year he had noted the many arguments in favor of maintaining a "proper *nationality* in American Letters; but . . . what this nationality *is*, or what is to be gained by it," he continued, "has never been distinctly understood. That an American should confine himself to American themes, or even prefer them, is rather a political than a literary idea."

Poe's outrage over the politics of publishing manifests itself in his first reviews in a sarcasm that seemed to his contemporaries unnecessarily vicious—though the reviews sold copies of the *Messenger* and called attention to the "tomahawk man" of the South. Poe took dead aim at the Boston and New York literary establishments, especially for their habit of "puffing" the books of friends and colleagues. One of their favorite devices was to announce a new book by an anonymous author of great talent, then to advertise the book in the papers they controlled with a guessing game about his or her identity. As early as 1835, Poe attacked this practice. Noting that the *New York Mirror* had identified the author of *Norman Leslie* as Theodore S. Fay, and that Fay was an editor of the *Mirror*, Poe blasts the novel as the "silliest" book he has ever read—"a monstrous piece of absurdity and incongruity," with an incomprehensible plot and characters that "have no character." But Poe's superlative could be overridden in the face of a more dismal example: reviewing Morris Matson's *Paul Ulric*, another clique-sponsored novel, Poe observes that "when we called Norman Leslie the silliest book in the world we certainly had never seen Paul Ulric." Such books, he asserts, "bring daily discredit upon our national literature."

A few months later, in response to the criticism of his scathing reviews that was being printed in the *New York Mirror* and other Northern papers, Poe prefaced his assessment of the poems of Joseph Rodman Drake and Fitz-Greene Halleck with remarks on "the present state of American criticism." At one time, he says, Americans "cringed to foreign opinion" and would not read an American book without European sanction. But now we have gone too far in the opposite direction: we "often find ourselves involved in the gross paradox of liking a stupid book the better, because, sure enough, its stupidity is American." Praise from personal, regional, or national bias brings no credit to American literature. Only honest and unprejudiced criticism will gain the respect of the world.

A decade later Poe was fighting the same fight. In the March 1845 *Broadway Journal,* he suggests that what is really appreciated by the general public is a "pungent impartially"—witness his having increased the circulation of *Graham's Magazine* from 5,000 to 52,000 in little over two years. As he had ten years before, he asserts that his own practice as critic derives from a "set of principles" and is not the product of a temperament given to habitual faultfinding. Never, he writes, has he rendered an opinion, positive or negative, "without attempting, at least, to give it authority by something that bore the semblance of a reason."

This point of the critic's responsibility to give reasons for his judgments Poe had begun to address three years earlier in "Exordium to Critical Notices." The original concept of a book review, he wrote then, was to "convey a just idea of its design," to "survey the book, to analyze its contents, and to pass judgment upon its merits or defects." But present-day reviewers, hiding behind anonymity and paid by the line, substitute instead a "digest" with "copious extracts" and "random comments." Perhaps worse, the review becomes a pretext for a "diffuse essay" on some other topic. Although Poe admits the value of "a good essay," these generalized effusions, he feels, "have nothing whatsoever to do with . . . *criticism*"; for criticism "is not, we think, an essay, nor a sermon, nor an oration, nor a chapter in history, nor a philosophical speculation, nor a prose-poem, nor an art-novel, nor a dialogue." Criticism is itself an art of high importance, a genre of "clearly ascertained limit," which is "comment on *Art*." The critic's concern is with "*the mode*" of a book: and "it is only *as the book* that we subject it to review." The critic has "nothing to do" with "opinions" of a work except as they relate to the work itself.

Although his critical recognition is marked by strong disagreement over the intrinsic merit of his work, Poe's achievement in poetry and fiction, criticism and magazine journalism, is historically impressive. As a man of letters in a country that was seeking Old World acceptance, Poe tried in his career to unify the many roles of a writer staunch in his independence. In his personal life he was described by his contemporaries as a Southern gentlemen. In his writing, a certain Old Virginian condescension to the "mob" comes through from time to time, an attitude perhaps derived from the Southern mythos of a hierarchical society and cosmos. Otherwise, he conceived of himself as a man of letters on a broader scale, answering the call for a Southern man of letters in his own terms. Rarely does he employ Southern locales or character types; he does not embroil himself in the issue of slavery; he does not address matters of Southern autonomy and separatism; he does not confront Southern with Northern personages; he does not cast Southern leaders as knights in quest of glory. Rather, he focuses on the integrity of the work of art in terms of the ideal—a metaphysical ideal of "pure" poetry, an aesthetic ideal of total unity of effect in both poetry and fiction. These were the true concerns of the true man of letters as Poe conceived the role of the professional writer.

G. R. Thompson

William Cullen Bryant and the Fireside Poets

Reflecting the nineteenth-century passion for gathering specimens and artifacts, anthologies of poetry flourished in young America. Mostly designed for gift presentation or for schoolroom recitation, these collections were intent on validating to a provincial society the existence of a national literary culture. The political and economic independence of the new nation had been achieved; now it was time for American writers to turn to American themes and models. Nationalism was the watchword, patriotic and moral excellence the achieved expectation. Poetic merit and genuine literary value, however, were things the compilers were unable to be so careful about. Still, in the course of time, they predicted these would follow. American singers would arise equal not only to the immortal bards of Europe but also to the promise that was America, both of her glorious and heroic history as well as of the sublimity and majesty of her landscape. Among these collections, Samuel Kettell's *Specimens of American Poetry*, a three-volume work published in 1829, is still valued for the thoroughness of its editor's historical researches. Others, such as John Keese's *The Poets of America: Illustrated by One of Her Painters* and William Cullen Bryant's *Selections from the American Poets*, both of which appeared in 1840, retain distinction either for the beauty of their formats or for the literary authority of their compilers.

By far the most popular of these anthologies, and an excellent index to the poetic tastes and achievements of early nineteenth-century America, is Rufus Griswold's *The Poets and Poetry of America* (1842). Gathered within its nearly six hundred large, quarto-sized pages were extracts from the writings of some hundred and fifty persons, nearly all of them contemporary to the volume's publication. Few of these writers were poets by profession. Law, politics, medicine, journalism were their common occupations; versification, a pastime. Even fewer of these Sunday poets are remembered today. Though able readers in the 1840s might have doubted that the merits of the elder Richard Henry Dana, Fitz-Greene Halleck, or Charles Sprague, whose portraits served as a frontispiece to the volume along with those of William Cullen Bryant and Henry Wadsworth Longfellow, would in time go unnoticed, reviewers of Griswold's anthology did not, on the whole, mismeasure the value of the work it represented. While not all were so unkind as the writer in the *Democratic Review* (1843) who thought that Griswold should have titled his work "The Poets, Poetry, and Poetasters of America," nearly every commentator noticed that the verse Griswold had collected was of vastly uneven quality and that most of the authors represented in the collection would not long trouble the literary world with their momentary impositions and fleeting talents. Typical was the writer in *The North American Review* (1844) who recognized that in every civilized country there are a great many minor poets who possess both "a moderate share of the poetical faculty" and a good deal of "poetical feeling." In the United States, especially, there were a great number of such persons; "the ease with which a moderate skill in versification is acquired, and the copious flood of poetic expression which is poured into the minds of every schoolboy, enables most men of taste and feeling to write what is called respectable poetry with great facility."

The exceptions to this literary malaise in the 1840s were the generally distinctive poetic voices of Bryant and Longfellow, Edgar Allan Poe and Ralph Waldo Emerson, and to a lesser extent John Greenleaf Whittier, Oliver Wendell Holmes, and James Russell Lowell. Poe, through the good fortune of translation and the vagaries of literary history, and Emerson, at least in his theories if not always so successfully in his poetical deeds, have retained without interruption their central places won so early in the tradition of American poetry. The others, however, commonly labeled the Fireside Poets or the Schoolroom Poets, have in recent years increasingly become afterthoughts—though they once seemed secure in the American literary canon. Even their framed, sepia-tinted likenesses that used to hang on schoolroom walls or over the mahogany bookcases of the genteelly elect have faded from the common memory, leaving behind only the superstitions of gray beards and dusty leather bindings. Anthology makers give fewer and fewer pages to their poetry; biographical and critical studies of them and their works are publishing anomalies. Still the echo of the Fireside Poets has somehow survived the benign neglect and active assault that has too commonly been their common share; their minor but real achievement remains a genuine problem for the historian of literature, a challenge for the pedagogue, an annoyance for the fashionable critic. The question that is framed, both by their works and by the memory of their literary days, is that of Robert Frost's "Oven Bird": What can one make of such "a diminished thing?"

Except for Longfellow, none of these men ever fully measured the public worth of his life simply in terms of his poetry. Bryant was a lawyer by profession, and by occupation a journalist of national importance. Editor of the *New York Evening Post* for nearly fifty years, he wielded enormous influence in regard to the civic and political questions of his many days. And his days were many: when he was deep into his seventies he translated the *Iliad* (1870) and the *Odyssey* (1871–72), labors that testify both to his learning and to his desire to bring the classics to readers he had long since made his own. Also a journalist, Whittier dedicated his quiet life to reform movements, which in his view and that of many of his contemporaries would do far more to redeem their age and nation than could ever be effected by the versifier's craft. Lowell, as ardent a reformer in youth as friend Whittier, later won international acclaim for his literary scholarship and practical criticism, and during his term as United States minister to Great Britain did much through the grace of his person and the distinction of his public deeds to heal the wounds that had for too long existed between the two nations. Farthest of all from the purely literary life was the career of Dr. Holmes, for years a hardworking professor of anatomy and physiology at Harvard who carried among the remedies in his medicine bag the laughter and wit of which he so manifestly proved himself a master. Even Longfellow served his apprenticeship in the lecture room at Harvard, and for some years after a fortunate marriage and an unparalleled literary popularity had provided him with a princely independence of means, he still retained his position as Smith Professor of Modern Languages and Belles Lettres at the Cambridge institution.

Such divided loyalties were only in part the result of economic realities. While the patronage provided by a democratic readership never has proven any more predictable than the whimsy of autocratic princes and while few poets in America have ever been able to make their way merely by the flow of their pen, these writers seemed intent on defining their lives by a great variety of enterprise. Perhaps this was owing to that lingering distrust of the imagination that each had to some extent inherited from his common-sense ancestors and that had been reinforced by the utilitarian basis of the American middle-class society of which it seemed so essential to each to be a part. Poets, like preachers, were decidedly of secondary importance in nineteenth-century America; essentially decorative, their roles and acts were part of public ritual, valued and honored only if conducted within the established order. Fortunately for them, none of these writers appear greatly to have wished the situation otherwise. Limited by both talent and temper, they were nonetheless found by their times adequate to their tasks, a measure of their worth that even today should not appear entirely unjustified.

Long before the others had fully realized their powers, William Cullen Bryant defined the character and tone of poetry in America during the early nineteenth century both in his verse and in his criticism. Although Bryant was something of a prodigal, his early popularity, particularly the success that greeted the publication of "Thanatopsis" in 1817, found American readers finally susceptible to those romantic sensibilities that had long ruled literary taste in Europe. "Inscription for the Entrance to a Wood" (1817), "To a Waterfowl" (1818), "To the Fringed Gentian" (1832), "Earth" (1835), "Oh Mother of a Mighty Race" (1847), "The Flood of Years" (1876), among other of his poems, not only won the praise of his literary peers and the reading public but have continued to wear well. Sometimes called "the American Wordsworth," Bryant in his most memorable poems looked to nature and the American landscape for evidence of the divine. Whether it be that "still voice" that speaks to the poet in "Thanatopsis" or those groves that were "God's first temples" in "A Forest Hymn" (1825), his religious naturism was stylish and benign. Romantic critics from the very beginning noted the want of "fire" in his verse, that "very rashness" of a poet who is "overflowing with inspiration." In place of this, one finds restrained lyricism, verse (in the words of Washington Irving) marked by "purity of elevation and refinement of thought, terseness and elegance of diction." Few American poets have excelled Bryant in his description of nature. Drawn though he was to the solitude of the woods, his stoic, melancholy reflections on human mortality and the transience of all things are countered by a liberal faith in the sanctity and benevolence of progress. His thoughts are rarely deep, but they suited remarkably the needs of his generation.

As a writer of political propaganda, John Greenleaf Whittier won praise from only a small, albeit eloquent, group of contemporaries. Active among the abolitionists and other liberal reformers, this gentle Quaker frequently found his fiery emotions strangely at odds with the quiet demeanor dictated by his religious beliefs; still, few of his reform poems have manifested any staying power. Even the masterful "Ichabod" (1850), so perfectly achieved in its tonality and biting irony, barely outlived the memory of Daniel Webster's infamous support of the Compromise of 1850. It is rather as a regional poet who recorded the ways and memories of New England folk life that Whittier won the happy reputation that favored the final decades of his life and made his seventieth-birthday party an occasion for reverence (curdled into embarrassment by Mark Twain's iconoclastic fable about three seedy imposters posing as Longfellow, Emerson, and Holmes). "Snow-Bound" (1866), "Maud Muller" (1854), "Abraham Davenport" (1866), "Skipper Ireson's Ride" (1857), and the "Prelude" to *Among the Hills* (1869) are in their literary way akin to the genre paintings popular at the time, homely, commonplace idylls.

Henry Wadsworth Longfellow, by far the most celebrated of the group, enjoyed a reputation that reached as far as the printed text could travel. His work was translated into every civilized tongue, and no poetry before or since has enjoyed a more loving and uncritical acceptance than that which greeted his verse. The easy regard his work seemed to invite undoubtedly accounts for the disturbing contradictions one finds in Longfellow's poetic life and literary reputation. An extremely learned and cultivated man, he came to represent in the popular literary mind of the early twentieth century the facile mindlessness of Victorian culture in America. Although he was at times a fine lyricist, his best-known work, that verse which most appealed to his hordes of encouraging readers, is banal in its poetic craftsmanship, at times nonsensical in its linguistic and metaphoric incoherence. And underlying what countless readers have found to be his "conscious, cheerful faith" is a melancholy at times hopeless and painfully cognizant of the essential meaninglessness of human endeavor. The author of "The Psalm of Life" (1838), "Excelsior" (1841), and "The Village Blacksmith" (1840) won the praise of his day and the damnation of afterdays, a rejection that has unfortunately all but hidden the poet of "The Tide Rises, the Tide Falls" (1880), "My Lost Youth" (1858), "The Jewish Cemetery at Newport" (1852), "The Cross of Snow" (1879), and several sonnets, especially those he composed on the occasion of his masterful translation of Dante's *Divine Comedy* (1864–67). Along with Irving and the romantic historians of the mid-nineteenth century, Longfellow also helped create in his patriotic verse and historical narratives a national myth that exists apart from his personal reputation, as is evidenced in the common currency of "Paul Revere's Ride" (1860), "The Courtship of Miles Standish" (1858), "Evangeline" (1847), and even "The Song of Hiawatha" (1855). Winston Churchill, a careful student of American culture, well knew the enduring value of Longfellow's popularity with Americans when he greeted the United States on its entrance into World War II with lines from the poet's "Building of the Ship" (1849).

Very few with a talent so limited in range as that of Dr. Oliver Wendell Holmes have managed to use it so splendidly. A social, urbane man of engaging wit and clear-minded intelligence, Holmes published during his long, happy life nearly four hundred poems, the great majority, as he said, written "to order." These occasional poems greeted foreign visitors, dedicated libraries, opened jubilees, entertained the American Medical Association (as well as the National Sanitary Association), celebrated birthdays, and eulogized the dead. Long an admirer of Holmes, Ralph Waldo Emerson found these poems always justified by their "wit, force, and perfect good taste." Holmes's reputation as a writer, however, is founded not on his occasional verse and still less on his three "medicated novels" (of which *Elsie Venner* [1861] is the most intriguing) but on a dozen or so poems written in the comic mode and on two or three religious poems. His comic stance is unmistakable. Never profound, it is instead brilliantly intelligent and refreshing. The careful balance in such poems as "The Last Leaf" (1831) and "My Aunt" (1831) between satirical cruelty and sentimental humor before the pathos of the situations he depicts is remarkably successful. "The Chambered Nautilus" (1858) and the lesser-known but superior poem "Our Limitations" (1850) are examples of Holmes in a more serious but no less effective mood. Together with his *Breakfast Table* books and a handful of essays, these poems reveal him as one of the truly wholesome figures in literature. His writing, done in those spare moments he was happy to steal from his medical practice and the lecture room, was in the fullest sense a social act, an affirmation of the values of civilization as he knew it.

Never enjoying the popularity won by the others, James Russell Lowell was also the least effective in mastering a poetic voice, especially in the lyrical mode. The deficiencies that characterized his work in youth are never entirely absent from his more mature performances: technical infelicities and irregularities, didacticism, muddleheadedness, and excessive literariness. As much aware of his limitations as were his critics, he frequently expressed to friends his misgivings. His reference to the volume of poems *Under the Willows* (1869) as "Under the Billows or dredgings from the Atlantic" is not only a masterful pun (many of the poems had first appeared in the *Atlantic Monthly*) but is very close to the truth. But as a public poet— either in his Pindaric odes or in his satiric verse—Lowell has few equals in American literature. Drawn into the antislavery movement in the early 1840s, he wrote during that decade scores of articles and poems in defense of abolition and other reform causes. His shrewdness and wit found their natural expression in satire, and while his times greatly and rightly praised such poems as "The Present Crisis" (1845) and "On the Capture of Fugitive Slaves near Washington" (1845), it is *The Biglow Papers* (1848) that has endured. Purporting to be the collected verses of Hosea Biglow, a Yankee farmer who is vehemently opposed to the Mexican War, and the prose commentaries of the Reverend Homer Wilbur, the quintessence of what Holmes would later call the Brahmin caste of New England, the book is a wonderful medley of voices and moods, prose and verse, classic English, Yankee speech, and tortured Latin. Some of it is dated, as one would expect of occasional satire, but much is timeless, universal in its depiction of man-kind's matchless venality. Yet the book is an aggressively hopeful, modestly reserved defense of man's ability to control his dreams and destinies.

Though courageous, well-meaning readers have tried, it has proven impos-sible to reclaim the reputation of these poets in terms of modern literary values and current standards of academic taste. Absurdity, irrationality, elliptical compression, multivalences of symbolic meaning, solipsistic ag-ony: such is the coinage honored in the modern literary marketplace. Time will undoubtedly prove this currency as soft as any other that critics have dealt in, perhaps as soft as the pieties that generally ruled at the time the works of the Fireside Poets were celebrated. Theirs was an age that saw no reason to fear sentiment in art. Clarity and even simplicity of expression, good feeling, and hopeful expectations were the virtues celebrated in good writing and right thinking. Typically, Longfellow caught both the spirit and the tone of these poets' popular appeal in these stanzas from his poem "The Day Is Done" (1844):

> Come, read to me some poem,
>   Some simple and heartfelt lay,
> That shall soothe this restless feeling,
>   And banish the thoughts of day.
>
> Not from the grand old masters,
>   Not from the bards sublime,
> Whose distant footsteps echo
>   Through the corridors of Time.
>   . . . .
> Read from some humbler poet,
>   Whose songs gushed from his heart,
> As showers from the clouds of summer,
>   Or tears from the eyelids start;
>
> Who, through long days of labor,
>   And nights devoid of ease,
> Still heard in his soul the music
>   Of wonderful melodies.

Such unabashed sentiment and soft-minded engagement with the problems and powers of literary art are common enough in every age. During the nineteenth century in America, however, they prevailed. The attitude was a comforting one for readers convinced that they were heirs to an age more confusing than their forebears had ever known. The world, indeed, was too much with them, and they found in reverie and nostalgic retreat a stasis of meaning and value. The old homestead, the pastoral memory of the lost virgin wilderness, and especially the fireside: these were already by the time of the Civil War the materials of an American classical vision.

One of the common elements in these poets' work is the light of the fireside; its glow, as in the work of Nathaniel Hawthorne, helps to create a neutral ground where the poet and reader alike can find imaginative delight and melancholy instruction. This is the light that unites the company of Longfellow's travelers in *Tales of a Wayside Inn*, that sustains their tales and dreams:

> Around the fireside at their ease
> There sat a group of friends, entranced
> With the delicious melodies;
> Who from the far-off noisy town
> Had to the wayside inn come down,
> To rest beneath its old oak trees.
> The fire-light on their faces glanced,
> Their shadows on the wainscot danced,
> And, though of different lands and speech,
> Each had his tale to tell, and each
> Was anxious to be pleased and please.

It is in the homely glow of Huldy's hearth-fire that Zekle first catches a glimpse of his lady love in Lowell's New England pastoral, "The Courtin' " (1867); the vision transfixes the simple Yankee fellow:

> 'Twas kin' o' kingdom-came to look
>   On sech a blessed cretur,
> A dogrose blushin' to a brook
>   Ain't modester nor sweater.

And undoubtedly the most memorable moment in Whittier's poetry is when, at the end of "Snow-Bound," the poet invites the reader to

> Sit with me by the homestead hearth,
> And stretch the hands of memory forth
>   To warm them at the wood-fire's blaze!
> And thanks untraced to lips unknown
> Shall greet me like the odors blown
> From unseen meadows newly mown,
> Or lilies floating in some pond,
> Wood-fringed, the wayside gaze beyond;
> The traveller owns the grateful sense
> Of sweetness near, he knows not whence,
> And, pausing, takes with forehead bare
> The benediction of the air.

There can be no question that these writers were hampered by their limited appreciation of the range and possibilities of poetry. Too easily their opinions and ideas led them to the view that art was at best an escape from life; at worst, mere decoration and the idling away of time. Bryant wrote in 1826 that poetry differed from prose "by excluding all that disgusts, all that tasks and fatigues the understanding, and all matters which are too trivial and common to excite any emotion whatsoever." Poetry, Longfellow later remarked, should "fill up the interludes of life with a song, that shall soothe our worldly passions and inspire us with a love of heaven and virtue." Unreadable in the broad daylight of the marketplace, the Poet's verses assume meaning only in the "revelations" of the moon's light. Even the ardent and courageous reformer, Whittier, a quiet rebel who cared intensely about the riddle of this painful earth, would at times defend his art as an escape from the cares and labors of life:

> Let none upbraid us that the waves entice
> Thy sea-dipped pencil, or some quaint device,
> Rhythmic and sweet, beguiles my pen away
> From the sharp strifes and sorrows of to-day.

His failure as a poet, he tells us in "Proem" (1847), was that life got in the way, that duty and labor made his song unskilled and harsh. Certainly in such a context of attitudes it is easy to agree with the good Dr. Holmes when he observes: "How small a matter literature is to the great seething, toiling, struggling, love-making, bread-winning, child-rearing, death-waiting men and women who fill this huge, palpitating world of ours!"

Still, within the limits of what might be called a Fireside poetics one finds essential values and saving graces, particularly in the common view of the beneficial role poetry plays in the world of human affairs and sympathies. Like the Emersonian poet, the Fireside Poet was representative, apprising "us not of his wealth, but of the common wealth." There is a significant difference, of course: neither a seer nor a "liberating god," the Fireside Poet was representative because his work typified values and desires that in the minds of thoughtful men and women in the nineteenth century were synonymous with culture or civilization. Insofar as these writers desired to create a great national literature, it was not to be done by radical innovation but by transporting to these desert shores the best of all cultures as manifested primarily through literary expression. Their song was neither the bardic yawp of Whitman nor the Orphic riddle of Emerson, but rather an embodiment in verse of ancient, hearthside truths, eternal verities that mankind did so poorly without. For the Fireside Poets, such truths were not so much to be found in some splendid, mysterious moment of transcendent enlightenment as to be achieved through a reliance on tradition and culture, the entire record of experiences distinctively human. They tried to answer positively the inquiry of whether human nature itself has a center. Underneath or outside of that illusion of change called history, there were, they insisted, the permanent elements of human nature; the successful human life is that which embodies a decorous, harmonious relation to this unchanging human center and manifests in its words and deeds the virtues of moderation and poise.

Lowell appeared to be speaking in behalf of his contemporaries' regard for the poet's role when he wrote: "Surely the highest office of a great poet is to show us how much variety, freshness, and opportunity abides in the obvious and familiar. He invents nothing, but seems rather to *re*-discover the world about him." Or elsewhere: "The poet's office is to be a Voice, not of one crying in the wilderness to a knot of already magnetized acolytes, but singing amid the throng of men, and lifting their common aspirations and sympathies . . . on the wings of his song to a purer ether and a wider reach of view." Ideas as ancient as Pindar; sometimes out of fashion, perhaps, but never out of date.

Until the twentieth century, poetry performed in American culture an important social function: as a public event it gave expression to the values, the aspirations, and the pride of the community; as ritual it dignified the proceedings occasioning the poem; as language it had the power to inspire and entertain. Attempts to revivify this ancient tradition have been unsuccessful, and it is difficult for modern readers even to appreciate its values. The poet spoke from the public sector of his mind to the public sector of the reader's mind. His faith assured himself and others that the particular was typical, that the common was universal. If he wrote of his own interests, Holmes observed, it was "not because [those interests] are personal, but because they are human, and born of just such experiences as those who hear or read what I say are like to have had in greater or less measure. I find myself so much like other people that I often wonder at the coincidence."

Almost every memorable Fireside poem earns its victory primarily because of its successful adherence to these public principles. Lowell's magisterial "Commemoration Day Ode" (1865), Holmes's magnetic occasional verse, Bryant's frequently sublime "libertarian" poems, Longfellow's heroic narratives and elegiac reveries—in all their variety, these poems evidence a unity of purpose and public success. Solace was to be found in the old forms: comfort in the familiar, the tried and true. The great charm of poetry for Whittier, as well as for the others, consisted "in its simplicity, and genuine, unaffected sympathy with the common joys and sorrows of daily life. It is a home-taught, household melody. . . . It is the poetry of home, of nature, and the affections." And it is precisely for these very reasons that "Snow-Bound" charms and endures. As Robert Penn Warren has so brilliantly pointed out, this poem could have emerged only from a society that had made the first, irreversible step from agrarian life to the urban, industrial pattern. The new America—with its "larger hopes and graver fears"— the new order of "throngful city ways" demanded that the poet find in the timelessness of art the security that appears to have vanished with the old ways and customs. In Warren's words, Whittier seeks "in the past not only a sense of personal renewal and continuity, but also a sense of the continuity of the new order with the American past."

It is perhaps unfortunate that the nineteenth century sometimes lavished excessive praise on Bryant, Longfellow, Whittier, Holmes, and Lowell, especially when it did so at the expense of Walt Whitman, Jones Very, and Frederick Goddard Tuckerman (though the evidence shows that the Fireside Poets were more judiciously measured by their contemporaries than prejudiced memory wishes to record). Nineteenth-century America was intensely conscious of itself as a literary culture, and it made as much as it could, certainly more than it should, of its "singing strength." The poets and readers of the twentieth century have justified American culture in ways their forefathers could not and dared not have imagined. But these latter-day successes should not obliterate the earlier melodies of the Fireside Poets.

Thomas Wortham

The Rise of the Woman Author

Between 1814 and 1840, the profession of authorship in America took on
the shape we know today, becoming a part of the business of selling identical copies of the same printed work for profit to the largest possible number of buyers. A century before Henry Ford's assembly line began producing automobiles, the publishing industry pioneered mass production in the
United States. The industry addressed a huge audience of avid readers created by population growth, urbanization, and a rising standard of living.
The improvement of technologies of papermaking and bookbinding, the invention of the rotary press, the development of dependable road and rail
networks, the adoption of a special mailing rate for books by the Post Office
Department—these and other changes permitted national distribution of vast
quantities of cheap printed matter.

In a society whose business was already business, the entrepreneurial
publisher, at once idealist and opportunist, emerged to provide the newspapers, magazines, and books that people desired. The new audience wanted
a different kind of writing from that which authors in earlier times had
created for their small readership of relatively privileged men who, often as
not, were friends or acquaintances. The educated gentlemen readers of earlier times expected literature to display verbal ingenuity, wit, knowing allusion, and erudition that would certify the author as one of their own kind;
such standards, however, had no pertinence for a mass audience. Educated
gentlemen readers, for that matter, became ever more scarce in nineteenth-
century America; as a general rule American men of wealth and leisure did
not devote themselves in any significant way to preserving or enhancing
American cultural life. Both by numbers and by default, therefore, women

and young people increasingly formed the chief audience for imaginative literature in nineteenth-century America. The publisher had to find and cultivate authors who could write for them.

Male authors of traditional stamp were likely to be scornful of this task, or unsuited to it. Inevitably, perhaps, publishers found their authors among women. We cannot understand the phenomenon of female authorship at this time unless we discard the notion that a woman writer was considered a sexual monster by her culture. On the contrary: publishers and editors in the popular press vigorously encouraged the literary ambitions of their women readers. They treated both successful and aspiring women authors with critical seriousness and esteem. Love of popular literature, viewed democratically, could be interpreted as an intermediate stage in the formation of true taste and appreciation. A writer willing to provide material for this stage could be praised for helping to inculcate, in a rude and heterogeneous population, aesthetic and moral standards appropriate to an enlightened citizenry. The advent of female authorship itself could be, and was frequently, perceived as a sign of a rise in general standards of culture.

Nor did authorship for women run afoul of conventions of female propriety, because such conventions applied more strictly to the workplace than to the work itself. (For example, women were assigned to the sick-chamber, but barred from the hospital.) Respectable or genteel women did not work in public, but writing posed no problem—it was done at home. Too, women were advised to write only in the popular, "lighter" forms—sketch, familiar essay, tale, novel (the genre had not yet been transformed into high literature), lyric and occasional poem—rather than to attempt sermon, oration, treatise, history, or epic. Women generally complied, so that cultural assumptions about feminine nature were not disturbed; indeed, many women authors held quite conventional views about women's place and sexual difference and would have been shocked to think of themselves as unfeminine in any way. In book after book, story after story, young heroines think of authorship as a vocation that is appropriate for them should they prove to have the talent and determination.

Certainly, hostility was occasionally expressed toward a group that Nathaniel Hawthorne was to call, in exasperation, "scribbling women." But Hawthorne's much-quoted remark occurs in a letter to his publisher; it was not meant for general circulation. And a month after writing it, he retracted it in a burst of enthusiasm for Fanny Fern's novel *Ruth Hall*. The casual comment was resuscitated as the centerpiece of a later campaign against female authorship. For, beginning after the Civil War and continuing to our own time, antagonism toward women writers has been institutionalized on the literary scene.

No matter what mode of writing the women authors of this period used, they imbued it with an ideology appropriately labeled "domestic." Such an ideology does not require that home be the only subject of representation, or that home be unreservedly exalted as earthly paradise. Many works of fiction by women were exciting adventure stories or exotic melodramas and many were sharply critical of American homelife. The critique, however, rose from the conviction that the values presumably fostered by the home— affiliation, intimacy, and altruism—were at risk in American society because the home had neither support nor influence in the public sphere. The Northern male returning exhausted and embittered from work every night (after a stop at his club for brandy and a cigar), the Southern male lounging on his verandah day after day hoping for excitement (rifle at the ready), were a continuous worldly presence in the home, as the home appeared in women's writing. The unstable national economy (there were serious recessions in 1817, 1837, and 1857) made rich homes into poor, poor into rich, overnight. One husband's death or bankruptcy turned a pampered lady into a struggling milliner, another man's successful speculation turned his millhand daughters into debutantes. How were women to instill the domestic virtues in homes whose foundations were so insecure? Then again, it was hard to maintain home as haven in the crowded cities. And, if every household item had to be bought, how could home escape commercial values and pressures? If household help was always drawn from the poor or the immigrant population, how could home be sealed off from politics?

Social life in women's writing of this period is usually represented from a middle-class and white Anglo-Saxon perspective. Willing, even eager, to accept the poor and foreign into the fold, women's writing made the acquisition of gentility a precondition for such acceptance, and demonstrated little sensitivity to alternative cultures. Moreover, the writing of women exposes another kind of tension: as it pleads for a greater influence of the home on public life, it shows that the direction of influence was actually all the other way—public values of competitive individualism, aggressive consumption, and financial advancement contaminate family life and produce domestic misery. And though the women believe that the flow ought to be reversed—had to be reversed for national survival—they had no other means to suggest for achieving that reversal than the power of individual influence. In this respect, their ideology was less an alternative to that of the dominant culture than they may have imagined. But despite the implications of their own testimony, women writers continued to suggest that American society could be transformed by making the home the locus of national values and by giving women true sovereignty therein. Such a transformation would leave women in the home but give them influence in all aspects of public life. Women's future lay in accepting the leadership that the new social order would confer, and in preparing for it. Of course, to "publicize" home values as this writing did was precisely to bring them into the public, the male arena, and in this way the women authors did not contradict their own preachments by their professional careers.

The promulgation of a domestic ethic was only part of the women writers' announced aims. More practically, they sought to set before youthful readers a series of models to help them become the men and women of a reconstituted domestic nation. And more broadly, they sought to record in their works the customs, manners, characters, and features of the national life as they observed it. Thus, among women writers before the Civil War, we find an intense preoccupation with representing the surface details of everyday life—in effect, a practice if not a theory of literary realism—and an idea of writing as a patriotic activity that obliterated the category of "female writing" as distinct from male authorship. Finally, less seriously but no less importantly, these writers saw themselves as purveyors of wholesome entertainment and supporters of play and imagination in a culture too readily given over to extremes of work and dissipation.

Even as women authors worked within an ethic of enlightened domesticity, envisioning American society reconstituted by powerful homes, their own success and prominence pushed them into the commercial and public world. As early as the 1820s women began to edit magazines as well as contribute to them. Sarah Josepha Hale was for many years editor and editorialist of the influential and popular woman's magazine, *Godey's Lady's Book*. Opposed to woman suffrage, deeply committed to women's education, she may well have hindered the one reform movement and helped the other. As correspondents for journals, women provided regular letters and columns that required them to go out into the world and observe it. They gave and attended literary parties that were written about in the papers. Their portraits were featured in popular magazines, along with adulatory biographical sketches. Their opinions were solicited on questions of the day, they were asked to support a range of charitable causes, they were visited by fans. When the publisher Robert Bonner desired to ensure the success of his weekly fiction paper, the *New York Ledger*, he did so by engaging E. D. E. N. Southworth for exclusive serialization of her novels and the humorist Fanny Fern for weekly columns—and by publicizing the high fees he was paying these women. By 1858 the *Ledger* had a circulation of over 400,000. Almost in spite of themselves, then, these women became personages, making the presence of women in the public sphere more acceptable.

A commonality of ideas and literary practices among these women did not mean that they all fitted one pattern. Four strikingly different literary careers will illustrate the variety to be found among women of letters before the Civil War. Our first highly successful woman author, Catharine Maria Sedgwick, was comfortably situated in a distinguished and prosperous old Massachusetts family. Whatever her private motives for writing may have been (frequently depressed, she probably began to write as a form of therapy), she offered her early works to the public on behalf of patriotism, religious rationalism, and womanly self-reliance. Along with James Fenimore Cooper, Sedgwick was praised by critics in the 1820s as a major creator of an emergent national literature, and certainly her style surpasses his in elegance and clarity. In the mid-1830s she abandoned novel writing and began to produce tracts on behalf of such causes as religious and social tolerance, women's education, the abolition of dueling, improved housing for the urban poor, and prison reform. This move, if a loss for imaginative literature, clearly shows how a woman might utilize her status on behalf of public causes.

Sedgwick's literary reputation rests on her five early novels, each one strikingly innovative and an important, if neglected, precursor for later American literature: *A New England Tale* (1822), a story of contemporary small-town life and religious bigotry; *Redwood* (1824), an ambitious treatment of regional types; *Hope Leslie* (1827), an "Indian story"; *Clarence* (1830), a novel of manners; and *The Linwoods* (1835), a Revolutionary story. Running through all these books is a preoccupation with the idea of national identity and an ideal of the women citizen. Emotional denominationalism is scrutinized from a rationalist point of view; regionalism from a nationalist perspective. Sedgwick values rationality and consistently advances an antisentimental heroine notable for common sense, self-reliance, and moral courage.

In the crisis of a Sedgwick novel the heroine must usually prove her principles by carrying out an act of rescue that is both morally correct and physically daring: Hope Leslie rescues an Indian woman from prison; Ellen Bruce *(Redwood)* saves her rival from drowning and rescues another young woman from the Shakers; Gertrude Clarence rescues Emilie, her best friend, from a dissolute suitor by abducting her during a masked ball. Sedgwick's last novel, *Married or Single?* (1857), cautiously approaches some of the issues publicized by the new women's rights movement. Its story of an upper-class heroine who almost marries a libertine because she has no alternatives is an argument for the education of all women for life outside of marriage.

The pattern Sedgwick set in her career had an influence on other women writers. Her family connections and exemplary life certainly helped establish authorship as a respectable profession for women, and helped guarantee that women's writing would receive serious critical attention. Her polished style, her gifts for description and characterization (at least of minor figures), her historical research, and her contemporary social realism merited the aesthetic praise that they received; and her morality and patriotism called for respect. Ostensibly nonpolitical, her works advanced Jeffersonian values in a Jacksonian age, and thus showed how women might comment, albeit covertly, on public life. But her example was also used to denigrate the motives of women writers who seemed to be writing for themselves, whether for pleasure, wealth, or ambition. Since these motives have always been allowed, even esteemed, in men, Sedgwick's case could define female authorship as different in kind from male authorship.

Lydia Maria Child was, like Sedgwick, a Massachusetts native and a Unitarian, but she lacked Sedgwick's family connections and made no bones about the professional nature of her ambition. She devoted the bulk of her literary career to editing and writing for magazines and to producing books of advice for women. Her first published work was a very popular historical novel, *Hobomok* (1824), which featured a cross-racial love between an Indian man and a white woman. She wrote only two more novels: *The Rebels* (1825—treating the American Revolution) and *Philothea* (1836—set in ancient Greece). In both of these we find very strong women characters as well as abiding friendships among women.

But Child departed radically from the sphere of women's writing by publishing *An Appeal in Favor of That Class of Americans Called Africans* in 1832. Her argument, evident from the title, is that as Americans, blacks deserve the full protection of the law as well as equal professional and educational opportunities. The work earned her a very high place in the nascent abolitionist movement, but curtailed her literary career for close to a decade; she regained popularity, however, as a correspondent for the *Boston Courier* in the early 1840s. Revised and collected as *Letters from New York* (1843–45), her columns afford excellent examples of the essay of personal observation, providing wide-ranging and thoughtful accounts of life in New York City. The occasional essay suited her individualism, for, as she remarked when resigning from a brief term as editor of the *National Anti-Slavery Standard*, "I am too distinctly an individual to edit the organ of any association." Her independence kept her apart from the women's rights movement as well. With her own life as proof that energetic women could make their way in the world, Child concentrated her rhetorical energies on behalf of two groups she thought to be much more viciously discriminated against than women—blacks and American Indians.

A third pioneering woman of letters was Ann Sophia Stephens. Looking back on her successful career, she recalled that she had resolved to write stories and make books in her earliest childhood, even before she knew what an author was. Her husband was publisher of the *Portland Magazine* in Maine, and Stephens worked with him as editor and contributor. After a move to New York City in 1837 she became associated with such important and popular women's magazines of the day as *The Ladies' Companion,* *Graham's,* and above all *Peterson's Magazine,* where most of her novels were initially serialized. Among more than two dozen novels, two of particular significance are *Fashion and Famine* (1854) and *The Old Homestead* (1855). Along with highly exciting stories, both of these novels featured meticulously detailed contrasts of life among New York City's poorest and wealthiest classes and expressed outrage at the conditions in which the urban poor were not merely allowed to live but forced to live. Manifestly influenced by Charles Dickens and Eugene Sue, both of whom had been extremely popular with American readers in the 1840s, these were muckraking novels half a century before the form, according to standard American literary history, came into existence in this country.

Whatever her didactic intention or moral point, Stephens's greatest talents were for the colorful and melodramatic. And in this manner she escaped the double bind wherein the woman writer is simultaneously restricted to the pure and the purely didactic, and laughed at as a schoolmarm. Insisting that excitement and entertainment, blood and gore, were as much a woman's province—woman writer and woman reader alike—as home and hearth, Stephens claimed a license for the woman writer that her popularity vindicated. Launching its famous series of dime novels, the publishing house of Beadle reissued an early Stephens work, *Malaeska: The Indian Wife of the White Hunter,* as its first volume. Stephens wrote six more dime novels; nor was she the only woman contributor to this series, which is supposed by many cultural historians to express exclusively masculine values.

Among influential women of letters before the Civil War one must give a special place to Margaret Fuller. A Massachusetts woman of formidable intelligence and energy, she was educated by her father and had free access to the books in his extensive library. Although she longed to improve herself and to join the intellectual world, she was required to stay home and help raise her younger sisters and brothers. In time, however, she persuaded her family to move closer to Boston. There she began a "career" as conductor of "conversations" among women in their homes. These were formal group meetings at which she introduced a philosophic topic and guided the ensuing discussion. Women whose talk was usually limited to household matters found these sessions exhilarating and remembered Fuller with love and gratitude throughout their lives.

Margaret Fuller next became a close associate of Ralph Waldo Emerson and Henry David Thoreau and an important figure in the transcendental movement. She edited and wrote many of the essays in *The Dial*, including a piece called "The Great Debate." Expanded and published as *Woman in the Nineteenth Century* in 1846, this work makes a strong feminist statement two years in advance of the first women's rights convention. Fuller claims for women the inherent divinity that transcendentalists like Emerson had reserved for men; she holds that until men recognize women as equal, their own claim to divinity is suspect. Though convinced that men will eventually accept women as human partners, Fuller argues that for the time being women will have to rely on themselves and each other if their lives are to improve. Her transcendental, masculine commitment to self-cultivation and self-expression is balanced by a feminine belief in cooperation and relation. She believed that no man was exclusively "masculine," as the culture defined the term, and no woman exclusively "feminine." To force such stereotypes on real people was to diminish all humankind.

The sexual stereotyping in the pronouncements of such major transcendentalists as Emerson and Thoreau came to weary her, as did their (unmanly) preference for talk over action, and she accepted a position on Horace Greeley's reformist and widely read newspaper, the *New York Tribune*, late in 1844. After a few years as columnist and reviewer, she went to Europe as the paper's foreign correspondent, met numerous literary and political figures, and eventually settled in Rome, where she became engaged in revolutionary politics. She also had a child by Giovanni Ossoli, a Roman aristocrat whom she may have married. Returning to the United States after the failure of the Roman Revolution of 1849, she, Ossoli, and their son drowned in a shipwreck off the New York coast. Friends collected many of Fuller's writings in memorial volumes that were as much apology for her wayward individualism as praise for her role in American intellectual life. What she had done for women and as a woman was ignored, and her centrality to the transcendental movement in this country was overlooked.

Between 1800 and 1850 at least eighty American women published books of poetry, and more than twice as many published poems in the magazines.

Poems were reprinted time and again in newspapers around the country; after appearing in books, favorite poems were extracted and gathered again in anthologies and yearbooks. Although Henry Wadsworth Longfellow was the most popular single American poet of the antebellum period, most of the native poetry read and remembered by Americans was the work of women. Three of the best-known writers were Lydia Huntley Sigourney, Elizabeth Oakes Smith, and Frances Osgood. Their works deploy different poetic strategies and taken together show diversity within the territory they share.

Sigourney is the most important poet of the three, not only because she was the most popular but also because, as the "first," she (like Catharine Sedgwick) had a powerful influence on other women writers as well as on the way in which women poets were perceived. She published her first collection of poems in 1815 and continued active for half a century, appearing in all the major journals and eventually producing about sixty books. Her 1834 *Poems* was reprinted many times; in 1849 a volume of her poetry appeared in a lavishly produced series that also included William Cullen Bryant and Longfellow. As a poet who elected to "write as a woman," she defined opportunities and limits controlled by a literary representation of gender still powerful today. For Sigourney, to write as a woman meant to remain chiefly in the emotive realm, to be engrossed in immediate personal relations and above all in motherhood. Women exist to be mothers, and their existence is meaningful only when they are immersed in the nurturant role.

Yet, Sigourney's way of treating the ideal is continually to situate it in a threatening context. Most threatening, of course, would be the rupture or termination of the mother-child relation, and accordingly the subject of most of Sigourney's poetry is the death of mothers or children. Such poetry has little kinship with meditative poetry where the thought of death leads to general reflection on the course of human life; or with heroic elegies on the death of prominent persons. Death here is something that happens to ordinary, obscure people and is conceived of chiefly in connection with its devastating impact on those who survive.

Today's trained readers will repudiate this poetry in part because such open emotionality is now scorned; and in part because its vocabulary and imagery are severely impersonal. Sigourney makes no attempt to bring the events home to her own experience, and does not seek wording that will bestow the significance of uniqueness on the recounted event. On the contrary, private experiences are represented in a public language that all can share; the merely personal is sifted out and the inward grief becomes externalized in standard turns of speech. Modern ears discern greeting-card verse here, not serious poetry. Sigourney used a variety of verse forms, favoring the ballad or nursery-rhyme stanza of four-line units with alternating four and three beats. This is also Emily Dickinson's preferred form; but whereas Dickinson uses the form as the foundation for her own idiosyncratic poetic acrobatics, Sigourney simply affirms that foundation, remaining faithful to the exact beat and the perfect, predictable, rhyme. The poet is interested in producing accessible, useful poetry that can be taken to heart by numerous readers.

Elizabeth Oakes Smith wrote novels and essays as well as poetry; her reputation as a poet came chiefly from her seven-part narrative poem, "The Sinless Child" (1843). This is a meditation on the spirituality of woman, and its story is of the child Eve whose wondrous nature is snuffed out when she bestows her first kiss—a chaste one, on the forehead—on a man. As with Sigourney, Oakes Smith advances an ideal of woman in the situation that most threatens it; the situation here is sexual connection. And women's spirituality does not survive; the ideal exists only as a dream of what one used to be in childhood. The poem combines simple ballad prosody with a highly abstract diction deemed suitable for its allegorical content.

The major breadwinner in her family, married off by parents when she was only sixteen (to a man she did not care for who was almost twice her age), Oakes Smith was greatly attracted to the women's rights movement. A series of her essays on the topic appearing in the *New York Tribune* was collected in 1851 as *Woman and Her Needs*. The essays argue that in the fallen, male-dominated actual world, women must have the same opportunities as men in order to have the freedom not to marry. Since marriage is woman's only choice, it is no choice at all; but if women could marry or not as they wanted, there would be no bad marriages, and the institution would be a force for good instead of a hypocritical facade. On the other hand, if our world were not fallen, Oakes Smith added, women would not require equal opportunity, for men and women really are intrinsically different: men are material, women ethereal. Thus, even as she advocated equal rights, Oakes Smith was unwilling to abandon faith in an essential female nature that made women spiritually superior to men.

Frances Osgood came from a comfortable Boston family and began to publish poetry in juvenile magazines at the age of fourteen. When she and her husband, a society painter, settled in New York City in 1839, she became an active contributor of poetry to major American periodicals, publishing a half-dozen or more books of verse and prose. She was deeply involved in the social life of New York "literati" and especially close, for a while, to Edgar Allan Poe. Her poems are all short; bold in their use of complicated stanzas and metrics; predictable in diction and in imagery; enlivened by witty rhymes (refusal, usual; get through, undo) and a general tone of mockery that we see again in the "light verse" of twentieth-century women like Dorothy Parker, Edna St. Vincent Millay, and Phyllis McGinley. For this poet, writing as a woman meant writing mostly about love in the first person. But the implicit bathos of this content is avoided by the wry tone and the use of various dramatis personae. Woman as continuously lovelorn is asserted as subject but then denied by rhetoric and form. In one of her longer poems, "A Flight of Fancy," the poet aligns herself with Fancy, a "strange little spright" allegorized as a bird or butterfly, with luminous, multicolored wings, who abashes graver folk (men, reason, logic) by waltzing, whirling, singing, and escapes all attempts to pin her down, to fix her.

Among scores of other poets, the sisters Alice and Phoebe Cary were singled out by contemporaries because they had begun to write in conditions of extreme poverty and hardship on the frontier. From a poor farm north of Cincinnati, then a recently settled territory, these two young women endured the difficulties of westering life and the deaths of their beloved sister and mother. They wrote prose and poetry by the light of tallow candles and were published in Western journals where Eastern editors discovered and reprinted them. Alice Cary's 1852 volume, *Clovernook*, which collects some of her Western sketches, is, after Caroline Kirkland's 1839 *A New Home, Who'll Follow?*, the most important literary representation of settlement life as women experienced it, and of the settlement ideals that survived difficult actuality. Following the publication of *Poems of Alice and Phoebe Carey* in 1850, the sisters came to New York. For fifteen years their Sunday night receptions brought together artists, writers, intellectuals, and activists. Dedicated abolitionists and suffragists, they were energetic in numerous other progressive causes; like many women writers of the era, they felt that their prominence gave them the opportunity and obligation to be active in doing good.

In 1850 the publication of *The Wide, Wide World* by Susan Warner initiated the most important trend in antebellum women's writing. The rest of the decade saw numerous imitations of this novel, many as successful as the original. They were all about the female transition from child to young adult, about the forging of an identity that is individual, independent, and yet feminine in a culturally acceptable way. Formula plots follow the actions of poorly prepared young women who are denied expected emotional and financial support and forced to make their way in a hostile world. In novel after novel the heroine's "trials" lead to "triumph" as she achieves

what was then called "self-dependence," and now might be called autonomy or independence. Her story is often counterpointed by subplots about
weak, passive women who cannot rise to the test that misfortune brings, or
about manipulative women who exploit their attractiveness for a dazzling,
yet inevitably transitory, success.

Novels sharing this general plot can be classed as more domestic or more
melodramatic. It is particularly in the domestic fictions that we find the
fully developed commitment to a realistic literary practice. The formula
plot had to be diversified to be used over and over; variations were achieved
through careful depiction of particularized settings and supporting characters. In contemporary reviews many of these books were praised precisely
for their notation of everyday life and manners in different parts of the
country. Melodramatic versions of the fundamental story featured unusual
settings and extreme plots. Heroines found themselves in dangerous, exciting situations, with opportunities for displaying manly heroism instead of
winning female graces. The books were rhetorically ornate (we would say
they were overwritten). But their settings in city and wilderness achieved a
convincingness of their own, and the books shared the domestic values of
their more demure sisters; it could be argued that their ebullient heroines
made an even stronger statement about female ability and independence.
Domestic or melodramatic, these novels all allowed an author to display
individual qualities, and despite a recurrent didacticism, few of them can be
reduced to a single moral or message without jettisoning most of the work.

For example, *The Wide, Wide World*, the best-selling book of 1850, expresses the author's deeply felt Evangelical pietism as it tells of an orphan
achieving emotional self-sufficiency. Ellen's mother dies and her father
abandons her; she is raised in poverty on a small upstate New York farm
by a well-meaning but narrow-minded aunt with little understanding of
children and outright hostility to Ellen's well-bred city ways. While the
often inadvertent cruelties of the plainspoken aunt engender strong reader
sympathy for Ellen, Warner also stresses the child's inner failings—willfulness, selfishness, temper—and offers faith as a tool for gaining self-control
as well as for standing up to external ill-treatment and winning respect from
one's adversaries. But the message is not all; there is a richly detailed depiction of the rural locale—so much so that leading journals of the time saw
the book as a sovereign contribution to an American literature. Along with
the earnestly treated major characters, Warner offers a variety of minor and
amusing characters whose vernacular, individualistic speech patterns are
certainly contributions to the development of the native voice in our prose
fiction.

Maria Susanna Cummins wrote two extremely popular works, both based on Warner's formula; yet these novels are different from *The Wide, Wide World* and from each other. *The Lamplighter* (1854) draws its heroine, Gerty, from a city slum and many of its characters from the urban working class. Whereas Ellen had found strength in a private and tenaciously held religious belief, Gerty found it rather in a community of friends. Though her great moment of triumph comes when she is sufficiently self-supporting to take rooms in a Boston boardinghouse, she readily gives up independence to take care of those who had helped her overcome her background as street hoyden. The heroine of *Mabel Vaughan* (1857) begins life as a rich city girl but, after her family loses all its money, has to learn to live in poverty. The novel ends with successful transplanting of the family, now headed by Mabel, to the garden of the Midwest, bringing in timely themes of pioneering, settlement, and the American future.

Altogether different from these two Northern novelists is the Southerner E. D. E. N. Southworth, the most popular and perhaps most prolific fiction writer of her time. In contrast to their studied plainness of style, Southworth's novels burst with overstatement and energy. The very willfulness and passion that Cummins and Warner deplored were virtues to Southworth; and where the crises in Warner were apt to center on whether or not one was allowed to stay up late, those in Southworth involved suspenseful chases and close escapes. She is satirized in Louisa May Alcott's *Little Women* as Mrs. S. L. A. N. G. Northbury, whose story in the fiction papers is accompanied by an illustration of "an Indian in full war costume, tumbling over a precipice with a wolf at his throat, while two infuriated young gentlemen, with unnaturally small feet and big eyes, were stabbing each other close by, and a dishevelled female was flying away in the background, with her mouth wide open."

Southworth's most popular novel, *The Hidden Hand*, was serialized in the *New York Ledger* in 1859; its heroine, Capitola, runs away from a wicked guardian, dresses as a boy, fights duels, performs many brave deeds, uses slang expressions, and generally outmans all her opponents. Capitola, like all Southworth's heroines, is a real hero. She is larger in spirit than any of the petty, selfish, and childish men who surround her, and is an implicit argument—as her name suggests—for a national order in which women were appreciated as natural rulers. In the midst of fun and excitement, Southworth suggested that contemporary sociosexual arrangements destroyed women and men alike; the subordination of women, besides wasting human talent and denying human aspiration, encouraged men to act as self-indulgent and childish tyrants. Her work can be read for its gallery of diverse women—certainly she created the widest number of female types in mid-century American fiction—as well as for its descriptions of social institutions and life in the antebellum South. In all, Southworth wrote about forty novels and remained immensely popular well into the 1880s.

Another Southern woman novelist is Augusta Evans Wilson, whose fiction blended Warner's religiosity and decorum with Southworth's elaborate plotting; her heroines were distinguished not only by their rectitude and moral strength but by their passion for learning and scholarship. Skilled in all the ancient languages, they were intellectual matches for any erudite man. Wilson's first novel, *Inez: A Tale of the Alamo* (1855), was set in early nineteenth-century Texas and contributed a rare picture of life there to the growing collection of antebellum local color treatments of the American scene. It also involved extensive treatment of Protestant-Catholic religious controversy, arguing the Protestant side equally with melodrama and Scripture. *Macaria; or, The Altars of Sacrifice* (1864) was among other things a fascinating description of life for Southern women during the Civil War; and *St. Elmo* (1867) was an almost archetypal rendition of the story of the young girl of ferocious willpower making her way alone, rejecting friends and enemies alike in the struggle to achieve absolute "self dependence." *St. Elmo* was one of the most popular American books of the century.

There were many other widely read women novelists in the 1850s. Caroline Lee Hentz was a New Englander transplanted to the South; the anguished heroine of her best-selling *Linda* (1850) runs away from home to escape harassment by relatives and has adventures bloodier than those of Huckleberry Finn. Hentz also wrote several novels defending slavery by showing the happy community it fostered, the most widely read of which was *The Planter's Northern Bride* (1854). *Ernest Linwood* (1856), a novel recounted in the first person, is an advanced psychological study of the anguish a young woman endures after marrying a man who is pathologically jealous, under the mistaken impression that jealousy is the same as love. Mary Jane Holmes had a lively style and a good ear for dialect. *Tempest and Sunshine* (1854) takes place in the backwoods of Kentucky, as do several other of her works; in *The English Orphans* (1855) the heroine spends a good deal of time in a New England poorhouse. "Marion Harland" (Mary Virginia Terhune) set many of her novels in Richmond and showed a side of Southern life rarely treated in fiction before Ellen Glasgow.

A writer who did not attain popularity, probably because her work disregarded certain formulaic requirements of typical women's fiction, was Elizabeth Stoddard, whose novel *The Morgesons* (1862) is a striking work of gloomy local color, harsh and revealing in its depiction of New England life. The novel also inverts the moral scheme of most women's fiction, centering its depiction of the home on bitter and sexually charged family politics, and celebrating a predatory heroine who sees women as rivals and men as conquests. An earlier creator of eccentric plots is Caroline Chesebro', whose novels celebrated a variety of unorthodox female characters—in *Isa* (1852), for example, a couple lives happily out of wedlock, while in *The Children of Light* (1853) two superior women who have been jilted by inferior men form a couple; and in *Getting Along* (1855) a number of unconventional women find places for themselves outside the confines of the ordinary.

One should not neglect to mention the appearance, in novel form, of numerous tractlike works by women advocating various reform causes: pro- and antislavery, sectarian, and (above all) temperance. Nor the development of a thriving literature for children, much of it written by women. One of these children's books, Louisa May Alcott's *Little Women* (1869), has remained in print continuously until our own day. Once read, it is never forgotten. Jo March is an unequaled representation of adolescent tensions and the constricting force of idealized womanhood. Jo wants to develop freely as her talents dictate—which means, in her society, to be male—but also to remain a child forever in the nest of her family and to become a mature social woman. Her story runs parallel to those of her three less complicated but still attractive sisters; all are sustained by the community they form, a matriarchy governed by "Marmee," who combines teacher and nurturer in one image.

But the lessons of this book, there for all to see, are not Marmee's lessons; in fact they fly in the face of her dictates. They are: first, that maturity destroys the family, because "family" to each person means the natal family, and in adulthood one achieves only melancholy imitations of that earlier paradise; and, second, that "women" are not born but are culturally produced. To shape the varied material of human nature into more or less identical female adults is an arduous and unremitting task, to which the lifelong dedication of Marmee is barely adequate. The marriage of Jo to Laurie, both androgynous characters, is rejected for the daughter-father marriage of Jo to Professor Bhaer. One becomes an "adult" woman by accepting women's place as inferior. The many readers who wept when Jo did not marry Laurie mourned not only the loss of romance but the loss of self in the imperatives of role.

Alcott, daughter of Bronson Alcott (the minor transcendentalist), was full of talents that her class and gender prohibited her from exercising. She wanted to be an actress; she wrote exciting melodramas (like E. D. E. N. Southworth's) that she published under an assumed name; she was a splendid athlete. But acting was unacceptable in her class; melodramas were unacceptable to the gentility of her surroundings; and women athletes did not yet exist. Hence we have *Little Women,* and a host of similar books almost as popular, by which she supported her parents, her sisters, and their families.

In their continual preoccupation with the dilemmas of women and the inevitably personal, circumscribed nature of these dilemmas, these books by and for women have seemed narrow to many who look for a certain kind of scope in fiction, a scope that expresses itself in rapid strategic moves to "universals." No such accusation, however, can be brought against the most sensational and sensationally popular American book of the age, *Uncle Tom's Cabin,* by Harriet Beecher Stowe. Later tradition described the novel as an accident produced by an amateur, but in fact Stowe was a professional writer who had been publishing for more than a decade when *Uncle Tom's Cabin* began its serial run in an abolitionist journal. Republished in book form in 1852, it combined all the elements of fiction that American critics of the age were looking for: a diverse group of memorable characters, some hateful, some lovable; a tremendously exciting story; scenes of great pathos and scenes of humor; meticulous depiction of the customs, manners, and scenery of various regions in the country on a scale unequaled by any American work of fiction to that date. In addition, the book defined writing in general, and the novel form in particular, as a kind of visionary and prophetic mode, thus making women authors equal to the highest literary tasks. And beyond this, it dealt with an inflammatory political issue in a highly partisan spirit. Far from disqualifying the work in the eyes of readers (though its politics made critics deeply uneasy), these ambitious elements obviously made it all the more compelling. The public accepted the book on Stowe's terms. It was printed and reprinted, dramatized, illustrated; millions who had not read the book still knew about Uncle Tom, Eliza crossing the ice, saintly little Eva, mischievous Topsy, and the monster of evil, Simon Legree. What effect the book finally had on public sentiment is impossible to know, but people at the time were certain that it had played a crucial part in making slavery morally and intellectually indefensible.

The vision of *Uncle Tom's Cabin* is deeply religious; Stowe was the daughter of one of the age's most famous (and one of the last) orthodox Calvinist preachers, Lyman Beecher, and all five of her brothers became ministers in their turn, including another generation's most famous, Henry Ward Beecher. The whole family was immersed in theological speculation; and Stowe came over time to reject the stern Old Testament God of wrath in favor of the

New Testament God of love. Her opposition to slavery carries a particular theological charge, as she chronicles the defeat of charity by secular greed. We are to read Tom's decision not to run away when he is sold downriver, and his eventual martyrdom standing up to Simon Legree, not as submission to the secular world, but as triumph over it. As well as "Christian" in this broad sense, Stowe's book is "matriarchal" in the particular values it espouses—emotive over rational, relational over individualistic—and the repeated crises at its core: the breakup of families and the separation of mothers and children form the repeated matter of its suspenseful efforts. It does not, however, parcel out its good and bad qualities according to gender: the book is full of good men, and in Marie St. Clair it creates a memorably vicious woman. Moreover, beyond its Christian or proto-feminist protest, *Uncle Tom's Cabin* mounts an attack on American capitalism, north and south: slavery is the ultimate expression of a culture dedicated to buying, selling, and accumulation.

Stowe published a second antislavery book, *Dred: A Tale of the Great Dismal Swamp* (1856), but her career was not engrossed by the slavery issue; after the Civil War she wrote a series of novels depicting New England life of the past and present, important as examples of local color realism, as meditations on doctrinal questions prominent in New England theological disputation, and as instances of searching and self-conscious inquiry into the New England mind and character. These books are: *The Minister's Wooing* (1859), *Pearl of Orr's Island* (1862), *Old Town Folks* (1869), and *Poganunc People* (1878).

It is probably no exaggeration to say that close to half of the literature published by Americans in the period between the War of 1812 and the Civil War was written by women. It is certainly the case that, in its own time, this writing was taken seriously and women writers were respected as well as successful. Their subsequent removal from the record is part of the literary history of a later day when exponents of various literary movements—especially post–Civil War realism and post–World War I modernism—found it convenient to allegorize women authors as exemplars of all that was wrong with literature, all that the new writers were committed to correcting and erasing.

Nina Baym

Forms of Regional Humor

There was much complaint in Jacksonian literature about the lack of ruins. Washington Irving, James Fenimore Cooper, Edgar Allan Poe, Nathaniel Hawthorne, romantic fabulists, had to create their own ruins, to find them in old embroidery, in the last Mohican. The New World was raw, its culture recent. "There are no annals for the historian; no follies (beyond the most vulgar and commonplace) for the satirist; no manners for the dramatist; no obscure fictions for the writer of romance; no gross and hardy offences against decorum for the moralist; nor any of the rich artificial auxiliaries of poetry"; so wrote Cooper in *Notions of the Americans* (1828). Walter Scott, who had all these things, advised Irving, his bereft American compeer, to consider America's "vast aboriginal trees" as its "monuments and antiquities," and though Irving knew better, having been "brought up in a country overrun with forests, where trees are apt to be considered mere encumbrances, and to be laid low without hesitation or remorse," he nonetheless took the suggestion and made an effort. In an American forest that had been ravaged by a tornado, Irving would look upon the "vast havoc made among these gigantic plants" and see "something awful," something that looked like tumbled pillars and wrecked statuary, "magnificent remains, so rudely torn and mangled, and hurled down to perish prematurely on their native soil." Jacksonian writers worked hard to discover romantic objects in their immediate landscape. They filled in the perceived blanks with wild scenery and wild Indians, and gave the scene and the Indian the look and feel of marble. They ransacked their shortage of history for what Hawthorne called the "atmosphere of strange enchantment." Hawthorne took hold of the Puritans, Irving the antique and irrelevant Dutch, Cooper the French and Indian Wars, the pre-Revolutionary period.

The Civil War provided real ruins, the ruins of Atlanta, the ruins of

Richmond, the ruination of the old South. It sealed off and preserved the entire South, its speech, its customs, as a ruin. The North became the nation, the South a region, and as the North, progressive, modernizing, expansive, turned westward in 1866 to build its transcontinental railroads, it left the South behind as something of a cultural appendix. The South was the sad place where visible history, moldering, crumbling, still spoke its object lesson about vanity. When Shreve McCannon, "the Canadian, the child of blizzards and of cold," has heard the whole of Thomas Sutpen's tragedy in William Faulkner's *Absalom, Absalom!* (1936), he sits back in wonder. There is "something awful" here. Sutpen's desire to build a Domain, to found a lineage, has created a "vast havoc" and left only ruins. Quentin Compson, "the Southerner, the morose and delicate offspring of rain and steamy heat," Shreve's roommate at Harvard, has largely told the tale, turning over old letters, conjuring the spectral voices. He would hate to come from the South, Shreve tells Quentin, to have been raised amid ruins, always feeling their oppression. "I just want to understand it," he explains, "if I can and I dont know how to say it better. Because it's something my people haven't got. Or if we have got it, it all happened long ago across the water and so now there ain't anything to look at every day to remind us of it." Canadians do not have "bullets in the dining room table," an impressive past, a lost cause, present ruins, "always reminding us to never forget." What do Canadians have? Trees, vast, aboriginal trees. So Shreve, fascinated, constantly prods Quentin: *"Tell about the South. What's it like there. What do they do there. Why do they live there."* And of course Shreve can only know the half of it, Quentin's side of Sutpen's story. He does not see the ruins in Faulkner's style, the literary relics, the fragments, this piece of folklore, that piece of legend. He doesn't know what is in Sutpen's name. He doesn't hear a certain song Quentin silently sings, which Quentin gets from Poe: *"Nevermore of peace. Nevermore of peace. Nevermore Nevermore Nevermore."* Faulkner's reconstruction of Southern speech in *Absalom, Absalom!* is loving, an act of preservation, and yet, at the same time, even as he renders the voices in that speech, plays the music, he negates its mythic value, marks its excesses, its entrapment. A larger language, lucid, ironic, contains Quentin's melancholy, contains Shreve's fascination for "it," the awful news from darkest Mississippi, the great ruin of Sutpen's grand house.

Like Shreve, who has a future, who is going to become a practicing surgeon in Edmonton, Alberta, we know that Southern speech is ruinous talk. It is antique, reactionary, racist. It is preindustrial, pretechnological, confined to the countryside, to hamlets and towns, to manorial life. It is a construction that is fixed, finished, eroding. Such is the presentation of Southern speech in nineteenth-century American literature, the mythic speech that is ready for Faulkner's composition. Of all the idioms that figure in that literature, Southern speech is the only one that is polyphonic, has modes: patrician, poor white, black, child-fool-idiot, the only one that constitutes a full discourse. Huck Finn instructs us in the niceties of its representation, shows us, long before Quentin Compson appears as our interlocutor, how capably this Southern speech expresses Nevermore. Huck Finn not only delivers "the Missouri negro dialect; the extremest form of the backwoods South-Western dialect; the ordinary 'Pike-County' dialect; and four modified varieties of this last" in the *Adventures of Huckleberry Finn* (1884); he also reports the speeches of the Colonels Grangerford and Sherburn, recites lugubrious Southern poetry, catches Shakespeare on the fly, and does this all in his own homespun composition. He has his sad refrain, not from Poe, but from Emmeline Grangerford: "And Art Thou Gone Yes Thou Art Gone Alas." Mark Twain, Faulkner, these writers give us the classical transcription of Southern speech, even as they transcend it, lift their styles from the limiting category of regional writing. What Shreve learns at Harvard about the South, that it is tragic, cursed, Huck Finn tells us at the end of his tale. He doesn't want to go back. He wants the territories, the not-South, where he can start over, begin afresh, be free. Of Quentin, Shreve asks: "Now I want you to tell me just one more thing. Why do you hate the South?" The answer, given "in the cold air, the iron New England dark," is a redoubled negative: *"I dont. I dont! I dont hate it! I dont hate it!"* It is what we ask of Mark Twain, of Huck Finn.

The double stroke that is in mature Southern writing, humor and horror, love of place, hatred of place, an ambivalence that constantly poses the problem of its regional writing, gives the Southern text its exceptional status in American literature. Where and how did Southern regional writing get this ironic mechanism? In the South, long before the Civil War imposes its awful realities, the genre is deceptive, complex. New England, 1830–60, cherishes its nooks and crannies, its vales and ponds. Its regional writing is appreciative, exacting in its fidelities. The South, from the start, is ingeniously lying, and not just to itself.

Within the context of a regional writing, a colloquial style, Southern writers create the tall tale, invent, as a form of ironic hyperbole, the stylistic phenomenon of tall talk. This form, as we shall see, subverts the project of the local sketch, enables the writer to play with that urgent Jacksonian desire for the romantic subject, the picturesque. Writers of tall tales typically use an observing intelligence, a literate interlocutor, to frame the tale, to contain it, and then trap this detached folklorist with a duplicitous tale, a tale full of sound and fury. What also occurs in the tall tale is the definition of two exemplary voices, patrician and poor white. They are contraposed, writer and speaker, two different sensibilities, and their problematic relation is what, to some extent, the tall tale is about. It is a relation that undergoes successive transformations in Southern writing, one of which is Huck Finn's relation to "Mr. Mark Twain." The significant history of colloquial writing in American literature therefore begins in the Jacksonian period, and its principal subject is Southern speech.

A certain character appears, Colonel Nimrod Wildfire in James Kirke Paulding's popular *The Lion of the West* (1830), "Davy Crockett" in the several Crockett narratives and almanacs. David Crockett, an ambitious Whig politician from Tennessee, shapes this character, that of a rough-hewn, loquacious backwoodsman, and produces an artful tall talk that is mesmerizing. Paulding appropriates something of Crockett's manner and speech in his presentation of Colonel Wildfire: "My name is Nimrod Wildfire—half horse, half alligator and a touch of the airthquake—that's got the prettiest sister, fastest horse and ugliest dog in the District, and can out-run, outjump, throw down, drag out and whip any man in all Kaintuck." Other writers simply took up "Davy Crockett" entire, some for the purest relish, others as a job of work. Whig politicians were quick to see the usefulness in Crockett's celebrity and sought to keep him and his anti-Jackson populism before the electorate. He was their primitive, their droll version of the shaggy Democrat in the White House, Andrew Jackson. Crockett soon had writers working up material for him and something of a production staff. James Strange French's *Sketches and Eccentricities of Colonel David Crockett of West Tennessee* (1833) is for pleasure. The authorized "Life," *A Narrative of the Life of David Crockett* (1834), which Crockett told to, wrote with, Thomas Chilton, is political. William Clark's *An Account of Colonel Crockett's Tour to the North and Down East* (1836) strains to enhance Crockett's national reputation and is full of political asides and campaign issues. Richard Penn Smith's *Col. Crockett's Exploits and Adventures in Texas* (1836) is a patriotic melodrama that contains a journal Crockett supposedly kept while in the Alamo. In *Davy Crockett's Almanack of Wild Sports of the West, and Life in the Backwoods* (1835), Crockett's tall talk is perfectly stylized, a system of gestures, a common property.

As Constance Rourke so vividly showed us in her pioneering work, *American Humor: A Study of the National Character* (1931), a host of mythic characters suddenly appear in the 1830s, characters of region and race: the Gamecock of the Wilderness, the Yankee Pedlar, Jim Crow; but they do not have, as she implies in her treatment of them, an equal standing. It is this character, "Davy Crockett," the mythic speaker in all these different texts, that immediately matters in American literature. "Davy Crockett" is indeed "half horse, half alligator," hybrid, trusty, treacherous, and his devious, often curiously deep tall tales provide an apt model for the definitive tales that emerge in the 1840s.

There are two episodes in the history before us. The first begins with the invention of "Davy Crockett," with the formation of the tall tale, and encompasses the brief flourishing of Southwestern humor in *Georgia Scenes* (1833), "The Big Bear of Arkansas" (1841), "The Indefatigible Bear Hunter" (1850), and *Some Adventures of Captain Simon Suggs, Late of the Tallapoosa Volunteers* (1845). In these exemplary texts, at once regional and colloquial, the South considers its territories, the frontier in Georgia, Alabama, Louisiana, Mississippi, Arkansas, and discovers there the rude figure of the poor white. The Southern response to the meaning of that figure is the tall tale. The second episode begins with Harriet Beecher Stowe's *Uncle Tom's Cabin* (1852), with what might be called the irruption of the real. In this widely read novel, banned in most Southern districts, Stowe not only refutes every conceivable Southern alibi for slavery but breaks into Southern writing to do so, enters its space, appropriates its speech, its locales, rewrites its characters, and adds one. She thoroughly wrecks its composure. The genial, beaming Southern master we see in a certain Southern text is here the languid dependent, Augustine St. Clare. Johnson Jones Hooper's happy rascal, Simon Suggs, turns out to be Simon Legree. With St. Clare's discourse, which is composed of long, self-justifying speeches, Stowe takes the sweetness of the patrician Southern sensibility, that benign, ironic quality, and slowly, carefully, empties it. A Northerner, a minister's wife, an abolitionist, it is she who writes the first major Southern novel. *Uncle Tom's Cabin* changes everything in Southern writing. Every mode of Jacksonian discourse (legal, political, academic, literary) is disrupted in the 1850s, made contentious. Regionalists, writers of sketches and occasional essays, colloquial humorists North and South, begin angrily to take the measure of their respective differences. Here is George Washington Harris's *Sut Lovingood's Yarns* (1847–67), Southern rage, and there is James Russell Lowell's *The Biglow Papers* (1847–66), Northern disdain. When Jim Crow forces his way into regional writing in 1852, comes to speak in the colloquial text, for himself, all the humor in Southern writing turns immediately black. "I'se so wicked," says Topsy in *Uncle Tom's Cabin*.

"I Outwit a Yankee," by "Davy Crockett." A cautionary tale, this one. During the election of 1835, at a backcountry place called the "Cross Roads," a "large posse" of backcountry voters has gathered "to get a taste of the quality of the candidates at orating." Crockett is present to address the assembly, wearing his hunting shirt, carrying his rifle on his shoulder, but before he can speak the crowd demands he stand them to a drink. Nearby is the grog-shanty of Job Snelling, a "gander-shanked Yankee," a trader known in those parts to be "sharp as a steel trap, and as bright as a pewter button." He has hung a sign above the bar: *Pay to-day and trust tomorrow*, hard words in the cash-poor backcountry. Crockett does not have the ready cash to pay for a quart of Job Snelling's New England rum, so he dashes out into the adjoining woods, shoots a raccoon and skins it, returns with the pelt as barter, and secures his quart. Busily engaged, Job Snelling wedges the skin between the logs supporting the bar. When Crockett realizes he must buy a second round to keep his crowd, he is forced to the expedient of snatching the first skin and using it again. Before the day is over, Crockett has so circulated his single coonskin that he has had ten quarts of rum for his thirsty constituents and effectively won the election. The coonskin story, Crockett reports, "soon circulated like smoke among my constituents, and they allowed, with one accord, that the man who could get the whip hand of Job Snelling in fair trade, could outwit Old Nick himself, and was the real grit for them in Congress."

Such a man, wearing a hunting shirt, carrying a rifle on his shoulder, who can get round the sign *No Credit*, is indeed the poor white's tribune. We immediately recognize the populist hero, the populist villain, the populist fantasy. It is all there, brilliantly exposed, in *The Sound and the Fury* (1929). Faulkner reestablishes the ancient enmities, reconvenes the old adversaries, the Gamecock of the Wilderness, the Yankee Pedlar. Jason Compson rails against the "damn eastern Jews" who control the stock market, who keep the little man, the small farmer, profitlessly toiling. He orates: "They fill the farmer full of hot air and get him to raise a big crop for them to whipsaw on the market, to trim the suckers with. Do you think the farmer gets anything out of it except a red neck and a hump on his back?" Jason is himself a cheat and a luckless speculator. He hatefully envies the "smart-money boys" with their "inside dope." "You'll admit that they produce nothing," he tells his audience in the town diner, a single woebegone salesman. "They follow the pioneers into a new country and sell them clothes." Jason's complaint was doubtless heard at the Cross Roads in 1835. Who were these Yankees, "geniuses" at making money, but a race apart, a type—manufacturers, capitalists. There stood Crockett in his homespun shirt, nobler by far than Faulkner's Jason Compson, but with the same ideas. He knows what Job Snelling's product is. "Job, himself, bragged of having made some useful discoveries; the most profitable of which was the art of converting mahogany sawdust into cayenne pepper, which he said was a profitable and safe business; for the people having been so long accustomed to having dust thrown in their eyes, that there wasn't much danger of being found out." Crockett addresses that red-necked feeling of bitter resentment in the tale and in his political career. Southerners knew the Yankee trader, the short count, the hand on the scale, knew his sign *No Credit*, and here is Crockett's counting: one coonskin, ten quarts, told with an almost childish glee.

The "Davy Crockett" who tells this story is Richard Penn Smith, writing in *Col. Crockett's Exploits and Adventures in Texas*. Smith takes it from the extant legend that is based on Crockett's original performance of "Davy Crockett," a performance that was, by all contemporary accounts, carefully crafted, fairly practiced. John Gadsby Chapman, who painted two portraits of Crockett in 1834, watched Crockett improvise for visitors, tell stories, assume the manner "half horse, half alligator," and then, after the visitors had left, abruptly turn from the "dramatic pose," shake off the character, and become once more a grave, deliberate man. What was Crockett doing in that performance? In his buckskin fringes and fur cap, as Chapman painted him, Crockett symbolically bespoke the cause of the rural poor, of those without book learning or professional training. In Washington, D.C., he projected their frontier guile, their frontier resourcefulness. He was the one who gave that dubious coonskin to Job Snelling, who could outwit the traders and dealers, whose tall talk mesmerized the propertied and purse-proud. To this extent, Crockett was the real thing. There was "real grit" in the performance.

In the authorized *Narrative*, which is singularly free of posturing and exaggeration, Crockett takes some pains to assert the integrity of his "true" character. Here are the facts of his life, his humble origin, the struggle to rise in the world, and here, too, constantly before us, is what he stands for, the statement of his politics. Crockett's congressional record is, after all, substantial. He initiated and fought for the Tennessee Vacant Land Bill, legislation that would have protected the property rights of poor white farmers. He opposed Jackson's infamous Indian Removal Bill (1830), which deported the Cherokees. An exemplar of the commons, Crockett was in Washington to proclaim Jackson's betrayal of the farmer and the working-man. All this is clearly set forth in the *Narrative*, and was part of the performance. But if this "Davy Crockett" had specific political meaning, there was still another who had his eye on the newspapers, the periodicals, the almanacs, the book trade. Crockett's principal writers—French, Chilton, Clark, Smith—had always that difficulty in treating "Davy Crockett." Their narrative typically alternates the partisan material and the entertaining stories. It is where we find "Davy Crockett," in these makeshift versions, "half horse, half alligator," to use Paulding's epithet. Of Crockett himself as a writer, there are only letters, and none of these are in the character and speech of "Davy Crockett." Chapman painted two portraits: a sober gentleman in broadcloth, the congressman, and the backwoodsman, rifle in hand, with dogs, on the hunt.

Readers of "Davy Crockett" are thus left holding a dubious coonskin, contemplating the trace of Crockett's self-effacing grin. The grin is in French's *Sketches and Eccentricities*. Crockett is again on the campaign trail, giving stump speeches, contending this time with a candidate known for his winsome smile and endearing manner. He can't match this person's "good humored smile," Crockett tells the crowd, but he does own a grin that enthralls raccoons, brings them tumbling down from the trees, swooned, prostrate. His story is Aesopian. The grin is infallible, and yet one bright moonlit night it seemed to fail him. A treed coon resists Crockett, doesn't tumble no matter how he concentrates his loony grin. Exasperated, Crockett fetches an axe and brings the tree down. No coon at all. "I found that what I had taken for one, was a large knot upon a branch of the tree—and, upon looking at it closely, I saw that I *had grinned all the bark off, and left the knot perfectly smooth.*" A message is appended to this tall tale: Be wide awake, "look sharp," consider "my opponent's countenance," his smiling manner, "and do not let him grin you out of your votes." Appearances are deceiving. Crockett's grin bares that truth. It strips the bark from the knot; it unmasks that trustworthy smile. What seems to be there is not. The coonskin and the grin, these are the emblems of "Davy Crockett," and they give us the peasant cunning that is at the center of Crockett's performance. They give us that something that resists mythic transformation, that goes on grinning right through the glaze of mythic speech. Look sharp, says the tall tale, myth exaggerates, myth lies.

The Southern humorists who come after Crockett in American literature write their tall tales in the shade of his celebrity. They evoke Crockett's figure and speech in their bear hunters and tall talkers. They occupy his locale, the Southern backcountry. They write for a public he had largely created. "There must be something in me, or about me," Crockett muses in the *Narrative*, "that attracts attention, which is even mysterious to myself." Half-domesticated, half-wild, Crockett embodies at once the duplicity and the ambivalence of the tall tale. Writers of the tall tale observe the drama of that appropriation, that resistance, and draw from it a series of questions, not all of which they meet. It is, in any case, the question to ask of the tall tale: what is appropriated, what resists? Other questions soon follow. Why is this odd form, this lie exposing itself, the South's principal usage in its pre-Civil War regional writing? What cultural strategies, what issues of class and ideology, inform this exemplary text? There are Northern humorists just as popular and colloquial as Crockett in the Jacksonian period. Seba Smith, who created Major Jack Downing, an ambitious, office-seeking Down Easterner let loose in Jackson's office-dealing Washington, enjoyed a considerable vogue in the 1830s and 1840s. But his work is no longer in use. Of Jack Downing all that remains is his lanky figure, his striped trousers, his duck-tailed coat, and his top hat. He is the model for the cartoon figure of Uncle Sam. It is in the South that the tall tale prospers, accumulates value, renders a stylized speech that is still before us, garrulous, poetic. There are two significant modern reincarnations of "Davy Crockett." In the 1950s Walt Disney would have an immense success exploiting the "Davy Crockett" of the *Almanack*, the simple Davy. In the 1960s, swaggering, boasting, Cassius Clay would become Muhammad Ali, "float like a butterfly, sting like a bee," and reanimate the sociopolitical complexity of the original populist figure. Indeed, it is in this period, during the civil rights struggle, that the South again takes on the fearsome aspect it showed in the Jacksonian period.

As every important European visitor to Jacksonian America noted, the South was the place, the region, where the lie of American democracy stood forth, revealing, glaring. Here was slavery, a semifeudal society, the "Dark Corner" in American life. Coming upriver on the Mississippi in 1828, Frances Trollope stood by the steamboat rail and keenly observed the faces of the backwoodsmen as they stood grouped on the shore with their families watching her boat slowly pass by. "These unhappy beings are invariably the victims of ague, which they meet recklessly, sustained by the incessant use of ardent spirits. The squalid look of the miserable wives and children of these men was dreadful, and often as the spectacle was renewed I could never look at it with indifference. Their complexion is of a bluish white, that suggests the idea of dropsy; this is invariable, and the poor little ones wear exactly the same ghastly hue." This is the true condition of the American Adam in the Southern Bower of the New World. "I never witnessed human nature reduced so low," Mrs. Trollope writes, "as it appeared in the woodcutters' huts on the unwholesome banks of the Mississippi." She is then told a story, which she gullibly repeats in the *Domestic Manners of the Americans* (1832), of the immense crocodiles that prey upon these woodcutters, devouring entire families. In *Life on the Mississippi* (1884), Mark Twain scornfully relishes this tall tale: "They told Mrs. Trollope that the alligators—or crocodiles, as she calls them—were terrible creatures; and backed up the statement with a blood-curdling account of how one of these slandered reptiles crept into a squatter cabin one night, and ate up a woman and five children. The woman, by herself, would have satisfied any ordinarily impossible alligator; but no, these liars must make him gorge the five children besides." *Slander* is the curious word in Mark Twain's outburst. He ignores the context, Trollope's direct sighting of the poor whites assembled on the shore, that assembly of Finns, to which she merely appends the story as an example of their short, nasty, and brutish life. It is her attitude, her desire to see what she sees, and the tone of her representation, that infuriates him. What do "these liars" do? They slander the reptile, they make it out to be far worse than it actually is, they come upon her exaggeration ("I never witnessed human nature reduced so low") and expose it. "Unfortunate tourists!" With that epithet, Mark Twain commences his exposure. In this turning of Trollope's "slander," still another movement in the tall tale discloses itself. The tall tale does not deny or conceal the misery of the squatter. It attacks a certain response to that misery, a certain appropriation of its meaning, and, even as it does this, it displaces the feeling such misery should evoke, deflects the import of the object.

"Tell about the South," Shreve insists in *Absalom, Absalom! "What's it like there. What do they do there."* Not now, but formerly, Augustus Baldwin Longstreet begins in *Georgia Scenes,* there was a place in Lincoln County called the "Dark Corner," a place of "vice and folly." His narrator, Hall, is walking in the springtime woods marveling at "its sportive streams, its vocal birds, and its blushing flowers," when he hears the fierce commotion of a violent fight, boisterous voices, awful oaths, grunting and thrashing, and finally the outcry: "Enough! My eye's out!" It is a red-necked plowboy, Hall discovers, wrestling with himself in the forest glade, doing all the voices, enacting a town fight before the courthouse. The youth sullenly explains himself to Hall, then returns to his plow in the adjoining field. "I went to the ground from which he had risen," Hall tells us, "and there were the prints of his two thumbs, plunged up to the balls in the mellow earth, about the distance of a man's eyes apart; and the ground around was broken up as if two stags had been engaged upon it." "Georgia Theatrics" is the best piece in Longstreet's book. "The language of the narrator is as urbane as Addison's," Kenneth Lynn writes in *Mark Twain and Southwestern Humor* (1959); "the cool elegance of the diction, the measured rhythms, the familiar yet reserved tone, are the credentials of an impeccably civilized man." So the South, in 1835, is told, in this patrician voice, in that opposed peasant voice. "You brute!" says Hall, coming upon the youth. "You needn't

kick before you're spurr'd," he insolently replies. "There a'nt nobody there, nor ha'nt been nother. I was jist seein' how I could 'a' *fout*."

There are sharp and smooth sketches in Longstreet's text. Some are perfectly written in the voice of that Whiggish sensibility, are written in silvery Augustan prose, and the subject is sentimental, antiquarian. In others—"Georgia Theatrics," "The Horse Swap," "The Fight"—Longstreet keeps a certain distance from the fluent Addisonian voice. "Georgia Theatrics" is a cautionary tale about rage. "Enough! My eye's out!" And it looks again, past Hall's discomfiture and wonder, at the seeming savagery of the poor white ("You brute!"), this raw creature risen from the ground, half-bestial, this fellow who is desperately struggling with himself. In "The Fight," Longstreet is unsparing in his gore. As the fight ends, one combatant has his left ear and a large part of his left cheek bitten off. The other has lost a third of his nose. Hall's disclaimer at the end of the sketch draws a nervous line around this barbaric backwoods violence. "Thanks to the Christian religion, to schools, colleges, and benevolent associations, such scenes of barbarism and cruelty . . . are now of rare occurrence, though they may still be occasionally met with in some of the new counties. Wherever they prevail, they are a disgrace to that community." *Georgia Scenes* has its dark pictures of Southern life, but they are framed, rationalized. Longstreet's Southern squires know where the "Dark Corner" is, know of it, but they are never in it, never participate in its barbarism and cruelty.

There are other versions of these Southern scenes, narratives where the "Dark Corner" is the world, where the Addisonian narrator is often a figure of inhibition, of blindness. In Johnson Jones Hooper's *Some Adventures of Captain Simon Suggs* (1845), Lynn observes, "we drift loose from the familiar assurances of the Whig universe into a featureless world of nightmarish sounds." Suggs's motto—"IT IS GOOD TO BE SHIFTY IN A NEW COUNTRY"—is unchallenged in Hooper's text. The writers of these tales are, properly speaking, the Southwestern humorists, and they constitute something of a circle, share a common style. William T. Porter's *Spirit of the Times: A Chronicle of the Turf, Agriculture, Field Sports, Literature and the Stage*, founded in 1831, published in New York, effectively became the home journal for Southwestern humor in the 1840s. The Southern writers Porter collected, notably William Tappan Thompson (Major Jones), Charles F. M. Noland (Pete Whetstone), Hooper (Simon Suggs), Henry Clay Lewis (Madison Tensas), and Thomas Bangs Thorpe, happily created an intertextual parlance in the *Spirit of the Times*, referred familiarly to each other's tales and characters, were at play with a common style, a shared form. It was Porter who found the colloquial jewel in Jacksonian regional writing, Thorpe's "Big Bear of

Arkansas." He published it in 1841, realizing, as did many of his readers, that this tale was somehow definitive. But what did it tell of the South? It positively discouraged travel to Arkansas.

A transplanted Northerner who had moved to Louisiana for his health, a sometime painter of portraits and wildlife who had studied with John Quidor in New York, Thorpe had a certain intellectual and artistic distance from the Southern lie exposed in the Southern tall tale. In 1854, living once more in New York, he would publish an antislavery novel, *The Master's House: A Tale of Southern Life*. Thorpe brought to his humorous writing a painterly sense of the formally arranged composition. It was indeed the literary finish of "The Big Bear of Arkansas" that most impressed Porter and elicited congratulation from the other humorists. Henry Clay Lewis was one of those who admired Thorpe's tale, and yet he saw clearly the awful message Thorpe had tucked into his tale. *For its overweening pride, its moral blindness, the South was to suffer castration and humiliation*. In "The Indefatigible Bear Hunter," which reinstates the heroic Southern countryman Thorpe had demystified, Lewis would briefly answer that "slanderous" judgment. Of Mike Hooter, known as Mik-hoo-tah in the text, Lewis writes: "The 'Big Bear of Arkansas' would not have given him an hour's extra work or raised a fresh wrinkle on his already care-corrugated brow." Moreover, this hunter, "though almost daily imbruing his hands in the blood of Bruin," had "not become an impious or cruel-hearted man." Dismasted, having already lost one leg to a bear, Lewis's hunter returns indomitably to the hunt and kills his bear with the splintered stump of his wooden leg. He is a proto-Ahab, indefatigable, the sign of Southern mettle. Thorpe understood the double movement of the tall tale, the duplicitous nature of its exchanges, understood the nature of the contradiction (the pious killer) that would simply reappear in Lewis's response. He was an outsider who had gotten inside, who was not a tourist, not hatefully disposed. Thorpe intuitively grasped the logic of the tall tale's ambivalence. He had studied the Southern intelligence that operated in the tall tale, saw its blindness, its bafflement, and, in 1841, half Northerner, half Southerner, he perfectly caught the poignance of its constrained thinking.

This, then, is what the tall tale offered Thorpe. In this form, and in this form only, the South put at risk the issue of its cultural identity, considered its alibi. What was urbane, genial, at ease with country manners, in Southern life, this storied Southern civility displaced to its backcountry everything that was mean, amoral, sadistic, and drew round its villainous speech a discursive containment, the relaxed, rational Addisonian voice. Ideally these two voices, these two persons, appeared in their proper relation. Yet the patrician writer who depicted the poor white was imaginative enough to catch in that rough country speech the true wit of a bitter knowledge, could see the native speaker's sardonic grin peel the pose from the interlocutor's Addisonian stance, and so was himself uncertain, ambivalent. There was a power in the subtext, in the framed story. The compulsive drive of the Jacksonian ego spoke here, in plainest English, of its desire, its disillusion. "This here's a mighty hard world," Simon Suggs reflects, "to git along in. Ef a feller don't make every aidge cut, he's in the background directly." Lewis's bear hunter is determined to get his name "put in a book with a yaller kiver," and it is for that reason he stands alone in the woods, drives his wooden leg into the ground, and prepares to meet the onslaught of a grizzly bear. "I warn't a genus, Doc, I nude that, nor I warn't dicshunary," the hunter confesses to the interlocutor. "So I determined to strike out in new track for glory and 'title myself to be called the 'bear hunter of Ameriky.' " It was, in fact, this active voice, and not the interlocutor's leisurely voice, that often bespoke the writer's secret perspective, his desire.

Everything the tall tale is about is displayed and realized in "The Big Bear of Arkansas." Here is the steamboat, the *Invincible*, sister ship to the *Fidèle* in Herman Melville's *The Confidence-Man* (1857), a company of planters, pedlars, merchants, farmers, and among them the "half horse half alligator species of men, who are peculiar to 'old Mississippi,' and who appear to gain a livelihood by simply going up and down the river." Here, too, is our interlocutor, "a man of observation" who likes "to read the great book of character so favorably opened before him." And there, stepping into the story, declaring his title, his legend—"Hurra for the Big Bear of Arkansaw!"—is the curious figure of "Davy Crockett." His name in this text is Jim Doggett. Behind the bearish bluster, he is simply a dogged man, and that is how Thorpe divides his enclosed tale. First the "Big Bear" performs in the bar, regaling the crowd. Then, prompted by a question from the interlocutor, the "Big Bear" explains his name. All the awfulness that is so brilliantly turned in the first section, defiantly lied about, returns in the second, and is not turned. This part of the tale expends itself in two anticlimaxes, in a double bewilderment.

In the first section, the "Big Bear" ranges from question to question, deftly seizing each one and immediately converting it. In some such way, warmed with whiskey, Crockett must have improvised. Doggett's tall talk exposes the misery of life in Arkansas, this "creation state" that is "without fault." Its mosquitoes "are rather *enormous*," he admits, but then "mosquitoes is natur, and I never find fault with her. If they ar large, Arkansaw is large, her varmints ar large, her trees ar large, her rivers ar large, and a small mosquito would be of no more use in Arkansaw than preaching in a cane-brake." In the second section, Doggett's tall talk misfires. He had become the "best bear hunter" in his district, Doggett tells the assembly, and was enjoying his mastery when a certain bear begins to mark the sassafras trees. The marks indicate monstrous size. It is indeed the Creation Bear, and this bear not only eludes Doggett in the hunt but, after a while, begins to hunt Doggett. Obsessed, frustrated, Doggett begins to waste away. He loses his forest sense, can't manage his musket, thinks on one hunt that he has killed the Creation Bear only to discover that he has shot a "she-bear." Then, one morning, as he is in the woods near his house, squatting to defecate, the Creation Bear suddenly appears. "Stranger," Doggett says, "he loomed up like a *black mist*, seemed so large, and he walked right towards me." With his pants down around his ankles, tripping, Doggett dishonorably shoots the bear.

How, then, is the interlocutor to frame this tale, to draw his relation to Jim Doggett, to the "Davy Crockett" hidden in the story? Thorpe tells us this much: Doggett has falsely appropriated, for the sake of his performance, the meaning of the Big Bear. He is in drinking company. Here's a bearskin, the famous grin: "Hurra for the Big Bear of Arkansaw!" Yet Doggett knows the true story. The meaning of the Big Bear is Nemesis. He is the presiding spirit of that Southern "natur," immense, unforgiving, capricious. Between Doggett and his desire (his title), a *"black mist"* intervenes. Besmeared, the hunter stands over the carcass of the Creation Bear. Although Doggett takes the trophy, makes a bedspread of its skin, takes its name, he knows all the same that it is history, social encroachment, something else, certainly not his effort, that makes the bear give up, choose its perishing. This bear was *"unhuntable,"* he allows, *"and died when his time come."* The interlocutor's response is to mythicize, to attribute Doggett's mystification to "superstitious awe," a feeling "common with all 'children of the wood,'" when they meet with any thing out of their every-day experience." A silence falls. The story ends. What is to be read in this Southern book of Southern characters? Both interlocutor and native speaker, patrician and poor white, are blind to the meaning of their lie.

In 1851–52 *Uncle Tom's Cabin* appears. Harriet Beecher Stowe transforms Southern writing with this novel, divides Southern literature into two branches, relevant and irrelevant. She teaches Southern writers their subject, and those who learn it, Mark Twain, Faulkner, prosper. Those who avoid her instruction, who go on fantasizing, mystifying, embellishing the lie, Thomas Nelson Page, Margaret Mitchell, do not. It is a book of answers, *Uncle Tom's Cabin*, unerring. This is what the Southern novel must do. Here are its characters, white and black, a perfect matching of pairs, and this is what, in love and anger, they must say to each other. *Uncle Tom's Cabin* exhibits the Southern alibi in its best spokesman, the exemplar of Southern civility, Augustine St. Clare, whose interlocution we abruptly lose near the end of the novel. St. Clare tries to separate two fighters in a bar and is stabbed with a bowie knife. Into the place of his mastery, his control, steps another. This one is all hard edges, amoral, vicious. Simon Legree will show his fist twice, first to Uncle Tom, whom he has just bought, and then to the uneasy gentry who are standing nearby on the steamboat. "Just feel of my knuckles, now; look at my fist. Tell ye, sir, the flesh on 't has come jest like stone, practising on niggers,—feel on it." Hard fist, hard words. If Southern writers had diversely pondered in the tall tale the relation of these two figures, St. Clare and Legree, had shifted and weighed their difference, *Uncle Tom's Cabin*, with a single blow, showed what they had in common—Uncle Tom. As St. Clare's silvery discourse disappears, so much mist, Legree's hard fist emerges. Southern identity, as Stowe sees it, is the coincidence of these two persons, these two voices, and it is the awful one that must finally dominate. In the conclusion to *Uncle Tom's Cabin*, Stowe appeals to her Southern readers, appeals to Southern women, to search their own "secret souls" and "private conversings." "Is *man* ever a creature to be trusted with wholly irresponsible power?" That is the clincher in *Uncle Tom's Cabin*.

In the 1850s regional writing is adversarial. Northerners go South and depict horrors. Southerners describe the factory towns of New England, behold the slaving Irish in the slums of New York. When Frederick Law Olmsted rides through the deep South in 1854, he does not find a single clever Southerner. Everyone he meets has suffered a kind of brain damage, is morally retarded, intellectually disabled, either a lout or a lump. George Washington Harris would send a belligerent Sut Lovingood to New York in 1858. Sut would find the city full of queer dandies. "They haint neither man nur 'oman," he reports, not much good at fighting. He took also into account the radicals and free-lovers. *"Who's in New York tu tame me?"* Sut wants to know.

Northern satirists had indeed begun their fire in 1846–47, attacking the war with Mexico, which many Northerners saw as a Southern adventure, a reach for territory and power. It is Lowell who directly expresses, in a colloquial voice, liberal political feeling in the North. Hosea Biglow, a simple New England farmer, begins to write verse letters for the *Boston Courier* in 1846, and from the start Lowell aims at "them Southun fellers." Lowell would subsequently try to broaden the scope of Biglow's letters, to enhance their regional flavor. He would stress their literary value as colloquial writing, add characters: Parson Wilbur, a pedantic minister, Birdofredum Sawin, a rural lout; but from the First Series to the Second Series, which ends in 1866, the political line dominates. Jaalam, Lowell's invented village, with its antiquarian parson, its thriving, commonsensical farmer folk, its town meeting and churchgoing, is picture-perfect, eminently fit to pass judgment on "them nigger-drivin' States."

Everything awful the North saw in the South—its stupidity, its sexual license, its violence, its bestiality—Harris defiantly publishes in *Sut Lovingood's Yarns*. Sut bursts into Harris's text, "a queer-looking, long legged, short bodied, small headed, white haired, hog eyed, funny sort of genius, fresh from some bench-legged Jew's clothing store, mounted on 'Tearpoke,' a nick tailed, bow necked, long, poor, pale sorrel horse." His reckless spirit rules this Southern countryside. Sut has a clear, cold understanding of "natur." "Whar thar ain't enuf feed, big childer roots littil childer outen the troff, an' gobbils up thar part," he tells us. *Sut Lovingood's Yarns*, Edmund Wilson distastefully observes in *Patriotic Gore* (1962), "is by far the most repellent book of any real literary merit in American literature."

Harris began writing sketches for the *Spirit of the Times* in 1843. In his early work, stories about racing and frontier fights, he is very much in the ongoing Southwestern literary mode. "The Knob Dance, a Tennessee Frolic" (1845), shows Harris's debt to Longstreet's *Georgia Scenes*. Sut is his discovery, and with Sut, who first appears, as we have just seen him, in the sketch "Sut Lovingood's Daddy, Acting Horse" (1854), Harris begins to alter significantly the form and style of Southwestern humor. The Lovingoods are this poor: Sut's Dad must be harnessed, must pull the plow. He acts horsey, kicks at the bridling, makes Sut labor with the plow. In the midst of his prankish horseplay, Dad stirs up a hornets' nest, takes flight, heads for the creek, jumps in, Sut following with joyous rapture. It is a piece of knockabout physical comedy, visually specific, just that. Stung, Dad "fotch a squeal wus nur ara stud hoss in the State," and explodes into action. "When he cum tu the fence, he jis tore thru hit, bustin an' scatterin ni ontu seven panils wif lots ove broken rails. Rite yere he lef the gophers, geers, close, clevis, an' swingltress, all mix'd up, an' not wuf a durn." In the sketches that follow, mostly written for the *Nashville Union & American*, Harris, it might be said, brings the Southwestern tale to its end. The Southern rage, the Southern cruelty, that Longstreet had contained in *Georgia Scenes* is here set off in a series of demolitions.

Sut's tales are not, properly speaking, tall tales. They are something else.

Sut calls them "skeers." Each "skeer," both in the tale and the telling, is carefully crafted, painstakingly constructed. Harris had numerous careers: mechanic, planter, merchant, factory owner, superintendent of a glass-works. He was, it would seem, above all, a mechanic, something of an engineer curious about the production of "special effects." He liked to imagine things splintering, breaking, smashing. He liked to write about things flying apart. Sut looses an enraged bull upon a wedding party, and it produces this splendid explosion of things: "Pickil crocks, perserves jars, vinegar jugs, seed bags, yarb bunches, paragorick bottils, aig baskits, an' delf war—all mix'd dam permiskusly, an' not worth the sortin, by a duller an' a 'alf."

Harris's interlocutor, "George," has only the barest existence in these sketches. It is understood that "George" admires Sut's "genius," knows what Sut is about, what Sut's scare is. We may see Sut as the trickster, the scary spirit of this mountainous place in eastern Tennessee, its cruel demigod, see him as the South reduced, missing a vowel, a consonant, and its conscience, as the South unpenned, almost out of its genteel frame, its patience, the furious South, the vengeful South, the scary South; but for "George," who relishes the pure scathing intensity of Sut's released aggression, Sut is primarily a "funny sort of genius," an estimable artist at creating havoc. Harris's work effectively asks us to dissociate our moral and visual attention. Just as we might watch, and appreciate, beautifully engineered disasters in movies, car crashes, buildings collapsing, just as we might watch outrageous physical comedy, the Three Stooges at their mayhem, so we might read Harris's tour-de-force sketches: "Old Skissim's Middle Boy," "Mrs. Yardley's Quilting," "Sut at a Negro Night-Meeting," and not be necessarily "skeer'd."

In the *Yarns*, Harris's colloquial style liberates vision, speaks the thing. What is this South like? What do they do there? These are the hard questions the Southern regional writer had to answer in the Jacksonian period. A tall tale is one response. This is another: explicit revelation, scary, told in the blackest of humors. Sut's tales, proudly presented, barely bracketed, relate sadistic pranks, acts of vandalism, practical jokes that humiliate and injure the victims, and they are vividly told in a mean hard voice. "I kotch a ole bull frog once an' druv a nail thru his lips inter a post, tied two rocks tu his hine toes and stuck a darnin needil inter his tail tu let out the misture, an left him there tu dry." The text itself is hard: Harris's rendering of Sut's dialect is unremitting in its difficult orthography. Sut's talk is a spew of hateful epithets. He hates the "hook-nose Jews," the "pot-gutted, ball-heded Baptis' bull nigger," the "roach-maned, wall eyed Irishman." He hates the sheriff, the parson, the itinerant pedlar, the suspect freemason, and, most of all, he hates the Yankee. He hates Hosea Biglow. From this Suttish boiling, this superabundance, Mark Twain gets Pap Finn, Faulkner gets Thomas Sutpen, Jason Compson, Mink Snopes, and others. Of all the colloquial writers in the Jacksonian period, Harris is the strongest, and the most problematical.

Jacksonian writers had wanted ruins. It got them from Sut. After his devastation of Mrs. Yardley's quilting bee, Sut visits the site to inspect the damage: "I tracked the route that hoss tuck in his kalamantus skeer, by quilt rags, tufts ove cotton, bunches of har (human an' hoss), an' scraps ove gridiron jackid stickin ontu the bushes, an' plum at the aind ove hit, whar all the signs gin out, I foun a piece ove watch chain an' a hosses head." Blown to tatters, that earlier Jacksonian desire for picturesque ruins, for the bucolic scene, and the peasant in his colorful outfit. So, too, is the duplicitous tall tale. "George" has nothing to say about this "kalamantus skeer." It is Sut who has come directly to speak for Harris, to express him. American ruins, Harris had discovered, look like wreckage.

Neil Schmitz

A New Nation's Drama

As popular culture texts, the plays of early America lend themselves to valuable contextual study in a way that little else in American literature does. For this was an art form that captured the spirit of the hour, at the extreme, turning the theater that it fed into a notoriously violent place. Often even before a real-life drama reached its denouement, a dramatic version of the same event was being read or played on stage. The special circumstances of early America—its turbulent politics, its uncertain cultural identity, its short history and budding political drama—often seemed to blur the line between art and life. As history invaded drama and drama created history, the theater of the battlefield and town-hall seemed scarcely distinguishable from the stage version of the same events. Ample illustration is provided by the events surrounding theater riots and the dramatization of battles and political intrigue during the American Revolution while the war was still in progress.

Most of the plays have scant intrinsic literary interest. The critic to do a new critical or poststructuralist literary study of the dramas of early America has not yet appeared, nor is ever likely to appear, given the character of the plays. The kinds of literary scholarship that they inevitably do generate with some regularity are bibliographies, thematic studies of frequently recurring character types—the Indian, the frontiersman, the spunky heroine, George Washington—and considerations of particular dramatists as prologue to the realists of twentieth-century America. The nature of literary criticism of America's early drama has to be understood in light of the supreme irony of the American stage: that while its *theater*, recognized for its liveliness and artistic merit, constitutes one of the most active chapters of national cultural history, only the most modest claims can be made for the literary excellence of its *drama*.

Colonial circumstances did not augur well for rapid development of a great English-language theater or drama in the New World. Obviously, the earliest dramatic performances were tribal dances of the first Americans. Records of Mexico, the Southwest, and Canada indicate that sixteenth-century French and Spanish communities were able to view biblical dramas presented or encouraged by the Roman Catholic church. Such was not the case in the English-speaking New World where the expurgation from the church of the theatrical tradition, inherent in the sacraments and other high ritual, was fundamental to radical protestantism, notably Puritan and Quaker sects. The well-documented animosity to the stage was not new in America, but the overwhelming predominancy of the Puritans and Quakers meant that the disapproval of drama was felt more keenly in America than it was in the broader and older European and English intellectual tradition. The legal prohibition of the drama by American churches was founded on a variety of beliefs that actually slowed the development of all the literary arts, but especially drama: the distrust of the imagination as a faculty susceptible to Satan's use and to the temptation to create fictional worlds; the power of the Protestant Ethic, by means of which art and entertainment were branded as idle; the distrust of drama in performance as a tool by which emotions were manipulated; the ribaldry and irreverence traditionally found in many plays; and finally the immorality of the playhouse itself, which supported a bar and a third tier for prostitutes.

From the colonial period until the twentieth century, American drama, defined here as plays written by playwrights living in America, lagged behind theater, which was kept lively by British and European plays and performers. Even in the seventeenth century, American theater was putting down roots in areas, like South Carolina and Virginia, dominated by the Church of England and settled by colonists with sympathies and tastes more cavalier than those of New England Puritans. However, the dramas as well as the church in these areas were English.

The self-conscious groping to identify a drama that could be labeled American and to establish an American dramatic tradition became a national exercise in self-definition that interested some colonial writers, frequently occupied nineteenth-century seekers of cultural independence, and obsessed those who were to write the drama's history. As a consequence, a description of early American drama is often a compendium of landmarks, somewhat on the order of a baseball hall of fame, but it also gives some idea of what dramatic events originated when: *Ye Bare and Ye Cubb* (1665), attributed to a Virginian, William Darby, and two other performers, is the first play written by an American in English and presented in what is now the United States; Robert Hunter's *Androboros* (1714) is the first known published play by an American resident; Major Robert Rogers's *Ponteach; or, The Savages of America* (1766) is the first play to treat a Native American subject seriously; Thomas Godfrey's *The Prince of Parthia* (1767) is the first original play by a native author to be professionally produced; William Dunlap's *The Father; or, American Shandy-ism* (1789) is the first play written by an American-born theater professional. As grandiose and confusing as such lists can become, they suggest the ways used to begin building, from the ground up, a national dramatic tradition independent of English letters.

In light of widespread disapproval, it is not surprising that the first flowering of that tradition, *Ye Bare and Ye Cubb*, was nipped in the bud when its three author-performers were briefly detained immediately afterward on grounds of immorality. Not until the eighteenth century did American drama begin to sustain some momentum, actually rising in level of activity coincident with the rising discontent with England. Even here it is difficult with assurance to classify many of the recorded eighteenth-century works as either dramas or American. A number were written and performed by Tories or British officers for English troops, "American" in the loosest possible sense. Into this group fall Jonathan Sewall's 1774 *The Americans Roused, in a Cure for the Spleen*, General John Burgoyne's 1776 *The Blockade*, and an anonymous play of the same year entitled *The Battle of Brooklyn*. It is interesting that works generated at this time by authors of anti-Revolutionary, pro-British sentiment are far more playable than those of their adversaries. Revolutionaries, on the other hand, were inclined to write dramatic argument with little potential for stage success. Into this category fall works of America's foremost Revolutionary playwright, Mercy Otis Warren, who dominated the field of blatantly propagandistic poetic dialogues that predate the proliferation of American drama suitable for staging. *The Adulateur: A Tragedy, as It Is Now Acted in Upper Servia* (1773) and *The Group* (1775) were provocative satires of the political scene leading to the Revolution; *The Blockheads; or, The Affrighted Officers*, attributed to Mrs. Warren, was written during the war, in 1776, as a response to General Burgoyne's *The Blockade* of the same year.

To find American pioneers in a form indisputably intended for stage performance, drama historians must turn elsewhere. Two outstanding examples are *The Fall of British Tyranny*, a 1776 chronicle drama attributed to John Leacock, and *André* (1798), one of several original plays by the father of American drama, William Dunlap. Both make dramatic use of the American Revolution and George Washington, popular subjects on stage well into the nineteenth century. Otherwise, the two plays are vastly different, *The Fall of British Tyranny* being a blatantly propagandistic piece written about the war while it was in progress. As an early American chronicle, it is loosely and episodically constructed around several major events, including the battle of Bunker Hill and the death of General Richard Montgomery. The proximity of real drama and stage drama is impressive because the history portrayed in the play was being made at the time of the play's appearance, the outcome of the war and of the play still undecided at the drama's close. Not only is this tedious play an early type of the Revolutionary War drama, it also has many elements of popular stage panoramas that amused nineteenth-century audiences.

William Dunlap's *André*, performed in 1798, reveals just how far the Revolutionary War drama had come in twenty-two years. By comparison with *The Fall of British Tyranny*, Dunlap's play was tightly constructed, with a time span of twenty-four hours and four settings and with a cast of only ten speaking characters. It is a more sophisticated study of a very complex situation, a war play essentially without villains. Both the condemned spy, John André, and his adversary, General Washington, are heroic figures in their own way. André's personal heroism is in sharp contradiction with his betrayal of a cause. Washington's actions are also open to question in that, heroic as he seems, he is willing to sacrifice to the cause (and from vengeance) two men of quality, one of whom is totally innocent. Although Dunlap was a thoroughgoing Federalist who venerated Washington, his sympathy with André, a fellow stage artist and sometime actor, was ill-concealed. The extraordinary effect of the play comes from the creation of a heroic drama on a classical scale of action with mythic characters involved in a timeless conflict between allegiance to an individual and allegiance to a cause—and Dunlap did it, not with Greek and Roman sagas, but with materials of his own time. His mythic warrior, George Washington, also an avid playgoer, was still alive when the play was produced, and fights erupted outside the theater after the play ended, necessitating some rewriting in order to save the reputation, not to mention the hide, of the actor who had to challenge Washington in the play.

Ponteach, written by the famous Indian fighter, Major Robert Rogers, is obviously playable but was never staged. Rogers used drama to mythologize events of his own experience. However, he accomplished this in a very unexpected way. Ironically, every white character of every nationality, without exception (including a priest), who, like the playwright, had had any association with Indians, is an unscrupulous blackguard, while Rogers's hero is an Indian chief. *Ponteach* was the first of a popular American type that saturated the nineteenth century with glorified noble savages whose excessive breast-beating made them targets of very successful parody.

The ideals attributed to unsullied nature, reflected in the typical Indian drama, were also present in another play of the eighteenth century, *The Prince of Parthia* (1767), by Thomas Godfrey, one year after *Ponteach*. Despite the later play's heavy debt to Elizabethan tragedies and histories and its setting in the first century B.C., it is very like *Ponteach* in situation, psychology, and ideals. Both celebrate heroes of noble blood who belong to a pre-Christian golden age in the process of disintegration. Although warriors in each play must do battle with enemies external to the tribe, the greater danger issues from within the family, between rival brothers in a reenactment of the enmity between Cain and Abel on the outskirts of paradise. Ponteach, renouncing forever the civilized Christians' butchery of nature and provocation of treachery within the tribe, heads West like Huck Finn. Both plays turn on the seduction of innocence and end tragically with the murder and suicide of lovers.

The Contrast (1787) by Royall Tyler is in the tradition of the English comedy of manners, taking as its subject, however, the contrast between trivial-minded slaves to European fashion and a solid, down-to-earth, serious-minded American patriot. It is a contrast in cultures, one shallow and one substantial. Tyler used the form of Richard Sheridan's *The School for Scandal* (1777) for his American subject, even having his rustic Jonathan, the prototype of many rural stage Yankees to follow, give his own hysterical interpretation of Sheridan's play, which Jonathan has mistaken for an actual occurrence. Tyler's smooth, witty, quick-paced play still reads and plays as if it were from the pen of a seasoned theatrical professional instead of an attorney who, previous to its composition, had had very little experience with the stage or drama.

The Contrast led the way for the American society comedy that was most apparent in fashionable theaters of nineteenth-century America. But low comedies were also a major part of nineteenth-century drama, especially in working-class theaters. The early play that prefigures America's taste for slapstick and ribaldry is the first published play in America, New York Governor Robert Hunter's *Androboros*. The interplay of dramatic action with historical action takes an interesting turn in this play in that Governor Hunter includes himself as a character. New York politicians are ridiculed with raucous and effective tricks of broad comedy including outrageous names, dialects, malapropisms, nonsense legislation, and scatology. The play includes scenes in which the title character, identified as General Francis Nicholson, is shoved into a collapsing chair, soaked with a bucket of sludge, belched on, sprayed with a mouthful of ale, and has snuff thrown in his eyes.

Despite many literary protests on the part of Ralph Waldo Emerson, Edgar Allan Poe, Washington Irving, and others that America was capable of producing and supporting superior native art independent of England and Europe, the American stage in the nineteenth century was decidedly colonial, attested to by the overwhelming number of Shakespearean productions supported by upper- and lower-class audiences alike, largely rendered by English actors, and by the popularity of adaptations of European works. Dramas written by American authors constituted a very small part of theatrical activity, but subjects and character types chosen by American playwrights were largely native: serious Indian plays, frontier and rural dramas, Yankee plays, temperance plays, minstrel afterpieces, burlesques, and melodramas.

A review of the emergence of these types in the context of theatrical landmarks and national history indicates the extent to which drama engaged national issues of the day. In the first two decades of the century, when Jeffersonian Republicanism widened democracy and power began to shift from New England westward and southward, when British impressment of seamen, among other antagonisms, brought on an embargo of British manufactures and the War of 1812, national pride ran high, bringing with it further dramatic interest in promulgating the natural, which is to say, national values represented by the American rustic and frontiersman. Along with Westward expansion between 1814 and 1824 came such plays as *She Would Be a Soldier; or, The Plains of Chippewa* (1819) by James Nelson Barker and *The Forest Rose; or, American Farmers* (1825) by Samuel Woodworth. The frontiersman and the rustic were to be the most enduring types on the American stage in the nineteenth century, right up to James A. Herne's 1892 production of *Shore Acres*.

Despite the Seminole War of 1817 and the formation of Andrew Jackson's Indian solution in the 1830s, the romantic impulse to idealize the man of nature, which James Fenimore Cooper had given way to with great success, contributed to another distinctive type—the Indian play, the first produced being *Tammany* written in 1794 by Anne Kemble Hatton. American dramatists had written plays about Indians since the Revolutionary period, but with the production of *Metamora; or, The Last of the Wampanoags* by John Augustus Stone, the demand for Indian plays really began. Its 1829 production resulted from a contest offered by Edwin Forrest, the first male star of an American stage that had been dominated by English actors. In an attempt to find himself a vehicle with which to further native drama, Forrest offered a prize of five hundred dollars for "the best tragedy, in five acts, of which the hero or principal character, shall be an aboriginal of this country." An expression of the author's and the actor/sponsor's national sentiments was voiced in the prologue and epilogue, which pled for support of native plays. The prizewinning drama reinforced a pattern for Indian plays that can be discerned in an 1830 production, *Pocahontas; or, The Settlers of Virginia*, by George Washington Parke Custis. Both plays open with an Englishman, left behind in the New World for many years, who rejoices at the arrival of English explorers. Both plays turn on the threat of an arranged marriage distasteful to the women protagonists. In both plays the Indian's world is a paradise that falls with the arrival of the white men greedy for gold and land. The earlier play signals the demise of a whole culture in the murder/suicide of Metamora and his wife. *Pocahontas* shows one Indian character, Metacoran, choosing not to accept an "alliance with the usurpers of his country." Instead he flees west where "there rolls a western wave . . . on the utmost verge of the land." His rival and Pocahontas's father, Powhatan, blesses a union between the best of natural and traditional cultures in the marriage of Pocahontas and John Rolfe. Edwin Forrest made a fortune from *Metamora;* his dramatist, John Augustus Stone, received five hundred dollars and a handsome tombstone that Forrest had placed on his grave after Stone's suicide. As important as *Metamora* and the events surrounding its production were in America's struggle for cultural independence, the play's place in the literary history of American letters is curious and typical of many other nineteenth-century plays: though it spawned more Indian dramas and, itself, continued to be played throughout Forrest's career, even withstanding devastating burlesque, it vanished entirely as soon as it was no longer produced on stage, only an incomplete version having been available for publication in 1841.

The 1840s and 1850s were probably the most theatrically significant decades in the century. Vital to what was happening in drama were the political events of the period. In the background was the Whig victory of 1840, following in the wake of the 1837 financial crash and widespread unemployment. Growing urban areas and an immense increase in immigration led to the nativist movement and labor agitation for better wages and working conditions. Between 1830 and 1840 railroads opened much of the frontier to settlement. What would be the two most energetic areas of English-language theater outside New York City were beginning to be settled: California in 1849 and Salt Lake City in 1847. The 1830s and 1840s were the years of "the Benevolent Empire," when religious societies attempted to effect moral and social change in education, women's rights, temperance, prisons, and asylums, aiming to reform the poor in America as well as savages abroad. Although abolition had already been brought to the public's attention in 1831 with William Lloyd Garrison's spirited attacks in *The Liberator*, the issue heated up in 1850 with the enforcement of the Fugitive Slave Act, the publication of Harriet Beecher Stowe's *Uncle Tom's Cabin; or, Life among the Lowly* in 1852, and John Brown's raids in Kansas in 1856 and on Harpers Ferry in 1859.

Like the masterpieces of the American Renaissance, milestones in American drama also cluster in the 1840s and 1850s. A segment of the theater joined the Benevolent Empire's moral crusade in 1843 when *The Drunkard; or, The Fallen Saved* by William Henry Smith, based on a novel, was produced in the Boston Museum. This first of many temperance dramas drew into the theater a class of patrons who had previously shunned the stage as disreputable. Members of the Temperance Society in America, which, through women's rights efforts, had been growing in strength since its founding in 1826, were only too pleased to have an ally as effective as the stage, only too pleased to have the use of a play as persuasive as *The Drunkard*. On the one hand, *The Drunkard* borrowed all the stage gimmicks that entertained Americans in other plays in the theater: a buried will, a secret identity, a last-minute rescue from an attempted assault, a forgery, and a hissable villain. On the other hand, its melodrama did not diminish the almost clinical credibility of the main character's alcoholism.

In 1845 the nineteenth century's first and most successful American comedy of manners was staged, encouraging a group of less well executed social satires. Anna Cora Mowatt was already a prolific writer with a broad classical education and extensive experience as an amateur actress and playwright at the time she wrote *Fashion; or, Life in New York. The Autobiography of an Actress* (1854) is her rare early account of the translation of a drama from paper to stage. The form of *Fashion* is thoroughly European, in the mode of the eighteenth-century bourgeois play. Even the tone is British in its sophisticated ridicule of the *nouveaux riches*—their laughable past lives as clerks and cooks, and their inability to command proper French pronunciation or dress stylishly. This undermines its stated message, which, like its forerunner, Tyler's *The Contrast*, pits francophilic pretenders against independent, truthful patriots—disciples of fashion against disciples of nature. Both villains and heroes are American, foolish or laudable by means of their response to Europe. After the opening of *Fashion*, Mowatt, with great reluctance, went on stage as an actress, several times thereafter taking the part of Gertrude in *Fashion* and the part of Blanche in a second play she authored, *Armand, the Child of the People* (1847).

With the exception of Mercy Warren and Anna Cora Mowatt, standard drama histories do not include discussion, rarely any mention, of women playwrights before the twentieth century. The failure of American women to write plays for the early theater, if it is to be believed, would be especially mystifying for several reasons: women were extremely prolific novelists; plays about women and domestic dramas were popular; playwriting was the least censurable theatrical activity for a woman; and the stage gave many women lives of independence and fulfillment, as did no other segment of nineteenth-century life. These were years of what has been derisively called "petticoat management," the heyday of female stars and formidable managers who commissioned vehicles for the display of their talents. Notable among them were Charlotte Cushman, Laura Keene, Catherine Sinclair, Adah Menken, Mrs. John Drew, Lotta Crabtree, and Clara Morris. Their theatrical activity refutes any suggestion that literary contributions by women were nonexistent, and records of professionally produced plays in America before 1900 belie standard histories. Even a cursory investigation uncovers over 250 plays written by American women. Far from being amateur pieces written for small, out-of-the-way community groups, all of these plays were professionally produced, the large majority opening in New York, Philadelphia, Boston, and San Francisco theaters. Furthermore, among these dramatists were prolific playwrights, including Susanna Rowson, also the novelist-author of *Charlotte Temple*, whose seven plays were professionally produced between 1793 and 1810, and Louisa Medina, whose twenty-one plays were produced between 1829 and 1849. Throughout the century prominent actresses continued to write vehicles for themselves or their companies: Mrs. Sidney Bateman wrote five plays in the 1850s; Laura Keene, six in the 1850s and 1860s; Fanny Herring, eight in the 1860s and 1870s; Olive Logan, nine in the 1870s. Several women who were prolific and popular playwrights at the end of the century now have virtually no place in America's theater history: Marguerite Merington; Madeline Lucette-Ryley; Charlotte Blair Parker, whose *Way Down East* (1898) ran for two decades (an indication of its success: one actress played the lead in Parker's play 4,000 times); and Frances Hodgson Burnett, an Englishwoman whose eight plays produced in America between 1881 and 1897 included one of the century's favorites, *Little Lord Fauntleroy* (1888), a dramatization of her own novel. Martha Morton, who is an obscure figure now, was in her lifetime regarded as the "dean" of women dramatists, in part because she was one of the first women to be commercially successful in the field and to articulate the difficulty women had in writing for the stage. Among her canon of thirty-five plays are nine written in the 1880s and 1890s.

The women mentioned here are only the most prolific writers, selected to illustrate the triumph of silence. The research to be done in this area will present interested scholars with a formidable challenge, for few of the plays and virtually none of these literary reputations have survived.

In the late 1840s, with the rise of cities and working-class audiences, a new American stage type created by Benjamin A. Baker and based on the Bowery fireboy, tagged the Bowery "Bhoy," began appearances in numerous plays. Playing to the same working-class audiences, John Brougham, an English actor who had immigrated to America, halted the proliferation of Indian plays with his 1847 burlesque, *Metamora; or, The Last of the Pollywogs*, ironically inaugurating a burlesque craze that became more extensive than the Indian craze. *The Last of the Pollywogs* was followed in 1855 by his even more successful Indian burlesque, *Po-ca-hon-tas*. Brougham acted in most of his plays. Ironically, burlesque, which was also standard fare in English music halls, was more American in spirit than Indian dramas that made use of native materials. Sympathetic characters in Indian dramas were invariably white English aristocrats and Indians of noble birth, and the emotional force of the dramas arises from their bloodlines and background. Burlesques, on the other hand, were democratic expressions of contempt for all high culture, anything aristocratic, everything pretentious. Any sacred cow was fair game, not just Indian plays. Burlesques, of which John Brougham was the undisputed master, began to flower in the 1840s working-class theater, especially in William Mitchell's Olympic Theater and William Burton's Chambers Street Theater, both in New York City. Parodists seemed most fond of burlesquing their own anglophilic profession, particularly the plays of William Shakespeare, on which British actors still seemed to hold a monopoly. Burlesques diminished regal members of the patrician classes of England and America by placing them in rough, tough American landscapes and putting them to washing dishes, waiting tables, and getting drunk on moonshine. To make Othello a Southern slave, to prepare to ship off Desdemona as the fat lady in P. T. Barnum's museum, to make Julius Caesar a petty New York politician or Kate a suffragette was to deflate a whole category of uppity Englishmen. Some sense of the staggering popularity of burlesques in America can be had by combing the *Annals of the New York Stage* (1927–49) by George C. D. Odell for the number of burlesques written and the number of times they were performed.

Burlesques of English actor William Charles Macready figured prominently in the 1849 Astor Place Riot caused by heated nativist resentment of the British and of upper-class Americans, represented by Macready who was feuding with America's working-class hero, Edwin Forrest. Burlesques, especially one entitled *Macgreedy*, served, according to Odell, as "light artillery" in a theater riot that left twenty-two people dead and thirty wounded.

Much of the rage for burlesques can be attributed to an American institution, the minstrel show, to which was added in the 1850s a final comic playlet, usually a burlesque, called an afterpiece. Despite the minstrel show's debt to European and African entertainments, it has been accurately labeled as the most American art form. Not only the subjects and attitudes of minstrel burlesques but the composition of them constituted exercises in folk democracy, as did nothing else in the theater. Most minstrel burlesques were true collaborative efforts by the entire cast, much of the result impromptu and some of it contributed by the audience during performance. By the 1860s, with over one hundred minstrel groups in the country, the large majority of them consisting of Northern white men in blackface, minstrel techniques had become infused in more traditional American dramas, such as those written for actress Lotta Crabtree.

One of the many ironies of American drama is that the minstrel show, a parody of black people as grotesques, gave blacks opportunities to enter the profession that they otherwise might not have had. Only a few black playwrights, most of their names now lost, contributed plays that predate the minstrel show. Original plays were written between 1821 and 1823 for New York City's African Grove Theater, founded by Henry Brown and supported by actor James Hewlett to provide a stage for black talent. *King Shotaway*, the first play written by an Afro-American, probably Henry Brown, was staged here. The play no longer exists, and its dates are unknown. Two American men of the theater found opportunities for serious theater in Europe that they could not have in America. One was actor Ira Aldridge, who did several adaptations, the one extant play entitled *The Black Doctor* (1847) having been adapted from the French for the London stage. The other black expatriate was New Orleans-native Victor Séjour, who lived in Paris from the age of nineteen and saw twenty-one of his plays produced for the French stage.

The Escape; or, A Leap to Freedom (1856), a notable play something in the style of *Uncle Tom's Cabin*, was written by William Wells Brown, the ex-slave who wrote *Clotel* (1853), the first novel published by an Afro-American. *The Escape*, a dramatization of his autobiographical slave narrative, as well as a second play, *Experience; or, How to Give a Northern Man a Backbone,* written by Brown in the same year, was frequently presented as a reading. Like *Uncle Tom's Cabin, The Escape* is a protest drama, a harsh indictment of religious hypocrisy, with heavy borrowings from minstrel show comedy and a great escape, in this play based on Brown's experience. Records indicate two other plays written by Brown in the 1850s that were neither published nor performed: *Life at the South* (185?) and *Miralda* (1855).

When companies of all-black actors began to form in the late 1850s, identities of black dramatists were submerged in the usual collaboration of the entire troupe in the writing of the piece. Only at the very close of the century did individual black playwrights emerge from the minstrel tradition: *A Trip to Coontown* (1898) by Bob Cole; an afterpiece, *Clorindy, the Origin of the Cake Walk* (1898) by Marion Cook and Paul Laurence Dunbar; and *Senegamian Carnival* (1898) by showman Jesse A. Shipp were sketches that borrowed from the minstrel show's racial parody, at the same time that they began breaking the minstrel show's hold on the musical.

One black writer who had some success as a serious playwright in an age dominated by minstrel shows was William Easton. His verse drama, *Dessalines, a Dramatic Tale; a Single Chapter from Haiti's History*, was produced in Chicago in 1893.

The minstrel show, including the character of Jim Crow, which was first popularized in America by Thomas D. "Daddy" Rice, had been in great demand for over ten years when Harriet Beecher Stowe's first installment of *Uncle Tom's Cabin* appeared in 1851. So it is not surprising that when George L. Aiken dramatized in 1852 the play that would generate great sympathy for black slaves, he would incorporate routines from minstrel shows. Aiken's was not the first drama based largely on Stowe's novel, nor would it be the last, but its success was the most spectacular dramatic event of the century. The play had an astonishing number of performances, was seen in every conceivable place to which theater could be introduced, spawned hundreds of "Tom" companies (in the 1890s there were five hundred), and brought into the theater thousands of people who had earlier been convinced that the theater was literally the devil's den. Aiken not only incorporated the minstrel breakdown and banjo music, he also borrowed from several other popular types of dramas: the tableau (with which his scenes end), the spectacle (of Eliza crossing the ice), the coincidence of melodrama (as when St. Clare is killed just before he can free Tom), the comic rustic, the sadistic villain, the dramatic social commentary (Mr. and Mrs. Howard, the leading actors, had also worked in *The Drunkard*), and the use of a variety of dialects. The play, like the novel, venerates, in romantic fashion, those least corrupted by society—the child and the black slave. Although the Quakers, Little Eva, and Tom find instruction and comfort in a nonintellectual Christianity removed from the religious establishment, perpetuators of the slave system are Christian hypocrites who teach slaves that it is God's will to acquiesce to slavery.

The theater of 1855 ran from the sublime to the ridiculous. In that year were produced John Brougham's "Pokey" and *Francesca da Rimini* by George Henry Boker, a romantic tragedy in blank verse widely recognized as the finest literary achievement by a nineteenth-century American playwright. Taking his plot from Dante's *Inferno*, Boker proved himself the equal of any European or English master of poetry and stagecraft of his day. It was one of the few original plays by an American that did not exploit an American setting or uniquely American issues.

The years following the Civil War brought a surge in industrialism, urbanization, and concentration of wealth as well as changes in the nation's theatrical system. "Single-play combinations," companies formed to take one play on extensive tour, dominated the scene that had once belonged to the star system and the resident and touring repertory company. At the turn of the twentieth century there were some five hundred combinations on tour. In the 1890s big business invaded dramatic art when a syndicate assumed iron-fisted control of theater in America. Drama was also influenced during these years by spectacular technical advances that served both melodrama and realism, allowing Augustin Daly to bring a locomotive on stage in *Under the Gaslight* (1867) and introducing an elaborate system of treadmills, horses, and chariots in the 1899 production of *Ben-Hur* based on the novel by Lew Wallace.

Having weathered the nationally painful and theatrically moribund years of the Civil War during which theater people were generally and regularly suspected of sympathizing with the South, and having survived the disgrace of Abraham Lincoln's assassination in Ford's Theater by an actor, American theater established an alliance with the public by means of two popular plays about American heroes: *Rip Van Winkle* (1865), inspired by Washington Irving, and written jointly by several men including Dion Boucicault and Joe Jefferson, America's favorite actor, who played the lead; and *Davy Crockett; or, Be Sure You're Right, Then Go Ahead* (1872) by Frank Murdoch. A wounded nation wept and raged at the melodramas of Owen Davis, throughout the seventies and eighties laughed at the Mulligan plays about the urban Irish by Edward Harrigan, and allowed itself to be diverted for thirty years by *The Black Crook* (1866), a mindless spectacle by Charles M. Barras, sometimes credited with being the first American musical. The nation also continued casting longing glances backward on a dying American

Eden in plays like *The Old Homestead* (1886) by Denman Thompson and George Ryer.

The most significant literary development from the Civil War to 1900 was the move in the direction of realism from domestic melodrama. Two prominent American writers of realistic fiction, Henry James and William Dean Howells, were occasional playwrights. Gifted playwrights, several of whom learned stagecraft as professional actors, and whose plots and characters remained in the older tradition of melodrama, nevertheless inclined toward realism. Regional dramas like *Davy Crockett* and *The Poor of New York* (1857) often introduced realistic detail in setting and dialect, and even the most sensational melodramas exploited the new mechanical advances to create technical realism. Arising naturally from Steele Mackaye's grounding in the Delsartian system of natural acting was a dialogue in *Hazel Kirke* (1880) more realistic than that to which audiences had been accustomed, and under Mackaye's influence the understated performance lent realism to this enormously successful play. Even so, *Hazel Kirke* is cluttered with the unrealistic trappings of coincidences, asides, interjected songs, and a case of hysterical blindness.

One playwright in particular is notable in the last two decades of the nineteenth century for experimenting with realism and naturalism that went beneath the surface (of technical effects and acting techniques) to involve, more fundamentally, his development of characters and situations. James A. Herne was drama's representative in the new literary camp of realists that included Hamlin Garland and William Dean Howells. Although Herne's work was not free of melodramatic devices, with encouragement from American fiction writers and the inspiration of Henrik Isben, whose plays he had read but not yet seen, Herne showed that he was capable of developing dialogue that reflected the way people actually spoke and plots that were believable and unified. Despite the direction that American fiction had already begun to take, in 1890 his play *Margaret Fleming* was considered radical by audiences and the theatrical establishment. Although the play is recognized as the first important attempt at the kind of realism being encouraged by Howells and Garland, both of whom attempted, with little success, to help Herne secure a hearing, it never fared well. The then taboo subject that frightened theater managers was a woman's decision to bring her wealthy husband's illegitimate infant into her home to rear, to nurse the child with milk from her own breast, and to deplore the double sexual standard that would exact her forgiveness for actions that, had they been hers instead of his, would have damned her forever. Melodramatic coincidences are minimized to allow the play to proceed from forces within the environment of characters. The play had only intermittent and brief runs during Herne's lifetime, even after he altered the ending to secure a measure of appreciation. The original play ended with what he saw as the inevitable separation of the husband and his unforgiving wife. The revision allowed a happy reunion. For all its innovation, *Margaret Fleming* did not readily secure a place in literary history. The only copy of the original version was destroyed in a fire in 1909, and the play now available is the second version, with happy ending, which was reconstructed from notes and memory by Mrs. Herne in 1929.

Two years after *Margaret Fleming* first opened, Herne's *Shore Acres* (1892) was as well received as *Margaret Fleming* had been rejected by audiences and managers. Critics concluded that, whereas the newer play was pleasant, the older one was unpleasant. Audiences and critics alike were less offended by a father who tries to ensure that his eloping daughter will wreck in a ship and drown than by a man who fathers an illegitimate child and has a wife who takes the child in. Be that as it may, *Shore Acres* is a much more satisfactory play than Mrs. Herne's reconstruction of *Margaret Fleming*. There are, it is true, many of the old well-made-play devices: superfluous local color sequences, the revelation of a long-kept secret, coincidences, the manipulation of plot for dramatic effect, and the abrupt reformation of the hardhearted father. Still, a significant contrast between *Shore Acres* and earlier plays is seen in Herne's graceful and realistic dialogue that is said to make almost any actor look good. The play's most striking contribution to realism in drama appears in Herne's extensive stage directions, which are designed to assist the director and actors in the interpretation of characters and scenes; for example, "This must be worked very gradually," and, "Here the staccato changes to a deep ominous murmur."

Furthermore, Herne hung his plot on a conflict of ideas somewhat reminiscent of Pastor Manders and Mrs. Alving in Isben's *Ghosts* but, unlike *Margaret Fleming*, skirting the question of sex and the New Woman. The action affirms the traditional values of hearth and home, family and land, certainly one reason for the play's success. But a person reading the play almost one hundred years afterward appreciates a certain irony: the speculations that raise the humanity of the hero will eventually present a devastating challenge to the very values recommended by the play, going beyond the realism of Eugene O'Neill to the Absurdism of the existentialist playwrights. The physician hero, under the influence of Herbert Spencer, Charles Darwin, and William Dean Howells, is driven to the freedom of the West by his prospective father-in-law, whose life is run by "dead men's laws and dead men's creeds." Here is a world in the process of being disillusioned.

No longer is it possible or desirable to "let the scarlet runners chase you back to childhood," as Denman Thompson and George Ryer wrote in 1886 in *The Old Homestead*. In *Shore Acres*, Darwin and Spencer have given larger meaning to young Nat's line, "I tell yeh there ain't no Santy Claus."

The work of three other playwrights at the turn of the twentieth century pointed the way for a professional theater increasingly free of the limitations of nineteenth-century theatricality: Bronson Howard, Clyde Fitch, and William Vaughan Moody. Even though Howard was a playwright of some eighteen plays, only one of which is now anthologized, and is sometimes misleadingly referred to as the dean of American drama, his importance more accurately belongs in the history of theater rather than drama. The reputation of his major success, *Shenandoah* (1889), has survived the passage of time as a good play, but like Howard's other work, it is the heart of melodrama. One need only note such devices as a case of hidden identity uncovered only at the play's close, other final act revelations, last-minute instantaneous changes of heart, and a scene in which the infant of the dead, once misunderstood son unites the hero's widow and his father. Still the play occupies a critical place in theater history in having launched the theatrical business empire of Charles Frohman, its producer. Theater began to be big business with *Shenandoah*. Howard's chief contribution to the drama was not so much the literature that he wrote as it was the high level of professionalism he sought for practitioners of his craft. As a former journalist he used his access to the press to encourage high regard for American plays and for playwrights whose reputations had frequently suffered by comparison with British and European dramatists. His financial success was also distinct encouragement to the profession, as was his founding of the American Dramatists Club in 1891.

William Vaughan Moody occupies a prominent place in the history of American drama even though his primary genre was poetry and only two of his plays were ever produced, for like the plays of Clyde Fitch and James A. Herne, Moody's work is a transition between nineteenth-century theatricality and the modern theater. *The Great Divide* (1906), which ran for 238 performances, is a realistic and experimental treatment of an older theatrical subject, chiefly the conflict between the American East and West. In both of Moody's prose plays the conflicts between freedom and discipline, between genuine emotion and religious and intellectual dogmatism have the complexity of the modern theater rather than the simple black-and-white morality of melodrama. Moody's experimentation is in his effective use of lyricism and subtle use of symbolism, not unexpected in a poet who had written three verse plays.

The influence on the modern theater of Clyde Fitch also rests on only one or two plays, despite the considerable number and popularity of his works. The general estimate of historians and even critics of his time is that both Moody and Fitch died at the beginning of what well may have been extremely significant developments in their careers. During the last four years of his life, after having become very popular and fairly well-to-do with over fifty plays to his credit, most of which were reviewed as morally simplistic and contrived, Fitch came under the influence of William Dean Howells and Henrik Ibsen. Only in a play entitled *The City*, produced in 1909 after Fitch's untimely death, did critics see a power and genuineness that could only have come from his willingness to forgo some of his more characteristic theatricality. To the persistent American theme of city versus country life he added shockingly naturalistic elements: coarse language of a kind that had not been heard on stage before (one of the actors felt it necessary to turn upstage to speak "goddamn") and a climax so highly charged that it sent members of the audience into hysterics. The taboo subject matter, somewhat reminiscent of *Ghosts*, was incest. The graphic, violent on-stage action included attempts at suicide and a groom's shooting of his bride before her older brother can reveal to her that she has committed incest.

Looking back over the eighteenth and nineteenth centuries, one sees the nation's struggle for a broader democracy and cultural independence reenacted on the stage by American types in native dramas. Taking center stage are the dispossessed of Europe, the unenfranchised, the powerless, who inevitably endeavor to come to terms with tradition and authority: the savage usurped by a civilized warrior; a youthful freethinker persecuted by his community; a black man bought and sold by whites; a simple rustic tricked by sophisticated city slickers; a frontiersman outwitting aristocrats; and always, and repeatedly, a young girl dreading a marriage arranged by an elderly parent who bargains her away "like a bale of goods."

The reiterated myth in which those outside the corridors of power played leading roles belonged especially in the theater, itself an outcast subculture, viewed by a church-powerful nation as the devil's drawing room (as Jonathan calls it in *The Contrast*), a counterforce determined to compete with the church for time, money, and souls. Yet the relationship of the stage to the larger society of which it was a part was as intimate as it was hostile, for in no other art form were the issues of the century more immediately and consistently engaged; its subjects were the American Revolution, slavery, the Civil War, the Indian question, political corruption, temperance, women's rights, native art, immigration from Europe, evolution, the higher criticism, and virtually every other issue of national import.

Even after the national fall into experience called the American Civil War (the bullet that "undeceives," as Herman Melville put it), the nation's drama was reluctant to relinquish the pastoral dream. Dramatists were not ready to take a straight look at the unhappy underside of the nation and the self that for some time would seem to have been inescapable, a lesson the theater could have heard from its old Puritan antagonists long before the Civil War.

But it is neither for unflinching realism nor for artistry that early American drama constitutes a compelling chapter in literary history. It is rather because for two centuries, from the birth of the Revolution to the advent of modernism, what was written and rewritten, rehearsed, staged, and revised, to play in theaters across the country, were multiple versions of one play—a play called America.

Claudia Johnson

III. Intellectual Movements and Social Change

Social Discourse and Nonfictional Prose

Between the years of Thomas Jefferson's presidency and Jefferson Davis's rebellion, the United States expanded from the eastern seaboard to the Pacific Ocean. When James Monroe became president in 1817, the Louisiana Territory was already the scene of a mass migration, as if the Mississippi River were a magnet drawing Americans into its vast central basin. Among the many forces propelling this geopolitical expansion was the spread of a market economy fueled by cotton profits. By 1830, cotton was a "King," served both by the "lords of the lash" and the "lords of the loom." It not only accelerated commercial growth in both the North and the South but also greatly stimulated the spread of slavery. As William Faulkner would put it a century later, neither "the rifle nor the plough . . . but Cotton" settled the West, binding "for life them who made the cotton to the land their sweat fell on." The conjunction of cotton and slavery, dramatic and tragic, highlights the two poles of the nation's experience in the first half of the nineteenth century: economic expansion and the social and psychic costs it exacted. As the era's most prominent form of public discourse, public oratory registers the attraction of both poles.

Expansion in its various forms drew from the age's politicians a celebratory glee that marks not only the speeches of the most famous orators, Edward Everett, Daniel Webster, and Henry Clay, but those of stump speakers throughout the nation, whose espousal of Manifest Destiny embodied the nation's pride as well as its sense of a divinely ordained mission. Everywhere they looked, political speakers saw evidence of progress. In 1830, Everett spoke of the Lowell mills as the sign of a "holy alliance" between capital and labor, showing the world that industrialization need not resemble the British example. In 1847, Daniel Webster looked at a newly opened railroad in Massachusetts and saw in it the "indomitable industry of a free people" spreading throughout the land. In what Leo Marx has aptly called the rhetoric of the technological sublime, Americans celebrated an industrial progress that had brought 100,000 "operatives" to work in the textile mills of New England by 1815. Eastern industry and Western migration alike provoked a bombastic oratory, replete with self-congratulation over the nation's expansion.

As market capitalism carried Americans west, the Jacksonian ideology of individual freedom and the self-made man overwhelmed all of Whiggery's efforts to contain it within traditional boundaries. At the same time, however, the social and psychic costs of such rapid expansion surfaced. One can catch the note of anxiety in Abraham Lincoln's 1838 address to the Springfield, Illinois, Young Men's Lyceum. Lincoln registers his alarm over a recent incident in which abolitionist editor Elijah P. Lovejoy had been killed by an antiabolitionist mob. Whether or not one agrees with Edmund Wilson's argument that Lincoln's plea for the rule of law is a prophetic warning against a tyranny Lincoln would one day embody as war president, it is clearly a law-and-order speech, forceful because of the social fears it both speaks to and expresses. "Reverence of the laws," Lincoln admonished his audience, should "become the political religion of the nation." Mob violence against abolitionists was only the most recent example of what Lincoln viewed as a "mobocratic spirit" at loose in the land. Nor was he expressing any Whig disdain for the unruly masses; Lincoln never displayed such contempt, and by the late 1830s his party could not afford it. Social violence was simply pervasive, and the sources of its provocation were unpredictable. In 1849 it would break out in New York City over a British actor's antidemocratic rendition of *Macbeth*.

The mob violence that Lincoln feared would undermine fealty to the government is only one sign of an undertow of anxiety that menaced the American flood-tide of expansion in the period from 1810 to 1865. Whether we focus on the decline of New England's farms and the gradual breakdown of the household economy, on the brutal "removal" of Native Americans from their land, or on the spread of slavery from Virginia to Texas, there is ample evidence that the nation's expansion was purchased at a high price, both externally, in the numbers of human beings exploited, and internally, in the mounting anxiety over the future and guilt over the past.

The most powerful expression of anxiety is to be found in the growth of evangelical religion, most markedly in the Second Great Awakening, spearheaded by Charles Grandison Finney, which spread west and south of the "burnt-over district" of western New York in the 1830s and 1840s. Despite opposition from orthodox Congregationalist and Unitarian churches, the resurgence of evangelical religion spawned a host of reform movements in the Northeast in the 1840s. Even the relative orthodoxy of a Lyman Beecher could not withstand the force of evangelicism. Indeed, the religious and reform enterprises of Beecher and his children can serve as an emblem of the social consequences of evangelical religion in this period. In her *Treatise on Domestic Economy* (1841), Catharine Beecher transformed the religious travail provoked by her father's conversion demands into an engine for running the American home along lines whose efficiency would parallel and support its moral sanctification. Her younger sister Harriet transformed the domestic novel into an astonishing piece of political propaganda with the bestselling *Uncle Tom's Cabin* (1852).

Evangelical religion sent women out of the home to petition against slavery, to reform prostitutes, and to organize temperance societies. Even when they were attacked by the orthodox ministry, as were the Quakers Angelina and Sarah Grimké, a religious energy drove and sustained their reform efforts. Indeed, the power of evangelical reform as a social force in this period is incalculable, second only in its effects to that of the antislavery sentiment it fostered. William Lloyd Garrison, the nation's most controversial abolitionist, was inspired (not to say driven) by his evangelical faith. Arthur and Lewis Tappan, New York City's leading abolitionists, pursued their goals out of a religious commitment less radically perfectionist but no less zealous than Garrison's.

As evangelical faith infiltrated American lives, it also penetrated social discourse. No major form of discourse escaped its influence in this period: it is thus hardly surprising that the language of religious faith finally displaced the older secular language of republican ideology, which had long fastened on the American Revolution and the Declaration of Independence as its central sources of authority. In the nineteenth century, the authority of the Declaration of Independence, especially, continued to be invoked for a host of contradictory ends, from workers' autonomy to women's rights to Southern secession, so that by 1865 the rhetorical power of the document had been dispersed in virtually direct proportion to the number of times its opening clause had been reinterpreted. In the process, the secular historical authority of the Revolution was displaced by the sacred, providential purpose to which God had committed the nation. As anxiety overtook and reshaped American republican faith, a "political religion"—though not exactly the one for which Lincoln called in 1838—became a reality. The change assumes dramatic clarity in Lincoln's own oratory.

Perhaps the most secular public man of the age, Lincoln clung with fierce loyalty to a republican ideology rooted in the eighteenth century. As late as 1863, he could still speak in its terms. His words at Gettysburg border on the anachronistic, so secular is the republican faith upon which he called. He defined the war simply, as a test of the initial claim of the Declaration of Independence "that all men are created equal," and his one reference to God was added as he spoke: "under God" does not appear in the original drafts. The simplicity and the cleanness of line for which the Gettysburg Address has long been praised are due in no small degree to the purity of its direct appeal to an earlier, republican ideology.

Far more representative of the period, and of the direction in which even Lincoln was compelled to move, is his second inaugural address of 1865. Here, America is not merely a "nation, under God," but a nation destined to carry out his purposes. The war is not a test of a political experiment in social equality, but a punishment. As at Gettysburg, Lincoln remains concerned that the war is still to be won; now, however, it is not merely "unfinished work" the nation faces, but prolonged penance for national sin. Like Christ at Gethsemane, Lincoln wishes this cup to be taken from him. "Fondly do we hope—fervently do we pray—that this mighty scourge of war may speedily pass away"; but like Christ, he is resigned to God's providential plan, since "the judgments of the Lord are true and righteous altogether." The exorbitant cost of the American project, now on bloody display, could only be accounted for in the language of religious apocalypse. The generation that made the war relentlessly instructed those who fought in it, as well as those who were to lose it, in the providential meaning of their suffering. Sinners all, they were being punished so that the nation might then rise to fulfill its appointed destiny as God's Chosen. As Sacvan Bercovitch has shown, the American jeremiad returned to the fore with a vengeance in the years leading up to the Civil War.

To follow the prose discourse from 1810 to 1865, then, is to listen to a dialogue fueled by guilt, anxiety, and anger, a dialogue that only God's voice could bring to an end. In using the term dialogue, I want to underscore two features of American discourse as it developed in this period: (1) the remarkable expansion of the public forum in the 1830s to accommodate a new diversity of voices; and (2) the gradual polarization of these voices by the 1850s.

Applying this lens to the period's nonfictional discourse necessarily excludes much from our view, but it serves to bring into focus the social process that made such discourse recognizably American in the antebellum years. As the economy got up steam—both literally and figuratively—after the War of 1812, pressure grew for a unifying and inclusive national ideology. By the 1830s, thanks to improved printing and distribution technologies and a rapidly growing rate of literacy, Americans were tied together not only by "cotton thread"—as Emerson caustically remarked—but also by the threads of a discursive fabric they had come to weave themselves. By 1850, the question of what pattern would prevail in this national crazy-quilt of talk had become itself the subject of vociferous discussion. By 1865, that question had been answered. The dominant voice was not God's but it came close to resembling the nation's concept of God. It was the voice of the white, Protestant male, and whatever its origins, it spoke with a Northern accent.

No ideology, of course, is total; voices of opposition may be displaced or absorbed, but they are never completely silenced. Our primary goal is to understand how many voices were reduced to two, the North's and the South's, and how the former prevailed as "American." But before proceeding, we need to recall that the voices diffused in the course of this polarization were to be heard again. For women, Afro-Americans, and working people all participated in the national conversation that emerged in this period, and their voices were only temporarily subdued by that of the dominant culture.

Women won the right to a public voice by the 1840s. Although they achieved this victory largely in the name of "domestic" virtues, the campaign for women's rights formally begun at Seneca Falls, New York, in 1848 yielded political fruit by the end of the nation's next war. The ranks of laboring men and women who organized and published their own newspapers in the 1820s and 1830s would be swelled by immigrants; together with Populist farmers in the West, these voices would compel recognition by the 1890s. Finally, the Afro-American slaves whose narratives were heralded in the abolitionist press won their freedom but lost much of their claim on the national public forum after 1865. Of all the voices to emerge clearly in the national dialogue during the prewar period, those of Afro-Americans were the most thoroughly repressed by the dominant ideology of the white North that prevailed after 1865. As we shall see, this is hardly surprising, given the racism on which that ideology was built. Accordingly, having explored the expansion and contraction of the public forum between the 1830s and the 1860s, we shall return to focus on the slave narrative. Even though it was only one of many forms in which Afro-Americans expressed themselves, it can serve to represent their active participation in the nation's dialogue. Further, its fate can serve to indicate how narrow, and narrowing, was the view of American identity implicit in the national ideology of 1865.

The polarization of North and South that made this national ideology possible is usually dated by historians as beginning in 1831. Garrison's *Liberator* first appeared on January 1, 1831, and Nat Turner's rebellion took place in the same year, provoking a debate on abolition in the Virginia legislature. In an influential account of this debate, not only did Thomas R. Dew attack the abolitionist proposals of younger legislators from the western part of the state but he did so on the basis of a new approach to the slavery issue. Rather than merely apologize for slavery, Dew actually defended it as a positive good. John C. Calhoun soon took a similar position, giving the "positive good" argument broad political authority in the South. Garrison's approach also represented a new departure, even though antislavery sentiment was by no means new when Garrison began publishing *The Liberator*. By the 1820s there were more than 100 abolition societies in the South, where the nation's first abolitionist newspaper, Elihu Embree's *Emancipator*, had appeared. What distinguishes the abolition discussion of the 1830s from its precursors is signaled by Garrison's demand for "immediate emancipation on the soil." The idea of immediate emancipation marked a decisive shift in goal; when combined with Garrison's attack on colonization in *Thoughts on African Colonization* (1832), it not only threatened Southern slaveholders with the sudden loss of their property and their labor force but also confronted Northerners with the specter of over three million freed slaves flooding into their cities and spreading across the new lands in the West.

In short, a debate on abolition opened in both North and South in the early 1830s, but it took another twenty years for pro- and antislavery voices to polarize themselves irremediably on a North-South axis. Not all Northerners, of course, were against slavery, or all Southerners for it. Some Southerners, like George Fitzhugh and James Henry Hammond, became aggressive defenders of slavery, while others, such as Francis Lieber and Hinton Rowan Helper, allied themselves with the North. But by the 1850s a Northern voice had achieved dominance, and the South was reduced to the position of the silenced Other.

Southern spokesmen contributed mightily to this effect. George Fitzhugh's *Cannibals All!* (1857) and *A Sociology for the South* (1854) have received much attention in recent years because of Fitzhugh's incipient Marxist analysis of Northern capitalism, but his defense of Southern feudalism only served at the time to confirm the emerging view in the North that Southerners had been deranged by their despotic power. In many ways, the most intelligent of the Southern defenders of slavery was John C. Calhoun, and yet even he sounded absurd when he argued against the proposition that all men are born free because "men are not born. Infants are born. . . . They are not born free. While infants they are incapable of freedom." While the South was reduced to such logic-chopping on the Declaration of Independence, the Bible, and the Constitution, the North responded to the threat of amalgamation with mob violence. Obviously, the social fears that came to focus on racial amalgamation had complex origins; but such fears acquired ideological force because of a new journalistic forum. By examining key features of journalism in this period, we can appreciate why a movement spearheaded by Garrison's *Liberator* (whose subscribers numbered a mere 500, largely Afro-American, in 1832) could generate such volatile responses in both North and South. We can also begin to see how the expansion of the public forum exacerbated the social anxieties of Northern white men for whom amalgamation represented a threat to the crucial distinctions of class, gender, and race, on which their social identity rested. Finally, we should be able to see how the South as silent Other provided a screen on which such men could project all that they wished to repress, deny, and purge from the national body politic.

Nothing signals more clearly the expansion and growing diversity of the public forum in Jacksonian America than the growth of periodical publishing. According to Frank Luther Mott, the number of magazines grew from 100 to 600 between 1825 and 1850, ranging from *Godey's Lady's Book* to *The American Agriculturalist*. Women, children, farmers, and specialized professionals all found magazines that addressed their interests. But while C. F. Briggs could remark in 1845 in his *Broadway Journal* that "the whole tendency of the age is magazineward," foreign visitors were more often impressed with the spread of newspapers. In 1833, Thomas Hamilton remarked in *Men and Manners in America*, "In truth, nine-tenths of the population read nothing else. . . . Every village, nay almost every hamlet, has its press." Again, figures are necessarily rough, but Mott estimates that by 1833 there were three times as many newspapers being published in the United States as in France or England. Most important, the first penny daily, the *New York Sun*, appeared in 1833, followed shortly by the most famous, James Gordon Bennett's *New York Herald* in 1835. Although most newspapers continued to be owned and operated for either political or commercial purposes, the penny press expanded the newspaper's range in both subject matter and audience. Bennett's *Herald*, in particular, initiated financial and human interest columns and indulged in a bravura of indiscreet exposé.

The new journalism met with vast success; by 1850, the *Herald* had a circulation of 30,000.

Bennett's success rested in part on his shrewd combination of sensationalist titillation and moral arrogance. Speaking only "the words of truth," Bennett announced that he had "seen human depravity to the core" and set out to reveal "the deep guilt that is encrusting our society." A proslavery Democrat, he aimed to expose the evils not of slavery but of pretension and "humbuggery." Yet his statement curiously echoes that of Garrison in the first issue of *The Liberator:* "I will be as harsh as truth, and as uncompromising as justice. . . . I am in earnest—I will not equivocate—I will not excuse—I will not retreat a single inch—and I will be heard." It may seem perverse to ally Garrison and Bennett, especially in light of the latter's anticlericalism, but as editors they shared a habit of sensationalist exposé and self-congratulatory zeal. They shared as well a talent for exploiting the social and technological forces set loose in the Jacksonian era. Although their ends were opposed, their means were similar, and similarly dependent upon deep and pervasive changes in the public forum they helped to broaden.

As universal white male suffrage spread to every state, the political links joining "gentlemen of property and standing" were short-circuited by the results of the very "internal improvements" such men had so often supported, especially in the Northeast. A mass culture had begun to form, in which organic ties of class and family were eroding in the wake of an economic flood-tide carrying young adults away. Where once only a few established gentlemen had been heard speaking to, and arguing with, each other, now a host of new voices addressed a growing audience.

Such a development presented a threat to upper-class men like James Watson Webb, whose responses reveal a good deal about the changing context of American discourse in the 1830s, particularly about the sources of Northern hostility toward abolitionists. Webb was editor of the *Courier & Enquirer,* until the rise of the penny press the daily with the largest circulation (4,000) in New York City. A staunch traditionalist, Webb was prone to invoke his Massachusetts lineage and also prone to violence. Among his enemies was James Gordon Bennett, whose *Herald* indulged in such outrageous abuse of the *Courier* and its editor that Colonel Webb, as he liked to be called, twice attacked Bennett on the street. In 1840, Webb employed a more civilized method of attack when he organized a boycott of the *Herald* among the "respectable people" of all the major Northeastern cities. But Webb had already defined his position on social matters: in 1833 he had organized an antiabolitionist mob that attacked William Lloyd Garrison in New York City.

Webb's adverse relations with both Bennett and Garrison are telling. For what made Webb an enemy of both men (regardless of their own political opposition) was his ardent opposition to the class subversion their journalism was fostering. An expanding popular press was bypassing the traditional voices of authority. As Harrison Gray Otis put it to an antiabolitionist meeting in Boston's Fanueil Hall in 1835, abolitionists were spreading their "dangerous" ideas not only among men but among women and children as well. "Sewing parties" had become "abolition clubs," complained Otis, and children's hornbooks were teaching that "A B stands for abolition." Additionally, racial lines were being threatened by an abolitionist press that spawned hundreds of antislavery societies by 1840. The spread of abolitionist journalism in the 1830s forced a recognition of what white Americans, North and South, had successfully repressed—that over three million Afro-Americans were alive in the nation's midst. And as women mounted platforms to speak and working people formed unions with their own newspapers, social boundaries of all kinds seemed threatened.

Such boundaries had to be redrawn and reinforced if any "Union of these States" was to be preserved. Or at least that became the view of the men who joined voices in the 1850s to support the new Republican party. The consensus upon which that party depended resulted from a gradual process of ideological reformation in which the boundaries of race, class, and gender blurred in the era's journalistic forum were reconstituted around the binary opposition of North and South.

George Templeton Strong, the Wall Street lawyer whose *Diary* articulates the emerging viewpoint of the North as vividly as Mary Chesnutt's represents that of the South, wrote in 1856, "We at the North are a busy money-making democracy, comparatively law-abiding and peace-loving, with the faults (among others) appropriate to traders and workers." By no means an opponent of slavery, Strong moved in measured steps toward a decision to vote for Lincoln in 1860. Yet by the time he wrote this entry, he had already absorbed the views of the North upon which the Republican party drew. He expresses clearly the terms on which a variety of feelings came to be blended into an ideology that incorporated the views of Western farmers, of Brahmin aristocrats, of white urban workers—of a Wendell Phillips and an Abraham Lincoln. Such diverse groups came to see themselves and their interests reflected in the aspirations and values on which Republican party propaganda drew. What made such political consensus possible was the objectification of the South as Other. The Republican party did not create this polarized framework; it simply exploited the terms of opprobrium that had solidified by the 1850s.

Strong again provides a telling example when he dismisses Southern claims of aristocracy and remarks that "Southern Gentlemen" are "a race of lazy, ignorant, coarse, sensual, swaggering, sordid, beggarly barbarians, bullying white men and breeding little niggers for sale." The specific lines along which ideological opposition had formed are clear: civilization versus barbarism. Even Nathaniel Hawthorne was not immune to such attitudes. In his piece for the *Atlantic Monthly* in 1862 ("Chiefly About War Matters"), Hawthorne took a typically ironic line, casting doubts on the sacred, providential purpose ascribed to the war in the North. Yet he viewed the imprisoned Southern soldiers he saw in Virginia as "peasants, and of a very low order; a class of people with whom our Northern rural population has not a single trait in common." Hawthorne confesses that he had "seen their like" in other parts of the world, but had not imagined such people "to exist in this country." In this instance, the South has become alien, a land of European peasantry.

Of course, a tendency to look south and see a strange country is already apparent from the opening decades of the nineteenth century, but it is not until the 1830s that a critical boundary began to develop between an enterprising, vigorous, and civilized North, and a lazy, decadent, and barbaric South. By the 1850s that boundary had acquired further definition. And the most crucial pattern in its development saw the South becoming identified as black. Charles Eliot Norton, for example, referred to the South as a "transatlantic Africa," and George Templeton Strong called the region a "niggerocracy." Just as Southerners called Northerners "Black Republicans," Northerners came to see both slave owners and slaves as black. The racial lines threatened by the abolitionist campaign beginning in the 1830s were thus reconstituted as a sectional boundary in the discourse of both North and South.

Further, as a result of the nexus between race and gender in antebellum discourse, the South in Northern eyes was not only black but to a remarkable extent female as well. As the work of social historians has made clear, nineteenth-century Americans came to embrace a domestic ideology of separate spheres for men and women. Women were enshrined in the private sphere of the home so as to neutralize the threat to masculine control presented by a social scene in which women were increasingly visible—as part of a volatile labor force, as outspoken abolitionists, or as the popular novelists whom Hawthorne disparaged as "scribbling women." Ascribing to women the innate traits of a natural Christian—moral purity, passive obedience, and a habit of maternal self-sacrifice—domestic ideology in effect feminized them. Given abolitionists' roots in evangelical religion, it is not surprising that many critics of slavery readily extended the same virtues to Afro-Americans. By the 1840s, the identification of Afro-Americans and women on the grounds of their shared feminine traits was a common theme among antislavery clergymen. Liberal Unitarians such as James Freeman Clarke and William Henry Channing, for example, delivered sermons espousing a view of the "Negro" as inferior "in some faculties," as Clarke put it, but "in others superior," specifically in a "strong religious tendency" and the consequent capacity for "self-denial and self-sacrifice." Thus the Afro-American would pose no threat once emancipated, according to Channing, who claimed "there is no reason for holding such a race in chains," since "they need no chains to make them harmless."

This brand of romantic racism flourished in the North, where it not only figured centrally in nonresistant abolitionist arguments but entered the broader framework of antislavery discourse, ultimately inspiring the era's most famous feminine figure, Uncle Tom. By the time the war had begun, the ideological feminization of both women and Afro-Americans was a rhetorical staple of speeches as well as sermons. At Cooper Institute in 1863, Theodore Tilton concluded, "The negro race is the feminine race of the world."

Such appropriations of domestic ideology, however, proved problematic for militant abolitionists like Theodore Parker. As early as 1841, Parker delivered a sermon in which a note of contempt can be heard for the slave's alleged docility. "If the African can be so low that the condition of slavery is tolerable in his eyes, and he can dance in his chains," Parker said, "then it is all the more a sin in the cultivated and strong, in the Christian, to tyrannize over the feeble and defenseless." Parker is trying to accept the common conclusion to which romantic racism led—that if Afro-Americans are innately feminine, all the more reason to protect, not exploit, their innocence. However, his apposition of "cultivated and strong" with "Christian" registers an implicit protest against the alliance of Christian and feminine traits on which domestic ideology depended.

After John Brown's raid, however, men like Parker and his friend Thomas Wentworth Higginson no longer minced words. In 1861, Higginson wrote, "If the Truth were told, it would be that the Anglo-Saxon despises the Negro because he is not an insurgent," and he added that there was "more spontaneous sympathy with Nat Turner than with Uncle Tom." By this time, the fault line within romantic racism had opened up to reveal what its feminization of Afro-Americans and women had served to neutralize—a deep-seated threat to white male authority. For, at bottom, what women and Afro-Americans shared was not any common docility but a common threat—that of social and sexual energies out of control.

Women's rights advocates had comprehended this threat for some time. When Margaret Fuller argued in *Woman in the Nineteenth Century* (1845) that the abolitionist principle against one man holding another in bondage should logically apply to gender relations as well, she drew the kind of startling conclusions about women's legal and political equality that George Templeton Strong found so alarming. Meanwhile, Parker came to define the Anglo-Saxon race in masculine terms—as rational, aggressive, and dominant. Acknowledging that "the Anglo-Saxon tribe" had "exterminated the Indians" and "taken a feeble tribe of men and made them slaves," Parker could not help displaying his pride in the very traits he criticized, traits that inhered in, and served to ally, the "Anglo-Saxon" race and the male gender.

By the late 1850s, the threats to social boundaries defined by gender and race had grown intolerable, especially for upper-class men like Strong. While Strong blamed extended suffrage, Charles Eliot Norton and Francis Parkman focused more obsessively on the emasculation of the aristocratic class and welcomed the impending war as an opportunity to test and reaffirm the vigor of its young men. But it was Francis Lieber, German émigré, Southern intellectual, and now a Northern Republican, who sounded the keynote for the ideological resolution of the internal contradictions in Northern white ideology. In approving of John Brown's raid, Lieber said that "Brown died like a man," while "Virginia fretted like a woman."

If the North now understood itself to represent the progressive force of the Anglo-Saxon race, while the South embodied blackness and barbarism, the North also saw itself as masculine and the South as a woman—fallen, out of control, and in need of domestication by the forces of law and order. In 1853, Wendell Phillips not only registered this image but took credit on behalf of the abolitionist movement for creating it: "To startle the South to madness, so that every step she takes in her blindness, is one step more toward ruin, is much. This we have done." Phillips liked to refer to the South as "one great brothel." Even the Fireside Poets adapted their didactic vision to the prevailing image: John Greenleaf Whittier saw the South as a ruined white woman, and James Russell Lowell talked of the "orgies of loquacity" emanating from a South Carolina that talked too much of her virtue. The younger generation could express itself more violently, as a remarkable comment made by Salmon Chase in 1841 indicates. Chase wanted to force "the system of slavery to be stripped of her veil, to be exposed in all her monstrous deformity, and to perish amid [destruction] of them whom she has so long deluded and betrayed."

The ideological polarization increasingly evident in political oratory, sermons, diaries, and essays drew upon the energies of other prose genres as well. The major American historians of the period steadily produced volumes (fifty, in all) on Spanish, Dutch, Franco- and Anglo-American history that collectively charted the providential role of the Anglo-Saxon race in bringing about Western progress and human freedom. As David Levin's *History as Romantic Art* demonstrates, William H. Prescott, George Bancroft, Francis Parkman, and John L. Motley shared a perspective in which the noblest forces of history were embodied in what Parkman called "the masculine race." In the sturdy yeomen of New England (according to Bancroft and Parkman), the steadfast William the Silent (as presented by Motley), and the heroic Cortés (celebrated by Prescott), masculine vigor joined natural law to foster history's progressive victory over both the effeminacy of decadent civilizations and the barbarism of infidel races. In *The History of Ferdinand and Isabella* (1838), for example, Prescott attributes the Moors' defeat by the Spanish to a mixture of "effeminate indulgence" and savage barbarism. Along with the other historians, he resolves the apparent contradiction between barbarism and decadence by pointing out their common ground in sensuality. Motley's fierce account of the Spanish Inquisition in *The Rise of the Dutch Republic* (1856) adopts a similar perspective toward savagery and refinement as does Parkman's treatment of pagan and priest from *Pioneers of France and the New World* (1865) through *Montcalm and Wolfe* (1884).

The historians' view of progress as dictated by natural law made manifest in Anglo-Saxon masculine vigor was refracted through different political lenses, but among the educated readership they mainly addressed these writers helped to legitimate the dominant ideology emerging in the North. Prescott opposed the doctrine of Manifest Destiny that Bancroft actively fostered as Secretary of War in 1845, but even in his stateliest prose Prescott voiced the common faith in the rise of liberal principles from Anglo-Saxon origins. Although his *History of the United States* (1834–76) tends to sentimentalize the Native Americans whose culture struck Parkman as the scene of filth and degradation, Bancroft like Parkman viewed the American "Indian" as noble only insofar as he demonstrated a masculine vigor by courage and endurance. Parkman's *Jesuits in North America in the Seventeenth Century* (1867) blatantly assumes connections between the sensual, the material, and the female body; the "Huron woman," Parkman remarks, is a "wanton" before marriage and a "drudge" afterward. In short, the ideological opposition of North and South along the lines of race and gender found a ready source of intellectual authority among the historians. For their work relentlessly pitted the natural against he decadent and artificial, the masculine against the effeminate, and the white against the dark races.

Two other prose genres, finally, deserve special attention, not only because of their significant impact on subsequent American literary history but also because they demonstrate at close range how voices of opposition were either incorporated into, or silenced by, the dominant discourse of a white, male North. The first of these is the slave narrative.

In addition to the thousands of accounts that appeared in the periodical press, more than fifty book-length slave narratives were published in the half-century before emancipation. By the 1840s, some of these narratives were achieving large sales. Among the most notable were: *Narrative of William Wells Brown, a Fugitive Slave, Written by Himself* (1847); *Narrative of the Life of Frederick Douglass, an American Slave, Written by Himself* (1845); *The Life of Josiah Henson, Formerly a Slave, Now an Inhabitant of Canada, as Narrated by Himself to Samuel Eliot* (1849); *The Narrative of Lunsford Lane* (1842); Austin Steward's *Twenty-Two Years a Slave and Forty Years a Freeman* (1857); *A Narrative of the Life of Reverend Noah Davis, a Colored Man* (1859); William Craft's *Running a Thousand Miles for Freedom; or, The Escape of William and Ellen Craft from Slavery* (1860); and Harriet Jacobs's *Linda: Incidents in the Life of a Slave Girl, Written by Herself* (1861).

Historians have used these and other accounts of bondage for decades as source materials on American slavery, but only in recent years has the American slave narrative received the full critical attention it deserves as literary discourse. While the slave narrative can be linked generically to a variety of forms—from seventeenth-century captivity narratives and eighteenth-century autobiography to the domestic novel of the nineteenth-century into which it was incorporated by Harriet Beecher Stowe and others—it assumed a specific identity in the thirty years before emancipation, when the abolitionist press ardently sponsored the publication of testimony by fugitive slaves for its propaganda value.

Since abolitionists also edited many of these narratives, historians have long debated their reliability. From a literary viewpoint, however, the question of authenticity serves not to raise doubts about evidence but to generate insight into form. By the 1840s, when the slave narrative had become a staple of abolitionist propaganda, it was common for such narratives to be prefaced by an editor's testimony, even when they had been written by the slave himself. The slave's voice, in short, had to be authorized by a white voice, a fact of which every slave narrator was keenly aware. Even Frederick Douglass's *Narrative*, the finest example of the genre, was prefaced by letters from Garrison and Phillips. The issue of authorization became inscribed in the form, and not merely as a question of literary authorship; for the slave there was also the crucial matter of authoring the self. If many fugitive slaves could attach with accuracy the claim "written by himself" to their narratives, the emphasis they placed on their own literacy went far beyond title pages to the very essence of what they wrote.

As Douglass would discover, there was a conflict of interest between the white abolitionists, who wanted to use slave narratives as they were using slave lecturers, and the ex-slave writer, who had a good deal more at stake. Douglass later recalled that abolitionists liked to introduce him as "chattel," as a "thing," and then assure the audience that "it could speak." For these abolitionists, the slave's literacy testified to his humanity, even as the struggle it had entailed testified to the slaveholder's inhumanity. Beyond that, they were not usually concerned. According to Douglass, his instructions were to "give us the facts," with the supposed assurance that "we will take care of the philosophy." But Douglass was not alone in feeling that the "philosophy" in question belonged properly to the slave himself. Thus, when he, like Lunsford Lane and a host of other fugitive slave narrators, highlighted his hard-won efforts to learn the alphabet, he did so not merely in response to the abolitionists' propaganda needs but also out of his own desire to establish the origins of the only identity he had in the eyes of his white audience—that which his literacy gave him. The slave's struggle to become, as Austin Steward put it, a "Freeman and a Brother," not only constitutes the story he tells but often culminates in its telling. For to represent the self in the authorized language of a white audience is to enact a rite of passage from slavery to a problematic freedom, a ritual for which the passage from illiteracy to literacy embedded in the narrative serves as synecdoche.

Such a rite is signaled in Douglass's *Narrative* when the author refers to the first time he rose to address a white audience: "The truth was, I felt myself a slave, and the idea of speaking to white people weighed me down. I spoke but a few moments, when I felt a degree of freedom, and said what I desired with considerable ease." As we know, freedom of speech had long been an abolitionist issue; for Douglass at this moment, however, speech *was* freedom. The level at which white abolitionist ideology affected the fugitive slave's discourse thus lay well beneath the merely propagandistic. In addressing a white audience, the slave incorporated its ideology; but he often did so in ways that exposed its limits.

Those who find in these narratives a lamentable dependency on the central themes of white American ideology, such as the self-made man's rise to fame and fortune or the sanctity of motherhood and family values, have failed to appreciate the difference made when the voice reiterating these themes is that of an ex-slave. For example, countless narratives testify to a fact that white abolitionists refused to acknowledge—that the path from slavery to freedom lay through the cash nexus. The Garrisonians' harsh response to Douglass's decision to allow his freedom to be purchased reveals more than their insensitivity to his circumstances, exiled both from his nation and from his family. It indicates as well the degree to which the white antislavery North refused to see slavery as an economic institution at all, except insofar as it had allegedly proved retrograde when compared to a free labor system. But a narrative such as Lunsford Lane's articulates the economic basis of slavery in terms that expose the emphasis on money that lay at the foundation of both Northern and Southern society.

Lane's narrative is not unique in sounding Franklinesque in its record of how self-discipline and an enterprising inventiveness can foster the accumulation of money and independence, but his is a more detailed account than most. Lane tells how he finally acquired the $1000 necessary to buy himself out of bondage. He began by selling peaches at thirty cents a basket and ended up selling pipes of his own design and tobacco mixed to his own specifications, both at prices that undercut his competitors. But the central fact of Lane's entrepreneurial career is that it is motivated by the desire not to *make* but to *buy* himself. In the hands of the ex-slave narrator, the harsh facts of a commodified society are blurted out. Lunsford Lane's narrative internalizes the authority of his white audience by speaking within the terms of its ideology; at the same time it refracts that ideology through a language peculiar to a man who has been a slave—a language in which both manhood and freedom have a precisely stated price.

The cash nexus was also exposed in the slave's narrative treatment of domestic ideology. The famous scene in Douglass's *Narrative* in which he looks on in painful impotence as his Aunt Hester is whipped finds parallels in almost every slave narrative of the period, although the woman being beaten is usually a mother. Whether depicted as losing their children through sale, or as lost to their children through an untimely death attributable to slavery, slave mothers emerge in these stories as the source of love and the center of the family, from both of which the slave child is alienated early. A sense of impotence and a sense of loss at the dispersal of the family are thus joined together in the most resonant image, that of a slave mother being beaten for too loudly lamenting the sale of her child.

Given this image of the family's destruction, it is not remarkable that the domestic novelist could so easily incorporate the slave's story into the framework of sentimental fiction. No doubt many slave narratives were themselves influenced by the conventions of such fiction, but when Stowe's *Uncle Tom's Cabin* ushered in a decade of slave novels in the 1850s, the most radical implications of the slave narrative's treatment of the family were lost. A significant exception was Harriet Wilson's *Our Nig; or, Sketches from the Life of a Free Black* (1859). As its subtitle indicates, Wilson's fusion of slave narrative and sentimental fiction was aimed at exposing Northern racism. Stowe's novel was far more representative—and of course far more influential. It exploited the sentimental power of the feminized and dying black man while leaving the insurgent mulatto to pursue self-colonization in Africa. This was not what Douglass had in mind when he designated his defiance of the slave driver, Covey, as the beginning of manhood. But more telling than her distortion of slave narratives, five of which she cited as sources for *Uncle Tom's Cabin*, is Stowe's effort to separate home and family from the contamination of economic forces. By showing how the cash nexus operated at the heart of the slave system, she exposed paternalist ideology as a ruse, but her book stopped well short of exposing what both *Our Nig* and the slave narrative revealed—the extent to which the hallowed sanctuary of the family required the very financial connection that threatened it. That is, as recorded in slave narratives, the experience of the Afro-American family made clear what both Northern and Southern ideologies had long served to deny—that the cash nexus had already penetrated and commodified the family.

If the forces of the marketplace had operated to break up the slave family, leaving mothers without children and fathers without families, it was by their efforts to appropriate those same forces that slave narrators set out to found, or reunite, families. Noah Davis was not alone in expressing a desire to sell his narrative in order to "buy" the members of his family who remained in bondage. When they commodified their experience as narratives, fugitive slave writers responded with stunning candor to the price tag put upon their families. They joined the marketplace world in order to *purchase* family unity, thereby revealing the commodification of an entire society.

The themes we have addressed so far should be understood as primarily characterizing male slave narratives, which far outnumbered those published by female writers before emancipation. But female slave narratives did exist: among them, the richest is Harriet Jacobs's *Linda: Incidents in the Life of a Slave Girl*, which focuses on the sexual exploitation of Linda Brent, as the narrator calls herself. Linda hid in an attic for seven years in her effort to avoid the abuse of her white master, finally escaping to the North and freedom. Her story is patterned quite differently from those of the male narrators, for reasons that also help to explain its rarity. While male narrators focus on their impotence at watching the mother beaten or abused, they conventionally regain their manhood by winning possession of themselves. But because her very body as well as her labor is alienated, the slave woman's plight is "far more terrible," as Jacobs puts it. Lunsford Lane buys his way out of bondage by finding ways to profit by his own labor, but Linda Brent can only go so far as to find the means for turning her children (and herself) into commodities to be purchased by the white man—not her master—who is their father. In becoming free, male slaves become men; but Linda never possesses herself. She can determine only who will possess her and her children.

In this light, there is a telling irony in one of the last popular slave narratives to be published before emancipation, *Running a Thousand Miles for Freedom*. Here the fair-skinned mulatto, Ellen Craft, poses as a white, male slave owner traveling north with his slave, William Craft, her husband. It would seem that the only way the slave woman could be fully represented as winning her own freedom was as a white man.

Like the slave narrative, the travelogue proved a seminal literary form, spawning some of the greatest American writing of the nineteenth century. In *A Week on the Concord and Merrimack Rivers* (1849), Henry David Thoreau evokes the possibilities of interior exploration by merging travel and essay. In *Moby-Dick* (1851), Herman Melville transforms travel to epic meditation. And in "Song of the Open Road" (1856), Walt Whitman, inhaling "great draughts of space," celebrates the expansive freedom of the American self. Long before Henry James and Mark Twain appropriated the travel narrative for their own purposes, it had enriched American letters in a variety of ways.

So protean is the travel writing of the antebellum period that only in the loosest sense can one call it a genre. In *Two Years Before the Mast* (1840), Richard Henry Dana, Jr., did adopt the form of what he called "personal narrative," a form to which Parkman's *The Oregon Trial* (1849) added historical resonance. Very different in purpose and scope was Frederick Law Olmsted's *The Cotton Kingdom* (1861), a condensed version of his earlier *Journey in the Seaboard Slave States* (1856), *Journey Through Texas* (1857), and *Journey in the Back Country* (1860); Olmsted's book was less committed to narrative than to a set of extensive sociological "observations" and "investigations." Beyond these extremes lay the long tradition of scientific travelers' reports continued by Darwin and parodied by Melville and Poe. But whatever pattern travel writing took, reviewers insisted that it be objective. In practice, however, a travel writer's credibility derived not from his objectivity but from the degree to which he maintained the distinction between "us" and "them." In *Typee*, Melville blurred the boundaries between civilization and savagery, lost credibility, and became the "man who had lived among cannibals." In *The Cotton Kingdom*, however, Olmsted reinforced the boundary between North and South and was praised for his dispassionate objectivity.

Olmsted's "investigations" were vast and various, but they served always to demonstrate that the conjunction of cotton and slavery bred poverty—economic, social, and cultural. Best known for designing New York City's Central Park, Olmsted was also executive secretary of the United States Sanitary Commission, which served as the springboard for the postwar bureaucratizing of organized charity—charity being understood as something to control, not to dispense. Olmsted, then, was one of the nation's first and most effective bureaucrats. Perhaps more decisively than any other single book, *The Cotton Kingdom* registers the voice of the dominant white North that would prevail after the war. Olmsted's belief that "the prosperity of a country can be estimated from the character of the roads" became a fixed principle; Henry Adams was still appealing to it fifty years later. But the principle itself simply expressed the difference between North and South on which the entire book relied.

A relentless observation of this difference marks *The Cotton Kingdom*, as does a continual distaste at sights such as that of "swine, hounds, and black and white children . . . commonly lying very promiscuously together on the ground" around Southern homes. Notably, the term "promiscuous" was also applied to audiences in which both men and women were present. Such assemblies, like anything that threatened boundaries, offended gentlemen of property and standing like Olmsted, who repeatedly noted a "closeness of intimacy" between the races in the South "that would have been noticed with astonishment, if not with manifest displeasure, in almost any chance company in the North."

Vital and original in many of its manifestations, travel writing of the antebellum years could also reaffirm the prevailing ideology of the North, all the more convincingly because of a reputation for objectivity to which we still pay unexamined tribute. Olmsted, for example, continues to be described in *The Oxford Companion to American Literature* as a man "noted for his unbiassed travel books." Yet, thanks to Afro-Americanists' scholarship, the slave narrative has at last begun to receive the tribute it deserves, not only as a literary genre, but also as the irrepressible voice of those who "made the cotton" in the first place.

Carolyn Porter

The Transcendentalists

New England transcendentalism was the first American intellectual movement to inspire a substantial number of literary classics: the best essays of Ralph Waldo Emerson and Henry David Thoreau, Thoreau's *Walden* (1854), and the first edition of Walt Whitman's *Leaves of Grass* (1855). To proclaim transcendentalism's impact, however, is easier than to define it, for the movement was loosely organized and its boundaries were indistinct. Nathaniel Hawthorne's whimsical image of transcendentalism as an enigmatic, shapeless giant was not altogether wrong.

Partisans and enemies each had an interest in keeping transcendentalism vague. Detractors baptised the movement with what they took to be a piece of outlandish jargon from Immanuel Kant in order to dismiss it as foreign mystagoguery. The popular mind duly came to associate transcendentalism, as one bemused witness put it, with "everything new, strange, and unaccountable." Nor did the transcendentalists themselves seek to define their tenets minutely, since one tenet was resistance to all creedal formulas. They favored instead a rhetoric of oracular pronouncements; and they encouraged the image of themselves as prophets of change while seeking to counter attempts to lump them together with less reputable "isms."

Up to a point transcendentalism should indeed be seen as one among many manifestations of the era of so-called romantic reform in America, particularly in the Northeast. The movement's heyday, from the mid-1830s through the late 1840s, also saw the burgeoning of abolitionism, feminism, sectarianism, communitarianism, temperance, and dietary reform. In all of these, various transcendentalists were deeply involved, thus giving the movement a protean look, although it began and achieved its most notable successes as a religious ferment that expressed itself most memorably in literary form.

American transcendentalism's geographical base was the Boston area. Most transcendentalists were drawn to the movement as young (under thirty-five) men and women of genteel, well-educated background if not of great affluence, who had come within the orbits of Harvard College (attended by most of the men) and the Unitarian church, which had split from the main Orthodox Calvinistic Congregational trunk in 1815. Many of the men were trained for the ministry; some remained Unitarian clergymen lifelong. Most of the nonclerics pursued related, often overlapping, vocations as teachers, lecturers, journalists, writers.

Although the line between "transcendentalist" and "nontranscendentalist" is hard to draw, a core of several dozen figures may be identified, through whom the movement achieved a notoriety and impact far beyond eastern Massachusetts, particularly in a handful of urban centers: in Cincinnati during the 1830s, in Providence during the 1830s and 1840s, in New York during the 1840s and 1850s, and in St. Louis after mid-century.

Ralph Waldo Emerson, then as now, was considered transcendentalism's most seminal force. A Harvard-trained Unitarian minister who became restless with clerical routine and convinced that religious intuitions were more authoritative than the institutionalized church, Emerson resigned his pulpit in 1832 to become a lecturer, essayist, and poet. His Concord neighbor and sometime disciple Henry David Thoreau, self-taught in the mysteries of nature that Emerson praised in more theoretical terms, put Emersonian principles into more rigorous practice in his individualistic style of living, his style of prose, and his work as surveyor and lifelong observer of Concord's natural history.

Amos Bronson Alcott, father of novelist Louisa May Alcott, was a Connecticut farmer's son turned educator who removed in 1840 to Concord, after the collapse of his experimental school in Boston, for a life of fitful projecting and long talks with Emerson. Alcott became a kind of institution on the lyceum circuit, delivering semimonologues he thought of as "conversations." As one of the longest-lived of the original transcendentalist group he helped to organize and preside over the Concord School of Philosophy (1879–87), a summer lecture-discussion forum that was the movement's last significant organized activity.

George Ripley was, like Emerson, a Harvard-trained Boston pastor who became in later life a man of letters. As a transcendentalist, however, Ripley was chiefly notable as a more systematic philosopher of religion than Emerson and as the founder of transcendentalism's most successful communitarian experiment at Brook Farm (1841–47), on Boston's outskirts. When Brook Farm failed, and Ripley's fortunes with it, he left the region and the movement for New York City, where he became one of the nation's leading book reviewers and co-compiler of America's first major encyclopedia.

Pioneer feminist Margaret Fuller also left Boston in the 1840s for the world of New York journalism and a post on the same newspaper Ripley later joined, Horace Greeley's *New York Tribune*. Previously, however, Fuller had made her mark on the movement as one of its most forceful personalities, and as the first editor of its leading periodical, *The Dial*. Fuller became transcendentalism's most cosmopolitan figure. In New York she helped to communicate its ethos outside the tribe, as she had previously done in Providence during a period of schoolteaching in the 1830s, while also becoming weaned away from Boston-Concord provincialism. Near the end of her life, Fuller journeyed to Europe and became involved in the Italian republican struggle under Mazzini, one of whose partisans became her lover, possibly but not certainly her husband—to the consternation of some New England acquaintances.

Two others whose careers also show the pattern of dispersal after a period of intense involvement were Frederic Henry Hedge and Augustus Orestes Brownson. Hedge, a Unitarian minister who Emerson once thought might become the group's leading intellect, was an early spokesman whose ardor cooled after his 1835 removal to a parish in Bangor, Maine. Brownson, a brash and mercurial non-Bostonian born on the Vermont frontier, became prominent in the late 1830s as preacher, as editor of the most trenchant transcendentalist journal (*The Boston Quarterly Review*, 1838–42), and, most important, as author of a series of social reformist essays (especially "The Laboring Classes" [1840]) that show a proto-Marxist awareness of the class basis of social conflict beyond that of any other transcendentalist social critic. In 1844, however, Brownson dismayed his colleagues by converting to Catholicism, later becoming its leading New England apologist.

The other firebrand among the major transcendentalists was Theodore Parker, also by no coincidence of nongentry origins, though educated at Harvard. Parker became the boldest critic of traditional Christianity among the Unitarian clergy, which tried in vain to expel him, as well as transcendentalism's most learned theologian, thus in a sense filling the place left by Hedge. Parker was a champion of the slave and the urban poor as well as a militant antisectarian. In the constancy and strictness with which he pursued his chosen commitments, Parker along with Thoreau stands out among the movement's leading figures. Both dramatize different extensions of Emersonian initiative that made the relation between Emerson and each a relation of mutual wariness as well as mutual respect, and that make Emerson to twentieth-century eyes seem at once the more timid and the more balanced figure.

Among other transcendentalists two overlapping groups stand out: a group of literati, whose accomplishments will be surveyed below, and—more prominent then than today—a number of liberal Unitarian ministers who at different periods in their careers actively furthered the movement. Chief among these during transcendentalism's heyday were Emerson's lifelong friend William Henry Furness, whose *Remarks on the Four Gospels* (1836) gave support to the transcendentalist reinterpretation of Scripture; James Freeman Clarke, close friend of Fuller and Emerson, sometime editor of transcendentalism's first periodical, the Cincinnati-based *Western Messenger* (1835–41); and Clarke's editorial successor, William Henry Channing, a peripatetic advocate of many reformist causes until his removal to England in mid-life. These and many other transcendentalists were inspired by the example of Channing's more famous uncle, William Ellery Channing, whom Emerson called "our bishop." Among Unitarianism's early leaders Channing evinced the greatest confidence in human possibility, the greatest impatience with sectarian restraints, the greatest inspirational eloquence in relation to analytical rigor, and the greatest tendency to prize likeness to God above moral restraint as the key to religious life.

Indeed, transcendentalism may be said to have achieved movement status in New England during the 1830s as a reform impulse within Unitarianism by younger clergy and laypersons who, in the spirit of Channing's bolder utterances, sought to build both upon and against the liberal ferment that had provoked the 1815 split within Congregationalism. Transcendentalism accepted Unitarianism's most important anti-Calvinist claim, that human nature is improvable through nurture and self-culture rather than corrupt beyond hope without conversion through a special act of divine grace. But transcendentalist radicals then carried this optimism further by questioning the Unitarians' continuing reliance on the authority of revelation and historical Christianity as checks on human reason, thereby turning against their elders one of the great weapons the latter had wielded against Calvinist doctrine: the historicism of the Higher Criticism in biblical studies, which approached revelation as culture-specific human construct rather than as divine given. At the same time, the transcendentalists reacted against the Lockean epistemology underpropping that historicism, according to which the scope of human perception is limited to the empirically knowable. The Unitarians had found the philosophical psychology of John Locke and his Scottish rationalist successors a valuable weapon against Calvinist "superstition." The transcendentalists worried about the opposite problem: that Lockean empiricism seemed to deny the possibility of direct spiritual experience and thereby cut humankind off from God. Against Unitarian epistemology, therefore, but building upon Unitarian optimism concerning human nature, the transcendentalists held up a model of human nature as inherently divine, and a model of divinity as accessible to and immanent within human nature itself. Emerson once stated that he had only one doctrine, "the infinitude of the private man." That indeed was his great argument, and the movement's as well, either as a point of advocacy or (as in Emerson's later work, and the work of transcendentalist moderates) as the central point of inquiry and examination.

Transcendentalism, then, was at once a theological position, combining elements of liberal rationalism and visionary mysticism; an anti-empiricist epistemology; and an incipient program of church reform, valuing spiritual experience above religion's institutionalized structures.

Transcendentalist theology was best encapsulated in Emerson's Address delivered to the graduating class of the Harvard Divinity School in 1838 and in *A Discourse of the Transient and Permanent in Christianity* (1841) by Parker, who had been one of Emerson's admiring auditors. These two manifestos, respectively, precipitated and brought to a climax the so-called Miracles Controversy between moderate and radical Unitarians over the importance of Jesus' supernatural deeds, as against his inspirational teaching and exemplary spirituality, in establishing his divine authority, and over Jesus' claims to preeminence as a spiritual authority, above those of other prophets and of the religious intuitions of the ordinary individual. (Conservative Unitarians held that Jesus' miracles furnished crucial testimony to the validity and uniqueness of the Christian revelation, transcendentalists that the authority of Jesus and other prophets rests not on reports of their supernatural deeds but on the appeal of their lives and teachings to the religious sentiment.) The transcendentalist *summa theologica* came with Parker's lengthy *A Discourse of Matters Pertaining to Religions* (1842), which attempted a systematic, scholarly historical and theological presentation of the transcendentalist position. During the 1840s Parker and the more moderate Clarke also ushered in a series of attempts among the radical Unitarian clergy to encourage greater autonomy, openness, and inclusiveness in their congregations.

Others were more notable for elaborating the epistemology that underlay transcendentalist religious iconoclasm. Best known are a series of Emerson essays that explore the grounds of human knowledge nontechnically but with remarkable sophistication, in view of Emerson's long-standing reputation as a shallow philosopher. Especially important are *Nature* (1836), "Self-Reliance" (1841), "Intellect" (1841), and "Experience" (1844), though of some interest as well is Emerson's late-life attempt to codify his first principles in two series of Harvard lectures (1869–70), given after his powers had begun to fail and posthumously arranged for publication as *Natural History of Intellect* (1893). Closer to qualifying as philosophers in the conventional academic sense were Hedge and Ripley. Both were influential during the early stages of the movement in introducing their compatriots to the methods of recent Anglo-European moral and mental philosophy. Hedge's groundbreaking 1833 article on Samuel Taylor Coleridge and German philosophy for *The Christian Examiner*, Unitarianism's chief intellectual organ, was the most important among several works in which Hedge, the transcendentalist's leading Germanist before Parker, helped ensure that the movement would not imbibe Kantian philosophy strictly from British sources. Ripley's *Discourses on the Philosophy of Religion* (1836) was the most sustained exercise in methodical argumentation produced during the movement's early stages. Along with Brownson, Ripley also became the transcendentalist most responsible for promoting among his compatriots so-called French Eclecticism—a compound of Scottish common-sense philosophy and German idealism—with his translations of Victor Cousin, Theodore Jouffroy, and Benjamin Constant for his 14-volume collaborative *Specimens of Foreign Standard Literature* (1838–42).

Even so brief a survey as the foregoing sheds light on two vexed questions: Should transcendentalism be considered a philosophy or a religion? and was transcendentalism essentially native or imported in its character? The answer to each question is "both." American transcendentalism as an organized movement began as a response within a particular American religious sect to its perceived ideological limits; and transcendentalism remained strongly religious in its themes. Thus it is partially justifiable to categorize the movement as an intellectual descendant of New England Puritanism, representing both a stage of secularizing apostasy beyond Unitarianism and a sort of recrudescence of Puritan pietism. In this sense, transcendentalism looks like a variant form of Second Awakening revivalism. The crisis of conviction that gave rise to the movement, however, had to do with a philosophical question about the nature and grounds of human knowledge that native theological models did not instigate and could not resolve. Thus Emerson, in an 1842 lecture on transcendentalism, ascribed the movement's origin not to Channing or the Puritans but to Kant. To Emerson and his cohorts, Kant stood for the triumph of idealism over the skeptical tendencies inherent in Locke.

Actually, Kant and his continental successors were less directly influential for most transcendentalists than their literary refractions in Goethe and in the semipopularized British interpretations of German idealism by Thomas Carlyle and especially by Samuel Taylor Coleridge. It was from the reworking of Kantian categories in Coleridge's *Aids to Reflection* (1825) that most transcendentalists derived the distinction between "Reason" (which they tended, reversing Kant himself, to define as that capacity of higher intuition enabling humankind to apprehend and participate in divinity) and "Understanding" (which they defined as the empirical, rational faculty that allows us to make sense of the world in Lockean terms). The "discovery" of the Reason was the great intellectual breakthrough that allowed the transcendentalists to reinvent the domain of higher spiritual consciousness and escape from the trap of empiricism that Unitarian epistemology seemed to have set.

The cautiously advancing rationalistic empiricism of the Unitarians and the intuitionalist response of the transcendentalists were variations on themes shared in common with their more orthodox adversaries as the dogmatic structures of traditional Protestantism began to erode throughout the Western world in the post-Enlightenment era. The first American disciple of Coleridge's religious thought, for example, was not a Unitarian but a moderate Calvinist, James Marsh, whose edition of Coleridge's *Aids* (1829) is sometimes taken to mark the start of American transcendentalism as an intellectual force, though Marsh seems to have felt only scorn for the movement he helped inspire.

As a coordinated endeavor, transcendentalism may be said to have begun in 1836 as a small discussion group of four Unitarian clerics, including Emerson, Ripley, and Hedge, who convened during the Harvard bicentennial to discuss the current religious and philosophical situation. This was the germ of what later became known as the Transcendental Club, which met irregularly over the next four years to discuss such issues as "American Genius," "Does the Species Advance Beyond the Individual?," "Pantheism," and "The Character and Genius of Goethe." The membership was immediately broadened to include laymen—and women; and all the eight major figures profiled above attended on at least one occasion. The Club was the first and most famous of a series of forums that served during the next few decades as social gathering points, though even more important were the less structured encounters afforded by Emerson's more or less ongoing hospitality at Concord, which became the movement's magnetic center.

The year 1836 also marked the emergence of transcendentalism as a public force in magazine, monograph, and lyceum. From this year until 1850 the movement never lacked a journalistic voice: *The Western Messenger* under Clarke, Christopher P. Cranch, and Channing; *The Boston Quarterly Review* under Brownson; *The Dial* under Fuller and Emerson; *The Present* and *The Spirit of the Age* under Channing; *The Harbinger* under Ripley; and *The Massachusetts Quarterly Review* under Parker. Though relatively short-lived and uneven, together these magazines fulfilled the Transcendental Club's most tangible objective, to found a journal. Their agendas were in good part anticipated by five manifestos, all produced during the *annus mirabilis* of 1836, outlining transcendentalist positions on epistemology (Emerson's *Nature*, Ripley's *Discourses*), theology (Furness's *Remarks*), institutionalized religion (Brownson's *New Views of Christianity, Society, and the Church*), and pedagogy (Alcott's *Conversations with Children on the Gospels*). Finally, Emerson's lectures were coming into vogue as a rallying point for the younger Boston intelligentsia and as an example of a genre and a means of livelihood that a number of his admirers tried to follow.

Transcendentalism thus emerged as a consciousness-raising project fomented by a group of loosely linked intellectuals whose chief mode of action was the written or spoken word. Beyond mere proclamation, however, most leading transcendentalists also sought to instigate permanent changes in selected social institutions if not in the structure of society as a whole. Their first major effort, not surprisingly, was their essentially parochial challenge to the parochial limits of Unitarianism, culminating in the Miracles Controversy of the late 1830s but continuing for several more decades as a struggle between radicals and moderates over polity as well as doctrine. But by the early 1840s, if not before, transcendentalism had clearly become much more than a sectarian movement.

The most unequivocal signs of this were two communitarian experiments of the 1840s, the first at Brook Farm, the second at Fruitlands, near Harvard, Massachusetts. The first became a flourishing enterprise that, despite a rather traumatic shift to Fourierist regimentation, might have lasted longer than its six years except for a disastrous fire in the uninsured main building. Today the community is known best through the satirical retrospects of Hawthorne's *The Blithedale Romance* (1852) and Emerson's "Historic Notes on Life and Letters in New England" (1883). Yet Brook Farm proved that at least to some extent the transcendentalist vision could take a corporate as well as an individualistic turn. It thereby lent support to the minority position (developed by Brownson and others in dissent from Emerson) that the divinity of human nature is fulfilled within the collectivity rather than within the individual. Fruitlands seemed to prove the contrary. Incompetently managed by Alcott and an English colleague, Charles Lane, it failed to last out its first winter.

More fundamental to the transcendentalist impulse than utopianism, however, was educational reform. Brook Farm's most distinguished institution was its school. To a considerable extent Emerson's works amount to a gospel of self-improvement to which Thoreau's writings are a corrective and a guide. So far as education in a stricter sense is concerned, the key figures are Alcott, Fuller, and Elizabeth Peabody. Alcott, with Peabody as a somewhat reluctant assistant, achieved notoriety in the mid-1830s with an experimental Boston school where a degree of emphasis was put on freedom of speculative inquiry (especially on religious topics) that shocked public opinion when the results were published in Peabody's *Record of a School* (1835) and Alcott's *Conversations*. For Alcott, as for a number of his colleagues, a Wordsworthian fascination for the intuitive perceptions of childhood followed from their central doctrine; and he paid the price of unemployability for this conviction. Neither collaborator abandoned the commitment to education, however; Peabody became an activist in the kindergarten movement, Alcott in adult education.

Another controversial educational project was the discussions for women, later opened to men as well, conducted in Boston by Fuller from 1839 to 1844. In these sessions, Fuller combined general intellectual cultivation with feminist objectives and developed some of the themes later expounded in her most ambitious work, *Woman in the Nineteenth Century* (1845), America's first landmark feminist treatise. Interweaving historical and social commentary with wide-ranging and arrestingly original interpretations of mythology, Fuller sought to adumbrate models of human nature and excellence that recognized and affirmed women's potential equally with men's.

Fuller was only the most gifted among a number of able women (Peabody was another) drawn to transcendentalism for the encouragement it seemed to give to strenuous intellectual endeavor regardless of sex, although the actual thinking of her male associates did not prove so bias-free as their first principles. This Fuller found from her friendship with Emerson and posterity can see from the *Memoirs of Margaret Fuller Ossoli* (1852), compiled by Emerson, Clarke, and William Henry Channing after her premature death by shipwreck while returning home from Europe.

Transcendentalism also gave support to abolitionism, to the principle if not always the organized enterprise. The movement has even been blamed with having driven antebellum Northern public opinion beyond the point of compromise with the South. Parker became a staunch antislavery activist; Emerson publicly urged defiance of the Compromise of 1850; Alcott helped in one famous attempt to rescue a fugitive slave; John Brown became Thoreau's greatest hero. By and large, however, transcendentalist support for organized abolitionism tended to be reluctant before 1850 and sporadic thereafter. Emerson, Thoreau, and a number of others were notoriously fastidious about endorsing reformist institutions of all kinds as opposed to virtuous individual action—one sign, perhaps, of the Federalist-Whig background of most transcendentalists. But their instinct was always to support freedom, including freedom for the slave.

Transcendentalism's greatest long-range impact, however, did not lie in any of the various areas mentioned so far. The social reforms in which individual transcendentalists took part did not absolutely hinge upon their contributions. In the areas of philosophical and especially religious inquiry, transcendentalism's influence was greater but still rather limited to its particular place and time. Emerson is justly considered as having helped inspire the growth of America's one distinctive philosophical tradition, pragmatism. But except for William James and John Dewey, America's serious philosophers have not looked to Emerson or transcendentalism for models. In theology, transcendentalism had a crucial impact on Unitarianism, pushing it away from its cautious fusion of reason and revelation toward a more secularized ethical idealism. In the process transcendentalism also helped further the study of comparative religion in America and to prepare the way for the Social Gospel movement of the turn of the twentieth century. Yet transcendentalism's influence on American religious structures remained strongest within the limited sphere of Unitarianism, which never in numbers or in territorial influence became more than a splinter sect compared to the leading Protestant denominations. Though Unitarian intellectuals exerted, throughout the nineteenth century, an impact disproportionate to the size of their church (partly because of its high level of education, wealth, and social status), their role as the vanguard of American religious liberalism was eventually preempted as the much larger, more conservative churches began to liberalize.

Finally, it was on literature that transcendentalism had the greatest and most permanent influence. Whereas in philosophy, theology, and social reform transcendentalism achieved fewer and less frequent breakthroughs after the mid-1840s than in the preceding decade, its most important literary results were yet to come, although Emerson and others had prepared the way.

From the start, the movement had a markedly aesthetic cast. The young Emerson based his choice of the ministry as his vocation on the hope that he could attain the eloquence of a Channing. Throughout his life he conceived of his public role as essentially that of a speaker and writer (though "scholar" was his preferred term). No other major transcendentalist except Fuller and Thoreau showed Emerson's commitment to letters, and some were even suspicious of what they took to be the frivolity of Emerson's aestheticism. But all were at least marginally interested in the cultivation of effective expression (a necessity for ministers, of course); most at some time or another tried their hand at literature (Parker wrote poetry, Brownson two novels, Alcott a collection of poems and two nonfictional volumes of ruminative Concord chitchat); and even the more programmatic transcendentalist periodicals, like the Fourierist *Harbinger*, contained large infusions of poetry and literary criticism.

Transcendentalism's aesthetic bent was partly a matter of individual temperaments, partly a matter of principle. Unitarian culture tended to endorse the arts as instruments of spiritual growth, over against the Calvinist fear of the evils of "unsanctified" recreations. The transcendentalist framework was even more hospitable to the former line of thinking. It regarded all doctrinal structures as created artifacts. Beyond this, it was strongly influenced by the Miltonic-Romantic idea of the great artist as prophetic seer. Once having defined intuitive experience and creative expression as the essence of religious practice and discourse, transcendentalism naturally became drawn to the idea that the theologian and the denominational preacher are less credible vessels of spirituality than the inspired artist. It was likewise natural that Walt Whitman, simmering with the ideas that were to congeal into the first edition of *Leaves of Grass*, should have received Emersonianism primarily as a stimulus for a new poetic.

In New England as well, Emerson's influence seems to have been strongest on younger transcendentalists of literary aspirations. Among these, of greatest note were the two mentioned previously: Thoreau and Fuller, whose conversation surpassed her writing but who nevertheless stands out as a significant literary critic and intellectual pioneer. One sees this not only from *Woman in the Nineteenth Century* but also from *Summer on the Lakes* (1843), a descriptive account of Midwestern travels, and from her collections of essays and other miscellaneous pieces, of which *Papers on Literature and Art* (1846) and *Life Without and Life Within* (1860) are the most notable. Emerson, Thoreau, Fuller, and semiliterati like Alcott, Parker, and Cyrus Bartol (*Pictures of Europe* [1855], *Radical Problems* [1872]) developed a distinctive prose style: strongly didactic, much given to reflection on moral and spiritual truths, aphoristic, dependent on example and analogy rather than on sequential argument, fond of paradox, highly reiterative yet sometimes compressed to the point of mysteriousness. Individual practice varied widely, however, from Alcott's fondness for high abstraction to Thoreau's meticulously precise descriptions of Concord settings; from Emerson's oblique, sometimes transitionless lapidary style to Parker's bluntness; from the tendency Alcott, Bartol, and Fuller often displayed for fulsome periods to the comparative terseness of the other three.

On the whole, literary transcendentalism was more enduringly important for its ideology than for its actual literary achievement. As an ideology that privileged poesis as spiritually inspired, transcendentalism provided the most aggressive crystallization of romanticist premises in nineteenth-century America: through the writings of Emerson, Thoreau, and especially Whitman it set the tone for the emphasis put by American poetics on the writer's potential role as social prophet and on the priority of original genius to tradition-based craftsmanship. The literature the movement itself produced did not always measure up to its high hopes. Except for the work of Emerson and Thoreau, transcendentalist prose is distinguished only in patches. But as a symptom and model of a more aesthetic consciousness emerging from the didactic-utilitarian background of New England literary history— a model combining intellectual seriousness with imaginative play—it is a landmark achievement.

Next to nonfictional prose, the transcendentalists' favorite genre was lyric poetry. The best of Emerson's uneven verse, collected in *Poems* (1847) and *May-Day and Other Pieces* (1867), shows a gnomic jaggedness that anticipates Emily Dickinson, who may have been influenced by it. Even less the poetic craftsman than Emerson, Thoreau produced a few lyrics of real delicacy and enough total output to fill a posthumous volume of *Collected Poems* (1964). More significant poets of the movement, however, were two other Emerson protégés, Jones Very and William Ellery Channing II.

Very, a shipmaster's son trained at Harvard as a classical scholar and Unitarian minister, specialized in sonnets on religious themes, although he wrote sensitively about nature as well. The most evangelically inclined of the transcendentalists, Very composed his most striking poems during a period of "insanity" in the late 1830s when he thought himself to be Christ returned to the world to call humankind to conversion. Very at his worst is a formulaic, repetitious ventriloquizer of biblical tags; but his best sonnets are powerful, intricate, luminous. Emerson, whom Very came to consider disappointingly secular-minded, oversaw the publication of his *Essays and Poems* (1839). Shortly thereafter, Very's productivity declined, as he retired to his native Salem to live out his life as occasional poet and part-time supply preacher.

Channing, today better known as Thoreau's first biographer (*Thoreau: The*

Poet-Naturalist [1873]), was the most prolific of the transcendentalist bards. His gift for image and epithet won him a feature article by Emerson in the second number of *The Dial*. But Channing was too volatile and self-indulgent to discipline his style; he remained a poet of noteworthy passages who wrote far too much. The best among his half-dozen volumes is scattered throughout *Poems* (1843), *Poems: Second Series* (1847), *Near Home* (1858), and *The Wanderer* (1872): the first two consisting largely of short lyrics, the latter two of longer descriptive-meditative poems. Sadly but justly, Channing eventually came to represent for antitranscendentalists an exemplum of the transcendentalist as ne'er-do-well, just as Very seemed the transcendentalist as wild-eyed mystic. Settling in Concord in 1843 after marriage to Fuller's younger sister, Channing proved a lively conversationalist but a poor husband, father, and breadwinner, and an increasingly disappointed, lonely, and embittered man.

Mention should also be made of several other transcendentalist literati. Christopher P. Cranch, remembered today for whimsical cartoons of Emersonianisms like the transparent eyeball passage in *Nature*, was also a painter and lyric poet of considerable skill. His several volumes of poetry, which reveal a somewhat more social, "Victorian" muse than Channing's or Very's, are perhaps at their strongest when exploring the difficulties and nuances of human relationships, as in "Enosis" (*Poems* [1844]), and "Veils" (*The Bird and the Bell* [1875]). John Sullivan Dwight, also trained for the Unitarian ministry, was a Brook Farmer who went on to become Boston's leading music critic and music historian, founder and editor of *Dwight's Journal of Music* (1852–81). Elizabeth Peabody was a memoirist, student of linguistics and history, and sometime publisher as well as educational reformer, confidante and intermediary for many among the movement. The roster could be extended further by including three other categories. First, such lesser participants in the main enterprises of the 1830s and 1840s as Ellen Sturgis Hooper and her sister Caroline Sturgis Tappan, both of whom contributed poetry to *The Dial*, the former leaving at her death a sheaf of poems still not sufficiently appreciated; minister-poet-translator Charles T. Brooks; and diarist Charles King Newcomb. Second, peripheral groups like the Providence romantics, including among others poet Sarah Helen Whitman, the friend of Edgar Allan Poe, and jurist-essayist-poet Job Durfee, author of an idealistic poetico-philosophical treatise (*The Panidea* [1846]). Finally, the younger legatees of transcendentalism who reached literary maturity during the years of the Civil War or thereafter, like Emily Dickinson's mentor Thomas Wentworth Higginson and Concord-circle memoirist Franklin Benjamin Sanborn. Well before 1860, however, the contours of the transcendentalist aesthetic were clear.

Transcendentalist aesthetics were, first of all, to a marked degree verbally oriented, although certain individuals like Cranch and Dwight displayed a keen interest in music, art, sculpture, and dance. Within the literary realm, the transcendentalists' interest was also selective. Other than for Fuller, the leading figures were rarely attracted to drama except as readers of ancient and Renaissance classics. To prose fiction of the more instructive sort they were sometimes drawn as consumers, but they wrote little themselves, and what they did tended to be heavy-handedly didactic, like Brownson's thinly disguised narrative of his spiritual progress, *Charles Elwood; or, The Infidel Converted* (1840). Significantly, the two closest approximations to successful "transcendentalist novels" were written by individuals who considered themselves, respectively, as peripheral and as opposed to the movement: *Philothea: A Romance* (1836), a classical fable by Lydia Maria Child, abolitionist sister of moderate transcendentalist minister Convers Francis; and *Margaret: A Tale of the Real and Ideal* (1845), a pioneering work of regional realism (despite cloying homiletics) by Unitarian minister Sylvester Judd. The visionary nature of the transcendentalist gospel lent itself to poetry and, even more, to rhetoric better than to narrative or to drama; and in particular to poetry and rhetoric of a high order of moral seriousness. It allowed for the development of satire and invective—Parker, Thoreau, and even Emerson were masters at both—but not, on the whole, for comedy of the lighter sort. Emerson's droller passages, as in "New England Reformers" (1844) and "Historic Notes," are almost by definition antitranscendental; Ellery Channing and Christopher Cranch had a gift for light caricature, but one must go to their manuscripts, not their published works, in order to find the best of it.

This inventory of transcendentalism's aesthetic proclivities reveals that notwithstanding the movement's iconoclasm, it remained solidly within the framework of New England thinking, which had traditionally valued literary refinement more highly than the cultivation of the other arts; which set rhetoric and poetry above the other genres, approached poetry as a species of rhetoric, and encouraged a high moral tone whereby sparing dramatizations of the comic and the sensuous were contained within a prevailing intellectual seriousness. Under these circumstances it is not surprising that transcendentalism's chief contributions to American literary history consisted in such legacies as the Emersonian reformulation of the Miltonic-Romantic idea of the poet-prophet, which through Whitman's influence became crucial to the work of modern American poets as diverse as Hart Crane, Ezra Pound, William Carlos Williams, and Allen Ginsberg; and in Emerson's and Thoreau's meditations on nature as setting and as symbol, which helped to dictate the terms of modern American pastoral. What is more surprising is that a movement in some respects so parochial could have had such a far-flung effect on subsequent American letters, and to a considerable extent on a number of other aspects of American thought as well.

It is tempting to credit the impact to the genius of transcendentalism's leading figure, Emerson. Such an explanation would be a fitting tribute to the person who once described institutions as the lengthened shadows of individual men. But it would be true only in part. That the transcendentalist strain in American culture derives most fundamentally from Emerson's central doctrine of self-reliance, which was also the movement's central doctrine, seems incontestable. But Emerson's achievement in itself represents a fortuitous confluence of Euro-American intellectual currents coming to convergence not in the mind of a solitary person but within a community of intellectuals.

For brevity's sake this chapter has been forced to underdramatize the duration and extent of that ferment. More attention could well be paid to the attempts of the Massachusetts transcendentalists to extend their impact beyond their Concord-Boston base, to the range of transcendentalist intellectual/literary magazines, and to independently generated analogues of transcendentalism like the liberal ferment within orthodox Congregationalism and the scientistic mysticism found in transcendentalist-hater Edgar Allan Poe's *Eureka* (1848). Likewise, the efforts of a new generation of New England radicals to sustain and reshape transcendentalism in the 1860s and after—including figures like orientalist and universal religionist Samuel Johnson and philosopher-editor William Torrey Harris, sometime Alcott disciple and co-founder of "St. Louis Hegelianism" and the Concord School of Philosophy—deserve more than the short shrift they usually get in historical surveys, including this one. This chapter has, however, at least begun to show why Hawthorne was moved to remark in the preface to "Rappaccini's Daughter" that the transcendentalists "under one name or other" seemed "to have their share in all the current literature of the world." If the so-called American literary Renaissance in literature can be said to have one reference point more crucial than any other, transcendentalism is it.

Lawrence Buell

IV. The American Renaissance

Ralph Waldo Emerson

At the International Exposition at Paris in 1863, American products and manufactures seemed to one visitor notably inferior to European ones. Yet the American exhibit could boast a different sort of attraction. "At the end of the section were Bierstadt's picture of the Rocky Mountains, Church's Niagara, and close to these, a fine portrait of Emerson."

That the arrangers of the American exhibit saw fit to group Ralph Waldo Emerson's face with paintings of America's most celebrated pieces of natural sublimity as things worthy to attract the curiosity and admiration of Europeans suggests better than anything else the commanding position Emerson occupied in the cultural landscape of mid-nineteenth-century America. We now know, of course, that the landscape was hardly as empty as it then seemed. Many of the greatest works of the American Renaissance—*Walden, Moby-Dick, Leaves of Grass*—were in existence but were then ridiculed or neglected (though Emerson himself had tried hard to win recognition for Walt Whitman and Henry David Thoreau, at least). Still, at a time when few American authors were known outside the borders of their own country, Emerson's essays had been translated into French and German, reviewed in the London *Times*, and respectfully discussed in the *Revue des deux mondes*.

The rising literary fortunes of his contemporaries have removed Emerson from his position as lonely sentinel, but the temptation remains to treat him more as a phenomenon, like Niagara, than as a man of letters, like Nathaniel Hawthorne or Oliver Wendell Holmes. He has always been hard to classify. He was by profession first a minister, then a public lecturer, but a comparison of his addresses with Daniel Webster's shows how intimate, how eerily private his voice can sound, just as a comparison of his essays with Charles Lamb's shows how much longing for the collective ecstasies of oratory remains beneath the decorum of his printed page. In recent years philosophers have argued for his claim to be taken seriously as a philosopher, yet the verbal brilliance of his textual surface, the feline shifts of tone and stance, seem always to be pushing him back in the direction of literary artistry. But literary artists have often been offended by Emerson's frank love of the didactic, his consistent preference for the artist's genius over any of the works it has produced, and his contempt for mere craftsmanship. He was certainly a kind of social critic, and in his own day heard himself denounced as a dangerous radical, yet some modern interpreters have read his texts as covert defenses of a declining Whig aristocracy, siphoning off in its imagery the raw energy of the Jacksonian democracy he both despised and envied.

The elder Henry James accused Emerson of being a man without a handle. It might be more accurate to accuse him of having too many. As the witty self-portrait he sketches at the end of the essay "Nominalist and Realist" suggests, he recognized his own close resemblance to John Dryden's Zimri, the self-thwarting genius of *Absalom and Achitophel*, who was "everything by turns and nothing long." He once boasted that after thirty years of teaching he had not a single disciple, since his aim was to bring men, not to him, but to themselves; and the sincerest compliment his protégés paid him was rejection. As Whitman said: "The best part of Emersonianism is, it breeds the giant that destroys itself."

Little in Emerson's early life suggested the equivocal eminence of his later career. He was born in Boston in 1803, in an era he later referred to as "that early ignorant & transitional *Month-of-March*" in New England culture. His father, who died when Emerson was eight, was a Unitarian clergyman who dabbled in polite literature and fostered the intellectual ambition of his sons. His death left the family in desperate straits; they managed to survive by running boardinghouses and taking charity, but the experience left its mark on Emerson. His word for the final state of spiritual misery or intellectual dessication was always "poverty."

Mrs. Emerson managed to see that her sons attended Harvard. Ralph Waldo entered at fourteen, the second of the brothers to enter the school. His career there was undistinguished; he lacked the steady diligence of his brother William or the brilliance showed by his younger brothers Charles and Edward. The most significant thing he did there, in fact, was to begin his lifelong practice of keeping a journal (these journals and manuscript notebooks—182 in all—have been published in sixteen volumes by Harvard University Press). At first Emerson used his journals for long compositions:

trial essays, or parts of essays, for his college courses or competitions. But gradually the journal entries began to take on the form they were to have throughout Emerson's maturity. A stray thought, a chance observation, a fact from a scientific journal, or a paragraph from a philosopher—something catches Emerson's attention. He meditates on it, analyzes it, explores the unexpected analogies it reveals with other facts of his experience. When he has reached the end of his thought—sometimes in a few paragraphs, sometimes in a few sentences—he stops.

Unlike the turgid essays with which he had attempted (unsuccessfully) to win the admiration of the Harvard faculty, the journal entries he was writing by the early 1830s are short, intense, and vividly written. The practice of journal keeping freed him from the necessity for "methodical writing" (something he knew he had little talent for) and gave him the license to pursue whatever thought he found most interesting at the moment. In doing so, it gave him not only the material he used in his sermons, lectures, and essays (which are essentially anthologies of passages from the journals) but the ideology he repeatedly expressed in them. Only what is genuinely interesting to you can ever be interesting to another, he says; "the soul's emphasis is always right." The curious fact that "Self-Reliance," Emerson's most militant essay about personal integrity, is also about composition may have its origins in his unhappy experience at Harvard. Self-reliance is like writing in one's journal; conformity, like trying to please a professor on an assigned theme.

His first public compositions were neither wholly free nor wholly determined. Like many of his ancestors, Emerson chose to study for the ministry—a profession he desired not so much for its pastoral duties as for the scope it gave him for the practice of "eloquence." He later recalled that the discipline of the weekly sermon helped give him the habit of steady productivity he depended upon in later life. He was already learning to draw upon the paragraphs composed in his journal for a large portion of the sermon he had to produce each week; the practice gave his style a surprising freshness and an intriguing discontinuity, particularly noticeable in an era when sermons and orations were usually written according to plan. Emerson loved addressing audiences, and by all reports was both a popular and a powerful speaker; his prose style even in intimate essays never entirely loses the oratorical flavor of the sermons and speeches he and his brothers extravagantly admired and frequently memorized.

The Unitarians were a liberal denomination, and the scope they afforded Emerson for the expression of his ideas was wide—many of his sermons read like trial versions of the iconoclastic essays of his maturity. But he grew increasingly restless, and chafed under the restrictions of any creed, however generous in spirit. He never lost faith in the existence or accessibility of the divine mind, but he came to feel that all attempts to ground religious belief in external "proofs"—miracles, testimony, even Scripture itself—were doomed to fall before the corrosive effects of nineteenth-century philosophy, natural science, historical criticism, and comparative anthropology. (Emerson's older brother William had gone to study theology in Germany; he returned home so shaken by what he had learned of the new "historical" criticism of the Bible that he abandoned the ministry for the law.) Emerson chose instead to argue that the only proof of faith is the experience of faith in the individual's own soul, which can *confirm* the truths of doctrine but never be *convinced* by them: conviction emanates only from the soul. Upon the rock of this internal faith Emerson founded his life, and the immediate conviction of his soul's connectedness to godhead gave him both the courage and the serenity by which he was best known to his contemporaries.

With the death of his young wife in 1831 Emerson's ties to conventional modes of living were loosened: a legacy from her estate made it possible for him to contemplate life outside a regular profession, at least for a while. He resigned his position with the Second Church in Boston, then left for a tour of Europe, during which he paid visits to a number of the literary giants whose works he had admired from the other side of the Atlantic: Landor, Coleridge, Wordsworth, and Carlyle. Most of these meetings were comically disappointing (he gave an account of them much later in the first chapter of *English Traits*). But the meeting with Thomas Carlyle, then a struggling writer living in the wilds of Scotland, marked the beginning of a lifelong friendship and a mutually fruitful correspondence.

Emerson returned from Europe eager to publish something and begin acquiring that literary fame his journals show him passionately desiring. On the sea voyage home he confidently refers to a "book about nature" he is planning; his only anxieties concern "where and how" he is going to live. Providentially, the growth of the American lyceum movement (an adult education movement in which subscribers pooled money to hire lecturers) coincided with Emerson's need to find a way to support himself. For the next twenty-five years he spent nearly every winter season delivering lectures on the lyceum circuit, beginning first in New England and New York, but eventually traveling as far south as St. Louis and as far north as Montreal. His financial rewards from the lectures were sometimes pitifully small, but the forum the lyceum provided for the development of his ideas was invaluable. His curiosity had always been wide-ranging, and his mind worked best by analogizing; now he could lecture on topics like natural history (his very first lyceum lecture is entitled "Water"), as well as on more familiar subjects like biography or English literature. Emerson found in lecturing precisely the right blend of discipline and freedom. He could choose his topics, so long as he kept to a certain length and had the manuscript ready by the scheduled date of the lecture. The stimulus to production was just what he needed; most of the essays we now have in his published works had their origin in lyceum lectures, and in their startling juxtapositions of ideas and shifts of tone we can see residues of the techniques Emerson first developed to hold the attention of an audience.

Three years after he first confided his plans for a little book to his journal, Emerson's first book appeared. *Nature* (1836) was a small book, but its ambitions were vast. Like Edgar Allan Poe's *Eureka* (1849), Emerson's book aims to present nothing less than a theory of the universe, of its origin, present condition, and final destiny. Emerson asks us to consider nature from a variety of perspectives—as material benefit, as aesthetic object, as preceptress of stoicism—then hold out the intoxicating possibility that the vast "riddle" of nature might someday be solved by man and that the "kingdom of man over nature" prophesied since the beginning of the world might then organize itself around our organs of perception.

We have two clues to help us in solving the riddle of the Sphinx: ecstasy and science. The former dissolves us in moments of joy in which our usual state of alienation from nature is revealed as an aberration; the latter shows us that nature must emanate from a mind like our own, since we are able to penetrate its secrets both deductively and intuitively. If Immanuel Kant tried to demonstrate how synthetic propositions could be knowable *a priori*, Emerson is more interested in the conclusions that follow from the fact that they are thus knowable. He embodies these conclusions in a fable contained in *Nature*'s apocalyptic closing chapter. Man is "a god in ruins," nature his alienated consciousness, frozen into symbolic form by the failure of his outflowing creative energy. But the world is full of hints that man is gradually resuming the power he had mysteriously abandoned. With the "influx of the spirit" the world will heal itself, and "the kingdom of man over nature" will give man "a dominion such as is now beyond his dream of God."

Nature had been published anonymously, but its authorship was soon guessed (a Boston joke ran: "Who is the author of Nature? God and Ralph Waldo Emerson"). Emerson's next significant productions, on the other hand, were public—in fact, notorious—events. In 1837 the Harvard chapter of Phi Beta Kappa invited him to deliver the annual address to the Society at the Harvard commencement festivities. The topic of his address, "The

American Scholar," was a conventional one: laments for America's cultural backwardness, calls for a national literature, attempts to define the place of the scholar in a democratic and mercantile society.

But Emerson's treatment of these shopworn themes was anything but conventional. He chose to treat genteel subjects like "tradition" and "inspiration" in metaphors borrowed from military science or venture capitalism. Tradition, he argued, *tyrannizes* over later writers; genius *monopolizes* inspiration. "Genius is always sufficiently the enemy of genius by over influence. The literature of every nation bears me witness. The English dramatic poets have Shakespearized now for two hundred years." The way out of this subservience of debt is by adopting an aggressiveness equal to tradition's own. When "the mind is braced by labor and invention," we read the great works of the past with a light that emanates from us, not from them: "the page of whatever book we read, becomes luminous with manifold allusion." This sudden burst of inner light makes the domineering masterpiece seem less formidable. "We see then, what is always true, that as the seer's hour of vision is short and rare among the heavy days and months, so is its record, perchance, the least part of his volume." The aggressive reader decides which parts of his author constitute the "authentic utterances of the oracle" ("authentic" is deliciously circular) and rejects the rest. His guide in this radical act of appropriation is the same "self-trust" Emerson had urged in rejecting the external "proofs" of Christianity for a faith wholly interior; it might be regarded as the literary application of the same spiritual principle.

The language of power and monopoly is one thing applied to literary history, quite another applied to religion itself. The Harvard authorities who submitted to being mildly shocked or mildly titillated had quite a different reaction to the address Emerson delivered the next year to the tiny graduating class of the Harvard Divinity School. To resent "coming into nature, and finding not names and places, not land and professions, but even virtue and truth foreclosed and monopolized"; to rebel against the voice that seems to say "You shall not own the world," sounds like admirable self-assertion when the monopolist is Plato or Shakespeare, something rather different when the monopolist is Jesus Christ and the prohibiting voice belongs to his church.

Emerson's friend and fellow transcendentalist Theodore Parker remembered once being present at a meeting of gentlemen who spent the evening debating the question "Whether Ralph Waldo Emerson was a Christian." They decided that he was not, "for discipleship was necessary to Christianity," and Emerson's whole life was a passionate rejection of the ideal of discipleship. Willing to accord Jesus respect as the man who spoke with perfect candor the truth that "God incarnates himself in man," Emerson nonetheless insists that whoever pays undue reverence to the *person* of Jesus turns Christianity from a sublime "provocation" to a mere "Cultus" or "mythus" like the religions of Greece or Egypt—myth rather than truth.

The chief fault of all forms of what Emerson dismisses as "historical Christianity" (including the Unitarian) lay in its murderous insistence that the liberating words of Christ be quarantined and canonized as merely another deadly Sacred Text. Emerson deplores the "assumption that the age of inspiration is past, that the Bible is closed," and argues that "the office of a true teacher" is "to show us that God is, not was, that he speaketh, not spake." He urges each of his hearers to account himself "a newborn bard of the Holy Ghost" and to "acquaint men at first hand with the Deity." As Jesus added a new testament to the Hebrew Torah, so might some American Messiah do the same, with a gospel for his age's own desperation and unbelief. "I look for the hour when that Supreme Beauty, which ravished the souls of Eastern men, and chiefly of those Hebrews, and through their lips spoke oracles to all time, shall speak in the West also."

If D. H. Lawrence, writing in *The Dial* for 1926, could express dismay at Emerson's call for "a hundred million American godlets," Emerson's own contemporaries were even unhappier. It was difficult to be a Unitarian heretic, but Emerson discovered he had managed the feat. Andrews Norton, the formidable head of the Divinity School, blasted Emerson in the public newspaper, a vigorous pamphlet war (in which Emerson himself refused to take part) went on for some time, and Emerson was banned from speaking at Harvard for thirty years.

This "storm in our washbowl" (as Emerson described it in a letter to Carlyle) had two very important results: it drove Emerson to rely completely on secular writing and lecturing for a living—he had continued to function as a substitute or "supply" preacher after resigning his pastorate—and it revealed to him the inadequacies of his earlier model of revelation. It was not enough to lie in the lap of Infinity and utter piercing truths; the success of the prophet's message, he had discovered, depends partly upon the hearer's willingness to receive. What forces aid the communication of truth, and what forces obstruct it?

Analysis of the struggle between power and resistance informs many of the essays gathered together in the volume Emerson published in 1841 (now entitled *Essays: First Series*). The essays are made up of passages intricately interwoven from the journal passages and lectures of the preceding years; many of them clearly grow out of his experience of social opposition following the "Divinity School Address." Most of the essays in this aggressive volume stress power rather than obstruction. "Spiritual Laws" speaks of the "willingness and self-annihilation" that makes a man the "unobstructed channel" of divine energy, just as "The Over-Soul" explores the region from which that energy flows, the gigantic heart without valve, wall, or intersection that rolls its blood uninterruptedly in "an endless circulation through all men."

Such ecstatic affirmations led Lawrence to grumble that Emerson "was only connected on the Ideal Phone." They were certainly responsible for the precipitous decline his reputation took in the middle decades of the twentieth century, when it became fashionable to belittle Emerson as a bloodless optimist who lacked a Vision of Evil. In fact, the most famous essays in this first volume derive their energy from the conflicts they explore between the arrogant assumption of spiritual power and the clear-sighted listing of all forces ranged in opposition to that power, not the least of which are forces emanating from another region of the seer's own mind.

In the celebrated "Self-Reliance" the forces opposing self-assertion are mainly social. Mental timidity is a reflection of the moral cowardice of the crowd. "Society everywhere is in conspiracy against the manhood of every one of its members. . . . Self-reliance is its aversion." Hence the anarchic advice: "Whoso would be a man, must be a nonconformist." If most societies initiate young men *into* the group, Emerson envisions an alternative elite chosen chiefly for its power to reject. "I shun father and mother, wife and brother, when my genius calls me. I would write on the lintels of the door-post, *Whim*. I hope it is somewhat better than whim at last, but we cannot spend the day in explanation."

The brio of the essay is largely generated from its fantasies of insouciance. Emerson delights in imagining insults to the church, good society, philanthropists, abolitionists (here conceived of merely as another species of do-gooder), lovers of conformity, and even his own past beliefs, in favor of a strenuous self-expressiveness that can "bring the past for judgment into the thousand-eyed present, and live ever in the new day."

In its constant metaphoric equation of youthfulness with virtue, "Self-Reliance" is in danger of making regeneration seem too easy, as if evil, obstruction, and misery were only stodginess. "Circles" is more trenchant in its analysis of the obstacles to desire. Attempting to locate a controlling pattern beneath the constant warfare of old and new in intellectual and cultural history, Emerson finds it in the circle, that emblem both of perfection and of limitation. "Our life is an apprenticeship to the truth, that around every circle another can be drawn; that there is no end in nature, but every end is a beginning; that there is always another dawn risen on mid-noon, and under every deep a lower deep opens." That last clause, with its phrases borrowed from both innocent and diabolical speakers in *Paradise Lost*, shows how equivocal Emerson's voice has become in this essay. In place of the tingling exhortations of "Self-Reliance" we hear a cooler analyst, who no longer thinks the world can be divided simply between the creative and the ossified, but who has come to see ossification itself as the inevitable end of every creative impulse. "For, it is the inert effort of each thought having formed itself into a circular wave of circumstance,—as, for instance, an empire, rules of an art, a local usage, a religious rite,—to heap itself on that ridge, and to solidify, and hem in the life. But if the soul is quick and strong, it bursts over that boundary on all sides, and expands another orbit on the great deep, which also runs up into a high wave, with attempt again to stop and bind." Though the essay as a whole is electric and expansive, it contains within it an explicit confession that limitation follows power as its eternal antagonist and inescapable twin.

By the time Emerson published his first series of *Essays*, his style had achieved the distinctive form from which it never subsequently varied. A series of short, declarative sentences, whose logical relationship to one another is left deliberately unarticulated, will suddenly flower out into illustrative metaphors and periodic sentences, then return to conclude in a tart epigram. It is a stimulating style (many nineteenth-century readers spoke of Emerson as if he were a kind of tonic), but it can also be a tiring one, in the amount of aggression it directs against the reader and the amount of sustained attention it demands from him. As O. W. Firkins (1915) mildly complained, "Emerson's feet are all spondees." The journals are much easier to read for long stretches than the essays; there is a good deal of random observation and humorous reflection is interspersed between the paragraphs of concentrated thought. Yet a comparison of paragraphs from the *Essays* with their originals in the journals shows how little internal revision was needed to make them publishable; the tense, highly wrought style of the *Essays* had become for Emerson a medium as natural as thought itself.

Power was Emerson's True Grail, but power had always been an elusive commodity. His own inner life seemed to ebb and flow; he complained in "Circles" that he sometimes felt like "a God in nature" and sometimes like "a weed by the wall." In the years immediately following the publication of the first series of *Essays* a number of things had increased the time he spent in the latter of those conditions. The death of his greatly beloved son from his second marriage left him devastated, first by grief, then by the more terrible numbness that succeeded it. The arrival of his fortieth birthday in 1843 outwardly confirmed his growing sense that youthful opti-mism, like youthful energy, was disappearing. A certain weariness suffuses the second volume of *Essays* he published in 1844.

Even "The Poet," the opening essay of the volume and its most celebra-tory, shows signs of the change in mood. Emerson praises the poet extrav-agantly for the insight that reveals to him that "the Universe is the exter-nization of the soul" and gives him a speech that "flows with the flowing of nature." The poet sees everywhere in nature evidences of that central mys-tery Emerson terms, simply, "the metamorphosis"—that all things are in flux, that all created things are only the temporary incarnation of a divine energy always on the brink of transformation into something else. Like the prisoners in Plato's cave, we live blinded to the truth of our condition. "We are symbols and inhabit symbols; workmen, work, and tools, words and things, birth and death, all are emblems; but we sympathize with the sym-bols, and being infatuated with the economical uses of things, we do not know that they are thoughts." By using symbols to reveal the symbolic nature of reality, the poet frees us from false belief in its substantiality, and hence deserves to be called a "liberating god." "The use of symbols has a certain power of emancipation and exhilaration for all men. . . . We are like men who come out of a cave or cellar into the open air."

But "The Poet" is not content with a poetry that awakens and liberates men. The old hope that had animated *Nature*—that poetry, by translating natural symbols into linguistic ones, could serve as a new Scripture—re-turns to plague and baffle the argument of "The Poet." If it is really true that "the sea, the mountain-ridge, Niagara, and every flower-bed, pre-exist, or super-exist, in pre-cantations," then the poet is reduced from the status of liberating god to more or less faithful scribe, and his once-vaunted indi-viduality (praised in "The American Scholar" and "Self-Reliance" as the only path to immortality) suddenly is cast as villain of the piece: "we lose ever and anon a word or a verse and substitute something of our own" in our attempts to hear and capture these pre-cantations, "and thus miswrite the poem." (Emerson did not finally resolve this fundamental contradiction at the heart of his poetic theory until he was willing to relinquish his hope of a fixed natural symbolism merely waiting for the poet's transcription in favor of an emphasis on the poet's role as symbol *maker* and dialectician. In the late, brilliant essay "Poetry and Imagination," published in *Letters and Social Aims*, he argues that all symbols were meant to hold only for a mo-ment, and that it is the poet's capacity to transfer significance endlessly from one symbol to another that makes him the emblem of human thought.

"All thinking is analogizing, and it is the business of life to learn metonymy.")

The contradictions visible beneath the brave affirmations of "The Poet" surface in a different and more dangerous way in the next essay in the volume. "Experience" is one of Emerson's greatest essays; it is also one of his most shocking, shocking because so much of its aggressivity is now directed against the self. Even in tone it is quite unlike anything Emerson ever wrote. It begins in weariness and exhaustion, rises in places to intense bitterness, or sinks into a Gallic cynicism. Of course there are more familiar accents too: declarations of hope, of courage, of faith in the "subright Mecca of the West" that still reveals itself, in flashes, to the pilgrim. But in no other essay does Emerson allow so much space to the negative forces before vanquishing them, and in no other essay does the victory finally obtained leave so many casualties behind on the battlefield.

What "Experience" offers is an extended meditation upon the fact of subjectivity, and a devastating candor about the moral and psychological corollaries that follow from the fact that it is inescapable. First Emerson lists all the things that keep us locked in the "prison of glass" that is our own selfhood. He describes with clinical precision the "flux of moods" that renders the very notion of personal "identity" a bitter joke; he analyzes the necessary bafflement of a creature trapped in a temporal succession that renders all his efforts at knowledge futile and ensures that what pitiful wisdom he achieves will be only retroactive. As if this were not chilling enough, he then proceeds to detail, with frightening honesty, the corollaries that follow from our inescapable self-centeredness—the ease with which we outgrow books, friends, lovers; the indulgence we always extend to our own crimes, real or contemplated; the sham quality of all those emotions, like grief or guilt, that depend upon a belief in the real existence of other people.

Against this radical skepticism "Experience" can offer only a few practical defenses—a reliance on common sense, on small pleasures; an acceptance of custom; patience in waiting for those eruptions of the old power that never entirely deserts us; resigned acceptance of the self-reliance forced upon us by the fact of our isolation; a gentleman's courteous determination to treat the ghosts and shadows we live with "as if they were real."

These are only palliatives, and are offered as such. What takes the place of hope in the essay is the courage with which its unpleasant truths are faced, a courage that keeps it from seeming depressing even when those truths are bleakest. As Maurice Gonnaud has said: "The greatness of an essay like 'Experience' lies, I suggest, in our sense of the author's being engaged in a pursuit of truth which has all the characters of faith except its quality of radiating happiness."

Of the remaining essays in the volume, "Character" still retains some of its power to shock. By "character" Emerson means what we should probably call "charisma," and he coolly asserts that Jesus of Nazareth didn't have enough of it—since his Crucifixion (which Emerson labels "a great Defeat") was a victory only for the soul, not yet for the senses. The millennarianism that had prompted the closing chapter of *Nature* returns here, as Emerson, still bitterly refusing to accept a universe that could engineer the death of his son, rejects as incomplete any Messiahship that fails to restore paradise and immortality. "Nominalist and Realist" is memorable for the shrewd Yankee wit of some of its epigrams ("Every man is wanted, and no man is wanted much") as well as for its attempt to give an ontological justification for one of Emerson's favorite rhetorical devices: the paradox. "No sentence will hold the whole truth, and the only way we can be just, is by giving ourselves the lie. . . . All the universe over, there is but one thing, this old Two-Face, creator-creature, mind-matter, right-wrong, of which any proposition may be affirmed or denied." And "New England Reformers" combines an affectionate nostalgia for the goofy idealism of the decade just past with wry portraits of the visionaries, reformers, social schemers, religious fanatics, and campaigners for improved nutrition who had made New England both a national mecca and a national joke. Despite Emerson's earlier assertion that a prosperous middle-aged man has "ripened beyond the possibility of sincere radicalism," he is still cheerfully insisting that men are conservative only when they are "least vigorous," radicals whenever "their intellect or their conscience has been aroused." The "rankest Tories" in Old or New England, if exposed to "a man of great heart and mind," will begin to thaw, to hope, to "spin and revolve." And he affirms the belief that lies behind all schemes of reform and survives even the depredations of skepticism: "Men in all ways are better than they seem."

After the publication of *Essays: Second Series* Emerson found himself in need of new material for a winter course of lyceum lectures. A single lecture he had written on Napoleon suggested the possibility of a lecture series with "a biographical basis." By the winter of 1845 he was ready to begin this new series, entitled "Representative Men," and including lectures on "Plato; or, the Philosopher," "Swedenborg; or, the Mystic," "Montaigne; or, the Skeptic," "Shakspeare; or, the Poet," "Napoleon; or, the Man of the World," "Goethe; or, the Writer." As the lecture titles and series title suggest, Emerson is choosing his heroes not merely because they were great but because each embodied one attribute of that central divinity Emerson saw as the birthright of every man. Plato's vision, Goethe's courage of thought, Napoleon's executive genius, Shakespeare's brilliant facility in making the material world the servant of his thought, Montaigne's dispassionate weighing of truths and opinions in the scales of an unbiased intellect, Swedenborg's mystical insight into the symbolic nature of reality—all are incarnations in mortal form of that godhead whose distribution into individualities Emerson had marveled over as long ago as "The American Scholar." But this distribution has its dark side as well; the human vessels into which this genius is poured are often weak and sometimes wicked; a catalogue of genius is necessarily also a catalogue of partiality, deformity, even madness. Each lecture begins with a cascade of praise, and then, in a savage about-face, begins attacking the shrine it has just constructed. Plato is too intellectual to possess real spiritual authority; Swedenborg falls into the monstrous egotism that bedevils all religious fanatics; Montaigne's skepticism, while an admirable defense against "bigots and blockheads," still leaves us thirsting after righteousness and truth; Napoleon's executive genius is finally useless without common honesty and some vision higher than the sensual; Shakespeare, the greatest poet in the world, was at last content to be nothing more than "the master of the revels to mankind"; the worldly Goethe, for all his ambition to know everything knowable, is finally too self-conscious, too devoted to mere culture, to reach the highest regions of the spirit. The Representative Man these fragments of godhead might compose, if divorced from the defects of their virtues, will never wholly materialize, yet from these fragmentary lobsided mortals (as Emerson once called them) we can compose his figure.

The lectures in this series were finally published in 1850 as *Representative Men*. Earlier volumes had drawn heavily on lecture material, but this was the first of Emerson's books to consist of a single course of lectures, revised only slightly for publication. As Wallace E. Williams has pointed out, the "freedom and daring" of the lecture hall are evident in the book's style, which is racier, more colloquial, less lapidary than in the two volumes of *Essays*. The language of *Representative Men* deserves the compliment Emerson pays to the language of Montaigne: "Cut these words and they would bleed; they are vascular and alive."

In 1846 Emerson published a volume of *Poems*, the fruit of thirty years of poetic activity. His ambitions in this area had always been high—he once said, "I am more of a poet than anything else"—and his earliest notebooks and journals show him experimenting with forms and styles. As a schoolboy and Harvard undergraduate he had confined himself chiefly to the approved neoclassical couplets, though his favorite aunt's passion for Byron

had led him into a few sallies of Romantic melancholy, of which little memorable remains except the delicious line, "I will shake hands with death and
hug Despair." His first response to Wordsworth, to whom he was introduced while at college, was strongly contemptuous, but gradually Emerson
became a convert to the new mode: intimate, reflective, autobiographical.
While a student at the Divinity School he became a passionate admirer of
Coleridge, who in turn introduced him to the seventeenth-century lyric
masters: Herbert, Donne, Jonson, Marvell. Later still he learned to admire
Goethe and the Persian and Arabic poets he read in German translations.

Traces of all these enthusiasms are visible in the *Poems* of 1846. Emerson
admired the tetrameter couplets of Milton and Marvell for their capacity to
reconcile compression and fluency, to seem gnomic without seeming epigrammatic, like the far more discontinuous pentameter couplet of neoclassical verse. Emerson uses the tetrameter line for meditations on nature ("The
Humble-Bee"), on human life and human emotion ("Initial, Daemonic, and
Celestial Love"); he uses it for moral lessons ("The Visit"), for dramatic
monologues ("Alphonso of Castile"), for parables ("The Sphinx"), and for
excursions into myth ("Bacchus," "Merlin").

It is easy to see why Emerson liked the tetrameter line. At best, it allows
him to write verses as unforgettable as a witch's spell, as in the closing lines
from "Merlin":

> Subtle rhymes, with ruin rife,
> Murmur in the house of life,
> Sung by Sisters as they spin;
> In perfect time and measure they
> Build and unbuild our echoing clay.
> As the two twilights of the day
> Fold us music-drunken in.

But the tetrameter line is far less forgiving of metrical roughness than the
longer pentameter, and Emerson's self-confessed inability to master the
mysteries of rhythm leads to line upon line of frankly unmetrical verse.
Worse still, the sureness of taste that never seemed to desert Emerson in
the wildest of his prose experiments deserts him frequently in verse, and
the result is a bathos deeper than anything in Wordsworth:

> I cannot shake off the god;
>   On my neck he makes his seat;
> I look at my face in the glass—
>   My eyes his eyeballs meet.
>   ("The Park")

Mercifully, these lapses of taste and of meter disappear from Emerson's blank-verse poetry, to be replaced by the quiet assurance of "Musquetaquid," or by the descriptive exuberance of "The Snow-Storm," with its loving portrait of the "mad wind's night-work" and of the suddenly isolated house-dwellers in their "tumultuous privacy of storm." In most of these poems Emerson is content to employ verse rhythms that descend from the descriptive poetry of the eighteenth century, but in places he is clearly experimenting with the possibility of a tougher-sounding, "native" pentameter line, as in the opening lines of "Hamatreya":

> Bulkeley, Hunt, Willard, Hosmer, Meriam, Flint,
> Possessed the land which rendered to their toil,
> Hay, corn, roots, hemp, flax, apples, wool and wood.

The wit that plays off the monosyllabic or strongly trochaic rhythm of the Yankee farmers' names against the smooth "English" pentameter of the line that follows anticipates the metrical virtuosity of one of Emerson's greatest twentieth-century admirers, Robert Frost.

Some of Emerson's best poems are examples of a genre not very easy to define. "Uriel," "Saadi," "Bacchus," and "Merlin" are visionary or emblematic fables loosely modeled on Coleridge's "Kubla Khan" and on German mythological lyrics like Goethe's "Prometheus" or Holderlin's "Patmos." If, as the Higher Critics argued, all religion was essentially mythological, then modern poets had as much right to invent gods and fables as the Greeks or the Hebrews had. Like his European predecessors, Emerson uses figures drawn from literary or mythological tradition to embody new impulses of the spirit for which received tradition had no name. Emerson's visionary lyrics are intended to do what Emerson praised Goethe for having accomplished—creating, in Mephistopheles, the "first organic figure that has been added for some ages" to European mythology. In a series of brief narrative poems, written mostly in some combination of tetrameter lines, Emerson gives us Uriel, whose terrifying vision of the Law of Compensation ("Evil will bless and ice will burn") shakes the heavens, but who is himself crippled by excessive self-knowledge; Saadi, whose joyous wisdom survives all the ascetic lobbying of the Fakirs; Bacchus, who demands an intoxication great enough to restore man to innocence and nature to joy; Merlin, incarnation of the individual poetic will, who is grimly ready to accept the fatality in nature if only he is given access to her frightening power.

The decade of the 1840s had been a period of intense productivity: two volumes of essays, a volume of poems, the lecture series on representative men. But in the latter half of the decade Emerson had begun to feel both exhausted and stale, in need, as he said, of a whip for his top. He boarded a ship for England in October 1847. The following nine months were spent in an exhausting but exhilarating tour of Scotland and England, with a brief trip across the Channel to France, then in the midst of revolutionary excitement. He was then at the height of his fame, lionized everywhere (though his native shyness made that British institution, the evening party, a torment for him). He revisited such old friends as Carlyle and Alexander Ireland; he paid a final call on Wordsworth; he met Matthew Arnold, Arthur Hugh Clough, Francis Jeffrey, Thomas De Quincey, and Alexis de Tocqueville, as well as a number of famous scientists and mathematicians.

Once home again Emerson began lecturing on his experiences in Britain, lectures that eventually were revised into *English Traits*. As Alfred Kazin remarks, the book is notable for being "worldlier, shrewder, wittier, than anything else by this god-intoxicated man." Emerson is warmly admiring of English skill and self-reliance, gently amused by English eccentricity, and everywhere fascinated by a culture whose historical roots are vividly evident in the smallest customs of the people. He is critical, too: of the squalid poverty that haunts the spectacular wealth of the island, of the fondness for cant that Emerson sadly judges to be the constitutional vice of the Anglo-Saxon race, since it is as visible in Old England as in the New. His chapter on the Anglican church is as trenchant a criticism of the hypocrisies of nineteenth-century Christianity as the "Divinity School Address"; it is also slyly but devastatingly funny. Indeed, the whole book has a complexity of tone and attitude familiar enough to a reader of Emerson's journals, but rarer in the published works, where moods are made to alternate rather than coalesce. Emerson had frequently been ironic; in *English Traits* he is finally urbane.

The keener interest in political questions that Emerson had brought back from Europe was soon given native fodder. In 1850 the government in Washington enacted a series of measures designed to secure California's admission to statehood, something Southerners opposed. To pacify the South, legislators (led by Massachusetts' own Daniel Webster, one of Emerson's heroes) agreed to the passage of a tough Fugitive Slave Law, whose provisions included a demand that Northern citizens aid in the capture and remanding of fugitive slaves who had escaped into free states. These events catapulted Emerson from his scholarly retirement into violent public activity. He denounced Webster and the Fugitive Slave Law in speeches whose vitriol was not lessened even by Webster's death; he stumped for Free-Soil candidates; he addressed Anti-Slavery Society meetings and called for abolition; he urged his fellow citizens to break "this filthy enactment" at the earliest possible opportunity.

Yet a private pessimism about the efficacy of reform in the face of the cruelty and wastefulness of nature recurs frequently in his journals, along with a growing awareness that for the vast mass of suffering humanity— the urban proletariat, the black slaves—his customary exhortations to a life of romantic self-expansiveness were bitterly irrelevant. "Ask the digger in the ditch to explain Newton's laws; the fine organs of his brain have been pinched by overwork and squalid poverty from father to son for a hundred years." "The German and Irish millions, like the Negro, have a great deal of guano in their destiny. They are ferried over the Atlantic and carted over America, to ditch and to drudge, to make corn cheap and then to lie down prematurely to make a spot of green grass on the prairie."

These ugly sentiments come from the essay "Fate," first in a volume entitled *The Conduct of Life*, published in 1860, but based on a series of lectures first written in the turbulent years 1850–52. The opening paragraph of "Fate" suggests the helplessness Emerson then felt as he tried to resolve the huge "question of the times" into a "practical question of the conduct of life." "We are incompetent to solve the times. Our geometry cannot span the huge orbits of the prevailing ideas, behold their return and reconcile their opposition." Yet only part of the book really fits this announced plan of retreating into a private world. The middle essays— "Wealth," "Culture," "Behavior," "Considerations by the Way," and "Beauty"—can certainly qualify as recommendations of the genteel values of the Boston aristocracy, and "Worship" offers the same private answer to the loudly debated question of the "decay of religion" that Emerson had been advancing since the "Divinity School Address": religions do not decay, only the outward forms of religions do; the great truths are always adequate to us, whether or not we are adequate to them. And "Illusions," the final essay, is as private as a one-man polar expedition, and almost as cold; it describes all of human existence as a "snow-storm" of private fantasies, which lifts only occasionally to reveal the gods sitting on their thrones, staring down at the solitary mortal—"they alone with him alone."

But the book's opening essays—"Fate" and "Power"—show Emerson attempting the very task he claimed to have renounced: a solution to the riddle of the times by working out its permutations on a slate as large as the cosmos. "Fate," the grimmest essay he ever wrote, lists all the forces hostile to human freedom, both natural and social; "Power," the other great fact of the world, recoils against this catalogue of horrors with a counter-assertion of the "affirmative force" with which the world is also saturated. Taken together, they are among Emerson's strongest essays, intellectually uncompromising, rhetorically violent. They reflect in their titanic opposition the moral dilemmas of a country moving closer to the agony of civil war.

After the war Emerson's career was nearly over. He published another volume of essays, the genial *Society and Solitude*, and another volume of poems, *May-Day and Other Pieces*. But a progressive deterioration of memory rendered him incapable of writing or lecturing, and his family had to call in the help of James Elliot Cabot to ready a collection of his earlier pieces, *Letters and Social Aims*, for the press. Emerson's physical health, however, remained good, and he was only a few weeks short of his seventy-ninth birthday when he died in 1882.

Emerson's reputation has undergone the usual cycles of inflation and crash in the century since his death. What he once called "the unstable estimates of men" are never likely to rest easy in their judgment of a man who combines lofty idealism with militant self-assertiveness, who assumes the authority to exhort without renouncing the instinct for outrage, whose style manages to be at once repetitive and elliptical. In his own day Emerson mystified or infuriated as many listeners as he exhilarated or convinced, and the ratios do not seem to have changed very much today. He took such hostility philosophically, believing that an author "elects" his readers as inexorably and mysteriously as the Calvinist God chooses the company of the saved. What he meant to the young men and women of his own time is best summed up in James Russell Lowell's nostalgic account of Emerson as a lecturer. "At any rate, he brought us *life*, which, on the whole, is no bad thing."

Barbara Packer

Henry David Thoreau

On August 30, 1837, Henry David Thoreau graduated from Harvard College. He was just over twenty years old and was thinking of a career in teaching, which he had tried out some two years before. Thoreau had less than twenty-five years left to live, his life so fraught with ironies, most of them self-engendered, that a blend of irony, curiosity, and ecstasy may be said largely to define it. One of those ironies can be seen at this major beginning point. On the day after Thoreau's graduation, as part of the same commencement exercises, Ralph Waldo Emerson spoke to the Phi Beta Kappa Society on the subject "The American Scholar," putting the emphasis in his address as much on the adjective as on the noun it modified. We have no certain evidence that Thoreau heard Emerson speak; yet none of Emerson's contemporaries would do better at exemplifying what he called for—that pairing of home-directed thought and stubborn originality, a hard look at local turf and a broad look at universal history—than Thoreau himself.

Those times held other beginnings as well. On October 22, 1837, Thoreau began a journal that eventually came to fill forty-seven manuscript volumes and contain over two million words. It was the major record of his thoughts and the course of all his works, a project so rich and compendious that it is, arguably, his finest achievement. On November 17 he wrote down the substance of a moment of present joy that echoed Goethe but also defined a thrust of self that was to occupy him to the end: "The smothered breathings of awakening day strike the ear with an undulatory motion— over hill and dale, pasture and woodland, come they to me, and I am at home in the world." Here, early and strikingly, is fundamental Thoreau, the radical act of his consciousness, a preoccupation so profound that it determined all he was to try as vocation as well as the attendant passions. Getting the self to be at home in the world became the main business of

Thoreau's life, the single and central vocation to which all other forms were subsidiary. All else was part of that act, an aspect of its performance, a gesture designed to accomplish its essential purpose. Rarely was the act so easy to accomplish as it seemed in the late months of 1837.

Thoreau's purpose was becoming clearer as he set about living in Concord. An effort at public-school teaching having failed (he did not know that he was supposed to whip the students), Thoreau and his brother John opened a private school, the tenets of which would now be recognized as those of progressive education. On August 31, 1839, between sessions of their school, he and John began a boat trip to the source of the Merrimack River. The gestures and imagery of that excursion gave the firmest substance so far to that radical practice of home-making that—he was now coming to see—could be acted on as well as pondered. And if it could be acted on it could also be written about. Indeed, he was also coming to see that living and writing, in fact the whole business of working in language, were not only cooperative acts but, in part at least, the same act when viewed in a special perspective.

Thoreau began to explore these and related matters in his first important essays, "The Natural History of Massachusetts," solicited by Emerson for *The Dial* in 1842, "A Walk to Wachusett," published elsewhere later in the same year, and "A Winter Walk" and "The Landlord," both published in 1843. Together these essays play out early versions of the intricate relations of self, place, and text that were to follow in Thoreau's finest work. The Nature of "The Natural History of Massachusetts" is a place of elemental joy, the qualities of which must determine the essential qualities of being: "surely joy," he wrote, "is the condition of life." But Thoreau was too lucid and canny, too hard-nosed and perceptive, to continue such sentimentality for long; even in this early essay he set about making the requisite adjustments. The things of nature typify, suggest, and represent, and thereby turn nature into a text to be read. If the old idea of typifying was put to wonderful contemporary work in Emerson's *Nature* (1836), Thoreau played harder and more profoundly with his own special sense of the way the things of this world speak to each other and bring the world into intricate converse by imitating each other in a gesture he always called "answering": "Every tree, shrub, and spire of grass, that could raise its head above the snow, was covered with a dense ice-foliage, answering, as it were, leaf for leaf to its summer dress." But there are kinds and kinds of converse, more levels and hierarchies than were broached in Emerson's essay, all manner of modes of awareness that have their own sort of elocution. If Thoreau compares the written to the preached word, nature's joy to our wailing, he can also say, in a clumsy early poem to Walden Pond (entered in the *Journal* in 1838), that "our converse a stranger is to speech." To be at home in the world is to know *all* of its modes of converse, not only its various ways of "answering" but the questions to which "answering" is one sort of response.

The self that asks and answers, probing nature for its felicities as well as its facticity, finds all manner of relations to nature in the early *Journal* and essays. Taking a firmly Emersonian stance, it can query nature about its usefulness and get a response that does not come from nature but from the pressure of the self's own needs: "Let us not underrate the value of a fact," Thoreau wrote in "The Natural History"; "it will one day flower in a truth." Thus is the flow of a river "a beautiful illustration of the law of obedience." Natural facts become instruments of intelligibility, the world a more coherent place for our reading of them. There, too, nature is a text. And yet it speaks of itself to us in more subtle ways as well. In "A Winter Walk" we hear of a surprising fact that blossoms into a number of truths: "There is a slumbering subterranean fire in nature which never goes out, and which no cold can chill." At this time of the year there is a curious bifurcation in nature, a cold external purity that weeds out all except that which "has a virtue in it"; but there is also a warmth within, a condition that we imitate not only in the hearths within our homes but in the warm centers within us, centers of self that reveal and sustain a bifurcation of self and substance. The poem that begins "The Natural History of Massachusetts" speaks of "the verdure of my mind," green and warm within while the world is white and pure and cold. Thus does nature speak to us of the linkage that ties us to it, the bifurcations we share with it. Thus do we find (or forcibly make?) a place for ourselves in the natural context. In one of our many aspects we are the counterpart of that which we love and inspect and slowly learn to see in all its facets and facts, in what it can offer us as symbols for our lives, in that awesome self-generation that it performs for itself.

Yet if there is a sense in which such love and linkage help us to locate ourselves in the world, our relations are too complex to be contained in these matters alone. If we have learned to locate ourselves we can come upon dislocation and find that it is really not so bad: "And when he has done, he may have to steer his way home through the dark by the north star, and he will feel himself some degrees nearer to it for having lost his way on the earth." Bifurcation is not only between self and substance, the warm core and the exterior chill, but, in certain conditions, between ourselves and where we are grounded. We can go on excursions not only to local locations but *in the direction of* ("toward" rather than "to") places that now can only be glimpsed. The play of sharing and difference, likeness and otherness, that these bifurcations show is so basic to Thoreau that his sense of placement in the world cannot be understood without it. Some local places speak, even smell, of our terrestrial origins: a strong odor of musk recalls that wildness from which we all have come and that still hangs about our borders. Yet on the same page of "The Natural History of Massachusetts" Thoreau speaks not only of the sights and sounds around us but "a quite new note, which has for background other Carolinas and Mexicos than the books describe." In the passage of the *Journal* from which this thought is taken the words had been "many a Carolina and Mexico of the soul," locations of the self that can never be shared with the sights and sounds of nature the books describe (March 4, 1840). "A Walk to Wachusett" begins with a poem about mountains seen in the west, "unhewn primeval timber . . . the stock of which new earths are made." This is the westering Thoreau extols throughout his career, the destiny of his country as it moves toward the Pacific, that mapping of the unhewn and primeval that makes more ground for the location of American selves. Yet in that essay he also speaks of climbing Mount Wachusett and finding in "the subtler and purer atmosphere of those elevated places" a solemn and solitary remoteness "removed from all contagion with the plain." At such an altitude he glimpses that place where he cannot yet go ("from the summit he beholds the heavens and the horizon"), but there is no overt sense of uneasiness about the glimpse. For at this point in Thoreau's life he could leave such limits untouched. Three years later, by the time of the writing of *A Week on the Concord and Merrimack Rivers*, the ambivalence had grown so potent that he could not put it by, and the experience of another mountain evoked the same ideas and sights but took on quite a different tonality.

Little of that ambivalence showed in Thoreau's life in Concord, which was as undramatic in externals as it was dense with the tensions and glories of consciousness. John's death in 1842 shook Thoreau deeply, but it had no lasting effect on the main business of his life, seeking the self's at-homeness. The inspection of the things of this world, the transformation of nature into consciousness—into language as well as that which words could never enfold—kept Thoreau's time fully occupied when he was not making a living. He lived for a while with the Emersons as friend and handyman, wrote for *The Dial* and other journals, lectured to the Concord Lyceum, became a successful maker of pencils, and, for half of 1843, tutored Emerson's brother's children on Staten Island. But as often as he could he walked, trying for at least one excursion a day and such longer walks as he could manage. Excursions had come to constitute much of the essential business of Thoreau's life and writing. Both the act and the word (he always used it with complex precision) had much to show and say about the world's effect on him and his on it. An excursion into unmapped places (and no map of Concord showed the new things that he found there daily) was an act of demarcation, a defining of the undifferentiated. It was as though his walks inscribed his selfhood on the world, wrote on it in gestures that were more than bodily. And in fact there is plentiful evidence that he thought of excursions and writing and reading as parallel acts, each with the same sort of result. In the "Monday" chapter of *A Week* he tells of the movement of an old book as being like "a comment on the flow and freshet of modern books. The reader leaps from sentence to sentence, as from one stepping stone to another, while the stream of the story rushes past unregarded." In *Walden* he is even more pointed: speaking of his purpose in going to the pond, he tells of the need to "give a true account of it in my next excursion," the term enfolding, at once, both a walk and an essay. In fact, the term encompassed many of the moves he made in the world, whether outward and public, or inward and private, within the gestures that consciousness makes.

And yet it is impossible to separate the moves without and those within. If they are at certain times seen to be the same, at others different but parallel, they are always indissolubly linked even when they may well take contrary ways. Consider the complexities of *A Week* and the irony of the conditions under which it was written. Thoreau went to Walden Pond in part to make a house—the fittest act imaginable to set the self at home in the world—and in part to write a book about the quest for two sorts of origin, terrestrial and transcendental. The search for the former origin was successful and anticlimatic, the search for the latter a failure this time around. The record of a trip with his brother (who comes into the text only as part of an occasional "we") turns into a tale about all sorts of history, human, natural, aboriginal, and teleological, a tale of us and our places, of where we and those places began and where we in particular will end. It was not the longest of Thoreau's excursions but what he saw within it made it the most complex and, in certain ways, the most frustrating. The boat they chose, like all effective boats, was "a sort of amphibious animal," related both to fish and bird through its hull and its sail, combining aspects of both in its build and its business. Like the blue-green sheen of Walden Pond beside which he was writing *A Week*, the boat takes in both water and sky. Yet, with this perfect union established as an entering tone of the text, the narrative needs only one page before the journey of the body on the river and the concurrent journey of the mind move not only on different errands but in different directions: "our reflections had already acquired an histori-cal remoteness from the scenes we had left."

With this split the book begins on an interplay of history and immediacy whose energy is to carry the passengers into the New Hampshire hills and then back to their own Concord and the first touches of fall. Indeed, that final gesture in the book is only the culmination of a complex of interflow-ing cycles: those of the day, the week, and the seasons; the circular journey on the river; the journey of the water itself from sea to cloud to river to sea; and finally the journey of the soul from the place where it began and back to that place (the last the only one of the cycles that had not yet been rounded out). Each of these cycles can be immediately experienced. Each contains its own segment, its own parcel of inscriptions, of all the histories the text contains. As a traveler Thoreau works very much like Byron's Childe Harold: he is a reader who sees the world, civil and uncivil, as the text he has to take in, interpreting the inscribings of man on nature and of nature on itself. Sometimes the inscribings are literal, especially those remnants of old home places that Thoreau always finds fascinating. He searches out locations like "the foundation of an Indian wigwam" or a site near Salmon Brook ("a favorite haunt of the aborigines") where he still can stand in the dent of an ancient settler's cellar and converse with one "whose grandfather had, whose father might have" talked with the original settler.

Much of *A Week* is about such a sense of proximity, such tentative touch-ing. Yet there are sites crucial to our understanding of what and where we are that still can be touched, fully and firmly, in all their immediacy. The trip took these passengers with the current, the natural flow, the flow that images history, to the source of their native stream at "the summit of AGIO-COCHOOK." But human beings have other sources as well, sources other than natural. At the beginning of the "Tuesday" chapter Thoreau tells the tale of a mountain ascent that took place in 1844, five years after the trip re-corded in *A Week*. Though it is out of historical sequence it fills a need that the ascent to Agiocochook, the *natural* climax of the excursion on the rivers, could not satisfy. Watching the day break at the top of Saddleback Moun-tain, he felt that "as I had climbed above storm and clouds, so by successive days' journeys I might reach the region of eternal day beyond the tapering shadow of the earth"; but "owing as I think to some unworthiness in my-self" that time of absolute purity had not yet come and "I sank down again into that 'forlorn world,' from which the celestial Sun had hid his visage." It is the same sort of event that had taken place on Mount Wachusett; but it is seen now in terms of a radical split between what the body is able to do (go up to the natural source) and what the soul cannot yet do (make contact with its ultimate origin). The ideal blend imaged in the boat that is bird as well as fish cannot, it seems, remain intact when we seek to favor the source of our higher selves.

Traveling up toward sources is not the only way to conduct such business. The narrative of Thoreau's river excursion and of his probing of all sorts of history took its essential shape in the hut at Walden Pond, the hut he had borrowed an axe to build and into which he had moved on July 4, 1845. *A Week*'s probing of history was matched and countered by the deep probing of immediacy that characterized his life at the pond as well as the *Journal* entries that recorded it. It is as though Thoreau needed the one to offset the other, as though his permanent instinct to seek out binary truths and live both truths at once was at work here, too. In *Walden*, the book that resulted from the two years at the pond, he offers several statements of purpose. The longest of them tells as much about what he will not do as what he does: the first two sentences contain five "not"s and a "nor," showing how often his activities compel him to say "no" until he can finally say "yes." He would make similar points about what we do not have to do in the essay that was eventually entitled "Civil Disobedience": "It is not a man's duty, as a matter of course, to devote himself to the eradication of any, even the most enormous wrong. . . . I came into this world, not chiefly to make this a good place to live in, but to live in it, be it good or bad."

Thoreau rewords his purpose again and again, seeking to make clear that all the undoing is for the sake of the purest sort of doing. The "not"s and the "nor"s turn up, directly and indirectly, in all of his statements of purpose, in and out of *Walden*. Speaking, in *Walden*, of the night he spent in jail because he did not pay a tax to the state, he says, "I had gone down to the woods for other purposes." Earlier he had said that "my purpose in going to Walden Pond was not to live cheaply nor to live dearly there, but to transact some private business with the fewest obstacles." The "not"s and the "nor"s undo obstacles, remove encumbrances, take away all that stands between us and the quest for what *is*. Reduce your affairs, unload the baggage of goods and desires that makes us tools of our tools, eat less, eat less elaborately. The chapter "Economy" that properly begins the book is actually about an interplay of economies, material and spiritual (again, Thoreau's way of seeing in binary terms), and the inverse ratio in which they relate to each other. As we favor the one so do we disfavor the other. Practice "simplicity, simplicity, simplicity" to the point where all obstructions have been removed. So that we may "drive life into a corner, and reduce it to its lowest terms," having pared away all that stands between us and knowing what those terms are. To simplify is to act out a "not" and a "nor." It is to perform in our lives what we do in the language of our statements of purpose. Our language and the acts of our lives work together so closely because they are instruments of the same essential quest, the quest for what *is*, the knowledge we must have before we can be at home in the world. Our language is, indeed, one of the major acts of our lives. Thoreau made much of that point.

He used the capacities of language as a means of defining his position in relation to the town and, through that, to all that the town does not yet know. Telling in a wry but appropriate way of his decision to build by the pond, he plays with the language of the bookkeeper's ledger, using its words to subvert the context in which those words habitually move: "I determined to go into business at once, and not wait to acquire the usual capital." Thoreau does not set himself up directly as an antagonist to the values of the town or even claim, overtly at least, that his are exemplary acts. He did not, as he says, live by some calculated plan of expense or with a mode of attack in mind, but to take care of some private affairs with the least possible hindrance. Yet his way of turning the words upon themselves, of implicating language by language as he does when he first speaks of his purpose, shows that in his *telling* of his actions he is practicing exemplary subversion.

Put into proper context, shown for what they portend for all our economies, Thoreau's private actions could be subversive of the town's established ways. Yet the line between the public and the private was never very clear in his acts by the pond, whatever the direction of his intention. (He could have gone much farther away, where no one would have seen him, had he wanted to separate public and private more emphatically.) On display in his daily business, he knew that the private act of home-making would have to draw the town's attention and eventually have to end up in words: "I should not obtrude my affairs so much on the notice of my readers if very particular inquiries had not been made by my townsmen concerning my mode of life." Whatever the direction of his intention, what he was doing for his own purpose could be turned to the purposes of others: "I would fain say something, not so much concerning the Chinese and Sandwich Islanders as you who read these pages, who are said to live in New England." So much of importance lies in how we stress those last words: shall we say "who are said to *live*"? Bookkeeping language, all unwittingly, is never very far from concern with the essentials of being: when Thoreau writes, "I did not wish to live what was not life, living is so dear," the "dear" puts the matter precisely. One of the results of his business by the pond (to understand what Thoreau tried to do we must distinguish carefully between "result" and "purpose") was a text that showed us how to keep the books for others' economies, economies that had a language of their own that we would have to learn to read.

Better, we would have to learn to hear within those languages the questions—about self and nature and the cycles of each, as well as the relations of each to home—to which "answering" is a response. *Walden* is, as much as *A Week*, a narrative of the hunting of sources, and it puts the same questions as the earlier book though with different gestures and in different directions. Whereas *A Week* sends Thoreau up rivers and mountains, *Walden* sets him down in place. "What do we want most to dwell near to?" he asks, and answers: "to the perennial source of life." And though "this will vary with different natures . . . this is the place where a wise man will dig his cellar." Thus, he will set the foundations for his home here, at the place of the perennial source, because this is where he can most be at home in the world. Thoreau's acts beside Walden Pond are exemplary in this way, too. He dug down to a fine sand to make his cellar ("it was but two hours' work") and built a home over that foundation that took him comfortably through all the seasons. In the deep of winter he drew up his selfhood within the house, its vital heat the answering counterpart of that within his selfhood that always kept him warm. The likening of self and home means, of course, that the self is, in a very important way, its own home, a point that Thoreau suspected early and that, by the time he settled in at the pond, had come to be crucial to him. Here is an essential Thoreauvian paradox, or rather a set of them. *Walden* is a text obsessed with place, the texture and weather of place, and the relations of these to the self; and yet Thoreau can say, on the very next page after his comment about the wise man's cellar, that "any prospect of awakening or coming to life" is so important that it "makes indifferent all times and places. The place where they may occur is always the same." The perennial source, one sees, is to be found everywhere. The tools with which we find it are with us wherever we go, and therefore we need no local home. In the essay "Walking" he says that "the secret of successful sauntering" is "having no particular home, but [being] equally at home everywhere."

With all its richness of attention to the world at his feet, *Walden* carries on what we have seen as Thoreau's radical instinct to search out binary truths and live both truths at once; to seek out all sorts of sources, just as he does in *A Week*. For if Thoreau is a student of local places he is also a most successful saunterer who is at home everywhere, a maker of perennial excursions who hears converse in various languages and knows how to read in each. In *Walden* the first paragraph of the chapter "Sounds" shows him exploring modes of language, human and natural, then moves to the statement, "Read your fate, see what is before you, and walk on into futurity." In the last two paragraphs of the book he brings together *A Week* and *Walden*. He tells, first, how "the life in us is like the water in the river" and how he sees "far inland the banks which the stream anciently washed"; then he recounts the story of how an egg deposited in a living tree hatched many years later "to enjoy its perfect summer life at last!" The narrative as a whole ends with a reminder of old origins and with the prospect of new ones in the "futurity" he spoke of in "Sounds," an undemarcated distance as yet uninscribed by the self but where it will surely make its mark.

When he left the cabin by the pond Thoreau spent a year in Emerson's house, caring for Emerson's family while he was abroad, and then returned to his parental home where he lived out his final years. He took to surveying for a living, demarcating the lands of others while he spent the better part of his time making maps of the self, charts of the inner world that were segments of the "home-cosmography" he spoke of in the last chapter of *Walden*. And there were other cartographies as well, outer phenomena that became inner as the landscapes of Maine and Cape Cod, Minnesota and Canada, became the stuff of the self's home places. On call for occasional lectures, given largely at the invitation of friends and a few disciples, he saw his speech take on special passion when the sickness of slavery became more than a distant, generalized ill. In 1850 Congress passed the Fugitive Slave Law and Thoreau broke it occasionally and eagerly, helping to slip slaves into Canada. "Slavery in Massachusetts," a speech of 1854 arguing for violation of that law, showed that the play of prophecy and privacy by which he had lived his life, his sense of his personal acts as gestures of homegrown business that may well have exemplary functions, turned fully outward to the world.

In 1857 Thoreau met John Brown in Concord. On October 16, 1859, Brown captured the United States arsenal in Harpers Ferry, Virginia. Two weeks later Thoreau spoke out in "A Plea for Captain John Brown," calling once again for resistance to civil government but in a tone never heard from him before, though it had been hinted at in "Slavery in Massachusetts." He turned the language of "Economy" into bitter parody: "I hear another ask, Yankee-like, 'What will he gain by it?' "; and he stated that though "a man may have other affairs to attend to" (an echo of *Walden*) the times may well call out for his own violent involvement. But he was to be involved only with the spiriting of slaves and the language of his lectures. These were moments of special passion in a life of limited but intense passions. He did not write a biography of Brown, he said, because he was far too deeply absorbed in studying Indians, having thought for at least a decade about doing a book on them. That book remained undone, and no others were to be published in his lifetime.

Thoreau died on May 6, 1862, a few months short of his forty-fifth birthday. His last clear words were "moose" and "Indian," key concepts in the essays on his travels to Maine that were to be published as *The Maine Woods* in 1864. Three essays record three trips, their result an extraordinary study whose quality and place in Thoreau's thought have never been fully acknowledged. *A Week* had pondered long on the history of the settlements along the rivers. *The Maine Woods* shows settlement as a present and immediate gesture, settlement being enacted much as it is in *Walden*, though with a far different tonality. Dwellings of all sorts became what they nearly always are for Thoreau, instruments in the inscribing of the civil on the wild and thus of the self's achievement of at-homeness in the world. "Every log hut in these woods," he wrote, "is a public house."

The importance of hospitality in a life devoted to excursions had always been apparent to Thoreau but never more so than in these woods, where even the Indians are only visitors. "Ktaadn" takes as its center a trip that culminates in a classic encounter with the terrestrial source of things, the top of the mountain that is the place of primeval Chaos, pure and original matter that man may learn to use "if he can." "Chesuncook" still unsettles with its description of a scene of moose-hunting whose coarseness rubbed off on Thoreau and qualified his view of our ways in the wilderness. If the skills of men who make centers of the civil define much of his reading of the woods in "Ktaadn," he sees those same skills turned to slaughter in "Chesuncook." In "The Allegash and East Branch" this encounter of the civil and uncivil takes personal shape in his finest character portrayal, the study of their Indian guide Joe Polis, who can contemplate buying more acreage to add to his holdings and yet speak intelligibly to muskrats. Polis, whatever else he owns, still owns "the red face of man," through which we can glimpse, if only dimly, the mists that cover origin.

And it was in some way to part those mists that Thoreau took these obsessive journeys to a place where he could never quite shake his uneasiness, never quite locate his selfhood. *The Maine Woods* is, as much as *A Week* and *Walden*, a tale of a quest for origins. More precisely, it offers three versions of such a tale, the first finding the site that precedes genesis, where nature is wholly and only itself, the second and third picking up from some observations about Indians in the first and exploring the qualities of the Indian guide as well as the textures of the place where his ancestors hunted. Thoreau nearly always calls his guide "the Indian," seeking through his language to depersonalize him in order to study him (a seeking that the rich personality of Polis tends to rebuff). Yet he gets closer to the origins of nature than to those of the human sort, never quite able to part the mists into which Indians disappear, even so civil a one as Polis. True to his long-standing fascination with the way language locates us in our worlds, Thoreau listens closely to Indian speech, but he cannot get through to the way it places Indian selves in their contexts. Early in the first essay he points out how the capacities of our language to name and therefore to identify and therefore to demarcate cannot work "in the midst of the unnamed and unincorporated wilderness." So much the less can the language the guide speaks with his fellows work for Thoreau, a copious language unaltered from its origins, unintelligible to the white man. When Thoreau hears that language it puts him "as near to the primitive man of America" as any of the discoverers had gotten; but that is not very near at all. If *Walden* is, in part, about physical and spiritual economies, *The Maine Woods* is, in part, about physical and spiritual geographies. To be standing among the building blocks of nature, the place from which it begins, is not the same as to be standing next to a man who answers "out of that strange remoteness in which the Indian ever dwells to the white man." The quests for origin that define the essential work of *The Maine Woods* were, like those in *A Week*, dual; and, again like those in *A Week*, only one had any sort of success. The origins of nature turn out to be more accessible than the origins of man. Some of the grandest of Thoreau's excursions remain open-ended, their conclusion beyond the reach of even this most attentive walker.

Cape Cod, published in 1865, is a lesser book that comes most fully to life when paired with *The Maine Woods*. Together, the two show a nature profoundly inimical to man, inhospitable and often deadly, the interplay of the books revealing its extremes. The Cape is narrow, flat and barren, houses as scarce upon its strip of land as they are in the broad and thick Maine woods. Its sterility contrasts ironically with the "inexhaustible fertility" of the sea that wrecks man's works. Here, as in Maine, Thoreau felt himself to be alien, the dense woods as difficult to cope with as the vacant landscape on the narrow spit. Here, as in Maine, nature is fully Other, however affecting in all its dreariness. And in this book, too, there are three trips, the first beginning with the horror of a shipwreck whose flotsam included bloated and broken bodies. And yet the Cape, like Maine, is a place where men have "at length, learned how to live," how to *be* in their worlds.

That sort of nature and that sort of learning show how far Thoreau had come from "The Natural History of Massachusetts" and the setting of his earliest excursions. He had grown to see the significance of Act and how all our essential acts are acts of making—of a perfect staff, an exemplary text, the freedom of a slave, a house on the eternally shifting sands. And he had also grown to see how those acts, when properly done, become gestures in the making of self and thus of the self's at-homeness in the world. Which is not to say that all the people of Concord were aware of the import of Thoreau's acts, however curious they were about them. The best-known gesture of Thoreau's life is not the settling-in at the pond, which mimics, in an act with manifold ironies, the settlement of this wild continent. It is, rather, that refusal to pay poll tax, in protest of slavery and the Mexican War (1846–48), which got Thoreau arrested, late in July 1846, by his friend the constable Sam Staples. But to understand this gesture fully we must see it in its fullest context, which means to read the words of "Resistance to Civil Government" (Thoreau's title for the essay, first published in 1849, that was later to be called "Civil Disobedience") as carefully as Thoreau put them down, letting them mean all they can say. We have already noted the statement, in that essay, that he "came into this world, not chiefly to make this a good place to live in, but to live in it, be it good or bad." The operative words are "not chiefly." This man does not, mainly or ordinarily, set about directly to right society: "It is not a man's duty, as a matter of course, to devote himself to the eradication of any, even the most enormous wrong; he may still properly have other concerns to engage him." And yet this is not to say that one ignores the enormous wrong, but, rather, that duty is to be found wherever and however we turn: "it is his duty, at least, to wash his hands of [the enormous wrong] and, if he gives it no thought longer, not to give it practically his support." There are other sorts of duty that Thoreau must perform, the performing of which might make him look "harsh and stubborn and unconciliatory." Yet, however it makes him look, the performance of his duties treats "with the utmost kindness and consideration the only spirit that can appreciate or deserve it." We can gather the essence of that spirit from his insistence that *he* is, in fact, his own principal business, and that if he goes about this business properly he will necessarily go right to the center of the enormous wrong: "If *one* HONEST man, in this State of Massachusetts, *ceasing to hold slaves*, were actually to withdraw from this copartnership, and be locked up in the county jail therefor, it would be the abolition of slavery in America." By going about his homegrown business, the business of his selfhood, in the most appropriate manner, "a single man can bend [the American government] to his will." The way to bring on the right is to do what we have to do for ourselves, to learn how to be in the world, to make the self at home in the world. Even in the moments of passion brought about by the business of John Brown, the making of self that is finally the making of the self's location never ceases to be Thoreau's main gesture, never becomes less than his single and central vocation.

In "Life Without Principle," published the year after his death, Thoreau says that "the aim of the laborer should be, not to get his living, to get 'a good job,' but to perform well a certain work." In "Reform and the Reformers," first published in 1973, he says that "we would have some pure product of a man's hands, some pure labor, some life got in this old trade of getting a living—some work done which shall not be a mending, a cobbling, a reforming." The apt and successful performance of one's single and central vocation, the "certain work" of "Life Without Principle," is the encompassing and sufficient act that takes in all one's other acts; that, in getting itself accomplished, gets all the others accomplished as well. We tend too often to see only some of those others and think them the encompassing whole. But to see less than all of Thoreau, less than Thoreau at the central business that takes in all the subsidiary business, is to see him fractionally, factionally, sentimentally, not as he is but as we would like him to be. That was always a problem for Thoreau, who never acceded to what the bookkeepers wanted him to be nor even what Emerson thought best. It may be the clearest sign of his greatness that he still gives us such trouble.

Frederick Garber

Nathaniel Hawthorne

During the 1950s, the age of the "New Criticism" in literary scholarship, critics spoke repeatedly of the "ambiguity" of Nathaniel Hawthorne. Now, decades later, this term is likely to strike us as inadequate. *Our* Hawthorne is a figure not so much of ambiguity as of paradox and profound contradiction: a *public recluse*, openly and even sociably proclaiming his own isolation and alienation—a *mild rebel*, at once a conformist to the literary and social pieties of his day and an ironic underminer of these pieties. First published in ladies' magazines and annuals, whose editors' tastes he cultivated throughout his literary career, he was also praised by Herman Melville, in an 1850 review entitled "Hawthorne and His Mosses," for subverting these pieties by appealing to "that Calvinistic sense of Innate Depravity and Original Sin, from whose visitations, in some shape or other, no deeply thinking mind is always and wholly free." In 1851 Melville would dedicate his masterpiece, *Moby-Dick*, to Hawthorne, "In Token of My Admiration for His Genius." It was no small accomplishment, in mid-nineteenth-century America, to appeal simultaneously to the canons of "genteel" literary respectability and to Herman Melville's ultimately antisocial conception of "Genius."

The essential paradox at the heart of Hawthorne's life and writing is nowhere clearer than in his frequent public comments on his own career. Indeed the very frequency of these autobiographical excursions is itself paradoxical, since their point is usually to insist on the author's retiring nature—even on his personal and social insignificance. What is most striking in these prefaces to volumes of tales and sketches and later to novels is Hawthorne's public insistence on his *literary* insignificance. For instance, in his preface to an 1851 edition of *Twice-told Tales*, a collection originally issued in 1837 (and expanded in 1842), Hawthorne expresses surprise that his tales "have gained what vogue they did," while noting that this "vogue" was in any case "so little and so gradual." He then goes on to enumerate the defects of his tales—to write, in effect, a hostile review of his own work. He also insists that he was never "greatly tormented by literary ambition," by a "craving desire for notoriety."

Hawthorne's self-effacing pose was by 1851 characteristic, but by 1851 it was also at the very least disingenuous. Although *The Scarlet Letter*, which had appeared in 1850, was not exactly a best-seller, it had firmly consolidated Hawthorne's literary reputation; in fact, his publisher chose to reissue *Twice-told Tales*, in 1851, in order to capitalize on its author's newfound fame. Nor should Hawthorne's disavowal of "literary ambition" and a "craving desire for notoriety" be taken at face value: few of his American contemporaries in the first half of the nineteenth century pursued a literary career with such single-minded application over such a long period of time. Behind Hawthorne's public disavowal of ambition lurks a sense of dedication bordering on obsession; and obsession and the concealment of obsession were, from first to last, Hawthorne's great literary subjects.

Hawthorne was born on the Fourth of July, 1804, in Salem, Massachusetts, into a family descended from influential seventeenth-century New England Puritans. Four years later, his sea-captain father died at Surinam, and young Nathaniel grew up in genteel poverty, often dependent for support on his more prosperous maternal relations. This support enabled him to attend Bowdoin College from 1821 to 1825, where his classmates included Henry Wadsworth Longfellow, who would become the most popular American poet of his generation, and Franklin Pierce, who would serve as President of the United States from 1853 to 1857. In an 1821 letter to his mother Hawthorne announced his literary plans with a characteristic mixture of ambition and self-deprecation: "What do you think of my becoming an Author, and relying for support upon my pen. Indeed I think the illegibility of my handwriting is very authorlike. How proud you would feel to see my works praised by the reviewers. . . . But Authors are always poor Devils, and therefore Satan may take them."

Following his graduation in 1825, Hawthorne returned to Salem to live in his mother's house and pursue his literary career. In 1828 he published, anonymously, a novel, *Fanshawe*, which he would later seek to suppress; but he devoted most of his energies to short tales and sketches. These began appearing, also anonymously, in 1830—most frequently, in the early 1830s, in Samuel G. Goodrich's *The Token*, an annual published in Boston. Although Hawthorne planned at least three book-length collections, he could persuade no publisher to take the risk of issuing them, and it was not until

1837, twelve years after he initially set out to become a writer, that his first published collection, *Twice-told Tales*, brought his name before the public. This was not an auspicious moment to seek a living through literature; 1837 was the year of a great financial panic in the United States, and the literary marketplace—with book prices depressed by the competition of cheap, pirated editions of foreign works—was in even worse shape than the general economy. Not very surprisingly, *Twice-told Tales* achieved only a modest success; 600 or 700 copies, of an edition of 1,000, were sold in two months, but then sales pretty much stopped. Still, the collection received favorable reviews—including high praise in Boston's *North American Review* from Hawthorne's former classmate, Longfellow.

In an 1837 letter thanking Longfellow for this review, Hawthorne recalled the years of his anonymous apprenticeship with something close to bewilderment:

By some witchcraft or other—for I really cannot assign any reasonable why and wherefore—I have been carried apart from the main current of life. . . . I have secluded myself from society; and yet I never meant any such thing. . . . I have made a captive of myself and put me into a dungeon; and now I cannot find the key to let myself out—and if the door were open, I should be almost afraid to come out. . . . For the last ten years, I have not lived, but only dreamed about living.

Thus began Hawthorne's cultivation of the myth of his "solitary years" of writing in Salem. This myth has been challenged; it has been argued that Hawthorne exaggerated his seclusion and alienation, that between 1825 and 1837 he was in fact involved in a number of significant social activities and relationships. What matters, though, is that Hawthorne chose to cultivate and promulgate this myth of self-isolation.

And what is most interesting about the letter to Longfellow is the way Hawthorne dissociates himself from his own activity: if he chose literary seclusion, he nonetheless "never meant any such thing." Writing is here viewed as a form of unmotivated, even compulsive behavior, and the voice that speaks to us stands far outside of this behavior. Hawthorne's application to literature—carried on for more than a decade with no public recognition and little financial reward—suggests a powerful ambition; yet here, instead of admitting this ambition, he attributes his literary seclusion to "some witchcraft or other." This stance of what we might call self-dissociation—this radical separation of the voice that speaks to us from the subjects about which it speaks, this separation of the sociable *speaker* from the antisocial *person*—lies at the heart of the narrative strategy of much of Hawthorne's best fiction. As Hawthorne himself put it in his preface to the 1851 edition of *Twice-told Tales*, his stories "have none of the abstruseness of idea, or obscurity of expression, which mark the written communications of a solitary mind with itself. They never need translation. It is, in fact, the style of a man of society."

The publication of *Twice-told Tales* in 1837 marked, in any event, a turning point both in its author's career and in his personal life. Hawthorne continued to publish tales and sketches in annuals and magazines, even though his income from these sources remained minimal. When he became engaged to Sophia Peabody of Salem in 1839, he was obliged to seek some reliable means of financial support. Very few American writers, before the Civil War, were able to earn anything close to a living from literature, and Hawthorne was never one of this select few; he had to find other work and hope to write in his spare time. So in 1839–40—while he worked at the Boston Custom House, a patronage appointment secured through his Democratic political connections with Franklin Pierce and others—he sought to tap the potentially lucrative market for children's literature by writing three small volumes of children's history, published in 1840 and 1841 as *Grandfather's Chair*, *Famous Old People*, and *The Liberty Tree*. A fourth volume, *Biographical Stories for Children*, was added to the series in 1842. Hawthorne briefly joined the transcendentalist utopian community of Brook Farm (in West Roxbury, Massachusetts) in 1841. In 1842 he published an expanded version of *Twice-told Tales* that, although it sold even less well than its predecessor, elicited a highly favorable review from Edgar Allan Poe, in which Poe first formulated his well-known argument for the "unity of effect" of short fiction.

In the same year Hawthorne and Sophia Peabody were married, and they settled at the Old Manse, in Concord, Massachusetts. Here they lived for three years, and here Hawthorne wrote many of the tales collected in *Mosses from an Old Manse* (1846). This brief experiment in literary self-sufficiency ultimately proved unsuccessful; in 1846 Hawthorne was still unable to support himself by his writing, and reviewers increasingly spoke of him, even in praise, as an author unlikely to reach a broad public. But he was by now well known, at least in "cultured" circles, and generally admired; the self-proclaimed recluse of 1837 had become a husband, a father, a writer of some reputation, and a public figure with valuable Democratic political connections.

These connections led to Hawthorne's appointment in 1846 as Surveyor of Customs at Salem—an appointment made famous in 1850 by "The Custom-House," the autobiographical preface to *The Scarlet Letter*. Hawthorne and his family lived with his mother in Salem, and while there was little time for writing he was at least able to support his wife and children. Then, in 1849, things changed dramatically. In January, the Whigs having defeated the Democrats in the previous year's national elections, Hawthorne was dismissed from his customhouse position. Six months later, his mother died. At this point—with no means of earning a living, and profoundly affected by his mother's death—he returned to his writing, with new dedication. The result was *The Scarlet Letter*, completed in February 1850, and published in March. In May the Hawthornes moved to Lenox, in the Berkshire hills of western Massachusetts, where, in August, Hawthorne first met Herman Melville, who was living nearby in Pittsfield.

Hawthorne had originally planned to include *The Scarlet Letter* as a long tale in yet another story collection, to be called "Old Time Legends," but his new publisher, James T. Fields, convinced him to publish the work (together with the "Custom-House" preface) as a novel—Hawthorne's first novel (except for the suppressed *Fanshawe*) after twenty-five years of writing fiction. While sales were not spectacular, they were better than those of any of Hawthorne's earlier books—perhaps because of the novel's scandalous theme of adulterous love and because of the preface's attack on the Whigs who had dismissed him from the customhouse. In any case, spurred on by the success of the book and by Fields's constant encouragement, Hawthorne in the next few years pursued literature at an almost frantic pace. He produced two more novels (or, as he called them, "romances"): *The House of the Seven Gables* in 1851 and *The Blithedale Romance* (based very loosely on his experience at Brook Farm) in 1852. There were also works for children: in 1851 *True Stories from History and Biography* (a revised collection of the children's histories originally published in 1840–42) and two new books of mythology for young readers, *A Wonder-Book for Girls and Boys* in 1851 and *Tanglewood Tales for Girls and Boys* in 1853. Fields sought to cash in on the reputation of *The Scarlet Letter* by reissuing *Twice-told Tales* in 1851, and *The House of the Seven Gables* was followed in 1852 by a new collection (mostly of earlier, previously uncollected stories) called *The Snow-Image, and Other Twice-told Tales*. And in 1852 Hawthorne published a campaign biography of his friend Franklin Pierce, who was running for President on the Democratic ticket. Meanwhile, in November 1851, the Hawthornes had moved once again, from the Berkshires to West Newton, Massachusetts, just outside Boston.

It has been argued that Fields exhausted Hawthorne by forcing him to produce so much material so rapidly, but while it is certainly true that Hawthorne would never match this pace again, he had reasons other than exhaustion for turning away from literature after this flurry of activity. Franklin Pierce won the election of 1852, and in 1853 he rewarded his friend and campaign biographer by appointing him American consul at Liverpool, a truly valuable bit of patronage. By the time Hawthorne left this position in 1857, he had managed to *save* $30,000—which one might compare to his total lifetime *earnings* from American sales of *The Scarlet Letter* of $1,500.

Following their four years in Liverpool, the Hawthornes spent two years in Italy, living in Rome and Florence. Here, as in Liverpool, Hawthorne's writing was confined to his notebooks; he was storing up materials for future "romances." Ultimately he managed to extract only one more "romance" from this horde: *The Marble Faun*, set in Italy, appeared in 1860. Following its publication the Hawthornes returned to the United States, to the "Wayside" in Concord, where Hawthorne wrestled with his increasingly intractable materials until his death in 1864. He did get a book of social observation out of his English notebooks—*Our Old Home*, published in 1863; but except for *The Marble Faun* his fictional exertions in the late 1850s and 1860s produced only confused fragments. Portions of these unfinished manuscripts were published posthumously as *Septimius Felton; or, The Elixir of Life* (1872), *The Dolliver Romance* (1876), *Dr. Grimshawe's Secret* (1883), and "The Ancestral Footstep" (1883).

"An old man," says a character in *Dr. Grimshawe's Secret*, "grows dreamy as he waxes away. . . . But I should think it hardly worth while to call up one of my shifting dreams more than another." One suspects that this character speaks for his author. In 1837 or 1851 the disavowal of literary ambition had been for Hawthorne a paradoxical or ironic pose. By the 1860s, following the years of financial and social success in England and Italy, this pose had apparently become a reality; Hawthorne could no longer remember, it would seem, what he wrote for, why he had called up his "shifting dreams" in the first place. Having forgotten this, having finally disguised his ambition and the sources of his inspiration even from himself, he could no longer write. Following a long period of illness and depression, he died on May 19, 1864, at the age of fifty-nine, while visiting the White Mountains of New Hampshire with his friend Pierce.

In his laudatory 1837 review of the first edition of *Twice-told Tales*, Longfellow described the book in terms characteristic of the way Hawthorne would come to be valued and understood by most of his contemporary admirers. Longfellow praised Hawthorne for his "bright, poetic style," for revealing the "poetry" of the commonplace; and, like most of Hawthorne's readers in the 1830s and 1840s, he preferred the fanciful sketches or essays—for instance, "The Vision of the Fountain," "Sunday at Home," "A Rill from the Town-Pump"—to the "tales" (what we would now call the "short stories"). Of these latter, Longfellow's favorite was "The Great Carbuncle," an allegory of the search by "a party of adventurers" for a legendary jewel in the White Mountains. He did not mention, that is to say, the works modern readers most admire and anthologize—for instance, "The Gray Champion," "The Minister's Black Veil," "The May-Pole of Merry Mount," "The Gentle Boy," "Wakefield," "The Prophetic Pictures." A review of the 1837 *Twice-told Tales* in New York's *Knickerbocker Magazine* expressed what would soon become near-consensus even more explicitly. Singling out for special praise "A Rill from the Town-Pump," a light sketch "spoken" by the pump at the corner of Essex and Washington Streets in Salem, the reviewer went on to mention "Sunday at Home," "Mr. Higginbotham's Catastrophe," "The Gentle Boy," and "Little Annie's Ramble"—while noting that " 'The Minister's Black Veil,' and 'The Prophetic Pictures,' are less to our taste."

In 1850, at the close of his "Custom-House" preface to *The Scarlet Letter*, Hawthorne caustically imagined that future citizens of Salem might "sometimes think kindly of the scribbler of bygone days, when the antiquary of days to come, among the sites memorable in the town's history, shall point out the locality of THE TOWN-PUMP!" Still, Hawthorne deliberately cultivated the taste he here mocks; he was careful to leaven the more somber works we now tend to admire with the lighter sketches most of his readers apparently preferred. Indeed, among the tales already published in magazines and annuals by 1837, and therefore available for collection in *Twice-told Tales*, Hawthorne passed over some of the grimmest ones, stories now considered to be among his finest works. "Roger Malvin's Burial" (1832) and "Young Goodman Brown" (1835) were not collected until 1846, when they appeared in *Mosses from an Old Manse*. "My Kinsman, Major Molineux" (1832) was not collected until 1852, when it was included in *The Snow-Image, and Other Twice-told Tales*. Of *Twice-told Tales* Longfellow wrote in 1837, "A calm, thoughtful face seems to be looking at you from every page; with now a pleasant smile, and now a shade of sadness stealing over its features. Sometimes, though not often, it glares wildly at you, with a strange and painful expression." Hawthorne was usually careful to keep such "painful expressions" to a minimum.

A few contemporary readers, however, dissented from the general preference for the "calm, thoughtful" Hawthorne of the sketches. Poe—in his 1842 review of the expanded edition of *Twice-told Tales*, published in Philadelphia's *Graham's Magazine*—objected to the "*repose*" of the sketches and insisted on the superiority of the tales. "Of Mr. Hawthorne's Tales," he wrote, "we would say, emphatically, that they belong to the highest region of art." Eight years later—in "Hawthorne and His Mosses," published in New York's *Literary World*—Herman Melville observed that "where Hawthorne is known, he seems to be deemed a pleasant writer, with a pleasant style— . . . a man who means no meanings." But Melville vigorously rejected this view. "The world," he insisted, "is much mistaken in this Nathaniel Hawthorne," some of whose stories "are directly calculated to deceive—egregiously deceive—the superficial skimmer of pages." Melville then went on to praise "Young Goodman Brown" (which Hawthorne had kept out of both the 1837 and 1842 editions of *Twice-told Tales*) for being "deep as Dante."

"Young Goodman Brown," however uncharacteristic it may be of what Hawthorne's contemporaries admired, is in many respects typical of what most readers now value in his best fiction. For one thing, it is concerned with the great theme of many of the stories first published in magazines and annuals in the 1830s, New England's colonial past. Hawthorne turned away from this theme in the 1840s, the "Old Manse" period, but at the end of the decade he returned to Puritan history in his masterpiece, *The Scarlet Letter*. Critics used to argue (as many, in fact, still do) that Puritan history in Hawthorne is only incidental to his more "universal" moral or psychological concerns. More recently, however, a number of scholars—most notably Michael Colacurcio, in *The Province of Piety* (1984)—have shown how Hawthorne's fiction demonstrates among other things a serious and coherent interest in, and understanding of, the history of colonial New England. Their point is not so much that Hawthorne "used" or "drew on" New England's past as that in many of his best historical tales, especially if we take them together, we can perceive an underlying *interpretation* of colonial history. The general lines of this interpretation are perhaps clearest in an 1849 sketch, "Main Street" (collected in *The Snow-Image, and Other Twice-told Tales*). Of the first generation of Puritans, those who migrated from England in the 1630s and 1640s, Hawthorne here writes that "the zeal of a recovered faith burned like a lamp within their hearts." However, he continues, this generation was able to transmit only "its religious gloom, and the counterfeit of its religious ardor, to the next. . . . The sons and grandchildren of the first settlers were a race of lower and narrower souls than their progenitors had been."

A few of the historical tales collected in 1837 relate incidents—in effect heroic legends—of the nobility of the first-generation Puritans. In "The Gray Champion," a story set in Boston in 1689 (and first published in 1835), the Royal Governor's effort to subdue a restless crowd of Puritans is successfully resisted by the appearance of a mysterious figure who turns out to have been one of the judges who condemned Charles I to death during the Puritan Revolution in England. This "Gray Champion," we are told at the close, "is the type of New-England's hereditary spirit," of its tradition of resistance to "tyranny." In "Endicott and the Red Cross" (1838), based on an event that took place in Salem in 1634, John Endicott dramatizes the spirit of New England by cutting the red cross from the British banner used by the Salem militia. Here again, for Hawthorne, seventeenth-century history prefigures the spirit of liberty, of the American Revolution.

Such patriotic filiopietism, however, is not altogether typical of Hawthorne's historical tales, and even in "Endicott and the Red Cross" the main focus is elsewhere. The scene in Salem is dominated by tokens of Puritan intolerance and persecution of those whose ideas of "liberty" differ from Endicott's: a suspected Catholic (confined in the pillory), a boisterous drinker (in the stocks), a woman who has spoken against the elders of her church (forced to wear a cleft stick on her tongue). There is also a young woman (a brief preliminary version of Hester Prynne in *The Scarlet Letter*) "whose doom it was to wear the letter A on the breast of her gown" in token of having committed the sin of adultery. Hawthorne's general view even of the first generation of Puritans is at best mixed.

And many of Hawthorne's historical tales (including the ones now generally most admired) focus not on the founders but on those "sons and grandchildren of the first settlers" who, as he writes in "Main Street," "were a race of lower and narrower souls than their progenitors had been." In "The Gentle Boy" (1835), the title character, whose mother is a Quaker unwelcome in the colony, ultimately dies, a victim to the persecution of second-generation Puritans. In "Roger Malvin's Burial" (1832), the young protagonist—one of the few survivors of a disastrous Indian battle that he fled with his dying father-in-law (whom he abandoned while still living)—works out his guilt many years later by killing his own son. In "My Kinsman, Major Molineux" (1832), a Boston crowd defying the authority of the colonial government in the 1730s is portrayed as an unruly mob, whose cruelty provides the backdrop for the problematic coming of age of the young protagonist, Robin Molineux. And in *The Scarlet Letter* the patriarchal community of the founders—of a Boston "which owed its origin and progress, . . . not to the impulses of youth, but to the stern and tempered energies of manhood, and the sombre sagacity of age"—is repeatedly contrasted with the "tremulous" and "melancholy" weakness of the "young minister," Arthur Dimmesdale.

At the beginning of "Young Goodman Brown" (1835) the title character, a naïvely pious third-generation Puritan, leaves his new wife to visit a witches' sabbath in the forest outside Salem village. In the forest, perhaps in a dream, he sees the "shapes" of the civil and religious leaders of the colony, of his father, and finally of his wife, Faith. As he calls to Faith to "resist the Wicked One," the whole scene disappears. Brown returns to Salem village, and lives out his days "a stern, a sad, a darkly meditative, a distrustful, if not a desperate man," convinced that all those in whose virtue he had believed have joined in worshiping the devil. Like the judges who condemned "witches" to death in Salem in 1692 (including Hawthorne's famous ancestor, Judge John Hathorne), Brown accepts what was known as "specter evidence"; he blames his wife and neighbors for what he has seen their "shapes" (or "specters") doing. The deeper irony is that he clings to his own "virtue" by blaming them for doing what he, after all, was also doing; the one fact he ignores is the only one he can know with certainty, that *he* chose to visit the forest. Thus is Brown's piety revealed to be but a "counterfeit," as Hawthorne puts it in "Main Street," of the "ardor" of the fathers.

If "Young Goodman Brown" is typical of Hawthorne's fiction in its concern with Puritan history, it is typical in at least one other sense as well: the mode of "Young Goodman Brown," as of many of Hawthorne's tales and romances, is the mode of *allegory*. Objects and characters, in Hawthorne, often seem to matter less for what they *are* than for the ideas they *represent* or *illustrate*. Losing his wife, Brown loses his "Faith," just as we are told at the beginning of *The Scarlet Letter* that the town Beadle, leading the procession, "prefigured and represented in his aspect the whole dismal severity of the Puritanic code of law"—or as we are told of the scaffold, on which Hester Prynne's shame will soon be made public, that "the very ideal of ignominy was embodied and made manifest in this contrivance of wood and iron." Many readers, including Poe, have complained about Hawthorne's reliance on allegory, but there is something peculiar we should recognize in these examples. While Faith, the Beadle, and the scaffold represent ideas, they do not represent *Hawthorne's* ideas. It is young Goodman Brown, not Hawthorne, who loses his "faith" when he thinks he sees his young wife at a witches' sabbath, and it is the Puritans of Boston, not Hawthorne, who have made the Beadle and the scaffold into allegorical symbols of their own strict social code. It is Hawthorne's characters who are allegorists, who try to find meanings in symbols or to turn others into symbols by imposing meanings *on* them. Thus in *The Scarlet Letter* the story turns on the conflict between Puritan Boston's literal effort to subsume Hester Prynne's "individuality" under the symbol of the scarlet *A* and Hester's efforts to reconcile her "individuality" with this imposed allegorical identity.

Such a dehumanizing, allegorical tendency is not confined to Hawthorne's historical fiction; it is also the besetting sin of the characters in many of the best tales of the "Old Manse" period. In "The Birth-mark" (first published in 1842), it is the scientist, Aylmer, who sees in the birth-mark on the face of his wife Georgiana a shocking symbol of "earthly imperfection," and who kills her in his effort to remove it. In "The Artist of the Beautiful" (1844), it is the artist, Owen Warland, who considers his mechanical butterfly a representation of "the intellect, the imagination, the sensibility, the soul, of an Artist of the Beautiful," and who turns from life to the perfection of this symbol. And in one of Hawthorne's greatest stories, "Rappaccini's Daughter" (1844), it is Giovanni Guasconti, a young man in many respects similar to Goodman Brown, who becomes obsessed with the poisonous qualities of Beatrice Rappaccini, and who kills her, as Aylmer killed Georgiana, in his effort to "purify" her. Beatrice's final words might stand as a condemnation of all of those characters in Hawthorne who substitute allegory for human sympathy. "Oh," she says to Giovanni as she dies, "was there not, from the first, more poison in thy nature than in mine?"

Yet if Hawthorne, as narrator and moral historian, stands outside the obsessions of his characters, if his style (as he put it in 1851) is "the style of a man of society," the obsessions of these characters are still remarkably similar to his own—or at least to the way he characteristically described his own behavior, to what was earlier called his posture of self-dissociation. One of the most striking and even comic features of "Young Goodman Brown" is that Brown himself never recognizes or even thinks about *why* he is going to the forest to meet the devil. While his whole experience may be a projection of the "poison" in his own "nature," this is precisely what he never permits himself to understand. In his 1837 letter to Longfellow, we might recall, Hawthorne expresses a similar bafflement about his previous twelve years of supposed literary seclusion: "I have secluded myself from society," he writes; "and yet I never meant any such thing." "I have been carried apart from the main current of life," he insists (two years after the first publication of "Young Goodman Brown"), "by some witchcraft or other—for I really cannot assign any reasonable why and wherefore." This is not to say, however, that Hawthorne's vision of Puritan history, or of moral history generally, is simply a projection of personal psychological conflict or neurosis. Rather, it would seem that Hawthorne's understanding of himself and of his need to conceal this understanding provided him with an acute comprehension of the experience of others.

The titles or subtitles of the four full-length fictions Hawthorne published between 1850 and 1860—*The Scarlet Letter: A Romance; The House of the Seven Gables: A Romance; The Blithedale Romance;* and *The Marble Faun; or, The Romance of Monte Beni*—identify these works as "romances" rather than "novels." In a well-known passage from the preface to *The House of the Seven Gables* Hawthorne sets out to explain this distinction:

When a writer calls his work a Romance, it need hardly be observed that he wishes to claim a certain latitude, both as to its fashion and material, which he would not have felt himself entitled to assume, had he professed to be writing a Novel. The latter form of composition [that is, the Novel] is presumed to aim at a very minute fidelity, not merely to the possible, but to the probable and ordinary course of man's experience. The former [that is, the Romance]—while, as a work of art, it must rigidly subject itself to laws, and while it sins unpardonably, so far as it may swerve aside from the truth of the human heart—has fairly a right to present that truth under circumstances, to a great extent, of the writer's own choosing or creation.

For Hawthorne, this is to say, the romancer, unlike the novelist, is not tied to conventional reality ("the probable and ordinary course of man's experience"); he has the freedom (or "latitude") to depart from novelistic realism.

In the 1950s and 1960s, many literary scholars—most notably Richard Chase in *The American Novel and Its Tradition* (1957)—used Hawthorne's terms to distinguish generally between the supposed "romance" tradition of American fiction and the "novelistic" tradition of Great Britain. American fiction-writers, they argued, should be judged by standards different from those we apply to Jane Austen or George Eliot. In spite of the great value of their insights into the literature they discussed, these scholars were often rather vague (as they were often far from agreement) about just what qualities distinguished a "romance" from a "novel"; and Hawthorne's *Seven Gables* preface provided surprisingly little help. While Hawthorne tells us what the romance does *not* deal with ("the probable and ordinary"), he says almost nothing about what *does* constitute its distinctive subject; although he identifies the romance with the romancer's "latitude," he still does not say what this "latitude" is *for*.

Hawthorne, one should note, often uses the term "romance" pejoratively, as a way of describing the inferiority of his supposedly "insubstantial" works to the solid "reality" of the novels he always claimed to prefer. "It was a folly . . . ," he writes toward the end of "The Custom-House," "to insist on creating the semblance of a world out of airy matter, when, at every moment, the impalpable beauty of my soap-bubble was broken by the rude contact of some actual circumstance." This apology cannot help but seem a bit odd; terms like "airy," "impalpable," and "soap-bubble" hardly seem appropriate to the grim story of Hester Prynne and Arthur Dimmesdale; as has already been noted, Hawthorne's historical tales, and perhaps *The Scarlet Letter* above all, are deeply involved with "actual circumstance." Moreover, Hawthorne's most immediate importance to the history of fiction in English may be his development of analytic, psychological realism, foreshadowing (as he also influenced) the work of such later realists as George Eliot and Henry James. So his comments on "romance," for all their apparent forthrightness, may ultimately strike us as being at least a bit disingenuous.

One may get a better sense of what Hawthorne meant by "romance" by noticing some more casual comments in his prefaces. "If a man . . . cannot dream strange things, and make them look like truth," he writes in "The Custom-House," "he need never try to write romances." Of the setting of *The Blithedale Romance* he writes, in his preface, that he has chosen his memories of Brook Farm, not for the purposes of the novel, but "merely to establish a theatre, a little removed from the highway of ordinary travel, where the creatures of [the author's] brain may play their phantasmagorical antics." The "latitude" of romance, that is, is a latitude of *imagination*, of dreams. And romance allows the romancer both to release his private fantasies and to "make them look like truth"; Hawthorne's romancer, like so many of his characters, at once indulges "strange" fantasies and conceals this indulgence—as Hester Prynne, for instance, uses her scarlet letter simultaneously to express and to hide her forbidden "individuality."

One might note, too, Hawthorne's description of himself—in his preface to *The Snow-Image, and Other Twice-told Tales*—as one "who has been burrowing . . . into the depths of our common nature, for the purposes of psychological romance,—and who pursues his researches in that dusky region, as he needs must, as well by the tact of sympathy as by the light of observation." The key term here, one guesses, is "sympathy"—the opposite of the obsessively allegorical intolerance by whose means so many of Hawthorne's characters manage to disown their forbidden fantasies by projecting them onto others. The ideal romancer, the writer of "psychological romance," releases his own fantasies and dreams "strange things," but he does so in order to *understand* the fantasies of others—not as a form of "sin" or "poison" or "earthly imperfection" but as a token of "our common nature." The power of romance, unlike that of self-protective allegory, is above all the power of sympathy.

Hawthorne's insistence on the importance and mutuality of imagination and fantasy might seem to ally him with nineteenth-century "Romanticism" (a term closely connected to, and in fact derived from, "romance"), but Hawthorne's relationship to romanticism, like so much else in the case of this self-contradictory writer, is essentially paradoxical. The great Romantics—such figures as William Wordsworth in England or Henry David Thoreau in the United States—sought to turn from the artificial constraints of commercial civilization to what they saw as the superior truth of "Nature." The same movement occurs again and again in Hawthorne's fiction: young Goodman Brown journeys from Salem village to the forest; in *The Scarlet Letter* Hester Prynne and Arthur Dimmesdale meet in the forest to confess their abiding passion and plan their escape from Puritan Boston; in *The Blithedale Romance* a group of would-be idealists flees the "artificial life" of nineteenth-century Boston to begin "the life of Paradise anew" in a rural utopia. Yet Hawthorne hardly shares the Romantics' valuation of this movement from civilization to nature, or at least their confidence that such a return to nature is possible. Goodman Brown is destroyed by his wilderness experience, and the vows Hester and Arthur Dimmesdale exchange in the forest prove illusory. So do the reformist schemes of the idealists at Blithedale, whose dream of a natural society based on "familiar love" soon gives way to the nasty reality of sexual competition among the four major characters, Hollingsworth, Zenobia, Priscilla, and the narrator, Miles Coverdale.

As the Romantics valued nature and the natural, so they also valued sincerity—the direct, personal expression of *human* nature. Hawthorne's frequent autobiographical excursions might link him to this Romantic valorization of sincerity, but these prefaces are exercises more in personal concealment than in self-disclosure. As he writes of the author's "talk about his external habits, his abode, his casual associates, and other matters entirely upon the surface," in his preface to *The Snow-Image, and Other Twice-told Tales:* "These things hide the man, instead of displaying him." Or there is his comment, at the beginning of "The Custom-House," on his increasingly characteristic "autobiographical impulse": "we may prate of the circumstances that lie around us, and even of ourself, but still keep the inmost Me behind its Veil." And veils, as we know, occur repeatedly in Hawthorne's fiction. For instance, in "The Minister's Black Veil" (1836), Parson Hooper, another descendant of the Puritans, protests against secrecy, paradoxically, by covering his face with a veil—a veil he refuses to have removed even on his deathbed.

The transcendentalism of Ralph Waldo Emerson and his followers was, among other things, an American variant of European Romanticism, and Hawthorne, in the 1840s, had a number of associations with the transcendentalists. He joined the transcendentalist community at Brook Farm for six months in 1841, and he lived in Concord—where Emerson, Thoreau, Margaret Fuller, and Bronson Alcott were among his neighbors—from 1842 to 1845. Yet he regarded the thinking of these neighbors with the considerable skepticism that he recorded, for instance, in "The Old Manse" (1846), his autobiographical preface to *Mosses from an Old Manse*. "Never was a poor little country village," he writes of those who came to Concord to worship Emerson, "infested with such a variety of queer, strangely dressed, oddly-behaved mortals, most of whom took upon themselves to be important agents of the world's destiny, yet were simply bores of a very intense water." Hawthorne satirized the optimism of those who flocked to Emerson—particularly their easy denial of the reality of sin and evil—in a number of sketches, most notably "The Celestial Rail-road" (1843), and he gave full expression to his antitranscendental skepticism in *The Blithedale Romance*.

"Our age is retrospective," Emerson complained in *Nature* (1836). "It builds the sepulchres of the fathers." Emerson exhorted his contemporaries to reject this fealty to the past: "Let us demand our own works and laws and worship." Such an exhortation is echoed in the forest scene in *The Scarlet Letter* when Hester Prynne urges Arthur Dimmesdale to flee Boston: "Begin all anew! Hast thou exhausted possibility in the failure of this one trial? Not so! The future is yet full of trial and success. There is happiness to be enjoyed! There is good to be done! Exchange this false life of thine for a true one!" Even Hester's style here, relying on brief assertions and imperatives, echoes or parodies Emerson, an effect clearly quite deliberate on Hawthorne's part. Hawthorne, fully aware of the repressive intolerance of Puritanism, is more than a little sympathetic with Hester's aspirations, as he is sympathetic with similar aspirations expressed by women characters in his later romances—by Zenobia in *The Blithedale Romance* and by Miriam in *The Marble Faun*. The passionate *women* in these romances, in significant contrast to the often tremulous and even prurient defensiveness of the *male* characters, embrace with sincerity and passion the most revolutionary ambitions of Romanticism.

Nevertheless, these ambitions, in the romances of the 1850s, are always defeated by the force of circumstance and guilt and by the abiding pressure of the past. Hester and Dimmesdale do not escape; at the close Dimmesdale ascends the scaffold to confess his sin, and years later Hester returns to Boston, "of her own free will," to resume wearing the scarlet letter she had thrown off in the forest. *The House of the Seven Gables* relates a story of the working out of a seventeenth-century curse in the nineteenth century—illustrating "the truth," as Hawthorne puts it in his preface, " . . . that the wrong-doing of one generation lives into the successive ones." This sense of the continuing pressure of the past, of the futility or tragedy of efforts to escape its influence, sets Hawthorne apart from the forward-looking, revolutionary optimism of Emersonian Romanticism, and it lies at the heart, once again, of the last romance Hawthorne completed. In *The Marble Faun*, the artist Miriam seeks to escape a mysterious figure associated both with her own past and with the distant past of Rome. Sympathetic to her plight, an innocent Italian, Donatello, murders the pursuer. At the close, however, Donatello, increasingly wracked by guilt, has given himself up to the authorities, and Miriam, like Hester, has embraced a life of penitence. She is last seen kneeling in a Roman church, her face "invisible, behind a veil or mask."

It would be a gross distortion, however, to categorize Hawthorne simply as an anti-Romantic dissenter from the enthusiasms of his literary contemporaries. After all, Herman Melville, whose early career was fueled by precisely these enthusiasms, found in Hawthorne a fellow "Genius." Hawthorne's real scorn was not for Romanticism as such but for the bogus popular Romanticism, the easy "spirituality," which seemed to him to pervade the culture of his own nineteenth-century America, the culture portrayed with such telling irony, for instance, in *The Blithedale Romance*. If the voice that addresses us in Hawthorne's fiction, to return to the 1851 preface to *Twice-told Tales*, speaks in the sociable "style of a man of society," the subjects about which it speaks, in however "veiled" a fashion, are nevertheless the great themes of the great Romantics: alienation, solitude, nature and natural impulse, unconscious fantasy and dream. That Hawthorne sometimes viewed such things skeptically, and far more often in the light of tragedy, does not mean that he dismissed their power or their truth. "Truth," writes the narrator of "The Birth-mark," "often finds its way to the mind close-muffled in robes of sleep, and then speaks with uncompromising directness of matters in regard to which we practise an unconscious self-deception, during our waking moments." From first to last the tension between this sort of "truth" and the "self-deception" that resists such "uncompromising directness" constituted both Hawthorne's main subject and the most significant model for his art.

Michael Davitt Bell

Herman Melville

Reading Herman Melville in his fullness means attending to the peremptory inward development that impelled his most ambitious books, strained the confines of his literary forms, and gave his career an organic unity that subsumes and transcends the cumulative achievement of his works. Through the early 1970s at least, Melville's career was commonly figured as an eleven-year parabola that shot upward in *Typee* (1846), peaked in *Moby-Dick* (1851), and swiftly descended through the introversion of *Pierre* (1852), the retrenchment of the magazine pieces (1853–56), and the ironies of *The Confidence-Man* (1857) to the thirty years of prose silence broken only at the last by the unfinished *Billy Budd, Sailor* (posthumous, 1924). Subsequent criticism has revised the estimate of Melville's fiction after *Moby-Dick* but has been slow to recognize the richness of his later work, almost exclusively poetry. The full career spans forty-five years; it has twin foci, *Moby-Dick* and the long narrative and philosophical poem *Clarel* (1876); and it is distinguished for a half-dozen other works—not least of them *Battle-Pieces and Aspects of the War* (1866), Melville's volume of Civil War poems—that are both remarkable performances in their own right and acts in a spiritual drama as significant and absorbing as any American writer's.

Though Melville claimed he "had no development at all" till he was twenty-five, his writings are grounded in the circumstances and impressions of his early years, shaped intellectually in response to his later reading: the descent from two Revolutionary War grandfathers; the position as a second, apparently less brilliant son; the secure middle-class childhood in New York City that ended abruptly with the bankruptcy and subsequent death of his father, Allan; the straitened circumstances of the family and the blighted personal expectations; the sailor's voyage to Liverpool in 1839, undertaken partly for adventure, partly as an escape from hard times; and the more formative voyage to the Pacific that began on the whaler *Acushnet* in 1841 and carried Melville to the Marquesas, Society, and Sandwich Islands before returning him to America more than three and a half years later aboard the frigate *United States*. Biographers since Raymond Weaver (1921) have stressed Melville's projection of himself as an Ishmael deserted by his father, scorned by his mother, and eclipsed by a favored brother. What raised Melville's feeling of abandonment to cosmic status was the sailor's encounter with the blank immensity of the sea, sublime but appalling, and suggestive in its alienness of humanity's abandonment by God. Reinforcing this metaphysical estrangement were two features of Melville's Pacific experience that had permanent consequences for his social thought: the anomalous shipboard position that aligned him by birth and breeding with the genteel classes, by association and sympathy with the disinherited commons; and his contact with the pre- and half-civilized cultures of Polynesia, which gave him an outsider's perspective on the West and the rudiments of a vision of history.

Discharged from the Navy in October 1844, Melville returned home, his only capital consisting of four years of adventures and an engaging manner of recounting them. A chance word decided him upon authorship, the story runs, but in working up his benign captivity among the Marquesan Typees, Melville found it necessary to borrow from previous travelers and to exaggerate or invent incidents to form a loose plot. Melville's later observations in Tahiti and the Sandwich Islands also intruded upon his narrative, turning him from reminiscence to cultural reflection and charging his qualified admiration for Marquesan life with righteous anger at the predations of missionaries and imperialists in the Pacific.

Neither strict autobiography nor fictional romance, *Typee: A Peep at Polynesian Life* is an appealing mixture of adventure, anecdote, ethnography, and social criticism presented with a genial latitudinarianism that gave novelty to a South Sea idyll at once erotically suggestive and romantically chaste. The main critical issue is the book's divided attitude toward the natives. For Melville the traveloguer seeking to enliven his materials, the Typees were lurkingly sinister captors in a suspense plot that played on the horrors of cannibalism; for Melville the social critic at odds with America, they were carefree Arcadians whose cooperative anarchy exposed the contentiousness of laissez-faire capitalism and the repressions of genteel prudery. Competing literary purposes tend to blur *Typee*'s estimate of the "primitive," yet on balance Melville viewed the Marquesans with an appreciative, if sometimes baffled cultural relativism, admiring their harmonious adaptation to their world, drawing back from their mental puerility, and invoking the idea of the noble savage only as a rhetorical device for berating "the vices, cruelties, and enormities" of the civilized West.

Despite attacks in the religious press and his consent to a second, expurgated edition of *Typee*, Melville resumed his quarrel with missionary civilization in *Omoo: A Narrative of Adventures in the South Seas* (1847), a slighter but more professional book that sandwiched six chapters on the degenerate condition of Tahiti between an opéra-bouffe mutiny and the narrator's picaresque wanderings with a gentleman-scamp called Dr. Long Ghost. In *Typee* Melville had prophesied the destruction of Marquesan life by would-be civilizers who appropriated the products of the earth and turned the somnolent natives into day-laborers. *Omoo* depicts the genocidal results of this process in the Society Islands and broods on the inexorable triumph of Western asceticism over the sensuous harmony of primitive life. A critique of nineteenth-century consciousness is implicit in both books, yet lacking terms for his vision of the Westerner's alienation from nature, the community, and the self, Melville could only appeal ineffectually to Christian idealism, measuring profession against colonialist practice and watching history unfold as a disturbingly amoral play of force. Henceforward, the doomed innocence of Polynesia would hold largely metaphoric meanings for him: psychically, as a fount of instinct and fraternal affection that the civilized man needed to recover; and mythologically, as a paradise of peace and joy from which the restless seeker flees, only to be haunted long afterward by the nostalgia for simplicity that *Pierre* would call "the avenging dream."

In *Mardi: And a Voyage Thither* (1849) Melville put travel narrative behind him and plunged deeply into "the world of mind." Recently married to Elizabeth Shaw and living in New York City, Melville had begun the book as a "South Sea Adventure" of proven appeal but soon burst beyond it— first, to a romance of the narrator Taji and the lost maiden Yillah, then, in response to his initial bout of serious reading, to an allegorical voyage of the philosopher Babbalanja and his companions through the imaginary archipelago of Mardi.

Though conceived successively and only crudely joined, Taji's quest for Yillah and Babbalanja's for the ideal way of life are symbolic and intellectual complements in a myth of the Fall that would recur throughout Melville's career. Lapsed from Edenic happiness, whether through sin or the lure of thought, the Melvillean hero must struggle ahead through the fragmented world of experience and try to reunify it by knowledge or faith. *Mardi* is Melville's private enactment of this myth, borne forward energetically by his experimentation with new ideas, then focused with growing obsessiveness on the metaphysical dead-ends that would occupy him for a lifetime: the question of God's existence and nature; the problem of evil; the limits of knowledge; the indifference of Creation.

Mardi fails as a romance because it lacks the ballast of fact that would authenticate its ideas and the interest in character that would dramatize them. Yet more than any other American text, *Mardi* gives voice to the transatlantic moment when the romantic confidence in nature and the self yielded to a paralyzing despondency in the presence of an alien, God-bereft universe. What distinguishes Melville among skeptical Victorians is his resistance to any stabilizing religious and emotional compromise. A youth of Bible-reading tinged by Dutch Reformed sermons compelled him to theize the faceless Creation he met as a sailor and constrained his basically existential sense of life within a religious vocabulary as deeply felt as it was inapt. In *Mardi* the terms of Melville's religious thought coalesce and become fixed, and the dual endings Melville constructed for the book—Babbalanja's conversion to the Christian humanism of Serenia and Taji's Byronic "abdication"—anticipate the gestures of accommodation and defiance through which Melville would resolve in literature a spiritual crisis that enduringly defied resolution in life.

Exhausted by *Mardi*, Melville found new inspiration in Shakespeare and Emerson and was soon speaking of distancing the book by "ten miles." *Mardi* sold poorly, however, and to regain his literary independence Melville returned to his sailor experience and hurriedly composed *Redburn: His First Voyage* (1849) and *White-Jacket; or, The World in a Man-of-War* (1850), "two *jobs* . . . done for money" but within whose limits he spoke "pretty much" as he felt.

In *Redburn* Melville fashioned memories of his father's bankruptcy and death and his own youthful humiliations into a story of outward adaptation and inner impairment whose comic melancholy only partially masks the author's continued hurt. From its early initiation scenes in New York and at sea through its sketches of Liverpool poverty to the passage home when the emigrant-laden *Highlander* becomes an image of class society, *Redburn* is haunted by the economics of Adam Smith, whose *Wealth of Nations* Redburn wraps in his hand-me-down shooting jacket (a symbol of fallen gentility) and uses for a pillow. As Redburn matures, the book's depiction of social misery widens from the boy's personal hardships to the general condition of the laboring poor. Despairing of the efficacy of reform, however, all Melville or his scarred narrator can offer is a wistful humanitarianism and a tenuous hope that America will provide a haven and asylum to the world.

The greater sureness of *White-Jacket*'s social vision owes much to Melville's elaboration of a microcosmic form that allowed him to work outward from life aboard an American warship to a detailed and penetrating analysis of warring Christendom. Melville's plea for reform in the Navy is passionate and cogent, yet on the larger issue of societal reform his conviction of the rights and dignity of humanity is tempered by a practical acquaintance with human nature that leaves him wary of the revolutionary's assault upon social forms and contemptuous of the romantic's idealization of the oppressed. Not class itself so much as arrogance and brutality rankled Melville, whose political faith joined the Declaration of Independence and the Sermon on the Mount in an ideal of fraternal democracy that promised to regenerate the core of social relations while only modestly adjusting their institutional frame. What gives vibrancy to this belief in *White-Jacket* is Melville's new and tough-minded sense of the metaphysical foundation of democracy. As chapters on war, sickness, death, and the "armed neutrality" of fate darken the final quarter of *White-Jacket*, *Redburn*'s plea for a brotherhood of man under the fatherhood of God gives way to the mature Melvillean vision of a brotherhood of man asserted in the absence of God and represented on the *Neversink* by the community of topmen presided over by Jack Chase, liberal-hearted gallants who breathe what Melville would soon call the "unshackled, democratic spirit of Christianity in all things."

If *White-Jacket*'s robust democracy looks ahead to Ishmael's in *Moby-Dick*, also prophetic is the narrator's fascination with his saturnine shipmate Nord, one in a line of dark and withdrawn soul mates who allure Melville's heroes with their promise of hidden depths. A youthful infusion of Byron may have disposed Melville toward romantic melancholy, but by 1850 he had come to associate greatness with spiritual suffering and to identify himself with an aristocracy of thought-divers stretching across the centuries and united by a perception of sober truth. Feelings of kinship with universal genius helped sustain him after the failure of *Mardi;* however, the pride of the solitary thinker sat uneasily with his Christian democracy and raised a question of philosophical commitment that was also a question of literary identity: was he a nascent tragedian aloof from the common reader, even from the times, or was he a popular novelist with the distinctively American gospel of democratic fraternity?

For Melville, divided and intellectually alone, the discovery of Hawthorne in August 1850 was the stimulus for self-integration. During the fifteen months they were Berkshire neighbors—in September 1850 Melville bought a farm in Pittsfield, Massachusetts, a few miles from Hawthorne's cottage near Lenox—the nights of "ontological heroics" over brandy and cigars gave substance to Melville's vision of an earnest but genial brother-

hood of truth-seekers and provided a touchstone for his ideal of male friendship. In Hawthorne the man and writer Melville found the same conjunction of "blackness" and compassion he had marveled at in Shakespeare, and
brooding on its significance, partly through the medium of Thomas Carlyle's "The Hero as Poet," he grasped the relationship between tragedy and
democracy he had intuited in *White-Jacket.* "Love and humor" were "the
eyes" through which "a great, deep intellect" viewed the world, he proclaimed in "Hawthorne and His Mosses" (1850), because what the thinker
fathomed was a terrifying nothingness that united human beings as common victims. The tragedian was a democrat by the imperatives of his vision: he was even, Melville implied, a tragic hero himself, standing high to
receive the lightning bolts of truth while conducting them into his art only
disguisedly, for an elite, and presenting to the masses "a boundless sympathy with all forms of being." By most accounts, Melville's readings in Hawthorne, Shakespeare, and Carlyle led him to reconceive *Moby-Dick* during
the fall of 1850, more than six months after he began it. If so, "Hawthorne
and His Mosses" may represent the moment when Melville emerged from
the chrysalis of his early work confident of his vision and fired by the prospect of a brave and original American literature founded on "the great Art
of Telling the Truth."

Like so many American classics, *Moby-Dick; or, The Whale* is at once a natural outgrowth of its writer's themes and materials and a quantum leap in
achievement. As Ishmael's story, the book is a narrative of education that
follows its hero from his opening hypos through his conversion to brotherhood by the pagan Queequeg to his encounters with the sea, the whale,
and the white whale, linked images of Creation and the powers that govern
it. But Ishmael's quest for "the ungraspable phantom of life" is also the
quest of the reader, wrought up for the adventure by the prefatory Extracts
and genially commandeered by Ishmael as a companion in discovery. Even
without Ahab, *Moby-Dick* would rival *Walden* and *Leaves of Grass* in the mid-
nineteenth-century American literature of spiritual exploration. With its
maddened hero at the center, the book is a nineteenth-century apocalypse
that dramatizes the emergence of a new cultural order from the death-throes
of the old.

   The origins of Ahab's hunt lie deep in Melville's reading of 1849–50
(Pierre Bayle, Shakespeare, Goethe, Aeschylus, Carlyle, the Bible) as it fell
upon a mind checked by the metaphysical problems of *Mardi* and upon a
literary imagination groping toward some climactic gesture of defiance. A
"Job's whale," Moby Dick belongs with those primeval dragons and sea

monsters which embody the forces of chaos that rule over Creation; and Ahab, who is linked to such champions as Perseus and St. George, is a self-appointed redeemer who sets out to fulfill the prophecy of Isaiah (quoted in Extracts) and "slay the dragon that is in the sea." Within this universal myth Ahab is a mid-nineteenth-century thinker tormented by the gulf between experiential fact and human need but too intense to moderate his claims upon life and too theistic to ascribe the world's silence to empty materialism. His hunt is a Victorian fantasy of revenge in which the exasperated ex-Christian hurls himself against the universe for its betrayal of Christian promise.

In elevating his materials to match the grandeur of his theme, Melville overcame the absence of a native tradition of heroic literature by infusing Old World models with New World color and spirit. The magnitude of the whale was a natural source of epic sublimity, but Melville also invoked both the traditional heroic associations of war, royalty, Scripture, and myth, and the emerging ones of American amplitude and self-reliant individualism. A "poor old whalehunter," Ahab posed special problems of elevation and speech; and "denied all outward majestical trappings and housings," Melville presented his hero in the resonant idiom of Shakespearean tragedy and forged from Quaker archaism and romantic grandiloquence "a bold and nervous lofty language" that served as a homegrown analogue to blank verse. For the rest of his cast Melville sought the archetypal, peopling his whaler with vigorously drawn representative men assembled to form "an Anacharsis Clootz" deputation and raised to tragic accessories by his appeal to the "great democratic God," America's muse.

The subtlest challenge Melville faced was mediating between Ahab and the reader in such a way that Ahab's madness emerged from common humanity and his hunt took place in a recognizable world that shaded off insensibly into the mysterious and terrifying. The meeting point between tragic vision and insanity was a perception of nothingness so intense that it engendered a fantasy world where frustrations might be played out apart from the restraints of morality and sense. The chapters "Moby Dick" and "The Whiteness of the Whale" are Melville's efforts to portray the logic of cosmic paranoia and make it the reader's own. Having distanced himself from "crazy Ahab" and his rage at Creation, Ishmael leads us back to a wild but inescapable sympathy ("Wonder ye then at the fiery hunt?"), as if our horror at the snow-fields of universal emptiness found its vent in Ahab's delusion of an "audacious, immitigable, and supernatural revenge."

The counterpoise to *Moby-Dick*'s drama of defiance is its running tutorial on whales and whaling, raised by whimsical speculation to a tutorial on life. As a backdrop to Ahab's hunt, the cetological chapters bring forth a wondrous but alien world, treacherous in its surface benignity and lurking cannibalism. Outwardly the chapters seem plotless, yet Ishmael's encounter with the sea and its offspring is itself a thematic action as Ishmael discovers his cosmic orphanhood and responds with a "genial, desperado philosophy" vis-à-vis the universe and a fraternal solicitude toward humanity. Complementing sailor Ishmael's education is the narrator's investigation of the whale, a "portentous and mysterious monster" that evokes all Creation and perhaps the Deity himself—vast, dreadful, riddling, and mute. The effort to "hook the nose of this Leviathan" that begins bravely in "Cetology"—Ishmael would conquer Job's whale by knowledge, as Ahab would by force—ends with despair in "The Tail," but the comic virtuosity with which Ishmael salvages his defeat is a victory of the ever-inquisitive intelligence and a life-giving alternative to Ahab's rage to know.

Altogether, the narrative and thematic organization of *Moby-Dick* suggests Melville's effort to exorcise the Ahabian element in himself and his culture by giving it full expression and encircling it by the productive sanity of Ishmael. As Ahab grows more furious, the figure who began as humanity's redeemer becomes a scapegoat-villain who assumes our cosmic anger and is repudiated and slain. From the wreckage of the *Pequod*, the world-ship of nineteenth-century consciousness, rises Ishmael, temporarily unburdened of Ahab, as we are, and free to become the ludic sensibility who will narrate the tale and stand as the prototype for a new democratic man: exuberant, uncompromised, absurdist, humanitarian; delighting in the speculative play of mind upon fact and redeeming the world from emptiness through his own inexhaustible creative energy.

That *Moby-Dick* remains, emotionally and dramatically, Ahab's book may be owing to the deeper levels of Melville's involvement with his hero. Beneath *Moby-Dick*'s rhetoric of an ethical protest against Creation lies the drive to compel a recognition of spiritual kinship from the withholding Father. Ahab grasping the lightning chains in "The Candles" is an image of this core fantasy, soon to be recast in *Pierre*'s myth of the Titan Enceladus. The vision in both books is of man, a creature of earth and spirit, disinherited by God and bent on proving his divine worth by storming the heavens. Parallels between *Moby-Dick* and Melville's letters to Hawthorne from the spring of 1851 reveal how deeply Melville had come to identify imaginatively with Ahab, much against his philosophical allegiance to Ishmael. The ending of *Moby-Dick* was a temporary catharsis for Melville—"I have written a wicked book, and feel spotless as the lamb," he told Hawthorne—but what would happen when Melville awoke from the dream of an exhilarating god-defiance to the mundane encumbrances of creditors, critics, and family?

Some such appeal to Melville's inner life is needed to explain the diablerie of *Pierre; or, The Ambiguities*, the book that severed Melville from the novel-reading public and raised doubts about his sanity. Conjecture has it that Melville began *Pierre* as a popular romance designed to please a largely feminine audience while insinuating its deeper meanings to an elite. Far from disguising its dark themes, however, *Pierre* insists on them from the start and seems bent on antagonizing its readers by a tortuous, parodic style and a promise of scandalous discoveries ahead. The form Melville chose for his book was equally forbidding: a densely analytic *Bildungsroman* whose hero leaves the circle of common life to champion his illegitimate half-sister Isabel only to entangle himself in "unique follies and sins." *Pierre* is the Melvillean quest retold in a bizarre version of sentimental romance, but this time Melville addresses his hero ironically and resolves his sublime poses into an infinite regress of unconscious motives and soul-impugning determinisms.

Pierre's turn from metaphysics to psychology marks a striking new emphasis in Melville's writing; the book's air of perversity comes from the mingled contempt and regret with which Melville exposes the underpinnings of heroic enthusiasm, as if he were excising a deep-rooted part of himself. Incest is the vehicle Melville uses to illustrate the psychic clay that taints even the noblest actions; more deeply, incest is a symbol for the narcissism with which the truth-seeker fondly pursues an idealized image of himself as a demigod fronting the spiritual world. Having sacrificed his mother and his fiancée Lucy for Isabel, "willing that humanity should desert him, so long as he thought he felt a far higher support," Pierre comes to realize that "the gods do likewise despise him, and own him not of their clan." The writhing honesty of *Pierre* (whose autobiographical parallels are numerous and detailed) is Melville's recoil from the questing impulse on which he too had staked his life, trusting to the course of his intellectual journey and imagining himself with men like Hawthorne "forming a chain of God's posts" scattered through "the boundless, trackless, but still glorious wild wilderness." Hawthorne left the Berkshires in November 1851, however, and for reasons one can only guess—the anticlimax of surviving a too-close identification with Ahab; a discovery that laid bare the psychic origins of his hunger for truth and God; a debilitating skepticism wrought by "Sudden onsets of new truth"—Melville came to feel betrayed by a development that only multiplied the conundrums of knowledge and was now circling back to question the sovereignty of the knower. In *Pierre* Melville's fancy of "God's posts" becomes a nightmare of God's fools, as Melville unmasks his hero with a frankness that would be brutal if it were not also so visibly pained.

Melville's plan in *Pierre* was apparently to lead his character to his own position of nihilism and self-distrust through a succession of awakenings—the first, moral and metaphysical (the sinfulness of the world; the beckoning mysteries of creation); the second, psychological (the layered depths of the self); the third, epistemological ("the everlasting elusiveness of Truth" that mocked the earnest writer). As Melville addressed Pierre's career as a "juvenile author," however, he disrupted the progress of his book with a satiric account of the literary establishment, initiating a countermovement that would eventually recast Pierre as a heroic truth-teller assailed by poverty, exhaustion, and the "universal Blearedness and Besottedness around him," much as Melville himself was. By the time of its climactic vision of Enceladus hurling himself at the sky, *Pierre* has turned its aggression outward and reaffirmed the spiritual heroism it set out to expose. Yet missing from Melville's grim self-apotheosis is any dream of divine acknowledgment, prospect of human community, or confidence in the future discoveries of his mind. Aspiration has been frozen into a posture of solitary and hopeless resistance toward the heavens and society.

By mid-1852, the most rapid and exuberant phase of Melville's unfolding had run its course, and though Melville's vision would deepen and expand as he aged, growth would mean a sober settling in to life, not the chartless voyage of an ardent, self-dramatizing "I." Estranged from his audience and close to nervous collapse, Melville found refuge in the moderately paid anonymity of *Putnam's* and *Harper's* magazines, in which he published fourteen tales and sketches between 1853 and 1856, along with the serialized narrative *Israel Potter*. The magazines exacted their compromises—"Nothing of any sort to shock the fastidious," "nothing weighty," Melville assured the owner of *Putnam's* about *Israel Potter*. Forced to tread lightly on his readers' sensibilities yet determined to have his say, Melville mastered the art of covert insinuation, managing his ironic or unreliable narrators with such subtlety that readers still dispute which (if any) of the narrators voice his own opinions and which are objects of satire or detached psychological interest. Within a year and a half of *Pierre*, Melville refounded his work on the intellectual discovery that had vexed him most: that all perceptions of truth are rooted in temperament and life history, and are therefore more amenable to the dramatist's sidelong art than to the truth-seeker's propositions.

Though mostly comic in mode, the stories abound with spectacles of failure, beleaguered compromise, and unrelieved misery. Bartleby's scaled-down Ahabian defiance ("I would prefer not to") is a triumph of sorts; but more typical of the stories' themes is the lawyer-narrator's "Ah, Bartleby! Ah, humanity!"—an epitaph for the entire gallery of life-battered figures who at their highest (as in Hunilla from "The Encantadas") endure with a quiet humility that is now the mark of Melvillean heroism. Seldom are the stories overtly metaphysical; the heavens' silence, an object of discovery for Ishmael and Pierre, forms an unobtrusive backdrop for the moral or physical suffering of the characters and for the opposition of overly bright and dark visions of life that gives the stories their dramatic and philosophical tension. Interpreters may argue whether Melville the fabulist writes of humanity or of the times, but in the best of his tales the levels of meaning blend together in a vision of tragedy more poignant than *Moby-Dick*'s or *Pierre*'s because it is more keenly responsive to the lived human condition. The walls that oppress Bartleby are at once socioeconomic, psychological, and existential, just as the horrors of the Devil's Dungeon paper mill in "The Paradise of Bachelors and the Tartarus of Maids" are simultaneously those of the New England factory system, the biological processes of gestation and birth, and the ponderous, mechanical regularity of nature.

"Bartleby, the Scrivener" is unquestionably the masterpiece of the short fiction, but two less familiar stories, "Cock-a-Doodle-Doo!" and "I and My Chimney," are superb comic performances themselves, as "Benito Cereno" is superb in a dense, brooding vein that anticipates Joseph Conrad. When the stories disappoint it is generally through a flimsiness of plot that suggests Melville rummaging for materials or settling for the modest piece well done.

In *Israel Potter: His Fifty Years of Exile* (1855), the narrative of a Revolutionary War veteran, Melville skirted the problem of sustained invention by his literary borrowings and hand-to-mouth picaresque structure; but crimped by the demands of magazine publication and Melville's depleted energies, the book is an accomplished potboiler that rises to distinction only when Melville turns to the sage-conjuror Benjamin Franklin or evokes Potter's later years of misery in London. A dry, resourceful Yankee to whom things happen, Potter comes to represent the universal commoner exploited by the two faces of war—the deviousness of Franklin and the vainglory of John Paul Jones—and then ground down by the Malthusian imperatives of poverty, family, and heartless competition. Laboring in an English brickyard, Potter even becomes an image for Creation's stolid brickmaker-god. Against Henry David Thoreau's exultant question of 1854—"What is man but a mass of thawing clay?"—the Melville of the mid-fifties poses his own: "What is a mortal but a few luckless shovelfuls of clay, moulded in a mould, laid out on a sheet to dry, and ere long quickened into his queer caprices by the sun?"

Melville's last completed fiction, *The Confidence-Man: His Masquerade*, is as brilliant but convoluted in manner and theme as *Israel Potter* is engaging but thin. The book was suggested by the exploits of a mid-century sharper named William Thompson whose appeals for "confidence" gave a philosophical twist to the wiles of the swindler and offered Melville a device for exploring the paradoxes of belief and the reigning optimisms and hypocrisies of American life. Set on the Mississippi riverboat *Fidèle* between sunrise and midnight of April Fool's Day, *The Confidence-Man* is a version of the fictional anatomy—a form in which characters and events are used illustratively to examine mental attitudes, sometimes in light of a single many-sided idea—and consists mainly of dialogues between the confidence man in successive guises and his intended victims. Long mistaken for a flawed novel, the book is now admired as a masterpiece of irony and control, though it continues to resist interpretive consensus.

One traditional reading views *The Confidence-Man* as an allegory patterned after Hawthorne's "The Celestial Rail-road" in which the devil boards the microcosmic *Fidèle* to preach a bland, enervating optimism that lures its adherents to spiritual death. By contrast, later discussions have turned from the identity and motives of the confidence man to his role in exposing the philosophical confusions of his victims, with author Melville practicing his own verbal confidence-game on the fuddled reader. From a third perspective the book seems Melville's exhaustive comic reflection on the theme of Christianity versus the world that had occupied him since *Typee*. Within the terms established by his opening chapter—the lamblike man's "Charity thinketh no evil" and the barber's "No Trust"—Melville uses the confidence man to force the issue of religious and moral belief in all its tangled contradictions. The root paradox is that while "the too-sober view" of life "is, doubtless, nearer true than the too-drunken," as the skeptic Pitch remarks, an insistence on darkness breeds a withering misanthropy. The pivotal dialogue between Pitch and the Cosmopolitan (the confidence man in his most subtle and charming disguise) poses the practical question of the book, which had also become the practical question of Melville's life: Should the dark-visioned man live "lone and lofty" or surrounded by the false but mellowing coin of assumed conviviality?

Though *The Confidence-Man* supplies no answers, it directs its strongest assaults against those who pretend to have reconciled philosophical optimism and worldly prudence: Charlie Noble, a riverboat scamp whose affirmations of friendship hide a cynical heart; Mark Winsome, a mythy-shrewd philosopher (modeled on Emerson) whose lofty speculations have their practical face in the selfish calculation of disciple Egbert; and the *Fidèle*'s barber, a typical man of the world who professes confidence and acts from distrust. Against these smug hypocrites, the Cosmopolitan Frank Goodman may seem an ideal of forthrightness and benevolence, yet in Melville's world no goodness is genuine that averts its eyes from darkness on the ground of pained sensibilities. Neither does Melville endorse the Indian-hating Colonel John Moredock, whose fierce, ascetic resistance to evil is an antidote to the mealymouthed temporizing Melville despised in the age but by no means a model itself. In spirit Melville is closest to the gruff but tender-minded Pitch, a "surly philanthropist" whose disillusion would blossom into faith with life's small encouragement. Where Pitch defends his vulnerable idealism by prickliness, Melville shelters his by an irony that disclaims commitment and resolves every aspect of confidence into an artful but paralyzing neither/nor. By the close of *The Confidence-Man* no further stories seem worth telling because nothing productive can possibly be said.

When Melville finished *The Confidence-Man* in the summer of 1856 he was barely thirty-seven years old and had a second creative life before him, though nothing could have seemed less probable when, urged by a family grown desperate over his nervous irritability, he embarked that fall on a journey of seven months to Europe and the Near East.

Random in content and ordered only by the logic of his itinerary, the journal Melville kept during his travels unfolds like one of his quest narratives and records a vision of diminution and blight that would evolve over the next twenty years into a reading of history. The heart of the journey, four weeks in Egypt and Palestine, was a pilgrimage backward to the origins of the Judeo-Christian tradition and a venturing into God's wilderness akin to Ishmael's going to sea. The "fearful" emptiness of the desert confirmed Melville's intuition of barren divinity; but after the horrors of Judea and the shabbiness of Jerusalem's shrines (later recalled in *Clarel*), Melville revived on the journey homeward, stirred by the splendors of the Italian galleries. Reflection came later during the fall of 1857 when he organized his thoughts in the lecture "Statues in Rome," the first of three touring performances he would give through successive winters now that he had abandoned fiction. Alienated from his readership and contemptuous of the modern world, Melville turned inward in "Statues in Rome" and transferred "Utopia" from historical time to the imagination, opposing the new iron age—scientific, utilitarian, shallowly progressive—to the "heroic tone peculiar to ancient life" and located now in the private aspiration toward beauty. Though too rarefied to content him for long, the theory of art and civilization Melville drew from his travels helped reorient him during the painful interregnum between careers: it channeled his personal bitterness about American life into a historical skepticism that became the bedrock of his social thought, and it stimulated his experiments with a more formalized, less mimetic craft—poetry—in the late 1850s.

Of Melville's first poetic manuscript (1860) very little is known, though some of the poems, revised years after the collection had been rejected, probably appeared in *Timoleon* (1891) as "Fruit of Travel Long Ago" and in the posthumous *Weeds and Wildings* (1924). Almost certainly the poems were slight, and fresh from Chapman's Homer and Matthew Arnold's preface to his 1853 *Poems* Melville may have doubted whether a heroic subject were possible in the modern world. "But battle can heroes and bards restore," he would shortly write, finding in the Civil War a complex of themes at once contemporary and timeless and a role as national writer he had not enjoyed since he turned upon his audience in *Pierre*.

Composed largely after the fall of Richmond on April 3, 1865, *Battle-Pieces and Aspects of the War* takes the form of a polyphonic verse journal of the conflict. The volume begins spectacularly as the image of John Brown's shadow darkening America's green yields to anguished meditations from the months before Sumter, then to the grisly pastoral of Northern boys frolicking toward Manassas. Enclosing the poems is a vision of the impending war as a fall into knowledge. The question *Battle-Pieces* asks is how to live with wisdom and magnanimity in the convulsive world of history, and the fear that haunts the collection is not that the Union will perish but that it will survive "stronger for stress and strain" yet with "Power unanointed."

As a collection of individual poems, *Battle-Pieces* is uneven; its achievement lies in the interplay of voices and moods through which Melville patterns a shared historical experience into formative myth. With the sixth poem ("Lyon"), the troubled, reflective speaker of the opening gives way to a new persona, the laureate, who celebrates Northern victories and heroes in a tone of increasingly righteous jubilation. Though the laureate's Unionism is partly the author's, his fiery assurance of divine favor is consistently qualified by Melville's arrangement of the poems, by ironies within the triumphant poems themselves, by poems assigned to rival speakers, and by Melville's portrayal of the horrors of even a "just" war. As the fighting draws to a close and Northern sentiment grows shrill, Melville introduces a more sober, authoritative voice, that of the reconciler who would dissolve the issue of blame in a recognition of common tragedy. The permanent legacy of the war, it now becomes clear, is its instruction in darkness, which shatters America's dream of immunity from the cataclysms of history yet offers the compensating prospect of "Power dedicate" (Melville's answer to "Power unanointed"), "and hope grown wise,/ And youth matured for age's seat."

There is more than a casual relationship between the redemption through suffering Melville imagined for America and the vocational recovery he sought for himself. If the Civil War seemed to confirm his vision of betrayed national promise, it also summoned Americans from materialism to sacrifice and gave hope of educating them in the tragic foundations of fraternal democracy. The excitement of the war roused a genuine patriotism in Melville, but the commitment that shaped *Battle-Pieces* into a vehicle for persuasion rose from a more private belief that the imaginative writer might yet bring forth a nobler America and in so doing rescue himself from impotence and obscurity.

Any such hopes Melville harbored were defeated by the vindictive course of Reconstruction and the popular failure of *Battle-Pieces*, which returned him to the isolation that had marked his life since the late 1850s. Settled now in New York City, he accepted a position in the New York Custom House in December 1866 in what must have seemed as complete a self-redefinition as the writing of *Typee*. His intellectual life had deepened, but his discourse now was almost entirely with books and memories. In his solitude, the problem of belief returned in force. Thoughts of Hawthorne, recently dead, returned too as he sifted the revelations in Hawthorne's newly published American and English notebooks, among them impressions of himself that recalled the pain of a frustrated intimacy.

In *Clarel: A Poem and a Pilgrimage*, his autumnal masterpiece, Melville channeled his preoccupations of thought and feeling into a verse narrative of 18,000 lines that explored the crisis of modern civilization through the travels and conversations of an extraordinary set of latter-day pilgrims. Clarel himself is a young American divinity student who has come to Jerusalem to renew his faith and finds solace for the city's blank decrepitude in his love for Ruth, a Jewish emigrant from America. Clarel's urban wanderings occupy the early cantos, but as the party advances through the desert Clarel is eclipsed by the more complex and articulate pilgrims: Derwent, an urbane Anglican cleric who speaks for progress and liberal religion; Vine, an alluring recluse modeled on Hawthorne; Rolfe, an adventurer and perpetual seeker whose balance of earnestness and good-fellowship resembles the younger Melville's; Mortmain, a former revolutionary indignant at man and despairing of God; and Ungar, an embittered Southern officer who voices the poem's harshest criticism of the modern world. The drama of ideas is recapitulated in "The High Desert" as the pilgrims debate good and evil, science and faith, the mutability of creeds, and the future of Western democracy, "While unperturbed over deserts riven,/ Stretched the clear vault of hollow heaven." Though ideal for anthology purposes, the canto barely suggests the dramatic portraiture through which Melville converts a peripatetic seminar in philosophy into a study of the philosophers themselves, both individually and in their charged relations. Derwent, especially, is a full-blooded creation whose exchanges with the other pilgrims are subtler in their psychology, more attentive to nuances of gesture and tone—closer, in short, to the novelist's art—than any comparable scenes in Melville's fiction.

Interwoven with the poem's exploration of faith and doubt is Clarel's search for a soul mate, an action that focuses on his attraction to Vine and culminates in a bower by the Jordan when Clarel reaches out in spirit and is met by Vine's "rebukeful dusking." The sublimated eroticism of the canto recalls language from "Hawthorne and His Mosses" and the lyric poem "Monody" begun soon after Hawthorne's death, a confession of love and blameless estrangement. In *Clarel* Melville generalizes this failed communion into the failure of all communion and the powerlessness of human ties to relieve the agony of unbelief. Whatever the biographical origins of the Clarel-Vine relationship, the theme that unites the intellectual and erotic strands of the poem is the yearning for wholeness and refuge in an alien world.

With the appearance of Ungar late in the journey, *Clarel* develops into an analysis of the spiritual condition of modern democracy, with special reference to the New World. On one side a wilderness Ishmael who protests the horrors of laissez-faire capitalism, on the other a reactionary who rails at flabby meliorism from a conviction of original sin, Ungar voices the negatives in Melville's bifurcated social vision, grown crustier with time. The Ungar cantos are Melville's *Culture and Anarchy* poised between a nightmare of the coming "Dark Ages of Democracy" and a genial but tragically based humanitarianism embodied in the poem's model, Rolfe. Where Melville's Enceladan heroes had proved their godlikeness by storming the heavens, Rolfe's fate is to live undramatically at humanity's best without suspecting that this itself is divinity. Overwhelmed by doubts, Clarel finds Rolfe's agnosticism too demanding and, as the pilgrimage ends, would console himself in the promise of Eden with Ruth. But Ruth is dead, just as all Melville's paradises are irrecoverably lost; and Clarel's destiny—humanity's,

Melville implies—is to press onward through the fallen world of separateness and doubt, bearing his cross as best he can.

Ignored in its own time, *Clarel* has still to find its audience, yet it remains the great Victorian poem of faith and doubt, a work of keen human insight as well as philosophical depth, and a verse performance with a rare stony beauty peculiarly its own.

Externally, Melville's life from the publication of *Clarel* to his retirement from the customhouse in 1885, and onward through his death in 1891, is a near blank. If to family members Melville seemed calmer in his last years, though still prey to moods, to outsiders he was a gray, stalwart figure who cultivated obscurity as a defense and resisted all attempts to bring himself and his work before the public.

In the title poem of *John Marr and Other Sailors* (1888), the finest of his late verse collections, Melville projected his feeling of anachronism into the situation and musings of an aging ex-sailor living miles inland among an unsympathetic people and drawn in his loneliness to memories of his former shipmates. Nostalgia also colors "Jack Roy," a fictionalized tribute to Melville's comrade from the *United States*, Jack Chase, and "Bridegroom Dick," the rambling monologue of a retired petty officer that revisits the world of *White-Jacket* and turns Melville's mid-century protest into an elegiac tribute to past gallantry. Antithetical in spirit are the "Sea Pieces" that complete *John Marr*, verse anecdotes of shipwreck and disaster that caution the unwary about nature's treacheries and darkly moralize on life. The volume ends with a muted accommodation ("Healed of my hurt, I laud the inhuman Sea"), but the stoicism of the "Sea Pieces," so bleak after the camaraderie of the sailor poems, argues a divided vision that assigns all valor and magnanimity to the past while facing the present with grim endurance.

Timoleon (1891) is a looser collection whose most urgent poems explore the trials and rewards of truth's votaries, as if Melville were questioning his long dedication to art. "Timoleon" itself, elaborated from Plutarch's account of the Corinthian soldier and statesman, is a mythic projection of Melville's seventy years and a partial retelling of *Pierre*, but this time Melville ends his story with a fantasy of vindication. Estranged from a weak-hearted populace and abandoned by the silent gods, Timoleon emerges from retirement to rescue the state, then voluntarily returns to exile, scorning those who now applaud him as Melville in his minor way resisted the overtures of the New York literati. Together, *John Marr* and *Timoleon* show Melville still chafing at nature's indifference and society's neglect. The light pastoralism of his final collection, *Weeds and Wildings Chiefly: With a Rose or*

Two (posthumous, 1924), seems evidence of a deathbed reconciliation, but in fact most of the poems were drafted by the end of 1887 and some may date back more than thirty years. Dedicated to Melville's wife, *Weeds and Wildings* is the modest, landed complement to *John Marr*, its serenity a triumph of generic decorum, not a sign of psychic renewal.

The themes of Melville's late poetry are a crucial context for *Billy Budd, Sailor* (posthumous, 1924, 1948, 1962), an inexhaustible and perhaps indeterminate work which grew out of the ballad "Billy in the Darbies" that Melville apparently began around 1886 as a prose-verse composition along the lines of "John Marr." The original Billy was an older sailor sentenced to hang for plotting mutiny, but as the manuscript evolved through successive stages Melville altered the characterization of Billy, developed the figure of Master-at-Arms John Claggart, and elaborated the portrait of Captain Edward Fairfax Vere, in this last phase more than doubling the manuscript leaves of his near-finished narrative of 1888. Melville was still interpolating, deleting, and refining passages when he died, leaving behind a chronologically complete manuscript in such disarray that a reliable *Billy Budd* would not appear until the Hayford-Sealts edition of 1962, long after *Billy Budd* criticism had taken its shape.

In *Billy Budd* the nostalgia of *John Marr* is elevated to myth as the childlike Billy is impressed from the *Rights-of-Man* and introduced to "the ampler and more knowing world of a great warship," Melville's image, as in *White-Jacket*, for warring Christendom itself. In setting Claggart against Billy, Melville seems originally to have intended an illustrative tale on the fate of sensuous, good-natured innocence amid the mantraps of the world. As Melville sketched in the nature of Claggart, however, the undertones of Satanic malice became overtones and the narrative developed into a reenactment of the Christian Fall that raised the theological problem of evil, first explored by Melville more than forty years before in *Mardi*.

In the manuscript of 1888 Billy's execution followed closely upon his striking and killing Claggart; the turn toward questions of law and political morality occurred later, as if Melville completed his story only to discover a new and more absorbing set of issues. The long trial scene of Chapter 21, central to the narrative's political meaning, is a masterpiece of ambiguity and a virtual Rorschach test for its interpreters' commitments, with Vere in some readings an anguished but duty-bound representative of the state, in others a myopic servant of the god Mars. There is much of the late Melville in Vere's skeptical conviction that "forms, measured forms" are humanity's imperfect but necessary stays against nature's chaos, and yet Vere's particular forms are both brutally deficient in themselves and administered with a passionate insistence that divides our attention between the ethics of governance and the private psychology of the governor. Though readers commonly put Vere in the dock, Melville himself seems less intent on judging Vere than on presenting the example of a man with "sterling" but not "brilliant" qualities acting under the press of circumstances and compounding society's failures by inward limitations of his own, a theme Melville strengthened by late revisions that question Vere's unconscious motives and suggest the psychological ambiguities that attach themselves to any ethical or political judgment.

Reworked though it was, *Billy Budd* preserves the traces of its development in its movement downward from theological allegory to dramatic "case." In the closing scenes Melville puts politics and psychology aside and turns to the imagined spectacle of two men meeting the inevitable with magnanimity and strength. The Vere who had argued for coolness in the trial scene is humanized by sorrow and bent by the weight of a judgment made with full awareness of tragic sacrifice. Billy's role—to forgive Vere—is greater still, and his growth becomes visible at the last when, "spiritualized now through late experiences so poignantly profound," he becomes, not a symbol of Christ, but an example of humanity's Christlike capacity for self-transcendence. For some readers there is a pathos too terrible to bear in Billy's "God bless Captain Vere," and certainly it is wrong to take the words as Melville's deathbed affirmation. For a moment, nonetheless, the injustices of the human world and the silences of the divine seem suspended in a mood of hushed contemplation, as if Melville, securely beyond the vision of *John Marr*, were marveling at what victimized human beings were capable of achieving and what he, the writer, was capable of bringing to life. The narrative trails off into irony as plodding officialdom garbles Billy's story and the witnessing sailors fashion a cult of personality from a greatness it is theirs to imitate. Melville, however, has finished with the world and seems at the last to have dissolved the tortures of metaphysics and reputation in a conviction of inner sufficiency that is the closest he ever approached to peace.

Robert Milder

Walt Whitman

"If Whitman has taught me anything, and he has taught me a great deal, often against my will," the poet Robert Creeley wrote in 1973, "it is that the common *is* personal." Probably no other "confession" better explains away the so-called anxiety of influence that our most celebrated poet is alleged to have cast over those he addressed in "Poets to Come" (1871). Standing between Ralph Waldo Emerson and the modern age in America, Walt Whitman remains our most successful apologist for a literature that is universal because it is "native." Having nothing but himself, he extolled that self in a poem whose original version appropriately had no title. In subsequent editions of his poems it became "Poem of Walt Whitman, an American," then simply "Walt Whitman" until finally in 1881 it went almost full circle with itself and became "Song of Myself." *Leaves of Grass,* as Whitman later realized and reiterated, had "been the outcropping of my own emotional and other personal nature—an attempt, from first to last, to put *a Person,* a human being (myself, in the latter half of the Nineteenth Century, in America,) freely, fully and truly on record."

"Born here of parents born here from parents the same, and their parents the same," the poem said. Its rhythmical language brought to life at midlife a poet who hoped "to cease not until death." At age thirty-six Walter Whitman became Walt Whitman, who lived another thirty-six years. The first life was absorbed by the second, which looked back to discover that the self was everything and nothing. The poet born in *Leaves of Grass* was first born in the West Hills farming community of Long Island, New York, in 1819, the same year in which James Russell Lowell and Herman Melville were born. Lacking their relatively patrician backgrounds, Whitman absorbed an America largely overlooked by the literati of New England and New York. Of English and Dutch ancestry several generations into America, he was the second eldest of eight surviving children. His carpenter-father's patriotism is recorded in the names of three of his sons: Andrew Jackson, George Washington, and Thomas Jefferson. In an early sketch entitled "My Boys and Girls" (1844) the young and still conventional poet asks, "What would you say, dear reader, were I to claim nearest relationship to George Washington, Thomas Jefferson, and Andrew Jackson?" Correcting his father's agrarian preference for a chronology beginning with Jackson, Whitman would eventually conceive of a new breed of American middle class—a "divine average" who combined the wisdom of Jefferson with the practicality of Jackson to form a George Washington for all seasons.

Unlike the utopia of "Song of Myself," however, where the meal is "equally set," the reality of Whitman's sometimes harsh family life in Brooklyn, where the family resettled in 1823, suggested that the American character took many and diverse forms. The family that gave America its greatest poet also gave the world a few more failures. The eldest son Jessie died in an insane asylum, possibly the victim of an advanced case of venereal disease. The eldest daughter Mary married an alcoholic shipwright from Greenport, Long Island, and seldom saw her family; the younger Hannah never let her family forget the fact that she suffered hypochondria as well as connubial torment from her third-rate landscape painter of a husband. Andrew, the most impractical of all (nicknamed "Bunkum"), married a streetwalker and died of alcoholism and tuberculosis during the Civil War. And Edward, the youngest son, was both physically and mentally handicapped. By rather strong contrast George became a celebrated veteran of the war, and Jeff—Walt's favorite—became a successful civil engineer who ultimately helped supervise the laying of the St. Louis water system.

Whitman grew up in a microcosm of working-class America. Distant, often hostile, alcoholic fathers frequently headed such families in the nineteenth century, and Walter Whitman, Sr., was probably no exception. The poet's early fiction abounds in uncaring fathers, persevering mothers, and neglected sons. In the lachrymose "Reuben's Last Wish" (1842) the father is "a *drunkard*, habitual and confirmed," who finally agrees to sign a temperance pledge at the request of his dying and mistreated son. Perhaps with the protagonist of Nathaniel Hawthorne's "Roger Malvin's Burial" in mind, Whitman brought Reuben back to life as Bourne, a minor character in his temperance tract, *Franklin Evans; or, The Inebriate* (1842). Both of Whitman's tales echo Hawthorne's theme of guilt resulting from the unpardonable sin of betrayal. Taken in sequence, they also appear to be about the fear of *becoming* the father. Whitman's "Reuben Bourne," as it were, grows up to become as irresponsible as the father. In the autobiographical poem "There Was a Child Went Forth," the father is remembered as "strong, self-sufficient, manly, mean, anger'd, unjust." A lifelong bachelor in both the literal and the literary sense, Whitman probably never became a father himself. In old age he claimed to have sired six illegitimate children, but he no doubt had in mind his own brothers and sisters to whom he had indeed become a father figure following (and perhaps before) the death of his father one week after the first publication of *Leaves of Grass*.

Whitman's employments were numerous and various during his adolescence and early manhood. Off and on until the 1850s he dabbled in the housebuilding business, but as early as his sixteenth year he had completed training as a "journeyman-printer" and become a compositor in New York City. A year later he followed his family to Hempstead, Long Island, where it had relocated briefly, and began his short-lived career as a schoolteacher. In 1838 he turned his hand to journalism and founded the *Long Islander*, a weekly newspaper that operates today. The experiment no doubt whetted his appetite for the newspaper world with its opportunity to "filter" events through the medium of writing. Although there were further stints at teaching, by 1841 he had returned to the city and launched himself in the profession of journalism, which at that time in America was a scurrilous and unsteady business. Twopenny presses appeared and disappeared with the issues they championed. Although only two new papers started up the year young Whitman came upon the scene, nine had begun a year earlier and another nine would be added to their number in 1843. Twenty more newspapers entered the marketplace in 1845 to replace the many that had already folded. Beginning as a printer for Park Benjamin's *New World*, Whitman soon followed his interest in local politics and entered the editorial rooms of a series of newspapers with meteoric existences. By 1842 he became editor of the newly founded *New York Aurora* and in that capacity heard Emerson's New York lecture on "Nature and the Powers of the Poet."

Thirteen years later he would "simmer," as he may have told John Townsend Trowbridge in 1860, "to a boil" and publish the first edition of *Leaves of Grass*. Hearing an early version of "The Poet," which first appeared in Emerson's *Essays: Second Series* (1844), probably left its impression upon America's most "personal" poet. On the receipt of his complimentary copy of Whitman's book, Emerson obviously thought he saw his own ideas "originally drest" in Whitman as well as in Henry David Thoreau. He promptly greeted the poet "at the beginning of a great career which must have had a long foreground somewhere for such a start." Perhaps on purpose, Emerson mixed his metaphor to suggest how Whitman had put transcendentalist ideas on the broad canvas of the American imagination. In the now-famous letter of July 21, 1855, he both praised the "beginning" of Whitman's career and spoke of its "foreground." The first *Leaves*, Emerson instinctively knew, was a panorama with foregrounds and backgrounds from which new American lives were forever emerging from the old world of the Self. Indeed, its central poem—"Song of Myself"—is punctuated with beginnings. Its legion of characters that form the main character or composite voice of the poem keep waking up to their new identities in a present without end. They arise to discover that "there are millions of suns left" to guarantee their immortality. They awake to learn that "it is just as lucky to die" as it is to be born. They find themselves in catalogues in which everyone is a "novice beginning yet experient of myriads of seasons."

In his "letter of thanks" Emerson had also used "career"—a word not then in general use as a synonym for "profession." In other words, Whitman was at the beginning of the "full swing" of his literary powers. But this poet had always been at the beginning of a "career." In the 1840s he kept starting over in the world of journalism. Often those beginnings followed bad endings as the result of newspaper owners either going out of business overnight or dismissing Whitman for his political opinions. After an abrupt departure from the *Aurora* in the spring of 1842, he worked for a series of newspapers, including the *Evening Tatler*, the *Long Island Star*, the *Brooklyn Daily Eagle*, the *New Orleans Crescent*, and the "free-soil" *Brooklyn Freeman*. After a stormy decade as a journalist, Whitman was ready to begin another "career" as a poet. Already the author of a handful of mediocre short stories, quite conventional poems, and one temperance novel, he may have also already written out some of the ideas if not the trial lines of the first *Leaves*. In a notebook that may date back to 1847, he writes of the ignorant man who "is demented with the madness of owning things." In section 32 of "Song of Myself" the poet declares that he "could turn and live with the animals" because "not one is demented with the mania of owning things." Other parallels between notebook and poem make it plausible that Whitman began some of his lines as prose and then converted them to free verse. Such a process at the beginning of this great career was evidently gradual, for in many cases the language is present without the force of the poetic sentiment.

As the era of Whitman's journalism came to a close with the passage of the Fugitive Slave Law in 1850, the poet finally liberated himself from the literary conventions that had enslaved the American sense of self. Curiously, the oppressive political situation ushered in an exciting half-decade of literary freedom that began with *The Scarlet Letter* and *Representative Men*, continued with *Moby-Dick* and *Walden*, and concluded with *Leaves of Grass*. Although Whitman believed that fugitive slaves must be returned as long as the Constitution upheld slavery, there was something in him and the American literary character that could never be returned to bondage. As with the other American classics the half-decade produced, Whitman's book stood up for the civil liberties of the Self. This poet would stand up for both Body and Soul (as he also wrote in his early notebook), but as the political reality of the 1850s unfolded, Whitman saw that the body politic was threatening to eclipse the American identity of Body and Soul the founding fathers had stood—really posed—for. He feared for the cause of liberty under the presidency of Franklin Pierce, who was at best "soft" on slavery. In the 1855 Preface to *Leaves of Grass*, he notes an early stage in the demise of liberty when "the memories of the old martyrs are faded utterly away . . . when the large names of patriots are laughed at in the public halls from the lips of orators." Whitman chided the Union much in the way John Greenleaf Whittier had chided the South over slavery in his poem "Massachusetts to Virginia" because he feared it had forgotten the "good cause" of soul-liberty: the freedom to begin a great career with oneself in the New World.

The "good cause" had more to do with white slaves than black ones— "the true people, the millions of white citizens, mechanics, farmers, boatmen, manufactures, and the like" who were economically and politically harmed by the institution of black slavery in the New World. Whitman's antislavery "plan" would have freed the white man before the black, but poetized in *Leaves of Grass* it is an underground railroad to all those running away from the guilt of their existence. Just as the runaway slave is "pass'd north" in section 10 of "Song of Myself," so the "Americano" of *Leaves of Grass* is brought back from Virginia to Massachusetts—back from original sin to "original energy." "Nature without check" is the theme of the first edition of *Leaves of Grass*. The self was good, the average divine, when it was at the *beginning* of its career. Whitman's "password-primeval," his version of Emerson's concept of self-reliance, is "original energy." "Afar down I see the huge first Nothing," the poet announces. "I know I was even there." Adding tall-tale hyperbole to the romantic vision of the transcendentalists, Whitman is "afoot" in the poem with an idea wholly American. Half-Body, half-Soul, the self celebrated is larger than even the Slumbering Giant Emerson had imagined. It is "solid and sound," "plumb in the uprights," and "braced in the beams."

Another of Whitman's achievements in his first edition of *Leaves of Grass* was to advance Emersonianism or transcendentalism by contradicting it. To the American romantics, the world of the senses—particularly the Body—was but an emblem of the Soul. Indeed, even the pseudo-science of phrenology had taught the New York poet that a healthy and well-developed body was the signature of a harmonious and well-appointed soul. The idea or goal was to transcend the Body and become—in the neoplatonic sense—whole again in the mind of God. Whitman transcended, however, by finding in nature (and the language that celebrated its value) the same godlike reunion with the Oversoul. In the words of Roger Asselineau, "Instead of proceeding at once to a spiritualization, like the English romantics or the American transcendentalists, he never forgets that his body is the theater and the point of origin for his mystical states." In the famous section 5 of "Song of Myself," the Soul is beckoned earthward by the Body:

> Loafe with me on the grass, loose the stop from your throat,
> Not words, not music or rhyme I want, not custom or lecture, not even the best,
> Only the lull I like, the hum of your valvèd voice.

The poet beholds "God in every object," yet understands "God not in the least." The idea is self-contradictory, lacking all the logic that romanticism borrowed from eighteenth-century rationalism, but so is the poet who contains "multitudes."

Whitman also departed from his transcendentalist precursors in his use of the American vernacular. "Cut these words, and they would bleed," Emerson had said in comparing the speech of Montaigne to that of blacksmiths and teamsters and other "men about their work." Whitman knew such language firsthand: in the 1840s he had befriended many such "roughs"; he had accompanied stagecoach drivers atop their omnibuses during twenty-hour shifts up and down congested Broadway. Whitman therefore wrote the *spoken* language, that of the Body as well as the Soul. He was—as he described himself in an anonymous puff for the first *Leaves*—"An American bard at last! One of the roughs, large, proud, affectionate, eating, drinking, and breeding, his costume manly and free, his face sunburnt and bearded, his postures strong and erect." The poet signed his first edition with just such a portrait of himself. The frontispiece is a steel engraving that showed not the conventional writer dressed from head to foot in black but one in workingman's clothes—shirt open at the throat, head disrespectfully cocked to one side. He stood with hand on hip, oratorlike as if he were delivering the 1855 Preface as a speech. Seeing America as "essentially the greatest poem," its "veins full of poetical stuff," he vows never to allow literary language to stand between him and the thing he celebrates.

Leaves of Grass celebrated the spontaneity of an American "renaissance" already grown torpid in New England. Its spirit had moved south to New York by the middle of the 1850s and Whitman was its spokesman, drawing out from Concord such Emersonian confidants as Thoreau and Amos Bronson Alcott. The utopian community of Brook Farm (1841–47) was but a dim memory, having fallen first into the hands of socialists and finally into extinction. The transcendentalist organ, *The Dial* (1840–44), was also gone— along with its original editor, Margaret Fuller, who had drowned off the coast of New York. *Leaves of Grass* reminds us of the protean vitality of what we call the American Renaissance. Whitman's "language experiment" saved American literature from the bondage of New England culture. He freed its slaves by democratizing its tropes—by filtering and "fibering" its blood. Originally, Emerson had forsaken the "culture" of the Bible for that of (his own) nature, but by the 1850s the ex-minister had become the Concord Philosopher. He had turned (or returned) to something other than himself, and it was Whitman's job to teach America how to go and live with the "animal" in itself again. It was the poet's job, he wrote in his Preface, "to cheer up slaves and horrify despots."

The despotic tendency of New England culture, its literary Brahmanism, had again threatened to make slaves of its subjects in the post-Emersonian period of the 1850s. Even Emerson was talking of the limits of self-reliant action in his lecture "Fate" (c. 1850). In what has come to be regarded as a preface to the second edition of *Leaves of Grass* (1856), Whitman boasted that his thirty-two poems resumed "Personality, too long left out of mind. Their shadows," he said, "are projected in employments, in books, in the cities, in trade; their feet are on the flights of the steps of the Capitol; they dilate, a larger, brawnier, more candid, more democratic, lawless positive native to the States, sweet-bodied, completer, dauntless, flowing, masterful, beard-faced, new race of men." This "Open Letter" to Emerson was meant to remind him (and America) of what the New Englander had called for in such earlier essays as "Self-Reliance" (1841) and "The Poet"—a literature that celebrated the "national character" instead of America's literary charter from England and the Continent. Whitman also upset the conservative New England tradition by reviewing his own work and by inventing the "puff" or dust-jacket copy. Who understood the merits and demerits of *Leaves of Grass* better than the author? he asked in later defending the practice to his Boswell, Horace Traubel. He reviewed himself anonymously in the first edition, but it was on the spine of the second that he had embossed in gold lettering (and without permission) the words, "I Greet You at the Beginning of a Great Career   R W Emerson." Making Emerson *ipso facto* the endorser of a book of poems he had not—with the exception of the original twelve of the first edition—seen, Whitman both astonished and angered the admirers of *Essays* (1841) and *Essays: Second Series* (1844), who had never imagined that the doctrine of self-reliance would allow a poet to go so far as to equate Body with Soul, democracy with divinity, and sexuality with spirituality.

Yet Whitman was not finished with his "Programme" to replace the "neuter gender" in our literature with something virile and fecund. "This filthy law [against sexual allusions in literature] has to be repealed," he declared in the second edition. "There should not be infidelism about sex, but perfect faith." Accordingly, as the third edition of *Leaves of Grass* (1860) swelled to 146 poems, it included the "Children of Adam" and "Calamus" sequences. The first sang of "libidinous joys only," "native moments" when the Body spoke for the Soul. These were poems of man's love for woman, but as one critic has observed, Whitman appears in them to be addressing the inhabitants of Mars. That is to say, such pieces—"Once I Pass'd through a Populous City," for example—underestimate the complexity of human affairs, which consist of more than a "casually met" assignation. The idea, however, that these poems are merely (or too) hedonistic may be as wrongheaded as was the Victorian standard that originally condemned them. In the case of "Children of Adam," Emerson himself may have agreed that the subject matter was taboo—at least if one hoped to offer his book for sale to the general public. Whitman, for his part, insisted that the poems were crucial to the thematic integrity of his book. Their theme was that the sex act brought catharsis and rebirth of the spirit. "After the child is born of woman," he had already announced in "I Sing the Body Electric" (1855), "man is born of woman." In other words, it is through coitus, not by its suppression, that man as the child of Adam wends his way back to the Garden of Eden.

In the earlier editions Whitman borrowed terms from phrenology to label concepts he was trying to define in his poems. Whereas "Children of Adam" celebrates "Amativeness," the "Calamus" sequence (also expanded and reordered from 1856) explores the ecstasies and agonies of "Adhesiveness," or manly love. Resembling in theme and form the Elizabethan sonnet sequence, "Calamus" reveals the secrets of the poet's "nights and days" as a lonely and unrequited lover. These poems perhaps ring truer than "Children of Adam." Their thematic appeal is finally more "personal." Apparently, "Calamus" was not originally composed as a sequence, but most of the poems were written during the late 1850s, at a time when Whitman had descended from the emotional heights of his first two editions and confronted the hard facts about his existence. At one point in 1857 he may have even thought of writing a long, religious poem intended to replace the

Bible, but the reality he faced at the end of his most successful decade as a poet was that Emersonian self-reliance denies personal love. One could not have it both ways and become (or remain) the Poet of the Body and the Poet of the Soul. Rather, life presented one with a choice between projected wholeness in the Oversoul and perpetual halfness in search of a lover to "complete" oneself in the fleeting here and now.

In the third edition of *Leaves of Grass* the poet who felt divine "inside and out" in 1855 admits "that the soul of the man I speak for rejoices in comrades." It has been argued that a "religious purpose" lay at the heart of Whitman's best poetry, but the evidence for this assertion is generally limited to the poet's retrospective statements about his art. Later he would adopt the pose of the more conservative "Emersonian" poet and seek "a passage to more than India!" but in "Calamus" we find him on a passage to nowhere except the doubts and fears of personal—and very possibly homosexual—love. In his forty-first year the poet declares,

> I proceed for all who are or have been young men.
> To tell the secret of my nights and days,
> To celebrate the need of comrades.

The forty-five poems in this sequence trace the lover's peregrination through the streets of his experience in search of a satisfactory relationship with another. They may well represent Whitman's last on-the-scene account of his experience with experience. Whereas "Out of the Cradle Endlessly Rocking" and "As I Ebb'd with the Ocean of Life" frame the experience or occasion of the poem for the possibility of resolution, the "Calamus" poems hardly get the protagonist beyond the chaos or crisis of the experience itself. In "Calamus" the poet begins ever and anon at the beginning rather than waking up to experience *in medias res*. This "aftering" or belatedness of the later poems both denies the poet the power of Emersonian self-begetting and allows him to fulfill—as he states in "Out of the Cradle"—the true vocation of the poet:

> Now in a moment I know what I am for—I awake,
> And already a thousand singers—a thousand songs, clearer, louder, more sorrow-
>   ful than yours,
> A thousand warbling echoes have started to life within me,
> Never to die.

Whitman's ultimate theme in 1860 is the fusion of Love and Death.

It is fairly clear that "Out of the Cradle" and "As I Ebb'd" were "farewell" poems to the power of poetry (or transcendentalist Reason) to charm the Understanding out of its fear of death. Poetry had become for Whitman in 1860 an instrument toward confronting the conflict between Life and

Death. The conflict remains unresolved, of course, but at this point it is fully recognized and even studied. Such a development may account for the general poignancy of the third edition. As Roy Harvey Pearce has observed, "This is a Whitman who confronts us on a ground neither of his nor our choosing, the ground of our lives lived day to day." Having come through the Dark Night of Experience, the poet rests satisfied with its memory now recorded in the truest song of himself. Life's painful paradox is also proof that experience is never more than half over.

The publishers of the 1860 *Leaves of Grass* had hoped for a healthy sale (planning a paperback and deluxe edition), but they were unable to collect their Southern credits after the outbreak of the Civil War and went bankrupt before Whitman's book could prove itself. The war seemed to consume almost every other activity—even the poet's preoccupation with Love and Death. In September 1861 (a few months after the firing upon Fort Sumter and his brother George's enlistment in the Union Army), Whitman published what has come to be regarded as his recruiting poem, "Beat! Beat! Drums!" Not inclined to combat himself and really too old at forty-three for the soldier's life, he nevertheless followed the war closely through newspaper accounts and reports in letters from his soldier-brother. When it was reported in 1862 that George had been wounded at the battle of Fredericksburg, Whitman went immediately to the front. There his heart went out to the soldiers both Union and Confederate. He returned north in a few weeks but only as far as Washington, D.C., where he secured a part-time position as a clerk in the Army Paymaster's Office and spent the rest of his time visiting wounded and sick soldiers in the more than fifty wartime hospitals set up in the Union capital.

Whitman's wartime experience marks an important juncture in his life as Walt instead of Walter. In a poem written in 1871 and placed prominently in the definitive 1881 edition of *Leaves of Grass*, the poet declares: "My book and the war are one." The retrospective introduction of wartime emotions into the great poetry written before 1860 may account for many readers' preference for the earlier editions. Even revised poems such as "Out of the Cradle Endlessly Rocking" ("A Word Out of the Sea") lack some of the tensions that marked the original versions. By the time Whitman had settled upon the final arrangement and character of his poems, he had become "The Good Gray Poet." The sobriquet comes from the title of a forty-six-page pamphlet by William Douglas O'Connor in 1866. Written in response to the poet's dismissal from the Department of the Interior allegedly for being the author of an obscene book, the polemic waxes panegyrical in its affectionate description of the poet grown gray in the service of his country.

Also grown slightly gray, however, was the muse. Whitman may have had his head turned a bit by O'Connor's comparisons of the poet with Homer, Dante, Cervantes—even Christ. In any event, the poetry becomes less and less Emersonian (in the original sense) and so more and more acceptable to the genteel taste of the New England literary establishment.

Even *Drum-Taps* (1865) lacks the daring self-discovery of the earlier verse. Although the volume stands beside Herman Melville's *Battle Pieces* (1866) as one of the great literary responses to the Civil War, the poems come more from the head than from the heart. It took the national tragedy of President Lincoln's assassination shortly before the publication of *Drum-Taps* to bring the poet back to himself—for the last time—as America's most "personal" poet. Although "When Lilacs Last in the Dooryard Bloom'd" (published in the *Sequel* to *Drum-Taps*) is an elegy in the tradition of Milton's "Lycidas" and Shelley's "Adonais," its pattern of grief and reconciliation also afforded the poet another opportunity to return to the theme of "Out of the Cradle Endlessly Rocking"—the fusion of Love and Death. Indeed, Lincoln is a relatively minor player in this drama of the Self. The fact that he was not known personally to the poet (unlike the cases of Milton and Shelley) suggests that the slain president—though highly admired by Whitman—was merely the catalyst that sent the poet down the same stretch of "open road" he had traveled in the poems of the 1860 edition. This time, however, he has no illusions about the compatibility of self-reliance and personal love but instead is flanked by "the thought of death" and "the fear of death." The first represents love of life, while the second stands for death in all its inevitability.

Together, according to James E. Miller, Jr., "these two comrades are personifications of the basic conflict that has been present throughout the poem." Miller sees the poet's joining hands with both of them as a symbol of reconciliation between a love of life and a love of death. This reading, however, may be influenced by the desire to see Whitman's "Lilacs" as a traditional elegy (which it is in one sense). The poet, it should be remembered, holds hands with Love and Death but stands between them to underscore the meaning of the poem's basic symbols of "Lilac and star and bird." These represent the trinity of Life, Death, and Love. As the "western orb"—or star representing Lincoln's fall—sails through "the heaven," the poet relives the epiphany of "Out of the Cradle":

> Now I know what you must have meant as a month since I walk'd,
> As I walk'd in silence the transparent shadowy night.

Reconciliation of Love and Death is impossible because the "open road" of Life is always open-ended. In "Lilacs" the poet confronts the same conflict he had encountered in "Out of the Cradle," the one basic to all his great poems. It is the paradoxical duality of experience, which is visualized as Body and Soul in "Song of Myself," the lover and his memory in "Calamus," the man and his reminiscence in "Out of the Cradle," and the opposite shores in "As I Ebb'd with the Ocean of Life." Read strictly as a threnody, the poem does not conclude on a note of reconciliation: the poet's grief over Lincoln's death is assuaged by the hermit-thrush's chanting apostrophe to death. But as the poet departs, he leaves behind a "lilac with heart-shaped leaves" to indicate that the same old conflict between Love and Death continues for the mourner if not for the mourned.

Drum-Taps and its *Sequel* were absorbed into the 1871–72 (fifth) edition of *Leaves of Grass*. Whitman had brought out the fourth edition in 1867, and he would publish, in all, six editions of his expansive book (1855, 1856, 1860, 1867, 1871–72, 1881–82). The others—such as the "Author's Edition" of 1876 and the "death-bed edition" of 1891–92—are more strictly defined as issues or printings. After the war the poet also returned to prose and published *Democratic Vistas* in 1871, *Memoranda During the War* in 1873, and *Specimen Days* in 1882. Because it complains of the excesses of materialism in America, the most interesting of these titles is *Democratic Vistas*. It is probably correct to say that Whitman wrote no truly great poems after "When Lilacs Last in the Dooryard Bloom'd," but certainly one of the most important later poems is "Passage to India," which was first printed as an annex to the second issue of the 1871–72 edition. The poem was occasioned by the completions of the Suez Canal, the Union Pacific Railroad, and the Atlantic Cable, but in the words of Gay Wilson Allen, "Passage to India" is a great deal more than a celebration of engineering facts—"though no other poet of the age seems to have so fully appreciated these materialistic achievements." Seeing these events as evidence of the potential brotherhood of the world community, Whitman also views the global connection as the first step toward a "Passage to India!"

> Reckoning ahead O soul, when thou, the time achiev'd,
> The seas all cross'd, weather'd the capes, the voyage done,
> Surrounded, copest, frontest God, yieldest, the aim attain'd,
> As fill'd with friendship, love complete, the Elder Brother found,
> The Younger melts in fondness in his arms.

According to the preface to the 1876 *Leaves*, Whitman came to regard this poem as the launching song for a volume of poems that would do for "the unseen Soul" what the earlier ones had done for the Body. Four years earlier in the preface to "As a Strong Bird on Pinions Free" he had maintained that "the religious purpose" had underlain his work since the beginning.

Just what exactly he intended, therefore, with such poems as "Passage to India" and its (weaker) sister "Proud Music of the Storm" is difficult to discern. Whatever the case, Whitman soon realized his poetic powers had waned: the poetry—like the theory—becomes abstract and allusive.

Missing are the psychological connections and half-connections of "The Sleepers" (1855) or the paradoxical symbolism of "Crossing Brooklyn Ferry" (1856). Indeed, Whitman may be lamenting the loss of his original energy in "Prayer of Columbus" (1876), where he assumes the persona of the forgotten explorer:

> A batter'd, wreck'd old man,
> Thrown on this savage shore, far, far from home

Not only did he feel the decline of his power, but he believed (rightly) that the work of his strong years was being consciously overlooked by the literary lights of his day. "All the established American poets studiously ignore Whitman," the poet wrote anonymously of himself in a *West Jersey Press* article that would set off the 1876 Anglo-American debate over the shabby reception of *Leaves of Grass* in America. "The omnium gatherums of poetry, by Emerson, Bryant, Whittier, and by lesser authorities, professing to include everybody of any note, carefully leave him out." Particularly painful to him must have been his exclusion from Emerson's *Parnassus* (1874), though the sting of this slight would have been easier to endure had he known the anthology was mainly the work of Emerson's family and not of the man who had first hailed Whitman as a great poet.

Throughout the 1870s Whitman was generally regarded by the American literary establishment as the proverbial prophet without honor in his own country. Only in Europe had he received the critical attention he deserved. In 1868 in England William Michael Rossetti published his selected edition of *Leaves of Grass*, and later Anne Gilchrist, after reading the English edition, published "An Englishwoman's Estimate of Walt Whitman" in the *Boston Radical*. Other appreciative essays followed from Ferdinand Freiligrath of Germany and Rudolph Schmidt of Denmark. But the turning point for Whitman's reputation in his own country came in 1880 with Edmund Clarence Stedman's article on Whitman in *Scribner's Monthly*. Without overtly approving the sexual allusions in *Leaves of Grass*, Stedman was the first American critic outside Whitman's circle of acquaintances to give the book unstinting praise. Probably because of this favorable criticism, the Boston firm of Osgood & Company offered Whitman a contract to publish the sixth edition of his book. The opportunity was good news to the poet who had enjoyed the luxury of a commercial publisher only once before, in 1860.

But it was also a mixed blessing because, not long after the volume was released, the Boston District Attorney charged that it violated the obscenity laws and ordered it withdrawn. The controversy that ensued gave Whitman both the notoriety of having perhaps the first book to be "banned in Boston" and (when the edition was reissued the next year by a Philadelphia publisher) the best sale *Leaves of Grass* received in the poet's lifetime.

By this time the poet was "house-tied" in his brother's home in Camden, New Jersey. A paralytic stroke in 1873 had forced his retirement from the Washington job he had held since the war. He suffered at least one more stroke and never regained completely the good health he had celebrated in *Leaves of Grass*. With the profits from the sixth edition he was able to purchase his own house in 1884. It was in this modest row house in a working-class district of Camden, not far from the Philadelphia ferry that brought visitors to his door from other states and other nations, that Whitman spent the rest of his days. In 1879 he had journeyed to the Western states he had vicariously explored in *Leaves of Grass*. But in fact the poet who boasted of having roamed his land and emerged with his vision had traveled very little in his country and never abroad. In 1848 he had spent three months in New Orleans editing the *Crescent*, but in the main the "travel" upon which his book was based was not that much more extensive than the shops, offices, and fields of Concord that took Thoreau around the world. During the final decade of his life such travel consisted mainly of reminiscences and letters, many of which are recorded in Horace Traubel's multi-volume *With Walt Whitman in Camden*. In his old age the poet became the primary vendor of the book he had been writing for almost half his life and sold copies through the mail. The fact that a New York printer was selling counterfeit copies of the 1860 edition (from plates sold at auction in the 1870s) no doubt increased the poet's desire to be read according to the final (1881) arrangement. In the "Complete 1892" printing Whitman carefully listed the copyrights in effect for all previous editions and issues. He also insisted that since "there are now several editions of L. of G., different texts and dates, I wish to say that I prefer and recommend this present one, complete, for future printing, if there should be any."

There have been many printings, of course, not only of the 1891–92 arrangement but of the earlier editions as well. No other serious American poet has been printed so widely. Yet as late as the 1940s Henry Seidel Canby, the author of the Whitman chapter in the *Literary History of the United States*, felt compelled to ask whether his subject was a great poet. Writing at a time when the celebratory was considered naïve and shameless, Canby found it necessary to chide Whitman for "his too urgent sense of importance." Of course, *Leaves of Grass* survived the insistence of the New Critics for the well-made, rigorously impersonal poem. Today the book that grew as the nation grew is the subject of both traditional and deconstructionist analysis. It remains our central literary text because it paradoxically links the American quest to European tradition by cutting the connection between the two literatures. "There is no art of poetry save by the grace of other poetry," William Carlos Williams observed. "So Dante to me can only be another way of saying Whitman. Yet without a Whitman there can be for me no Dante." In this sense, the emergence of a great literature in the United States in the nineteenth century was truly an American "renaissance."

Reborn to the possibilities of what Emerson called "an original relation to the universe," Whitman at mid-life had plunged *himself* into the heart of the American experience of new worlds and second chances. He had descended into himself and emerged not simply with the subliminal experience of his countrymen but with "the thoughts of all men in all ages and lands." The Columbus of our literature, he had set out for India and discovered the new world of himself in the old world of experience. "Song of Myself," the central poem and indeed the heart of *Leaves of Grass*, dramatizes this quest for the "supreme fiction" of the Self. Without the poem, Whitman's book would be simply Whitman's collected works; with it, the psychic work of this poet is collected into a force that can never be scattered among the ruins of a genteel literature. In fact, as Whitman expanded and rearranged his book, he came to regard *Leaves of Grass* as a "single poem"—one that grew out of "Song of Myself" and its drama of discovery. In "So Long!" the poet says of his book and himself:

> Camerado, this is no book,
> Who touches this touches a man

"So Long!" concludes all editions of *Leaves of Grass* beginning with the third, but the farewell was not premature even in 1860 because the poet had already made the work for which we most honor him. The result consisted mainly of waiting for the message to produce its meaning with regard to the poem and his people:

> When America does what was promis'd,
> When through these States walk a hundred millions of superb persons,
> When the rest part away from superb persons and contribute to them
> When breeds of the most perfect mothers denote America,
> Then to me and mine our due fruition.

Jerome Loving

Part Three

1865–1910

I. Signs of the Times

Literature and Culture

Considered in terms of its most noted writers, the change in American literature between the earlier and later halves of the nineteenth century is strongly marked. With the deaths or retirements from authorship of the generation of Hawthorne, Melville, Emerson, and Poe in the 1850s and 1860s, then the emergence, just after the Civil War, of such new figures as Henry James, William Dean Howells, and Mark Twain, American literature undergoes one of the most thoroughgoing changes of the guard in its entire history. But fully to understand the difference in American writing between the pre– and post–Civil War periods we need to look behind individual authors to the changing life of literature itself as a cultural institution. For the fundamental change that takes place at this time is a change not just in who American authors are but in the terms in which it is possible to *be* an author in America; a change that derives not from the writers' works alone but from the changing place made for their work in the world of American life.

In the early nineteenth century, we need to remember, American literature had the character very largely of an unsupported activity. Literature itself had a place in American life, even a prominent one: the first national culture to come into existence after the early modern literacy revolution, America was already a nation of readers in 1800, and there is hardly an account of the life of that time in which literature fails to appear. (Alexis de Tocqueville, we might recall, first read Shakespeare's *Henry V* not in a European school or library but in a hut on the American frontier.)

But the sizable American consumption of literary works did not much extend, at first, to native productions. The cultural legacy of America's colonial situation was that America continued to import both its literature and the terms by which it judged its literature from England long after it had achieved its political independence. Indigenous institutions of the sort that would eventually be able to produce and support an indigenous American literature—publishing houses, literary magazines, and so on—begin to be founded in the early decades of the nineteenth century, but typically these institutions were, well into the 1840s, geographically limited, economically vulnerable, and short-lived.

Authors of extraordinary power emerge at this time, but since they have to rely on such imperfectly developed institutions to win their work its public life, authorship as they know it is always an insecurely supported practice. They write, but without the confident presumption that they can earn a living through the work of writing. (Paid at the rates that prevailed for native authors, Nathaniel Hawthorne earned $108 for the entire literary output of a productive year in the 1830s; of all American writers only one, James Fenimore Cooper, was able to support himself wholly by the proceeds of his literary labors prior to 1850.) Similarly they address a public, but without confident expectation that their work will be brought home to the audience meant to receive it. The minute circulations achieved for Hawthorne's *Twice-told Tales* (1837), Poe's *Tales of the Grotesque and Arabesque* (1839), and Thoreau's *A Week on the Concord and Merrimack Rivers* (1849) illustrate the fact that American writing of the earlier nineteenth century is a virtually *undistributed* literature; the voice of a Whitman, whose poems address everyone, and a Dickinson, whose poems address no one, might be thought of as joint reflections of a situation in which the writer does not know with much certainty who in particular he could be addressing.

For the next literary generation, things have changed. These writers live in a world where American writing, even rather specialized forms of it, has sizable and well-identified audiences, and reliable means of reaching its audience. Not coincidentally these writers work in a world in which writing is, for many if not for all aspirants, a remunerated activity—and a source of reliable public standing, even of power and prestige. We name the great difference in this generation's situation when we say that it knows literature as something already *established*, not something trying to *be* established: as a cultural system whose place is well-provided for, and whose meaning— however much writers might want to dispute or rework that meaning—is well assured.

If we ask how American literature became established in this sense, the answer is that it was established in not one but several cultural forms, each with its distinct cultural history. If by establishment we mean the creation of a secure public for literary writing, secure channels by which to reach that public, and a secure public value for the work so received, then the first phase of American literature successfully to establish itself was that associated with popular fiction written by women. Literary historians have often noted the sudden advent, around 1850, of a group of novels—Susan Warner's *The Wide, Wide World*, Maria Cummins's *The Lamplighter*, and Mrs. E. D. E. N. Southworth's *Retribution* are examples—that achieved sales of unprecedented dimensions. The rise of such best-sellers has long been read as a sign of literary slippage into vulgarity of baleful feminization. But we would understand such books better if we read them as products and agents of a process of literary establishment: a process in which certain forms of writing succeed in so involving themselves with the values and concerns of a social group that such writing becomes one of that group's regular needs. The 1850s best-sellers had the success they did because they spoke so directly and comprehensively to the new world created for women and for family life with the institution of new middle-class norms of domestic propriety. And in their success, such books helped crystallize patterns for future exchange: helped identify the novel as the staple entertainment of domestic leisure, and helped organize the world of domestic leisure into a market authors could regularly trade on.

This mid-nineteenth-century conjunction of women's writing and a middle-class domestic audience is an event of central importance in American literary history, understood as the history of literature's whole life in the social world. This conjunction helped establish both the circle of readers and the reading tastes and habits by which the great bulk of literary production was consumed in later nineteenth-century America. The most widely read writers of the post–Civil War decades, we should remember, were not Howells or James but domestic writers like Mrs. Southworth, Caroline Lee Hentz, and Mary Jane Holmes, figures who commanded readerships literature has seldom matched since. (Augusta Evans Wilson's *St. Elmo* [1866] is reported to have been read by a million people—out of a national population of thirty-six million—in the year of its publication alone.)

But what might be called the domestic establishment of American literature is not the only cultural operation of its time to have organized an ongoing literary audience on a mass scale. The appearance of mass journalism or the "penny press" in the 1840s gave quick rise, among its other products, to a kind of newspaper that published fiction in place of news. This new vehicle of literary production was developed in the 1850s first into the story-paper, then into the mass-produced cheap book. The marketing ventures of Erastus Beadle (publisher after 1860 of Beadle's Dime Novels) and his competitors in this line crystallized, alongside the domestic novel, another popular literary form: the short and sensational tale of adventure and social rise.

They opened up a cultural and economic role for another kind of writer: the writer as proletarianized worker, stamping out a standardized product at a maximized productive rate. (Beadle author Prentiss Ingraham, author of six hundred novels, is said to have written one thirty-five-thousand-word piece in a day and a night.) And they established such writing just as deeply in the everyday life of another audience, as large as or larger than the domestic one. A mass audience of youths, factory workers, and others at a lower level of leisure and literacy purchased five million Beadle novels between 1860 and 1865 alone.

Such developments, taken together, are responsible for having made prose fiction what it peculiarly becomes in nineteenth-century America: a daily presence on an unprecedented scale, even something like the public entertainment of first resort. But from the point of view of literature more strictly considered it is a third development of this time that is of crucial importance. For the same mid-century decades that saw the formation of these domestic and low-literate audiences also witnessed the formalization or establishment of another literary zone: a well-marked and well-supported cultural place for high or "serious" authorship.

We get a good sense both of the principal figures in this development and of the power with which it imposed itself on those within its sway from William Dean Howells's bittersweet reminiscence "My First Visit to New England" (1894), collected in the volume *Literary Friends and Acquaintance* (1900). This essay is Howells's account of his coming, as an aspiring young writer from the Midwest in 1860, to what seems to him the seat of American literary greatness: Boston, the home of such literary giants as James Russell Lowell, Oliver Wendell Holmes, and Nathaniel Hawthorne. But Boston as he describes it is not just a place where great writers reside. Quite palpably, it is a place where a new and extraordinary kind of value is being conferred upon authors. Lowell and Holmes—and even their publisher James T. Fields—take on an aura of almost sacred power in the mind of this caller. (To visit an author, in this book, is "to come within his presence.") They are placed in a position of such eminence that Howells's instinctual response is not to think of them as equals but to subordinate himself, to prostrate himself in reverent respect.

The Boston Howells visited, as he fully recognizes, was the center from which the new American literary high culture was being fashioned and spread. The new cultural prestige being created for "high" authorship is what he is encountering and documenting in the story of his literary pilgrimage. If his essay is useful, it is because it suggests so fully what kind of value was made for literature in this process, and from what cultural base this assertion proceeded. Historically the promoters and custodians of this high culture were, like the figures Howells calls on, of old and established gentry background, presuming to the leisure not just of the new middle-class housewife but of secure wealth and quasi-aristocratic removal from financial concern. This group was secularized in outlook, mentally removed from the urgencies of a religious piety still intensely active in other parts of American culture. It was cosmopolitan in range, looking to the European cultural world—more than to socially remote areas of American life—as an extension of its sphere. It cared about the traditional high arts and letters—indeed, it located in the domain of the arts the sort of founding or elemental value no longer located in religion. And, believing that concern for such values was the base of civilization itself, it felt entitled and even obliged to try to impose this sense of value throughout its society: to disseminate culture so conceived throughout the land, and so to win minds to that reverence for elevated art that Howells had so perfectly displayed.

In the gentry thus described, mid-nineteenth-century America had a group doubly defined by its authentic care for literature as a supreme value and by the sense of its right and duty to impose this care on groups with other values. (Typical of such imperialism, when Beadle's Dime Novels caught on as a mass entertainment, Charles Eliot Norton, cosmopolite Harvard art historian and early champion of the aesthetic, tried to persuade Beadle to print dime Shakespeares instead of dime novels: a transparent move to expropriate a "vulgar" means of cultural production and use it to bring the vulgar many into high culture.) Working from this double imperative, in the 1860s and afterward the members of this class took hold of many of the most powerful existing institutions for the administration of literacy, and also fashioned powerful new ones to further their cause. They moved, at this time, into the administration of libraries, where they worked to form and raise the taste of less highly literate classes through control of their reading habits. (A new model library rule of these years, stating that the patron can take out only one book at a time, or two if one is not a popular novel, shows the librarians' aim of re-forming readers' mental literary cultures.) They moved, as well, into American schools—the liberal arts colleges and universities, newly elaborated at this time, in which figures of this background became professors of literature; and more powerfully still the elementary schools, which, following Horace Scudder's textbook reforms of the 1880s, delivered an enormous audience of heterogeneous American schoolchildren to the compulsory reading of "classical" American writings. In a century in which most literary reading was done in magazines, they moved too into editorial control of prominent magazines, identifying periodicals such as *Harper's Monthly*, the *Atlantic Monthly*, and *Scribner's Monthly*, (later *The Century*) as "quality" journals over against their popular competitors.

The version of literary culture these agencies strove to establish has been known since the turn of this century as "genteel," and to the extent that it has been discussed at all it has been dismissed without further curiosity as a kind of institutionalized insulation-system, an attempt to keep the literary field clear of references to disturbing social or sexual subjects. Allowing for its native-born Protestant cultural basis, in fact the official literary culture of the Gilded Age was much less closed than its detractors make out: in the 1860s the *Atlantic*, the most self-consciously "cultivated" of the high-culture periodicals, published not only Holmes and Lowell but also Whitman's "As I Ebb'd with the Ocean of Life," Rebecca Harding Davis's pioneering industrial novel *Life in the Iron Mills*, Thomas Wentworth Higginson's polemic against differential education for the sexes "Ought Women to Learn the Alphabet?," and Mrs. Melusina Fay Peirce's *Cooperative Housekeeping*, an important early critique of the middle-class cult of domestic privacy, to name no more.

In truth this literary culture was neither open nor closed but, like every organization of culture, open to some things and closed to others. What really separates it from other nineteenth-century literary establishments is not its greater narrowness of horizon but the superior power of cultural definition it succeeded in achieving. The high-cultural organization of literature of the mid-nineteenth century did not make women stop reading women's novels, or boys adventure stories, but it did make the great mass of readers defer to it as the realm of "literature" proper. More than that, working through the schools and libraries and magazines, it succeeded in gathering its own large audience around the matter of serious writing. (*The Century*, if not so widely sold as a Beadle's novel, reached a circulation of 200,000 and a readership of perhaps a million in the 1880s.) And it succeeded in getting literature to be taken seriously by large masses of Americans of quite other cultural traditions than the gentry's. The fact that the citizens of Jefferson, Ohio, gathered to hear Howells tell about the great Boston literati when he returned from his trip in 1860, or that many American homes were decorated with pictures of these same authors (the American classics, as they were then regarded) at the end of the century, reminds us of the value this movement succeeded in establishing for literature, in the minds of ordinary men and women.

The literary institutions under gentry control in the later nineteenth century succeeded in creating, it may be, the closest thing to a coherent national literary culture that America has ever had. And at the same time that they did so, they also created a new kind of world for authors to work in. Virtually all of the major authors of the post–Civil War generation supported themselves financially by publishing in the new journals of this new literary establishment, and supported themselves artistically by appealing to its system of cultural values. Edmund Clarence Stedman, the laureate of late nineteenth-century poets now remembered, if at all, as the poet-stock-broker who used Keats and Shelley as code words for purchasing orders, was a creature of these arrangements for literature's cultural place. So were a host of other nineteenth-century figures regarded as important men of letters in their time, but now recognized only as products or tools of their literary establishment: the novelist-editors Thomas Bailey Aldrich and Charles Dudley Warner are examples of this type. But Howells, we should note, was just as fully a creature of these literary-cultural arrangements. Howells found his first great position as editor of the *Atlantic*. His novels were published serially first in the *Atlantic*, then in *The Century*, then in *Harper's*. His campaign for literary realism was conducted in the Editor's Study column of *Harper's*, to the audience *Harper's* had assembled and with the backing of House of Harper's lucrative payments. And realism itself in the Howellsian conception, while partly aiming to expose and reach beyond the limitations of a gentry conception of culture, has the marks of that conception pressed deep inside it: especially in its belief that literary reading is the chief gauge and sustainer of a culture, and so that debased writing must be driven out by superior work to preserve civilization from collapse.

Henry James is another product of these same arrangements. Less interested than Howells in what might be called the administrative aspect of literary creation (he was never an editor), James nevertheless published virtually all of his work in the *Atlantic*, from his earliest stories through *The American* and *The Portrait of a Lady* to *The Aspern Papers* and *The Spoils of Poynton*. And while his supporting artistic creed is in one sense his own creation, in another sense he derives this support too from the gentry literary culture of the 1860s, 1870s, and 1880s. James brings to the intensity of an authentic personal faith the group ethic that locates the supreme good in the cosmopolitan, aesthetic creation, and the civilizing powers of the artistic imagination.

And James and Howells are not the only notable authors this system supported. George Washington Cable, the recorder of Creole culture in novels like *The Grandissimes* (1880), found a place for his work in *The Century*, and found help in learning how to do his work from *The Century's* editor, Richard Watson Gilder. Writers like Sarah Orne Jewett, author of the superb *The Country of the Pointed Firs* (1896), and Constance Fenimore Woolson, best known as the woman Henry James loved less than art but in fact a writer of considerable distinction, produced their work through the "quality" periodicals and identified with their cultural ethos—suggesting that when women authors began to assert themselves as something other than domestic writers after the Civil War, they were enabled to this assertion by the support they derived from the gentry establishment of a "serious" literary realm.

Many of the dominant literary forms of the post–Civil War decades, similarly, have this set of arrangements as their cultural base. Considered in terms of its place of production and the audience it therefore reached, American realism is largely a product of this high culture of letters—so much so that three of its classic texts, Twain's *Adventures of Huckleberry Finn*, James's *The Bostonians*, and Howells's *The Rise of Silas Lapham*, all ran in the pages of *The Century* in 1884 and 1885. Regionalism, the staple literary form of the postwar decades, has as its social background the draining of life from an old agrarian culture to the new cities, and the supersession of local cultures by the new national culture modern transportation and marketing opened up. But in terms of its cultural production the literature of regionalism is a product more particularly of the high-cultural literary establishment. Jewett's and Mary Wilkins Freeman's tales of northern New England were printed not in northern New England but in *Harper's* and the *Atlantic*. Mary Noailles Murfree's *Prophet of the Great Smoky Mountains* (1885) registered the folkways of eastern Tennessee, but it too did so for *Atlantic* readers. Cable's fictionalized Louisiana was disseminated from New York, in the pages of *The Century*. Hamlin Garland found his subject in the hard-bitten farm life of the upper Midwest, but he looked to the East's literary establishment to validate his work: having a story accepted in *The Century*, in the words of his memoir *Son of the Middle Border*, was like receiving a "diploma" for Garland, institutional certification of his literary adequacy.

In sum, if the high-cultural literary establishment of the post–Civil War decades functioned in one sense as an imperialistic social institution, coercing a mixed and various populace into sharing the values of an elite civilization, this same establishment served in another way to create a space where serious art could be practiced, and the artist protected while he did his work. It performed both of these functions with impressive power during the decades that this system thrived. But while it had taken on a massive public solidity in the 1870s and 1880s, this establishment began to be challenged at that peak of its apparent power; and its full history is also the history of its eventual supersession.

The causes for its supersession were in place from the time of its origin. When Howells came to Boston in 1860, as "My First Visit to New England" records, there were really two new developments there to attract the eye. Howells wanted to meet America's new literati, but the sponsor who paid his way East wanted him to go see the new manufacturing processes of the New England mills. For Howells the pilgrim New England was a cultural landscape, but just over the hill, he keeps reminding us, was another, industrial landscape: in his travels Howells came to the Concord of Emerson and Hawthorne direct from the Lowell of the modern factory. What this means is that although it bore no visible traces of this fact, the high literary culture spread out from New England after the 1850s arose contemporaneously with, and even in sight of, those processes of capitalist industrial development that would transform every aspect of American life by the nineteenth century's end.

The decades in which this literary establishment extended its sway over American letters were exactly the ones in which this other process of development extended its sway over American economic life. What is crucial for the cultural history of literature is that at a certain point in the late nineteenth century this economic development began to impinge much more directly on the literary realm: began to call forth its own instruments of literary production, and so to establish a rival culture of letters organized on quite different grounds. This intrusion can be seen in a decisive way in the world of magazines. By the mid-1880s, the "quality" magazines like *Harper's* and *The Century* had built up circulations of one to two hundred thousand. But in the late 1880s and early 1890s a new kind of magazine appears—*Ladies' Home Journal*, *Munsey's*, *McClure's Magazine*, and the revamped *Cosmopolitan* are examples—attaining to circulations three or four times that size. These magazines were significantly cheaper than the older kind of monthly—fifteen cents or even a dime, as in the case of *Munsey's*, as against a quarter or thirty-five cents. They could be cheaper because they financed themselves in a different way: instead of supporting themselves by subscription fees, they dropped fees, built massive circulations, then sold space to advertisers at a price based on the size of the audience the advertiser could thereby reach, using advertising revenue as their financial base.

What this means is that such magazines had changed not just their price but the whole relation of the magazine to the economic realm. They had become marketing instruments as well as sources of verbal and visual entertainment, vehicles through which large-scale manufacturers could create and maintain markets for their commodities. Or we might say that they now put verbal entertainment in the service *of* commercial interests: since in the act of delivering reading matter *to* the reader they also delivered him *over* to manufacturers, advertisers, and the world of commercially created needs. Such magazines literally embedded literary writing in the writing of commodity culture. Unlike, say, the text-heavy pages of the *Atlantic*, these magazines ran columns of text through areas of much more eye-catching ads. They used the lure of literary imagination to pull the mind into a commercially imaged world: tailing or ad-stripping, the custom of printing a continued story between columns of advertisements, perfected in the *Ladies' Home Journal* in the mid-1890s, makes the story line an engine literally to drive the reader forward through consumeristic space.

From their first accession, these new magazines began to encroach on American high culture's established literary domain. *Cosmopolitan* managed to hire Howells for its editorial staff after he had resigned from *Harper's;* Edward Bok, advertising and promotional genius of the *Ladies' Home Journal*, bought up the rights to two future Howells works as one of his first editorial moves. (Bok's plan to pay Howells $10,000 for an autobiographical serial, then to spend $50,000 promoting the serial, reveals both the economic tactics of the new magazine and its sense of literature's relative value.) More critically, from their first accession these new publications began to dispute literary high culture's hold on its most cherished power: the power to control the reading habits of the populace at large, and so to mold its sense of collective value. We read this encroachment and the anxieties it produced in the growing obsession, in American literary writing of the 1880s, with an aggressive popular-print culture devoted to commercial ends—as in Howells's *A Modern Instance* (1882), where Bartley Hubbard's circulation-boosting, advertising-sensitive brand of journalism is strongly linked to the decline of traditional American community values; or in James's *The Bostonians* (1885), where the popular-print media are associated with a menacing assault on the civilized value of privacy.

From the point of view of the older establishment, as such books show, these new instruments of literary production looked like the enemies of culture itself. But from a more detached point of view they can be recognized not as corroders of culture in some absolute sense but as the agents of a different version of culture: the establishers of literary writing in the lives of another audience, grouped around other—consumer-culture, not gentry-culture—values. This new establishment did indeed sap the social position of its high-cultural rival: after 1890 the older literary establishment became much more narrowly elitist and reactionary, except where it managed to accommodate itself to the methods of its more commercially successful competitors. But at the same time this new order also created, as its predecessor had, a new cultural place the writer could practice in.

Theodore Dreiser's case is instructive here. Born a generation after Howells (in 1871), in an immigrant and working-class environment, Dreiser formed his first aspirations as a writer on the basis not of a Boston-centered literary circle but of Chicago's popular newspapers. As Howells had with the *Atlantic*, Dreiser first established himself by writing for and managing the new publishing organs of his time. In the 1890s Dreiser cranked out feature articles on random subjects for such advertising-heavy journals as *Ainslee's*, *Demorest's*, and *Success;* after the turn of the century he became managing editor of *The Delineator*, a fashion-pattern magazine (this one with glorious advertising graphics) of immense circulation. Dreiser's literary work is not wholly determined by the literary culture he worked out of, any more than that of Howells or James is; but his writing too bears, deep in its literary nature, the marks of its culture of origin. The prose of a book like *Sister Carrie* (1900) is writing not strongly identified, any more, with cosmopolitan consciousness of tradition or the display of highly deliberated craft. Instead it is associated with straightforward or rapidly processed communication, minute attention to contemporary appearances, and deep knowledge of the desires created by commodities: the concerns, that is to say, of the magazine world of the 1890s.

Dreiser's connection with the new mass media of the late nineteenth century is especially close, but in a sense he is exemplary of the new literary training those media produced for writers of this time. The other new writers of his generation are united really less by the fact that they believed in the creed of literary naturalism than by the fact that they wrote out of the same literary-cultural situation. Authors like Stephen Crane, Frank Norris, and Upton Sinclair also took their literary bearings in the world of the commercialized journalistic media, and they too bear the marks of this origin in their work.

But to think of the older, high-cultural literary establishment as having been replaced by a commercialized, mass-media establishment tells only part of the story of American writing at the end of the nineteenth century. For what begins to emerge at the end of the century is not just another organized world of authorship but several parallel literary worlds, a new variegation of the literary scene. A full study of the gentry-based establishment of the 1870s and 1880s would show it, two decades later, trying to recoup its control over literary value through renewed efforts of institutional assertion. The National Institute of Arts and Letters (founded in 1899) and its artistic inner sanctum, the American Academy of Arts and

Letters (created in 1904), are clear attempts to institutionalize the fact that the older establishment's authors *are* America's literary greats, and to debar other writers from the literary realm. (Howells, Henry James, Charles Dudley Warner, Stedman, Aldrich, and Charles Eliot Norton—but certainly *not* Dreiser or Edward Bok, and still not popular woman novelists—were among the Academy's first members.)

Such structures represent one new world of authorship—this one converting authorship into a closed club of the officially certified—arising contemporaneously with the mass media's. But this is not the only literary world the older establishment helped produce at this time. If part of its energies went into such schemes for prestige-support and literary exclusiveness, other aspects of the older establishment took on new life in these years, as they caught on to the business techniques of their commercially oriented rivals and relaxed their wish to enforce the values of a narrowly defined social group. In the 1890s and afterward the traditional literary publishing houses took new lessons in literary marketing and the creation of literary demand. (When the House of Harper's went into receivership in the 1890s, Colonel George Harvey, trained by Joseph Pulitzer in the world of mass journalism, was put in charge of its publishing operations. Harvey ruled the resuscitated firm with a portrait of the firm's new patron—the financier J. P. Morgan—hung on his office wall.) The result of such crossings is the emergence, at the beginning of this century, of publishing institutions that work to join the appreciation of the literary with the commercial cultivation of mass markets, instead of treating these interests as antithetical. Edith Wharton could illustrate the difference this arrangement makes from the author's side. Unlike the works of such artistically similar but historically earlier authors as Jewett or James, Wharton's works became best-sellers; unlike the works of such best-selling writers as Warner or Cummins, Wharton's works sold as literature. She demonstrates the stabilization, made possible by the convergence of high-cultural literary institutions and their more market-oriented competitors, of a new literary category of the late nineteenth and early twentieth centuries: serious writing made commercially successful on the basis of its quality *as* serious writing.

As portions of the older literary establishment enter into this new form of collusion with their commercially minded rivals, they also become, in very marked measure, less committed to the idea of literary exclusiveness. The concepts of a special "high" grade of authorship and of a value-fraught separation between "high" and popular authorship become less zealously insisted on in the mainstream literary culture that begins to emerge at the turn of the century. Similarly, traditional communication-systems begin to open themselves, at this time, to varieties of voice and experience they had not been receptive to earlier. Houghton Mifflin, the high Bostonian publishing firm par excellence and the chief promoter of the idea of standard author and classical text, published the stories and novels of Charles W. Chesnutt, the first black literary writer to find a regular white audience in America, beginning in 1899. In the previous year this same concern had published *The Imported Bridegroom, and Other Stories of the New York Ghetto* by Abraham Cahan, the first major Jewish-American author and the first immigrant writer (Cahan was born near Vilna, in Lithuania, in 1860) to assert a strong American literary voice. (The fact that Cahan helped create major publishing institutions of New York's Jewish immigrant culture—Cahan edited a socialist weekly in the 1890s, and later the *Jewish Daily Forward*—can remind us of how many literary establishments besides its dominant ones America began to have at the end of the nineteenth century.)

But paradoxically, the same years that saw a new popularization of writing centered in the mass media, and that saw this new democratization take place within the literary realm proper, gave rise, as well, to a new version of elite literary culture in America. The same decade that produced the cheap magazine like *Munsey's* or *McClure's* also produced another new kind of magazine, of which *The Chap-Book* (printed from 1894 to 1898) is the chief example: the art magazine, expensively printed, without advertisements and relatively indifferent to circulation management, featuring work that is interesting to those in the know. *The Chap-Book* and the company that lay behind it—Stone and Kimball, first American publishers of Ibsen, Shaw, Maeterlinck, and the French *symbolistes*, publishers too of James's *What Maisie Knew* (1897), Kate Chopin's *The Awakening* (1899), and a Beardsley-illustrated edition of Poe—represent a new kind of publishing institution in American literary history. Like all such institutions, they need to be thought of not as journals or companies merely but as agencies that express a certain conception of culture and that help group a real audience around that conception. The vision these new ventures promote is obviously at odds with the consumer-culture vision projected in the late nineteenth-century mass media; but it is equally opposed, really, to the older high-cultural scheme it obviously descends from. The culture these instruments project is intensely, even aggressively, cosmopolitan—England, France, even Norway are within its reading purview; but now it is the modern, the daring, the disruptively experimental, not monuments of classical achievement, that are sought on foreign shores. The culture these magazines and books project is that of the few, not the many; but now there is no wish to spread an elite civilization to the many: "the distinguished class of readers and collectors" or "the *illuminate*" is how *The Chap-Book* names its intended audience. Above all, literature is a supreme good in the culture these vehicles publish, but now it is presented much more as a good in itself, a source of purely *aesthetic* pleasure, not as part of a larger program of moral and civic values and obligations: the selection of Poe as the American classic, not Lowell or Holmes, forcefully registers this change.

The different literary-cultural worlds that we see emerging in the last years of the nineteenth century have one thing in common: they have not yet attained, at the end of the century, the cultural power fully to support the new forms of authorship they appear to enable. Chesnutt was printed by a prestigious, main-line publisher, but in spite of his and his publisher's vigorous promotional efforts his books did not reach a large enough audience to make him feel validated in his choice of career. Chesnutt accordingly retired from the literary vocation, returning to his legal and legal-stenography practice in 1905. Literary institutions based on an antipopular ethic of daring and the flouting of respectability were sufficiently well-developed in 1900 that Chopin's *The Awakening* could be published, but they were insufficiently strong to create a body of taste that would approve of her efforts in the face of more traditional readers' disapproval; lacking such validation, Chopin too retired from authorship in the wake of *The Awakening*'s hostile reception. The literary form of *Sister Carrie* may reflect the consumer-oriented magazine world Dreiser was trained in, but that does not mean that this world sustained Dreiser's more strictly literary efforts: Dreiser too gave up literary authorship for several years in the aftermath of *Sister Carrie*'s failure to find a public, earning his living from mass-circulation magazines but finding no support for his literary career there.

We could think of the new American writers of the late nineteenth century as reliving the plight of America's earliest literary authors, that of writing without cultural machinery that could establish adequate support for the writer's work. But if they remind us of this past, their much more genuine connection is with American literature's future. For such writers attempt under pioneering conditions forms of authorship that have since become more fully established. Charles Chesnutt did not become a central American writer by writing out of the Afro-American experience and tradition. But writers of this century have become just that; and the literary possibility they have realized was first explored, and the cultural conditions for that possibility first tested out, in Chesnutt's aborted career. Similarly, the kind of authorship a Chopin failed to sustain in the late nineteenth century has been practiced in this century—and has been *made* practicable by later developments in the literary culture she encountered in its incipient phase. The elite or anticonventional literary world that could not yet support a Chopin in 1900 is the same world the American modernists took their bearing in, somewhat later: *The Chap-Book*, a weak vessel in itself, has its real meaning as the progenitor of the "little magazines" the modernists found publics through in the 1910s and 1920s; just as the publishing house of Stone and Kimball has its historical meaning as the disseminator of the literary texts—late Ibsen, late James, and the French *symbolistes*—the modernists would immerse themselves in and on which they would form their anticonventional ideas of what literary expression could be.

All of which is to say that the consequences of America's literary history in the nineteenth century are not confined within the boundaries of that century. One achievement of this time is the creation of the more securely grounded world of letters late nineteenth-century authors practiced in. But in just as real a sense the chief creation of the late nineteenth century is the world of literary possibilities—in the forms both of literary expression and of such expression's cultural position—that twentieth-century American authors would go on to explore. The history of literature's cultural life is never the history of its establishment alone, but always too of its continual reestablishment in changing cultural positions. Twentieth-century writers could mount the quite new literary projects that they mounted, and could find the new forms of public support that they found, at least in part because of what had come before: because of the arrangements that begin to be made for literature's place in America at the nineteenth century's close.

Richard H. Brodhead

Culture and Consciousness

In any modern society or era the intellectual life bearing directly on literary creation is, broadly speaking, twofold. There is the collateral territory where philosophers, scientists, members of the certified intellectual professions do their work; it is chiefly against the rivalry, if not active resistance, of this other realm of published discourse that "defenses of poetry" have seemed required of every new literary movement and epoch. So Nathaniel Hawthorne had felt in offering ironic apologies for being a mere writer of storybooks, and so too in the generation that came of age after the Civil War did those writers of fiction—most consequentially William Dean Howells and Henry James—who published defenses of the initially controversial tactics of literary realism. But there is also the booming, buzzing world of popular understanding, its expressed transactions less ordered or rationalized than those of trained intellect but more unintermitting in actual influence; a world that through its corresponsive participation in all the languages of human exchange has its own decisive ways of both stimulating literary ambition and holding it to moral account. In the uncertain years after the Civil War each of these vital streams of national consciousness, the professional and the popular, appeared to have gone rather abruptly over its banks. Each had entered a critical phase of displacement and redirection, for which the turmoil of the war itself was both portent and effective cause.

It would be Gertrude Stein's judgment, sixty years later, that with the Civil War America had begun creating the twentieth century. In more ways than one the great convulsions of 1861 to 1865 became—as the historians Charles and Mary Beard were to argue in the 1920s—a "second American Revolution," and our first evidence for continuing to think so is in the testimony of those who lived through and beyond it. Historians looking back over the whole cycle of conflict can sort out its moments and actions of decisive significance and identify what in the aftermath proved to be the important new trends. The understanding voiced by contemporaries is likely to be less particularized and differentiated but nonetheless grounded in reality. Above all, through the half decade of the Civil War, there was simply the immense effort of concentrating material resources, productive capacity, and the practical and spiritual energies of whole populations upon the continent-wide struggle; an effort that, reempowered in the victorious North by a systematic program of national consolidation and expansion (railroad building, the massive subsidies of wartime contracts, the new release of public lands signalized by the Homestead Act), committed the country to the most rapid material, industrial, technological development possible.

It was a development, a cultural as well as economic transformation, that may be traced not merely in census reports but in the imaginative experience of living people. Its principal victim was the old localized, sectarian-provincial ordering of consciousness, now inexorably shunted into margins and backwaters of social influence. Not of course without confusion and strain, not without counterviolences of resistance and repudiation that a century later have not yet reached resolution, the epoch-defining processes subsumed in what historians have latterly called the *nationalization*, the *incorporation*, the *reinstitutionalization* and, concurrently, *professionalization* of American life and culture were now set on an irreversible course. Decade by decade after 1860 both reasoned understanding and popular feeling moved forward in the United States under the coercions of a steady and prodigious growth—financial panic or depression in every decade between 1870 and 1910 hardly broke the ascending curve of it—in societal wealth, numbers, integration, and power.

A handful of instances must serve to document, for the war period itself, this suddenly materializing sense of change, overwhelmingly confirmed in the years that followed. Looking back half a century to the bleak winter before Gettysburg and Vicksburg, Henry Adams, in the *Education*, recalled the astonishment that from his diplomatic outpost in London he had felt at, across the Atlantic, the "first faint flush" of a new and specifically "imperial" consolidation of energy. "Little by little, at first only as a shadowy chance of what might be . . . one began to feel that somewhere behind the chaos in Washington power was taking shape; that it was massed and guided as it had not been before." The military consequences of such power became apparent soon enough as the campaigns of 1863 and 1864 unrolled. The long-term organizational and, ultimately, moral consequences forcibly caught Adams's attention on his disillusioned return, at the end of the 1860s, to the America of General Grant's administration and the Erie Railroad and

Gold Conspiracy scandals. These newest patterns of Washington and New York life were a clear signal that the rules of social action had somehow changed since the time when men of virtue like Adams's presidential grandfather and great-grandfather could win high office and rationally oversee the country's development. They were not a bit less disturbing to Walt Whitman, whose exalted hope for an America that would exemplify "the sanest, highest freedom" he now perceived as under massive assault by formidable new antagonists: the depravity of the dominant business classes, the associated corruption of government service and the tainting even of the judiciary, the robbery and scoundrelism—"respectable as much as non-respectable"—of everyday city life and its thickening miasma of hypocrisy, fraud, and hollowness of heart. (The harsh terms were Whitman's own, in his 1871 manifesto, *Democratic Vistas*.) To Whitman both the spiritual purgation of the war years and the precious legacy of an "all-varied, all-permitting, all-free theorem of individuality" were in danger of systematic betrayal, leaving behind only the headlong material expansion.

Much the same judgments fill out the panorama of contemporary life in which, two years later, Mark Twain and Charles Dudley Warner made the liveliest and bluntest of responses to the novelist John W. De Forest's call in 1867 for a "great American novel," a novel addressing itself comprehensively to the national condition. In nothing perhaps is *The Gilded Age* (1873) more remarkable than in providing a definitive name for a cultural era that had just begun to make clear its dominant character. A generation later the New York critic and social analyst John Jay Chapman was in no doubt about the historical logic of these years. If "the salient fact in the history of the last quarter-century," Chapman wrote in *Causes and Consequences* (1898), "is the growth and concentration of capital" (made feasible, Chapman noted, by the new railroad and telegraph networks), the underlying strategies of concentration for purely material advantage, and of corporate organization and countrywide monopoly, were arts acquired and initially mastered in the Civil War. The corruption of public life followed as a matter of course. Power itself, in every compartment of society, had simply, by virtue of the war experience, been "condensed and packaged for delivery," a phenomenon not lost on those bent on securing the advantages of power in postwar society.

This unprecedented condensing and packing in the essential organization of life—this long march of plutocratic centralization, as Brooks Adams celebrated it in the hard-edged historiography of *America's Economic Supremacy* (1900) and *The New Empire* (1902)—inevitably took toll of private sensibilities. A new civilization seemed to be generating a new order, or new aggravation, of human uncertainty and discontent. At the same time older attitudes fundamental to the distinctive American-democratic ethos recoiled seemingly out of control upon a population that had grown up under their bracing stimulus. What during Andrew Jackson's presidency the French observer Alexis de Tocqueville had already identified as a feverish national "restlessness" (*Democracy in America*, II, II, xiii) now fixed itself in popular consciousness as a social pathology requiring scientific treatment, as with the "American nervousness" diagnosed in 1881 by the New York neurasthenist Dr. George Beard. And what the revived Protestant introspection of the transcendentalist era had held up as a supreme ethical model and goal, a rule of "every man for himself," the new monopoly capitalism sealed into place as the private discipline best suited to its own suprapersonal fulfillment. Emerson himself, though with different circumstances in mind, left behind a name for the new ethical order—an "age of severance, of dissociation," tending to all the rigors of occupational "solitude" ("Historic Notes of Life and Letters in New England")—but in a still pastoral Concord Emerson had not imagined this ethic's ruthless promotion by the legal and moral apologists for economic expansion, or its actualization in the congested mill cities, the laissez-faire tenements and sweatshops, the debt-swamped farm communities of the new monetary-industrial leviathan.

An oppressive consciousness of displacement and separation, and of the betrayal of birthright political promises of happiness and free opportunity, lay in wait for nearly everybody not wholly in thrall to the new business-coup mentality. (Mark Twain's burlesque of this mentality in the entrepreneurial fantastications of Colonel Sellers, of *The Gilded Age* and an 1892 sequel, *The American Claimant*, did not miss its underlying pathos.) Howells's point-for-point diagnosis of the national condition in *A Traveler from Altruria* (1894) merely put into plain words what his readers were coming to know as a fact of experience: that a new gulf had opened between the advantaged and disadvantaged in American life, and that more than ever fear and suspicion dominated the everyday relations of classes and interest groups. Whatever cohesion of spirit had been achieved in the crucible of the Civil War had not outlasted the victory bonfires. Beset by historical changes of this magnitude, men and women at every level of life—educated elite as well as popular masses—characteristically reach out for familiar models of consolation and recovery, or restitution; and in the America of the later nineteenth century that other grand force beside the "spirit of liberty" that Tocqueville had seen as the wellspring of American democratic behavior, the historic "spirit of religion," put its distinctive stamp on nearly every new upsurge of popular resistance, every reasoned proposal for reform and reconstruction.

Well past 1865 the old Protestant-sectarian determinations of American thought continued to shape speculative inquiry and grassroots dissidence alike. Even the new secular philosophy of widest currency, the dour cosmic libertarianism of Herbert Spencer—whose main lesson for American disciples like the pioneering Yale sociologist William Graham Sumner was that any interference with the natural laws of social evolution, any legislated attempt to soften their impact on individual lives, threatened the welfare of the whole species—was taken up, after publication of *First Principles* in 1862, with the fervor of fresh religious conviction. In America Spencer's ponderous rationalism took on the familiar character of a popular revival movement, denouncing as immoral one after another institutional overgrowth or ill-advised scheme of public intervention. (In fairness it should be observed that Sumner's own table of forbidden practices included business trusts and the new geo-political imperialism of the Spanish-American War as well as fair-employment legislation and tax-funded charities.) Darwinism itself and the alarming principle of the "survival of the fittest," though widely interpreted as denying the authority of religion, coalesced neatly with the inherited outlook of New World Calvinism. Religious confidence may well have been shaken if not dissolved by Darwin's science, but the vision of created life conveyed in *The Origin of Species* (1859) and *The Descent of Man* (1871) could also reinforce old certainties that only a few extraordinary souls were to be favored in life with creaturely success, and that all others somehow deserved their fate. In popular understanding the system of Darwinism came across morally as Calvinism with a scientific face—just as Social Darwinism's main ideological opponent, the altruistic socialism attractive to Howells and others (until events like the brutal stock-market collapse of 1893 and the 1894 Pullman strike forced them to choose political sides), could be shrewdly characterized by John Jay Chapman as a "religious reaction going on in an age which thinks in terms of money."

Calvinism itself, among old-stock Americans, had lost ground decade by decade to softer and easier theologies—to Deistic and Unitarian rationalism, to the revived upper-class Episcopalianism of the principal towns and cities, and to the periodic revival fervors of Methodists, Baptists, New-Light Congregationalists, and their pentecostal, perfectionist, utopian, and humanitarian offshoots. More and more after 1865 a generalized humanitarianism, a blurred faith in progress and collective benevolence, settled into place as the religion of those pretending to taste and education. (This is the popular background for a series of problem novels of the decade 1886–96—among others, Howells's *The Minister's Charge*, Edward Eggleston's *The Faith Doctor*, H. H. Boyesen's *Social Strugglers*, and Harold Frederic's *The Damnation of Theron Ware*—all dramatizing the retreat of the old faith before the constrictions, and temptations, of the new materialism.) The old Puritan moral severity, however, held fast as a weapon of last resort; new social frictions promptly brought it out of its scabbard. Julia Ward Howe's Grand Army of the Republic anthem—"He has loosed the fateful lightning of his terrible swift sword," "He is sifting out the hearts of men before his judgment seat"—spoke intimately to a population that still addressed itself to conflict in the exalted though not always clarifying language of Revelation, projecting every crisis as a return to Armageddon and every public campaign as a struggle for the nation's soul. The tenacity and persistence of this inherited frame of judgment best explain the primacy in both popular and professional thinking of millennialist and utopian responses to the institutionalized depravity, as it seemed to others besides Whitman and Mark Twain, of the new age.

During the 1880s and 1890s three books in particular, each a best-seller, tapped the enduring American instinct for, at once, prophetic outrage and evangelical hopefulness. To Henry George millennial anticipations were as natural as breathing, and they were equally so with his popular audience. Admirers of *Progress and Poverty* (1879) were not simply persuaded by George's arguments about economic inequity. They were converted to them, and to promises of a future when neither business cycle nor survival of the fittest but the Golden Rule would regulate human exchange. Conversions, however short-lived, followed also on the experience of reading Edward Bellamy's futuristic romance, *Looking Backward* (1888). There the nightmare (literally, for the protagonist) of 1880s capitalism vanishes before the heavenly city of A.D. 2000, a property-owner's paradise of technological innovation and obedience-disciplined efficiency—its wage laborers as docile as servants. The degree to which Henry Demarest Lloyd's exposé of Standard Oil, in *Wealth Against Commonwealth* (1894), spoke to the same evangelical-utopian habit of mind is apparent in a contemporary reviewer's praise of its "noble argument on behalf of industrial Christianity." The melodrama of Lloyd's indictment, sharpened by his vigorous phrase-making—his model for style was Emerson's epigrammatic plainspokenness—was ultimately in the service of one more American vision of social redemption. Like the old Calvinism, it gave voice in particular to an odd undercurrent of yearning for an escape from solitary powerlessness through sublimation within some larger massing of historical/universal force, some reawakening of the dream of a wholly covenanted life. (May we not observe a comparable imaginative plot in Henry James's *Portrait of a Lady* and the paradoxes of his heroine's search for a significant life, or in the recondite speculations of Henry Adams, who searched boldly for a single rule or law to unriddle all history but never stopped feeling that the highest personal good would be to submit intelligence to some overmastering historical purpose?)

Lloyd, who at Columbia College in the 1860s had subscribed to Professor Francis Lieber's economic liberalism, was alone among these reformer-prophets in being seriously attracted to the cause and ideology of socialism, though put off by what he saw as the rank material-mindedness of its American adherents. Beyond specific proposals for reform, socialism's great appeal was its suitability to the spiritual crisis of the new corporate-industrial age. Its transcendentalizing promise was of a new mass consciousness in which, Lloyd wrote late in life, all particular reforms would be for the sake of one loftier reform, "the self-creation of a better individual [by] putting him to work as his own God at the creation of a better society." (Knowing the apprehensions of those who would have money to buy his books, Lloyd also argued for socialism as the best way of regaining "social control.") With George and Bellamy, on the other hand, visions of a re-formed future have on examination an odd resemblance to structures of relationship in the fast-disappearing preindustrial past. An evident subtext in their writings is an unsubduable nostalgia for some "world we have lost." What after all supported the social equity each prophesied if not certain idealized memories of preindustrial New England village life or of the bluff freemasonry of new Western settlements before profiteering took absolute command? A comparable nostalgia became a staple of the new prose fiction. In Mark Twain's Mississippi Valley writings and George Washington Cable's Creole tales, in the New England genre studies of Harriet Beecher Stowe and Sarah Orne Jewett, but equally in the American evocations of Henry James's *Washington Square* and *The Europeans*, a warmth of affection for the relative stability of earlier manners more than balances the satirizing of provincial narrowness. So, too, Howells and Edith Wharton, in late novels like *The Vacation of the Kelwyns* and *The Age of Innocence* (each published in 1920 but set in the 1870s), are essentially forgiving of rigidities of attitude they had earlier pilloried. Sooner or later, in the bewildering onslaught of contemporary history, certain stranded formations and obsolete simplicities of human coexistence reentered political and storytelling imaginations alike as possessions dangerously squandered and essential to recover.

A new sense of chronic social crisis; unprecedented challenges to paramount beliefs and values, most of all to the old balance of monitored selfhood and historical, or evolutionary, expectation; a secularized evangelicalism that instinctively measured events and prospects against some transcendent perfection of justice, along with new scientized ideologies that seemingly opposed spiritual aspirations with hard biological fact; a pervasive nostalgia, matching a pervasive civil anxiety, for the simple egalitarianism attributed to times past—these intuitions and themes suffusing popular consciousness in the United States after 1865 were equally preoccupying to that first generation of university-based scholars who in the same years were systematically carrying out the professionalization, and full secularization, of the life of disciplined inquiry.

In background and early experience the men, as they almost exclusively were, of this intellectually rededicated generation were much like their more popular—and populist—contemporaries. (George, Bellamy, and Lloyd all at some point in the 1890s, like Hamlin Garland and Edgar Lee Masters among the younger writers, nourished hopes of an alliance with the Populist insurgence in national politics.) The resemblance is closest with those who established in American universities the new degree subjects of history, sociology, personality psychology, and—in inchoate form—cultural anthropology. Bellamy and Lloyd were sons of clergymen; so also were the influential Chicago sociologists William I. Thomas and, theological school training behind him, Albion Small. William Graham Sumner was ordained as an Episcopal minister before introducing Spencerism at Yale (where the maverick Thorstein Veblen heard him lecture); Sumner's chief ideological antagonist, Lester Ward (U.S. Geological Survey and Brown University), was a clergyman's grandson; the fathers of Richard T. Ely (Johns Hopkins, Wisconsin) and Simon Patten (Pennsylvania), prime movers in the founding of the American Economic Association and in the attack on laissez-faire fundamentalism, had been rigidly devout Presbyterians. The father of the labor economist John R. Commons (Wisconsin) was a Quaker abolitionist and, eventually, Christian Scientist; Commons himself, along with the Chicago social philosopher (and clergyman's son) George Herbert Mead, had attended Oberlin College in Ohio—where Thomas taught briefly in the 1890s—and Veblen, Carleton College in Minnesota, each a stronghold of Midwestern Congregationalism. It may be noted that the members of this generation who became the most influential administrators within the new university system—Presidents Eliot of Harvard, White of Cornell, Gilman of Hopkins, Harper of Chicago, Carey Thomas of Bryn Mawr—were, by contrast, the children of merchants and public officers.

It is impossible to mistake the evangelical trace across this "cognitive revolution," as it has been called, in late nineteenth-century American thought. (One product was the natural though politically undeveloped alliance between university-based social activists and the Social Gospel movement in liberal Protestantism.) Richard Ely, whose *Social Aspects of Christianity* appeared in 1889, spoke for the majority in remembering his initial sense of mission as "a burning desire to set the world right." More specifically he defined his generation's intellectual task as one of "fulfill[ing] the Second Commandment"—but fulfilling it scientifically, through empirical investigation. The moral utopianism of his vision of reform comes over clearly enough in its leading principles: "Distribution must be so shaped . . . that all shall have assured incomes, but that no one who is personally qualified to render service shall enjoy an income without personal exertion"—this moral extremism, to be fair, in a popular article for *Forum Magazine* in 1894. Similarly, in Ely's draft platform for the new American Economic Association, unmodified laissez-faire doctrines are identified as not merely "unsafe in politics" but "unsound in morals." (Ely's personal commitment each summer to the Chautauqua movement in regenerative popular education was much in keeping.) Given both popular and educated-genteel resistance to a social science that embraced evolution and cultural relativity as axiomatic, a certain missionary zeal and stubbornness were indispensable simply to professional survival. Sumner's position at Yale was put in peril in the 1880s by the objections of the university's philosopher-president Noah Porter to classroom use of Spencer's *Principles of Sociology*. A decade later Ely himself—target of a prolonged attack in E. L. Godkin's liberal-purist weekly, *The Nation*—was brought to public trial, at Wisconsin, for the alleged subversiveness of his social welfare thinking; at Leland Stanford in 1900 the Hopkins-trained sociologist E. A. Ross was dismissed outright for lending scholarly support to a populist-progressive legislative program. One particular impiety charged to the new empirical methods of social inquiry was "materialism," a term of denunciation also leveled in the mid-1880s at the narrative realism of *A Modern Instance* and *The Rise of Silas Lapham*.

In one decisive respect, however, the new professional and academic intelligentsia had an inestimable advantage not only over popular prejudice but over rearguard defenses of idealism and cultural gentility. This was in its increasingly informed relation to contemporary European learning. (The counterpart in prose fiction was a new critical openness to the methods and moral temper of Balzac and Flaubert, George Eliot, Zola, and Tolstoy.) America's extraordinary economic and technological expansion meant, inevitably, a continual broadening and intensifying of contacts with world culture and with movements of thought elsewhere initiated and developed. In the 1780s no one would have thought of inviting Immanuel Kant to transport his revolutionary philosophic message to the New World republic; no one in America knew there was any such message to be received. Sixty years later the American vogue of Thomas Carlyle came about only through the accident of Emerson's enthusiastic promotional effort, and Emerson himself could never persuade Carlyle of the advantages on both sides of an American lecture tour. But by 1909, even before *The Interpretation of Dreams* was translated into English, Sigmund Freud had come to lecture at Clark University, the New England Johns Hopkins. As after 1900 there would not again be a major international war without American intervention (beginning with Theodore Roosevelt's peacemaking between Russia and Japan in 1905), so there would not again be an important development in European thought or expression without, promptly enough, its American adaptation.

Among the founders of university-level inquiry in the United States after 1865 nearly everyone had studied at a German university and had returned armed with the archival realism of German historical scholarship and, not less important, a keen admiration for the new imperial-German commitment to a guided social welfare policy. The Germanic model, trained intelligence offering its professional findings to the whole civil commonwealth as well as within its own circle of learning, was a main influence in the fundamental late-century shift in sociocultural authority from a localized legal and ministerial elite to a national meritocracy of competitively trained specialists. But it was an influence that also worked to reinforce common expectations. The new disposition blended frictionlessly with the long-established tenor of American intellectual life as Tocqueville and others had perceived it: activist, practical, and oriented toward immediate material improvement and well-being. The same service-culture orientation and activist elitism are comfortably in place in 1875 in the program announced for the founding of Johns Hopkins University by its first president: "to prepare for the service of society a class of students who"—wherever situated—"will be wise, thoughtful, and progressive guides." It was a public fulfillment of what a dozen years earlier Henry Adams had privately called for from the world-historical perspective of his father's London embassy: "a national school of our own generation . . . to start new influences not only in politics, but in literature, in law, in society, and throughout the whole social organism of the country."

Not surprisingly the most influential American philosopher for nearly a half-century after 1900, John Dewey, would make collective human betterment his guiding purpose at every stage of a long, honorable life of speculation and advocacy; not surprisingly popular education, democratically conceived, was the cause nearest Dewey's heart. (His major treatise, *Democ-*

racy and Education, in 1916, was preceded in 1899 by *The School and Society*.) Dewey himself did not study in Germany. But he was at Johns Hopkins during its heroic early years, when the philosopher-genius C. S. Peirce and the experimental psychologist G. Stanley Hall taught there in company with the new-model social scientists, and when Veblen, Woodrow Wilson, and the historian Frederick Jackson Turner took advanced degrees. It was at Hopkins that Dewey began his transformation from an abstruse Hegelian idealism to the view—epitomized in his 1908 address, "Intelligence and Morals"—that philosophy's ultimate task is "to obtain more equable and comprehensive principles of action . . . in the interests of a common good," and that its practitioners are not to be content with serving merely their own discipline but must accept responsibility to the life and welfare of a society "whose conscience is its free and effectively organized intelligence."

Of Dewey, though, it must frequently be said that his arguments as written slide somewhat too easily between analysis and prophecy and tend to state as proved or given what may only be nobly desired. In the peroration just quoted on society's "conscience," both "effectively" and "is" are promissory rather than factually descriptive. They tell us what is wanted, not what has been shown to be the case. Such use of formulated conceptions to help bring about the state of mind necessary to some desired organization of things was, of course, of the essence of American pragmatism in its popularized form (much to the annoyance of its exacting founder, C. S. Peirce, who rebuked William James for terminological frivolousness and dismissed Dewey's contributions to the 1903 Chicago volume, *Studies in Logical Theory*, as so much idealized "natural history"). Pragmatism of this broader kind was as heartening a philosophy as transcendentalism had been to an earlier American era. It could not fail to give aid and comfort to writers, artists, makers and inventors of every species, who necessarily deal in unproved assessments and imperfectly verifiable propositions. Certainly pragmatism matched and confirmed the speculative outlook of the innovative architects Louis Sullivan, whose homiletic "Kindergarten Chats" date from 1901, and Frank Lloyd Wright, whose 1941 compilation *On Architecture* restates ideas worked out forty years earlier, and equally of the Connecticut composer Charles Ives—though all three, as in the pungent essays Ives wrote to accompany his *Concord* Sonata (1900–1915), tended to go directly to the Emersonian fountainhead for confirmation rather than to the newer, professionally framed arguments of Dewey and William James.

But pragmatism, Peirce's rigorous version excepted, is also the grand modern instance of a tendency the Spanish-born Harvard philosopher George

Santayana, from his invaluable outsider's perspective, attributed to the American mind in general: the tendency to entertain all its important ideas in the form of "premonitions and prophecies" and to let thought be dictated not by logical requirements but by what has accidentally forced itself on the thinker's personal attention. To Santayana, arguing the case in *Character and Opinion in the United States* (1920), the American intelligence displayed, all around, a settled "incapacity for education" in matters not directly touching "[its] own spontaneous life." ("United with great vitality," Santayana added, not without malice, "incapacity for education . . . is one root of idealism.") Such minds characteristically fail to distinguish their intellectual intention from "the potency in [themselves] and in things which is about to realise that intention." As mood directs, they "oscillate between egotism and idolatry"—or, as to method, between materialism and magic—and disconcertingly identify the swervings of private willfulness, which they idealize, with reality itself. The tough-talking naturalism of the newest American thought was, to Santayana, merely the newest form of this premature spiritualism.

Santayana's is a telling indictment. It played its part in the flurry of national self-examination that followed the breakdown of Progressive-era confidence during and after World War I. (An endorsement of this acidulous model of the self-entrapping American will would come in the life histories chronicled after 1920 by novelists from two younger generations: Willa Cather in *A Lost Lady*, Theodore Dreiser in *An American Tragedy*, F. Scott Fitzgerald in *The Great Gatsby*, William Faulkner in *Absalom, Absalom!*) Santayana's own coolness toward a problem-oriented liberal humanism, with its trust in instant educability, lingers in the expressed outlook of writers as different—among those who heard him at Harvard—as Wallace Stevens and Walter Lippmann, T. S. Eliot and John Reed, none of them especially notable (as a poet like Thomas Hardy, a social analyst like the precocious Randolph Bourne are notable) for warmth or discrimination of insight into conditional human selfhood. The cost of such studied coolness can be a troubling detachment from the actual passion and travail of mind under which, in modern society, the common life of men and women must be enacted. Given the immense new overgrowth of institutional life and the speculative constrictions of Darwinism, Marxism, anthropological or psychoanalytic determinism, to say nothing of Nietzschean inhumanism (rapidly coming into vogue toward the end of this period), what margin of freedom was left for ordinary individuality and purposefulness? On such a question Santayana—whose *Reason in Society* (1906) entrusts social health to a guardian-supervised change of heart among ordinary citizens—had relatively little to contribute. He only (it is of course philosophy's first task) helped clear the ground, keeping speculation alert to its own unsubduable appetite for self-delusion and error.

Two whose contributions in these years did rise from an intense and sustained personal engagement were the social-work pioneer Jane Addams and the black sociologist-historian W. E. B. Du Bois. Each, as member of a subpopulation effectively denied legal and vocational equality, was acutely sensitive to modern society's enormous power of exclusion. The radical split in the national mind that Santayana identified in "The Genteel Tradition in American Philosophy" (1911) as between aggressive material enterprise and high-minded abstraction, Jane Addams perceived as a corrupting "duality of conscience." Its power "to stifle the noblest effort in the individual because his intellectual conception and his achievement are so difficult to bring together" was grounded, she wrote in *Democracy and Social Ethics* (1902), in the social order itself, above all in "the separation of the people who think from those who work." (The heroine of Louisa May Alcott's 1870 novel, *Work*, identifies much the same experiential gap as a major obstacle to effective reform.) Jane Addams had—as did, *a fortiori*, the sociologist Du Bois in his passionate reconstruction of the "spiritual world" of American blacks in *The Souls of Black Folk* (1903)—a richer and more immediate understanding than most philosophers of the obdurate economy of human weakness and vulnerability. She had seen at first hand how men and women living too long under the threat of destitution and economic obsolescence can lose their capacity for self-government, and how young children forced into subsistence labor can be deprived not simply of physical health but of their evolutionary birthright. She saw also, in teaching experiments carried out at Hull House in Chicago, the residual capacity of the so-called dangerous classes to reassume the civil and moral powers men and women are born to. The visionary Tolstoy of *What to Do Then* touched Jane Addams as he had touched Howells, and led her to require of all education that it "free the powers of each man and connect him with the rest of life." A truly popular education would thus perform the comprehensive function Du Bois eloquently claimed for the Negro churches (*The Souls of Black Folk*, ch. X), giving both personal and collective expression to the ethical life of a whole people.

By comparison the more conventionally articulated social and behavioral thought of the liberal publicist Herbert Croly—whose manifesto, *The Promise of American Life* (1909), projected a transformation of the Progressivist impulse into a politics of national reconstruction—and even of the humanely eloquent Josiah Royce in philosophy, is likely to seem synthetic and, in application, more wishful than realistically observant. (Nobly wishful, in Royce's case; humankind would indeed be better off if by acts of will it could march down the path outlined in Royce's 1901 *summa*, *The World and the Individual*, toward a fulfillment at once individual and social.) Croly, who inherited notions of a rationally engineered human solidarity from his father's dedication to Auguste Comte's mid-nineteenth-century religion of humanity, feared one consequence in particular of the modern division of labor and the drive toward corporate concentration; this was the massive subdividing of the civil population into specialized functions and groups without capacity of their own to negotiate "a wholesome national balance." He thus identified a modern dilemma for which, soon after, fascism would emerge in Europe as the unacceptable solution. In contrast, Croly's own proposals for technological and managerial efficiency were designed to make democracy work, not to replace it.

Whether democracy remained workable under the aggrandizements of modern industrial capitalism is a question that seems less important in the writings of Thorstein Veblen (though Veblen does ask it) than a cultural anthropologist's quizzical curiosity about the process itself of institutional adaptation and change. Allied to the rhetorical irony that concentrated attention on such phenomena of modern life as "conspicuous consumption" or—defining industrial sabotage—"the conscientious withdrawal of efficiency," Veblen's neo-Darwinian analyses of the behavior of business society's leisure class (1899) and of American business enterprise as an ideological system (1904) quickly became part of the new century's enduring folklore. His moralized distinction between *engineer*, hero of disinterested creativity, and *financier*, manipulative and parasitic, has the imaginative authority of great fiction, and his celebration of the human species' indestructible "instinct of workmanship" mythopoeically balances the world-historical pessimism of his 1914 treatise bearing that title. Little wonder that as much as any other figure Veblen became the moral hero of the dispiriting panorama of John Dos Passos's 1930s trilogy, *U.S.A.*

Something of the same difference in force of understanding can strike us in comparing the philosophic legacy of Royce and of his older Cambridge (but not Harvard) contemporary, Charles Sanders Peirce. Much of Peirce's writing was too rigorously specialized to claim general attention—though his important early essays, "The Fixation of Belief" and "How to Make Our Ideas Clear," appeared in 1877–78 in *Popular Science Monthly*, the organ of the American Spencerians. (The mass of Peirce's difficult thought, once regarded as eccentric, is under admiring reexamination in our own semiology-fixated era.) Writing discursively, Peirce considered it a matter of methodological probity to argue by means of opaque neologisms whose sheer ugliness would repel anyone looking for short cuts. When his friend William James transformed "pragmatism" from a rule in logic into an all-purpose intellectual attitude, Peirce at once renamed his concept "pragmaticism" and reproved James for being insufficiently attentive to "the moral aspect of terminology."

On the great emergent issue of existential trust, of whether the individual consciousness could keep its bearings and organize its own destiny against the depersonalizing expansions of modern history, Royce, who gratefully borrowed Peirce's mathematics in postulating how individual selves might hold position within an infinitely expanding totality, fell back for psychological and ethical support on a "philosophy of loyalty" (1908). Loyalty—to some truth or truths, to the human collectivity, to existence itself—is affirmed as a vital and sufficient *principle* of behavior chiefly because, unlike the ethical "inner check" coincidentally propounded at Harvard by the self-proclaimed new humanist Irving Babbitt, it is so evidently a primal human *need* and *appetite*. All Royce's considerable forensic skill goes to establishing loyalty as the best because most natural solution to both spiritual and societal alienation, though contradictorily one whole chapter is devoted to the necessity of extended training in such loyalty, in the surrender of selfhood to causes outside itself. (Another who in these years fixed attention of the problem of reattaching human selfhood to some greater experiential whole was the University of Michigan social psychologist Charles Horton Cooley, whose *Human Nature and the Social Order* [1902], on the socialization of personality, explores the double premise that "a separate individual is an abstraction unknown to experience, and so likewise is society when regarded as something apart from individuals.")

But Peirce had realized from the beginning that a behavioral truth needing so much explanatory inculcation would not in and of itself stave off confusion and doubt. Peirce's starting point was the recognizably Emersonian, and Kantian, principle that what we are obliged to do in our sentient and intellective life we are—so far as may be known—already constituted to do. By formidable reasoning his 1903 lectures on pragmatism arrive at his own version of Emerson's intellectual *point d'appui* in the crucial sixth chapter of *Nature* (1836), which was simply that "God never jests with us." Everywhere in existence, Peirce declares, we will find "an element of Reasonableness to which we can train our own reason to conform more and more. . . ."

. . . we need not wait until it is proved that there is a reason operative in experience to which our own can approximate. We should at once hope that it is so, since in that hope lies the only possibility of any knowledge.

For Peirce as for Emerson, such "hope," which in the vernacular seems frail and unstable—"the thing with feathers," Emily Dickinson's meditation on it begins—is nevertheless the very engine of active, creative being.

So was it also for William James, the man "born afresh every morning" (his sister Alice's double-edged appraisal). It is fitting that an account of American intellectual life during the half-century after the Civil War end with James, who became as ebulliently persuasive a writer of speculative prose as America has produced, a master of both technical and popular exposition. James's insistence on submitting every reflective issue to the test of common experience was already established in 1880 when, precisely as regards hope and its painful contraries, he announced to the Harvard Philosophical Club that "the permanent presence of the sense of futurity in the mind has been strangely ignored by most [philosophic] writers" ("The Sentiment of Rationality"). "The fact is," he continued, "that our consciousness at a given moment is never free from the ingredient of expectancy." How consciousness actually behaves at given moments was William James's life-long preoccupation. It regulates both of his masterworks, *Principles of Psychology* (1890), with its brilliantly specific evocations of ordinary mental behavior, and *The Varieties of Religious Experience* (1902), the abounding open-mindedness of which rises from an intensely personal sense of the "inner authority and illumination" characterizing spiritual transactions however disconnected they may seem from the rest of life. James was so respectful of experienced reality that in a later essay, "Does 'Consciousness' Exist?" which Alfred North Whitehead saw as completing the long revolution out of Cartesian positivism, he could deliver an unabashed *no* to the question whether consciousness-as-such could be treated by speculative thinkers as any sort of substantial or unitary entity.

The power to make robust negations, even at one's own vital expense—to say *no* in blood as well as in thunder—was for William James a test of intellectual maturity, and a prerequisite to productive thinking. "It seems almost as if it were necessary to become worthless as a practical being," he wrote in "On a Certain Blindness in Human Beings" (1899), "if one is to hope to attain any breadth of insight into the impersonal world of worths as such." No more than in his brother Henry's fictional narratives of the "finer grain" of consciousness and feeling are social and historical concerns commonly at issue in William James's writing. Yet he understood very well how it is in the interest of institutional and collective health as well as of private satisfaction that "the energies of men," title of his presidential address to the American Philosophical Association in 1906, find full and natural release. So in a characteristically provocative address at the end of his life he defined the whole issue of human survival in the new era of global imperialism as one of developing not a mass instinct for "pacificism"— something against the grain of the human spirit—but a "moral equivalent of war" (1910). (*Ad bellum purificandum:* thus would his truest American inheritor, Kenneth Burke, inscribe his own monumental study of the varieties of human expressiveness.)

Extraordinarily different in temper and style from either Peirce's argumentative severity or Veblen's implacable moral naturalism, William James's thinking wonderfully complements theirs in its open-minded candor. And in its unflagging grace of style it articulates all the more directly the supple intellectual courage that within their American generation broke essential ground for the renaissance in imaginative literature of 1912 and after—for the confident, self-planted originality of Stein, Lewis, Hemingway, Fitzgerald, and Faulkner in prose fiction; of Eliot, Stevens, Frost, Pound, Williams, and Marianne Moore in the art and understanding of poetry.

Warner Berthoff

II. Genre Deliberations

Realism and Regionalism

Because their edges blur and their central meanings shift, the categories "realism" and "regionalism" cannot be conveniently separated. A simple division between the urban realism that accompanied the growth of industrial America in the post–Civil War period and the several regional literatures that flourished at the same time would lose sight of the complex aesthetic, social, and economic entanglements between them. If we instead judge realism from the 1870s through the early 1900s as a developing series of responses to the transformation of land into capital, of raw materials into products, of agrarian values into urban values, and of private experience into public property, then the city appears as one region among others, part of the national network of modernization actualized as much by the ties of language and literature as by new railroad lines and telegraph wires.

The transformation from muscle to mechanical power, wrote Josiah Strong in *The Twentieth Century City* (1898), "has separated, as by an impassable gulf, the simple, homespun, individualistic life of the world's past, from the complex, closely associated life of the present." By the same token, he noted, it now takes sixty-four men to make a shoe. Such ironic complication in modern life can be observed throughout the fiction of the period, which records a revolutionary change in the order of life comparable to that depicted by the great European and Russian novelists of the period. In the United States, as in parts of Europe, the nineteenth century was both an era of industrial progress and heightened materialism, and one of great colonial movements and migrations. In the case of America, this involved heavy European immigration and significant movements of the population from rural to urban areas in the East and Midwest; whereas the West experienced the significant immigration of Asian laborers and the continued dispossession of former Mexican landholders in the aftermath of the 1848 war. The growth of communication and transportation following the Civil War linked the regions of the country and made them newly aware of differences in speech and customs. Vernacular writing by Mark Twain, Sarah Orne Jewett, Hamlin Garland, and others is one manifestation of the variously held American theory (reflecting that of Hippolyte Taine in France) that realistic literature must embody the race, the milieu, and the historical moment of its author. In their often nostalgic attention to diverse regional customs eroded by standardized urban society, American regionalists share with European writers of the period like Thomas Hardy, Ivan Turgenev, and Knut Hamsun the belief that a work's "realism" resides both in its local details and in the larger transfigurations of national ideology to which it responds.

As it initially appeared in French aesthetic theory, "realism" designated an art based on the accurate, unromanticized observation of life and nature, an art often defiant of prevailing convention, as in the prose of Gustave Flaubert or the paintings of Gustave Courbet, whose authentic depictions of lower-class life and of nudes were banned from the Paris Exposition of 1855 but exhibited privately in the "Pavilion of Realism." To the European insistence on precise description, authentic action and dialogue, and moral honesty, the American tradition deriving from Walt Whitman, Nathaniel Hawthorne, Harriet Beecher Stowe, and Herman Melville adds a democratic openness in subject matter and style that breaks down rigid hierarchies even as it may indulge in imaginative disorder or utopian fantasy in order to probe the limits and power of a prevailing social or political reality. At times, as in William Dean Howells or Robert Herrick, there is a Balzacian attempt to give a comprehensive picture of modern life in its various occupations, class stratifications, and manners; at times, as in Stephen Crane or Theodore Dreiser, there is a fascination with the city as a region of mystery such as one finds in Charles Dickens, Feodor Dostoevsky, or Emile Zola. Such examples tempt one to argue that realism belongs with what is brutal or sordid, or with the open portrayal of class struggle. In this definition, where realism verges on a more overt naturalism, the "real" is identified as something biologically internal (what Frank Norris called the "red, living heart of things"), psychologically subconscious, or socially and economically oppressed. Accordingly, a muckraking classic like Jacob Riis's *How the Other Half Lives* (1890), because it exposes a terrain of vice and poverty while turning it into an "alien" spectacle, is easily parodied by Crane's *Maggie* (1893), in which city life seems a modernist theatrical experiment.

The narrative strategies by which the alien is made either brutish or exotic reflect in literature the imperatives of foreign colonialism and Progressive reform observable in the social and political thought of the period, which stressed the homogenization of American life through a process of economic control and cultural improvement. One result, increasingly evident in the realism of both city and country, is an anthropological dimension in which new "regions" are opened to fictional or journalistic exploration and analysis. The country's continued spirit of Manifest Destiny, peaking in imperial adventurism at the turn of the century, along with a sudden rise in anxiety about immigration, is not unrelated to the developments of capitalism but rather is its engine of power. For this reason, economic or political power can itself be seen to be definitive of a realist aesthetic, in that those in power (say, white urban males) have more often been judged "realists," while those removed from the seats of power (say, Midwesterners, blacks, immigrants, or women) have been categorized as regionalists.

As it links urban fiction to the colonized regions of "local color," realism thus participates in the rising spectator culture promoted by newspapers, magazines, advertising, photography, and later motion pictures. It shows America's psychological space, like its open range and developing city space, being mapped and marketed. Likewise the development of bureaucratic modes of social organization, rational theories of efficient production, mass marketing strategies, and new techniques for "reproducing reality" over wires or on records and film all have vital consequences for the novelist's theory and practice. The energetic transformations of the period serve to unite writers whose subjects and styles seem divergent but who all claimed to practice the new realism. Chief among them was William Dean Howells, who battled long to establish an audience for fiction attuned to the moral difficulties of a society threatened with rapid change. Because he linked American literary realism to its European counterpart and defined its means and range, Howells became the center and circumference of realism in America.

Together with his voluminous literary and cultural essays, the three dozen novels and short-story collections of Howells are a full record of the theory and practice of realism in America. Although they lack the innovative style that distinguishes Twain, Crane, and Henry James, or the mastery of urban psychology in Dreiser, Howells's works are punctuated by moments of great power. His centrality, moreover, derives as well from his influential role as the author of hundreds of essays and reviews in America's leading magazines and especially as editor of the *Atlantic Monthly* (1871–81) and resident critic for *Harper's* (1886–92), in both of which he promoted the work of the best European novelists and of other American writers, among them James, Crane, Garland, Twain, Herrick, Jewett, John De Forest, Frank Norris, Abraham Cahan, and Charles Chesnutt.

In 1872 Howells reviewed Taine's *History of English Literature* and the following year Turgenev's *Dimitri Roudine*. Between the theorist and the novelist, Howells may have found his own aesthetic: the realistic novel, unlike the historical romance or the sentimental melodrama, would be anchored in its own time and place, accord psychologically mimetic attention to the customs and actions of common people, and rely on observation and a "neutral" dramatic method of narration. Howells's realism focuses on the rising middle classes, while treating upper and lower classes largely as raw material for observed spectacle, and avoids indulging in either sentiment or naturalistic degradation. A passage from an 1895 essay on the Spanish realist Benito Pérez Galdós succinctly captures the implications and limits of Howells's theories: "Realism at its best is not tendencious. It does not seek to grapple with human problems, but is richly content with portraying human experiences." This aesthetic of observation also characterizes Howells's most extensive critical statement, *Criticism and Fiction* (1891), which was constructed of columns appearing monthly as "The Editor's Study" during his years at *Harper's*. Fiction, Howells argues, must be "true to the motives, the impulses, the principles that shape the life of actual men and women"; while it should avoid the clichéd morality of popular fiction, it must be infused with an ethical sense that will counter the rampant materialism of contemporary life. Although the volume is Howells's longest sustained work of criticism, it is less insightful and coherent than his best individual essays—for example, "Mark Twain: An Inquiry" (1901), "Henrik Ibsen" (1906), or "Henry James, Jr." (1882).

In his criticism, as in his fiction, realism often seems a means of middle-class regulation, even repression, rather than a liberating force. Yet while Howells believed that Dreiser's *Sister Carrie* failed in its moral duty to scrutinize Carrie's casual sexuality and that Norris's fiction was one-sided ("Life is squalid and cruel and vile and hateful, but it is noble and tender and pure and lovely, too"), he was quick to applaud Flaubert, Tolstoy, Hardy, and Ibsen for what he considered their morally exacting dramatizations of tragic passion. The fiction of Zola he considered often "filthy and repulsive," but he defended him as the "greatest poet of his day," surpassed only by Tolstoy, whose embracing Christian humanism and view of the moral course of the contemporary world influenced Howells from the mid-1880s on.

Howells's moderation in the treatment of both sexual and political themes was dictated in part by personal taste, in part by the taboos of magazine publication in America, and in part by his conviction that his own country still lacked the necessity of more radical treatment. A novel such as *Crime and Punishment* could hardly be imagined in America, he remarked, since "very few novelists have been led out to be shot, or finally exiled to the rigors of a winter at Duluth." When Howells sought to translate his awareness of the potential violence of American class conflict into fiction in *A Hazard of New Fortunes* (1890) he created a masterpiece defined in part by its flaws. The novel's power arises out of its fine characterization and panoramic observation, but Howells's refusal to call for revolutionary reform— to write as Dostoevsky or Zola would—creates an ideological paralysis that is characteristic of his work. Set in New York City, where he had moved from Boston in 1888 after taking over "The Editor's Study" for *Harper's*, the novel is the symbolic center of Howells's career. Because he had become the leading figure in the world of New England letters, his move to New York represented the transformation of American culture that occurred during the age of realism. In the last decades of the century the genteel, largely Anglo-Saxon tradition of American letters gave way to challenging representations of a more ethnically diverse, urbanized culture, a change that Howells portrayed with simultaneous approval and apprehension.

When Howells left Boston he was midway in a career that was an archetype of success for the American man of letters in an increasingly commercial literary world. Following his childhood and youth in Ohio, a period recalled in a number of candid and psychologically revealing volumes, notably *A Boy's Town* (1890) and *Years of My Youth* (1916), Howells set out for New England in 1860 at age twenty-nine as an experienced journalist and an aspiring poet. There he met Hawthorne, Emerson, Lowell, Holmes, and Thoreau, experiences later recounted in *Literary Friends and Acquaintance* (1900), and laid the basis for his career. Written just prior to the Civil War, his campaign biography of Abraham Lincoln led to an appointment as consul in Venice lasting until 1866. The Italian travel sketches he published in *The Nation* and the *Atlantic* were later collected in two popular volumes, *Venetian Life* (1866) and *Italian Journeys* (1867). When Howells turned to longer fiction in the next decade, in such novels as *A Foregone Conclusion* (1875) and *The Lady of the Aroostook* (1879), he continued to explore the conflict of American and European values in the popular Italian setting used also by Hawthorne, James, and Henry Fuller.

As an assistant editor of the *Atlantic* (1866–1871), Howells began his ascent in Boston literary culture. It was at this time that he began lifelong friendships with James (who would always think of Howells as *the* American novelist) and Twain, about whom he would later write the wonderful memoir, *My Mark Twain* (1910). It is also the period during which he began to perfect his fictional talents with a group of articles entitled *Suburban Sketches* (1871) and a travel novel, *Their Wedding Journey* (1871), which introduced Basil and Isabel March, characters modeled in part on Howells and his wife who would reappear throughout his work. Like the suburban sketches, the novel displays signs of Howells's fascination with the observation of city life, which peaks in *A Hazard of New Fortunes*. In the later novel, Basil March, now like Howells a magazine editor in New York, searches the squalid urban landscape for "picturesque" material, indulging his sense of sympathy for the immigrant poor while at the same time framing the "real" within his carefully cultivated point of view.

Because Howells appears cautious (if not anxiously timid) in comparison to the naturalists who extended his vision, it is possible to mistake his accomplishment and ignore the resistance his call for realism encountered from both genteel and popular audiences, the one eager for idealism, the other for what Howells called the "opium-eating of conventional romantic fiction." "The whole business of love, and love-making and marrying, is painted by novelists in a monstrous disproportion to the other relations of life," says the Reverend Dr. Sewell in *The Rise of Silas Lapham* (1885), a novel that attacks sentimental self-indulgence in love as fiercely as it does corruption and dishonesty in business. Silas Lapham's moral rise, accompanied by his financial fall and return to rural Vermont, depicts the victory of self-regulation over temptation, of rural values over urban; while his two daughters' romantic lives depict the triumph of rational marriage over the punishing conventions of sentimental fiction. Howells's examination of American sexual morality had been even more frank and provocative in *A Modern Instance* (1882), which released the creative tension that grew from such circumspect stories of conventional passion and courtship as *A Chance Acquaintance* (1873) and *A Fearful Responsibility* (1881). Although the novel ends by taking a peculiarly reactionary stand against liberal divorce law, it begins with a powerful display of the tragic compulsions of Euripidean drama suggested in Howells's original title for the book, "The New Medea." This discrepancy, though, may indicate the book's deepest tragedy: the social and sexual freedom of the complexly drawn New England heroine, Marcia Gaylord, is sacrificed first to her increasingly dissolute husband, second to the crippling prudery of her potential lover, and finally to the anxieties of her authorial creator. Despite the novel's troubled ending, lamented by Edith Wharton as an example of Howells's "incurable moral timidity," it remains a landmark in the American treatment of marriage under pressure from the decline in religious faith and the advance of commercialism.

Following *The Rise of Silas Lapham* there appeared in Howells's fiction in the mid-1880s a more vigorous insistence that realism directly confront the moral and material problems of society. Both his initial reading of Tolstoy in 1885 and his recoil from the execution of the Haymarket Square anarchists, whom he had publicly defended, sparked this growth of moral consciousness. The humanitarianism Howells found in the Social Gospel movement (which practiced charitable Christian reform work) was reflected during the 1890s in such essays as "Are We a Plutocracy?" and "Equality as the Basis of Good Society." In fiction he espoused his evolving theory of "moral complicity" in *The Minister's Charge* (1886) and in the powerful *Annie Kilburn* (1888). The latter is a novel of labor unrest in which the heroine, a philanthropic heiress, discovers that patronizing charity must give way to an aggressive fight for justice. These and subsequent novels probe the decay of moral values that seemed to Howells to accompany the industrialization of agrarian America. Providence becomes "accident" or "chance," as in *The World of Chance* (1893), in which an aspiring novelist resists the efforts of a socialist to show him his obligated role in a world "where luxury and misery are armed against each other." *A Traveler from Altruria*, a utopian novel written the following year in response to the worsening depression, imagines a bloodless revolution in which greed has disappeared and peaceful communism flourishes. Of the several hundred utopian novels that appeared from the 1880s through the early decades of the twentieth century, Howells's is much less significant than Edward Bellamy's *Looking Backward* (1888) or Ignatius Donnelly's *Caesar's Column* (1891). But it registers his sympathetic reaction to the economic hardships of the 1890s and adds a hopeful, if visionary, perspective to *A Hazard of New Fortunes*, in which Howells's ambivalence about the role literary realism should play in bringing about social justice is most evident. As though to illustrate his contention that he considered himself "a theoretical socialist and a practical aristocrat," Howells in *A Hazard of New Fortunes* turns away from the realities of labor violence much as he turned from the realities of divorce in *A Modern Instance*. But if the novel fails to meet head-on the conflict between wealth and justice, it does so by critically portraying in a series of taut, fully dramatized scenes the writer's own self-conscious conversion of what is alien and dangerous into the materials of voyeuristic literary exploitation.

The position of the artist's compromised integrity that Howells took up in his essay "The Man of Letters as a Man of Business" (1893) characterizes both Basil March and the magazine he edits; like the magazine, Howells's hero could appropriately be called the "missing link between the Arts and the Dollars." Although Howells disliked Balzac's melodramatic tendencies, he too was an enormously productive writer whose novels are often linked by repeated scenes and characters. Perhaps more important, he too (like his alter ego Basil March) took a businesslike approach to his writing. He negotiated handsome royalty agreements for himself and objected that the spread of public libraries would reduce the commercial value of books. Although Twain advertised himself more flamboyantly, Howells also skillfully marketed his talents and his written products, and in doing so made his art part of the commercial spectacle he dramatized.

None of Howells's later works matches *A Hazard of New Fortunes*, but several are noteworthy: *An Imperative Duty* (1891) for its portrayal of miscegenation; *The Landlord at Lion's Head* (1897), a naturalistic novel of manners split between feminine sensitivity and masculine, immoral power; *The Son of Royal Langbrith* (1904), which depicts the destructive illusions engendered in his family by a powerful dead father; and *The Leatherwood God* (1916), which anticipates Sinclair Lewis's *Elmer Gantry* (1927) in its combined exploration of religious mania and sexuality. Ironically, though Howells is his most obvious literary ancestor, Lewis among others considered Howells's realism somewhat tame, even quaint, by the time of his death in 1920. Yet no one had done more, as editor and as practicing novelist, to define the terms of American realism. However inadequate his theory and practice would come to seem—whether because of his timidity about human passion, his reluctance to write more openly about social ills, or his conservative sense of plot, style, and character—during his lifetime Howells *was* literary realism in America.

Howells's novels built around the contrast between rural, familial values and urban, corporate values echo the portrayal in much of the period's regional fiction of a sense of crisis or loss, a breakdown in the comparatively close-knit communities of pre–Civil War America. In a world increasingly defined by calculated zones of time and labor, and technologies of measurement and regulation, the sparsely populated, flawlessly sketched landscapes of the local colorists came to seem a lost world. The combined aura of timelessness and irrevocable decay that marks the genre's New England masterpiece, Sarah Orne Jewett's *The Country of the Pointed Firs* (1896), appears to the west in Hamlin Garland's *Main-Travelled Roads* (1891), and achieves a brilliant apotheosis in Willa Cather's *My Ántonia* (1920). As a literature of memory, local color often has elements of the historical novel; yet it strives to delineate not history's great figures or movements but the scant record of time's passage left when a simpler way of life succumbs to one more complex.

In the fiction of the most important New England local colorists, Sarah Orne Jewett and Mary Wilkins Freeman, memory is often lodged in the vestiges of a world of female domesticity. The country's internal migration of younger men and women to new urban areas has left behind a ghost world of spinsters, widows, and bereft sea captains. Myth, colloquial narratives, and riveting emotion animate Jewett's work, creating in her Maine landscapes an effect of natural simplicity merged with exquisite craft: a scene of trout-fishing in "The Dunnet Shepherdess," an epilogue story to *The Country of the Pointed Firs*, suggests nothing so much as Ernest Hemingway, in whom local color sentiment and the shock of modernist realism would be combined in the next generation.

In the preface to her early collection of stories, *Deephaven* (1877), Jewett speaks of her desire to find "some trace of the lives which were lived among the sights we see and the things we handle." Widely read in European literature and later a figure in Boston literary circles, Jewett nevertheless devoted her writing life to recording the traces—formal customs, speech, legends, everyday habits and manners—of a native American life disappearing from view. She did so by publishing her stories in the nation's leading magazines after the initial encouragement of Howells (who wrote her, "Your voice is like a thrush's in the din of all the literary noises that stun us so"). Her work is thus representative of a paradoxical effect of much local color writing, namely, that the same communication and transportation developments that closed the nation's sectional divisions following the Civil War and brought isolated communities closer also began to destroy rural "islands" of life. Local color records in part the rustic border world rendered exotic by industrialism but now made visible and nostalgically charged by the nation's inexorable drive toward cohesion and standardization.

Also praised by Howells (for her resemblance to Turgenev), Freeman surpasses Jewett in her ability to combine contemporary social problems with a stylistically detailed apprehension of regional character. In the most representative stories in *A Humble Romance* (1887) and *A New England Nun* (1891), a latter-day Puritanism can destroy emotional growth but result as well in ambivalent power among the women who are most often its victims. "A New England Nun," "Sister Liddy," and "The Revolt of 'Mother'" portray the determined resistance of women to pain inflicted upon them by foolish or crude men. Her novel *Pembroke* (1894) stands between Hawthorne's stories and Edith Wharton's brilliant New England works, *Ethan*

Frome (1911) and *Summer* (1917), as a study of the "dreadful warping of a diseased will" that tears apart two lovers and their families. *The Portion of Labor* (1901) belongs to the popular genre of labor-romance novels also written by Howells, Isaac K. Friedman, Winston Churchill, and others during the period. Those, like Freeman's, especially concerned with the family and the lives of women can be traced to Rebecca Harding Davis's uncanny industrial romances, *Life in the Iron Mills* (1861) and *Margret Howth* (1862), Louisa May Alcott's *Work* (1873), and more pedestrian sentimental novels like Elizabeth Phelps's *The Silent Partner* (1871) and Amanda Douglas's *Hope Mills* (1880). The heroine of *The Portion of Labor* is a young girl who resembles little Eva in *Uncle Tom's Cabin* in her childhood awareness of "the awful shadow of the labor and poverty of the work world," and she thus represents an overt translation of the abolitionist benevolence Stowe's child heroine had made famous into the new arena of industrial "wage-slavery," and of the archetypes of antebellum romance into the social realism of America's emerging cities.

Comparable to Jewett and Freeman in her use of local setting and manners is the Tennessee writer Mary Murfree, who wrote under the pseudonym Charles Egbert Craddock. Her popular story "The Dancin' Party at Harrison's Cave" appeared in Howells's *Atlantic* in 1878 and was collected in *In the Tennessee Mountains* (1884). Like other regional work both in the South and in New England, Murfree's sought to record local material threatened with extinction. Her several dozen stories and eight novels combined careful research with tall-tale humor, often depicting the proud and superstitious lives of Tennessee mountain dwellers. *The Prophet of the Great Smoky Mountains* (1885) verges on natural mysticism, while *In the "Stranger People's" Country* (1891) displays the archaeological stance of much local color in its tale of an urban outsider whose study of the burial ground of prehistoric mountain pygmies leads to an involvement in a local romantic rivalry. Murfree's fiction, along with Jewett's, offers a window into secluded territory receding into a past paradoxically contemporaneous with the urban worlds of Howells and Crane. With Garland and Bret Harte in the West, Murfree and Jewett defined local color as a fictional region at once curiously alien and yet entirely familiar to the native American imagination.

The South stands apart from other regions in that the history of its literature from the end of the Civil War to the early 1900s is of necessity an account of continued sectional pride, conflict with the laws and customs imposed on it during Reconstruction by a Northern government, and participation in the slow process of national healing. Like that of New England, the South's literature is also one of memory, although in its case the remembered way of life disappeared in a bloody military defeat, never to return in actuality but often to return over the next century in the magnificent dreams probed with both tragic sympathy and devastating irony by such writers as Mark Twain, William Faulkner, and Robert Penn Warren.

Just as the great urban realists were often foreign or native newcomers, so several of the most important writers about the South in the postwar period were Northerners who saw the lost Confederate world and its Reconstruction aftermath within a different field of vision. The first of them, John William De Forest, ended his career as he began it, with rather conventional romantic novels, even though his one lasting work of fiction, *Miss Ravenel's Conversion from Secession to Loyalty* (1867), prompted Howells to say of him that he was "a realist before realism was named." Howells thought the novel comparable to Tolstoy's *War and Peace*, and it is easily the most impressive fictional treatment of the Civil War next to Crane's more stylistically innovative *The Red Badge of Courage* (1895). Moreover, the magazine sketches based on De Forest's experience as a Union officer that appeared in *Harper's* in the 1860s (posthumously collected in 1946 as *A Volunteer's Adventures*) are a brilliant account of the actuality of battle and the likely source of much of Crane's best material. De Forest did not flinch from the war's toil and carnage, and in *Miss Ravenel's Conversion* he made his Southern heroine's conversion to the cause of union emblematic of the war's divisive wounds. Besides two other strong novels, *Kate Beaumont* (1871), the naturalistically detailed story of feuding Southern families, and *Honest John Vane* (1873), a satire on the political corruption of the Crédit Mobilier, De Forest is often remembered for originating the search for "the great American novel" in his essay of that title (1868), in which he argued that *Uncle Tom's Cabin* was to date the most likely candidate.

A second posthumous volume of sketches follows De Forest's career as an officer in the Freedman's Bureau in South Carolina, but it adds little to the controversial picture of the postwar South drawn by Albion Tourgée. Tourgée's novels are sometimes blind to Southern integrity and to their own impractical doctrines of equality; but if realism is measured by the fusion of historical materials and imaginative action, Tourgée, a Northern lawyer who became active in the Reconstruction politics of North Carolina (a carpetbagger par excellence), has few peers. *'Toinette* (1874; reissued in 1881 as *A Royal Gentleman*) employs the story of tragic love between a mulatto servant and an aristocratic Confederate officer in order to attack the destructive caste pride that, as Tourgée saw it, had "its root in slavery, but its flower and fruitage in freedom." White pride of caste is attacked as well in *Bricks Without Straw* (1880), which argues that black cultural advance and material progress is thwarted by the violent tactics of the Ku Klux Klan. To his most important novel, *A Fool's Errand* (1879), Tourgée even appended a short volume entitled *The Invisible Empire*, which, like Stowe's *A Key to Uncle Tom's Cabin*, bolsters the fictional assault on racism and the Klan by a compilation of journalistic, congressional, and official Klan documents. As a work that combines precisely observed detail with philosophical speculation, and that presses at the very limits of fiction's manipulation of historical materials in its explosive critique of both Northern and Southern policies, *A Fool's Errand* belongs in the category of such visionary works of nineteenth-century realism as *Moby-Dick* and *A Connecticut Yankee in King Arthur's Court*.

Tourgée's later work, like De Forest's, declines in power, in his case perhaps because the harrowing work and ultimate failure of Reconstruction drained his best energies. By the 1880s, moreover, the sections of the country were becoming reunited culturally and economically if not politically, so much so that Tourgée could write in "The South as a Field for Fiction" (1888) that American literature had become "distinctly Confederate in sympathy." A Northern cultural campaign to "Americanize" the South began soon after the war, and by the 1880s, loyalty to the Union and nostalgic celebration of the Lost Cause, strikingly enough, had merged in much popular entertainment and serious literature. Leading Northern magazines offered work by George Washington Cable, Joel Chandler Harris, Murfree, and others to a more urban Northern audience intrigued by the exotic South. Southern themes and characters appeared in the work of Howells, James, and Constance Fenimore Woolson. The more ideologically charged remembrances of leisured plantation life and contented slaves by writers devoted to racial superiority also appealed to an audience embroiled in the social and economic questions of racial equality. Questions about the place of blacks in American society that emancipation had produced were reflected in similar racist reactions to Jews, Irish, Italians, Asians, and others among the large new groups of immigrants seeking to become Americans. The nostalgic cult of the Confederacy that accompanied the South's literary revival beginning in the 1880s thus reflected both sectional and national anxieties about modernization and the blurring of racial boundaries that it entailed. The stage dramatizations of Thomas Dixon's defenses of the Klan, *The Leopard's Spots* (1902) and *The Clansman* (1905), were immensely popular, as was D. W. Griffith's 1915 film version, *The Birth of a Nation*. But the artistically wooden melodrama of Dixon's overtly racist novels pales beside the age's most brutal and darkly comic critique of racism, Twain's *Pudd'n-*

head Wilson (1894), which ridiculed Confederate nostalgia and adumbrated the Supreme Court's tragic decision in favor of a "separate but equal" policy in *Plessy* v. *Ferguson*. In a nation of contending racial voices, Twain's burlesque suggests, "reality" inheres as much in the imagined narratives that constitute a culture as in the "fictions" of law and doctrine one people promulgates to control another.

The role of black writers in American realism is thus special, not only because, like European and Asian immigrants of the period, they added a distinctive voice to American fiction, but also because their assimilation continued to challenge the extent of democratic freedoms on which realism was based. Dialect stories like Charles Chesnutt's *The Conjure Woman* (1891), an ironic variation on Joel Chandler Harris's Uncle Remus tales, and Paul Laurence Dunbar's *Folks from Dixie* (1898) were often trapped between an authentic presentation of folk materials and the distorting expectations of a largely white audience. But Dunbar's novel *The Sport of the Gods* (1901), naturalistically portraying the breakup of a black family driven to the urban North after a wrongful criminal charge, presages Richard Wright; while W. E. B. Du Bois's *The Quest of the Silver Fleece* (1911) mirrors Northern labor novels in its depiction of blacks in conflict with the cotton economy of the modern South. Best known for his sentimental tragedy of "passing," *The House Behind the Cedars* (1900), Chesnutt answered the picture of Reconstruction produced by Southern conservatives in an exceptional novel, *The Marrow of Tradition* (1901). Its story of tangled social and cross-racial familial violence, built around an actual 1898 race riot in Wilmington, North Carolina, reveals that "our boasted civilization is but a veneer, which cracks and scales off at the first impact of primal passions." With similar power, Pauline Hopkins's *Contending Forces* (1900) links antebellum slaveholding violence in the Caribbean and the South to contemporary racial oppression by means of a chronicle of several generations of the black American family. Her title page quotes Emerson: "The civility of no race can be perfect whilst another race is degraded."

Even if Reconstruction served to strengthen the Confederate myth, Dixon and the more able Thomas Nelson Page were perhaps no more biased in their account of it than Tourgée. Page's social essays, collected in such volumes as *The Old South* (1892) and *The Negro* (1904), are often defiant and racist in tone, but they also contain reasoned attempts to correct Northern misconceptions about the relationship between the Confederacy and the New South. Although punctuated by virulent racism, his best novel, *Red Rock* (1898), follows the then widely accepted argument that the Klan arose originally as a defensive organization and depicts the destruction of cherished

Southern values by discontented blacks aroused by a militant carpetbagger government. As a reply to Tourgée the novel has merit, but its artistry is less impressive than that of the dialect stories Page collected in *In Ole Virginia* (1887). Among the most influential and significant, "Marse Chan" is an ex-slave's sentimental reminiscence of antebellum life; but "No Haid Pawn," an exciting if improbable story of a haunted 1850s plantation, reveals the race nightmare buried within the benign myth. The most popular Southern writer, throughout all parts of the country, was the Georgian Joel Chandler Harris. His newspaper sketches of a former slave named Uncle Remus, who narrated the tales of Brer Rabbit and Brer Fox, grew into a brilliant exploration of black dialect and folklore that generated an immediate, more ironic reply in Chesnutt's Uncle Julius in *The Conjure Woman* and would influence later writers like William Faulkner and Ralph Ellison and permeate American popular culture. The stories of Uncle Remus, collected in such volumes as *Uncle Remus: His Songs and Sayings* (1881), *Nights with Uncle Remus* (1883), and *Uncle Remus and His Friends* (1892), do not entirely whitewash the Old South but maintain a taut balance between minstrel humor and a subversive critique of slavery and racism. While Harris's other short fiction and novels—for example, *Free Joe and Other Georgian Sketches* (1887) and *Gabriel Tolliver* (1902)—speak with moderation of Reconstruction and its aftermath, the Uncle Remus stories offer an instance of popular work grounded in local folklore that is more psychologically revealing than sophisticated narrative and speaks with an authentic and original American voice.

At once Southern and cosmopolitan, New Orleans produced some of the nation's best literature in the last decades of the century. The work of Grace King collected in *Balcony Stories* (1893); the Cajun stories of Kate Chopin in *Bayou Folk* (1894) and her lyric novel of discovered sexual freedom, *The Awakening* (1899); and Lafcadio Hearn's beautifully evocative Gulf Coast novel *Chita* (1889) all combine regional materials with artistic craft. Hearn's New Orleans and Caribbean sketches, along with his several important volumes of tales based on the folk stories of Japan, show the merging of *fin-de-siècle* aestheticism with local color's precise observation. Most notable of the New Orleans writers, however, is George Washington Cable, a Confederate cavalryman who wrote successfully in several fields and genres. His 1885 argument for black rights in "The Freedman's Case in Equity"—a view expanded the same year in *The Silent South* and later in *The Negro Question* (1890)—aroused the indignation of Southerners; and his publication of slave and Creole musical scores had an important impact on the development of American jazz. Both the commitment to equality and the painstaking interest in local customs mark Cable's fiction as well. Like his stories in *Old Creole Days* (1879), and his nonfiction in *The Creoles of New Orleans* (1884), his novels were often based on hours of research into municipal records and newspapers. His great work, *The Grandissimes* (1880), is set before the Civil War, a strategy Twain also employed in *Adventures of Huckleberry Finn* and *Puddn'head Wilson* in order to measure ironically the similarities between antebellum slavery and postwar racial conflict. Its dense social texture, its violent tale of miscegenation and fratricidal betrayal, its lurid account of Bras-Coupé, an African king reduced to humiliating bondage as an American slave—all these elements raise the novel above sheer regional interest and, as later in Faulkner, suggest an intensification into mythic, psychological realism. Rivaling Cable's fiction in a sympathetic portrayal of the black man's plight is the work of Opie Read, a native Tennessean whose novel *My Young Master* (1896) powerfully attacks slavery, effectively undermines the ideology of white supremacy, and poignantly depicts the dilemma of the mulatto.

The alliance between South and West that accompanied the rise of Populism in the early 1890s did not produce a Southern version of Hamlin Garland. The Kentucky novelist James Lane Allen, though hardly a Populist, may be seen as a peculiar fellow traveler. His attack on the genteel tradition of Howells and James in "Two Principles in Recent American Fiction" (1897) advocates a masculine naturalism mixed with idealism, as in *The Reign of Law* (1900), a Hardyesque tale of shattered Victorian ideals set in the Kentucky hemp fields. *The Choir Invisible* (1897), a popular pioneer romance; *Summer in Arcady* (1896), which tells of a young girl's pastoral maturation; and *The Bride of the Mistletoe* (1909), a mythically fraught portrait of modern marriage, suggest Allen's broad scope and locate him midway between a regionalist and modernist sensibility. The same might be said of Amélie Rives, a Virginian aristocrat whose romantic novels and tales often treated the lower classes sympathetically and created strong, assertive women characters. Her impressionistic short novel *The Quick and the Dead?* (1888) is a bold psychological study of a young widow's sexuality that anticipates the work of Chopin.

In her fictional exploration of changing social roles and depiction of strong women characters, Rives also anticipates Ellen Glasgow, for whom the transition between Old and New South is a constant theme. Although Glasgow is best known for later novels such as *Barren Ground* (1925) and *Vein of Iron* (1935), her early work includes novels of bohemian New York, a fine Civil War novel, *The Battle-Ground* (1902), and *The Deliverance* (1904), the haunting story of a family dispossessed of their estate by its former overseer. Glasgow's ability to deal with a range of characters is even more evident in *The Voice of the People* (1900), which is concerned with complex class relations and the rise of lower-class whites in postwar Virginia. Glasgow once said of her novel that it was the "first work of genuine realism to appear in Southern fiction." This may claim too much, but there is no doubt her clear-eyed view of social and economic realities in the emerging New South elevated her above her romantic predecessors. "I had not revolted against the sentimental fallacy in order to submit myself to the tyranny of the Northern genteel tradition," she later wrote, echoing both Allen and the urban naturalists in her thrust at Howells. Like her predecessors, however, Glasgow portrayed a South rich in folk and intellectual materials, at once unique, proud, and anxious to reassert in literature, as in political and economic life, its vigorous and undiminished traditions.

Glasgow's desire to probe the "harsher realities beneath manners, beneath social customs, beneath the poetry of the past, and the romantic nostalgia of the present," allies her with Crane, Dreiser, and Garland. Like Glasgow, Hamlin Garland in turn represents in his fiction the conflict of a native reservoir of land with a modern commercial order. His lecture "Local Color in Fiction," for example, was delivered at the 1893 World's Columbian Exposition in Chicago, where technology and America's great natural resources were equally celebrated. Garland's lecture may have been a less significant event than Frederick Jackson Turner's expounding of his famous frontier thesis in the same arena, yet it too marks symbolically the union of the agrarian and urban traditions in a city and on an occasion that quickly became symbolic of America's cultural and industrial progress.

The Western tradition of which Garland is a more complex exponent can be traced to frontier writing early in the century, but its first representative in the age of realism is Bret Harte, whose brief career coincided with the nation's fascination with a West opened up by the transcontinental railroad in 1869. The editor of the *Overland Monthly* in California, Harte became famous overnight in 1868 with picturesque gold-country stories like "The Luck of Roaring Camp" and "The Outcasts of Poker Flat," and was able to command from Howells the royal sum of $10,000 in 1871 for work in the *Atlantic*. He helped to create a lasting audience for dime western novels as well as for historical romances of American Indian and pioneer conflict like Helen Hunt Jackson's *Ramona* (1884). In his use of local dialect and landscape he also initiated the vogue of Western "local color" that by the end of the century would be the subject of highly stylized satire in Crane's "The Bride Comes to Yellow Sky" (1898) and "The Blue Hotel" (1899). During the same period the West Coast also witnessed the significant development of an often oppressed Asian community, whose urban experience was first recorded in the short stories collected in *Mrs. Spring Fragrance* (1912), by the British-born Chinese American Edith Maud Eaton writing under the pen name Sui Sin Far.

From the Homestead Act of 1862 through the ascendance of Theodore Roosevelt, the West embodied the dream of America's Manifest Destiny and defined the nation's political and economic course in critical ways. Goaded by gold-inflicted debts, railroad corruption, and fears of corporate manipulation and foreign conspiracy, the Populists of the early 1890s both embodied and capitalized on the failure of America's garden utopia, the lost Jeffersonian world fallen prey to industrial advances. Out of this despair came powerful revivalist-tinged writing that challenged the pastoral ideal. But by the end of the century the agricultural and industrial recovery, along with the nationalist pride evoked by the Spanish-American War, gave the West a fresh mythic dimension exemplified in the raw power of Frank Norris's *McTeague* (1899) and *The Octopus* (1901), the Western landscape writing of Joaquin Miller, John Wesley Powell, and John Muir, such masculine adventure tales as Richard Harding Davis's *Soldiers of Fortune* (1897), and Theodore Roosevelt's celebration of Anglo-Saxon virtues in *The Winning of the West* (1889) and *The Strenuous Life* (1900).

Of special value as an index of the demise of Mexican power in the face of new Anglo settlement are the numerous *mexicano* autobiographical narratives collected in Hubert Howe Bancroft's *History of California* (1884–90), as well as independent works such as Mariano G. Vallejo's unpublished five-volume "Recuerdos historicos tocante a la alta California" (1875).

To the extent that the new Anglo-Saxonism arose from the territorial conquests of the Mexican War and directly influenced attitudes toward later immigrants, especially East European Jews crowding into New York, the idea of the "West" can be understood in the context of growing debate over the power of the supposedly superior race to determine the course of American destiny. But it may also be viewed as an arena for the struggle between economic progress and fading ideals of male independence and self-reliance. Owen Wister's *The Virginian* (1902), dedicated to Roosevelt, portrays the vanished world not of Eastern America but of nineteenth-century Wyoming. Yet its tale of the naturally aristocratic cowboy transplanted from Virginia to the West makes his courage, his enterprise, and his rugged individualism the signs of a true democracy disappearing under pressure from corporate and alien forces.

Equally influential in the development of a regionalist aesthetic was the group of Midwestern writers whose work leads toward Booth Tarkington's elegaic drama, *The Magnificent Ambersons* (1918), and Sinclair Lewis's stinging satire, *Main Street* (1920). The first of them was the circuit rider and Bible salesman Edward Eggleston, whom Garland would call "the father of us all." His novels, influenced by Taine's theories of race and milieu, show a careful attention to the dialect and manners of frontier Indiana, Illinois, and Ohio. *The Hoosier Schoolmaster* (1871) and *The Circuit Rider* (1874) are for the most part adventurous entertainments; but *The End of the World* (1872) and *Roxy* (1878) are striking critiques of religious fanaticism. An influential Chicago literary figure who wrote significant histories of that city, Joseph Kirkland was also praised by the younger Garland, who thought his fiction "as native to Illinois" as Tolstoy and Turgenev were to Russia, and who sought him out in Chicago when starting his own career. Kirkland's *Zury* (1887) and its sequel *The McVeys* (1888) are enlivened by the coarse prairie language of their hero, Usury Prouder, whose greed teaches a Populist lesson: "Money-making . . . is like climbing a chimney that grows narrower toward the top; one reaches a place where he can get neither up nor down, and is enveloped in dirt and darkness till he dies." An even darker picture of Midwestern life appears in the work of Kansas newspaperman Edgar Watson Howe, whose eerie *The Story of a Country Town* (1884) looks forward to Sherwood Anderson and Carson McCullers without rising to their level of craft. Malice and insanity pervade this tale of a failed agrarian dream, which was based on Howe's own memories and observations of small-town rural America and elicited the praise of Howells, Twain, and Garland. Howe's brutal picture of family betrayal and psychic collapse is moderated, however, in the formally experimental *A Man Story* (1888) and *The Anthology of Another Town* (1920), as well as the autobiographical memoir *Plain People* (1929).

The achievement of Hamlin Garland that crowned the Midwestern realist tradition was based on his theory of "veritism" articulated in *Crumbling Idols* (1894). The essays in that volume heralded the native qualities of local color and demanded that American literature, in order to be both great and national, "deal with conditions peculiar to our own land and climate." Garland's aesthetic follows Whitman in calling for a democratic art that breaks with corrupt and dying European traditions in order to explore the "new fields" of Midwestern and Far Western America. His theories drew strength from memories of his youth, when his family migrated from Maine to Wisconsin (where Garland was born) to Minnesota to Iowa and finally to South Dakota. But that experience also showed him the bitter toil and loneliness of rural life. Exacerbated by the guilt he felt about leaving his family to

move to Boston in 1884, the difficulty of Garland's escape from rural hardship became the theme of his best fiction, which was warmly promoted by
Howells and collected in *Main-Travelled Roads* (1891) and *Prairie Folks* (1893).
Just as his criticism may be seen as the next step from Howells's "commonplace" realism to the unguarded exploration of hardship and vice by the
naturalists, Garland's short fiction, in wrenching stories like "A Branch Road,"
"Up the Coulee," or "Lucretia Burns," depicts common life in the combined humility and degradation that he would recall from an 1887 return
visit to South Dakota: "The houses, bare as boxes, dropped on the treeless
plains, the barbed-wire fences running at tight angles, and the towns mere
assemblages of flimsy wooden sheds with painted-pine battlement, produced on me the effect of an almost helpless and sterile poverty."

His popular autobiographical volumes *Boy Life on the Prairie* (1899), *A Son
of the Middle Border* (1917), *A Daughter of the Middle Border* (1921), and two
others recalled his frontier childhood and mature life as a writer. In their
illustration that "free land was receding at railroad speed," they offered in
popular, often romantic form the radical argument Garland made in lectures on Edward Bellamy, Herbert Spencer, and Henry George, in his
campaign for the Populist cause in Iowa, and in two novels of political
corruption set against a background of Populist revolt, *Jason Edwards* (1892)
and *A Spoil of Office* (1892). Later works that reflect his travels in the Far
West and the nation's renewed interest in the spirit of the frontier include
The Eagle's Heart (1900), a heroic romance of Colorado; *The Captain of the
Gray-Horse Troop* (1902), a tale of war with the Teton Sioux, praised by
Roosevelt; and *The Book of the American Indian* (1923), a book of finely rendered tales and legends. *Money Magic* (1907) and *The Moccasin Ranch* (1909),
mixing naturalism with elements of romance, recast the figure of the oppressed pioneer woman but are less effective than his short stories and his
striking 1895 novel, *Rose of Dutcher's Coolly*, which was attacked for its open
depiction of a young girl's sexual awakening. The brilliant first half of the
later novel equals Thomas Hardy and D. H. Lawrence in its revelation of
Rose's burgeoning natural desires; her life in Chicago, where she must balance her writing career against her prospects for marriage and her remembrance of plains life, is less engagingly portrayed but anticipates Dreiser's
Sister Carrie and Cather's *The Song of the Lark* (1915) in its view of the magnetic attraction of Chicago upon the artistic Western personality. With Crane,
Garland may be said to have carried forward Howells's realist aesthetic. He
introduced the "gaunt, grim, sordid, pathetic, ferocious figures" (as Howells wrote in his review of *Main-Travelled Roads*) that the next generation of
writers would take as their central characters, and he recorded with pano-

ramic intensity and acute historical consciousness the dissolution of America's Western garden.

The breakdown of the agrarian myth occurred in relative proportion to the rise of the corporation, with its dramatic new social and economic pressures acting to reform American beliefs and manners. Capitalism's transfiguration of material reality—what Joseph Schumpeter called its process of "creative destruction"—produced an array of fiction devoted to economic life in the industrial mill, the ghetto sweatshop, the skyscraper, and the board of trade. Some of the most striking is set nowhere at all—that is, in a utopian future like that of Edward Bellamy's immensely popular *Looking Backward* (1888), which contrasts a collectivist paradise of the year 2000 with the urban misery of the 1880s, or Bradford Peck's *The World a Department Store* (1900), which envisions a cooperative business utopia, or Ignatius Donnelly's *Caesar's Column* (1890), which forecasts a fascist apocalypse symbolized by a monumental tower of corpses and cement. Utopian fiction extended the largely romantic treatment of labor in such novels as Thomas Bailey Aldrich's *The Stillwater Tragedy* (1880), John Hay's *The Breadwinners* (1884), and Edward King's *Joseph Zalmonah* (1893) into the arena of prophetic fantasy. Inspired by the rise of American socialism between 1900 and 1912, the best of labor fiction, Isaac K. Friedman's *By Bread Alone* (1901) and Winston Churchill's *The Dwelling Place of Light* (1917), combines powerfully drawn descriptions of immigrant millwork with naturalistic tragedy and cross-class socialist romance.

Such a diversity of responses to the problems of labor and technological progress indicates that no one strategy of "realism" seemed adequate to portray the effects of capitalism across the spectrum of American life. Especially important were novels of political corruption like Henry Adams's *Democracy* (1880) or H. H. Boyesen's *The Mammon of Righteousness* (1891), and chronicles of the competitive business world like Howells's *The Quality of Mercy* (1892) or Will Payne's *The Money Captain* (1898). Indeed, when Howells reviewed Thorstein Veblen's sociological study *Theory of the Leisure Class* in 1899, he concluded that the "evolution of the American magnate" was a great field for the novel, since it "sums up and includes in itself the whole American story: the relentless will, the tireless force, the vague ideal, the inexorable destiny, the often bewildered acquiescence." Just this mix of critical realism and native admiration appears in the period's best business novels, Dreiser's *The Financier* (1916), Herrick's *The Memoirs of an American Citizen* (1905), and Abraham Cahan's *The Rise of David Levinsky* (1917).

In his 1889 essay "Realism," Cahan, editor of the *Jewish Daily Forward*, called for an art of social revelation and protest that would represent the virtues of Howells and Tolstoy. Applauded by Howells along with Crane's *Maggie* as a new urban fiction, Cahan's *Yekl, a Tale of the New York Ghetto* (1896) and *The Imported Bridegroom* (1898) merge urban "local color" with socialist protest. His masterpiece, *The Rise of David Levinsky*, the first-person narrative of a Jewish garment manufacturer, initially began as a series of sketches for *McClure's* in 1911. It follows the life of Levinsky from poverty in Russia to success in New York, examining with complex power the problems of assimilation and "Americanization," anti-Semitism, and the entanglement of business aspirations and familial obligations. Measured against the background of fears about "race suicide" through unchecked immigration voiced by Josiah Strong, Francis Walker, and Theodore Roosevelt, and the triumphant Anglo-Saxonism of Norris and London, Levinsky's struggle to survive in a cutthroat world and to balance the conflicting identities of his past and present creates a troubled record not just of immigrant life in America but of the very substance of American "reality." Like James Weldon Johnson's *The Autobiography of an Ex-Coloured Man* (1912), Cahan's brilliant novel depicts the American self as a masquerade of values that are constantly cast into new forms by turbulent social and racial pressures.

Also influenced by Howells in his contrasting portrayals of New York wealth and ghetto life was the Norwegian immigrant H. H. Boyesen, often best remembered for his claim in "The American Novelist and His Public" (1884) that the American girl is an "Iron Madonna who strangles in her fond embrace the American novelist." Boyesen's most significant novel, *The Social Strugglers* (1893), is a fierce satire on the struggle for position among the upper classes, whose view of tenement life in carriage-driven slumming parties results in one shocking scene in which the heroine confronts a poor woman who would "like to strike her nails into her face, and disfigure it with hideous gashes." The philanthropically inspired romance that unites a couple from disparate classes at the conclusion of Boyesen's novel also characterizes *The Lawton Girl* (1890), an unorthodox romance by Harold Frederic of labor in conflict with inherited wealth. Frederic's unusually diverse work embraces both regional and urban scenes, and combines accurate detail with romantic, sometimes mystical elements. His late novels set among the British aristocracy, *Gloria Mundi* (1898) and *The Market-Place* (1899), derive from his flamboyant years as London correspondent for the *New York Times*. Earlier, as a reporter and editor in Utica and Albany, he gathered material for *Seth's Brother's Wife* (1887), which mixes plots of marital infidelity and political corruption, and anticipates Garland in its contrast of the new "century of cities" to the "living death of mental starvation" of rural

existence. *The Damnation of Theron Ware* (1896), a critical and popular success crossing Howellsian moral realism with a provocative psychology of
sexual and spiritual desire, stands with James's *The Turn of the Screw* (1898)
as an exploration of the disintegration of Victorian beliefs and values. In
his seduction by sensual aestheticism and philosophical scientism, the young
Methodist minister Theron Ware harks back to Hawthorne even as he anticipates the spiritual wasteland of modernism.

Given the symbolic power of the World's Columbian Exposition as an
expression of America's simultaneous material progress and class upheaval,
it is appropriate that Chicago, transformed from wilderness into a metropolis in a few generations, be *the* city of realism, counting Kirkland, Garland,
Dreiser, Fuller, Herrick, Jane Addams, and Upton Sinclair among its great
writers. Henry Fuller's *The Cliff-Dwellers* (1893) is set in a skyscraper, the
self-enclosed organism of the urban world stratified into levels of hierarchical power. Carved from the city's landscape where "the rushing streams of
commerce have worn many a deep and rugged chasm," the building is a
microcosmic version of American commercial development, a rather ironic
salute to Louis Sullivan's expressive theory of office-building architecture
and the 1890s "upward movement" of Chicago culture. Considered by Dreiser
to be "the father of American realism," Fuller divided his efforts among
genteel Italian travel-novels, literary criticism like "Howells or James?" (1885),
which debated the advantages of American over European material, and
fiction set in Chicago's high financial circles, such as *With the Procession* (1895),
a novel of Howellsian generational conflict. His contemporary and a teacher
at the newly created University of Chicago, Robert Herrick inscribed his
own attack on social climbing within a broader view of middle-class professionalization and modern marriage. In illustration of his belief in the variety
of available native materials spelled out in his essay "The Background of
the American Novel" (1914), Herrick's fiction covers a number of professions, including medicine, banking, engineering, art, architecture, and
teaching. But his fascination with professions arose as well from his belief
that personal and family ideals were being displaced in modern life by bureaucratic loyalties. *The Web of Life* (1900) attacks the world of finance, while
The Common Lot (1904) follows an architect's moral decay. His best novel,
The Memoirs of an American Citizen, is the success story of a Chicago meat-
packer modeled in part on the lives of Philip Armour and Gustavus Swift.
While it stops short of the view of packing labor as mechanized death found
in Sinclair's *The Jungle* (1906), the first-person narrative employs great symbolic events like the trial of the Haymarket anarchists, the World's Columbian Exposition, and the Spanish-American War to give national dimension

to the mixed idealism and corruption of its hero's life, which is made representative of the American market expansion of "God's great world."

The novel of business inevitably raised the issue of sexual roles; its masculine world of finance and production created the world of conspicuous consumption supposedly governed by the habits and tastes of women. Like Winston Churchill in *A Modern Chronicle* (1910), Robert Grant in *Unleavened Bread* (1900), David Graham Phillips in *The Hungry Heart* (1909), or Edith Wharton in *The House of Mirth* (1905) and *The Custom of the Country* (1913), Herrick found the phenomenon of the "new woman" a paradoxical mix: at once "a neurotic slave" to the ideal of material success and an independent, aggressive personality. The translation of domesticity into the new consumer culture of advertising and corporate routine suggested to Herrick, Dreiser, Wharton, Veblen, and Charlotte Perkins Gilman—and to James in a more complex international setting where "luxury" and "style" became synonymous—that "prostitution" was not simply a last resort of the lower classes but a metaphor for modern business and modern marriage. The same message appeared in the radical drama of Henrik Ibsen and August Strindberg, which found enthusiastic American audiences beginning in the 1880s and 1890s. The crusade against prostitution in the early Progressive period mirrored both actual economic depravity and middle-class anxiety about the commercial destruction of family morality; in both cases market values intrude into private life and defiantly question the meaning of "woman's work" in the capitalist order. Although melodramatic works like Reginald Kauffman's *The House of Bondage* (1910) or Estelle Baker's *The Rose Door* (1912) had been parodied in advance by Crane's *Maggie* and rendered simplistic by Dreiser's characterization of Carrie Meeber and Jennie Gerhardt, the age's most significant work on prostitution, David Graham Phillips's *Susan Lenox* (1917), is in many ways equal to Crane and Dreiser in its clarification of the links among acting, marriage, and prostitution. Along with Phillips's many muckraking novels of political and financial corruption—for example, *The Great God Success* (1901) or *The Deluge* (1905)—*Susan Lenox* provides a searching indictment of the parasitic entanglement of sexuality and economy in the early twentieth century.

The small towns or farms left behind by the protagonists of Garland, Howells, Herrick, Phillips, or Dreiser when they come to the new cities of iron and glass live as flickering memories, signs of a seemingly vanished order. In the journey between the regions of rural and urban life, most of all in the tension that binds them together, lies the substance and spirit of American realism. Held in balance by the emerging techniques of industrial labor, by racial and class antagonism, and by the twin energies of commerce and social progress, the period's fiction speaks eloquently of the moral complexity and paradoxical freedoms of modern American life. In that fiction what is "real" resists easy categorization but belongs instead to the rich profusion and often idiosyncratic detail of the diverse regional and ethnic voices of which America was being composed.

Eric J. Sundquist

Naturalism and the Languages of Determinism

Toward the end of the nineteenth century, an international movement dislodged a primary assumption of classic literary realism: that characters were autonomous agents, more or less responsible for their behavior. The "naturalists" committed themselves instead to the premise of "absolute determinism," and wrote novels in which particular motives mattered less than conditions that dictated events. No longer did it seem appropriate to treat characters as if they were morally accountable, and the naturalists now imagined traits and circumstances that deprived individuals of responsibility. Or in the words of their self-proclaimed spokesman, Emile Zola, when in 1868 he touted his first novel: "I chose characters completely dominated by their nerves and their blood, deprived of free will, pushed to each action of their lives by the fatality of their flesh."

Yet Zola's rallying cry fell upon deaf ears outside France. Indeed, it is safe to say that most intellectual upheavals in Europe went unnoticed by the American naturalists who came of age in the following quarter century. Frank Norris alone read Zola, Stephen Crane professed to have read virtually nothing, and only later in their careers did Jack London and Theodore Dreiser turn to Darwin or Marx. Unlike their counterparts abroad, moreover, these authors lacked any sense of common purpose that might have made them a self-conscious "school." Few of them knew each other's work, none persevered in the mode through his career, and those who theorized, did so badly. On first glance, in fact, the American naturalists seem to have had little more in common than their historical context. That context was nonetheless a powerful one, and particularly so for young writers, who came to share as never before a scorn for the conventional pieties.

Many of them turned away from traditional models of ethical behavior, attracted instead by philosophical determinism as a premise for understanding the late nineteenth century. What a few authors made of that slippery premise has come to define the movement known as American literary naturalism.

"Determinism" itself was a new term, appearing in print no earlier than 1846, and the concept's very freshness explains its availability to multiple interpretations. Individuals previously may have felt subject to religious necessity or the "hand of fate," but the scientific concept of determinism implied constraints that were more insidious, in part because pervasively economic and psychological. The distinct advantage of the concept, however, was that for the first time those constraints might be understood. Auguste Comte had pioneered a positivist "science of man" as early as the 1820s, and his sociological explanations contributed to a revolution in the understanding of everyday behavior. Thereafter, developments in biology, chemistry, and physics further transformed common sense, altering events themselves by altering the ways in which they were conceived. Individuals no longer appeared as morally independent actors in a Christian universe; rather, like filings aligned by magnets, they succumbed to the logics of heredity and environment. And greater study promised to reveal the laws underlying all thought and action, since it was becoming apparent that behavior was less a mystery of life than a problem for science.

Realists might continue to trust to an inherent spark of moral divinity, but in the 1890s the naturalists directed attention to innate traits and socialized habits. Instead of dramas of choice, they centered their fictions in scenes of coercion, since moral dilemmas mattered not at all in a universe that enmeshed characters logically, even predictably. Moreover, chance events could not truly occur in a world where all causes were knowable, since it is only one's uninformed point of view that can make an event seem fortuitous. It is precisely that point of view, however, that is manipulated in any narrative, and the failure to avoid what *seems* like chance can be used to reveal limits to one's will. Even when they did not appear to do so, the naturalists inverted realist strategies in order to enliven their philosophical premises. The willing self keeps reappearing as a pleasant fiction we tell ourselves, cherished by characters and sometimes by readers but at odds with the vision each artist presents.

How could literary naturalism have thrived in a country so committed to personal liberty that its national character is presumably one of rugged individualism? Why, more pointedly, did the seemingly arid concept of social determinism fascinate those American writers who came of age in the 1880s? The answer lies at least in part in the rapid industrializing of American society, which as never before displayed practices fully at odds with its republican ideals. Seemingly overnight, an agrarian nation became an industrial giant, webbed together by millions of miles of railroad lines and telephone wires. An unprecedented influx of immigrants contributed to a boom in population, as farms became mechanized, Big Business grew bigger, and a new consumer society evolved. Tremendous funds of capital were concentrated in cities that struggled as never before to keep pace with rising demands, and as expectations were disappointed, a mood of unrest began to trouble the nation. Social and economic dislocations had of course induced qualms before in America's citizens, as well as skepticism among the thoughtful about the relevance of their political ideals. But similar turmoil in the 1840s had also renewed hope in institutions and inspired an unprecedented number of movements for reform of daily American life. Those disrupted by the late nineteenth century no longer felt sanguine in their hopes, perhaps because the old and familiar seemed displaced far too radically by the new and uncertain.

Henry George was hardly the first to point out the link between "progress and poverty," but as never before, Americans grew convinced that that link was a mutually dependent one. A land of unequaled economic growth seemed to require that farmers grow inured to "hard times" and that the jobs of workers in general should depend on a wildly fluctuating global economy. The irony did not go unnoticed that the period's most concerted celebrations of national "progress"—the 1876 Philadelphia Centennial and the Chicago World's Columbian Exposition of 1893—both occurred in the midst of the most severe economic depressions Americans had yet experienced. The new Big Business made millionaires out of the Goulds, Carnegies, Armours, and Rockefellers, but it pressured the overwhelming majority of Americans into an industrial working class. And the increasing violence of strikes simply spoke to diminishing possibilities for labor mediation. Agrarian suffering fueled a brief-lived movement of Populist reform, but it too came to seem an ineffectual expression of general discontent. The political scandals that riddled national administrations following the Civil War did nothing to inspire the citizenry, who began to sneer at a Gilded Age of graft and corruption. True, the middle class voted Republican with annual regularity, in part because they thought of "business" as the prime mover of American life. Yet even they could not ignore the costs incurred by economic gain, particularly in the diminished control that most could wield over the events of everyday life. In less than a generation, international forces had appeared as if from nowhere to mold American society.

Perhaps it was the pressure of these forces that brought a nearly intolerable stress to bear on the traditional "explanation" offered by republican ideology and Christian values. Religious faith failed to sustain the younger generation as it had their parents, and few now shared a secular belief in agrarian independence or civic stewardship. At the same time, a convincing alternative had emerged in the powerful new claims for science. The paleontological investigations of Georges Cuvier in the first quarter of the nineteenth century, followed in the second by the geological revelations of Sir Charles Lyell, and then most dramatically, Charles Darwin's 1859 evolutionary theory of natural selection: all combined to undermine a faith in older religious assurances and to lend to scientific discourse a power that continues in the present. When the Englishman Herbert Spencer grafted Darwin's biological thesis onto a social model, he found an eagerly receptive American audience that in the 1870s made his name a household word.

Well before Darwin, Spencer had coined the phrase "survival of the fittest," and in a long career he used it to legitimate laissez-faire attitudes about economic conditions. He advocated a supposedly "natural" evolution of business enterprise free of government interference. Gross inequities would continue to occur between the privileged few and the laboring masses, but however unfair, Spencer excused them as simply the by-products of a longer-term welfare. According to his theory of Social Darwinism, the weak and stupid would fall victim in the natural course of events to economic forces— as they should, if civilization were to profit from the "go-getting" energy of the best and the brightest. Or as Andrew Carnegie complacently wrote in 1889, "While the law may be sometimes hard for the individual, it is best for the race, because it insures the survival of the fittest in every department. We accept and welcome, therefore . . . great inequality of environment." Going on to explain the irrelevance of individual well-being to human progress, Carnegie's well-known essay "The Gospel of Wealth" celebrates a universe of force. One need not be cynical to recognize in Social Darwinism a self-serving logic that was especially attractive to self-made millionaires like Carnegie.

It is probably true that Spencer's logic would have seemed less convincing in less troubling times. And the new fascination with science was itself not enough to divert novelists from scenes of moral responsibility. Contributing as well to the emergence of naturalism was the curious vocational fact that neither before nor since have so many American authors been journalists first. Crane, Norris, and Dreiser each cut their prose teeth on newspaper assignments, as did others whose fiction anticipated the determinist patterns of naturalism: Ambrose Bierce, Abraham Cahan, Edward Eggleston, Harold Frederic, Edgar Watson Howe, and David Graham Phillips. They were journalists, moreover, precisely when the profession itself was being transformed. Joseph Pulitzer and William Randolph Hearst had turned to a new style of front-page sensationalism, winning readers with a "yellow journalism" that catered to the lowest intellectual denominator. One could not help but feel a certain contempt for the news now fit to print, a contempt that was only compounded by the popular muckraking exposés of business chicanery and government corruption. And even when the public delighted in flag-waving slogans, pulpit pieties, and idealizing editorials, hardened journalists were more likely to recognize these bromides for what they were meant to do: simply ease the troubling news of labor violence, imperialist ventures, and urban dissatisfaction.

Wherever one happened to turn in the popular fiction of the day, however, such pieties proliferated, confirming anew the divided response of Americans toward their transforming society. Most middle-class readers enjoyed sentimental melodrama, no less then than now, and especially delighted in historical romances like Lew Wallace's *Ben-Hur* (1880) and Thomas Nelson Page's *In Ole Virginia* (1887). By the 1890s, inspirational novels began to top the list of best-sellers, including William Thomas Stead's *If Christ Came to Chicago!* (1894) and Charles Sheldon's *In His Steps* (1896). These works distracted readers from their lives as well as from current events, and for some even seemed to ameliorate the starkly materialist dogmas of Spencer and Ernst Haeckel, Max Nordau and Cesare Lombroso. Critics concluded that that was precisely the danger of such fiction, especially consumed on so large a scale, and the phenomenal success of the sentimental novel prompted the major American realists to declaim against it. Mark Twain, William Dean Howells, and, to a lesser extent, Henry James condemned their contemporaries' delight in spun sugar. Instead of fantastic plots, embellished prose, and moral triviality, they insisted on a direct engagement with the issues and experiences of everyday life. Their own fiction offered a viable alternative and argued (if with decreasing confidence) for traditional moral prerogatives in a society being altered beyond recognition by amoral forces. Howells even theorized, moreover, that American novelists were obligated to depict those prerogatives by concentrating on middle-class people living in simple, commonplace conditions. When fiction ceased "to lie about life" and instead focused on ordinary human experience, he felt it would then achieve its true mission of defining patterns of acceptable action.

The naturalists shared this contempt for romance and yet dismissed the realists as far too "genteel," rebelling against Howells in particular, whom Norris found "respectable as a church and proper as a deacon." Moral imperatives seemed quibbles to them, irrelevant in fictional worlds that were governed by far more pervasive and impersonal energies. Characters might believe in an ethical order and occasionally even assert it openly, but the overall thrust of the novels themselves contravenes any such logic. The naturalists felt even more disaffected than the realists from their society's idealizations, out of a genuine excitement at the demands that industrialization was placing on American life. No longer did older assurances about the effectiveness of deliberation and choice seem adequate, and ethical considerations seemed therefore irrelevant to people as they actually lived and worked. Adapting narrative devices the realists had somehow assumed their own, the naturalists attempted a more accurate view of contemporary experience by portraying characters who were not responsible in a world they had not made.

Few American writers ever declared themselves literary naturalists, which sometimes creates a problem in classifying a particular work. Even so, one negative test would seem to apply: any sure evidence of effective choice, of free will or autonomous action, makes a novel something other than naturalistic. Realist texts present a wide variety of individuals, but each one has the ability to choose, and characteristically does so through scenes that enact a process of deliberation—a weighing of alternative actions through a consideration of consequences. Take Huck Finn's climactic decision to "go to hell" on behalf of Jim, or Silas Lapham's nightlong contemplation of bribery as a means of saving his business, or Isabel Archer's vigil before the dying embers as she accepts responsibility for a bad marriage: these form perhaps the classic moments in American literary realism. And they do so because possibilities for the "self" are conceived in terms of responsible choice. However much circumstances otherwise compel us to act in a particular way, we have the power to choose another, and then to act on that choice.

Curiously, however, not one of these prominent scenes leads directly to the act that is contemplated, suggesting that what distinguishes realist from naturalist texts is restraint, not action itself. After all, naturalist characters act out of a similar set of motives and desires, and they differ from their realist counterparts only in being unable to resist the conditions that press upon them. The moral heroism that Huck, Silas, and Isabel achieve is the result of a decision in each case *not* to act as desires dictate at the moment. None of them behaves as one might have predicted on the basis merely of circumstance. Or conceive the distinction another way: the kind of character familiar to realism is a more or less unified self, subjectively whole and self-consistent. What naturalism imagines instead is that this self may be no more than an illusion. The dynamic forces that constrain one's actions from within as well as without do not simply overwhelm an otherwise integrated self but rather *are* that self in a fragmented state. No disjunction actually exists between outer events and inner disposition, and since circumstances are the source of character in naturalism, contingency comes to seem unimportant. Alternative courses of action are no longer entertained by the narrative, and the category of tragedy is therefore entirely excluded from the naturalist mode. Precisely because the realist hero might always act differently in circumstances that destroy him, he can attain a tragic stature. Not so, the naturalist character.

Sharply as it is possible to differentiate the two modes, some texts still resist classification, as do careers that have otherwise seemed straightforwardly realist. Mark Twain's excoriations of man's "contemptible" moral sense would lead to a confused necessitarianism in "The Mysterious Stranger," the manuscript unfinished at his death in 1910. Yet aspects of that fierce late nihilism appear as early as *Adventures of Huckleberry Finn* (1885), when a bewildered Huck is compelled to assist Tom Sawyer in setting a "free nigger free." Hank Morgan feels even more entrapped in *A Connecticut Yankee in King Arthur's Court* (1889). The nightmare of history in which he is mired evinces his contempt for all human behavior—contempt expressed in terms that are distinctly deterministic:

Training—training is everything; training is all there is *to* a person. We speak of nature; it is folly; there is no such thing as nature; what we call by that misleading name is merely heredity and training. We have no thoughts of our own, no opinions of our own; they are transmitted to us, trained into us.

Henry James viewed the coils of circumstance from a less single-minded perspective. And his early masterpiece, *The Portrait of a Lady* (1880), is a realist tragedy precisely because manipulation is tempered by choice and characters refuse to be swallowed by circumstance. Isabel Archer's willful idealism makes her more than partially responsible for an unhappy marriage into which she is tricked. Two decades later, *The Wings of the Dove* (1902) would shape Kate Croy more forcibly through poverty, her aunt's expectations, and the shabby selfishness of her sister and father. Even the plot she comes to imagine for Milly Theale and Merton Densher ends by committing her, unlike Isabel, to a foreclosure of absolutely all she has wanted. More than Maisie Farange in *What Maisie Knew* (1898) or Fleda Vetch in *The Spoils of Poynton* (1899), Kate is enmeshed in an elaborate web. She may seem responsible for effecting the end of her relationship with Densher, but the narrative voice remains troublingly divided. James's conception far exceeds the bounds of philosophical neatness, here as elsewhere, which may explain why he expressed fewer doubts about determinism than Twain or even William Dean Howells.

Howells was certainly the most conspicuous proponent of American realism, even though two of his finest works toy with a strikingly determinist vision. *A Modern Instance* (1882) describes Marcia Gaylord's insight into her husband's amoral selfishness as a desire "to resist, but she could not try." That inability to "try" leads another character later to conclude: "I do believe that if she were free to choose from now till doomsday she would always choose Bartley Hubbard, bad as she knows him to be." Bartley too is compelled to act on occasion against his will, and otherwise feels that "the mute, obscure forces of habit . . . were dragging him back to her." At the crisis of the novel, when he again decides to reconcile with Marcia after a bitter quarrel, his return to her is prevented by the theft of his wallet. The manuscript here breaks off (and Howells broke down in nervous collapse) with an assertion that seems to confuse choice with chance: "Now he could not return; nothing remained for him but the ruin he had chosen." A pickpocket's success has become the improbable measure of Bartley's will. Later in the decade, as Howells grew more pessimistic about the possibilities of responsible choice, he had Basil March observe that "accident and then exigency seemed the forces at work." Characters in *A Hazard of New Fortunes* (1890) repeatedly act as if at the mercy of overpowering forces, either psychological or circumstantial—whether Dryfoos's destructive relationship with his son or Beaton's and Alma's undisciplined sparring. By the end, Basil comes to sound much like Twain's Hank Morgan as he "fatalistically" wonders if anything alters us. Yet despite the strong elements of determinism, Howells explored its narrative implications no more consistently than had his two friends, Twain and James.

That the major American realists succumbed to certain determinist possibilities suggests why the philosophy should even more fully have attracted four authors who are also not naturalists. Ambrose Bierce, Edith Wharton, David Graham Phillips, and Upton Sinclair each fictionalized circumstances that variously deprived their central characters of autonomy. Bierce, for instance, anticipated Stephen Crane with narratives so violent that the will seems annihilated. In the stories collected as *Tales of Soldiers and Civilians* (1891) and *Can Such Things Be?* (1893), he sketched a modern wasteland of poverty and war in which the future seems foreclosed. "An Occurrence at Owl Creek Bridge" best illustrates this impulse in presenting a hopeful narrative of escape that is at last revealed as simply the brief final thoughts of an executed man.

Bierce's sardonic tone was echoed, surprising as it may at first seem, by none other than Edith Wharton. In *Ethan Frome* (1911), she grimly depicted a failed suicide attempt that locks Frome, his wife, and the woman he loves into an irremediable triangle of despair. And in two other novels, characters are entrapped as fully as in any by Dreiser or Norris. Brought up to be merely a social butterfly, an impecunious Lily Bart repeatedly acts against her own best interests in *The House of Mirth* (1906). Her long slide from house-party high-life to tenement struggle results from an inability to match intention with inclination, or will with desire. Nearly everyone else in the novel, moreover, shares this inability, including the philandering Gus Trenor, the feckless Lawrence Selden, and the crudely excessive Gormers. Likewise in *Summer* (1917), Charity Royall feels "too unequally pitted against unknown forces" and finally marries a guardian she does not love out of shame at a background she cannot help. Neither Lily nor Charity discovers ways to escape the hypocrisy of her society, and both at last ironically become their societies' uncomprehending representatives.

Bierce and Wharton condemned America with no expectation of social repair. Upton Sinclair and David Graham Phillips criticized instead to effect solid reforms, much as Jack London would also do in a career of social activism. The very titles of Sinclair's *The Jungle* (1906) and Phillips's *Susan Lennox: Her Fall and Rise* (1908) suggest two of naturalism's recurrent concerns: social systems that destroy and dehumanize, and individual trajectories of failure or success. Both novels anatomize society through chronicles of victimized careers and reveal possibilities for altering the social structure through a fictional form of investigative muckraking. As it happened, Sinclair's nightmarish narrative of the immigrant Rudken family instigated a series of legislative measures that were highly successful. His lurid scenes of a meat-packing industry that ground both rats and fingers into sausage aroused the middle class to demand sanitary conditions for food preparation. Yet far less effective by comparison was his severe indictment of the working conditions that regularly reduced laborers to impoverished insanity. As Sinclair later wryly observed, "I aimed for the heart and hit the stomach of America." Phillips's successful novel fictionalized the career of a woman forced into prostitution, and discredited the middle-class society that morally condemned and yet economically encouraged her behavior. The narrative patterns of both novels form a clear denunciation of laissez-faire capitalism, illustrating for the middle class the toll of modern life on the powerless.

Even earlier, less accomplished writers had fumbled with the implications of determinism, and they warrant at least a brief glance for their fictions of factory, farm, and urban life. They experimented with subjects as well as techniques, and despite an insistent strain of melodrama, their work revealed new dimensions to the drama of human will-lessness. Indeed, by emphasizing as never before the effect of setting, circumstance, and temperament, they pioneered narrative possibilities the naturalists later would develop. Rebecca Harding Davis is often cited as the first "realistically" to depict factory life, but her story "Life in the Iron Mills" (1861) can more aptly be said to anticipate a determinist vision. The story illustrates an ineluctable pattern much like that which Upton Sinclair would detail, in the worker-hero's vain aspirations for art, his unpreventable suicide, and the mineowner's callousness toward his workers.

Conditions on the farm were not substantially different from those in the factory, contrary to Bret Harte's popular romanticizing. And among writers alert to the similarities were Edward Eggleston, Edgar Watson Howe, Harold Frederic, Hamlin Garland, and Joseph Kirkland. Each experimented with grim fictions of life on the middle border, where local conditions were no longer mere backdrops to action but compelling forces in their own right. Another group of writers devoted their attention to just as coercive urban environments, recognizing determinist possibilities in the violent impersonality of Chicago and New York City. The three most prominent of these were Henry Blake Fuller, Abraham Cahan, and Robert Herrick, each of whom fictionalized the flotsam and jetsam adrift in a modern city: the eager ward heelers and ambitious businessmen, the strolling consumers and beleaguered poor. Shrewd natives were no more secure than the transplanted farmboys and bewildered immigrants who tumbled improbably upwards and downwards on and off the ladder of success. The overwhelming pressures of urban life, at least as these writers depicted them, make either hope or regret seem irrelevant.

The concept of determinism inspired new narrative conceptions of setting and character, and by the turn of the century four American authors had incorporated these possibilities into their work. Stephen Crane, Frank Norris, Jack London, and Theodore Dreiser each began by rejecting certain illusions about individual choice—illusions elaborately sustained in the popular tradition of literary romance. Instead, they depicted experience in completely materialist terms. Those terms varied from writer to writer, given their divergent understandings of determinism, and yet the work of these four defines the movement we know as American literary naturalism.

The most bleakly nihilistic of the group, Crane compiled a body of fiction that also remains the most clearly self-consistent. It is as if he had known his aims from the beginning and, in H. G. Wells's words, "sprang into life fully armed." His career spanned little more than half a dozen years before he died of tuberculosis at twenty-eight, but his relatively small body of fiction is nonetheless a profound inquiry into norms of behavior. Repeatedly, the perspective he offers is one of a fundamentally indifferent universe, in which institutions lack any intrinsic validity and human endeavor comes to seem futile. Crane invariably posed his characters in situations that exceed their smugly humanizing judgments. At the end of *The Red Badge of Courage* (1895), Henry Fleming complacently assumes he has become a "man"; the Easterner sums up the action of "The Blue Hotel" (1898) with a rebuke to the cowboy that is itself mistaken; and the final clause of "The Open Boat" (1897) makes a curious claim for the shipwrecked survivors: "they felt that they could *then* be interpreters." The misplaced adverb asks to be read as "therefore," not "now," suggesting that the men will assume once again their survival was more than merely fortuitous. In each case, the narrative questions the comforting impulse to "interpret" oneself, and thereby to adopt a false significance by standing outside the remorseless patterns of history.

Directly contradicting those realists who felt that moral claims redeemed the starkness of experience, Crane depicted the world as inherently amoral and irredeemable. Nature provides no haven in his fiction, nor are its processes altered by desire. The oiler's drowning in "The Open Boat," like the rescue of the correspondent through "a miracle of the sea," suggests that survival cannot be earned but is simply a matter of accident. The Swede's death in "The Blue Hotel," like the gambler's imprisonment and Johnny's beating, are unfortunate and even pathetic but finally of no intrinsic importance; nor are the deaths of Jim Conklin in *Red Badge* or of Maggie Johnson in *Maggie: A Girl of the Streets* (1893). The world, as "The Blue Hotel" defines it, is merely "a whirling, fire-smitten, ice-locked, disease-stricken, space-lost bulb" to which men and women cling like lice.

In order to intensify this vision of a thoroughly unaccommodating universe, Crane dramatized the emptiness of deliberation and choice. His settings of war, shipwreck, and blizzard obviously preclude quiet contemplation, but even did they not, inner forces would still dictate behavior. His characters seem in the end enslaved no less by conventions than by circumstances. Maggie is destroyed by her slum environment, but she is also as much self-victimizer as victim, imprisoned by her own ready acceptance of a false social code. Likewise creating the worlds they find, however inadvertently, are Henry Fleming, the correspondent of "The Open Boat," and the Swede of "The Blue Hotel." It is not that Jim Conklin or Wilson or even Henry acts as heroically as he hopes, but rather that *Red Badge* makes the very conception of heroism seem irrelevant to the reiterated advance and retreat of battle. Sheer impulse governs all, leaving no one in control of events or themselves. And even those few temporarily capable of appreciating this wisdom do so uncertainly, as the conclusion to "The Open Boat" suggests.

Part of his characters' inability to take responsibility for experience results from the unusual form of Crane's presentation. His "nervous" style contributes to a radical questioning of the very concept of a self, by making the integrated ego disappear amid a welter of conflicting assumptions and desires. By breaking up normal syntax and disrupting habitual patterns of expression, Crane effectively presents to his readers an analogue of the experience his characters face: an ambivalent welter of details that ever require a tentative interpretation. Any conclusion we make about his writing depends upon our own socialized expectations, illustrating once again that both reader and character cannot fail but impose interpretations on experience. His persistent delight in questioning conventions suggests, moreover, why Crane liked to parody literary genres themselves, whether the Horatio Alger slum tale in *Maggie*, the war novel in *Red Badge*, the sea story in "The Open Boat," or the shoot-'em-up western in "The Bridge Comes to Yellow Sky" (1898). Indeed, it may be the short story's very resistance to a larger order that explains his attraction to the form. The absence of strong plots in his fiction, combined with the fact that characters often lack names, forms a tacit repudiation of conventional labels and predictable judgments. Crane's narratives, that is, call into question all causal assumptions and compel us to recognize how any conclusion can only emerge from predetermining expectations. We are always enmeshed in a series of conventions that dictate action, foreclose alternatives, and limit what characters and readers can ever know.

Literary naturalism has often been narrowly identified with the phrase "pessimistic determinism," as if the words somehow required one another.

The clichéd label may happen to fit the characteristically dark vision of Crane, but it is now worth recalling that nothing about the concept of necessity need be pessimistic. Other naturalists adopted quite different assumptions that evolved no less logically from determinism. Frank Norris, for instance, subscribed to a Social Darwinism of inevitable human progress. Characters in his four naturalist novels demonstrate no greater capacity for responsibility than do Crane's, and yet in the end they supposedly contribute to an overall social amelioration. Norris's youthful enthusiasm for Zola had led him to this progressive view of determinism and encouraged him to transplant onto native soil the French novelist's unconventional material. Ironically, much as he differed from Crane (who had no similar literary influence), the two were the first American authors to embrace the Darwinian notion that brutish impulses dictate human behavior.

Although Norris also resembled Crane in dying young (at thirty-two), his equally brief career can nonetheless be divided into three distinct parts. The first is defined by two novels he wrote but failed to get published in the early 1890s: *McTeague* (1899) and *Vandover and the Brute* (1914). In order to gain a popular audience, he then wrote three more conventional novels that nonetheless extended his central concerns: *Moran of the Lady Letty* (1898), *Blix* (1899), and *A Man's Woman* (1900). This middle period helped prepare Norris for the fiction of economic conditions he had long wanted to write, and before his death he completed two parts of an intended trilogy devoted to "The Epic of the Wheat": *The Octopus* (1901), which described the production of grain, and *The Pit* (1903), its commercial marketing ("The Wolf" would have dealt with its distribution worldwide). Norris's "epic" at last made explicit his lifelong belief in the human race—that collective behavior was inherently more significant than any individual crisis, and that the local and pathetic invariably mirrored the universal and typical. For Norris, all was leading inexorably toward the perfection of human society.

The glorious future of the race notwithstanding, the here and now of late Victorian society could not disguise man's innate animality. And in an animal world, the weak or stupid or misdirected are supplanted—just as Vandover, McTeague, even Annixter are finally sacrificed to the progressive flow of history. Fighting one another, McTeague and Marcus Schouler bite ears and break arms, driven by the same brutish impulse that impels McTeague to kiss his unconscious dental patient, Trina Sieppe ("Suddenly the animal in the man stirred and woke"). After their marriage, he will likewise be impelled to gnaw her fingers sadistically, and finally to bludgeon her to death. Greed, lust, rage, and envy are no longer sins but inherited traits that some can sublimate, others cannot. Even that difference, moreover, results from simply a fortuitous conjunction of circumstance and temperament, leaving everyone to submit to forces larger than the will.

Norris did not share Crane's belief that culture actively constitutes behavior, believing instead that conventions were no more than garments draped over man's animal nature. Moral codes formed no more than invidious labels on basic instincts, and Victorian mores in particular suppressed the sexual desires men and women normally feel. In *Vandover and the Brute*, the "social disease" that precipitates Vandover's physical decline aptly exposes society itself as diseased in its moral values. After all, he has been educated to reject as "evil" what are otherwise natural impulses, including the instinct for survival and for sexual consummation. Vandover's casual disregard of the woman he seduces, much like the tortured self-regard that leads her to suicide, results from an inability to recognize sexuality as anything other than a sign of sin. Whereas a stupid McTeague remains merely the lumpish victim of hereditary forces, Vandover's very sensitivity to social nuance leads him to conspire in his own victimization. Like Crane's Maggie and Dreiser's Clyde Griffiths, his unconsidered acceptance of the society that destroys him exposes all the more fully the inadequacy of its codes.

Norris's three middle novels invert this theme of cultural repression by showing how men and women in exile from conventional society at last discover their innate strengths. In *Moran*, for instance, socialite Ross Wilbur is shanghaied, endures shipboard discipline, and returns to reject the futilely demeaning life of San Francisco high society. Clearly marred as these middle works are by the formulaic demands of the popular romance, they nonetheless illustrate the fundamentally Spencerian logic that characterizes Norris's vision throughout.

The Octopus, Norris's most ambitious novel, attempts to reveal a global pattern to economic forces by fictionalizing the actual Mussel Slough massacre of 1880. That episode had pitted California ranchers in a rate war against the Southern Pacific Railroad, and the novel dramatizes the actual dispossession of the ranchers by the railroad. Here more than ever, Norris takes a long historical view and suggests that the railroad's victory forms nothing more than a temporary achievement (as its president, Shelgrim, wisely realizes). Everyone else mistakenly attempts to wrest control of a process that is larger than any human institution, with the ranchers compounding this misassumption through arrogant self-righteousness. If at first they seem less immoral than the railroad, it is simply because the novel is narrated from their point of view. Their "bonanza" farming is equally speculative, equally oriented to short-term profit, and suggests neither love of the land nor a particular concern for future generations. And as if to confirm their moral equivalence with the railroad employees, they too finally stoop to bribery and violence to achieve their self-serving ends.

The conflict of rancher and railroad is clarified through the major subplots of *The Octopus*, in the depiction of three men's growing awareness of forces that transcend the self. The rancher, Annixter, learns through love to acknowledge the legitimate bonds of community; the shepherd, Vanamee, bears witness to the material effects of a spiritual realm; and the poet, Presley, realizes that only just such respectful awareness as Annixter and Vanamee achieve can free him from the usual forms of social and psychological exploitation. Yet universal reform is not soon likely, and such highly charged scenes as the rabbit hunt and barn dance serve to remind the reader that the weak must still be weeded out. Force ever drives human behavior, as Norris blithely concludes, and individuals must be sacrificed to the race's ongoing progress.

Falseness dies; injustice and oppression in the end of everything fade and vanish away. Greed, cruelty, selfishness, and inhumanity are short-lived; the individual suffers but the race goes on. Annixter dies, but in a far-distant corner of the world a thousand lives are saved. The larger view always and through all shams, all wickedness, discovers the truth that will, in the end, prevail, and all things surely, inevitably, resistlessly work together for good.

These well-known concluding lines sum up Norris's determinist credo, even as they disguise the problematic terms in any Social Darwinist vision. Like Spencer, he ignores the question of how the recognitions that Presley and Annixter have had will now be repeated in others, or of how the greater good will assuredly, necessarily emerge from any blind conjunction of forces.

Similar questions arise at the conclusion of *The Pit*. Specifically, how will Laura Jadwin use her newly won independence to alter the plight of women in a culture still dominated so thoroughly by men? She will not even be better able to escape her own social powerlessness, or to integrate her experience any more fully with that of her husband. Likewise, Curtis Jadwin's late "conversion" from the evils of market speculation offers no solution for the inherent dynamics of a capitalist economy, nor any prescription for more conscientious activity in the Chicago Board of Trade. Norris once again fails to justify his Spencerian belief, by proving that present activities work for the better, or that the "better" is equivalent to true social excellence. How can one know that the "fittest" will be any kinder or more generous instead of simply more ruthless than those they survive? As elsewhere, Norris here slighted the salutary role of culture in a world of force.

Or rather, he failed to allow that force exists always already shaped by culture.

Crane's pessimism and Norris's optimism are but two of the responses determinism can elicit. Another attitude hearkens back to Zola's reasons for first extolling naturalism: an affirming belief in social reform. Given that individuals are determined by society, restructuring institutions so as to curb excesses will improve the environment that still conditions behavior. Through the use of fiction to interpret the effects of economic conditions, those effects might someday be altered through education and reform, and instead of quiet submission to Spencer's jungle law, we would have found the means of transcending it. Clearly, this is the least consistent of the attitudes associated with the naturalist mode, since at the very least, any determinist premise would seem to contravene possibilities for choice or deliberate effort. And predictably, "reform" determinism attracted writers of thoroughly contradictory enthusiasms, including Upton Sinclair and David Graham Phillips. It was Jack London, however, who was most notably self-contradictory in his simultaneous commitments to a super-race and yet to a classless society—convinced of Nietzsche's individualistic will-to-power even as he signed letters to Marxist friends, "Yours for the revolution."

Such inconsistencies did not trouble London, perhaps because his compulsive regimen kept him otherwise engaged: for seventeen years he wrote a thousand words a day, completing more than forty-nine volumes altogether. In part, he was trying to keep written pace with a life more multi-faceted than that of any other American writer—from his teen-age days as an oyster pirate with his mistress "Queen" on San Francisco Bay; then as seaman on a sealer, cross-country hobo, and socialist speaker; and later, as hopeful prospector in the Alaska gold rush. Returning empty-handed, he began to write about his Klondike experiences, and soon won the enormous popularity that made him the first millionaire novelist. London's best efforts came relatively early, and include *The Call of the Wild* (1903), *White Fang* (1906), and his finest story, "To Build a Fire" (1908), which dramatizes an unnamed man's attempts to reach camp in the sub-zero Yukon. Progressively unable to exert his will or to control his rapidly benumbed limbs, the man is nonetheless debilitated less by freezing conditions than by a distinctive narrative style. The very prose in which he is immersed makes it seem that his death has been determined from the beginning.

In general, the most vexing problem faced by naturalist authors is that readers habitually extend a capacity for agency to characters, whether they warrant it or not. We find it just as difficult to allow that characters are determined by forces beyond their control as we do in imagining ourselves or our friends somehow similarly constituted. London occasionally avoided this problem by using dogs as central figures, making questions of deliberation and free will seem to disappear. And by doing so, the consequences of heredity, temperament, and innate capacity were more easily isolated, allowing success in these fictions to be simply defined as an adaptation to circumstance—a coordination of inner energy and external force. In *The Call of the Wild*, Buck is stolen from a California estate to serve on a sled team in the Alaskan trade. Removed from civilized comfort, the dog soon apprehends the true "law of life," and a series of trials develop innate strengths that at last free him from domestic standards. In *White Fang*, London reversed the process through a plot that dramatizes "the thumb of circumstance," as a young wolf-dog is trained to lead a sled team before becoming a California house pet. For London no more than for Crane or Norris do natural forces always overpower the individual, but survival for each of them is determined by factors that always do lie beyond one's control.

Even more than it had for Norris, the conflict between conventional values and natural force fascinated London, and in *The Sea Wolf* (1904) and *Martin Eden* (1908) he again plotted movements respectively away from and toward the codes of civilization. Like *The Call of the Wild* (and Norris's *Moran*), *The Sea Wolf* portrays Humphrey Van Weyden's growth from dilettante to self-sufficient seaman. Rescued from shipwreck by Captain Wolf Larsen, who ruthlessly initiates him to life aboard a sealer, he comes to appreciate the logic of amoral individualism in a world of force. When cerebral cancer debilitates Larsen, Van Weyden is aroused at last to defiance and to an abandonment of his vapid social ethos. The plot of *Martin Eden* is precisely the opposite, following the title character from rough-and-ready obscurity on the San Francisco docks to fame as best-selling author and intellectual. The most autobiographical of London's novels, it most fully elaborates the conflict between a class-oppressed society and the model implied by a Spencerian vision. Ruth Moore, Martin's sometime fiancée, embodies cautious propriety, and the clash between his desire for marriage and yet his Promethean resistance to compromise figures forth the larger antithesis between defiant individualism and a faith in class struggle. Unable to resolve this inner conflict and yet desperate for inner peace, Martin finally drowns himself.

London's faith in social determinism stood, like Martin's, in conflict with his avowed commitment to collective action. He later told Upton Sinclair, for instance, that he had actually written *Martin Eden* as "an attack on individualism"—this, despite its title character's Byronic personality. And to confuse the issue even further, London's letters and speeches espoused social reform in ways only fleetingly suggested by the larger body of his fiction. To gather evidence for his devastating indictment *The People of the Abyss* (1902), he disguised himself as a pauper and lived for two months in the notorious East End of London. Five years later he portrayed an "intellectual swashbuckler" who leads a future revolution against now-fascist America in *The Iron Heel* (1907). The novel's conclusion guarantees the promise of a glorious socialist age, despite both Ernest Everhard's execution and the fact that the "Iron Heel" still maintains power. In the decade that followed this unusual novel, London's career declined in part because he churned out pages he seldom deemed fit to revise. His own probable suicide at forty meant that he too failed to resolve the tensions so clearly exemplified in his fiction. And with his death, naturalism in America became identified with one man.

Theodore Dreiser was no less a hybrid practitioner than other major American naturalists, and his important works elude clear classification as "pessimistic," "optimistic," or "reform." It is true that occasional passages in his novels do confidently proclaim a Spencerian optimism and also true that, toward the end of his life, the philosophy he espoused was mildly reformist. Yet his narratives themselves fit neither alternative in their concentration on the irremediable helplessness of the present. Claims for the ultimate triumph of "good" and for society's eventual perfection are illusory in novels that everywhere else undercut the promise that the future will improve on the past. Dreiser's plots, in other words, subvert the sanguine beliefs expressed by his narrators—that, for instance, "we have the consolation of knowing that evolution is ever in action, that the ideal is a light that cannot fail."

The first major American writer raised on the wrong side of the tracks, Dreiser was also, as Ellen Moers observed, the first Catholic, the first to hear a foreign language at home, the first whose family was impoverished and disreputable. Such a background brought him as a child to realize the irrelevance of middle-class standards, a realization later reinforced by his study of Spencer's and Haeckel's sociology, Elmer Gates's biochemical research, and, still later, Sigmund Freud's psychoanalytic theories. It was primarily his wayward family, however, that offered him material for his novels and, more important, a perspective on moral dictates that made them seem beside the point. In Dreiser's novels, impersonal energies always engulf desire, which becomes cause for neither the nihilism of Crane nor the enthusiastic assurance of Norris. Success and failure merely form opposite sides of the same coin, and while some of his characters live comfortably, even virtuously, none possess traits that might sustain a consistent self. Because everyone acts directly in response to a sequence of impulses and temptations, no one is left able to deliberate or choose. Settings no longer constrain desire, but now express it fully, if only to confirm in the end that desire itself can never be satisfied. And in identifying desire with urban settings, described in unprecedented detail, Dreiser became the greatest chronicler of America's cities.

His first novel, *Sister Carrie* (1900), struck such a blow at contemporary expectations that for more than a decade it was virtually ignored. Young Carrie Meeber rises from farm-girl innocence to theatrical stardom not only despite, but because of, living out of wedlock with two men: first the "masher," Drouet, and then the married George Hurstwood. Yet Dreiser's flouting of literary convention is itself less radical than Carrie's easy acceptance of her improprieties. She may think she believes in the customary forms of marriage and gentility, but she is incapable of feeling guilt or of considering herself a "fallen woman." Her attention is engaged not by moral considerations but by the seductive goods that a consumer culture displays in department stores up and down Broadway. In a society that also gives lip service to morals, Carrie finally succeeds because she is unwittingly able to act out desires and expectations shared by everyone else. In the right place at the right time, with a glint in her eye and a fetching smile, she wins both recognition and riches. Conversely, the saloon manager Hurstwood loses status as well as comfort by being at the wrong place, in front of an open safe that happens to be full of money. Neither character can be considered responsible for rising or falling in a world so fully shaped by circumstance and disposition.

This chance alignment of desire and environment recurs throughout Dreiser's work. *Jennie Gerhardt* (1911) and *An American Tragedy* (1925) present youths much like Carrie in background and psychology who drift from place to place, person to person, according to a similar pattern. Yet simply because her circumstances differ, Jennie is brought to a different end. Lower-class constraints mold a yielding disposition that at once attracts men and yet discourages them from marriage. Both Senator Brander and Lester Kane flout social conventions, but Jennie's compliancy inspires neither one to jeopardize career immediately for "love" (in the way that Carrie's stalwartness spurs Hurstwood). Clyde Griffiths is likewise shaped by a culture that images his desire for success in sexual terms. And his experience in *An American Tragedy* is emblematic in its failures, as he woos a series of women who represent what lies always just beyond his reach, from Hortense Briggs to Sondra Finchley. Ever placing him in the path of disaster, the novel repeats sometimes point for point events and contexts beyond Clyde's control—all in a repetitive narrative pattern that stresses his lack of will. He no more than Jennie or Carrie has technical responsibility for the events of his life, whether for a car accident that leaves a girl dead or a boating accident that kills Roberta Alden. Circumstances alone enmesh him, driving him relentlessly to the executioner's chair.

More than any other naturalist, Dreiser dramatized chance as a means of compelling characters to pay or gain for actions not their own. An onstage Carrie blurts out a comic line that leads by a curious sequence to stardom. Jennie merely happens to observe Lester Kane with Letty Page, culminating a number of fortuitous episodes that have brought her and Lester first together, then apart. Perhaps predictably, the two most famous scenes of chance occur in Dreiser's two finest novels, *Sister Carrie* and *An American Tragedy*. When Hurstwood stands in front of the unlocked safe at Hannah and Hogg's, musing drunkenly on the available cash, the scene marks the novel's turning point. And when the safe door happens to slam shut, foreclosing the resumption of his managerial career, the event seems to deprive Hurstwood of any choice. Similarly, when Clyde strikes Roberta at Loon Lake, he precipitates her death and ultimately his own. Yet the injury is an inadvertent one that occurs despite his confused intention, representing simply another accident in a series that extends to the novel's opening.

In his "Trilogy of Desire," Dreiser offered the contrast of a "success" to the examples of those who drift downward—the desiring Hurstwoods and the Clydes who are foredoomed by disaster. *The Financier* (1912), *The Titan* (1914), and *The Stoic* (1947) detail the turn-of-the-century career of the fictional robber baron Frank Algernon Cowperwood. In the famous opening sequence, Cowperwood observes "the bitter struggle" of a squid being destroyed by a lobster. "That's the way it has to be," he concludes. Later, his ruthless success in high finance seems to result from this early recognition that "things live on each other." No more than anyone else, however, is Cowperwood able to act autonomously. He is "a financier by instinct" alone, whose compelling desires for business deals, women, houses, and prestige all undercut any suggestion that he makes a conscious series of choices, or that he might not have led the career that he has. His success has been no less a matter of chance than Carrie's, nor any different in kind from the failures of Clyde and Hurstwood.

While subsequent writers have borrowed from the fiction of Crane, Norris, and London, it has been the adaptations from Dreiser that more recently have made the tradition seem to continue. John Dos Passos and James T. Farrell, John Steinbeck and Norman Mailer, even William Faulkner and Ernest Hemingway: all at one time or another have seemed to resemble Dreiser in technique or material. Yet it is worth recalling that naturalism is distinguished by no particular attitude or assumption, no specific technique or style. Crane's "impressionistic" vignettes hardly call to mind Dreiser's lumbering prose, and Norris's epic span could not be further from the canine allegories London conceived. American literary naturalists are bound together by historical context and philosophical determinism—a philosophy that on its face suggests nothing of the range of possibilities available to the mode.

Few writers since the turn of the century have acknowledged the full implications of determinism, perhaps because the historical conditions seem no longer ripe. The particular constellation of influences at work on writers now thought of as naturalists disappeared with World War I. By contrast, realism is generally agreed to transcend a specifically historical era, since it has seemed to depend on a set of mimetic conventions coterminous with the life of the novel. Definitions of naturalism instead have depended on specifically historical influences that for a brief period encouraged an unusual philosophical view. That the movement was so short-lived simply testifies to the unique conditions it required. Few literary generations have dramatized what it might mean to be deprived of personal autonomy, as if choice no longer mattered in a world dead to moral considerations. The naturalists' triumph was to take from a period of dislocation so circumscribed a vision, and then in various forms to make that vision of human possibility come alive.

Lee Clark Mitchell

III. Literary Diversities

Literature for the Populace

In 1782, J. Hector St. John de Crèvecoeur asked, "What is this American, this new man?" It is a question that neither he nor anyone else has answered satisfactorily. The question, of course, is not the same as asking "Who am I?" For some of our writers, Who am I? What am I? echoes violently against a wall of silence and indifference. Melville and Hawthorne, for all their differences, were more concerned with understanding the Self than the American Self. Others—Emerson, Thoreau, Whitman—wanted to define the nature of the American, but could best do so by making clear what was wrong with America. Not so deeply struck by the power of blackness, they nevertheless recognized the heart of darkness that was the New World's. From Emerson's rhetoric of self-reliance to Thoreau's search for an honest man to Whitman's ever-increasingly solitary singer, the voice of the writer makes clear America's unsettled state. The problem is political, sexual, and, above all, moral. Nietzsche's Zarathustra would not announce God's death until 1892; but, in America God (if not religion) had long been dead. We were, Ben Franklin made clear—and William James would codify for us—a pragmatic people. There was neither time nor need for an I-Thou dialogue; the chief business of the American people, Calvin Coolidge would inform us in 1925, was indeed business. Business, money, power: these we have come to see are the urges that define the American. And consequently, our questions are questions about these matters. Emerson made clear how ingrained anti-intellectualism is in American life when he wrote, "our America has a bad name for superficialness. Great men, great nations, have not been boasters and buffoons, but perceivers of the terror of life, and have manned themselves to face it." However one might want to define a "great nation," it is clear that as a people Americans seldom have been "perceivers of the terror of life." Those writers who have concerned themselves with this terror have seldom attained great popularity. They may rage against the heavens and tell us to say No! in Thunder or they may complain about those "scribbling women" who wrote domestic novels, but for the most part we listen to different voices—voices that may not speak to and for us as Lear and Job did for others, but voices that, just because they are different, may get us closer to answering Crèvecoeur's haunting question.

Of course, the American of whom Crèvecoeur wrote—the "new man"— was to be radically transformed as America itself would undergo its most radical change. Crèvecoeur spoke prophetically when he wrote that in America "individuals of all nations are melted into a new race of men, whose labours and posterity will one day cause great changes in the world." But he could not foresee that the first great change would take place in America itself— that increasingly events would challenge his contention that "we are the most perfect society now existing in the world." No event so dramatically challenged that contention as did the Civil War. Even before then, how- ever, writers as different as Washington Irving, Henry David Thoreau, Lydia Sigourney, and Susan B. Warner were expressing their discontent with aspects of this "perfect society." The official rhetoric of Jacksonian America—which always invoked the virtues of a white democratic repub- lic—could not hide the disquiet caused by the movement toward an urban society that was increasingly becoming more mechanized, industrialized, and middle-class. So, when Alexis de Tocqueville visited America in 1833, he, like Crèvecoeur, commented upon the energy and independence of this new person now known as an American. But by now this new race of men that had so impressed Crèvecoeur was no longer a perfect society; despite its enormous potential for personal comfort and mobility, Tocqueville feared that democracy would make Americans among the loneliest of people. And indeed, with the onset of the Civil War, loneliness and separation became ingrained in the cultural sensibility of America. The more American tech- nology provided ways of unifying the country—the transcontinental rail- road, the telegraph, national circulation magazines—the more intense be- came the image of Americans caught in their own progress; like Theodore Dreiser's Carrie Meeber, they would be attracted by the city, money, and success, yet would find themselves little more than "waif[s] amid forces."

This sense of disorder and uncertainty, made more complex by the writ- ings of Darwin, Marx, and Freud, was addressed in various ways. In Vic- torian America, as has frequently been noted, an American gentry (mainly white middle-class Protestants from the Northeast) made a conscious at- tempt to instill a sense of social responsibility and personal morality in

American life. Industry and integrity, they argued, would build character; without it, there would be neither peace nor progress. The Civil War may have been over, but as Henry Ward Beecher was to tell his parishioners in 1872: "We are to be warriors still, but warriors for peace; warriors against the forces of nature that resist us, until we subdue the nations to the blessed condition of industry, as well as social and civil conquest."

In marked contrast to Beecher's stentorian tones, but no less concerned with a search for order in post–Civil War America, are the works that express the popular culture. In myriad written and visual works, the popular artists spoke to the changing nature of America—to its fears and hopes, as they both reflected and created those fears and hopes. Unlike Beecher and the reformers for whom he so brilliantly spoke, the popular artists did not speak *at* the new urban middle class; they spoke *to*, as well as *for*, them.

If many of our writers and critics have been concerned with defining this new person, "this American," most people living in the United States during the nineteenth century seem not to have been particularly worried about "the national character." Rather, as Henry Seidel Canby generalizes in *The Age of Confidence* (1934), his memoir of life in the 1890s, that decade may have been the last time in living memory "when everyone knew exactly what it meant to be an American." Despite the Civil War, and all the changes that took place subsequently, that confidence about being an American permeated the entire period. And nothing strengthened that confidence more than the popular literature of the time, especially the dime novel.

Although the first dime novel, Ann S. Stephens's *Malaeska: The Indian Wife of the White Hunter*, was published in June 1860, it was neither the first inexpensive book to be published in the United States nor, in fact, was it even the first publication of *Malaeska*. Stephens's novel originally was serialized in *The Ladies' Companion* in 1839; but it is as "Beadle's Dime Novels No. 1"—for which Erastus Beadle paid Mrs. Stephens $250 for reprint rights—that *Malaeska* is remembered. Ironically, *Malaeska* is hardly a representative "dime novel." Less lurid and fantastical than many, it is also more somber and brooding than most.

The cover of the first issue of *Malaeska* proclaimed Beadle's intention: here, for a dime, were "Books for the Million!"; here one would find "The Choicest Works of the Most Popular Authors." A notice from the publisher also prefaced the story:

We take pleasure in introducing the reader to the following romance by Mrs. Ann B. Stephens. It is one of the most interesting and fascinating works of this eminent author. It is chosen as the initial volume of the Dime Novel series, from the chaste character of its delineations, from the interest which attaches to its fine pictures of border life and Indian adventure, and from the real romance of its incidents. It is American in all its features, pure in its tone, elevating in its sentiments, and may be referred to as a work representative of the series that is to follow—every volume of which will be of the highest order of merit, from the pens of authors whose intellectual and moral excellencies have already given the writers an enviable name, in this country and in Europe. By the publication of the series contemplated, it is hoped to reach all classes, old and young, male and female, in a manner at once to captivate and to enliven—to answer to the popular demand for works of romance, but also to instil a pure and elevating sentiment in the hearts and minds of the people.

Ann Stephens had indeed attained some eminence by the time Beadle selected her novel to inaugurate his series of books for the millions: she had been the editor of *The Ladies' Magazine* and *The Ladies' World*, and had authored *Fashion and Famine* (1854; her first novel) and *The Old Homestead* (1855). *Malaeska*, however, did not foreshadow the works Beadle was to publish in the series. And the work *is* very much a romance of its time—as sentimental and moralistic in its plot as it is ornate in its language. (When Malaeska's white husband returns to her after an absence of many days, Stephens writes—not untypically—of Malaeska: "The feelings which in civilized life are scattered over a thousand objects were, in her bosom, centered in one single being; he supplied the place of all the high aspirations—of all the passions and sentiments which are fostered into strength by society, and as her husband bowed his head to hers, the blood darkened her cheek, and her large, liquid eyes were flooded with delight.") But the suicide of Malaeska's own son, William Danforth, when he learns that she, an Indian, is his mother, Malaeska's death—"the heartbroken victim of an unnatural marriage"—and the final desolation of Danforth's fiancée Sarah Jones, who goes back "to her useful life, without a murmur against the Providence that has made it so lonely," make *Malaeska* very much a work in character with the domestic novels of Susan B. Warner, E. D. E. N. Southworth, and Catharine Sedgwick. *Malaeska* may also have been the first of Beadle's dime novels, but it was really Edward S. Ellis's *Seth Jones* that was representative of the works to come.

Seth Jones was in fact the eighth novel to be published in E. F. Beadle's new series. Within three weeks of the publication of *Malaeska*, Beadle published a sea tale by the pseudonymous "Harry Cavendish," which was followed in quick order by another novel by Ann Stephens, as well as works by Metta V. Victor, Colin A. Barker (Henry J. Thomas), Mary A. Denison, and Cavendish again. Then came *Seth Jones*, preceded by an impressive advertising campaign. In an introduction to a 1907 reprint of his novel, Ellis recalls that Beadle's first step was to "placard the country with 'dodgers' and posters, composed of the simple question, 'who is Seth Jones?' A few weeks later these placards gave place to a big picture of a hunter, in coon-skin cap and border costume, with a rifle resting easily on one arm, and the announcement, 'I'm Seth Jones,' adding the interesting information that the book with that title could be purchased of all newsdealers for ten cents."

An estimated 400,000 copies were purchased that year, and by December 1860 Beadle & Co. announced that Ellis would devote his best labors exclu-sively to their service: "The resources of our early history, of our frontier settlements and experiences of Indian life and character, offer a field of inexhaustable [*sic*] richness to the writer whose knowledge of that field is accurate and thorough, and whose talent is especially adapted for that ex-citing yet historical narrative." A series "of splendid romances and of fron-tier, Indian and trappers life has been arranged for." Ellis did indeed pro-vide the firm with numerous works, though years later he would claim that they were "early ill-constructed works." But even so, Ellis noted, "no crit-icism could be made upon their moral tone." Critics tended to agree: what-ever their failings may have been, these early dime novels "did not pander to vice in the remotest form." Moreover, a writer like Ellis deserved his popularity: he shows "variety and originality in his characters; and his In-dians are human beings, and not fancy pieces."

Today, such judgment seems arcane at best. Such stories as *Seth Jones* may not have pandered to vice, but their moral effect was pernicious in a way that Ellis never understood. For just as minstrel shows of the time not only attained their popularity by caricaturing blacks but reinforced the de-humanizing images of blacks permeating white America, so works like *Seth Jones* not only failed to show Indians as human beings but established their popularity by insisting on the moral superiority of white Americans. Thus, Ellis tells his reader that his woodsman hero—Seth Jones from New Hamp-shire—"was a splendid specimen of nature's nobleman. . . . His features were regular and strongly marked. The nose was of a Roman cast and the eyes of glowing blackness." It is this splendid specimen, created by a twenty-year-old New Jersey schoolteacher, who gravely warns: "You oughter know that it's never safe to trust a redskin; try to put your finger on 'em, and by gracious they're elsewhere." To prove the point, Ellis has a small group of Mohawk Indians make off with the young and innocent Ina, who was "a perfect type of what a young woman should be in a physical sense." Ina, of course, is eventually saved by Seth Jones, but not before Ellis had occa-sion to inform the reader, "It has been said that the American Indian never forgets an injury or a favor. This may be true, but when he remembers later, it is to repay it with horrible ingratitude." The American Indian wants nothing more than to tie the dangling scalp of a white man to his girdle. If this seems harsh, Ellis informs his reader, "ask any man who has had dealings with the Apaches, Comanches, Sioux, Utes or other tribes of the present day."

The differences inherent in Ann Stephens's *Malaeska* and Edward Ellis's *Seth Jones* are telling. In *Malaeska*, Stephens clearly separates her attitude toward Malaeska as woman *and* Indian from that of her white male characters; in *Seth Jones*, Ellis's voice is inseparable from his hero's hatred for American Indians. It is not insignificant to note, therefore, that while *Malaeska* is best remembered as the first dime novel, *Seth Jones* is the far more representative work of the House of Beadle and Adams. *Seth Jones* has none of *Malaeska*'s moral ambiguities. Like many of the popular novels that were published before 1860 by such figures as "Ned Buntline" (E. Z. C. Judson) and Emerson Bennett, as well as the large majority of works published by Beadle and such competing firms as Street & Smith, Frank Tousey, and Munroe, the dime novel offered a clear and unambiguous vision of America: it was a nation of strong, resourceful people who loved adventure, space, and mobility, and who were not bound by either class or location; it was a nation, too, in which rugged white males could make their way in the world, assured that being white and male in America made them morally unassailable against all those who might be "other."

The image of America that the dime novels conveyed should not be glossed over too readily. Movies may have been the first true form of mass amusement in the United States, but the dime novel was the first and most influential of the democratic art forms to be produced in this country. And as movies would provide millions of immigrants with a way of seeing—and knowing—America, so the dime novel provided the new working class with tales of adventure and excitement that were as implicitly political in their nationalism and patriotic fervor—as well as their racism and sexism—as were the films to come by Frank Capra and John Ford. That the popular novels of the period, especially the dime novels, created an illusory rather than a real past is precisely the point: these works were not intended to tell their audience who they were, but who they ought to be. Illumination of what made us, as Henry Canby notes in *The Age of Confidence*, was not the concern of most popular novelists. But Canby misses the point when he than asks: "Is illusion, however, ever less powerful for being essentially false?" For surely the very importance of these words—and the influence most popular art exerts on a culture—stems from the very fact that illusion is all the more powerful just because it is false.

The popularity of the dime novel, however illusory its basic vision, was the result of concrete events that unalterably were changing the way of life in America: the steam press (which allowed for quick and inexpensive mass production); the rise of the middle class; school laws resulting in an increased literacy; urbanization. Numerous other factors as well dictated the success of Erastus and Irwin Beadle's 1860 publishing venture. By pricing the novels at 10 cents rather than 25 cents, the usual price for a novel, Beadle made the works affordable to the working class, which like the young men who were soon to be fighting in the Civil War, needed a form of entertainment that was not only entertaining but also accessible. Later in the century, to quote Canby again, when many of the people "were content, but never enthusiastic," when their "intellects were being cramped into a routine" without any emotional outlets, when the community made the people "in its own likeness and [they] were exactly fitted to its narrow philistinism," the dime novel and its literary extensions continued to provide temporary escape from the "banality of most middle-class experience in America."

During this thirty-year period, from 1860 to 1890, the dime novel underwent numerous changes. Beadle's Dime Novel series, with books of 100 pages, 6¼" × 4", and a burnt-orange cover, lasted for 321 issues; it then became Beadle's New Dime Novels, which issued 309 volumes, all reprints from the earlier series. At the same time that the House of Beadle underwent numerous transformations, other publishing houses competed for the new reading audience. George Munro, a former employee of Beadle, brought out "Munro's Ten Cent Novels" and Robert De Witt "DeWitt's Ten Cent Romance." In 1877, a sixteen-page pamphlet, 8½" × 12½", with black and white illustrations on the cover, appeared. Beadle inaugurated two new series, "Beadle's Dime Library" and "Beadle's Half-Dime Library"; these were joined by Frank Tousey's "Wide Awake Library," George Munro's "Old Sleuth Library," and Norman Munro's "Old Cap Collier Library," and Street and Smith's "Tip Top Weekly" (which featured Frank Merriwell in addition to a cover in color).

As publishers, formats, and series titles changed, so did the focus of interest. Early tales about the Revolutionary War, the War of 1812, and frontier life began to give way to tales about life in the West: in 1869 Street & Smith published two serials by Ned Buntline about Buffalo Bill and in 1877 the story *Deadwood Dick* was the first work issued in "Beadle's Half-Dime Library." During the next two decades, stories about crime and detection became increasingly popular. Although the tales about such figures as Buffalo Bill continued to attract a considerable readership, they were now joined by various detectives—Old Cap Collier, Old Sleuth, Young Sleuth, and Nick Carter—as well as by the notorious "James boys," Frank and Jesse. Other outlaws—Billy the Kid, for example—gained some popularity with the readers of dime novels, but with the exception of Edward L. Wheeler's fictional Deadwood Dick none really rivaled the Jameses. In their daring if sometimes brutal actions, they foreshadowed the popularity in the 1960s of such figures as Bonnie and Clyde and Butch Cassidy and the Sundance Kid, who also spoke to a generation of Americans frustrated by the way in which people in power frequently seemed to abuse the rule of law. Like many of the outlaws and criminals who have become folk heroes, Frank and Jesse James came to represent that strain in American society that recognized the need to stand outside the law in order to respond to the insidious power of those who represented that law.

But the need even to vicariously violate the law in order to protect oneself against those people who in actuality made the law was to meet with considerable moral outrage. And no one was to suffer from the severity of this outrage more than the best known of all the novelists, Horatio Alger, Jr.

It was not until 1866, as Alger acknowledged in "Writing Stories for Boys" (1896), that he "scored a decided success." That success was *Ragged Dick; or, Street Life in New York*, first serialized in *Student and Schoolmate* in 1867 and published in book form in May 1868. It is the work that made Alger's reputation, the work that became the prototype of the "rags-to-riches" novel; it is a work, however, that, for all its simplicity, has been strangely misread. The rags-to-riches ideology for which *Ragged Dick* and its author are best known has little to do with the novel itself. What Alger in fact stresses in *Ragged Dick* is not riches but respectability.

Young Dick Hunter, a prototype of the street Arabs Alger had befriended when he came to New York, is dirty and impoverished when he is introduced to the reader, but he also is honest and hardworking. Although Alger felt compelled to note that he did not consider Dick a model boy, there were some good points about him nevertheless: "He was above doing anything mean or dishonorable. He would not steal, or cheat, or impose upon younger boys, but was frank and straight-forward, manly and self-reliant. His nature was a noble one, and had saved him from all mean faults." Moreover, like many American fictional heroes, Alger's bootblack "looks honest. He has an open face, and . . . can be depended upon." He understands that in America "a good many distinguished men have once been poor boys." There's hope for a young boy like Dick Hunter, but only if he tries: "Telling you won't make it turn out so, Dick," the bootblack is counseled at one point. "If you'll try to be somebody, and grow up into a respectable member of society, you will. You may not become rich—it isn't everybody that becomes rich, you know—but you can obtain a good position, and be respected." Because he is honest and hardworking—because he is a boy with pluck—he also has some good luck. He saves a young child from drowning and is rewarded by the father with a new suit and a good job. This modern day Visible Saint has indeed found favor with Providence; his "lucky stars . . . shinin' pretty bright now," Ragged Dick the Arab street urchin has finally become Richard Hunter, Esq.—"a young gentleman on the way to fame and fortune."

But "fame and fortune" are the words of Dick's friend Fosdick. Alger did not share such a lofty vision for Dick Hunter or any of the young boys in the Ragged Dick series. He was, in fact, very much a part of his time; the urge for Alger—at least as he projected it in his fiction—was for middle-class respectability, not great wealth. The act of "Struggling Upward" (the title that Alger gave to his 1886 novel about Luke Larkin) was worth the effort not because one would go from a "boyhood of privation and self-denial" to one of riches; an adulthood of "prosperity and humor" was all Alger desired—whether the focus of attention was on the bootblack Dick Hunter or the young janitor, Luke Larkin, the son of a carpenter's widow.

In 1900, a year after Alger's death, Theodore Dreiser was to publish *Sister Carrie*, that extraordinary novel that turns the basic Alger story upside down and inside out. (As, even later, Ernest Hemingway would excoriate Alger's "All labor is respectable, my lad, and you have no cause to be ashamed of any honest business" in his 1925 short story, "Soldier's Home"— as indeed Dreiser that same year would again devote his attention to the Algerian sensibility in *An American Tragedy*.) Ironically, it was at just this point that Alger's popularity began to reach a new high; by 1910 it was estimated that more than a million copies of his books were being sold annually. Yet it was only a few years earlier that Alger found several of his works under attack for their sensationalism and was to learn that libraries were either lending his books only to adults or removing them altogether from their shelves.

The problem for Alger began when he, like many other dime novelists, began to write tales about the West. These adventure tales were far more sensational and lurid than the Ragged Dick series, and it was not long before Alger found himself being attacked for his "blood and thunder" novels. Young boys who want "fighting, killing, and thrilling adventures," one critic noted, often turn to the novels of Horatio Alger; and another critic, reviewing *In a New World* (1893), wrote: "One's patience fails long before reaching the end of *In a New World*, the latest volume from the too prolific pen of

Horatio Alger, Jr. One feels indignant not only with the writer, who might do something better than pour forth this unceasing stream of sensationalism, impossible literature, but with the boys who persistently read, enjoy, and talk over them." This came just ten years after Anthony Comstock's virulent attack on half-dime novels and story papers in his notorious *Traps for the Young.* "Trick and device, lying and deceit, dishonesty and bloodshed, lawlessness and licentiousness, is the lesson taught in most of these stories," warned the founder of the New York Society for the Suppression of Vice. Virtue and honesty must be instilled by the parent: "The child's mind must be protected from the virus of putrid imaginations. The passions of the child must be kept subdued, and wholesome restraint ever maintained over youthful desires and whims. Evil communications must be shunned." No wonder that by 1896 Alger would himself comment, "Sensational stories, such as are found in the dime and half-dime libraries, do much harm and are very objectionable. Many a boy has been tempted to crime by them. . . . Better that a boy's life should be filled with humdrum than with such dangerous excitement." (When Alger's books were reprinted in inexpensive editions by Hurst & Co., the jacket of the uniform series noted, "Few boys live who, at some period of their youth, have not read with intense interest, some of the writings of this famous author. Alger is original; his stories enthuse and invigorate the reader, yet they are devoid of sensationalism.")

Coincidentally, but not insignificantly, Alger's comment about the sensational aspects of the dime and half-dime novels appeared the same year as the first publication of Gilbert Patten's "paragon of the paperbooks," *Frank Merriwell; or, First Days at Fardale.* Patten—using the name of Burt L. Standish—went on to write more than 900 tales about Frank and Dick Merriwell. Although the Merriwell stories by the man who was perhaps the last of the major dime novelists were not devoid of adventure and some sensational aspects, they differed considerably from the novels of Horatio Alger and reflect the changes that were taking place in America. Patten, like Alger, settled in New York to become a writer. But, unlike Alger, city life was not of particular importance to his tales; nor was he interested in the boy who was *Strong and Steady* or *Making His Way* or *Shifting for Himself.* If anything, as Patten was to write later, he wanted to make his books beneficial "without allowing them to become namby-pamby or Horatio Algerish." Because he believed that "the old-fashioned dime novel was on the way out," he decided to set a new style with his stories and "make them different and more in step with the times."

Actually, the idea for the Frank Merriwell stories did not originate with

Patten. Street & Smith, still one of the most successful publishing houses in the 1890s, apparently wanted to capitalize on the current success of a series of school stories that had emanated from Great Britain. The basic idea of the series, which was to appear in Street & Smith's "Tip Top Library," was "to interest young readers in the career of a young man at a boarding school, preferably a military or naval academy." It was essential, publisher O. G. Smith informed Patten in a letter dated December 16, 1895, that the initial episodes deal with life in the academy. After about twelve issues, the hero would leave the academy, come into a considerable sum of money, and begin to travel. Twenty or thirty episodes later, "we would bring the hero back and have him go to college—say, Yale University; thence we would take him on his travels again to the South Seas or anywhere." It would be an advantage to the series, Smith told Patten, "to have introduced the Dutchman, the Negro, the Irishman, and any other dialect you are familiar with." Moreover, "a little love element would not be amiss, but this is not particularly important."

The point of Smith's letter was to engage Patten as the author of the series that would be, as the advertising soon announced, "AN IDEAL PUBLICATION FOR THE AMERICAN YOUTH." Patten, of course, accepted the invitation, and began to think of a catchy name for his hero. He decided upon Frank Merriwell because it was "symbolic of the chief characteristics I desired my hero to have—*Frank* for frankness, *merry* for a happy disposition, *well* for health and abounding vitality." Because the first issues were to be stories of American school life, Patten saw in them an opportunity to feature all kinds of athletics, with baseball, about which he knew most, predominating. Such stories, Patten has written in his autobiography, *Frank Merriwell's "Father"* (1964), would give him "an opportunity to preach—by example—the doctrine of a clean mind and healthy body." And so he did, providing Street and Smith with one episode a week for the next three years. Alger's insistence on middle-class respectability has here been replaced by a quest for personal excellence. Like Alger's characters, Patten's heroes do not smoke or drink, but they are—ironically—tougher than Alger's street children. No longer will pluck and an honest face bring the intervention of Providence. The moral sensibility has changed yet again. This is a more strenuous, a more personal and individual, period. It is no longer urging a struggle to reach the middle class but is one *of* the middle class. It is the America of Theodore Roosevelt, Thomas Eakins, Jane Addams, Henry Ford, and Thomas Edison. It was also, however, a period marked by Frederick Jackson Turner's declaration that the frontier was closed, when the availability and meaning of space had to be rethought and redefined. Technology may have been creating new ways of dramatically using space, but for the people who were part of Jacob Riis's *How the Other Half Lives* (1890) or Upton Sinclair's *The Jungle* (1906) or Charles Chaplin's not too-distant *Modern Times* (1936) the sense of enclosure—despite the rhetoric of the newly inaugurated president—was a formidable fact of life. For some, the turn of the century may have been an Age of Confidence; for others, a 1906 letter sent by a "Constant Reader" to the editor of the *Jewish Daily Forward* speaks of a different America: "I read the troubles of family life in your 'Bintel Brief' each day very attentively. But my own troubles are so great, so enormous, that I will not even ask you for your permission to print my few words in your paper, as others do, but simply, I ask you right on the spot: Help!"

No doubt there was little that the editor of the *Forward* could say to such despair. There was little, too, that popular culture as yet had to say to most of America's immigrants. The world of P. T. Barnum, of vaudeville and sports, was there to entertain all who could afford to attend, but popular literature spoke primarily to a white Protestant audience, frequently extolling a Christian morality. In the works of such writers as Alger and Patten, whose readers and heroes were largely male, this morality was implicitly stated. In the works of numerous women writers, however, Christian morality was not only explicitly expressed but was in fact central to the authors' vision. Nowhere is this more apparent than in Martha Finley's enormously popular series about Elsie Dinsmore.

Finley, who frequently used the name "Farquharson," began to write *Elsie Dinsmore* during the Civil War. Bedridden and dependent upon her stepbrother for support, she prayed for the strength and ability to write a novel that would allow her to support herself. Her prayers were apparently answered, and she worked on the novel for the next three and a half years. The manuscript was then submitted to M. W. Dodd, who cut the work in half: *Elsie Dinsmore* was published in 1867 and *Elsie's Holiday at Roselands* in 1868. As was the case with Alger's *Ragged Dick*, *Elsie Dinsmore* became the prototype for the volumes that were to follow.

Unlike Alger's stories for boys, in which the young hero seeks the support and patronage of an older man, Elsie needs only the love of her father and, above all, Jesus. When Elsie is unjustly punished by her teacher, she bemoans her failure to endure the punishment in silence: " 'Oh!' she sobbed, 'I—I did not do it; I did not bear it patiently. I was treated unjustly, and punished when I was not to blame, and I grew angry. Oh! I'm afraid I shall never be like Jesus! never, never.' " It makes Elsie's heart ache "to read how the Jews abused our dear, dear Saviour." It also makes her heart ache that her father, who went to Europe shortly after her birth and her mother's death, and has just returned to his home in Roselands, does not love Jesus as much as she, and at first does not seem to love his daughter. But Elsie perseveres, and soon her demanding father begins to cherish her too. Still, despite the hugs and kisses and Elsie's sitting on her father's knee, there is trouble between the two. For although Elsie never hesitates to tell Horace Dinsmore that she loves him more than anyone save Jesus—"It was Jesus I meant papa; you know he loves me even better than you do, and I must love Him best of all; but there is no one else that I love *half* so much as I love you, my own dear, dear precious father"—Dinsmore insists that Elsie do "just what I bid you, nothing more nor less." So, when her father bids her to sing a song on the Sabbath, Elsie is torn between her father and her Father, and refuses to do as she is asked. As punishment—for punishment is inevitable—she must sit where she is until she obeys. Elsie will not obey, will not sing on the Sabbath, and sits until she faints. Dinsmore carries his young daughter to her bedroom where she insists on praying before going to sleep. She tells her father that she loves him "so very, *very* much," but not better than everybody else. "No papa, I love Jesus best; you next"—a reply that does not entirely please Dinsmore, for he is "not quite willing that she should love even her Saviour better than himself." Nevertheless, Horace and Elsie enjoy their life together and the tears that Elsie sheds as she goes to sleep thinking that her father may remarry are wiped away by Horace, as "he longed to tell her that all her fears were groundless, that none other could ever fill her place in his heart."

Finley went on to fill many more pages with Elsie's story. In all, the Elsie Series (1867–1904) comprised twenty-eight volumes. When that seemed not to satisfy the public's interest in her creation, Finley supplemented the Elsie stories with the Mildred series, seven volumes devoted to Elsie's cousin, Mildred Keith. Critical response to Finley's work was by no means unanimous. To some, she had destroyed childhood itself and substituted "the precocious melancholy of a prig"; to others, she was to be praised for "her simple womanliness and Christianity," which made her "a type of the best in American spinsterhood." But however the critics may have disagreed about Elsie and her cousin Mildred, Martha Finley remained one of America's most popular writers of juvenile fiction. If Elsie's piety caused some to see her as "a morbid, introspective, and self-conscious child," her piety certainly was not unknown to the post–Civil War readers, especially those who were female. Harriet Beecher Stowe's *Uncle Tom's Cabin* (1852), with the saintly little Eva, had been adapted into the most commercially successful of all American plays; Louisa May Alcott's *Little Women* (1868–69) was published the year after *Elsie Dinsmore* first appeared; one could even hear overtones of Elsie in *A New England Girlhood* (1889), the autobiography of Lucy Larcom, poet and former Lowell factory worker: "The first real unhappiness I remember to have felt was when some one told me, one day, that I did not love God. I insisted, almost tearfully, that I did; but I was told that if I did truly love him I should always be good. I knew I was not that, and the feeling of sudden orphanage came over me like a bewildering cloud. Yet I was sure that I loved my father and mother, even when I was naughty. Was He harder to please than they?" But most of all, and whatever the differences between juvenile and adult fiction, Elsie was a part of the women's sphere that formed the subject of the domestic novel.

During recent years the question of the authorial intention of many of the women writers of the nineteenth century has become a matter of considerable scholarly contention. As the more widely debated issue of the scholarly canon begins to dominate much of the literary discussion of the 1980s, so too does the question of whether the domestic novels of the previous century were "any good." In the heat of the debates about intention and quality, attention no longer was given to the domestic novels as works of popular literature. But they are as representative of women's struggles to deal with the restrictions of a society dominated by men as the fiction of Alger, Owen Wister, and Zane Grey would project fantasies of male power and supremacy.

Not that the fiction of so many women writers of the nineteenth century was not impelled by a need for power and control. To the contrary: whether the writers were but "scribbling women" who, as Sarah J. Hale said of herself, wrote only "to obtain the means of supporting and educating her children in some measure as their father would have done" or whether they were more consciously intent on subverting male domination, their novels are about dominance and subjugation. For men, our popular literature insists, this power was defined by money, a six-shooter, or the power of silence; for women, at least in the nineteenth century, this power was almost always tied to the will of God. If home and husband were too restrictive, Jesus and Heaven were not: "It is not till one looses one's hold of other things and looks to Jesus alone, that one finds how much he can do," Mrs. Vawse says in Susan B. Warner's *The Wide, Wide World* (1855). A woman may no longer have any friends to lean upon but that is of little matter: "My home is in heaven, and my Saviour is there preparing a place for me. I know it—I am sure of it—and I can wait a little while, and rejoice all the while I can wait."

Waiting is what women do in most of the works by nineteenth-century women writers. In Warner's *The Wide, Wide World* Mrs. Vawse waits to go to her new Home, while the novel's heroine, Ellen Montgomery, must "wait" until she has learned to control her desires before her home can, in effect, become a heavenly home on earth. In Harriet Prescott Spofford's short story "Circumstance" (1860), the nameless protagonist waits, pinned in a tree, for a panther—the "Indian Devil"—to strike. The story, as sexually wrought as it is racist, makes clear that it is God not man who will save women from the clutches of "the great King Death." When first assaulted by the panther, the protagonist does not think to call upon God: "She called upon her husband. It seemed to her that she had but one friend in the world; that was he; and again the cry, loud, clear, prolonged, echoed through the woods." But when her husband does not come to rescue her—the panther fawning "his fearful head upon her," scoring "her cheek with his tongue"— she remembers that she is in God's hands and that "if this were in his great plan of providence, was it not best, and should she not accept it." She begins to sing softly of God's glory, and so singing soothes the passion of the beast until her husband finally arrives to kill the panther that would ravage her body. But there is no longer any home to which wife and husband can return; the destruction of the panther has taken place while "tomahawk and scalping-knive" have left their home in smoking ruin. Whatever the meaning of the experience in the forest, of the encounter with the "Indian Devil," there was only "desolation and death" to be found in the domestic sphere; "beneficence and life" were in the forest, and "for the rest,— the world was all before them, where to choose."

The attitude toward men that is projected in many of the works by women during this period is as ambiguous as it is in the novels of Martha Finley and Spofford's "Circumstance." In some works, perhaps best exemplified by E. D. E. N. Southworth's enormously popular *Ishmael; or, In the Depths* and its sequel *Self-Raised; or, From the Depths* (published in two volumes in 1876), the central male character was highly regarded because he was a true benefactor to women. Ishmael Worth, whom Southworth told her publisher she loved more than any other character she created, is the ideal male. Indeed, these two works, originally serialized in the *New York Ledger* in 1863–64 as *Self-Made; or, Out of the Depths*, were like most of Southworth's other novels except for the character of Ishmael. He was an "experiment" for her, and a most successful one. Ishmael was born to serve the needs as well as the rights of women. He begins life with little; he has no parents, no place in the world; "He has nothing—nothing but the eye of the Almighty Father regarding him." As is the case with Alger's heroes,

however, that is more than enough for a boy with integrity and perseverance. Ishmael becomes a respected lawyer, living "to honor, to vindicate,
to avenge" his mother. And he does so by honoring all women, "loving,
feeble, and oppressed from the beginning of time." As Alger hoped that his
young readers would "find something in [Ragged Dick] to imitate," so
Southworth hoped the youth of every land would take Ishmael for a guiding star, "to show them that there is no depth of human misery from which
they may not, by virtue, energy, and perseverance, rise to earthly honors
as well as eternal glory."

Most domestic novelists, however, had a less glorified view of men. Most
men were sterner and more demanding, like Horace Dinsmore, or more
distant and unavailable, like the husband in "Circumstance." Frequently,
the resolution of the novel came only with the male's conversion, as it did
in one of the most popular novels of the nineteenth century, Augusta Evans
Wilson's *St. Elmo* (1867). St. Elmo is morally bankrupt, but he is rich,
virile, and mysterious. When the novel's heroine, Edna Earl, first meets
him, "A painful thrill shot along [her] nerves, and an indescribable sensation of dread, a presentiment of coming ill, overshadowed her heart." St.
Elmo's face had once been singularly handsome, but now "the fair chiseled
lineaments were blotted by dissipation, and blackened and distorted by the
baleful fires of a fierce, passionate nature, and a restless, powerful, and
unhallowed intellect." Before long, "with bitter shame and reproach and
abject contrition, she realized that she had begun to love the sinful, blasphemous man." Yet she will not marry him. Instead, she goes to New York
to become a writer; here, she publishes a novel that the critics snarl at but
"the mass of readers warmly approved." She turns down numerous offers
for marriage and refuses to see St. Elmo. But, as Wilson would have it, St.
Elmo reforms and becomes a minister. Now, Edna is prepared to marry
him. He, for his part, will "snap the fetters" of her literary bondage. The
public that loves her so well will have to "whistle for a new pet," for she
belongs solely to him. And as they kneel before the shining altar, Edna
knows that "his dedication was complete; and now to be his companion
through all the remaining years of their earthly pilgrimage, to be allowed
to help him and love him, to walk heavenward with her hand in his; this—
this was the crowning glory and richest blessing of her life."

Here, then, was a world made clear and simple. Despite Seneca Falls—
to some degree, no doubt, because of it—despite Jane Addams, Susan B.
Anthony, Lillian D. Wald, and Elizabeth Cady Stanton, despite, in some
cases, their own lives, most of the domestic novelists echoed the plea of
Augusta Wilson in *Beulah*, a work published eight years before *St. Elmo*.

Fearful that husbands, sons, and brothers would leave home for "the altars of mammon," Wilson pleaded that women prove themselves "worthy of the noble mission for which [they] were created." It was their responsibility to provide a moral light; the domestic sphere had to be the sphere of women. It was a strenuous task, one that required the help of God: "God help the women of America!," Wilson pleaded. "Grant them the true womanly instincts which, in the dawn of the republic, made 'home' the Eden, and the acme of all human hopes and joys." This cry, which reverberates through much of domestic fiction, is telling: women were to be the moral center of America, but it was the men who established (and then violated) the moral temper. What the domestic novelists have given us, then, is an inversion of Puritan piety. The Victorians became *the* Puritans, establishing an emotional response to God; serious metaphysical discourse was replaced by God as a *deus ex machina*, bringing salvation to those who wanted to move into the wide, wide world but who found that world, in actuality, to be narrow, restrictive, and menacing.

By the end of the nineteenth century, it was not just the domestic novelists who were responding to the restrictiveness of American society. The piety of these writers, it now seems clear, was but a variation on the adventure fantasies of the dime novelists. Order and meaning had to be established, and popular culture addressed that need. In the most basic sense, there was little difference between the Heaven yearned for by Susan Warner and the open spaces of the West that attracted many dime novelists in the 1870s and 1880s: what they provided was the illusion of a meaningful structure.

Few events better underscored just how illusory that sense of order actually was than the Chicago World's Columbian Exposition of 1893. Intended to be a display of America's great achievement and to delineate its dreams for the future, White City coincided with the onset of an economic panic and the Pullman strike of 1894. It offered a dazzling display of technological innovations and cultural forms, so much so that Owen Wister was moved to write in his diary that "before I had walked for two minutes, a bewilderment at the gloriousness of everything seized me." But for all the fair's fascination with technology and culture, it showed little interest in the lives of the people who were being affected by these innovations. Unlike Wister, Edward Bellamy was moved to write of this utopian vision: "The underlying motive of the whole exhibition, under a sham of pretense of patriotism is business, advertising with a view to individual money-making."

White City refused to recognize some of the central changes taking place in the United States. It paid homage to America's technological powers, but ignored the social and cultural displacement felt by many—blacks, Indians, as well as newcomers who were immigrating to America in unprecedented numbers. Not surprisingly, however, it was the popular culture that reflected many of these changes. First, there was, as there had to be, a fading away of old forms. The dime and half-dime novels slowly gave way to the pulps, and by the 1880s piety was less central to the concerns of the domestic novelists. The once-iconoclastic Phineas T. Barnum died in 1890; and Buffalo Bill, who reached the apex of his fame at the Chicago World's Columbian Exposition, soon after began to struggle to keep the public interested in the character he and "Ned Buntline" had created, and was to die in 1917. Just as much of the popular poetry and illustration of the post–Civil War period focused on reunion and rebirth, so the popular images of the 1870s and 1880s were reconstructed during the next two decades to address the issues confronting the new middle and working classes.

Buffalo Bill, as E. E. Cummings would write, may have been defunct, but the cowboy was not. Cody—and of course James Fenimore Cooper's Leatherstocking—were transformed into Owen Wister's *The Virginian* (1902), Zane Grey's *Riders of the Purple Sage* (1912), and Clarence Mulford's Hopalong Cassidy (beginning with *Bar-20*, in 1907). Wister, enamored by White City, was distressed by the changes taking place in America as a result of its new populace, and created perhaps the best known of all Western heroes to uphold traditional values; as agile with words as he is with a gun, the Virginian stands for the glory of the once-virgin West—for all the patriotic images that the name Virginian conjures up—as he stands for a rejection of an urban, immigrant East. Wister's audience, however, like that of Mulford and Grey (whose books were on the best-seller list for almost ten years), was largely urban. The western provided city dwellers with a vision of space and freedom—a place where men were not bound by buildings, clocks, and social responsibility. In the city, men had to bear the responsibility of work and home; in the West, they could be cowboys—just "great big simple boys," as Zane Grey had one of his characters say in *The Light of Western Stars* (1914).

A need for space and a sense of the past—pervasive subjects almost from the inception of this country—dominated the popular imagination at the turn of the century. The Revolutionary War, the most popular subject of the early dime novelists, received new treatment at the hands of Winston Churchill, whose 1899 *Richard Carvel* was a best-seller. So was *The Crisis*, Churchill's 1900 novel set during the Civil War. Both novels, of course, provided the reader with a sense of the past, as well as with a sense of space. But, ironically, as large numbers of people—particularly in cities—were attending sports events, amusement parks like Coney Island, or such public parks as Central Park and Prospect Park in an attempt to get "out of doors," many of the same people were going indoors to be entertained, to think about the past, to escape from their own enclosures. The movies, which had their first official United States public showing for a paying audience in 1896, were about to become the most popular, accessible, and influential of all the popular arts. Between 1908 and 1910, for example, seventy films were produced having the Civil War as their setting. Before long, these films about America would be made by people who had but recently come to this country. In New York, first- and second-generation Jews like Irving Berlin, Sammy Cahn, Dorothy Fields, Ira Gershwin, E. Y. Harburg, Lorenz Hart, Richard Rodgers, and Arthur Schwartz were growing up and soon would dominate the field of popular songwriting. (The enormous popularity of Charles K. Harris's 1892 song, "After the Ball," frequently has obscured the fact that an earlier song, "Bake That Matzoth Pie," denotes his ethnic background.) Minstrel shows, like Buffalo Bill's, were defunct (though not popular stereotypes of either blacks or Native Americans), and black musicians were beginning to play for audiences who were "steppin' out" to have a good time and fulfill their fantasies. It was an America that Martha Finley never dreamed of and that Owen Wister feared. Pious children and noble cowboys would remain with us, but there were now new voices to be heard, voices that would drastically alter and reshape the way we would respond to Crèvecoeur's haunting question.

Jack Salzman

Immigrants and Other Americans

In Mark Twain's novel *A Connecticut Yankee in King Arthur's Court* (1889) the forces of pseudomedieval community (which bears some features of the pre–Civil War South and some of pre-emigration Europe) and modern American capitalist society clash head-on, as the Yankee entrepreneur and Colt arms-factory manager Hank Morgan anachronistically brings to Camelot a whole array of nineteenth-century innovations—telegraph, telephone, sewing machine, bicycle, dynamite, typewriter, and, most interestingly, a newspaper. The first issue of the Camelot *Weekly Hosannah and Literary Volcano!*, announced by "one greater than kings . . . the newsboy," is a paper "too loud" for Arthur's sixth-century Britain: "It was good Arkansas journalism, but this was not Arkansas." Hank Morgan's "hunger" for news contrasts with the unsuitability of an undisturbed feudal system for sensationalist news reporting. Thus the *Hosannah*'s "Court Circular" column reads:

COURT CIRCULAR

On Monday, the King rode in the park.
   " Tuesday,   "   "   "
   " Wednesday   "   "   "
   " Thursday   "   "   "
   " Friday,   "   "   "
   " Saturday   "   "   "
   " Sunday,   "   "   "

No wonder that the Yankee's modern and at times catastrophic activities make all the headlines. As Benedict Anderson has emphasized, drawing on an idea expressed by Alexis de Tocqueville, an aristocracy did not need newspapers. The rise of modern bourgeoisies, of capitalism, and of national and ethnic identifications was intricately interrelated with the emergence of the press. The specificity with which newspapers and periodicals brought together on the same page or in the same issue the most diverse yet concrete items, *this* marriage announcement with *that* story, *this* commodity price with *that* sketch or vignette, *this* historical sidelight with *that* editorial opinion, *this* advertisement with *that* letter to the editor, Anderson writes, created "communities by reverberation."

Print capitalism participated actively, not only in the emergence of an American national life, but also in the creation of ethnic and regional "imagined communities." As Tocqueville put it, "Newspapers make associations, and associations make newspapers." In the period of the "incorporation" of America (Alan Trachtenberg's phrase), divergent identities were also being generated, and "minority voices," too, supported the modern constructions of imagined ethnic and national communities. Whether immigrants from diverse hometowns and with dramatically different dialects began to perceive themselves as "Norwegian-Americans" and "Italian-Americans," whether religiously heterogeneous newcomers learned to think of themselves as "German-Americans," whether former Moravians, Bohemians, and Silesians came to describe themselves as "Czech-Americans," whether traditionally free or formerly enslaved, light- or dark-skinned ethnically diverse inhabitants of the United States thought of themselves as "Afro-Americans," whether the different original dwellers on North American soil conceived of themselves as intertribal "Indians," or whether readers of the most varied ancestries learned to view themselves as "Americans"—in all these cases literature, print culture, and most especially newspaper and periodical writing played a crucial role in shaping and identifying various modern ethnic communities. Newspapers provided orientation, "nationalized" and "ethnicized" readers, created national unity as well as ethnic divisions, and promised revelations across ethnic boundaries, yet also affirmed the existence of "veils" around ethnic groupings. Specific forms of concrete attachment to a village, a place, or a kinship network had to be generalized as widely recognizable imagined group affiliations. The establishment of imagined communities was facilitated by print media "organs" (a naturalizing metaphor for periodicals first recorded in 1826); these organs of the community were often known by nicknames such as "grandma" (for the *Commercial Advertiser*) or "hellhound of the opposition" (for the *New York World*). What gave the project of community construction added meaning was the high influx of immigrants—23 million came from 1880 to World War I alone—and the intensified process of urbanization—in 1870 only a quarter of all Americans lived in towns and cities, by 1920 more than half did.

In nineteenth- and twentieth-century America a large number of writers from all backgrounds worked as journalists, editors, correspondents, and contributors to the vastly expanding newspaper and periodical market. This development started well before the Civil War (which is a poor divider in nineteenth-century cultural life), but accelerated and intensified toward the turn of the century. The eighteenth-century patron saint of American journalism was Benjamin Franklin, whose role as a founding father, inventor, and self-made man was nicely supported by his identification as a journalist, which Franklin himself celebrated in his *Autobiography* (first published in its entirety in 1867): " Our first Papers made a quite different Appearance from any before in the Province, a better Type & better printed." With Franklin, Benedict Anderson writes, "the printer's office emerged as the key to North American communications and community intellectual life." The "Franklin Press," for example, was so named in 1856 because its inventor received his inspiration from Franklin in a dream. Franklin's establishment of his own press, his founding of the newspaper that became the *Pennsylvania Gazette* in 1729, and of the *General Magazine* in 1741, were stories often retold, on which many nineteenth-century journal writers and newspaper men and women modeled their own careers, as they engaged in a double quest for print literacy and divergent nationalisms and ethnicities. The forces of advancing capitalist technology made possible not only modern warfare, communications, industrialization, urbanization, and centralization but also the proliferation of diversity through the creation of communities by reverberation.

Major nineteenth- and twentieth-century writers such as Edgar Allan Poe, Walt Whitman, Mark Twain, Stephen Crane, Theodore Dreiser, and Ernest Hemingway did significant work as journalists. Such work, however, was not limited to white native-born Americans. The extent to which immigrant and minority intellectuals participated in journalistic endeavors is surprising, and it is hardly an overstatement to say that the newspaper and the periodical formed the central arena of the writers' activities and shaped themes and forms of their literature. It is therefore appropriate to focus an account of America's polyethnic literature not merely on the development of books but on the centrality of journalism in the literature of practically all ethnic groups.

Newspapers functioned as an orientation device. When the enslaved Frederick Douglass heard the word "abolition" for the first time he tried to ascertain its meaning. A dictionary definition, "the act of abolishing," proved useless, but a city paper, the *Baltimore American*, instructed him that it was slavery and the slave trade that were to be abolished. He writes in his *Narrative of the Life of Frederick Douglass, an American Slave, Written by Himself* (1845): "From this time I understood the words *abolition* and *abolitionist*, and always drew near when that word was spoken, expecting to hear something of importance to myself and fellow-slaves." His owner's wife, Mrs. Auld, understood and resented the power emanating from newspaper reading: "Nothing seemed to make her more angry than to see me with a newspaper. She seemed to think that here lay the danger. I have had her rush at me with a face made all up of fury, and snatch from me a newspaper, in a manner that fully revealed her apprehension." Douglass retained his love for the press. As a resident of New Bedford, after his escape from slavery, Douglass was given a copy of William Lloyd Garrison's paper *Liberator*, which "took its place . . . next to the Bible," a phrasing that resonates with Hegel's view of newspapers as a substitute for prayers. Douglass writes in *My Bondage and My Freedom* (1855): "I not only liked—I loved this paper, and its editor." After a two-year trip to the British Isles Douglass made plans to start a newspaper of his own: "[A] tolerably well conducted press, in the hands of persons of the despised race, by calling out the mental energies of the race itself; by making them acquainted with their own latent powers; by enkindling among them the hope that for them there is a future; by developing their moral power; by combining and reflecting their talents—would prove a most powerful means of removing prejudice, and of awakening an interest in them." Following the North Star—the old escape route from slavery—received a new meaning for Afro-American readers after Douglass founded the newspaper *North Star* (1847), followed by *Frederick Douglass's Paper* (1851), in Rochester.

In the German-American novelist Theodore Dreiser's *Sister Carrie* (1900), newspapers have a great metaphoric importance, as Philip Fisher suggested. Hurstwood reads them, Carrie wants to be featured in them. For Carrie, succeeding in the theater is only a step toward publicity in the press. Hurstwood, in his decline, reads about Carrie in out-of-date newspapers, and, at one point, he is literally "buried in his papers." The newspapers also tell Hurstwood about Carrie's absence in a direct way: "He knew that Carrie was not there not only because there was no light shown through the transom, but because the evening papers were stuck between the outside knob and the door."

Some newcomers were among the ardent innovators in print journalism from the times of the revolving cylinder press in the 1850s to the arrival of the typewriter in the 1880s. The German-American Ottmar Mergenthaler perfected the invention of the linotype in a Baltimore basement, an invention that was soon adopted by Stilson Hutchins's *Washington Post* and Horace Greeley's *New York Tribune* and came into general use by the 1890s. (In 1886 the enterprising Mark Twain, who also marketed books on the newspaper model, by subscription, planned to inspect the invention in Baltimore, but put his money on the rivaling Paige typesetter that lost out.) Carl Schurz, a German participant in the 1848 revolution who emigrated to the United States in 1852, embarked on a long career in liberal politics and journalism. Apart from his activities as Union brigadier general and Missouri senator (1869–73), he worked as correspondent of the *New York Tribune*, for which another revolutionary of 1848, Karl Marx, had covered the European scene from 1851 to 1862. Among Greeley's other European correspondents was Margaret Fuller, whose thirty-three dispatches to the *Tribune* from 1847 to 1849 included detailed accounts of the events of the Italian 1848 revolution, posthumously collected in the volume *At Home and Abroad* (1856). Carl Schurz continued his career as co-editor of the German-language *St. Louis Westliche Post* and the *New York Evening Post*, and as contributor to *Harper's Weekly*. His three-volume *Reminiscences* (1907–8) contains interesting passages on his Americanization in Philadelphia, where he lived in a circle of German immigrants centered on the weekly paper, *Die Locomotive*. Schurz learned English, without a grammar, by resolutely beginning to read the daily *Philadelphia Ledger:* "Regularly every day I worked through editorial articles, the news letters and despatches, and even as many of the advertisements as my time would allow." The process of Americanization was completed in 1859 when he gave the speech "True Americanism" at Boston's Faneuil Hall, praising the United States as the place where all members of the human family might meet and mix on the basis of equality, advocating suffrage without Know-Nothing restrictions, and invoking a noble history that included Bunker Hill and "Benjamin Franklin's birthplace." The Hungarian-born Jewish journalist Joseph Pulitzer came to America in 1864 and wrote for Carl Schurz's *St. Louis Westliche Post*. Later, Pulitzer made the *New York World*, which he acquired in 1883, the popular modern newspaper that ran the first comic strips. Richard Felton Outcault's humorous "Origin of a New Species, or the Evolution of the Crocodile Explained" (1894) was soon followed by the serial "Down Hogan's Alley," set in the New York slums and printed in color. Because of the hero's large yellow shirt (yellow was the hardest color to reproduce with the new technology), the strip was renamed "The Yellow Kid" (on February 16, 1896); alluding to this cartoon, Charles Anderson Dana of the *New York Sun* gave the sensationalist press the name "yellow journalism." In 1897 the German-

American Rudolph Dirks contributed the first long-running comic strip, "The Katzenjammer Kids," to Pulitzer's competitor, William Randolph Hearst's *New York Journal;* this strip featured two German-accented boys in a fantasy-Africa and was based on Wilhelm Busch's German children's book *Max und Moritz.*

The immigrants Edward Bok (from Holland), S. S. McClure (from Ireland), and Jacob Riis (from Denmark) actively participated in the establishment of a national journalism. Riis, who had the crime beat at the *New York Tribune,* became *the* reporter of the *New York Evening Sun,* developed the use of the flashlight for muckraking photographs and published the famous volume *How the Other Half Lives* (1890), which describes his journalistic struggle against tenement conditions in New York City. (In the pages of the *Commercial Advertiser,* the Russian-born journalist Abraham Cahan satirically viewed the search for the "Other Half" as the concern of an "amateur slumologist.") McClure and Bok were the central figures to create syndicated journalism (in 1884) and mass circulation magazines. *McClure's Magazine* first appeared in 1893 with contributions by Hjalmar Hjorth Boyesen, Sarah Orne Jewett, Joel Chandler Harris, and Robert Louis Stevenson and with the interview feature, "Real Conversations." It was sold at the startling price of only 15 cents, opening a magazine war with *Munsey's* and *Cosmopolitan.* Bok gave shape to the *Ladies' Home Journal,* of which he became the editor in 1889, by imagining the magazine as an "authoritative clearinghouse for all the problems confronting women in the home," giving "light and leading in the woman's world." Bok created a new advertisement-oriented market and established himself as a name editor, a personality, and a leader.

Riis, McClure, and Bok emphasized the deep significance of their journalistic endeavors in widely read autobiographies, Riis's *The Making of an American* (1901), McClure's *My Autobiography* (1914), partly ghostwritten by Willa Cather, and *The Americanization of Edward Bok: The Autobiography of a Dutch Boy Fifty Years After* (1920). The books, modeled on the life story of Franklin and on Horatio Alger's popular success stories of shoeshine boys and, of course, newsboys in the Ragged Dick (1867 ff.), Luck and Pluck (1869 ff.) and Tattered Tom series (1871 ff.), sketch amazingly parallel life patterns from lowly beginnings in the Old World to wealth or national fame by way of print media. The thrust of subjugating varied and concrete lives to the generalized and community-supporting pattern of Franklin is also visible in Edward Bok's account of the life of his father-in-law, Cyrus Curtis. The famed owner of the *Ladies' Home Journal* had founded his own first paper, *The Young America,* at age fifteen in 1865 and, in 1897 and for $1,000, bought Franklin's *Pennsylvania Gazette*, now called *Saturday Evening Post*, and appointed as editor George Horace Lorimer, who wrote features such as "Letters of a Self-Made Merchant to His Son." The journal reached the unheard-of circulation of more than a million copies by 1900. Bok entitled the book about his father-in-law, *The Boy Who Followed Ben Franklin* (1926).

The son of an Irish laborer, Joel Chandler Harris joined the *Atlanta Constitution* in 1876, from which his Uncle Remus tales made him famous. *Uncle Remus: His Songs and Sayings* (1880), *Uncle Remus and His Friends* (1882), and *Nights with Uncle Remus* (1883) now form a rich repository of nineteenth-century black folk tales, including such influential ones as "The Wonderful Tar-Baby Story," "Brer Rabbit's Riddle," "Mr. Possum Loves Peace," and other precursors of blues heroes. Uncle Remus's animal fables of outwitted powerful adversaries are now largely considered in the same light that Harris presented them: "Not one of them is cooked, and not one or any part of one is an invention of mine. They are all genuine folk-tales." Harris's sense of accurate reporting made his books part of a new canon of American folk collections in the period that reported specific idioms, yet helped to create a shared sense of Americanness.

Black folk music is mentioned and described in Frederick Douglass's *Narrative* (1845), and in the first Afro-American novel, William Wells Brown's *Clotel; or, The President's Daughter* (1853). In her *Diary from Dixie*, written in the Civil War years and published in 1905, Mary Boykin Chesnut describes the centripetal power of a camp meeting. In 1867 Thomas Wentworth Higginson, who had led a black regiment in the Civil War, published the article "Negro Spirituals" in the *Atlantic Monthly*. In the same year W. F. Allen's collection, *Slave Songs of the United States*, appeared in print. Indian materials were collected by the journalist George Copway (Kah-ge-ga-gah-bowh) in *The Traditional History and Characteristic Sketches of the Ojibway Nation* (1850) and by Daniel Brinton in *Myths of the Americas* (1868). In 1854 Thomas B. Thorpe published "The Big Bear of Arkansas," a story supposedly told on a Mississippi steamboat and a source of William Faulkner's *Go Down, Moses* (1942). The folk collections, at times assembled by journalists, in turn inspired other reporters and writers.

One of the most brilliant authors of the period, Charles W. Chesnutt, started his literary career in New York in 1883 as a reporter for Dow, Jones, and Company and, reputedly, as a gossip columnist for the *New York Mail & Express*, which covered the lives of the Vanderbilts and the Morgans. In the second year of McClure's syndicate Chesnutt contributed "Uncle Peter's House" (1885), followed by many short stories and sketches; and in 1887 his best-known story, "The Goophered Grapevine," was accepted by the *Atlantic Monthly*, then under the editorship of Thomas Bailey Aldrich. Narrated by the Ohio Yankee grape-cultivator John who, together with his wife Annie, goes to North Carolina after the war, the frame story soon leads to an encounter with the former slave Uncle Julius. Julius's inside tale describes the magical transformation of the slave Henry—who ate goophered grapes from the very vineyard John wants to purchase and cultivate—into a living grapevine whose seasonally fluctuating market value was advantageously utilized by his owner. Despite the story of the goophered grapevine, John buys the vineyard: Yankee modernizers may not be superstitious, but they can be greedy. Chesnutt wrote fourteen interrelated conjure stories from 1887 to 1900, seven of which were collected in *The Conjure Woman* (1899). William Dean Howells reviewed this volume and the collection *The Wife of His Youth and Other Stories of the Color Line* (1899) in the *Atlantic Monthly*, comparing Chesnutt with Henry James, Ivan Turgenev, and Guy de Maupassant and revealing that the author was an Afro-American. The conjure tales, however, are also reminiscent of Mark Twain—who is mentioned in "Baxter's Procrustes," a story Chesnutt published in the *Atlantic Monthly* in 1904. In *Conjure Woman* as in *Connecticut Yankee*, a postbellum Northern entrepreneur confronts preindustrial people whom he misunderstands and modernizes violently. In Chesnutt's universe, however, the Afro-American narrator of the inside tale gets equal time, and, ideally, much of the reader's sympathy. Chesnutt, who tried to succeed in "the author business," published a biography, *Frederick Douglass* (1899), as well as the novels *The House Behind the Cedars* (1900), *The Marrow of Tradition* (1901), and *The Colonel's Dream* (1905). Chesnutt's interest in modernization included the new life of the colored middle class in urban centers such as Cleveland; and his talents as a social satirist of that milieu are striking. The denouement of "A Matter of Principle" (in *The Wife of His Youth*) reveals that the light-skinned Mr. Clayton's race prejudice against darker-skinned Afro-Americans has thwarted a possible matrimonial connection between his daughter Alice and a desirable spouse. Significantly, Clayton learns the bitter truth from an article on the local page of his morning paper.

Indian, Afro-American, and immigrant autobiographical books not written by journalists also illustrate and stress the importance of the press in the period. *O-Gî-Mäw-Kwĕ Mit-I-Gwä-Kî (Queen of the Woods)* (1899) was an early American Indian novel by chief Simon Pokagon, a Potawatomi author who had printed the pamphlet *Red Man's Greeting* on birch bark for distribution in Chicago at the World's Columbian Exposition in 1893 in order to remind Americans that "the land on which Chicago and the Fair stands, still belongs to [the Potawatomis], as it has never been paid for." Chief

Pokagon's partly autobiographical sentimental novel—which used much Algonquin vocabulary with parenthetical English translations—was published posthumously, and the publisher appended a fairly extensive collection of newspaper clippings to the text from which one learns that the author's and Pocahontas's name were derived from the same Algonquin root, "Poka" (shield). Another note of the publisher testifies that Simon Pokagon "has furnished many contributions to such leading magazines as the *Arena, Forum, Chautauquan, Harper's Magazine, Review of Reviews*, and many others . . . [and] has been called by the press, 'the red-skin bard,' the 'Longfellow of his race,' and the 'grand old man.' "

The Afro-American founder of Tuskegee Institute, Booker T. Washington, included a variety of adulatory newspaper clippings from Boston, Buffalo, Chicago, and New York papers in his best-selling autobiography, *Up From Slavery* (1901), which was originally serialized in Lyman Abbott's *Outlook*. It is another life of a self-made man, one who traverses an enormous social distance from slave cabin to nationwide public distinction as educator and power broker. Washington's incorporation of the *New York World*'s description of his accommodating Atlanta Exposition address of 1895 as coming from a "Negro Moses," or a *Boston Transcript* account of the powerful oratory of "this man of culture and voice and power, as well as a dark skin," suggested the high esteem in which the author was held and how he strengthened his "image" as a black authority and leader.

A Jewish-immigrant woman from Polotzk (Russia), Mary Antin, described her rebirth as an American in her popular autobiography *The Promised Land* (1912), which had previously been serialized in the *Atlantic Monthly*. In a chapter entitled "My Country," which marks the ethnic turning point of her life, Antin portrays her new self-understanding as an American citizen. "Naturalization," she writes, "with us Russian Jews, may mean more than the adoption of the immigrant by America. It may mean the adoption of America by the immigrant." This process of reciprocal adoption neared completion when she wrote a patriotic poem in school on her imaginary fellow citizen George Washington and "invaded" Boston's newspaper row because the poem "ought to be printed." Making her way through an urban melting-pot scene and passing a tall newsboy who bellowed "Herald, Globe, Record, *Tra-avel-er!*" she approached city desks until the *Boston Herald* agreed to publish the poem. This made her father so proud that he bought up all the *Heralds* he could lay his hands on "and distributed them gratis to all our friends, relatives, and acquaintances; to all who could read, and to some who could not." Her name in print gave her the confirmed identity of an *author* and made her a public celebrity in the eyes of people who pointed her out and said: "That's Mary Antin. She had her name in the paper." Her passage to America was completed, and in her plea for tolerance toward immigrants, *They Who Knock at Our Gates: A Complete Gospel of Immigration* (1914), she called the heroes of the American Revolution "our Fathers" and described newcomers as Mayflower-like pioneers and self-made men.

The very act of newspaper reading could suggest a certain group identification. Kate Chopin, the daughter of an Irish immigrant and a French Catholic woman, who started her literary career as a contributor to the *St. Louis Post-Dispatch*, the *New Orleans Times-Democrat*, *Vogue*, *Atlantic Monthly*, *American Jewess*, and the American Press Association syndicate, described Edna Pontellier's husband Léonce at the beginning of her important novel, *The Awakening* (1899), as a member of the group of privileged men who, when they are bored, can withdraw from concrete society and enter imaginary communities by smoking and reading their (even day-old) newspapers. "He was already acquainted with the market reports, and glanced restlessly over the editorials and bits of news which he had not had time to read before quitting New Orleans the day before." This introduction to Mr. Pontellier as the typical husband-who-deserves-to-be-deserted prepares the reader for the modern story in the course of which Mrs. Pontellier, an Emerson reader, fatally searches for a fuller, cosmic identity. The contrast with Douglass's experience also suggests that Mr. Pontellier's gesture is one of free manhood that could be denied to a slave.

Print identity could be conveyed by positive as well as by negative images; communities by reverberation could thus emerge or be strengthened by a bad press. The psychological process of negative group identification is developed by the fictional narrator of the novel *The Rise of David Levinsky* (1917), written by Abraham Cahan, the most interesting Jewish author of the period. The novel, an earlier version of which was serialized in *McClure's* in 1913 under the title "The Autobiography of an American Jew," contains an episode in which the capitalist narrator is made the target of an attack by the Yiddish socialist weekly, *Arbeiter Tseitung*. Levinsky finds himself denounced as a former union member who has become a traitor, and reacts to reading the paper with "mixed rage and pain": "and yet the sight of my name in print flattered my vanity, and when the heat of my fury subsided I became conscious of a sneaking feeling of gratitude to the socialist editor for printing the attack on me. For, behold! the same organ assailed the Vanderbilts, the Goulds, the Rothschilds, and by calling me 'a fleecer of labor' it placed me in their class. I felt in good company."

Levinsky's description of his own reaction is also an illuminating point of departure for an understanding of the popularity of "muckraking"—the name of which was inspired by a character in John Bunyan's *Pilgrim's Progress* (1678). Ida Tarbell's exposé of the Standard Oil Company and Lincoln Steffens's indictment of municipal mismanagement in *McClure's* of 1897 provided no less an orientation device about America than did the more euphoric writings in other issues and journals. Muckraking contributed to a process that one may describe, in George Devereux's term, as antagonistic acculturation. Assailing, being attacked, and reading the results of investigative reporting may all contribute to imagining a community. The newspapers and magazines conveyed a sense of ethnic belonging not only by the creation of a positive sense of reverberation and by political muckraking but also by hostile images, by "stereotyping," a telling metaphoric adaptation of a printing preparation technique—casting plates for printing—which was given its name around 1800 by Firmin Didot and came into widespread use in the nineteenth century. The literature of ethnic stereotypes between the Civil War and World War I was voluminous, ranging from collections such as *Cooper's Yankee, Hebrew, and Italian Dialect Readings and Recitations*, and anonymous jokebooks such as *Wehman Bros. Book of Minstrel Jokes: Gags and Conundrums*, to works by authors who specialized in that genre, such as Charles Follen Adams's *Leedle Yawcob Strauss and Other Poems* (1878).

The reaction of immigrants and minorities is often imagined along the lines of Mark Twain's Arthurian observers of the *Weekly Hosannah*. Early reviewers of *Connecticut Yankee* drew analogies between the Yankee's confrontations with sixth-century Britain and American technology vis-à-vis indigenous people, such as Indians. Apropos of Hank Morgan, the *Boston Sunday Herald* reminded readers on December 15, 1889, that "when Frank Hamilton Cushing astounded the Zuni Indians with an acoustic telephone constructed of two tomato cans and a string, they deemed him a magician, and tried him for witchcraft." The *Herald* also suggested that Mark Twain's characterization of medieval savages "might apply equally well to a tribe of Dakota Indians, to their hardly more civilized foes, the cowboys of the plains, to the mountaineers of Tennessee and Georgia, or even to the savages in our great slums." The march of nationalization and the Americanization of newcomers and minorities have been portrayed as the modernization of premodern people; and the ethnics were viewed along the lines of the awed medieval "readers" of the *Hosannah*: "What is this curious thing? What is it for? Is it a handkerchief?—saddle blanket?—part of a shirt? What is it made of? . . . Is it writing that appears on it, or is it only ornamentation?"

Yet this is not the whole story. What is rarely fully described is that—unlike Mark Twain's ignorant Arthurian public—Americans of all races and backgrounds did create a lively periodical press in the nineteenth century that invited readers in many different languages and idioms to think of alternative, or at least complementary, imagined communities. Some Afro-American, German, and Yiddish papers have already been mentioned, but the number of foreign-language and English-speaking ethnic and minority serials, their circulation figures, and their cultural significance in nineteenth- and early twentieth-century America are impressive.

In 1922 the Chicago sociologist Robert Park estimated the total circulation of the foreign-language press to be as high as 10,000,000 and found the quantitative dimensions of newspaper-reading an American phenomenon. He observes, for example, that out of 312 Russian immigrants "only 16 have regularly read newspapers in Russia. . . . In America all of them are subscribers or readers of Russian newspapers." Literary texts helped to establish print identity among nineteenth-century immigrant and minority readers; and the periodicals are a rich resource for ethnic readings long before the more familiar book publications started. In 1897 approximately 1,200 foreign-language periodicals appeared in the United States: 788 German, 139 Scandinavian, 57 Spanish, 50 French, 35 Czech, 34 Polish, and 29 Italian ones among them. This number probably needs to be corrected upward; it also does not include ethnic newspapers and journals in English. The following examples can only be suggestive of a more exhaustive treatment.

In nineteenth-century Boston, New York, Washington, D.C., Philadelphia, New Orleans, Key West, Tampa, and other cities, 250 Spanish-language periodicals have been identified. Outstanding among them were the early *El Correo Atlantico* (Mexico City and New Orleans, 1835–36) and *Las Tres Américas* (1893–96). *La Revista Ilustrada de Nueva York* (1886–93), called "el *Harper's Magazine* nuestro" (our *Harper's*) by its editor, Elias de Losada y Plisé, carried many Spanish and Latin American literary contributions as well as a series on six American women novelists (including Harriet Beecher Stowe and Helen Hunt Jackson) and translations of Poe and Mark Twain. Mariano Azuela's famous novel about the Mexican revolution, *Los de abajo* (The Underdogs), first appeared in 1915 in an El Paso newspaper.

According to the writer and journalist Shakuma Washizu, the first Japanese paper in this country, *Nineteenth Century*, and the first magazine, *Ensei* (Explorer), were published in 1892 in San Francisco. Because of attacks on the Japanese government, some issues of the mimeographed *Nineteenth Century* were confiscated in Japan. Next year the editors sent for some Japanese type, and enterprises such as the *Golden Gate Daily* and *Jiji* (Chronicle) followed; the poet Yone Noguchi handled the circulation. The comic paper

Agohazushi (Open the Jaws) appeared in 1896 with contributions from Ooka, Watanabe, Satsuke, Yamada, Yoshita, Ishimaru, Kobayashi, Fukase, Yone Noguchi, Yamada, Ito (the editor of the Japanese-American *New World*), Sakakami, and the artist Takahashi. Other periodicals were the *Japan Herald*, later *Japan News*, and the *North American*, which merged to form the *Japanese-American News* in 1900.

The *Connecticut Yankee* reviews notwithstanding, another little-known publishing flurry came from American Indians who also established print communities with the new methods, though they are often cast as the "silent" minority. Before 1900, 250 Indian papers appeared, 320 between 1900 and 1910. The first paper, published on February 21, 1828, was the *Cherokee Phoenix (Tsa-la-ge-Tsi-hi-sa-ni-hi)*, founded—in protest against the Indian removals—by the Cherokee National Council and edited by Elias Boudinot. In 1829, the year that John Augustus Stone's popular play *Metamora* was produced on stage, it became the *Cherokee Phoenix, and Indians' Advocate*, with a poetry department in English and Cherokee (using Sequoyah's syllabary), and with subscribers in Britain, France, and Germany. In Lydia Maria Child's *The First Settlers of New England* (1829), the character of the Mother mentions the Cherokees' paper with praise. In 1844 the *Cherokee Advocate* was published, authorized by the Cherokee National Council; its editor was William P. Ross, a Princeton-trained nephew of the chief. Renamed *Indian Journal*, the paper lost its intertribal focus when the Choctaws established the *Choctaw News* (1878). Other periodicals were the *Choctaw Telegraph* (1848–49); (George) *Copway's American Indian* (1851), devoted to American literature and Indian culture, and proud of such contributors as William Gilmore Simms, Henry R. Schoolcraft, William Cullen Bryant, Washington Irving, and Lewis Henry Morgan; the *Tahlequah Telephone* (1887), printed in the Cherokee capital and edited by B. H. Stone, a photographer married to a Cherokee woman; and the *Tomahawk* (1903—later the *Calloway Tomahawk*), edited by Gustave H. Beaulieu, one-quarter Chippewa. In the pages of the Indian press appeared the first creations of Alexander Lawrence Posey, a Scotch-Irish and Creek Indian–descended poet and humor columnist. Posey was typesetter for the *Bacone Indian University Instructor*, worked as editor for the *Eufaula Indian Journal*, created the humorous dialect character "Fus Fixico," and published his collected poems in 1910.

The beginnings of American ethnic literatures and periodical journalism are often intertwined. According to Clinton Machann, Czech journalism in America had its beginnings in a short-lived attempt by Frantisek Korizek, *Slowan Amerikansky* (January 1, 1860, in Racine, Wisconsin); *Narodni noviny* started to appear January 21, 1860, in St. Louis. In 1875 August Geringer, the publisher of the daily *Chicago Svornost*, issued the weekly *Amerikán* (with a circulation of about 40,000 by 1913) with an annual literary almanac. Thus the 1900 edition contained a novella by Hugo Chotek, "Z Dob Utrpeni" (From the Time of Suffering), in which Texan Czechs were suspected of being Yankee sympathizers during the Civil War because they had subscriptions to "Northern" newspapers (in Czech, of course).

Hutchins Hapgood's classic account of the Lower East Side, *The Spirit of the Ghetto* (1902), contains vivid sections on the Yiddish theater, on writers, and on "The Newspapers." Hapgood argues that the Yiddish press "has helped essentially to extend the intellectual horizon of the Jew beyond the boundaries of the Talmud, and has largely displaced the rabbi in the position of teacher of the people," another Hegelian interpretation of print community as a sacred institution. In 1870 Z. Bernstein started the first Yiddish periodical in the United States, *The Post*, for which Hebrew type had to be imported. In 1881 the first Yiddish daily, the *Tageblatt*, appeared. In 1903 the Polish-immigrant woman Rose Pastor (who gave advice to the lovelorn in the *Forverts*) interviewed the millionaire Graham Stokes for the *Tageblatt*, and in 1905 they announced their marriage. Abraham Cahan, the Russian-immigrant author of the novella *Yekl: A Tale of the Ghetto* (1896)—acclaimed by Howells in Pulitzer's *New York World*—contributed a piece to the *New York World* in 1883, wrote short sketches of life on New York's Lower East Side for the *New York Sun and Press* (1884–86), and worked as a staff writer for Lincoln Steffens's *Commercial Advertiser* (1897–1901); he also established the Yiddish weekly, *Die Neie Tseit* (The New Era; 1886), was editor of the *Arbeiterzeitung* (1891–94), and, in 1897, founded the *Forverts* (Jewish Daily Forward), of which he was editor from 1902 to 1946; *Forverts*, the largest Yiddish daily, reached a peak circulation of 200,000 copies. His letter-to-the-editor column, "A Bintel Brief" (A Bundle of Letters), contains many queries by immigrants that are of cultural, literary, and historical interest; several selections have been translated into English and reprinted.

Gunnar Myrdal perceptively described the function of Afro-American periodicals: "*The press defines the Negro group to the Negroes themselves.* The individual Negro is invited to share in the sufferings, grievances, and pretensions of the millions of Negroes far outside the narrow local community. This creates a feeling of strength and solidarity. The press, more than any other institution, has created the Negro group as a social and psychological reality to the individual Negro." *Freedom's Journal*, the first Afro-American newspaper, appeared in 1827; the first magazines, *Mirror of Liberty* and *National Reformer*, in 1838. The *African Methodist Episcopal Church Magazine* commenced publication in 1841. Before joining Frederick Douglass to launch the *North Star*, Martin Robison Delany had published the Pittsburgh newspaper *Mystery* (still in print today as the *Christian Recorder*); Delany, a Harvard medical student, wrote an interesting tract, *The Condition, Elevation, Emigration, and Destiny of the Colored People of the United States* (1852), which praised Douglass as self-made man, paper editor, and "sole proprietor of [a] printing establishment." Delany also was the author of an early Afro-American novel, *Blake; or, The Huts of America*, a militant answer to *Uncle Tom's Cabin*, serialized in the *Anglo-African Magazine* (1859–60), Thomas Hamilton's periodical that was dedicated to printing the work of black writers and that also published Frances Ellen Watkins Harper's short story "The Two Offers" in 1859. After emancipation the black periodical press proliferated. In 1887 T. Thomas Fortune began editing the *New York Age*, which shaped Booker T. Washington's image; in 1900 the *Colored American Magazine* appeared, which serialized Pauline Hopkins's romantic "Winona: A Tale of Negro Life in the South and the Southwest" (1901); and in 1901 Monroe Trotter founded the *Boston Guardian*. In the year 1890, 154 Afro-American periodicals were counted.

By far the largest foreign-language press was that written in German. In 1732, among Franklin's early advertisements in his *Pennsylvania Gazette*, appeared the announcement that the first American German-language paper, the biweekly *Philadelphische Zeitung*, was to be published. Among the hundreds of daily, weekly, and monthly papers that succeeded it were such literary efforts as the *New York Belletristisches Journal* (1852–1911) and titles as evocative of origins as the *Cincinnati Deutscher Franklin* (1835–37). A particularly flamboyant editor was Emil Klauprecht of the *Cincinnati Republikaner* who also published an early German-American novel, *Cincinnati; oder, Geheimnisse des Westens* (Cincinnati; or, Mysteries of the West [1853–54]), partly set in the journalistic milieu of German-American Cincinnati.

Klauprecht's title echoed Eugène Sue's feuilleton novel *Les Mystères de Paris*, serialized in the *Journal des Débats* in 1842–43, which had promised to reveal to its readers the lives of urban Indians (Paris lowlifes), in the acknowledged tradition of James Fenimore Cooper. Sue was translated and adapted to many urban settings, and his American followers included George Lippard's *The Quaker City; or, The Monks of Monk Hall* (1844); *The Mysteries and Miseries of New York: A Story of Real Life* (1848) by "Ned Buntline" (Edward Zane Carroll Judson); the anonymous *Geheimnisse von Philadelphia* (1850); Heinrich Börnstein's *Die Geheimnisse von St. Louis* (1851); and the Italian-American novelist Bernardino Ciambelli's *I misteri di Mulberry* (1893), *I misteri di Bleecker Street* (1899), and *I sotteranei di New York* (1915). Though Ciambelli is all but forgotten now, the *New York Recorder* once declared that

Ciambelli had "the realism of Zola and the fantasy of Poe," a statement used by the publisher as a "blurb." Serialized in the *National Era*, Harriet Beecher Stowe's *Uncle Tom's Cabin* (1852)—subtitled "Life among the Lowly"—also followed Sue's strategy of revealing to the readers a hidden world, providing them with panoramic views of American slavery.

Uncle Tom's Cabin generated many successors, from M. Eastman's Southern *Aunt Phillis's Cabin* (1852) and William Wells Brown's Afro-American *Clotel; or, The President's Daughter* (1853) to Thomas Dixon's viciously racist novel *The Leopard's Spots* (1902), the working title of which was "The Rise of Simon Legree"; the book was followed by *The Clansman* (1905), Dixon's novel that formed the basis for D. W. Griffith's film *The Birth of a Nation* (1915). *Uncle Tom's Cabin* was the direct source of Afro-American poems such as Frances E. W. Harper's "Eliza Harris" and "Eva's Farewell" and of Harper's narrator Aunt Chloe in *Sketches of Southern Life* (1872). Harriet Beecher Stowe's novel inspired much literature about "the lowly": Alice Rollins, *Uncle Tom's Tenement* (1886); Edward Fuller, *The Complaining Millions of Men* (1893); Edward Townsend, *A Daughter of the Tenements* (1895); James Sullivan, *Tenement Tales of New York* (1895); Jacob Riis, *Out of Mulberry Street: Stories of Tenement Life in New York* (1898); Hutchins Hapgood, *Children of the Ghetto* (1902); O. Henry, *The Four Million* (1906); *Three Lives* (1909), by the German-Jewish Gertrude Stein (who remembered seeing George Aiken's dramatization of *Uncle Tom's Cabin* early in her life); James Oppenheim, *The Nine-Tenths* (1911); Morris Rosenfeld, *Songs of Labor and Other Poems* (1914); and many, many other books, often developed from newspaper and magazine publications. "Lowly" could simply signal the downward glance of a teacher or a doctor or the sideward look of more established ethnics. The Irish teacher Myra Kelly wrote about her "58 little children from Israel" under the title *Little Citizens: The Humours of School Life* (1904). James Oppenheim's *Dr. Rast* (1909) is a novel about a German-Jewish physician who works among new Jewish immigrants from Eastern Europe. Frances N. S. Allen's *The Invaders* (1913) is set among Polish and Irish immigrants in the Connecticut valley; and Jack London's *The Valley of the Moon* (1914) takes place among Croatian applegrowers in California. Paul Laurence Dunbar's *Lyrics of Lowly Life* (1896) and *Poems of the Cabin and the Field* (1899) alluded to Harriet Beecher Stowe, to whom he also addressed one of his poems. Dunbar's less well known fiction includes attempts to retell popular stories with a different slant; thus he took on the Horatio Alger tales in a short story, "One Man's Fortunes," in *The Strength of Gideon* (1901).

The language of social historians of the second half of the twentieth century was anticipated by such volumes as the Irish-American autobiography *From the Bottom Up: The Story of Alexander Irvine* (1910) and *The Life Stories of Undistinguished Americans as Told by Themselves* (1906), a rich collection of sixteen interesting autobiographical sketches ranging from Rocco Coresca, an Italian bootblack, and Sadie Frowne, a Polish sweatshop girl, to Ahnen-la-de-ni, an Indian masseur, Lee Chew, a Chinese laundryman, and, anonymously, a Negro peon, an Irish cook, and a Japanese servant; the selections in *Life Stories*, representing the "humbler classes in the nation," were chosen from among seventy-five previously published in *The Independent* and edited by Hamilton Holt. Hutchins Hapgood dedicated a whole chapter to "Literature in Low Life" in his *Types from City Streets* (1910). Albion Tourgée's novel *A Fool's Errand* (1879) was called "the *Uncle Tom's Cabin* of Reconstruction." A reviewer of *The Melting-Pot* (1909), the Anglo-Jewish writer Israel Zangwill's successful play, wrote in *The Living Age* (1914) that Zangwill's Christian-Jewish intermarriage plot "was calculated to do for the Jewish race what *Uncle Tom's Cabin* did for the colored man." The Jewish-immigrant author of *Hungry Hearts* (1920), Anzia Yezierska, reported in *Red Ribbon on a White Horse* (1950) that she had worked in Hollywood on the "*Uncle Tom's Cabin* of the Immigrant."

The rhetorical gesture of revelation and initiation often went along with a fully developed image of a veil that separates insiders and outsiders and prevents a fuller vision of America, sometimes a combination of the journalist's promise to present "the inside story" and an allusion to Paul's second letter to the Corinthians (3:13–18). Kristofer Janson's Norwegian-American novel *Bag gardinet* (Behind the Curtain) simply explains that there is "much in Minneapolis that goes on behind the curtain." The Afro-American abolitionist, journalist, poet, and temperance activist Frances E. W. Harper published her novel *Iola Leroy; or, Shadows Uplifted* in 1892. Francis La Flesche's autobiographical account of life in a Presbyterian mission school in northeastern Nebraska during the Civil War years, *The Middle Five: Indian Schoolboys of the Omaha Tribe* (1900), explicitly intended to "reveal the true nature and character of the Indian boy." W. E. B. Du Bois, the Fisk- and Harvard-educated Afro-American intellectual and editor of *The Crisis* (from 1910 to 1932), used the image of the veil pervasively as a leitmotif and with a variety of meanings in his landmark collection of essays, *The Souls of Black Folk* (1903), a book that also explicitly invoked *Uncle Tom's Cabin*. Du Bois was the central Afro-American figure of the period and published voluminously, from his postdoctoral study *The Philadelphia Negro* (1899), a pioneering work in urban sociology, to autobiographies and the novel *The Quest of the Silver Fleece* (1911). One of Du Bois's most influential concepts emanated from his ethnic adaptation of Ralph Waldo Emerson's famous notion of a "double-consciousness" that separates our "two lives," "of the understanding and of the soul" ("The Transcendentalist"). In Du Bois's *Souls of Black Folk* this "double-consciousness," "an American, a Negro," described the psychological experience of the social veil. Abraham Cahan worked on, but never finished, a project entitled "The Chasm." The Norwegian-American author Hjalmar Hjorth Boyesen speaks of a "gulf" in his *Tales from Two Hemispheres* (1881); and Anna-Maria Thibault articulated the doubleness in *Les Deux Testaments* (1888), set among French Canadians in New York City's Yorkville. Du Bois's "double-consciousness" is an enlightening explanatory category for the many intellectuals who were involved in constructing two, at times complementary but often conflicting, communities by reverberation.

Charles Alexander Eastman, a Santee Sioux educated at Dartmouth, and the author of the autobiography *Indian Boyhood* (1902), revealed *The Soul of the Indian* in 1911. The publisher's preface to the novel by the Atlanta- and Columbia-educated Afro-American writer James Weldon Johnson, *The Autobiography of an Ex-Coloured Man* (1912), promises that in "these pages it is as though a veil had been drawn aside: the reader is given a view of the inner life of the Negro in America, is initiated into the freemasonry, as it were, of the race." The readers' initiation includes the recognition that American culture, while promising an artistically exciting fusion of the black and the white, is not yet able to accept its own syncretism. At the end of the novel the narrator, who has abandoned his career as a synthesizer of ragtime and Chopin, of European classical and Afro-American folk music, regrets that he, unlike Booker T. Washington or Mark Twain, is socially inactive and cowardly. Johnson's ironic tale of racial passing, published anonymously, sounded so plausible that the author once met a man who tacitly claimed authorship of the book; later Johnson felt obliged to write his own autobiography in order to fend off questions concerning his imaginary character. What Johnson shared with his protagonist, however, was the belief that *Uncle Tom's Cabin* was an "eye-opening" novel, and that among the most distinctively American artistic products were the spirituals, the Uncle Remus stories, the cakewalk, and ragtime. Johnson spent much time working as a journalist. In 1895 he purchased a flatbed cylinder press and started the *Jacksonville Daily American*, in which he admonished readers to heed Benjamin Franklin's advice, "We must all hang together, or assuredly we shall hang separately." In 1914 he became the editor of the *New York Age*, which he defined explicitly as a "race paper." Johnson's many contributions to American music and letters include "Lift Every Voice and Sing" (the Afro-American national anthem), "Under the Bamboo Tree," and the autobiography *Along This Way* (1933), which contains an episode that illuminates Johnson's cultural efforts in the period of segregation. When James Weldon Johnson worked in the New York music scene with his brother Rosamond and with Bob Cole, Edward Bok published half a dozen of their compositions in the *Ladies' Home Journal*. When Bok announced a little later the forthcoming publication of compositions by a Georgia Negro, he received a letter of protest from a white woman reader from Georgia who doubted that Negroes had the ability to do anything worthy of getting into the *Ladies' Home Journal* and concluded her letter with the request that Bok "give us some more of those little Negro classics by Cole and Johnson Brothers" (who she presumed had to be white). Ethnic boundaries and print identity are more fluid than many readers may assume.

There was, of course, room for fake revelations, sometimes of a sensationalist nature, and for writers who specialized in trying other ethnic voices than their own. Henry Harland, who was later associated with the *Yellow Book* in Britain, published a series of successful "Jewish" novels under the pen name Sidney Luska. In *As It Was Written: A Jewish Musician's Story* (1885), an orphaned German-Jewish violinist, Ernest Neuman, is the first-person narrator who becomes the unwitting agent of an ancestral curse and kills his fiancée Veronika Pathzuol; the book also contains a virtual paean to the American melting pot and its Jewish ingredients, expressed by Neuman's friend, the poet Daniel Merivale who smokes and reads newspapers. Harland published two more novels as Luska, *The Yoke of the Thorah* (1887) and *Mrs. Peixada* (1886), in which a young New York lawyer of Anglo-French background unwittingly entraps the title heroine—a German-Jewish beauty with a dark strain in her past who has become his wife—by placing an advertisement for a client in the newspaper. (In the novel this procedure is still considered shady and unconventional for a New York lawyer, though missing-persons ads had appeared in American newspapers at least since October 1, 1831, when the *Boston Pilot* ran an inquiry by an Irish immigrant woman about her husband.)

Paul Laurence Dunbar, best known for poems such as "We Wear the Mask" or black dialect poetry such as "When Malindy Sings," also experimented with Irish dialect poems ("Circumstances Alter Cases"—a poem that shares its title with the sixth section of Abraham Cahan's *Yekl*). The production of dialect literature in all tongues was stimulated by the proliferation of periodicals, from Thomas Nelson Page's sentimental plantation stories in *Century*, *Scribner's*, and *Harper's*, collected under the title *In Ole Virginia* (1887), to Joel Chandler Harris's Uncle Remus tales in the *Atlanta Consti-*

tution, from George Washington Cable's Creole sketches in the *New Orleans Picayune*, *Scribner's* and *Appleton's*, gathered in *Old Creole Days* (1879), to Finley Peter Dunne's humorous sketches on the Irish saloonkeeper Mr. Dooley, first published in the *Chicago Journal* and then collected in many volumes, starting with *Mr. Dooley in Peace and in War* (1898). Where dialect seemed less appropriate, for example in suggesting "Yiddish" in the English language, or "English" in Czech writing, the texts often display an intriguing mix of vocabulary. Thus, an early Italian-American New York ghetto novel, Luigi Donato Ventura's *Peppino* (1885; 1913), was written in French, interspersed with fragments of English ("at a minimum") and Italian ("al paese," "dolce far niente"). The book centers on the author's encounter with Peppino, a twelve-year-old shoeshine boy from Viggiano who now works on Prince Street. The narrator, also an impoverished Italian immigrant, shares the popular belief that in America the streets are paved with money ("je croyais que l'Amérique était un pays où l'argent couvrait les rues")—as they were in the Celestial City of Bunyan's *Pilgrim's Progress*. Ventura tries to break into journalism, but has no luck at James Gordon Bennett's *New York Herald* or Charles Anderson Dana's *New York Sun*. *Peppino's* linguistic mix parallels the ethnic neighborhood on Crosby Street that is described as "pêle-mêle des êtres et des choses sans nom" (hodgepodge of nameless beings and things).

The motif of melting-pot interaction was probably the most popular one of the period. In one of the early Norwegian newspapers, the Racine, Wisconsin *Democraten* (No. 1, June 8, 1850), the editor advises Scandinavians not to regard themselves "as a separate nation in this soup pot ('suppe-gryde') for all people and languages." The Norwegian-American Waldemar Ager's book *Paa veien til smeltepotten* (On the Road to the Melting Pot) appeared in 1917. Stories of many different intermarriages and attachments pervade the literature of all ethnic groups, from Nils Kolkin's Norwegian-American epic poem *Winona* (1878) to Charles Chesnutt's ironic story "Her Virginia Mammy," in which the foundling Clara Hohlfelder—a living allegory of the United States, perhaps—is unable to recognize her racially mixed background, though the Yankee Winthrop, her future husband, understands it and loves her. Edward King's *The Gentle Savage* (1883) is about the love between the half-Cherokee Pleasant Merrinott and the white woman Alice Harrelston. Emma Wolf's *Other Things Being Equal* (1892) and Elias Tobenkin's *Witte Arrives* (1916) are Jewish-Gentile intermarriage stories. In the *Cincinnati Commercial* (August 22, 1875), the Irish-Greek journalist Lafcadio Hearn sketched the racial mix of "Bucktown," where "all are Ishmaels bound together by fate" and where white women "have conceived strange attachments for black laborers, and live with them as mistresses." The vision of a polyethnically mixed America appears in the Mississippi steamboat tales from the Irish-American Mayne Reid's *The Quadroon* (1856) and Herman Melville's *The Confidence-Man: His Masquerade* (1857) to *The White Rose of Memphis* (1885), a popular romance that went through thirty-five editions and was written by William Clark Falkner, William Faulkner's Scotch-Irish (or Huguenot?) grandfather.

Journalistic endeavors shaped American forms of literary and cultural consciousness in the nineteenth and twentieth centuries. This is true not only of the thematic and biographical interconnections between "mainstream" and "ethnic" writing and the periodical press but also of literary form. Playwrights like the Irish immigrant Dion Boucicault not only used newspaper scenes—as in the hagiographic *Franklin* (1856) or the problem piece *The Octoroon* (1859)—but also designed theater playbills in the familiar newspaper format, complete with scandalous headlines. The short story, theoretically defined by the journalist Edgar Allan Poe, was a genre that thrived in and on periodicals and has been considered the American genre par excellence. Serialized fiction intensified the sense of community between writer and audience as well as among the readers themselves. Brander Matthews wrote *Vignettes of Manhattan* (1894); Stephen Crane's sketches were collected in *Wounds in the Rain* (1900); William Dean Howells published *Imaginary Interviews* (1910); and writers as diverse as Mark Twain and Gertrude Stein collected newspaper headlines for possible use in their writings. In *The American Scene* (1907), Henry James—who in 1888 published the little-known newspaper novel, interestingly entitled *The Reverberator*—observed that the "sense of the elements in the cauldron—the cauldron of the 'American' character—becomes thus about as vivid a thing as you can at all quietly manage" and wondered "what type, as the result of such a prodigious amalgam, such a hotch-potch of racial ingredients, is to be conceived as shaping itself?" Perhaps the various print communities that were established by stereotype and linotype provide the beginning of an answer.

Werner Sollors

Women Writers and the
New Woman

"Molly Donahue have up an' become a new woman!" So begins Finley Peter Dunne's satirical "Mr. Dooley" sketch "On the New Woman" (1898), in which the Irish Molly has sorely tested her husband by riding a bicycle, demanding to vote, and "wearin' clothes that no lady shud wear." Now Molly proclaims "she'll be no man's slave." Henceforth a woman like her will "wear what clothes she wants [and] earn her own livin'," no longer to be given over in marriage to a "clown" who makes her "dipindant" on male whims.

Mr. Dooley's sketch, which pivots on the reversal of traditional male-female roles, ends in Molly's capitulation to her husband and a reassertion of the status quo in which women will "stay at home an' dredge in th' house wurruk." But if Molly is mollified for the price of a new shawl, her cause is not so easily set aside. When Mr. Dooley spoofed the new woman of the 1890s, he affirmed her importance. The Chicago-based Dunne, America's foremost political-social satirist, acknowledged the status of "the New Woman" when he gave her equal space with such topics as American imperialism in the Philippines, military adventurism in Cuba, Populist politics, and the Dreyfus case.

In fact, the new woman demanded attention because, as Dunne recognized, she was a powerful social-literary figure by the late nineteenth century. She both embodied new values and posed a critical challenge to the existing order. And she affected the national literature. From the 1890s the new woman—independent, outspoken, iconoclastic—empowered the work of Kate Chopin, Alice James, Charlotte Perkins Gilman, Edith Wharton, Ellen Glasgow, Willa Cather, and the young Gertrude Stein, even if Wharton denounced "the new theories . . . that awful women rave about on platforms." The new woman, moreover, was incumbent in American literature in the previous decades. Wharton disparaged the "rose-and-lavender" pages of Sarah Orne Jewett and Mary E. Wilkins Freeman, but the idea of the new woman occupies an incipient, covert place in their careers and writings, which have subversive thematic implications.

In literature and social history the new woman comes to mind most readily in the familiar image of the 1920s Jazz Age flapper with the bobbed hair and boyish figure that proclaimed the personal freedom foreclosed to her grandmother. The new woman, however, had a decades-long developmental background. By the 1890s she was an important part of the era's flouting of middle-class convention. Women on both sides of the Atlantic were challenging the foundations of a patriarchal society.

It is fair to say that from the 1880s the new woman in theory and fact changed the canon of American literature, affecting writers' lives and invigorating the national literature with new fictional design in character, form, and theme. At a period when the men's *Bildungsroman* was urban and industrial, and based upon such scientific "laws" as Darwinism, the ethos of the new woman engendered a fiction of what must be called women's regionality. It sought to establish alternative bases of consciousness and to show how consciousness itself could be deployed for women's empowerment. Its design was iconoclastic, challenging the very premises on which men's fictional worlds were constructed.

Alice James, for instance, challenged the presumptions of a patriarchal culture in her diary and her letters spanning the period from the 1880s until her death in 1892. James offers a running commentary on various male physicians baffled by the symptoms from which she suffered for most of her adult life. James's doctors, representatives in her mind of social authority and expertise, prove to be vapid and mechanical. As a patient, James learned that these male authorities, "all terrible," presented "a spectacle of paralysis. . . . talking by the hour without *saying* anything."

James's contemporaries were also challenging the received wisdom on courtship, marriage, and the family, rejecting such "truths" as the maternal instinct and the role of child-rearing as the highest duty of women. One of Sarah Orne Jewett's characters in *A Country Doctor* (1884) remarks acidly that it "cannot be the proper vocation of all women to bring up children, so many of them are dead failures at it." And in *The Awakening* (1899), Kate Chopin, a widow and mother of six, brought biographical experience to bear when she presented a character who disparaged "marriages which masquerade as the decrees of Fate," and satirized the "women who idolized their children, worshipped their husbands, and esteemed it a holy privilege to efface themselves as individuals and grow wings as ministering angels." Like-minded feminists proposed that women's health would improve if sports and rational dress replaced the whalebone of the conventional middle-class woman, a point that Gilman argued in her fiction of the 1910s.

The new woman proposed to seek personal fulfillment through work instead of matrimony. In *A Country Doctor*, Sarah Jewett's young female protagonist wishes "she had been trained as boys are, to the work of their lives!," then feels like "a reformer, a radical, and even like a political agitator" as she decides to forgo housekeeping and enter a profession. Rhetorically she asks, "Would you have me bury the talent God has given me?" Jewett was not alone. In *Virginia* (1913), Ellen Glasgow wrote sarcastically of the Southern woman bred for genteel idleness even in the era of the postbellum industrial South. How humiliating, she says wryly, for a mother "to train her daughter in any profitable occupation which might have lifted her out of the class of unskilled labour in which indigent gentlewomen by right belonged." Through their own commitment to professional writing, figures like Glasgow, Jewett, and others were able to understand, and to propound, the importance of self-fulfilling work outside the sphere of domesticity.

Central to literary portrayals of the new woman was the idea of women's sexual freedom, including the right to abstain and to choose sexual partners in or out of marital relationships. By the 1910s, when Margaret Sanger had opened her birth-control clinic in New York City, journalists proclaimed "sex o'clock in America." Certain literary texts, meanwhile, had argued that sexual freedom was a woman's prerogative. Such was the erotic life Chopin chronicled in her (posthumously published) story of a married woman's afternoon affair with a former suitor: "Her firm, elastic flesh . . . was knowing for the first time its birthright" ("The Storm"). A woman's extramarital sexual pleasure, Chopin suggests, can coexist with a satisfying domestic life.

From the 1890s, then, the new woman had a recognizable identity, one derived largely from the rational, analytical demystification of the "fair sex." Like Mr. Dooley's Molly, the new woman could resolve to earn her own living, as did Freeman, Gilman, and Cather, and, like Glasgow and Stein, be confident of personal fulfillment outside the marital or familial relationship, which she viewed as a form of slavery. Ellen Glasgow remarks on this point. Her Virginia Pendleton "let her mother slave over her because she had been born into a world where the slaving of mothers was a part of the natural order, and she had not as yet become independent enough to question the morality of the commonplace."

As Glasgow's statement indicates, the idea of conscious choice in and of itself was a hallmark of the identity of the new woman, who was very much a middle-class figure, since women lower on the socioeconomic ladder, laborers for decades as domestics and as factory operatives, were not at liberty to shape their lives according to such principles. For the privileged new woman, however, the principles were paramount. Her modernity was neither whimsical nor idiosyncratic, but based upon intellectually informed (and personally distressing) analyses of woman's place in contemporary society. Kate Chopin's character from *The Awakening*, Edna Pontellier, an upper middle-class wife and mother, determines to have her "own way," knowing "that is wanting a great deal . . . when you have to trample upon the lives, the hearts, the prejudices of others." Early in life Edna understands the duality of the "outward existence which conforms, the inward life which questions." But the new woman was not content to continue the duality nor to sustain its terms of conformity and concealment. Because her priority, like Edna's, was in large part sexual, the new woman posed serious challenge to the status quo, for she could not be dismissed as a prostitute or a fallen woman. Her radicalism was a matter of personal decision. It did not take the form of an organized political movement. No congresses or conventions mark its history. In this sense it was individualistic, operating in the spheres open to personal choice, from sexual preference to dress.

Sketched in this light, the new woman can seem a model of enablement for aspirant women writers like Chopin, Gilman, Cather, Wharton, Glasgow, and others, all of them middle-class figures (with the exception of the upper-class Wharton) who ranged in age from their twenties to their forties when Mr. Dooley's "New Woman" appeared in American newspapers. For these writers, additionally, the new woman pertained directly to the matter of literary succession. Their female predecessors in nineteenth-century American literature, best-selling authors like Louisa May Alcott, Susan Warner, and Harriet Beecher Stowe, had prospered with fiction only covertly insurrectionist, fiction congenial to an era that idealized the values of the virtuous, home-loving woman in her proper domestic sphere. In hindsight it seems inevitable that this new generation of American women writers would undertake revisionist fiction formulating the viewpoint of the new woman.

Wharton, Cather, Glasgow, and the others did seize this opportunity, but not without struggle. Powerful socioliterary forces defended older traditions in ways subversive of the new woman. For if the new woman was an enabling figure, she could also verge on caricature, a quality evident in the Mr. Dooley sketch. Some of the women writers recoiled from so blatant, so peremptory a figure. Edith Wharton exhibited hostility toward her Miss Verney (*Sanctuary* [1903]), who is "patently of the 'new school': a young woman of feverish activities and broad-cast judgments, whose very versatility made her hard to define." Wharton was not alone in her critical stance. Ellen Glasgow's *Phases of an Inferior Planet* (1898) includes a vignette of three feckless Southern belles posturing as new women in New York. They imagine their Alabama aunts "grounded in the belief that the new woman is an *edition de luxe* of the devil." But the young Southern women's conversation shows that their new-woman commitment is cosmetic, literally skin-deep. One remarks that to take men seriously, that is sexually, is to "sit at home and grow shapeless and have babies galore." Shapelessness, she concludes, "is a more convincing argument against [love] than all the statistics of the divorce court." These vignettes are indicative. The new woman—in Wharton a schemer, in Glasgow a posturer who puts fashion first—is subjected to the novelists' skeptical scrutiny, even as the novelists themselves push into the new woman's territory with such subjects as adultery, marital breakdown, and female careerism.

Writers like Wharton, Glasgow, and the others worked against additional burdens, a point that must be acknowledged. It is no wonder that to some extent they kept their distance from the figure of the new woman; some of their most distinguished male counterparts made an example of her, but only to affirm her traditional femininity or to punish her for defying it. Such writers as William Dean Howells, Jack London, and even Henry James engaged the figure of the new woman; but they portrayed her, like Mr. Dooley's Molly, as an upstart or rebel who would be brought to heel by male authority and by her own susceptibility to fashion, frippery, and, above all, social convention. For instance, in *The Iron Trail: An Alaskan Romance* (1913), the best-selling novelist Rex Beach shows a tough-talking new-woman journalist dispatching stories from the Alaskan bush—but proving her womanliness by housekeeping for the hero and secretly decorating her own Yukon tent in pink tulle and satin.

The artful male writers were subtler, but equally subversive of the new woman. They essentially portrayed her in ways that denied her power. In James's *Portrait of a Lady* (1881), the new-woman journalist, Henrietta Stackpole, is bumptious and crass. Like a roaring express train, James says, she represents the future of motion and crude energy. In James's fictional world Henrietta's traits in and of themselves diminish her importance, in fact marginalize her—while in the same novel the free-spirited protagonist, Isabel Archer, apparently a really formidable version of the new woman, ultimately shows herself to be a traditionalist, not a new woman at all. She returns to a stultifying marriage because, James suggests, she is essentially conventional and because she is no match for the male sexuality represented by her longtime suitor. Isabel is a conformist, while Henrietta often verges on the ridiculous. In both cases, the new woman is conceptually subverted.

Henry James was not alone. His friend Howells equally undercut his new woman. In *Annie Kilburn* (1888), the gentlewoman Annie, the title character, resolves not to lead an "idle and vapid" life. She is told, "If you want to have a mind of your own and a heart of your own, all you've got to do is have it." But this adviser, like all others in the novel, is an authoritative man. Annie heeds male counsel in one instance "like a young girl with an invitation to a ball," the image itself showing Howells's need to keep his new woman in check. Politically Annie becomes a socialist and works for a pilot project in cooperative living. Yet Howells insists that her own style of life remain thoroughly conventional. He so tightly circumscribes the new woman's field of action that she most resembles heroines of domestic fiction.

A different fate awaited the nontraditional new woman in the hands of the male writer. In the Nietzschean, Darwinian world of Jack London's *The Little Lady of the Big House* (1916) we meet Paula Destin Forrest. She is womanly pride incarnate, a master horsewoman, high diver, portrait painter, pianist. She plays Rachmaninoff "masterfully, like a man." She is frank, outspoken, steely, passionate, irresistible. Every man is in love with her; and she is in love with two, her husband and his friend. She must choose between them, yet cannot. London prepares readers for a spirited woman's struggle to shape her life without regard for social convention. But what is the author's solution to her problem?—suicide. Faced with inflicting pain on one she loves, this nonconformist new woman sacrifices herself, which is to say that London consigns her to the deathbed of the conventional true woman. She shares the fate of centuries of her errant fictional sisters. Having created a new-woman heroine, London retreated from the implications of his act.

Even the woman writer seeming to present the new-woman viewpoint could in reality carry the banner for conservative traditions. The novelist and short-story writer Margaret Deland, author of *The Awakening of Helena Ritchie* (1906) and *The Iron Woman* (1911), is an excellent case in point because she exploited new-woman themes essentially to argue against them and to ratify the conservative status quo. Personal fulfillment, Deland emphasized, is a dangerous goal. Her women characters who pursue it, one a suffragist and the other an industrialist, are grotesques. The higher, authentic fulfillment, Deland argues, lies in commitment to marital, parental, societal duties that sustain traditional institutions.

The new-woman writers, faced with such conservatism, steered a careful course, risking rejection, even outrage. The hostile reception of Kate Chopin's *The Awakening*, attacked as "sex fiction," indicates their obstacles and suggests, additionally, why the earlier new-woman writers, Jewett and Freeman, should mask their radical impulses. For distinguished male writers were not the only critics of the new woman. Conservative women writers, too, were vigilant in defense of tradition. They opposed the new woman by proclaiming the sacred doctrines of domesticity. A sampling of turn-of-the-century women's advice books suggests how resistant the American mainstream could be to the literary new woman, who needed to win readers from that very culture. Contemporary fiction by men dealt overtly with business corruption, divorce, human brutishness, and grinding poverty (in the work of Howells, Stephen Crane, Frank Norris, and Hamlin Garland). But women's fiction in the era of the new woman abounded with romantic sweet stories of imperiled damsels rescued by gallant knights. Titles like Mary Johnston's *To Have and to Hold* (1900) and Gertrude Atherton's *Patience Sparhawk and Her Times* (1895) exemplify the continuing tradition of the sentimental romance.

Numerous texts, moreover, enjoined women to seek an ineffably higher plane of spiritual-intellectual life. Dr. Mary R. Melendy's *The Perfect Woman . . . A Complete Medical Guide for Women* (1901) is a good case in point. Its preface advised:

Woman's labors and successes, in the various fields and affairs of life, are calling daily for more and more attention. While we admire her in her new role, with her efforts toward success in society, literature, science, politics, and the arts, we must not lose sight of her most divine and sublime mission in life—womanhood and motherhood.

The author, a woman holding dual doctorates in medicine and philosophy, emphasizes that only physical, mental, and spiritual perfection will enable a woman to remain "permanently secure on her lofty throne." That ideological throne is implicit in Lillian Whiting's *The World Beautiful* (1897), which devotes a chapter to "The Modern Corinna," the career woman "identified with the professional or the industrial world." She is urged above all to be ladylike and transcendently lofty in thought. "In the increasing avenues of industrial labor opened to women and preempted by them," writes Mrs. Whiting, "there is not one in which refinement, delicacy, and courtesy will not prevail over self-assertion, aggressiveness, selfishness, or rudeness." Why, the author asks, should women renounce the "higher and finer prerogative to descend into strife and demands?" If things go wrong, she advises, "bridge over the defect by laying hold resolutely on higher states. Transmute falsehood to truth, irritability to pleasant speech, doubt and distrust to faith."

The woman writer comes in for direct address in Marion Harland's *Eve's Daughters; or, Common Sense for Maid, Wife, and Mother* (1902). This how-to book urges women to seek fulfillment in marriage and maternity, but addresses "those of us who might be eloquent with tongue or pen. . . . women after Emily Brontë's kind." That "kind," however, proves to be the traditional woman at her needlework. Her "poetic fancies flow" on a manuscript "white work" page of muslin and linen, which the pen hems and backstitches on its surface. The author's message is clear: at the turn of the twentieth century, women's writing must assume the protective coloration of the sewing basket.

In fact, these images of writing as hemming and backstitching imply something other than a safe self-identification of women writers with domestic life. The figure of the writer-as-seamstress implies the need to conceal or to deny that writing is an intrinsically aggressive act. The woman narrator in Charlotte Perkins Gilman's "The Yellow Wallpaper" (1892) recounts that she persisted in writing even though the effort was exhausting and met with "heavy opposition" from "them," the family's men. As Gilman knew, "strife" and "demands" are the writer's stock in trade. "Refinement," "delicacy," and "pleasant speech" are inherently inimical to literary truth. The new-woman writer understood this point. Mary Wilkins Freeman admired Emily Brontë because she was able "to comprehend the primitive brutalities and passions," because "she handles brutality and coarseness as another woman would handle a painted fan." Chopin concurred, bringing her Edna to understand that because love and sexual drive coexist without connection, life is a "monster made up of beauty and brutality."

Wharton similarly understood that the writer must confront all base human drives, which verbal nostrums only work to deny. In *Madame de Treymes* she identified the writer's antagonists in the figure of the sheltered matron who proclaims, "When there is so much that is beautiful to dwell upon, we should try to ignore the existence of . . . horrors." This "warm drip of platitudes" is "petrifying." Glasgow says the suppression of reality comes from misconceived notions on women's upbringing. In *Virginia* she scorned the postbellum genteel Southerners who raised their daughters on expurgated Shakespeare and "sweet stories," who cherished "the naive conviction that to acknowledge an evil is . . . to countenance its existence," and whose educational theory was "that the less a girl knew about life, the better prepared she would be to contend with it."

Of course the new woman's writing criticized and defied traditional values, but the fate of Kate Chopin speaks volumes about the cultural retribution on the woman writer whose literary treatment of her subject offended convention by daring to give readers "the unaccustomed taste of candor." Reaching her full powers in *The Awakening*, a novel explicitly concerned with women's sexual passions, Chopin was devastated by the audience rejection, which took the form of hostile reviews, librarians' refusal to circulate her novel in her native city of St. Louis, and the snubbing by that city's Fine Arts Club, which declined to make her a member. Friends shunned her as reviewers called *The Awakening* morbid, poisonous, and vulgar. One friend said Chopin was "crushed," and she wrote very little in the remaining five years of her life. She felt "left by the wayside" as she herself wrote in a short sketch—"struck mute" as Larzer Ziff has so accurately written.

Thus the new-woman writers walked a narrow line between frankness and the ostracism that frankness might incur. They rejected the camouflage of domesticity but gained acceptance, many of them, under another rubric—regionalism. Until recently, which is to say until feminist critics began reevaluation of their work, Jewett and Freeman, together with Chopin, Glasgow, and Cather, were considered to be regionalists or even local colorists, writers faithful to particular geographical areas whose cultural patterns of speech, manners, and habits they accurately reflect, often in tones of affectionate nostalgia. In this light Jewett and Freeman become memorialists of a faded New England, Glasgow of the Virginian South, Cather of the pioneers' Nebraska where she grew up, and Chopin of French Creole Louisiana. Wharton, metaphorically a regionalist of the terrain of High Society, also brought the dark naturalist's focus to bear upon New England in *Ethan Frome* (1911) and *Summer* (1917).

The regionalist label was in part justified. Jewett vivified the world of rural Maine, while Freeman's collections, such as *A Humble Romance* (1887) and *A New England Nun* (1891), feature the artifacts of a New England fast disappearing in metropolitan America: calico, patchwork quilts, braided rugs, the garden patch, the domestic memorabilia of "brown loaves and flaky pies—the proofs of . . . love and culinary skill." So in Glasgow we find Virginian honeysuckle, cornmeal "soap," loyal darkies, mint juleps, fox hunts, while Chopin's fiction abounds with the accoutrements of French-Creole Louisiana, where women sip wine and spirits, smoke cigarettes, and enjoy men's risqué stories. Chopin's *Bayou Folk* (1894) and Cather's *O Pioneers!*

(1913) indicate the regional appeal to readers leading increasingly urbanized lives in a metropolitan America looking nostalgically upon its past. Under cover of regionalism, however, these women writers explored the territory of women's lives. Their essential agenda in the era of the new woman was to map the geography of their gender. They were regionalists—but not solely in the ways critics have conventionally thought. The geography of America formed an important part of their work, but essentially they charted the regions of women's lives, regions both without and within the self.

For these new-woman writers argued that "the inner life which questions" must be given full rein. Thus they were avid, not so much for that education achievable by formal schooling, but for consciousness and the knowledge that can follow from it. The premise here is that a woman's life can be her own only if she is first in full possession of her mind. So elementary a point would not seem deserving of emphasis had the writers themselves not insisted upon it. They knew that the ethos of the enthroned "perfect woman" functioned to deny and suppress consciousness, itself the "imaginative power and habit of story-making," as Gilman termed it in "The Yellow Wallpaper," the story in which the rationalist physician-husband drives his wife insane by working to immobilize her, body and mind.

Chopin addresses the problem of consciousness in terms of a primordial state of being. The beginning of the human world "is necessarily vague, tangled, chaotic, and exceedingly disturbing," she writes. "How few of us ever emerge from such a beginning! How many souls perish in its tumult!" In Chopin's terms, to perish, especially in marriage, is to exist without consciousness. Chopin's Edna initially does so, "unthinkingly, as we walk, move, sit, stand, go through the daily treadmill of the life which has been apportioned out to us." This is the woman automaton, in Glasgow's term, "born to decorate instead of to reason." She emerges in Wharton's Anna Leath (*The Reef* [1912]), who spends her childhood in a household in which "the unusual was regarded as either immoral or ill-bred, and people with emotions were not visited." Wharton re-created this figure in May Welland (*The Age of Innocence* [1920]), whose fiancé knows "it was his duty, as a 'decent' fellow, to conceal his past from her, and hers, as a marriageable girl, to have no past to conceal." May is "trained not to possess . . . experience, versatility, freedom of judgment," and is "doomed to thicken," like her mother, "into the same middle-aged image of invincible innocence."

In full revolt against specious "innocence," these writers concerned with the "regionalism" of female consciousness used that consciousness to construct iconoclastic fictions. This diverse group, from Jewett to Wharton, evades any one comprehensive statement on technique, style, or thematic center. Yet to become conscious, to come into being, is to achieve the vision destructive of disabling myths. From Freeman to the young Gertrude Stein, these women writers exposed the myth of the "perfect woman" and thus of its complementary obverse, patriarchy. It is fair to say that consciousness of the new woman stirred all these writers into a fiction of iconoclasm, a scathing indictment of the status quo and the values serving to maintain it.

Freeman, whose productive years began in the 1880s, is an instructive case in point because she could not benefit from the generalized, prevalent new-woman ideology of the 1910s or 1920s and was thus limited in her literary field of action. "Little female weapons," she calls the powers of one of her characters, speaking inadvertently of her own. In the story "Christmas Jenny" (in *A New England Nun*) Freeman warns about the exercise of women's authority in a patriarchal culture. In defense of a neighbor considered to be eccentric, a woman gets so "carried away by affection and indignation" that she "almost spoke in poetry" and, in the eyes of the men, "became so abnormal that she was frightful." Indirectly, Freeman reveals her own literary predicament. The passions of the woman writer must be roused—but formally constrained lest she be judged frightfully abnormal by the devotees of the women's advice books and by the men (represented by such figures as ministers, lawyers, and propertied farmers) who constitute established power. Literary defiance must not exceed their criteria for normality.

Thus Freeman becomes a covert revolutionist, as a number of her stories reveal, among them "The Village Singer," "Sister Liddy," "Christmas Jenny," "A Church Mouse," and "The Revolt of 'Mother.' " All deal with the triumph of women's will. Each features a woman whose quiet life conceals "the elements of revolution." Such characters as Candace Whitcomb, Polly Moss, Mrs. Carey, Hetty Fifield, and Sarah Penn all revolt. "Men git in a good many places where they don't belong . . . jest because they push in ahead of women," says Hetty Fifield ("A Church Mouse"), a homeless woman who crosses gender roles and, with the support of community women, claims a place on men's terrain. Sarah Penn ("The Revolt of 'Mother' ") wins a territory of her own when she moves the family out of their crowded box of a house into the spacious new barn. Sarah is "overcome with her own triumph," triumph that, in Freeman's fiction, leaves the men momentarily disempowered, helpless as Sarah's weeping husband.

But Freeman limits women's revolution. Or, to put it another way, revolution itself limits Freeman's literary course of action, given her need not to be offensively "abnormal." Her insurrectionists, however modest their New England villages, call for the overturn of the old order and for a reformation of society according to the new consciousness they have brought to themselves and others. Freeman, however, was committed as a writer to "normal," nonfrightening fiction. (Her most passionate revolutionaries are too old to incite others to rebellion or to be sexually driven.) Caught in a formal and thematic dilemma between the status quo and its threatened overturn, Freeman often preserves the integrity of her insurrectionist women by mooting her own deepest thematic points.

Sarah Orne Jewett, another precursor of the new-woman movement, also sought acceptable forms in which to assert the power of woman's consciousness. Jewett's feminist politics took shape when, as a Maine doctor's daughter, she considered the study of medicine and realized the extent of societal enmity to be incurred by a woman in that or in any professional role. *A Country Doctor* contains Jewett's manifesto of the feminist principles she codified and continued to follow as a professional writer.

The pastoral treatment of her literary subject matter, however, formally limited Jewett's new-woman themes. Her commitment to the conventions of pastoral literature guaranteed that Jewett's fiction would not trumpet new-woman themes in polemical tones. For instance, her acknowledged masterwork, the novella *The Country of the Pointed Firs* (1889), divides characters along issues of gender. The men of the coastal Maine village are superannuated, weak, addled. In Jewett's world, vision and initiative are the monopoly of the women, especially Almira Todd, the generous, bountiful, incisive, gregarious, independent, philosophical, fair-minded *genius loci* of the novella, who stands "grand and architectural, like a *caryatide*"—more, like an "oracle," as both Medea and Antigone. Jewett's country of the pointed firs is, to borrow a title from Charlotte Gilman, "herland."

Yet Jewett's voice never rises to feminist militancy. She softens her new-woman material by working primarily in the tradition of the pastoral idyll. "Mrs. Todd might belong to any age," she writes, "like an idyll of Theocritus." The third century B.C. Greek poet had depicted the simple, rustic life in Sicily to please the sophisticated Alexandrians, just as the well-traveled, worldly Jewett presented rural Maine to America's urban intelligentsia. Her elegaic tone and her fidelity to the pastoral idyll blunt the new-woman feminist "principles" Jewett had stated militantly as personal doctrine in *A Country Doctor*. Formally, the idyll makes her a gentle iconoclast.

By the 1900s, however, the American new-woman writers were abandoning formal and tonal constraints on consciousness. In *The Age of Innocence*, set in 1870s New York, Wharton brought forth the woman who is literally the embodiment of consciousness itself. The American-born Countess Ellen Mingott Olenska has "had to look at the Gorgon" and can never again repose in "blessed darkness." Hers is the iconoclastic vision that rejects the naïveté of the married man who wants to flee with her. More experienced than he, more conscious of the claim of society, she knows that the social structure turns romance into squalor. The scenes between the two of them throb with sexual energy, but Wharton never retreats from Ellen's socio-cultural insights.

The new-woman iconoclastic consciousness, however, could be problem-atic, as Chopin's *The Awakening* reveals. The protagonist, Edna Pontellier, a New Orleans businessman's wife and the mother of two young sons, knows she would sacrifice her life but not her self for her children. Edna's route to consciousness includes an unconsummated extramarital love affair, a tryst, and, on Chopin's part, an elaborate use of the sea as a symbol of release from social constraints.

Some readers see Edna as a flamboyant romantic to the end. In this read-ing a romantic Edna ultimately drowses to her death in a dream of self-fulfillment via romantic Love and Art. According to this interpretation, it is not Edna but the author-narrator who achieves the real awakening into critical analysis of society and romance.

Those who see Edna Pontellier as a triumph of the new-woman con-sciousness, however, find her to be an iconoclast of romance, motherhood, and marriage because she thinks the unthinkable in authoritative terms that the author supports. Edna thus can function as a figure knowledgeably con-scious of a woman's inner life. Discursively she offers the disinterested and authoritative critique of culture, at the same time opening the psyche of the woman and demystifying romance, marriage, and motherhood. To awaken is, by definition, to leave those shibboleths behind. Edna says, "Perhaps it is better to wake up after all, even to suffer, rather than to remain a dupe to illusions all one's life."

The Awakening, however, brings up a crucial problem of the new-woman fiction. Once consciousness is achieved and deployed against pernicious myths, what remains? Beyond iconoclasm, what is the ultimate use of con-sciousness?

Chopin's novel enacts this problem. In form it argues that beyond awak-ening there is no transcendence because a woman like Edna is caught in a double bind. In youth she is romantic, but in awakened maturity inevitably jaded. She can do nothing with her hard-won knowledge, her very con-sciousness. To step beyond the newborn's miasma or off the routinized treadmill of unconsciousness is to enter the world of this bind, which only becomes clear to Edna (and to the reader) in the closing pages of the novel, at which point Edna yields irrevocably to the embrace of the sea, having concluded that there is no transcendence but only a cruel awakening from illusion and the prospect of an unlivable life ahead. The story has enacted the disjunctive movement from romantic illusion to the abyss.

We are meant to see Edna's ultimate, suicidal swim as an existential act in a culturally and psychologically unlivable life. But because ennui prompts it, and because it obliterates Edna's hard-won consciousness, the death-swim focuses the very question of the use of consciousness. Edna becomes, inadvertently on Chopin's part, a precursor to F. Scott Fitzgerald's shallow Daisy Buchanan in *The Great Gatsby*, who asks, "What'll we do with ourselves this afternoon . . . and the day after that, and the next thirty years?" In fact, Chopin had no answer. She had charted Edna's developing consciousness and the knowledge gained from it. After that she did not know what to do. The ostensibly triumphant death-swim, which works at the level of high melodrama, only masks Chopin's dilemma, which is the dilemma of the new-woman writer facing the problem of the burden of consciousness itself.

The iconoclastic new-woman writers engaged this problem in diverse ways. But all asked, How can consciousness be empowering, and what forms can manifest the power of women? This quest for formal structures adequate to the new-woman consciousness took multiple forms, from the diary to the utopian novel and quasi autobiography. The locus of consciousness also varied in the writings of Gilman, Wharton, Glasgow, Cather, and Stein. Seeking alternatives to the urban, industrial, scientific male *Bildungsroman*, these writers also sought alternatives to the cul-de-sac enacted in *The Awakening*, which argued that to come to life as a woman is necessarily to choose death.

Alice James did both, paradoxically choosing to die yet articulating, in a voice of ironic objectivity, the terms of her life in the interval before her death. As a sister of the acclaimed novelist Henry, and the equally acclaimed psychologist William, Alice evidently chose death as the area of her expertise and of her family competition. In a voice of ironic detachment that echoes that of Emily Dickinson, a writer she admired, James made herself a study in "get[ing] myself dead," especially when the discovery of a cancerous breast tumor gave her the "palpable disease" that "fulfilled" her "aspirations." In a "scientific spirit" expressed in the hard-edged irony soon to flower in modernist art, James refused, as she said, the "seduction" of a vaporous "float . . . into the deep sea of divine *cessation*", thus rejecting the way of Kate Chopin's Edna even in the face of imminent death. Her image of the tumor as "an unholy granite substance in my breast" and of her heart as a "bewildered little hammer" instance James's objectification of consciousness in concrete things and her rejection of the decayed transcendentalism of the late nineteenth century. James's voice in and of itself repudiated the decayed romantic style urged upon women writers by the "perfect woman" advice books.

Alice James stands virtually in polar opposition to Charlotte Perkins Gilman, who developed and propounded ideas on the social transformation of the patriarchal culture. James penetrated its inequities, as had Freeman; Gilman proposed programs to eliminate them. Like Alice James, Gilman suffered from psychiatric illness all her life and would readily have agreed with James's deathbed remark that "moral discords and nervous horrors sear the soul." Gilman's consciousness, however, turned outward from the body and self into social, utilitarian expression. Her fiction is programmatic, presupposing that a restructured society can alleviate, in fact eliminate, psychic pain. Gilman's stories, including "When I Was a Witch," "If I Were a Man," "The Cottagette," and "Turned," in addition to the utopian novel *Herland* (1915), show the possibilities for transformed surroundings, including central kitchens and day-care centers (baby gardens, as she calls them), courteous social intercourse, physical freedom in dress, and satisfying work for both sexes. Gilman's plots have happy endings, not as anodynes but as reassurance that individual and social change is possible. Admittedly, she sidesteps the psychological and social process by which the self is formed. Gilman argues that women's power is rational and humane, and can legislate new lives and new worlds.

Not every new-woman writer insisted upon socioeconomic reformulation. Ellen Glasgow brought her consciousness to bear upon the possibility for a female *Bildungsroman* in which a woman might triumph on the same terms as a man, achieving financial and sociopolitical power in the wider world. In so doing, Glasgow undertook the exploration of the process of woman's self-formation and self-assertion. She took on a subject broached by several of her new-woman cohorts, Freeman included, who were concerned about women's abilities to survive and to prevail in the larger world beyond domesticity, a man's world made "abnormal," says one of Wharton's characters in *The Custom of the Country* (1913), because men prevent women from sharing "in the real business of life" and so make them a mere "parenthesis."

Glasgow, like the others, argues that a "room of her own" must be correlated with a bank account of her own. Such novels as *The Romantic Comedians, Virginia, They Stooped to Folly, Life and Gabriella,* and *The Builders* all broach the subject. But *Barren Ground* (1925) most aggressively pursued the issue of woman's independence in the character of a young farm girl who, without money, a sheltering family, or marriage, single-mindedly bends land and society to her will in a triumph of fortitude—and renunciation.

Barren Ground recounts the adult life of the Virginian Dorinda Oakley, whose strength of will, appetite for work, and managerial intelligence thrust her into power as a kind of agricultural and social empress. Her marriage to a miller-storekeeper unifies commerce and agriculture, though it is one of mutually respectful convenience without sexual involvement, and thus seems virtually a test of character designed to verify women's independence of all men, even those bound to them by marital contract and daily domestic custom. Indeed, Dorinda is as tough-minded as the hardest businessman—which may in fact be Glasgow's point as she sets out to repudiate all feminine dependency. In *The Country of the Pointed Firs*, Jewett's matriarch, Mrs. Todd, rules by the power of sympathy; but Glasgow's Dorinda dominates because she exerts the will to power. *Barren Ground* works to show that a woman can be triumphantly self-sufficient, independent, and, within reasonable human expectation, fulfilled.

If a number of the new-woman writers avoid sexual entanglements in their writings, Edith Wharton insisted that sexual drives could not so easily be set aside, that they were primary motives of self and society. Like Chopin, Wharton made sexuality a crucial focus of her literary consciousness. Heterosexual passions lie at the heart of all of her major fiction, defining characters' relationships and forcing crucial turning points in their lives.

Sexual politics enter Wharton's first important novel, *The House of Mirth* (1905), when an impecunious, single young society woman, Lily Bart, flirtatiously seeks financial advice from a friend's husband, a crude business mogul. Warming to her advance, he promises to invest on her behalf, soon appearing with her Wall Street "earnings." Lily, because she cannot admit, not even to herself, the sexual dimension of her overture, avoids him—"when she made a tour of inspection in her own mind there were certain doors she did not open." The man corners her one night to complain, in business language freighted with sexual innuendo, that she is "dodging the rules of the game" and owes him "interest" on the investment. Within moments he is prostrate in self-abasement, which Lily finds loathsome, escaping his presence only to face the fact of her complicity. Suddenly she is "alone in a place of darkness and pollution." Sex, Wharton suggests, is central to power in relationships. It is, to echo one of her own, biblical titles, the fruit of the tree of knowledge.

Wharton subsequently enlarged her focus upon sexuality. The compass points here are *The Reef* (1912), *The Custom of the Country* (1913), *Summer* (1913), and *The Age of Innocence* (1920). Her Anna Leath, Undine Spragg, Charity Royall, and Ellen Olenska all define their lives in the sexual terms that, Wharton argues, are integral to America's powerful business culture and to civilization itself. Given the prominence of Wharton's sexual themes, it is not surprising that her biographer, Cynthia Griffin Wolff, discovered the sexually explicit fragment, "Beatrice Palmato," which describes a scene of father-daughter incest in utterly graphic language. Wharton, whose reputation once rested on her ability to memorialize old New York culture with its peculiar manners and mores, and to expose the hypocrisies of the wealthy, warrants further critical attention as the writer of sexual consciousness in the era of the new woman. Sex, she insists, is central to woman's personal and social power.

Willa Cather recast the terms of women's power from the sexual to the sensual. Cather's primary locus of consciousness is the landscape of preindustrial America. In her work the American landscape itself bears the burden of consciousness. "The great fact was the land itself" (*O Pioneers!*). Other new-woman writers identified women with territory. Jewett's matriarch presided over coastal Maine, while Glasgow's Dorinda dominated the acreage of Tidewater Virginia. Cather's claim for women, however, is bolder, vaster. Her women are identified with the West, that America undefiled by industrialization and urbanization. It includes the Nebraska plains where she grew up and the Arizona and New Mexico desert that she visited repeatedly in adulthood.

A fiction of the American land evidently represented Cather's reaction against the male novel of industrial, urban America. The novelist turned instead to the natural landscape as the material from which to fashion an alternative women's aesthetic. Against the masculine, constructed world, Cather posed an organic realm of the fecund land. If bridges and factories represented the power of a masculine civilization, the biologic and geologic energies inherent in the land expressed a power far greater than that of so-called modern civilization. Cather allied herself with the energies of the land, and identified them as female. Thus on the Continental Divide a young boy (*O Pioneers!*) can feel that the fierce and savage land "wanted to be let alone." Yet with the heroine's "human face set toward it with love and yearning. . . . the Genius of the Divide . . . bent lower than it ever bent to a human will before." It is crucial that the Continental Divide responds to the female will. Cather says that "the history of every country begins in the heart of a man or a woman," but her best novels insist that the woman's heart is really the sole province of that history.

The American land, then, is the center of woman's power in Cather's fiction. Her heroines—the "Amazonian" Alexandra Bergson of *O Pioneers!*, Ántonia Shimerda of *My Ántonia*, Thea Kronborg of *Song of the Lark*—all embody its characteristics. They enact its generative values, its natural cycles, the moods of its changing weather, its very spatial expensiveness.

It is perhaps startling to realize that Willa Cather's years of birth and death virtually coincide with Gertrude Stein's. Cather, a romantic, insisted that the artist sing the song of an organic world of vegetative and bodily being; but Stein allied herself with the modernists, who identified the artist as a designer and insisted that the work of art be defined as a construction. Accordingly, objects bear the burden of consciousness in Stein's work. A onetime student of the psychologist William James, she believed knowledge was gained from experience of the concrete. Cultural objects, therefore, were primary texts for consciousness, especially in *Tender Buttons* (1914), her abstract word-portraits of "Objects," "Food," and "Rooms." Stein's critics agree that she attempted to create, in words, the abstractionist paintings of such friends as Pablo Picasso and Juan Gris. Her nonlinear, disjunctive texts invite interpretation from a Cubist perspective. The objects in *Tender Buttons* may suggest the traditional concerns of women involved in domestic life, but Stein is working anew in the genre of the still-life painting. Hers is a mandarin domesticity. And her exertion of woman's consciousness and power may lie ultimately in her erection of structures of language that defy critical penetration and the possessive assimilation that comes with the understanding of difficult texts. Stein built a fortress of language that was virtually unassailable by the powerful, principally male, critics and writers who admired and learned from her. This new-woman writer became the matriarch of modernism.

The achievement of Stein, as of all the new-woman writers, has been increasingly recognized in recent years. It prompts renewed appreciation when we recall the quandary in which one early twentieth-century new woman, Jane Addams, located her contemporaries. In *Democracy and Social Ethics* (1902), Addams, thinking of younger women, admitted that families customarily regarded daughters as "a family possession. . . . fitted to grace the fireside," while modern education moved them in a contrary direction to develop "individuality" and the "powers for independent action." Addams had in mind the family, the home, and the wider social world in a period of important change—as she put it, of "reconstruction." The situation, she added, "has all the discomfort of transition." Addams urged that women not succumb to the old traditions but work from a new consciousness to reconstellate the family and the wider social environment. In American literature that was exactly what the new-woman writers achieved.

Cecelia Tichi

IV. Major Voices

Emily Dickinson

When Emily Dickinson died of Bright's disease, a kidney disorder, on May 15, 1886, her brother Austin listed her occupation as "At Home" on her death certificate. The fifty-five-year-old poet died in the same house in Amherst, Massachusetts, in which she was born and lived her entire life. Soon after her burial in the family plot, her sister Lavinia found forty-four sewn packets or "fascicles" of poems that Emily had written, as well as several others on scraps of paper or loose sheets. Only a few of these 1,775 poems were published in Dickinson's lifetime and the others might never have become available to the public had Lavinia and Mabel Loomis Todd, Austin's mistress and family friend, not made it their mission to find a publisher for them. In spite of her obscurity during her own lifetime, Dickinson is one of the most important American poets, and even today, more than one hundred years after her death, she continues to be a source of inspiration and new ideas for contemporary poets.

Emily Dickinson is the ghost that haunts American literature. The legend of the white-robed spinster recluse who wrote poems in the upstairs room of her father's house where Dickinsons had lived for almost a hundred years has been embellished until she has been largely obscured by the myths. Dickinson was a complicated woman and poet, so much so that scholars who have written about her have created widely varying portraits. Some of the interpretations of her life are dramatic, many are distorted, others are damaging to our understanding of one of the most accomplished American poets. She has been described as neurasthenic and morbidly afraid of men; as a repressed lesbian; as an agoraphobic; as a person who projected her active self onto Austin and his wife Susan and was content to let them function in the world on her behalf; and as having suffered psychological and physical problems resulting from an illegal abortion.

Recently, feminist critics have analyzed Dickinson's work and life in the context of the constraints placed on women in the traditional New England society in which she lived. These new interpretations demonstrate quite convincingly that she was a dedicated and disciplined poet whose relative isolation was a self-imposed strategy that gave her time and space in which to write. She was able to make such a profound contribution to American literature because of her radical questioning, reworking, and often rejection of conventional language, poetic style, theology, feminine roles, and attitudes toward her world. To protect herself from more conventional opinions, she largely divorced herself from her social context and created a very private life that suited her artistic needs, and her strikingly original perceptions are clearly visible in her poetry and letters.

As a young woman Emily Dickinson experienced a series of conflicts with powerful male figures from which she gained a sense of herself as an independent thinker and writer. In order to achieve psychological and artistic autonomy, she had to undergo a "civil war" of the self against the very authorities—religious, familial, literary—she sometimes sought to follow.

Her first skirmish in the battle for self-reliance was with the traditional religious concept of an all-powerful God who laid claim to her soul. As an adolescent she resisted being converted during the religious revival that swept through Mount Holyoke Seminary where she was sent to school from 1847 to 1848. In her sermons the headmistress, Mary Lyons, skillfully applied the fire-and-brimstone rhetoric used a century earlier by the Puritan preacher Jonathan Edwards. Most of Dickinson's classmates responded, but Dickinson remained impenitent. For meeting after meeting, she was the only student described as having "no hope" of salvation. Even the conversions of her father and sister in the revival in Amherst in 1850 did not sway her, and she wrote to her close friend, Abiah Root, "I am standing alone in rebellion."

For Dickinson, submission to Christ as her "Master" meant relinquishing her attachment to life on earth as well as her individuality. After more than a year of spiritual turmoil, she admitted to Abiah, "I know not why, I feel that the world holds a predominant place in my affections, I do not feel I could give up all for Christ, were I called to die." But even though she resolutely resisted conversion, Dickinson felt extraordinarily guilty: "I am one of the lingering *bad* ones, and so do I slink away, and pause, and ponder, and ponder, and pause, and do work without knowing why—not surely for *this* brief world, and more sure it is not for Heaven." Alternating between self-possession and self-abnegation, Emily Dickinson ultimately embraced the risks and rewards of spiritual autonomy. "The shore is safer," she wrote to Abiah Root in December 1850, "but I love to buffet the sea."

Ultimately, Emily Dickinson rejected a theology based on the absolutes of salvation and damnation, vice and virtue, and instead accepted the experiential discontinuity and linguistic ambiguity that characterized her life. With a mixture of curiosity and skepticism, she questioned theological and secular values, even to the extent of challenging the accepted meanings of words. Her radical dissent was the basis of her startlingly experimental poetry that continues to be a major force in American literature.

Having put the matter of conversion to rest, Emily Dickinson faced a second crisis when she struggled with her father for intellectual independence. A stern and emotionally inaccessible man, Edward Dickinson had not permitted his daughter to continue her studies at Holyoke, where she had been an outstanding student, because he was convinced that academic work was harmful to her health. Mr. Dickinson apparently subscribed to the nineteenth-century belief that mental exertion damaged woman's physical well-being. As Emily Dickinson observed, "Father. . . . buys me many Books—but begs me not to read them—because he fears they joggle the Mind." It was commonly believed that the womb and the brain were inversely related and that excessive thought injured the reproductive organs; domestic, not intellectual, activities were considered appropriate for the female constitution. Dickinson's plaintive letter to her friend Abiah Root captures this painful contradiction: "I am now working on a pair of slippers to adorn my father's feet. . . . We'll finish an education sometime, won't we? You may then be Plato, and I will be Socrates, provided you won't be wiser than I am."

Emily's relationship with her brother Austin was also problematic during this period—she resented the preferential treatment he received from their father because he was the eldest and the only son, and she felt competitive with him about writing poetry. As adolescents all the Dickinson children wrote poetry, but what she saw as Austin's encroachment on her territory angered her:

> And Austin is a Poet, Austin writes a psalm. Out of the way, Pegasus, Olympus enough "to him," and just say to these "nine muses" that we have done with them!
> Raised a living muse ourselves, worth the whole nine of them. Up, off, tramp!
> Now, Brother Pegasus, I'll tell you what it is—I've been in the habit *myself* of writing a few things, and it rather appears to me that you're getting away my patent, so you'd better be somewhat careful, or I'll call the police!

In this passage Emily Dickinson asserts her dominance by relegating Austin to the instrumental role of Pegasus, the winged horse ridden by the Muses. And she does not define her creativity according to male convention; she rejects passive inspiration and has "raised" her own "living muse"—a tenth muse in the tradition of Anne Bradstreet. When the complicated skirmish for identity among the Dickinson children was over, Emily claimed the role of willful, eccentric, rebellious artist, Lavinia emerged as the "angel in the house" and professed to be content to serve her family in the traditional role of caretaker, and Austin ultimately accepted his role as lawyer and provider for his wife and children.

Finally Dickinson was acknowledged by her family and friends as having creative genius. As Lavinia observed, Emily "had to think—she was the only one of us who had that to do." She gained access to her father's library and also won exemption from schedule. Thereafter, she often worked late at night in the large bedroom that overlooked the main street of Amherst. Emily Dickinson marked these victories in a note of thanks that she wrote to her father in 1858, thanking him for her *"morning-hours, viz—3AM. to 12PM."* Dickinson cherished and zealously guarded the hard-won privacy that gave her time to think and write. Her niece, Martha Dickinson Bianchi, describes her aunt Emily as being fiercely proud of her ability to seclude herself in her room; pretending to lock the door, she said to her niece: "It's just a turn—and freedom, Matty!"

Dickinson's third crisis centered on the issue of psychological autonomy. In a process paralleling her religious agony, she reclaimed the energy that she had invested in the ideal of the romantic hero. Just as she had come to believe that there was no Heavenly Savior, she eventually understood that no man would be her protector on earth. During this phase of her life in the early 1860s, Dickinson wrote three letters in which "Daisy" expresses an almost worshipful love for her "Master," who remains aloof. There has been an extraordinary amount of speculation about the identity of the "Master" to whom Dickinson addressed these letters. Some critics have argued that the Reverend Charles Wadsworth was Emily Dickinson's beloved, but this seems unlikely in view of the fact that Wadsworth and Dickinson rarely encountered each other (he lived in Philadelphia), and in the only extant letter that Wadsworth wrote to Emily Dickinson he misspells her name, addressing her as "Miss Dickinsen." Other critics argue that the "Master" letters were written to Samuel Bowles, the editor of the *Springfield Republican* and close friend of the Dickinson family. Bowles was a handsome, flirtatious man whose wife, Mary, was one of Emily Dickinson's best friends; he was a frequent guest in the Dickinson household, and if the letters were written to a specific person, it was probably Samuel Bowles.

Whoever may have been their real or imagined recipient, the "Master" letters express Dickinson's conflicting needs for independence and protection. Written from the perspective of a penitent child who begs for attention, these letters reveal a desperate need for approval:

Master—open your life wide, and take me in forever, I will never be tired—I will never be noisy when you want me to be still. I will be . . . your best little girl—nobody else will see me, but you—but that is enough—I shall not want any more—and all that Heaven only will disappoint me—will be because it's not so dear.

Dickinson's self-abnegating letters are strikingly similar in style and emotional stance to those of Charlotte Brontë written a few years earlier to her schoolmaster, Constantin Heger. Both women cast themselves in the role of vulnerable and insignificant creatures who are at the mercy of powerful men for emotional survival. Although this female version of the Byronic mode is masochistic, these letters describe a struggle for psychological wholeness. By experiencing the extremes of longing, rejection, abject humiliation, and despair, Emily Dickinson works through her self-denial and ultimately discovers her own strength. A poem written during the period of the "Master" letters expresses her effort to relinquish the habit of excessive dependence. It begins "I'm ceded—I've stopped being theirs—" and concludes "With Will to choose, or to reject,/ And I choose, just a Crown—." With this poem, Dickinson signals that she no longer serves the needs of others and now commands her own energies. The image of the Crown represents this self-possession, and it refers to the laurel wreath traditionally awarded to poets as well as to regal control.

Dickinson's fourth and final struggle centered on her efforts to receive validation as an artist. Soon after the noted literary critic Thomas Wentworth Higginson published an article of advice to young writers in April 1862 in the *Atlantic Monthly*, Emily Dickinson sent him four of her poems with a note asking, "[Is] my Verse alive?" Again submitting herself to the judgment of a powerful male, she begged him to tell her "how to grow—or is it unconveyed—like Melody—or Witchcraft?" And again, she is self-effacing: "I could not weigh myself—Myself—My size felt small—to me." Having survived her religious, intellectual, and romantic crises, she shifts her attention to her destiny as a poet. When Higginson advises her to "delay" publication, she responds that publication "was as foreign to my thought as Firmament to Fin" and demurs that she is not interested in fame. Nevertheless, her agitation is evident: "You think my gait 'spasmodic'—I am in danger—Sir—/ You think me 'uncontrolled'—I have no Tribunal." As in her "Master" letters, Emily Dickinson diminishes herself: "I have a little shape—it would not crowd your Desk—nor make much racket as the Mouse, that dents your galleries." Although her ambition is concealed by her diminutive pose, Emily Dickinson again experiences conflict between her need for external approval and her inclination to trust her own judgment.

Higginson acknowledged Emily Dickinson's genius even though he did not encourage her to publish. After she repeatedly declined his invitations to attend literary events in Boston, he wrote her, "Yet it isolates one anywhere to think beyond a certain point or to have such luminous flashes as come to you—so perhaps the place does not make much difference." After visiting Dickinson in Amherst in 1870, he was deeply affected by her sensitivity and her total commitment to poetry, so much so that he recorded her observations in letters to his wife. For example, he was fascinated by her definition of poetry:

If I read a book [and] it makes my whole body so cold no fire can ever warm me I know that is poetry. If I feel physically as if the top of my head were taken off, I know *that* is poetry. These are the only way [*sic*] I know it. Is there any other way.

Overwhelmed at times by Dickinson's intensity, Higginson described her to his wife as "half-cracked" and confessed that it drained his "nerve power" to be near her for any length of time.

After a period of intense self-doubt Dickinson found her own ground, and one of her letters to Higginson in 1862 presents her subtle but emphatic declaration of independence:

When much in the Woods as a little Girl, I was told that the Snake would bite me . . . but I went along and met no one but Angels, who were far shyer of me, than I could be of them, so I have not that confidence in fraud which many exercise.

Through her often painful struggle with Higginson, Emily Dickinson learned not to project her strength onto authoritative men but to reclaim her energy for her work.

In her later years, Emily Dickinson created her own version of self-reliance in the tradition of Benjamin Franklin, Ralph Waldo Emerson, and Andrew Jackson. Unlike her male counterparts Walt Whitman, Emerson, and even Henry David Thoreau, all of whom participated in public life, Dickinson committed herself to the private sphere and evolved her poetic vision there. Paradoxically, by simplifying her world, by remaining single, and by shunning conventional social life, Emily Dickinson remained receptive to the intricate patterns of her experience; she decided that she could best engage in the adventure of life and death by staying at home.

In the protected space of the Dickinson household, which she described as "the Infinite Power of Home," Emily Dickinson wrote almost two thousand poems and probably as many letters, of which a thousand are extant. Instead of becoming a fixed point for a husband whose duty it was to navigate the uncertain currents of a burgeoning industrial economy, Dickinson embarked on an adventure of self-discovery: "Within is so wild a place," she wrote. Having rejected the traditions of evangelical Christianity, male dominance, and redemptive femininity, she recorded her discontinuous emotional states; by mapping points of consciousness she discerned larger patterns of experience that she described as "Circumference." As far as Emily Dickinson was concerned, the public self required reified responses that narrowed consciousness.

Observing that she was "born for Bachelorhood," she understood that the responsibilities of traditional nineteenth-century marriage would have given her little time to write poetry. Even as a young woman, she feared that her artistic energy might be destroyed by marriage. When she was twenty-one, she expressed this concern in an often quoted letter to Susan Gilbert, her future sister-in-law:

How dull our lives must seem to the bride, and the plighted maiden, whose days are fed with gold, and who gathers pearls every evening; but to the *wife*, Susie, sometimes the *wife forgotten*, our lives perhaps seem dearer than all others in the world; you have seen flowers at morning, *satisfied* with the dew, and those same sweet flowers at noon with their heads bowed in anguish before the mighty sun; think you these thirsty blossoms will *now* need nought but—*dew?* No, they will cry for sunlight, and pine for the burning noon, tho' it scorches them, scathes them; they got through with peace—they know that the man of noon, is *mightier* than the morning and their life is henceforth to him. Oh, Susie, it is dangerous, and it is all too dear, these simple, trusting spirits, and the spirits mightier, which we cannot resist! It does so rend me, Susie, the thought of it when it comes, that I tremble lest at sometime I, too, am yielded up.

Critics have noted that Dickinson describes the flower as helplessly tracing the sun's course, and that Dickinson's use of the passive "yielded up" reveals that she perceives marriage as a sacrifice. For Dickinson, then, the single life represents emotional autonomy and artistic integrity.

At first Emily Dickinson stayed home because her father insisted that she lacked the stamina to survive in a larger world. However, another factor in Dickinson's choice to remain "At Home," one that has almost entirely been overlooked by Dickinson's biographers, was her eye problems. These visual difficulties were sufficiently severe to require two six-month trips to Boston for treatment, in 1864 and 1865. During her visits she stayed in a boarding-house and was cared for by her cousins Louise and Emily Norcross. Her doctor was Henry W. Williams, a respected ophthalmic surgeon and Harvard professor whose books on the medical and surgical treatment of eye disease were standard references in the field. Emily Dickinson described her visits to Dr. Williams as "painful" and complained in her letters to friends that bright light bothered her. Dickinson's sensitivity to light may explain her propensity for remaining indoors most of the time. Medical evidence indicates that Dickinson probably had exotropia, a deviation in the alignment of the eyes characterized by eyestrain, blurred vision, and difficulty with reading. Dickinson's letters reveal that she was unable to use her eyes for prolonged periods, and her poems about sight and vision take on deeper meaning in the context of her visual difficulties. For example, her poem "Before I got my eye put out," which is traditionally interpreted as a poem about narrowing of vision and the loss of understanding, is obviously more than metaphoric:

> Before I got my eye put out
> I liked as well to see—
> As other Creatures, that have Eyes
> And know no other way—
>
> (#327)

Emily Dickinson was a highly visual person and poet. She was deeply attached to the phenomenal world, but, like Emerson, she felt that it was a poet's responsibility to penetrate surfaces, to see more completely; much of her poetry is concerned with the relationship of physical sight to poetic vision, and her eye problems must have been terrifying to her.

In later years, Dickinson was needed at home to help care for her mother, Emily Norcross Dickinson, who was an invalid from the time Edward Dickinson died in 1874 until her own death in 1882. With Lavinia, Emily was responsible for the elaborate household while their mother was bedridden. Because her father had been a prosperous lawyer and legislator, the Dickinson domestic life was comfortable, if sometimes cumbersome. The Dickinson family lived in a large house and could afford servants; the Dickinson gardener, MacGregor Jenkins, describes Emily Dickinson as a gentlewoman in the traditional sense of the word:

One summer morning . . . Miss Emily called me. She was standing on a rug spread for her on the grass, busy with potted plants which were all about her, . . . a beautiful woman dressed in white, with soft, fiery, brown eyes and a mass of auburn hair. . . . She talked to me of her flowers, of those she loved best; of her fear should the bad weather harm them; then, cutting a few choice buds, she bade me take them, with her love, to my mother.

One of Dickinson's dreams during her father's lifetime reveals that she knew that her privileged life depended on her father's financial success: in her nightmare, "Father had failed and mother said that our rye field which she and I planted was mortgaged to Seth Nims." Her fear underscores the abject dependence of the traditional woman on men for financial protection.

Although these pressures caused Emily Dickinson to conform to the nineteenth-century code of female domestic seclusion, what began as a necessity became a virtue for her. Ultimately she subverted the tradition of true womanhood to serve her own poetic mission. As an adolescent, Dickinson parodied the standards of "female propriety or sedate deportment." Later, like Mark Twain, who wore white suits, in part, as an ironic response to the tradition of the cavalier gentleman, Emily Dickinson mocked the ideal of frail and angelic femininity with her long white dresses. In addition, Dickinson's white robes signaled her dedication to the "white heat of poetry," which was her secular version of salvation.

Turning the definition of woman as a private creature to her advantage, Dickinson used the Victorian confinement of women to the home to create a space for her poetry. Even as a young woman Emily Dickinson recognized that living at home provided her with an opportunity for self-determination. At twenty-one she wrote, "I'm afraid I'm growing *selfish* in my dear home, but I do love it so." Paradoxically, her reclusive life became a measure of her self-possession, *not* her self-denial. Above all she was an artist who was intensely involved with the world around her; she was a rebellious intellectual, not a neurotic recluse, as many critics have erroneously claimed.

Dickinson found freedom from excessive sociability in solitude and in nature. For her, the continual round of parties, picnics, concerts, lectures, fairs, sleighrides, receptions, levees, temperance dinners, church socials, weddings, baptisms, and funerals that constituted the social life of Amherst prevented awareness of larger existential patterns. Because "the Homestead" was located on one of Amherst's busy main streets and was near two churches, a railroad intersection, and the town hall, Dickinson had to go to great lengths to protect her privacy—it was even risky to visit her brother and his family because Sue Dickinson was an unusually active hostess. In the privacy of her room and garden, Dickinson achieved a measure of freedom; as the forty-year-old Dickinson wrote to her friend Elizabeth Holland, "The Fence is the only Sanctuary."

In spite of her refusal to participate in the reflexive sociability of Amherst, Emily Dickinson was nevertheless involved in major intellectual and social issues of her day. Her own household was charged with political excitement: her father was elected to the general court of Massachusetts and then to the United States Congress, and close family friends Samuel Bowles and Josiah Holland were prominent editors who discussed political events with the Dickinson family. Dickinson's mentor, T. W. Higginson, was a nationally known critic and was active in the antislavery and feminist movements.

Although she scoffed at patriarchal politics ("George Washington was the Father of his Country '—George who?' That sums up all Politics to me—," she quipped), she was deeply affected by the Civil War, the assassination of Abraham Lincoln, the antislavery movement, and the increasing industrialization of New England. Her letters are full of references to the Civil War battles, and her poetry uses considerable military imagery. When a family friend, Frazer Stearns, died in combat, Emily Dickinson was disconsolate, and she was never able to reconcile herself to what she felt was the arbitrary carnage of the war. Some critics have suggested that the war also functioned as a metaphor expressing Dickinson's conflicting needs for achievement and dependence, as well as the tension she experienced in her effort to forge an identity in her father's household.

As Emily Dickinson grew older her home increasingly became a focus for her energy: "Home is the definition of God," observed the forty-year-old Dickinson. Subscribing to the nineteenth-century belief in the sanctity of the home, she felt that domestic life protected love and friendship, which were superior to business and politics. The domestic sphere functioned for Dickinson, as it did for many nineteenth-century women, as an arena of activity that emphasized the superiority of emotional concerns over financial values—as a place where empathy and loyalty were more important than ambition or profit. Many nineteenth-century women were convinced that the domestic tradition with its emphasis on mutual support and cooperation offered a superior alternative to the competitive world of the marketplace. Some critics have contended that this emphasis on feminine purity and piety not only trapped women but excluded them from defining the larger society. But along with other defenders of the domestic tradition, Dickinson was convinced that women attained a deeper understanding of life because their energies were not narrowly defined by male notions of economic necessity. For Dickinson, the female sphere with its emphasis on nurturance made civilization possible. Convinced that women possess "the skill of life" *because* they are exempt from competition in the marketplace, she insisted that "Remoteness is the founder of sweetness."

Dickinson prized her friendships with women, but very little attention has been given to her enduring relationships with her cousins Louise and Frances Norcross and her close friend Elizabeth Holland. Holland's loyalty to Dickinson sustained her as an artist, just as her early friendships with Abiah Root, Jane Humphrey, and Susan Gilbert helped her to think of herself as a serious poet. Emily Dickinson's deepest tie, however, was with her sister Lavinia, on whom she became increasingly dependent. Their relationship was intensely symbiotic: "Vinnie is sick to-night, which gives the world a russet tinge usually so red . . . when she is well, time leaps. When she is ill, he lags, or, stops entirely." Lavinia was the lifeline that enabled her sister to enter uncharted emotional terrain, to evolve the contradictions that undercut androcentric abstractions, and to create a woman-centered cosmology.

Rejecting the idea of subordination, Emily Dickinson explored relationship and interconnection. Dickinson's rendering of disparate states of consciousness challenges masculine linguistic hierarchy. In her poetry she frequently used the oxymoron to capture existential ambiguity: "Stolid Bliss," "numb Alarm," "Confident Despair," "Heavenly Hurt," "Infinities of Nought," "the Scant Salvation," "Sumptuous Solitude," "a piercing Comfort," and "abstemious ecstasy." Dickinson's images are drawn from daily life, and her emphasis on the quotidian results in a radical subjectivity that is the source of unusual metaphors. For example, frost is described as "the blonde Assassin"; sin as "a distinguished Precipice"; the moon as a "Chin of Gold."

Dickinson's synaesthetic descriptions interweaving sensory experience are startling: "A circus passed the house—still I feel the red in my mind though the drums are out" or "the lawn is full of south and the odors tangle, and I hear today for the first the river in the tree." While Dickinson rejects what she perceived as male epistemology in which the mind dominates the body and reason the senses, her deliberate fusion of sensory perceptions invigorates her diction. The ambiguity and the astonishing range of Dickinson's poetry are the result of her understanding that language itself simplifies reality and, at best, can only approximate experience. In part, Emily Dickinson's disrupted phrases, metrical variations, and inverted syntax reflect her effort to create a world by adapting established forms to serve her often startling linguistic experimentation.

Dickinson developed an aesthetic that was, in part, intended to demolish patriarchal poetic conventions. Although she claimed to be unresponsive to nineteenth-century feminist activism, she understood the politics of gender very well indeed. Dickinson's counter-poetic is characterized by lexical surprises, frequent use of oxymoron and synaesthesia, which create a world of resonant possibility intended to overturn the utilitarian priorities that she associated with traditional masculinity. What seems evanescent in her poetic style is a deliberate indeterminacy that expresses her transient and provisional sense of the world—a world at once multidirectional and relational at the boundary between the familiar and unknown. The many variants of her poems constitute tacit acknowledgment of the primacy of process. Similarly, her refusal to use traditional punctuation constitutes an antideclarative stance; her dashes signal an urgent immediacy that undercuts the possibility of an absolute cultural hegemony; her phrases referring simultaneously backward and forward permit the reader to make connections and create the ambiguity necessary to create new modes of perception.

In spite of her father's dictates to the contrary, Dickinson was a voracious reader, and her poems were deeply influenced by her extensive reading in classical and contemporary literature. She read the Bible, Bunyan, Milton, Shakespeare, Sir Thomas Browne, Ruskin, Carlyle, Dickens, the Brownings, the Brontës, George Eliot, Byron, Shelley, Goethe, Tennyson, Longfellow, Bryant, Hawthorne, Emerson, and Thoreau, as well as popular fiction by such writers as Harriet Spofford and Donald G. Mitchell, whose pseudonym was "Ik Marvel." Not only is her poetry peppered with biblical references and phrases and images from romantic poetry, but she derived much of her unusual syntax from Latin grammar, and her original rhythmic structure is often a syncopation of conventional scansion.

Dickinson's irregular or inverted syntax often confuses readers, but many of her unusual constructions are adaptations of Latin rules outlined in *A Grammar of the Latin Language: For the Use of Schools and Colleges* (Boston, 1843), which she used as a student. Her stylistic innovations—odd inversions, "Rekindled by some action quaint"; omission of auxillary verbs, "Before it [can] see the Sun!"; use of adjectives and verbs as nouns, "We talk in Careless—and in toss—"; use of adverbs as nouns, "I lingered with Before"; conclusion of sentences or clauses with verbs, "Nor what consoled it, I could trace"—are actually taken from classical forms of grammar such as hyperbaton, anastrophe, hysteron, proteron, hypallage, syncrisis, enallage, aphaeresis, parenthesis, and ellipsis. Her idiosyncratic syntax, then, is based on traditional usage, not ignorance or whim, as many critics have suggested.

Dickinson's unpredictable poetic rhythms caused T. W. Higginson to complain that her meters were "spasmodic." However, he failed to understand that she was deliberately syncopating established metrical patterns—especially of the hymnist Isaac Watts—in an effort to create a flexible, organic style. Satirizing strict scansion, her poetry was based on the phrase, not the traditional foot; instead of an inexorably regular stress pattern, she used dashes to indicate pauses. Dickinson's innovations influenced William Carlos Williams, who called her his "patron saint," and his "variable foot" based on the inflection of American speech—the breath as a unit to determine the length of phrases and lines—was inspired by her poetics. Dickinson's creation of new syntactic and rhythmic possibilities had a tremendous influence on many important twentieth-century poets, including Ezra Pound, Marianne Moore, Robert Lowell, and Adrienne Rich.

In addition to these stylistic influences, many of Dickinson's poems are either a response to or a direct reworking of her reading, and her work often contains dramatic renderings of scenes from specific novels. For example, Dickinson's poem "I rose—because He sank—" (#616) is her recasting of the chapters in *Jane Eyre* (1857) where Jane and Rochester are reunited. Rochester has been partially blinded in his unsuccessful effort to save his insane wife Bertha from the fire that demolished Thornfield Hall. In the novel, Charlotte Brontë describes the effects of Jane's efforts to cheer Rochester, to make him "less sad": "Blind as he was, smiles played over his face, joy dawned on his forehead." When Rochester urges Jane to marry him immediately, she teases him for being "stiff about urging his point" but rejoices that "the sun has dried up all the rain-drops." In the second and third stanzas of the poem, Dickinson actually incorporates Brontë's language to portray Jane's triumph:

> I cheered my fainting Prince—
> I sang firm—even—Chants—
> I helped his Film—with Hymn—
>
> And when the Dews drew off
> That held his Forehead stiff—
> I met him
> Balm to Balm
>
> (#616)

In addition to being a direct response to Brontë's novel, this poem describing Jane's increasing strength and control is a paradigm for Emily Dickinson's emotional growth in general. The concluding lines "And Sinew from within—/ And ways I knew not that I knew—till then—I lifted Him—" articulate Dickinson's acceptance of her own power.

An analysis of the flower imagery in Emily Dickinson's poetry illuminates this transition from passive femininity to autonomous womanhood. She often uses the flower to represent female consciousness and sexuality, as well as nature's plenitude. In her early poems, labiate blossoms tend to be decorative, seductive but helplessly dependent on the male sun, bee, or admirer for completion:

> I tend my flowers for thee—
> Bright Absentee!
> . . . .

Geraniums—tint—and spot—
Low Daisies—dot—
My Cactus—splits her Beard
To show her throat—

(#339)

In later poems, the flower is important in its own right and must resist destructive climatic conditions in order to bloom. The male bee is depicted as an intruder or marauder:

The Rose received his visit
With frank tranquillity
Withholding not a Crescent
To his Cupidity—

(#1339)

Finally, blossoms represent the totality of awareness free of traditional gender limitations; these flowers are associated with a comprehensive vision of life—the diverse aspects of the universe in which human beings are but a part. They are often the symbol of the unfolding moment, "the moment immortal" in Dickinson's poetry.

Dickinson's work habits reflect her commitment to process and her immersion in the present. In his introduction to the standard edition of her poetry, Thomas Johnson tells us that she often wrote on scraps of paper, on flaps or backs of envelopes, discarded letters, wrapping paper, edges of newspapers—on anything that came to hand. For her, revision was a continual process, and her writing technique resembled patchwork quilting, in which the larger pattern became evident through the repetition of a design or motif. Often, she transposed phrases from her letters into her poems. Emily Dickinson sewed her poems into small packets that her sister Lavinia called *fascicles*, a botanical term that describes her sister's arrangement of her work, in which she conceived of each poem as a petal, each packet a flower. With the recent publication of an edition of her poems that restores the original order of the fascicles, it is becoming increasingly clear that Dickinson's poems have thematic groupings, with each packet constituting a coherent narrative.

Very few of Dickinson's poems were published during her lifetime. Five were published in the *Springfield Republican*, a local newspaper, although Dickinson complained that the editor corrupted the text of "The Snake" (#986). Only one Dickinson poem was presented to a wider audience. Interestingly, it was the popular poet Helen Hunt Jackson who insisted that Emily Dickinson submit her work. At first she refused Jackson's repeated pleas, but after much cajoling, Dickinson relented and permitted Jackson to include "Success Is Counted Sweetest" in *The Masque of Poets*. Dickinson must have taken great pride in the fact that the *New York Times* reviewer singled out her poem for special praise. Her syncopated rhythms and unusual imagery contrasted dramatically with the insistent cadences and sentimental themes of popular women poets: Lydia Sigourney ("the sweet singer of Hartford"), Fanny Fern, Caroline Kirkland, and Helen Hunt Jackson herself. Unlike many of her contemporaries, Dickinson did not indulge in an idealization of pastoral life, and she avoided the excesses of the romantic Sublime and the cult of scenery. Accepting nature's capacity for horrible destruction, Dickinson wrote about death and devastation as well as plenitude and ecstasy.

In the tradition of protest and reform that characterizes American experience, Dickinson is the pivotal poet between the Puritans and the moderns. Anticipating the work of the modernists with its awareness of mortality and lack of absolute certainties, her poetry also recapitulates the Puritan mission to build the New World Jerusalem. Borrowing images and phrases from Saint Matthew and Revelation, adapting classical syntactic devices, and syncopating the meters and stanzas from hymns, she created a vision of an early paradise in which nature and friendship were sacred.

Dickinson's meditative poetry has its roots in Puritan contemplations on the divine testing of the human spirit as well as on the meaning of life. Like her New England ancestors who committed themselves to serve God's "calling," Emily Dickinson consecrated herself to poetry. As the following lines reveal, language was sacred to her: "A Word made Flesh is seldom/ And tremblingly partook" (#1651). And her extraordinarily complex poetry discloses emotional patterns as intricate as Puritan conversion with its phases of sanctification, justification, and grace. Recording the entire range of her experience from joy to sorrow, anguish to celebration, she was what the Puritans called a "heart's rememberancer." By accepting all of her feelings, however contrary, Dickinson created a cosmology in which consciousness functions as the soul, ecstasy is the equivalent of grace, human love replaces sanctification, and the community of friends constitute the visible saints. For Dickinson, home is heaven and nature is paradise.

For her, generativity in all of its forms was more important than the quest for eternal life: "Redemption leaves nothing for the Earth to add," she remarked. Unwilling to trivialize the quotidian, she insisted on reverence for daily life: "O Matchless Earth, We underrate the chance to dwell in thee." A close family friend, Clara Newman Turner, observed that Dickinson was profoundly attuned to nature's rhythms: "Her events were the coming of the first birds;—the bursting of a young chrysalis;—the detection of the first fascinating spring fuzz of green in the air—the wonderful opening of the new world in every little flower; an unusual sunset; the autumn changes—and the inexhaustible life." Reshaping the Puritan ideal of the city on a hill into a vision in which "Nature is Heaven," she said, "I find ecstasy in living—the mere sense of living is joy enough."

Nothing was more frightening or fascinating to Emily Dickinson than death, which she referred to as the "flood subject." Throughout her life she grieved deeply for the loss of those she loved. As an adolescent, she was profoundly depressed by the deaths of her friend Sophia Holland from consumption and of Austin's friend Frazer Stearns who was killed in the Civil War. When her Aunt Lavinia died in 1860, Emily Dickinson wrote:

Blessed Aunt Lavinia now; all the world goes out. . . . I sob and cry till I can hardly see my way 'round the house again; . . . it is dark and strange to think of summer afterward: how she loved the summer; the birds keep singing just the same. Oh! the thoughtless birds.

Her father's death fifteen years later rekindled deep anxieties about the fate of the soul:

I dream about father every night, always a different dream, and forget what I am doing daytimes, wondering where he is. Without any body, I keep thinking, what kind can that be?

This emotional crisis had important metaphysical implications—in a universe without God, what principles gave meaning to life and death? The epistemological and theological complexities in the questions of the existence of an all-powerful god and the relationship of the spirit to the flesh, or the mind/body problem, repeatedly surface in Dickinson's work, and her best poetry expresses the intense anxiety she experienced in her effort to resolve these issues. Ultimately, Emily Dickinson realized that life after death consists of the memories of the deceased cherished by their loved ones: "Show me eternity, and I'll show you memory," she declared.

During her mother's invalidism, Dickinson learned lessons daily about physical frailty and the process of dying. In the final phases of her mother's illness, Dickinson seems to have accepted death as an inevitable conclusion of life:

Brave Vinnie is well—Mother does not yet stand alone and fears she never shall walk, but I tell her we all shall fly so soon, not to let it grieve her, and what indeed is Earth but a Nest, from whose rim we are all falling?

When Emily Norcross Dickinson died, her daughter wrote, "She slipped from our fingers like a flake gathered by the wind, and now part of the drift called 'the infinite.' " When her much-loved eight-year-old nephew Gilbert died in 1883, Dickinson succumbed to "nervous prostration" and experienced a "revenge of the nerves." Upon the death of Otis Lord, a family friend with whom Emily Dickinson had a long-distance courtship from 1881 until 1884, her profound sorrow deepened her understanding of her own mortality.

Some of Dickinson's most powerful poems express her firmly held conviction that life cannot be fully comprehended without an understanding of death:

> The Zeroes—taught us—Phosphorus—
> We learned to like the Fire
> By playing Glaciers—when a Boy—
> And Tinder—guessed—by power
> Of Opposite—to balance Odd—
> If White—a Red—must be!
> Paralysis—our Primer—dumb—
> Unto Vitality!
>
> (#689)

Paralleling life and death, these opposites—heat and cold, light and dark, health and sickness—exist in a reciprocal relationship creating meaning for each other. For Dickinson, this "Compound Vision," "the Finite—furnished/ With the Infinite," lends depth and meaning to the present moment. Eternity is not a specific destination but the enfolding present, or, as she observed, "Forever—is composed of Nows—"

Repeatedly, Dickinson insists that it is a mistake to represent the concept of eternity as a place: "The Blunder is in estimate./ Eternity is there/ We say, as of a Station" (#1684). Dickinson often uses the word "estimate" to underscore the misguided efforts to measure and delimit existence: "I fear we think too lightly of the gift of mortality, which, too gigantic to comprehend, certainly cannot be estimated," she wrote when Samuel Bowles was dying.

Ultimately, Emily Dickinson learned to see death as an "Adventure," concluding that "Dying is a wild Night and a new Road." With her acceptance of the inevitability of death came a deepened reverence for life:

> Did life's penurious length
> Italicize its sweetness,
> The men that daily live
> Would stand so deep in joy
> That it would clog the cogs
> Of that revolving reason

Whose esoteric belt
Protects our sanity.

(#1717)

Anticipating modernists like Marianne Moore, Theodore Roethke, Wallace Stevens, and William Carlos Williams, Dickinson believed that death intensifies life: "Uncertain lease—develops lustre/ On Time," or as she observed in another poem, "That it will never come again/ Is what makes life so sweet."

Instead of relying on the comforts of the conventional religious doctrine, Emily Dickinson responded to mortality by creating a cosmology that was centered on nurturance and generativity. Her playful working of the Trinity expresses her priorities: "In the name of the Bee—/ And of the Butterfly—/ And of the Breeze—Amen!" Sardonically remarking that she "wished the faith of the Fathers didn't wear blue Brogans and carry Umbrellas," Dickinson often parodied religious pieties and took an ironic view of orthodox beliefs: "The Bible is an antique Volume—/ Written by faded Men." With no theological certainty to comfort her, Dickinson was sustained by her love of family, friends, and nature. Love, not power, was at the core of Dickinson's cosmology: "Pardon my sanity in a world *in*sane, and love me if you will, for I had rather *be* loved than to be called a King in earth, or a lord in Heaven," she wrote to Elizabeth Holland in 1856. For her, the tenderness embedded in the female tradition was superior to the control and power traditionally prized by men.

Describing herself as being on "an errand from the heart," Dickinson demonstrated extraordinary courage in her rejection of the promise of salvation and the threat of damnation and in her celebration of earthly existence. Describing her life, Emily Dickinson wrote her own epitaph:

But awed beyond my errand—
I worshipped—did not "pray"

The rebellious girl who dared to pick "Satan's flowers" became a major poet who was rewarded with the revelation of the moment.

Wendy Martin

Mark Twain

In 1861 at the age of twenty-six Samuel Clemens deserted the Company of Missouri Volunteers; in effect, "resigning" from the Civil War in its opening days. He set out for the territory of Nevada to spend the years of the war prospecting for silver, loafing in bohemian ease, and learning the newspaper world of the booming West. He had, by means of his flight, decided that his was to be the generation that lived in the shadow of the gold rush rather than that of the Civil War. His would be the age of suddenly worthless silver-mine shares rather than the aftermath of the assassination of Abraham Lincoln. Samuel Clemens would be part of a generation rotating dizzily around the pole of wealth rather than that of race.

Presided over by P. T. Barnum, but also by the seemingly endless and lucrative inventive fertility of Thomas Edison, its fortunes tied to oil and railroads, steel and coal, Clemens's generation used up reality in double time. It raced from the steamboat age of a canal-, river-, and waterway-linked republic of the 1840s and 1850s, through the continental spree of railroad building after the Civil War, to the onset of democratic private transportation: Henry Ford's Model T passenger car of the 1900s. The railroad boom meant the collapse of the steamboats and canals just as, later, the highways, buses, automobiles, and trucking industry would bring down, in their turn, the railroads. It was Ralph Waldo Emerson's image come to life: each new circle was only formed to be, yet again, encircled.

Both wealth and fame had a magical and dangerous aspect in the years between the Civil War and 1910, the year of Clemens's death. That magic and that danger gave him the armature for his major works. The Clemens family lived in the dream, from which Sam at an early age distanced himself, that the 20,000 acres of so far worthless Tennessee land to which they held claim might someday, overnight, make them rich. Magical, possible wealth from this land became a dream that sapped the life energy of Clemens's brother Orion and sister Pamela. Even Sam's various talents were in some ways always seen by him as his own, private Tennessee Land, assets that tottered between fabulous wealth and mere claims.

For the United States in these years wealth had an aspect of treasure for which the gold rush was an accurate preview. Oil, coal, gold, silver, or iron ore might be just out of sight, underground, like the money found by Tom Sawyer and Huck Finn in the cave at the end of *The Adventures of Tom Sawyer* (1876). The largest fortunes were still made by selling and reselling the land itself in city lots or rural sections. The linking of the continent into the European economic system had converted scenery into real estate, dirt into land. Accidental rights-of-way where railroads had drawn a line on the map multiplied the value of every adjacent cornfield. Inventions like Clemens's own easy-stick photo album, the thought of a few minutes, earned him more than his books for a year or two. The Horatio Alger qualities of luck, alertness, and daring paid off at a faster rate than hard work, thrift, and patience. The nation became one large exchange, a world of "prospectors," "claim-holders," and traders in imaginative schemes. It was a world of future values.

Shares, speculations, and political giveaways turned paper into fortunes, but just as often turned fortunes back into worthless paper. When Clemens was a publisher, his luck and timing brought him the memoirs of Ulysses S. Grant, for whose widow he made a fortune. Then, within a few years, Clemens's own fortune had been thrown away in the same publishing business on his speculative backing of the Paige automatic typesetting machine, which in his typically manic style he thought of as potentially the greatest invention in human history and, incidentally, one that would make him fabulously wealthy. His bankruptcy only ensured that Clemens, like his entire generation, would know both sides of the cycle of boom and bust. In *Roughing It* (1872) we see in miniature the sudden dreamlike shifts that would shape Clemens's life as a whole. In one set of chapters he is rich for ten days, but within a few pages we find him down and out in San Francisco nursing his last dime. His life led him to make and waste fortunes. He married an heiress, spent fortunes on his gaudy Hartford, Connecticut, mansion, chased gimmicks and inventions all his life, and signed on again and again for ruinously exhausting but lucrative lecture tours to recoup his finances.

Clemens knew that the man that corrupted Hadleyburg did so with the promise of wealth. Often his plots involve a poisonous gift. Three of his best late stories, "The $30,000 Bequest," "The £1,000,000 Bank Note," and

"The Man That Corrupted Hadleyburg," turn on spectral wealth that remains untouchable or decays in the hands. In *The Tragedy of Pudd'nhead Wilson* (1894), the slave woman Roxy's gift to her child of a life as a white man produces only destruction. The treasure found at the end of *The Adventures of Tom Sawyer* becomes a prison for Huck in the book that follows, one that he has to stage his own death to escape from. This should make us reconsider even Huck's gift to Jim of his freedom because in each of Clemens's tales the gift of self-transformation (whether in the form of freedom, wealth, or whiteness) turns in the aftermath to poison. And yet magical, unearned release, like the silver wealth of Nevada, was always at the heart of what Clemens meant by action.

His story of the 1890s, "The £1,000,000 Bank Note," is an allegory of the anxiety of talent, an uncashable bank note that nonetheless can work as wealth. The note leads to fame, newspaper attention, public belief or amusement, credit, and finally to secondary wealth, true love, marriage, and social position just as Clemens's own talent had. Yet the note is never spent, only exhibited for the eyes of others. The story is an unusually candid study of the commercialization of talent in a world of dupes and worshipers of wealth. The artist's life is viewed as a bunco scheme, a pyramid sales fraud in which the pleasure of being entertained leads the public to buy worthless shares. The public world of Clemens's allegory is an inch-thick crust of reality on which only the brave walk to success or fall through to bankruptcy. The story's hero has the elated feeling of having pulled something off or of having gotten away with something. The world in which he moves is one in which people buy each other's worthless shares and all get rich together on faith. They float together in the insubstantial air of a society of massive credit, debt, risk, and collapse.

The magical and treacherous qualities of wealth under these unique American circumstances came to seem aspects of reality itself for Clemens. The manic confidence in which all reality seemed to be play, ready to be made into the limitless forms of the imagination, turned for him later in life into the nightmare of depression in which the boys at play are suddenly seen as puppets jerked mechanically by a malicious and cruel power whose game or toys they all along had been.

A world relying on the imagery of sudden wealth and financial collapse is alternately a comic and an embittered one. The economic swing from boom to bust or from expectation to disappointment has formal elements in common with the style of humor on which Clemens relied. The hoax, the fraud, the stunt, the practical joke are all comic forms based on speculation and collapse. Boasting, bragging, mock-heroic exaggeration, and inflation, along with their subsequent collapse into fact, are verbal and formal equivalents to the greatly inflated promissory economics of boomtowns and boomtimes, to silver strikes and grand schemes that are mere projections from small beginnings.

The strategy of hyperbole, of exaggeration and its subsequent contraction to the merely real, becomes endemic as a comic form wherever the real is "not yet" real. Exaggeration describes the necessary part that daring, imagination, self-confidence, dreaming, and projection play in bringing about reality where most of reality remains unfinished. Colonel Sellers in *The Gilded Age* (1873) is Clemens's most lively version of this necessary type for societies in their youth. Such speculators are the opposite of liars. A lie looks back to the past that it alters verbally. Speculators look forward by means of descriptions that human will, energy, and luck will vindicate. In making reality happen the pioneer is cousin to the trickster. World builders and frauds share common ground, and it is this ground that the comic art of Clemens makes visible. Large numbers of values within such a world come to count in the future in a speculative way. The price of a share of stock involves a guess about future earnings; the worth of an acre of land takes in the future town that will be built around it and the train that will someday connect the town to Chicago. Every riddle or joke plays on this rhythm of speculation followed by collapse back into the ordinary. When Tom Sawyer stages his heartless phony rescue of Jim at the conclusion of *Adventures of Huckleberry Finn* (1884), a speculative reality is evoked and then collapsed, but not without real wounds. Tom's staging, in *The Adventures of Tom Sawyer*, of his own funeral, at which he then puts in a surprise appearance, involves a similar jokelike speculative reality and collapse. Fraud, trickster, inventor, and imaginative agent of civilization, along with the humorist and the criminal salesman of nonexistent realities, are, in Clemens's work, all blood brothers.

The comic plots of greed and speculation, fraud and dreams, unmasking and pretense are ones that center on the moral problem of honesty rather than that of courage As a writer, Clemens was driven both toward play and toward a directness and candor that had to be rescued from a world of play indistinguishable from inflation, fraud, and, finally, delusion. Clemens's single greatest creation, Huck Finn, at least always knows when he lies, exaggerates, hides facts, plays tricks, or masquerades. He knows the difference between an alias and a name, a "story" and a story. At the same time, he makes use of all of them.

Huck's opposite, and Clemens's single other great character, Colonel Sellers of *The Gilded Age*, was a dreamer within the mazelike world of promotion and flamboyant, exaggerated salesmanship, as his name's pun on "seller" points out. Sellers is the master of the widest use of what in the silver-mining West were quite rightly called "claims." He lived always halfway between what reality was and what it might be. In this he shared one essential part of the outlook of a generation of major capitalists and world builders. He was one of those enthusiasts or braggarts or liars (depending on the outcome) who could see railroads where an ordinary man sees a ditch, but who often do, in the end, make a railroad that turns out to fit nicely right alongside what used to be the ditch, making out of worthless land a "site" for depot, town, house lots, views, parks, and, out of all of these, money.

The material world of wealth, which had been both accelerated and mystified by the new machinery of shares, claims, and inventions, and by the simple fact of the unfinished state of American society, had its parallel in the immaterial world of fame that had been compressed and speeded up in the public world of Clemens's lifetime. Clemens lived through three larger-than-life American presidencies. The differences among them register the new forces for the magnification of the self in American life. Born in 1835 in Florida, Missouri, Samuel Langhorne Clemens was a child in Hannibal, Missouri, during the presidency of Andrew Jackson, who democratized and gave a populist turn to political imagery. The years of Abraham Lincoln coincided with Clemens's years of apprenticeship in the newspaper world and with his invention of his public identity, Mark Twain. His final decade was passed in the era of Theodore Roosevelt, who had managed to surpass even Twain himself to become the "most famous man in the world."

These three very different but equally popular presidencies gave distinct and novel meanings to the public world in which Clemens sought, as Mark Twain, to insert himself. Jackson's was a public world best expressed by symbolic sculptural figures, most often of military leaders like George Washington, Napoleon, or Jackson himself. Each leader was mythically frozen in equestrian statuary and set in outdoor civic space.

Lincoln's was a world of the voice, of the debate platform, of the common visage best captured in Brady's photographs, tragic but ordinary, an ugliness and integrity fit for a world of realism. Lincoln's was a world of photographs instead of sculpture, but above all it was a world of short, noble speeches fit for the most solemn moments of national history.

Forty years later, Teddy Roosevelt's was a world of the new fame of newspaper cartoons and headlines, and of the early movies that would soon define the mechanism called stardom. Slogans, bluster, distinctive, memorable, and infinitely variable signature traits: equipped with these Roosevelt embodied the new public world of advertising. It was a projectable, thin fame of stylistic touches and unforgettable identity that could be said to make a man or a product "stand out" from the crowd that society had become.

Samuel Clemens's life overlapped the worlds of Jackson, Lincoln, and Roosevelt, and in his public persona, Mark Twain, he drew on elements of public style and self-promotion from each of the three realms of popularity. William Dean Howells once called Mark Twain the Lincoln of our literature. It would be equally true to see him as the frontiersman Jackson, the great democrat of our literature, conquering the Eastern establishment and making our literature, for the first time, a national rather than a provincial New England affair. At the same time Twain was the Teddy Roosevelt of our literature, its first newspaper and media personality, its first cartoon figure who knew how to grab publicity with his flamboyance and his wit, and then turn that publicity to good use for the ongoing business that was Mark Twain, Incorporated. He was, in effect, our first modern literary politician. Only Ernest Hemingway would equal him in the generation that followed.

Samuel Clemens is the only significant American writer to be known by a pen name: Mark Twain. Earlier English writers had used pen names to indicate aristocratic embarrassment about taking up the low role of author, or for moral caution in an age of censorship, or, as was the case with George Eliot, to express a woman's unwillingness to have her books dismissed as mere "female novels." The name "Mark Twain" differs because it is more like a brand name in a commercial world of celebrity, advertisement, and packaged products like Ivory Soap, Coca Cola, and Winchester rifles. "Mark Twain" was an enterprise that included popular travel writing, coast-to-coast lecturing, door-to-door subscription sales of his books, a publishing house, and speculations in various inventions. The name was a trademark, secured by constant public witticisms and cartoons, and stabilized by a fixed and well-known eccentric appearance. His bushy red (later white) hair and mustache, black suits, or, later in life, white suits, and the distinctive costumes like his sealskin coat worn inside out and his honorary Oxford gown that he wore on every possible occasion made him recognizable on the streets or in the few strokes of a newspaper cartoon. His flamboyant Hartford mansion, recalling a Mississippi River steamboat, was a form of highly visible corporate headquarters, not different from the many skyscrapers in New York or Chicago that caught the eye and stood for the corporate identities of newspapers, banks, and the new giant industrial corporations. Clemens was so well known that he only had to walk slowly onto the stage and stand silent for the audience to begin to laugh.

The newspapers that Twain began by writing for as a cub reporter in San Francisco, and then, back East, edited and owned, and finally as a famous personality of the day became an endless series of stories for, were at the peak of their power to define public reality. Joseph Pulitzer and William Randolph Hearst created the mass circulation newspaper in the 1880s and 1890s as an everyday "best-seller" with sales in the millions of copies. The newspaper was an organ of celebrity and notoriety that lived off ever new heroes and ever more sordid scandals and political exposés. The newspapers turned nobodies into celebrities and likewise turned yesterday's celebrities into has-beens with the same speed that the penny stocks and worthless claims became wealth and then mere paper. The forty-year love affair between Mark Twain and America was carried on through the new structure of celebrity and fame that had as its center the newspapers and their new mass audiences.

Three features of American culture in the late nineteenth century fed into the uniquely popular and commercial vitality of Clemens's work: the newspaper, the lecture platform, and the new national market made possible by the door-to-door salesman, and later by the Sears, Roebuck Catalog. Clemens himself was an overnight success as a writer when his story "The Celebrated Jumping Frog" (1865) was reprinted in newspapers across the land. This initial success was symbolic, for Clemens was in effect America's first coast-to-coast writer whose books were known and read from literary Boston to the tiniest rural areas reached by the army of subscription salesmen through whom his books were marketed. If the newspaper was one side of his contact with a mass audience, the door-to-door salesman was the other, but each fed on the chemistry of personal contact that Clemens established in his many lecture tours. It was the overwhelming success of his lecture tours in the late 1860s that made him a national figure.

The lecture platform had been the source of Emerson's public fame and the place of decisive political encounters like the Lincoln-Douglas debates. It was an elevated space in which the American crowd was roused by the abolitionists, the suffragists, or by temperance advocates. From the platform the public was brought to patriotic fervor by Fourth of July oratory and urged to repent by fire-breathing or gentlemanly preachers of the day. This lecture platform was, in Twain's day, undergoing a transformation from a medium of politics and culture to a source of entertainment. Still, it was the primary medium of public life, as the television would be a century later in the 1960s and 1970s, or as the newspaper would be for most of the years in between.

Americans heard rather than read the stories of travelers. The latest religious or political ideas came fused with the seductive or the trumpeting voice. Lincoln and William Jennings Bryan were its masters, but the Reverend Dwight Lyman Moody was its P. T. Barnum. American philosophy itself from Emerson to William James performed in public. The lecture platform was a culture of the voice and the ear. Many of its best-loved speakers—Dickens, Kipling, and Twain, for example—were writers who were meant to be read aloud.

On the stages of America Clemens was a performer rather than a lecturer, and yet his appearance continued that lyceum tradition in which Emerson had given his public performances of American philosophy or in which the serious issues of the day had been aired. By Clemens's day the great educational mission of the lecture platform had begun to give way to entertainment. Humorists like Artemus Ward and Petroleum V. Nasby had replaced Henry David Thoreau and William Ellery Channing. Travel lectures supplanted philosophy and antislavery agitation. In fact, by the 1860s when Clemens's career began, the American stage was already halfway between lyceum and vaudeville.

Yet, in spite of what might be seen as the decline to entertainment, Twain shared with Emerson an extravagance of language and a play with those extremes of exaggeration that lead to mystical wisdom or to laughter. Twain begins where Emersonian loftiness meets the tall tale. Both men lectured and wrote in episodic forms of staged excitement. Twain moves from one punch line to another following the energy of the crowd in just the way that, on a philosophical plane, Emerson's pith and epigrams, his local intensity and explosiveness, gave to his lectures and essays a formlessness that was in effect philosophical thrill-seeking in search of sudden breathtaking prospects. Those huge cliffs over which Emerson invited his listeners to peer had their equivalents in Twain's breathless stunts, his wild stories that led only to the next even wilder story.

Throughout his career Twain worked in bursts of energy. He was a man made for tirades, for set-piece descriptions, for loving enthusiastic sketches or venomous denunciations. As a result, even his best books are made up of patches of extraordinary writing. Incidents or episodes that are nearly perfect are lodged with structures that lurch from matter to matter. Dozens of energies are ignited only to fizzle out. His books work in four- or five-chapter units. The book then jumps to new settings, new complications. In Twain's work there are no plots, only local complications.

The lecture circuit from which Twain, like Emerson in the previous generation, earned his living laid the ground rules, in combination with the newspapers, their cartoons, and the emerging art of photography, for a popular culture of celebrity and media dominance that would, in the twentieth century, move to Hollywood and later to television. In his late nineteenth-century world Mark Twain was what we now call a "star." By 1905 he shared with that former Rough Rider, President Theodore Roosevelt, our first headline and cartoon president, the honor of being the best-known American of his generation. Twain was the funniest man in the English-speaking world.

Just as Twain's first lectures propelled him to the center of the lecture circuit, so too his first book, *The Innocents Abroad* (1869), an expanded version of his newspaper columns that reported on the events of a grand tour of Europe and the Holy Lands, became a best-seller. Sold by subscription salesmen in the small towns of America, the book locked in a genuinely democratic national audience for Twain's subsequent work. Twain supplied that audience with what might almost be called, in the commercial sense, a "product" for approximately thirty years.

Twain's awareness of his audience and of the many fads within the book market led to a calculated positioning of his secondary books. He followed every move of the best-seller market. *The Prince and the Pauper* (1882) and *A Connecticut Yankee in King Arthur's Court* (1889) exploited the popularity of children's books and European romance fantasies. *Personal Recollections of Joan of Arc* (1896) was written in the years that saw Lew Wallace's *Ben-Hur* and Henryk Sienkiewicz's *Quo Vadis?* become widely discussed best-sellers as religious, historical costume romances. *Pudd'nhead Wilson* (1894) picked up many of the devices of the detective-story fad in the wake of Arthur Conan Doyle's Sherlock Holmes, who first appeared in 1891. Even the very special attention to dialect and Southern voice in *Adventures of Huckleberry Finn* responded to the craze started by the Uncle Remus stories that Joel Chandler Harris had published in 1881. Of course, the travel books and the lecture platform persona were modeled on distinct popular and lucrative commercial opportunities of the moment.

Setting out to write in the late 1860s, Twain found himself in the shadow of the unprecedented popularity of Charles Dickens, whose American reading tours in 1842 and 1867 were models for Twain's own. Just as James Fenimore Cooper had Americanized the historical novel of Walter Scott by importing the techniques of description, setting, national history, and the adventure-novel form into the American novel of the 1820s, so too did Twain and his contemporaries Bret Harte and Harriet Beecher Stowe take their start from the novel as designed by Dickens, the central novelist of the English-speaking world. Whereas Scott's was a novel of place and landscape, its finest passages being descriptive and atmospheric, the novel of Dickens was a novel of the speaking voice. Both narrator and characters came to life by means of unique, garrulous torrents of inventive language. It was this that Twain learned from Dickens: voice was the key to a comic, dramatic novel of picturesque individualities. In his *Martin Chuzzlewit* (1842) Dickens had shown American writers how to do America by means of its bragging, exaggerating, florid voices, its colorful characters with their energy and oddness.

Twain's many great speaking voices, which range from the riverboat pilots to Colonel Sellers, the King, and the Duke, are men made real by their flow of talk. Dickens invented the novel as a gallery of voices and it was just such a gallery that the greatest of Twain's works would be: books that can be heard as they are read. The set of distinct authorial voices from the canny narrator of "The Celebrated Jumping Frog" through *The Innocents Abroad, Life on the Mississippi,* and *Adventures of Huckleberry Finn* to the cranky, sarcastic voices of the final books: these voices add up to Mark Twain, the signature by which he is best recognized.

Naturally, one of Twain's greatest achievements was to write the most important first-person narrative in American literature, the novel told in the uniquely honest and vital voice of Huck Finn. In Huck, Twain invented a richer autobiographical voice than the comparatively weak first-person voices of Dickens. In *David Copperfield* and *Great Expectations* it is in the central voice of David or Pip that Dickens's art lacks character. It was just here that Twain went beyond Dickens. Dickens needed to set his picturesque figures at a distance where they can be seen externally, like actors of their own identity on the novel's stage. In this visual distance Twain created Colonel Sellers, his most obviously Dickensian character. Twain, in the naïve voice he assumed in *The Innocents Abroad,* in the deepened voice of fervid admiration in "Old Times on the Mississippi," and in his greatest voice, that of Huck Finn, enriched the Dickensian pattern. He played off the gallery of figures and voices against a central voice that was both poetic and humorous, capable of reaching unexpected and fanciful passages that were as strongly etched as the characters themselves. Twain made it possible to become intimate with the Dickensian character, knowing it from the inside. He shattered the doll-like mechanical externality of Dickens's figures by staging his books around the inner life of an appealing central narrator whose voice and idiom had a freshness that created anew the entire observed world and charged it with moral drama and play.

The experience that gave an essential form to much of Twain's work was the experience of travel. In motion from place to place, alternating excitement with the boredom or exhaustion that tells the travelers to move on, Twain created in his travel work the model of a novelist who, whenever he runs dry, turns to a new chapter or that of a humorist who pauses and begins an unrelated anecdote whenever he feels his audience becoming restless. Travel is made up of a set of episodic events and encounters with what Twain would always call "characters." What holds the loosely assembled episodes together is the fresh descriptive point of view of the traveler himself. The series of clearly audible narrative voices that give both texture and tension to his works was one of Twain's greatest achievements. Its climax was the extraordinary speaking voice of Huck Finn. The reliance on a central, distinctive guiding voice was a consequence of the travel form where the fresh angle of vision holds the reader's interest, where there is neither a plot nor any characterization that is more than momentary.

From *The Innocents Abroad* (1869) through *A Tramp Abroad* (1880) to *Following the Equator* (1897) Twain produced what were literally travel narratives, but the inner logic of travel shaped his more important works as well. *Adventures of Huckleberry Finn* describes a journey down the Mississippi undertaken by two fugitives, Huck and Jim. Their episodic set of encounters lets the reader sample the small-town world of America and survey the social world from the bank of the river that runs through the heart of the country. Twain's autobiographical *Bildungsroman, Roughing It* (1872), works first of all as a story of successive apprenticeships in which young Sam Clemens turns prospector, reporter, lecturer in the process of finding himself, or rather, finding himself to be Mark Twain. This story Twain superimposes onto a travel narrative of a journey that works its way farther and farther west through Nevada to San Francisco to Hawaii. The journey west, like the journey south undertaken by Huck Finn, is at the same time a journey toward identity. Going west and growing up, rafting south and finding moral identity are both stories told by means of the loose, bit by bit structure of travel.

Twain's other great autobiographical work was the work known as "Old Times on the Mississippi" when it appeared month by month in the *Atlantic Monthly* in 1875. Later expanded to make up the book *Life on the Mississippi* (1883), it was the most concentrated and fervid of his books of memory. The story of his boyhood ambition to become a riverboat pilot, it too, like *Roughing It,* was a novel of education and apprenticeship, and it too was told in terms of journeys, this time up and down the Mississippi. The young man masters the river, learning it like a book whose every word and comma he memorizes while, in the process, growing into his dream. He passes from the boy on the small town's wharf looking with awe at the steamboat to the young man who has become a pilot. Like many of Twain's books about dreams, *Life on the Mississippi* is the story both of a dream achieved and of a dream shattered. The boy becomes a pilot, but the Civil War ends the brief days of glory on the river. In Twain's narrative the steamboat explosion that kills his brother Henry and ends the boyhood narrative substitutes for the larger explosion of the war itself. The journeys up and down the miles of the river in which its every danger is memorized are then replaced by journeys of memory in which the middle-aged writer revisits the river as the scene of his youth.

In Twain's own work the outward travel of the novel of education that had yielded *Roughing It* and *Life on the Mississippi* gave way to the inward travel of memory and recollection that, in the aftermath of the later chapters of *Life on the Mississippi,* produced two of Twain's best books, *The Adventures of Tom Sawyer* and *Adventures of Huckleberry Finn.* In these classic accounts of small-town American boyhood, Twain, now married, successful, established in the wealthy Eastern suburbs of Hartford, travels back to a childhood that has to be protected from growth or education. Within the books one of the most powerful acts is the act of running away.

The Hawaiian, European, or world tours that lay behind Twain's successful lectures were only the most literal of his travels and travel books. His later fantasy books had as their premise travel in time instead of in space. These could best be seen as travel books through history rather than through either geography or personal memory. *A Connecticut Yankee in King Arthur's Court* (1889) literally transports, in the style of Jules Verne or H. G. Wells, the nineteenth-century Connecticut Yankee, Hank Morgan, back into the mythic days of King Arthur and Merlin. Time-travel takes the hero through an episodic experience of the feudal world comparable in structure to the experience of contemporary Europe in *The Innocents Abroad* or of the American West in *Roughing It* or of the South in *Adventures of Huckleberry Finn.* Twain's book for children *The Prince and the Pauper* (1882) and his historical novel *Personal Recollections of Joan of Arc* (1896) were more superficial examples of his narratives of time-travel. But it was not the journeys into the historical time of *A Connecticut Yankee in King Arthur's Court* or *The*

Prince and the Pauper that yielded Twain's most profound work. The central experience that produced "Old Times on the Mississippi," *The Adventures of Tom Sawyer*, and *Adventures of Huckleberry Finn* within the ten years between 1874 and 1884 was a journey back into personal memory that let Twain view his own boyhood as a country to be revisited and reported on to his extraordinary audience.

His late stories "The Man That Corrupted Hadleyburg" (1899) and the posthumously published "The Mysterious Stranger" represented, for the first time, the story of travel from the otherside of the telescope, that of the society invaded, disturbed, or finally destroyed by a traveler who mysteriously arrives and just as mysteriously disappears. Twain's normal point of view is that of the invader, the outsider, the traditional trickster of folk literature. Huck Finn is his Don Quixote and Odysseus all in one. Like every traveler, Twain's disappear, taking with them at least the story of their adventures from which they will profit elsewhere. Only in the final stories did he address the disruptive influence of the visitor, his power to toy with the world that he invades like a god, and, finally, his power to vanish when it suits his mood or purpose.

In his greatest work, *Huckleberry Finn*, Twain splits his outsiders into two pairs. The King and the Duke invade to plunder and con the many worlds along the river. Huck and Jim enter homes or towns because they must. To protect their freedom or their lives, they disguise themselves, lie, invent stories, and accept affection and hospitality in order to survive, while at their side, the King and the Duke duplicate their every ploy in the interest of hard cash. The King's first social disguise is in fact accurate. He is best described as a pirate, but not as the romantic pirate of children's literature. He lands to plunder. One of the most banal and squalid outlaws of American literature, he cashes in on every situation that he encounters. His loot, like many a pirate's, ends buried in a grave, and the only money he holds onto comes from the sale of Jim for $30. Huck's greatest danger in the novel is that he will be contaminated by those characters whose acts parallel, while differing in subtle ways from, his own. The King and the Duke draw him into their performances, which differ mainly in clumsiness and greed from his own earlier defensive ruses. Later, after Huck has escaped being tarred by the same brush that finally blackens the two villains, his adventures are juxtaposed to those of an even nearer twin: the artistic but innocent theatricalities of Tom Sawyer, whose very name Huck finds himself stuck with in his final impersonation. One of the extraordinary features of the structure of *Huckleberry Finn* rests on these nuanced moral differentiations made between closely parallel outsiders, tricksters, and frauds, outsiders and invaders who stir into visibility the many sleeping towns they slip their way into.

These literal and metaphoric travels anchor Twain's writing and design his narrator around the perceptions of the tourist, the visitor, the greenhorn, the innocent, the fugitive, or the demonic intruder. At the same time his many travel forms resonate with the wider social facts of the years between 1840 and 1910. His wise-guy reporter style, perfected in his first best-seller, *The Innocents Abroad,* parodied the rather solemn Victorian cultural pilgrimages in which thousands of Americans paid homage to the art and history of Europe. John Ruskin in his *Stones of Venice* or Henry James and Henry Adams in their travel writings or novels spiritualized the journey abroad, giving it, as Henry Adams was to do in *Mont-Saint-Michel and Chartres,* a quasi-religious, high-cultural tone that completed a new solemnization of art and history for which Ruskin, Walter Pater, James, and Adams were key figures. In contrast, Twain debunked and sassed his way past the masterpieces of Europe as though his struggle with Europe were something of a boxing match between two scrappy lightweights. He stood up to Europe, unlike James who looked up to it. He refused to be bullied by culture, and in so doing he defended democratic ordinariness with his arsenal of humor and sarcastic leveling against the cultural pressures to genuflect but also to buy up the treasures of Europe. Twain writes against the grain of Nathaniel Hawthorne's *The Marble Faun* or Henry James's novels from *The American* to *The Ambassadors.* Although Twain subtitled his book "The New Pilgrims Progress," what he defies with bravado is the American self-deprecation that the homage to Europe of Hawthorne, James, and Adams involved.

Twain did not locate himself purely as the antagonist of Victorian cultural stuffiness; he also positioned his travel books, especially *Roughing It* and *Life on the Mississippi,* within the rich nineteenth-century literature of exploration. Francis Parkman's *The Oregon Trail* or the earlier Journals of Lewis and Clark along with the exploration-like passages of Cooper's Leatherstocking tales are instances of a pragmatic and lyrical spirit that fused exploration with both realism and poetry. Thoreau's exploration and mapping of his own backyard in *Walden* and the best chapters of Twain's *Life on the Mississippi* and *Huckleberry Finn* are the essential lyrical masterpieces of American pragmatic exploration. Both Thoreau and Twain are surveyors who know the world through exact measurement and precise description. It is a world that he who knows, masters. The pilot, not the passenger, is the master of his fate on the river. It is a detail of great symbolic importance that in his greatest work, *Huckleberry Finn*, it is the more fragile and vulnerable raft, barely controllable and subject to many forces larger than itself, traveling mostly in the dark of night and carrying fugitives, that Twain substitutes for the lordly Mississippi steamboat, a regal dominating presence on the river. But from the pilot house of the riverboat the singular authority of the pilot takes dominion over the river as Thoreau did over his smaller world at Walden.

The exploration of the American West, described from the moment of the rush to settlement and land claims in Twain's *Roughing It*, went on simultaneously with the great European exploration of Africa, the Nile, and the Arctic. The travel works of Henry Stanley, David Livingstone, and Mungo Park describe the conquest of the few remaining unknown parts of the globe with which the exploration and settlement of the American West coincided. The look and feel of the entire surface of the earth, including its odd local customs and inhabitants, was being digested by a culture that had invented anthropology and had begun to measure the details of social life on a worldwide basis. Twain's *Roughing It*, especially its ludicrous Hawaiian chapters, was a minor masterpiece of the amateur, reportorial wing of a powerful intellectual hunger to know and to observe, to explore and record even the most remote cultures. The interest within literary realism in local color and regionalism, along with the authorial pride in recording dialects and local expressions, is the more conventional, provincial part of this wider narrative research.

From the genial, wisecracking pages of *The Innocents Abroad* to the pessimism of Twain's final stories, "The Mysterious Stranger" and "The Man That Corrupted Hadleyburg," one feature of what Twain himself called the "invasion" of another culture lay beyond the self-awareness of reporters, explorers, and anthropologists. Unlike them, he notes with stronger and stronger revulsion the outsider's disturbing presence, his revolutionary and destructive impact. We might say that he was the first of Western writers to be aware of the nihilism latent in the crossing of cultural borders.

Hank Morgan's visit to the world of King Arthur begins with the ordinary post-Enlightenment contrasts between cultures in which progress and backwardness, superstition and modern scientific technology are set in opposition. However, what begins as argument quickly degenerates into battle, then into warfare, and finally into cataclysmic slaughter. The truly portable knowledge that one civilization brings to another is the knowledge of killing. Finally, all cultural competitions come down to the machine gun versus the crossbow.

Hadleyburg is not observed, it is corrupted by its visitor. Twain's outsiders tamper, expose, and distort. They run experiments, often experiments in cruelty. In *The Innocents Abroad* we feel that Twain would rather tease Europe than record it as it is on its own terms. He has something of the small-town practical joker's point of view. He sets off firecrackers near sleeping cats or ties a tin can to a dog's tail to watch it run. The dog alone, asleep in the shade, doesn't interest him. He has to stir it up. In Europe Twain sets out to stir up some excitement, tease or play jokes on the guides or locals. He sees himself as the player in a game who is expected to be lied to or tricked out of his money. He plans to outwit the tricksters who take him for a fool. He is at heart a provocateur. Even Huck plays his cruel hoaxes and tricks on Jim, putting a dead snake in Jim's bedding to watch his alarm.

What are, in the early works, teasing experiments that trick reality into unwitting self-revelation, turning the tables on the con artists who for once go down to defeat at the hands of the greenhorn, are, in Twain's later stories, demonic, nihilistic paranoid plots. The early geniality of the outsider's trick has its best example in the story that made Twain famous, perhaps the best yarn ever written in America, "The Celebrated Jumping Frog of Calaveras County." The carefully trained frog is filled with buckshot when Jim Smiley is out of the room, and the absurd frog-jumping contest is reversed. In the stories written thirty years later, in the final years of the century, tempting inheritances or windfalls force to the surface the greed and veniality of otherwise respectable people, the kind of honest folk who have never, in Twain's view, been given the right opportunity to display just how vicious and grasping they really are. Hank Morgan "modernizes" or destroys Arthurian England. Even a benign parable like "The £1,000,000 Bank Note" of 1893, an intricate parable of Twain's own life and talent, in which a random stranger is given the use of an uncashable, large bank note for a month, involves an experiment on a human being that most likely will destroy him. From the story of the frog filled with buckshot to that of the man in the street handed a £1,000,000 bank note or the citizens of Hadleyburg tormented with a windfall that is dangled just out of reach in front of their eyes, Twain's plots turned on the outsider whose manipulation of reality has the character of a practical joke. In essence a practical joke is a small psychological experiment performed for an audience of insiders. The practical joke has deep structural ties to fraud or to the paranoid pessimism that darkened Twain's final years.

The intruder, the provocateur, the reporter, the explorer, the tourist, and the fugitive are all variants of the figure who enters or who moves between cultures. For American society between the Civil War and the stock-market crash of 1929 a number of major experiences at the core of the culture restate the same pattern of movement between cultures. It was the greatest age of European travel, and, in the other direction, the greatest period of immigration. Many writers from Henry James to Ezra Pound and Ernest Hemingway became expatriates, balancing two cultures as they went back to Europe, moving, in effect, against the stream of immigrants.

With his travel writing and the literary form of the journey, Mark Twain set his work in resonance with the entire complex cultural pattern. He followed Horace Greeley's well-known advice to "Go West, young man!" and found his vocation there. He traveled again and again to Europe, spending about a sixth of his entire life abroad. During the 1890s he was, in effect, an expatriate. He entered and conquered cultural worlds from the beginning to the end of his career.

In what might be called the first of his dark works, *A Connecticut Yankee in King Arthur's Court*, Twain's larger reflection on these many patterns led him to write one of the first parables of colonialization. In his novel he follows the journey from an advanced, confident civilization of a representative of modern technology and ideas who moves in time rather than in space into a historically backward, feudal society. Modernizing and destroying at the same time, Twain's enlightened cultural emissary is a slightly disguised version of his many contemporaries who were carrying what they called the White Man's Burden of colonial education and integration into the modern world system. The great fame of Rudyard Kipling, Twain's main rival as a popular author in his day, grew out of this colonial movement. The climactic barbarities of King Leopold's Congo, to which Joseph Conrad's *Heart of Darkness* as well as Twain's own journalism was a response, is already visible in *Connecticut Yankee*. Offering to develop the Arthurian world and rid it of superstition, Hank Morgan brings it war and destruction. Twain's book, like his great denunciations of the exploitation of the Congo in the early 1900s, was a thoughtful account of that most pressing of late nineteenth-century travel forms: the final mad scramble of the European powers to grab up and modernize whatever scraps were left of the underdeveloped world. Like his contemporaries Kipling and Conrad, Twain wrote, in *A Connecticut Yankee*, a parable of cultural arrogance and its self-destructive naïveté that has its place alongside Conrad's *Heart of Darkness* with its idealist turned savage, Kurtz.

The civilization of men at home nowhere, on the run, and running away was one of Twain's essential contributions. Linked to the collapsing worlds was the risky fiction of personal worth. He generalized the conditions of paper currency into the conditions of society itself. Money had been the eroticism and the scandal, the romance and the magic of his generation. He lived within, yet saw beyond this enchanted kingdom. *Tom Sawyer* ends with boys made rich; *Huckleberry Finn* with men made free.

Philip Fisher

Henry Adams

Henry Adams's role in American literary history has been shaped primarily by his most celebrated work, *The Education of Henry Adams* (1907), which he insisted not be taken as an autobiography. Nevertheless, the first trade edition of the *Education* (1918) appeared with the subtitle "An Autobiography," and critics devoted to Adams's genius have worked hard to correct this "error." Yet, even in its most avant-garde formulation as "anti-autobiography"—as a study of the *impossibility* of writing one's own life-story, the *Education* remains the quintessential *modern* autobiography. The very centrality of this work in our cultural memory testifies to our fascination with Henry Adams as a crucial archetype in the narrative of modern American culture.

Adams has been mythologized with some consistency according to the terms he himself used to describe his eccentric relation to America between the Civil War and World War I. Above all, he considered himself an "amateur," dabbling in a wide range of disciplines: history, anthropology, the natural sciences, political journalism, diplomacy, economics, biography, literary criticism, medieval scholarship, philosophy, linguistics, the novel, poetry, painting, sculpture, architecture, the philosophy and history of science. On the one hand, Adams's amateur status is a confession of failure, insofar as Adams acknowledges his marginal relation to areas of knowledge that in the early modern period became highly specialized disciplines with their own institutions and terminologies. Adams encourages us to think of him in the *Education* as the "manikin" who is unable to master any of these disciplines, each of them testifying to the growing complexity and fragmentation of the modern age. Adams's manikin leaps from one to the other, not always in an orderly manner, in the increasingly desperate hope that he might find a key to unlock the secret relations of them all. On the other hand, Henry Adams's "amateurism" is a deliberate pose he derived from the Enlightenment's "man of letters," the *philosophe*.

Against the fragmenting and alienating tendencies of empiricism, the *philosophe* pitted "right reason," which drew its authority from the presumably rational structures of Nature, the mind itself, and social institutions based on the proper relation of mind and Nature. Voltaire's and Jean-Jacques Rousseau's respective efforts to ground the social contract in natural rights, the social utilitarianism of Baron Holbach and Denis Diderot are familiar terms in the Enlightenment thought that evolved into European romanticism. The romantics would explore more closely the subjective and cognitive bases for such rationality, and some romantics would so stretch the eighteenth-century conception of reason as to render it utterly strange. Adams's debts are to the more conservative brand of romanticism. This commingling of Enlightenment and romantic intellectual history is the appropriate background for understanding Henry Adams's cultural heritage. Critics and historians often acknowledge Adams's inheritance of an Enlightenment system of values from his forebears, but they insist that he rebelled in the manner of the romantic idealist and poet against the "rationalism" of the Enlightenment. Yet, Adams's romantic gestures more often than not end up affirming the Enlightenment values of his family. This is not to suggest merely that Adams blindly recapitulates his ancestors' rationalism in some other guise. Even so, he drew much from the German idealists' romantic subjectivism. Like Kant, Adams believes that eighteenth-century rationalism could be reconciled with the profoundly subjective character of modern experience; like Kant, Adams assumes that human beings share similar faculties and cognitive capabilities, despite different histories and cultures. Like Hegel, however, he considers such faculties to be understandable only in their historical uses and applications. Adams's general view of historical degeneration in the nineteenth century always included his conviction that the subjective mind could and ought to become the rational basis for social organization. If history *betrayed* Adams, then it was in large part Adams's chosen labor to expose such treason and restore nineteenth-century America to the principles and virtues of human reason, as well as the social institutions best suited to develop such distinctively human powers. In his deepest despair, Adams resigned himself to a universe of chance and unpredictability, which nonetheless determined ultimately every social and historical effort at order and unity. In his more positive views, however, Adams was convinced that the randomness of natural forces permitted man to take some control of his own history. The central problem for Adams remained educational: how could modern man be led to assume such responsibility? In that final paradox rests much of the anxiety of the modern thinker and certainly the character of Henry Adams.

The much-celebrated *literary* turn in Adams's career, which begins with the novels *Democracy* (1880) and *Esther* (1884) and informs *Mont-Saint-Michel and Chartres* (1905), the *Education,* and even the late essays on the relation of science and history, encourages us to think of Adams as a writer who repudiated rationalism for the sake of symbolic mode expressive of man's essential irrationality. Yet, Adams's break with his past is greatly exaggerated. Our continuing interest in Henry Adams may well be a consequence of the ways his writings incorporate the shared concerns of the Enlightenment, romanticism, and modernism. Struggling to revive his own faith in the human mind, Adams discovered the psychological and linguistic aspects of reason that Emerson and other romantics would insist were active forces in every thought and action. Even in his most deliberately eccentric works, Adams still employed what might be termed "representative symbols," Virgin, Dynamo, Pteraspis, the Church of the Ara Coeli in Rome—these familiar symbols in Adams's later writings are more consistent with the Coleridgean Symbol—"the translucence of the Eternal through and in the Temporal"—than with the private and iconoclastic symbols of Adams's early modern contemporaries, the French Symbolist poets and English Decadents. Even when they *deny* human reason— as Pteraspis, Rome, and the Dynamo seem to do—these symbols still serve Adams's larger purpose of demonstrating the capacity of the human mind to recognize what exceeds it ("disorder") and to understand thereby its own rational limits. Adams's modern, paradoxical views, then, still reveal their dependence on Enlightenment assumptions regarding rational man and the universality of reason, even if Adams's romantic interests helped him to expand considerably the scope and complexity of such reason.

Born February 16, 1838, "under the shadow of Boston State House," Adams was also born under the shadows of his great-grandfather, John Adams, and his grandfather, John Quincy Adams, each of whom epitomized the values of the Enlightenment man of reason and letters: "Had he been born in Jerusalem . . . under the name of Israel Cohen, he would scarcely have been more distinctly branded, and not much more heavily handicapped in the races of the coming century." In 1838, no child in the Western world could be said to have had *better* chances of worldly success than the child born Henry Adams. That Adams did not succeed as a politician, political commentator, or diplomat is quite simply a consequence of his refusal to work seriously at those professions. Even the changed political climate of antebellum, Jacksonian America could not have kept such a scion of the Adams line from a significant career in government or politics, were it not for his own diffidence regarding these professions of his fathers. To insist as Adams did throughout his life that the "times" had passed him by was to insist upon remaining precisely what he did not wish to be: the *child* of an Enlightenment heritage, unable to transform that legacy to meet the exigencies of his own age.

As a child, Henry and his brothers benefited from the peculiarly American version of the Deism of their grandfather, John Quincy Adams, and father, Charles Francis Adams: "The children reached manhood without knowing religion, and with the certainty that dogma, metaphysics, and abstract philosophy were not worth knowing. So one-sided an education could have been possible in no other country or time, but it became, almost of necessity, the more literary and political." This is the Enlightenment background to the pragmatism we associate with William James and John Dewey, and it would seem an especially pertinent education for the historical drama Adams was preparing to enter. Complaining of his own effacement by the modern age, Adams could find nothing but dedicated, practical, self-effacing statesmen in his own distinguished heritage. From John Adams to Henry's father, Charles Francis Adams, these leaders had been "perfectly balanced," quietly authoritative, and confident even in great national crises—virtues that depended upon their faith in "rational man" rather than upon any personal willfulness. They themselves had been the "manikins" on which the styles and fashions of their times had been draped, and they had served such purposes with few complaints and considerable distinction. Such noble characterizations of his paternal ancestry, of course, are in part Henry Adams's own contributions to the American myth of the Adams Family, reaffirmed in this generation by the public television series *The Adams Chronicles*. If he recognized the great division between the strong public personality of an Adams and the private pessimism, despair, and tragedy of his several unsuccessful forebears, Adams still celebrated the abilities of the great Adams statesmen to maintain a crucial distinction between public and private. Even in his most rebellious moments, Adams still subscribes to the notion that an Adams must always be an exemplary or representative man.

Henry Adams, however, was intent upon distinguishing himself apart from this heritage. Although he went to Germany in 1858 to study law and thus complete his Harvard education in the manner best suited to his social position as an Adams, Adams committed himself early to a career as a general "man of letters." In many ways, such a career turned out to be a perfect compromise between his inescapable heritage and his need for individual authority, as well as a means of balancing Enlightenment values with romantic inclinations. By the same token, such a "balanced" identity often split into two voices—the rationalist and iconoclastic, which may often be heard in his subsequent writings. Adams's earliest published writings are his letters from Europe, which his brother, Charles Francis Adams, Jr., duly arranged to have printed in the proslavery *Boston Daily Courier*, under the initials "H.B.A." These letters ("Letter from Austria," "Letter from Italy," et al.) began appearing on April 30, 1860; they are travel impressions with a strong political cast. They are notable for Adams's treatment of personalities and "local" color, especially amid the excitement of the Italian Risorgimento's military actions under Garibaldi. Adams's "portraits" of famous or merely representative characters Adams met—an Austrian lieutenant aboard the Vienna express, King Victor Emmanuel II, the first king of a unified Italy, and Giuseppe Garibaldi—prefigure Adams's talents for rendering "representative men" as part of his later methods of historical analysis. His sympathies with the Italian republicans are in keeping with the Adamses' liberal democratic politics, just as his nostalgia for a vanishing European order of enlightened aristocratic rule betrays the elitism of a Boston brahmin.

Returning to America after two years, Adams affirmed his father's antislavery position by voting for Abraham Lincoln on November 6, 1860, in the same election in which his father defeated the Union candidate for Congress. Traveling as his father's private secretary to Washington, D.C., Adams arrived in time for the opening of the Thirty-sixth Congress. He also served as Washington correspondent for the *Boston Advertiser*, a position that Adams had to keep secret in order not to compromise his position as private secretary. The four letters he wrote as correspondent for the *Advertiser* certainly sharpened his talents as an observer of political events, and his writings continued to rely on characterization to give some personal dimension to the great events of the day.

On the basis of these letters for the *Advertiser*, Henry planned his first major political essay on the stormy congressional session of 1860–61. "The Great Secession Winter of 1860–61" is an excellent example of Henry Adams's early style. On the one hand, it merely describes the chaotic political events in Congress leading up to Secession. On the other hand, the essay distinguishes itself by setting the confusion of political figures and parties against the confidence an Adams properly has in the restorative and regulative powers of the Constitution. Unlike the tourist letters or early political correspondence for the *Advertiser*, this essay subordinates character to what may be termed the *authority* of the Constitution. A mistake had been made in the original drafting of the Constitution by avoiding the issue of slavery. For Adams, however, the Constitution invites, even requires, legislative revision according to historical needs: "What genius has ever yet described, or what nation has ever drawn from the cumulative wisdom of centuries, a system more strong, more elastic, more tenacious, more full of life and instinct with self-consciousness than ours?" In the best Enlightenment spirit, Adams finds "self-consciousness" and "genius" not in individuals but in the founding principles of the Republic embodied in the Constitution. It is on this basis that Lincoln "called the whole nation to arms," not with a confidence derived from the force of his personality but with a personality drawn from a confidence in rational principles supporting lawful government.

When his father was appointed in 1861 as American ambassador to England during the Civil War, Adams traveled with him again as private secretary and as a foreign correspondent, now for the *New York Times*. Once again he maintained the secrecy of his position as a journalist. Despite the difficulties of playing these two roles, Adams was hardly divided in his loyalties. The letters from England warned Americans of the potential importance of England's role in the conduct of the war, as well as of the general significance of foreign relations in a period when Americans seemed to have directed virtually all their attentions to domestic affairs. Such views were by no means at odds with the positions taken by Adams's father as the American ambassador. Adams's expectation that the English people would rally behind the Northern cause was hardly supported by fact; his misreading of the political situation in England—the English people were generally apathetic about the Civil War—is in part traceable to his lifelong insistence that historical actuality *ought to conform* to the terms of right reason. Recalling in the *Education* the London *Times*'s exposure of his identity as a foreign correspondent, Adams takes a certain ironic satisfaction from the fact that his criticism of the stiff and parsimonious formality in English high-society was the *cause célèbre* for the London *Times*, rather than the important political issues he had addressed. But this exposure by the *Times* of the "young Henry Adams, son of the Minister" was all the occasion he needed to give up his role as foreign correspondent for what he termed a "private correspondence" concerning the political events in England for family and friends.

It was at this time that he committed himself with special energy to the new science and the controversies surrounding Darwinian evolution, especially as those debates were brought to his attention by Sir Charles Lyell, a Northern sympathizer who frequented the American legation. Reading enthusiastically in the natural and physical sciences, Adams also discovered the extensions of such scientific methods to the social sciences, especially in the works of Auguste Comte and Herbert Spencer. By the time he left the legation for the Continent in 1868, Adams had committed himself to the study of those "scientific" methods, organized by Darwin's theory, that promised some unification of the different disciplines of human knowledge. That he had turned to such science as a consequence of his disappointment with political journalism is not incidental; science offered a scholarly method to confirm the principles of his eighteenth-century heritage and justify the "education" of human reason.

Adams applied his new studies in a review of the tenth edition of Lyell's *Principles of Geology* (1866) in the October issue of *The North American Review*. As in his early political sketches, Adams exhibits a curious blend of liberal and conservative thought in this essay. His criticisms of Lyell and Darwinian evolution in general were based on the "catastrophism" of his old professor at Harvard, Louis Agassiz, who had insisted upon the dramatic glacial and geological changes of the earth as fundamental to all natural change rather than the gradual and selective geological evolution Lyell adapted from Darwin's natural science. Lyell's effort to reconcile geology with the natural sciences smacked of the "modern," whereas Agassiz's theory of catastrophic geological change, radical as it was among nineteenth-century geologists, could be used to argue that the human species emerged suddenly and unexpectedly from the ruins of prehistoric ages. Behind Adams's surprisingly good command of the scholarship, the modern reader finds Adams's arguments against natural determinism his means of defending his eighteenth-century commitment to choice and judgment as the unique properties of human reason. As Rousseau had argued in his *Discourse on the Origin and Bases of Inequality among Men* (1754), human "nature" is defined by what *distinguishes* it from purely physical laws: reason and language.

In "The Gold Conspiracy," published in the *Westminster Review* for October 1870, Adams treats Jay Gould and James Fisk, Jr., the two capitalists who cornered the gold market and effectively caused the Panic of 1869 (memorialized in "Black Friday," September 4, 1869), as the modern antagonists to his notion of the "representative" man. Working solely for personal gain and power, Gould and Fisk illustrate the dangers Adams foresaw in abandoning too hastily the rational and moral percepts of the *philosophes*. Adams could still conclude this essay by claiming optimistically: "Messrs. Gould and Fisk will at last be obliged to yield to the force of moral and economical laws," but he must have known already that the equation of "moral and economical laws" had become less tenable to America's Gilded Age. The mere possibility of such power as that wielded by individual speculators like Gould and Fisk reminded him, as well as the rest of the country, that the economy of reason was rapidly giving way to the economies of unregulated individuals.

In 1870 Adams accepted a joint appointment as assistant professor of history and editor of *The North American Review* at Harvard. The fact that he accepted such a life of retirement, as he judged it, is some measure of his own desire to withdraw from a world that increasingly seemed dominated by Goulds and Fisks. From 1870 to 1877, Adams turned his attentions to medieval history in a quest not so much for some origin of the "modern"—that would be the task of *Mont-Saint-Michel and Chartres* much later—but rather for those principles of rational government that seemed to be rapidly vanishing from America. Adams committed his scholarly energies to the Middle Ages. The volume, *Essays in Anglo-Saxon Law* (1876), that he edited in this period represents his commitment to new German methods of precise legal and institutional history. The work included essays by three of his graduate students (including Henry Cabot Lodge) and one of his own ("Anglo-Saxon Courts of Law"), and it represents his effort to establish the source of democratic ideals firmly in medieval constitutional law. He also sent his students to the writings of Swift, Pope, Shaftesbury, and other eighteenth-century literary figures as the proper cultural complements to this legal tradition.

In the same year that he published this collection of essays, Adams delivered a Lowell Institute lecture in Boston, "Primitive Rights of Women." Generally, historians notice this essay as an anticipation of Adams's subsequent concern in *Mont-Saint-Michel and Chartres* and the *Education* with women of special distinction, whose abilities question the predominantly patriarchal values of nineteenth-century America. Yet, tempting as it is to use this essay to align Adams with contemporary women's rights movements and twentieth-century feminism, the essay typifies the curious blend of conservatism and liberal rebellion that characterizes this self-proclaimed "Conservative Christian Anarchist." The essay traces the relatively recent development of patriarchal societies in the West, documenting the power and authority of matriarchal societies in other periods and cultures. Adams energetically attacks the injustice of the Catholic church with respect to "women's social and legal rights," claiming that the ideal of the "meek and patient, the silent and tender sufferer, the pale reflection of the Mater Dolorosa, submissive to every torture her husband could invent" would be the church's perverse bequest to modern woman. Nevertheless, the vigor of Adams's argument in favor of women's rights vanishes unexpectedly at the end of the essay, and we are left with Adams's curiously energetic endorsement of the existing patriarchal order and the bourgeois family it sustains. There is perhaps some irony in Adams's claim "that the most powerful instincts in man are his affections and his love of property; that on these the family is built." But Adams's rather sentimental endorsement of the bourgeois family seems unequivocal: "The family is the strongest and healthiest of human fabrics; . . . it always has and probably always will trample every rival system under its feet." Indeed, similar sentiments about the "family" had caused many nineteenth-century liberals to hesitate to support American feminist politics in this period. Ralph Waldo Emerson's lecture "Woman," delivered in 1855 before the Woman's Rights Convention in Boston, reveals a similar contradiction of liberal sympathies for women activists and conservative insistence on the necessity of such patriarchal institutions as the bourgeois family.

In 1877, no longer challenged by Harvard, Adams accepted the offer made to him by Albert Rolaz Gallatin, son of Albert Gallatin, Secretary of the Treasury from 1801 to 1814: to edit the elder Gallatin's papers. This scholarly project resulted in Adams's biography *The Life of Albert Gallatin*, and three volumes of the edited papers, with the four-volume *The Life and Writings of Albert Gallatin* appearing in 1879. In his long and distinguished public career, Gallatin was an apt figure for any historian, especially since he had been so overshadowed by such monumental contemporaries as John Adams and Thomas Jefferson. Gallatin was also a man of letters, who published later in his life ethnological studies of the American Indians and in 1842 founded the American Ethnological Society. Self-made Pennsylvania gentleman-farmer, politician, economist, historian, and ethnologist, Gallatin was a kind of alter ego for Henry Adams, and Adams's study testifies to the eighteenth-century idealism Gallatin shared with Jefferson and John Adams.

Gallatin is also Adams's first figure in his extended history of the failure of Jeffersonian idealism in the practical conduct of American government. Jefferson's policy of American government during the Napoleonic Wars in Europe (1803–14) depended upon a strong domestic economy, the reduction of the national debt, and the peaceful neutrality of America in those conflicts. These very policies, however, were based on principles of government too rigid, too *a priori*, and finally too idealistic to address the political and economic realities of that chaotic period in Western history. Adams writes of Jefferson's enlightened system of government in *The Life of Gallatin:* "Far in advance, as it was, of any other political effort of its time, and representing, as it doubtless did, all that was most philanthropic and all that most boldly appealed to the best instincts of mankind, it made too little allowance for human passions and vices; it relied too absolutely on the power of interest and reason as opposed to prejudice and habit; it proclaimed too openly to the world that the sword was not one of its arguments, and that peace was essential to its existence." Despite admiration for and hereditary commitment to the values represented by Gallatin's fiscal policies and Jefferson's philosophical government, Adams realized how the failure of both helped precipitate the War of 1812 and jeopardize the very survival of American society. What Adams recognizes in *Gallatin* is that the *a priori* principles of Enlightenment reason would have to be made more pragmatic, more utilitarian, and thus more adaptable to the changing character of modern man and his social circumstances. Even so, Adams's insistence that the modern statesman become *more* pragmatic follows the utilitarianism of such Enlightenment figures as Voltaire and Holbach, rather than the more idealist inclinations of Rousseau and Jefferson. Insofar as Adams invokes the social utilitarianism that Jefferson expressly had attempted to overcome (for "self-interest," Jefferson substituted man's inherent "social disposition"), there is a reactionary quality to Adams's *Gallatin*. Adams's insistence upon more practical governmental policies appears to be an attempt to reconcile eighteenth-century values with modern political reality. Yet, his pragmatism is rooted in his pessimism regarding man's capacity to follow higher laws. In many of his writings, Adams expresses his conviction that man often follows the personal passions and appetites of a narrow self-interest. Like other great satirists, he cannot believe in human perfectibility.

The project that would occupy Adams for the next decade certainly took shape as he was writing and editing *Gallatin;* its motives are inextricably bound up with his entire education to this point. The nine-volume *The History of the United States in the Administrations of Jefferson and Madison* (1889–91) is, like *Gallatin,* a positivist history in the German manner that organizes its narrative according to the dictates of the numerous historical documents included in the work. The polemical aim of the *History* is ostensibly to defend American democracy and demonstrate in these two administrations its achievement of the economic, political, and cultural stabilities that would guarantee America's endurance and growth. In its own way, Adams's *History* attempts to demonstrate the ways America succeeded despite the reverses associated with the War of 1812 and the practical failures of Jeffersonian idealism. In addition, the *History* tells another story, which is the virtual subconscious of Adams's liberal optimism. Like *Gallatin,* the *History* analyzes the historical causes for the disappearance of the great statesman as a figure of exemplary or representative authority. Jefferson's philosophical temper and willful personality are often represented as at odds with the larger political forces he could no longer effectively control. Even as Adams acknowledges Jefferson's greatness, he insists upon Jefferson's uneasiness "in the position of a popular leader": "His instincts were those of a liberal European nobleman" and "his true delight was in an intellectual life of science and art." Jefferson is judged by Adams to be too idealistic and philosophical to rule effectively, but his failure is also the consequence of an America that has become too practical and commercial. In this regard, Adams distinguishes between the "self-interest" of utilitarianism and the more material self-interest of the Goulds and Fisks who thrived in the nineteenth-century industrial economy of the West.

Unlike Jefferson, James Madison effaced his own personality and ideals in the conduct of government, surrendering his authority to political parties and popular will. Madison typifies for Adams the "new" statesman who would become merely the "channel" or "circuit" for impersonal forces. In his "Epilogue" to the nine-volume *History*, Adams concludes rather pessimistically, amid his enthusiasm for the economic and political stability achieved in the aftermath of the War of 1812: "That the individual should rise to a higher order either of intelligence or morality than had existed in former ages was not to be expected, for the United States offered less field for the development of individuality than had been offered by older and smaller societies. The chief function of the American Union was to raise the average standard of popular intelligence and well-being, and at the close of the War of 1812 the superior average intelligence was so far admitted that Yankee acuteness, or smartness, became a national reproach; but much doubt remained whether the intelligence belonged to a high order, or proved a high morality." Despite Adams's obvious liberal and nationalist commitments in these works, *Gallatin* and the *History* establish the basic terms of his subsequent degradationist theories of modern history.

Fundamentally informed by the methods of German historiography, the *History* hardly can be said to concern principally the personalities of Jefferson and Madison. Yet, Adams's personal anxieties concerning the apparent failure of the enlightened statesman to exemplify the rational principles on which American democracy ought to be founded are involved centrally in the *historiographical* interests that govern his thought and writings from the *History* to the end of his career. Despite its Germanic concern with legal, economic, and institutional documents, the *History* still warrants F. O. Matthiessen's praise (in "Henry Adams: The Real Education") as "one of the greatest achievements of American historiography." The *History* depends upon several historiographical assumptions that Adams would explore in subsequent writings. First, Adams identifies the period 1800–1817 as a period of crisis—politically, economically, and socially—that will test the principles of government and social organization as embodied in the Constitution. Examining this "crisis" as a point of "origin" is Adams's way of analyzing subsequent historical forces and understanding their determining powers. Second, it is something of an eccentric or unexpected "origin" for modern America, offered in the place of the more obvious period of the American Revolution. Third, even as Adams effaces his own narrative voice and avoids the narrative personality of such "literary" historians as Francis Parkman and George Bancroft, he subtly offers the *historian*—in his knowledge of actual documents and with his analytical and synthetical powers—as a modern equivalent of the "representative man" of a vanishing eighteenth-century heritage.

In the decade between *Gallatin* and the publication of the *History*, Adams published two novels, *Democracy* (1880) and *Esther* (1884), and his study *John Randolph* (1882). It is at this stage in Adams's career that the critic may begin to identify *pairs* of works, which are related sometimes dialectically and at other times ironically. In any case, these pairs, ranging from *Gallatin* and *Randolph* through *Democracy* and *Esther* to *Mont-Saint-Michel and Chartres* and *The Education of Henry Adams*, exemplify, among other aspects of Adams's profession of letters, the dividend identity of the social anatomist and the would-be "educator" of the public concerning American reforms, prospects, and aims. Adams's method of "measuring" history in terms of the relations his analyses establish between contrary forces is already the active principle organizing the *History* in terms of the presidential administrations of Jefferson and Madison.

In the career of John Randolph of Roanoke, Adams gives us his most detailed portrait of "rational man" gone wrong, nearly mad. Randolph represents the cultural transition from Jefferson's philosophical idealism to the entrepreneurial spirit of Fisk and Gould. John Randolph embodies for Adams the paradoxes of modern individualism that could not be resolved with the customary antinomies of Enlightenment philosophy. Randolph had assumed the responsibilities of public service, and yet he had served only the cause of a small faction—the Quids, a splinter group of the Republican party—and had worked generally against nationalist aims in favor of states' rights.

For Adams, Randolph represents the minority party statesman who cannot compromise and fails to understand the larger social purpose served by the two-party system. For Randolph, the democratic drive for greater national solidarity in the early years of the nineteenth century was a corruption of the "pure" principles of Randolph's republican vision of decentralized government. By 1806, he considered all of his colleagues to have betrayed such purity, and he grew ever more eccentric, politically powerless, and isolated as he drifted into political solipsism. A congressional crank and faultfinder, Randolph in his later years served as a frightening reminder to Adams of how easily rational ideas could turn into *idées fixes*. Adams expresses surprising compassion for Randolph, who had been one of John Adams's bitterest antagonists. Randolph's failure was not so much the collapse of the Virginian theory of government under the pressures of a larger and more complicated Union; it was his personal failure to compromise and to avoid stubborn, even mad adherence to a faulty "theory." Adams's characteristic irony and self-deprecation in his later writings might well be viewed as psychic defenses, as well as rhetorical strategies, developed to avoid his own inclination to monomaniacal theories.

The Life of Gallatin and *John Randolph* are complementary books, which illustrate two alternatives for the Enlightenment statesman confronted with the dramatic changes of nineteenth-century America. As a public figure, Gallatin suffered many personal failures and yet still served with dedication and selflessness, whereas Randolph judged all compromise of his Virginian doctrines as treason and every political defeat as a personal injury. In retirement from government, Gallatin was still from 1830 to 1840 in "the prime of his life" and capable of immersing himself in the classification of North American Indian languages and other ethnological activities that would win him a small but enduring reputation as a scholar. Randolph lapsed into truculence, bitterness, and self-imposed isolation that some rumored was insanity, but Adams judged merely the consequence of a life lacking in "self-restraint"—*the* virtue of Adams's successful ancestors.

Democracy and *Esther* also deserve to be read together; both pursue a general inquiry into the foundations of human reason and the relevance of such reason for contemporary American society. *Democracy: An American Novel* was published anonymously in March 1880; Adams wrote it in late 1878 during his work on *Gallatin*. *Esther: A Novel* was published under the pseudonym Francis Snow Compton, in March 1884, during the research and composition of the *History*. The English novelist Mrs. Humphry Ward identified the author of *Democracy* as Adams, whose satire of post–Civil War American politics had considerable popularity in England. Although Adams's intimates knew he had written *Esther*, his authorship was not made public until Adams's death. Adams's effacing pose as a novelist is generally related to his characteristic self-deprecation, but it is also a consequence of his judgment that such work was somewhat beneath his dignity as an Adams and his ambitions as a philosophical "man of letters."

Madeline Lee in *Democracy* and Esther Dudley in *Esther* are in many ways feminine characters shaped by Adams's own personal concerns with modern politics and religion. They are autobiographical *caricatures*, in about the same sense that the youthful Stephen Dedalus offers a distorted reflection of James Joyce's aesthetic problems in *A Portrait of the Artist as a Young Man* (1916). These two women anticipate Adams's subsequent symbolization of Woman as a figure representing the art and imagination that the modern age needs as a complement to its scientific materialism. Yet just as Joyce ironizes himself in the portrait of an "artist as a young man," so Adams ironizes himself in these feminine characters. Madeline Lee's conscientious effort to discover the governing power behind American politics in *Democracy* brings her to Washington in the same spirit of enthusiasm as the young Henry Adams. What she discovers instead is the merely banal corruption of individual politicians, like Senator Ratcliffe, who use the appearances of statesmanship and government service to pursue personal interests. Indeed, *Democracy* turns on the difference between mere "personality" and the rational individualism exemplified for Adams by his own ancestors. The Virginia lawyer, Carrington, represents those values, but he is eccentric to the politics of the day; he only can observe the power struggles of Ratcliffe and his associates as battles waged without any true generals. Madeline's *desire* for some controlling agent or principle drives her ultimately from Washington to Egypt, from modern politics to ancient mysticism. Ironizing the transcendentalists' fascination with the mystical East and its supernatural lure, Adams shows how the failure of reason not only produces the corruptions of practical politics but also turns philosophy into mystical escapism or elaborate rationalization.

In *Esther*, Adams offers a short version of his developing theory of modern history, ranging from the thirteenth-century religious faith of the Reverend Stephen Hazard through the Renaissance humanism of the painter, Wharton, to the nineteenth-century scientific confidence of George Strong. More explicitly than *Democracy*, *Esther* displays a kind of existential *bathos*, punctuating the narrative with visions of nothingness: that is, the ungrounded essence of human history. Like Madeline, Esther longs for a governing principle that would connect the individual with some larger, transhistorical purpose; in *Esther*, it is figured in the natural energy of Niagara Falls, rather than ancient Egypt. *Esther* is in this regard a very romantic novel, which could be made quite consistent with the main themes of American transcendentalism, albeit the more extreme transcendentalism of Whitman and Dickinson rather than that of Emerson and Thoreau. It prefigures the modern, "literary" Adams by insisting that the relation of mind and matter, of individuality to personality, of natural law to human action may well be an *artistic process* that understands the fundamental *law* of human consciousness to be nothing more than the *desire* for unity. Yet, *Democracy* suggests that the intellectual problems in *Esther* may be insoluble simply because they have been divorced from the practical issues of politics and history. The "void" that Esther sees behind the religion, art, and science of the three male characters may be, like the "lack" experienced by alienated nineteenth-century American woman, merely a consequence of the historical forces that have alienated thought from action, philosophy from politics, virtue from practical conduct. Like his friend Henry James, Adams criticizes vehemently the separation of intellectual from practical spheres in nineteenth-century America.

Madeline and Esther are also partial portraits of Henry Adams's wife, Marian ("Clover") Hooper Adams, whom he married on June 27, 1872, during the years at Harvard. The two novels are *romans à clefs* with characters identifiable as Adams's friends, acquaintances, and enemies: Senator Ratcliffe is a satiric portrait of Senator James G. Blaine, implicated in the Mulligan Letters scandal of 1876; George Strong in *Esther* is a more friendly caricature of the Adamses' close friend, Clarence King, the geologist who was one of the familiars of the "Five of Hearts" group that met at the Adamses' house across from the White House. The two novels also include many small autobiographical details from the Adamses' married life. Madeline's longing for Egypt as a relief from the corruption of Washington recalls the Adamses' wedding trip to the Nile, where Marian, an accomplished amateur photographer, took some of her best photographs. The dramatic action of *Esther* revolves around the death of Esther's father, and how she will behave without his support. Adams had in mind the powerful authority that Dr. Robert William Hooper, a successful Boston surgeon, exercised over his daughter, Marian, whom he had raised by himself after his wife's death in 1848. It is tempting to say that life imitated art in this case, since Marian nursed her father through his last illness a year after *Esther* appeared. But such artistic "prophecy" is usually an effect of psychological insight, and Adams knew well enough that Marian would be strongly affected by the death of her father, who had played such a dominant role in her life even after her marriage.

Most historians leave Marian's suicide in December 1885 as the "silence" that Henry Adams made it in the *Education*—an unaccountable event that must tell a story either of acute, irrational depression following her father's death or even of some biochemical imbalance, such as is now associated with manic-depressive behavior. Marian was a nineteenth-century woman of considerable intelligence and curiosity, who had been given every advantage the daughter of a wealthy Boston family could have—as well as every *disadvantage*. The disadvantages were the excessively sheltered life that Marian led as daughter and as wife; like Alice James, she lived in the shadows of male authorities and may well have been driven to suicide (as Alice was driven to "illness" and Emily Dickinson to agoraphobia) by the conflict of her strong personality with the passive role required of a respectable young woman of Boston married to an Adams. Perhaps there is some belated recognition on Adams's own part of how much Marian shared his sense of eccentricity to the dominant male powers of the age in the mysterious figure he commissioned Augustus Saint-Gaudens to design and cast in bronze for their burial site in Rock Creek Cemetery in Washington, D.C. "Grief," as the sculpture was titled by Mark Twain, is quite consciously intended to be an androgynous or at least sexually ambiguous figure combining features of the Virgin, Kwannon, and Apollo. Adams insisted that the memorial remain unmarked by any title or epitaph, although Adams referred to it as "The Peace of God."

Henry Adams's modern character is often identified with the skeptical, detached, and observational attitudes that shape the narrative voice in the *Education*. Adams's world-weary tone in that work seems frequently to suggest some resignation to the determining forces of modern science and history that Adams could neither command nor escape. After Marian's suicide in 1885, Adams's despair regarding the recovery of any rational terms by which to understand modern life—personal or public—seems to dominate his skepticism and irony. It is just this tone and style that have mythologized a certain literary "Henry Adams," who prefigures the dominant existentialism of the twentieth century. In his later writings, however, Adams committed himself with renewed energy to those *exceptions* to the deterministic laws of science and the fragmenting forces of modern history that might offer alternatives to ultimate social chaos and entropy. In the *Education*, he compares himself with Lyell's *Pteraspis*, the first vertebrate that had survived unchanged through every stage of natural evolution. Yet, this apparently ironic expression of himself as anachronism also represents his lifelong commitment to discover some means of reconciling human reason and blind natural force. In many ways, this was merely Adams's replay of the age-old conflict between free will and determinism, but Adams was less interested in radical individualism than in some principle for human subjectivity that might enable man's knowledge to do genuine work. The Enlightenment offered the rational state as the proper end for man's knowledge of both himself and Nature; as complement or supplement to Nature, the rational state would justify man and provide the terms by which individuals might think, judge, and act.

Yet, the Enlightenment had also produced those Western nations that caused much of the political chaos of early modern Europe and America. A world-traveler in the years following Marian's suicide, Adams observed in the Far East and then in Polynesia the consequences of Western colonialism. His reactions, however, are not those of some twentieth-century liberal critic of imperialism; instead, Adams reverts to his Enlightenment values as the only means of restoring a balanced and rational social order. A kind of amateur—and very ethnocentric—anthropologist, Adams repeatedly insists upon the need for strong and enlightened leaders in whatever culture he visits. Traveling in Polynesia with a friend, the painter John La Farge, from 1890 to 1892, Adams writes in a letter to his close friend Elizabeth Sherman Cameron: "The chiefs interest me much more than the common-people do, for they are true aristocrats and have the virtues of their class, while the common people would sink to the level of the Hawaiians if the chiefs were to become extinct." In Tahiti, Adams and La Farge met Queen Marau, who had been married to and divorced from the titular king of Tahiti, Pomare V. Fascinated by the genealogical legalities of Tahitian royalty, especially as these issues were complicated under French colonial rule, Adams immersed himself in the oral history of genealogy, folklore, and Tahitian songs and poems that the old chiefess provided.

What was ultimately published privately (in ten copies) in Washington as the *Memoirs of Maura Taaroa, Last Queen of Tahiti* (1893) and then in a revised edition of 1901 as *Memoirs of Arii Taimai E* is hardly as exotic or eccentric to Adams's *oeuvre* as first appears. It is of special interest to students of the *Education* because it is a fictionalized autobiography, purportedly told to him by the old chiefess but clearly *composed* by Henry Adams. On the one hand, Adams appears to concentrate on the decline of the Tahitian people as a consequence of English and French colonialism. Like Gallatin, Jefferson, Randolph, and the Virgin, the Queen represents a coherent social order destroyed by the indiscriminate forces of modern history. On the other hand, as much as the modern historian would like to turn *Tahiti* into Adams's indictment of Western colonialism, it reaffirms the strong family relations and genealogically transmitted rights to rule that Adams associates with an enlightened aristocracy. Indeed, what makes *Tahiti* so clearly the work of Henry Adams is the frequent analogies it makes with European history, with special reference to noble Roman families and the importance of the family in Roman law. Adams does not indict Western colonialism in its aristocratic origins; instead he attacks the erratic policies of the nineteenth-century colonial powers.

In 1894 the American Historical Association elected Adams as its president, with special irony, one suspects, since Adams's previous service as vice-president had been entirely *in absentia*. Writing from Mexico on December 12, 1894, Adams sent his inaugural address in the form of "The Tendency of History," the first of his two public "letters" to American historians and the best introduction to the "dynamic theory of history" formulated in the *Education*. Together with "A Letter to American Teachers of History" (1910) and "The Rule of Phase Applied to History" (1909), "The Tendency of History" forms the posthumous volume edited by his brother, Brooks Adams, under the title *The Degradation of the Democratic Dogma* (1919). Tracing the lines of force connecting *Tahiti* with "The Tendency of History" is easier than may first appear, because Adams's reversion to his early interest in modern scientific theories is in "The Tendency of History" an explicit effort to establish an epistemological authority that might match the sociopolitical authority of his Enlightenment heritage. In psychobiographical terms, Adams's "turn" to scientific theories of history may also be viewed as his effort to rationalize some of the contradictions in his inherited system of values. What is of special interest in "The Tendency of History" is the direct address Adams makes to those very contradictions, even as he sees the "socialistic" and "communistic" alternatives to be even more unattractive. At the same time, the "science of history" that Adams urges his fellow historians to adopt is a curiously *active* and *causal* kind of history: "Yet we cannot conceive of a science of history that would not, directly or indirectly, affect all these vast social forces." This formulation of science as an active historical agent is all the more confounding when read in terms of Adams's appeal for methods of historical measurement that would be "absolute" and could be calculated with "mathematical certainty." Adams offers no theory at all in "The Tendency of History" and no clear idea of what a "science" of history would involve, save that it ought to perform actively by explaining to modern man just what means are available for overcoming the current "crisis" in world history. "A science cannot be played with," Adams writes; it has *authority*, which can be calculated and tested.

From "The Tendency of History" to his last writings, Adams found at last his proper discipline, even though it was one that would continue to expose contradictions of his eighteenth-century heritage and his modern circumstances. Many scholars have defined accurately the discipline of Adams's late writings as "historiography." As different as the essays collected in *The Degradation of the Democratic Dogma* seem to be from the more literary qualities of *Mont-Saint-Michel and Chartres* and the *Education*, all of these works develop a general theory of historical representation that combines science and myth as complementary forms of knowledge. In my view, Adams's *historiography* in this period may be more adequately defined as a *critical theory of history*. In the attention Adams pays to the ideological determinants of any theory of history, he avoids the objective "science" of his earlier German positivist methods. My specific description of Adams's later work in terms of a "critical theory of history" offers several advantages in viewing works that otherwise might be classified diversely as science, history, and literature. *Mont-Saint-Michel and Chartres* and the *Education* do not so much *combine* historical and literary forms as demonstrate the curious *competition* between these two modes of representation. And it is the *tension* between the competing claims of science and art that motivates the historical drama in both *Chartres* (St. Thomas versus the Virgin) and the *Education* (the Dynamo versus Adams himself).

Thus in "The Rule of Phase Applied to History" (1909) Adams's persistent irony undercuts his otherwise dogged effort to apply Willard Gibbs's thermodynamic "rule of phrase" to historical periods. Changes in chemical phases are consequent upon changes in the equilibrium of a system; by analogy, Adams seems to argue that changes in intellectual periods are consequent upon disturbances in the "equilibrium" or normative values of a culture. Adams knew, however, that the analogy fails when one looks closely at the "solution" or "system" of a historical period. When an "immaterial" substance—Thought—is substituted for the physicochemical substances governed by Gibbs's "rule of phase," then human psychology, the connotative character of language, and other subjective variables warp the "formula" beyond recognition and use. Nevertheless, what the ironic analogy of "thought" and "matter" accomplishes for Adams is a "critical reading" of science itself. Like Werner Heisenberg's "Uncertainty Principle," which argues for the unavoidable determinations of human perception in any scientific observation of natural phenomena, Adams's ironic "rule of historical phase" demonstrates the fallibility of any science that fails to take into account the agency of the scientist, the language he employs, and the historical circumstances in which he works.

It is just this entanglement of human psychology, language, and the desire for scientific accuracy that organizes *Mont-Saint-Michel and Chartres* and the *Education* into a "critical theory of history." They are, as Adams so explicitly tells us, a pair of works that "measure" history in relation to "thirteenth-century unity" and "twentieth-century multiplicity." It would seem simple enough to pursue this opposition of "unity" and "multiplicity" as the means of understanding a history of the West as the *loss* of some religious principle of unity—the Virgin of Chartres—and the consequent production of scientific multiplicity—the Dynamo Adams first contemplates at the World's Columbian Exposition of 1893 in Chicago. Yet, Adams's "medievalism" is not merely the nostalgia of his fellow Victorians for an age in which epistemic certainty could be established by faith. Nor is Adams's view of "modern multiplicity" explained simply as the modernist's reaction to the "dissociated sensibility" and "alienation" produced by indiscriminate industrialization and "balance of power" politics.

"Unity" and "multiplicity" are the dialectical terms governing both *Mont-Saint-Michel and Chartres* and the *Education*. Adams is especially canny in subtitling *Chartres* "A Study in Thirteenth-Century Unity" because it is the thirteenth century in which Adams's St. Thomas Aquinas attempts to give rational form to the religious and social power of the Virgin of Chartres, whose period of dominance is for Adams the *twelfth century*. In her own symbolic figuration, Adams's Virgin achieves a fragile equilibrium, balancing as she does the complex demands of medieval metaphysics with the emotional and practical interests of medieval man. The Virgin is a symbol of differences, a composite of different forces—the Trinity, masculine and feminine sexuality, lord and vassal, artist and scientist, thought and instinct, experience and desire, truth and fiction. She is unified only insofar as we recognize the tensions that support her, as structural tensions support the Cathedral's arches.

For Adams, Thomist metaphysics exemplifies the structural contradiction of human reason and any universal to which reason might appeal. Adams finds little difference between modern man and the "irrational man" defined by the theology of St. Thomas, "who insisted that the universe was a unit, but that he was a universe; that energy was one, but that he was another energy; that God was omnipotent, but that man was free. The contradiction had always existed, exists still, and always must exist, unless man either admits that he is a machine, or agrees that anarchy and chaos are the habits of nature, and law and order its accident." Insofar as Adams insists upon this "contradiction" in *Chartres* and the *Education*, he transforms his own modern dilemma into a metaphysical condition without resolution. In the myth of Henry Adams, this existentialist vision has often been invoked to link him with the development of literary modernism.

This structural contradiction of man and some larger natural or divine force is what ought to provoke man to constitute his own foundations for reason in social and historical forms. Like Swedenborg and Hegel, Adams believes that the security of being man cannot find in Nature or God might be constituted in those secular and communal forms that exceed individuals and yet remain essentially *historical*. In this regard, he is true to his Enlightenment heritage, insofar as he places his confidence in historical continuity and stability as the primary means of testing and justifying individual acts of reason. The mind of man confronts its own contradictoriness or its essential alienation only in those moments of historical crisis when the customary social foundations for thought lose their credibility or applicability, as they had done in St. Thomas's thirteenth century and in Adams's early modern period.

The *Education*, then, like the late essays on science and history, is Adams's effort to resolve the crisis of thought in his own period. His task has about it all the ambitions of John Adams or John Quincy Adams to lend America the image of a representative man, who would reconcile social law and individual action. In "A Dynamic Theory of History" (chapter 23), Adams accepts as a given that "two masses—nature and man—must go on, reacting upon each other, without stop, as the sun and a comet react on each other, and that any appearance of stoppage is illusive." Yet, this given merely argues for the necessarily *historical* context in which human meaning and value must be situated. In the moment that man relies "absolutely on forces other than his own, and on instruments which superseded his senses," then he abandons such history and submits either to natural chaos or deterministic force, whether the latter is understood as a law of nature or philosophy. The Virgin of Chartres remains an active, historical principle for human and social knowledge; Thomist metaphysics and modern science and technology produce the very alienation *from history* that they promise to overcome.

Understood in this context, Adams's *symbolic* mode in the *Education* has relevance more as a social and historical method of representation than as a literary strategy. The Virgin is just such a sociohistorical "symbol," which brings together man's desire for unity—for some foundation for his reason—and the multiplicity of his experience. The historical "symbol" gives particular form to man's essential division—soul and body, mind and matter, unity and multiplicity—in terms that are expressive of his specific historical moment. The expressive terms of a symbol like the Virgin are thus drawn from the discursive conventions of the particular cultural moment and yet respond to a universal dilemma. Such symbolism becomes "literary" only in a culture that has lost its confidence in its ability to represent itself, to provide itself with functional metaphors for its own identity. As an active cultural force, the Virgin is more *mythic* than *symbolic*. The representative man, who is the true statesman, provides in his own person just such an expressive figure for historical order. As ironic as Adams's characterization of himself as the "manikin" of education is, it is also intended to carry with it some trace of the Virgin's and his ancestors' power to organize and focus a culture's energies. The skepticism, intellectual curiosity, and cosmopolitanism of the "Henry Adams" composed by the *Education* offers some resistance to an increasingly chaotic modern history.

In his last work, *The Life of George Cabot Lodge* (1911), Adams confirms his faith in such individualism, even though his subject seems to mock any such claim for the structural integrity of reason or the coherence of a life. George ("Bay") Cabot Lodge was the son of Adams's former student at Harvard, Henry Cabot Lodge, who was serving the second of his three terms as United States Senator from Massachusetts when his son died of heart disease in 1909 at thirty-six. Adams had known Bay Lodge well since 1893, when Bay came to Washington with his father, who was then serving his first term in the Senate. There was much with which Adams could identify in the short career of George Cabot Lodge, who had started out like Adams fitfully filling posts arranged by his powerful Boston family. Like Adams, Bay rebelled against the role he was expected to assume as a Lodge, turning his energies to lyric and dramatic verse only after having tried careers as different as private secretary and naval gunner.

Like *Gallatin*, the biography of Bay Lodge was initiated at the request of the family, and thus has the usual limitations of such memorial biographies. Two volumes of Bay Lodge's poetry were published together with Adams's 200-page biography in the three-volume *Life, Poems and Dramas of George Cabot Lodge*. Lodge was a minor American poet, derivative from the extreme romanticism of Shelley and Byron, and it was with some difficulty that Adams found the proper tone to provide a memorial without celebrating poetry he knew to be in many respects youthful and unpolished. Nevertheless, Adams clearly admires the willful aggression and poetic self-reliance of the central characters in Lodge's two most accomplished works, the verse plays *Herakles* (1908) and *Cain* (1909). Both are typically romantic versions of their mythic prototypes, and they epitomize the sort of transcendent individualism that in Adams's and Lodge's *fin-de-siècle* moods could justify itself only in poetic action. In his often grudging admiration of the romantic will for self-knowledge and self-mastery dramatized in these two plays, Adams betrays again his own dream of transcendental individualism. As a young man, Henry Adams had judged Emerson "naïve," but much of Adams's later writing affirms the sort of manifold, ironic, metamorphic self that is mythologized in our culture as Emersonian man.

That Henry Adams's Enlightenment heritage found some refuge in an essentially transcendental concept of self-reliance tells us a good deal about the fate of eighteenth-century rationalism from Emerson to Adams and the early moderns. If reason could no longer be said to constitute the relation between individual and society, then the individual would have to create a "world elsewhere," an alternative "social" order in which the very predicates of "reason" would be redefined. In a sense, this is precisely the work of literary modernism, which turned inward to find the shape and limits of human consciousness. This noted inferiority, together with its characteristic distinction between everyday life and the "higher" reality of pure consciousness, would manifest itself in literary works with dominantly autobiographical qualities. Such "autobiographical" narratives by James Joyce, Ezra Pound, Marcel Proust, T. S. Eliot, Virginia Woolf, Wallace Stevens, and William Carlos Williams are also remarkable for their extraordinary irony toward their autobiographical subjects. It was the function of such irony to establish the necessary literary distance that would protect the world of the author from the intrusions of the real. On the one hand, Henry Adams's ironic mode in the *Education* provides a model for such literary modernism. On the other hand, Adams's struggle to develop a "critical theory of history" as a means of interpreting the social and historical grounds for human reason cannot be comprehended in either purely literary or historiographical terms. Adams's unfinished project for a multidisciplinary "sciences of man" has been taken up in our own period by structuralists, semioticians, and poststructuralists. It is *this* Henry Adams, rather than the ironic precursor to literary modernism, who deserves our contemporary interest and study.

John Carlos Rowe

Henry James

All fiction is in part autobiography, and any autobiography is partly a fiction—a great novelist's perhaps most of all. The small boy who appears in the opening chapters of Henry James's memoirs, "wondering and dawdling and gaping" as he rambles alone through the streets of old New York at mid-century, is at once the genesis of the future novelist and one of that novelist's most typical characters. The boy is a detached and solitary observer, peering eagerly at scenes in which he takes no part. He owes the leisure with which he wanders both to the privilege of childhood and to the wealth his family has inherited: the "chance feasts" he enjoys along the way satisfy his hunger for impressions, not for food. Looking back some sixty years later on the remarkable freedom with which his younger self was permitted to come and go unchaperoned, the aging writer found himself momentarily puzzled—only to realize that those at home must not have judged him sufficiently reckless or adventurous to worry about. His elders seem to have understood, he ruefully noted, that "the only form of riot or revel ever known to me would be that of the visiting mind." Like many of the narratives James would later write, the small boy's own story is in one sense that of experience missed: "He was to go without many things, ever so many—as all persons do in whom contemplation takes the place of action." But for this most representative of Jamesian figures, the adventures lost would abundantly prove the imagination's gain. Of the small boy's habit of dawdling and gaping, James himself quietly observed that "he was really, I think, much to profit by it."

The language of profit and loss is the nineteenth-century American idiom, and James's own writing is thoroughly grounded in its terms, even as he works to convert them into a different currency. He had been born in 1843, to a family wealthy enough to keep its distance from the financial struggle and to be skeptical of popular notions of success. The novelist's father, the elder Henry James, felt himself "leisured for life" by an income of $10,000 a year—though he had obtained his legacy only by breaking the will of his stern Presbyterian father, an Irish immigrant and self-made millionaire, who had distrusted the effects of inherited wealth on his offspring. "The rupture with my grandfather's tradition and attitude was complete," the novelist later wrote; "we were never in a single case . . . for two generations, guilty of a stroke of business." A philosopher and religious thinker deeply influenced by the work of Emmanuel Swedenborg, Henry James, Sr., was a prolific writer and lecturer, but his son would recall with affectionate irony the helplessness he and his brothers felt when trying to explain to their childhood playmates just what it was their father "*was*." Though the novelist would eventually earn the bulk of his income from his writing, and was not above some hard bargaining with his publishers, there is little question that he had been profoundly affected by the paternal injunction "just to *be* something, something unconnected with specific doing, something free and uncommitted"—and by the impulse to translate cash into the values of the imagination and the intellect. James's remarkable capacity to identify with his female characters has many sources, but if he felt an especial affinity for the figure of the heiress, it may have been because his culture had already made her the vehicle of such translation—assigning to woman the function both of purchasing culture and of representing it. Though a number of James's heroes have earned vast sums of money—Christopher Newman in *The American* (1877) and Adam Verver in *The Golden Bowl* (1904) have both made millions—how they have done so is rarely specified; when the stories of Newman and Verver open, they have already abandoned the business of accumulating wealth and are eagerly exchanging their dollars for the products of European civilization. Like Henry Sr.'s family, the Jamesian novel typically avoids any direct engagement with business itself. Much critical energy has been fruitlessly expended in trying to identify the "vulgar" item manufactured with great profit by the Newsomes in *The Ambassadors* (1903), an item that the novel's hero persistently refuses to name. Rather than vulgarly specify, James's language characteristically transmutes gold, turning the words that refer to it into metaphoric vehicles, figures for transcendent meanings. Yet unlike so many nineteenth-century novelists on both sides of the Atlantic, he rarely indulges in conventional pieties about the wickedness of wealth and the virtues of the poor. As was the case in his family's own history, wealth in James's fiction is frequently allied with a sensitive conscience and a romantic imagination—and like those endowments, it is at once dangerous and potentially liberating. Milly Theale, the ambiguously Christ-like heroine of *The Wings of the Dove* (1902) and a tribute to James's beloved cousin, Minny Temple, has "thousands and thousands a year." Such an income brings no exemption from betrayal and death—only a consciousness released from the petty distractions of most women's lives and free to concentrate fully on coming to terms with those ultimate constraints.

By raising both Henry Jr. and William James—the one son America's greatest novelist and the other its most influential philosopher and psychologist—Henry James, Sr., effectively confounded his own father's belief in the debilitating results of inherited wealth. Filial resistance met his ideas in turn, yet it is impossible not to sense Henry Sr.'s profound influence on both his sons' extraordinary achievements. The intellectual kinship between the mid-nineteenth-century Swedenborgian philosopher and the author of *The Varieties of Religious Experience* (1902) may seem relatively obvious, though William's sympathetic recording of his father's mystic experience never extended to any direct adoption of the latter's theological system. But if the younger Henry's relation to "Father's Ideas" was still more oblique, his autobiographical volumes—*A Small Boy and Others* (1913) and *Notes of a Son and Brother* (1914)—pay moving tribute to Henry Sr.'s personality and to the spirit in which he exercised his thought. Cultivating his children's moral sensitivities but detesting "prigs," he "only cared for virtue that was more or less ashamed of itself," his son recalled; and

nothing could have been of a happier whimsicality than the mixture in him . . . of the strongest instinct for the human and the liveliest reaction from the literal. The literal played in our education as small a part as it perhaps ever played in any, and we wholesomely breathed inconsistency and ate and drank contradictions. The presence of paradox was so bright among us. . . .

Mentally dining on "contradictions" was to prove abundantly nourishing to the mature writer, whose work would thrive on paradox and ambiguity, and whose tales of moral conflict would continually elude any moral system. Indeed, "the strongest instinct for the human" and "the liveliest reaction from the literal" might happily characterize the Jamesian novel itself. Of course this language from the memoirs *is* that of the mature writer, recalling a past more than fifty years gone; but if it is again impossible here to separate memory from fiction, that is only to emphasize how deeply the novelist's sense of his father was bound up with his conception of himself.

The education of the young Jameses was governed by an eccentric succession of tutors and institutions, as the restless father spent a decade, beginning in 1855, shuttling back and forth between America and Europe and moving about from New York to Newport and Boston. Henry Sr.'s resistance to "specific doing," his enthusiasm for educational and vocational experiment, and his tolerance of contradictions could be wonderfully liberating, but they were not without their price. The two younger sons, Garth and Robertson, struggled painfully to establish themselves on their own; Robertson especially was to lead a troubled and unsettled life. Immensely and variously talented, William himself was over thirty before he broke away from home and embarked decisively on a career; not until 1876 did he really settle into teaching at Harvard, and not until 1878, after much worrying of the question, did he finally bring himself to marry. Like their father, all the James children suffered from an assortment of nervous and physical ailments: both Henry Sr. and William underwent forms of psychological and spiritual breakdown, as did the youngest child and only daughter, Alice, who would spend much of her adult life an invalid. Henry Sr. himself had been partly crippled as an adolescent boy and wore a wooden leg, having received severe burns when he tried to stamp out a stable fire that he and some playmates had inadvertently set. And in *Notes of a Son and Brother*, his second son and namesake wrote of his own "horrid" if "obscure hurt," an injury he too suffered when as a young man of eighteen he attempted to put out a stable fire—and which he vaguely associated with "the huge comprehensive ache" of the Civil War then raging and his personal failure to enlist in battle. Though the evasive circumlocutions with which he recalled the incident once prompted speculation that he had been wounded sexually, it seems more probable that he had somehow injured his back. But what is most striking is the implicit identification with his father, the partial reenactment of his fate: to be thus obscurely wounded was somehow to be justified as a noncombatant, freed to remain in his turn a "student" of life. Whether as fact or as personal myth, the obscure hurt became for the writer a mysteriously enabling condition.

The novelist's memoirs depict him as a small boy forever lagging hopelessly "behind" his gifted elder brother (who was, in fact, only fifteen months his senior); yet of all the James children he seems to have arrived earliest and most confidently at a sense of vocation. Even while engaged in a brief and abortive attempt at the Harvard Law School, he was quietly wooing "the muse of prose fiction" and nourishing a "deeply reserved but quite unabashed design of becoming as 'literary' as might be." In 1864, when he was not quite twenty-one, he published anonymously his first short story, a melodramatic tale of adultery and misdirected murder bearing the imprint of his avid reading in French romance. In the same year he published his first piece of criticism, a review of Nassau W. Senior's *Essays on Fiction*, in which he imagines a prolific novelist defending himself from the charge of "grinding out" his inventions by announcing, "My *work* is my salvation." Though he would not produce his own first novel until the end of the decade, the next few years witnessed a considerable outpouring of stories, literary criticism, and travel sketches—all forms in which he would continue to exercise his talent for the remainder of his life. Appearing in such journals as *The North American Review*, *The Nation*, and the *Atlantic*—the last under the sympathetic editorship of William Dean Howells—these stories and reviews reveal the influence of his generously eclectic reading in contemporary American, English, and continental fiction; the critical voice is at once sensitive, shrewd, and brashly opinionated—the voice of an ambitious young man of letters, self-consciously cultivating and defining his art. The other side of James's seeming passivity as an observer is his extraordinary energy and confidence as a writer, increasingly eager to claim the authority of authorship. "I shall immortalize myself," he characteristically announced to his sister in 1874: *"vous allez voir."* He made this boast in a letter from Florence, where he was at work on the opening chapters of his first major novel, *Roderick Hudson* (1875), the story of two men—the extravagantly ambitious artist of the title and his anxiously watchful patron and friend, Rowland Mallet—who together struggle with the ambiguities of art, of observation, and of power.

Strictly speaking, James's first novel was *Watch and Ward*, published serially in the *Atlantic* in 1870, though not issued as a book until eight years later; an oddly Pygmalion-like tale of a Boston gentleman who raises a ward in order to marry her, the novel anticipates later James in its focus on a young girl's choice of suitors, and in its uneasy commingling of the acts of watching and love. But it is *Roderick Hudson* that first substantially develops several of his most typical preoccupations and themes: the artist-hero torn between the demands of his art and of "life," the New England puritans intoxicated and bewildered by their sensuous education in Europe, the American romantic who dreams of transcending the ordinary constraints of experience, the sensitive observer who loves in vain and seems doomed in the end to an ambiguous renunciation. Roderick himself is a promising but egotistical young sculptor, an American whose European adventures conclude in a spectacular fatality. Infatuated with the beautiful Christina Light, who is compelled to abandon him for an Italian prince, torn between grandiose visions of possibility and disgust at the limitations of his achievement, Roderick undergoes a kind of spiritual collapse, ultimately plummeting to his death during an Alpine storm. Though melodrama would continue to exert a powerful hold on James's imagination, his subsequent heroes and heroines rarely make so theatrical an exit: an Alpine disaster is more likely to figure in the later James purely as a metaphor for a crisis of consciousness. Even in *Roderick Hudson*, it is Rowland who survives to register the significance of Roderick's fall—and in looking back at the novel more than a quarter century later, James would characteristically locate its real center of interest not in the histrionic artist but in the "drama" of his patron's consciousness: "what 'happened' to him . . . was above all to feel certain things happening to others."

James himself had first made Roderick's intoxicating journey from New England to Italy some five years before writing the novel; his arrival in the imperial city in the autumn of 1869 had sent him "reeling and moaning thro' the streets, in a fever of enjoyment," as he reported to those at home. After a longer European sojourn in 1872–74, he had briefly attempted to establish himself in New York City; but in 1875 he returned to Europe, and by 1876 had decided to settle permanently in London. Like the hero of "The Passionate Pilgrim," an early international tale that lent its title to his first collection of stories (1875), the novelist arrived in England with dreams of possession—though the issue was not an American's claim to an ancestral estate, as in the story, but his imaginative grasp of a culture. "I take possession of the old world," he triumphantly announced to his family in a letter from London; "I inhale it—I appropriate it!"

It was once fashionable among American critics to argue that James's art had suffered from his deracination, that the growing abstraction and elaborate refinement of his later style could be traced to his unfortunate decision to deprive his imagination of its native sustenance. James's *Hawthorne* (1879) touched a sensitive nerve among his contemporaries by seeming to suggest that American culture was too aridly provincial to nourish a great artist; his famous catalogue of all the "items of high civilization" missing from American life ("No State. . . . No sovereign, no court, no personal loyalty, no aristocracy, no church, no clergy . . . no sporting class—no Epsom nor Ascot!") drove Howells to protest that "after leaving out all those novelistic 'properties' . . . we have the whole of human life remaining." Certainly James's account of Hawthorne was in part a defense of his own recent move to England, a statement that *his* novels would benefit from the thick texture of Europe—and in part simply a literary son's declaration of independence from a profoundly influential father. But James also knew that "it's a complex fate, being an American," as he wrote in a letter of 1872, "and one of the responsibilities it entails is fighting against a superstitious valuation of Europe." His list of all that America lacks concludes with a tribute to the native gift of humor, and the final allusion to the missing Epsom and Ascot carries its own subversive irony.

James's deep affinities with Hawthorne are apparent not only in the frequent echoes of the earlier novelist's themes and situations but in a subtle irony that delights more in the play of opposing attitudes than in recording the outcome of their struggle. Indeed, one of the principal uses of the international theme in James's fiction is to generate a splendidly ironic comedy—and it is by no means only the innocent Americans who are the object of the joke. Nor does James simply repudiate the American yearning to do away with the encumbrances of Europe. The heroine of *The Portrait of a Lady* (1880–81) will prove tragically naïve in her faith that "nothing that belongs to me is any measure of me; everything's on the contrary a limit, a barrier, and a perfectly arbitrary one"; but the Emersonian romanticism of Isabel Archer, her dream of a transcendent self, is finally more attractive than is the insistent worldliness of her opponent, Madame Merle, who cynically proclaims her own "great respect for *things*!" And James would argue many years later that he himself had surrendered to a vision of "experience liberated, so to speak; experience disengaged, disembroiled, disencumbered, exempt from the conditions that we usually know to attach to it," as he put it in a celebrated passage from the preface to the New York Edition of *The American* (1907). For all his desire to appropriate the expressive riches of the Old World, he discovered in retrospect that he had unwittingly turned the first novel he had composed after settling in Europe into an American romance.

The American (1877) opens with affectionate irony at Newman's expense, as the aesthetically ignorant millionaire is hoodwinked into vastly overpaying for a third-rate copy of a painting in the Louvre. As in the principal transaction he attempts in Paris—the buying of a wife—James's representative American proves at once vulgar and generous, credulous and honorable. In a typically Jamesian ending, the novel will at once deprive Newman of the woman he desires and grant him the ambiguous triumph of renunciation, when he abandons his chance to seek revenge on the proud French family that has spurned him as a son-in-law. Yet when James himself came to revise the novel for the New York Edition, he decided that the very plotting of his wealthy American's rejection by the French aristocrats betrayed his own unconscious surrender to romance: so intent had he been on the idea that Newman should be "ill-used," James confessed, that he had ignored the probable behavior of the Bellegardes, who would "positively have jumped" at marrying their daughter to so "rich and easy" an American. Rereading this novel forty years later, James thus associated his impulse toward romance with his wish to justify his American hero. He might also have argued that he had contrived a bit of gothic melodrama for the same end, since it is Newman's discovery that Madame de Bellegarde has secretly murdered her husband, and their daughter's decision to shut herself up forever in a Carmelite convent, that transform the Bellegardes from the blocking agents of comedy to the villains of melodrama. *The American* is an early work, and such shifts between genres are not without their strain, but in its very mixture of narrative modes, its simultaneous satire of and indulgence toward the hero, it anticipates some of James's most mature achievements.

"Daisy Miller" (1879) also ends with the ironic vindication of its protagonist: when James's charming American dies of the malaria she has contracted in the Colosseum, she figuratively succumbs to the bad air generated by the Old World's corruption—and the Italian admirer with whom she had appeared to carry on a scandalous flirtation declares her to have been wholly "innocent." James's greatest popular success, "Daisy Miller" established his reputation on both sides of the Atlantic and helped to make of the American Girl a celebrated cultural type. Yet given the light irony with which he drew the heroine of the tale, it is hardly surprising that readers were uncertain what to make of her and that some American ladies were said to have found her portrait "shameful." By compelling us to see Daisy largely through the eyes of Winterbourne, the expatriate American who hesitates to return her love, James characteristically shifts the focus from the heroine herself to the problem of knowing her. And even in so slight a sketch, he manages to suggest some of the ambiguities of innocence, its implication in its own destruction. If there is a sense in which the Americans usually prove the moral victors in James's early international fiction, it is also true that the value of such morality is always open to ironic question. The reader of *The Europeans* (1878) may well prefer the artful lies of its continental Baroness to the unvarnished sincerity of its straightforward New Englanders—or at least be tempted to suspend judgment. Stylish and urbane, the Baroness Munster fails in the end to win an American husband, but in her mannered elegance, her capacity to re-create herself and to make deception "right," she prefigures such an appealing representative of European civilization as Madame de Vionnet in *The Ambassadors*. The very elegance and wit of James's own style, its increasingly subtle discriminations, ally him with the artfully civilized, and suggest how deeply values other than moral compel his imagination.

The Europeans is something of an anomaly in James's canon: it reverses the usual trajectory of his international fiction by sending the representatives of the Old World to invade the New and it resolves their comic entanglements in a quartet of marriages. The muted conclusion of *Washington*

Square (1881) is more typical, with its sadly enlightened heroine, her dignity earned in disillusion, resigning herself to a lonely future as she deliberately locks the door against the man who once betrayed her love. Terminating in such gestures of renunciation, implicitly linking heightened consciousness with loss, refusing to forecast the characters' fates, James's narratives repeatedly defy the convention of the "happy ending"—what he would memorably describe in "The Art of Fiction" (1884) as "a distribution at the last of prizes, pensions, husbands, wives, babies, millions, appended paragraphs, and cheerful remarks." By entering a plea for Newman's successful marriage while *The American* was still running as a serial in the *Atlantic*, Howells merely became one of the first to protest the Jamesian sense of an ending. (Despite the objection of his editor and friend, James's novel would still conclude with Newman's loss of his fiancée.) The close of James's early masterpiece, *The Portrait of a Lady* (1880–81)—Isabel's refusal of escape with Caspar Goodwood, her flight from his passionate embrace, and her return to her unhappy marriage—has seemed especially problematic to many twentieth-century readers, who have found themselves troubled by Isabel's apparent fear of sexuality and skeptical of her view that marriage is a "magnificent form." Though Isabel's views are not necessarily her creator's, the distrust of sexuality that surfaces repeatedly in James's early fiction can doubtless be traced to his private history, his hesitant coming to terms with his own eroticism. And it certainly can be argued that *The Portrait of a Lady* is too ready to make marriage symbolize the necessity of commitment. But Isabel's final gesture should primarily be read in the context of the novel's extended exploration of the possible meanings of "freedom": from her original, prototypically American belief in an independence that defies all limits, Isabel gradually arrives at a sense of freedom that is largely a state of consciousness—the paradoxical freedom of a self that deliberately accepts its own constraints and faces responsibility for the choices that it makes.

The *Portrait of a Lady* makes use of a story that James would tell repeatedly, and that he had already sketched in the history of Christopher Newman: seduced by Europe, the innocent American awakens belatedly to the knowledge of a secret past, to the discovery of sexual intrigue and betrayal. Isabel learns that her husband and Madame Merle were formerly lovers, and that they had secretly conspired to arrange her marriage. But while it might be possible to read her history as that of an innocent victim, what Isabel herself comes to understand is how thoroughly she has been implicated in its plot. In this sense her recognition anticipates what James would later argue in his preface to the New York Edition of the novel (1908)— that "character" precedes "story," that James's sense of who Isabel was, and not a preexisting "plot," had determined what would happen to her. In this sense too *The Portrait of a Lady* represents a profound advance over the relatively mechanical contrivances of a work like *The American*—written only three years earlier—and a major turn in the direction of James's art. With Isabel's awakening to the meaning of her experience, James gradually transforms his international drama into a drama of consciousness; and it is only a slight exaggeration to say that the heroine's recognition scene, her fireside meditation in chapter 42 in which she first articulates to herself that something is terribly wrong with her marriage, marks the principal moment of transition. Not surprisingly, the later James singled out this scene as "obviously the best thing in the book."

In the novel's resonant opening chapter, the English aristocrat, Lord Warburton, tells the ailing American banker and expatriate, Daniel Touchett, that he fears to " 'take hold' of something" lest it be "knocked sky-high" the next moment. Touchett's reply—that "the ladies will save us"—is ironically fulfilled, as Isabel's consciousness comes increasingly to dominate a novel in which social institutions and their representatives have in some sense failed. Yet unlike the more intensely concentrated and inward novels of his later phase, James's first "big" novel, as he repeatedly proclaimed it, seems also to aspire to a comprehensive representation of its social world; from Warburton, the uneasily radical aristocrat, to the brashly inquisitive Henrietta Stackpole, the American reporter on a futile quest for Europe's "inner life," the novel approaches its various types with a typically Jamesian mixture of satire and sympathy. In the very thickness of its texture, its shrewd glimpses of social anxiety and change, even its sheer scale—as well as its subtle probing of its heroine's consciousness—*The Portrait of a Lady* bears comparison with the major achievements of nineteenth-century European fiction.

James's own wide acquaintance with the literature of his day continued to nourish both his practice and his theory of narrative. To his avid reading of the great mid-century novelists—Dickens, Thackeray, George Eliot—as well as a host of lesser writers on both sides of the Atlantic, he added a knowledge of the French unusual among the Victorians; more than any of his contemporaries, he brought French self-consciousness and theoretical sophistication to Anglo-American criticism of the novel. *French Poets and Novelists* (1878), the first published collection of his reviews, includes extended appraisals of George Sand, Balzac, and Turgenev, to all three of whose work he would return repeatedly in the course of his career. In the winter of 1875–76 he had frequented the circle of realists and naturalists gathered around Flaubert, Zola, and Edmond de Goncourt in Paris. Though all his life he would resist what seemed to him narrow and doctrinaire in their literary program (especially Zola's solemn assumption that reality was "necessarily allied to the impure," as James put it in an 1880 review of *Nana*), he would also strongly sympathize with their insistence on their freedom to choose their subjects and their seriousness about the novelist's vocation.

"The Art of Fiction" (1884), his celebrated reply to a lecture on the subject by the English novelist and man of letters Walter Besant, argues strenuously for the artist's freedom to choose his "*donnée*" and against any attempt to lay down prescriptions for the making of a novel. Though the essay identifies "the air of reality" as "the supreme virtue of the novel" and contends that "the only reason for the existence of a novel is that it does attempt to represent life," James's is not a programmatic realism: "reality" in his sense of the term "has a myriad forms," and its measure is "very difficult to fix." James's idea of representation is correspondingly flexible: it is characteristic that he should counter Besant's conventional wisdom that one must write from experience (specifically, that the rural lady novelist should not attempt a novel about army life) by suggesting that the sensitive artist's "experience" includes the capacity to imagine, to "guess the unseen from the seen," and to deduce an entire world from the most fleeting of impressions. While "The Art of Fiction" expresses pleasure at signs that the novel is beginning to have "a theory," its own theoretical procedure is typically to break down critical distinctions rather than to establish them— arguing, for instance, that "character" cannot be distinguished from "incident," or the "romance" from the "novel"—and to identify the quality of a novel with the quality of mind of its creator. James's essay had less influence on his immediate contemporaries than it has had on twentieth-century critics, for whom it has become a seminal text—anticipating both the New Critical approach to the novel as an "organic" form and the structuralist and poststructuralist focus on theory itself. In his own deliberately borrowed term, James's criticism began to make the English novel "what the French call *discutable*."

The two novels that follow "The Art of Fiction" are at once the most overtly "political" of James's works and skeptically detached from all fixed positions and ideologies. *The Bostonians* and *The Princess Casamassima*, both published in 1886, raise issues that have still seemed topical to many twentieth-century readers. After World War II, American intellectuals reread *The Princess Casamassima* for its study of the conflict between a love of culture and a commitment to revolution; more recently, a new generation of feminists have turned to *The Bostonians* to reconsider its satire of New England's agitating women. Yet if James's sympathy for both his European anarchists and his American feminists now seems stronger than many critics once assumed, neither text readily lends itself to political appropriation. In their struggle for the allegiance of Verena Tarrant, the gifted yet oddly vacuous heroine of *The Bostonians*, the "reactionary" Southerner Basil Ransom triumphs over his zealous opponent, Olive Chancellor, and the novel concludes with Verena's abandonment of public speaking and the cause of women for marriage to Ransom. But Basil—who believes that women "were delicate, agreeable creatures, whom Providence had placed under the protection of the bearded sex"—is as much the object of James's satire as are the Northern reformers; while Olive, with her fierce self-suppression, her ardor for Verena at once erotic and impersonal, is lucidly, if rather coldly, understood. And the apparently conventional resolution of the novel's plot is subverted by the narrator's dry allusion to the "far from brilliant" union on which Verena is tearfully embarked, and his final prediction of the many future tears she will shed. Indeed, the "deathly silence" with which the public seemed to greet *The Bostonians* may be in large part explained by the very consistency of the novel's ironic detachment, its sustained refusal to indulge its readers' emotional expectations. Neither *The Bostonians* nor *The Princess Casamassima* was a popular success.

"I am quite the Naturalist," James reported to a friend after spending a morning at London's Millbank Prison, "collecting notes" for *The Princess Casamassima*. *The Bostonians*, he boasted to another correspondent, "is something like Balzac!!!" Though the sociological concerns of the French realists and naturalists clearly influenced both novels, the prison scenes of *The Princess Casamassima* are also strongly reminiscent of Dickens—as is the novel's tendency toward genial caricature, especially of the lower-class figures. Whether or not the relative failure of *The Princess Casamassima* can be attributed to the novelist's personal detachment from political life, his inability convincingly to imagine the hidden world of anarchist conspiracy—as some have suggested—it seems clear that the very effort at naturalism was itself uncongenial to James. Certainly the illegitimate union of an English aristocrat and the Frenchwoman who murders him provides an improbable origin for the fine Jamesian consciousness with which the novel's hero, Hyacinth Robinson, is endowed—and that fine consciousness sorts uneasily with his role as a potential assassin. But as the conflict between an essentially aesthetic and a moral approach to experience, the split that torments him is nonetheless an extreme version of a familiar Jamesian dilemma, and Hyacinth's eventual suicide a melodramatically violent form of the novelist's typical renunciatory conclusions. Like *The Tragic Muse* (1890), the last of these large-scale and uneven social narratives, *The Princess Casamassima* dramatizes the conflict between the aesthetic and the moral as a struggle between culture and politics—though in *The Tragic Muse* the politics are those of parliamentary elections and diplomatic careers rather than of revolutionary conspiracies, and it is not so much civilization in general as the practice of art itself that competes for allegiance.

The preface (1908) to *The Tragic Muse* calls "the conflict between art and 'the world' " one of "the half-dozen great primary motives," but it might have been more accurate had James confined his claim to literature since the beginning of the nineteenth century—the imagined opposition between art and life being a peculiarly modern invention. James himself takes up the conflict as early as *Roderick Hudson*, though it is his fiction of the eighties and the nineties—especially the shorter tales of art and artists—that most deeply influenced modernist variations on the theme. The 1880s were of course the years of debate over Aestheticism in England and France, and by representing the exponents of the movement in the Pateresque person of Gabriel Nash, *The Tragic Muse* joins its two predecessors in satirizing contemporary ideologies. But to speak of the tension between art and "the world" in James, or between the aesthetic and the moral, is always to risk a certain distortion, since his own art continually works to subvert such simple oppositions, or at least to call them seriously into question.

Indeed, in a series of short stories, loosely grouped by critics as his "Artist Tales," James makes these problematic relations between art and life the very subject of his narratives. Though "The Lesson of the Master" (1888), for example, seems to turn on the need to choose between perfection of the life and of the work—as W. B. Yeats would later put it—the witty and disquieting reversals with which the tale concludes suggest that the lesson may prove ironic and the dichotomy false. The Master, Henry St. George, has apparently sacrificed his literary genius to an enviable marriage and worldly success. Having been persuaded by the Master that his is an example to be avoided, a promising younger writer decides to give up the girl he loves—only to discover that the Master has become engaged to marry her himself after the death of his first wife. The final lines of the tale even raise the possibility that this second happy marriage might rejuvenate the Master's art. "The Real Thing" (1890) plays ironically with the gap between representation and reality, as a painter's attempts to use a real lady and gentleman for models fail utterly, while he succeeds in transforming a tawdry pair of professional sitters into convincing images of gentility. But the painter's "innate preference for the represented subject over the real one" is partly countered by his recognition of the genuine nobility with which the impoverished lady and gentleman eventually accept their failure, in this sense at least proving themselves "the real thing" after all. While the paradoxes of representation do not always figure so openly as a theme, James's self-consciousness about the subject can be felt in much of his writing, particularly in the later novels. Several of their most resonant scenes turn on a character's consciousness of the relation between a represented image and "reality"—as when Lambert Strether in *The Ambassadors* feels as if he had stepped into the frame of a Lambinet landscape as he wanders in the country on a day's outing from Paris, or when Milly Theale identifies herself with the Bronzino portrait in *The Wings of the Dove.*

James's novels are rich in such pictorial analogies and allusions, though his later work also increasingly declares its kinship to the art of the theater. *The Tragic Muse* is James's only novel to take a professional actress for a heroine, yet it shares with its immediate predecessors an uneasy fascination with histrionic display, and anticipates the later novels' radical play with the metaphor of life as performance—a performance that becomes virtually impossible to distinguish from the underlying "truth" it might superficially be thought to conceal. But only the frustration and failure of James's own effort to woo a theatrical audience—an effort to which he largely devoted the half-decade following *The Tragic Muse* of 1890—seem to have liberated the theatrical possibilities of his narratives. He was drawn to the theater partly by a desire for the financial success that appeared more and more to elude him as a novelist and partly by the challenge of the dramatic form itself, as well as by a deep if ambivalent infatuation with the popular stage that dated back to the Shakespearean performances, the adaptations of Dickens and *Uncle Tom's Cabin*, that he had witnessed as a small boy in New York. His theatrical version of *The American* (1890) enjoyed a brief success in its provincial run, but the comedies with which he followed it were never produced, and his career as a dramatist ended in a painful moment of public humiliation, when he was exposed to the catcalls and jeers of the gallery at the opening performance of *Guy Domville* in 1895. That play dramatizes its hero's vacillation between the demands of the world and the monastery to which he finally retreats, and the story of James's own unhappy relations with the theater seems to have been shaped by a similar conflict—an inability to reconcile a longing for popular acclaim with a profound distrust of vulgarity and self-display. Though he never wholly abandoned his efforts to gain a larger market for his work, James's failure in the theater intensified his sense of isolation from the mass audience; and the growing difficulty and even obscurity of his later fiction appear in retrospect as signs of the widening breach between high and popular art that has characterized modern culture. Yet by drawing on his theatrical experiments in the fiction to which he now returned, James succeeded not only in easing his own pain, but in radically rethinking his art, at once clarifying and deepening its psychological power.

James's Notebooks provide a moving record of the process by which he re-created himself as a novelist. "It is now indeed that I may do the work of my life," he wrote a few weeks after the *Guy Domville* fiasco. "And I will." Beginning with an entry the next month in which he triumphantly alights on the "divine principle of the Scenario," the Notebooks document James's growing confidence that the novel might achieve the compression and the "SCENIC intensity" of the drama. In his detailed "scenarios" for *The Spoils of Poynton* (1897) and *What Maisie Knew* (1897), he repeatedly exhorts himself to adopt "the *scenic* method" and "to stick to the march of an action"; in their deliberate patterning and the relative economy of their form— *The Spoils of Poynton* was originally plotted in three "Acts"—both novels bear the imprint of the "well-made play," a tightening of structure especially noticeable after the comparatively loose and sprawling narratives of the previous decade. Well before his theatrical ventures, James had protested the "suicidal satisfaction" with which Anthony Trollope seemed to intrude his reminders that "the story he was telling was only . . . make-believe," thus destroying the illusion that the events were "real" and his narrative a "history." But now the analogy of the dramatist supplants that of the historian and entails a far more thoroughgoing suppression of the narrator. In *The Awkward Age* (1899) James would experiment with a novel that was virtually all dialogue, denying himself the privilege of "going behind" the characters, as the preface later put it, to render consciousness or to explain.

Such experiments, it should be noted, were never conducted as rigorously as James's retrospective account of them in the prefaces—or as some of the twentieth-century criticism derived from those prefaces—liked to suggest. Even *The Awkward Age* relies on a narrator to record appearances and gestures, and occasionally resorts to the device of recounting what a sensitive observer "might" have seen or guessed had he been present to register the action. In James's late masterpieces dialogue alternates once again with description and summary—"scene" with "picture," in the deliberately borrowed terminology of the prefaces—but by restricting the narrative to the point of view of a single character and by subtly refining the free indirect style, James could continue to conceal the narrator's presence, or at least fuse him imperceptibly with the consciousness of the protagonists. The dramatic bias of James's later fiction and of the theory implicit in his practical criticism and prefaces can be clearly traced in the poetics of the novel that began to be formulated in England and America in the twentieth century—especially in the modernist reaction against intrusive narrators and the widespread celebration of "showing" as opposed to "telling" as a mark of superior realism and mature narrative technique. Though recent practice and theory have largely abandoned the realist illusion for deliberate fictionality and self-conscious narrative play, the very force of the reaction is a measure of the power that the Jamesian creed long exerted.

James's extraordinary capacity for representing and identifying with a female consciousness, apparent at least as early as *The Portrait of a Lady*, becomes especially evident in the fiction of the 1890s. Leon Edel has argued that the novelist's heightened sense of his own vulnerability after his failure in the theater prompted this identification with young women; though causal relations in such matters are never simple, his affinity for the female point of view may also have been evoked in part by his increasing consciousness of his own homoerotic feelings. Almost from its inception, James's fiction had represented the innocent's awakening to knowledge as the uncovering of a secret, like Newman's discovery of Madame de Bellegarde's murder of her husband or Isabel Archer's belated recognition of the past affair between her husband and Madame Merle. But from *What Maisie Knew* through *The Golden Bowl* (1904), James's narratives dwell with a new intensity on the mystery of passion itself, and sexual transgression becomes *the* secret that the innocent protagonist must confront. Eager witnesses (or perhaps inventors) of sexual scandals in which they themselves do not participate, at once frightened by and avid for the "facts," the governess of *The Turn of the Screw* (1898) or the female telegraphist of "In the Cage" (1898) are typical late Jamesian figures, and types of the novelist's own ambivalent fascination with the problem of sex.

Indeed, the nineteenth-century convention that the ideal woman was ignorant of sexuality, innocent not merely in act but in thought, made the female consciousness a particularly apt vehicle for Jamesian drama. Both *What Masie Knew* and *The Awkward Age* turn not on the possible violation of the young woman's body (as in many eighteenth-century narratives) but on the violation of her mind, her acquisition of knowledge. And if the very existence of such texts negates the innocent heroine's "classic identity with a sheet of white paper," as *The Awkward Age* puts it, much of their energy nonetheless derives from the force of the ideal they thus violate. In *What Maisie Knew* James exploits the ironic gap between the reader's understanding of the events that the child heroine witnesses and the terms into which she herself innocently translates them—as Maisie, who has no mental language for adult sexuality, struggles to make sense of the dizzying couplings and uncouplings of her adulterous parents and stepparents. And in *The Awkward Age*, the adolescent Nanda Brookenham finally loses the man she loves because he believes her tainted—not by any sexual license of her own, but by too much knowledge of the sordid world he and she both inhabit. The climactic sign of this knowledge is her public admission that she has read a French novel, and James's own accounts of his French counterparts betray the pervasive ambivalence about the representation of sexuality that so profoundly shapes his later fiction. It is characteristic that his early review of Zola's *Nana* should complain of the "monstrous uncleanness" of that work—even as it deplores the informal yet effective censorship of the Anglo-American novel—and simultaneously argue that despite their self-imposed restrictions, the English were finally "better psychologists" than the French. And it is also characteristic that when James's influential essay "The Future of the Novel" (1899) laments what it calls "an immense omission in our fiction," the very language in which it does so at once calls attention to the missing sexuality and keeps the secret.

The notorious ambiguities of James's late fiction arise in part from this double impulse to uncover and conceal—from the tension between an avid curiosity about the "vulgar" facts and a wish to keep them at a distance, to sublimate them into what the narrator of *The Sacred Fount* (1901) calls "a perfect palace of thought." Though the later fiction frequently dramatizes the obsession with a secret, Jamesian ambiguities can best be approached by viewing them not as concealing some hidden "truth" that the reader must decipher but as enacting the problematic nature of interpretation itself. Perhaps the most radically undecidable of James's texts, both *The Turn of the Screw* and *The Sacred Fount* have as their protagonists first-person narrators who seem obsessed with sexual relations from which they are excluded—relations, however, which may in each case simply be the fantastic projections of the narrator's own anxieties and longings. Neither work allows the reader to choose definitively between a belief in the objective existence of those relations and the assumption that the narrator is in fact mad.

Probably because it continues to exert the primal fascination of a ghost story, *The Turn of the Screw* has inspired a livelier—if apparently interminable—critical controversy. What began as a debate between those who took the ghosts to be genuine manifestations of the supernatural and those who insisted that they were merely hysterical products of the governess's repressed sexuality later developed into a sophisticated theoretical argument about the inevitable indeterminacy of all interpretation. But *The Sacred Fount* is finally the more instructive case, for the narrator of the novel, who takes a self-conscious pleasure in spinning out an elaborate theory about the adulterous affairs of his fellow guests at a country-house weekend, seems a revealing surrogate of the artist himself. The narrator's hypothesis of a vampirish reciprocity between lovers, in which one gains in beauty or wit by drawing on the "sacred fount" and depleting the resources of the other, has the symmetry and metaphorical resonance of fine art. By raising the possibility that the entire theory is pure fantasy (as one of the other guests stoutly maintains) and leaving the question unresolved, the novel seems to dramatize the artist's anxiety about the impossibility of representation, the unbridgeable gap between imagination and reality. Yet it also suggests that such a gap is precisely what makes art possible, since the principal condition of the narrator's theory-spinning is his absolute refusal to peer through the keyhole and get directly at the "truth" of the others' private lives.

James himself insisted that both these problematic texts were essentially jokes, forms of sophisticated play—calling *The Sacred Fount* "the merest of *jeux d'esprit*" and *The Turn of the Screw* "an *amusette* to catch those not easily caught." Yet if they ultimately lack the emotional power and human seriousness of *The Wings of the Dove* (1902), *The Ambassadors* (1903), and *The Golden Bowl* (1904), they anticipate the later works' epistemological excitement, their delight in the imagination's freedom and power. Though the late masterpieces do not finally leave the reader quite so baffled as to the essential "facts," their narratives continue to turn on mystery and delayed revelation: much of their drama derives from the tension between the characters' longing to know the vulgar truth and their terror of it, between the impulse to uncover the "literal" and the wish to rename and transform it. And that drama is reflected, indeed created, by the very rhythms of James's prose style, which was to become an extraordinarily subtle medium for the representation of his characters' double consciousness. With its metaphoric indirections, the hesitations and qualifications of its syntax, the late style dramatizes the impulse toward evasion and postponement, articulating the space of imaginative free play; while the momentum of verbal association and the seemingly compulsive extension of metaphor simultaneously enact the drive toward discovery. Fully to appreciate the excitement of James's late style is to approach it not as an opaque screen for some underlying story—as literal-minded readers have sometimes attempted—but as in great measure the story itself.

At least as early as *What Maisie Knew*, James had exploited not merely his protagonist's distance from the facts but her power innocently to imagine them otherwise: "appearances in themselves vulgar and empty enough," in the words of the preface, "become, as she deals with them, the stuff of poetry and tragedy and art." In the later novels consciousness similarly works to transmute the raw material of the world, both by delaying recognition of disturbing truths and by consolingly renaming and thus remaking them. So in *The Ambassadors*, for example, Lambert Strether long manages to avoid conscious knowledge of Chad Newsome's illicit affair, preferring to believe Chad's elegant mistress a "good" woman and their liaison, in Little Bilham's polite phrase, "a virtuous attachment." And so Milly Theale in *The Wings of the Dove* refuses to acknowledge that she is dying, instead declaring herself "all right" and choosing to believe that survival is a question rather of the will than of the flesh. Yet if Milly nonetheless must die and Strether must finally admit the sexual facts he has been evading, the effect of such reversals is not merely ironic, nor are the beautiful fictions the characters project thereby proved merely fiction. Labeling the attachment as "virtuous" has enabled Strether to see and sensuously to appreciate its virtues; comically forced to abandon his belief in the lovers' technical abstinence from sex, he continues to imagine possible referents for "virtue" well beyond the narrow construction of the term in Woollett, Massachusetts. Although she has pronounced herself "all right" and willfully trusted in the good faith of those who deceive her, Milly dies with the knowledge of her betrayal; but her romantic assertions posthumously work to create their own truth, as Merton Densher makes his "lies" good by falling in love with her memory.

If "the real," as James defines it in the preface to *The American*, represents "the things we cannot possibly *not* know, sooner or later, in one way or another," then the structure of late Jamesian narrative repeatedly places illicit sexuality and betrayal, like death itself, among those real things we must inevitably know. But if "the romantic stands, on the other hand, for the things that . . . can reach us only through the beautiful circuit and subterfuge of our thought and our desire," then the very evasions and indirections of James's late style are that "beautiful circuit and subterfuge"— vehicle of "the things that . . . we never *can* directly know." In this sense James's late novels do not so much resolve the conflict between the romantic and the real as enact the interplay between them, paradoxically celebrating the power of art and language to "*make* life"—as he put it in a famous letter to H. G. Wells (1915) less than a year before his own death—and insisting on the inescapable conditions of life itself, stubbornly resisting the transforming power of art.

In these late masterpieces, James returns to the international theme with which he began, at once simplifying the essential structures of his earlier fiction, elaborating the drama of consciousness that now subsumes them, and intensifying their realist surface toward metaphor and symbol. With remarkable economy he redeploys old character-types and situations—the effort to exchange New World capital for Old World culture, the American innocents abroad and the European sophisticates who betray them—even as he translates them into the fully developed idiom of the late style and thus radically alters how they are to be read. The triangular relation of Isabel Archer, Madame Merle, and Gilbert Osmond in *The Portrait of a Lady*, for example, can be seen as the prototype of the central triangles in *The Wings of the Dove* and *The Golden Bowl*: in each case an innocent American heiress falls victim to a pair of lovers, themselves too poor to marry, who conceal their own past relations so that the man can woo the wealthy girl; in each case her discovery of the lovers' secret precipitates the crisis of the young woman's history. But the moral terms in which it still is possible to comprehend the earlier text seem profoundly inadequate for the later ones; by representing the consciousness of both "villain" and "victim" alike, and by granting even the most limited of characters a romantic imagination, the late style converts the moral and social conflicts of the earlier novels into dramas of knowledge, of vision, and of power. To read a character like Kate Croy as a mere hypocrite, whose beautiful surface conceals ugly depths, is to ignore the degree to which surface *is* depth in the late James—and to fail to appreciate Kate's "wonderful" plan as itself a "beautiful circuit and subterfuge," a means of sublimely transcending the inevitable limits her world imposes.

Of all the late fiction, *The Golden Bowl* makes most evident this move beyond moral judgment, as the unresolved critical debate over good and evil in the novel perhaps attests. By dividing his narrative into two nearly symmetrical "books," obliging the reader to view the adultery first through the eyes of the lovers and then of the injured wife, James compels a double perspective. Like Kate Croy and Merton Densher, the adulterers of *The Golden Bowl* have a way of beautifully naming and justifying their acts, and even more than *The Wings of the Dove*, the later novel demonstrates the culpability of the "innocent" victims: for a father and daughter to marry without giving up their intimacy with one another, purchasing with their American millions a sophisticated Prince as the daughter's husband, is virtually to ensure their own betrayal. But once she has discovered that betrayal, the heroine of *The Golden Bowl* differs from almost all her Jamesian predecessors by refusing the innocence of renunciation. Unlike Lambert Strether, for example, who preserves his superiority over the world he confronts by vowing "not, out of the whole affair, to have got anything for myself," and unlike

Milly Theale, who "turns her face to the wall" and dies, Maggie Verver chooses to fight for the husband she desires. The very intensity with which she does desire her husband, the fact that this heroine moves toward rather than away from sexual fulfillment, marks the novel's departure from its predecessors and James's own coming to terms, personally and imaginatively, with physical passion. Mastering the actress's art, learning willfully to manipulate and deceive, Maggie finally triumphs over Charlotte Stant— her husband's lover and her father's wife—by out-maneuvering and out-"humbugging" her rival. Though the symbolic golden bowl of the quartet's harmonious relation has been shattered, the Princess restores its gilded surface by pretending not to know what she knows—preserving the fiction of harmony by speaking of it as unbroken even as she leaves the reader uneasily aware of the price such harmony exacts. In this turn away from the search for knowledge toward the reimposition of an ambiguously consoling fiction, *The Golden Bowl* reverses the usual direction of Jamesian narrative, at the same time intensifying the vertiginous identification of surfaces and depths that the late style produces. And the titular bowl itself—read both as a slightly disreputable object and as a triumphant symbol—is at once a culminating instance of the novelist's own metaphor-making and a token of the characters' engagement in analogous acts of imaginative "conversion."

The second half of *The Golden Bowl* offers a rereading, a revision of the first, and in the last decade of his life James himself was multiply engaged in acts of revision: returning to the land of his origins in 1904–5 and recording its unsettling transformations in his ironic elegy, *The American Scene* (1907); selectively rewriting his earlier novels and tales for inclusion in the collected edition of his works, later known as the New York Edition (1907–17); retrospectively analyzing and accounting for the origins of those works in the prefaces that accompanied them; and looking back to his own beginnings in his autobiographical works—*A Small Boy and Others* (1913), *Notes of Son and Brother* (1914), and the uncompleted *The Middle Years* (1917). Indeed, the composite Portrait of the Artist that emerges from these revisions and from the prefaces to the New York Edition is arguably one of James's most influential achievements—a "work" that has not only shaped the terms of subsequent James criticism but deeply marked the twentieth century's idea of the novel, of literary criticism generally, and of the relation of the artist to his art. The image of the artist as a detached and sensitive observer, the celebration of fine consciousness, and the prefaces' more technical argument for restricting narrative point of view, all helped to shape modern literary theory and practice. Yet it is always important to recognize that James's own critical tenets, and certainly his narrative practices, were more subtle and various than some later systematizers would imply and that the prefaces themselves are neither summaries of the novels and tales to which they are attached nor even straightforward accounts of their origins, but supplemental fictions.

The New York Edition had its predecessors in the collected works of Honoré de Balzac and of Sir Walter Scott, but it is the self-consciousness and sophistication of the prefaces, the seriousness with which they took the novelist's work, that mark the transformation of storytelling into high art. The shaping of the New York Edition was in part a deliberate act of monument-making. But it would be an ironic legacy of James's achievement if the "Master of nuance and scruple," in W. H. Auden's splendid phrase, should be viewed too simply *as* the Master, the embodiment of aesthetic intelligence and civilized control. Like his near-contemporary, Sigmund Freud, Henry James understood that to study civilization was to investigate its anxieties and discontents—and the greatest of his works are intensely moving, even disturbing, representations of what he discovered.

Ruth Bernard Yeazell

Part Four

1910–1945

I. Contexts and Backgrounds

The Emergence of Modernism

"Modernism" now seems oddly remote, since the literary period it refers to is thought to have ended in the late 1930s or early 1940s. The word was first widely used in Germany in the 1890s, the decade in which modernism is said to have appeared. Unlike such terms as "romanticism" or "classicism," it does not refer to the qualities of works of art in a given period but simply suggests that they represent a break with the past. Since no such break can be complete, we must ask, when considering the various movements given this name, what it proposed to get rid of, what ideas about art and its place in society it employed, and what techniques were most often used by those associated with it. Historians assume that modernism is the consequence of the transformation of society brought about by industrialism and technology in the course of the nineteenth century. It was in the great urban centers of Europe that the pressures of modernity were most intensely felt, and it was in these cities that what many people viewed as the extravagant or shocking works of modernists were produced. The expressionists of the 1890s in Germany offer an example: here were city dwellers who took to the fields and shed their clothing in an almost parodic effort to shake off the social molds they found stifling and to recapture a primal freshness in experience.

In the Europe of the two decades before World War I, and at an accelerating pace thereafter, publicly recognized authority lost legitimacy, while the arts took on more and more of the job of defining the human horizon. The challenge they posed to church and state was less direct, but rather more effective in the long run than that of anarchists and social revolutionaries. Such movements as expressionism produced paintings and plays that startled their audiences, music that provoked riots. These outbursts testify to a lively awareness among the public that cherished conventions were threatened. Some of the impulses eddying out of expressionism found their way into politics, as in the satirical drawings of George Grosz in Germany. Other developments seemed totally nihilistic, attempts to break out of all existing social forms, shapes, and values at once, as in Dada, the creation of Tristan Tzara. Carried from Switzerland to Paris, where it became the progenitor of surrealism, it even reached New York in 1915, where, however, it hardly caused a ripple. Not all modernism was primitivist or an attempt at a blanket rejection of bourgeois reality. Marinetti's futurism went to the other extreme, cherishing technology as the promise of a new kind of consciousness.

We may glimpse the variety and intensity characteristic of European modernism in a passage on his childhood in Paris from Jacques Barzun's *The Energies of Art:* "To be born near the beginning of the decade before the first world war and at the center of the most advanced artistic activity in Paris is an accident bound to have irreversible consequences on the mind." As a youngster, Barzun had been surrounded by cubist paintings, had heard Stravinsky's music, been exposed to futurist and simultanist poetry, "modernistic" architecture, and had visited the studios of Duchamp and Villon, Gleizes and Metzinger. He describes what went on at home:

Every Saturday and Sunday and sometimes oftener, the stage was full: Marinetti acting and shouting, Archipenko making Léger roar with laughter, Delaunay and Ozenfant debating, Paul Fort declaiming his ballads, Varèse or Florent Schmitt surrounded at the piano. . . . On view at close range were also: Ezra Pound, Cocteau, Severini, Bérard, Kandinsky, Copeau, Bosschère, Polti, Milosz, Poeret, Brancusi, La Fresnaye, and many others fleeting or unremembered. Unquestionably, art and the discussion of art were the sole concern of all who counted in that particular universe.

Our curiosity is aroused by the presence of Ezra Pound. Can we distinguish what the experience of this scene might have meant to him, and to other Americans, as opposed to Europeans whose modernist impulses were reactions to, or efforts to break off from, European traditions?

A brief answer is that those usually spoken of as our early modernists, Henry James, Ezra Pound, T. S. Eliot, Gertrude Stein, William Carlos Williams, and others, inherited an American past that both empowered and constrained them in discernibly different ways. As far back as Emerson, who was born in 1803 and died in 1882, those Americans whose chief concerns were moral, intellectual, and literary had made wide claims for the capacity of individual human beings to define themselves through their own inner resources and create their own vision of existence without help from family, fellow citizens, or tradition. In Emerson's day, American culture was approaching imaginative domination by those who lived for money and profit. Possessed of the most fully endowed slice of the continent, and licensed by democracy and egalitarianism, the citizens of the United States had unequaled opportunities for the acquisition of personal wealth. Yet Emerson insisted that the individual who exploited his own inner powers could claim a far wider empire. Family ties and practical necessities were felt to be secondary concerns. Emerson's extravagant claim for the visionary self as against the acquisitive one is representative of an uneasy standoff that haunted Americans with intellectual and literary aspiration into the modernist period. One had to acknowledge the need to get a living, but it was held that those who put it first obscured and distorted their capacity for a wider vision of things.

To the extent that relationships with one's fellows were defined in monetary terms, rather than those of the family, the community, or the nation, each person's capacity to see others as fully present characters on a common stage was reduced. The answer both explicit and implicit in an Emerson is to say that the resulting isolation is native to us, rather than enforced by social conditions; that it is in fact the basis of our self-fulfillment: each of us must create a picture of the world for himself, and only after doing so may we hope—as Emerson liked to put it—to "meet again on a higher platform."

The making of a picture of the whole of things such individualism required was a lonely affair, and it has an important resemblance to the loneliness of the man seeking monetary profit: both are led to think of ties to other people and of the society at large impersonally; to distance themselves from others. This attempt to stand outside or above a culture to which one was nonetheless bound persisted into our own century, and shows up unmistakably in our early modernists. Writers who, like Nathaniel Hawthorne in his century, or William Faulkner among our modernists, see people as inescapably tied to each other are striking exceptions. For these two writers the human condition is as fatally distorted by those who claim an all-inclusive vision of things as by those who view the community chiefly as a set of conditions offering occasions for profit.

What for most of our early American modernists was seen as a continuing individual struggle was for European modernists an imaginative encounter with climactic historical change. What now appears to have been the essential aspect of that change—that Western civilization was more and more dominated by the search for profits—was, and for American writers had long been, a settled aspect of their condition. In this sense they were post-modern before modernism began in Europe.

No American may be said to have done what is characteristic of some of the greatest European modernists: so written as to enforce a realization of the bearing of the Western past on the present. As Stephen Spender puts it in describing European modernism: "This confrontation of the past with the present seems to me . . . the fundamental aim of modernism. The reason why it became so important was that, in the early stages of the movement, the moderns wish to express the *whole* experience of modern life." Another way of putting this is to note that the presumption that artists *could* offer a wholesale judgment of the Western past, while not unprecedented, had now become widely diffused. In James Joyce, Thomas Hardy, Joseph Conrad, Thomas Mann, and others there is an inclusive effort to encounter and assess the Western inheritance.

Americans who, like Henry David Thoreau and Herman Melville, had framed their work in nature, or in a judgment of the human condition in general, anticipate the impulse of our early American modernists to detach themselves from a culture in which, to adapt Melville's exacerbated protest, dollars damned them. This was not the declaration of a man inwardly an expatriate, who cherished the sense that he might find community elsewhere. All Melville's work testifies to his sense that all human beings were as alone as he. If public space had been preempted by money-getting activities he might still reach them in their solitude by writing about their common plight, a stance that later appears in writers as different as T. S. Eliot and Ernest Hemingway. European modernism was, by contrast, intensely aware of being in the forefront of momentous shifts in the cultural horizon, and eager to define the views of the past these shifts implied.

In Marcel Proust the effort to encounter the past is played out on the scale afforded by the growth of a single consciousness in which a social scene is reflected and its transformations are observed. In Thomas Hardy our recession from an assured sense of our relation to the cosmos in classical times is a recurring theme. In James Joyce's *Ulysses* and in much of the work of Thomas Mann, the represented scene is a culmination, the end result of a process that refers us back to Western origins. Joyce's novel created so strong an impression that the Western past had been imaginatively summed up and rendered that readers were led to speak of it as putting a full stop to the novel as a literary form—as if Joyce had landed us gasping in an eternal present. Misleading as this conclusion was, it was an understandable response to a book so successful in illluminating the presence of the past in daily life without appearing to diminish either past or present for the reader.

There were many other modes of registering a sense of profound cultural change, as the examples of Franz Kafka and Rainer Maria Rilke show. Although European modernism often conveys a sense that Western civilization is in a bad way, this conviction was compatible with, or perhaps provoked, the release of an extraordinary array of artistic energies.

Our early American modernists are far less enclosed by the awareness of changes in society, and rather more likely to echo the mid-nineteenth-century focus on the human condition. They wrote, as Lionel Trilling observed, at a greater remove from the idea of society. To see this continuity between Emerson, Thoreau, Whitman, and Melville and our first modernists, we require a fuller description of those who had earlier tried to define themselves without help from human others. What provoked these efforts, which Thoreau spoke of as the attempt to "build a self"?

The "commercial republic" foreseen by James Madison in *The Federalist* had indeed come into being, but neither Madison nor his contemporaries could have anticipated the speed with which the recognition of individual merit implicit in the republican ideal gave way to the impersonality of commercial transactions in the Jacksonian period. It was Alexis de Tocqueville who, in *Democracy in America* (1835–40), first saw that democracy and egalitarianism, beneficent in many ways, offered individuals radically diminished chances of securing a sense of their own inner worth, a satisfying identity. He concluded that, driven back on themselves, they would be forced to take refuge in the family, and that public recognition could only be assured by amassing money and property.

Emerson, Thoreau, and Whitman pushed this conclusion about the predicament of individual Americans to its limits. In works published from the mid-1830s to the 1850s they offered an extraordinarily inclusive countering assertion. They proposed that each individual was potentially capable of fashioning himself and building a total conception of the world. This was the social meaning of what we call "transcendentalism." These three held that their activity as speakers and writers might encourage others to realize themselves as well.

To write and speak as if one were at least potentially able to survey the human condition as a whole, and to claim that "nature" revealed it, involved the equally extravagant claim that the family and the community, no matter how much one might cherish some of their members, worked to fragment and distort the self's vision of the whole. Those whose world was defined by the parts they played on a social scene were thought to limit each other's capacities to embrace the whole of things.

The assertion that one was the child of some universal condition—of nature or of a divine power rather than of one's family or of the community—was not, of course, literally realizable. Yet it had important practical meanings. It made a virtue out of what might otherwise have seemed an isolation imposed on those who refused to define themselves in the ways the culture afforded. Another important consequence was that in granting the chance to realize a full humanity to individuals alone, the whole world became an object for the single self, the garden in which you alone were experiencing what was essential. If your example fired others they too would be isolated by their quest. Meanwhile they were denied a full humanity. As I have noted, "transcendentalism" shares the impersonality of the practices it opposed, the impersonality characteristic of the search for profits.

Thoreau's presumption that to see the world truly each individual must find a way of obtaining a subsistence that did not blur his vision of things offers a suggestive contrast with the assumptions of Karl Marx. In the 1840s Marx was beginning to work out his tremendous social drama, which was to climax in a new social order that, having guaranteed food, clothing, and shelter to all, would free people to pursue their highest interests. In the same decade, Thoreau, living at Walden Pond, was preparing to write the book in which he details his success in securing food, clothing, and shelter on terms that free him (and him alone) to carry out an exemplary expansion of his capacity to grasp reality, a reality that those who allow acquisition to absorb them cannot glimpse.

The Civil War demonstrated that the social arena could after all engulf those who had tried to keep aloof from it. Emerson and, even more emphatically, Thoreau found that an armed power based on slavery was a threat to their very conception of the individual's capacity to embrace the whole of things. Emerson called down blood and destruction in his journal, and Thoreau was a vehement subscriber to the murderous ethos of John Brown. Whitman, in the first two editions of *Leaves of Grass*, so completely identified the nation with himself, as a physical manifestation of his vision, that he tried frantically to imagine a way to hold it together, slavery and all. By the time war came he had surrendered his total vision. As his later editions and prose writings show, he had taken on the roles of lover and citizen, and had become a far shrewder commentator on the fate of the nation than Emerson or Thoreau. Yet, as Whitman and his literary intimates were aware, the "new man" he had loosed on the world in those first two editions of his poems, the poet who had proclaimed the "interior American republic," loomed over everything he subsequently wrote and said. As in the case of Emerson, it is Whitman's earlier and more assertive phase that gives him a representative importance in the history of our culture.

Despite the intervening literary movements we call "realism" and "naturalism," it was the imperial or world-possessing stance of Emerson, Thoreau, and Whitman that most of our early modernists adopted in judging American circumstances. This was hardly the result of direct emulation of these predecessors; it was rather the consequence of the persisting and increasing pressure to distance themselves from a commercial culture. We must, however, credit the mid-nineteenth-century figures with a fuller assurance as to the possible effects they might have on individual listeners or readers.

What they did was to put the struggle with acquisitiveness within the self, to turn a public issue to a private one, rejecting the hopes for a glorious collective destiny that many people still voiced before the Civil War. The question: what sort of values ought to define our nation? becomes in their writings: how can each of us found a self free from individual greed? Clearly, the majority of the population was too busy getting a living to be much burdened by such a question, but the relatively self-conscious minority whom Emerson addressed were pleased to be told that they had inner resources sufficient to construe the world in a way that firmly subordinated the marketplace.

But if only the socially unfettered individual could apprehend universal values, it followed that the self was sole arbiter on questions of morals, politics, and—not incidentally—relations between the sexes and the nature of manhood and womanhood. Since Emerson could not conceive of women except as bound to the reciprocal duties imposed by motherhood and the care of the household, he saw them as fatally immersed in the society and incapable of self-reliance. This denial of a full humanity to women sometimes embarrassed him, as his journal shows. The fact that he clung to it is an index of his desperate need to believe in the possibility of a wholly independent selfhood. Another formidable contradiction of the realities of the life he and others were living lay in the fact that he and his audience were inescapably involved in the world of work. Like Thoreau and Whitman, he praised the energy, skill, and imagination of the individuals who were taking possession of the continent, while deprecating the search for profits that motivated so much of their effort. He thought of individuals as both visionary and practical, but the middle ground of associated life, the scene of history and fiction, was, as far as possible, canceled and swept bare.

Whitman had written fiction in his prentice years; Emerson's early journals show that he was as saturated in Walter Scott's novels as his contemporaries. But both writers came to feel, as did Thoreau, that fiction entangled the almost godlike self in the web of social roles, and blinded one to universal truths. Like history, fiction implied that, since you were determined by the past, you could not build your own world. What these three said and wrote aimed at the exemplary rather than the dramatic. What they offered others was an example of the creative self taking imaginative possession of the world on its own terms. Emerson called this "provocation," as distinct from instructing others, which implied coercion; Whitman spoke of "indirection," that is, of offering a sample of the awareness evidenced by his "new man"; Thoreau's *Walden* is an extended illustration of one man's unaided effort to achieve the fullest possible grasp of his world.

Moby-Dick is a fiction, yet it shares the bias against dramatic encounter within society as the scene of significant human activity. Although Melville gives a very full account of the practical activity of whaling, his primary stress is on the attempts of individuals to construct the world for themselves. Both Ishmael and Ahab are visionaries. Such dramatic encounters as we find in the novel, between Ishmael and Queequeg, Ahab and the crew, and the final scene between Starbuck and Ahab, are firmly subdued to the display of exemplary attitudes.

Most of the first generation of American modernists were forced, like their mid-nineteenth-century predecessors, to create identities removed from the world of business. It is not surprising that the first American whom students of the period usually call a modernist, Henry James, furnishes the most important link between modernism and the generation of his father and Emerson, since the novelist was committed to an art that reveals the spiritual poverty of the greedy. His absorption in European accomplishments gave rise to an exquisite awareness of what was beyond Emerson's ken: he could see just how the artist's execution produced its effects. But his judgment of works of art was focused less on their place in history than on their exhibition of something relatively timeless, the generic qualities of humanity, the kinds of consciousness discernible in their makers and admirers.

He was led to feel that our humanity might safely be confided to the keeping of art, that formal expression was the best evidence we had of the possibilities of human fulfillment. He became the first modernist to appropriate European culture for the uses of American individualism. This was a step beyond the horizon open to Emerson or Thoreau, who had no such faith in the powers of art; it was also a retreat common to American modernism: Emerson and Thoreau had tried, as had Whitman, to offer nothing less than an inciting example of self-creation. What James did share with them was the belief that the quality of our individual consciousness—*how* we know—is more important than any inventory of what is out there to be known.

James, then, is as modernist as he can be, since he believes in the capacity of art to institute a civilization; he is also an American in the mode of Emerson because he was determined to represent individual consciousness as triumphing over acquisitive impulses in the self and society. Like his "transcendentalist" predecessors he had been born into a culture in which one's relation to money values, to the commercial character of the society, was more determinative of one's outlook than citizenship, organized religion, or any other aspect of the life of the nation. One defined oneself through accepting or endeavoring to reject business as the predominant force in the country's life.

As a young man James had had hopes that the independent spirit and the "moral spontaneity" he found among his countrymen, and, in still higher degree, among his countrywomen, might prevail over business. But on his return to the United States in 1904 after an absence of nearly a quarter of a century, he came to feel that democracy and egalitarianism had removed all the barriers to the ascendancy of commerce, the barriers that "squire and parson" were still trying to preserve in England. The phrase occurs in *The American Scene* (1907), a book founded on his tour.

James makes an excursion to the New Jersey shore and observes that the large, bewindowed houses of the vacationing rich all face outward as if to show themselves as expensive rather than to provide their owners with "the supremely expensive thing," a "constituted privacy"—or, we may put it, a richly furnished interior life of their own. James finds an "illustrative importance" in the spectacle:

For what did it offer but the sharp interest of the match everywhere and everlastingly played between the short-cut and the long road?—an interest never so sharp as since the short-cut has been able to find itself endlessly backed by money. Money in fact *is* the short-cut—or the short-cut money; and the long road having, in the instance before me so little operated for the effect, as we may say, of the cumulative, the game remained all in the hands of its adversary.

If, as James has it, an achieved civilization is represented by buildings and works of art that testify to distinctive human powers, what is one to make of a country whose most prominent structures, New York's skyscrapers, are erected for profit, and then demolished the moment they cease to pay?

For James, the American use of the "short-cut" so apparent in his country's speech, manners, press, architecture, and destructive treatment of its landscape was far from being a fresh revelation. The "match everywhere and everlastingly played" had all along been his central theme. Since the 1870s he had aspired to the splendid unselfishness of the artist as described by his father: the artist abandoned all personal claims on the world and sought to dissolve the selfishness native in all of us by creating forms that widened and enriched the consciousness of his readers.

The elder Henry James, a theologian who was a contemporary and friend of Emerson, devoted his life to the effort to describe the extended process of creation, not as the work of six days, but as the history of mankind: our common destiny was to rid ourselves of individual greed and come to the apocalyptic realization that God had descended into each of us so that we might all come to see that the whole world was a reflection of our own glorious nature—a possession shared by everybody.

The elder Henry James was often impatient with Emerson because he had no conception of the greed that shadowed and enclosed all people from birth, until they realized that what lay about them was not to be owned but to be loved and celebrated. The novelist described his father's millennial hope as a moment in time when, with "a turn of the inward wheel," we were all to realize our godhead in a universal spiritual socialism. The elder James found Emerson an innocent; he saw him as blithely unconscious of this passage from selfishness to selflessness, since Emerson assumed that if each of us simply looked within he would find himself already elected a celebrant of the universal rather than a possessor. Nonetheless, Emerson's goal and that of the novelist's father have much the same consequence: everybody is in the end to enjoy an imaginative possession of everything.

The novelist Henry James is not simply the first American whom we describe as a modernist; he also carries forward what was central in the work of Emerson, Thoreau, Whitman, and Melville: the assumption that the individual could attain a kind of secular transcendence, could judge the world from a perspective wider than that offered by society and history. The overriding need to assert such powers in the self is even more directly visible in James than in his mid-century predecessors: the struggle between the greedy and those who offer the world a widened consciousness is at the heart of those works of his that are now most highly praised. To understand how this thematic concern is related to James's fictional technique in these works, and to see how they relate to modernism and its emphasis on the separate realm of art, we must consider the fictional technique known as the "point of view."

The term was used by J. W. Beach in 1918 to point to James's use of a fictional device: the narration of the work through the consciousness of a single character, or a succession of such characters within the work. In James such narrators are not neutral registers of an action but participants in a situation; their particular qualities are very much in question. What James has done is to shift the focus of the novelist's concern from attention to the events of a fictional world to the question: how is this scene being perceived? The connection of this device with the writer's fundamental beliefs, and the moral question it raises, are often ignored. Laurence Holland, one of James's most accomplished readers, did maintain that James had indeed sacrificed himself to his work with moral and political ends in view, but Holland denied that this had anything to do with the beliefs of the elder James or a distinctive American attitude. But it is in fact James's use of "point of view" that seals the connection between him and his father and Emerson, as well as between him and other members of the first generation to react strongly to America's commercial culture.

Locating a surrogate "author" within the work was, James argued, a way of preserving the integrity of narrative form, which is shattered by the interpositions of an omniscient author, or by the author's creation of a fictional scene in which a number of ways of rendering experience appeared together, reflecting not a single intelligence, but the randomness or incoherence of daily life. If a character within the work is made responsible for the reader's sense of it, the narrative is safely enclosed from the surrounding chaos of existence. The method is singularly adramatic, in the sense that it subdues all other centers of consciousness to their reflection in the one that is seeking a grasp of the whole situation. Yet in James's hands the accretion of awareness on the part of this central sensibility, now foiled or deliberately blocked by the acquisitive characters, and again opening out into a fuller vista on the situation, culminates in a command of the widest awareness available to the inner author James has circumscribed for us. This becomes a fascinating game: a peopled sample of the "match everywhere and everlastingly played," between the generous creative consciousness and those who take the "short-cut," in pursuit not simply of money but of every form of acquisitiveness. For James acquisition takes many forms: sexual, as in the appropriation of women; moral, as in self-righteousness; social, as in the claim to fixed status; and still other kinds of spiritual hoarding, like that of the tourist who boasts of impressions, or clutches at Shakespearean memorabilia at Stratford, as if the genius of Shakespeare could somehow be owned.

The acceptance on the part of American readers of James's extraordinary panache—his proposal of the superiority of the point of view as a mode of fictional construction—which carries with it the thoroughly Emersonian presumption that only the consciousness that embraces the whole presented scene deserves our assent and respect—is an acceptance that tells us something about his American admirers as well as about James. They delighted in the triumph of a lone consciousness over acquisitiveness. What, after all, was James objecting to when he condemned the novels of his contemporaries as messy, random, and incoherent?

What James objected to was not simply acquisitiveness but those reciprocal ties between people which make up the life of society. The authors who, as James saw it, made concessions to the incoherence of experience were in fact testifying to their immersion in concerns their readers shared with them: the love affair, marriage, material or political success, births, deaths, inheritances, the life one led in a newly urbanized world, the conduct of business, and so on. James's internal authors subordinated these matters to an Emersonian individualism, a world that could be judged simply on the basis of a single issue: which view of the situation represented in the narrative widens consciousness, and which is expressive of self-serving desire?

Far from being simply technical, James's device serves an end similar to one we find in Emerson, Thoreau, and Whitman; it too offers an exemplary assurance that we can overcome our acquisitive instincts. James uses point of view to bring us nose to nose with the horrors greed gives rise to within and around us. He poses the infinite claims of consciousness, which unites us all, against the horde of merely personal desires.

The wonderful variety and precision of James's capacity to catch and render the appearance and atmosphere of people and places has been often and properly praised. But his fiction characteristically avoids direct presentation of such deep personal commitments as that of husband to wife or parent to child, except as these are expressive of love or greed within the single self. Thus denatured, women could be put to emblematic use as greedy Eves, who practice and counsel acquisition, like Kate Croy and Charlotte Stant, or as such self-sacrificing figures as May Bartram in "The Beast in the Jungle," Alice Staverton in "The Jolly Corner," or Milly Theale in *The Wings of the Dove*, who stand ready to become a loving conscience that replaces selfish impulses in the men to whom they are attached. James did not employ the device of the central consciousness in all his works, but he chose to cap his career with a novel in which two emblematic Americans finally resolve the struggle between loving creativity and personal acquisitiveness.

The Golden Bowl (1904) contributes a happy ending to James's account of the career of consciousness. It is a tale of triumph over a commercial culture and its root in individuals, a greed generic in the species. The end of this "novel" realizes the moment when, in Emerson's phrase, "we shall meet again on a higher platform," and rejoice in a world that reflects a nature common to us all. James's final American, Adam Verver, once more marries an "Eve," Charlotte Stant, who is, when the book ends, compelled to sing the praises of wholly unselfish creation, represented by the massed works of art in Adam's supreme collection, housed in "American City." Prince Amerigo, whose family history exhibits centuries of unbridled acquisitiveness, is wholly informed by his love for Maggie, Adam Verver's daughter. A descendant of Amerigo Vespucci, he becomes the true discoverer of America, or rather, the discoverer of the true America. He is redeemed by a vision of humanity transformed by love—that is, by seeing himself, an epitome of all mankind, through Maggie's eyes.

In this novel James permitted himself to imagine an end to "the match everlastingly played" between creative love and the world of money. If we are to enter into the fable we must be content to imagine ourselves bundled into the Prince, our universal representative. Since the Prince has been subdued to Maggie, as Charlotte has been to Adam, and since James is the maker of the whole affair, we must think of him as claiming an imaginative dominion no less extensive than those Emerson and Thoreau aspired to, and that Whitman liked to say he had already won. Like these forerunners, James offers his readers a position from which they may grasp the whole scene, at the expense of sacrificing all reciprocal relationships. James offers, that is, a prospect contrived for the single viewer, for an Emersonian American. Society as we know it in the European novels of Balzac, Flaubert, and Zola barely appears. A lone writer is addressing readers who share an Emersonian remoteness from their society. The "difficulty" many readers find in the prose of the late James—and in much modernist poetry—is a hedge that announces and defends an isolation that both writers and readers feel as their actual situation in the culture.

Henry James's contemporary, Henry Adams, offers an illuminating contrast. Adams, a scion of ambassadors and presidents, wrote an excellent narrative history of the early American republic (1891). He had, perhaps inevitably, associated his identity and the significance of the work he did with the development of the republic his family had served. Overtaken by domestic misfortune, and what he regarded as the disastrous decline in public integrity that accompanied a rising industrialism, he wrote the two books by which he is now best known, *Mont-Saint-Michel and Chartres* (1904) and *The Education of Henry Adams* (1907). In the first of these two books a magnificent concretion of distinctively human energies focused on the Virgin results in the building of Chartres; in the second Adams is confronted by a society that is undergoing a rapid dehumanization, symbolized by the impersonal force of the dynamo. Within this antithesis, however, is a more immediately felt personal predicament: the disappearance of public life as a basis for the writer's identity. Adams's response to his life was rather widely shared among fortunate and cultivated Americans at the end of the century, some of whom made similar efforts to find in other cultures or in early times—that of Dante, for example—more humanly fulfilling models of society.

Our first modernists are much more closely akin to Emerson, Thoreau, and Whitman. Their kinship shows in their common assumption, so different from that of Adams, that they were not caught up in their culture, which they tended to view ahistorically and *en bloc*. What separated them from it was their determination not to be defined by its commercial character. When, late in Henry James's career, such representative American modernists as Ezra Pound, Gertrude Stein, and T. S. Eliot appeared, the American writer who meant most to them was James, in whom the practice of his art was united with a character of unwavering integrity.

The seriousness, the degree of dedication, these three and certain others brought to the craft of writing (notably two who were close to Pound before he settled abroad, William Carlos Williams and Hilda Doolittle—the poet known as "H. D."—as well as Robert Frost) cannot be fully explained. The example of Henry James counted for something, but knowledge of French poets and critics was perhaps more important. Some credit ought surely to be given to the institution Pound was so fond of denouncing, the university; all five of those named had for varying periods of time gone either to the University of Pennsylvania or Harvard. They shared the conviction that art mattered profoundly, but, unlike Henry James, they did not begin their work with any inclusive assurance about the set of values art served, and their American origins made it inevitable that finding such an assurance was not, as it was for European artists, defining a place within—or against— one's own historical epoch. Nor was it to begin where Emerson had, as a member of the first generation to offer an inclusive denial of the values of the commercial republic. Yet their relation to the country was just as much a problem, since the United States had not so much changed its character as intensified that aspect that Emerson had rejected two generations before.

The solutions Williams, Pound, and Eliot found to the question of their identity and the significance art had in the world were in each case distinct, yet they shared a common root. What did it mean to be a writer in, or from, if you lived abroad, the United States? You saw yourself as set apart from a nation predominantly concerned with business. A Frenchman, Italian, or Englishman might well have found it difficult to make such a wholesale judgment, but the commercial republic was in fact a less complicated spectacle. A sense of their detachment was, at any rate, the response of these three writers, who might well have agreed with Henry James's remark that in turn-of-the-century America the office of the language was chiefly that of facilitating commercial transactions.

William Carlos Williams, the most self-consciously American of these three poets, wrote one of the books that most fully expose the stressed state of those who sought to be both Americans and poets in his time. *In the American Grain*, a prose work of 1925, ranks with D. H. Lawrence's *Studies in Classic American Literature* (1922) and Constance Rourke's *American Humor* (1931) as an early effort to describe a nation in which individuals had observably been forced to do more of the work of self-definition for themselves than was the case in Europe. The writers of these three books were arrested by a sense of the isolate quality of the American's personal existence. Williams's book attempts to overcome that isolation; it eroticizes the very landscape. Figures capable of touching and making love take on a heroic evaluation in contrast with the hard impermeable shells that surround individuals whom Williams thinks of as repressed "Puritans," a derogatory label current in the 1920s. His countrymen are seen as incapable of living in accord with the glorious spectacle of generative life that the continent had once offered them, and might still if they would stop befouling it with the sludge of moneymaking.

In the American Grain is an attempt to close the gap that separates us from each other, an almost frantic burrowing into the past for instances in which heroic figures had achieved an imaginative grasp of the continent and its original inhabitants, and for men and women whose union might serve as an example of form-creating energy—the kind of union Williams suggests in his account of the meeting of Aaron Burr and Jacataqua, leader of her Indian tribe. He associates the defeat of sexual energy with a blockage of the imagination; he is especially vehement about the denial and distortion of the capacities of women. He writes in his exclamatory vein: "Emily Dickinson, starving in her father's garden, is the very nearest—starving—Never a woman: never a poet. That's an axiom."

We may feel less assured now than Williams did in 1925 that the release of sexual and imaginative energy will create a culture that will erase the gap between us. But we recognize what has widened the gap and hardened the shells that enclose us when he writes, two paragraphs further on:

Our life drives us apart and forces us upon science and invention—away from touch. Or if we do touch, our breed knows no better than the coarse fiber of football.

Though Bill Bird [a publisher he had met in Paris] says that Americans are the greatest business men in the world: the only ones who understand the passion of making money: absorbed, enthralled in it. It's a game. To me it is because we fear to wake up that we play so well. Imagine stopping money making. Our whole conception of reality would have to be altered.

A conception of reality rooted in "money making" had permeated the language; Williams undertook to scrub off these accretions so that people and things could once more be seen clearly, called forth by a use of words as bright, hard, and shining as pebbles on the bed of a brook.

Williams's exemplary uses of words have the effect of clogging his effort to convey the flow of life and the transformations of human energy in his long poem, *Paterson*, published in sections (1946–58). From Whitman's viewpoint it would be judged a failure because its pages are strewn with verbal artifacts, made things detached from the omnipresent maker who presides in Whitman's work. We cannot imagine Whitman sharing our pleasure in the wonderfully grainy and evocative flashes with which things and people present themselves in Williams from the 1920s on. But he would have been in fundamental accord with Williams's search for an American "measure," a verse form to supplant those to which, as Williams thought, T. S. Eliot remained tied. This is a signal likeness to Whitman because it carries a crucial implication: this vast object, the United States, is in the process of formation as a whole, a thing to be apprehended by an equally comprehensive subject. If a contemporary European had voiced such an ambition he would have appeared ridiculous, but Williams persists in the search for a national measure, for a voice that complements the whole she-bang. This is not definitive of his accomplishment as a poet; rather it points to the effect of a limitation: seeing one's country as an object, one has to invent a maker sufficient to cope with that totality. Williams is both freed and constrained by this demand, which is also apparent in two modernists who did not stay in this country but were likewise affected by it, Ezra Pound and T. S. Eliot.

That both carried such an individualistic limitation abroad with them, and were on that account "postmodern" when they met European modernism, is a fact Lyndall Gordon and others have established in the case of Eliot, though the issue remains largely unexplored in the case of Pound, whose admirers generally feel that Pound's American origins count for little. The prime fact about the cultural situation in Europe when Pound arrived there in 1909, and Eliot in 1914, had been shaping individual American lives for at least two generations. It was nothing less than a cultural horizon almost ringed by questions of money.

The youthful Ezra Pound, our first self-conscious modernist, was equipped with a remarkably keen ear for the qualities of verse. He had ransacked the Western past for voices he judged alive in a number of languages, and was a tireless advocate of the talents of contemporaries he found worthy. His own considerable merits as a poet are less in point here than his faith in language as a medium of exchange, and the relation of that faith to his American birth and upbringing. Long sections of his major work, *The Cantos* (1925–59), are devoted to American figures, Thomas Jefferson, John Adams, and Martin Van Buren among them. But Pound's admirers have been too much interested in his achievements as a poet to bring his relation to American culture into focus, in particular his conviction that the struggle with the National Bank conducted by Jackson and Van Buren was the crucial event in nineteenth-century American history. For Pound, language was like money in that both were means of exchange, and both could be debased; our humanity depended on the transmission of meaning or significance, that is, on exchange, whether of words, goods, or money.

Pound's view of what language does for us may be called naïve in the extreme, not because it is wholly wrong, but because it asks more of language than it can ever give. One may put it simply: neither works of art nor other ways of transmitting significance like dollars and computers can ever adequately define us because we are as a species still busy changing ourselves and our world. Yet in *The Cantos* our humanity depends wholly on a currency of meanings sufficiently stable to hold our world together: meanings that make up a realized or fulfilled humanity. Pound did not feel that such a structure of awareness was wholly inclusive; it might be but a shining platform in the surrounding darkness, but there was no other standpoint, our endowment was fixed. Emerson had asked us to transform ourselves in order to possess the world in vision; Pound's attention falls not so much on the potentialities of individuals as on our employment of the social means that bind us together. Both writers make an inclusive demand on us; they are equally exorbitant in claiming that our sense of reality must be reshaped, and equally ready to gut history for timeless examples that accord with their views. But, unlike Emerson, Pound finds himself enclosed by a society in which, as he sees it, a false monetary currency contends with genuine exchange, and broken and distorted verbal meanings must be replaced by full and precise meanings. He has no quarrel with the use of a medium of exchange that represents actual goods that fulfill human needs. His most scathing denunciations of the power of money are directed at those who create values out of thin air, as bankers do by lending more than they have.

Pound's tacit claim to power, the extent to which he appropriated both past and present for his imaginative use, seems no less inclusive than Whitman's, and quite as representative of American individualism. Whitman, however, insisted that we emulate him while Pound contended with social practice. Convinced that nothing less than the absolute power of a Chinese emperor could enforce the stability of meanings required to preserve and enhance our humanity, Pound moved steadily toward fascism. Even in this impulse we recognize something American; we have long been inclined to make disproportionate claims on reality precisely because of our fear of being saturated by economic motivations.

T. S. Eliot's relation to his American origins, masked by his deliberate assumption of English traits, is less easy to discern, although he is actually closer to Emerson than to Pound, in whose imagination the quality of our immediate social surroundings had a much more important place. Both men had an indubitable influence in the history of English modernism; both served as catalysts, provoking change, first Pound, who had been busy for five years when Eliot arrived, and then—with an effect that endured longer—Eliot. Before they appeared in London they had, in their separate ways, been profoundly affected by recent French poetry and criticism. Their discovery of fresh possibilities in the use of language and of critical opinions that cut through the fog of encumbering poetic practices proved immensely enlivening to them. Having carried to Europe the sense of detachment or distance from history that the relatively undifferentiated spectacle of their own culture had inspired in them, they found the European past a wonderful warehouse, a resource open to exemplary uses by a poet seeking an identity. Like Emerson, both Pound and Eliot tended to see history as meaningful primarily as a parable of their own "being and becoming."

The part Eliot played in the modernist ferment of his time turns out in retrospect to have been misleading to many people on both sides of the Atlantic. When *The Waste Land* appeared in 1922 it was felt not simply to be a great poem but a testimony to a cultural despair that marked, as did the work of European modernists, the recognition of a profound social change, the end of a historical epoch. As recent studies have shown, however, Eliot's life exhibits a continuing struggle for religious assurance. This preoccupation with the manifestations of the eternal in the Western past consorts with his American individualism and reminds us of the youthful Emerson's efforts to assure himself of the sufficiency of Christianity. Eliot was not so much testifying to a sense that an epoch was ending when he wrote *The Waste Land* as illustrating the fact that when a poet of genius sets about showing that the world is vicious and empty without God any age will offer abundant evidence.

In Eliot's plays as well as in his poems, we encounter characters who claim nothing less than a total view of the human condition. Eliot's emphasis, like Emerson's, is always on an individual's inward transformation. Emerson, Thoreau, and Whitman had limited themselves to the exemplary mode, largely forgoing the effort to act directly on others, primarily because their claim to a wider sense of things than was available within society meant that it was meaningless to contend with society at all. They were passive in relation to public issues, a tendency in which they anticipate both Eliot and his uniquely illumined central characters.

Yet there is an important difference between Eliot and these earlier Americans. Eliot had taken refuge in England, hoping that Christian aspiration would continue to be given public recognition there. When this hope proved delusive Eliot's exacerbated sense of the need to preserve authority that might foster belief led him to proclaim himself "classicist in literature, royalist in politics, and Anglo-Catholic in religion." This set of labels both acknowledges tradition and—because it is strikingly out of accord with the times—distances Eliot from his historical moment. It makes a claim on reality that rivals the extravagance of Emerson's assertion of total self-reliance. Despite Eliot's assumed Englishness, what remains clearly visible is his persisting American need to make a self removed from the aspect of the Western world that the United States had first come to embody, in which, as Eliot put it, "the acquisitive, rather than the creative and spiritual instincts are encouraged."

Modernism is a term open to attack in an age that questions the prevailing literary canon as too narrow and exclusive. Few writers are called modernists, and those few have been given the status of an elite. This chapter offers evidence that the gap between individual Americans lamented by William Carlos Williams was present in Emerson's time as well as his own, and that it was bound to widen in a commercial republic with no strong opposing tendencies. The visionary who claimed a grasp of the whole did not close that gap. He simply proclaimed that his vision was the source of an authentic identity that could not be gained from seeking possessions. The mid-nineteenth-century writers, and those modernists who share their world-possessing position, do not, in this light, appear an arbitrarily chosen elite, but, rather, representatives of a recurrent response to an underlying cultural condition: to oppose the mere piling up of bits of the world and mortgages on its future, they asserted imaginative possession of the whole.

No such imaginative leap had been taken in Europe. The ascendancy of commerce, which, although growing fast, was but a single aspect of the culture in Europe, loomed over all others in the United States, and became so pervasive that neither Christianity nor the republican ideal could withstand it. Americans were more alone with money than were Europeans. They had a much greater measure of personal freedom, but its exercise was increasingly limited to the marketplace. Nineteenth-century European literature is of course shot through with brilliantly realized studies of the effects of commerce and industrialism on society and the individuals who composed it. Yet these works, and those of the modernists who succeeded them, were launched *within* a social milieu, and directed to it, whether their aim was a wide assessment of the past, an assault on outmoded conventions or social injustice, or an attempt at wholesale cultural destruction.

The Americans whose response to their culture was to deny that family, society, and history were the compelling sources of their awareness of the world had, from the European point of view, discarded all there was to think or write about. Europeans could hardly have guessed how massive and undifferentiated a few percipient Americans found the spectacle of their culture. Yet it is difficult to see how those few could have responded to what they saw with anything less than a massive blanketing assertion of their own. A self sufficiently commanding could create a picture of things in which possessions were insignificant. History might then appear, as Emerson put it, an account of "one's own being and becoming."

Except for certain writers whose representation of life is direct and dramatic (I would include Emily Dickinson in her century, and William Faulkner and Robert Frost in our own), our early modernists were limited as well as freed by their efforts to stand outside our culture. William Carlos Williams saw this half a century ago. In *In the American Grain* he insists that only those who are in touch with each other and the past can hope to deal with the dominance that possessions have assumed in the imaginations of Americans.

Quentin Anderson

Intellectual Life and
Public Discourse

In March 1939, as the American people struggled with the Great Depression and tottered on the edge of a second world war, the United States proudly unveiled a world's fair on an open marshland along the outer reaches of New York City. The 1939 New York World's Fair celebrated a streamlined future in exhibits that included a model of a rocket capable of shooting a projectile from New York to London, a television set as the cultural center of the American home, and a preview of "Democracity," an elaborate model of "a perfectly integrated, futuristic metropolis," in which average Americans would devote unprecedented amounts of leisure time to highly organized, socially engineered activities rather than to what its designers called the "dissipated idleness or carousing" of previous generations. Yet the fair's most popular exhibit was the General Motors building, featuring a richly detailed projection of American life in 1960. In a fifteen-minute simulated flight over the United States, visitors observed ultrasophisticated—and ultrasonic—modes of transportation, vast stretches of glass-covered ripened orchards, and skyscrapers piercing the clouds over futuristic cities. Although they clashed with the chaotic financial and social realities that loomed beyond the gates of the fair, these exhibits proclaimed the American people's deep faith that technological prowess would ensure their bright future. In addition, the exhibits also demonstrated just how extensively the nation's cultural consciousness had been transformed during the first four decades of the twentieth century.

Even as it expressed the collective commitment of the United States to building a productive consumer society in which every citizen, in principle if not in practice, would have equal access to the benefits of the country's prodigious technological power, the 1939 World's Fair belied a host of un-settling transformations, involving unprecedented redefinitions of self-iden-tity as well as radically new ways of experiencing time, space, work, and leisure. Virtually everything seemed uncertain in the new consumer society that was emerging, including the difficult task of securing a reliable sense of one's own "place" in the world.

The public discourse of the period at once engaged and reflected the difficulty of fashioning a functioning, durable self in a culture driven by corporate entrepreneurial interests. This difficulty found powerful expres-sion in the literature of the period—in the fiction of Theodore Dreiser, Frank Norris, Sherwood Anderson, Jack London, Sinclair Lewis, John Dos Passos, F. Scott Fitzgerald, Ernest Hemingway, Nathanael West, and Zora Neale Hurston; in the poetry of "H. D." (Hilda Doolittle), T. S. Eliot, and Ezra Pound; and in the works of a host of minor novelists, poets, drama-tists, and writers of popular literature. Yet what is most striking is the extent to which this issue pervaded virtually every aspect of the daily life of both intellectuals and ordinary citizens—in print, on the air, and on the screen.

Of all the tensions in American life, one of the most basic was that be-tween an agrarian America that drew its values from a domestic tradition of nineteenth-century Jeffersonianism and an urban, industrial America that drew its values from an international network of rapidly changing eco-nomic, technological, and social developments. The intellectual currents of the period were infused with the tension between production and consump-tion, between earning and spending, between work and leisure, between abundance and scarcity. Corporate enterprise helped spread the spirit of consumption throughout American culture, and it played a major role in altering the general public's ways of thinking about self-identity and artic-ulating personal values. Eventually, even culture itself became a commod-ity. In the early decades of the new republic, America had searched anx-iously for a distinctive, indigenous culture; in the early twentieth century it became a highly self-conscious society, absorbed in itself, eager to read about and to discuss itself, its problems, and its potential.

During the early decades of the twentieth century, American intellectual life and public discourse displayed all the symptoms of a mid-life crisis. On the surface, signs of material and social progress were everywhere apparent. By every measurable standard, Americans were better educated, better paid, and generally "better off" than at any other period in the nation's history. This was, as Thorstein Veblen had suggested in *The Theory of the Leisure Class* (1899), an era of "conspicuous consumption." Even during the years of the Great Depression, Americans produced—and consumed—more goods, including manufactured experiences, than any people in the world. A collective will to believe in their own potential unified the American people. Yet beneath the booster spirit and the veneer of public confidence there lurked old, irrepressible anxieties about the nature, purpose, and direction of individual and collective identities, values, and actions. "We are unsettled to the very roots of our being," the critic and cultural commentator Walter Lippmann observed in *The New Republic* in 1914. "There isn't a human relation, whether of parent and child, husband and wife, worker and employer, that doesn't move in a strange situation."

The nation's youthful confidence in its political ideals and its naïve faith in traditional cultural values had begun to weaken during the Civil War and continued to erode during the flush times of the Gilded Age. By the outbreak of World War I, Americans' traditional relationship to nature, for example, had changed substantially. As Lewis Mumford has demonstrated in his remarkable four-volume analysis of the physical and social transformation of the city into the "megalopolis" (see especially *Technics and Civilization* [1934] and *The Culture of Cities* [1938]), the vast expanses of land that had served for well over three centuries to shape the American character no longer remained the primary locus for defining this nation's distinctive experience. The once open, horizontal stretches of the countryside were giving way to vertical, multileveled office towers and smokestacks. In the new nation, economic growth depended more on an industrial worker's punching a daily time-card than on a farmer's cultivating the land in harmony with nature's slow-paced seasonal clock. The ideal of the self-reliant, rugged individualist of the American frontier tradition yielded to the ideal of the faithful employee—a resolute breadwinner whose self-identity was often determined by the corporate interests he labored to serve.

Harriet Monroe, the founding editor of *Poetry* magazine, described this tension in an editorial in the journal's first issue, in October 1912. "The world grows greater day by day," she observed, "as every member of it, through something he buys or knows or loves, reaches out to the ends of the earth." Monroe's efforts to create a public role for poetry in modern life presupposed "a world whose great deeds, whose triumphs over matter, over the wilderness, over racial enmities and distances, require [poetry's] ever-living voice to give them glory and glamour." Yet Harriet Monroe also recognized just how fragile self-identity could be in early twentieth-century America, at a time when "things precious to the race, things rare and delicate, may be overpowered, lost in the criss-cross of modern currents, the confusion of modern immensities." In the decades leading to World War

II, public discourse chronicled the nation's efforts to come to terms with these confusions by positing a renewed and more durable sense of individual and collective identity amidst what William James called "a teeming multiplicity of objects and relations."

James's words might well also be read as symptomatic of the dramatic shift in American culture that spanned the late nineteenth and early twentieth centuries. During most of its first century, the United States had been a nation in which people searched for products in order to survive. By the mid-1920s, however, the United States had become a nation in which products were being pushed on people from every side. What one consumed suddenly seemed more important than what one produced. In the course of these exchanges, American culture itself became a purchasable commodity. In the section on "Commodity" in his essay *Nature* (1836), Ralph Waldo Emerson had offered a magnanimous view of America's "useful arts" in serving its citizens and ministering to their needs. "The private poor man hath cities, ships, canals, bridges, built for him," Emerson observed, before he proceeded to envision a world in which everyday chores are simplified by a combination of American energy and ingenuity. By the early twentieth century, however, at least one of Emerson's propositions in this essay—"A man is fed, not that he may be fed, but that he may work"— seemed well on its way to being reversed. By trading on this double image of the worker both as producer and as consumer-purchaser, American corporate inventiveness established, bit by bit, the foundation of a consumer society.

Gradually, mass production itself became one of the principal spurs to American inventiveness. In 1932, two General Motors executives defined what they called a "New Necessity": "We cannot reasonably expect to continue to make the same thing over and over. The simplest way . . . is to keep changing the product—the market for new things is infinitely elastic. . . . The whole object of research is to keep everyone dissatisfied with what he has in order to keep the factory busy making new things." As a result, America had become, as the historian Daniel Boorstin has noted, a "democracy of things."

By October 7, 1913, when the first Model T Ford rolled off the assembly line, Eli Whitney's century-old theory of interchangeable parts had become one of the dominant principles of everyday life in America. Anxieties about the anonymity of urban industrial life were intensified by the worker's faceless presence on the assembly line. Soon workers were as interchangeable as the parts they assembled. As one writer for *Collier's Weekly* put it: "Those who make the parts do not know what functions they perform in a car;

those who assemble the engines cannot adjust them." The "place" and the importance of the individual in a system of mass production is a recurring theme in both the intellectual discourse and the popular culture of the period, including, for example, such films as Charlie Chaplin's *Modern Times* (1936).

As the number of assembly lines and conveyor belts increased, threatening individuality and weakening pride in personal accomplishment, a surge of nonconformity sprang up in the arts. From ragtime's elaborately syncopated rhythms to architecture's radically restructured relationships between form and function, the arts embarked on a series of revolts against formalism. The photographer Alfred Stieglitz spoke for many artists and writers when he declared that an individual's work must be marked by "honesty of aim, honesty of self-expression, honesty of revolt against the autocracy of convention." In architecture, for example, Louis Sullivan and Frank Lloyd Wright repudiated the prevailing classical precepts and encouraged a functional relationship between structure and space.

An attack on conformity surfaced as the unspoken theme of the controversial Armory Show in 1913, in which such avant-garde painters as Arthur Dove, Marcel Duchamp, John Marin, and Joseph Stella turned New York City's 69th Regiment Armory into a gallery of "modern art." Their work attacked the conservative standards of the nation's most prestigious art galleries and rejected the "polite" subjects and traditional forms of their predecessors. Whitmanesque contemplation of the commonplace by such artists as George Bellows, Edward Hopper, Charles Scheeler, and John Sloan embraced saloons, prizefights, street scenes, and even bedrooms as proper artistic subjects. A new emphasis on the individual's response to experience quickly made "expressionism" one of the hallmarks of modernism.

In literature, the imagist poets—most notably Amy Lowell, Hilda Doolittle ("H. D."), and Ezra Pound—rebelled against standard poetic material and forms as well as traditional expressions of sense experience, advocating instead the direct presentation of feelings in exquisite images. Many writers were preoccupied with cultivating their own artistic freedom and so resisted what they saw as the vagaries of mass culture. Some were disillusioned enough by the pervasive materialism of American culture in the years following World War I that they left for Europe: among others, Ezra Pound, T. S. Eliot, E. E. Cummings, F. Scott Fitzgerald, Ernest Hemingway, and Gertrude Stein. Although they were collectively dubbed the "lost generation," they were bound together more by their artistic sensibilities than by a set of common beliefs. Furthermore, though some writers involved themselves in social, political, and business issues of the day, a group of critics and thinkers—including Walter Lippmann, Edmund Wilson, H. L. Mencken, Lewis Mumford, and Reinhold Niebuhr—provided much of the intellectual leadership in the United States during the period, often through the essays and articles they wrote for national magazines.

Small magazines flourished in this age of intellectual irreverence. *The Masses* (1911), *Poetry* (1912), *The New Republic* (1914), *The Seven Arts* (1916), and *The American Mercury* (1924) were among those that printed their first issues during this period, and each served as an important outlet for cultural criticism, fresh political views, and avant-garde aesthetic principles. The editors of *The New Republic*, for example, declared that the purpose of their journal was "less to inform or entertain its readers than to start little insurrections in the realm of their convictions." *The Seven Arts*, founded by novelist and critic Floyd Dell, featured many of America's major new literary voices—including Sherwood Anderson, John Dos Passos, Theodore Dreiser, Robert Frost, and Amy Lowell—as well as such cultural commentators as Randolph Bourne, Van Wyck Brooks, and John Reed.

Other small-circulation journals with long-standing reputations for incisive cultural criticism and political opinion participated eagerly in the intellectual controversies of the time. *The Nation*, founded in 1865, continued to serve as the leading liberal voice for political, social, and literary experimentation during the editorship of Paul Elmer More (1909–14) and Oswald Garrison Villard (1918–33). The revived *Dial* had started in Chicago as a conservative literary magazine in the late nineteenth century. In 1916 the journal moved to New York, listed Randolph Bourne and Van Wyck Brooks among its new contributing editors, and cultivated a more radical readership by publishing such controversial authors as Charles A. Beard (best known for *An Economic Interpretation of the Constitution* [1913]), John Dewey (*Democracy and Education* [1916]; *Experience and Nature* [1925]), and Thorstein Veblen (*The Theory of the Leisure Class* [1899]). By the 1920s, *The Dial* was widely recognized as the most distinguished literary monthly in America, and its contributors included such renowned international writers as Thomas Mann, Jules Romains, and William Butler Yeats, as well as the latest poetry of the expatriate T. S. Eliot. The poet Marianne Moore served as *The Dial's* final editor from 1925 to 1929 and published E. E. Cummings and Hart Crane, among many other newly celebrated American writers.

The relatively small circulation of magazines such as *The Dial* and *The Seven Arts* did not deter their editors from recruiting the major intellectuals of the time. In 1913, Willard Huntington Wright, the new editor of *The Smart Set*, promptly declared that the magazine would "provide lively entertainment for minds that are not primitive." H. L. Mencken and George

Jean Nathan, who succeeded Wright, repeatedly satirized what they called the "booboisie" and provided a major public forum for a new generation of social critics who, like Joseph Wood Krutch, assessed the impact of science and technology on American society and decried the cultural values promoted by big business. Mencken and Nathan founded *The American Mercury* in 1924 to provide "a realistic presentation of the whole gaudy, gorgeous American scene." Skepticism and satire dominated, however, as Mencken delighted in fulfilling what he described as his "agreeable duty to track down some of the worst nonsense prevailing and do execution upon it."

In a period still grappling with the implications of the late nineteenth-century intellectual rebels—including Darwin, Marx, Nietzsche, and Freud—orthodox belief in virtually every aspect of American life remained suspect. Politics proved no exception. Emma Goldman's *Anarchism and Other Essays* (1910), as well as such journals as *The Masses* (edited by Floyd Dell and Max Eastman) and *The Liberator* (founded in 1918 and edited by Dell and Michael Gold), helped create a climate of radicalism by encouraging public debate on such issues as pacifism, feminism, birth control, and individual rights. An era that witnessed the arrival of the Ku Klux Klan, the "Red Scare" of 1919, the Palmer raids of 1920, when A. Mitchell Palmer formed a special Justice Department division to seek and destroy radical and "Communist" factions in America, as well as the trial and execution of Sacco and Vanzetti (1920–27), also saw the founding of the American Civil Liberties Union (1920). Despite the monstrous violence and enormous casualties of the Great War, the quest by progressives and radicals for social reform met with less and less support. By the mid-1920s, amidst America's postwar booming economy, social and political reform seemed a distant prospect. The Jazz Age "had no interest in politics at all," F. Scott Fitzgerald declared. Such interest would not be rekindled until the New Deal politics of the 1930s.

The diverse challenges to individual identity in America occurred, ironically, within a commercial context dependent on corporate novelty and inventiveness. The conflict between the machines that produced an array of new gadgets and the people who operated them created an audience of new readers eager to imagine attractive alternatives to the crowded urban and factory conditions in which they lived and labored. The general reading public devoted unprecedented attention to reading about the "unspoiled" natural world and to mobilizing to preserve it. Such enormously popular fictional folk heroes as Paul Bunyan and Casey Jones attracted a large readership by repeatedly demonstrating that they were larger than any machine and could overcome any mechanical invasion of the natural world.

Membership rolls swelled in organizations dedicated to preserving and expanding the nation's parks, wildlife, and wilderness. The Sierra Club, founded by John Muir in 1892 in California, filed numerous legal challenges to corporate interests. "These temple destroyers, these devotees of ravaging commercialism," Muir argued, "seem to have a perfect contempt for Nature, and, instead of lifting their eyes to the God of the mountains, lift them to the Almighty Dollar." Through its nationally distributed publications, the Sierra Club was instrumental in the early decades of the twentieth century in helping to create the National Park Service and the National Forest Service.

Another response to the general public's interest in the "wild" was the creation of botanical and zoological "gardens" designed to attract people who could afford neither the money nor the time to explore pristine nature firsthand. Zoos in particular served to recall an even more primitive frontier than the one about which Frederick Jackson Turner had written his famous obituary in 1893. A similar nostalgia was echoed in the titles of such immensely popular novels as Jack London's *Call of the Wild* (1903) and Edgar Rice Burroughs's *Tarzan of the Apes* (1914). The "primitive" values celebrated in the popular fiction of the period found more "civilized" expression in the creation of such organizations as the "Sons of Daniel Boone," the "Bay Pioneers," and especially the Boy Scouts.

By the outbreak of World War I, the image of the independent, self-reliant American clearly had begun to crack. The vast majority of American workers exercised little control over the results of their own labor; more often than not, they judged their work to be an insignificant element in an impersonal system of production. Unnerved by Chaplinesque assembly lines and the shuffle of invoices, workers' self-esteem began to depend more on take-home wages than on the nature of either the work they performed or the goods they produced. Earning a "decent wage" became the most widely advertised sign not only of success but even of "manhood." Many men responded by equating their own personal welfare with that of the corporation, in an early anticipation of what in the 1950s would be called "the organization man." Others became "burnt-out furnaces of energy," as one advertisement put it. Talk of heart disease, ulcers, alcoholism, and a host of illnesses filled the factories and office corridors. During the Depression, a popular cereal advertisement made the cruel point dispassionately clear: "a sick man has no place in business." A painful irony was surfacing: American businesses both promulgated the drive to succeed and made money on prepackaged remedies when efforts failed.

To compensate men for diminished individual independence, American corporate interests endorsed the collective image of working men as "masters" of their personal and domestic lives. Such an image served as a form of cultural indemnification. The popular press and magazines addressed the father and "breadwinner" with a deferential tone that had little to do with either the working lives or the domestic realities of most Americans. In the late nineteenth century, a foreign visitor, here to observe "aristocracy in America," noted that "the family, which is a monarchy in the old world, has become, like everything else, a republic in the new. The father is not king; he is simply a president." By the mid-1920s, the father's authority had been reduced further and was associated primarily with voicing approval when the family decided to make a major consumer purchase.

By 1907, one in ten American homes could boast of electricity; by 1929 that ratio had soared to nearly seven in ten. As electricity transformed American homes into self-contained technological units, the fabric of daily life began to change, and with it the nation's reading habits. Even the distinction between "night" and "day" began to blur, increasing productivity at work and at home. One of the recurring topics in the popular press focused on what women would do with their "free time" once electricity had liberated them from the drudgery of household chores. Advertisements depicted such laborsaving devices as the washing machine, stove, refrigerator, iron, and carpet sweeper as solutions to "the servant problem." In a 1917 essay entitled "The Woman of the Future," Thomas Edison portrayed American women as liberated by inventions. "Neither a slave to servants nor herself a drudge," he solemnly intoned, the woman of the future "will be rather a domestic engineer than a domestic laborer. . . . This and other mechanical forces will so revolutionize the woman's world that a large portion of the aggregate of woman's energy will be conserved for use in broader, more constructive fields."

As the number of products increased, additional retail outlets were needed. "Department stores" began springing up across the country, selling standardized, mass-produced goods in larger and larger quantities. Although not an American innovation, these consumer "palaces," as they were called, distributed the latest fashions in ready-made clothing and home furnishings as well as countless gadgets. In the process, as the French novelist Emile Zola observed, the American department store "democratized luxury." Shopping became a national pastime as well as a communal activity. In a similar vein, advertisers depicted the supermarket "chain" not only as "a land of adventure" but also as a gratifying expression of democratic principles. "Make your own decisions," consumers were urged, "linger or hurry as you please."

Manufacturers cluttered American experience with an astonishing array of laborsaving "appliances" and "revolutionary" counter-top gadgets. Although some inventions raised the standard of living, many others trivialized experience. In 1913, having made a fortune on 5 & 10 cent stores, F. W. Woolworth paid $13 million in cash to build America's first skyscraper, the Woolworth Building in New York City—the kind of "temple spire of the religion of business" that Sinclair Lewis would later fictionalize as "austere towers of steel and cement and limestone, sturdy as cliffs and delicate as silver rods." The Woolworth Building contained fifty-eight stories and office space for 14,000 workers and helped irrevocably to redistribute the American work force to urban corporate centers.

The telephone helped to unify a dispersed, and isolated, rural population. It also quickened the pace of business transactions by linking sellers and buyers in networks that accelerated the nation's economic growth. In the process, it intensified the psychological need for immediate results, in personal as well as business affairs. Like the typewriter, the telephone redefined work, providing numerous jobs, many of them for women, in the skyscrapers that were beginning to fill the American horizon.

Women entered the urban work force in substantial numbers in the first four decades of the twentieth century. In 1880, only 4 percent of all employed women worked in offices while the remainder were concentrated in agriculture. By 1890 the percent working in offices had risen to well over twenty. Thirty years later, women represented nearly 50 percent of all bookkeepers and accountants, and over 90 percent of all typists and stenographers. As the distinguished cultural historian David Potter has observed, "As a symbol, the typewriter evokes fewer emotions than the plow, but like the plow it played a vital part in the fulfillment of the American promise of opportunity and independence. . . . The city was the frontier for American women and the business office was what gave them economic independence and the opportunity to follow a course of their own."

Yet women soon found themselves as confined by the typewriter as men had been by the plow, and the majority of them also remained economically dependent on their wage-earning spouses. The fundamental inequality that afflicted American middle-class women in the early twentieth century is nicely summarized in Charlotte Perkins Gilman's observations in *Women and Economics* (1898):

All that she may wish to have, all that she may wish to do, must come through a single channel and a single choice. Wealth, power, social distinction, fame—not only these, but home and happiness, reputation, ease and pleasure, her bread and butter—all must come through a small gold ring.

The evidence from American culture throughout much of the twentieth century confirms the accuracy of Gilman's appraisal. Despite the political emancipation decreed by the Nineteenth Amendment, the advantages of marriage remained an unchallenged assumption in the vast majority of poems, novels, and dramas, as well as in films, songs, popular magazines, and on radio programs. In a delightful exception, Dorothy Canfield Fisher's novel *The Home-Maker* (1924) depicts a wife whose failure as a mother and house-wife prompts her to exchange roles with her husband, who has been equally unsuccessful at business. Both prosper in their new identities. But the pop-ular media resisted such scenarios, preferring instead to reinforce America's familiar female stereotypes: the winsome and determined single girl, the blissful and triumphant bride, the cheerful and gossipy wife, the diligent and nervous mother.

Although the needs of World War II changed these tradition-bound and corporately managed images of women, the war represented more an inter-ruption than a revolution. Between 1942 and 1945, more than six million women joined the ranks of workers who manufactured the materials essen-tial to secure victory. Two million women worked in heavy industry as welders, riveters, lathe operators, and the like. Such popular periodicals as *Life* and *Look* recounted the wartime exploits of the Women's Air Force and Air Corps, and advertisers traded on the feats of such corporate creations as "Molly Pitcher" who "gallantly fill the breach left by their fighting broth-ers-in-arms." Yet once the war was over, women found themselves forced out of the workplace and back into idealized images of women who found fulfillment by catering to their husbands' needs. As late as 1946, the pollster Elmo Roper could report that 25 percent of the women he interviewed declared that they would rather have been born male.

Black Americans fared even worse in the popular media, being relegated to servile and menial roles. Such caricatures as the foot-shuffling faithful old servant or the simpleminded and lovably oversized maid dominated the popular magazines, the movies, and the airwaves. Before 1945 virtually the only widely circulated image of blacks other than as servants was the white entertainer in blackface, a minstrel show tradition that became a standard feature of the vaudeville routines of such entertainers as Al Jolson and Ed-die Cantor. Even the slow-witted but endearing characters in *Beulah* and *Amos 'n' Andy*, two of the most popular radio shows in history, were played by whites.

As large numbers of blacks migrated from the rural South to the indus-trial North, the percentage of blacks living outside the South rose from approximately 10 percent in 1915 to 25 percent in 1940. Segregation forced most to live in slum areas and work at low-paying, menial jobs—as janitors, bootblacks, and dishwashers. The painful realities of growing up in these circumstances are powerfully evoked in the works of many black writers, most notably in the distinguished fiction of Richard Wright (*Native Son* [1940] and *Black Boy* [1945]), as well as in the remarkable poetry and prose of Jean Toomer and Langston Hughes. Whites panicked when blacks settled in the more attractive parts of Northern cities. During the 1920s, for example, 117,000 whites fled Harlem as 87,000 blacks moved in, bringing with them an extraordinarily rich cultural tradition that found powerful expression in such indigenous American musical forms as ragtime and jazz, as well as in the poetry and prose of the Harlem Renaissance.

During World War II, black Americans were still regularly seen in popular magazines and wartime propaganda in servile roles. Despite the impressive gallantry of black regiments, the prevailing image remained that of the faithful porter tending to the needs of white G.I.s on their way to battle. Even such prominent black magazines of the late 1940s as *Ebony* and *Jet* repeatedly featured advertisements for skin lighteners and hair straighteners, grim reminders of the "costs" of being born black in white America.

In 1920 the census revealed that for the first time in American history more than one-half the population lived in cities. By 1930, 115 American cities could boast of populations exceeding 100,000. Living in these "new" urban centers were large numbers of both recent immigrants and black Americans.

The immigrant population helped to diversify American literature. Their experiences became the subject of much literature, as did the lives of working-class Americans. From Frank Norris's *The Octopus* (1901) and Upton Sinclair's *The Jungle* (1906) to Max Eastman's *Venture* (1927) and Josephine Herbst's *Pity Is Not Enough* (1933), writers established a strong tradition of proletarian literature advocating social reform. As Clifford Odets's play *Waiting for Lefty* (1935), John Steinbeck's *The Grapes of Wrath* (1939), and Thomas Bell's *Out of This Furnace* (1941) suggest, this tradition received new impetus during the Great Depression. The nation's first major ethnic writers surfaced during the period between the wars, among them Abraham Cahan (*The Rise of David Levinsky* [1917]), Anzia Yezierska (*Bread Givers* [1925]), O. E. Rölvaag (*Giants in the Earth* [1927]), and Henry Roth (*Call It Sleep* [1935]).

Print—the dominant medium in nineteenth-century America—soon found itself facing unprecedented competition from both motion pictures and radio. By the late 1920s, many Americans were learning their morals and manners—and in some cases their modes of misbehaving—from the celluloid exploits of Saturday matinee heroes and heroines. An eighteen-year-old college student writing in the 1920s offered a provocative view of the effects of motion pictures on American popular taste and behavior:

These passionate pictures stir such language, desires, and urges as I never expected any person to possess. Just the way the passionate lover held his sweetheart suggests so many beautiful and intimate relations, which even my reacting to a scene does not satisfy any more. I cannot believe that I am "I" any more.

The darkened movie house also served as a refuge from urban loneliness and anonymity. In his *The Art of the Moving Picture* (1915), Vachel Lindsay, vagabond poet and champion of what he touted as the "higher vaudeville," described the irresistible power of motion pictures: "Forced by their limited purses, their inability to buy a Ford car, and the like, [people] go in their loneliness to film after film till the whole world seems to turn on a reel."

The possibility that moviegoing might prove harmful stirred much public debate in the 1920s. Too many films ended tragically, one critic decried. Too many subverted traditional values, others charged, especially by treating such controversial subjects as unwed mothers and women's rights. Still other critics feared that the dark interiors of movie houses might promote wayward longings. Women in particular, one male critic argued, should be wary of the "dim auditorium which seems to float on the world of dreams . . . [where] an American woman may spend her afternoon alone" and "let her fantasies slip through the darkened atmosphere to the screen where they drift in rhapsodic armours with handsome stars." But such warnings fell largely on deaf ears.

As a form of entertainment for the working class, motion pictures rapidly expanded their audience. The immigrant population quickly became one of the principal audiences of the silent pictures featured at the many "nickelodeons" that dotted urban areas. Even those who neither spoke nor understood English could enjoy the silent screen artistry of such filmmakers as D. W. Griffith, Harold Lloyd, and Mack Sennett. In 1922, over 40 million Americans bought tickets to the movies. With the addition of sound in 1927, movies became even more influential. Billed as an outgrowth of the telephone, "sound pictures" were advertised as heralding a "new art in entertainment." Audiences were urged to "hear and see the world's greatest personalities." What they at first heard was so crudely contrived that Charlie Chaplin "came away from the theatre believing that the days of sound were numbered." Soon, however, sound dominated the industry and expanded it. In 1929, over 100 million people purchased movie tickets. As if to confirm the notion that invention breeds invention, the first experiments with television were soon under way. By the 1939 World's Fair, a working television model was attracting substantial interest as people sensed for the first time the cultural potential of transmitting visual experience instantaneously.

A good deal of American corporate inventiveness in the first several decades of the twentieth century was directed toward establishing instant relationships among people, places, events, and products. The radio empowered people to communicate instantly over vast distances. By the 1920s the airwaves were alive with the sounds of news, weather reports, entertainment, and "commercials." By 1939, nearly 48 million bulky radio sets were giving Americans access to major political and cultural events, democratizing knowledge as well as entertainment. The radio also helped to break down the distinctions between here and there, and between then and now. Yet, from its inception as a mass-produced cultural commodity, radio triggered spirited public debates both in print and on the air about the effects of transmitting commercials directly into what sponsors called "the privacy of your own home." Radio—as well as film—enabled immigrant and other "marginal" segments of American society to participate in the nation's culture. In his 1938 broadcast based on H. G. Wells's *The War of the Worlds*, Orson Welles also demonstrated that radio had enormous potential as the nation's "theater of the air."

In early twentieth-century America, everyone—and everything—seemed to be in motion and in the service of commerce. But more than any other commodity, the automobile remained the most visible indication of America's prosperity and social mobility. Spurred by federal legislation creating a national highway network, seven million consumers bought automobiles in 1919. By 1929, that number had soared to well over 27 million. In 1940, the figure increased to 32 million. Installment plans, a by-product of automobile sales, irrevocably changed America's buying habits. The back seats of automobiles offered the nation's young adults a new place to experiment with America's changing mores.

Putting more Americans on the road and in the driver's seat also helped to change the relations between people and the spaces around them. Mobility had long played a major role not only in America's history and literature but also in its conception of freedom. The automobile became an important factor in redefining luxury and status, and it added many new settings to American literature—including the diner, the gas station, and the motel, as well as the open road. In a broader sense, it even extended the boundaries of self-identity and rearranged the borders among city, suburbs, and countryside.

Suburban Great Neck, Greenwich, Shaker Heights, Grosse Point, Beverly Hills, as well as Johnson and Marin counties, owe at least part of their social status to the automobile. Like Fitzgerald's Gatsby, suburbanites used their cars to drive *to* the city, not, as in later years, to escape *from* it. The standards and aspirations of middle-America seemed no different. In *Middletown*, the famous 1929 study of an "average" American community, Robert and Helen Lynd documented the social status of owning an automobile. Of twenty-six working-class families without an indoor toilet, twenty-one owned an automobile.

By the mid-1920s, the general public found reading less attractive than such ready-made and seductive alternatives as listening to a new phonograph recording or dancing to the latest popular music on the radio. Yet this reduction in the time the general public spent reading was to a large extent offset by the dramatic increase in the number of people who were learning to read. Statistics gathered by educators suggest startling national gains. From 1910 to 1940, for example, the number of students attending high school increased 540 percent, and the number enrolling in college increased 321 percent. In both high schools and colleges, faculty who subscribed to the principles of such educational theorists as John Dewey encouraged their students to be more assertive, to express more intellectual initiative, and to exercise greater responsibility for the quality of their lives.

Curriculum innovation also flourished during period. Special studies and honors programs found receptive audiences among students at all levels of instruction. And in a similar vein the number of options available to students in selecting the institution they wanted to attend also increased. Research universities, professional schools, liberal arts colleges, community colleges, extension courses, and adult education programs provided students different ways of educating themselves. For the first time, unions and corporations began offering instruction to their employees.

The nation's investment in educating its people accelerated both book production and local library circulation. The number of publishers increased markedly. Led by such distinguished new imprints as Alfred A. Knopf and Boni and Liveright, and such established houses as Houghton Mifflin and Harper and Brothers, publishers initiated aggressive efforts to discover major new voices—Sherwood Anderson, Theodore Dreiser, Willa Cather, Jean Toomer, Sinclair Lewis, Gertrude Stein, F. Scott Fitzgerald, Ernest Hemingway, John Dos Passos, Katherine Anne Porter, John Steinbeck, William Faulkner, and Richard Wright, to name a few. Much the same can be said of the major new poets of the period: Edwin Arlington Robinson, Robert Frost, Hart Crane, Robinson Jeffers, T. S. Eliot, Ezra

Pound, Langston Hughes, William Carlos Williams, and Wallace Stevens. Reassessing American literature preoccupied several major critics of the period, including John Macy (*The Spirit of American Literature* [1913]), Van Wyck Brooks (most notably in *America's Coming of Age* [1915], and *The Flowering of New England* [1936]), and Lewis Mumford (*The Golden Day* [1926]). The poetry of Edward Taylor was discovered, the work of Emily Dickinson reevaluated. Herman Melville's significance in American literature was reconsidered, as was the work of many other nineteenth-century writers. More generally, an increasing public interest in reading prompted a 60 percent increase in book production between 1920 and 1929, much of it attributable to a rash of best-selling works—ranging from F. Scott Fitzgerald's *This Side of Paradise* (1920) and H. G. Wells's *Outline of History* (1920) to Erich Maria Remarque's *All Quiet on the Western Front* (1929) and Lloyd C. Douglas's *Magnificent Obsession* (1929).

Over the course of the first two decades of the twentieth century, popular magazines evolved into the intellectual counterpart of the retail department store. America's prestigious and inexpensive mass market magazines steadily increased the number of special features designed to satisfy the particular interests of different readers. To a considerable extent, reading for information began to replace reading for pleasure and literary experience. In a January 1913 editorial entitled "Scientific Management in Reading," the publisher of *The Independent* declared that more streamlined articles were needed to summarize efficiently "what is now important to be known of what the world is doing and thinking." The "gentle reader" who had provided the primary audience for such periodicals as *Harper's*, the *Atlantic*, *Scribner's*, and *The Century* seemed harder to locate as magazines struggled to maintain or enlarge their circulation base. Soon magazines were reserving more space for presenting information about the world and for offering advice about how to conduct and improve life.

Frederick Taylor's principles of scientific management, so influential in American corporate enterprise, also infiltrated the ways in which many Americans organized their domestic lives and managed their intellectual relations with the world around them. "Time-on-task" became a watchword for personal behavior. Advertisers, for example, began encouraging the public to start each morning with a "hurry-up breakfast." Lunch was soon measured more in terms of the time taken than of the food consumed. This principle of time management also invaded the nation's reading habits. Highly readable condensations of political and business affairs began to appear in such aptly named weekly magazines as *Time* (founded in 1923), *Fortune* (1933), and *Life* (1936)—each, until recently, an anonymous collective effort ostensibly designed to supply enough "facts" about an issue to enable readers to make informed judgments. Those who had neither the time nor the patience to choose and read full-length novels or books or to keep pace with experimental magazines could purchase the *Reader's Digest* (founded in 1922) or join the Book-of-the-Month Club (1926). In the 1930s, Robert M. Hutchins and Mortimer J. Adler launched the Great Books of the Western World series. When these fifty-four "superbly bound volumes" were published as a unit in the 1950s, they were accompanied by a two-volume "Syntopicon," an "idea index that took eight years and over a million dollars to build." Purchasers of the Great Books were encouraged to use the Syntopicon to "trace every thought in the Great Books as easily as you can look up words in your dictionary." Culture had finally taken its place as an indexable commodity in a world of consumption.

As the demand for timely knowledge increased, more and more magazines were created to satisfy the specialized informational needs of different audiences. When this happened, the circulation base of such large-scale weeklies as *Saturday Evening Post* and *Collier's* shrank. Widely circulated magazines were forced to match the news summaries of more specialized magazines, the entertainment "value" of radio and motion pictures, and the sensationalism and celebrity watching of tabloids and daily newspapers. For some magazines—such as *Collier's*—the competition was too formidable, and they folded. Others countered by trying to provide an intellectual supermarket within their covers.

This reshaping of popular American magazines sounded a clear challenge to the personal essay as a widely read literary form. In search of new information, many readers lacked the time and curiosity required to ponder a writer's eloquent reflections on the world. Other readers preferred more open forms of literature—the novel and the long poem—that seemed better able to accommodate sweeping, large-scale themes. Still others found the essay less entertaining than its popular competitor for magazine space, the short story. H. L. Mencken, James Thurber, Edmund Wilson, Walter Lippmann, and E. B. White, among others, tried to revive the essay as a literary genre. But the formal restrictions of the essay were not easily adapted to the shifting terms and structures of twentieth-century consciousness. In America's consumer culture, the essay was often relegated to the nonliterary task of conveying useful information.

The little magazine remained the primary outlet for twentieth-century intellectual discourse and debate. Such distinguished literary journalists and cultural critics as H. L. Mencken, George Jean Nathan, John Jay Chapman, Walter Lippmann, Lewis Mumford, Floyd Dell, Harriet Monroe, Alice Corbin Henderson, Randolph Bourne, Paul Elmer More, Van Wyck Brooks, Reinhold Niebuhr, Henry Seidel Canby, Joseph Wood Krutch, V. L. Parrington, Max Eastman, F. O. Matthiessen, and Edmund Wilson turned little magazines into lively centers for intellectual exchange. Many of these writers were generalists, humanists of the first rank. All retained abiding faith in the potential of American experience, and each took seriously the work of creating a public role for the intellectual within American culture. Having immersed themselves in American culture, they wrote with a fierceness and integrity never quite matched since. Perhaps it was because they remained so skeptical of the commercialism of American culture that they were able to maintain secure intellectual identities in the free exchanges that constitute a democracy of ideas. Through their commitment to such exchange and their refusal to convert ideas into commodities, they presented enduring alternatives to the wonders of the mechanical world displayed at the 1939 World's Fair. Their work stands as a principled expression of the theme of that fair—"unity *without* uniformity."

Donald McQuade

Literary Scenes and Literary Movements

Halley's comet aroused no ancestral fears in the United States when it flashed across the skies in 1910, but although it was disregarded as a portent of future wars, coincidental events might have suggested to some astute astrologer that the nation was passing into a new phase. To gloomy Mark Twain, who died in April, and to pessimistic Henry Adams, who proclaimed six months later that "our America has no longer any virginity to lose," the future offered little to live for.

But in 1910 the country was deaf to dire prophecies and receptive to change. In that year, New York voters elected the first socialist ever to sit in the national congress and sent young Franklin Delano Roosevelt to the state senate. His cousin, Theodore Roosevelt, flexing his political muscles after a restless hiatus out of office, demanded a "square deal" for the people. W. E. B. Du Bois joined the newly formed National Association for the Advancement of Colored People (NAACP) and announced in the first issue of its organ, *The Crisis:* "This is the critical time in the history of the advancement of men."

The color line was not about to fade, as Du Bois quickly discovered, but many of the other constraints inhibiting social and cultural innovation had begun to weaken. A talismanic word, "new," set the tone for a good deal of thought and expression during the next few years. Americans learned about the "New History," the "New Woman," the "New Theater," the "New Poetry." Although the presidential campaign of 1912 signaled the victory of Woodrow Wilson's "New Freedom" over Theodore Roosevelt's "New Nationalism" (leaving President William Howard Taft, the Old Guard Republican incumbent, with nothing "new" to offer), both Democratic and

Progressive philosophies were liberationist in spirit, however different their political and economic programs. Both appealed to new expectations among the electorate, notably recent immigrants, women, and social dissenters heretofore denied, they felt, the promise of American life. A sentence in Wilson's inaugural address caught the cultural as well as political meaning of the "New Freedom":

We have been proud of our industrial achievements, but we have not hitherto stopped thoughtfully enough to count the cost . . . of lives snuffed out, of energies over-taxed and broken, the fearful physical and spiritual cost to the men and women and children upon whom the dead weight and burden of it all has fallen pitilessly the years through.

From 1912, the *annus mirabilis*, until 1917 when the United States entered World War I, the literary and artistic community expanded in an atmo-sphere of confidence. To call this period a "renaissance" may exaggerate its effulgence, but those who lived through it remember it as a "joyous sea-son," an intense historical moment marked by its "sharp and probing qual-ity, its insatiable lust for knowledge, its determined self-analysis."

Such moments are rare in American history and their causes hard to determine. They have occurred at times, neither torpid nor inflamed, when a rebellious league of youth (often the beneficiaries of the persons and insti-tutions they challenge) reject the values of their elders. The rebels aim to unsettle, not destroy. They find corroboration for their rebellious impulses in the works of foreign thinkers and writers and seek outlets for their reformist zeal in redressing the wrongs of defenseless and exploited individuals, groups, and classes. They start new magazines, new communities, and work out personal problems in public ways. These bursts of insurgency peter out as experience chills and unanticipated events smother idealistic hopes. The story of the New England "renaissance" of the mid-nineteenth century fol-lows a similar scenario, and so does the story of the "little renaissance" that blazed for a half-dozen years in the 1910 decade.

The latter was, if not the first, then the most sustained uprising against the "genteel tradition"—a term coined in 1911 by the philosopher George Santayana—that had guided the directors of American cultural life since the last third of the nineteenth century. The much-abused "genteel custo-dians," too varied a lot to fit into a stereotype, included men and women of culture and taste who did their best to mitigate the crudities of the Gilded Age. But as a group, they lacked boldness, glanced back nostalgically to the myth of unspoiled homogeneous America, and shrank from the squalor, violence, and vulgarity of their own times. The condition of the industrial working class quickened their fears, not their sympathies; the streams of immigrants aroused ancestral dread of unassimilable strangers taking over the land. With few exceptions, they seemed incapable of addressing, much less comprehending, the critical issues of their times (technological innovation, the race question, urban problems, science, the new role of women, trade unionism) or of mediating the silent conflict, as novelist and critic Ludwig Lewisohn put it, "between the sense of life and scale of values brought by the yet inarticulate masses of immigrants."

As editors of magazines for the middle-class readership (the largest and most influential part of which were women) or as essayists and critics, they could not hope, and did not try, to reach the populace; they could and did uphold the beacons of Beauty and Idealism and enforce the standards of "good taste." Even men of letters who chafed at editorial censorship—Henry James and William Dean Howells, for example—were compelled by the facts of American life, and very likely by their own inner reticences, to disguise their departures from the going codes. The majority plumped for unchanging moral values and traditional culture. They closed ranks against naturalism, literary experimentation, and social heterodoxy, against any movement that might endanger, in the indicative phrase of the very "genteel" Henry van Dyke, "the spiritual rootage of art."

By the end of the century, however, a handful of journalist-critics—among the more lively, Percival Pollard, Edgar Saltus, and James Gibbons Huneker—were promoting a different kind of culture. These cosmopolitan iconoclasts and importers of illicit foreign ideas and tastes lived in their respective bohemias (New York, San Francisco, Chicago, or abroad) and did what they could to shake up the cultural establishment. The burden of their criticism, also implicit in their translations of foreign authors, came to this: the arts in America were tepid, provincial, prudish, old-fashioned, and didactic; art and literature were to be enjoyed like sex and food and drink; aesthetic experience transcended morality and politics. Thanks to them, the names of Friedrich Nietzsche, Henrik Ibsen, and George Bernard Shaw were already hallmarks in 1910; symbolism, impressionism, anarchism, familiar concepts; and the philistinism and materialism of the middle class, legitimate targets for satire. Younger counterparts of these cosmopolitans preached a similar gospel, notably in Chicago, a cultural haven for "the splendidly pagan" escapees from small Midwestern towns, where, according to Van Wyck Brooks, impassioned discussions over "the life-force, art and socialism and the finer emotional forces that were to prevail in the future" evoked the mood of New York's Greenwich Village. A comparable if less vital atmosphere infused the San Francisco scene from the days of Ambrose Bierce, Jack London, and Frank Norris until the early twenties.

The imminent intellectual awakening Ezra Pound predicted in 1913 derived in part from the aesthetic journalists, but it embraced a broad range of social issues absent or subordinated in their writings: education, feminism, Freudian psychology, birth control, penology, industrial unionism. The new radicals, like Ralph Waldo Emerson's young transcendentalists, had "knives in their brains." They flung off "old systems, old morals, old prejudices." Pound called the awakening a "Risorgimento," by which he meant "a whole volley of liberations." And it is the word "liberation" that sounds a refrain throughout these years: liberation from chauvinistic and sheeplike provincialism and from the pedantry and insipidness of academic culture. A notorious figure of the liberation, Mabel Dodge, remembered 1913 as a year when "barriers went down and people reached each other who had never been in touch before; there were all sorts of new ways to communicate, as well as new communications."

These excited "communications" produced as much dissonance as harmony. The dissenters, a mix of idealists, pragmatists, anarchists, pagans, aesthetes, seekers, often clashed over their respective tastes and goals. But they had a common enemy in what they loosely and inexactly labeled "Puritanism," a catchall term for everything that appeared to them arid, repressive, and joy-denying in American life. "Puritanism," Huneker declared, taught "that the entire man ended at his collarbone." According to H. L. Mencken, Huneker's disciple and friend, Puritanism fired Anthony Comstock's lifelong crusade against "bad books" and permeated the genteel class, which for a half-century had monitored the country's laws, literature, education, religion, and morals.

Mencken, the most belligerent of the antipuritan polemicists, was already a veteran journalist when he and George Jean Nathan became editors of *The Smart Set* in 1914. His influence would not peak until after World War I, but his controversial book on Nietzsche (1908) and his defense of the American "Grendel," Theodore Dreiser—like himself of German extraction—earned him a fearsome reputation during the prewar years. Cheerful, irreverent, hating censorship of all kinds, he banged away at the "civilized and denatured Brahmins," deaf, he charged, to everything "honest, interesting, imaginative, enterprising" and hostile to anyone radiating "an alien smell." Even so, he was a dubious ally to the young insurgents. He treated them genially enough, yet his distaste for Greenwich Village radicals—"the birth controllers, jitny Socialists, and other such vermin," he called them—and his contempt for democracy itself, placed him outside their orbit. *The Smart Set*, catering to "civilized adults in their lighter moments," occasionally published serious writers, for example, James Joyce, Joseph Conrad, and Ezra Pound. But although Mencken defended the realism of Dreiser and sneered at the "pecksniffery" of "smut-hounds" like Comstock, he took no interest in the "happenings" that epitomize the spirit of this anarchic era: the confident manifestos of little magazines; the "terrific and blinding" dances of Isadora Duncan, priestess of women's sexual emancipation; the controversial exhibits of modern art; the productions of George Cram Cook's Provincetown Players; the "evenings" at Mabel Dodge's Fifth Avenue Salon where "all who had a notion that characterized the moment" might congregate.

These and other episodes, symptomatic of the time, in spite of the political and aesthetic disagreements of their promoters, were attempts to upset or reshape the old, to "make it new," to "try things out." Poets impatient with tiresome didacticism, vague eloquence, and hackneyed poetic forms and subject matter found outlets in *Poetry: A Magazine of Verse*, launched by the Chicagoan Harriet Monroe in 1912, with Ezra Pound as foreign editor; or in the more experimental little magazines like Margaret Anderson's *The Little Review* (1914) and Alfred Kreymborg's *Others* (1915). *The Masses*, edited by Max Eastman between 1913 and 1917, backed away from the poetic revolution but opened its columns to every other kind of revolutionary impulse. It featured brilliantly indecorous drawings and cartoons and assailed with passion and humor capitalism, racial bigotry, war, and organized religion, all at odds with its commitment to the gospel of "Comrade Jesus," the "workingman of Nazareth." For the less romantic and more pragmatic reformers, *The New Republic*, founded by Herbert Croly in 1914, offered what seemed to the progressive publisher and his talented editor, Walter Lippmann, a practical program to fuse art and politics. Their admitted failure to achieve this blending encouraged a group of visionary and optimistic "cultural nationalists" to publish the short-lived *Seven Arts* in 1916.

To a degree, all who savaged the Genteel Tradition, even Mencken, opted for invigorated national culture. They might swear by Nietzsche, Bergson, Freud, and Marx and snap at the Puritans for resisting the liberating influences from abroad, but they had high hopes that something wonderfully fresh might emerge from the American ferment as the black voices of Claude McKay, Jean Toomer, Walter White, James Weldon Johnson, and Langston Hughes began to be heard (the Harlem Renaissance was only a few years away) and the new immigrants, heretofore restricted to a kind of cultural Ellis Island, challenged the Anglo-Saxon overlords. "The future American poet," declared the Irish critic Padraic Colum, "may be the child of a Syrian or a Swede, or a Greek or a Russian." He might also have added, "the descendant of slaves." In Walt Whitman and Mark Twain and, with some reservations, Emerson, the movers and shakers had "usable" literary models from the American past, the first two respected for their rootedness in American life and language, the last for his warning to shun "the courtly muses" of Europe. All three (with Nathaniel Hawthorne, Henry David Thoreau, and Edgar Allan Poe sometimes added) pointed alternative courses to the radical artist: he could follow the safe and level byways laid out by conventional designers, investigate the wild and less traveled roads frequented by artistic and intellectual brigands, or cut a path for himself.

Van Wyck Brooks and Randolph Bourne spoke the most eloquently for a national culture. Both took to heart the complaints of Shaw and Yeats that American literature was not American enough, that it consisted of stale cribbings from Europe. No "true revolution" was possible, Brooks thought, until "a race of artists, profound and sincere, have brought us face to face with our own experience." Bourne, more truly cosmopolitan, rejected the "melting pot" metaphor and fostered in its stead the ideal of "trans-nationality," which he defined as "a weaving back and forth, with the other lands, of many threads of all sizes and colors." A good many artists and intellectuals shared the hopes of Brooks and Bourne. The expectation of a new and exciting development in American arts and letters animates Pound's little book *Patria Mia* (written but not published in 1913) and Brooks's famous overview of American literary culture, *America's Coming-of-Age* (1915). The emphasis was on the word "coming." Few would maintain that American culture had "arrived."

No event dramatized the oppositions and contradictions of the period more clearly than the exhibition of international modern art held in the New York Armory in 1913. Postimpressionist European painting had been shown as early as 1908 in the gallery of photographer Alfred Stieglitz, but never before had American museum-goers been presented with so many examples of modern painting and sculpture. The Armory Show provoked a hullabaloo in both radical and conservative circles and was misrepresented by both. The latter were predictably repelled by its violation of "ideal forms" and "noble subject matter"; to them the deformations of the human body were barbaric and immoral. But avant-garde artists and writers, given their abandonment of tradition, their intense individuality, their use of vernacular materials, their fascination with movement, might have been expected to be elated by this flouting of rigid standards and authority. A few of them were. The revolutionist John Reed, who had reported the campaigns of the Mexican bandit leader Pancho Villa in 1913 and later the earthshaking Russian revolution of 1917, equated futurism with socialism. Mabel Dodge, briefly Reed's inamorata, drew an analogy between Pablo Picasso's cubist painting and Gertrude Stein's fractured prose. Both, she felt, revealed "inherent meanings," and she concluded: "To worship beauty as we have known it may be to worship a corpse. Only death is ugly." Art began where imitation ended.

Such notions, however, troubled the bohemian socialists, artists and writers alike, for whom art was by definition social and democratic. They had thrown over genteel prescriptions of subject, the superrefined, the ideal, but not the representations of images or other precious legacies of their craft. It had seemed to them at first as if all innovations poured out of the same revolutionary fount. The Armory Show underscored the irreconcilable gulf between the formalists, preoccupied with technique and deadly serious about their work but indifferent to politics, morality, and society, and the party of the socially concerned who were unable to divorce art from ideas and from the living world around them. The latter rejected Mencken's dichotomy of boobs and patricians and aimed rather at narrowing the gap between the antitheses "highbrow" and "lowbrow," phrases inspired by Santayana and coined by Van Wyck Brooks. The first signified etiolated culture, the second "catchpenny realities." Brooks and his like-minded friends wished to conflate "highbrow" and "lowbrow" into a "middlebrow" blend of Henry James and Mark Twain. Formalists objected to this compromise. Their model was the "artist," personified in hard-boiled yet refined technicians like Ezra Pound and Ernest Hemingway.

Pound's select company survived the war pressures more successfully than the romantic rebels who either bowed to political necessity or went down with guns blazing. The group around *The Masses* and *The Seven Arts* saw their magazines literally driven out of circulation by government agencies because of their opposition to a war that for them had rung down the curtain on the "joyous season" and ended the dream of social and cultural transformation. Fittingly, Randolph Bourne, the most hopeful and responsible of the "League of Youth" and its true martyr, pronounced a sad and bitter elegy on the defeat of "the effort of reason and the adventure of beauty." Now in 1917 he predicted a spiritual impoverishment of the country as sentiment drained "into the channels of war" and emotional as well as financial capital was swallowed up in the general annihilation.

The interlude referred to as the "Little Renaissance" and the "confident years" cannot be separated from what followed or preceded it. Some of its principal participants were veterans of campaigns fought several decades before 1910; others were new recruits who resumed the struggle after the war was over, only to discover that conservatism (now entrenched in the places of political and economic power) had regained lost ground. Once it had seemed as if the spontaneity and experimentation of the Wilsonian years had quickened the entire country, turning America into an expanded Greenwich Village. In fact, the vast majority, especially outside the large cities, remained untouched by the rebellion. Only a few years after its happy inauguration, the repressive forces gaily lambasted by *The Masses*—ethnocentrism, chauvinism, censorship, economic and political reaction, racial and religious bigotry—had acquired new vigor.

Both the tough pragmatists and the romantic bohemians of rebellion, inheritors of a common culture, had been close enough to their adversaries to make a dialogue possible. They left few masterpieces, to be sure, and failed to introduce any original or profoundly radical ideas, yet their achievement was substantial. The movements and experiments they supported not only shook up the orthodox; they also supplied some of the cultural nutriment for the creative generation that came of age during the Great War.

Many of the writers who figure prominently in the literary annals of the 1920s had written near or at the top of their bent before 1917 and belong outside the group Gertrude Stein dubbed the "lost generation." In 1918, the war's end, Theodore Dreiser was 47, Robert Frost 44, Sherwood Anderson 42, Wallace Stevens 39, H. L. Mencken 38, William Carlos Williams 35, Ezra Pound and Sinclair Lewis 33, Van Wyck Brooks 32, T. S. Eliot and Eugene O'Neill 30. None had taken part in the war, though several had been marked by it.

The writers born between 1890 and 1910, it is often said, were a different breed from their older contemporaries—less idealistic and hopeful, more private and professional, and unresponsive to the high-minded social aspirations of the "League of Youth." As projected in the early works of writers as diverse as Ernest Hemingway, John Dos Passos, E. E. Cummings, William Faulkner, and Katherine Anne Porter, the war had exposed the power and ubiquity of military, government, and business bureaucracies. It simply added a sinister dimension to the "old tyrannies" against which Eastman and Bourne had buoyantly contended. After "Mr. Wilson's War" to "save democracy" and the fiasco at Versailles, disenchanted writers found good reasons to debunk the hollow abstractions of professional patriots. They set up enclaves where, in Malcolm Cowley's words, they could "free themselves from organized stupidity" and establish a place "in the hierarchy of talent." For those unable to breathe in Babbitt-ridden prohibition America (the Eighteenth Amendment had gone into effect in 1920), Europe offered a congenial last resort.

This picture of the 1920s, of course, is grossly simplistic: prewar writers

were not unmitigated optimists nor were postwar writers unconstrained he-
donists devoid of social concern. The very intensity with which they indicted American values and institutions—see, for example, *Civilization in
the United States: An Inquiry by Thirty Americans* (1922), edited by Harold
Stearns—argues the contrary. Santayana, who reviewed this symposium,
attributed the outrage of its contributors to society's failure "to approximate
the scale of greatness they had set up." What surprised him, however, was
not so much the vehemence with which they revealed their "affronted ideals" but their vitality. Surely the country was not "entirely at a low ebb" if
thirty lively critics could be mustered so quickly to condemn it.

Santayana was right. The energy of the nay-sayers qualifies the negativ-
ism of their message. The characterizations of the decade—the "Jazz Age,"
the "Roaring Twenties," the "Era of Wonderful Nonsense"—suggest not
only its frivolity but its power as well. The war veterans, all the sad young
men, might agree with Eliot's gloomy assessment of the contemporary world
in *The Waste Land* (1922) and cite any number of enormities to justify their
disgust. But all the evidence they presented, all the grimy and ridiculous
incidents sensationalized in the press during the Harding, Coolidge, and
Hoover administrations, foddered their imaginations and left traces in the
prose and poetry of the next twenty years.

F. Scott Fitzgerald inserted the "Black Sox" scandal of 1919–20 (players
on the Chicago White Sox took bribes to throw the world series) into *The
Great Gatsby* (1925). Upton Sinclair based his novel *Oil* (1927) on the Teapot
Dome affair, which involved a member of President Harding's cabinet in a
fraudulent oil deal. Aimee Semple McPherson, a popular evangelist who
preached her "Foursquare Gospel" to thousands from her Hollywood pulpit
and whose patently spurious tale of being tortured by fiendish kidnappers
filled the tabloids in 1926, figured prominently in Sinclair Lewis's novel
Elmer Gantry (1927). John O'Hara's *Butterfield 8* (1937) drew heavily on the
Starr Faithful "murder" case that filled the headlines in the summer of 1931
and inspired vacuous editorial homilies. John Dos Passos, the most histori-
cal-minded of all the twenties writers, packed the violence, banality, corruption, and injustice of the decade into his great trilogy, *U.S.A.* (collected
1938).

Overseeing this gaudy and squalid public scene was the impressario of
buncombe, H. L. Mencken. With his literary partner, George Jean Nathan, in association with the publisher Alfred A. Knopf, he had founded
The American Mercury in 1924 after a ten-year stint editing *The Smart Set*.
For the remainder of the twenties, he delighted his disciples, the alleged
"intelligent majority," and pressed his assault on the "yokels" and "gaping

primates" of the "Bible Belt"—the butts of his series *Prejudices* published between 1919 and 1927. At this stage, as conditions conspired with his genius and furnished him a subject matter and an audience, Mencken became less the literary critic and man of letters than the parodist and humorist. The America he excoriated and delighted in spread out before him, part zoo stocked with amusing specimens of national fauna—the "Quack," the "Boob," the "Gabbling Simian"—and part circus sideshow where calliopes blared and snake-oil salesmen from President Harding on down barked their wares. In these years he reached the top of his influence. He had not forgotten the anti-German campaign when war patriots urged that the word "coleslaw" be changed to "liberty cabbage." He remembered the "Red Scare" of 1919–20 when Attorney General A. Mitchell Palmer saw "anarchists" and "Bolsheviks" with scraggly beards and smoking bombs lurking underneath every bourgeois bed—and now he scoffed and laughed. He relished American vernacular speech as much as Whitman did but drew less flattering conclusions about the common man, whose salient traits he exaggerated into caricature. His slam-bang essays, satires, burlesques might have been collectively titled "Mencken's Funny Papers" and illustrated by popular comic strips of the twenties, "Boob McNut," "Happy Hooligan," "Andy Gump," and "Mutt and Jeff." His United States was a Yahoo land

engaged in a grotesque *pogrom* against the wop, the coon, the kike, the papist, the Jap, the what-not—worse, engaged in an even more grotesque effort to put down ideas as well as men—to repeal learning by statute, regiment the arts by lynch-law, and give the puerile ethical and religious notions of lonely farmers and corner grocers the force and dignity of constitutional axioms.

Mencken had in mind such events as the celebrated "Monkey Trial" of 1925. A publicity stunt staged by two enterprising merchants in Dayton, Tennessee, it focused world attention on the state law against the teaching of evolution in the public schools and brought the famous Clarence Darrow, lawyer for the defendant, John T. Scopes, and the aging fundamentalist and presidential aspirant, William Jennings Bryan, into widely publicized conflict. Mencken's outrageously slanted reports on the Dayton "show," a brilliant antipastoral on the rural South, climaxed the derisive set of commentaries he had started in 1917 with his newspaper piece "The Sahara of the Bozarts." Mencken's jibes had spurred Southern intellectuals to establish cultural oases in Charlotte, Richmond, and Nashville. Now Mencken's reflections on the Scopes trial prompted an even stronger reaction, especially among the Southern writers associated with *The Fugitive* (1922–25): John Crowe Ransom, Donald Davidson, Allen Tate, and Robert Penn

Warren. By 1930, their regional patriotism had solidified with a collective counterattack against Northern capitalist society, *I'll Take My Stand*.

During the prosperous twenties, Mencken had little good to say about democratic institutions or the qualifications of American businessmen, for him an *arriviste* plutocracy lacking "all the essential characteristics of a true aristocracy: a clean tradition, culture, public spirit, honesty, courage—above all—courage." Yet like his friend Sinclair Lewis, he shared a good many of the assumptions and values of the types he ridiculed. Moreover, their antics and idiocies furnished substance for his satirical pieces. The United States, he said, was "the only really amusing form of government ever endured by mankind." It never occurred to him, as it did to so many of the "lost generation," to leave it.

The migration to France in the early 1920s had little in common with the star-struck quests of nineteenth-century literary pilgrims, or even with the "wanderers" who had gone abroad to look, compare, enjoy, and criticize before or during Wilson's first term. For them, America was always the homeland, a place of possibilities. The new migrants also remained belligerently American, but they took off for Europe neither to explore hallowed ground nor with the intention of civilizing America on their return. They left because they were restless, or because they hoped to study, or to find a cheaper place to live, or to work out personal or artistic problems, or to escape Mencken's asinine public in favor of one that valued art more. "Lost generation" and "expatriate" are misleading clichés and much too vague to subsume the diverse group of writers and artists, the serious ones and the fakes, who lived abroad for varying lengths of time between the armistice and the stock-market crash of 1929. Put in the simplest terms, Berlin or Rome but chiefly Paris provided the fugitives with a cheap and attractive setting, a humane and tolerant climate. Most important, as Gertrude Stein observed, Paris was "where the twentieth century was" and where the most interesting modernist experiments were taking place. Sinclair Lewis's image of the drunken, sex-obsessed "expatriate" haunting the cafés of Montparnasse ("standardized rebels" fleeing "from the crushing standardization of America") has some basis in fact, but it shifts attention from the valuable literary consequences of what Ernest Hemingway remembered as a "moveable feast."

Europe (largely Paris) not only permitted writers to drink legally; it also gave them a congenial atmosphere in which to refine their craft. Some, like E. E. Cummings, John Dos Passos, and Ernest Hemingway, had fallen under the spell of Paris during the war and returned as soon as they could, drawn, as were those who came a few years later, to the center of avant-garde movements, the city of James Joyce, Ezra Pound, and Gertrude Stein. There they formed part of an American enclave and contributed to the advanced magazines that did so much to spread the news of dadaism and surrealism and to print the work of Hemingway, William Carlos Williams, and Hart Crane before most American publishers dared to take them on. Without the examples and direct influence of Paris-based intellectuals and artists, without such little magazines as *The Transatlantic Review* (1924), *The Little Review* (1924–29), *This Quarter* (1925–32), *transition* (1927–38), it would be hard to account for the experimental styles and international appeal of the best pre–World War II American writing.

The most impressive effort to combine international modernism with the native American strain occurred in 1919 with the revival of *The Dial* (1920–29), still widely considered the finest American journal of literature and the arts ever published in the United States. Among the new magazines of the early twenties, only *The Freeman* (1920–24), edited by the quirky and gifted Albert J. Nock, even approximated its quality. Both magazines had ties with the critics of *The Seven Arts*. *The Freeman* featured Van Wyck Brooks's fervent articles in which he warned American writers against a "sterile aestheticism" and summoned them to "project images of a beautiful, desirable, and possible social order." Scofield Thayer and J. S. Watson hoped to instill the spirit of Randolph Bourne into *The Dial*, but in contrast to Nock and Brooks they also opted for literary experimentation and were readier to follow the injunction of T. S. Eliot: "to maintain the autonomy and disinterestedness of literature." In keeping with their promise not to turn *The Dial* into an "organ of a clique or group," Thayer and Watson welcomed the aesthetic and ideological differences of their contributors and featured writers of antithetical literary tendencies in the pages of their magazine. The much discussed *Dial* awards went to Sherwood Anderson, T. S. Eliot, Van Wyck Brooks, Marianne Moore, E. E. Cummings, William Carlos Williams, and Ezra Pound—in short, to cultural nationalists and internationalists, to formalists fascinated by technical innovations, and to artists and thinkers preoccupied with social issues.

Almost immediately *The Dial* established a transatlantic communication line with distinguished English and European artists and writers and eventually scheduled monthly letters from foreign capitals. Readers at home and abroad praised its energy, tolerance, good humor, and high standards, as well as its elegant reproductions of modern drawing, painting, and sculpture. More cautious than *The Little Review*, which was forced to relocate in Paris after it was brought to trial in 1921 for publishing a "dirty" chapter of Joyce's *Ulysses*, *The Dial* editorially attacked censorship but took care (as

Thayer wrote to Joyce) not to fall under the "sinister shadow" of the post office. Over the decade it offered a neutral ground on which contending literary and intellectual camps could present their views and their work to its conventionally cultivated readership. It ceased publication in July 1929, just two years before the onset of nationalism and divisive political wrangling made the climate unsuitable for a magazine committed to catholicity and fairness.

No one followed the scenes and movements of the twenties and early thirties more attentively than Edmund Wilson, literary journalist, poet, critic, and novelist. Before he began to write steadily for *The New Republic* in 1925, his felicitous and intelligent reviews, his learning and integrity, made him a figure respected by all groups and factions. His work had appeared in *The Liberator*, *The Freeman*, *Vanity Fair*, and *The Dial*, magazines spreading across the entire literary and social spectrum. Sympathetic to the cultural nationalism of *The Seven Arts* and alert to the significance of Einstein and Freud for his literary generation, Wilson was also an early and appreciative reader of Joyce's *Ulysses*, Eliot's *The Waste Land*, and Hemingway's early short stories. He had pertinent things to say about the theater and the popular arts. Literature, he once said, "demands not only all one can give it but also all one can get other people to give." Hence he kept in touch with disparate groups of writers and artists, encouraging and criticizing their contributions, adjudicating their quarrels. He evenhandedly reported "discordant encounters" between the proponents of rival literary schools, and although immersed in the cultural turbulence of the twenties, he remained a disciplined moralist, condemning the "mean ambitions" and commercialism of the times and recording ominous signs of an impending earthquake.

One of these signs was the trial and electrocution of two anarchists, Nicola Sacco and Bartolomeo Vanzetti, in 1927, an event that inspired a reaction in literary circles somewhat comparable to the shock of John Brown's execution (1859) on his literary contemporaries. Wilson pronounced the Sacco-Vanzetti case "the most important and significant event that had happened in this country for some time," one that anatomized American life "with all its classes, professions and points of view and raised almost every fundamental question of our political and social system." His friend John Dos Passos strongly agreed. For them and for other writers of their age and background, the case symbolized the widening breach between themselves and the complacent middle and upper classes. On the eve of the execution, a group of writers—among them Dos Passos, Edna St. Vincent Millay, Michael Gold, and Katherine Anne Porter—kept vigil outside of Boston's Charlestown prison. Soon after, the stories of "the shoemaker" and "the fish peddler" were memorialized in elegies and polemics, in cartoons and paintings, in plays, poems, and novels. The death of the anarchists, John Dos Passos wrote later in his trilogy *U.S.A.*, polarized "two nations," setting the old-stock xenophobes and power-dealers against the underclass of "greasy foreigners" who spoke broken English and did the menial jobs.

Two years after this drama of social dislocation, the great stock-market crash of 1929 ushered in a long period of economic depression. It took several years to politicize American writers and artists, but the marshaling of forces was already detectable in another movement that peaked in 1930— the New Humanism. By this time the republic of letters was riddled with ideological dissension. Founded in 1926, *The New Masses* at first displayed something of the gay rambunctiousness of its namesake, *The Masses*, but it soon revealed its Communist party affiliation. As the promulgator of serious socialism and the class struggle, it turned its heavy guns against the "reactionary" doctrines of the New Humanism.

The New Humanists espoused no economic or political program but were nonetheless defenders of property—"*more important*," Paul Elmer More asserted, "*than the right to life.*" He and his friend, Irving Babbitt, had attracted few disciples outside the academy before the twenties. In time, however, they became more militant, and in 1930 they captured public attention with the publication of their manifesto, *Humanism and America*, which argued for social order, self-discipline, and a responsible elite while criticizing uncontrolled individualism, hedonism, and sentimental humanitarianism. To Michael Gold, one of the editors of *The New Masses*, the New Humanists were simply fascists. His bruising assault on the novels of Thornton Wilder in November 1930 (whom he incorrectly pegged as the quintessence of New Humanism) touched off a six-month free-for-all in the columns of *The New Republic* where it had appeared, and marked for Edmund Wilson "the eruption of the Marxist issues out of the literary circle of the radicals into the field of general criticism." Although Wilson took little stock in the social and aesthetic principles of Babbitt and More, the contrasting philosophies of New Humanism and communism still seemed to him the only systematic attempts "to deal with large political, social, moral, and aesthetic questions in a monumental and logical way." Yet once the New Humanists and a loose coalition of anti-Humanists had fired their ineffective salvos, the New Humanist cause sank from public sight. Its program for spiritual rehabilitation and emotional restraint had little appeal for Depression America.

The awarding of the Nobel Prize to Sinclair Lewis in 1930, the first American author ever to win it, offended both the New Humanists (who had pushed hard for their own candidate, Paul Elmer More) and the supporters of Theodore Dreiser, Lewis's only American contender. But it also upset many American critics who ranked Lewis far below Hemingway, Sherwood Anderson, Eugene O'Neill, or Willa Cather. The Swedish Academy, however, regarded Lewis as a symbol of a new and powerful American literature even though his best work was behind him. His novels had bolstered European preconceptions about American commercialism and complacence, the gulf between America's material and intellectual achievements, but they were also unsolemn, liberal, iconoclastic, and energetic. In his acceptance speech, Lewis unfairly lampooned many of his illustrious predecessors (to whom he owed unacknowledged debts), took a swipe at the American Academy of Arts and Letters, and ridiculed the "nebulous cult" of the New Humanists and their "chilly enthusiasms." But he generously saluted his literary contemporaries and expressed his joy "in being not too far removed from their determination to give to the America that has mountains and endless prairies, enormous cities and lost far cabins, billions of money and tons of faith, to an America that is as strange as Russia and as complex as China, a literature worthy of her vastness."

Lewis delivered his peroration as "billions of money and tons of faith" were evaporating in American coffers and minds. The business panic of 1929 presaged greater disasters to come. Urban breadlines lengthened, factories closed, and farmers burned unmarketable crops. The suddenness of the debacle caught writers, as well as the rest of the nation, by surprise, even those who had moved to the left during the apogee of the Great Bull Market in the late twenties. Now many more agreed with Edmund Wilson that the collapse "of that stupid gigantic fraud" pointed to a socialist solution and that it was time for intellectuals to leave their ivory towers and pitch into the job of social reconstruction.

Reformers of all kinds proffered cure-alls, but throughout the thirties the theory and programs of the Communist party attracted a considerable number of writers, artists, and intellectuals. In 1932 fifty-two of them—including Sherwood Anderson, Sidney Hook, Lincoln Steffens, Erskine Caldwell, Langston Hughes, Malcolm Cowley, and Edmund Wilson—signed an open letter backing the Communist presidential ticket. Thereafter socially concerned writers of differing political persuasions worked with communist-organized committees investigating violations of civil rights. They wrote articles, poems, and plays on behalf of the eight "Scottsboro boys" convicted in 1931 of the rape of two white women and sentenced to death by a kangaroo Alabama court (a decision later reversed by the Supreme Court);

they publicized the plight of the striking coal miners of Harlan County, Kentucky, embroiled in a bloody war with the operators; they joined such organizations as the national John Reed Clubs (named after the former Greenwich Village "playboy" and author of *Ten Days That Shook the World* who was buried in the Kremlin) and the communist-managed League of American Writers formed in 1935 to enlist support of unattached liberals in a "United Front" against fascism.

The "literary scenes" and "movements" in the thirties took on an increasingly public complexion as writers expressed, and masked, their personal anxieties in political metaphors and symbols. They pictured a final struggle looming between fascist Germany and the Soviet Union, bastion of international revolutionary socialism. Their emotional vision of a Soviet utopia, already under attack in the mid-thirties by anti-Stalinist radicals as well as conservatives, pretty well disappeared in 1939, but the dream died hard and left a bitter legacy. Leftist writers engaged in fierce sectarian wars and contributed to a dismal politicizing of culture. Doubters were pressured to take sides; critics probed for latent ideological heresies. All the same, this time of leagues, congresses, appeals, demonstrations, marches, manifestos, exposes, benefit performances could bring out the best as well as the worst in the participants.

One cultural-political episode—the birth, death, and revival of the *Partisan Review*—can be read as a microhistory of the literary left in the thirties. The conflicting accounts of its founding in 1934 and the sincerity of its revolutionary commitment, if not its literary significance, are still disputed. The young editors of the review were less amenable than their mentors on *The New Masses* to aesthetic directives from the Communist party and readier to profit from two decades of modernist innovation. The party at this stage conceived of art as a weapon to be employed in the war against capitalism, and it laid down criteria for revolutionary or "proletarian" writing. *Partisan Review* editors wanted to adapt the experiments of Joyce and Eliot to their "revolutionary tasks." They resisted party warnings against "Bohemian individualism and irresponsibility" and "the official idea of art as an instrument of political propaganda." Talented unattached writers, they argued, would not be lured into the progressive camp if subjected to the crude formulas of party philistines.

The first *Partisan Review* folded in 1936. Reorganized in 1937, it quickly repudiated Soviet communism for its own brand of anti-Stalinist Marxism and printed the work of writers heretofore unwelcome. In pages once reserved for unknown proletarian authors, steeped in the realities of the Depression and equipped to provide what orthodox communists considered "the real stuff of proletarian literature," there now appeared the alien names of Wallace Stevens, T. S. Eliot, Allen Tate, and W. H. Auden. It had been a short step from ideological to aesthetic deviation.

The Moscow "show trials" further splintered the American literary left. Staged by Stalin to purge the remnants of his political opposition, they featured "confessions" of penitent old Bolshevik "traitors." In revulsion, a number of disenchanted radical writers turned to the brilliant revolutionary leader, theorist, and historian, Leon Trotsky, exiled in Mexico and denounced by Stalin as the master-plotter of the fascist "imperialists." The American Communist party tried to justify the trials but only hardened the opposition of anti-Stalinists like Dos Passos who now accused the Communists of playing a dirty game in Spain.

The Spanish civil war had broken out in 1936 after the forces of General Francisco Franco, aided by Mussolini and Hitler, rebelled against the legitimately elected Republican government. In the United States, every antifascist group across the political spectrum rallied to the Loyalist side. At the second American Writers' Congress (1937), Archibald MacLeish linked the cause of Spain with the cause of democracy and morality. Ernest Hemingway described fascism as "a lie told by bullies" and asserted that "a writer who will not lie cannot live or work under fascism." In the next few years, the war in Spain prompted an outpouring of antifascist literature: fiction, plays, poetry, reportage, films. For the majority of writers, and particularly for those who fought in international brigades, Spain was the last great cause.

The collapse of the Spanish Republican government (March 1939) made all other historical events of that year—even the "sellout" of Czechoslovakia at Munich and the stunning nonaggression pact signed by Stalin and Hitler—seem anticlimactic. Save for a handful of diehards, the "pact" virtually killed Communist party influence over the intellectual community of the United States.

In sum, the impress of the Communist party on writers and intellectuals was real enough, but its impact on American culture as a whole and on American letters in particular was of less moment than that of home-bred movements and currents of thought. The party shaped and focused dissent, and yet, as it belatedly recognized, it had to project its public image in democratic rhetoric and American symbols to make any headway beyond a small and committed following. Communist leaders blundered when they dismissed the New Deal in its early phase as "social fascism." Only by adopting the slogan "Communism is twentieth-century Americanism" and by incorporating Tom Paine, John Brown, Walt Whitman, and "Abe" Lincoln into its revolutionary pantheon did it succeed partially in tapping the nationalist vein uncovered by the New Deal.

What is noteworthy about this allegedly "Red Decade," then, is not that some writers passed in and out of the Communist party or as "fellow travelers" followed the "party line," but that so many of them found "more life in the debris of democracy" than they had anticipated in the nadir of the Depression. Roosevelt's landslide victory in 1932 did not immediately cheer them. Literary radicals neither expected nor wanted capitalism to survive and at first interpreted New Deal reforms as an anodyne for "the profit-squeezing class." Not surprisingly, albeit from a conservative perspective, Mencken repudiated the President's men, calling them a "gang of professional politicians advised and abetted by a gang of half-educated pedagogues, non-constitutional lawyers, starry-eyed uplifters." Nor did Edmund Wilson ever reconcile himself to Franklin Roosevelt's "unctuous" speech and "Boy Scout smile." But he was not alone in welcoming the "defeat and consternation" of Roosevelt's enemies and, rather grudgingly, acknowledging his "benevolent influence." John Dos Passos remained skeptical of Roosevelt's style "of whiting the sepulchre with fair phrases and handouts," but he still preferred it to the Hitler-Mussolini style of "capitalist consolidation." In 1927, on the night Sacco and Vanzetti had been executed, Dos Passos seceded from the United States; in the early days of the New Deal he announced his return.

Benevolent or not, influences emanating from the White House and the New Deal offices were bound to affect maverick intellectuals. The government's initiation of what amounted to a cultural rescue operation resulted in an outpouring of literature, films, recordings, graphic art, photography. It has been rightly called "the most overwhelming effort ever attempted to document in art, reportage, social science, and history the life and values of the American people." The most remarkable feature of this efflorescence is not so much its quality (which is still debated) or its newness (its origins long antedated the thirties) but rather the conditions and circumstances that brought it into being.

First and foremost was the Depression itself. The Depression weakened popular faith in the ethos and ethics of business and in its crucial stage gave credence to the President's declaration that only concerted group action would enable the people to surmount the economic peril he likened to a foreign invasion. Second was the advent of a new communications revolution. Radio, talking pictures, musical recordings, and photographs not only dramatized the breadth and depth of the national crisis; they were also instruments employed by administration leaders to unify a disintegrating society and to raise popular hopes through a sophisticated evocation (Roosevelt's foes said "manipulation") of national myths and symbols. This surge of nationalism was too deep and widespread to be diverted by sporadic outbursts of nativism and xenophobia.

With the possible exception of Senator Huey Long, whose proposal to make every man a king had won masses of converts by the time of his assassination in 1935, the personalities and promises of demagogues posed little threat to the jaunty Roosevelt. Despite liberal fears that fascism "could happen here" and Communist allegations that it already *had* happened here, right-wing coups d'etat "happened" only in the fantasies of novelists like Sinclair Lewis and Nathanael West. Would-be Hitlers, the "night-shirt" fringe, made no headway with the public at large; rank and file Americans uncovered no scapegoats. The hysteria that in the previous decade lay behind "Red Scares," the deportation of "anarchists" and "bolsheviks" and the crusades of the Ku Klux Klan, did not break out in the thirties.

Perhaps the very magnitude of the Depression deadened for a time racist and ethnic phobias. A great leveler, the Depression put millions of "forgotten men" in the same leaky boat, among them the ethnic groups, once the targets of both rabble-rousing and genteel nationalists. In 1924, after a half-century of agitation, the "Nordic" anti-immigrationists pressured the Congress to slash the quotas of the so-called unassimilable breeds. By 1930, the "off-scourings" of Southern and Eastern Europe, of Asia and Latin America, had acquired a proprietary feeling for the United States and responded positively to Roosevelt's call to collective effort. For American culture as a whole, and for literature in particular, the importance of this multi-ethnic constituency cannot be exaggerated.

The onset of the Depression abruptly reversed the debunking style so prevalent in the twenties. One illustration of that change can be seen in the frequent and even fervent evocation of the "people"—a word that Mencken had associated with the inmates of zoos. Now the "people" were appealed to seriously and were depicted without condescension or satirical intent. The country had suffered an "earthquake" and a series of aftershocks. Literary journalists who set out to explore and report the effects of the devastation on the underlying population, and to assess the anger and bewilderment it had caused, emerged with a new respect for the resilience and toughness of ordinary Americans. Soon writers were giving a new resonance to phrases like "the American way of life" and "the American dream," as well as "the people." This is not to say that they and the rest of the artistic and intellectual community subscribed wholeheartedly to the poet Carl Sandburg's folksy celebrations of the Common Man's wit and wisdom (his book-length free verse poem, *The People, Yes*, published in 1936, is a somewhat excessive tribute to American speech and folkways), or to the New Dealish affirmations of Archibald MacLeish. But most writers in the thirties dealt with the American present or past without flippancy or cynicism.

In their retrospective mood, moved by a kind of cultural isolationism, writers and scholars located enduring national values precisely in those areas of the South and Midwest the Menckenians had scoffed at: small-town and rural America, the nation's heartland. A spate of biographies of the country's "fathers" and "grandfathers" restored their desecrated reputations and showed, in the words of a thirties reviewer, "that the past is a living part of the present." Exemplary lives of Benjamin Franklin and Thomas Jefferson, Andrew Jackson, Walt Whitman and Mark Twain, each of whom became the subject of poplar biography in the age of Roosevelt, could be read as apotheoses of the Common Man, epiphanies of the homespun. The historical past also furnished byways for escape, as the success of Margaret Mitchell's *Gone with the Wind* (1936) attests. This novel, published the same year as William Faulkner's extraordinary but virtually unnoticed tale of a doomed South, *Absalom, Absalom!*, further inflated the myths of the Civil War and Reconstruction, a period of domestic trial that commanded special interest among the history-minded in the 1930s.

The drift away from regionalism and toward national consensus is evident in the government-funded Federal Writers' Project (1935–42), a section of the Works Progress Administration (WPA) headed by Harry Hopkins (renamed the Work Projects Administration in 1939). The FWP's most significant achievement was a series of state guidebooks, the production of which involved an army (about 12,000 in all) of researchers, writers, and administrators. More than a compendium of towns and cities and collections of road tours, the American Guide Series constituted a new kind of human and historical geography, a Whitmanesque kaleidoscope that disclosed to discerning readers the "real" United States hidden "behind billboards and boosterism." A few professional writers in the Project—John Cheever, for example, or Conrad Aiken—resented the anonymity of their contributions and the limited time allotted to them to do their own work and therefore quit as soon as they could afford to. Yet to them and to many still unrecognized writers, the Project offered a haven and an opportunity. The tasks of digging into folklore and ethnic culture, and the exposure to other kinds of Americana, according to one of the Project's historians, "turned out to be the most effective measure that could have been taken to nurture the future of American letters." Richard Wright and Ralph Ellison were two among the Project's notable beneficiaries. Recalling his debt years later, Saul Bellow wrote: "This was the day before gratitude became obsolete. We never had expected anyone to have any use whatsoever for us. With no grand illusions about Roosevelt or Harry Hopkins, I believe they behaved decently and imaginatively for men without culture—which is what politicians necessarily are."

It has been plausibly argued as well that the New Deal's focus on the South (in Roosevelt's words, the "Nation's No. I problem") created a wider audience for Southern writers already or soon to be at the height of their powers. Government-sponsored photographs of share-croppers and factory hands in Southern mill towns; the guidebooks to Southern states; the New Deal–inspired studies of Southern rural life and folk culture; the publicity generated by the Tennessee Valley Authority (TVA); journalistic surveys; and, most of all, the fiction of writers as different as Ellen Glasgow, William Faulkner, T. S. Stribling, Eudora Welty, Erskine Caldwell, and Thomas Wolfe—all corrected simplistic notions of the South and of Southern character. Instead of the stereotypical "South," an unspecified territory inhabited by grotesques and throbbing with violence, Southern writers and publicists in the thirties depicted many "Souths," each resisting or struggling to accommodate their ways to modern America. It was in this decade, too, that the greatest writer of them all, William Faulkner, put his "own little postage stamp of native soil" on the map of world literature.

The New Deal's subvention of the arts can also be seen as an attempt to heighten further the national consciousness by encompassing the shared historical experience of a people. In the course of surveying the national legacy, the Federal Art Project documented in photographs and films what could happen when even a nation as rich as the United States abused its human and physical resources. The documents gave marginal Americans, blacks and "native sons," their long-denied recognition, and thereby affected the cultural climate of the post–World War II years. The men and women who decorated public buildings and painted the urban and rural landscape; who transcribed the stories of former slaves, compiled an index of American design, and recorded folk music; who produced a Harlem adaptation of *Macbeth* with a West Indian setting and a black *Swing Mikado;* who collected little-known facts for state and local histories—they were themselves an ethnic and racial conglomeration, old stock and new stock, representing, like the New Deal, a new consensus.

The most sensational social protest novel of the decade, John Steinbeck's *The Grapes of Wrath* (1939), managed to capture this consensus. In contrast to the trilogy by John Dos Passos, *U.S.A* (1930, 1932, 1936; collected 1937), a technically inventive, biting, and pessimistic story of American commercialism and exploitation between 1900 and 1930 and one of the major literary achievements of the thirties, Steinbeck's slicker and more sentimental novel was positive and hopeful. It aroused humanitarian indignation in the teeth of a conservative reaction without undermining confidence in the redeemable republic. Based on the epic trek of Oklahoma and Texas families who, driven off their lands by dust and drought, drifted like lemmings toward the Promised Land of California, *The Grapes of Wrath* orchestrated much of the experience and many of the themes of the thirties. The Joad family is part of a migrant army, one of the many "armies" marching through the "Angry Decade." The novel abounds in disasters, celebrates the bravery and essential goodness of ordinary people, exhales the moral urgency of the period. Most important, it binds the Depression, the overwhelming fact of the thirties, to America's democratic heritage.

Far more persuasively than the Communist writers, Steinbeck put his radical-sounding statements in the American vernacular and framed his accounts of social injustice in scenes a large cross-section of the public could grasp. Communist reviewers praised Steinbeck for writing a revolutionary book, but plainly *The Grapes of Wrath* was New Deal, not Stalinist, art. It condemned "economic royalists" rather than "capitalist exploiters"; it owed more to the evangelical progressivism of nineteenth-century reformers than to Karl Marx. Even the novel's symbolism was New Dealish (the migrants' only place of refuge is a government camp); and Steinbeck conveyed his apple-pie radicalism without recourse to left-wing clichés ("toiling masses," "capitalist lackeys," and the like) so alien to American ears. His stagey dialogue and narrative at times bordered on the maudlin, but his theme—that Americans must put aside private greed and cooperate to save the country and their souls—won a favorable response even from readers out of sympathy with his recipe.

The thirties are not usually thought of as years of unusual creativeness, and few literary masterpieces composed during the decade can be attributed to New Deal influences. In fact, the great literary accomplishments—Robert Frost's *A Further Range* (1936); Wallace Stevens's *Ideas of Order* (1936) and *The Man with the Blue Guitar* (1937); Ernest Hemingway's *Winner Take Nothing* (1933); and William Faulkner's *As I Lay Dying* (1930), *Light in August* (1932), and *Absalom, Absalom!* (1936), to name a few—seem remote from Depression issues. Some remarkable works of the period, however, undervalued when they appeared, more obviously addressed the conditions of a sick society: for example, the savage and brilliant novels of Nathanael West; Henry Roth's powerful and stylistically modernist story of a ghetto child,

Call It Sleep (1934); and *Let Us Now Praise Famous Men* (published in 1941 but begun five years earlier) by James Agee and photographer Walker Evans. The last, ostensibly a study of cotton tenantry in Alabama, was both an exhaustive account of a few impoverished dirt-farmer families and a lyrical celebration of the human spirit. These books suggest that in the strife-ridden and agitated thirties, even those writers obsessed with grim and tragic themes were surprised by their own and their country's unsuspected vitality.

The Great Depression of the 1930s cast a giant shadow over the whole decade. The overwhelming event of the forties was World War II. It took the Japanese bombing of Pearl Harbor (1941) to propel the country officially into war, but United States abandonment of strict neutrality began soon after Germany's invasion of Poland in 1939. With Roosevelt's domestic program stalled by an increasingly conservative Congress, the economy still sputtered, but on the eve of America's entrance into the war against the Axis powers it had begun to revive. "Dr. New Deal," the President announced, had done his work. Now "Dr. Win-the-War" would take over, prepared to woo the mulish opponents of his policies and to form a workable coalition against the Fascist machine. Between 1941 and 1945, the entire country, including most writers and intellectuals, donned real or metaphorical uniforms in "the fight for national survival."

Before Pearl Harbor, the literary community did not unanimously support intervention. Communist writers (for whom the war had been "phony" or "imperialist" until the Germans invaded the Soviet Union in June 1941) were volubly hostile to it. Even nonaligned liberals, clearly antifascist and sympathetic to the beleaguered British but still bitter over the "betrayal" of Spain and Czechoslovakia to the Nazis, hesitated to renounce the principle of neutrality. The fall of France in 1940, however, alarmed all who had hoped to see Hitler's Third Reich collapse without American involvement. The prospect of a quick German victory impelled writers like Van Wyck Brooks, Lewis Mumford, and Archibald MacLeish to press for direct aid to the Allies before German armies conquered Europe and enslaved the world.

One ringing testament for intervention, MacLeish's "The Irresponsibles" (1940), precipitated a hot literary debate. America's writers and artists, he charged, had over the years created a moral vacuum by casting doubts on political and cultural ideals and thereby weakening the nation's resistance to poisonous foreign ideologies. The novels of Hemingway and Dos Passos in particular, he charged, had "done more to disarm democracy in the face of fascism than any other single influence." MacLeish's mournful rebuke of the two novelists he acknowledged to be "the best and most sensitive of my generation" drew caustic replies. Edmund Wilson dismissed the accusation as poppycock. He especially resented MacLeish's plea to American writers not "to weaken the validity of the Word even when the deceptions of the Word have injured them." Dwight Macdonald, then a *Partisan Review* editor, denounced MacLeish's "totalitarian" argument, and like-minded critics spoke out against literary thought-controllers who would "turn literature into a certain Stars and Stripes Forever."

The flurry over the MacLeish offensive on behalf of a positive life-affirming literature can be seen as another episode in the drawn-out contest between the literary nationalists and the literary formalists, as well as an extension of the old thirties debate on the compatibility of art and propaganda. The menace of fascism had transformed the literary interventionists, according to their adversaries, into "critic-patriots" unable to distinguish between the artist as citizen and the artist as artist. This failure, so the argument ran, made them inadvertently the allies of geopoliticians like Henry R. Luce, publisher of *Time*, *Life*, and *Fortune* magazines and unsavory prophet of America's coming economic and political hegemony. Forgotten was Randolph Bourne's warning to writers to shun the dangerous embrace of the state.

Still, signs of the state's coercive power on the literary mind were less evident in 1941 than in 1917. In 1917, Wilson's government recruited "publicity talent" and passed harsh laws in its efforts to stifle dissent. In 1941, all parties and all classes mobilized without prodding against a common enemy, and soberly took part in the war effort with no illusions about the coming "Century of the Common Man." The war fiction presented American soldiers as an amalgam of the best and the worst, and as remaining quite unmoved by ideology. The first reports of battles and invasions from war correspondents, Hemingwayesque in style and spirit, bristled with unadorned facts and were studiedly devoid of patriotic flourishes. Ernie Pyle's poignant battle diaries, Ira Wolfert's and Richard Tregaskis's accounts of the ferocious Pacific war, and Martha Gellhorn's hospital scenes anticipated the postwar novels that were already incubating in the minds of writer-soldiers like James Jones, Norman Mailer, and Joseph Heller. The nightmare panorama of a battle-stricken world challenged untested beliefs in the innocence and essential goodness of human nature and seemed to document the neo-Calvinist reassertion of original sin.

Reinhold Niebuhr, a prominent theologian, sanctioned this dark view of the human condition in a series of widely discussed books and lectures. An early advocate of democratic collectivism and a qualified believer in the possibility of beneficent social change, Niebuhr had looked for ways to approximate a tolerable society without reliance on utopian blueprints. After Munich, his conviction deepened that "the inevitable tragedy of human existence, the irreducible irrationality of human nature," must be faced up to. Institutions were evil because men were evil.

The stories that poured in from the war theaters—of destroyed cities, of annihilated armies and civilian populations, of millions disposed of in crematoriums—proved for many intellectuals the truth of Niebuhr's speculations on original sin and the inadequacy of purely secular solutions to social problems. Although Niebuhr continued to advocate social justice and to support liberal programs, his writings fueled the assault against what the critic Lionel Trilling later called the "liberal imagination." In time, Niebuhr's central terms ("irony," "the tragic sense," "complexity," and "ambiguity") reappeared in the vocabulary of the postwar New Criticism, an influential approach to literature that was buttressed by the political and religious orthodoxy of T. S. Eliot. In circles in which the doctrine of "man's fallen nature" gained currency, the naturalism predominant in the thirties quickly passed into disfavor.

Paradoxically, and unbeknownst to the intellectual community, a popular expression of a philosophy even more anticollectivist than that of the aroused literary traditionalists, but antireligious as well, began to attract a large underground readership in the early forties. This was Ayn Rand's *The Fountainhead* (1943), a crude biographical novel with a Homeric soap-opera plot about the travails and ultimate triumph of a Nietzschean architect, a triple-pronged foray against collectivism, altruism, and mysticism, and a celebration of "rational self-interest." To vindicate his individuality, the hero blows up his own housing development, because "second-raters" have viciously tampered with his designs. He is improbably exonerated by a jury who swallow his un-Niebuhrian thesis that happiness is an inalienable right.

In 1945, two years after Ayn Rand's hymn to freedom, President Roosevelt died, and a real bomb exploded over Hiroshima. Roosevelt's death closed one era; the atomic bomb inaugurated another. During the fifteen years between 1930 and 1945, Americans had grown accustomed to Roosevelt's reassuring presence; he had embodied their confidence and their modified hope that "the forgotten man" could get his due and that government could be made accessible to all. During the years since Hiroshima, the "Bomb" has proved far more portentous than Halley's Comet. It continues to haunt the world.

Daniel Aaron

II. Regionalism, Ethnicity, and Gender: Comparative Literary Cultures

Regionalism: A Diminished Thing

Asked to name the regions of the United States, almost everyone would probably reply: New England, the South, the Midwest, and the West (or possibly the Far West). These, after all, are what we might say constitute the traditional regions. They really are not quite that traditional. In his monumental *History of the United States During the Administrations of Jefferson and Madison*, Henry Adams, looking back from 1885 to the state of the nation in 1800, divided the young country into three parts: New England, the middle states, and the Southern states. Beyond the original thirteen states, there were only Vermont, Kentucky, and Tennessee (Ohio would not be admitted until 1802). The two latter states were, in effect, the western United States. To the north of them was the Northwest Territory, to the south, the Old Southwest, consisting of what is now Alabama and Mississippi. The rest of what is now the country was actually international in identity, belonging to Spain and, slightly later, to France. Thomas Jefferson, looking to the mountains from Monticello, saw only the west stretching beyond them, and he engineered the Louisiana Purchase to claim all the west he could for his country. After the Missouri Compromise in 1820 drove the old Mason-Dixon line westward between free and slave states, the country changed from an east-west to a north-south axis, leaving Jefferson in his old age to foresee the ultimate division of the union. The North expanded into the Northwest Territory, the South into the Southwest, each competing to add states on its side of the fatally surveyed line. This competition greatly accelerated westward expansion at the same time that it intensified the regional conflict.

With the admission to statehood of California in 1850, there was at last a West beyond the west, though not yet a Midwest. That, as we know it today, came after the Civil War, and when it came it was not the real Midwest at all but more or less the old Northwest Territory. The Old Southwest disappeared into the defeated Confederacy, which, after its disastrous experiment at nationhood, came to include every state that had been in it. The border states—Kentucky and Tennessee—did not make it into the Midwest but, in the national mind and even to themselves, remained more Southern than Northern. Then there was the West, transforming itself from territory into new states beyond the free states that existed before the Civil War, creating a Midwest behind it that seemed more Eastern than it ever had before. As the country drove toward the Pacific, the countercurrent of cultural memory drove east, so that Virginia and New England became almost for westerners what England had been to the colonists.

To begin to glimpse the volatility at work in the making of what seem to be traditional regions is to recognize the pressures still at work on our regional vision. New England, which never quite surrendered its identity to the North in the polarization of the Civil War, is at the point of being overwhelmed by the tyranny of compass designations, as it becomes merely a part of the Northeast. The chief force operating to produce the change is the emergence of a new Southwest—the Sun Belt—made possible by air conditioning, which has in turn made possible industrial expansion and retirement communities in that region. The burgeoning of the Sun Belt has taken Texas, never wholly in the South, into the Southwest, and made the Old South the Southeast. Not that these lines of force are totally new. The land from the beginning ran southwest, following the Appalachian range from the White Mountains to northern Mississippi. It is well to remember that Thoreau, a surveyor as well as a writer, always set his compass southsouthwest when he went walking.

So much for the emergence of regions. Regionalism in literature, though associated with political and geographical regions, is a different thing. First of all, it involves language, and language is a problem in the United States. The nation was from the beginning and through its life but a dialect, a region, of the English language. It was textually intruded into the world of nations, and the texts—the Declaration of Independence and the Constitution—were English. The difficult issue facing the American writer was the effort to make a national literature for a country without a native language, just as the chief difficulty for scholars and literary critics has been to distinguish between American and English literature. To acknowledge so much does not mean that there is no American literature. If American writers were burdened with the act of writing in English, their glory was both their wish and their determination to be *American*. America *was* their region, and however many dialects existed within the nation, from the perspective of England—an outside perspective—all writers were American.

From an inside perspective, there was a great difference. The regions, or sections, within a country "regional" in its language but national in its identity, still had the revolutionary possibility of themselves being nations. Until the Civil War settled the issue by force, there was the chance, however risky and undesirable, of secession on the part of states or sections of the union. New England had pondered such a decision at the Hartford Convention when a faction of the Federalist party met to consider secession. As long as secession was a possibility, sectionalism of a fierce and independent sort could smolder. It finally burst forth, not in New England but in the South. The Civil War permanently annihilated that possibility, though not until the South had diastrously experimented with four years of nationhood. If freedom from slavery was won in the war, the possibility of secession was permanently lost.

After the Civil War, which is to say both after the war was being won and after it was won, regions, as we think of them to this day, displaced the fierce sectionalism that had led to the national conflict. Regions, in this post–Civil War sense, are sections that have lost not merely national political power but the political power to be nations. There is the "diminished thing" of my title. The sectional strife preceding the war reflected much more than the growing determination of the South to secede. It revealed in the North, and particularly in New England, a corresponding claim to be the essence of the nation. John Greenleaf Whittier could write "Massachusetts to Virginia" with an untrammeled conscience, assured that there were "No fetters in the Bay State—, no slave upon our land!" Abraham Lincoln's own rhetoric tended toward logical division of the nation coupled with a national moral imperative of *union* (and, later, freedom) as the unconditional principle of the nation.

Looking back from 1900 upon the literary situation in New England when he had come there just before the Civil War, William Dean Howells could write in *Literary Friends and Acquaintance:*

Certainly the city of Boston has distinctly waned in literature, though it has waxed in wealth and population. I do not think there are in Boston to-day even so many talents with a literary coloring in law, science, theology, and journalism as there were formerly; though I have no belief that the Boston talents are fewer or feebler than before. I arrived in Boston, however, when all talents had more or less a literary coloring, and when the greatest talents were literary. These expressed with ripened fulness a civilization conceived in faith and brought forth in good works; but that moment of maturity was the beginning of a decadence which could only show itself much later. New England has ceased to be a nation unto itself and it will perhaps never again have anything like a national literature; and it will probably be centuries yet before the life of the whole country, the American life as distinguished from the New England life, shall have anything like a national literature. It will be long before our larger life interprets itself in such imagination as Hawthorne's, such wisdom as Emerson's, such poetry as Longfellow's, such prophesy as Whittier's, such grace as Holmes's, such humor and humanity as Lowell's.

However we might revise Howells's valuations of the particular writers— only Hawthorne and Emerson would remain in *our* canon—his observation about New England is remarkable. Coming from a writer who entered that commanding literary environment and not only succeeded in it but literally succeeded it, Howells sees with great precision both its regional and its national nature. Moreover, he sees that the era of his own succession represents a decline in power and authority of the region. The decline has occurred between 1865 and 1900, the years when literary realism, regionalism, and local color became the dominant aspects of American literature, aspects that Howells himself powerfully championed. The implications of his vision are clear. Literary realism and regionalism not only have accompanied a decline of regional power; their fidelity to regional life has failed to sustain their power to be a national literature.

Howells significantly resorts to an agricultural metaphor to explain New England's decline, observing that the region had arrived at a ripened fullness marking the beginning of decadence. Since he is writing a personal history, his metaphor is perhaps adequate for his purposes, yet he is a part of a much larger history. The New England maturity he speaks of is historically the moment of Civil War, which ended New England dominance almost as much as it spelled defeat for the South. Where sections had been there were now regions. In this historical context, regions become the imaginative space created by the loss of national potentiality. What was political possibility becomes literary possibility, what was expansiveness becomes closure, what was a future becomes a past. These are the losses—and these the gains—registered in the conversion from section to region.

Here the career of a single writer, Harriet Beecher Stowe, assumes immense significance. She began writing as a regionalist in the old republic. Her first work, entitled "A New England Sketch," was published in 1834 in James Hall's *Western Magazine*. In the second paragraph of that slight yet significant beginning, the author, expressing her determination to eschew the exotic settings of romance in favor of the homely yet honest plainness of her native land, calls her own effort "a little breeze of patriotism." In that assertion, the identity of regionalism and nationalism, which Howells remembered at its height of power, is already evident. By 1843 Mrs. Stowe was able to publish a collection of New England sketches, entitled *The Mayflower*, indicating in a volume depicting the moral virtues and droll humor of simple New England life and character her claim to the Pilgrim past. But with *Uncle Tom's Cabin* in 1852, she broke away from regional character sketch into the melodramatic novel form at the same time she took up the central political issue of her day. In the process she paradoxically succeeded in annihilating sectionalism, finding in the South a present historical and social evil upon which she at once focused and exorcised the sense of evil she had inherited from her Puritan forebears. If the Southern planter was directly condemned by her vision, the arbitrary masculine God of Calvinism, as merciless as planters in taking suitors away from young women and infants away from mothers, was implicitly attacked.

She had no sooner completed *Uncle Tom's Cabin* than she began work on a New England novel, only to be caught in the storm of events her novel had reflected, forecast, and in no small way precipitated. Not until 1859 did she complete *The Minister's Wooing*, her first New England novel, and in the years following she continued to write novels set in New England. Her ambition was to write a novelistic history of New England, covering the years between the American Revolution and the disestablishment of the Connecticut theocracy in 1818. Not that she approved the theocracy; she did not. But, admiring the strength of its moral austerity, she felt that its disappearance signified that the true heart of the region had died. Though there was a corollary contention that the past was the continual and continuing inheritance of the region, the only hope in the contention rested on the claim that the upright character of New England had been diffused to enrich the nation. If she had anticipated the Civil War with her passionate melodrama, she anticipated post–Civil War regional literature with her imaginative recognition that the region, having provided the possibilities of a patriotic national literature, was now about to become an exemplary past to be chronicled in romances. The turn in her intentions is well registered in 1855, the year of *Leaves of Grass*, when she brought out a new edition of her regional sketches, this time entitled *The May Flower*, as if to emphasize the transformation of the sturdy Pilgrim identity into the delicate and fragile flower that blooms in the stony soil cultivated by the stern old settlers.

In any event, Mrs. Stowe was prophetic for a second time. The triumph of the Union meant that the old sections and the separate states were subordinated to the federal government in a way that would have made Jefferson tremble for his country as much as he trembled for it in the face of slavery. The two polarized sections, New England and the South—around which the sectional strife had dramatized itself—were left politically and economically stricken. Political power that had, in national elections, centered in Massachusetts and Virginia went to Ohio, from which president after president came until the person of Warren Gamaliel Harding enabled the nation to bid goodbye to all that.

All of which brings us back to William Dean Howells, who, coming from Ohio, was made assistant editor of the *Atlantic Monthly* in 1866, a year after his return from Italy, where he had spent the war years as Venetian consul, a post he received in return for having written the campaign biography of Lincoln. Ambitious in the extreme, Howells, who, under the cover of an official trip to report back to his Columbus newspaper the nature of New England industry, had made a personal pilgrimage to the land of his literary idols, returned to what he knew was the strongest literary base of operations in the country. Whatever New England was losing in the aftermath of the war, its literature remained. If the strength of the rising Midwest is reflected in its having nurtured such a talent as that of Howells, the strength of New England lay in the powerful opportunity it could offer such a writer. In the twenty-three years of his residence in Boston before moving to New York, Howells established himself as one of the strongest writers of his period. More important, he became the most powerful editor in the history of American literature—powerful because he fully understood the American literary situation, because he recognized the strong writers of his generation, because he kept himself abreast of literature on an international scale, and because he assimilated, practiced, and championed the dominant literary movement of his time—realism. Determined to attract the best literature of the nation to the pages of the *Atlantic*, he immediately recognized Mark Twain and Henry James, both of whom subverted the genteel New England establishment—the first with a bedrock hostility to conventional morality, the second by transcendent refinement of form.

That still left the region of New England itself, which Howells, as much as any Midwesterner with genuine literary vision, could see had shrunk to the status of province in a union that was expanding to the Pacific. The fact that, as a friend of Rutherford Hayes and James Garfield, he had the political influence to get his old friend and patron, James Russell Lowell, the position of ambassador to England, could hardly be lost on a person of Howells's social and regional awareness. And he could see, in the deaths of

Longfellow, Emerson, and Whittier, how rapidly the mighty were falling. Yet it was Howells's commitment to realism coupled with his ambition to make it the ideology of a national literature for his generation that enabled him to appreciate and support literature from the provinces. Regionalism became, in the long battle being waged by realism against romanticism and the sentimental romance, a subordinate order of realism. In the literary history that Howells was helping so much to make, regionalism constituted a small-scale representation of the larger reality of national literature, reflecting as it did the diminished order of things rather than the grandiose and exotic claims of romance. Moreover, the local color movement provided a field in which Howells's adopted region of New England could continue to lead the country.

The writers who contributed most to the movement were, significantly, women. It is not too much to call them the literary daughters of Harriet Beecher Stowe. Like hers, their setting was New England, and like her they had an eye for regional scene and, more important, an ear for regional speech. But they brought to the form a self-consciousness of art resembling the efforts of Irving, Hawthorne, and Poe. Dramatic irony and psychological motivation displaced sentimentality and conventional morality. Regional type was strengthened through individuation of character. The general picture of New England in the work of Sarah Orne Jewett, Mary E. Wilkins Freeman, and Alice Brown is one of recessiveness, disclosing the isolate individual at the edge of eccentricity in the process of resisting change on the one hand and outmoded traditional social and religious pressures on the other. The old loneliness of Hawthorne is there, but the allegorical element is gone. Stereotypes are there, but dialect, description, and characterization are sharpened and refined. These writers gave one last cultivation to the region, but it is a region whose nature has grown thin, whose economy has grown stingy, whose society has grown small.

Beyond these achievements, however, the values of these writers rest too comfortably in the national ethos of freedom to enable them to escape the gentility of the male literary establishment that patronizingly encouraged them. Their region was a refuge for imaginative expression, yet it was also the enclosure that kept them in their place. If they were accorded the status of artist by the editors who supported them and were no longer seen as the scribbling women of whom Hawthorne complained, they were just as surely being defined as minor writers representing a region no longer able to hold its own against the major economic and political forces of the dynamic Union. Lincoln, the very embodiment of those forces, had called Harriet Beecher

Stowe a little woman but in the same breath had said she started the big war. There was no war of that scale to start under the tutelage of E. C. Stedman, R. W. Gilder, or, for that matter, W. D. Howells.

What of this New England regional movement in the last third of the nineteenth century? First, it represented the national regional movement in literature following the Civil War. Second, it gave continuance to the forms of sketch and tale, so vital a part of American literature. Irving's *Sketch Book* had signaled the aptness of the form for a nation that was but a region of the English language. Hawthorne had followed Irving, and Poe, in a review of Hawthorne's *Twice-told Tales*, had provided a critical rationale for the tale, elevating it to the status of art. Third, the movement opened an avenue for women to compete in the arena of *literature*, an avenue that has remained open ever since. Finally, these writers provided a model for other regional writers to follow so that, by the turn of the century, there was a much greater sense of regional identity in the country. In the South and Midwest, however, though there were practitioners of regional art, there was neither the strong tradition of literature nor the presence of a literary center like Boston to give the sense or the image of a truly literary region. Though a Southern writer like Thomas Nelson Page mastered dialect, he could never plot his way out of historical romance. He displayed the congenital Southern penchant for an outmoded romanticism, which, though it formally reflected his defense of the Southern past, left him engulfed in the novel form and at the same time cut him off from the dominant ideology of realism. Mary Noailles Murfree could write about the Southern mountains; Kate Chopin and Grace King about New Orleans; Joel Chandler Harris could immerse animal fables in wonderful black dialect. Yet the very specificity of locale and dialect made them truly local colorists. In the Midwest, Edward Eggleston's Hoosier Schoolmaster showed a realism of character and speech yoked to a romantic plot; and Hamlin Garland, following Howells's "major" ideology of realism—he called it veritism—attempted a large-scale chronicle of the region that lacked the fine compression of regional form.

This highly truncated account of the regional movement makes clear how much New England, even as its literary force was waning, remained the dominant region in American literature until 1900. It had a coherent body of writing reaching back to William Bradford's *Of Plimmoth Plantation*; it had in Emerson, Hawthorne, and Thoreau the strongest writers of the nation, and in Longfellow, Lowell, Holmes, and Whittier proof that American poetry could successfully emulate the English poets. The fact that these poets came to be called the Schoolroom Poets indicates how profoundly the *idea* of New England saturated the nation's schools; and it had in the distinguished Harvard faculty the means of creating an intellectual history of the country showing that New England settlers had been the originating force of American freedom. More than any other region, it had defined and articulated the free union that was reborn in civil war.

Still, the region was losing power. If it had the power to attract Howells and Mark Twain, it nonetheless needed the influx of energy they brought. Having become a world in which body yielded to mind, life was secondary to learning, nature was superseded by culture, and passion was dominated by morality, the region was, in a word, genteel. Impressive in its standards and general conduct, it was finally complacent in its self-approval.

The best evidence of what had happened to life and literature in the home of Emerson, Hawthorne, and Thoreau was the Concord Library's decision in 1885 to remove *Adventures of Huckleberry Finn* from its shelves on grounds that the book was offensive to both taste and morals. The next year the true genius of the region, Emily Dickinson, died in Amherst, unpublished and unknown. Finally, in 1889, Howells left Boston for New York, a date that could mark the end of New England's preeminence as the leading literary region.

Howells's decision also revealed the supremacy of New York as the literary capital of American literature from that time to this. It would be—and has remained—the place for aspiring writers like Howells to go in search of the literary life. It had never been a sectional or regional center as Boston had been. It was expansive, volatile, and embodied the dynamism of capital growth. As a literary capital, it in no way represented regional identity. Its great writers gave a clue to its meaning. Irving's *Sketch Book* reflected the impulse to tour England, promising Irving's later tour of the prairie. Cooper envisioned Natty Bumppo moving westward with an all-conquering civilization even as he elegiacally recorded the extinction of Indian civilization that fatally accompanied it. The dying Bumppo could say "Here!" in the far Dakotas, at once answering the heavenly roll call and asserting an indefinite location in the endless expanse of the west. Melville wrote of the Pacific with its thousand leagues of blue into which he sent an epic captain and crew on a nihilistic voyage bound round the world. Whitman, his feet firmly on the granite of Manhattan, embraced the universe, determined to find a passage to India. James had much of New England gentility in him, but his cosmopolitanism came as much from Irving as from James Russell Lowell. Certainly the expeditionary force of questing Americans he sent into Europe had much more to do with the New York than the Boston spirit. It is hardly surprising that he crowned his career with the New York Edition of his works.

New York was at once intensely American, international, and modern. In its polyglot population, its capacity to renew itself, its unquestioned position at the head of capital investment, and its accelerating drive into the future, it was the essence of naked American energy. It was, to borrow a phrase from Harold Rosenberg, the tradition of the new. Add to all this the fact that it was, and was to be, the undisputed center of publishing and communications, and one has a notion of its identity. Far from representing a region as Boston had done, it was the very antithesis of the regional—a consuming threat against which the regional spirit would have to define itself as best it could. The relationship of the regions to this city would have to be resistance. New York might publish them but it would not nurture them.

Still there were regions at the turn of the century. A succinct way to define them in relation to each other is to measure their stereotypical image in terms of an economic model exchange, seeking to gauge their political, cultural, and moral resources. New England was politically poor, yet, on the face of things, culturally and morally rich—a wealth that enabled it to make a virtue out of its relatively skimpy economic base. Already in industrial and agricultural decline, its mills leaving for the Midwest and later the South and its farmers continuing to leave for the Midwest, it would pride itself on its Yankee ingenuity of making do with little. It still had Harvard University, which Robert Frost, Gertrude Stein, T. S. Eliot, Conrad Aiken, Wallace Stevens, John Dos Passos, E. E. Cummings, James Gould Cozzens, Charles Olson, Robert Lowell, and Norman Mailer—to name but a few—were to attend. Harvard was thus as dominant in its capacity to attract future writers as it was in influencing the historical interpretations of the past. Most important, however, was New England's capacity to preserve its rural identity against the tide of urban expansion into Connecticut, Rhode Island, and Massachusetts. The essentially rural world of New England was shrinking into the picturesqueness of Maine, New Hampshire, and Vermont, where the unchallenged whiteness of the racial situation matched the whiteness of the steeples and the snow, yet New England made that shrinking image stand, in the eyes of the nation and in its own eyes, as a place of nature and villages where individual rights were still sacred. There were deep-seated reasons for the prevalence of an essentially rural New England. Emerson and Thoreau had made the village of Concord stronger than literary Boston. Equally important, the relation between Boston and rural region was one of economic and cultural reciprocity. Summer people have been invading New England for a hundred and fifty years; urban artists have been capitalizing on the landscape of mountains and coast for just as long. At the same time, farmers and village folks have been able to reap enough financial benefits from the annual incursion of summer people (and, more recently, winter people!) to look upon vacationers as one more cash crop. Then too, the vacationers and newcomers to the region take pride in the stereotype, cultivating it into a postcard image of itself as a means of preserving the past in the present.

That very past, however, left New England ill-prepared to flourish in a nation whose literary center was New York and in a century whose literary revolution would be that of modernism. There is only one major writer from New England (and he was born in San Francisco) whose work everyone would recognize as both major and regional: Robert Frost. True, Edwin Arlington Robinson preceded him. And, until "Ben Jonson Entertains a Man from Stratford" launched him on a journey that eventually took him into the toils of King Arthur's Court, Robinson had, in Tilbury Town, created a series of portraits that strike the true chord of New England. Robinson's strength was his ability to truncate narrative into lyric and sonnet form in such a way as to make background and character a haunting inferential foreground for the reader. But it was Frost who, through a long life, truly occupied the region. The title of his first book, *A Boy's Will* (1913), coming as it did from Longfellow's "My Lost Youth," signaled what its romantic lyrics tended to obscure—the depth of Frost's relation to the region. *North of Boston* (1914) was a different book. It not only laid out Frost's position in a rural New England shrinking *north* of Boston but disclosed in dramatic monologues and narratives the lonely, broken, desolate lives of people not quite or just barely holding their own in a marginal economy and on marginal land about to be reclaimed by nature. The subject matter was deeply akin to the short stories of Jewett, Freeman, and, particularly, Alice Brown; the spirit and detail owed much to Emerson and Thoreau. But the form involved a bending of blank verse—as if the traditional English pentameter were as supple as a birch tree being subjugated by a boy's will—toward the nature of New England earth and speech. If Frost's form bent the parent English line to the region, it lifted informal and colloquial speech into the realm of poetry. Throughout a life of poetry, Frost continued his conversion of an inescapably recognizable New England into all the traditional forms of English poetry. Blank verse narrative, dramatic monologue, sonnet, lyric, rhymed narrative, eclogue, satire, and epigram all yielded to the sway of Frost's genius. In the process his relation to his region came to have the magnitude of Mark Twain's relation to the Mississippi. Like Mark Twain, Robert Frost became a national institution unto himself who spoke for the country with a wisdom rooted in humor. Though Frost was not cursed with the identity of humorist that Mark Twain periodically lamented, his work displays a current of humor flowing right through the common sense of his down-to-earth speakers.

Contending that he was not a regionalist but a realmist, Frost was not so much resident as proprietor of his region. He assimilated both English poetry and a dying New England into a new poetry that yet seemed an inheritance of all the past. Howells, in reviewing Frost's work, said that it was the old poetry as new as ever, yet he might well have said that it was a new poetry as old as ever. New in its rhythm, in its fine skepticism that freed it from the morality and aridity of the genteel tradition, it penetrated the common speech of the region, lifting it to heights of tenderness, wisdom, and beauty that no poet in America had been able to achieve. To read the wide range of Frost's poetry is to feel—almost to know—that this was the final fruit of New England's literature, or, to put it another way, the end of the New England line.

The Midwest, unlike New England, was just coming into its own. If New England at the turn of the century was culturally and morally rich yet politically poor, the Midwest was politically and morally rich yet culturally poor. It had attracted from dwindling New England a whole supply of able people who recognized the fecundity of soil twenty feet deep. Then too its eastern border was made up of western New York and Pennsylvania. The New York Central and Pennsylvania Railroad systems having fanned out through the region, the Midwest was in certain respects a westward extension of those two middle states, the one the capitalistic nerve center of the country, the other symbolically the keystone of the nation—the place of the Declaration of Independence and the Constitution, of Valley Forge and Gettysburg. Equally important, Pennsylvania's rich deposits of coal and petroleum put it at the front of basic industry. With Philadelphia on the coast and Pittsburgh near the western border, the state defined the spirit of the fortieth parallel running through the middle of the country all the way to California, just as Benjamin Franklin, D. H. Lawrence's snuff-colored man who stood between the patrician John Adams and the aristocratic Thomas Jefferson, defined what Henry Adams called the Pennsylvania mind—a political force that no Adams could ever master. Directly in line with that force, the Midwest—rich in soil, water, coal, and iron—was in a perfect position to take advantage of the conversion from steam to electric power. Its broadened industrial base was evident not only in its major cities of Cleveland, Detroit, and Chicago, but in dozens of minor cities. Thoroughly identified with the national ethos of freedom, the region was able to couple its moral well-being and Protestant religious values into a complacent and oppressive civic ethic celebrating moral growth and industry. For all its urban and industrial growth, the region retained a sense of itself as farming country, but this rural image was planted not so much against as with the growth of industry. Farming in the region was as much a business as it was a way of life, involved not so much in growing crops as producing them.

All these forces combined to create a region true to its geographical designation: a middle west absolutely occupied and defined by the middle class. The English and Europeans had always seen the American as essentially a commercial person. Henry James had rooted his Christopher Newman precisely in that identity and called him The American. The strategy enabled older societies to sustain ideals of high culture and at the same time exclude the rising middle class from it. Older regions did the same—New England implicitly with its Brahmin patrician class, the South explicitly with the institution of slavery and a planter class. In this context, the Middle West, for all its political power and moral wealth, was culturally impoverished. Its chief literary activity, in the age of Howells, had been the pursuit of the subordinate order of regionalism. Lowell had encouraged Edward Eggleston to work on dialect; James Whitcomb Riley produced homely versions of *The Biglow Papers* in his Hoosier poems. Such literature would have made the Midwest a diluted version of New England.

Yet in the period following the Civil War, the writers who were to dominate American literature during the first thirty years of the twentieth century were being born for the most part in the Midwest. Dreiser, Gertrude Stein, Anderson, Eliot, Lewis, Hemingway, Lardner, Fitzgerald, and Willa Cather (born in Virginia, but thoroughly identified with Nebraska) are but the beginning of a list of writers who sprang out of the country's heartland. They came of age at precisely the moment the revolution of modernism in literature and art was taking place in Europe. They were not to be regionalists in the post–Civil War sense of the term, yet they participated in the making of modern American literature; they were from the region; and they were from the middle class.

Viewed stereotypically, the middle class is forever averted from both the present and the past in its pursuit of upward mobility. Both the originator and the victim of the myth of progress, it sees the past as something from which it is escaping and the present as but a rung on the ladder to something better, either for it or for its children. Holding hard to the work ethic and Franklin's program for self-improvement, it is at home with the practical rather than the fine arts. Instinctively suspicious of, even hostile toward, high art, the middle class at best can acquire art as a badge of respectability, the designation applied by high culture to middle-class pretensions.

What is a person, fated or determined to be an artist, to do in such a class? I think that the true emotion of middle-class, Middle Western writers was one of estrangement from the flat landscapes, towns, and society on which they looked. They felt a hunger for art and the knowledge of art almost as abstract as the surveyor's grid that had laid out and laid off the land that enclosed them.

What characterizes the dominant literature from the Midwest in this century is its essential noninterest in the land, as if the writers fully comprehended how much the land had become a means of production rather than a realm of freedom. Dreiser, for example, set the stage in the first year of the century by showing Sister Carrie leaving the small town for the city. Moving through this novel of seduction and feeling hemmed in by the middle class, Carrie rocks between love and need. In that space Dreiser saw that glamor, not nature, was the aesthetic of middle-class desire. The sheen and glitter of manufactured material objects constitutes the spirit of the city, which, like a magnet, attracts Carrie from the inertia of farm and village life. In the city the larger laws of nature are at work. Guilt and innocence become irrelevant in the face of a longing larger than hunger, whose rhythm is embodied by Carrie in her rocking chair, moving yet stationary. Fitzgerald, for all his differences from Dreiser, also pursued an aesthetic rooted in glamor. Nature and land hardly exist in Fitzgerald's work, except as stage properties—lawns, trees, and beaches—assuming animation in the syncopated rhythm of a world whose final magic is money. The height of nature in such a world is its transformation into a mythic image drawing the imagination backward to the recess of memory.

Sinclair Lewis retains the realism so deeply necessary for regionalism, but it is under the eye of satire that loves to hate. Satire is the representative literary form of nations that have achieved imperial power. Augustan Rome got Horace; the France of Louis XIV got Molière; England, after the Duke of Marlborough's great victories, got Swift. Lewis, as a writer from the Midwest and as an American writer at the moment of America's victorious return from World War I, was able to take the traditional towns and rising cities of the region and expose, in a world totally devoted to business, the sterile conclusion of regional morality and gentility. Land is not even a means of production in Lewis's world; it is real estate. Nature is nothing more than empty space between towns or a spot one visits on vacation. As if that were not enough, Ring Lardner brought a new vernacular vision out of the region, disclosing a world in which men have turned the child's game of baseball into a business arena, as they pursue the "World's Serious." Even Willa Cather, the one writer who hymns the actual land, sees it already under siege by the railroads and the business interests following in their wake, as the frontier spirit is overtaken by capitalism. Cather's narrators and sensitive characters all but self-consciously realize that their capacity to appreciate the beauty of the land cuts them off from the original energy and courage required to subdue it.

If all these writers, whether naturalistic, realistic, or romantic, gave a recognizable sense of a region whose very nature was becoming business, they seem to me no more Midwestern than the modernists who came from the region. Gertrude Stein, in Paris by way of birth in Allegheny, Pennsylvania and youth in Oakland, strikes the modern middle-class chord when she insistently asserts, "I write for myself and strangers." "There is no there there," she said of Oakland, which could well be said of everything west of Harrisburg on the fortieth parallel, and of the Midwest, and of the middle class. Having lived in the Midwest for twenty years and being helplessly middle class (as all Americans surely are, most of all those who cannot quite stand it), I of course know that there is a there at precisely the same time I know exactly what Gertrude Stein means when she says there is not. She sought in writing to produce the "continuous present" that absolutely defines the middle class yet from which it is forever estranged. In *The Making of Americans* (1925), she wrought her vision in a steady, sturdy, simple prose so impenetrable that it can hardly be read—a style equal in its abstraction to the deep firm squares of Midwestern land that were, from the air, to resemble the cubist art emerging at just the time the airplane was being invented by two brothers from Dayton.

Add to her radical modernism that of Eliot (from St. Louis) and Pound (from Hailey, Idaho and Philadelphia) and you get a notion of the full estrangement of the middle class in poetry as well as prose. These two revolutionaries reorganized not merely the present of English poetry but also its past. Realizing that English insularity had cut American literature off from French literature, Pound and Eliot, behaving as if they were Jefferson, Franklin, and Adams in Paris during the time of the American Revolution, reasserted the French connection—and beyond it the Italian and the classical connections as well. In terms of their substance they could be considered reactionary, but in terms of form they succeeded in overturning the

English literary establishment. In their work discontinuity prevails, not in terms of an abstracting continuous present maintained by a repetition of present participles affirming endless beginnings, but by form made discontinuous by democratically juxtaposing present and past. The past, broken into shards of traditional poetry, abruptly intrudes into the present, breaking it in turn and leaving the reader's solitary consciousness to attempt a reconstruction of continuity that is at once a necessary yet mocking illusion—a step on the way to recognizing that the breakdown of old conventions is the eternal reality of both present and past. We might, deluded into the prejudice that they are "elitists," forget that Pound's very name signaled his relation to the sound money he wanted to redeem in a world of usury, just as we might fail to remember that he got Eliot a job in a bank.

I realize that Stein, Pound, and Eliot will not seem like regionalists, since they are so indisputably modern, yet I hold their form, its attendant emotion, and their enterprise to be the essence of the middle-class American as artist, whose homeless home is the Midwest and whose relation to its cultural poverty is one of estrangement, self-making, and cultural imperialism. They are true descendants of those New York writers, Walt Whitman and Henry James.

That leaves two writers, Anderson and Hemingway, who, in *Winesburg, Ohio* (1919) and *In Our Time* (1925), wrote books that are indisputably both regional and modern. Their form of linked short stories owes much to Joyce's *Dubliners;* their substance is unmistakably Midwestern, even as their commitment to the short story puts them sharply in relation to the form most suited to regional literature. Anderson creates a town peopled by grotesques, isolated not only from each other but estranged from themselves. Wing Biddlebaum's hands—the hands that pick berries—seem not a part of him, as if they held the story that he cannot touch. And one after another Anderson's sensitive figures have stories they cannot tell. It is the adolescent poetic moment, precarious and frail, within them that, untold, they want to tell, yet fear telling, lest by telling they destroy all the self they have. And so they survive—mute, tentative, groping—as emblems of an individuality they cannot reach, alone with the poem of their lives.

In Our Time, in its discontinuous yet linked stories, catches the deliberate rhythm of Gertrude Stein's work and couples it with the juxtaposition of two time frames characteristic of Eliot's poetry. It thus verges on a continuous present and simultaneously registers discontinuity of sequence. But Hemingway moves to recover both realistic representation and naturalistic determinism. By having the "chapters" of his book compressed into explosive vignettes of World War I battle action, violent confrontations between city police and gangsters, and bullfight scenes, he achieves relative expansion of the short stories of Nick Adams's youth in Michigan. These very short stories, the hallmark of "minor" regional writing, become the larger "interchapters," displacing the "major" convention of the novel. The two-part "Big Two-Hearted River," which so brilliantly concludes the book, details Nick Adams's return, for a fishing trip, to the land of his youth and young manhood, but bearing a consciousness taut with deliberation, holding on to the fact of landscape and the act of fishing in order to hold off all the thought rising like an abyss beneath it, an abyss that is the nothing coming after the end of something. Here indeed is the wounded Fisher King, yet so precisely individuated, so firmly present in a solid landscape that even to attribute symbolic meaning to the figure is to violate the hard, pure clarity of the prose. Here at last is no mere theme of estrangement but its *emotion*, at once strange or, better, *funny*, like the sensation of touching one's own scar tissue where severed nerves of a deep lesion still lurk beneath the healed and hardened flesh. Here is literature at once regional and modern, set in the heart of the country.

Then there was the South. If we think of it as beginning with Williamsburg, it was the oldest English-speaking region of the country. But if we think of the moment it became a dominant region in literature, it succeeds the Midwestern surge of the 1920s. We could even name the year, 1929, when both *The Sound and the Fury* and *Look Homeward, Angel* were published, and, of course, when the Depression began. The coincidence is hardly accidental. It is not too much to say that when the country entered the Great Depression it was doing no more than arriving at where the South had been since 1865. Whereas New England had emerged from the Civil War politically poor but morally and culturally rich and the Midwest culturally poor but politically rich, the South had emerged poor on all fronts. With the failure of Reconstruction in 1877, the region did manage to gain some political strength out of its very solidity, since both the Democratic party and the country could count on it as surely as they could count on death and taxes. Yet even with political reconciliation, the rest of the country could do little more than patronize it.

But the South did have a past. Whatever "culture" and "politics" meant, Washington, Jefferson, Madison, and Monroe were cultured politicians. Its real culture and literature had in fact been political. When, during the romantic movement that followed the American and French revolutions, literature was more and more separated from politics—when it became literature rather than letters—the South was poor indeed. William Gilmore Simms

had made an effort at historical romance, but as the sectional strife intensified, he had surrendered to the tyranny of Southern political ideology. Poe,
the Bostonian fallen into the South, was the section's one strong writer,
save for the humorists of the Old Southwest. Poe prefigured the South, as
he prefigures so much else, in "The Fall of the House of Usher." Ruin,
disease, incest, collapse, and hallucination were the gothic possibilities of
the section. And humor—humor rooted in wildness, loss, hopelessness, violence, poverty, and ignorance—made unforgettably plain by the Southwestern humorists. In a deep way the South was lost before the war, and
it was wilder always than New England, being so much later in time and
so far west in space. Few Americans realize to this day that Atlanta is as
far west as Detroit.

After the war the full hopelessness of the region materialized. Its defensiveness, evident in the romances of Thomas Nelson Page, its defiance embodied in the exaggerated chivalry of John Esten Cooke, might do for old-
fashioned readers but not for a literature moving into realism. Mark Twain
and George Washington Cable, making terms with the liberal North on the
crucial issues of slavery and race, were able to capitalize on the humor and
dialect of the region. Indeed, Mark Twain, drawing on Southwest humor
and comic journalism, achieved a humorous vernacular vision that exposed
the possibility that slavery itself, underlying the confident and arrogant illusion of freedom, might be the ground reality of the universal human condition. That perception showed what a bold writer might do with the negative identity of the region.

The negative identity was, finally, the region's possibility. It was evident
in the rich dialect of the South—in the talk of black sharecroppers, the poor
whites, the soft tones of a fallen planter class, the mountain twang. These
well-defined dialects gave voice for a range of stereotypes so vitally necessary for all literature, since the stereotypes force the writer to work harder
and harder to catch as well as mime the intonations of speech. The wide
range of stereotypes also indicated the remarkable diversity within the region—from plantation, through a wide belt of piedmont, and on to mountains still wild, and beneath all this on a wall map the deep South of black
belt, where dark soil and race produced cotton.

Here was truly a backward region, half recoiling on itself in abject surrender, half defiant against a Union that had defeated, defined, and judged
it. Such a region felt itself to have a separate history in a nation that would
proudly boast of never having lost a war. Having driven itself directly against
middle-class, capitalist, democratic progress and lost in unconditional surrender, having endured twelve years of military occupation, and having

been morally judged for both its treason and its slavery, the South was unquestionably a different region. It had pursued agriculture rather than industrial growth, seeing ownership of land as the surest seal of freedom in a society that had instituted slavery in a nation conceived in freedom from tyranny. It had dreamed of honor and aristocracy in a country based on equality. Finally, it was reduced to economic poverty in what seemed the richest nation in the world. When it took up the New South policy of attracting industry, it was greeted with the Great Depression.

With its lynchings, its mountain feuds, its courthouse fights, its fundamentalist religion, it seemed more violent than any settled region of the country. The Civil War had proved to the North that it was the place to go if you wanted to fight. In a country devoted to getting ahead it seemed to fall further behind; in a nation where industry was a virtue, it seemed lazy. Beyond that, in its commitment to racial segregation it was preventing the nation from achieving a spotless freedom and equality. All this loss, resistance, poverty, violence, backwardness, and defeated gentility gave the region both its unity and its identity. Lewis Simpson is surely right in observing that the South's loss and subsequent resistance to middle-class industrial progress put its writers in intimate touch with the alienation of modernism.

William Faulkner, more than any Southern writer, realized the loss and the possibilities of loss within the region. Thomas Wolfe's Eugene Gant, struggling to get out of the South but unable and almost perversely refusing to get the South out of himself, carried it with him to the North, extravagantly spending emotions in an effort to fuse the anguished division within his mind. The fusion took the form of a torrent of poetic prose, as if Gant were one of Anderson's grotesques who, starting to release his story, could never stop. Sixty years after Appomattox, Wolfe made a Whitmanian effort not for union in the face of division but for reunion after mortal separation. Small wonder that Eugene's origins were centered in his father's childhood experience of watching Southern soldiers approaching Gettysburg; small wonder too that his passion to reach and express the nation should have taken Eugene to Brooklyn.

Faulkner's achievement was of a different order. Following Anderson, who had encouraged him as a young artist in New Orleans, Faulkner invented not a town but a county, Yoknapatawpha—its county seat Jefferson—deep in Mississippi. The process of invention was almost as endless as Wolfe's but the sequence was a series of discrete and self-contained novels and stories related to each other through the blood lines and property lines that form the life and deeds of his region. Hemingway had cut his prose to the bone, achieving narrative in the form of strict account; Faulkner worked through a process of addition, emerging with narrative as endless relation. Hemingway's characters guard their emotional bank account to avoid the overdrawals that result in false emotions; Faulkner is Keynesian in his emotional economy. His whole world is in debt from the beginning, having inherited the loss of the past. His characters literally spend themselves in order to save the loss that is their life and land. Saving that loss made Faulkner not only the writer of the South but the writer of the Great Depression, in which and out of which he wrote his best work. The reappearance of old characters in new works of Faulkner's emerging saga of families, beyond enabling the author to discover their stories in an expansive new relation, provided him the opportunity of using them over again rather than casting them aside.

Anyone who has read *The Sound and the Fury* knows how daringly Faulkner enacted his vision. Instead of thematically defining his world, he emptied the narrative of temporal sequence, displacing it with the voices of three brothers all of whom are obsessed with the loss of their sister who has run away. The result of this bold, discontinuous form is that readers directly experience the loss of time before they realize all that the characters have lost. They have lost so much. Benjy the idiot has lost his manhood, having been castrated. Quentin has lost his life by taking it at Harvard. Jason has lost not only the inheritance he never received but both the money he has saved and the money he has stolen. The reader, forced to find his way by reconstructing the time of this whole lost region, comes to know the essential selfishness of all three brothers and at the same time feels the pain as well as the poetry of their lives. Even Jason, probably the meanest figure in literature except for Iago, is in pain. Proof of his humanity should be the fact that his section of the book is as richly humorous as anything in Mark Twain. Then there are the blacks, a society at once separate from yet intimately bound to the freer whites. For the reader, their generations are the means by which temporal sequence is recovered and the order of action discovered. They literally mark the time of the Compson generations. Rising out of the voices of the three brothers, an omniscient narration is reborn to view, as if from above, the servant Dilsey taking Benjy to the black church on Easter Sunday, and we begin to know the history of a time and place and family. Beginning to know is the feeling, the emotion, of knowledge that comes out of the remembered voices behind us. The landscape— a pasture turned into a golf course, a branch running near the house, a pear tree by a window, plowed fields lying outside the town, fences, gates, and bridges—gradually emerges not as scenery but as the vital landmarks by which time and place and action can be recognized, and can be recognized as interlaced.

Even this glimpse of Faulkner's form should give a sense of his achievement as a regional writer. By seizing upon the discontinuity of modernism, he was able to resolve the contradiction besetting the regional writer. Past writers had seen literary possibility in regions, but the form they brought involved them in miming regional speech, yet resorting to literary discourse in describing, framing, and analyzing action. Such a strategy, whatever the writer's intention, patronizes the region—whether in praising, defending, explaining, or judging it. Mark Twain had eluded the trap by having the deviant vernacular of a boy throw him out of the book and take over the entire narrative. Faulkner's form, by being uncompromisingly resistant, difficult, and modern, paradoxically leaves his characters firmly in place and at home. They are truly different from us, and to reach them we have to leave the conventions of temporal sequence and causation so often used to contain characters. Lost in their world, we have to find out the most primitive facts: Where are we? What time is it? Who is speaking? What is happening? What has happened? Reduced to these primordial questions, freed from conventional novelistic suspense about what is going to happen and from the narrative confidence about what has happened, we at once recover and discover the *relation* of time.

That relation is nothing less than the presence of all that Faulkner was to do as he reconstructed the South through a whole series of related narratives. To read his work is to enter a wilderness of loss and degeneration replete with ruin, defeat, decay, venality, guilt, and shame, yet imbued with honor, courage, struggle, and endurance as it dies into our possession. Language and land are so intricately entangled in Faulkner's South that the entire region emerges as our inheritance as we pursue the narrative threads connecting blood and property lines through all the wills, deeds, ledgers, memory, and legends constituting the transactions of its people.

Much as Faulkner achieved, he was by no means alone in realizing the possibilities of the region. There were the Southern women who proved themselves superior to their New England forebears. Ellen Glasgow began things in the early years of the century by bringing realism into her Virginia novels and breaking the Southern penchant for romance that had so exasperated Mark Twain. Even so, both her realism and her form, the plotted novel, worked against true regional space. It remained for Katherine Anne Porter, Eudora Welty, and Flannery O'Connor to pursue the classic regional form—the short story. As a convention, the novel, with its federalizing plot, tends always to subordinate the parts to the whole, whereas the collection of short stories does precisely the opposite. Though Faulkner is rightly denominated a novelist, his breakthrough involved decentering the temporal sequence of plot, displacing it with rhetoric and voice. The rhetoric lay in repeated efforts to tell a story through isolated voices— efforts that Faulkner later claimed were failures requiring new efforts to tell the same story. Both rhetoric and voices sought the lost relations of their life and land.

Katherine Anne Porter's Miranda stories were, in their clarity and authority, more on the order of Hemingway's Nick Adams sequence, yet in their attention to family and land they were inescapably Southern. Stories like "The Grave" and "The Circus" portray young Miranda's consciousness in momentous transition between childhood and a glimmeringly ominous awareness of adulthood. Their author was able, in such unforgettable moments, to remake her own life at the same time she grasped the vulnerability and innocent courage of childhood. Miranda's awareness registers her relation to her family and at the same time glimpses a future in which she will be solitary in a strange land. The emphasis on family relationships and the insistent assertion of family history serve to Southernize what would otherwise be a Western landscape. There are the inevitable Southern components—the blacks, the memory of family pride in the face of straitened circumstances, and above all the sense of place making an immovable stability against all the past mobility that has brought the family to this Texas place and all the future mobility that will take the central consciousness away, leaving an indelible memory not so much in the mind as in the heart.

Eudora Welty brought to the art of the short story both a magic and a humor relatively absent from Katherine Anne Porter's work. The magic is most evident in *The Golden Apples* (1949), a set of linked stories that, dispensing with the subordination of part to whole, achieve a sequence that creates the mythical small town of Morgana, Mississippi, and at the same time reflects the volatile and tender experience at play in the community of isolated individuals that echoes a whole past of myth and magic. Reminiscent of Winesburg, Morgana is intertextually connected to the poetry of Yeats, to the world of fairy tale and Arthurian legend, and, as the title makes unmistakably clear, to Greek mythology.

But it is in stories such as "Why I Live at the P.O." and "The Petrified Man" that Welty strikes the truly regional note. "The Petrified Man" miraculously transposes the world of Ring Lardner's "Haircut" into a woman's beauty salon, and at the same time transforms it from dramatic monologue into a conversation reflecting the malice of small-town gossip, perfectly catching in the process the intonation of regional speech. Whereas Lardner's story retained the element of sadism in its humor, Welty dissolves the malice into the improverished competition of Depression capitalism expressing itself in the economy of helpless humor.

Flannery O'Connor goes behind malice and sadism to the humor of violence. Writing out of her identity as Catholic and Southerner, she sets forth a fundamentalist, bigoted, backward South against the modern world, as if she knew that all her readers, wherever they might come from, would fatally be enlightened, secular "Northerners," committed to life, not death; to art, not religion; to time, not eternity; to mercy, not judgment; to hope, not grace. That is the world against which she sets her South—a South of place much more than a South of time, a South that has lost not to the North but to itself. Its people are truly alienated—from themselves, from the reader, and even from their author. Their compelling reality has its source in the moral breach O'Connor creates between us and them. Recognizable as they are in their adherence to Southern stereotypes—they possess a strong comic regional vernacular—they are exceptions in the moral order. Confronting us as freaks and cripples who wear their physical and mental deformities like badges, they measure a grotesque distance between their region and the liberal, secular, moral universe. Multilated, impoverished, judged, and punished though they are, they may at any moment be given the gift of true vision, of bearing witness. They have access to revelation because God can come to them as truly Other—in his power and his terror and his glory. He comes to them not because they are good (that would be the sentimentality our weakened religious sensibility would wish for) but because he is real. His grace may strike them dead, as it strikes Mrs. Shortley dead in "The Displaced Person." Her angry heart explodes in the very moment of contemplating for the first time the frontiers of her true country. Discovering in the inertia of her region and her characters the ground that keeps them backward from the modern world threatening to displace them, Flannery O'Connor was able to imagine a violent God nearer to them than to the encroaching secular world. The violence of her vision both measures and expresses the reality from which secular modernism is averted. Her achievement lay in taking the secular form of the short story, which Poe had imagined as a vision violently separating art from religion and morality, and violently reestablishing a relation between the two worlds.

All these Southern writers—Faulkner, Porter, Welty, and O'Connor—have touched the old sectional fire, largely banked by the rise of regionalism, and given us a living region from which to read and recognize our spiritual displacement. In the face of our helplessness in the face of national as well as international mobility and mobilization, their writing has not lamented but saved the loss of all that helplessness in the form of a worn land and place representing both the ruin of and resistance to the civilization it has survived. In precisely such resistant ruin is the beauty and power of their art.

All this may sound as if the South has ended. In a certain way it has, its resistance finally broken. Even as the South came into the nation's literature, the nation's economy came into the South. Beyond this process, regions are always ending. That is the fate of their imaginative space before the ever-encroaching Union. But the point is that they are *always* ending, which is to say that ending is their eternal process. In the South, for example, black Southern writers already show the promise of inheriting the possibility of all their loss and their resistance to the region. In the face of the national will to make them representatives of its "progress," they yet have a resistance more than passive to everything in America that would possess them. It is in their language, their loss, their humor (which, like all humor, is the economy of loss), their silence. Why should they not be in position to possess the region that so long possessed them? What better place than the South for the defiance, outrage, humor, patience, and language of loss?

That leaves the West, which is really not a region in my context. It is all future and mobility—it is America. Two new states—Alaska and Hawaii—have recently been added to it, both of which are so far away from it that they but emphasize its boundlessness. The fact that one of these states is characterized as an island paradise and the other as wilderness indicates, as John Seelye once pointed out to me, just how American rather than regional the West remains. As if that were not enough, the Western writer perpetually confronts the impasse of the Western in literature, a formulaic convention assuming the rigid identity of a popular literary genre dominating the national mind and defining the whole space as either a book or a movie. These art forms convert the West always ahead of time into a romance or a dream. Land in the West is either space or corporate farm. Workers are migrants. How much that word tells us. Not only are Eastern Americans being drawn to it; so are the orientals, the true Easterners. The day when this space and this attraction becomes a region will mark the end of the nation that has left the other regions behind it.

James M. Cox

Afro-American Literature

Most histories of Afro-American writing are extrinsic histories. Written from a distant—and presumably objective—vantage point, they have focused on the existence of the literature more than on the practice of it. These histories have been useful, especially since the task of informing large, otherwise literate readerships of the presence of Afro-American writing remains unfinished. (One of the most literate persons I know recently told me he had just discovered Ralph Ellison's *Invisible Man.*) However, since the display of literary facts is essentially a bibliographical activity, and since the repair of one bibliography (say, that of American writing in a specific period) usually creates little more than another bibliography (say, one of American writing revised to include Afro-American authors), we must recognize that extrinsic histories are severely limited. In some larger sense, they are scarcely histories at all. Although they meld fact and chronology, they do not risk the acts of narration and fictionalization that necessarily figure in the larger business of *writing* (as opposed to *assembling*) *history*, especially literary history. Moreover, even when these acts are risked, problems occur. Some historians, confronting ignorant or hostile audiences, rely on outmoded and tiresome strategies of protest-writing. Others engage in self-authenticating strategies in which the fact of the literature authenticates the historian, who in turn authenticates the fact—without realizing that only the authors of such histories are likely to find them compelling.

Afro-American literary historians in the 1980s must move beyond both extrinsic histories and protest narratives. New audiences exist, including some who encountered Afro-American literature at a young age and already know many texts and many black selves in literary form. Some extrinsic historiographical work remains to be done, of course. Bibliographical repairs can sometimes initiate revisionist history. But the larger tasks are intrinsic.

The intrinsic history, like the extrinsic, seeks facts, but it asks different questions and hence seeks different answers. There is, for example, a profound difference between asking, as the extrinsic historian tends to do, "What is the Afro-American contribution to literary modernism?" and asking whether literary modernism, as traditionally conceived, can "contain" Afro-American writing or give form to any part of its history. The first question accepts literary modernism as an established canonical entity that is to be refined or embellished, and then assumes that our task is to identify black confreres or "equivalents" of, say, Eliot, Hemingway, and Mencken. The second assumes that we should focus on those black writers who followed paths of their own, and in effect challenged, by resisting them, the impulses and models of modernism.

For present purposes, I shall pursue both types of inquiry, but my aim is in the main intrinsic. I assume from the start that a history of Afro-American writing between the wars is basically a history of the Harlem Renaissance. But I join the work of others—notably Sterling A. Brown and Arthur P. Davis—in arguing that the Harlem Renaissance is more properly termed the New Negro Renaissance or the Modern Negro Renaissance.

A wider view of the Harlem Renaissance must begin with a sense that the history of the notion of a "Renaissance" is a part of our literary history. Why, since the late 1960s, have teachers and scholars organized courses, assembled anthologies, and composed histories around this particular historical construct? How, in an academic climate of dissent and revision, has this particular construct continued to be so uncritically embraced?

To answer these questions, we need to observe, first, the extent to which standard histories and chronologies have conspired to suggest that, in the modern era, there were few Afro-American writers of note—certainly not enough to establish a "conversation" with each other, to constitute a movement, period, or generation, or to redefine a genre. Students of the 1960s were often directed to study the seemingly comprehensive chronology of key publications and literary events in Thrall, Hibbard, and Holman's *A Handbook to Literature* (revised edition, 1960), in which the only Afro-American text listed was Richard Wright's *Native Son* (1940). Another, more widely used research tool of the era, *Literary History of the United States* (third edition, revised 1963), edited by Robert Spiller *et al.*, was almost as useless to the student of Afro-American literature: of its fifteen hundred or so pages, two needed to be consulted. On one page, in the chapter "Humor," we find a brief discussion of dialect, Negro humor, and blues. Paul Laurence Dunbar and James Weldon Johnson are the authors most prominently cited, though Countee Cullen, Langston Hughes, Sterling Brown, and Zora Neale Hurston also make an appearance—in a list that is as good as the context is suspect. The bare mention of these writers, in a pause between relatively substantial commentaries on Joel Chandler Harris and Finley Peter Dunne, assigns them to a small corner of a minor scene. The second page appears in Section X ("A World Literature"), Chapter 77 ("A Cycle of Fiction"), where James T. Farrell and Richard Wright are given almost equal attention. But even this concession loses its force when the discussion of Wright becomes another hasty, canonizing aside dominated by a formula in which a brief discussion of a prominent author (here, Wright) is used to introduce the names of a motley group of apparent fellow travelers that includes such "critics, poets, publicists, novelists, and scholars" as W. E. B. Du Bois, James Weldon Johnson, Countee Cullen, Claude McKay, Roi Ottley, Zora Neale Hurston, Adam Clayton Powell, Chester Himes, Edwin Peeples, St. Clair Drake, and Horace Cayton.

Had this assembly been put forth as part of an interdisciplinary or multigeneric search for the modern Afro-American canon, we might accept and even hail it. After all, Wright, Drake, and Cayton did in a sense collaborate on a 1940s study of black urban life, and Du Bois's remarkably varied writings include three novels. But something else is afoot. Literary artists are being viewed and valued in extraliterary terms, as purveyors of what Albert Murray witheringly terms "social science fiction." To include Adam Clayton Powell, for example, in a discussion of Afro-American literature is to patronize, confuse, and diminish that literature. Such an act comes across finally as a grasping at straws—the sort of thing literary historians do when they feel obliged to mention writers they do not know well enough to respect.

Afro-Americanists might well have hoped to find a fresher, more broadly American idea of literary history in Alfred Kazin's *On Native Grounds*. Published in 1942 and widely read for more than twenty years, *On Native Grounds* begins with a bold preface in which Kazin announces that for him "the single greatest fact about our modern American writing [is] our writers' absorption in every last detail of their American world together with their deep and subtle alienation from it." Yet, in five hundred pages, Kazin mentions only one Afro-American prose writer, Richard Wright, whom he includes in a discussion of the "fellowship of proletarian naturalism." Given the influence of *On Native Grounds*, it is fair to say that Kazin has played a major role in promulgating some of the most familiar formulations about Wright, including those that name him Afro-American literature's true progenitor. In this important regard, Kazin anticipates the historical interpretations of critics as various as Irving Howe and Addison Gayle.

If indeed the 1920s saw a flourishing of Afro-American art and culture so great that we strain to call it a "renaissance," we might at least expect histories of the 1920s to provide some account of that activity. But when we turn to Frederick J. Hoffman's classic study, *The 20's* (1949; new, revised, Collier edition, 1962), we discover that the omission of things Afro-American, including the revisionist construction of "the Harlem Renaissance," is almost total. The names of Brown, Hurston, Cullen, Hughes, Johnson, Jean Toomer, and Jessie Fauset are not even mentioned in the tweed of names that appears on the cover. Even more interesting is what we find in their place. Although Hoffman ignores Negro writers, he acknowledges the "Negro theme"—by glancing at minor novels such as Waldo Frank's *Holiday* (1923), Carl Van Vechten's *Nigger Heaven* (1926), and, in a note, Ronald Firbank's *Prancing Nigger* (1924). Although these novels may have a place in our literary history, they do not represent Afro-American literature during the fertile decade of the 1920s. In Hoffman we find no suggestion that 1923 is more impressively represented by Jean Toomer's *Cane* than Frank's *Holiday*, or that Toomer and Frank should be discussed together—they knew each other well and Frank wrote the introduction to *Cane*. Nor is there any hint that 1926 saw the publication of Langston Hughes's *The Weary Blues* as well as Van Vechten's *Nigger Heaven*. Such blind omissions account in part for the corrective activities that began in the 1960s and early 1970s, in a whorl of intellectual anger, revisionist fervor, and missionary zeal.

Over the last two decades, revisionism has generally assumed one of two forms: it has sought to supplement the prevailing histories, and it has endeavored to compose the missing history—in this instance, black literary history. Since supplementary histories and "other" histories rarely create new history, however, the prevailing history has been left largely intact. What we have today is a proliferation of histories—black, chicano, women's, mainstream, to name a few. But we do not have a new American history. Supplementation rather than reconstitution has dominated not only bibliographies but also anthologies—which provide an especially interesting case study because they not only add new names and new texts but also strive to contextualize their additions in periods and movements. Anthologies, in short, are more emphatically about the business of proposing canons and identifying significant instances of particular genres.

And what is the state of supplementation in the anthologies of our time? For the most part, they participate in the sense of history that Spiller, Holman, Kazin, and Hoffman reached decades ago. *The Norton Anthology of American Literature*, for example, now includes four Afro-American writers in its 1914–45 unit (Zora Neale Hurston, Langston Hughes, Countee Cullen, Jean Toomer), with three of the four reappearing in the shorter edition. While it is encouraging to see a woman writer, Hurston, accorded a level of representation usually reserved for male writers, the coverage of Afro-American writing as a whole remains cursory. Toomer, for example, is probably the most experimental, enigmatic, and hence the most usefully difficult writer of this small group, yet it is he rather than the more traditional Countee Cullen who is cast aside in the shorter edition. Moreover, Richard Wright, who arguably wrote his best work in the late 1930s and early 1940s *(Uncle Tom's Children* [1938]; *Native Son* [1940]; *Black Boy* [1945]), is relegated to the section on the prose since 1945, a decision in which editorial and historical judgment merge. One questionable effect of this arrangement is that both novice and seasoned readers are discouraged from considering Wright with Hughes and Hurston, on the one hand, or with Ernest Hemingway and William Faulkner, on the other. By removing Toomer from the 1920s in the shorter edition, and Wright from the 1930s and early 1940s altogether, the editors freight the most recent Norton volumes with reactionary canonistic and historical assertions that sustain old interpretations of American writing instead of creating new ones.

The latest edition of *The American Tradition in Literature* (fifth edition, 1986), despite its claims of comprehensiveness based on a new historical awareness, joins the Norton shorter edition in including only three Afro-American writers in the period under review. *The American Tradition* employs thematic categories that could, under proper force, open up the canon and history alike. But no black writers appear in the "Fiction in Search of Reality" section, and poet Countee Cullen is the only black author in the unit "The Attack on Convention." Langston Hughes and Richard Wright are featured only in the narrow context of "The Literary Expression of Social Thought: The Thirties and Forties"—an arrangement that corrects the *Norton Anthology*'s removal of Wright from the 1930s and early 1940s only to ignore Hughes's lively presence in other decades and to disregard all of his writing that is not distinctly "social."

So many accomplished black writers are excluded here—particularly the women—that one is tempted once again to list them. But it is more telling to describe what is made of the three who are included. Countee Cullen, for example, is a curious selection for the "Attack on Convention" section, for while he was obviously a serious and frequently anguished observer of *social* conventions, he was also an unquestioning and for the most part uninventive practitioner of established *poetic* conventions. In other words, though his quarrel with society yielded moving expressions of anger and irony, they did not instigate a comparable, idiosyncratic skepticism about the shape a poem might take. New themes came, but new forms did not. Cullen— not the two "black Whitmans," Toomer and Hughes—is useful in supplementation activities precisely because his poems, in their traditional formality, are recognizable as poems, and because in their conventionality they tend to support two enduring conceptions of Afro-American literary achievements. The first is that technical virtuosity—say, with the sonnet— is evidence enough of black literary accomplishment and therefore justification enough for the inclusion of black authors in anthologies. This notion dominates the earliest assessments of Phillis Wheatley, reappears in discussions of Paul Laurence Dunbar, and continues with peculiar vitality in twentieth-century appraisals of Cullen, Melvin Tolson, the early Gwendolyn Brooks, among others. The second is that whereas Afro-American writers have been both within and outside literary movements and periods, both American and black American, giving their themes an air of significant *social* unrest, their forms have rarely been at the cutting edge of what Ezra Pound called the new wood. In short, their significance is more social than literary.

The American Tradition's embrace of Cullen, in the context of conventions attacked, sustains old histories far more than it suggests new ones, particularly in its implicit endorsement of the "perception" that Afro-American writers are in the main social and not aesthetic agitators. Something of the kind is also reflected in its treatment of Hughes and Wright. The context to which they are assigned implies that they are social science fiction writers and not much more. In *The American Tradition*, old boats are polished but not rocked.

Why this should be so deserves more than one answer. It is easy to declare that the editors of the *Norton Anthology* and *The American Tradition* are uninformed, but it is probably more accurate to describe them as inhibited and embattled. On one side, they want to maintain the traditional American literary canon. In response to a host of intense and persuasive contemporary pressures, they tinker with the canon. But on a deeper, unspoken level, they want not only to conserve but to possess it: each editor feels that some reach of the canon must be deemed unassailable, and in committee, this results in almost every reach being so designated. Moreover, too much new history suggests the need for new historians. How many "old" historians (however young) are willing to announce that they must either retool or delcare themselves obsolete?

It is also likely that the new anthologies have supplemented the old histories so minimally because the other form of supplementation—composing the missing history—has proceeded at such a rapid pace. I am reminded here of a former colleague who, according to student reports, told students who questioned his modern American novel syllabus that, if they wanted the "other" stuff—fiction by women, blacks, etc.—there were plenty of "other" courses down the street. Obviously, this colleague was conserving and possessing in the manner I have described above. But he was also acknowledging, as today's anthologists have, first, that the new and intimidating array of texts, histories, and critical studies would require vast work to master; and second, that courses built on them are suddenly quite close by: why do more than the minimum when full acts of supplementation are a shelf or a classroom away?

In truth, however, the rapid composition of the missing history is something of a myth, a specter. For while we do have some fine new anthologies, histories, and critical studies, it is more accurate to say that the missing history has been newly collected or assembled as opposed to freshly written. Consider, for example, the extraordinary effort in the late 1960s to reprint both primary and scholarly Afro-American texts, an effort that resulted in sizable collections of works readily available to libraries and individuals alike. By 1969, for instance, the Dover Black Rediscovery Series listed eleven titles, the Atheneum Studies in American Negro Life series included seventeen, and the Arno collection—The American Negro: His History and Literature—offered thirty-one. Even publishing houses that shied away from large series rushed to reissue titles they had published earlier. Thus, Harper & Row proudly brought out all the Richard Wright fiction it could, reminding us that Wright had been one of its authors well before the onslaught of Black Studies and the revision of American literature reading lists.

But publishers were not solely responsible for the barrage of new information and texts. Even a casual trip to a reasonably well-stocked library could produce startling results. Inquisitive readers found a body of Afro-Americanist literary criticism ranging back at least to the Benjamin Brawley, Alain Locke, and Vernon Loggins essays of the 1920s. They found that certain anthologies of American writing from years past *did* in fact include Afro-American authors in greater depth and variety than more recent collections (the Anderson and Walton *This Generation* [1939], for example, includes eight poems by Sterling Brown, who nowadays appears only in Afro-American collections). They found anthologies of Afro-American writing dating from the 1920s that were in many ways more honest and provocative in their assessments than newer volumes (Alain Locke's *The New Negro* [1925], James Weldon Johnson's *The Book of American Negro Poetry* [1922], and Sterling Brown's *Negro Caravan* [1941] are especially notable in this regard). And they found that the complete *oeuvre* of certain black authors, like that of certain white authors, commands our attention (Zora Neale Hurston is a prime example here, as is Langston Hughes).

Such trips to the library might have provided another insight as well: that much of Afro-Americanist literary scholarship before the late 1960s was conducted in a remarkably democratic spirit. In his *Negro Poetry and Drama* (1937), for example, Sterling Brown includes sections on "White Poetry of Negro Life before 1914" and "Contemporary White Poets on Negro Life." Comparable efforts appear in the Langston Hughes and Arna Bontemps volume, *The Poetry of the Negro* (1949). These are not, as some might argue, evidence of the subjugation of the Afro-American or the near colonization of his or her critical intelligence. Brown, Hughes, and Bontemps all argue implicitly, though not entirely in unison, for a comprehensive American literature canon, a canon that begins to emerge when one hazards the thought that, within our national circumstance, black and white writers alike have necessarily been compelled to write of things Negro.

The democratic spirit of Brown and Hughes, which we find in their anthologies and critical overviews as well as in some of their poems of the 1930s—Brown's "Sharecroppers," for example, which concludes " 'We gonna clean out dis brushwood round here soon,/ Plant de white-oak and de black-oak side by side' "—was a strong force. But it was not the spirit that inspired most black writers and Afro-Americanist scholars of the 1960s and 1970s. These writers and scholars were, of course, aware of Hughes and Brown. Had Hughes been alive, the celebration of his "rediscovery" certainly would have matched those accorded Brown, Gwendolyn Brooks, and other living "ancestors." But, the militant democratic spirit of Hughes and Brown was not embraced because it ran contrary to several strong needs. Some writers and scholars wanted to declare that Afro-American literary history was only beginning (or that Afro-American literary history was over and *black* literary history was now emerging); others wanted to mine from that history something more nationalistic or at least "blacker" than Hughesian pronouncements of "I, too, sing America"; still others sought to mesh these two inclinations. This is my sense of what Donald Gibson (in introducing his *Modern Black Poets* [1973]) means to suggest when he declares that "the poetry of black Americans" has not been a "unified poetry . . . except during relatively recent times of great social stress—in the twenties, for example, and in the sixties and early seventies . . . when a genuine black poetry [what he elsewhere calls "a definable black poetry"] has emerged."

With all this in mind, several things should be clear. First, the prevailing history of Afro-American writing between the wars is after all a *particular* history of the *Harlem* Renaissance—not of the New Negro Renaissance, or of Addison Gayle's configuration, the New Negro Renaissance Movement, or of some larger shaping in which the Renaissance is but a part. Second, this prevailing history of the Harlem Renaissance is particular in at least four key ways. First, it is a history bound to the needs, including the need to possess a history, of the "Second Black Renaissance" of the late 1960s and early 1970s, a renaissance that is better termed the "third," since, as William L. Andrews and others argue, the first was surely that of the 1840s and 1850s. Second, it stresses the literary events of the 1920s more than those of surrounding decades, in part because it submits to extraliterary definitions of its periodization (for example, by beginning with the end of World War I and ending with the stock-market crash of 1929). Third, it represents a search for the beginnings of a "genuine" or "definable" black art—a Black Aesthetic—that necessarily misreads the cultural integrationist impulses of the 1920s, the democratic proletarianism of the 1930s, and the Du Boisian explorations of the American Negro's "twoness" throughout the era. And fourth, it is a history that logically results when the missing literary history is seen to be the other history, not the new history, principally because the proliferation of other histories is less threatening than the formation of a new consensus.

What I would like to offer in the remaining pages is the outline of a newer history that suggests consensus without diminishing Afro-American literary accomplishment.

A. Periodizing the Period. The issue: Afro-American writing between World War I and World War II is often construed simply as Harlem Renaissance writing, and the period of the Renaissance is assumed to be the decade of the 1920s.

Revision here begins with the formulation and plotting of literary, as opposed to more social or cultural, history. This point is hardly new; Robert Bone urged it years ago in his *Down Home:* "The Story of the Harlem Renaissance is by now a twice-told tale. Yet no one has attempted a literary history of the period. We have had intellectual, cultural, and political histories, but not yet a truly literary interpretation. For literary history . . . is a history of literary forms." This said, Bone goes on usefully to discuss the "predominance" of the picaresque and pastoral strains in modern Afro-American writing. Though brief, his discussion is fascinating in its implications for literary history. Bone sustains the preeminence of Claude McKay, Jean Toomer, Langston Hughes, and Zora Neale Hurston as major writers of the period. But he does so by concentrating on their practice of specific literary forms and conventions, one result being that certain often overlooked texts (for example, Hughes's *Not Without Laughter*) finally enter our literary history of the Harlem Renaissance. With the entry of such texts into the history, the textual canon of the period is reconstituted and the period *qua* period is reformed: fully half of the texts that must be cited fall outside the strict confines of the 1920s. Moreover, emphasis on the picaresque and the pastoral, rather than on genre *per se*, introduces multigeneric considerations. Although Bone is writing about fiction, his categories force him to cite poetry and autobiography. Literary history here becomes a history of genre practices, in their weave and confluence.

Bone studies fiction, but histories of fiction-making are not the only histories that burst the bonds of conventional periodization. Indeed, it is nearly impossible to think of a modern Afro-American genre practice that is logically periodized by the 1920s decade. Once again, though familiar, this argument has been variously suppressed or misread. Regarding poetic practice, for example, J. Saunders Redding argued decades ago (in *To Make a Poet Black* [1939]) that the new Negro verse began as early as 1912, when Claude McKay first arrived from Jamaica. After stopping along the way in the 1920s, to valorize the art of Toomer, Hughes, and the usually unsung James Weldon Johnson, and to vilify the "bloodless" craft of Countee Cullen, Redding concludes by praising the "spiritual and physical return to the earth" (roots, heritage, and indigenous artistic impulses) of Sterling Brown's *Southern Road* poems (1932) and the complementary tales, prose poems of a sort, in Hurston's *Mules and Men* (1935). The French scholar Jean Wagner, in his *Black Poets of the United States* (1962; English translation, 1973), seems to second Redding's assertion that literary history must push forward into the 1930s to include Brown, though his definition of the poetic is not sufficiently elastic to embrace Hurston. He also proposes an even earlier date for the new poetry's initiation, 1906, the year in which Paul Laurence Dunbar died and Du Bois composed his "A Litany at Atlanta." For me, Redding's history is the more pleasing and plausible, but Wagner's extends Redding's early assertion that the 1920s simply do not periodize modern Afro-American poetic practice or achievement. To some extent, furthermore, both writers demonstrate that certain "conversations" between poets, conducted within and across the demarcations of the modern decades, are viable points of departure for substantial literary history.

One such exemplary conversation is the pre-1920 exchange between Paul Laurence Dunbar and James Weldon Johnson regarding the efficacy of Negro dialect in American poetry, a conversation reconducted and revised in exchanges between Johnson and Sterling Brown during the late 1920s and early 1930s. Both conversations are noteworthy for having taken place in person as well as within poems, essays, and autobiographies. Yet another conversation is that between Du Bois and Alain Locke; indeed, most of Locke's key points in *The New Negro* (1925) rephrase Du Boisian pronouncements in *The Souls of Black Folk* (1903). Another major pairing involves Langston Hughes and Zora Neale Hurston: confined mostly to the 1920s, it offers a tale of friendship and collaboration between black authors complicated by the intrusions of white patrons. The conversation that pairs Claude McKay and Sterling Brown is especially noteworthy since it has a way of taking in the entire period from 1912 to the 1930s. When Brown acknowledges McKay's influence (which seems unlikely at first, since McKay's verse is so relentlessly formal), he is suggesting, I think, that McKay's fierce militancy was a source of his own "critical realism." This conversation is at least as important as the one Redding celebrates between Brown and Toomer.

As the period expands, so does its geography. If Bone is right about the predominance of the picaresque and the pastoral, it is hard to confine Renaissance writers to Harlem alone—unless one doggedly argues that the writers only *wrote* picaresquely and pastorally, only imagined the travels and landscapes and personages they recount. But in fact the biographies of McKay, Toomer, Hurston, and even Hughes do not support this: they wrote of vagabonds and were vagabonds. Harlem *was* a crossroads, a mecca, but most pilgrims to most meccas travel with round-trip tickets, whether they know it or not. Alain Locke comes to mind here: he was a singular figure of the era, an integral part of what we might call the Harlem event, but he never really left Washington, D.C., or his professorship at Howard University.

The conversations and pairings suggested above are geographical chartings as well. Langston Hughes and Zora Heale Hurston, for instance, most certainly colluded and collided in uptown New York, and that supports the notion of a *Harlem* Renaissance. But a fuller and truer literary history (richer in texts, years, and dominion) becomes available when Hughes and Hurston are "allowed" to journey forth, as they did—Hughes to wherever, and Hurston to her home in Eatonville, Florida. The period under review featured Northern migrations followed by Southern returns; the literature of the period expresses this variously and richly, and histories of the literature should do so as well.

B. Historicizing Afro-American Genre Practice. The issue: Afro-American literature appears to be rich in content but not in form; Afro-American writers are social, not aesthetic, agitators.

Revision here must begin with a decision to avoid easy, fraudulent distinctions between what is social and what is artful. To repeat the obvious: a literature can be both social and artful; a text that is formally crafted can be deeply social in both content and form; a text that is conspicuously social, replete with hortatory or didactic qualities, can also be artful.

These are things to keep in mind when looking, for example, at the modern Afro-American practice of sonnet forms. The general view of this practice is that it provides evidence of black writers displaying their "mastery" of a set of forms and conventions; or of black writers "escaping" from their culture and "passing" into the world of Art; or of black writers pouring "black content" into "white forms"; or of black writers, caught in some sort of time warp, writing sonnets while the world of poetry is undertaking fresher tasks. Such views may describe a few particular instances, but any literary history based on them would confirm the insidious idea that some people are supposed to write sonnets and others are not. In fact, when we *read* the sonnets of Claude McKay and the early Gwendolyn Brooks, works that mark the beginning and end of the period under review, we discover poems, such as McKay's "White Houses" and Brooks's "Gay Chaps at the Bar," that are strong both socially and aesthetically by virtue of the inventions—the subversions—that are worked on the sonnet forms that they appear to embrace—Shakespearean in McKay's case, Petrarchan in Brooks's. What attracts Afro-American poets to the sonnet, particularly the Petrarchan or Italian sonnet, often has little to do with displaying technical mastery. For example, it can be said that the basic logic of the Italian form *invites* black poets to explore what Du Bois would have called the "twoness" of the Afro-American condition: two citizenships, two "warring souls," two ways of seeing reality, two time frames—one past and one present, or, better, one present and one future.

The tensions seen in the modern Afro-American poet's practice of the sonnet are also played out in other forms and in the entire work of individual writers. Very few modern black writers are exclusively social or aesthetic, any more than they are accomplished only in one literary genre. Of special interest is the play or counterpoint within a given author's writings between "received" forms (the sonnet at one aesthetic extreme, the ballad at the other) and "indigenous" forms (blues, folk sermon, etc.). Those writers who most delighted in (or most agonized over) this counterpoint also tended to play central roles in the literary history of the period: Dunbar, Johnson, Hughes, Hurston, Brown, the early Margaret Walker, Gwendolyn Brooks, and Richard Wright. This list does not revolutionize modern Afro-American literary history, but it does revise it, especially in terms of how that history is reflected in Americanist anthologies: Dunbar becomes a modernist for reasons other than the date of his death; Johnson and Brown finally enter history; the Margaret Walker of the late 1930s and early 1940s is recognized for something other than her friendship with Richard Wright.

In Johnson's *oeuvre*, we find fiction, Edwardian anthems, and sermonic poems owing much to the poetics of black folk preachers. In Walker, we find sonnets, ballads, new free forms, and after 1945, a novel. But we must also look to those texts that display a radical admixture of forms, not to uncover literary experiments, but rather to discover whether the mixing of genres creates a distinctive literature, a contribution to literary history. Several texts come to mind here: Jean Toomer's *Cane* (1923), Johnson's *God's Trombones* (1927), Hughes's "Seven Moments of Love: An Un-Sonnet Sequence in Blues" (1942), Hurston's *Mules and Men* (1935), Robert Hayden's "Middle Passage" and Brooks's "Sonnet Ballad" (both of the period, though published in 1945 and 1949 respectively). From this perspective, a reassessment of Johnson is overdue. To the extent that forgotten texts can alter our perceptions of their authors, Hughes and Brooks may yet be seen anew within our history.

I have touched upon experiments with the sonnet as well as the pursuit of new forms principally to urge that traditional and novel genre practices both figure in a given culture's literary history. Since some individual texts are singularly both traditional and novel and hence deserving of special attention, I also want to suggest that, despite the need for a certain briskness of narration, literary histories should slow down long enough to examine some texts in detail. However, since literary history must be more than a sequence of close readings, other historiographical strategies must be employed, including contouring and author pairing.

To borrow and simplify the arguments of Claudio Guillen, contours are episodes, often brief, of intense aesthetic debate or intense experimentation with a literary form. Such literary activity calls attention to itself because it fails to conform to literary history as we would like to package it: authors begin to defy labels, texts begin to burst generic pigeonholes, debates begin to spill messily out of one period into another. For me, the signal contour in modern Afro-American writing is the debate, carried on in texts of all sorts, over the efficacy and the means of creating an Afro-American written literature out of the vernacular art forms of the folk. The centrality of this contour, the extent to which it nearly constitutes a history, can be seen in Dunbar's agonies and Wright's renunciations, which together mark the beginning and the end of more than an episode. The peculiar intensity with which this debate is joined in the work of Dunbar, Johnson, Brown, and Hurston makes it a dominant feature of our historical landscape.

When the subject is genre practice, authorial pairing often crosses racial lines. It is simply insufficient to compare, say, McKay and Cullen as sonneteers or Hurston and Wright as fictionalizers of Southern black experience, as though any such comparison could provide a basis for measuring fully a given author's achievement. What modern black author acknowledges only black precursors and confreres? In short, when the subject is genre practice, the historian must accept the challenge of comparing Toomer and Hughes with Whitman; Brown with Frost, Robinson, and Sandburg; Wright with Dreiser; Brooks and Tolson with Eliot; Dunbar and Johnson with Tennyson and Kipling. The anxiety that such comparisons might diminish the accomplishments and innovations of Afro-American authors helps to explain why Afro-American literary history continues in such flux and crisis.

C. The Canon Received. The issue: The canon appears to include several men, principally Claude McKay, Countee Cullen, Jean Toomer, and Langston Hughes, and one woman, Zora Neale Hurston. Yet, as soon as we focus on authors *writing*, the canon widens, not for arbitrary reasons, but because more authors and more texts enter our ken. I have argued for the inclusion of Dunbar, Johnson, and Brown, as well as the early Margaret Walker, Richard Wright, and Gwendolyn Brooks. Although these writers may be seen as belonging to other periods, they were in fact strong presences in the era between the wars: in some instances, their writings prompted major literary achievements (consider here Dunbar's "prompting" of Johnson, Brown, and others); in other instances, their writings became major instances of those achievements.

It is perhaps controversial to include the early Walker and Brooks among the major women writers of the era and to exclude Jessie Fauset, Nella Larsen, Georgia Douglas Johnson, and others. But when one seeks out those writers who explore the play between "received" and "indigenous" forms, Walker, Brooks, and Hurston emerge as the major women writers of the age. This is not to say that Fauset, Larsen, and Johnson have no place in literary history. Obviously they do. Rather, it is to suggest that their place shrinks when our attention focuses on matters of form and invention.

Like the canons of other literary historians, my own is a special distillation of literary history—a construct accounting for some but not all of the literary activity of the era. The literature appeared not just in books but also in the pages of journals and little magazines. Moreover, modern black writers published both in "black" journals such as *The Crisis, Opportunity,* and *The Southern Workman,* and in "white" journals such as *Poetry, The New Masses,* and *The Dial.* This reflects the peculiarly diverse experiences of Afro-American writers within the tumultuous literary world of modern America. Canons need not account for this, but histories must make the attempt; hence, the particular challenge before the Afro-Americanist historian of the 1980s.

Robert Stepto

Mexican American Literature

Mexican American literature can be said to date from 1848 when the treaty of Guadalupe Hidalgo ended nearly two years of warfare between Mexico and the United States. In the treaty, Mexico ceded its northern territories—the present states of California, Nevada, Arizona, Utah, New Mexico, and half of Colorado—to the United States, while the region's 80,000 Mexican residents were given a choice between remaining in place with the guarantee of American citizenship or moving southward across the new national boundaries. Virtually all the Mexicans elected to remain in their homelands, thus becoming, in a single political stroke, Mexican Americans. But culture and literature seldom change in rhythm with politics, and so for several generations after Guadalupe Hidalgo these new American citizens were not significantly distinguishable in customs or literature from their brethren to the south.

Mexican American literature took shape in the context of a hybrid (Spanish, Mexican, Indian, and, eventually, Anglo*) frontier environment marked by episodes of intensifying cultural conflict. Across the Southwest, Mexican Americans maintained Mexican traditions as long as they could; only in response to irresistible Anglo influences did they develop a distinctive culture and literature. In the second half of the nineteenth century, when a distinctly Mexican American literature began to emerge, it followed a line of development common among frontier cultures. Historical and personal narratives predominated, many of them apologetic in tone. Mariano Vallejo and Pio Pico composed histories of California to show, as Vallejo put it, that their people "were not indigents or a band of beasts." Similar works issued from New Mexico and Texas. Mexican Americans also produced a

*The term *Anglo* is commonly used in the Southwest to refer to non-Latino Caucasians.

considerable volume of verse, much of it ephemeral and derivative. Oddly enough, so far as we now know, little sustained fiction was produced, perhaps because the harsh environment of the Southwestern frontier discouraged prolonged periods of creativity. Nevertheless, there were two notable novels by Eusebio Chacón: *El hijo de la tempestad* (The Son of the Storm) and *Trans de la tormenta la calma* (The Calm after the Storm), both published in Santa Fe in 1892.

Although publishing houses could be found in many Southwestern towns, the major outlets for early Mexican American writing were the dozens of Spanish-language newspapers that contained literary pages filled with essays, poems, and stories, or excerpts or serials of longer works. In addition to publishing works by Mexican Americans, these newspapers also published works by prominent Mexican, Latin American, and Spanish authors, enabling older writers to follow literary developments abroad and younger ones to find new models to emulate. Through their newspapers, Mexican Americans sampled the romanticism of the Spaniard Gustavo Bécquer and the *modernismo* of Rubén Dario and Manuel Gutiérrez Nájera. Despite the conventional view that early Mexican Americans were culturally isolated, their newspapers demonstrate that they maintained cultural and literary ties with Mexico, Latin America, and Spain. Chacón's novels are written in the picaresque tradition of Cervantes, but they also manifest a familiarity with contemporary literary movements in Latin America.

Despite the considerable volume of writing in the early period, oral forms command greater attention. The numerous newspapers of the period indicate a significant degree of literacy in the population, but Mexican Americans preferred oral forms of literature such as the folktale, folk drama, legend, and, most notably, the *corrido*.

A form of ballad that had evolved in Mexico, the *corrido* was embraced by Mexican Americans as the instrument most expressive of their particular cultural circumstances. Like ballad forms in other countries, the *corrido*—"a poem set to music"—flourished amid cultural conflict. As greater numbers of Anglos settled in the Southwest and antagonisms between them and Mexican Americans increased, hundreds of *corridos* emerged from across the American Southwest as a literary and musical chronicle of Mexican American experience.

The most fertile ground for Mexican American *corridos* was the border region of south Texas where relations with Anglos were especially volatile. As early as the 1850s, *corridos* were composed (usually anonymously) to celebrate those border Mexicans—from either side of the Rio Grande—who resisted Anglo injustice. The classic Mexican American *corrido* "Gregorio

Cortez" is an account of a Mexican-born *vaquero* who kills a Texas sheriff in 1901 for shooting his brother. The many variants of the Cortez *corrido*—still well known in Mexican American communities—compose a kind of Mexican American epic that pulls together the basic themes of contemporary Mexican American writing: ethnic pride, a forceful rejection of unflattering Anglo stereotypes, and, through celebration of Cortez's marvelous *vaquero* skills, an affirmation of the Mexican American's rootedness in the Southwest. The Cortez ballads remind their listeners that much that is widely admired about Southwestern culture was of Mexican origin. And because they are composed and sung in Spanish, a language with a longer history in North America than English, the ballads emphasize the importance of Spanish in preserving Mexican American culture.

Despite periods of relative decline, the *corrido* has endured as one of the key forms of Mexican American expression. During World War II, Mexican American soldiers composed *corridos* about MacArthur's campaign in the Pacific. In the 1960s, farm workers celebrated the exploits of César Chávez with a series of ballads. In the 1980s, *corridos* lamenting the massacre of patrons (some of them Mexican American) at a McDonald's restaurant on the border near San Diego have been heard. As an expressive tradition, *corridos* have acquired an importance in Mexican American culture equivalent to that of the blues in Afro-American culture. And like the blues, *corridos* have influenced other art forms. A recent play by Luís Valdez consists of a series of dramatizations of popular ballads and is in fact entitled *Corridos*.

By 1900, Mexican American literature had emerged as a distinct part of the literary culture of the United States, especially in the Southwest, where it has left an indelible imprint. Its origins were Mexican, its primary language was Spanish, and its religious sensibility was Roman Catholic. Given the proximity of Mexico, Mexican Americans could maintain ties to the homeland with relative ease, an advantage other ethnic minorities did not enjoy. People moved back and forth across the border frequently, invigorating both cultures. After 1910, when the Mexican revolution and labor shortages in the United States intensified immigration, Mexican contributions to the development of Mexican American literature increased. Julio Arce, a prominent newspaperman originally from Guadalajara, settled in San Francisco in 1915 and resumed his career as an editor and essayist. Ricardo Flores Magon, one of the leading Mexican intellectuals of the revolutionary period, fled first to San Antonio and then to Los Angeles, and in both cities became a major political and literary figure as well as the publisher of the newspaper *Regeneracion*. Less prominent refugees also left their marks on the Mexican American literary record, contributing tales of economic struggle, legends of the revolution, and *corridos* about the pain of immigration and acculturation. Once again, oral materials played a critical role in developing a literary sensibility that sought to locate enduring values and nobility not in the bourgeoisie but among working people.

During the thirty years between the start of the Mexican revolution and the coming of World War II, Mexican American literature continued along established lines of development. Historical and personal narratives, short fiction, poetry, and folklore predominated, with New Mexico as the center of activity. Of all Southwestern states, New Mexico prided itself most on its Spanish heritage. From 1598, when Juan de Oñate established a colony there, New Mexicans had done what they could to preserve and celebrate Spanish traditions. New Mexican hispanicism clearly manifested ethnic and regional pride, but it also represented a calculated effort to counter the consequences of widespread Anglo resentment of Mexicans and Mexican Americans. In Anglo eyes, Spaniards were the least of Europeans, but they were considerably superior to the mongrelized, treacherous, and shiftless Mexicans of American historical studies and popular fiction.

At the forefront of New Mexican hispanicism stood Aurelio M. Espinosa, a prolific folklorist who argued that New Mexican oral traditions were thoroughly Spanish, being virtually untouched by Indian, Mexican, and Anglo influences. Espinosa's claims had vast implications for New Mexican culture in general, but they spoke with special force to writers struggling under the weight of anti-Mexican sentiment. Examples of New Mexican "hispanic" literature include *Las primicias* (First Fruits), a collection of carefully wrought lyrical poems by Victor Bernal published in 1916; *Obras* (Works), a collection of both poetry and fiction by Felipe Maximiliano Chacón issued in 1924; and *Old Spain in Our Southwest* (1936), by Nina Otero Warren. Probably the most talented champion of New Mexican hispanicism has been Fray Angélico Chávez who, not surprisingly, has identified the Spaniards' establishment of Catholicism as their greatest accomplishment in the state. Chávez's major works include *New Mexico Triptych* (1940), a collection of religious tales, and *Eleven Lady-Lyrics and Other Poems* (1945). In addition to perpetuating hispanicism, the books by Otero Warren and Chávez signaled the appearance of a growing number of works by Mexican Americans in English.

Through World War II, Mexican American literature retained several deeply romantic qualities: a love of nature and rural life; a celebration of common folk such as farmers and *vaqueros;* a nostalgic longing for an idealized past in which life was simple and unhurried and cultural traditions and values were unthreatened; a defensive patriotism; and an almost willful simplification of contemporary problems. The supreme example of Mexican American literary romanticism is *Mexican Village* (1945), a beautifully written and immensely entertaining collection of ten closely related stories by Josephina Niggli. *Mexican Village* focuses on the American-born Bob Webster, the illegitimate son of a Mexican mother and an Anglo father who rejects the boy because of his manifestly Mexican appearance. After a long period of wandering, Webster settles in Hidalgo, the home village of the grandmother who raised him, to satisfy a "nostalgia of the blood." Although he has never before lived in Mexico, Webster comes to feel comfortable there, connected to the culture and the people by his remembrance of his grandmother's stories. In the end, he assumes his mother's family name, having discovered his essential and inescapable self.

Mexican Village was the first work of fiction by a Mexican American to reach a large Anglo audience. Recognizing the American public's meager understanding of Mexican experience, Niggli sought to convey an authentic sense of Mexican culture. An expert folklorist, she created fictional situations out of Mexican tales and legends and provided her characters with a large assortment of proverbs. Through the extensive use of Spanish syntax and idioms, she managed to approximate the rhythms and flavor of Spanish in English. The result of all these devices is a rich portrayal of village life in the mountains of northern Mexico.

But Niggli's greatest accomplishment was her delineation of Bob Webster and Mexican American duality. On the one hand, although Webster claims Hildago as his home, he remains unassimilated; his American qualities—his informality, egalitarianism, and independence—prevent his assimilation. On the other hand, he is even less an American than a Mexican. His memories of his father's bigotry have left him suspicious of American values and resentful of American attitudes. Webster, quite simply, is an archetypal Mexican American who fashions his identity out of the materials of two cultures.

In effect, *Mexican Village* epitomized the romantic qualities of an era that World War II brought to an end. The war thrust Mexican Americans into the national culture to an unprecedented extent. Tens of thousands of Mexican Americans either moved to large cities to take defense-related jobs or served in the armed forces. Both experiences, particularly the second, encouraged assimilation. Having made large contributions to the war effort, Mexican Americans emerged from the war with heightened expectations, but often found themselves frustrated and disillusioned.

Changes in Mexican American literature became visible as early as 1947, when Mario Suárez began to publish a series of stories in the *Arizona Quarterly*. Suárez's "chicanos"—a short way of saying *mexicanos*, as Suárez explains—live in a Tucson barrio. At first glance they seem to resemble the paisanos of John Steinbeck's *Tortilla Flat*. But, far from imitating Steinbeck, Suárez repudiates him. His chicanos are not childish and primitive stereotypes but authentic, fully realized characters. In "Señor Garza," Suárez presents a barber who closes his shop when business is heavy. Garza, living in American culture but not quite of it, recognizes the dangers of capitalism and determines to avoid them. Suárez ends his story with these lines: "Garza a philosopher. Owner of Garza's Barber Shop. But the shop will never own Garza."

Suárez's sharp portrayals of barrio life are enhanced by his effective rendering of *caló*—a combination of English and Spanish particularly popular among teenagers. To the dismay of his parents, a character called Kid Zopilote uses terms such as "watchar" and "syleacho" instead of their proper Spanish equivalents. The vocabulary of Suárez's stories represents yet another result of the Mexican American writer's concern for linguistic accuracy, a concern that had previously manifested itself in the use of standard Spanish and hispanicized English (as in Niggli's work). Suárez's use of *caló* reflects the continuing evolution of Mexican American speech and, by extension, of Mexican American culture.

In the decade after the publication of Suárez's stories, Mexican American literature languished, as if to gather energy for the rapid growth just ahead. In 1959, José Antonio Villarreal published *Pocho*, a work that not only stimulated a surge in Mexican American literary activity but also helped to shape its discourse. *Pocho* traces the experiences of a family from the time when its patriarch, Juan Rubio, quits the Mexican revolution and settles in California to a time when he watches helplessly as American influences transform and nearly destroy his family. The focus of the novel quickly turns to Richard—Juan's only son—as he struggles to achieve an identity that blends those elements of Mexican and American cultures that he admires. Richard's struggle proves agonizing in part because his father wants him to remain uncompromisingly Mexican, and in part because American culture is so intolerant of ethnic loyalty. Richard finally responds to these pressures by joining the Navy at the beginning of World War II.

Such events might seem trite were they not so paradigmatic. As the articleless title indicates ("pocho" refers, somewhat pejoratively, to an Americanized Mexican), Richard epitomizes the second generation's experience of assimilation as a process of alienation. The thoroughness of the process is evident in his decision to join the Navy: what better proof of one's absorption into a culture than by showing one's willingness to die for the country that produces it? The assimilationist nature of *Pocho* can be seen further in its style and technique. Its language, so important an indicator in Mexican American writing, is, with only scattered exceptions, standard English. Furthermore, nothing about *Pocho*'s shape or feel as a novel suggests a significant link to any literary tradition other than Anglo American. *Pocho* is an American book with Mexican American characters and themes.

To its largely Anglo readership, *Pocho* was a moving portrait of a necessary if painful process of assimilation. To a Mexican American audience, awash in a rising tide of ethnic pride, however, *Pocho* was a story of terrible loss. Far from being a story of desirable assimilation, it was a story of people victimized by insidious bourgeois institutions, most notably the educational system. In the 1960s, works of art were expected to be instruments of political and cultural change; writers were not just artists but social activists and apostles of ethnic awareness. *Pocho* was precisely the kind of book a new generation of Mexican American writers neither admired nor wanted to write.

Nothing exemplified the integration of literature into a program of Mexican American cultural and political activism more than the Teatro Campesino, which was established in 1965 when Luís Valdez seized an opportunity to combine his theatrical ambitions with the goals of César Chávez's farm workers' union. Under Valdez's direction, the Teatro merged traditional Spanish and Mexican dramatic forms with contemporary agitprop techniques to create powerful and entertaining skits in support of farm worker issues. Performed in open fields as well as university halls and theaters, the Teatro's *actos* attacked greedy farmers, dishonest labor contractors, brutal policemen—in short, all the enemies of the farm workers' union—with deadly wit. More than any other development of the time, the Teatro Campesino demonstrated to Mexican Americans the manifold potential of literary expression.

Stimulated by the Teatro Campesino, Mexican American literary activity expanded rapidly. In 1967, Quinto Sol Publications opened its doors in Berkeley for the sole purpose of issuing Mexican American writing. Although diverse, the authors associated with Quinto Sol shared certain assumptions and goals. They wanted to create a body of work that remained free of stereotypes while remaining faithful to their Mexican folk and belletristic traditions; they wanted to find forms and techniques compatible with the social, political, and cultural needs of their people; and they wanted, like their predecessors, to confront the language issue and the question of voice. In addition, however, they displayed new pride in their Indian heritage by evoking Aztec thought and culture. The notion of *Aztlan*, the ancestral home of the Aztecs believed to be located in the American Southwest, became a controlling metaphor for many writers. Aztlan freed Mexican Americans from the onus of being recent, displaced immigrants and provided them a sense of place and continuity. With the concept of Aztlan, the Southwest became theirs again.

The Quinto Sol writers were experimenters, using multiple narrators, combining poetry and prose in single works, and obliterating boundaries between fiction and nonfiction. Such innovations helped to generate new vitality and excitement among Mexican American writers. In poetry, the most interesting experimentation involved bilingualism or code-switching. The best Quinto Sol poets, such as José Montoya, blended English and Spanish, locating first in one and then in the other the most appropriate phrase or image. Poems by Montoya such as "Pobre Viejo Walt Whitman," "El Louis," and "La Jefita" exemplify vividly the leap in perceptual and aesthetic power available to the bilingual poet.

Quinto Sol introduced three extraordinary writers of prose: Tomás Rivera, Rolando Hinojosa-Smith, and Rudolfo Anaya. Like other writers associated with Quinto Sol, these three were animated by their ethnic sensibilities and their desire to depict vividly some essential part of Mexican American culture. Rivera's major work is ". . .y no se lo tragó la tierra" (And the Earth Did Not Part), published in 1971. In a series of fourteen related stories and sketches, Rivera delineates the Mexican American immigrant farm worker's experience in a spare, detached manner that is reminiscent of the Mexican master Juan Rulfo. No recent Mexican American writer has more effectively matched style and technique to subject matter. In vernacular Spanish that intentionally verges on artlessness, Rivera poignantly conveys the difficulties his characters experience in expressing themselves and in handling ideas. His stories and sketches, shorn of explication, reflect the meagerness of the farm workers' lives. His major character is an unnamed boy who struggles through bigotry, violence, and abject poverty. In some stories the boy is the narrator of the action, in others he is the subject of it. But throughout, his anonymity enhances his representativeness. Trapped, at least momentarily, at the bottom of the American social and economic hierarchy, he must learn not only self-respect and self-reliance but the larger lesson that every life is worth living well. By effacing his authorial presence as much as possible, Rivera gives his protagonist the run of his stories.

While Rivera's work seems rooted in the compact, harshly ironic narratives of Juan Rulfo, Rolando Hinojosa-Smith's stories draw on the *costumbrismo* movement of Latin America. They are steeped in the anecdotes, manners, and oral traditions of a particular region; yet they are also attuned to human idiosyncrasies. They seem in fact to share an aim earlier articulated by the Colombian master of *costumbrismo*, Tomás Carrasquilla: "to describe man in his milieu." Like Rivera, Hinojosa-Smith preferred to write in Spanish, to use Texas settings, and to favor the sketch as a literary form. Both writers disdain authorial explication, and both refuse to pronounce moral judgment on their characters. But Hinojosa-Smith's Spanish is much more buoyant and playful than Rivera's, his Texas settings are populated by a broader range of characters, and his sketches are often literary snapshots of two or three paragraphs.

Perhaps the most prolific of contemporary Mexican American writers, Hinojosa-Smith established the nature and trajectory of his most important fiction in his first two books: *Estampas del valle y otras obras* (Sketches of the Valley and Other Works [1972]) and *Generaciones y semblanzas* (Generations and Biographies [1977]). Although both works feature the same characters (Rafa Buenrostro and Jehú Malacara), the true heroes in Hinojosa-Smith's fictions are Mexican Americans who endure hardships and transcend vicissitudes. In this way Hinojosa-Smith joins Rivera and other writers in identifying the common people as the primary guardians and bearers of culture, without romanticizing or idealizing them. In Hinojosa-Smith's seemingly random collection of good-natured stories, the attentive reader discerns carefully wrought depictions of cultural values, ethnic relations, and economic issues that are of vital concern to Mexican Americans.

It is of signal importance that two of the finest Mexican American writers to emerge in the 1970s selected Spanish as the language of their art. Although Rudolfo Anaya, the youngest of the distinguished Quinto Sol group, writes in English, he too has advanced Mexican American literature. Of his three novels, several short-story collections, and plays, Anaya's best-known and most satisfying work remains his first novel, *Bless Me, Ultima* (1972). Set in a central New Mexico community at the end of World War II, the novel explores the transformation of the rural Mexican American culture subjected to both internal, conflicting forces and outside cultural pressures. One of the key symbolic events in *Bless Me, Ultima* is the testing of the atomic bomb in 1945 at White Sands. Without comprehending all its ramifications, Anaya's characters recognize the explosion as a sign of massive and irresistible change.

In *Bless Me, Ultima*, Anaya rejects the contrived hispanicism of an earlier generation of New Mexico writers. He sees contemporary New Mexican culture as a complex of traditions—Spanish, Indian, Anglo—not always coexisting in harmony. For Antonio Marez, the young protagonist of the novel, the task is somehow to forge a personal identity from this bewildering array of cultural values. His tutor in this experience is the magical Ultima, a *curandera* or healer whose power derives from her mastery of folk medicine and the oral traditions that have shaped the local culture. Having taught Antonio that individual choice is the way of knowledge, she bequeaths to him as a legacy the body of legends, tales, beliefs, and healing practices that have granted her not only great authority but also freedom.

By the mid-1970s, when the Quinto Sol house began to wane, its major objectives had been achieved. It had nurtured a group of writers who helped to determine the literary agenda for years to come. Whatever their differences of sensibility and perspective, Rivera and Hinojosa-Smith reaffirm the importance of Spanish as a factor in cultural preservation and the need to retain, through literature or any other means, ties with Mexico and Latin America. Anaya, on the other hand, demonstrates the inexhaustible vitality of oral traditions—Spanish, Indian, and Anglo—as a basis of elaborate, sophisticated fictions.

In the years since the demise of Quinto Sol, Mexican American literature has grown and diversified. Clearly, Mexican American writers no longer feel bound to the program of cultural preservation and political activism of the 1960s and early 1970s. Richard Rodriguez's autobiographical *Hunger of Memory* (1981), which accepts as inevitable—and deems ultimately desirable—the process of assimilation, makes this clear. The range of perspectives on cultural issues now spanned by Mexican American literature can easily be seen by comparing *Hunger of Memory* to the sometimes brilliant, always outrageous denunciations of contemporary American culture by Oscar Zeta Acosta in *The Autobiography of a Brown Buffalo* (1972) and *The Revolt of the Cockroach People* (1973).

The range of perspectives in Mexican American literature now includes a lively variety of feminism, a major development in a literary tradition not conspicuously attentive to women. Sandra Cisneros has used the *estampa* form brilliantly in her chronicle of a young woman's coming-of-age in *The House on Mango Street* (1984). Lorna Dee Cervantes's collection of poems, *Emplumada* (1981), treats women's issues, often with brutal eloquence. In *Loving in the War Years* (1983), a remarkable collection of poems, stories, and essays, Cherrie Moraga traces her growing awareness of herself as a "Chicana lesbian" against the background of her frequently misogynous Mexican American heritage.

In the last decade, Mexican American writers have tended to turn away from sweeping cultural perspectives and broadly representative characters toward introspective self-examination. Some of the most rewarding products of this development can be found in the poetry of Cervantes, Omar Salinas, and Gary Soto. Salinas's fierce talent is most visible in *Darkness*

Under the Trees/Walking Behind the Spanish (1982), a collection of poetic responses to such varied experiences as walking in a park to "lecture sparrows" and contemplating the ghost of Emiliano Zapata. Much of Salinas's power derives from the courage and honesty with which he confronts his own frail and flawed psyche. Soto is less wrenchingly intimate but, in his four volumes of poetry, he frequently looks back to his childhood in a Fresno *barrio* to locate his formative experiences.

In many ways, Soto's poetry exemplifies the best of current Mexican American writing. His ethnic consciousness animates his work without circumscribing it. Moving easily across national boundaries, he traces the lines of continuity between Mexicans and Mexican Americans. Although his most vivid characters are highly individualized, they identify strongly with their communities. Like Niggli, Suárez, Rivera, and Hinojosa-Smith, he shapes his art out of ordinary materials and experiences; his best poems are invariably his most accessible. In the title poem from his latest collection, *Black Hair* (1985), Soto recalls going to a neighborhood playground to watch baseball. Though unathletic, the poet watches in admiration the exploits of Hector Moreno until he comes to imagine himself circling the bases with Moreno, his face "flared," his hair "lifting/ Beautifully, because we were coming home/ to the arms of brown people."

It is of course noteworthy that Soto writes in English and grew up watching baseball. In other poems, he recounts watching television and other ways of being shaped by American popular culture. Recently, Rolando Hinojosa-Smith has been publishing regularly in English, presumably to reach a wider audience. Like all ethnic writers in the United States, Mexican Americans face formidable assimilationist pressures. Yet, of all ethnic groups, they almost certainly have the best chance of retaining their unique heritage. For the most part, they live where they have always lived, in the Southwest where Mexican traditions and influences are inescapable; they live within easy reach of Mexico; and they mingle regularly with thousands of Mexican immigrants—legal and otherwise—who help them to retain not only Spanish as a language but the culture that Spanish makes accessible. In many respects, the Mexican and Mexican American cultural presence in the Southwest has intensified recently, not diminished. It is likely, therefore, that Mexican American literature will continue along its distinctive course, in both Spanish and English, redefining and enlarging itself even as it intersects with the American mainstream.

Raymund A. Paredes

Asian American Literature

As writers of all ethnic and racial minority groups in the United States have noted, it is difficult to publish from a perspective that is American but not white, English, and even Protestant. This difficulty has been especially intense for Asian American writers—in part because a great ocean separates the United States from Asia, and even more because a great cultural gap separates Asian American writers from readers who lack solid information about Asian cultures and their peoples. One of the big problems facing Asian American writers has been the tendency of readers to view their works as sociological or anthropological documents rather than as literary ones. Too often Asian American works are taken to be representations of entire groups rather than expressions of individual artists. Given the large role that political and military issues have played in relations between Asian peoples and the United States, most critical assessments of Asian American literature have been influenced by political concerns.*

Only in the last decade has criticism begun to place social and literary issues at the center of interpretations of Asian American literature, exposing its texture, topography, tensions, and beauty. What has been revealed is that, from a historical perspective, Asian American writing mirrors the evolving self-image and consciousness of an often misunderstood and increasingly significant racial minority group, not only by documenting the experiences of Asians in the United States, but also by giving powerful expression to individual experiences and perceptions through the particular voices of Asian American artists.

Autobiography has been a popular genre among Asian American writers,

---

*Asian American literature is defined here as published creative writings in English by Americans of Chinese, Filipino, Japanese, Korean, and Southeast Asian (for now, Burmese and Vietnamese) descent about their American experiences.

largely because it has been the most marketable. Given the popular image of Asian Americans as perpetual foreigners, some publishers preferred writings with anthropological appeal over fiction. Others encouraged Asian American writers to present their work as autobiographical even when it was not. Carlos Bulosan was persuaded to write *America Is in the Heart* (1946) as personal history because it seemed likely to sell best that way. Although Maxine Hong Kingston's *The Woman Warrior* (1975) is fiction, it has been classified and sold as autobiography, or more broadly as nonfiction.

During the latter part of the nineteenth century, scholars and diplomats, who had been exempted from exclusionary legislation, published a number of "life stories" intended to counter negative views of Asia and Asians. For the most part, these writers used charming superficialities of food and dress, or ceremonies and customs, to appeal to the benign curiosity of Western readers. The first published works of this kind were Lee Yan Phou's *When I Was a Boy in China* (1887) and New Il-Han's *When I Was a Boy in Korea* (1928), narratives about upper-class childhood in China and Korea respectively.

Perhaps the best-known interpreter of Asia to the West is Lin Yutang, a self-styled cultural envoy who during four decades published a score of books on subjects ranging from "the importance of living" to tracts against communism to the feel of American life from a "Chinese" point of view. Lin's best-known work, *My Country and My People* (1937), enjoyed enormous popularity in Europe and the United States, although Chinese critics have pointed out that Lin ignored the everyday life-and-death struggles of the Chinese people under foreign domination. In contrast, Younghill Kang's quasi-autobiographical *East Goes West* (1937) marks a transition from the viewpoint of a visitor acting as a "cultural bridge" to that of an immigrant searching for a permanent place in American life. *East Goes West* is a vivid portrait of the life of Korean exiles—their work, their aspirations, and their exclusion from American social and intellectual life.

These early autobiographical works disclose a marked dissociation between their authors and the common people of both Asia and the West. Even their tentative apologetic pleas for racial tolerance are made primarily for members of the authors' own privileged class. Publishers and readers accepted them as representing all Asian Americans, but with few exceptions these works ignored the large numbers of laborers recruited for agricultural and construction work in Hawaii and the American West between 1840 and 1924.

One exception is Carlos Bulosan's quasi-autobiographical *America Is in the*

Heart. A self-educated Filipino migrant worker, Bulosan wrote in order "to give literate voice to the voiceless one hundred thousand Filipinos in the United States, Hawaii, and Alaska." Bulosan's work comes to us almost by accident: he was able to study and write while recuperating from tuberculosis in a California charity hospital. *America Is in the Heart* describes the lives of the Filipino migrant workers who followed the harvest, laboring in the fields and canneries from Alaska to the Mexican border during the 1920s and 1930s. The book, which emphasizes the promise of democracy against fascism, has been translated into several European languages and was hailed by *Look* magazine as one of the fifty most important American books ever published.

Among the first published works by American-born Asians are two Chinese American autobiographies, Pardee Lowe's *Father and Glorious Descendant* (1942) and Jade Snow Wong's *Fifth Chinese Daughter* (1945). These appeared in print at a time when Chinese, like Filipinos, were viewed as American allies and enjoyed unprecedented popularity. Both Lowe and Wong attempt to claim America as their own country, Lowe because he is so very American and Wong because she is uniquely yet acceptably Chinese. In *Father and Glorious Descendant*, Lowe describes Chinese objects as "alien" and "strange," Chinese customs as "old junk," and Chinese people as "emotionless automatons." America, on the other hand, with its schools, libraries, bathtubs, toilets, and railroad trains, Lowe presents as "God's own country." In *Fifth Chinese Daughter*, Wong introduces the reader to exotic and harmlessly interesting aspects of Chinese American family and community life. Assuming the role of an anthropological guide, she takes the reader on a tour of San Francisco Chinatown, even offering recipes for tomato beef and egg foo yung, complete with exact measurements and instructions. Both books are presented as evidence of how America's racial minorities can "succeed" through accommodation, hard work, and perseverance; and both more or less blame Chinese Americans—their families, their communities, their race—for whatever difficulties they face or failures they suffer.

While publishers encouraged writers like Lowe and Wong, they discouraged or even suppressed writers who insisted on going in other directions. Toshio Mori's *Yokohoma, California*, which indirectly challenged the views of writers like Lowe and Wong, was scheduled for publication in 1941 but did not appear until 1949, after World War II had ended. By 1953, when Monica Sone's *Nisei Daughter* was published, the Japanese had long since been released from wartime detention camps and were no longer concentrated in ethnic enclaves as they had been before the war. At first glance *Nisei Daughter* appears to be a cheerful Japanese version of *Fifth Chinese*

Daughter—a reassuring picture of the appealing qualities of a recently maligned group. On closer reading, however, it becomes a story of the enormous price exacted from second-generation Japanese Americans by politics and racism. In *Nisei Daughter*, the warmth and harmony of Japanese American family and community life are totally disrupted by the relocation experience.

In spite of such protests, however, during the 1970s, when the effects of the civil rights movement were being felt all across America, Japanese American "success" stories were widely publicized as evidence that racial minorities should blame themselves rather than external factors, such as racial discrimination, for social inequality. In particular, Japanese American "success" stories came to be regarded as examples that blacks and other minorities should follow. In this climate, major American publishers welcomed Japanese American autobiographies, and among those published were Daniel Inouye and Lawrence Elliott's *Journey to Washington* (1967), Daniel Okimoto's *American in Disguise* (1971), Jim Yoshida and Bill Hosokawa's *The Two Worlds of Jim Yoshida* (1972), and Jeanne Wakatsuki Houston and James D. Houston's *Farewell to Manzanar* (1973).

When it was first published, John Okada's *No-No Boy* (1957) was not favorably received. *Fifth Chinese Daughter* had been read by a quarter of a million people and was still being used in junior high and high school literature classes in 1975 as the best example of Chinese American literature. The first edition of *No-No Boy* had still not sold out when Okada died in 1971. Far from being another "success" story, *No-No Boy* explores the devastating effects of racism on the Japanese American community of Seattle just after the end of the war. Depicting a people incapacitated by uncertainty and self-hatred, Okada refuses to celebrate Japanese Americans as merely patient, hardworking, law-abiding, and long-suffering. To the contrary, he presents them as disfigured by the experience of relocation and racial hatred. In the *nisei* world of *No-No Boy*, no sacrifice is too great for the prize of social acceptance: the people in the community envy the war veteran who has lost his leg because his "patriotism" is evident at a glance. In Okada's confused and torn world, no one is complete: brothers betray brothers, children turn against their parents, parents turn to alcohol or suicide, husbands desert their wives, and wives commit adultery with their husbands' friends.

In many stories that portray Asian American community life, there are no white characters at all simply because segregated existence excluded them. As a result, issues of racism and race relations are submerged. In *Yokohama, California* and *The Chauvinist and Other Stories* (1979), Toshio Mori presents

Japanese American community life—featuring new immigrants and American-born characters of both sexes and all ages, farmers, laborers, small business owners, housewives, and students—in vignettes that bring out what he sees as deeply human joys and sorrows.

In half a dozen remarkable short stories published between 1949 and 1961, Hisaye Yamamoto offers a vivid picture of prewar family and community life among Japanese Americans on the West Coast, with a particular focus on women's perspectives. Yamamoto's stories concentrate on the relationships between immigrant husbands and wives and those between immigrant parents and their American-born children. Marked by subtle irony and understatement, Yamamoto's style juxtaposes two currents that reflect one of the quintessential qualities of Japanese American life. Beneath an apparently placid surface, often represented by a wholesome young *nisei* narrator, there are hints of hidden tragedy, usually tinged with death and violence. Sometimes, as in *Seventeen Syllables* (1949), Yamamoto accomplishes this by presenting fleeting glimpses into the mother's dark past and repressed desires through the half-uncomprehending eyes of the narrator daughter.

Milton Murayama's *All I Asking For Is My Body* (1975) is a powerful critique of authoritarianism and tyranny among Japanese Americans in Hawaii during the years immediately preceding World War II. Unquestioning acceptance of hierarchical authority thwarts the human freedom of dutiful sons who obey their fathers and of plantation workers who accept exploitation. The fictional company town of Pepelau is structured exactly like a pyramid: the plantation boss's house is built on top of the hill, followed by the houses of the Portuguese, Spanish, and *nisei* lunas (plantation foremen). Below these are the identical wood frame houses of the Japanese laborers, and at the bottom of the hill, where the toilet pipes and outhouse drainage ditches empty downhill, are the run-down shacks of the Filipino workers.

Both Lin Yutang's *Chinatown Family* (1948) and Chin Yang Lee's *Flower Drum Song* (1957) present euphemistic portraits of Chinatown, and both quickly earned popular and financial success. By contrast, Louis Chu's *Eat a Bowl of Tea* (1961) offers a more realistic insider's view of the daily life, manners, attitudes, and problems of the Chinese American community—and it failed to gain readers or make money. Focusing on the hypocrisy and self-deception that governs Chinese American life, Chu, like Murayama, presents the picture "with love, with all the warts showing." The vital quality of Chu's portrayal results in part from his ability to appreciate the spoken language of a people who regarded verbal skill and witty exchanges as a social art.

In recent decades, the Asian population in the United States has grown and diversified primarily as a result of changes in immigration and naturalization laws. Contemporary Asian American literature reflects this increasing diversity. Both greater social integration and new ethnic awareness have stimulated Asian American writing, in part by giving today's writers new confidence, and in part by creating markets that are less circumscribed by mainstream expectations. Some contemporary Asian American works are privately published; others appear in Asian American or minority journals and anthologies; still others are published by small presses interested in ethnic literature. But major publishing houses have also begun to express interest in the literature emerging from the Asian American community. Having first been performed for Asian American audiences, David Henry Hwang's plays became successful in New York theaters. In 1983, four of Hwang's works appeared together under the title *Broken Promises*, making him one of the first Asian American playwrights to be published.

In a growing spirit of self-determination, contemporary Asian American writers are experimenting with genre, form, and language to express sensibilities that are uniquely their own. Poetry presentations and dramatic readings with music and dance are flourishing in community forums. Recent writers blend drama with prose and poetry, fiction with nonfiction, and literature with history. Maxine Hong Kingston combines history, folk legends, and fictional interpretations, no one form dominating her work. Janice Mirikitani writes short stories that blend prose with poetry and poetry that is written to be accompanied by *koto* music and dance interpretations. Bienvenido N. Santos's *You Lovely People* (1965) combines the short-story and novel forms in a collection of self-contained short episodes that come together like a novel through the counterpointing of two narrative voices representing different aspects of Filipino American identity. The prose and poetry in the late Theresa Hak Kyung Cha's *Dictee* (1982) is presented in English and French and is illustrated with graphics derived from old photographs of Korea. Many writers, especially poets, are experimenting with Asian American colloquialisms. In *Yellow Light* (1982), Garrett Kaoru Hongo combines Japanese words with colloquialisms used in Japanese American communities in Hawaii and Gardena, California. The novelist Milton Murayama presents dialogue that combines direct translations of formal Japanese with both standard English and the pidgin spoken in Hawaii. *Sansei* poet Ronald Tanaka mixes traditional Japanese poetic forms with Japanese American expressions in the *Shino Suite* (1981).

Since the 1970s, Asian American writers have been concerned with filling in spaces, mending rifts, and building bridges across generations. Self-determination means telling the Asian American story from an Asian

American perspective, "restoring the foundations" of a culture that has been damaged or denied by racism. Such efforts, especially the search for historical foundations, have involved not only searching for works by little-known Asian American writers but also locating and translating works written by immigrants in their native languages. *Island: Poetry and History of Chinese Immigrants on Angel Island* (1980) consists of poetry discovered on the walls of the Angel Island Detention Center barracks. The editors present this poetry as "a vivid fragment of Chinese American history and a mirror capturing the image of the past." In *Island* we hear the voices of thousands of immigrants that might otherwise have been forever lost.

Chinese American writer Laurence Yep helps repair the foundations of the Asian American heritage in *Dragonwings* (1975)—a historical novel based on a newspaper account of the Chinese Fung Joe Guey, who invented and flew a biplane in 1901. Lacking information about Guey, Yep fashions a complex character, filled with apprehensions and motivated by dreams and longing, who proves to be capable of intense love and loyalty.

Rewriting Asian American history in literature from an Asian American perspective has given life to new heroes and heroines. Playwright David Henry Hwang's *The Dance and the Railroad* (1982) is about the 1867 Chinese railroad workers' strike, and the two main characters are railroad laborers. A number of contemporary Japanese American writers have re-created the World War II era in their works to show the effects of internment on individual lives. Lawson Inada's poetry anthology is titled *Before the War* (1971), reminding us that many Japanese Americans were marked for life by the relocation experience. In *kibei* Edward Miyakawa's *Tule Lake* (1979) and Jeanne Wakatsuki Houston's *Farewell to Manzanar*, contemporary Japanese American writers probe the effects of the camp experience, as does the Japanese Canadian poet and novelist Joy Kogawa in *Obasan* (1981).

Attempts to reconstruct the lost past have also involved exploring the half-buried mysteries of parents' and grandparents' experiences. Today's Asian American writer is often forced to seek the meaning of the past in shreds of stories heard in childhood. In Wing Tek Lum's "A Picture of My Mother's Family" (1974), a poet searches for the significance of each detail in an old photograph of his family, hoping to piece together a relevant story about his half-forgotten ancestors. Similarly, Filipino poets Al Robles and Presco Tabios have devoted years to collecting the life stories and oral histories of the Filipino elderly of San Francisco—men who, like Carlos Bulosan, immigrated to America as youths and then spent their lives laboring in fields and canneries. Bienvenido N. Santos, a Filipino expatriate who has lived in the United States since 1982, says that he has tried to write about the recent immigrant community but that his attention returns continually to "old-timers among our countrymen who sat out the evening of their lives before television sets in condemned buildings." Santos continues to write about the old exiles *(You Lovely People* [1965]; *The Day the Dancers Came* [1967]; *Scent of Apples* [1979])* because "now I realize that perhaps I have also been writing about myself."

The paucity of female characters in early writings by Asian American men reflects the harsh realities of the bachelor life created by American exclusion and antimiscegenation laws. Aside from Toshio Mori, few Asian American male writers have attempted multidimensional portrayals of Asian American women, focusing instead on defining themselves as men and on exploring their status as members of a minority. With the exception of the mother in the Philippines, most of Carlos Bulosan's women are either non-Asian prostitutes or idealized white women who represent the America that the narrator seeks to enter. The Chinese woman named Mei Oi in Louis Chu's *Eat a Bowl of Tea* is part seductress and part child, which makes her intrusion into the confines of the male-dominated Chinatown ghetto of the late 1940s profoundly disruptive. But the novel is about the men. Although Mei Oi reminds us that the men have failed as husbands and fathers, she lacks their dimensions as a character: she fails to understand, let alone consciously influence, the forces that shape both her life and theirs. The female characters in John Okada's *No-No Boy* are also stick figures. In the early 1970s, Frank Chin and Jeffery Paul Chan argued that Asian American men in particular were victims of "racist love" in American society. Citing the popular image of Asian men as asexual and the popular image of Asian women as wholly sexual, imbued with an innate understanding of how to please and serve men, they noted that both images served to bolster the notion of the white man's virility. But even when female characters play significant roles, as they do in the works of Frank Chin and Jeffery Paul Chan, they usually emerge either as domineering wives or mothers or as empty-headed girl friends who provide little more than an ironic audience for the metaphysical angst of male protagonists.

Although men are sometimes portrayed compassionately and convincingly in the writings of Asian American women, they generally remain in the shadows. Hisaye Yamamoto's men are conventional and colorless compared with the spirited women who must be subdued by husbands and fathers who resemble jailers. Unable to protect, inspire, or even understand women, many male characters in Asian American women's writing tend to seek emotional or physical escape rather than confront the things that limit them. The would-be lover in Eleanor Wong Telamaque's *It's Crazy to Stay*

Chinese in Minnesota (1978) departs for China, leaving the heroine to battle her problems alone. Sometimes there are striking contrasts between female characters who are triumphant boundry breakers and male characters who are too narrow and inflexible to flourish in American society. The brother in Wendy Law Yone's *The Coffin Tree* (1983) had been the strong one in Burma, but it is the sister who survives in America. The brother dies insane, leaving his sister in an alien world as the family's sole survivor.

Among both men and women writers today, intense longings for reconciliation persist. The narrator in Wakako Yamauchi's "That Was All" (1980) is haunted by her vision of the slim brown body and mocking eyes of the man whom she sees, as an aging woman, in a fleeting dream. In "The Boatmen on River Toneh" (1974), the female narrator is "swept against the smooth brown cheeks of a black-haired youth . . . and into his billowing shirt" only in death. Yet a mending of the rift may be at hand. The narrator in Shawn Hsu Wong's *Homebase* dreams of the woman he loves, while in David Henry Hwang's play *FOB* (1979), the gap between the immigrant and the American-born Chinese is bridged. During the play, the legendary woman warrior Fa Mu Lan teaches Gwan Kung, god of warriors and writers, how to survive in America; and at the end of the play Gwan Kung goes off with Steve, the immigrant. Perhaps Hwang, who says he was inspired by both Maxine Hong Kingston and Frank Chin, is consciously attempting to bridge the gap between Kingston and Chin, who have often been characterized respectively as writers for women or men.

In Asian American writing, gender has many dimensions. The "failure" of fathers is a favorite theme in Frank Chin's plays and short fiction and in Jeffery Paul Chan's short stories. Deprived of a masculine image and marked by their experience in a racist culture, male writers have struggled to destroy the myths that threaten their identities as men. The identity crises of the young stems in part from the complicity of older generations of Chinese Americans, who cling to "mildewed memories" of China or cater to tourists' exotic fantasies. Chinatown is a place of death, a "human zoo," an "elephant graveyard," and its people are like mechanical wind-up toys. Both the self and the family disintegrate, making flight the only possible means of surviving a suffocating environment. The young protagonists find establishing a new identity almost impossible, in part because the older men refuse to relinquish illusions that have limited their lives, preventing them from becoming real men. Both Chin's *Chickencoop Chinaman* (1974) and Chan's "Jackrabbit" (1974) focus on failed father-son relationships. One variation on this theme occurs in Shawn Hsu Wong's lyrical short novel, *Homebase* (1979), where the narrator seeks and finds his true American identity through the reconciliation of a father and son who share American roots as well as a Chinese American heritage. By claiming America as his own while reaffirming the love that connects his life to the lives of his father and forefathers, the narrator affirms his American identity. Wong's Chinese American is like a wild plant commonly "condemned as a weed" that survives to bear flowers, creating beauty and shade in the most difficult conditions.

The quest for a place in American life is a recurrent theme in Asian American literature. Contemporary writers, however, focus not on accommodation or racial self-negation but on the ideal that Carlos Bulosan articulated in the 1940s, of an America of the heart, where it is possible to be both American and nonwhite. Indeed, several contemporary Asian American writers express kinship with other nonwhite Americans, especially blacks and Native Americans, who frequently appear in their works. It is a Native American who tells the narrator in *Homebase* that he must find out where his people have been and see the California town he is named for before he can claim his home, his history, and the legacy of his forefathers in America. "Soon the white snow will melt," writes poet Al Robles, and "the brown, black, yellow earth will come to life."

During the late 1960s and early 1970s, many Asian American writers began to reject assimilation into what they view as a sterile and spiritually bankrupt white American mainstream that demands nothing less than denial of one's ancestry and heritage. The war in Vietnam strengthened such attitudes, as we see in "Japs" (1978), by Janice Mirikitani, a third-generation Japanese American:

if you're too dark
they will kill you
if you're too swift
they will buy you
if you're too beautiful
they will rape you
Watch with eyes open
speak darkly
turn your head like the owl
behind you

Young Asian American writers have also been moved to portray the recent immigrant experience. In "Song for My Father" (1975), a poem by Jessica Tarahata Hagedorn, the narrator is caught between America, "the loneliest of countries," and the land of her father, islands of music and tropical fruits. In a satirical story titled "The Blossoming of Bongbong" (1975), Hagedorn, who emigrated from the Philippines at an early age, traces the experiences of a young Filipino immigrant in a hostile America.

Consciousness of cultural conflict is also a major theme in the work of the Korean immigrant writer Kichung Kim, whose short story, "A Homecoming" (1972), depicts the confusion of a young Korean who returns to his homeland after ten years in the United States. In Ty Park's *Guilt Payment* (1983), many of the Korean immigrant characters fail to escape the haunting memories of the life they left behind. Of the few works of fiction in English by refugees from Southeast Asia, most focus on Asia. The protagonist of Tran Van Dinh's *Blue Dragon White Tiger* (1983) is a Vietnamese who has lived in America, but the novel itself is set largely in Vietnam. *The Coffin Tree*, an important novel by Burmese immigrant writer Wendy Law Yone, tells the story of a female protagonist who moves from Burma to America, only to face a contrast so severe that she almost loses her mind.

Although familiar themes still dominate it, Asian American writing has followed Asian American experience in accommodating an ever-widening range of perspectives. The poetry of Mei Mei Berssenbrugge *(Random Possession* [1979]), Alan Chong Lau *(Songs for Jadina* [1980]), James Mitsui *(Crossing the Phantom River* [1978]), and John Yau *(Crossing Canal Street* [1976] and others) demonstrates that Asian American writers cannot be confined by "Asian American" themes or by narrow definitions of "Asian American" identity. Their writings are all the more "Asian American" because they contribute to the broadening of what that term means. The most effective poems in Cathy Song's *Picture Bride* (1983) are not the ones replete with images of jade sour plums; they are those that explore the relationship between the persona and her family, from whom she ventures forth and with whom she is eventually reconciled.

Asian American writers are stronger today than ever before, and they deserve greater recognition and support, particularly as they strive to explore aspects of Asian American experience that remain misunderstood and unappreciated. Meanwhile, as they continue to celebrate the complexity and diversity of Asian American experience, they will also contribute to the emerging mosaic of American literature and culture.

Elaine H. Kim

Women Writers Between
the Wars

"I never was a member of a 'lost generation,' " the poet Louise Bogan wrote to her friend Morton Zabel in the 1930s, trying to account for the problems she was facing in her career. Bogan meant that she had not belonged to the famous group of literary pilgrims who fled the United States in disillusionment after World War I, to cultivate their Muse in London or Montparnasse. Yet in another, and more important sense, Bogan and her female contemporaries *were* members of a generation lost to literary history and to each other. For—despite the presence of Gertrude Stein, Katherine Anne Porter, and other women—the postwar literary movement that we have come to call the Lost Generation was in fact a community of men. In the 1920s, according to the critic John Aldridge, "the young men came to Paris. With their wives and children, cats and typewriters, they settled in flats and studios along the Left Bank and the Latin Quarter." Functional and anonymous as typewriters to male literary historians, the wives of the expatriates were nonetheless often ambitious writers themselves. Their marginalization, moreover, paralleled the dilemma of other American women writers who stayed at home. While the "lost generation" of Ernest Hemingway and F. Scott Fitzgerald became literary legend, another generation of American women writers suffered a period of conflict, repression, and decline.

For the literary women who came of age in the 1920s, the postwar hostility to women's aspirations, the shift from the feminist to the flapper as the womanly ideal, and especially the reaction against the feminine voice in American literature in the colleges and the professional associations made this decade extraordinarily and perhaps uniquely difficult. American society's expectations of modern womanhood were strikingly at odds with its image of artistic achievement. Women writers who had established their careers in the earlier part of the century found themselves out of touch with the new ideals; as Willa Cather would later remember, "the world broke in two in 1922 or thereabouts"; and for many women of her older generation it was impossible to cross the divide.

In order to understand the problems of American women writers in the 1920s and 1930s, we must also look at what was happening to American women generally during this period. First we need to look at the feminist crash of the 1920s—the unexpected disintegration of the women's movement after the passage of the Nineteenth Amendment. The 1920s were feminism's awkward age. The political coalitions of the suffrage campaign had dissolved into bitter and warring factions. While the suffragists had prophesied that an enfranchised female electorate would bring sweeping social reform to the United States, they were grievously disappointed when women did not press *en masse* for an end to war, prostitution, and poverty. To many feminists, moreover, Democratic and Republican party politics seemed crude, boorish, and mundane after the heightened utopian rhetoric and ennobling sense of sisterly mission conferred by suffrage activism. By the mid-1920s, it was widely acknowledged that the women's vote had failed to materialize. Women did not seem able to deliver a united vote that would give them power at the polls; instead they voted like their fathers and husbands, or simply stayed at home. Even one of the new female politicians, Democratic committeewoman Emily Newell Blair, acknowledged that the ballot had not brought women either power or political solidarity: "I know of no woman today who has any influence or political power because she is a woman. I know of no woman who has a following of other women. I know of no politican who is afraid of the woman vote on any question under the sun."

As articles began to appear in the popular press on the "failure" of women's suffrage, there were also signs of failure and disillusion on the personal level. The feminism of an earlier generation had been forged in the intense personal relationships of women's culture. Many female intellectuals and activists of the prewar generation—women like Jane Addams or Sarah Orne Jewett—had been raised to believe that women were the purer sex, blessed with little sexual appetite. The novelist Mary Austin recalled in 1927 that in her youth "nobody, positively *nobody*, had yet suggested that women are passionately endowed even as men are." Many ambitious women had forgone marriage and satisfied their emotional needs in intimate friendships with other women, or in communal female living in women's colleges or settlement houses. What they sacrificed in sexual passion they made up for in independence and the freedom to devote all their creative energies to their work.

But "modern" women read Freud and struggled to liberate themselves from outmoded sexual inhibitions. The heroine of the Jazz Age became the flapper, with her bobbed hair, short skirts, bathtub gin, and easy kisses. The feminism of the suffragettes seemed irrelevant or dated to the young women of the 1920s, who had been exposed to the messages of psychoanalysis, advertising, and Hollywood. The women's colleges that had been the avant-garde for the previous generation felt the shock wave of major changes in the 1920s. No longer intellectual sanctuaries where bright girls were initiated into intense female communities, they became sites of struggle over regulations and restrictions about heterosexual mixing. Even Bryn Mawr, the last holdout, offered tea dances by 1929 and allowed Princeton students to play the men's parts in student plays. The rituals and traditions that had united women students as a group withered away as students demanded more personal freedom and interaction with men. Ambitious women of the 1920s expected that they could have careers of their own, without surrendering the traditional feminine experiences of romance, marriage, and motherhood. "By the time I grew up," the playwright Lillian Hellman recalled, "the fight for the emancipation of women, their rights under the law, in the office, in bed, was stale stuff. My generation didn't think much about the place or the problems of women."

But these fantasies of lives that successfully balanced love and work were premature in a society where the husband's role was unexamined and unaltered, where wives were still expected to serve their men and their families, where in fact women's reproductive, marital, legal, and vocational rights were few. Encountering the real tensions between their writing and their personal lives led to disillusionment for women of Hellman's generation. Older feminists too felt bitter and betrayed. The younger generation did not seem to recognize their sacrifice or wish to emulate it. For a pioneer of women's higher education like Wellesley's Vida Scudder, the 1920s were "the bleakest years of her life."

While this shift in female attitudes toward personal achievement caused anxiety and conflict for women planning literary careers in the 1920s and 1930s, hostility toward female authorship and feminine values in academia and the literary establishment further stigmatized women's writing. A country taking new pride in its cultural heritage after the war saw only weakness and sentimentality in the contribution women had made to our national literature. In the years following the war, women writers were gradually eliminated from the canon of American literature as it was anthologized, criticized, and taught. In 1921, for example, the novelist Joseph Herges-heimer wrote the essay "The Feminine Nuisance in American Literature" for the *Yale Review*, in which he claimed that American literature was "being strangled with a petticoat." A similar essay in 1929 by Robert Herrick at-tacked women writers for their "feminization" of American literature. As the critic Paul Lauter has pointed out, these attacks reflected the concern of the age "that a truly American art [should] embody the values of masculine culture."

We can see the signs of this devaluation of women's writing as public honors for a few celebrated token figures were accompanied by mockery of women readers and writers in private literary correspondence and exclusion of women's literature from serious critical consideration. Although Willa Cather received an honorary degree from Princeton in 1931—the first woman to be so honored—her critical reputation, like that of her contemporary Edith Wharton, diminished. Both women were scorned by critics of the 1930s as decorous relics of a bygone age. While at the beginning of his career Fitzgerald acknowledged the influence of such important novelists as Cather and Wharton, he also complained that the American novel was being emasculated by female conventionality and propriety. Yet there was little tolerance for female unconventionality, originality, and impropriety from the very men who lamented the dictatorship of feminine prudery. Heming-way, for example, learned what he needed from Gertrude Stein, but could not imagine her being part of his literary circle. "There is not much future in men being friends with great women," he wrote in his memoir of Paris, *A Moveable Feast* (published posthumously in 1964), "and there is usually even less future with truly ambitious women writers."

Perhaps the worst casualties of the interwar period were the women poets. The image of the woman poet, or "poetess," as she might still be called, was much more stereotyped and limiting than that of the novelist. The pop-ular image of the American "female lyrist" was that of a "sweet singer" with three names, a pretty, youthful creature who wrote about love and renun-ciation, in a song as spontaneous, untaught, and artless as the lark's. After the war, however, American women poets needed to search for precursors who could define the shape of a serious woman poet's career as she matured and grew in artistry, range, and technique. Some, like Sara Teasdale, Edna St. Vincent Millay, and "H. D." (Hilda Doolittle), looked to Sappho, the Greek lyricist whose work existed only in fragments; and indeed reinvented her to provide a poetic matrilineage for themselves. Many turned to the

English poets Elizabeth Barrett Browning and Christina Rossetti. Others welcomed the rediscovery of a uniquely American female poetic voice, heralding the critical revival of Emily Dickinson in the la<e 1920s. Amy Lowell championed Dickinson's poetic genius and praised her unorthodox meters and rhymes during a period when mainstream critics regarded her work as eccentric, and her place in American literary history as inconspicuous. Genevieve Taggard's biography of Dickinson in 1931 was one of the first written outside of the poet's family circle, and Taggard was editing a collection of Dickinson's poems and letters when she died.

Yet none of these precursors seemed wholly satisfying either in their personal lives or in their poetic careers. Amy Lowell's poem "The Sisters" (1925) summarized her generation's sense of marginality and eccentricity:

> Taking us by and large, we're a queer lot
> We women who write poetry. And when you think
> How few of us there've been, it's queerer still.

Reviewing the work of her "older sisters" in poetry—Sappho ("a leaping fire"), Barrett Browning ("squeezed in stiff conventions"), and Dickinson ("she hung her womanhood upon a bough")—Lowell regretfully concludes that none offers her a model for the kind of poetry she wants to write:

> Goodbye, my sisters, all of you are great,
> And all of you are marvellously strange,
> And none of you has any word for me.
> I cannot write like you.

American women poets like Lowell were particularly troubled by the advent of a modernist poetic aesthetics. Before the war, there had been a place for the female poet in American culture, albeit a limited and sentimental one. But T. S. Eliot and Ezra Pound, among others, proclaimed the need for a severe poetry that transcended personal experience and emotion—precisely the modes in which women lyric poets had been encouraged to specialize. Serious, or "major," poetry, Eliot, Pound, and their disciples argued, was intellectual, impersonal, experimental, and concrete. Furthermore, they believed, women were by nature emotional creatures who could inspire major poems but lacked the genius to produce them. As John Crowe Ransom declared in an essay entitled "The Poet as Woman" (1936), "A woman lives for love. . . . safer as a biological organism, she remains fixed in her famous attitudes, and is indifferent to intellectuality." Even laudatory reviews of particular women poets frequently included derisory generalizations about the deficiencies of women's poetry as a genre; Theodore Roethke, for example, provided a lengthy catalogue of "charges most frequently levelled against poetry by women": "lack of range—in subject matter and emotional tone—and lack of a sense of humor . . . the embroidering of trivial themes; a concern with the mere surfaces of life . . . lyric or religious posturing . . . lamenting the lot of the woman; caterwauling; writing the same poem about fifty times, and so on."

Even when women produced feminine versions of modernism, reimagining myths, for example, from female perspectives (such as Bogan's "Cassandra" and "Medusa," Millay's "An Ancient Gesture," describing Penelope, and "H. D." 's "Eurydice"), as James Joyce and T. S. Eliot had modernized the myths of Ulysses and the Grail, their experiments were ignored or misunderstood. As they attempted to forge a new tradition for themselves against this patronizing aesthetic, American women poets struggled with the conflict between their ambitions to create and their internalized obligations to behave as beautiful and selfless Muses for men. This conflict can be seen as the common thread in a number of otherwise disparate poetic careers.

Sara Teasdale was one of the most famous female poets of her era. Yet she had been raised to believe in the romantic feminine myth of love as woman's whole experience, and she could never allow herself to acknowledge a primary commitment to art. "Art can never mean to a woman what it means to a man," she reassured an admirer. "Love means that." Believing that "a woman ought not to write . . . it is indelicate and unbecoming," Teasdale sought to curb her poetic ambitions, as she also repressed her sexual energies. Her early poems were wistful love lyrics that corresponded to her sense of feminine delicacy and decorum. When Teasdale married in 1914, her businessman-husband boasted that "she has put the duties of her womanhood (motherhood and wifehood) above *any* art and would I believe rather be the fond mother of a child than the author of the most glorious poem in the language." A rejected suitor, the Populist poet Vachel Lindsay, foresaw a new role for Teasdale in which her "woman heart" would express itself in verse that was both maternal and modest in scope: "You ought to make yourself the little mother of the whole United States," he enthusiastically suggested.

Yet marriage did not bring the ecstasies that she had anticipated, or the motherly role men envisioned for her. Only a few years later, Teasdale had an abortion, unable to imagine maternity and poetic creativity as other than antagonistic roles. In the 1920s she retreated into isolation and psychosomatic illness, as her poetry took up themes of frustration and suffering. As a young woman, Teasdale had believed that the woman who wished to be a poet should "imitate the female birds, who are silent—or, if she sings, no one ought to hear her music until she is dead." In 1933, convinced that her lyrics had become unfashionable, but unable to develop a new and strong poetic voice, she took her own life.

Another strategy for American women poets of the period seeking to reconcile femininity and creativity was the celebration of the miniature and the decorative, in exquisitely crafted sonnets and lyrics. Elinor Wylie, for example, specialized in images of whiteness, crystal, ice, glass, porcelain, and jewels. Unlike that of Teasdale, Wylie's life had been full of scandal, including adultery, divorce, and the desertion of her son. The precision of her poetic forms and the chilliness of her imagery helped Wylie defend herself against charges of overwrought feminine emotionalism and sexual promiscuity. Her most famous poems, such as "Velvet Shoes," about walking in the snow, and a series of sonnets about winter landscapes, established her persona as a daughter of the Puritans devoted to austerity, silence, and self-denial. In such books as *Nets to Catch the Wind* (1921) and in her essay "Jewelled Bindings" (1923), Wylie presented her view of the lyric poem as a "small jeweled receptacle" in two or three well-polished stanzas. The image associated the female lyric with the female body itself, especially since Wylie was celebrated for her silver gowns, dresses like a kind of metallic armor, in which her slender body reminded Van Wyck Brooks of "some creature living in an iridescent shell."

The themes of reticence, confinement, and silence so prominent in the work and personae of Teasdale and Wylie can be seen as the dominant ones of the modernist women poets; and we can understand them as in part a response to anxieties about female creativity. In the Imagism of "H. D." and the ellipses of Marianne Moore, subjective elements were made ambiguous or obscure. Moore's difficult and allusive poems withheld any hint of a self behind the text; the critic Hugh Kenner's remark that Moore was a "poet of erasures" for whom deletion "was a kind of creative act" suggests that the aesthetic of reticence demanded vigilant self-control. Léonie Adams and Louise Bogan also chose a severely impersonal poetry, dissociating themselves from what they saw as the sentimental excess of much women's writing. Bogan was outspoken about her contempt for a female tradition in poetry, although she did not recognize the self-hatred behind her stance. Rejecting a proposal to edit an anthology of women's verse in 1935, she wrote that "the thought of corresponding with a lot of female songbirds made me acutely ill. It is hard enough to bear with my own lyric side."

Yet these cautious choices also seemed to restrict the poets to minor status. Writing about Marianne Moore in the *Literary History of the United States* (1948), for example, a critic remarked that "she is feminine in a very rewarding sense, in that she makes no effort to be major." While Moore's self-effacement might seem rewarding in contrast to the bawling ambition of her male contemporaries, this is a revealing statement about the way in which femininity and minority status were linked in the critical mind. For many women poets of the period, feeling *"very* minor," as Bogan noted, was a painful reminder of their dilemma. At the same time that Bogan pursued her austere credo of withdrawing "her own personality from her productions," she envied male poets their scope, ambition, variety, and freedom to express personality. Often Bogan's sense of creative inhibition was expressed personality. Often Bogan's sense of creative inhibition was expressed in physical images of size and weight. In a review of Edna St. Vincent Millay's poetry, Bogan noted that "women who have produced an impressively bulky body of work are few." Just as she lamented the absence of a female precursor with a substantial body of work, Bogan longed to write "fat words in fat poems," like her friend Theodore Roethke, instead of the spare, chiseled, even anorexic verses she could allow herself.

At the beginning of her career, Edna St. Vincent Millay showed promise of becoming the most daring and successful presence in her generation of women poets. After her widely publicized youthful debut in 1912, when her poem "Renascence" won a prize sponsored by a poetry society, Millay became as notorious for her love affairs as for her art. Her first book, *A Few Figs from Thistles* (1920), established her as a bold voice for the New Woman. Such flippant lines as these from "First Fig"—"My candle burns at both ends;/ It will not last the night; But ah, my foes, and oh, my friends—/ It gives a lovely light!"—suggested that Millay would insist upon the kind of sexual freedom and emotional independence that had always been the prerogative of men. Raised by a strong mother in a family of loving and talented sisters, and a student at Vassar during the height of the suffrage movement, Millay became a passionate lifelong feminist. Unlike some of her contemporaries, she took pride in the achievements of other women. "Isn't it wonderful how the lady poets are coming along?" she wrote in delight after reading Louise Bogan. Millay dedicated her powerful sonnet-sequence *Fatal Interview* to the memory of Elinor Wylie, and even in unsuccessful poems like "Menses" she made a daring attempt to explore taboo female sexual experience and bring it into the realm of acceptable poetic subjects.

Yet Millay, too, suffered from the period's critical resistance to the first-person lyric as a serious art form. Working with such traditional poetic genres as the ballad, lyric, and sonnet, she was patronized by critics favoring formal and linguistic experimentation. In the 1930s, as she sought to incorporate her political interests into her writing, she disappointed an audience that expected her to remain a romantic laureate. Like Teasdale, she suffered a series of breakdowns as her popularity waned.

Millay was not the only woman poet of this generation who found it increasingly difficult to create as she grew older. Many seemed to run out of suitably "impersonal" subjects, and were finally silenced by years of self-censorship. Léonie Adams, having published two widely praised volumes of "metaphysical" poetry in the 1920s, virtually stopped writing by 1933. Louise Bogan simply could not imagine a woman poet who survived as an artist when youth, beauty, and romance were past: "Has there ever *been* an old lady poet?" she sadly inquired. Between 1941 and 1968, Bogan wrote only ten poems and was frequently hospitalized for depression.

One way to resist the label of "minor woman lyricist" was to write poems reflecting the political struggles of the Great Depression. Genevieve Taggard began her career with *For Eager Lovers* (1922), a book of poems about love, courtship, and pregnancy that reminded reviewers of Teasdale and Millay. Yet Taggard, a socialist and radical who had written for *The Masses* and who was active in left-wing organizations and writers' groups, became impatient with this limited cultural role. "I have refused to write out of a decorative impulse," she explained, "because I conceive it to be the dead end of much feminine talent." Neither could she accept the impersonal mask of the modernist aesthetic. Acknowledging the importance of Eliot as a poet, she nonetheless sharply criticized his elitist politics, his anti-Semitism, and his contempt for women. Believing that the most personal lyric could reveal the feelings of a whole community, Taggard used the form to write about the experience of the working class, in collections that critics promptly denounced as mere propaganda.

Ironically, women poets like Taggard and Millay who turned to politics in the 1930s as a way of establishing their strength and universality found themselves condemned by yet another set of double sexual and literary standards. As the historian Elinor Langer has noted, "the radical movement of the 1930s was a male preserve." Like other left-wing groups, the Communist party of America welcomed women into its ranks but elevated few to leadership and presented few as candidates for public office. Leftist groups saw feminist issues as not only potentially divisive but also as less important than the struggle of the working class. Women's roles and needs were subordinated to those of workers, and women organizers were expected to sacrifice personal ambitions, family, and children for the good of the party. Political work—picketing, demonstrating, writing and distributing party leaflets and tracts—demanded enormous commitments of women's time and energy.

Moreover, as the historians Alice Kessler-Harris and Paul Lauter have pointed out, "The cultural apparatus of the Left in the thirties was, if anything, more firmly masculist than its political institutions." Women were only token members of left-wing cultural and literary organizations such as the John Reed Clubs, and they were also underrepresented on the editorial boards and pages of radical journals: six women were listed among fifty-five editors and writers on the masthead of *The New Masses*. At the *Partisan Review*, also, male editors expected women to be frivolous, less than intellectually and politically serious. Mary McCarthy recalled that when she started writing for the *Partisan Review* she was given the job of drama critic because "I was a sort of gay, good-time girl from their point of view. . . . They thought the theater was of absolutely no consequence."

Finally, the literary and aesthetic values of the Left favored male writers, male protagonists, and masculine themes. In "Go Left, Young Writers," an editorial for *The New Masses* in 1929, Michael Gold described the advent of a new kind of American writer, "a wild youth of about twenty-two, the son of working-class parents, who himself works in the lumber camps, coal mines, and steel mills, harvest fields and mountain camps of America." The vogue of this tough-guy artist implicity cast doubt on the more private or domestic subject matter of women's fiction, even though for men, too, the lumberjack role was often a pose. In addition, the insistence that left-wing art should focus on economic oppression and the workplace created special problems for women. Only 25 percent of all women, and less than 15 percent of married women, worked outside the home during the 1930s; and few of these worked in the coal mines or steel mills. Once more women's special experiences were devalued or ignored.

What were the effects of political involvement for women writing during the 1930s? Despite their difficulties, some women felt nourished and inspired by the urgency of the issues before them and by the excitement of sharing revolutionary goals with male and female comrades. They found encouragement, communion, and fellowship in left-wing organizations. For the novelist Meridel LeSueur, for example, the thirties were a period of satisfying literary productivity and of "nourishing" associations with political men and working women. From her point of view, the decade was "a good time to be a woman writer, or any other kind of writer." Like other politically active women in the decade, such as Josephine Herbst, Martha Gellhorn, Tillie Olsen, and Mary Heaton Vorse, LeSueur developed new forms of reportage, combining journalism with a committed personal voice that made the work a precursor of the "nonfiction novel" of the 1970s. Her best-known essays are outspoken, colloquial, graphic vignettes of female experience during the Depression. "Women Are Hungry" (1934) describes the special anguish of women on the breadlines: "The women looking for jobs or bumming on the road, or that you see waiting for a hand-out from the charities, are already mental cases as well as physical ones. A man can always get drunk or talk to other men, no matter how broken he is in body and spirit; but a woman, ten to one, will starve alone in a hall bedroom until she is thrown out, and then she will sleep alone in some alley until she is picked up."

Yet there were other women on the Left trying to write about gender as well as class, who were isolated from each other, and who had no support either from women's groups or Communist party networks. Furthermore, as LeSueur admitted, the party demanded a particular style of writing from its members and had little tolerance for other literary forms. Most Marxist literary critics were hostile to the formal and linguistic experiments of modernist writers such as James Joyce, D. H. Lawrence, and Virginia Woolf; they dismissed such aesthetic preoccupations with language as bourgeois or decadent. Instead they advocated "proletarian realism," the theory that literature should describe and celebrate the lives, struggles, and triumphs of working-class people under capitalism. Literary innovation was to take the form of recording the language and dialect of the working class, or the "folk," extending reportage and documentary into a narrative form.

But even LeSueur had been profoundly influenced by Lawrence, whose writing about sexuality helped her overcome the puritanism of her Midwest upbringing and gave her a model for some of her lyrical short stories of the 1920s about female sexuality and pregnancy. Such subjects, however, were taboo among left-wing critics in the thirties, as were the styles and subjectivities of women's writing. When left-wing women writers moved away from the permitted subjects to discuss private female experiences, their work was harshly condemned by radical male critics. Whittaker Chambers rebuked LeSueur for the "defeatist attitude" of her essays about women, and other reviewers disparaged her fictional efforts to describe women's feelings and their sexuality. LeSueur struggled during the decade to purge her fiction of what she called its "narcissistic" elements; but later she ruefully recalled that the Communist party tried "to beat the lyrical and emotional out of women."

We can see the effects of this pressure on the development of her writing during the period. In her early work, LeSueur had been drawn to explorations of women's awakening sexual consciousness in the tradition of Kate Chopin's *The Awakening* and Edith Wharton's *Summer*, and to almost mythic projections of the cycle of separation from the mother, reproduction, and death. "Persephone" is a haunting allegory about a young girl's abduction from her mother, a Demeter-figure identified with nature and fertility. In subsequent stories such as "Wind" and "Annunciation," LeSueur described female rites of passage, including sexual initiation and pregnancy. Yet her major fictional work of the 1930s, a novella called *The Girl* (1936), which describes a community of women from different backgrounds who help each other to survive the Depression, was rejected by her publisher and remained unpublished until 1971.

Tillie Olsen has written in her book *Silences* (1978) about the periods of creative paralysis that beset writers and especially women writers, listing among the causes the moments when "political involvement takes priority." Olsen's own experiences in the thirties are a case in point. Coming from a socialist immigrant background in Nebraska, Olsen grew up aware of the sufferings of women and the poor, and familiar with both a radical and a feminist literary tradition. She had read the work of Rebecca Harding Davis, Willa Cather, Olive Schreiner, and Agnes Smedley, as well as that of John Dos Passos and Langston Hughes. When she joined the Young Communist League as a talented young writer in 1931, Olsen was assigned to a series of political tasks in the Midwest, including organizing women in factories and writing skits and plays for the Communist party. During these years, too, she was working at a series of low-paid jobs and taking care of two daughters. For Olsen, "it was not a time that my writing self could be first." Her writing self, indeed, had to be postponed until many years later, and in some sense it has never been fully recovered; a prizewinning book of short stories, *Tell Me a Riddle* (1961), and an unfinished novel, *Yonnondio* (1974), are fragments of a career that was damaged by long deferral.

Yonnondio, like *The Girl*, was begun in the 1930s and only published forty years later. Like LeSueur's book, it is about the struggle for survival: a family moving from mining to tenant farming and finally to the slaughter-houses and packing plants of Omaha. Yet the novel also has a strong sub-jective and experimental quality. It is the story of the daughter, Mazie, an autobiographical heroine who, in Olsen's original plan, was to have become a writer, and her mother Anna. But Olsen was never able to finish the book. In the tradition of feminist writers like Olive Schreiner, she wanted a place for the lyric, the personal, the mythic, and the fantastic. But her immersion in the aesthetic of proletarian realism made it difficult for her to develop the psychological elements of her story—the wrenchingly intense mother-daughter bond, the conflicts of sexual desire and feminine respectability, and the power struggles of marriage. These had to be suppressed in favor of a more impersonal account of the struggle between workers and bosses. Olsen was silenced by her internal conflicts as well as by the external pressures of family and work.

Josephine Herbst was another significant novelist on the Left whose work was both nourished and distorted by the formulas of the thirties. While Herbst was never an active feminist, her life and career were shaped by her profound feelings about other women. Her mother's stories first stimulated her imagination and made her want to become a writer; in the early 1920s her favorite sister's death after an abortion was a never-to-be-forgotten blow. Although Herbst was married to the left-wing writer John Herrmann, she also had two profound love affairs with women. Deep friendships with other women writers, especially Katherine Anne Porter and Genevieve Taggard, gave her a stronger base in a female literary community than Olsen or LeSueur had enjoyed. Herbst's political radicalism was also an important part of her life, although at many times she recognized that she was being marginalized or used as a token woman.

For Herbst's fictional development, however, the times were mixed. In 1920 she had an affair with Maxwell Anderson, then a married young reporter; when she became pregnant, he insisted on an abortion. The bitter novel she finished in 1922, "Unmarried," was never published. In a trilogy of novels based on her family's history in America, Herbst later tried to avoid the "constricted 'I'" deplored by Marxist critics and to submerge autobiography in an epic story of America society. But the documentary devices and the mixture of social consciousness and personal narrative that worked for male writers like Dos Passos struck readers as less significant when the central protagonists were women. Herbst's reputation declined, and although she worked for many years on a memoir of her life in the 1920s and 1930s, when she died it was found unfinished.

Another neglected writer of the thirties was Tess Slesinger. The daughter of a cultured and prosperous Jewish family, Slesinger studied writing at Swarthmore and Columbia. In 1928 she married Herbert Solow, assistant editor of the *Menorah Journal*, and through him met many of the young left-wing New York intellectuals of the period. The couple was divorced in 1932, and Slesinger drew on this experience for her only novel, *The Unpossessed* (1934). Like LeSueur and Olsen, Slesinger was drawn to the literary experiments of the modernist writers, and her novel was strongly influenced in its style and narrative technique by Katherine Mansfield and Virginia Woolf; its stream-of-consciousness technique is especially akin to Woolf's

Mrs. Dalloway (1925). Slesinger uses two heroines to represent the modern woman of the 1930s: Margaret Flinders, the working woman married to a Marxist intellectual, and Elizabeth Leonard, a boyish art student, who has bohemian love affairs and reads *Ulysses*. Through her account of the founding of a left-wing journal, Slesinger satirizes the sexism of the literary Left. One intellectual leader proclaims that "the point about a woman . . . is her womb"; and the women heroines wonder how to reconcile their desires for marriage and motherhood with their intelligence and their political ideals. In the bitter concluding section, "Missis Flinders," Margaret is made to have an abortion by her husband Miles, who fears that becoming parents would make them soft and bourgeois. The death of their child is clearly a signal of the death of their marriage, and perhaps also of their political movement. Slesinger ends with a despairing image of Margaret's barrenness and emotional sexlessness: "She had stripped and revealed herself not as a woman at all, but as a creature who would not be a woman and could not be a man." Published independently of the book, "Missis Flinders" was one of the first stories about abortion to appear in an American magazine.

But Slesinger's insistence that personal relationships as well as political ones needed to be revolutionized was lost on her male contemporaries. While the mainstream press generally praised her book, the work offended male radical critics, such as Philip Rahv, who complained in the *Partisan Review* that it lacked "a disciplined orientation for radicalized intellectuals"; Joseph Freeman in the *Daily Worker* called it "bourgeois and reactionary." In the late 1930s, Slesinger went to Hollywood as a film writer and became active in the Screen Writers' Guild. Her last, unfinished novel, left in fragments when she died of cancer in 1944, was a study of Hollywood written from the perspective of the film industry's workers, rather than its tycoons or stars.

The frustration, fragmentation, and silencing that plagued women poets and novelists generally during the 1920s and 1930s were especially acute for black women writers, who struggled not only with personal conflicts but also with racism and with pressures to conform to the aesthetic ideals of the Harlem Renaissance. As in the Left, the cultural theory and practice of the Harlem Renaissance was strongly male-dominated. Influential critics of the period, such as Alain Locke in *The New Negro* (1925), argued that the black writer should strive for positive expressions of black culture and for racial uplift, as well as for pure art. In the 1930s, when some leading black intellectuals such as Richard Wright joined the Communist party, they argued that the black artist had a primary responsibility to portray racial oppression and struggle. Women were expected to provide loving maternal nurturance for the new movement and its artists, not to lead it. The novelist Dorothy West recalled how in 1926 she joined a literary group in Harlem, but because she was "young and a girl . . . they never asked me to say anything." The highly educated and sophisticated women writers who participated in the movement often felt estranged from the working-class black community whose experiences they were expected to represent. Insulted by racist stereotypes of the black woman as erotic and primitive, they also felt hampered by family and religious pressures to deny their sexuality.

One of the most gifted women of the group the Harlem Renaissance called the "ultrarespectables" was the novelist Jessie Redmon Fauset. Educated at Cornell, where she was elected to Phi Beta Kappa, Fauset went on to graduate study at the University of Pennsylvania and the Sorbonne. From 1919 to 1926 she was the literary editor of the NAACP journal *The Crisis*. Fauset's male contemporaries admired her intelligence and culture, especially in her conventionally feminine role as the mentor or "midwife" for young black writers. Langston Hughes recalled her parties for the black intelligentsia in which conversations about literature sometimes took place in French. Claude McKay praised her for being "as prim and dainty as a primrose." But her refined hyperfemininity affronted those fighting oppression or defending the folk sources of black consciousness. Fauset's novels were as deeply concerned with problems of female sexual identity as with racial conflict; they show how race and gender together create permutations of power and powerlessness. Yet her romantic plots were mocked as "sophomoric, trivial and dull," or as "vapidly genteel, lace-curtain romances." Even McKay called her novels "fastidious and precious," and to critics of the Harlem Renaissance, Fauset is sometimes described as the "Rear Guard."

Fauset's own relationship to her literary community, however, was more critical and innovative than these condescending terms would suggest. On the one hand, she deplored the cult of primitivism and the limits that white publishers set on the portrayal of blacks in fiction. Most publishers, she wrote in protest, "persist in finding only certain types of Negroes interesting and if an author presents a variant they fear that the public either won't believe it or won't stand for it." Indeed, Fauset's first novel, *There Is Confusion* (1924), was rejected by publishers because it contained "no description of Harlem dives, no race riot, no picturesque abject poverty." "White readers just don't expect Negroes to be like this," her publishers complained.

On the other hand, Fauset's portraits of black middle-class women, struggling with sexual politics as well as with racial tensions, challenged the stereotypes of black male readers. Fauset's most important novel, *Plum Bun* (1929), uses a contrast between two sisters, the light-skinned Angela and the dark Virginia, to dramatize the temptations of "passing" for her gifted black women. For Fauset, the theme of "passing" has a double meaning; it refers both to the racial conflicts of the mulatto who can enter the white world and to the divided sensibility of the woman artist who must conceal or sacrifice her vision in response to social definitions of femininity. As one character in the novel remarks, "God doesn't like women." Each sister represents an aspect of Fauset's own identity. Through the vivid Jinny, a teacher in Harlem, she describes the intellectual world of the Harlem Renaissance and its male idols, like the spellbinding theorist Van Meier. Through the gifted artist Angela, who studies in New York and Paris, Fauset shows the steady subversion of female talent by myths of romance and domesticity. Whether she is courted by the cynical white playboy Roger or the idealistic black painter Anthony, Angela fears that she will risk losing love and security if she appears strong or insists on putting her art first; to be beloved and feminine she must be "dependent, fragile . . . to the point of ineptitude." In marrying Anthony, she determines to make his happiness her career: "At the cost of every ambition which she had ever known she would make him happy. After the manner of most men his work would probably be the greatest thing in the world to him. And he should be the greatest thing in the world to her."

Similar themes of female sexuality and frustrated ambition are explored in the remarkable novels of Nella Larsen. The daughter of a Danish mother and a West Indian father, Larsen studied at Fisk University and the University of Copenhagen, and trained as a nurse in New York. Later she became a librarian. Her literary career was brief and intense. On the basis of her two novels, *Quicksand* (1928) and *Passing* (1929), she was offered a Guggenheim Fellowship for creative writing in 1930—the first black woman to be so honored. But Larsen never finished another book. After her return from Europe, as she dissolved her marriage to a prominent black physicist, her career ended in silence and obscurity.

We may look for the clues to Larsen's unhappy career in the tensions of her two novels about cultivated women of mixed parentage trying to find a place for themselves in the Harlem art world, in white society, or in the black rural South. In *Quicksand*, the mulatto heroine Helga Crane is intellectual and cosmopolitan, but she feels alienated and alone wherever she goes. At the black Southern college where she teaches English, she is repelled by the caution of her black colleagues and by their self-denying emphasis on racial uplift. In Harlem, she is both intrigued by the glamor and imagination of black society and irritated by its obsession with race. Yet when she goes to live with relatives in Denmark, Helga misses the company of other blacks, experiencing a belated sense of racial identity she had not even known she possessed. Resisting marriage, moreover, she is tormented by the intensity of sexual desires that are unacceptable in all her social worlds. Larsen imagines a grim resolution to Helga's dilemma; wandering into a black revivalist prayer meeting in New York, she finds a release for her stifled emotions in the Bacchic frenzy of worship and song. "In the confusion of seductive repentance," she marries the evangelical preacher and goes to live with him in Alabama, a marriage that sentences her to permanent imprisonment in childbearing and poverty. Although she is gifted with intelligence and beauty, Helga seems doomed by both her sexuality and her race.

The most important and productive woman writer of the Harlem Renaissance, Zora Neale Hurston, experienced similar conflicts in her life, but managed to transcend them in her work. Raised in the all-black community of Eatonville, Florida, where her father was the mayor, Hurston grew up with the direct experience of rural Southern society that writers like Fauset and Larsen from the urban Northeast had missed. In 1925, however, having begun to establish a reputation in Harlem as one of the most talented and irreverent young writers, Hurston won a scholarship to Barnard College, where she was the only black student. Trained as an anthropologist by Franz Boas, and subsidized by a wealthy white patron of black writers whom she called "Godmother," Hurston returned to the South with the eyes of an observer, and with the methods of a social scientist rather than an artist. The tall tales of her childhood had been redefined as "folklore," and her task was to collect and analyze them. Yet Hurston kept her aesthetic identity intact; she survived both the pressure of the academic community to distance herself from black culture and the pressure of the white literary community to romanticize it. The books she wrote in the 1930s— most notably *Mules and Men* (1935), *Their Eyes Were Watching God* (1937), and *Moses: Man of the Mountain* (1939)—are memorable for what Hurston called "a Negro way of saying," a subtle, pungent, and original style that draws force from the black vernacular but is carefully crafted and influenced by literary models as well. However, Hurston's determination to write from inside black culture and to withstand fashionable issues of racial tension or oppression ("I do not belong to the sobbing school of Negrohood," she wrote in "How It Feels to Be Colored Me") antagonized her male contemporaries. Richard Wright, Sterling A. Brown, and Ralph Ellison accused her of pandering to a white audience and attacked her use of dialect humor as "minstrel technique." Like Fauset and Larsen, Hurston had to make her way as an independent and strong female artist in the face of male opposition.

Hurston's finest book, *Their Eyes Were Watching God*, blends several traditions of American writing. In technique, it is a modernist novel that incorporates surreal elements into its realism, and that alternates between the sophisticated verbal range of an omniscient narrator and a more intimate folk idiom that represents the consciousness of the heroine, Janey. Hurston's use of dialect, folklore, and a mulatto heroine roots her in the Afro-American literary tradition as well. But the novel is primarily the story of a woman's evolution from loneliness to independence. In what it includes and what it leaves out, it demonstrates Hurston's commitment to traditions of female narrative. Unlike her predecessors in the 1920s, Hurston was not afraid to make female sexuality a central theme in her fiction. Janey's growth to personal maturity is reflected by the sexual as well as emotional terms of her three marriages, which represent three stages of her inner development. Married at sixteen to an older man for whom she feels no desire and who would turn her into a "mule" (one who carries a burden passed by white men to black men to black women), she bolts. Her second marriage, to the domineering and possessive Joe Starks, becomes a power struggle that ends with her silencing and subordination. After Joe's death, Janey chooses Tea Cake, a younger man, who insists that she "partakes wid everything," that she share both his work and his play. Tender and affectionate, Tea Cake teaches her to fish and to shoot; he cooks for her and encourages her to tell stories with the men. Yet at the end of the novel, after Tea Cake has been bitten by a rabid dog, Janey is forced to shoot him.

Why does Hurston arrange her plot so that her heroine is forced to destroy a loving and egalitarian hero, if not because her heroine's survival meant more to her than romantic love? Having learned how to speak and to work, Janey must end on her own, free to make her own way in the world. Hurston's strong resistance to saddling her heroine with domestic burdens, however idealized, is made clear by the fact that despite three marriages, in two of which sex plays an important role, Janey has no children; in fact, the novel seems deliberately constructed to make us look away from this striking omission, to make us ignore such a lapse in its realism. In *Quicksand*, Helga Crane ends up pregnant and immobilized with her fifth child; in *Their Eyes Were Watching God*, Janey remains unencumbered and so is free to realize her dreams.

The 1930s did not end happily for American women writers. Within the

academic institutions of American literature, women were increasingly marginalized. In 1935, the first edition of a standard college textbook, *Major
American Writers*, included no women at all. Even the great best-sellers of
the decade, such as Pearl Buck's *The Good Earth* (1931) and Margaret Mitchell's *Gone with the Wind* (1936), were taken as confirmations of women's
talent for a popular literature that could never compete with male art. During the last years of her life, Zora Neale Hurston moved from job to job,
forgotten and neglected. When she died in 1960, she was living in a welfare
home, working as a maid. Her grave was unmarked.

Yet despite all the difficulties and defeats, American women writers in
the 1920s and 1930s produced an important body of work that has finally
become influential, as we begin to incorporate it into a three-dimensional
understanding of American literary history. Although the feminist movement waned during these decades, many strong women writers resisted the
pressures to abandon their own visions and voices. In every genre—poetry,
the short story, the novel—women writers between the wars advanced the
honest exploration of female experiences and female lives. Moreover, many
revised the aesthetic techniques and narrative strategies of their male contemporaries, in order to record uniquely female perspectives. As the feminist critics Sandra Gilbert and Susan Gubar have noted, the sonnet sequences of Wylie and Millay expressed female sexual desires within a genre
traditionally devoted to the expression of male desire. The more experimental poets of the period—Gertrude Stein, "H. D.," Marianne Moore—contested the linguistic, syntactical, and thematic conventions of what Stein
called "patriarchal poetry." Women novelists on the Left infused the stiff
formulas of proletarian realism with psychological nuance and lyric force.
And the women writers of the Harlem Renaissance insisted on telling their
own stories despite neglect, condescension, or critical abuse.

Ultimately, the value of the literature of the past has to be measured in
terms of its continued impact on readers, writers, and critics. No book is
ever lost as long as there are new generations of readers to enjoy it, new
generations of writers to be stimulated by it, new generations of critics to
reveal its fuller meanings. By this standard, women writers between the
wars have already established their place in our literary tradition. Ignored
or misunderstood in their own day, they often died in disappointment. Several of their most ambitious books were left incomplete. But their achievement has survived, making them significant precursors of the world in which
we live as well as the one in which we read and write. Like the contemporary renaissance in American women's poetry and fiction, the development
of a female tradition of political writing has been founded upon the work

of women writers of the 1920s and 1930s. Perhaps the fate of Zora Neale Hurston, in many ways the most painfully "lost" member of a lost generation, can serve as an example for all. When Hurston died, her books were out of print; histories of Afro-American writing ignored or disparaged her work; aspiring young writers studied American literature without even encountering her name. But today she is recognized not only as the most gifted black woman writer of the century but also as what the novelist Alice Walker, who made a pilgrimage in the 1970s to put a headstone on Hurston's grave, called "a genius of the South." For Walker and for many of the leading women writers, black and white, of the 1980s, *Their Eyes Were Watching God* has become one of the most important books in a literary tradition that continues to inspire them and to enable their work. As we continue to enlarge that tradition, the lost generation of American women's writing may offer further surprises and riches. We must not let it become lost again.

Elaine Showalter

III. Fiction

The Diversity of American Fiction

The early 1910s were a promethean moment in Western art. Artist bohemias were springing up in Greenwich Village and Chicago, and the promise of creative and personal freedom made Paris and London magnets for talented writers. In London, Ezra Pound and the expatriate Imagists were initiating a whole new era of poetic experimentation. Meanwhile, word was filtering back to America that European painters were in the midst of a visual revolution. When the first postimpressionist exhibition reached the United States, in the famous Armory Show of 1913, these rumors were more than confirmed. The fauvist, cubist, and early futurist works were palpable evidence that the individual artist could be the perceptual, intellectual, and ideological leader of the day.

Floyd Dell and John Reed, like Upton Sinclair and Jack London, took this notion of the artist quite literally in what Joseph Freeman was to call "the Lyric Year 1912, when the search for new values in life and art seemed to lead logically to the socialist society." At this time, nothing was more fundamental to American art than its opposition to previous culture and status quo society. Even in the political mainstream there was sympathy for this artistic disaffection. Theodore Roosevelt's anticapitalist rhetoric had deprecated the single-minded pursuit of wealth at the expense of humane values, and in 1912, when the more intellectual Woodrow Wilson became president, it seemed that politics and the world of ideas had become one. Women were on the way to winning suffrage, and a tremendous sense of vitality prevailed. As Eric Goldman wrote, "The New Freedom spawned a hundred other . . . escapes from the past—The New Poetry, The New History, The New Democracy, The New Art, The New Woman, the new anything so long as it . . . gave an intoxicating sense of freedom." Such feelings of energy and power led Pound to predict an artistic "Risorgimento."

Yet this excitement was strangely absent from the American novel. In the period from 1910 to 1914, two major tendencies appear: one, the finely crafted summarizing of nineteenth-century confidence, order, and constraint in the work of Ellen Glasgow, Willa Cather, and Edith Wharton, and the other, the tail end of naturalism, in, for example, Theodore Dreiser's *The Financier* (1912) and *The Titan* (1914). Novelistic controversy was largely a matter of values: the proper, "dimity" world of settled class and gender roles versus the realist crudity of poverty, crime, and capitalist ambition. If these had stylistic correlates, they were elegant finish versus plainness, ponderousness, and rough edges.

By the teens, both these possibilities looked tame next to developments in contemporary poetry, painting, and music. Poetry, it was widely assumed, would dominate the next age. Instead of debating dimity versus determinism, experimentalist poets were investigating the most fundamental relations between language and meaning. Moreover, there was good reason for skepticism about the novel's place in the modernist ethos. Modernism was intent on constructing a universal culture—an amalgam of East and West, of past and present, of sophistication and "primitivism"—whereas the novel was strongly rooted in nation, period, region, and class, and saw its mission as reflecting or forging a merely national identity.

Yet despite these indications, prose fiction did not wither away in the modern period. Quite the contrary, the interwar years witnessed the transformation of the American novel from a parochial anachronism to a world power. Even in the prewar years some seeds of this transformation can be detected. One of the most notable was the influence of Gustave Flaubert, whose stylistic discipline and innovation can be traced in writers as different as Edith Wharton and Gertrude Stein. Wharton's *House of Mirth* (1905) and Stein's *Three Lives* (1906) were written almost simultaneously. Both emulated Flaubert (*Three Lives* being an adaptation of *Trois Contes*), both depicted women and ideals defeated by their milieus, and both had melodramatic plots. With Flaubertian precision, Wharton's characterization of Lily Bart closes on the plot like a steel trap, and when Stein has Melanctha die of tuberculosis, the plot resolution merely formalizes the wasting of emotion that marked Melanctha's nature. The title of another of Stein's works, *Q.E.D.* (1903), reflects this mathematics of character and action.

But despite their shared source in Flaubert, it is hard to imagine a more incongruous pair than Wharton and Stein: the best-selling Wharton, on the one hand, with her elegant chronicles of the demise of American gentility, and the nonconformist Stein, on the other hand, with her shockingly experimental prose and her all too human characters, working class or poor, black or immigrant, repressed or sexually aware. Stein carried out her technical experiments at the expense of conventional novelistic ends, whereas Wharton's lesson from Flaubert went only as far as characterization and formal control. Generally speaking, it was not until the twenties that American novelists truly became an avant-garde, able to fuse their representational aims with original technical innovation.

The connecting of literary style to authorial personality was also part of Flaubert's legacy. In a preface written in 1907, Henry James echoed this idea, postulating "the perfect dependence of the 'moral' sense of a work of art on the amount of felt life concerned in producing it." Though such modernists as T. S. Eliot and James Joyce would define modernism as an impersonal art, with the writer an unmoved catalyst or a detached observer off in the corner paring his fingernails, in American fiction the relation between the artist and the work of art was seen as more direct. The artist was the modern protagonist par excellence, as Jack London's autobiographical *Martin Eden* (1909) suggests, with his Nietzschean striving against the uncultured, money-grubbing establishment.

London's story of the individual's transcending of class origins was in fact a modernist Horatio Alger plot with the artist rather than the businessman as hero. The rise in fortune was not a triumph, however, but a bitter revelation of the barrenness of America's financial and political elite. Social striving in *Martin Eden* culminates in the ultimate act of independence and power—suicide. Thus, the plot of social ascent, seemingly the antithesis of the descent charted in Wharton's *House of Mirth*, involves the same notion of individual control, for Lily Bart's exquisite morality determines not only her life but her self-inflicted death. The moral to be drawn from both works was that modern society had made these brilliant mergers of ethics and aesthetics untenable.

Such semiautobiographical novels were the forerunners of works by Ernest Hemingway, F. Scott Fitzgerald, and Henry Miller in the twenties and thirties. Their appeal was not merely their merit as works of art but the teasing similarity they bore to their artists' well-publicized lives. In the age of publicity, artists' personal images became as compelling fictions as their novels, and the temptation to see the two as reflexes of each other was all but irresistible. At the same time, James Weldon Johnson's *Autobiography of an Ex-Coloured Man* (1912) played on the fallacies of linking artist and text. This first-person novel masquerading as autobiography emerged through "a sort of savage and diabolical desire to gather up all the little tragedies of my life and turn them into a practical joke on society." The modernist fascination with the author-text relation produced other practical jokes of this sort, such as Stein's *Autobiography of Alice B. Toklas* (1933), and indicates the uneasy relationship in American letters between the artist's image and his or her art.

But of all the forces shaping the modern novel, undoubtedly the most powerful was World War I. Artists' responses to the calamity followed very closely the division between conservative and naturalist values expressed in their fiction. Edith Wharton's *Fighting France* (1917) described the war's cleansing effect on modern decadence. "It is as though [the soldiers'] great experience had purged them of pettiness, meanness and frivolity, burning them down to the bare bones of character, the fundamental substance of the soul." Mary Brecht Pulver's "The Path of Glory," published in *The Saturday Evening Post* (March 10, 1917), tells of a poor family who gain their community's respect when their son dies heroically as a battlefield ambulance driver. Ellen Glasgow's *The Builders* (1919) stresses the positive value of the opportunity to fight for democracy. Writing in *The Bookman* in April 1916, H. W. Boynton summarized the idea behind most war novels as "the purifying influence upon the individual and national character of devotion to a cause, to the large cause of patriotism, and the larger cause of humanity."

No doubt a good deal of this pro-war writing was aimed at provoking the United States to come to the aid of the Allies. Certainly, Richard Harding Davis's story "The Deserter" (1916) had this end in view, with its thin allegory of a volunteer who wants to quit, but decides to stay on to fulfill his commitments. Henry James explained his well-publicized switch to British citizenship in 1915 by the claim that only Britain was standing up for Europe. And certainly the barrage of writing supporting the Allies' declaration of war proved instrumental in ending American neutrality.

Nevertheless, such literary patriotism was a far cry from the shattered despair of younger novelists. For them, naturalism provided a more accurate vision, and the war came to symbolize human depravity and weakness in the extreme. Just as Frank Norris's *The Octopus* (1901) had pictured "progress" through the image of innocent sheep run down by the heartless might of a train, so Henry Miller's "Walking Up and Down in China" (1936) depicted "the boys from the north side and the boys from the south side— all rolled into a muck heap and their guts hanging on the barbed wire. . . . The whole past is wiped out."

The death of aesthetic promise, Pound's "Risorgimento," was also implicated in this tragedy. "War stops literature," wrote William Dean Howells in 1914. "It is an upheaval of civilization, a return to barbarism; it means death to all the arts." Though the war years yielded little enduring fiction, they did produce several works of grim power. Ellen N. LaMotte's stories of her experience as a nurse in France, *The Backwash of War* (1916), were so horrifying that sale of the book was prohibited in England and France. Josephine Preston Peabody's *Harvest Moon* (1916) dramatized the misery and absurdity of women's raising sons only to have them die as soldiers. Marice Rutledge's *Children of Fate* (1917) showed soldiers duped into battle by false information and outdated values. "There died a myriad," wrote Pound, "And of the best, among them,/ For an old bitch gone in the teeth,/ For a botched civilization."

This bitter analysis polarized the generations, the sexes, and the aesthetic orientations of everyone concerned. The parents who had proudly sent their sons to die for their country, the women who rejoiced in the nobility of soldiers' blasted experience, and the traditionalists who eagerly embraced the war as a lesson in morality and propriety were equated with the cause of the war itself—"an old bitch gone in the teeth," "a botched civilization." By the end of the war, the avant-garde revolt against tradition, which had begun in America as a youthful defiance of prudery and atrophied conservatism, became a grim exposure and destruction of every value supporting the past, and the novel became a privileged vehicle for performing this task.

Though America did not enter the war until 1917, an extraordinary number of future writers fought or served as volunteers in ambulance corps and other war-zone forces. Malcolm Cowley, John Dos Passos, Ernest Hemingway, Julian Green, William Seabrook, E. E. Cummings, Slater Brown, Harry Crosby, John Howard Lawson, Sidney Howard, Louis Bromfield, Robert Hillyer, Dashiell Hammett, Charles Bernard Nordhoff, and Edmund Wilson all saw the horrors of war firsthand. Others, like William Faulkner, felt cheated in having missed them. Some wrote stories that deal directly with the battlefield, while others focused on the return from war and the ensuing dislocation from family, past, and culture. John Dos Passos's depiction of dead youths in *One Man's Initiation . . . 1917* (1920) anticipates the imagery and disillusion of Eliot's *The Waste Land*: "The wind came in puffs laden with an odour as of dead rats in an attic. And this was what all the centuries of civilization had struggled for." His *Three Soldiers* (1921) was equally despairing. In *The Enormous Room* (1922), E. E. Cummings transforms his experience as a political prisoner into an image of society as an absurdist nightmare. The nineteenth-century dream of progress expressed in the plot of social ascent had suffered a death blow. Gertrude Stein, herself an ambulance driver in the war, dubbed the young men who survived a "lost generation."

The dislocation brought on by World War I, the fact that even the winners came home to a world they could not live in, provoked a profound analysis of the phenomenon of victimization. Woodrow Wilson's argument for neutrality had been based on the need to avoid the dynamic of physical battle, on the grounds that the difference between winner and loser was too slight. The United States, he claimed, could not "fight Germany and maintain the ideal of government that all thinking men share. . . . A ruthless brutality will enter into the very fibre of our national life." Fitzgerald's epigraph to *The Beautiful and Damned* (1922), "The victor belongs to the spoils," put the matter more cogently. In *Dark Laughter* (1925), Sherwood Anderson wrote: "In war or in peace we do not kill the man we hate. We try to kill the thing we hate in ourselves." Hemingway's prolonged examination of violence in *In Our Time* (1925), *The Sun Also Rises* (1926), and *Death in the Afternoon* (1932) follows this idea of victimization in war, love, hunting, fishing, bullfighting, and writing, developing a personal morality surrounding the rules of such interchanges. Love, sex, art, war—all subject-object interplays—were susceptible to this interpretation, and all were doomed to the unsatisfactory roles dictated by violence.

Black soldiers, doubly victimized by the European enemy and by white American soldiers, suffered discrimination and brutality abroad and upon their return home. For them, the war dimmed any real hope of assimilation. Their alienation from the land they had fought to preserve was confirmed by the bloody riots of the summer of 1919.

Leftists suffered a similar defeat at this time. In 1917 John Reed had traveled to Russia to observe and promote the Bolshevik Revolution, producing the brilliant reportage of *Ten Days That Shook the World* (1919). But though the Communist experiment gave heart to American leftists, the possibility of their pursuing such ends in the United States was severely curtailed after World War I. In 1919 Emma Goldman, Alexander Berkman, and two hundred other "undesirables" were deported to Russia. The persecution of "reds," "anarchists," and "unionists" climaxed in the 1920s in the execution of Nicola Sacco and Bartolomeo Vanzetti after prolonged appeals and the anguished outcries of leftist writers and intellectuals. Dos Passos memorialized the deportation of radicals in his fictions, and depicted Communist organizers speaking out for social justice with touching eloquence. Upton Sinclair's *Boston* (1928) spelled out the injustice of the Sacco-Vanzetti case. But nothing could halt the official suppression of leftist radicals and the fall of progressive hopes after the war.

One of the most frequent responses to the general cultural dislocation was expatriation. From the twenties into the forties, Paris was at least as important an American artists' colony as New York. Gertrude Stein had left the United States just after the turn of the century and lived in Paris for the rest of her life, where her apartment became a meeting place for American and European artists. Other writers, such as Ernest Hemingway, Edith Wharton, Robert McAlmon, Henry Miller, Djuna Barnes, Anaïs Nin, and later Richard Wright, were residents of Paris for several years, and Sherwood Anderson, William Faulkner, F. Scott Fitzgerald, and Katherine Anne Porter stayed for months at a time to write. In 1919 Sylvia Beach established her bookshop, Shakespeare and Company, as a center for expatriate Americans. The brilliant life and favorable exchange rate made Paris a haven for artists, a second country that provided an alternative to the lost home of the United States.

The year 1922 was a time, Stein wrote in *The Autobiography of Alice B. Toklas*, when all the young men were twenty-three. Indeed, the youth of these writers and their experience of battle set them apart from the prewar generation. Moreover, whether at home or abroad, writers were now able to make a living with their pens in journalism, advertising, the movies, or scholarship. John Dos Passos, Thornton Wilder, Glenway Wescott, Louis Bromfield, Thomas Wolfe, Hemingway, and Fitzgerald were all self-supporting authors by their thirties. Jack London had set the example for this professionalization of writing by earning $75,000 per year.

One of the major sources for this support was the flourishing magazine industry. In the interwar period a now familiar division emerged—the pulps, the slicks, and quality journals. The pulps (for example, *True Confessions*), named for their cheap paper, carried popular fiction such as westerns, crime, adventure, science fiction, or sex stories. Slick publications—*Woman's Home Companion*, *Saturday Evening Post*, *Collier's*, *American Magazine*, *Ladies' Home Journal*—printed "higher" fiction, but kept within rather limited formulas for the short story. Serious, successful writers would be more likely to publish in the quality journals: *Atlantic Monthly*, *Harper's*, or *Scribner's*.

But a fourth category of periodicals was even more important to the development of modernist literature. This was the so-called little magazine of the late 1910s and 1920s, which did not create financial independence for its contributors but did provide a place for young or experimental writers to publish. *The Seven Arts* was started specifically to generate "a feeling of common cause, the sense of a community of writers building a new culture." Though most little magazines ran on a shoestring, appeared irregularly, and were short-lived, some had considerable success. One of the most famous was Margaret Anderson and Jane Heap's *The Little Review* (Chicago). The revived *Dial* (New York), which was edited in the twenties by Marianne Moore, had over 30,000 readers by the mid-twenties and was the most successful monthly art magazine in the country. The aim of these periodicals was openly revolutionary. *Broom, transition, Secession,* as well as the black magazines *Fire, Harlem,* and *The Messenger,* sought to sweep away all that was retrograde in art.

Layout was a major concern of many little magazines and reflected both their aesthetics and their politics. Robert Coady's *The Soil,* for example, juxtaposed selections from dime novels, photographs of skyscrapers, frames from Charlie Chaplin movies, drawings of machines, and "high" literature and art in a Whitmanesque simultaneity meant to imitate modern American life. Less dramatically, *The Dial* interrupted large stretches of prose with paintings and poems, implying a notion of the journal not as a mere collection but as a design totality. These experiments served as a formal analogue for fictional experimentation in the twenties and thirties, such as Dos Passos's *Manhattan Transfer* (1925) or James Agee's *Let Us Now Praise Famous Men* (1941), with their headings and texts interpolated from all levels of art and life.

Expatriate Paris and the little magazines, as alternative Americas, reflect a further characteristic of postwar art. The generational dislocation provoked by the war made the notion of place problematic. For naturalism, identity had been treated as a reflex of one's locale and one's society, but now a whole generation of Americans found themselves unable to live in or relate to their native land. Far from Ralph Waldo Emerson's picture language, the physical environment appeared hostile or blank: Fitzgerald's valley of ashes, Richard Wright's no-man's-land, John Dos Passos's machine-like Manhattan, or Hemingway's sterilely artificial Paris. Each of these writers opposed an Edenic alternative to the forbidding setting—the "fresh, green breast of the new world," the rural paradise of Spain—but these counter-worlds of fostering and fulfillment were either denied to their heroes or betrayed by them.

One of the most concentrated meditations on the image of America was William Carlos Williams's rhapsodic history, *In the American Grain* (1925). Though not a novel in the conventional sense, it invented an identity for America that was similar to that proposed in many fictions, and its disjointed, poetic style echoed the form of contemporary avant-garde novels. The aim of the book was to draw out life, "nameless under an old misappellation" because the various conquerors of the land had failed to see it as it was. Williams treats the relation between conqueror and land as paradigmatic of all subject-object relations in America, including the sexual. He pictures the mystery of the continent as a flower ravished by Columbus that then, become a poisonous apple, turns on him. The murder and enslavement of the Indians is the revenge of the Old World upon the "orchidean beauty" of the New, a revenge that redounds upon the conqueror. Similarly, the Puritans' thrift and repression abstract them from the land and from the language that should have expressed it, impoverishing their existence while filling their pockets. "Never a woman: never a poet" was Williams's verdict.

Such excursions into history and myth were, of course, the hallmark of modernist poetry, from Pound's *Cantos* to Eliot's *Waste Land*, Hart Crane's *The Bridge*, and Williams's *Paterson*. Indeed, the examination of the American locale through its history in *In the American Grain* was part of a general fascination with the past. H. G. Wells's *Outline of History*, with its confidence in human progress, was the most popular nonfiction best-seller of the twenties, attracting broad ranks of Americans not yet ready for Williams's more esoteric and negative account. The Southern Agrarians dug back into the national past to retell the lives of the South's great men: Allen Tate's biographies of Stonewall Jackson (1928) and Jefferson Davis (1929), Robert Penn Warren's of John Brown (1929), and John Crowe Ransom's *God Without Thunder* (1930). Willa Cather's novels were frequently set in earlier times, for example, *O Pioneers!* (1913) and *My Ántonia* (1918). After the shock of the war she retreated further back to historically remote periods in *Death Comes for the Archbishop* (1927) and *Shadows on the Rock* (1931). The popularity of historical fiction continued throughout the thirties and forties, with Hervey Allen's best-selling *Anthony Adverse* (1933), Margaret Mitchell's *Gone with the Wind* (1936), the novels of Kenneth Roberts and Esther Forbes, and the prodigious output of Howard Fast, including five novels set in American Revolutionary times.

Along with history, the social sciences (especially anthropology, sociology, and folklore studies) left their mark on the interwar novel. Mourning Dove (Hum-Ishu-Ma) became the first Native American woman to publish a novel, *Cogewea the Half-Blood: A Depiction of the Great Montana Cattle Range* (1927); she also collected and recorded numerous Okanagan tales and songs. Zora Neale Hurston was not only a fiction-writer but a trained anthropologist. Katherine Anne Porter, involved in Mexican politics from 1918 to 1921, presented the rural world of Mexico in "Flowering Judas" (1930) and other stories as offering the chance of salvation to Americans. To counteract their alienation and rootlessness, American interwar authors often wrote like amateur ethnologists, studying regional characters as products of geography and social habit, whether in the South, the West, the Midwest, or the great urban "regions" of New York, Boston, and Chicago.

This aesthetic anthropology can be seen most obviously in the preoccupation of modernist painting and literature with "primitive" models, particularly African sculpture. Black and white writers alike were fascinated with the image of Africa and the values of authenticity and freedom from inhibition that it came to signify. Marcus Garvey's Universal Negro Improvement Association posited Africa as the spiritual home of the blacks and advocated a back-to-Africa policy that expressed politically the artistic preoccupation with "primitive" cultural sources. One of the most noticeable elements of Harlem Renaissance writing was its use of dialect and folklore and its identification with the spirit of jazz. "Jazz was the symbol of the age," W. E. Bigsby writes, "because of its spontaneity, its creation of a cooperative method, and its assumption of an empathetic community." It authorized a distrust of rationalism, a celebration of sensuality, a separateness from conventional society, and a belief in improvisation and authenticity of feeling that were becoming the ideology not only of blacks but also of whites in this period that Fitzgerald made famous as the Jazz Age.

In works like Williams's *In the American Grain*, Waldo Frank's *Holiday* (1923), Sherwood Anderson's *Dark Laughter* (1925), DuBose Heyward's *Porgy* (1925) and *Mamba's Daughters* (1927), and Carl Van Vechten's *Nigger Heaven* (1926), black American culture became a kind of Africa for whites, an inaccessible homeland where all the passion and vitality kept in check by "Puritanism" were expressed. Yet, much as this image was embraced by the Roaring Twenties with its wild dancing, risqué sexuality, and bathtub gin, the anthropological identification was also threatening. A standard assessment of literary experimentalism was Laura Riding's critical essay "Hulme, the New Barbarism, and Gertrude Stein." And a literary scholar, A. C. Ward, after presenting an extremely positive view of black culture, feared that "it is possible to experience a profound emotional response to syncopated rhythms and at the same time to feel that jazz is for Europe and America a dance of death."

A very different fascination with history and mythology marks James Branch Cabell's writing, a kind of naughty boy's version of *The Waste Land*. Raided and suppressed by the Comstock Society, his *Jurgen: A Comedy of Justice* (1919) became an overnight sensation. H. L. Mencken claimed that "every flapper in the land has read 'Jurgen' behind the door; two-thirds of the grandmothers east of the Mississippi have tried to borrow it from me." Both its shock value and Mencken's extravagant praise of Cabell as "an imagist in prose" are hard to appreciate today, but *Jurgen*'s epitomizing of twenties concerns is quite extraordinary. The novel is presented as the medieval legend of a middle-aged poet-manqué who is transported back in time to his youth, though he maintains the mentality of a forty-year-old. This superimposition of a jaded, lecherous sensibility on the passion and beauty of youth is a perfect image for the Jazz Age, with its desperate celebration of youth and its simultaneous disillusion. Jurgen fulfills a panoply of sexual and artistic fantasies as he travels through the biblical and mythological past, including a battle between the Philistines, champions of realism, and Pseudopolis, the bastion of romance. In this arch, slick narrative, he discovers that all women he has loved are merely figments of his imagination and the only justice is poetic. Cabell elaborated these ideas in his other books, for example, *The Line of Love* (1921).

Cabell's cynicism, his flaunted learning, and his opposition of the realist philistine to the romance intellectual constitute an extreme but otherwise typical version of the sensibility of twenties artists. The split between intellectuals and the middle class had become acute, and writers constructed a lasting symbol of bourgeois piety and complacency: the Midwest. Sinclair Lewis's *Main Street* (1920) is a relentless mockery of the values of the Midwest (which nevertheless produced a large number of artists, female and male, novelists and poets, during the interwar period). H. L. Mencken, who edited, translated, and explicated Nietzsche, attacked the stupid *Herdenmoral* of the "booboisie." And the Harlem Renaissance writers found themselves similarly opposed to a "Negro Philistia," who believed that writing about improprieties endangered the future of black people.

The split between intellectual and bourgeois also expressed itself in an extreme hostility toward women. Though in the 1910s the literary conflict between traditional gentility and rugged naturalism had been roughly aligned with female versus male writers, both approaches seemed viable as aesthetic strategies and were treated as significant social assessments. By the twenties, women writers had been almost completely routed from all but the popular taste, and antifeminism had become a pervasive novelistic theme. As recent feminists have noted, Nathanael West's newsmen in *Miss Lonelyhearts* (1933) say that what lady writers like "Mary Roberts Wilcox" or "Ella Wheeler Catheter" "needed was a good rape." Scholars such as A. C. Ward treated women's writing as a separate category, often dismissing it with condescension: "The more accomplished American women novelists [of the 1910s] had hardly been lifted from the sandbank of sentimentality [in the 1920s] before they were cast away on the reef of intellectualism."

Robert Herrick's *Waste* (1924) and Sherwood Anderson's *Dark Laughter* (1925) blamed women's bourgeois values for starting World War I and halting artistic progress. In *I Thought of Daisy* (1929), Edmund Wilson's protagonist describes women as "the most dangerous representatives of those forces of conservatism and inertia against which [my] whole life was a protest." And Sinclair Lewis's novels contain some of the most virulent attacks on women in American literature. Critics took up the same theme. In the symposium *Civilization in the United States* (1922), editor Harold Stearns listed among the current evils of society the fact that "our cultural interests and activities have been turned over to the almost exclusive custody of women."

Alfred Kuttner, writing in the same collection, claims that the American husband, a victim of mother-worship, "becomes everything in his business and nothing in his home, with an ultimate neurotic breakdown or a belated plunge into promiscuity. The wife, on her part, either becomes hysterical or falls a victim of religious reformatory charlatanism." This sense of the breakdown of gender roles in the family is often associated in fiction with the confusion of sexual identity. In Fitzgerald's *Tender Is the Night* (1933), the film actress, Rosemary, is spoken of as "economically a boy." She has starred in a movie called *Daddy's Girl*, and like other women in this book consistently plays the child to her men. Ellen in Dos Passos's *Manhattan Transfer* (1925) grows up wanting to be a boy. "I hate women," she cries, determined to avoid female dependence and victimization. But despite her vitality and striving she ends up a cold, insensitive figure, compared ironically to the Statue of Liberty. Sam Spade in Dashiell Hammett's *The Maltese Falcon* (1929) swears, "I don't know anything about women," and calls his secretary "a damned good man, sister." And William Faulkner's *The Sound and the Fury* (1929) sets Quentin's "Father and I protect women" against Jason's "Once a bitch, always a bitch"; Caddy, the sexually aware sister who is the focus of their misery, is absent, unable to speak for herself.

During the twenties, the caricaturist John Held, Jr., became famous by inventing the image of the flapper for *Vanity Fair* magazine. This totally modern woman with her bobbed hair and short skirts, her car-driving and tennis-playing, her wild dancing and drinking, and her utter self-absorption, was presented as a fascinating trap for men. Lovely, expensive, and definitionally young, the flapper was at once the ideal and the cruel limitation of modern life. As the most famous flapper of them all, Daisy Buchanan, says in *The Great Gatsby* (1925), "That's the best thing a girl can be in this world, a beautiful little fool." "I'm p-paralyzed with happiness," she stutters.

The negative treatment of women was the result not simply of blind misogyny but of the symbolic baggage then surrounding women. *The Education of Henry Adams* (1918; privately printed 1907) gained wide prestige in the twenties with Adams's juxtaposition of the Virgin and the Dynamo as symbols, respectively, of medieval and modern values. In exchange for the wealth brought by the machine age, people had traded the purity, beauty, and fostering love gathered in the Christian image of womanhood. The recurrent choice of "Daisy" for the name of American heroines indicates the nostalgia for the old image, as does the condensation of art, transcendent value, and women in such novels as *The Maltese Falcon*. When all ideals prove hollow, the symbol of the ideal, woman, is equally disappointing.

For women, on the other hand, the late teens and twenties were in some respects a time of growing power. The Nineteenth Amendment was written into the Constitution in 1920, and the feminist drive for a transformed society was reflected in such works as Elizabeth Robins's *Ancilla's Share* (1924) and Dora Russell's *Hypatia* (1925). But during the twenties at least, established women writers as often as not reinforced male stereotypes of femininity. Ellen Glasgow and Willa Cather's narrators are consistently male. Though in *My Ántonia* Cather had idealized the fortitude and endurance of her heroine, in her later work women are frequently selfish, unnatural sirens. For example, her short story "Coming, Aphrodite!" (1920) shows a male artist of true originality temporarily bewitched by Eden Bower, a girl preparing for a brilliant career in opera. He watches her through a chink in his closet as she exercises in the nude before her mirror, and when he makes her realize that "woman's chief adventure is man," they have a short-lived affair.

In both this story and Cather's *The Professor's House* (1925), the investigation of anthropological origins produces an indictment against women. The artist in "Coming, Aphrodite!" tells Eden Bower the myth of an Aztec queen of insatiable sexual appetite. In *The Professor's House* Tom Outland discovers the well-preserved corpse of a woman as he excavates an Indian village. He is so moved by her that he names her Mother Eve, only to be told that she was probably killed by her husband for infidelity. Rather than uncovering a primitive image of beauty, he finds another confirmation of original sin. *The Professor's House*, whose protagonist can no longer bear to live with the conventionality and materialism of his wife and daughters, is full of such antifeminist jabs.

The relative sexual frankness of Cabell and Cather, Fitzgerald and Hemingway, indicates another important development in American fiction. Stein had disguised a lesbian triangle in her original conception of "Melanctha" with a heterosexual one in the final version, and invented some very euphemistic language for sexuality. Wharton's Lily Bart knew sexuality only as what society prohibits among the unmarried. The sudden inclusion of explicit sexuality in literature was part of a general assault on "Puritanism" waged by such essayists as Randolph Bourne in "The Puritan's Will to Power" (1917), H. L. Mencken in "Puritanism as a Literary Force" (1917), and Waldo Frank in *Our America* (1919). They blasted the hypocrisy of the American "who leads a sexually vicious life and insists on 'pure' books, draped statues, and streets cleared of prostitutes." Naturalism had done much to expand the "legitimate" subject matter of art, although grundyism and the Comstock Society were still powerful, and many books were criticized and some banned for their content.

Nevertheless, despite the burgeoning movements for free love and women's enjoyment of sex, it is hard to think of American novels in the twenties that celebrate the joys of physical love. *Manhattan Transfer* is full of disgust with sexuality, homosexuality, unwanted pregnancies, and venereal disease. In *The Maltese Falcon* and other hard-boiled detective novels, sex is dangerous; it is the weapon of women who are otherwise powerless in the world of money and violence they inhabit. Images of sterility appear everywhere, from Faulkner's Benjy in *The Sound and the Fury* to Hemingway's Jake Barnes in *The Sun Also Rises* to the homosexuals in *Tender Is the Night*, *Manhattan Transfer*, *The Maltese Falcon*, and much of Hemingway. Nella Larsen's *Quicksand* (1928) shows a heroine more or less victimized by her own sexuality. And even when sexuality is not a matter of tragedy or disgust, it is often the automatic or teasing accompaniment of flip "intellectual" smartness or rebelliousness, as in the work of Ben Hecht, Floyd Dell, Maxwell Bodenheim, or Waldo Frank.

The most important stimulus to the literary treatment of sexuality and primitivism was Sigmund Freud, whose works were widely discussed in the twenties. Freud's analysis of the artist as a neurotic who could objectify his or her illness by giving it aesthetic shape made art and sexual maladaptation correlates. Dick Diver in *Tender Is the Night* is both his wife's psychiatrist and an image of the self-destructive author, and he is surrounded by mother-fixated women, homosexuals, transvestites, and others whose inability to cope manifests itself in what the text portrays as sexual deviance. In *Manhattan Transfer*, a character undergoes psychiatric treatment for imaginary homosexuality, and Quentin's mind in *The Sound and the Fury* concocts a fantasy built on virginity, incest, and suicide. Conrad Aiken's *Blue Voyage* (1927), *Great Circle* (1933), and *King Coffin* (1935) were heavily indebted to Freud. Likewise, Edmund Wilson's influential *The Wound and the Bow* (1941) was a critical study of literature according to Freud's early theories of neurosis, the injury that both enables the concentration of creativity and undermines it.

The Freudian connection of illness and creativity added fuel to the auto-biographical tendency already manifest in the American novel. *Tender Is the Night* presents one side of a thinly veiled autobiographical story, while Zelda Fitzgerald's *Save Me the Waltz* (1932) presents the other. Since Zelda and Scott were also characters in Carl Van Vechten's *Parties* (1930), the fusion of public role and fictional image was rather extreme in their case. The *roman à clef* flourished at this time—everything from Djuna Barnes's *Ladies' Almanack* (1928), an outré fictionalization of Natalie Barney's lesbian circle, to Tess Slesinger's *The Unpossessed* (1934), a satire of the leftist Jewish intel-lectuals of the *Menorah Journal* in New York. This fictionalizing of the au-thor is carried even further in the multivolume *Diary* of Anaïs Nin and the novels and stories of Henry Miller. As Miller wrote in "The Third or Fourth Day of Spring," "For me the book is the man and my book is the man I am, the confused man, the negligent man, the reckless man, the lusty, ob-scene, boisterous, thoughtful, scrupulous, lying, diabolically truthful man that I am."

The author's public persona was not the only bigger-than-life image to intrude itself into the novel. Popular culture, advertising, and the movies were used to create a jarring counterpoint to the narratives in which they were embedded. Titles of popular songs provide ironic commentaries in such works as *The Day of the Locust* (1933), *Tender Is the Night*, and *Manhattan Transfer*, as do ads and journalistic headlines in a variety of texts. In the face of these mechanical, all-enveloping messages, Dos Passos's Jimmy muses, "If only I still had faith in words."

But of all popular culture, the movies exercised the strongest fascination over the novel. The number of movie theaters almost quadrupled between 1907 and 1915, and continued to grow steadily thereafter. In *Good-Bye Wis-consin* (1928), Glenway Wescott calls the movie house "imagination's chapel in the town," and the power of this art form is registered over and over in modernist fiction. Not only does *The Day of the Locust* show characters view-ing a pornographic film, but the entire novella takes place in a movie-set world in which scenes of the battle of Waterloo collapse into real-life disas-ters and the barriers dissolve between acting and life. The intercalary chap-ters of John Steinbeck's *The Grapes of Wrath* (1939) were directly influenced by Pare Lorentz's documentary films *The River* and *The Plow That Broke the Plains*. In Richard Wright's *Native Son* (1940), Bigger Thomas watches a film called *A Gay Woman*, which symbolizes the glamorous, closed world of white society. And in Ring Lardner's folksy "Haircut," Gloria Swanson's melodramatic performance in *The Wages of Virtue* provides the simple pro-tagonist with his idealized image of women. Faulkner, Fitzgerald, Hammett, West, Dorothy Parker, and many others wrote for the movies, the experience generally reinforcing their sense of the split between popular art and "serious writing."

The intellectual distaste for the "booboisie" and its culture was part of a larger polemic against the machine. During the first few decades of the century, "advances in technology" were suddenly felt not only in the workplace but in the home. The telephone, radio, cinema, automobile, and, after World War I, labor-saving devices for domestic cleaning and food preparation created profound changes in the way people lived, particularly in the way that families interacted. Fred B. Millett wrote somewhat apocalyptically in 1940 that these intrusions marked the end of reading, sustained conversation, and tranquillity in the home. As A. C. Ward put it, "Mass production led in time to the production of mass thinking, mass feeling, mass recreation. . . . The Machine was Lord of Prosperity and King of Pleasure—enthroned, worshipped, hated, and despised."

This theme of alienation is tied to the growth of industrialism, and in a sense virtually every novel produced in the modern period is dominated by it. More specifically, however, Sherwood Anderson's *Poor White* (1920), set in the Midwest between 1870 and 1910, describes the impact of a complex industrial economy on a simpler style of life, and Dos Passos's *Manhattan Transfer* creates a typology of modes of transportation—ferry, subway, taxi— to indicate the class and psychology of the characters conveyed by them. All these conveyances symbolize some sort of dehumanization, until Jimmy is left at the end striking off on foot for the country.

Inevitably, the plots of novels reflect alienation from people, history, place, and language. Perhaps the most typical story line is the subverted Horatio Alger plot, where success fails to provide satisfaction. Anzia Yezierska's novels of immigrant life in New York, *Salome of the Tenements* (1922) and *Bread Givers* (1925), and the short stories in *Hungry Hearts* (1920) tell of characters caught between the old values of their origins and the social mobility of their new lives. Hanneh Breineh, the immigrant heroine of Yezierska's "The Fat of the Land," cries, "It is I and my mother and my mother's mother and my father and father's father who had such a black life in Poland; it is our choked thoughts and feelings that are flaming up in my children and making them great in America. And yet they shame themselves from me!" A similar pattern can be seen in black novels of "passing": Walter White's *Flight* (1926), Jessie Fauset's *Plum Bun* (1928), and Nella Larsen's *Passing* (1929). Here blacks pass as whites and prosper in the white world, only to suffer a disillusionment that leaves them longing to return to their old communities. Fictional plots at this time typically open with a cultural disjunction—the eager immigrant faced with an alien society, the black naïf arriving in the decadent North, the young talent on the make in the bustling power structure of the city.

The fact that the alien world to be conquered is a repository of social values makes all these works subverted romances. And some are almost allegories of the conflict between realism and romance. In Cather's *The Professor's House*, the professor, Napoleon Godfrey St. Peter, has had two romances, one of the heart (his wife) and one of the mind (his scholarship), when a young orphan, Tom Outland, enters his life. A genius, Tom discovers and excavates a Pueblo Indian village, picks up an education, and invents a new aircraft engine. He is a self-made man, one of whose favorite books is *Robinson Crusoe*. But before he can marry St. Peter's daughter and develop his invention, reality enters, and he is killed in World War I. His invention then feeds the materialism and shallowness of St. Peter's family, and the ironies brought on by the fruits of his genius are more than St. Peter can stand. The romance of capitalism and individual striving is dashed by the violence and vulgarity of the real world.

Sometimes the romance-realism dialectic is reversed, when a "normal" life is suddenly exploded by adventure. The hero of Zona Gale's *Preface to a Life* (1926) becomes a businessman, has a family, and then, growing sick of all the pretense, "went delirious and escaped . . . into something real." Sherwood Anderson's *Many Marriages* presents a similar withdrawal, and Sinclair Lewis's *Babbitt* (1922) is probably the most famous story of the little man who suddenly revolts against convention, only to return to conformity at the end. This revolt is like Huckleberry Finn's "lighting out," except that it is doomed from the start.

Sam Spade tells the story of such a rebel in *The Maltese Falcon*, one Flitcraft, a banker who, almost struck by a beam during a lunchtime walk, jumps in his car, wanders about for a couple of years, and then gets himself a new job, a new family, a new house, and settles back into an orderly existence. "He adjusted himself to beams falling, and then no more of them fell, and he adjusted himself to them not falling." This short parable of the intrusion of romance into "real life" is inserted into Hammett's novel, whose plot follows the same pattern: the initial mundanity of Spade's life, the thrilling adventure with the Maltese falcon and Brigid O'Shaughnessy, and the final return to banality, pettiness, and tawdry liaisons. Jake Barnes's oscillation between the decadence of Paris and the Edenic world of Spain in *The Sun Also Rises* turns on a similar realist/romance conflict.

A variation of this plot is the manipulation of the naïve by the cynical con man. In Sinclair Lewis's *Elmer Gantry* (1927) or Countee Cullen's *One*

Way to Heaven (1932), clever opportunists turn religion, one of the few romance outlets for the workaday world, into a money-making proposition. In both cases though, love, the other intrusion into conventionality, undercuts their con games and provides them with moments of authenticity subversive to their cynicism. The ironic undercutting of one mode by the other leaves both realism and romance in an uneasy standoff.

One of the reasons for *The Great Gatsby*'s enormous appeal is that it combines virtually all of these plot variations. Nick Carraway is the Midwestern naïf faced with the sophistication of Long Island wealth. His friend, Jay Gatsby, is attempting to "pass" with the old wealth of East Egg. Gatsby deserts his own past and his immigrant origins and becomes a con artist, hinting at an Oxford education and noble parentage while remaining vague about his dubiously acquired fortune. His attractiveness lies in his absolute faith in the value of his ideals—Daisy, the things that money can buy, the capitalist dream. Through Gatsby, Fitzgerald generalizes the romance-realist clash into an image of America as a burgeoning paradise for its discoverers and a sterile waste for their heirs.

As we have already seen in Williams and Dos Possos, America's failed dream includes language itself. There is perhaps no more ironic line in twenties writing than Gutman's teasing toast to Spade in *The Maltese Falcon:* "Here's to plain speaking and clear understanding," for the general debasement of values is over and over again presented as the subversion of language. Artists responded by either dramatizing the emptiness of words or trying to return language to a perfect connection to things—tendencies that correlate with realist and romance ideologies, respectively, and often coexist in the same work.

The commonest techniques for expressing linguistic blight are fragmentation and what might be called literary montage, the frenetic interpenetration of one stretch of prose by another to suggest a disordered simultaneity. Dos Passos's *U.S.A.* trilogy is full of bits and pieces from newspapers, ads, songs, and poems. Hemingway's *In Our Time* is a series of disjointed little stories with abrupt beginnings and ends, whose connections must be fashioned by the reader. And Faulkner's magnificent imitation of mental flow produced paragraphs whose sentences belong to different worlds.

What Eliot had achieved in *The Waste Land* contemporary novelists were adapting to prose fiction, and the conflict between fragmentation and plot continuity produced some distinctive literary forms. Supported by an elaborate theory of the genre, Stein wrote well over one hundred literary portraits. Sherwood Anderson's *Winesburg, Ohio* (1919) presents a vision of an imaginary town through portraits of its inhabitants. Likewise, the first part of Jean Toomer's *Cane* (1923) consists of a series of descriptions of black women living on the Dixie Pike.

The conflict between fracture and flow pervades twenties prose. Daisy Buchanan stutters, whereas Sam Spade militantly refuses to do so. Stein, Faulkner, and Wolfe extended the sentence moment backward and forward to reduce the constant breaks—the stuttering—in normal prose, for Bergson's theories of temporal *durée* were almost as influential as Freud's views on the unconscious and dreams. At the same time, the example of James Joyce taught American writers that disjunction and illogical sequence can represent realities inaccessible to consecutive storytelling. The hallucinogenic ending of *Day of the Locust* or the narratorial switch into Nicole's deranged mind in *Tender Is the Night* are powerful examples of such experimentation.

In such works, the realist mimicry of blighted speech tended to merge with the idealistic desire to revitalize language, to remake prose so that it could again embody thought and emotion. Critics repeatedly praised the "imagism" of writers like Cabell or Elinor Wylie, whose care with language, when it did not descend into preciosity, suggested the minimalism and precision of the poetic Imagists. What Hemingway learned from Stein was largely verbal economy and simplicity. In *Death in the Afternoon*, he formulated an idea similar to Eliot's objective correlative: he wanted, he said, "to put down what really happened in action; what the actual things were which produced the emotion that you experienced." Writers used proverbial titles—*In the American Grain, In Our Time, You Can't Go Home Again*—in order to fill stock American idioms with contemporary salience.

Widespread experiments with dialect had a similar motivation. Ring Lardner's short stories not only turned folk humor and practical jokes into narrative plots but also transcribed the speech patterns of the regions and classes he was depicting. Sherwood Anderson did much the same with Midwestern accents in *Winesburg, Ohio*, as did Anzia Yezierska with the English of Polish Jews in New York. The use of Negro dialect in Harlem Renaissance novels produced a related merger of literary and political meaning, stressing the separateness of black English and the distinctiveness of "jive" slang. Williams was presenting a widely held view in *In the American Grain* when he claimed that Negro Americans were giving new life to the language.

Akin to this fidelity to the spoken language were experiments in the use of direct speech. Dorothy Parker published short stories in *Vogue*, *Vanity Fair*, and *The New Yorker* that were often written totally in witty, ironic dialogue. Sinclair Lewis's *The Man Who Knew Coolidge* was a novel in monologue, and, of course, Faulkner's writing is pervaded with speech unsupported by a narrator's contextualization.

In myriad ways, then, the prewar literary excitement about language, craftsmanship, and verbal experimentation—Pound's "Risorgimento"—bore fruit in the brilliant writing of the twenties and thirties. This extraordinary wealth of novels served to validate the youthful revolt against tradition and confirmed the belief that writers were at the beginning of a promising, if problematic, new age. However, the stock-market crash of 1929 posed an immediate threat to such thinking. Fitzgerald's Roaring Twenties gave way to the royal hangover of the thirties. *The Dial* stopped publication in 1929, and *The Little Review* closed down with the ad, "Wanted, a lost renaissance."

And yet, the demise of high living in the twenties was not universally regretted. In *Exile's Return* (1933), Malcolm Cowley describes the dissipation and confused shallowness of the times, concluding, "It was an easy, quick, adventurous age, good to be young in; and yet on coming out of it one felt a sense of relief, as on coming out of a room too full of talk and people into the sunlight of the winter streets."

This austere sunlight threw poverty and injustice into sharp relief. Black writers, as Robert Bone notes, moved their subjects from the crowded cabaret to the crowded tenement; depictions of agrarian and Southern life became more common than urban or foreign scenes; and jazz exoticism was replaced by social protest. White authors likewise turned away from the romanticizing of wealth and high times to a neonaturalism concerned with the plight of the poor and the unfortunate. This was the time of the great social novels: Erskine Caldwell's *Tobacco Road* (1932), Faulkner's *Light in August* (1932), and John Steinbeck's *Of Mice and Men* (1937) and *The Grapes of Wrath* (1939).

It was also the decade in which American writing gained international recognition. Sinclair Lewis received the Nobel Prize for Literature in 1930, and Hemingway, Dos Passos, Faulkner, and Thomas Wolfe became symbols of the diversity and power of American fiction writing.

Though leftist literature was certainly not absent in the twenties—Dashiell Hammett's *Red Harvest* (1929), for example, depicted gang war and labor organization—during the thirties American writing as a whole moved left. Hammett, Dorothy Parker, Lillian Hellman, Albert Halper, Leane Zugsmith, and Fielding Burke were radical writers, several of whom were later blacklisted. In 1931, as the harassment of unionists, anarchists, and black activists gained publicity, the National Committee for the Defense of Political Prisoners (NCDPP) was founded, with Dreiser as its chairman, Lincoln Steffens as its treasurer, and John Dos Passos, Suzanne LaFollette, Franz Boas, Floyd Dell, Waldo Frank, and Josephine Herbst as supporters. Emma Goldman, back in America again, published her autobiography, *Living My Life* (1931), and Michael Gold continued at the center of the leftist Jewish intelligentsia of New York. Purged of its hard-line Stalinists by 1937, the *Partisan Review* was an important organ of leftist art and opinion throughout the thirties, as was *The New Masses.* The journal *Challenge* (1934–37) explored the relevance of Marxism to black concerns, becoming more strident under Richard Wright's editorship as *The New Challenge* (1937). Edmund Wilson went to Russia in 1935 to learn about "that great international department of thought," Marxism, and returned to publish *To the Finland Station* in 1940.

At the same time, Robert Penn Warren and Cleanth Brooks, editors of *The Southern Review*, were joining with former Southern Agrarians such as Allen Tate and John Crowe Ransom in shaping the conservative ideology that emerged as the New Criticism. Its concern with the sensitive analysis of literary form and meaning contrasted sharply with the more historically and culturally oriented scholarship of F. O. Matthiessen. Early in 1929, Matthiessen had stressed the need for a new historian of American literature who would understand that "great literature is an organic expression of its age and nation," and would "take into account every side of American culture . . . [religion, education,] communication and travel, the 'movies' and cartoons, the Ford and the radio, the significance of the fact that the village reads Whittier and Longfellow, and the city, Whitman and James."

This call for a cultural history was answered most interestingly by authors employed by the Federal Writers' Project. A make-work program of the Work Projects Administration, the FWP hired hundreds of unemployed writers to compile guidebooks to each of the forty-eight states and Alaska. To these areas came teams of writers and photographers assigned to research and describe the people, land, history, and arts. The result was a massive accumulation of cultural information that intensified the nationalist focus of thirties writing. In documentary reports, biographies, histories, folklore compilations, and exploration accounts, FWP writing revealed how deeply the thirties experienced the need to recover what Alfred Kazin called "America *as an idea.*" "Out of the decade of unrelieved crisis and failure, of fumbling recovery and tension and war; out of the panic and extremism of so many of its finest talents; out of the desire to assess what could be known and to establish a needed security in the American inheritance, came the realization of how little . . . American writing had served the people and how little it had come to grips with the subject that lay closest at hand—the country itself."

The FWP was the training ground for black writers of the late thirties and forties: Richard Wright, Arna Bontemps, Roi Ottley, William Attaway, Margaret Walker, Ralph Ellison, Frank Yerby, and Willard Motley. The white FWP writers were perhaps not so notable a group, though their numbers included Edmund Wilson, Erskine Caldwell, and Archibald MacLeish. What was particularly striking about several documentary productions, including some sponsored by the FWP, was the collaboration between photographers and writers in a new and very interesting form of documentary, for example, Erskine Caldwell and Margaret Bourke White's *You Have Seen Their Faces* (1937), Dorothea Lange and Paul S. Taylor's *An American Exodus* (1939), and Richard Wright and Edwin Rosskam's *12 Million Black Voices* (1941).

The most famous of these joint ventures of pen and camera was James Agee and Walker Evans's *Let Us Now Praise Famous Men* (1941), which is particularly valuable for showing the persistence of twenties concerns in the socially committed literature of the thirties. As reportage, the book reflects in extreme form the ambiguity between fiction and nonfiction, novel and autobiography, that was the hallmark of the previous decade. The meaning of the sharecroppers, Agee insists, lies not in his presentation of them but in the bare fact that they exist, and his aim is to tease out "the cruel radiance of what is." But since Agee is just as much a fact as the sharecroppers, the narrative becomes highly autobiographical, forced by the "honesty" of the narratorial stance to explain the consciousness responding to the rural Alabamans. In terms of style, the book employs all the fragmentation and disjunction of Dos Passos, the endless lists and extravagant sentence flows of Walt Whitman, and a large array of popular culture references. Sexuality is crucial here—both that of Agee and that of his subjects—for it is a privileged case of the subject-object relations that dominate the book. In this meditation on perception, knowledge, and communication, the ethical status of Agee's role as observer, snoop, voyeur, and spy is a torment, and he speaks of the obscenity of prying into the "lives of an undefended and appallingly damaged group of human beings, an ignorant and helpless rural family, for the purpose of parading the nakedness, disadvantage and humiliation of these lives before another group of human beings, in the name of science, of 'honest journalism' (whatever that paradox may mean), of humanity, of social fearlessness, for money." The transformation of rural misery into human nobility, the sensitive reading of the anthropological sign, requires of Agee a self-examination and self-exhibition of humbling frankness.

The weaving of leftist sympathies into the structure of *Let Us Now Praise Famous Men* reflects the influence of the Communist party of America on the literature of the 1930s. However, the differences between leftist American writing and Soviet art are worth noting. Socialist Realism involved an extreme determinism in which an individual was a direct product of his or her class, and plot was a manifestation of history as the story of class struggle. American novelists seldom adhered to this model, and indeed the mixture of influences that converged in their radicalism would make such ideological purity difficult. For example, Mencken had at least as important an effect on Richard Wright as the FWP. In *Native Son* Wright depicts the white leftist sympathizer, Mary, as an overprivileged college girl impressed with her own nobility who uses her commitment as an opportunity to skip classes and play with liquor and sex. She is, in fact, a thirties version of the flapper—beautiful, self-involved, expensive, but ever so concerned with the plight of poor blacks. Wright is critical not only of such a posture but of his black protagonist, Bigger, who allows himself to be victimized by his social position.

Indeed, it might be more accurate to speak of the thirties not as a return to naturalism but as an exploration of the romance of realism, of the triumph of the individual in spite of the constraints of reality, or sometimes because of them. The enormous success of Pearl S. Buck's *The Good Earth* (1931) and Margaret Mitchell's *Gone with the Wind* (1936) indicates the power of this theme in the popular imagination.

Even the hard-boiled detective novel, whose unsentimental analysis of American society crystallized in the Depression, can hardly be seen as a determinist form. Despite the corruption and depravity that the detective wades through, he still manages to uncover the truth about things, and to go on surviving. The central organ for detective writing was H. L. Mencken and George Jean Nathan's periodical *Black Mask*. Having supported the work of Sinclair Lewis and Carl Sandburg in *The American Mercury* during the 1920s, Mencken and Nathan continued to make their elitist influence felt through this new magazine. And similarly, though Hammett, Chandler, and James M. Cain were popular successes, they were also valued by the sophisticated audience of French existentialists, whose fiction might be considered antideterminist in its detachment of cause from effect and motive from action. Albert Camus, for example, claimed that he had modeled *L'Etranger* (1942) on Cain's *The Postman Always Rings Twice* (1936).

The prevalence of violence in hard-boiled detective novels and other thirties fiction also anticipates existentialism, providing another view of the victim-victimizer relation. Depression novels are pervaded with violence—the smashing in of heads in Steinbeck's *In Dubious Battle* (1936) and *The Grapes of Wrath*, for example, or the nightmarish decapitation and burning of Mary in *Native Son*, where Wright depicts the transformation of Bigger's fear of whites into a physical humiliation of his black friend. In so many of these works, as in fiction of the previous decade, violence entraps the oppressor along with the oppressed in a determinist symbiosis.

But other novels stressed the possibility of individual triumph despite the desperate misery of everyday life. Thomas Wolfe's *Of Time and the River* (1935), *The Web and the Rock* (1939), and *You Can't Go Home Again* (1940) recapitulate the plot of the naïf in the crushing but fascinating city. In language that stretches the bounds of lyricism and graphic horror, Wolfe pictures the striver defeated and returning to fight again.

Zora Neale Hurston also resists a determinist analysis of class and gender. She herself had overcome forbidding obstacles to obtain an education and to write, and her fiction follows this pattern of bucking social constraint. Her short story "Sweat" (1926) is built on the classic plot of the victim turning the tables on her oppressor: a woman kills her husband with the snake he has used to terrify and humiliate her. In Hurston's magnificent novel, *Their Eyes Were Watching God* (1937), the heroine Janie goes through two wretched marriages and the tragic death of her beloved third husband before she escapes the chains of her grandmother, of men, and of social expectations. At that point she can say with satisfaction, "Ah done been tuh de horizon and back and now Ah kin set heah in mah house and live by comparisons." In a brilliant and for thirties fiction unprecedented image of fulfillment, the book closes: "Here was peace. She pulled in her horizon like a great fish-net. Pulled it from around the waist of the world and draped it over her shoulder. So much of life in its meshes! She called in her soul to come and see."

Such writing and even the most militantly documentary works of the time contrast sharply with the scientific naturalism of Crane, Norris, and Dreiser. By 1936, Willa Cather issued a call for a "novel démeublé"—a novel stripped of the elaborate furniture of naturalist detail—and Robert Penn Warren, in planning *All the King's Men* (1946), consciously tried "to avoid writing a straight naturalistic novel, the kind of novel that the material so readily invited." However gargantuan the descriptive excesses of Agee, Wolfe, and Henry Miller might be, they were excesses in the tradition of Whitman and not of Dreiser. Hence the puzzling contradictions in so much thirties fiction—that it is a literature of the people written in a style accessible only to the sophisticated, and that its explorations of cultural conditioning are so obviously products of unique, idiosyncratic individuals. Though the social commitment of these works is indisputable, novelists had not assimilated the act of writing as such into their analysis. They would hardly define themselves in opposition to the average person, as their predecessors had in the twenties, but their ability to express their disaffection from the system necessarily set them apart from other sufferers, and their imaginings generally focused not on social victims but on heroic nonconformists.

An exception is Eudora Welty, whose first novel, *Delta Wedding* (1946), was preceded by the short-story collections *A Curtain of Green* (1941) and *The Wide Net* (1943). In these, Welty portrays an astonishing array of people—field workers, town ladies, traveling salesmen, hairdressers, widows, children, murderers, suicides, the dying—re-creating their worlds with brilliant insight and intensity. The fitting of narrative voice to these characters is often extraordinary, as in "Powerhouse," where the news of the death of a jazz musician's wife is woven into his improvisations.

However, this unidealized exploration of the "ordinary" person is not the norm. Expatriate writers in particular demonstrate ironic romanticizing and fantasy that show their continuity with the twenties. Djuna Barnes's *Nightwood* (1937), praised by T. S. Eliot, is a dreamlike lesbian romance with a world-weary observer, one Dr. O'Connor. Its central concerns are linguistic and expressive, and it is full of puns, verbal exuberance, and sexual mystery and intrigue. In a 1934 preface to Miller's *Tropic of Cancer*, Anaïs Nin analyzes the modern predicament in the imagery of *The Waste Land*: "In the anaesthesia produced by self-knowledge, life is passing, art is passing, slipping from us: we are drifting with time and our fight is with shadows." Like Eliot's characters, Nin discovers a world with no awakening, a deadening morass of sameness in which the literary plot of transcendence, revelation, or revolution is a sentimental relic of the past. Gertrude Stein at this time was torn between the isolation of aesthetic discipline and the fame resulting from compromise. And Richard Wright, after completing his powerful autobiography *Black Boy* (1945), was preparing to leave America to associate himself with the intellectual life of France.

Perhaps Henry Miller best reveals the legacy of the twenties in American Depression writing. *Tropic of Capricorn* (1939) chronicles the passage from social commitment to individualism. Employed as a personnel manager at the Cosmodemonic/Cosmococcic Telegraph Company in New York, the narrator Miller dedicates himself to bettering the lot of his telegraph messengers, only to be subverted by his unfeeling vice-president, who then suggests that Miller write a Horatio Alger story about the Cosmodemonic messengers. "I'll give you an Horatio Alger book . . . just you wait!" Miller decides. "I will give you Horatio Alger as he looks the day after the Apocalypse, when all the stink has cleared away." Miller accordingly takes three weeks off to write. "I sat riveted to my desk and I traveled around the world at lightning speed, and I learned that everywhere it is the same—hunger, humiliation, ignorance, vice, greed, extortion, chicanery, torture, despotism: the inhumanity of man to man: the fetters, the harness, the halter, the bridle, the whip, the spurs." He quits the company and goes to Paris to write, "determined to wipe Horatio Alger out of the North American consciousness."

What Miller devises is not the subversion of the Horatio Alger plot, as we have seen it subverted from Jack London to John Dos Passos, but the end of that plot altogether and the embracing of aesthetic possibilities explored more in poetry at the time than prose. Indeed, Miller can be said to have brought the novel closer to poetry than it had ever come in America. There has probably never been so thoroughly anthropomorphized and self-reflexive a treatment of fictive setting than Miller's Paris in *Tropic of Cancer* (1934), in "Megalopolitan Maniac" or "Walking Up and Down in China" (*Black Spring* [1936]). As Miller says in the last, "The earth is one great sentient being, a planet saturated through and through with man, a live planet expressing itself falteringly and stutteringly." This is the very opposite of a determinist presentation of locale: a megalomaniacal assertion of control. The equanimity with which Miller contemplates the stuttering earth and his own "divine stuttering" in "The Third or Fourth Day of Spring" is the contrary of the fear of failed fluency in Fitzgerald or Hammett.

Moreover, Miller's capacity for flippancy and irony cuts him off from virtually every major novelist of the thirties, and connects him—like Stein—to postmodernism. His utter self-reflexivity in the two *Tropics*, his concern with the forward dimension of time in prophecy, and his image of the artist as proofreader reinforce this connection. Surrealist plots and language, technical virtuosity, and allusive richness produce sequences such as this passage from "The Fourteenth Ward": "O world, strangled and collapsed, where are the strong white teeth? O world, sinking with the silver balls and the corks and the life preservers, where are the rosy scalps? O glab and glairy, O glabrous world now chewed to a frazzle, under what dead moon do you lie cold and gleaming?" The Bible, *The Tempest*, Lewis Carroll, W. B. Yeats, and the thirties combine in one of the few American passages that one would compare to Joyce.

Miller's writing remains relatively unknown to the public because of its treatment of sex. The two *Tropics* and *Black Spring* stretched the limits of taboo to the breaking point and were banned in English-speaking countries. Outside of pornography, probably no one has ever presented women with less empathy or sex with less romance than Miller. And yet Miller's sexuality is so outrageous that it quickly becomes symbolic. "The wallpaper with which the men of science have covered the world of reality is falling to tatters. The grand whorehouse which they have made of life requires no decoration; it is essential only that the drains function adequately. Beauty, that feline beauty that has us by the balls in America, is finished. To fathom the reality it is first necessary to dismantle the drains, to lay open the gangrened ducts which compose the genitourinary system that supplies the excreta of art."

The urgency and even hysteria of Miller's writing reflect not only his personal idiosyncrasies but the political anxieties of the late thirties. The energy generated by Franklin D. Roosevelt's presidency had begun the country's recovery from the Depression, but the international developments of the mid- to late thirties gave little reason for confidence in a secure future. The show trials and purges in the Soviet Union and Stalin's pact with Hitler in 1939 caused a violent reorientation of political allegiance among American leftists. When Trotsky, the idol of writers such as James T. Farrell and Edmund Wilson, was assassinated by a Stalinist agent in 1940, the intellectuals' disgust with Soviet totalitarianism became extreme.

The rise of Nazism was, of course, even more unsettling. Kay Boyle's *Primer for Combat* (1942) and *Avalanche* (1944) chronicled the coming of Nazi terror. After the success of her *Pale Horse, Pale Rider* (1939), Katherine Anne Porter began work on a "moral allegory" about anti-Semitism, racism, and cowardice set in the thirties that was to become *Ship of Fools* (1962). The evils of dictatorship figure prominently in Robert Penn Warren's *At Heaven's Gate* (1943) and the acclaimed *All the King's Men* (1946), even though the latter, deeply grounded in its Louisiana setting, does not refer to the European war directly.

World War II, like the "Great War" before it, was a kind of literary hiatus, a pause between artistic generations. The period from 1937 to 1946 witnessed the deaths of not only the old guard—Theodore Dreiser, Ellen Glasgow, Edith Wharton, Sherwood Anderson, and Gertrude Stein—but of younger writers as well: Fitzgerald, Nathanael West, and Thomas Wolfe. "What we need, pal," says a GI in a 1945 story, "is Sherwood Anderson— he always knew how to write about people who were all mixed up inside— we need Sherwood Anderson, and he isn't around to help us out." Faulkner, Steinbeck, and Hemingway were still around—indeed, a good deal of war writing sounds like an unconscious parody of Hemingway—but many of the shapers of interwar fiction were not. In their place, a new group was beginning to publish—Carson McCullers, Eudora Welty, and Robert Penn Warren, whose writing came into its own in the forties, and John Hersey, Mary McCarthy, J. D. Salinger, Ralph Ellison, Norman Mailer, and William Styron, whose major achievements lay ahead.

What remains true of all the fictional works we have considered, whether expatriate or domestic, "Risorgimento" or "lost generation," conservative or avant-garde, is that the novel between 1910 and 1945 functioned as an assessment of possibilities, in life and in art. Naturalism had established a formula in which social forces limited individual freedom. Writers either reinforced or denied this economy, exploring the situation of women, blacks, the poor, immigrants, leftists, or "the average man" in a rich paradigm of possibilities. As "Puritan" constraints on subject matter and novelistic technique broke down, the novel emerged as the testing ground for new ideas, and stylistic innovation—the traditional province of poetry—now flourished in fiction. In the course of this transformation, the American novel for the first time became a leading force in international art, never again to take second place to British fiction. Along with the United States as a political entity, the novel experienced a perfect validation of its importance: that the most circumstantial analysis of the national situation was simultaneously a universal description. Though one might say the same of some classics of the American Renaissance, the full range of American fiction in the interwar period achieved this international relevance. The American novel had come of age.

Wendy Steiner

Ernest Hemingway, F. Scott Fitzgerald, and Gertrude Stein

No other novelists were, collectively, so influential in the development of modern American fiction as Gertrude Stein, F. Scott Fitzgerald, and Ernest Hemingway. Stein began early and continued long, often taking less-traveled roads; Fitzgerald triumphed commercially and almost accidentally; Hemingway managed to embody most of the diverse literary currents that bombarded young writers of his era. Together these three not only borrowed from but also created anew what Henry James had called the "house of fiction." As a result, they influenced writers of many genres and many nations, to whom their examples have been both a blessing and a challenge.

Having found the work of late Victorian writers dull and predictable, complete with telegraphed morals tagged to old structures, Stein, Fitzgerald, and Hemingway set out to create forms commensurate with the force of modern life. Organic form was their aim. "Free verse" or "*vers libre*" in poetry, "expressionism" in drama, or "lyricism," "impressionism," and "stream of consciousness" in fiction were terms for emergent styles and techniques. Hemingway's spare, laconic, yet intense prose became a hallmark of innovation. Although it echoed Mark Twain, Stephen Crane, Sherwood Anderson, Ivan Turgenev, and Ezra Pound, it struck twentieth-century readers as original and genuine, which was exactly the effect Hemingway sought. Like other modernist writers, he assumed that his art lay in the *way* he said what he said. Style, form, and meaning were parts of an inseparable whole.

During the aftermath of World War I, many traditional religious beliefs lost their force. Order and divine direction no longer seemed to characterize the world. In a changed situation, the task of the artist was to discover new meaning and create new forms. Ezra Pound, T. S. Eliot, and Ford Madox Ford, who among them wrote hundreds of reviews and essays between 1910 and 1930, kept hammering away at these maxims: "Literature is news that stays news." "The task of the artist is a task in the same sense as the making of an efficient engine or the turning of a jug or a table leg." "The Impressionist gives you himself, how he reacts to a fact; not the fact itself; or rather, not so much the fact itself."

As creative prophets, writers could hope to influence history. In the process they also had a chance to make large sums of money. As national income rose from $59 billion in 1920 to more than $87 billion in 1928, publishing burgeoned. Alfred A. Knopf was established in 1915; Boni and Liveright in 1917; Harcourt Brace in 1919; and Viking in 1925. It was a heady time to begin a literary career.

Stein and her contemporaries drew sustenance from philosophers—Henri Bergson, F. H. Bradley, John Dewey, William James—who were convinced that "knowing" grew from concrete experience and from dealing with the objects of a culture as well as its thought. Imagism, the poetic movement that published its manifesto in 1913, drew on these principles for its aesthetic. An Imagist poem consisted of clear visual images, often juxtaposed with other images, prompting the reader to an imaginative response that completed its meaning. As writers of both poetry and fiction discovered Imagism, the line between the genres blurred. Many modernists in fact wrote with little regard for genre. Hemingway, who began as a journalist, considered himself first a poet. Stein created new versions of every genre she appropriated. Like John Dos Passos and William Faulkner, both Hemingway and Stein wrote in different forms, borrowing techniques from one to use in another.

The fusion of many kinds of literature, drawn from many traditions—including Russian, Provençal, Greek, and Japanese, as well as Spanish, Italian, French, German, and English—brought new vitality to modernism. Given the rush of new materials, it was inevitable that writers would cite contradictory prototypes and principles. If the role of the modernist was to be a reporter, seeking an objective stance and tone, how could the selection of subject matter be impressionistic and subjectve? Hemingway thought of the interchapters of *In Our Time* as reports on things that he had seen during World War I and its aftermath. Yet he clearly shaped the reader's reactions by the way he told each story and the way he structured his narrative. None of the modernists was in any simple sense "objective."

In general, however, many of them did aim for objectivity, in part to avoid the charge of sentimentality. They concentrated on sensual presentations of images or scenes; they avoided direct authorial intrusion; and they used irony as a distancing device. In addition, they employed mythic and archetypal patterns—journey motifs, Grail quests, or struggles between fathers and sons—to add unexpected levels of meaning.

"Modernism" embraced painters, musicians, and sculptors as well as writers, and it fostered a belief in art as an avenue to self-fulfillment. Many writers had great difficulty living in the kind of country the United States was becoming, with its attempts to legislate morality, endorse prejudices, and make money an overriding preoccupation. Prohibition was one sign of the times; the Red Scare, the Palmer raids, the Sacco-Vanzetti trial, and the growing fascination with the stock market were others. In addition to fostering a belief in art as an avenue to self-fulfillment, modernism helped to explain why artists felt alienated from American culture.

Hemingway considered himself one of the best kinds of Americans: he mourned for his country more than he criticized it. But the origins of his alienation are clear. He was born in 1899, the first son and second child of a prominent Oak Park, Illinois, family. His father was a physician, his mother an opera singer and an early feminist. Both parents expected their son to excel, and their son complied. He made good grades in school; he wrote for the school paper and literary magazine; he participated in sports. With his father, he learned to hunt and fish. His older sister and younger siblings looked up to him. People found both his ingenuous manner and his convincing interest in them charming.

By the summer of his first birthday, Hemingway was spending part of every year at the family cottage on Walloon Lake, near Charlevoix, Michigan. Summers there allowed him to explore rivers, lakes, and the wilderness both with his father and alone, and later with Indian friends and lovers. Rowing alone across the lake with a storm coming up, fishing with friends, or hunting with his father: these and other early Michigan experiences, together with the sense of self that accrued from them, provided him with material that he drew upon for some of his best writing. Yet, early in his life, long before he went to Europe, he was looking for ways to escape the polite, effete, but curiously materialistic culture of his time.

After graduation from Oak Park High School in 1917, Hemingway left home to work for the *Kansas City Star*, covering the hospital beat and occasionally some crime stories. Within a few months he was combining a personal, storytelling style with a wry, almost slick tone. Despite his later emphasis on "objectivity," he was naturally more a feature writer interested in character than a reporter interested in events.

The next phase of Hemingway's education came not in college but in

Europe, in the American Red Cross Ambulance Corps during World War I. Having served briefly in France, Hemingway was transferred to Italy, where in the summer of 1918 he was badly wounded in both legs. During his convalescence, first in Italian hospitals and then for a winter in Petosky, Michigan, he began trying seriously to write, only to become further alienated from his family. By this time his father was depressed and irritable, near a breakdown, and his mother, who had assumed control of the household, was under economic pressures that Hemingway failed to appreciate. Urged by his mother to contribute to his own support, he left for Chicago, where he worked for a salary with the *Cooperative Commonwealth* while writing stories and poems that he tried to publish. There he also met, and then in 1921 married, Hadley Richardson of St. Louis.

Shortly after their wedding, the Hemingways left for Paris, where Hemingway wrote columns for the *Toronto Star* and played apprentice to Ezra Pound, Gertrude Stein, Ford Madox Ford, James Joyce, T. S. Eliot, and F. Scott Fitzgerald. In 1923, when Pound offered to publish one of his books *(Three Stories and Ten Poems)* with Robert McAlmon's Contact Press, Hemingway was composing both free verse and prose sketches, in a concerted effort to become a great writer. The series of one-page vignettes that first became the complete text of the lower-case *in our time* (1924) and then became the interchapters of *In Our Time* (1925) date from this period. Like the stories that he had been writing since his Petosky winter, these vignettes were the culmination of a word-by-word approach to writing through which he sought to endow prose with the density of poetry, making each image, each scene, each rendered act serve several purposes. Both the metaphoric titles of his early stories—"The End of Something," about a broken romance and a decayed mill; "Cat in the Rain," in which a questing wife comes to resemble a bedraggled and forlorn cat; "Soldier's Home," a poignant study of a young veteran almost devastated by his family's lack of understanding—and the resonances that the stories acquire from the larger structure of the book help to make *In Our Time* a masterful achievement. At age twenty-six, Hemingway suddenly acquired an enviable reputation.

When he wrote his first novel, *The Sun Also Rises* (1926), in a two-month period after he and Hadley had made a second trip to Pamplona to see the bullfights, he concentrated the many literary models he had absorbed in a work that was both technically and thematically revolutionary. Spare characterizations and taut relationships, drawn quickly in scenes at bars or over meals, serve a fast-paced plot line. One of his friends later told Hemingway that he had written "a travel book." Other readers praised *The Sun Also Rises* for its tight control of details and its metaphorical richness. Still others criticized it for the immorality of its "lost" characters. But the deeper stir that *The Sun Also Rises* created had to do with Hemingway's conception of his world-weary expatriates as redefining heroism.

Emasculated by a war wound, Jake Barnes tries to help Brett Ashley, whom he loves, find happiness with other men. Brett Ashley finally decides to relinquish her young bullfighter-lover in order to save him from her jaded life. Mike Campbell defies his various bankruptcies by trying to live the good life. Purified by his mastery of the art of bullfighting, Pedro Romero lives an almost spiritual existence. Robert Cohn's poorly repressed competitiveness and his insecurities make him simultaneously arrogant, self-centered, and childish. To middle-class American readers, saddled with prohibition and hounded by the desire to make money and earn respectability, *The Sun Also Rises* seemed shocking, its characters almost wholly "lost."

One of the most visible of modern novels, *The Sun Also Rises* is testimony to several of the difficulties of modern literature, including its implicit elitism. Although it is far less elliptical and elusive than Eliot's poems or Faulkner's novels, *The Sun Also Rises* still struck some readers as alien or difficult. One problem derived from its preoccupation with wealthy or at least well-to-do people, most of them male and some of them titled and privileged. How could such characters appeal or speak meaningfully to more restrained and less privileged readers? And how were readers, deprived of authorial intrusion, to measure accurately the moral distance between a character like Robert Cohn and one like Jake Barnes, when on so many counts they seemed similar?

Hemingway wrote *The Sun Also Rises* in part because he felt great pressure to write a novel. Many of his friends were novelists, and Pound had begun his long poem, *The Cantos*. A few readers enjoyed *The Sun Also Rises* because they recognized some of the models for Hemingway's characters—Duff Twysden, Harold Loeb, Cayetano Ordonez. But the book became a set piece of modernist art because it constitutes an almost perfect example of craft driving fragmentary scenes and provocative characters before it. Although it discloses the many ways in which the traditional principles of order and honor have disappeared from postwar life, and though it forces readers to confront disarray and ugliness, it also holds fast to the desire, the need, and the possibility of honor.

The difficult truth that Hemingway explored in *The Sun Also Rises* continued to engage him, first in the stories of *Men Without Women* (1927) and then in his second novel, *A Farewell to Arms* (1929). That truth, and the bleak life that it imposes, gave birth to the phrase "grace under pressure." In the code they seek to master, Hemingway's survivors mirror the honesty, the discipline, the restraint, and even something of the resonance that had come to mark his prose. By the end of the decade, Hemingway had surpassed F. Scott Fitzgerald, who had been far ahead of him in 1925, when *The Great Gatsby* was published, and had drawn so far ahead of one of his mentors, Gertrude Stein, that there seemed to be no race at all.

Gertrude Stein—"The Mother of Us All"—may yet catch Hemingway as well as Fitzgerald. Her work has continued to experience revival after revival and gain new audience after new audience. Except for Pound, no other American writer of this century has had greater impact on the writing world. Born in 1874, one of five children of wealthy Pennsylvania parents, Stein was educated at Radcliffe College where she studied with William James. She then spent four years in the Johns Hopkins Medical School. Although she left Hopkins without taking a degree, her specialty there, brain anatomy, was at once an outgrowth of her studies under James and a spur to two of her major literary preoccupations: characterization and the reader's perception of the text.

Once Stein's brother, Leo, had moved to Paris, however, she was eager to join him. In 1903 she moved to France and soon met her lifelong companion, Alice B. Toklas. She returned to the United States only once—for a highly successful lecture tour in 1934. Yet she always claimed America as her country (calling Paris her "hometown"), and much of her writing conveys her interest in American themes and subjects. Her career in Europe was as an art critic (as was that of her brother, who helped to discover Paul Cézanne) as well as a writer, and her salons were world-famous. Family money allowed both Steins to become patrons in the rapidly changing art world. Yet, though Gertrude Stein has been called "The Mama of Dada," and though Pablo Picasso's portrait of her (as well as her verbal portraits of many of the painters she knew) is justly famous, her most substantial accomplishment remains her writing.

Stein began writing seriously in 1903, but many of her works saw publication only years after their completion. *Three Lives*, published in 1909, was finished in 1904; *The Making of Americans*, published in 1925, was finished as early as 1911 or 1912. Other works remained unpublished at the time of her death in 1946 and have since appeared in eight volumes, published between 1951 and 1958. Although she wrote seriously from the age of twenty-nine, she did not have a major unsubsidized publisher until she was fifty-one. Among other things, her troubled publication history suggests how far beyond her contemporaries she was in unconventional and innovative methods.

To create a fresh impact on the reader, Stein relied on simple, commonplace words arranged in surprising ways. She admitted wryly to her close friend Sherwood Anderson that she was "fond" of sentences, and in much of her writing the sentence is the key unit of organization. The repetition that she is famous for occurs in the accumulation of separate sentences, as in this short paragraph from "The Good Anna," one of the three short stories of socially marginal women that constitute *Three Lives.*

Anna worked, and thought, and saved, and scolded and took care of all the boarders, and of Peter and of Rags, and all the others. There was never any end to Anna's effort and she grew always more tired, more pale yellow, and in her face more thin and worried. . . . The things that Anna really needed were to rest sometimes and eat more so that she could get stronger, but these were the last things that Anna could bring herself to do. Anna could never take a rest.

By achieving a kind of verbal "after-image," Stein believed she could penetrate the reader's consciousness—and evoke some genuine response—through her subversion of familiar literary technique. She intentionally used *un*literary language and diction, and wrote in unliterary structures.

Perhaps more important was Stein's insistence that writing should be about real characters, real objects, real scenes from American life. Unlike her contemporary William Carlos Williams, however, who achieves a similar aim by describing objects along straightforward lines, Stein forces the reader to complete the description. She draws the emotional states of "The Gentle Lena," "Melanctha," and "Matisse" but not their physical presence. She creates the salient—though perhaps nonvisual—characteristics of the objects described in *Tender Buttons* (1914), but avoids labels or names. As a result, though we remember Williams's red wheelbarrow, we remember Stein's phrasing. In her writing, *words* become the real.

Stein was a thorough maverick. Her wit and candor (and money) helped her to succeed in making her life a model of experimentation. By now it seems clear that she was years ahead of her time. Yet she was born in 1874, and though many critics have emphasized the differences between her work and that of the realists and naturalists who were her contemporaries, others have shown that she shared many of their concerns, including a focus on the ordinary and a reassessment of its "meaning." In addition, she treated women as separate entities, not as adjuncts to men, as Theodore Dreiser and Stephen Crane often did. And she used her knowledge of psychology to depict characters in fresh, unexpected ways.

Stein differed from most of her contemporaries by being female, Jewish, lesbian, and well-educated. A literal outsider as well as a metaphoric one, she fell into what recent feminist critics have called "disguising" tactics. *Lucy Church Amiably* and *Lifting Belly* are about lesbian experience, but uninitiated readers often fail to realize this. For all her apparent aggressiveness, Stein suffered the same "anxiety of authorship" that other women writers have described. She too made changes in the accepted forms of writing, partly out of a need to disguise the story she was writing. To view Stein as only an innovative modernist, then, disregarding the problems her gender and sexuality caused, is to simplify her artistic situation and diminish her artistic accomplishment. Given the many psychological barriers she faced, Stein's accomplishments are astonishing.

Her earliest works (*Things As They Are* or *Q.E.D.*, *Three Lives*, *The Making of Americans*, *Many Many Women*, *A Long Gay Book*) have been compared to Picasso's analytic cubism. In them she depicts characters whose basic motivation is emotional and—congruent with her belief that people have "bottom" natures—unchanging. The tragedy in Stein's early fiction comes when people eventually reach the end toward which they have been heading all of their lives. A more playful approach marks the somewhat later *Tender Buttons*, *Two: Gertrude Stein and Her Brother*, and *G.M.P.* (*Matisse, Picasso, and Gertrude Stein*), in which collages of single words or phrases and visual arrangements take precedence over narrative.

As Stein moved further from representation into more complex language structures, she began writing plays and using catalogues and lists as well as collections of phrases. Several of her most obscure works—from *Counting Her Dresses. A Play* (1917), through *Lucy Church Amiably*, *Patriarchal Poetry*, and *Four Saints in Three Acts: An Opera to Be Sung* (all in 1927), to *They Must. Be Wedded. To Their Wife, A Play* (1931) and *A Play of Pounds* (1932)—meld into *The Autobiography of Alice B. Toklas* (1933). Drawing on both her early work and the innovations of her later work, she wrote her fictional "autobiography" in prose so accessible that it attracted a more general audience. Through much of her later career, she continued to write in a more direct style: *Lectures in America* (1934); *Narration* (1935); *The Geographical History of America* (1935); *What Are Masterpieces and Why Are There So Few of Them* (1935); *Everybody's Autobiography* (1936); *Picasso* (1938); *Ida: A Novel* and *Mrs. Reynolds: A Novel* (both in 1940); *Wars I Have Seen* (1945); *Brewsie and Willie* (1945); and *The Mother of Us All* (1946). Yet, throughout these works, in their repeated experiment with discontinuous, circular, thought-connected verbal patterns, the influence of William James (who coined the phrase "stream of consciousness" in *Principles of Psychology*) continued to surface. Both the shape and the pace of much contemporary writing remain indebted to the innovations of Gertrude Stein.

Few writers differ more from Stein than F. Scott Fitzgerald. In 1920, when he broke on the literary scene at the age of twenty-four with his first novel, *This Side of Paradise*, and his first collection of stories, *Flappers and Philosophers*, Fitzgerald quickly became both a popular success and a spokesman for his age. Stein thought that Fitzgerald had more talent than all the other Lost Generation writers combined. Fitzgerald in turn stood in awe of Stein as well as of Edith Wharton, Willa Cather, Ezra Pound, and other writers who seemed to him able to delineate character effectively. Never confident of his ability, Fitzgerald struggled to carve out a reputation that would compensate for the failures he saw as dominating his early years: his father's business failures and his mother's chilled social hopes; unhappy years at boarding school; low grades at Princeton; and his lingering guilt about being a lapsed Catholic.

After leaving Princeton in 1917, without graduating, Fitzgerald spent two years in the Army and then went to New York to work in advertising. During these years he wrote several drafts of *This Side of Paradise*. Soon after the book's publication, Fitzgerald married Zelda Sayre of Montgomery, Alabama. Earlier, when he was stationed in Alabama, Fitzgerald had come to regard Zelda as the prototype of the rich, beautiful woman who figures so prominently in his fiction. Together, he and Zelda in turn came to epitomize the kind of Jazz Age style that his fiction portrays—of young glamorous people who try to live the American dream of money, success, and happiness, only to have their lives touched by sadness and even tragedy.

Fitzgerald's second novel, *The Beautiful and Damned*, was published in 1922. *Tales of the Jazz Age*, another collection of stories, also appeared in 1922, and *The Vegetable*, a play, in 1923. During these years, Fitzgerald also wrote scores of stories for high-paying magazines. By the end of his career he had published 178 such stories, including a few written with or by Zelda. So long as Scott's name appeared as author, the stories commanded fees of up to $4,000 each. Yet, as though on a binge, the Fitzgeralds ran through the profits so quickly that it horrified them as well as their friends.

Fitzgerald's 1925 novel, *The Great Gatsby*—a smaller financial success than his earlier fiction but a greater critical one—is a testimony both to Fitzgerald's seriousness about his writing and to his increased understanding of the directions that modern fiction was taking. The craft of the novel—its remarkable economy and its disciplined attention to details that acquire symbolical significance—marks it as a remarkable advance. In many ways, Fitzgerald's themes went back to his beginning in *This Side of Paradise*, with its concern for "a new generation grown up to find all Gods dead, all wars fought, all faiths in men shaken." But there were important differences in technique. Like Joseph Conrad in his Marlow stories and Willa Cather in *A Lost Lady*, Fitzgerald uses Nick Carraway as the narrative consciousness for Gatsby's story and thereby gives the reader contrasting perspectives that call both Gatsby's and Nick's motivations into question. The complex texture and structure of this short novel about the tragic consequences of America's native optimism make it evocative beyond its size.

T. S. Eliot called *Gatsby* "the first step that American fiction has taken since Henry James." Others praised it as the most American of this century's novels. Although Gatsby's life is more fabricated than fashioned, it acquires authority because Gatsby remains courageous enough to dream. Inheritor of an intensely American disposition that is simultaneously a blessing and a burden, Gatsby seeks to impose his private dreams on the social realities of his world. He persists despite the requirements of prudence, propriety, and even self-preservation, and in the process evokes a heritage that includes Ralph Waldo Emerson and Herman Melville: " 'Can't repeat the past?' he cried out incredulously. 'Why of course you can!' " Fitzgerald thus catches much of the complexity of American life and American culture in a brief, impressionistic novel. In the short, evocative chapters with which it begins and ends as well as in a series of vivid scenes, Fitzgerald merges the craft of the novelist with the craft of the imagist poet. Yet, for all its imagery and counterpoint, *The Great Gatsby* is an easy book to read. Chapter divisions set off a succession of interrelated scenes. Every line of dialogue pushes both action and character development forward—as when the dissatisfied Daisy says, "radiantly," "Do you always watch for the longest day of the year and then miss it? I always watch for the longest day in the year and then miss it." The tempo is rapid yet controlled, as each event contributes to the work's mounting irony.

In 1923 William Carlos Williams wrote what he called *The Great American Novel*. The book that deserves the title, *The Great Gatsby*, appeared in 1925, in Fitzgerald's depiction of what has come of the American dream. By a stroke of genius, Fitzgerald saw that that dream belonged, in its most intense form, not to the respectable, the educated, and the sensitive Nick Carraway (as it might in the hands of a nineteenth-century novelist) but rather to a fugitive, an outsider, a man born without a pedigree but with a great readiness for hope. In Gatsby, Fitzgerald shot the naturalists' theories into a cocked hat (while using some of their methods) and thus created a new version of the outrageous lowborn, even criminal, American "hero." Gatsby may well be descended from that earlier lowborn, Huck Finn. But Fitzgerald's creation is a new protagonist of great force who brings America's established social codes into direct confrontation with conflicting codes of human understanding.

Hemingway and Fitzgerald had met in 1924; they had borrowed money from each other; and they had "taught" each other about books and writing through long, sometimes cranky letters. Their aesthetic positions were very close. "God I wish I could see you," Hemingway once wrote Fitzgerald. "You are the only guy in or out of Europe I can say as much for." It is little wonder, then, that Hemingway was among those who found *Gatsby* impressive. Much of what Hemingway had achieved in his fiction—a concentrated yet seemingly effortless prose—Fitzgerald had sustained throughout an entire novel. Both men were still writing hard. In 1926 Fitzgerald published another collection of stories, *All the Sad Young Men,* and was working on *Tender Is the Night*. Hemingway was completing the stories collected in *Men Without Women* (1927). But things were already beginning to crumble for the Fitzgeralds. Zelda was writing her own novel, *Save Me the Waltz,* a story set in the South that covers many of the same events as *The Great Gatsby* from a woman's point of view. But she was already in need of occasional institutionalization, a condition that time would worsen. Scott was trying to give up hard liquor, but his financial circumstances would soon force him to move to Hollywood to write for the screen.

The thirties brought relentless decline for him, despite the appearance of *Tender Is the Night* (1934) and *Taps at Reveille* (1935), another collection of stories. In 1931 Fitzgerald was still making over $40,000 a year from his writing; in 1939 his royalties totaled $33. With the Jazz Age over, readers seemed to regard his fiction as dated and irrelevant, without realizing that he had been chronicling the malaise as well as the exuberance of the decade, showing how its fascination with material success was eroding values rather than confirming them. Although rich and glamorous people dominate much of his fiction, Fitzgerald remained loyal to an undercurrent of disillusionment, suspicious of happy endings, in touch with the deeper notes of his age. Ironically, though it had looked for a time as if he might live the dream of wealth and success, triumphing in life and in art, neither his life nor his career ended much better than Jay Gatsby's.

The thirties were a period of decline for Hemingway as well. During the 1930s new themes—having to do with human misery and the need for collective political action—seemed to call for new modes of expression. After *A Farewell to Arms* (1929), a powerful novel about Frederic Henry's alienation from patriotism and his search for love outside conventional norms, Hemingway continued to write good short stories. In 1933 they were collected as *Winner Take Nothing*. But he also began experimenting with other prose forms. His study of bullfighting and Spanish culture, *Death in the Afternoon,* appeared in 1932, and his treatise on big-game hunting and ecology, *Green Hills of Africa,* in 1935. To American readers mired in the Great

Depression, these books seemed escapist. Soon readers were asking why Hemingway, a writer who had insisted on looking unflinchingly at life, was abandoning American culture for distant and exotic lands.

In a sense, Hemingway was doing just that. Disillusioned with failed ideals, he felt a need to write about civilizations that were simpler and more immediate in their address to the crucial issues of life and death. When he was not living or traveling in other countries, he chose to live in remote parts of America. Even when he continued to challenge his rich country, in the hope of evoking its best responses, he remained as emphatic in rejecting the popular ideology of the 1930s as he had been in rejecting that of the 1920s. His preference for lands that were both simpler and more exotic might seem inexplicable, but it was almost certainly deliberate.

Gradually, his writing also changed. The tight control, the spare detail, the careful discipline of his early work gave way to work that rambled. Not until he closed the decade with the rough *To Have and Have Not* (1937); a play, *The Fifth Column* (1938); and the fruition of all his experimentation, *For Whom the Bell Tolls* (1940), were his new directions clear. Modernism prized continual growth. Writers like Carl Sandburg fell into disfavor when it became clear that their latest poems tended to resemble or repeat earlier ones. "Make it new" was the slogan Ezra Pound wore embroidered on his scarf as he walked through the streets of London and Paris. Finding ways to make writing new, however, grew harder as the years passed and one experiment followed another. Stein, insular in her demands and her audience, had perhaps the easiest time maintaining her personal direction. Much of the correspondence between Hemingway and Fitzgerald shows how difficult finding new directions proved to be for both of them.

By 1937, Fitzgerald was so ill from the effects of his alcoholism that writing had become almost impossible for him. When he died in December 1940 at the age of forty-four, after several heart attacks, he was struggling to complete *The Last Tycoon*. The seriousness of his vision in both *Tender Is the Night*, a complex novel of a psychiatrist and the woman he loves and fears, and *The Last Tycoon*, a story about Hollywood life, demonstrated once again how far Fitzgerald had moved from his early aim of making good money by depicting his culture. The gravity of his personal predicament comes through even more directly, however, in "The Crack-Up," published in *Esquire* in 1936—a three-part essay that horrified Hemingway, perhaps in part because he recognized too well the feelings Fitzgerald described there. After Fitzgerald's death, his friend Edmund Wilson edited both *The Last Tycoon* (1941) and *The Crack-Up* (1945), a collection that included several miscellaneous pieces.

Hemingway outlived Fitzgerald by twenty-one years, only to shoot himself during the summer of 1961, after prolonged treatment for depression and various other medical problems. During his last years, Hemingway wrote comparatively little, yet held fast to the notion that the writer must constantly strive to grow and develop. The critic Malcolm Cowley recalls seeing him stand almost motionless at his writing board, from early morning till afternoon, seldom able to write anything. Earlier Hemingway had written to Maxwell Perkins about Fitzgerald's 1936 essays, calling his friend's attitude "the shamelessness of defeat" and describing his anger with Fitzgerald for "giving up" ("What is he going to do? He can't have adopted being through as a career can he?"). But Hemingway's last twenty years were clearly dominated not so much by writing as by the need to write. In 1950 he published *Across the River and into the Trees*, a paean to military hardihood and virginal beauty that was denounced by critics. *The Old Man and the Sea* (1952) won the 1953 Pulitzer Prize for Fiction and led to the Nobel Prize for Literature a year later, but it failed to match his early work. *The Dangerous Summer*, an account of his last trip to Spain for the bullfights, a few scattered posthumously published works—*Islands in the Stream* and *The Garden of Eden*—as well as other unfinished manuscripts, date from earlier times. Yet they, too, fail to measure up to his best writing.

As represented by Stein, Hemingway, and Fitzgerald—a widely unread woman who remains notorious for her endless experimentation; a dispirited stylist who died by his own hand; and a romantic alcoholic who died young while trying to learn how to write screenplays—"modernism" may well seem to lose its aura. Yet we know that Stein, Hemingway, and Fitzgerald lived the lives that they lived and wrote the works that they wrote at least in part because of the high conception they had of the calling of the artist. Early in their lives, they clearly felt the excitement, the energy, the sheer joy of working in a milieu that both challenged and nurtured them. The joy of artistic creation is a part of their legacy, as is the conviction that the act of writing is a worthy way of spending one's days. The writer as a secular priest, creating an almost sacred text, and thus the act of writing as spiritual emprise, are parts of the credo of modernism. In action and reaction, this credo has influenced all aesthetic beliefs since.

When Fitzgerald describes his country at the end of *The Great Gatsby*, we sense the romantic awe he felt in contemplating the mystical newness of the new world:

the old island here that flowered once for Dutch sailors' eyes—a fresh, green breast of the new world. Its vanished trees . . . had once pandered in whispers to the last and greatest of all human dreams; for a transitory enchanted moment man must have held his breath in the presence of this continent, compelled into an aesthetic contemplation he neither understood nor desired, face to face for the last time in history with something commensurate to his capacity for wonder.

Fitzgerald's romance with America was not the same as Hemingway's. Yet both writers evoked the beauty of human promise through scenes in which nature provides an image of human potential. Here is Hemingway driving into a town and seeing

the heavy trees of the small town that are a part of your heart if it is your town and you have walked under them, but that are only too heavy, that shut out the sun and that dampen the houses for a stranger; out past the last house and onto the highway that rose and fell straight away ahead with banks of red dirt sliced cleanly away and the second-growth timber on both sides. It was not his country but it was the middle of fall and all of this country was good to drive through and to see.

Stein's wry pastiche, marked by humor and deft feints into the surreal, differs from both Fitzgerald's and Hemingway's art. Yet it provides another way of finding in words a way toward both the real and the mystical.

When we came away we came away to stay we came away steadily. And where are we. We are in the land of sky larks not in the land of nightingales. We do not mention robins swallows, quails and peacocks. We do not mix them. We murmur to each other, nightingales, we please each other with fruit trees.

According to Irving Howe, American literature is "a new idea . . . a new voice. Thought and language, idea and image fold into a new being, and we have the flowering of our literature." Modernism is one of several movements in the history of American literature that help give this "new idea" and "new voice" form and force. In novel after novel, poem after story, our modernist writers attempted—and sometimes achieved—aesthetically impossible possibilities. Through their considerable achievements they helped to bring American literature to full maturity. In that development, few were as seminal as F. Scott Fitzgerald, Ernest Hemingway, and Gertrude Stein.

Linda W. Wagner

William Faulkner

The first facts are the sentences, the act of style:

From a little after two oclock until almost sundown of the long still hot weary dead September afternoon they sat in what Miss Coldfield still called the office because her father had called it that—a dim hot airless room with the blinds all closed and fastened for forty-three summers because when she was a girl someone had believed that light and moving air carried heat and that dark was always cooler, and which (as the sun shone fuller and fuller on that side of the house) became latticed with yellow slashes full of dust motes which Quentin thought of as being flecks of the dead old dried paint itself blown inward from the scaling blinds as wind might have blown them.

—sentences (this one begins *Absalom, Absalom!*) that press forward even as they turn back, amending themselves with accretions of adjective and qualifying clause: refining, supplementing, substituting, digressing. Sentences that do not so much exhaust meaning as sustain its possibility within the proliferation of words. There is a violence here, to expectations of what words and sentences do as well as to rules of syntax and customs of clarity. One virtually loses the main clause—"they sat"—in the welter of where and how long. One must read what "Quentin thought" twice to realize that what is "blown inward" is not the proximate "paint" but "flecks," and the whole sentence twice to know that at its core is a "room"—the place where "they sat"—a room at once buried and freshly brought forth in the details of what it has been called and why it is so dim and hot and airless. For William Faulkner the origin of such sentences lay in a desire "to say it all . . . between one Cap and one period. . . . to put everything into one sentence—not only the present but the whole past on which it depends and which keeps overtaking the present, second by second." The desire resembles Tristram Shandy's attempt to catch up verbally with his life, and it has the same result of producing a kind of writing that seems to demonstrate and depend on the necessary failure of writing even as it pleads the value of its effort and its supreme hope.

Implicit to this prose is the larger structure of Faulkner's greatest novels—including *The Sound and the Fury, As I Lay Dying, Light in August, Absalom, Absalom!*—each one a series of voices, like the modifying elements of sentences, poised at odd intervals on the rim of a single event. At the center, resonant but incomplete, are the missing sister, the dead mother, the man without identity, the unexplained murder: mysteries that seem to inspire a potentially endless succession of tellings. Again there is the rebellion against a received tradition, as the classic narrative splinters into obliquely related fragments, chronological inversions, sudden shifts in perspective. The structure struggles for clarifications whose validity—and even desirability—it continues to question, as if fearing the loss of energy that mars any stay against confusion.

Then there is the myth, the people and places of Yoknapatawpha County, "a cosmos of my own." Behind the language that sometimes threatens to efface the reality it pursues lies an unmistakable referent, Faulkner's northern Mississippi home and history transformed into a world capable of being mapped, genealogically tabled, chronicled from past to present. Basic to that world is not only a region and society as substantial as James Joyce's Dublin, but the thick sense of a history already intact, preceding every event and word. Each new text, however resistant to its narrative tradition, thus becomes a return as well, deriving part of its voice from existing facts and fictions, acknowledging an order larger than and prior to itself.

These two dimensions of Faulkner's work—the dislocations of order, the creation of a fixed universe—are the dynamic poles of his achievement, representative forces opposing and generating each other: passions of talent and tradition, present and past, forgetting and remembering. Central to what may at first appear to be only stylistic disruptions of sentence and structure is a powerful confirmation of whatever is individual—indeed alien—even if it is an alienation that by its violation of language or design or communal code threatens to break through the boundaries of meaning and moral permissibility. Conversely, the substance and technique of the Yoknapatawpha world insist on an inherited context, inside of which the individual must act and understand. All of Faulkner's major (and many minor) characters enter the fiction trailing behind them clouds of familial and regional qualifiers: the grandparents, parents, and siblings, the hill country or bottom land or tidewater, whose cumulative significance is the indispensable background of identity.

It is easy enough, perhaps even at times necessary, to emphasize one of these dimensions at the expense of the other, to categorize Faulkner as modernist or traditionalist, caretaker of a fictional keystone or questioner of all utterance. The drama of his finest work is the meeting of the two. Faulkner's texts clearly demonstrate what Paul de Man has called the "deliberate forgetting" of the modern, its "desire to wipe out whatever came earlier in the hope of reaching at last a point that could be called a true present." But the inspiration of Yoknapatawpha County is the refusal to forget anything. Its characters and its fictional status dwell in reminiscence, as if living and writing were all reiteration.

To read Faulkner comprehensively is to attend to this dialectic of remembering and forgetting, and to realize that it is located not merely between but within each pole. On the one hand, the drive to abandon the received order can bring forth a design—a structure, a meaning, a stance—even if that design implies an impending collapse within its own compelling articulation. On the other hand, the memory of the past, the exploration of self through the inherited languages of family and history, can become a revision as well as a repetition—not an escape from the past or refusal of its facts but a re-creation of its meaning: a remembering that is also a forgetting.

Tensions such as these quicken the sentence with which we began. Much of it seems entrapped in stasis: the weight of "long still hot weary dead," the digressions backward in time; a room that is an "office" because someone (dead?) once named it that, blinds fastened because someone (dead?) once believed it useful. And yet the sentence moves as and where the scene does not. The sheer accumulation of modifiers brings paralysis to a new intensity; the afternoon advances, moves silently its six or so hours in the space between two prepositions—"from": "until." Finally, Quentin's thought infers motion in those specks of dust "blown inward . . . as wind might have blown them," disturbs the sentence with a metaphoric breeze. Not only does the past keep overtaking the present, but the present keeps drawing out like an infinitely expandable band the possibilities of the past. The sentence completes itself intelligibly, accepts with its period the limits of its desire to amplify meaning. But it allows loose ends to dangle—motes of dust or dried paint? air still or in motion? a present consumed by tradition or capable of re-creating it?—keeps itself alive, unfinished, to be rewritten and resolved.

The importance of Faulkner's life for an understanding of his fiction lies less in what he did than in what he was, simply by virtue of his birth: a native Mississippian and firstborn son of a family that had been prominent in his area for three generations. Born September 25, 1897, in New Albany, by 1902 William Cuthbert Faulkner had moved with his family to Oxford, Lafayette County, his principal place of residence for virtually the rest of his life. He grew up in a family shadowed by its own formidable history, a situation that set the stage for his conflict between the need to remember and honor the past and the need to create for himself a distinctive identity.

Anchoring the tradition was the figure of his great-grandfather, William Clark Falkner (Faulkner added the "u" as a young man), whom he never knew but whose extravagant life and career—lawyer, planter, soldier (a decorated officer in the Civil War), politician, railroad builder, novelist and poet—seemed to impose on all his heirs, even the most successful, a sense of their inevitable decline. Family deterioration was particularly vivid in the example of Faulkner's father, Murry, who failed in his ambition to take over the railroad of which his father was president, and who settled down in a position as secretary and business manager at the University of Mississippi in 1919 only after some fifteen years of drifting from one job to another.

By the age of twelve Faulkner had become an indifferent student, and never completed high school. Under the influence of his mother, however, a refined yet determined and even dominating woman, who valued education and the arts, he early became an avid reader in Shakespeare, Fielding, Voltaire, Dickens, Hugo, Balzac, and Conrad. Later his literary horizons were greatly expanded by his townsman Phil Stone to include the early modernists, such as W. B. Yeats, Ezra Pound, and T. S. Eliot, and the nineteenth-century English and French poets who had influenced them. Somewhat remote from and antagonistic toward his father—a taciturn man, prone to heavy drinking and occasional violence—William nevertheless learned from him to be a good hunter and woodsman, as well as a lifelong lover of dogs and horses.

Like some of the characters he would eventually create, however, the young Faulkner appears to us most memorably in the posture of listening: at his father's livery stable or the family's hunting cabin, his grandfather's house or Mammy Caroline Barr's cabin, listening to the tales of the old times and people. He could hear stories of the Civil War from men who had fought in it—members of his great-grandfather's Partisan Rangers—as well as from those whose words were their only weapons: the old aunts, "the women, the indomitable, the undefeated, who never surrendered . . . irreconcilable and enraged and still talking about it."

The example of a past grandeur, however exaggerated and sentimentalized, could not but be felt. Even Faulkner's more mature awareness of the injustice and violence implicit to the grandeur could not prevent its encroachment on his life in the present, threatening to paralyze it into pure nostalgia or arouse it to an alienating anger. The simultaneous need to emulate his ancestral past yet not be stifled by it took the form early in his life of a firm independence—a willingness to disappoint certain parental expectations and, subsequently, even provoke a degree of communal contempt—combined with the announced desire to be a writer, "like my great-granddaddy." This was an ambition that, despite the appearance well into his twenties of aimlessness and eccentricity, Faulkner seems never to have put completely aside. Writing became not only a means of asserting an identity (which yet linked him to the past), but a medium in which he could describe both the dynamics of decline—the pull of the past toward repetition—and the various possibilities of revision.

Faulkner's situation becomes further clarified if we see it in the larger context of his particular Southern generation, for whom, as Richard H. King has written, the Southern tradition "loomed distressingly distant and overpoweringly strong, insupportable yet inescapable." On the one side stood a tempting yet increasingly distant and questionable antebellum Southern ideal; on the other a modernity attractive in its call for an original vision, yet disturbing in its willingness to dismiss a past that—certainly for the Southerner—still constituted the very armature of thought and value. The result, in Allen Tate's terms, was an unusual situation of "double focus, a looking two ways," which while psychically difficult proved to be creatively fruitful. Out of this tension of imaginative modes Faulkner's generation created an authentic renaissance, of which his became the richest voice.

Joined to his Southern contemporaries by a common heritage and a common ambivalence, Faulkner was at the same time cut off from them, as he was from his literary contemporaries in general. Unlike many of the modernist writers, he did not attach himself to any coterie or school, did not travel extensively until much later in life, did not permanently uproot himself from the place where he grew up, even to settle in a different state. There were various forays into the world, but they never lasted for more than a year, and always culminated in his return to Oxford. In 1918, largely from disappointment over his sweetheart Estelle Oldham's engagement to another man, he visited Phil Stone in New Haven, and then volunteered for the British Royal Air Force, which sent him to Toronto for training. Much to his lasting regret, World War I ended probably before he had flown a plane, and certainly before he had seen combat. Following his discharge, however, driven by the demands of his heritage for a war record, he began concocting stories about plane crashes during flight training (sometimes shifted to combat in France), injuries to legs and hips, and a silver plate in his head. In 1921, after a year as a special student at the University of Mississippi, he spent a few months in New York, working in a bookstore. Of particular importance was his half-year stay in New Orleans in 1925, where he published a large number of prose sketches and stories and wrote his first novel, and where he associated with a vital group of artists and writers that included Sherwood Anderson. As he had listened earlier to tales of the Southern past, he now listened to talk of those who were establishing the grounds of modernism: of Conrad, Joyce, and Eliot; Freud, Frazer, and Bergson. In July 1925 he sailed to Europe, where he traveled and wrote for six months.

For the most part, however, during the formative years as well as the great ones, Faulkner remained in Oxford, where he eventually married Estelle, now divorced, and settled down in an antebellum house he renovated. There he worked in an isolation unique among major twentieth-century writers, gradually learning the lessons of the new modernism and what its encounter with the legacy of his family and region might come to mean.

For a period that began before he joined the RAF and lasted until he went to New Orleans in 1925 Faulkner was primarily a lyric poet, writing the bulk of the more than seventy poems he published. These included two volumes, *The Marble Faun* (1924) and *A Green Bough* (1933), as well as several unpublished, hand-printed poem sequences. Modeled largely on his reading in the late English romantics, the French symbolists, and the English writers of the 1890s, his poems tend to be formal, stylized, surprisingly mannered. Although generally "indecisive" in the symbolist fashion, their diction is too lacking in Paul Verlaine's crucial second requirement of "precision" to be genuinely suggestive. Faulkner's "Faun" would "from a cup unlipped, undreamt, unguessed" (and poetically unrealized) "Sip that wine sweet-sunned for Jove's delight"; his "Wild Geese" alludes to an origin and destiny it does not even vaguely evoke: "Over the world's rim, out of some splendid noon,/ Seeking some high desire, and not in vain."

The poems are of interest less for their own achievement than for what they tell us about Faulkner's long attraction to a poetry that attempts to move beyond the reality of things and conventional attitudes toward an essence of being and individual feeling that he later called the "universal." Under the pressure of poetic form, the word seeks to free itself from its referential function in order to imply not the object but its spirit. As Faulkner once put it, when asked to describe his ideal woman, "it's best to take the gesture, the shadow of the branch, and let the mind create the tree."

But Faulkner's poetry indicates more than an effort to forgo the description of a merely visible world; it suggests a momentary escape from virtually all the concrete realities of his life. To some extent this is the case even in the more representational mode of his first two novels, *Soldiers' Pay* (1926) and *Mosquitoes* (1927). Far more successful than most of the poems, these novels remain significantly unlocalized. Though set in the South, they largely relegate their characters and events into counters for some undefinable essence of postwar anguish, in *Soldiers' Pay*, or, in *Mosquitoes*, the foundations of Art.

Despite what may appear now to be a false start, Faulkner's apprenticeship to a symbolist tradition points toward a crucial feature of the later novels, namely, their willingness to challenge the solidity of that Southern context they so richly document. This challenge exists not only in the dramatization of particular characters such as Quentin Compson or Darl Bundren, desperate to suspend a "state of mind . . . symmetrical above the flesh," to loosen the word entirely from the deed; but in the more profound effort of whole texts to explore the vulnerability of both fact and time. It is the attempt to expose at the heart of the world an openness—what Stéphane Mallarmé called "the musicality of nothing"—that for the modernist confounds all language yet frees it to find again the truth it seeks. Like Yeats and Eliot, Conrad, Joyce, and Stein before him, Faulkner was in fact moving toward that fusion of symbolism and realism that Edmund Wilson early identified as central to modern literature: a literature grounded in a dense, palpable scene and language, yet striving to invent within those limits new dimensions of meaning.

Faulkner could begin to establish an original version of this fusion only when he turned to what Sherwood Anderson had referred to as "that little patch up there in Mississippi where you started from," a world deep and intricately textured, within (and against) which he could carry out the unique testings and expansions of his major fiction. Probably in late 1926, with the unfinished draft of *Father Abraham*, and then in 1927 with *Flags in the Dust*, which was first published in a much-edited version as *Sartoris* (1929), Faulkner began putting together the Yoknapatawpha world that would prove commensurate to his concerns and talent. Almost at once, he seized the essential features—topographical, generic, and thematic—that would define his fictional account of that world for more than a decade.

The focus of *Flags in the Dust* (original version published 1973) is the aristocratic Sartoris family, dominated by its now deceased founder whose flamboyant life (loosely modeled on W. C. Falkner's) remains the most commanding presence in the lives of his descendants. The mode of the novel vacillates between melodrama and aspirations to tragedy, as befitting its subject of a noble but doomed House; and its dominant theme and action is the need of successor generations to remember the past, in story and self-mocking deed. The town of Jefferson and its surroundings is primarily background to the narrative of family fatality and glory.

Father Abraham (published 1983) opens with the figure of Flem Snopes, but its real focus is not the pressures of descent but a place, Frenchman's Bend, and the loosely organized community that inhabits it. Comprising independent farmers, tenants, and sharecroppers, without aristocratic pretension to anything that might be called a heritage or a destiny, the people of Frenchman's Bend are far less bound and far less driven than are the illustrious families of Jefferson. Their memories are not compulsive but strategic. They recall the nameless founder whose alleged nationality has given the hamlet its name only for the house they can plunder for firewood and the treasure rumored to be buried in his now overgrown gardens. Thus the appropriate mode of their fiction is comedy: the broad, sometimes grotesque, yet often restorative humor of people who have learned to forget the history they cannot use. The theme is survival in a limited but unhaunted present.

Flags in the Dust and *Father Abraham* are the beginnings of the two strands of fiction that divide, somewhat unevenly, the Yoknapatawpha world between them: tragic and comic versions of the presence of the past and the responses to be made to it. Barely visible in these early conceptions of the past are the outlines of the complex social stance Faulkner developed in subsequent work. In Jefferson, particularly in *Sanctuary* (1931), *Light in August* (1932), and such stories as "Dry September" (1931) and "Uncle Willy" (1935) (as well as the non-Yoknapatawpha *Pylon* [1935]), the ordinary members of the community, who lack the prestige of long lineage yet live within its aura, can avoid the aristocratic drift toward catastrophe—but they replace it with the meaner alternative of respectability. The codes of honor and courage, the respect for an old frontier individualism, give way—once the ghosts recede from consciousness—to rules of propriety and a crushing conformity. The value of tradition declines to its distorted imitation, the value of convention. As a result there is a fundamental split within Jefferson's social fabric between white and black, group and individual, the community's stated rules and its repressed hungers. The violence that inevitably ensues, claiming its nonconformist victims, is the climax of a harsh critique of the social structure, however odd its juxtaposition to the texts' lasting regard for tradition.

The people of Frenchman's Bend have fewer ghosts, their own or anyone else's, to displace with decorum. And although in 1926 Faulkner did not get too far beyond his original condescending view of poor whites and the rising red-neck, eventually in *The Hamlet* (1940) he would establish in Frenchman's Bend a different kind of community, one in which a more flexible sense of the past seemed to make possible a less repressed and, for all its wild disruptions, a more vital and unified society.

In 1927, however, concerned precisely with the problem of a present become hostage to the past, Faulkner abandoned *Father Abraham* and went on to complete *Flags in the Dust*. The chief flaw of this novel is that uncritical reminiscence marks not only its theme but also its mode of execution. Its rhetoric echoes, with too little irony, the high-sounding despair of Sartoris self-imprisonment. "[T]he dark shadow of fatality and doom" trails every Sartoris male, who, if fortunate, ends up in "That Sartoris heaven in which [he] could spend eternity dying deaths of needless and magnificent violence while spectators doomed to immortality looked eternally on." The perpetual attack on the Sartorises by Aunt Jenny Du Pre serves only to glamorize their folly; she is at once the severest critic and the high priestess of the tradition. *Flags in the Dust* thus indulges in the very nostalgia that locks Bayard Sartoris into a repetition of history. The novel is not only *about* remembering, it becomes too one-sided an example of it.

The letter from Horace Liveright in November 1927 rejecting the manuscript of *Flags in the Dust* for publication was probably the greatest professional disappointment of Faulkner's life. Having written what he considered to be a major novel, he was told that it was "diffuse and nonintegral with neither very much plot development nor character development"; "The story really doesn't get anywhere and has a thousand loose ends." Faulkner's response, he would write a few years later, was to close himself off from the demands of publishers—and perhaps even readers: "because one day it suddenly seemed as if a door had clapped silently and forever to between me and all publishers' addresses and booklists and I said to myself, Now I can write. Now I can just write." But the novel he began a few months later was also an answer to the criticism. For here was a diffuseness that *Flags* had never dreamed of, a story that scarcely began, let alone one that would "get anywhere," and "a thousand loose ends" that readers would be tying up for decades to come.

The Sound and the Fury (1929) continues and intensifies the theme of imprisonment in the past of *Flags*, but voices it as a narrative revolution: a violation of fictional inheritance. The first three sections of the novel—in which each of the Compson brothers composes a private family history around a crucial trait of their now absent sister, Caddy—are difficult enough, with their abrupt scene shifts, looping chronology, and the perversely allusive prose of interior monologue. Far more disruptive, however, is the way in which each section conflicts with the others, questioning not only the interpretations they make but even the narrative modes they employ. The novel opens with the idiot Benjy's fragmented, strikingly objective images of Caddy's innocence and compassion; followed by Quentin's self-conscious, impressionistic prose transforming into the darker dream of incest the mundane fact of Caddy's promiscuity; followed by Jason's stand-up-comic rage, masking itself as realism, at Caddy's deception. Each of these voices advances a reading of experience that contrasts with and contradicts the others. And each is made slightly irrelevant by the fourth section, where Caddy practically disappears. A conventional, easily accessible narrative, this section is told by an outside narrator, providing a balanced, unobtrusive interpretation. And yet, freed from the turmoil of Compson consciousness, it has the eerie feeling of belonging to another novel, about the decline of a different family. The effect of these jarring shifts, as well as the sentence-to-sentence involutions, is that of a text mounting an assault on clarity itself—as if coherent utterance were the enemy, the tell-tale sign of surrender to the narrative tradition; as if writing could rid itself of the past only by denying all meaning whatsoever.

Enacting this prose of forgetting, however, are minds hopelessly trapped in reminiscence. Each brother encounters the present as some form of repetition, the double of a prior event that only Benjy, in his idiocy, can actually reenter in its original presence. Jason, scoffing at Compson pretentiousness, is perfectly capable of brandishing his heritage—"I says my people owned slaves here when you all were running little shirt tail country stores"—and spends his present compulsively arranging new versions of what he regards as an ancient pattern of personal injustice. Quentin is more aware of his obsession with the past. He converts his present life into theater, in which he recaptures what he regards as an original Compson grandeur through ritualized performances of it. He is a master of aristocratic gesture—scolding an errant sister, confronting the blackguard who has deflowered her, guiding a lost child home—while all the time determinedly indifferent to whatever human meaning the gestures and mores of the past may have possessed. This is especially apparent in those violations of the tradition that Quentin conceives as strangely confirming its validity: the incest with Caddy that he can only speak, not commit; the suicide that he carries out like a man reading a prepared script, carefully writing notes and packing belongings as if the import of the deed were not death but the accomplishment of its traditional details. Quentin's acts are acts of pure performance that achieve a kind of aesthetic permanence by hollowing out their own vitality.

The last section of the novel, with Dilsey at its center, knows nothing of bondage to the past or the violations of narrative that might be used to resist it. Dilsey and the narrative keep faith with the principle of a developing history. The present extends rather than repeats the past, taking its place within an emerging pattern of redemption just as each moment in a conventional novel serves the larger interest of its story. Yet the wholeness of the section, like Dilsey's life of Christian vision and patience, cannot establish a coherence for the rest of the text or convincingly disclose the secret of Compson decline.

The paradox of *The Sound and the Fury* is that the novel's ultimate refusal of coherence is the key to its freedom. The mysteries the text preserves in its discontinuous form are the price of its escape from fictional imprisonment. The result is a conflict so extreme as to produce an almost schizoid quality. On the one hand, there is a deferral of meaning, opening the text to further retelling; on the other hand, there is the paralysis of voices inscribed at the outset by their inheritance. The power of the novel depends upon this extraordinary tension of pure creative act bound to the highly localized imagery of a Southern family that remains trapped within its past.

Embedded in the tension is the dilemma not only of Faulkner's work but of literary modernism generally: how to confront the past without compromising the individual voice—or, put another way, how to free oneself from the language, the tradition, the experience of the given world without cutting oneself off from the hope of shared meaning. How to find proper words: to compose the text that disrupts the received order yet ends in the achievement of a durable but not static design.

All of the texts that follow the great breakthrough of *The Sound and the Fury* imply its dislocations and conflicts, yet their hope is to move beyond them. Having depicted the equal futility of an endless chaos of deferred meaning and a complacent acceptance of predetermined order, Faulkner began working toward the possibility of a creative relation with the past, one that would confirm the fact of derivation while—from the present—reopening its unrealized possibilities. The attempt is comparable to the efforts of such writers as Kierkegaard, Heidegger, and Freud to distinguish between a historical sense that duplicates a completed past and one that reexperiences the past, recovering from it or projecting onto it meanings that have been first realized only in the present.

A few months after reading proof for *The Sound and the Fury* Faulkner turned again to the situation of a deteriorating family, in *As I Lay Dying* (1930). With its major figure of unity dead and its remaining members in disarray, the Bundren family stands on the verge of spinning off into a series of alienated voices. This time, however, Faulkner locates the family in Frenchman's Bend, the place of humor in Yoknapatawpha, where all authority, present and past, is susceptible to reformulation. The result is a comic novel of the past revised. Even as they acknowledge the authority of the past, the Bundrens aggressively rewrite it.

The effective past in the novel is represented in the promise that Addie Bundren has exacted from her husband, Anse, in the name of a grimly fatalistic view of life: "And when Darl was born I asked Anse to promise to take me back to Jefferson when I died, because I knew father had been right"—"that the reason for living was to get ready to stay dead a long time."

The Bundrens fulfill the letter of Addie's request but revise its spirit to meet their own needs—which include both the individual desires that isolate them from each other and the core of common purpose that enables them to complete the journey. Anse's acknowledgment of the fact that Addie is dead—"God's will be done. . . . Now I can get them teeth"—is a callous but also a resourcefully comic rejoinder to the death and the journey it demands. Linked with him are Cash, Dewey Dell, and Vardaman, each of whom in distinctive ways subverts what seems intended as a punishment for Anse into a vehicle for potentiality. They transform a procession of the dead into a quest to fulfill the desires of the living. The climax of this transformation is to replace the source of authority herself, as Anse buries Addie on one day and takes a new wife on the next. The long dying, and the suffering it has imposed, are now revealed as the unlikely language of a comically contrived prothalamion.

Darl becomes the scapegoat of the comedy because Addie's rejection of him at the time of his birth has left him without any authority either to repeat *or* revise. He can neither submit to Addie's stated will nor become part of the comic reinterpretation of its significance. He is lost to the past— always in Faulkner a dubious freedom—mentally unanchored to the limiting facts of time and space, and thus open to the madness that eventually claims him. Finally purging themselves of Darl, the Bundrens—as well as the narrative—carry out a wayward progress that completes their quests, arriving at resolutions absent from *The Sound and the Fury*. *As I Lay Dying* achieves an order, however strange, of family and text, yet it possesses the bracing quality of release, of at least partial movement out of the paralysis of time.

In *Light in August* (1932) and *Absalom, Absalom!* (1936) Faulkner deepened the drama of meaning and the encounter with the past by adding the crucial factor of race. The most powerful image of the past becomes a racial conflict whose buried history only the present can tell. *Absalom, Absalom!* is a novel about the long, agonized invention of a mulatto as the means of understanding a legacy of violence and family decline; *Light in August* is about a mulatto's invention of himself in order to explain his own suffering, a major source of which is that he can never know whether or not he *is* a mulatto. In both novels the present moment discovers or projects a blackness hidden in the personal, regional, and national inheritance, and in that discovery declares its own autonomy—and its responsibility.

Light in August revolves around Joe Christmas, whose origins are a mystery, whose name documents only the day of his abandonment at an orphanage. Christmas confronts three choices, of ascending difficulty: he can forgo his problematic past, with its hints of possible black descent, and pass as white; he can accept his society's conventional reading of that past and assume the role of a black man; or he can transform the past into a new narrative, one that resists any definition, "black" or "white," that diminishes what he ultimately affirms as his full identity. The security of clear meaning is always available to him, most notably at the hands of the white woman, Joanna Burden, who, first as his lover, then his patron, requires of him an unequivocal blackness. Always, however, Joe declines what he regards as the simplification of his being: "If I give in now, I will deny all the thirty years that I have lived to make me what I chose to be." Instead, he takes hold of the conflicting strands of his potential origins and unifies them into a single design, the meaning of which outrages the community whose very understanding of reality he has challenged: "He never acted like either a nigger or a white man. That was it. That was what made the folks so mad."

By embracing his racial ambiguity, Joe Christmas moves toward an integration of several fundamental oppositions of the Western mind: black and white, female and male, freedom and restraint, mercy and justice, the unconscious and the conscious. He becomes the embodiment of a fictional meaning that affirms its wholeness and the action of its making; he is neither black nor white but the process of both callings—just as he is a present enfolding a past without yielding to it. Locked within the totality of his inevitable destruction, Christmas nevertheless asserts his freedom by drawing out of the past meanings only potentially there, like the god-man his name forces upon us: who heals the contradiction of the divine and the human, adapts a prior narrative to his own messianic desire.

Releasing *Light in August* from its nearly unbearable tensions is Lena Grove, who mirrors Joe's tragic transformations of the past with comic ones. Like the peasants of Frenchman's Bend, Lena's great talent is to reverse the paradigm that has been given her. Although in fact the unwed mother-to-be of a narrative of desertion, she insists that she is really inside a narrative of unorthodox conjugal fidelity. By substituting Byron Bunch for Lucas Burch, the fleeing father of her child, she re-creates her cautionary tale of promiscuity and its price into a new version of the holy family and its reward—a rewriting of the ancient story that is also a rewriting of the destiny of the child as Joe Christmas has reenacted it. Lena encloses Joe Christmas's tragic story in a comic one.

Light in August, like Christmas, refuses to accept a clarity unmarked with contradiction; yet it completes the twin trajectories, Lena's and Joe's, of its meaning, forfeiting neither the freedom of its discontinuities nor the force of its denouement. The narrative of Lena, oddly fulfilling her faith that a family "ought to all be together when a chap comes," seems to emerge from that of the victim it does not touch, as if her son's "pa was . . . the one in jail, that Mr. Christmas." And the narrative of Joe Christmas, never resolved, is nonetheless fixed in the vision of those who witness the catastrophe of his death and castration: "soaring into their memories forever and ever. They are not to lose it. . . . It will be there . . . of itself alone serene, of itself alone triumphant."

Unable to complete *Absalom, Absalom!*, having already discarded two pairs of narrators, Faulkner resuscitated Quentin Compson to become the central vantage point of the story of the rise and fall of the Sutpen family. Once the classic example of paralysis, Quentin develops over the course of the novel into Faulkner's most profound and moving version of the creative encounter with history.

Absalom, Absalom! is a novel entirely of interpretation, the attempts of several characters—Miss Rosa, Mr. Compson, Quentin, and Shreve—to explain the past, the meaning of Thomas Sutpen's astonishing climb from poor white to plantation owner, and the murder of Charles Bon, his prospective son-in-law, by Sutpen's son Henry, which is the enigmatic turning point of the history. For all their passion and imaginative ingenuity, however, the various narratives expose themselves as strategies of evasion and self-justification. Thus Miss Rosa's demonic interpretation of history, with a Satanic Sutpen as its center, explains *"why God let us lose the War"* by finally recalling Sutpen's brutally candid marriage proposal to her—suggesting they have a child first, then marry if it is male. The proposal both epitomizes the human violation behind the South's defeat and constitutes an apologia for Rosa's aborted life, frozen by the insult of forty-three years ago. For Mr. Compson, disillusioned and cynical, the Sutpen story emerges as merely one further instance of a blind fatality: "a horrible and bloody mischancing of human affairs." He carefully locates in Charles Bon a cynicism that surpasses even his own, as he imagines Bon attempting to mollify Henry's dismay that Bon has an octoroon mistress (and son) by asking, "Have you forgotten that this woman, this child, are niggers? You, Henry Sutpen of Sutpen's Hundred in Mississippi?" Mr. Compson even undermines Bon's apparent sense of honor in refusing to give up the mistress, by attributing it to Bon's fatalism. Bon's every act, in other words, becomes in Mr. Compson's retelling a warrant for his own nihilism, his deep conviction that nothing really matters, or means: "perhaps that's it: they dont explain and we are not supposed to know."

That part of the narrative in which Quentin and Shreve identify Bon as the half-brother of Henry and Judith and the threat of incest as the reason why Henry kills him is equally self-indulgent and self-justifying. The story of star-crossed lovers and valiant brothers doomed to destroy each other— these are the Byronic fantasies of adolescent boys, who vicariously enjoy their own love and rebellion in the guise of historical interpretation.

What all these fictions and their creators share is the desire to confront the past without risking the commitment on which valid meaning, however conjectural, depends. Claiming a quest for truth, they resort to defensive illusion; they gain a spurious freedom for the present by refusing its responsibility for the past. For the narrators, the violence and decline they have inherited originate elsewhere, prior to their existence and beyond their control: in the father—who is the brutal agent of Miss Rosa's paralysis and the tyrant who drives brave, devoted brothers to fratricide. If the father is not the origin, then it is only because "Fate, destiny, retribution, irony— the stage manager, call him what you will," is the true master of history. Even Sutpen, who lived these events, makes himself an interpretive stranger to them. He is curious only as to his "mistake," dismissing the moral dimension necessary to understanding: "Whether it was a good or a bad design is beside the point."

By denying that responsibility for the past that can be the only means of their involvement in it, the narrators also deny meaning. Their narratives do not persuade—they do not persuade Quentin, who listens to them all—because they do not pass from fictions of evasion to fictions of engagement. They cannot explain the past because they will not perform the leap that, in Kierkegaard's phrase, will make them "contemporaneous" with it: will enable them to recover the past out of their recognition of its significance for themselves.

Quentin's life is the product of these narratives—*"I have been told too much; I have had to listen to too much, too long"*—yet he is also the interpreter who breaks free from their pattern of declined responsibility. The last conjecture, with little basis in what the novel purports to be fact, is Quentin's: the claim that Bon is part black. The source of this conjecture is never made clear. Perhaps it is gleaned from Quentin's very act of reconstructing the several tales; or from the terror he sees in Clytie's face, "who didn't tell you in the actual words . . . [but] all of a sudden you knew"; or from the meeting of imaginations in his relationship with Shreve. The effect of this final attempt at explanation is to rewrite the Sutpen story yet again, this time as the narrative of racial violation in which the white man murders his mulatto half-brother, repeating and defending the father's rejection of his mulatto son.

Quentin's revision of the Sutpen history is also the revision of his own. His death, looming from the novel's appended chronology as his necessary end, is not so much the result of his agony over his sister Caddy as the agony over the moral tragedy he has exhumed from the past. That tragedy becomes his own by means of his complicity in the racial hatred he infers. By imagining the threat of miscegenation as the only adequate cause for murder (yes, a man would kill for that, although not for incest), Quentin implicitly defends Henry's act. Moreover he repeats it in the present by turning against his own "brother" Shreve, his Canadian collaborator in interpretation. For the long penultimate chapter of the novel, during which they elaborate the brotherhood of Bon and Henry and assert the former's black origins, Quentin and Shreve have been co-narrators, at one with each other and the young men whose meaning they so urgently seek: "They were both in Carolina and the time was forty-six years ago, and it was not even four now but compounded still further, since now both of them were Henry Sutpen and both of them were Bon." At the end, however, with Shreve's northern background as echo of Bon's alleged blackness, Quentin, like Henry Sutpen, must expel the intruder from the domain, must insist on driving Shreve from these Southern matters: "You cant understand it. You would have to be born there." In the process of imagining the dread secret of the Sutpen past, Quentin has been drawn into its reiteration, as if validating his conjecture by enacting it in the present.

Quentin is the only interpreter of the story who sacrifices his innocence to his need for meaning, probing the past for self-knowledge rather than self-exoneration. He transforms himself from the paralyzed inheritor of a past to which he can add nothing, to which he can *mean* nothing, into the creator of that past, its source and namer—and the bearer of its terrible consequences. Through his interpretive leap, he joins past and present together, binding them within a narrative that has occurred in the past but whose motive has only been realized in the present. Quentin bestows a new intelligence on the history that has engendered him. He discovers what the past *does not know about itself*, what the past has been waiting for the present to remember. Like Joe Christmas before him, Quentin creates the history that culminates in his identity.

Like *Light in August, Absalom, Absalom!* completes its sequence of voices in a design that preserves the problematic darkness of its center. Bon's blackness, like Christmas's, remains the human conjecture that orders history into a signifying whole, yet reopens it into its old and abiding mystery.

The years 1929 to 1942, from *The Sound and the Fury* to *Go Down, Moses*, were a time of extraordinary literary output for Faulkner, unequaled in modern American fiction for its consistently high level of excellence and abundance. Yet the period was touched by tragedy: the death of his first child in January 1931, only a few days after her premature birth; the death of his youngest brother Dean in November 1935 as the result of a crash in a plane Faulkner had sold him. It also saw the continuation of the occasional drinking bouts, at times ending in a sanitarium, that would recur for the rest of his life. There was, moreover, a significant amount of personal and professional frustration. Faulkner's marriage to the woman who had once rejected him proved to be, on the whole, an enduring but unhappy one, characterized by disagreements over money, possibly sexual difficulties, and the basic temperamental differences of a woman who desired an active social existence and a man bent on a privacy even beyond that normally necessary to the practice of his craft. In addition, despite the remarkable literary achievement of those years, Faulkner found that he could not support himself and his family on the earnings from his novels.

His discontent with his marriage led him eventually into a series of love affairs; and the generally poor sales of his novels, although they were often reviewed with respect, led him into other forms of writing. One was the writing of screenplays, the other was short fiction. In the years 1932 to 1937 and 1942 to 1945 Faulkner spent several periods of varying length in Hollywood, working on over forty film scripts, eighteen of which were eventually produced. While generally regarded as competent, Faulkner's film work seems hardly a significant achievement in itself and, especially in 1932–37, took many months away from his novel writing when he was at the peak of his powers.

The short fiction is a more complicated matter. Faulkner sometimes disparaged his stories, resentful of the time and energy they took from his novels as well as the very fact that they could be more financially rewarding than work he regarded as superior and more suitable to his talent. And yet, while the more than one hundred stories he published are not as consistent in quality, originality, and interest as the novels, they deserve more attention than they have received, not only for their illumination of the longer fiction but as a contribution to the modern short-story form. At their best—as in "Red Leaves" (1930), "That Evening Sun" (1931), or "Barn Burning" (1939)—they combine Faulkner's novelistic methods of characters and events set in a context of prior history, of meaning accumulating through the abrupt juxtaposition of fragments, with the greater economy and intensity of the short story.

As in the novels, Faulkner often arranges his fragments around vacancies: events referred to but not described. Neither Emily Grierson's poisoning of Homer Barron in "A Rose for Emily" (1930) nor her sleeping with his remains for thirty years is actually represented by Faulkner; and in "Dry September" (1931) the details of Minnie Cooper's accusation against Will Mayes, as well as his murder, are never filled in. The stories revolve around and gain much of their power from these silences, from the repeated fact that "none of them . . . knew exactly what had happened."

Yet there is an important difference between the sustained deferral of meaning in the novels—in which the mystery of family decline or an uncertain blackness survives to keep the narrative tentative and open—and that of the stories, in which the undescribed ultimately blends into a definitive resolution: a final, realized clarity, perhaps seen as necessary to the short-story form, that spills back across each of the story's fragmented details.

Despite, however, the additional money Faulkner could earn in Hollywood or through sales to the popular magazines, by the early 1940s his financial situation had become increasingly dire, and his outlook increasingly bitter over the disparity between his achievement and both his earnings and his reputation. In 1942, for example, his royalties from Random

House came to $300; by 1944 only one of his seventeen books was in print. It was not until after 1948, following the interest generated by the publication of Malcolm Cowley's *The Portable Faulkner* (1946), and the sale of the film rights to *Intruder in the Dust* (1948) to MGM for $50,000, that Faulkner finally achieved financial security. It was also after 1948 that he began to receive wide acclaim: election to the American Academy of Arts and Letters, the Academy's Howells Medal for fiction, the Nobel Prize, two National Book Awards, a Pulitzer Prize. He saw most of his books come back into print, traveled extensively—several times as a goodwill ambassador for the State Department—and even managed to overcome his shyness and strong sense of privacy to become something of a public figure, speaking out on current issues such as integration and submitting to numerous interviews concerning his work. By the time of his death in 1962 his reputation was still rapidly climbing, to the point where perhaps the majority of readers of modern fiction were ready to concur with a judgment Faulkner had made over two decades before, while working on *The Hamlet:* "I am the best in America, by God."

Following *Absalom, Absalom!* (1936), a new phase of Faulkner's career had begun to emerge. The conflict between past and present and the possible responses to it reach a climax of consciousness within the struggle of Quentin Compson to take imaginative possession of the history that precedes him, as well as a climax of narrative form in the struggle of *Absalom, Absalom!* to organize its separate voices into the design that does not wholly silence their differences. Most of the fiction that follows *Absalom, Absalom!* manifests a new sense of time: time as a completed whole, seamless, an already achieved history within which individual mind and fictional fragment take their prepared places. This acceptance by the present of a position within an abiding structure, whose origins, progression, and end are intact, is not a surrender to the past—as with the Sartorises of *Flags in the Dust* or the Compsons of *The Sound and the Fury*—but a recognition of, and a faith in, the total history of which the past is merely the beginning. Implicit to this new understanding is the absolution of the past, transforming it into a stage of a larger, redemptive pattern. The responses of earlier texts toward a past at once overbearing and remote are now replaced by belief in a oneness of present and past that makes struggle unnecessary, exposes forgetting as a form of ignorance, and enhances remembering into an anticipation of that which is still to be fulfilled.

The sense of wholeness permeating the fiction from *The Hamlet* (1940) to *The Reivers* (1962) resides not only in a new conception of unbroken history but in a sense of homogeneous community. Portrayed formerly as repressive and intolerant, community becomes in the later fiction a far more generous context, unifying rather than dividing its inhabitants, while permitting a new freedom and vitality. This shift in Faulkner's depiction of the community coincides with his return in *The Hamlet*—inspired in part, perhaps, by the creation of the Tall Convict in *The Wild Palms* (1939)—to the yeoman farmers and tenants of Frenchman's Bend. Initially described in the 1926 fragment *Father Abraham*, these people are sensitive to family ties, yet essentially they replace the notion of identity founded on inheritance with identity as a function of the community itself. The centrality of the family in the Frenchman's Bend novel of 1930, *As I Lay Dying*, gives way in *The Hamlet* to the centrality of a social structure: a loose, expansive, yet determinate set of conventions that generates and defines virtually all human activity.

The codes of Frenchman's Bend govern everything from the swapping of horses and tales to the satisfaction of sexual desire; the highest injunctions are to defend one's honor and mind one's own business. The codes are not immune to the distortions of Flem Snopes, who subverts the spirit of trade by focusing exclusively on its material end rather than the pleasure of its performance (and anecdotal recounting); or to the supreme exaggerations of desire and honor of the love-sick idiot Ike and the murderer Mink Snopes. Yet the community, utterly helpless against Flem and forced to curb the passions of Ike and Mink, nevertheless survives as a sustaining, invigorating context. Even in defeat at the hands of Flem, it confirms its fundamental identity. The men of Frenchman's Bend are never more themselves, their horse-trading dreams, their fierce individualism—or their own tall-tale subject matter—than in their hopeless pursuit of Flem's wild ponies, which they have just purchased at auction, over the Yoknapatawpha countryside. And the community is never more intact, more the unified members of a distinct way of life, than in their awed, respectful fascination with Henry Armstid, duped by Flem into an insane quest for imaginary treasure. The communal framework, like the seasonal cycle to which it is tied, remains whole: a given order of being, not to be invented, regretted, or revised, but only to be lived out exuberantly with an intuitive awareness of its meaning and value.

By the time of *Intruder in the Dust* and the two novels, *The Town* (1957) and *The Mansion* (1959), that conclude the Snopes trilogy—which make more emphatic the strong communal identity—Faulkner could find even in Jefferson a comparably homogeneous and resilient context for individual behavior. Jefferson comes to authorize an occasional rebelliousness against its own customs, and even seduces its great exploiter, Flem Snopes, into becoming its defender. The need for "respectability" robs Flem of his earlier unbridled rapacity and compels him to drive out of Jefferson those Snopeses who still practice it.

Counterpart to the community of these novels is the sense of history that presides over *Go Down, Moses*. In many respects Faulkner's last fully realized work, *Go Down, Moses* looks back to *Absalom, Absalom!* in its concern with racial violation and the idea of present responsibility for past acts, but it puts forth a vision of history as a sequence of human affairs whose origins can be definitely known, and that culminates in a future redemption. The strife within history and the strife between the makers and the interpreters of history are both healed. The story of the McCaslins and the South appears to confirm only a pattern of inevitable evil, as each generation repeats the sins of the father and founder, Carothers McCaslin. From Ike McCaslin's perspective of a completed history, however, this pattern is only partial, for its meaning is transformed by a larger design of immanent salvation. He sees history as a narrative of deliverance, every action of which—the enslavement of the blacks, the destruction of the wilderness, the sexual exploitation of the black kinswoman—becomes one of its necessary phases. As a result, even the violations become images of their own salvation, their ultimate rescue from the very crimes they repeat.

For Ike, whose experience as a boy in the woods is the crucial background of his subsequent determination to give up the land tainted by slavery, the most accessible version of such an image is his participation in the hunt. Carried out within the context of an elaborate ceremonial, his shooting of his first buck becomes the celebration of its survival: "since the buck still and forever leaped, the shaking gunbarrels coming constantly and forever steady at last, crashing, and still out of his instant of immortality the buck sprang, forever immortal." Ike's faith is that the long, continuing exploitation of the black race contains within it the same paradoxical resolution: that freedom for the blacks is intrinsic to their oppression, that redemption for the whites is already enfolded in their violations. His forfeiture of his land—like the rituals circumscribing the hunt with "love and pity for all which lived and ran and then ceased to live"—is at once the utterly ineffectual gesture and the promise of freedom and redemption.

Ike's stance here parallels a Christian view of history, at the heart of which is the ambiguity that, as the philosopher Karl Löwith has put it, "the time is already fulfilled and yet not consummated"; "where everything is 'already' what it is 'not yet.'" The story of Ike McCaslin and much of *Go Down, Moses* resonates in that ambiguity, discovers and resolves a series of contradictions. Ike pleads against the purpose of his own relinquishment, "Yes. Binding them for a while yet, a little while yet"; the land, destined for some mystic renewal, "free of both time and space," still yields to the continuing onslaught of civilization; the black McCaslin woman, of the race that "will outlast us," is still taken and dismissed by her white McCaslin lover. These contradictions are at the core of a text that envisions a history that each moment substantiates and denies, violates and fulfills.

In the novels that follow *Go Down, Moses*, the deliberate passivity of event and narrative form that distinguishes that text becomes far more prominent. Characters are willed by their contexts into preestablished identities and actions; consciousness is not so much the creator of its reality as the witness to it. Fictional fragments no longer seem either to drive toward some secret, impervious to language, or to coalesce in structures always on the verge of collapse. Rather, they unfold as a stable, historically rooted design. To readers nurtured on the high modernism of Joyce, Eliot, and Stevens—as well as earlier Faulkner—the novels from *Intruder in the Dust* to *The Reivers* have often proved disappointing, but this is at least in part a product of inappropriate expectations. The high modernist quest for a "true present" that liberates itself from all that is past is a quest that has become irrelevant. In fact, as early as *The Hamlet* and *Go Down, Moses*, Faulkner is trying to incorporate the very contexts the modernists so radically questioned: an available history and community, some fixed order that subsumes individual character and creation.

Dismayed over the outbreak of World War II, more intensely aware of the continued oppression of blacks—and occasionally discouraged by what he recognized as a loss of power and energy in his writing—Faulkner moved away both from the modernists and from the Emersonian call for that "original relation to the universe" that sets the tone of so much of American literature. The late fiction reflects a spirit closer to that of Eliot's *Four Quartets* (1943), another text that veers sharply from an earlier vision. The *Quartets* also situates itself within a series of contexts—musical, historical, literary, religious—within which it seeks to reveal, among present moments of violence and injustice, the consoling pattern of history: "The complete consort dancing together."

Even within criteria suited to their intention, however, it seems undeniable that Faulkner's late fiction is uneven in quality, its dependence on context often declining into stylistic and moral complacency, as if mere allusion to an intact world were sufficient to summon its power. There are, of course, exceptions: the historical sweep of parts of *Requiem for a Nun* (1951), the conception and intricate patterning of *A Fable* (1954), the powerful retelling and extension of Mink Snopes's story in *The Mansion*.

In the final passages of *The Mansion* Faulkner describes the death of Mink, once the violent sharecropper murdering from ambush, now, having spent thirty-eight years in prison, the unlikely agent of the community's exorcism of Flem. After shooting Flem—who, "immobile and even detached," meets his death with the passivity characteristic of these novels—Mink himself succumbs at last, not so much to the weakness of the body as to the strength of the earth, drawing him down to the place where "wouldn't nobody even know or even care who was which any more, himself among them, equal to any, good as any, brave as any, being inextricable from, anonymous with all of them: the beautiful, the splendid, the proud and the brave, right on up to the very top itself among the shining phantoms and dreams." The passage reminds us of what is at the heart of all of Faulkner's fiction, the grand challenge to hierarchy and decorum: the sharecropper as "good as any," the writing that insists on risking all—whether embodying the dissonances between past and present or dissolving them into oneness. The single sentences rush forward in their dream of inclusiveness; each consciousness, however common, seizes its moment as the center of a vision; the local and contained—"the little patch . . . where you started from"—reaches out to encompass the world.

Donald M. Kartiganer

IV. Poetry and Criticism

The Diversity of American Poetry

The modern American poetry we are most likely to encounter—the poetry most regularly anthologized, taught, reprinted, read, and written about—is the poetry of a limited number of figures that many people now consider to be the major poets of the period, including T. S. Eliot, Ezra Pound, Wallace Stevens, and William Carlos Williams. Yet the processes by which these poets have been elevated and others marginalized or forgotten are increasingly being scrutinized and challenged. As it happens, the period of 1910 to 1945 was actually an incredibly productive and diverse one in American poetry. The purpose of this chapter is to recover some of that diversity, as well as some of the social and literary context that is often ignored when we produce literary histories that are at once more narrowly *literary* and focused on the major figures in the canon.

In the received version with which we are all familiar, and in which Robert Frost, among others, plays a major role, twentieth-century poetry took a while getting started, as though both writers and readers of the first decade spent their time in a kind of cultural and ontological limbo—waiting for modernism to begin. Attempts to correct this model of early twentieth-century poetry—in which the birth of modernist poetry is taken to be the only story worth telling—have sometimes taken the even more dangerous route of constructing a contest between an aesthetically ambitious but elitist and apolitical modernism and a tired tradition of genteel romanticism. Had these been the only alternatives in play, that version of modernism would have deserved to win the battle. But in fact they were not.

It is true, of course, that no reading of modern American poetry is complete without a sense of the traditions Eliot, Pound, Williams, and others were reacting against. The problem is that the two-part contest model creates a logical structure that *seems* complete; it is a rhetorical construct that encourages us to think it does justice to the whole range of the poetries of the period. Yet there were actually other vital poetries and other engaged audiences for poetry in this time. Recently, we have begun to recover some of the partly forgotten poetry of this period—including black poetry, poetry by women, the poetry of popular song, and the poetry of mass social movements. But much remains to be rediscovered, including the realization that the recovery of forgotten and excluded traditions must entail more than a series of adjustments or additions to the canon.

What we need to recover and to learn how to value is not only poetry we can recognize as excellent (the criteria for which are always changing and always ideological) but also poetry of significant historical interest— poetry that helped shape American history, poetry that offers alternative visions of American culture, poetry that contextualizes the major achievements of literary movements. If literary history merely serves the continuing process of evaluation and the formation of the canon, we may regularly revive forgotten poets—as we are doing now—but we will also engage in the far more risky practice of reassigning some careers to oblivion. It can be taken as axiomatic that texts that were either widely read or influential at key moments need to retain their place in our sense of literary history, whether or not we happen, at present, to judge them to be of high quality. Thus the role of the canon is unlikely to be entirely eliminated, since we will continue to make evaluative judgments, though the aesthetic assumptions the canon embodies will change as other kinds of texts are valued once again. But the canon should never be equated with literary history, and it will not represent the whole range of works we read and teach and value. Seemingly ephemeral literature that once empowered large numbers of readers, significant subcultures, or a few key writers may once again become important. In some cases, poetry traditionally excluded from modern literary history will be seen as having played a powerful role in changing American lives.

One striking case is the legendary *Little Red Song Book* published by the I.W.W. (Industrial Workers of the World), which includes some of the famous songs by Joe Hill that contain phrases that have since entered the American lexicon. It was Hill, in a famous phrase repeated in the chorus of "The Preacher and the Slave," who sardonically assured us we need not worry about social conditions on earth, since we will receive "pie in the sky" when we die. First published in 1909, but soon revised and expanded, the *Little Red Song Book* sold hundreds of thousands of copies before World

War II. If, to take another case, we canonize the poetry of Langston Hughes, which was strongly influenced by spirituals, jazz, and the blues, on what intellectual grounds do we exclude (as nonliterary) the lyrics of, say, Gertrude "Ma" Rainey or Bessie Smith? The distinction is defended by claiming that Hughes merely uses blues rhythms. But if Zora Neale Hurston is correct, Hughes sometimes appropriated passages from such sources virtually unchanged. If the challenge posed by Hughes's poetry to the canon's view of literariness is not yet widely recognized, it is because the canon presently exists as a form of liberal pluralism whose contradictory assumptions have not been confronted.

Some of the more narrowly ideological grounds of the canon are gradually becoming apparent. If we fault Carl Sandburg's studies of working-class Americans for failing to present fully realized individual human beings, we may say as much about the power that romanticism has over our sense of poetry as we do about Sandburg's project. Like that of many activist poets, Sandburg's aim was to articulate and humanize certain socially constituted subject positions, to depict types not individuals. He sought to make these types available to a popular audience—not so they could be regarded with self-congratulatory empathy but so they could be reoccupied with a newly politicized self-awareness. Critics who fault him in this endeavor may feel uncomfortable with the argument that what we are as people has as much to do with our socioeconomic status as with any unique individuality we may possess.

Finally, when literature is contextualized—both within its own broader history and within American social history as a whole—some well-known failures in modern poetry become as interesting as the established successes, and some nearly forgotten poets become genuinely exciting again. Indeed, we need to stop thinking of artistic failure as a statement only about individual tragedy or the weakness of individual character and begin to see it as culturally driven, as the result of the risks of decisions made in a network of determinations. Then Vachel Lindsay's doomed fantasy of a fully public, participatory, democratic poetry becomes as important to our sense of the culture as T. S. Eliot's virtually decisive co-option of modernism in *The Waste Land*. The dadaist and surrealist dislocations of Else von Freytag-Loringhoven (a German national who was part of the American scene for a time), never collected in a book, which ranged from miniature effects that explode Imagism's referential claims ("be drunk forever and more/ with lemon appendicitis") to long poems in an exclamatory style ("Chiselled lips harden—shellpale skin coarsens—toadblood oozes in reddish pale palms"), make the risks other poets were taking in long poems seem almost tame. The unpre-

dictable, brilliantly inventive antiromantic love songs of Mina Loy take on
a central role in defining the modernist sensibility:

> Spawn of fantasies
> Silting the appraisable
> Pig Cupid   his rosy snout
> Rooting erotic garbage
> 'Once upon a time.'

The intricately theorized provocations of Abraham Lincoln Gillespie, finally gathered into a book thirty years after his death, are a conflation of
pop culture and reflections on the nature of language; they define the outer
limits of experimental writing. These passages, from his 1928 "Textighter
Eye-Ploy or Hothouse Bromidick?," suggest that postmodernism was with
us earlier than we usually admit:

> sweettrustmisery-Eyed hurtbyherMan-Woman
> motherready-responsewarmth
> cashregisterAnnote dissemINFO . . .
> tender-regretreminiscEcho LETTUCE-crunch . . .
> The necessity of 'impressionistic' begin-the-incarceration-
> of-Grammar changes in Language-functivity may seem questionable.
> A further step, then, is to suds a Fels-Napth at the
> Express-Shirt of precipiThinking, commence-examining its
> PhraseFront for Wot's-it-matter-how-much-the-Reader-is-
> Overt Insulted bleedpleadCommunicate.

Similarly, the dadaist poems published by Walter Conrad Arensberg, the
series of poems on death written by Walter Lowenfels, and the irreverent,
self-consciously staggered lines of the final section of *Twenty-Five Poems* by
Marsden Hartley—a painter who exhibited with the Blaue Reiter in Berlin
in 1913 and who experimented with fauvism and expressionism—become
as necessary to our sense of historically available verbal resources as, say,
the familiar collage effects of Ezra Pound's *Cantos*. And the anonymous or
essentially anonymous poems distributed as part of the mass social movements of the past century—from the poems distributed in rural areas by
the Populist presses of the 1890s to the poems passed out on street corners
during the strikes that convulsed major cities through the first third of the
twentieth century—become crucial to our understanding of ourselves as a
people and our understanding of the major traditions in modern poetry.

In the period at hand there is in fact an almost inconceivable variety of
poetry at work in the culture. A kaleidoscopic passage across book titles
and manifestos gives some sense of the range of poetries in the period. By
1910, Carl Sandburg, Ezra Pound, Vachel Lindsay, and William Carlos
Williams had published their first (though not yet characteristic) books. Ed-

win Arlington Robinson was entering the final phase of his immensely productive career. Within a few years, several of the central discourses of modernism were already at work. In 1912, for example, Alfred Stieglitz's *Camera Work* published reproductions of paintings by Henri Matisse and Pablo Picasso, along with essays on their work by Gertrude Stein; Stein's pieces were offered as evidence of the postimpressionist spirit in prose. Harriet Monroe's *Poetry*, founded in Chicago in 1912, printed Pound's Imagist principles in 1913. "Use no superfluous word," he warned, and, in a famous phrase, defined an image as "that which presents an intellectual and emotional complex in an instant of time." That same year Stein's highly influential experimental prose poems, *Tender Buttons*, appeared in print, and what remains the most important single art exhibit in American history opened in New York, the Armory Show (officially, the International Exhibition of Modern Art). The Armory Show introduced American poets to postimpressionism, cubism, expressionism, and futurism—with an immediate impact. *Camera Work* published Mina Loy's "Aphorisms on Futurism" the following year. "LOVE the hideous in order to find the sublime core of it," she wrote, "the Future is only dark from outside. *Leap* into it—and it EXPLODES with *Light*." Imagist poems soon began appearing in journals, and "H. D." (Hilda Doolittle), Amy Lowell, and John Gould Fletcher published Imagist collections. Lowell's work, however, soon became too diverse to be classified in any single movement. With "H. D.," even in the early poems there is too much throttled self-expression displaced onto nature, too much rhythmic invention, for her work to fit easily within Imagism's more regularly anthologized mode of pictorial detachment. "Hurl your green over us," she calls to the sea in "Dread," "cover us with your pools of fir." Imagism's pictorial mode we can represent with Charles Reznikoff's description of spring, in lines typically *not* anthologized: "The stiff lines of the twigs/ blurred by buds."

During the same time, Robert Frost published his first two books, *A Boy's Will* (1913) and *North of Boston* (1914); Vachel Lindsay issued the poems for which he is best known, *General William Booth Enters into Heaven and Other Poems* (1913) and *The Congo and Other Poems* (1914); Edgar Lee Masters published *Spoon River Anthology* (1915); and Sandburg completed his *Chicago Poems* (1916). In 1918 Sherwood Anderson published his effective Whitmanesque poems about the land, *Mid-American Chants*, a book now rarely read, in part because Anderson is classed as a writer of fiction. It is not that the works of these poets lie outside modernism but rather that modernism is constituted differently within them. Frost, for example, adopted traditional forms but resolutely used colloquial language and the subject matter of everyday life; for that he was recognized as a modernist and credited (even in *The Masses*) as having a revolutionary impact. But there are other levels at which Frost's textuality is inescapably modern; his apparently straightforward verbal surfaces begin to disintegrate under the slightest interpretive pressure and the poems become widely, if not infinitely, interpretable. Of course certain elements of Frost's poetry work against that kind of recognition. The tightly controlled forms seem to master the pervasive thematic treatment of doubt and irresolution. Often consolations are offered to us. But other forces erode these stabilities, from his affection for Dickinsonian riddles to strategic self-deflations. If some of his poems appear to affirm a stable religious faith, we realize from most of the rest of the poetry that Frost in fact does not believe, and thus that the local resolution may be disingenuous. In "The Rabbit-Hunter" the final parenthetical admission that he himself has no comprehension of death suddenly deflates the preceding stylistic and structural confidence. "In Hardwood Groves" offers natural process as something one can be confident in, but then the speaker appears to be repelled by its power over him.

Thus, within a few years, one encounters multiple versions of the compressed Imagist poem, populist poems celebrating American life, a restrained and universalizing regionalism, and poems on the bankruptcy of American culture. Soon dadaist and surrealist poems also began appearing in journals. One would shortly see Lola Ridge writing in empathy with specific immigrants in the cities (*The Ghetto and Other Poems* [1918]) and, of course, Eliot consolidating a universal ruined modern landscape in *The Waste Land* (1922). Marianne Moore's first two books, *Poems* (1921) and *Observations* (1924), were published, establishing what would prove her unending and exemplary ambivalence toward language—as she meticulously arranged its dispersal in quotations and descriptions, while paradoxically pursuing her intricately nuanced disavowals of the self.

By then, the Harlem Renaissance had begun its sudden prolific period. It was made possible, in part, by an unusual social configuration. Both during the war and after, blacks in the rural South were actively recruited by Northern industries. They moved North in large numbers, thereby infusing Harlem with Southern black culture. There were also productive, influential, and disputatious relations with Marxist and socialist politics and cultural theory, many more options for publishing (especially once the federal government ceased its World War I suppression of black magazines), some patronage by interested whites (most of which did not survive the worldwide economic collapse of the 1930s), and the kind of conjunction of opportunity and social dislocation that often generates a need to write.

Claude McKay's *Harlem Shadows* (1922) gave black anger new specificity and a much greater rhetorical range. James Weldon Johnson's anthology *The*

Book of American Poetry, with an important preface urging black poets to find new forms to express their experience, appeared the same year. Langston Hughes began publishing poetry based on blues and jazz rhythms in journals like *The Crisis* and *Opportunity*. These impulses were soon consolidated in a series of books—Countee Cullen's *Color* (1925) and *The Black Christ* (1929), Hughes's *The Weary Blues* (1926) and *Fine Clothes to the Jew* (1927), Johnson's *God's Trombones* (1927), and a number of anthologies, including Alain Locke's *The New Negro* (1925), with its classic introduction, and Cullen's *Caroling Dusk* (1927). Yet one singularly interesting body of work produced by a black poet prior to World War II did not have its full impact until the following decade—Sterling A. Brown's *Southern Road* (1932) and the twenty-some additional poems he published in journals in the 1930s. Brown's second book, rejected by publishers at the time, did not appear until his *Collected Poems* of 1980.

In Brown, many of the major strains of modernism undergo a powerful realignment. The indictment of the modern social milieu in Robinson, the regionalism and ordinary language of Frost, the empowerment of working-class lives in Sandburg, the verbal concentration and mixed forms frequent in the poetry of the 1920s, all combine in Brown's carefully nuanced dialect poems. Brown's use of dialect, drawing on but exceeding Hughes's own advance on James Weldon Johnson, is an extraordinarily compressed register for an ironic sense of cultural difference, for pride in an alternative knowledge amidst racial oppression. With their enjambed lines, their hypermetrical rhythms, and their subtle blending of humor and malice, Brown's dialect poems simply do not read like anyone else's. Moreover, Brown uses dialect very differently in different poems, sometimes limiting it to a strategic line, sometimes adjusting its rhythms and impact in poem sequences. Consider the opening lines of "Scotty Has His Say," in which Brown playfully decides to personalize the vulnerability of the class in power:

> Whuh folks, whuh folks; don' wuk muh brown too hahd!
>   'Cause Ise crazy 'bout muh woman,
>   An' ef yuh treats huh mean,
>   I gonna sprinkle goofy dus'
>   In yo' soup tureen.

During this time, Louise Bogan also published her first two books, *Body of This Death* (1923) and *Dark Summer* (1929), showing immediately a talent for poetry of elegantly compressed force. "I am the chosen no hand saves," she declares in "Cassandra," "The shrieking heaven lifted over men,/ Not the dumb earth, wherein they set their graves." Simultaneously, E. E. Cummings had started his career, combining typographic and grammatical experimentation with romantic humanism and occasional social commentary

(*Tulips and Chimneys* [1923], *&* and *XLI Poems* [both 1925]), and Wallace Stevens had started his lifelong phenomenology of discourse about the imagination in poems like "The Comedian as the Letter C," "Sunday Morning," and "Sea Surface Full of Clouds" from *Harmonium* (1923). Cummings is a particularly instructive case in modern poetry, for he demonstrates a reliance on technique alone as a way of putting sentiment at a slight (and thereby indecisive) distance, as in these lines about childhood:

> In Just-
> spring   when the world is mud-
> luscious the little
> lame balloonman
>
> whistles   far   and wee

A recognition of this unstable relation between technique and sentiment in Cummings is potentially disabling for many modern poets.

This was also the moment when Amy Lowell's short but awesomely varied and productive career came to an end with her death in 1925. A champion of free verse—with a fine sense of how to generate public awareness—Lowell also wrote poetry that was consistently distinguished by wit, intelligence, and passion. Her reputation has since been one of the real oddities of modern literary history—formed, it seems, partly by Pound's hauteur once she took control of imagism and partly by critics' continuing obsession with her physical appearance and health. A reevaluation of her career might begin with a love poem like "The Weather-Cock Points South" (1919), whose reordering of the natural world in layers around a pursuit of intimacy heralds the deep image poetry of the 1960s:

> I put your leaves aside,
> One by one:
> The stiff, broad outer leaves;
> The smaller ones,
> Pleasant to touch, veined with purple;
> The glazed inner leaves.
> One by one
> I parted you from your leaves,
> Until you stood up like a white flower.

One might then move to some of Lowell's forgotten poems on social and historical topics to get a sense of her range and dexterity. There are few subjects and few kinds of language that Lowell did not experiment with and convincingly master, from the polyphonic prose poetry of *Con Grande's Castle* (1918) to the long narrative poems of *East Wind* (1926). Nor are the results she achieves easily anticipated; one expects that her "Twenty-four

Hokku on a Modern Theme" will be consistently imagistic, but it is not. Some of the poems in the sequence have the hauntingly aphoristic quality of Sappho's fragments.

Socially and politically engaged poetry continued to diversify and to be intensely debated through the 1920s and 1930s—most notably in journals like *The Masses, Liberator, The New Masses, Dynamo, The Rebel Poet, The Latin Quarterly, Morada, The Anvil,* and *Partisan Review* and in books by individual poets and collections like *We Gather Strength* (1933) and the annual volumes of *Unrest* (1929–31), but in fact through much of the poetry of the period, either directly or reactively. Michael Gold wrote manifestos urging a proletarian poetry. Lola Ridge, in the title section of *Red Flag* (1927), mixed intricate, radiant imagery with revolutionary fervor: "ice-fangs bristle in the cooled-off guns." Herman Spector produced self-consciously overwritten and polemical poems with wildly contrapuntal rhythms:

> . . . the tugs, *bloot* their egregious pride,
> and the scummy waters twinkle with light . . .
> in the brief white glare of the smart arc-lamps
> strange shadowshapes loom, and threaten, and pass.
>
>   . . . .
>
> the phosphorescent worms emerge
> like vacant, jangling trolleycars . . .
> the walls are eaten with decay.
> the eliots, the ezra pounds
> play jazztunes of profound regrets . . .
> fascism yawns,
>   black pit of death.

Richard Wright wrote Whitmanesque catalogues and broadsides of protest, including "I Have Seen Black Hands," "We of the Street," "I Am a Red Slogan," and "Child of the Dead and Forgotten Gods"; Kenneth Patchen mixed ordinary speech with hortatory flourishes; Kenneth Fearing began to write his frenetic, exuberant, Whitmanesque social satires:

> Foolproof baby with that memorized smile,
>   burglarproof baby, fireproof baby with that rehearsed appeal . . .
> He's with you all the way from the top of the bottle to the final alibi.
>
>   . . . .
>
> Where everything lost, needed, each forgotten thing . . .
> Gathers at last into a dynamite triumph, a rainbow peace, a thunderbolt kiss.

John Wheelwright combined Christianity with Marxism to produce a visionary poetry of politically grounded self-transformation; he also articulated perhaps the most rhetorically intricate negative apocalypse of the depression. In his "Paul and Virginia" the greed underlying industrial expansion is everywhere: "Unseen/ a hungered Octopus crawls under ground"; in "Plantation Drouth" the milieu of *The Waste Land* is rewritten for a particular landscape and a specific historical context:

It has not rained.
The fields lie powdered
under smoke and clouds.
The swamps are peopled
with smoldering cedar
reflected on black, hoarded water.
The furrow in the field
behind the negro's heels
smokes, as though the plowshare stirred
embers in the earth.

Genevieve Taggard wrote poems on most of the social and political issues of her day and often gave special attention to women's social conditions. In "Everyday Alchemy" she writes of the peace "poured by poor women/ Out of their heart's poverty, for worn men." Edna St. Vincent Millay regularly published poems on political subjects, as well as articulate, ironic, and sometimes antiromantic sonnets; Joy Davidman and Muriel Rukeyser produced strongly committed first books, *Letter to a Comrade* (1938) and *Theory of Flight* (1935), that were both published in the Yale Series of Younger Poets. Davidman's career followed one of the patterns now regularly invoked by critics aiming to marginalize the history of political poetry; she continued to publish poetry and fiction for a time but eventually turned her commitments toward Christianity. Rukeyser, however, wrote a historically and politically engaged poetry throughout her life. Yet one finally needs to make comparisons across the whole spectrum of socially conscious poetry, including work by poets whose efforts were mostly in other registers. Charles Henri Ford, for example, edited *Blues* and *View* and is often identified with surrealism; one poem ends with "BABY WITH REVOLVER HOLDS HURRICANE AT BAY." But he also wrote "Plaint," in which a black man speaks before a lynch mob in Kentucky:

Now I climb death's tree.

The pruninghooks of many mouths
Cut the black-leaved boughs.
The robins of my eyes hover where
Sixteen leaves fall that were a prayer.

Even Wallace Stevens in *Owl's Clover* (1936) tried to negotiate between the claims of the imagination and those of politics. And a conservative counterreaction took form amongst Southern poets publishing in *The Fugitive* (1922–25), including Donald Davidson, Allen Tate, John Crowe Ransom, and the young Robert Penn Warren. Some effort has been made since to universalize Tate's poetry, to detach it from its social context and treat it as emblematic of a universal modern wasteland. In fact, Southern despair of the time has its roots in a very specific sense of history that deserves to be preserved and credited. To gain a stronger grasp on Southern feelings of historical defeat, alienation from the nation, and connectedness to the past, one might read, say, Tate's famous "Ode to the Confederate Dead"—"The headstones yield their names to the element,/ The wind whirrs without recollection"—alongside Davidson's "Lee in the Mountains": "The hurt of all that was and cannot be . . . What I do now is only a son's devoir/ To a lost father."

The problems in Ransom's poetry are perhaps somewhat greater, for he does try to generalize on the basis of very specific cultural allegiances. Thus not all contemporary readers will consider Ransom's struggle to reconcile honor and passion, in "The Equilibrists," to be a timeless and universal problem. Ransom is generally credited with being preoccupied with dignified problems like mutability and the inevitability of death. More prosaically, his difficulty was clearly with women, for they consistently represent for him the transitoriness of physical beauty and the horror of spiritual emptiness. Sexual difference is the opposition that underlies the pervasive binarism in his work. The first two sections of his 1974 *Selected Poems* are titled "The Innocent Doves" and "The Manliness of Men." No attribution of ironic implications, in the end, can explain away poems like "The Cloak Model." There a young man is described (by an older speaker) as imagining a woman's "broad brow meant intelligence," that "her fresh young skin was innocence,/ Instead of meat that shone." The older man draws his attention to "God's oldest joke, forever fresh;/ The fact that in the finest flesh/ There isn't any soul." Yet the very inescapability of Ransom's obsessions in turn can help us focus generally on the politics of sexual difference in modern poetry, a politics that rearranges all the received schools and movements of American literature.

The range of poetry marked as "political" in this period was so diverse that the nature of the "political" is itself continually being extended and called into question. Especially in the 1920s and 1930s there simply is no obvious boundary to political subject matter—it ranges from responses to sexual difference to responses to fascism. In the social environment of the time, even the avoidance of the political was itself constitutive of poetry.

Meanwhile, radically experimental forms proliferated, sometimes consciously politicized, sometimes not. In 1929, Bob Brown published *1450–*

1950, his whimsical, instinctively deconstructive picture poems in holograph. The categories of high art, seriousness, representation, and literariness were all at risk in his project. Hart Crane's major work, *The Bridge*, a poem sequence welding a sometimes exquisitely idiosyncratic diction ("The basalt surface drags a jungle grace/ Ochreous and lynx-barred") and references to popular culture ("singing low *My Old Kentucky Home* and *Casey Jones*") with the broadest, mythic cultural ambitions, appeared in 1930. Aiming to counter Eliot's impact by writing a long, visionary, and affirmative poem about the modern world, Crane adopted the Brooklyn Bridge as symbol of transcendence:

> Through the bound cable strands, the arching path
> Upward, veering with light, the flight of strings,—
> Taut miles of shuttling moonlight syncopate
> The whispered rush, telepathy of wires.

Overtly Whitmanesque, the poem also displayed Crane's adaptations of French symbolism and cubism.

At the same time, Eugene Jolas edited *transition* (1927–38) and published manifestos, sound poems, and surrealist experiments, as in these opening lines from "Firedeath":

> crackleflame and the circle the snapop and the
> implosion the volleybang the whirtatoo in the sandring
> the man stood up and yawned his cheeks roseflickering
> his hands drumrapping the atlas and
> his hair began to simounflash it bonfired Africa red
> blazesheaves sweltered.

A series of Harry Crosby's ecstatic, obsessional, sometimes misogynist books were published posthumously in 1931. They include Whitmanesque chants and tirades as well as concrete poems. Crosby was driven to record all the changes he could ring on images of the sun: "1) Take the word Sun which burns permanently in my brain. It has accuracy and alacrity. It is monomaniac in its intensity. It is a continual flash of insight. It is the marriage of Invulnerability with Yes, of the Red Wolf with the Gold Bumblebee, of Madness with Ra. 2) Birdileaves, Goldabbits, Fingertoes, Auroramor, Barbarifire, Parabolaw, Lovegown, Nombrilomane." That same year Louis Zukofsky edited a special Objectivist issue of *Poetry* and in 1932 *An "Objectivists" Anthology* was published, thereby creating a new movement whose members had relatively little in common stylistically. Zukofsky began to publish portions of his major poem sequence, *"A"* (1979), a hermetic, musically counterpointed poem that juxtaposes autobiographical and historical references. Sometimes attacked at the time for being apolitical, "*A*"—we are only now beginning to understand—represents a specifically linguistic historical and political intervention. Other poets associated with Objectivism include George Oppen and Lorine Niedecker, both notable for their exquisite craft. Throughout this period, Pound continued to publish additions to *The Cantos*; Stevens published his next two books, *Ideas of Order* (1935) and *The Man with the Blue Guitar* (1937); Cummings, Williams, and Laura Riding issued collected poems in 1938. Eliot published *Four Quartets* in 1943, and "H. D." began her ambitious mythic narratives with *The Walls Do Not Fall* (1944) and *Tribute to the Angels* (1945).

Riding deserves special mention because her work is in some ways quite anomalous in modern poetry. The extraordinarily self-conscious pressure she places on language would seem to align her with the whole strain of modernism devoted to unstable linguistic experimentation. Yet her declared aim was to control and limit her poetry's meaning to a degree perhaps no other poet believed possible. "We must learn better," she writes in "The Why of the Wind," "what we are and what we are not." Poetry, she felt, could help us divest ourselves of sensory distractions and historical contingency and lead us to the deepest, universal human truths. Finding that her readers would not cooperate in reading her work the way she intended and that she herself could not wholly bend poetry to her will, she stopped writing it. Much of her poetry requires a knowledge of her theoretical work if one is to credit her intentions. Other poems, however, draw on issues in the air at the time and are more accessible. In "The Tiger" she warns that she is not at all the kind of woman patriarchal society would have her be:

Earlier than lust, not plain,
Behind a darkened face of memory,
My inner animal revives.
Beware, that I am tame.
Beware philosophies
Wherein I yield.

Finally, in the 1940s a new generation began publishing their first books. Margaret Walker's *For My People*, the 1942 volume in the Yale Series of Younger Poets, is worth special note. Composed of three sections in very different styles, it suggests, more than many other mixed collections, how a plural textuality can articulate the fragmented, conflicted subcultures of our society. In the first section, incantatory poems build on a historically imposed schizophrenia—alternating between enraptured affirmation and the weight of social oppression. The second section uses jazz and ballad rhythms as well as dialect to give folk heroes, workers, and outcasts opportunities for violent self-assertion. And the third section tries, problematically, as Claude McKay had twenty years earlier, to adapt the sonnet for a poetry of social conscience. Finally, by 1946 Theodore Roethke, Robert Hayden, John Berryman, Robert Lowell, Gwendolyn Brooks, Elizabeth Bishop, and Denise Levertov had published their first books.

In any anthology adequately representing this diversity, modernism would emerge, not as a single coherent development, but as a shifting mixture of alliances and rejections, innovations and counterreactions, with new poets frequently discovering what had already been anticipated in the careers of others. Indeed, modernism remains a contested terrain. If, for example, we consider two key (but by no means universal) elements of the modernist revolution—first, the shift to an emphasis on either the self-referentiality of poetic language or the overall coherence of language as the preeminent cultural system; and second, the increasing doubt about either the possibilty or the political wisdom of identifying a single, unified speaking subject as the voice of a poem—then it is, at least arguably, clear that the major poet of modernism is Gertrude Stein, most of whose poetry was published posthumously (*Bee Time Vine and Other Pieces* [1953] and *Stanzas in Meditation and Other Poems* [1956]) and none of whose poetry was included in the hefty 1973 *Norton Anthology of Modern Poetry*.

For all the critical effort devoted to debating the relative radicalism of the poetry of the other dominant modernists, no poetry more than Stein's— neither Eliot's nor Pound's—so thoroughly overturns language's representational claims while exploring its signifying power. Stein's career constituted a lifelong project in cultural semiotics, in its totality quite impossible to naturalize and domesticate in the way that much of the rest of modernism has been. Indeed, because her long poems depend on incremental repetition and variation, they are almost impossible to quote effectively or edit for anthologies. Her work is generically undecidable: sometimes feminist and sometimes lesbian, it remains wholly unassignable to a humanizing persona, and it remains more purely and powerfully devoted to an exploration of how language works than that of any other poet of the period. By 1914, her work had anticipated not only most of the linguistically experimental strain of modernism but much of postmodernism as well. These are perhaps at once the reasons why she deserves to be and the reasons why she is not yet considered to be a central figure in modernist poetry.

Stein, of course, is representative of only some of the key elements of the modernist revolution. But her work, like that of so many of the poets of the period, simultaneously synthesizes multiple existing tendencies and provokes others. Masterpieces like *Lifting Belly* (1915–17) and *Patriarchal*

Poetry (1927) can be grouped with feminist poetry, with the most radical linguistic innovation, with the effort to introduce ordinary speech rhythms into poetry, or with movements like dadaism. Such taxonomies are inevitable and necessary, but we risk serious distortion if we refuse to entertain multiple classifications for individual poets and even single texts.

By grouping the poets of the Harlem Renaissance of the 1920s together, despite their differences, we are able to emphasize their vital expression of black pride and recognize its independent and oppositional cultural force. But in the process we suppress certain other important aesthetic connections and political alliances that informed their work, both directly and indirectly. Grouping black poets and regional poets separately, for example, can blind us to the political significance of dialect poetry and help make it seem merely quaint and harmless; alternatively, we can see it as a continuing tradition of resistance to the dominant metropolitan culture. A taxonomy of mutually exclusive categories will also consistently falsify the history of aesthetic innovation. Jean Toomer's *Cane* (1923), with its mixture of poetry, prose poetry, fiction, and dramatic dialogue, is one of the triumphs of modernist mixed forms and should be discussed with William Carlos Williams's *Spring and All*, which appeared the same year. But one could also highlight the imagist element in *Cane*, or discuss its jazz rhythms, its cubist dislocations, its use of ordinary language. Because of his deeply troubled relation to his own racial identity, Toomer himself came to resent being classed as a black poet.

Other poets have specifically rejected the categories we habitually use to arrange literary history. Laura Riding, for example, objects to being viewed within experimental modernism. Langston Hughes, perhaps the most versatile political poet of the period, made a number of efforts to link the oppression of blacks with poverty and discrimination throughout American society. One might want to see him within the whole long populist tradition in American writing. Not to link Hughes with other socially conscious poets amounts to maintaining, by way of the discourse of literary history, the same racial and cultural divisions and antagonisms (some of which Hughes himself expressed in *Fine Clothes to the Jew* [1927]) that the capitalist class in America promoted to prevent the working class from organizing effectively. Writing and teaching literary history that way is not a neutral activity; it reinforces (and treats as transhistorical, even natural) some of the worst features of American society.

The first step toward reconstituting the history of the poetry of the period is to draw as close as possible to the actual publications of the period—the periodicals that poets published in, the individual books in which their works (in some cases) were collected. As objects, individual books provide a stronger sense of intervention in the culture and of the development of a poet's career. Collected works are often valuable—"H.D." 's *Collected Poems 1912–1944* (1983), for example, contains a substantial amount of unpublished work—but in some ways they are deceptive. From Robinson to Sandburg to Stevens to Millay to Moore, volumes of collected poems are not complete; uncollected poems often define the outer edges of a poet's enterprise—directions a poet pursued and then rejected. Lowell's collected poems omit her important prefaces to individual volumes that explain her aesthetic aims and provide historical contexts for the poems. In other cases, no collected poems were published. Langston Hughes's *Selected Poems* (1959), to cite an extreme case, is both incomplete and misleading, in part because it is arranged thematically rather than chronologically, but primarily because it was assembled after a convulsively reactionary period of American history and excludes most of his more radical poems. Some of these poems were never even gathered in his books and pamphlets; they remain in the journals of the time. Until *The Last Lunar Baedeker* (1982), editions of Mina Loy's selected poems essentially obliterated her long, uncollected poem sequence, "Anglo-Mongrels and the Rose," a remarkable synthesis of personal and public myth, which for years lay scattered, like others of her poems, in journals like *Others, Contact, Broom*, and *Rogue*. Loy's collected poems, however, regrettably normalize her spacing and punctuation.

For other reasons as well, it is essential to follow the journals of the period, ranging from *Fire!* (1926), which published only one issue—its revolutionary cultural criticism staged with art deco elegance—to *Hound and Horn* (1927–34), whose commitments varied from Southern regionalism to humanism to Marxism. In the highly interactive culture they helped to create, little magazines defined their enterprises not only in manifestos but also in commenting on one another. Especially in the 1920s and 1930s, running from *The Modern Quarterly* and *Hound and Horn* through *Blues, The Rebel Poet, Contact, Fantasy, Partisan Review*, and *Monthly Review*, magazines praised each other's accomplishments and critiqued each other's weaknesses. Even *International Literature*, published in Moscow but with assistance from American writers (and distributed here in an English-language edition), covered American little magazines in great detail; like *The Liberator* and *Kosmos* it also published an extensive letters column that fostered further interaction and debate.

By reading these journals we can also begin to grasp the strategic, dialectical, and exclusionary relations among poetry and other discourses of an era. It is actually quite impossible to recognize the discursive terrain poetry occupied—the social, political, and aesthetic functions that it served—if one reads only anthologies and books of poems. Charlotte Perkins Gilman authored a monthly journal, *Forerunner*, where she published her own essays, editorials, serialized books, and poetry. Reading only her poetry, we miss the way she used poetry in relation to her other work—the topics she addressed there, the stances she took, the metaphors and levels of generality possible in the poetry as opposed to the prose. Similarly, to read Langston Hughes's "Christ in Alabama" in context—in the December 1931 issue of *Contempo* devoted largely to the Scottsboro case, in which eight black men were sentenced to death for rapes they did not commit—is a different cultural experience from reading the poem in isolation. Hughes's poem is placed in the center of the page, under a stylized silhouette of a black man bearing three stigmata. Essays on Scottsboro by Lincoln Steffens, by a defense attorney, and by Hughes himself frame the poem. "Christ is a nigger," Hughes writes in the poem, "Mary is his mother":

Most holy bastard
Of the bleeding mouth;
Nigger Christ
On the cross of the South.

Clearly, the poem can aim for a condensed but multiple indictment—religious, humane, and mythic—that the essays cannot achieve. In one sense it says all that needs saying. But the essays in turn root the poem in an unyielding, pressing set of historical facts that cannot be transcended even by myth. Similarly, to read the new black poetry in journals like *The Crisis* and *Opportunity* is to see the poetry as part of a whole critical and transformative social project. Introducing another problem, *The Masses* (1911–17), despite its varied radical and liberal commitments, often published love poetry and descriptive poetry that was not political—in an effort to demonstrate, by way of a lyrical and universalizing humanism permissible specifically in poetry, that a radical political commitment did not preclude other kinds of human emotions. Indeed, these other human engagements might become morally more acceptable by virtue of the magazine's political prose. *The Masses* was also graphically stunning. Both its poetry and its prose gain from that powerful visual environment.

In some journals, even type face and size become important. *Blast*, edited by Wyndham Lewis in England, issued manifestos in an extraordinarily large, bold type face that lends each statement an aggressive, architectural presence. *View* mixed type faces on individual pages, making each page into a striking poster and making poems into structural elements of the page.

Such techniques alter the role language and poetry are expected to play in the culture, giving them a strongly material existence by insisting they can be part of our physical and visual environment. Many literary journals also printed photographs of paintings and sculpture, thereby invoking a general revolution in the arts and urging us to mark similarities and differences between the literary and visual avant-garde. To grasp this is not easy, however, because it runs counter to our disciplinary training. The challenge, in effect, is to read many of these journals as if they were themselves coherent mixed genres, as if they were books like *Cane* or *Spring and All* that meld and juxtapose traditional genres. Yet the counterreaction is also apparent. *The Fugitive*, for example, aimed to have almost no physical presence; anticipating the aesthetic that would dominate conservative magazines in the 1950s, its neutral typography and layout was designed to project the poetry it printed directly into the imagination. Poetry, for *The Fugitive*, was a spiritual not a material phenomenon.

If we read widely in the journals of the period, some of the competing and reinforcing styles of the time, invisible in the collected works of individual poets or the canon-reinforcing anthologies and literary histories, become apparent. In Margaret Anderson's *The Little Review* (1914–29), first edited from Chicago, the magazine celebrated for serializing James Joyce's *Ulysses*, one finds juxtapositions of what have become, for us, quite separate discourses. In 1916, for example, feminist editorials coexist with John Gould Fletcher's essays on Imagist poets and Amy Lowell's dialect poetry and Imagist prose; Emma Goldman writes from prison; Pound writes from London; Carl Sandburg publishes several poems; editorials appear on labor issues. In 1917 Pound becomes foreign editor for a year and publishes Eliot, Wyndham Lewis, Ford Madox Hueffer (later Ford); the following year, Wallace Stevens and William Carlos Williams appear, along with Marsden Hartley and Freytag-Loringhoven. During these years, at the height of modernism, the revolution in poetry seemed naturally to entail a commitment to social change; most if not all of the ferment and aesthetic innovations of the arts possessed political inflections. Within a few years, allegiances would begin to coalesce differently, and readers would have to turn to more explicitly political magazines to find a similar mix of aesthetic and social commitments. One lesson we may learn is this: that an aesthetic revolution need not necessarily be tied to radical politics. Pound and Eliot would, in time, turn more overtly toward racism and anti-Semitism; Eliot would commit himself to religion; Pound would become entangled in the greatest fascist evils of the century. But a second lesson is this: that an aesthetic revolution can be articulated to a social conscience—and, for a time, was. Furthermore, although political poetry is widely regarded as unimaginatively polemical, in fact many journals continued to publish political poetry that was experimental, rhetorically complex, and explicitly modernist.

What was operating, in the 1920s and 1930s, on the margins of the disciplinary history now fixed in our textbooks, was something that we cannot now recognize without the expectation of compromise and betrayal—an emergent alliance politics of resistance. From the most fleeting publications of the age to a celebrated journal like *The Masses*, the passion of educated liberalism, the rough outlines of social configurations that now seem beyond our reach, are apparent. In many of these journals the poetry of the feminist movement coexists with the poetry of the unemployed, the poetry of desperation on the farm, the poetry of the industrial workplace, and the poetry of black pride. Even when the feminist movement collapsed after suffrage was won, radical journals continued, through the 1920s and 1930s, to give special attention to women's issues. Although many men on the left regarded feminism as less important than the need for a general social revolution, radical journals still helped to keep feminist issues alive, empowering a number of women poets. An ability to devote special issues to women poets and black poets, while integrating their poetry into general numbers, is something we still find difficult to achieve in many domains. Yet, in the ordinary, individual literary practices of the period, such alliances were frequently reaffirmed. The *Suffragist* reprinted a poem from *The Masses*. Max Eastman, editor of *The Masses*, wrote the introduction to Claude McKay's *Harlem Shadows* (1922). The International Workers Order published Langston Hughes's *A New Song* (1938), with an introduction by Michael Gold, in a first edition of 10,000 copies.

In such examples as these, we can discover why it is not enough to seek redress for the individual disenfranchisements of the existing canon, severe and inexcusable though these may be. It is easy, but unsatisfactory, merely to search for a past that mirrors our own fractured image. For something more cohesive and broadly revolutionary was at work in the diverse conflation of the popular and the elite that characterized the left publications of the first few decades of the century.

There were precedents, of course. Through the second half of the nineteenth century, Whitman created a publicly committed and democratic poetry. During the 1890s, the rural Populist presses published hundreds of poems as part of an effort to create an alternative culture. Poets like Edwin Markham and William Vaughn Moody wrote poetry that was socially engaged and critical. Edgar Lee Masters and Carl Sandburg grew up on the edges of radical currents that clearly entered their poetry. In short, evidence of the need for cultural change had been felt even before the broad revolution in poetic style began.

Standard histories of the late nineteenth and early twentieth centuries note, quite accurately, that the era was one of enormous change—featuring a new wave of mass immigration, a shift toward consumer-oriented production, the rise of mass advertising, the spread of a communications network, the coming of the second industrial revolution, the appearance of radio, film, and the automobile. Literary historians tend to be quite comfortable with the claim that the rate and degree of cultural transformation left people baffled and troubled. But, as historians have shown, the negative consequences of rapid change were not just existential; they were material, and we need to inform our sense of the period with an understanding of that material reality.

The first decades of the twentieth century saw the age of reform come to an end. The corruption exposed in books like Upton Sinclair's *The Jungle* (1906) led to new laws. But reforms in law are not necessarily reforms enforced. The century in fact began with another in a sequence of imperialist projects, in this case the genocidal suppression of a popular rebellion in the Philippines—events protested in William Vaughn Moody's "An Ode in Time of Hesitation." At home, a similar enterprise was taking place in the West; by 1910, the U.S. Army's slaughter and suppression of the Indians of the Great Plains was largely complete. In the South, laws were in place disenfranchising black citizens. In the East and across the Midwest, farming was becoming more mechanized and a major population shift to the cities was under way, thereby concentrating people in conditions of more volatile discontent. From 1860 to 1914, New York City's population grew from 850,000 to four million people, perhaps half of whom lived in tenements, some of which were rat-infested. Hundreds of thousands of children aged ten to fifteen worked a sixty-hour week in mines and factories. In 1914, 35,000 workers were killed in industrial accidents and more than 100,000 permanently disabled. In the steel mills in Pennsylvania in 1919, an adult worked twelve-hour days six days a week in extreme heat, earning barely enough to survive. At times, wages were cut below survival level. When workers struck, police or troops suppressed them with force. That same year, in Ludlow, Colorado, the National Guard set fire to a tent city set up during a coal strike; men had been killed in strikes often enough before, but this time eleven children and two women were incinerated, provoking a public outcry. Meanwhile, in 1911 one Frederick W. Taylor proposed a division of labor in factories so that no worker would make an entire product. Production would be divided into simple tasks and workers would be inter-changeable. It seemed an ideal system for the new immigrant population, and work was rapidly commodified and dehumanized. In World War I, an economically motivated competition among the European powers, we en-counter the first full expression of the modern social formation; ten million people died on the battlefield; twenty million died of starvation and disease.

There were limited improvements during the 1920s, motivated by the realization that some sharing of the nation's wealth would promote social stability and thus ensure long-term profits. But "the jazz age" did not set everyone dancing. During the 1920s an average of 20,000 workers were killed each year in industrial accidents. The Harlem Renaissance coincided with the revival of the Ku Klux Klan, which had over four million members by 1924. There were, of course, also some important social achievements, most notably the conclusion of a century of struggle when women won the right to vote in 1920. But poverty was widespread, particularly in the South, even before the onslaught of the Great Depression of the 1930s.

When Edwin Arlington Robinson began, at the turn of the century, to write poems about the emptiness of American life, he was not, therefore, articulating a merely private sense of despair. He was inaugurating a major strain of modernism, responsive to actual social conditions, that not only diverged into a literature of protest and a literature of hopelessness but also underwent problematic totalization in the work of two very different poets. In a paradoxical consummation, Robinson's vision found both its most vis-ible exposition and its most definitive abstraction in Eliot's "The Love Song of J. Alfred Prufrock" (1915), *The Waste Land* (1922), and "The Hollow Men" (1925). But Robinson's vision also found expression in an uncompro-mising poetry of human emptiness, a poetry without underlying restorative myth or ultimate affirmation, written by Robinson Jeffers in a series of books throughout the 1920s, 1930s, and 1940s. In short, historically specific lyrics and in long, allegorical narratives, Jeffers evokes a fierce natural world that would benefit most if the earth were to be rid of all human presence. As a first step, he urged that the human mind be uncentered from itself. In solutions that are deeply radical, Jeffers both anticipates and preempts the postapocalyptic and ecological concerns of contemporary writing.

The standard explanations of the disillusionment that dominates much modern literature tend to emphasize both the loss of secure, shared religious beliefs and the loss of confidence in the power of human reason. Whatever managed to survive Nietzschean skepticism, so the argument goes, was more or less done in by the mounting influence of Darwin, Freud, and Marx, combined with the experience of World War I—the massive hypocrisy of governments and the mindless, apocalyptic slaughter of trench warfare. For many intellectuals, of course, Freud was a source of tremendous excitement, but the increasingly oppressive social fabric—dominated by the unsafe workplace and the squalid city environment—was more than disillusioning. Everyday life, admittedly, is more polymorphous and contradictory than intellectual history, but it almost certainly created many of the most intense pressures toward change that poets felt.

Why then, despite a countertradition, was poetry relatively slower than fiction and nonfictional prose in evoking the texture of everyday life? The answer, perhaps, lies in the social function of poetry—the place it occupied in the discursive formations preceding modernism. In promoting an elevated style of vague idealism, in reinforcing belief in the spiritual superiority and political irrelevance of high culture, the genteel poetry often published in the mass circulation magazines (from *American Magazine*, *The Century*, *Collier's*, and *The Saturday Evening Post* to *Harper's* and the *Atlantic*) gave a specific message to its readers—that whatever the vicissitudes of history a certain transcendent realm of atemporal values was always available to those deserving access to it. This suggests that poetry was articulated precisely in terms of the social formation—which means that a socially disengaged history of modern poetry merely repeats the ideological status that genteel poetry occupied before the modernist revolution. We err, then, in imagining that modernism wholly and permanently altered the structural place of poetry within society. Modern literary history, as practiced within the discipline of academic literary studies, often proves the contrary.

To begin to understand the modern history of an idealized view of the poetic, we need to draw a conclusion, uniquely available now, more than sixty years after *The Waste Land* first scandalized the bourgeois reading public. The history of interpretation surrounding this and other major modernist texts demonstrates that readings of modernist poetry are not only widely variable but also, in certain key respects, reversible. For many readers *The Waste Land* seemed merely a scattered dumping ground for literary allusions and images of urban dislocation and dissolution; others recognized a partly cubist collage, or a musical counterpointing of themes. In fact, readings that stress formlessness and readings that stress form both have ample textual support. We tend now to emphasize the poem's quest for a new mythic synthesis in part because the religious dimensions of Eliot's subsequent work have influenced our reading of his earlier poems. But the poem is now available to us both as a revolutionary, code-shattering text that helped to make disjunctive collage central to the modern literary sensibility and as a conservative, even reactionary, text that evokes the multiplicity of modern life only to condemn it and urge on us some reformulation of an earlier faith. If we step back from the history of readings of modern poetry, we realize that virtually every major poet has been subjected to similarly contradictory readings. At times, the debates are conducted as if such matters can be settled, as if it were simply a question of deciding the immanent, essential nature of the poems themselves. But what now seems increasingly clear is that these questions are not decidable—that once discursive practices are in circulation they become available to be rearticulated to suit the historical needs of different generations and different social groups. Having recognized that modern American poetry contains intrinsically contradictory elements, we must also recognize that we can and have put the poetry of our modernist past to very different, even contradictory, uses.

Modernism, then, has been continually reconstituted, with new movements rearticulating already existing writing practices. Thus the Fugitives, consolidated in *Fugitives: An Anthology of Verse* (1928) and in *I'll Take My Stand* (1930), a collection of essays, mixed traditional tastes in poetic form with an anti-industrial agrarianism that drew on a history of rural organizing and social advocacy but rearticulated it to positions that were largely conservative. Some of the members of this group, including Ransom, Tate, and Warren, gave the New Criticism, with its emphasis on ahistorical literary analysis, its initial impetus. In doing so, they drew on some of Eliot's critical essays and thereby reinforced a disciplinary inclination to view the isolated modernist text as a purely aesthetic object, its linguistic fragmentation purified of social influence and critique. In a remarkable reversal of the revolutionary strain in modernism, literary theory thereby covertly fused the disjunctive modernist poem with the idealized view of poetry in the genteel tradition.

Both the local and the systemic consequences of this complex rearrangement and reconsolidation of discourses often remain invisible to us. Let us take one poignant, ironic result: Ezra Pound's survival. From 1941 to 1943 Pound broadcast several hundred pages of original talks over Italian radio. The full text of these talks was not published until 1978 (*"Ezra Pound Speaking": Radio Speeches of World War II*), though a number of them had been widely available before then. Suffice it to say that these pro-fascist, vitriolic, and anti-Semitic talks—drawing on themes that had in fact begun to appear in his poetry and prose as early as 1914—are often despicable; if discourse alone can constitute treason, these texts meet most relevant criteria. Tracing the complex and multiple relations among these speeches, Pound's other political writings, and *The Cantos*, relations long suppressed by academic critics, will probably be the center of Pound scholarship for the next decade—a development that should help us to look more deeply at the general relations between poetry and power. After World War II, however, in the absence of full public disclosure of the talks, a number of poets and critics came to Pound's defense, arguing that Pound was primarily a poet and should not be brought to trial. Ironically, they relied for their persuasiveness on the still potent assumptions about poetry that dominated the genteel tradition at the turn of the century, assumptions Pound himself had worked to overthrow—that poetry is a harmless and impotent realm, unrelated to history and incapable of provoking real change.

The lesson, hidden for some time, of the diverse poetry written between 1910 and 1945 is that *none* of this is necessarily true—that poetry is not necessarily given in its essence to be apolitical or historically irrelevant. The social function of poetry has been a contested domain throughout the twentieth century, and its political meaning remains open to disputation, as any writing of its history must show. We must recognize, furthermore, that the gradual broadening of the canon that has overtaken the academy in the past two decades is an extension of that struggle—over who wrote the poetry worth remembering, over which audiences count, over what aesthetic and social criteria underlie our judgments, over what kinds of discourse and what subject matter constitute the poetic, over what kinds of competitive and mutually stimulating connections existed among different groups of poets—in short, over the social meaning and political significance not only of poetry but also of our interpretation of it. All readings of the period, including those that claim to transcend politics, necessarily enter this struggle and take stands on these issues.

Cary Nelson

Robert Frost

Robert Frost was a canny poet, given to sly self-parody and ironic implication, full of contempt for most of his contemporaries, and quite willing to mislead sentimental readers into thinking that they understood his poems. Perhaps because he received so little in the way of public attention until his late thirties, when his first two volumes of poetry (*A Boy's Will* [1913] and *North of Boston* [1914]) were finally published, he craved the spotlight ever after. This mania for attention undid him—as a poet—in the end. As William H. Pritchard notes: "The final two decades of his life were those of a man whose productions as a poet, for the first time in his career, took a position secondary to his life as a public figure, a pundit, an institution, a cultural emissary." Frost's late posturings—in the late poems as well as in his life—were detrimental to his reputation among academic critics, who preferred the more abstruse work of T. S. Eliot, Ezra Pound, and Wallace Stevens to Frost's apparently straightforward pastoral verse, which did not cry out for exegesis on the same scale.

Yet even when Frost's public and critical reputations were most desperately at odds, the most perceptive readers (many of whom were poets themselves), such as Randall Jarrell, Robert Penn Warren, Lionel Trilling, and W. H. Auden, wrote important essays that, in essence, suggested that the "real" Robert Frost—as opposed to the grandfatherly figure who read simple, moralistic poems to enthusiastic audiences across the country—was a complex, even difficult, poet of extraordinary power and lasting importance. In recent years, full-length studies by Reuben Brower, Richard Poirier, and William H. Pritchard have permanently settled the question of whether or not Frost was a "major" poet in the sense that we apply that term to, say, Eliot or W. B. Yeats. Frost was. In more than half a century of active composition, he lodged dozens of poems in the collective literary memory of this country: poems that, like all worthy poems, constitute a palimpsest of meanings, admitting a number of plausible readings. Perhaps more essentially, Frost's poetry stays in the mind, providing comfort and consolation, as well as a coherent sense of the world. As Randall Jarrell puts it in "To the Laodiceans," his famous essay on Frost: "When you know Frost's poems you know surprisingly well how the world seemed to one man." This, of course, is no small thing.

A Boy's Will, like so much of Frost, owes a great deal to the Words-worthian tradition. It was Wordsworth who insisted that a poet was no more (or less) than "a man speaking to men." With Coleridge and the other romantics, he urged poets to use the idioms of spoken English and, when possible, to rely on commonplace, even rustic, imagery. The romantics wanted to reconnect poetry to the folk tradition, to what Yeats referred to as "ballad, rann, and song." In basing his language on the speech of New England farmers, with its idiosyncratic diction and syntax, Frost was par-ticipating in one of the main trends in poetry since Wordsworth and Col-eridge published *Lyrical Ballads* in 1798.

The emphasis on poetry as spoken language had been diminished by the Victorians and Edwardians, who preferred a more inflated, even rhetorical, type of poetry that depended, for effects, on techniques such as syntactical inversion, pleonasms (as when Tennyson called grass "the herb"), and Latinate diction. Among the most popular poets in the first decade of this century, when Frost began to write, were G. K. Chesterton and Alfred Noyes, poets whose loose, rattling meters and superficially poetical diction (as in "Lo! the wind doth strip the harried trees!") owed little to the rhythms and textures of ordinary speech. The Georgian poets (Edward Marsh, W. H. Davies, Edward Thomas, Edmund Blunden, and others), who came of age in the second decade of this century, made a radical break with their immediate predecessors, favoring realistic, rural subjects and a direct, idiomatic lan-guage. Frost was in England when Edward Marsh's famous *Georgian An-thology* (published in five editions between 1912 and 1922) achieved popu-larity, and his closest friend at this time was one of that anthology's exemplary poets, Edward Thomas. Somehow, Frost was able to adopt the virtues of Georgian poetry without succumbing to the shallowness of feeling, the slightness of intellectual content, and the false simplicity associated with the Georgian school.

Frost certainly did not see himself as belonging to a school. Indeed, he enjoyed bragging about his originality. "I dropped to an everyday level of diction that even Wordsworth kept above," he boasted to a friend. In letters, essays, and public lectures he explained his self-conscious poetics, referring constantly to what he called "the sound of sense," a phrase that, as William Pritchard observes, can be read two ways, laying stress either on the word "sound" or the word "sense." The phrase sets up two poles between which meaning shuttles to highlight the poem-as-music or the poem-as-meaning. Frost believed that a good poem "says" something before it is understood (T. S. Eliot said much the same thing), writing to his friend John Bartlett that the best way to hear "the abstract sound of sense is from voices behind a door that cuts off the words." A poet, according to Frost, must learn to "get cadences by skillfully breaking the sounds of sense with all their irregularity of accent across the regular beat of the metre." This was nothing new, of course: poets have always understood that meter is an abstraction, and that one superimposes the rhythms of normal speech across the theoretical beat of the metrical pattern. Take, for instance, a passage from Milton's *Paradise Lost* (3.1–6):

Hail, holy Light, offspring of Heav'n first-born,
Or of the Eternal coeternal beam.
May I express thee unblamed? since God is light,
And never but in unapproached light
Dwelt from eternity, dwelt then in thee,
Bright effluence of bright essence increate.

If one were to scan this passage in strictly iambic terms, the first word, "hail," would not be emphasized. Nor would "dwelt" in the fifth line. One would have to distort the word "offspring" to favor the first, not the second, syllable. The word "of" would outflank "Or" in the second line. The word "thee" in the third line would be absorbed, unaccented. In fact, the abstract meter bears little relation to the spoken language. The poetry is, instead, a function of the difference between the abstract and the actual performance of the lines. Gerard Manley Hopkins labeled this common poetic ploy "sprung rhythm," as if he had discovered it. Frost invented "the sound of sense" to explain something he found himself doing that poets had always done: playing the acoustic baseline of the metrical line off the irregular melodies of idiomatic speech. Frost's real originality lay in the actual practice of verse writing, where he could accommodate the sound of sense to New England's rural speech, a dialect that had not previously been exploited in poetry.

One can find Frost's theories in action in even the earliest of his poems, such as "Storm Fear":

When the wind works against us in the dark,
And pelts with snow
The lower-chamber window on the east,
And whispers with a sort of stifled bark,
The beast,
"Come out! Come out!"—
It costs no inward struggle not to go,
Ah, no!

That lovely first line owes its force to Frost's colloquial rhythms working against the grain of the blank iambic line (in which stresses fall on "the" and "in," whereas "When" and "wind" remain unstressed). It is the blunt spondaic quality of "When the wind works," with its heavy alliteration, that attracts our ear. The line is also subtly mimetic, the rhythms and sounds suggesting the pull of the wind and the way the speaker would feel about going outside in such weather. In the seventh line, which is quintessential Frost, the colloquial use of "costs" (with its oddly and abstractly negative direct object, "no inward struggle") enchants the ear: "It costs no inward struggle not to go." There was nothing quite like this in English or American poetry before Robert Frost.

The poems of *A Boy's Will* and *North of Boston*, two of Frost's strongest books, together define his pastoral world. It was not for nothing that Robert Frost was once a high school Latin teacher: his poetry shows intimate familiarity with the pastoral tradition embodied in the poems of Theocritus, Virgil, and others. John F. Lynen defines the pastoral mode in relation to Frost in an incisive book-length essay on this subject called *The Pastoral Art of Robert Frost*. He writes: "The pastoral genre can best be defined as a particular synthesis of attitudes toward the rural world. . . . Pastoral comes to life whenever the poet is able to adopt its special point of view—whenever he casts himself in the role of the country dweller and writes about life in terms of the contrast between the rural world, with its rustic scenery and naive, humble folk, and the great outer world of the powerful, the wealthy, and the sophisticated." That is, the pastoral poet is *not* a rustic himself who writes simple poems for his country neighbors. He is a sophisticate himself who looks to the rural world for emblems, symbols, instances. He believes that the rural world is representative of human society in general, and he chooses to limit his poetic world to a specific place with a discrete number of objects for contemplation. Symbols taken from the pastoral landscape that implicitly refer to the great world beyond the rustic scene appear powerfully (and paradoxically) amplified by self-conscious limitation.

Among the subtlest poems in *A Boy's Will* is "Mowing," in every way a
typical Frost pastoral:

There was never a sound beside the wood but one,
And that was my long scythe whispering to the ground.
What was it it whispered? I knew not well myself;
Perhaps it was something about the heat of the sun,
Something, perhaps, about the lack of sound—
And that was why it whispered and did not speak.
It was no dream of the gift of idle hours,
Or easy gold at the hand of fay or elf:
Anything more than the truth would have seemed too weak
To the earnest love that laid the swale in rows,
Not without feeble-pointed spikes of flowers
(Pale orchises), and scared a bright green snake.
The fact is the sweetest dream that labor knows.
My long scythe whispered and left the hay to make.

The poem's narrator is a farmer at work with a scythe, which makes the
only sound the speaker can hear, even though (as Richard Poirier points
out) there surely must have been other sounds about: the rustle of wind in
the grass, birdsong, perhaps even a tractor in the distance. But Frost is a
thoroughly humanistic farmer, insisting that his own agency is crucial to
the process of signification, to *making meaning*. The narrator, no ordinary
farmer, meditates on the sound of his own mowing, wondering if the point
about the sound is the absence implied by the presence of the sound itself:
"Something, perhaps, about the lack of sound." He resorts, finally, to a
mundane (that is, earthly) resolution that doesn't answer the question but
puts the questioner at his ease: "Anything more than the truth would have
seemed too weak/ To the earnest love that laid the swale in rows." So far
so good. The fact of mowing (writing/speaking/thinking) needs no embel-
lishment; its actuality is not in question. The work is its own pleasure and
reward, its own meaning. Fine. But in that penultimate summary line of
almost infinite suggestiveness, Frost insists, "The fact is the sweetest dream
that labor knows." A fact is, indeed, not something tangible after all, as in
the stone that Dr. Johnson kicked to demonstrate to his friend Boswell that
matter existed. Facts are dreams, what Shakespeare called "airy nothings."
Frost has pulled the rug out from under us once again.

As with so many Frost poems, one thinks one "has it" but one doesn't.
In "Mowing," as in so many of these early pastoral poems, Frost invites the
reader into his world, saying "I shan't be gone long.—You come too." Once
into this world, however, we realize that the way out is not so simple. The
poet can only lead one to the complex image: the woodpile (in "The Wood-

Pile"), the man in the field with a pitchfork ("Putting in the Seed"), the old man in his cottage who can no longer "keep" a house ("An Old Man's Winter Night"), the edge of a dark forest ("Stopping by Woods on a Snowy Evening"). The act of interpreting this experience is left to the reader; the poet, much as the farmer in "Mowing," is content to walk away from his work and let it "make." The poet's job is not one of interpretation. He presents the image, which is drawn from a "truth" that is, of course, no more than "a dream," albeit a sweet one. Idealists such as Plato, Thomas Aquinas, or Bishop Berkeley would all, in their different ways, have applauded Frost for not allowing the concrete "fact" too much sway.

In spite of this incipient idealism, Frost thought of himself as a celebrant of earth, of "fact." Like the Georgians, he considered himself a realist, emphasizing the down-to-earth, the rueful laugh, a Yankee stoicism. *North of Boston* and *Mountain Interval* (1916) exude a philosophy of limitation, of groundedness. "Love has earth to which she clings/ With hills and circling arms about," he writes in "Bond and Free." "Earth's the right place for love," he says in "Birches," adding: "I don't know where it's likely to go better." Unlike his spiritual forebear, Ralph Waldo Emerson, Frost does not feel constrained to spiral off into some outer region. This does not mean that he rejects heavenly things, the realm of spirit; rather, his poems, as James M. Cox says, "become strongholds where imaginative leverage can powerfully be exerted—where, in other words, the earth itself seems sufficient ground on which to stand and does not have to be transformed into symbolic nature."

Frost's sense of limitations is nowhere more apparent than in the fierce little dramas of New England farm life presented in the early collections, such as "The Death of the Hired Man," "Home Burial," "The Hill Wife," and "Out, Out—." In "Home Burial," for instance, we encounter a tense family scene as a husband and wife are locked in silent battle after the death of an infant. Like black smoke, the question of who is to blame hangs in the air they breathe. The distraught wife pauses on the staircase, looking out to her baby's grave, which her husband digs too vigorously for her grief to bear. He works methodically, "Making the gravel leap and leap in air." In Frost's harsh rural world, man and nature seem inextricably bound to work out whatever Fate has ordained. In this, Frost exhibits an innate conservatism: reason is never exalted (indeed, it is ridiculed in poems like "The Bear"); people have only minimal control over what happens. Acceptance is all. "Three foggy mornings and one rainy day/ Will rot the best birch fence a man can build," says the father of the dead infant, much as the narrator at the end of "Out, Out—," having witnessed the unimaginable death of a young man in a chainsaw accident, says quite plainly: "No more to build on there." The response of his family is equally stoic, but not unfeeling: "And they, since they/ Were not the one dead, turned to their affairs."

The pastoral aspect of Frost is implicit in the above poems, too. "Out, Out—," for instance, with its specific allusion to Shakespeare, is not the work of a ploughman-poet. The title directs the reader back to Macbeth's famous soliloquy that follows upon his wife's suicide. Life for the tragic hero of Shakespeare's play comes down to nothing but "a tale/ Told by an idiot, full of sound and fury,/ Signifying nothing." Macbeth has not under-stood the meaning of death, nor that he is responsible for his wife's demise. The boy in Frost's poem, on the other hand, "sees all." He understands that in his agrarian world a boy without a hand would be dependent for his livelihood on others. He sees that his life has been radically, if accidentally, changed by the loss of a hand. Frost, like Virgil and Theocritus before him, comments on the larger world from a rural, "unsophisticated" viewpoint. But his emblems, his rural myths and dramas, radiate meaning, turning the limitations of the poem to his advantage in commenting on the human con-dition generally. One cannot help but think that Frost actually believes that the rural world is coherent, if not superior to the urban world. He appears, at least, to celebrate the doggedness of his country people, even if—as with the mad wives of "The Hill Wife" or "Home Burial"—the rural life exacts its pound of flesh.

Unlike Eliot, Pound, Yeats, or Stevens—his fellow modernist poets—Frost did not "develop" from book to book. That is, one can place a good early poem, such as "Mowing," next to a good late poem, such as "The Most of It," without finding obvious differences in approach, style, or even subject matter. It is true, overall, that Frost's work decreases in quality as the career lengthens and the poet becomes more of a public figure; one has increasingly to rummage among inferior poems to find poems of depth and power after the publication of *West-running Brook* in 1928. Nevertheless, Frost continued to produce poems equal to his best early work almost to the end. An argument could be made that several of his later poems—"The Most of It," "The Subverted Flower," "Design" (a late revision of an early poem called "In White"), "Directive," "The Silken Tent," and "Take Something Like a Star"—show, if anything, an increase in power and sub-tlety as Frost began to reckon the price he had paid for his art.

It was Lionel Trilling who first emphasized the dark side of Robert Frost at a party in New York on the occasion of the poet's eighty-fifth birthday. Trilling said: "I have to say that my Frost is not the Frost I seem to per-ceive existing in the minds of so many of his admirers. He is not the Frost who confounds the characteristically modern practice of poetry by his notable democratic simplicity of utterance: on the contrary. He is not the Frost who controverts the bitter modern astonishment of human life: the opposite is so. He is not the Frost who reassures us by his affirmation of old virtues, simplicities, pieties, and ways of feeling: anything but." Trilling goes on to compare Frost to Sophocles, "the poet people loved most . . . because he made plain to them the terrible things of human life."

Trilling drew attention to some of Frost's best work, such as "Design," "Acquainted with the Night," and "Desert Places," poems as chilling, as redolent of evil as anything Franz Kafka ever wrote. Indeed, "Design" takes the old argument—that the sheer existence of design in the universe argues for the existence of God—and turns it on its head, showing us a ghastly scene: a blighted spider killing a white moth on a bleached-out flower. "What but design of darkness to appall?" he asks, the word "appall" echoing through its Latin root, meaning to "make white." It would be nothing less than foolish to read Frost as a simple purveyor of homely truths and Yankee wisdom.

It would also be a mistake to imagine that Frost is easy to understand because he is easy to read. Even poems that focus on casual country scenes, such as "Spring Pools" or "The Road Not Taken," can be maddeningly difficult. They are certainly deceptive. The latter, one of Frost's most popular poems, is worth examining in detail.

> Two roads diverged in a yellow wood,
> And sorry I could not travel both
> And be one traveler, long I stood
> And looked down one as far as I could
> To where it bent in the undergrowth;
>
> Then took the other, as just as fair,
> And having perhaps the better claim,
> Because it was grassy and wanted wear;
> Though as for that, the passing there
> Had worn them really about the same,
>
> And both that morning equally lay
> In leaves no step had trodden black.
> Oh, I kept the first for another day!
> Yet knowing how way leads on to way,
> I doubted if I should ever come back.
>
> I shall be telling this with a sigh
> Somewhere ages and ages hence:
> Two roads diverged in a wood, and I—
> I took the one less traveled by,
> And that has made all the difference.

Usually quoted out of context, the last three lines are among the best known in modern poetry. They are commonly paraphrased as follows: "Life often presents two choices: the well-trodden path and the more rugged, unworn path, the path of individualism. Frost advises the reader to follow him, to take the unconventional route, since that—for him—made all the difference; that is, the poet's nonconformity accounts for his happiness and success." This is a crude but not uncommon summary of how many, perhaps most, readers have interpreted these lines. In public performances and interviews, Frost himself encouraged this kind of misreading. Nonetheless, one must listen to the advice of D. H. Lawrence and trust the tale, not the teller. A close look at the poem reveals that Frost's walker encounters two nearly identical paths: so he insists, repeatedly. The walker looks down one, first, then the other, *"as just as fair."* Indeed, "the passing there/ Had worn them really about the same." As if the reader hasn't gotten the message, Frost says for a third time: "And both that morning equally lay/ In leaves no step had trodden black." What, then, can we make of the final stanza? My guess is that Frost, the wily ironist, is saying something like this: "When I am old, like all old men, I shall make a myth of my life. I shall pretend, as we all do, that I took the less traveled road. But I shall be lying." Frost signals the mockingly self-inflated tone of the last stanza by repeating the word "I," which rhymes—several times—with the inflated word "sigh." Frost *wants* the reader to know that what he will be saying, that he took the road less traveled, is a fraudulent position, hence the sigh.

"The Road Not Taken," like so much in Frost, resists easy interpretation. The poet presents contradictory readings within the same poem, tempting the reader this way, then that. "Mowing," "Putting in the Seed," "Birches," "Two Look at Two," "Mending Wall," "The Grindstone," "Gathering Leaves"—each is, in its way, a poem about the process of discovery, what Richard Poirier calls "the work of knowing." The road to knowledge, in Frost's shifty poetics, is tortuous, and the outcome is never guaranteed, especially since Frost is the reader's guide and one "Who only has at heart your getting lost." That last line is from "Directive," a late poem that can be read as a roadmap to Frost's imaginary country:

Back out of all this now too much for us,
Back in a time made simple by the loss
Of detail, burned, dissolved, and broken off
Like graveyard marble sculpture in the weather,
There is a house that is no more a house
Upon a farm that is no more a farm
And in a town that is no more a town.

It seems one could never in reality approach this sacred place, lost in time, buried in language. The poet is our archaeologist and guide, unearthing the Holy Grail (the poem?), which is really nothing more than a goblet taken from a children's playhouse. Ever *homo ludens*, man-the-player, Frost plays with the rapt seriousness of a child. As with the ancient Hippocrene, the spring on Mount Helicon that fed the Muses, there is a brook on this imaginary property:

> Your destination and your destiny's
> A brook that was the water of the house,
> Cold as a spring as yet so near its source,
> Too lofty and original to rage.

One cannot help but hear in these beautiful lines Frost's churlish commentary on the poetry of his age, which he apparently took to be low and unoriginal and raging, unlike the high original calm of his own verse. Ever the didact, he is offering the world a "Directive." The poem, for him, is a means of controlling the chaos of ordinary life; it offers "a momentary stay against confusion," as he liked to say. In a time of increasing cacophony, when even the static begins to sound good, Frost's antidote is as powerful as ever. This is the essential Frost, the notoriously unreliable guide of "Directive" who—by his wit and guile—entices his reader to the secret playhouse by the brook, where he takes that unsuspecting follower by the collar and says, "Drink and be whole again beyond confusion."

Jay Parini

Ezra Pound and
T. S. Eliot

Ezra Loomis Pound was born on October 30, 1885, in the frontier mining town of Hailey, Idaho, and died in Venice on November 1, 1972. He was buried in the Protestant cemetery on the nearby island of San Michele, surrounded by the graves of other expatriates who had made Venice their spiritual home. Pound first saw Venice in 1898 while on a European tour and he returned to the city often, spending most of his last years there. His first book of poems, *A Lume Spento*, was published in Venice in 1908, and some of the most moving passages in *The Pisan Cantos*—written in 1945 while Pound was a prisoner in the U.S. Army's Disciplinary Training Center near Pisa—are formed from memories of the Venice he thought he might never see again. Recalling the Venice of 1908, Pound says: "things have ends and beginnings."

Thomas Stearns Eliot was born in St. Louis, Missouri, on September 26, 1888, and died in London on January 4, 1965. His ashes were interred as he had wished at the church of St. Michael's in the Somerset village of East Coker, the home of Eliot's ancestor who migrated to the New World in the seventeenth century. On the memorial tablet in the church are inscribed the mottoes that frame *East Coker*, the second of Eliot's *Four Quartets*, a poem about personal history and the sense of the past: "In my beginning is my end" and "In my end is my beginning."

The poetic lives of Pound and Eliot would appear to follow a classic pattern of expatriation, a return to "beginnings" that antedate the American experience. At the start of their careers they felt keenly, like Henry James before them, the "thinness" and provinciality of American culture. For a young American poet, the first years of this century were especially dispir-

iting. The generation after Walt Whitman had produced no American poet
with a distinctive voice, and the anthologies of the turn of the century are
filled with poems written in a weak style one might call "academic romanticism." Looking back on this period many years later, Eliot remembered
the irrelevance of contemporary British verse and then added: "there were
no American poets at all." If we look at the verses that Pound and Eliot
wrote at around the age of eighteen the lack of freshness is striking, although their models are quite different. Pound was, as he remarked later,
"drunk with 'Celticism,' " as in this imitation of the early William Butler
Yeats:

> I have heard a wee wind searching
> Thru still forests for me,
> I have seen a wee wind searching
>   O'er still sea.

Eliot's style is more Tennysonian, but equally derivative:

> The flowers I sent thee when the dew
>   Was trembling on the vine
> Were withered ere the wild bee flew
>   To suck the eglantine.

Both poets came to feel that an escape from these stylistic prisons could not
be accomplished unless they escaped from the American social and literary
scene.

   Those contemporaries of Pound and Eliot who chose to remain in America and create a native American modernism often spoke of the expatriates
as enemies of this enterprise who had renounced the American inheritance.
This was especially true of William Carlos Williams, who felt that the "academic" nature of Eliot's early poetry threatened to stifle a more spontaneous American form based on "the local conditions," and who compen-
sated for his own sense of isolation and belatedness by casting Eliot in the
role of a cultural traitor. In Book One of *Paterson* he "envies the men that
ran/ and could run off/ toward the peripheries—," leaving him and his companions to grapple with the task of creating a new poetic idiom out of
American speech. The contest he set up between an international style and
a native American modernism may have been necessary at the time if the
young poets were to define their aims, but from the perspective of over half
a century we can now see that Pound and Eliot were in many ways just as
"American" as Williams or Wallace Stevens, and that Williams and Stevens
were as "international" as Pound or Eliot. Pound chose Europe because he
felt it offered the cultural stimulation lacking in America, but his personal-

ity remained quintessentially American throughout his life. Even the tragic and perhaps unforgivable errors of his later years were committed in the name of America. From his early essays on American literature and society called *Patria Mia* (1912) through the autobiographical writing of *Indiscretions* (1920) to the American history cantos, Pound remained an American abroad, a man of only one country. The first section of *Patria Mia* opens with "America, my country" and ends: "If a man's work require him to live in exile, let him suffer, or enjoy, his exile gladly. But it would be about as easy for an American to become a Chinaman or a Hindoo as for him to acquire an Englishness, or a Frenchness, or a European-ness that is more than half a skin deep." Pound resembles in many ways the great nineteenth-century poets who believed they had a social as well as a literary mission. His mission was "to drive Whitman into the old world . . . and to scourge America with all the old beauty."

Eliot's "Americanness" is less obvious, but no less profound. Pound makes this argument in a 1920 exchange with Williams, where he shrewdly turns the tables by saying that Williams is the newly arrived "outsider" who is objective enough to survive the American environment, while he and Eliot are so deeply infected with the American virus ("Eliot has it perhaps worse than I have—poor devil") that they must "fight the disease day and night." While Pound remained to the end a rambunctious American abroad, Eliot assimilated British culture until he became superficially an Englishman. He chose British citizenship in 1927, and it is said that he valued the Order of Merit conferred upon him by the Crown in 1948 (the highest civilian award for a British subject) more than the Nobel Prize he received that same year—possibly because Henry James had also belonged to the Order. But Eliot knew that he was, as he once said of James, "everywhere a foreigner"; and just as he believed that only an American "can *properly* appreciate James," so no one can properly appreciate Eliot without understanding those deep attachments to the American landscape and the American past that are the imaginative sources of much of his best later work, especially *Four Quartets*.

Ezra Pound's father, Homer Loomis Pound, was the son of Thaddeus Coleman Pound, a prominent Wisconsin businessman who once served as lieutenant governor of the state. Shortly before moving to Idaho, where he was register of the U.S. Land Office, Homer Pound had married Isabel Weston of New York City. When Ezra Pound was two years old the family returned to the East Coast, and in 1889 Homer Pound was appointed assistant assayer of the U.S. Mint in Philadelphia. Ezra Pound attended local schools and in 1901 entered the University of Pennsylvania, where a year later he met William Carlos Williams, a fellow student who was to become his closest "poet friend." In 1903 Pound transferred to Hamilton College, where he studied Romance languages and began work on some of the poems later published in *A Lume Spento* (1908). While at Hamilton he read Thomas Lovell Beddoes's *Death's Jest-Book* and marked the following passage, which he would recall forty years later in *The Pisan Cantos*.

> I utter
> Shadows of words, like to an ancient ghost,
> Arisen out of hoary centuries,
> Where none can speak his language . . .

Pound's lifelong project was to translate into the modern world the speech of ancient ghosts, and it may have been at Hamilton that he first conceived the idea of a long poem "including history."

In 1905 Pound returned to the University of Pennsylvania to begin graduate work in Romance languages, and it was at this time that he met Hilda Doolittle ("H. D."), who would later join him as a member of the Imagist movement. After receiving an M.A. degree in 1906 Pound spent the summer in Europe pursuing research on the Spanish playwright Lope de Vega, but when he returned to the University of Pennsylvania he found that he was more and more at odds with the narrow tastes and philological interests of his teachers. In the summer of 1907 he abandoned graduate work and took up a teaching position at Wabash College in Crawfordsville, Indiana, where he soon began to think of himself as an "exile." The opening lines of "In Durance," written at this time, sum up his feelings:

> I am homesick after mine own kind,
> Oh I know that there are folk about me,
>> friendly faces,
> But I am homesick after mine own kind.

After a few months at Wabash his "Latin Quarter" behavior (which included befriending a stranded actress) led to his dismissal, and in early 1908 he sailed for Europe where after a summer in Venice he settled in London. A second volume of poetry, *A Quinzaine for This Yule*, was published in December 1908, and in the same month there appeared an announcement that a "Short Introductory Course on the Development of the Literature of Southern Europe" would be given in early 1909 by Ezra Pound, M.A. At last Pound felt that he had found a congenial place in which to live and write, and he soon formed a productive friendship with William Butler Yeats, "the only living man whose work has more than a most temporary interest." "Am by way of falling into the crowd that does things here," he wrote to his friend Williams. "London, deah old Lundon, is the place for poesy."

In spite of his great admiration for Yeats, Pound knew that in order to become a modern poet he would have to cast off the influence of the Yeats of the 1890s that had made so many of his early poems shadowy and diffuse. The story of his remarkable poetic development from 1908 to 1914 is one of a struggle toward clarity, precision, and a direct conversational diction, and he was delighted to discover that Yeats was also moving in that direction. But the process was not an easy one, and many of the poems in Pound's first important volume, *Personae* (1909), did not survive in *Personae: The Collected Poems* (1926). Ironically, one of these casualties is entitled "Revolt, against the Crepuscular Spirit in Modern Poetry," which fails because the attack on "twilight" poetry is made in a diction equally outmoded. In the poems Pound wrote before 1912 we find many of the ideas that inform his entire poetic career, but they are seldom expressed in language that would satisfy his post-1912 standards.

One of these ideas is that the modern poet can, from time to time, recapture the vitality of ancient myths, since the gods are still with us. "The Tree" (1908) begins "I stood still and was a tree amid the wood," and it is typical of Pound that he does not use a simile; the metamorphosis is still possible, the modern poet can experience it and make us feel it. I am sure Pound did not retain this poem as the program piece of *Personae: The Collected Poems* out of admiration for its style, but rather because it was his best early statement of a belief that would guide his entire poetic life. Related to this belief is Pound's notion of *personae*, or masks: the contemporary poet can sustain a dialogue between past and present by speaking through various personalities drawn from history or legend. A rudimentary example of this method is "Villonaud for This Yule" (1908), where Pound speaks with the voice of the fifteenth-century poet François Villon (using Villon's favorite *ballade* form), but in a manner that reflects his own contemporary situation. Furthermore, the refrain of the poem ("Wineing the ghosts of yester-year") is adapted from the refrain of Dante Gabriel Rossetti's famous nineteenth-century version of Villon's "The Ballad of Dead Ladies" ("But where are the snows of yester-year?"), thus "triangulating" the experiences of Villon, Rossetti, and Pound. This method was to culminate years later in Canto 1, where Pound retells the story of Odysseus's descent into the underworld from Book XI of the *Odyssey* in the compressed narrative form of a Renaissance Latin translator and in a style drawn from Anglo-Saxon epic verse. The historical overlays allow us to view the problems of the modern Odyssean poet from a complicated historical and literary perspective.

Pound's obsession with the literary past, his desire to revive ancient ghosts and their languages, lies at the center of both his early poetry and his early criticism; and for a time it seemed as if the "archaeological" impulse might smother his drive to "Make It New." Although in the preface to his first volume of criticism, *The Spirit of Romance* (1910), Pound had anticipated the argument of Eliot's "Tradition and the Individual Talent" (1919) with his declaration that "All ages are contemporaneous" and his call for a literary criticism that will "weigh Theocritus and Yeats with one balance," in the book itself his fresh perceptions are often obscured by the language and methods of conventional scholarship. A similar difficulty is evident in *Canzoni* (1911), which is in many ways the most remote of all Pound's volumes, partly because at the last minute he succumbed to "hyper-aesthesia or over squeamishness and cut out the rougher poems" about modern subjects. Some of the poems in *Canzoni* are brilliant imitations of past masters that form— in Pound's words—a "chronological table of emotions"; but the volume as a whole is marred by the stilted language that he would soon leave behind, partly under the influence of the novelist Ford Madox Hueffer (later Ford), who insisted that poetry should have the economy and precision of the best modern prose. When Ford read *Canzoni* he literally rolled on the floor in helpless laughter, and according to Pound this therapeutic roll "saved me at least two years, perhaps more. It sent me back to my own proper effort, namely, toward using the living tongue (with younger men after me) though none of us has found a more natural language than Ford did." Pound's motto soon became "Poetry must be *as well written as prose*," by which he meant the prose of Flaubert and Joyce. It must depart "in no way from speech save by a heightened intensity (i.e. simplicity)."

This drive toward a more contemporary speech and attitude was first evident in Pound's criticism. In 1911–12 he published a series of essays called "I Gather the Limbs of Osiris" in which he discussed the need to identify the essential "virtue" of a writer or literary period, and to translate that "virtue" into contemporary experience. The format of "I Gather the Limbs of Osiris" blends discursive commentary with poetic demonstrations, and its center of gravity is Pound's splendid rendering of the Anglo-Saxon "Seafarer," a work that although imitative of a remote style has the urgency and intensity of a contemporary poem. "Translation" for Pound is a dynamic act, a vital transaction between past and present in which both are affected. Robert Frost once remarked that "poetry is what is lost in translation." Pound believed just the opposite: he wished to discover "what part of poetry was 'indestructible,' what part could *not be lost* by translation."

As the form of "I Gather the Limbs of Osiris" demonstrates, Pound believed that criticism and poetic creativity are inseparable. In a later essay he divided criticism into five "kinds," listing them in ascending order of importance. The *first* is "Criticism by discussion," ranging from occasional reviewing to the formulation of general principles—everything we normally think of as literary criticism. This category would include Pound's thousands of reviews and essays and his vast correspondence, all of which has to be read against the background of contemporary literary needs as Pound saw them. The *second* category is "Criticism by translation," and under this heading would come not only "The Seafarer" but all of Pound's adaptations from the Chinese and the Latin languages designed to interpret one culture to another. The *third*, "Criticism by exercise in the style of a given period," reflects Pound's belief that the final test of a poet is his ability to recognize and re-create traditional styles. Pound's major poems are a museum of re-created styles, and these imitations are essential means for renewing the past and defining the present. The *fourth* kind, "Criticism via music," indicates the importance Pound attached to what he called "melopoeia," the music within words that directs their meaning. Whatever one may think of Pound's excursions into musical theory and composition (he wrote two operas), these efforts were a form of criticism. Finally, the *fifth* and highest form of critical activity is "Criticism in new composition." All of Pound's major works would fall under this heading, since everything he wrote was a form of creative criticism. This broad view of "criticism" often leads to a pedagogic or hectoring tone, and in Pound's later career the critical impulse took monstrous shapes; but it was also the source of the extraordinary unity that marks his poetic life.

Pound's talents as a poet-critic are on full display in the public and private history of the Imagist movement. *Ripostes* (1912) is a transitional volume, containing some poems that would not be out of place in *Canzoni* but others that bear the unmistakable stamp of what we now call "modernism." The conversational, direct syntax of "Portrait d'une Femme" and the lovely free cadences of "The Return" (which Yeats praised for its "organic rhythm") give *Ripostes* a distinctive voice lacking in Pound's earlier volumes, and in the appendix he announced that a new school of poets, *Les Imagistes*, had the future "in their keeping." This "school" was actually invented by Pound to publicize his new poetry and that of his friend Hilda Doolittle. When she submitted a group of her finely chiseled poems to *Poetry* magazine, which had recently named Pound "foreign correspondent," he insisted that she sign them "H. D., *Imagiste*," and two months after they appeared in the January 1913 issue of *Poetry* Pound followed with the essays "Imagisme" and "A Few Don'ts by an Imagiste" that sought to give the movement a theoretical underpinning. The slogans and rules laid out in these essays were to have a profound impact on the course of twentieth-century poetry.

1. Direct treatment of the "thing," whether subjective or objective.
2. To use absolutely no word that [does] not contribute to the presentation.
3. As regarding rhythm: to compose in sequence of the musical phrase, not in sequence of a metronome.

Imagism and its descendant Vorticism were, like most critical theories, *post facto* explanations of tendencies already well developed in practice. This is clear in Pound's two descriptions of how he came to write his famous Imagist poem "In a Station of the Metro":

The apparition of these faces in the crowd;
Petals on a wet, black bough.

The first account in June 1913 is a matter-of-fact history of how an intense visual experience was transformed into something resembling a Japanese haiku; the second and much longer account in the "Vorticism" essay of September 1914 provides an elaborate theory of the "one image poem."

Pound's interest in Imagism culminated in 1914 with the publication of his anthology *Des Imagistes*. After that the movement became "popular," a pejorative term for a poet who under Yeats's influence was rapidly developing the notion that great art belongs to a chosen few; and when the American poet Amy Lowell captured it Pound labeled the diluted form "Amygism" and turned to other causes. But Imagism had a lasting impact on his poetic language, as it did with Williams and Stevens, and also on his sense of the poet's mission. From the beginning of his career Pound had believed that the poet is the interpreter of the luminous and mystical forms that lie behind the physical world. Now this neoplatonic belief could be grounded in specific and concrete language, in the "luminous detail."

Imagism was, however, only one aspect of Pound's immensely energetic poetic life in the years 1912–15. Scanning the contents of *Lustra* (1916), one is struck by the topicality of many of Pound's subjects, his engagement—usually satiric—with contemporary social and intellectual life. Also prominent is a new interest in Chinese poetry, which was brought into focus in late 1913 when the widow of Ernest Fenollosa, the pioneering American orientalist, entrusted her husband's literary manuscripts to Pound. She had met Pound and read some of his poetry, and she must have felt that his new style was ideally suited to the works her husband had studied. In Fenollosa's analysis of the Chinese ideogram Pound found not only support for his new belief in the power of the concrete particular but a method for organizing images into larger patterns through juxtaposition. This offered the possibility of writing "a long imagiste or vorticist poem" that would exclude the transitional passages of lesser intensity usually found in the traditional long poem. Pound was impressed by the Japanese Noh plays, which are often organized around a single image "enforced by movement and music," and he began to translate Noh drama. He also began to translate Chinese poetry, using the notes Fenollosa had obtained from Japanese masters, and in 1915 collected his translations in *Cathay*. Many of the poems in *Cathay* have war, exile, and isolation as their themes, and are oblique commentaries on the Great War that threatened to destroy both the old social orders and the "new Renaissance" in the arts.

In his introduction to Pound's 1928 *Selected Poems* T. S. Eliot called Pound "the inventor of Chinese poetry for our time," a phrase which implies that every age re-creates the past through its translations and that Pound had a special affinity for the Chinese even before he mastered the rudiments of the language. When we compare a translation made by an early twentieth-century scholar, H. A. Giles, with Pound's version of the same poem (probably done before he received the Fenollosa materials), Eliot's point becomes clear.

> The sound of rustling silk is stilled,
> With dust the marble courtyard filled;
> No footfalls echo on the floor,
> Fallen leaves in heaps block up the door . . .
> For she, my pride, my lovely one, is lost,
> And I am left, in hopeless anguish tossed.
>
> ———————
>
> The rustling of the silk is discontinued,
> Dust drifts over the court-yard,
> There is no sound of foot-fall, and the leaves
> Scurry into heaps and lie still,
> And she the rejoicer of the heart is beneath them:
>
> A wet leaf that clings to the threshold.

Giles's translation is a weak poem cast in the "period" style that Pound had finally purged from his own writing; it gives no sense of the original. Pound's free version, with its direct diction, its startling but precise use of the "unpoetic" word "discontinued," and its Imagist closure, re-creates the sensibility of another culture. When we compare poems such as this with Pound's verses of five years before we get some measure of how far he had to travel in order to make himself into a modern poet.

In September 1914 "an American called Eliot" visited Pound in London, and soon after sent him a poem entitled "The Love Song of J. Alfred Prufrock." Pound immediately shot off an excited letter to Harriet Monroe, the editor of *Poetry*. "I was jolly well right about Eliot. He has sent in the best poem I have yet had or seen from an American. . . . He is the only American I know of who has made what I can call adequate preparation for writing. He has actually trained himself *and* modernized himself *on his own*. . . . It is such a comfort to meet a man and not have to tell him to wash his face, wipe his feet, and remember the date (1914) on the calendar." From 1914 until the publication in 1922 of *The Waste Land* (a work Pound called "the justification of the 'movement,' of our modern experiment, since 1900"), Eliot and Pound were essentially collaborators, and I shall treat this period as a single story. But first we must discover how Eliot "modernized himself *on his own*."

T. S. Eliot's grandfather, one of the founders of Washington University in St. Louis, moved to that city from Boston in the 1830s. He was a Unitarian minister, and the influence of Unitarianism—which has been described as Puritanism without theology—pervaded Eliot's childhood. His father was a successful local businessman with artistic tastes, his mother a cultivated woman who wrote poetry. Although the family had lived in the Midwest for over half a century, the ties with Boston and New England were strong. Summers were spent at Cape Ann, and this landscape had a lasting hold on Eliot's imagination. After schooling in St. Louis he was sent East to Milton Academy and then Harvard, where he received a B.A. degree in 1909. After a year of graduate study at Harvard in philosophy Eliot spent a year in Paris, attending Henri Bergson's lectures on philosophy and reading French poetry. In 1911 he returned to Harvard and continued graduate work in philosophy and Eastern religions. After completing course work for the Ph.D. degree he started a thesis on the philosopher F. H. Bradley that led him first to Germany and then, with the war approaching, to Merton College, Oxford, where Bradley was a Fellow.

During these formative years the event that "affected the course" of Eliot's life was not a personal crisis, although he was often under psychological stress, but his discovery in December 1908 of Arthur Symons's *The Symbolist Movement in Literature*, which led him to the works of the nineteenth-century French poets, especially Charles Baudelaire and Jules Laforgue.

From Baudelaire he learned of "the possibility of fusion between the sor-didly realistic and the phantasmagoric," of how the apparently antipoetic experiences of the modern city could be turned into materials for poetry. From Laforgue he learned to use irony to "split" the poet's personality, allowing him to be both a participant and a spectator. Symons's book had an impact on Eliot like that of a deep personal experience or a religious conversion. Within weeks he was writing poetry distinctively his own, and distinctively "modern." The little poem "Spleen," published in January 1910, could have been written by no other poet. It sets the tone for most of the poems in Eliot's first volume, *Prufrock and Other Observations* (1917), al-though Eliot chose not to reprint it.

> Sunday: this satisfied procession
> Of definite Sunday faces;
> Bonnets, silk hats, and conscious graces
> In repetition that displaces
> Your mental self-possession
> By this unwarranted digression.
>
> Evening, lights, and tea!
> Children and cats in the alley;
> Dejection unable to rally
> Against this dull conspiracy.
>
> And Life, a little bald and gray,
> Languid, fastidious, and bland,
> Waits, hat and gloves in hand,
> Punctilious of tie and suit
> (Somewhat impatient of delay)
>   On the doorstep of the Absolute.

Most of the poems in Eliot's first volume, such as "The Love Song of J. Alfred Prufrock," "Portrait of a Lady," and "La Figlia Che Piange," were written between 1909 and 1912, and are marked by freely cadenced verse that can be a vehicle for confession but is always controlled by a distancing irony. It is as if the nineteenth-century dramatic monologue had been fil-tered through the sensibility of Henry James. The opening lines of "Pru-frock" are typical:

> Let us go then, you and I,
> When the evening is spread out against the sky
> Like a patient etherised upon a table . . .

Here the third line ironically deflates our romantic expectations, and it is easy to understand what John Berryman meant when he said that with this line "modern poetry begins."

The remaining poems in *Prufrock and Other Observations* were written after Eliot came under Pound's influence, and have many affinities with the short satiric pieces in *Lustra*. The sharp impact of Imagism is clear, as in the opening couplet of "The *Boston Evening Transcript*," which imitates "In a Station of the Metro":

> The readers of the *Boston Evening Transcript*
> Sway in the wind like a field of ripe corn.

But in "Cousin Nancy" we find something more, a special use of allusion that would become one of the leading characteristics of Eliot's poetry over the next decade. The first two movements of this short poem present an ironic portrait of a liberated "new woman" whose "modern" attitudes are expressed in trivial actions; but the last three lines strike a different note.

> Upon the glazen shelves kept watch
> Matthew and Waldo, guardians of the faith,
> The army of unalterable law.

"Matthew" and "Waldo," as Cousin Nancy would fliply refer to them, are of course Matthew Arnold and Ralph Waldo Emerson, defenders of an older order now safely locked away behind glass. The change of tone comes with the last line, which has the ring of heroic poetry, and if we recognize it as also the last line of George Meredith's Miltonic sonnet, "Lucifer in Starlight," the irony of the poem is suddenly deepened, since Cousin Nancy's petty rebellion is juxtaposed with classic treatments of Lucifer's grand defiance.

Over the next few years this allusive interweaving of past and present became not only the central method in Eliot's poetry but the major theme of his literary criticism. In 1916 he completed his thesis on F. H. Bradley and it was accepted by the Harvard philosophy department, but Eliot chose to remain in England and not take the degree. Instead he turned to part-time reviewing while working in Lloyds Bank, and between 1917 and 1920 produced a remarkable body of literary criticism that was to have a profound effect on the course of twentieth-century literature. The essays collected in 1920 as *The Sacred Wood* are mainly concerned with the function of the critic and with those English writers, many from the seventeenth century, whose work Eliot found useful for the contemporary poet. Readers of this volume and its successor, *Homage to John Dryden* (1924), would think that Eliot was primarily concerned with defining the idea of "tradition" and reconstructing the literary past to accommodate those poets of Metaphysical wit and modern irony who had influenced his own work. These are exactly the critical perceptions that Eliot wished to drive home at that time, but if we survey all of his critical activity in those early years we find that he was involved with many other complex issues. The publication of *all* of Eliot's early criticism in a uniform edition would reveal a wide-ranging and often amusing poet-critic engaged as much with the contemporary scene as with the monuments of the past.

For the purpose of understanding Eliot's poetry of 1917–22 we can seize upon two themes from his most famous essay, "Tradition and the Individual Talent": the need for an "impersonal" or objective poetry in which the life of the writer is dissolved into his art; and the need to see past and present simultaneously, the two affecting each other in an endless and dynamic process where "the introduction of the new (the really new) work of art" alters the entire order of the tradition. To give a practical example, a reading of Joyce's *Ulysses* permanently changes our view of the *Odyssey* while at the same time the classical model controls our understanding of the modern work. Most of the poems collected in *Poems* (1920) are powerful expressions of what Eliot called the "historical sense" that "involves a perception, not only of the pastness of the past, but of its presence; the historical sense compels a man to write not merely with his own generation in his bones, but with a feeling that the whole of the literature of Europe from Homer and within it the whole of the literature of his own country has a simultaneous existence and composes a simultaneous order."

A few of the poems in *Poems* (1920) are written in French: these are partly a gesture toward internationalism, a rebuke of American provinciality, and partly an exercise in the language that had played a major role in shaping Eliot's sensibility. In them he is often personal and confessional, as if the foreign language could replace the screen of irony. But the volume is dominated by poems written in English and cast in tight quatrains, a form that served a double purpose for Eliot. Both Eliot and Pound believed that the poet-critic should through example criticize and redirect the course of contemporary poetry, and around 1917 the two poets decided that a new direction was needed. As Pound remembered it, "at a particular date in a particular room, two authors, neither engaged in picking the other's pocket, decided that the dilutation of *vers libre*, Amygism, Lee Masterism, general floppiness had gone too far and that some counter-current must be set going." Their remedy was to adopt the quatrain form of the nineteenth-century French poet Théophile Gautier, an "impersonal" form well suited to irony and satire that Pound would later use with great daring in *Hugh Selwyn Mauberley*.

In Eliot's quatrain poems the transaction between past and present is usually conducted through a network of allusions. "Burbank with a Bae-deker: Bleistein with a Cigar," for example, is almost entirely made up of allusions to the Venice of history and the literary tradition. In this poem and some of the others the present often seems a grotesque and mean fall-ing-off from the grandeurs of the past. The question asked in "A Cooking Egg," "Where are the eagles and the trumpets?," often demands the answer: buried beneath our modern fragmentation. But elsewhere, as in "Sweeney among the Nightingales," the transaction is more complicated, and the present modifies our view of the "heroic past":

> And sang within the bloody wood
> When Agamemnon cried aloud,
> And let their liquid siftings fall
> To stain the stiff dishonoured shroud.

Passages such as this look forward to *The Waste Land*, as does the program piece of *Poems* (1920), "Gerontion," which Eliot once thought of reprinting as a "prelude" to *The Waste Land*. In "Gerontion" the fully realized narrator of the traditional dramatic monologue has dwindled into a disembodied voice speaking of spiritual dryness and the futility of "interpretation." This poem leads directly into the surreal world of *The Waste Land*, but its nervous "discontinuous" structure also dramatizes the difficulties Eliot would have in organizing a longer poem. In order to understand the solution of these difficulties we must return to Pound's poetic life.

Two poems in *Lustra*, "Provincia Deserta" and "Near Perigord," are to-kens of Pound's continuing desire to write longer poems "including his-tory." Narrative in development, they combine autobiography with a sense that the world of the Provençal troubadours can still be re-created out of the present-day landscape. This method was employed at greater length in the original Cantos 1–3 (1917), which were later radically revised and rear-ranged, with the rendering of Odysseus's descent into the underworld moved from the third to the first canto. "Ghosts move about me/ Patched with histories" might be the motto for these early cantos, where Pound rehearses the literary and personal experiences that had shaped his art; but if the subjects of *Three Cantos* point forward to his later work, the form is discon-certingly loose and Browningesque, making the cantos look curiously old-fashioned in comparison with the poems in *Lustra*. Between 1917 and his departure from London in 1920 Pound continued to draft further cantos, but much of his energy went into *Homage to Sextus Propertius* (1919), a free "translation" of the Latin poet's elegies in which Pound uses Propertius as a persona for expressing his own growing dissatisfaction with the society around him, and into *Hugh Selwyn Mauberley* (1920), his "farewell to London." Pound would draw on the lessons he had learned in writing these poems when he virtually collaborated with Eliot in the rewriting of *The Waste Land*.

Hugh Selwyn Mauberley falls into two parts: the longer first part is a series of related short poems that brilliantly dramatizes the plight of the Odyssean artist in the modern world, and that traces the origins of the cultural attitudes that led to the Great War and its aftermath. The second part, "Mauberley 1920," is a crisp and ironic commentary on the forms and themes of the first part. The opening poems of *Hugh Selwyn Mauberley* present a world in which the aggressive side of Pound's personality, "E. P.," can no longer function as it had in the hospitable prewar London. "Mauberley 1920" develops an alternative persona, Hugh Selwyn Mauberley, who embodies Pound's fears of what he might become if he remained in England as an isolated stylist. If E. P. is a thwarted Odysseus, then Mauberley is a modern counterpart to Elpenor, Homer's man of "no fortune." At the most immediate level *Hugh Selwyn Mauberley* is, as Eliot later said, "the experience of a certain man in a certain place at a certain time," and paradoxically it is this deep engagement with the contemporary scene that gives the poem its lasting power. But *Mauberley*, like Yeats's "The Second Coming" and Eliot's "Gerontion," is also a more general expression of the historical moment, of postwar disillusionment; while on yet another plane it is a delicate reading of literary history from the Pre-Raphaelites through the poets of the 1890s to the present. All these diverse interests reinforce each other in a work where every detail of rhythm and imagery seems exactly right. *Hugh Selwyn Mauberley* is an enduring monument to all that Pound achieved during his London years.

In early 1916, after the first months of his disastrous marriage to Vivien Haigh-Wood, and with the war growing more oppressive, Eliot wrote to Conrad Aiken that he had "*lived* through material for a score of long poems in the last six months." Six years later, in *The Waste Land*, he would express his sense of personal and cultural loss in a poem that, like Joyce's *Ulysses*, became part of an age that cannot be understood without it. But before he could write such a poem Eliot had to find an appropriate form, and this was not easy with suffering so near. From this perspective we can see Eliot's strong emphasis in his criticism on "tradition," "order," and "impersonality"—and the aloof tone of the quatrain poems—as a defense against his deep feelings of disorder and anxiety. By temperament Eliot was a confessional poet in the Romantic tradition, and although his criticism often calls for classical restraint he always believed, like the Romantics, that poetry has its dark sources in the unconscious. The poet cannot determine, or even comprehend, the origins of his inspiration, and may when first writing a poem not even understand what he is saying. It is in rewriting, in the search for form, that the conscious critical mind comes into play.

These notions are brought into sharp focus when we examine the manuscript of *The Waste Land*, which was "lost" for many years but rediscovered and published in 1971. Reaching back to "The Death of St. Narcissus," a poem Eliot wrote sometime around 1914 but suppressed in proof, the false starts in the manuscript provide a record of Eliot's spiritual and psychological anguish during the early London years. In late 1921, while recuperating from a physical and nervous breakdown, Eliot began work on his long poem in earnest, piecing together some of the earlier fragments and writing new passages, sometimes in an almost trancelike state. He then turned to Pound for the kind of "editorial" help already provided with *Poems* (1920), and Pound's extensive cutting and revising earned him the poem's dedication as *il miglior fabbro*, "the better craftsman." It is a sign of Pound's genius that he saw the formal possibilities in Eliot's loose sequence. Under his hand the poem was transformed from a series of narrative and dramatic episodes into a "cinematographic" montage of images and incidents that is unified by a presiding sensibility. Whether we look at Pound's large structural changes or at his work on the details of language, we see the practical result of his long struggle to forge a modern idiom.

The tendency before the publication of *The Waste Land* manuscript was to read the poem as a magisterial critique of modern society; more recently, with new evidence before them, critics have emphasized the poem's personal and lyric qualities. As with *Mauberley*, both readings are valid and reinforce each other. We might say that the poem began as a personal confession and ended as a text for its time. Earlier critics, influenced by Eliot's comments on the "mythic method" in *Ulysses*, stressed the importance of the Grail legend as a controlling point of reference; many readers today would find Eliot's exact use of the topography of London just as important, since it enables him to intensify the power of the hallucinatory scenes by placing them against a familiar landscape. Reacting against the initial cry that Eliot was a poetic "Bolshevik" who had destroyed the tradition, Eliot's first defenders may have overstressed the poem's "order" and mythic unity while neglecting the distinctive voice that holds *The Waste Land* together. When Virginia Woolf heard Eliot read the poem aloud in late 1922 she said that she had not yet "tackled the sense": "I have only the sound of it in my ears. . . . But I like the sound." Anyone who has heard

Eliot's masterful reading of the poem will know that all the variations in tone and voice come from a single personality.

Two aspects of *The Waste Land* should be noticed as a basis for comparison with Eliot's later works, especially *Four Quartets*. One is the precision of the allusions, symbolized by Eliot's scholastic notes to the poem. When the speaker at the end of Part I watches the anonymous commuters moving toward the City of London, he says:

> Under the brown fog of a winter dawn,
> A crowd flowed over London bridge, so many,
> I had not thought death had undone so many.

Here Eliot (as his note indicates) expects the reader to recognize that the third line is from *Inferno* III where Dante encounters the trimmers, those who were never truly alive. As in the quatrain poems the reader must understand Eliot's particular use of the past in order to grasp his attitude toward the present. Part of the deliberate "difficulty" of the new poetry as practiced by Pound and Eliot, this method coerces the reader who has been captured by the poem's music to explore its origins in the tradition. In a very real sense the early poems of Pound and Eliot were written to *enforce* their critical ideas.

Another aspect is the essential psychology of the poem's many "spectators." From first to last in Eliot's career, from the undersea vision of Prufrock through the Hyacinth garden in *The Waste Land* to the rose garden in *Burnt Norton*, a quintessentially Jamesian experience lies at the heart of his work. The tragedy is that of someone who can perceive but cannot act, who can understand but cannot communicate: "I could not/ Speak, and my eyes failed, I was neither/ Living nor dead," says the spectator looking into the "heart of light" in the Hyacinth garden. He is like Tiresias, who knows all, foresuffers all, and can prevent none of it. This is the vision of personal isolation that Eliot shares with James. In his later works Eliot does explore ways of breaking "the closed circle of consciousness," through discipline or through grace. But in *The Waste Land* the only consolation lies in memory and the ordering of the past: "These fragments I have shored against my ruins."

The Waste Land appeared in October 1922 in the first issue of *The Criterion*, an influential literary journal that Eliot edited in the years between the wars. The preeminence of *The Criterion* during those years was a reflection of Eliot's own dominance in the literary world; by the time he wrote the last three Quartets he could speak with the authority of an unofficial laureate for two nations united as never before or since in a common cause.

Yet this fame did little to assuage the anxieties that are evident in *The Waste Land's* successor, "The Hollow Men" (1925). One of the epigraphs for "The Hollow Men" is drawn from Joseph Conrad's *Heart of Darkness* ("Mistah Kurtz—he dead"), but Eliot might even more appropriately have used the line from the same story that he once thought of affixing to *The Waste Land:* "The horror! The horror!" In "The Hollow Men" we have Eliot's bleakest description of the modern wasteland, unrelieved by the rich music and pawky humor of the earlier poems. It is the dead center of his career, after which there could come only silence or a turning toward something new.

That turning or conversion took place in 1927, when Eliot was received into the Church of England. A year later he announced in the preface to *For Lancelot Andrewes* that he was a "classicist in literature, royalist in politics, and anglo-catholic in religion." Those who had taken Eliot as the spokesman for a "Lost Generation" were astounded, but any close reading of his early life and art makes the decision seem inevitable. The poetic effects of this "turning" were immediately evident in the first of the *Ariel* poems, "Journey of the Magi," published in 1927. Unlike Yeats's magi, "the pale unsatisfied ones," Eliot's wise man is content with his discovery: "it was (you may say) satisfactory." The entire poem is written in a sustained narrative form that contrasts sharply with the nervous pastiche of *The Waste Land* or "The Hollow Men." Even the use of allusion is different: in "Gerontion" Eliot adapted these gnomic lines from one of Lancelot Andrewes's Nativity sermons:

> The word within a word, unable to speak a word,
> Swaddled with darkness.

In "Journey of the Magi" Eliot opens with a passage from the same sermon; but the tone is quite different, and we no longer feel that we have missed something essential if we cannot recognize the quotation.

> "A cold coming we had of it,
> Just the worst time of the year
> For a journey, and such a long journey:
> The ways deep and the weather sharp,
> The very dead of winter."

Here the strong narrative line reflects a new confidence, if not a new serenity.

Eliot's conversion led him to write in 1927–30 the most private of his poems, *Ash-Wednesday*, where the opening line ("Because I do not hope to turn again") announces his subject. Filled with imagery from Christian iconography and allusions to the Anglo-Catholic liturgy, *Ash-Wednesday* is a poem that assumes a sympathetic and Christian audience, whereas Eliot's criticism of that time (most notably his 1929 Dante essay) is concerned with the question of what (and how) we must believe in order to appreciate a religious poem. Is a provisional and imaginative belief held during the process of reading enough, or must we judge the poem by some extraliterary standards? Eliot was to explore the ambiguities of this question in the writing of *Four Quartets*.

In 1932–33 Eliot returned to America after an absence of twenty years, and the experience changed his poetic life. Like Spencer Brydon in James's story "The Jolly Corner," Eliot had spent his adult life in Europe "after strange gods," and he must have been aware (to quote from *The Family Reunion*) that "The man who returns will have to meet/ The boy who left."

Eliot spent most of the year in America at Harvard where he gave the Charles Eliot Norton lectures, later published as *The Use of Poetry and the Use of Criticism*. In these lectures, as in much of Eliot's criticism written after 1927, the form of his early essays has given way to a more loose and discursive style. The early essays are primarily literary in focus, and like the early poetry are organized around allusive "touchstone" quotations. Such a method was obviously unsuited for the public lectures that Eliot was asked to give as his fame increased, but the change in method also resulted from a desire to discuss broader cultural and religious issues, to define a "tradition" that was not solely literary. Eliot's Harvard lectures were rather cautious and academic in tone, as befitted the occasion; but in the spring of 1933 he journeyed to the University of Virginia to give the Page-Barbour lectures, and in the congenial and conservative atmosphere of Charlottesville he spoke much more openly about his personal convictions. The lectures were published as *After Strange Gods* (1934) but Eliot never reprinted them, obviously out of embarrassment at his reactionary attitudes, which included remarks about "foreign races" and "free-thinking Jews." Like so many modernist writers who had joined in a literary revolution, Eliot in the early 1930s responded to the social disorder of the time with an almost irrational "rage for order." The difference between Eliot and Pound is that Eliot soon drew back from his position, while Pound, working in virtual isolation, became even more disoriented.

The most interesting thing about *After Strange Gods* is not the social ideas but the sense of landscape that pervades the book. In his early poetry of urban life Eliot had suppressed his deep feeling for nature, but in 1932–33 his return to the American scenes of his youth led both to a quickening of his poetic imagination and to a rapprochement with the American inheritance that is a vital theme in *Four Quartets*. The man who gave the Harvard lectures thought his poetic life was behind him—his last words were "The sad ghost of Coleridge beckons to me from the shadows"—but soon he was writing landscape poems such as "New Hampshire" and "Virginia" that prepared the way for *Four Quartets.*

> Children's voices in the orchard
> Between the blossom- and the fruit-time:
> Golden head, crimson head,
> Between the green tip and the root.
> Black wing, brown wing, hover over;
> Twenty years and the spring is over . . .

Here in "New Hampshire" the tone is elegiac but the new music in the words speaks of a liberated imagination.

Burnt Norton, the first of the Quartets, was written in 1935. The setting is an English country house that Eliot visited "without knowing anything whatsoever about the history of the house or who had lived in it," and where he underwent the intense experience of landscape as a state of feeling, a prompt for memory, that motivates the poem. The burden of *Burnt Norton* is the difficulty of reconciling the timeless with that which lives and dies in time, and the poem is filled with Wordsworthian "spots of time" that offer intimations of how this may be accomplished. The poem is religious in tone but not specifically Christian in content, and stands in the great tradition of English landscape poetry. In writing *Burnt Norton* Eliot followed the pattern he and Pound had devised for *The Waste Land:* five sections like a five-act play, with the fourth a condensed lyric that "turns" the poem.

It is important to understand that when Eliot wrote *Burnt Norton* he did not have a sequence in mind. He had just finished *Murder in the Cathedral,* a stylized religious drama that rehearses some of the major themes of *Four Quartets,* and he went on to write his finest play, *The Family Reunion* (1939), where he—like Yeats—tries to revive the tradition of popular verse drama. Near the end of his life Eliot said that "if there hadn't been a war I would probably have tried to write another play." It was the dislocations of wartime London and the threat to his two cultures—one native, one adopted— that drove Eliot toward the last three Quartets.

East Coker (1940), set in the Somerset village of Eliot's ancestors, is a meditation on the personal and historical past. Like *The Family Reunion* it is a Jamesian drama of both what was and what might have been, and it contains some of Eliot's most personal poetry, as in the opening of Part V:

So here I am, in the middle way, having had twenty years—
Twenty years largely wasted, the years of *l'entre deux guerres*—
Trying to learn to use words, and every attempt
Is a wholly new start, and a different kind of failure

This passage, which ends "For us, there is only the trying. The rest is not our business," is paralleled by the personal statements that open Part V of each of the other Quartets, and this symmetry is both one of the great strengths and one of the weaknesses of the poem. Beginning with *East Coker*, Eliot sought to replicate the pattern of *Burnt Norton* in each succeeding Quartet, so that the entire work can be read either as a four-poem sequence or as a four-ply single poem.

The strain placed on Eliot by this need to follow a set pattern of themes and verse structures is most evident in *The Dry Salvages* (1941), the poem most readers find least satisfying, although the first movements rank with the finest poetry Eliot ever wrote. The "Dry Salvages," as Eliot tells us, "is a small group of rocks, with a beacon, off the N.E. coast of Cape Ann, Massachusetts," and this is Eliot's most "American" poem in which he recalls scenes of his childhood and youth. Whereas *East Coker* is concerned with historical time, *The Dry Salvages* examines all the orders of time under the aspect of the timeless Incarnation and prepares us for the more explicitly Christian experiences of *Little Gidding*. It is as if Eliot were conducting his reader through a series of more and more specialized initiations leading from the secular visions of *Burnt Norton* to the Christian epiphanies of *Little Gidding*.

Little Gidding is a sacred place, the site of a seventeenth-century community devoted to the religious life, and Eliot uses the associations hovering about the place to draw together *Four Quartets*. Many readers feel that the closure is a forced one, accomplished more through imagery and music than through the argument of the poem. Lacking Dante's unified culture and sympathetic audience, all Eliot can do is present the "hints and guesses" that have moved him to belief. But if the final section of *Little Gidding* is anticlimactic, the brilliant imitation of Dante in Part II is the crown of his poetic achievement. In this passage a lifetime devoted to the study of Dante and the poetic tradition is justified. The scene is one known to all readers of Eliot, an encounter with an alter ego, "a familiar compound ghost/ Both intimate and unidentifiable." It resembles the encounter with Stetson at the end of Part I of *The Waste Land*, but here the literary allusions (and there are many) have been subsumed in the narrative, doing their work from well below the surface. At the close Eliot's favorite image from the *Purgatorio*,

Arnaut Daniel's willing acceptance of the refining fire, is combined with Yeat's favorite image of wholeness, the dancer and the dance.

> From wrong to wrong the exasperated spirit
>   Proceeds, unless restored by that refining fire
>   Where you must move in measure, like a dancer.

In the twenty years after World War II Eliot wrote a number of important critical essays and three popular plays: *The Cocktail Party* (1950), *The Confidential Clerk* (1954), and *The Elder Statesman* (1959). But he never returned to lyric poetry after *Four Quartets*, and it seems fair to say that his great and lasting influence will rest on his work of the years between the two wars. Meanwhile his old friend Ezra Pound, in the Pisan detention camp and later in St. Elizabeths Hospital for the criminally insane, continued to work on his lifelong "record of struggle," *The Cantos*.

In the biographical sketch that Pound provided for his 1957 *Selected Poems* we find this entry: "1918 began investigation of causes of war, to oppose same." World War I was the decisive trauma in Pound's personal and poetic life. Some of his closest friends died in the trenches, most notably the philosopher T. E. Hulme and the young sculptor Henri Gaudier-Brzeska ("and they killed him,/ And killed a good deal of sculpture," Pound lamented in Canto 16). These deaths became for Pound symbols of all the war's other disasters that had by 1919–20, as *Mauberley* testifies, made him a marginal figure in London. In a sense all of Pound's later economic and political obsessions, including his anti-Semitism, date from this time. His prewar writings are remarkably free of the easy prejudices of his generation, but in the war elegies of *Mauberley* lines such as "usury age-old and age-thick/ and liars in public places" foreshadow the future.

From 1921 until 1924 Pound lived in Paris, where he tried to play the same role of instigator and literary entrepreneur that he had brilliantly performed in the London of 1912–18, when he helped to launch the careers of Robert Frost, Eliot, Wyndham Lewis, and Joyce. The Paris years were exciting ones, including the discovery of Ernest Hemingway and work with artists such as Brancusi and Leger, but in 1924 Pound moved to Rapallo, and Italy was to be his home for the rest of his life. He may have left Paris because he once again felt "marginal," but *A Draft of 16 Cantos* shows that he was also lured by a growing interest in Italian art and history. Among the many subjects of these cantos—the myths of metamorphosis, the Odyssean journey, Confucian ethics—was the career of the Renaissance prince Sigismundo Malatesta, who in the midst of economic and historical chaos built the great Tempio in Rimini. With its interlacing of pagan, Christian, and humanistic motifs, the Tempio might also be a model for *The Cantos;* and Pound admired Sigismundo as an "entire man" who, like Jefferson or Mussolini, could impose his vision on history (Pound later wrote a book called *Jefferson and/or Mussolini*). Understandable as this admiration might have been at the time, in the light of Pound's later support of fascism it strikes an ominous note.

Pound's life in Italy from 1925 until 1945 is a history of the writing of *The Cantos;* all his other prolific literary, economic, and social writings were adjuncts to this enterprise. *A Draft of Thirty Cantos* (1933) reflects his growing concern with modern avarice and usury, which are contrasted with the savage splendors of the Renaissance and the natural order celebrated in pagan myths and Chinese philosophy. In Cantos 31–41 he turns to American history, tracing the original vision of Jefferson and Adams, and Van Buren's opposition to a national bank. *The Fifth Decad of Cantos* (1937) continues the argument against modern exploitative economics, and at its center we find Canto 45, Pound's magnificent denunciation of USURA, which thwarts all natural processes.

> With usura hath no man a house of good stone
> each block cut smooth and well fitting
> that design might cover their face,
> with usura
> hath no man a painted paradise on his church wall
>   . . . .
>
> with usura the line grows thick
> with usura is no clear demarcation
> and no man can find site for his dwelling.

Pound believed that clarity and precision in life or art depend on a "clean" economy, and in the Old Testament measures of Canto 45 this conviction rings with ancient authority. But as the nature of European fascism became clear to others after the Abyssinian invasion and the Spanish Civil War, Pound began to lose touch with the reality behind Mussolini's "dream." The Chinese and John Adams cantos of the late 1930s reflect this growing disorientation, and during World War II Pound made hundreds of broadcasts over Rome Radio attacking the Allies and the economic conspiracy that, he thought, had caused another war. In 1945 he was arrested by the U.S. Army and spent nearly six months in the detention center at Pisa, confined for part of the time in a steel cage. He suffered a mental collapse, and when he was flown back to the United States to be tried for treason he was declared "mentally unfit for trial" and remanded to St. Elizabeths Hospital for the criminally insane. Pound lived in St. Elizabeths for twelve years, reading, writing, and receiving a host of visitors who ranged from famous writers to right-wing fanatics. In 1958 his friends finally obtained a release order and he returned to Italy, where he spent most of his remaining years in penitential silence.

During the time at Pisa and St. Elizabeths Pound continued to work on his long poem. *The Pisan Cantos* (Cantos 74–84) appeared in 1948, and when Pound received the Bollingen Prize for this work the controversy surrounding his imprisonment intensified. *Rock-Drill* (85–95) was published in 1955, followed by *Thrones* (96–109) in 1959 and *Drafts and Fragments* (110–117) in 1969. The poetry of *Rock-Drill* and *Thrones*, written out of the relative isolation of St. Elizabeths, often harks back to the attitudes of the 1930s; but *The Pisan Cantos* and *Drafts and Fragments* are filled with moving passages of great poetry that meditate on the tragic arc of his poetic life. The most famous of these occurs in Canto 81:

> The ant's a centaur in his dragon world.
> Pull down thy vanity, it is not man
> Made courage, or made order, or made grace,
>   Pull down thy vanity, I say pull down.

Yet at the end of this self-accusatory chant Pound recalls, as we must, the great accomplishments that make the word "tragic" possible:

> But to have done instead of not doing
>   this is not vanity
>   . . . .
>   To have gathered from the air a live tradition
> or from a fine old eye the unconquered flame
> This is not vanity.
>   Here error is all in the not done,
>   all in the diffidence that faltered,

The question that every reader of *The Cantos* must ask is the one that Pound himself repeats throughout *Drafts and Fragments:* does it cohere? He has no doubt that "it [the ideal world behind appearances] coheres all right," yet he is keenly aware that his own vision flares "fitfully and by instants." From the beginning of his work on a long poem he had called its sections "drafts," and in the last cantos he speaks of "my notes," "a tangle of works," a "palimpsest." Along the way Pound had thought of his poem as a fresco of many scenes, a fugue of intertwined melodies, an arena in which the drama of past and present is enacted; but in the end it turned out to be a personal voyage "as the wind veers," a record of the richest and most complex poetic life this century has witnessed. As Michael Alexander has said: "For all their wrong-headed politics and confusing form," *The Cantos* "present simultaneously an heroic imaginative openness to actual living and to nature" and an access to "certain cultural possibilities that cannot be reproduced."

A. Walton Litz

William Carlos Williams and Wallace Stevens

The life spans of William Carlos Williams and Wallace Stevens are about the same. They make a natural pair in the literary history of the United States. Both lived in the Northeast in small industrial and commercial cities, Stevens in Hartford, Connecticut, Williams in Rutherford, outside Paterson, New Jersey. Both were part-time poets and carried on demanding professional jobs, Stevens as the vice-president of the Hartford Accident and Indemnity Company, Williams as a physician with a busy general practice. Williams boasted that he had brought several thousand babies into the world. Stevens was a specialist in the insurance of cattle being brought to market. Each writer is a major figure in modernist American poetry. Each belongs in the line of Emerson and Whitman. Each attempted in a different way to develop a distinctive American poetry, with its own rhythms and themes, "unsponsored, free" of European influences, as Stevens puts it in "Sunday Morning." Yet each was indebted, almost in spite of himself, against the grain, so to speak, to English romanticism and to modern French poetry, symbolism and surrealism, and also to modern French practice in the arts, to impressionism, cubism, and futurism, to Matisse, Braque, Miro, Picasso, and others. The two poets were friends and thought of themselves as colleagues in a common enterprise. There is even an early poem by Stevens, "Nuances of a Theme by Williams," which cites a four-line poem by Williams and executes variations on it. Nevertheless, as that poem shows, the work of the two poets is fundamentally different. Their juxtaposition in this chapter will perhaps make possible a better identification of what is distinctive about each poet by way of stressing their differences, as well as by identifying similarities.

William Carlos Williams was born on September 17, 1883, in Rutherford, New Jersey. His father was English, his mother Puerto Rican. After
education through the eighth grade in Rutherford schools Williams was taken
abroad for schooling during 1897–99 at le Château de Lancy near Geneva
and later for a short time at the Lycée Condorcet. From 1899 to 1902 he
attended Horace Mann High School, where his grade average was C. In
1902 he was admitted by special examination first to the School of Dentis-
try at the University of Pennsylvania, then by transfer to the School of
Medicine. After receiving his M.D. degree in 1906, Williams interned at
the French Hospital and the Child's Hospital in New York City and studied pediatrics in Leipzig. In 1910 he returned to open a general practice in
Rutherford. In 1912 he married Florence Herman. They had two sons.
Williams practiced medicine in Rutherford until his first stroke in 1951 forced
him to retire. After a long life combining medicine with poetry Williams
died in Rutherford on March 4, 1963.

Williams's career as a published writer began with the twenty-two page
Poems of 1909, privately printed in Rutherford at the poet's own expense
("about $50.00"). But he had been writing since medical-school years at
least, most notably a long poem, now lost, entitled "The Wanderer" and
modeled on Keats's Hyperion poems. From the point of view of literary
history, Williams's life is the story of his various books, the influences on
them and their influence.

While studying at Pennsylvania he met Ezra Pound and through him the
poet Hilda Doolittle ("H. D."). Later he came to know New York–based
avant-garde poets, writers, and artists such as Kenneth Burke, Marianne
Moore, Louis Zukofsky, and a host of others. Throughout his long career
his work was sustained by these New York contacts. The essential context
for Williams's work is New York modernism of the 1910s, 1920s, and 1930s
in poetry, painting, photography, and criticism. It is the milieu of the Armory Show and of little magazines like *Others*, *Contact*, and *Blast*, the milieu
of Alfred Stieglitz's photographs and of Marcel Duchamp's "Nude Descending a Staircase" and his *objets trouvés*.

Williams's work falls into five major categories. He is most famous as a
writer of short, extremely laconic lyric poems on apparently trivial subjects.
The best known is "The Red Wheelbarrow." This poem, in its entirety,
tells how "so much depends/ upon/ a red wheel/ barrow/ glazed with rain/
water/ beside the white/ chickens." Other examples are "Spring and All,"
where the focus is on bushes, small trees, and weeds, such as "the stiff curl
of wildcarrot leaf," or "Between Walls," which names "the broken/ pieces
of a green/ bottle" lying in the cinders between the walls of the back wings

of a hospital. These poems are gathered in two volumes, *The Collected Earlier Poems* (1951) and *The Collected Later Poems* (1950, revised edition 1963). But they were originally published, often in early, unrevised versions, in a multitude of "little magazines," then collected in small volumes—from *The Tempers* in 1913 and *Al Que Quiere!* in 1917 and extending all the way down to the splendid *Pictures from Brueghel and Other Poems* of 1962, which earned Williams a Pulitzer Prize in the year of his death.

The second category of Williams's writing has only one example, the long poem *Paterson*, published in five books from 1946 to 1958, and then gathered in 1963 in a definitive edition, including notes for Book Six. Throughout his career Williams was inspired by the Whitmanesque idea of creating a distinctively American poetry with a distinctively American rhythm and idiom. A great national poetry, he thought, should have its great, ambitious long poems, inclusive records of the country's national life and ideals, just as the Greeks had the *Iliad*, Rome the *Aeneid*. *Paterson* was Williams's attempt to create such a poem, an American epic. It is, as he says in the epigraph, *a reply to Greek and Latin with the bare hands*. *Paterson* is a poem at once local, about the history of Paterson, that industrial city by "the filthy Passaic," near Williams's hometown of Rutherford, and at the same time universal: "To make a start,/ out of particulars/ and make them general," as he says in the first lines of the "Preface."

Williams saw T. S. Eliot as a man of great poetic talent who had sold out to Europe and who was therefore the enemy of Williams's project of creating an indigenous American poetry. Nevertheless, *Paterson* is deeply influenced by Eliot's *The Waste Land*. Like *The Waste Land*, *Paterson* is made of juxtaposed fragments—bits and pieces of Paterson history and of Williams's experiences as a doctor and citizen. Like *The Waste Land*, *Paterson* is organized around a shadowy mythological narrative, in Williams's case two giant figures in a sleeping embrace, the city and his beloved, the park: "Paterson lies in the valley under the Passaic falls/ its spent waters forming the outline of his back/ . . . And there, against him, stretches the low mountain./ The Park's her head, carved, above the Falls, by the quiet/ river."

Unlike *The Waste Land*, however, *Paterson* is not structurally governed as a whole by a single underlying mythological action. It is, rather, peculiarly American in being written gradually over time in a series of somewhat fortuitous and unpredictable findings or improvisations, as Williams puts down what comes to him or what is born in his imagination—bits of Paterson history and folklore, letters he has received, images from magazines or descriptions of people he has seen on the street or in the park on Sunday, lines that come into his head, slogans or meditations on poetry inspired, sometimes, by reading earlier parts of *Paterson*. *Paterson* constantly changes direction and constantly changes tone or register. It moves back and forth from the oracular or prophetic to the prosaic, from the satiric to the apocalyptic, and back again to the physician-poet's down-to-earth diagnosis of the condition of things and people he examines with his senses. Like the potentially endless listing of particulars of American life in Whitman's *Song of Myself* or like the seriality of Pound's *Cantos*, though in a somewhat different way from each, Williams's *Paterson* remains unfinished and unfinishable, like the United States itself, with fragments of Book Six found among the poet's papers at his death.

Though Williams is best known as a poet, he was also a distinguished writer of short stories, novels, and plays, the third category of his works. These too were initially published in little magazines. Many of the stories of the thirties, for example, appeared in Fred Miller's *Blast*. Williams's work in these other genres has the economical directness and earthy realism that is also a distinctive characteristic of his poetry. One of his plays, *Many Loves*, had a successful off-Broadway run in 1959. His plays were collected in 1961 in *Many Loves and Other Plays*. Williams's stories were also gathered in 1961 under the title *The Farmers' Daughters*. His trilogy of novels about his wife's family history was published in 1937 *(White Mule)*, 1940 *(In the Money)*, and 1952 *(The Build-Up)*.

The fourth category of Williams's writing covers literary criticism and literary theory. Here his influence and importance is almost as great (or ought to be) as it has been through the example of his poetry. From the "Prologue" to *Kora in Hell* of 1920 to late essays on his final theory of prosody and measure, the "variable foot" (for example, "On Measure—Statement for Cid Corman" [1954]), Williams produced a constant stream of essays. These define and justify his own practice and praise the practice of those friends and associates he admired. There are essays, for example, on Ezra Pound, Gertrude Stein, Marianne Moore, Kenneth Burke, E. E. Cummings, and Charles Sheeler, the painter and photographer. Like his poetry, his essays are consistently anecdoto as well as theoretical. In a celebrated slogan Williams asserts that there are "no ideas but in things"; in other writers and artists, in the concrete details of their lives and works, Williams finds occasions for assertions about what poetry is and what it can do.

Many of Williams's best essays were collected in *Selected Essays* (1954), but perhaps his most important book of critical theory is the admirable *Spring and All*. Published in Dijon in 1923 as a small blue-covered paperback of 93 pages, *Spring and All* has now been reprinted with other such prose in *Imaginations* (1970). In *Spring and All* Williams mixes theoretical speculation and polemic with some of his best, most famous, and most characteristic poems, including "Spring and All" and "The Red Wheelbarrow." In this fourth category might be put, finally, *In the American Grain* (1925), Williams's book about American history. In a series of sketches or portraits of distinctive American figures—such as the Spanish explorer Ponce de León; the Jesuit missionary in Maine, Père Sébastien Rasles; and Benjamin Franklin—Williams identifies what remained his basic sense of the special quality of the American imagination as well as of the qualities of its betrayers, whether in poetry and the arts, or in exploration, conquest, and political action. For Williams, the children of darkness are those who have imported and imposed false and inappropriate forms from Europe, the children of light those who have opened themselves to or have helped open up a radiance or "gist" present in the American soil and in the American landscape.

Finally, as the fifth category of his writing, Williams also excelled in anecdotal and autobiographical writing. His *Autobiography* (1951) is essential reading for those who want to understand what Williams thought he was doing in poetry, as well as for those interested in the history of literature and art during the modernist period in the United States. Williams in his *Autobiography* tells of his encounters with many of the important writers, artists, and critics of the period. Other writings by him in this genre include *I Want to Write a Poem: The Autobiography of the Works of a Poet* (1958), an account of how his poems were written and published; and *Yes, Mrs. Williams: A Personal Record of My Mother* (1959), a kind of extended prose poem in praise of the earthy, practical, poetic genius of his Puerto Rican mother, Raquel Hélène (Hoheb). In the same mode are his *Selected Letters* (1957). Williams was a pithy and sometimes angry or profane letter writer. Much about his thoughts and opinions, his day-to-day life, his stance toward things and people emerged in his letters.

Abundant additional material in all these genres, as well as major collections of published work, are in the Lockwood Memorial Library at the State University of New York at Buffalo, in the Beinecke Library at Yale University, and in the Rutherford Public Library. Much work is still being done to sift and evaluate these materials, for example, in articles published in the *William Carlos Williams Newsletter*.

In the end what matters most to literary history are Williams's lyric poems, more even than his admirable work in other genres. The occasions for writing these poems, often brief moments snatched from a physician's busy day, early in the morning or late at night, were themselves historical events of the most concrete and productive sort. Each reading of one of these poems, when it is "really read," is another historical event.

An image of history as a series of unpredictable and radically inaugural events in fact pervades Williams's own writing in all its themes and forms. Birth, the appearance of something new, unheard of, something rising out of a profound darkness and hiddenness, is the fundamental theme and act of Williams's work throughout. Sometimes the theme of the appearance of the new is expressed in the birth of all those babies the doctor-poet brought into the world. Sometimes it is the poking up of weeds out of the wet ground in spring. Sometimes it is what Williams calls the "birth" of some hidden and essential spirit in that language appearing around us every day in common speech, as in "Detail": "Doc, I bin lookin' for you/ I owe you two bucks," or in this bit from *Paterson:* "Geeze, Doc, I guess it's all right/ but what the hell does it mean?" Sometimes the theme of birth is expressed in that diurnal repetition, always the same and yet always new, of the birth of the sun. The sun for Williams rises as though out of the earth and seems almost to pull the trees, behind which it rises, out of the ground, so terrific is its energy, as in these lines from "Spring Strains" (where there is a pun on "strains" as music and as effort):

> But—
> (Hold hard, rigid jointed trees!)
> the blinding and red-edged sun-blur—
> creeping energy, concentrated
> counterforce—welds sky, buds, trees,
> rivets them in one puckering hold
> Sticks through! Pulls the whole
> counter-pulling mass upward, to the right
> locks even the opaque, not yet defined
> ground in a terrific drag that is
> loosening the very tap-roots!

As the reader can see, the event of birth for Williams, in this case the birth of the sun, is no easy delivery. It is marked by tension and violence. One mode of this tension is the pull among four contradictory orientations of Williams's poems. I shall demonstrate this by means of one example, a charming and beautiful poem in the form of a note the poet left for his wife Flossie:

This Is Just to Say

I have eaten
the plums
that were in
the icebox

and which
you were probably
saving
for breakfast

Forgive me
they were delicious
so sweet
and so cold

One dimension of this poem, as of Williams's poems generally, is its referential force. The poem describes straightforwardly the plums, their taste and temperature, or rather it describes an event, the poet's eating of the plums, or rather (to refine still further) the poem presents a document, the actual note, so it appears, Williams left as an apology to his wife. This is now turned into a poem by being broken into short phrases printed on separate lines. One use of language, for Williams, when words are purified, is to catch, preserve, and pass on to others the virtues of immediate experience in the present moment. In the case of "This Is Just to Say" the experience is the taste of those plums on the poet's palate. Any object or event, even the most apparently trivial, such as the poet's eating of the plums, is worth naming and preserving in this way.

A second dimension of this poem, already present in the first, is Williams's attention to careful notation of his own thoughts, feeling, and behavior. Williams is known primarily as an objectivist poet. He is admired as the poet of objects normally thought to be insignificant, those bits of broken bottle, sea trout and butterfish, parsley on a kitchen sink, a field of Queen Anne's lace, images of a girl picking up a coin in the street or of a crowd at the ball game. Nevertheless, the first-person pronoun is exceedingly frequent in Williams's verse, as in "*I* have eaten/ the plums" in "This Is Just to Say." The reader of Williams's poems is made constantly aware of the doctor-poet scrutinizing the world, appraising it, tasting it, responding in a strongly sexual way to the women he sees, even turning that field of Queen Anne's lace into a sexualized "white desire." One poem, "Smell!," is an apostrophe to the poet's nose: "Oh strong-ridged and deeply hollowed/ nose of mine! what will you not be smelling?" Another poem, "Danse Russe," describes the doctor dancing alone in his room: "I in my north room/ dance naked, grotesquely/ before my mirror/ waving my shirt round my head/ and singing softly to my self: 'I am lonely, lonely . . .' "

The third dimension found in "This Is Just to Say" seems to conflict with the other two, just as they seem to conflict with one another. This third dimension is the purely formal or rhythmic aspect of Williams's poetry. If Williams had a gross nose that would smell anything, he had an exquisitely delicate ear, perhaps the finest ear of any American poet before or since. Along with those first two dimensions of Williams's work, the naming of things as they are and the careful notation of the poet's subjective goings on, there is a contrary motive in his poetry. This is the detachment of words from their objective or subjective valences, so far as that is possible. The words are then put down in detached units on the page for the shapes of sound they make and for their shapes on the page. This detachment is particularly obvious in the separating out as individual lines of words that, taken by themselves, have no referential meaning, since they are not nouns, verbs, or adjectives but conjunctions, articles, relative pronouns, or participles. Such words—and, or, but, the, a, that, which—dangle nonsensically in the air, until the syntax of the sentence completes them and gives those particles of language meaning. In "This Is Just to Say" such lines are: "that were in," "and which," "you were probably," and "saving." "Saving," taken by itself, may be an adjective, a participle, or part of a verb, depending on the words surrounding it. The word remains fundamentally ambiguous or even senseless as long as it just hovers there on the page as a single line all by itself. There are a great many other examples of such lines in Williams's poems. The effect of such detachment of words from their semantic and syntactic meaning is strange. It turns words into something like pure sounds or pure shapes on the page. Words become the basic raw material of a poetry that arranges these sounds or shapes in delicately beautiful patterns. These patterns are to be enjoyed for their own sake, without any necessary concern for what the poems name either within the poet's mind and feelings or in the world of objects outside: plums, parsley, fish, bits of green bottle, or whatever.

How can these three to some degree irreconcilable modes of poetry be brought together? Or is their co-presence evidence of a fundamental incoherence in Williams's poetic theory, as well as in his practice? Williams defined a poem as "a machine made of words." It seems as though he were trying to build out of words three different machines at once, for three different incompatible functions. The answer is that all three of these uses of words in Williams's poetry exist for the sake of a fourth and even more fundamental use that they all cooperate in accomplishing. This is the use of words in one way or another as acts of revelation, the exposure of an "it" or "thing" that underlies even the most trivial things, those bits of broken bottle, for instance, or the plums Flossie has saved in the icebox. This "essence" underlies also each person's "I" with all its thoughts and feelings. Perhaps most important for Williams, the "it" also underlies the words and rhythms of common American speech. The right choice and arrangement of words in any of the three functions of poetry is necessary to release that "thing" or "it," "nameless under the old appellations." Though to label it abstractly is not the same thing as revealing it (that can be done only by poetry itself), Williams nevertheless uses various epithets to name the "it" in so many words. It is called sometimes "beautiful thing!," sometimes the "radiant gist," sometimes "a fiery light, too fiery for logical statement," sometimes a "luminous background," sometimes "that secret and sacred presence." Perhaps the fullest attempt to say what that "it" is occurs in an eloquent passage in the *Autobiography*. Here Williams locates the "radiant gist" in what is perhaps its most important place for him, in the common rhythms and idioms of American speech:

We catch a glimpse of something, from time to time, which shows us that a presence has just brushed past us, some rare thing—just when the smiling little Italian woman has left us. For a moment we are dazzled. What was that? We can't name it; we know it never gets into any recognizable avenue of expression; men will be long dead before they can have so much as ever approached it. . . . It is actually there, in the life before us, every minute that we are listening, a rarest element— not in our imaginations but there, there in fact. It is that essence which is hidden in the very words which are going in at our ears and from which we must recover underlying meaning as realistically as we recover metal out of ore.

At the end of his life Williams developed a new technique of verse, the arrangement on the page in triadic units of collocations of words he called "variable feet." In his great last poems, the poems of *Pictures from Brueghel*, particularly in the masterpiece among these late poems, "Asphodel, That Greeny Flower," these clusters of words rise, in a potentially endless stream, as if out of some fathomless depth that is at once objective, subjective, and within language itself. The words rise to appear there on the page as a continuous holding off of the poet's imminent death and as a continuous revelation and simultaneous forgetting of the "it":

> There is something
> 　　　　something urgent
>
> I have to say to you
> 　　　and you alone
> 　　　　　but it must wait

While I drink in
>   the joy of your approach,
>   perhaps for the last time.

And so
>   with fear in my heart
>   I drag it out

and keep on talking
>   for I dare not stop.
>   Listen while I talk on

against time.
>   It will not be
>   for long.

I have forgot

Though Wallace Stevens was a contemporary of William Carlos Williams, his friend and ally in the same poetic movement, that of New York–based American modernism, nevertheless their work is fundamentally different in ground and in orientation. One way to define this dissimilarity is to recognize a difference in the mixture of the local and the universal, the particular and the abstract, in the two poets. Williams, as I have said, takes as his fundamental poetic project appropriating the banal and trivial particulars of American life or landscape and making them universal, or revealing the universalities hidden within them. His poems notoriously stick close to an exact and literal naming of those particulars. Stevens's poetry, from the beginning, is much more obviously "abstract," philosophical, difficult. It is often more concerned with the operations within the mind of language than with the way words can take hold of reality.

"It Must Be Abstract" is the title of a section of one of Stevens's greatest poems about poetry, "Notes toward a Supreme Fiction." The first thing any reader of Stevens is likely to notice is that he certainly did obey that command. Part of the charm of reading Stevens, for an American reader, especially one from Pennsylvania or New England, is that she or he encounters familiar American place names: Perkiomen, Haddam, New Haven, Chocorua. These names are, however, likely to be encountered within a poem that, on first reading, is bewilderingly difficult. A trip to New Hampshire to climb Mt. Chocorua is not going to help one much in reading that admirably eloquent but also admirably abstract poem, "Chocorua to Its Neighbor." Here are a few lines from it:

He was a shell of dark blue glass, or ice,
Or air collected in a deep essay,
Or light embodied, or almost, a flash
On more than muscular shoulders, arms and chest,
Blue's last transparence as it turned to black . . .

If Williams's poetry is a challenge to the reader, teacher, or critic because its meaning seems so clear and obvious that it almost successfully resists commentary, the exhilarating challenge of Stevens's poetry is the opposite. What in the world, the reader, even the trained and expert reader, may ask, do these lines *mean?* Who is this "he"? How could a "he" be "a shell of dark blue glass, or ice"? What are the lines *about?* How could I say something adequate about them or explain them to someone else? How would I know if I had got them right? By what handle should I take hold of them? Let us note some basic facts about Stevens's life and work toward suggestions for answers to these questions as they might be raised by any lines from Stevens's poetry, early or late.

Wallace Stevens was born in Reading, Pennsylvania, on October 2, 1879. He came of Holland Dutch stock. His grandfather, Benjamin Stevens, was a well-to-do farmer, a member of the Dutch Reformed Church. His farm in a little place called Neshaminy was not far from the Perkiomen Creek, celebrated for its bass. Stevens later remembered this in two beautiful lines in "Thinking of a Relation Between the Images of Metaphors":

The wood-doves are singing along the Perkiomen.
The bass lie deep, still afraid of the Indians.

Wallace Stevens's father, Garrett Barcalow Stevens, left the farm to become first a schoolteacher and then a successful lawyer in Reading. Wallace Stevens grew up there with his two brothers and two sisters in a large brick row house. He was educated in Reading, first in a Lutheran parochial school, then in Reading Boys' High School, where he studied Latin and Greek, as well as mathematics and English. He flunked one year, possibly because of illness, and had to take the year over. He nevertheless graduated "with merit" in 1897 and entered Harvard College as a special student in September of the same year.

During his three years at Harvard, Stevens lived in a boardinghouse on Garden Street, studied English composition, French, and German, read widely in literature and philosophy, met George Santayana, began to keep a journal, wrote Shelleyan sonnets and Keatsian lyrics, and published poems in the *Harvard Advocate*, of which he became editor after a year on the staff. His first poem to appear there was in the issue of November 28, 1898.

Though there are anticipations of Stevens's mature poetry in these early efforts, on the whole they do not sound very Stevensian. In fact, the early journals, now in large part printed with commentary by Holly Stevens, the poet's daughter, in *Souvenirs and Prophecies: The Young Wallace Stevens*, have greater glimpses and flashes of the Stevens of *Harmonium* and "Notes toward a Supreme Fiction." He passed his own judgment on his early work in a letter of 1950: "Some of one's early things give one the creeps."

Stevens left Harvard for good in mid-June 1900. He moved to New York, where he worked at first as a newspaper reporter. After failing to make a living at that, he shifted to the law. On October 1, 1901, he entered New York Law School. He began work as a law clerk in the office of W. G. Peckham in the summer of 1902. He received his law degree and was admitted to the bar in 1904. Stevens's journals of this period are the record of long walks taken in the city and in the country (including notes made in the summer of 1903 during a camping, hunting, and fishing trip with W. G. Peckham in the wilds of British Columbia), of plays and concerts attended, books read, and of meals eaten. Part of the "poetry" of the journals (a weird indirect anticipation of the linguistic exuberance of the mature poetry) is in the naming of food, drink, and cigars:

I've just been reading my journal. A month or two ago I was looking forward to a cigarless, punchless weary life. *En effet*, since then I have smoked Villar y Villars & Cazadores, dined at Mouquin's on French artichokes & new corn etc. with a flood of drinks from crême de cassis melée, through Burgundy, Chablis etc. to sloe gin with Mexican cigars & French cigaroots. I have lunched daily on—Heaven's [*sic*] knows what not (I recall a delicious calf's heart cooked whole & served with peas—pig that I am).

It would be unfair to the journals, however, to suggest that they are no more than the record of youthful *gourmandise*. Stevens was a heroic walker from his childhood. The journals of his New York years are full of descriptions of long walks taken in the city and in the country around the city, as well as of walks taken in the country around Reading when he went home for visits. "Walking," he wrote, "is my only refuge from tobacco & food." The writing down in his journals of what he saw and heard on these walks was practice for that important dimension of his poetry that turns the appearances of the landscape into a way of naming the colors of the mind and of the imagination. Here is part of the entry for April 4, 1904, the description of a long hike to the Palisades, one of many such passages in the journals:

Extraordinarily brilliant day. A day for violet and vermilion, for yellow and white—and everything of silk. . . . Personally, I felt quite up to the mark; yesterday, I walked a score of miles sloughing off a pound at every mile (it seemed). There were any number of blue wings flitting down the round sides of the world. Saw a fiery robin & I know not what other birds; & noticed the first clucking of the wood-frogs, which sounded like the creaking of Flora's wain. The creatures seemed to be choking & no wonder; for some of the ponds were still filled with slush & rotten ice. Item: any fool could have found pussy willow in abundance. Some of the berry bushes had turned purple & there were plenty of green boughs of something or other. Spring comes this way, trait by trait, like a stage sunrise, *bien calculé*.

It was during an extended visit home to Reading, the summer after this journal entry was written, that Stevens met and fell in love with Elsie Viola Kachel, a native of that city. She was seven years younger than the poet. From 1904 to 1909, while he was practicing law in New York and living in New York or New Jersey, Stevens courted Elsie, mostly by letter. They were married in 1909. The young couple settled in an apartment on West Twenty-first Street in New York, which Stevens ultimately furnished with a baby grand piano for Elsie. Elsie was a delicate, temperamental woman, unable to stand the summer heat of the city. The young couple were therefore often separated during these years, though apparently amicably so. Much of Stevens's poetry of this period was addressed to Elsie or written for her.

By the time of his marriage Stevens had shifted from law practice to the insurance business. In the spring of 1916 he moved permanently with his wife to Hartford, Connecticut, where he joined the newly formed Hartford Accident and Indemnity Company. He became vice-president of that company in 1934 and remained with it until his death.

Shortly before leaving New York for Hartford, Stevens began publishing his first poems (after the juvenilia in the *Harvard Advocate*). Some poems, including five stanzas of "Sunday Morning," were published in Harriet Monroe's *Poetry*. Others appeared in less well known magazines, such as a journal called *The Trend*, edited by Pitts Sanborn, a friend from Harvard days. Some of these poems were written as early as 1909, as part of a birthday book for Elsie. Others were the first of Stevens's mature poems, poems that were to appear in his first book of poetry, *Harmonium*, published by Alfred A. Knopf in 1923. Knopf remained his major publisher.

The rest of Stevens's life, after the move to Hartford, is, from the point of view of literary history, primarily the story of the publication of his successive books of poetry and of his gradual recognition as one of the greatest of all American writers, in fact a great poet of world literature. Of his personal and professional life after the move to Hartford little need be said. His only child, a daughter, Holly Stevens, was born in 1924. She has served her father well as the editor of excellent editions of his letters, his early journals, and the standard paperback selection of his poetry, *The Palm at the End of the Mind*. Stevens became a successful insurance executive, specializing in the insuring of cattle being sent to market. There were annual trips to Kansas City for the cattlemen's meeting there, as well as frequent trips to Florida (without Elsie), and a famous early excursion by boat to Mexico (with Elsie). The last is reflected in "The Comedian as the Letter C" and "Sea Surface Full of Clouds," two notable poems from *Harmonium*. The poet's home life was not ideally happy, apparently, since Elsie was a difficult person. She would not, for example, allow him to have poet friends, such as William Carlos Williams, as house guests. He lived, on the surface at least, the ordinary life of a successful insurance executive, playing golf with colleagues and taking martini lunches at the Canoe Club in Hartford. He was by no means, nevertheless, universally liked by his colleagues at the office. He walked to work, and, so the story goes, composed his poetry on the way and dictated it to his secretary after he got to the office. Though Stevens never visited Europe, he collected modern French paintings and watercolors in a modest way. A notable poem, "Angel Surrounded by Paysans," is based on one of these paintings, a representation of some jars or pots by Tal Coat. Stevens kept up his friendships with some of the literary people he had met in New York—for example, William Carlos Williams—continuing to correspond with these literary associates and with others encountered during the years, some of whom had been encountered only by letter. Stevens was awarded the Bollingen Prize in Poetry in 1950. He won the National Book Award twice, in 1951 and 1955, and the Pulitzer Prize in Poetry in 1955. It has recently been revealed that he probably became a secret convert to Roman Catholicism at the end of his life. He died in Hartford on August 2, 1955.

Stevens was forty-four years old when *Harmonium* was published. During the rest of his life he continued writing poems, most of them first published in various magazines, that were periodically collected in the separate volumes that gradually earned him recognition as a major poet of our century: *Ideas of Order* (1936), *The Man with the Blue Guitar* (1937), *Parts of a World* (1942), *Transport to Summer* (1947), and *The Auroras of Autumn* (1950). All of these poems were collected, with a final section of recent poems called "The Rock," in a single volume published the year before the poet's death: *The Collected Poems of Wallace Stevens* (1954).

Stevens at first wanted to call his collected poems *The Whole of Harmonium*, to emphasize the continuity of his work. All of his poems are part of a single series, or they may even be thought of as one immense long meditative poem, broken somewhat arbitrarily into sections. This poem is the record of that unending dialogue of imagination and reality that was the life of the mind for Stevens.

A volume of essays, _The Necessary Angel: Essays on Reality and the Imagination_, had been published in 1951. After Stevens's death a miscellaneous volume of hitherto uncollected poems, plays, notebook adages, and essays was issued as _Opus Posthumous_ (1957). _The Letters of Wallace Stevens_ (1966), _The Palm at the End of the Mind_ (1971), a paperback selection of poems published in chronological order, and the volume of early journals and poems, _Souvenirs and Prophecies_ (1977), all edited by Holly Stevens, complete the writings by Stevens so far published.

In spite of anticipations of Stevens's mature poetry in his early poems and journals, there is little, after all, that prepares one for the appearance, in Stevens's forty-fifth year, of the magnificent ensemble of poems that make up _Harmonium_. Little even in _Harmonium_ prepares one for the admirable trajectory of the later poems following in a continuous stream. Those later poems deepen, darken perhaps, certainly make more complex, a poetic project whose contours already appear clearly in _Harmonium_. Stevens cannot be explained by anything antecedent to him, nor by contemporary movements in art and poetry, superficially helpful as identification of those filiations may appear to be. Neither his roots in Pennsylvania Dutch country, nor his education at Harvard, nor his personality as it may be encountered in journals and letters, nor the three main poetic filiations that may be identified helps much in explaining "Sunday Morning" or "The Snow Man," much less "Chocorua to Its Neighbor" or "The Owl in the Sarcophagus."

The filiations most often discussed by critics are those with English romanticism, especially Wordsworth, Shelley, Keats; those with the American tradition from Emerson to Whitman to the American pragmatists; those with the modern European tradition in poetry, painting, and philosophy from Baudelaire and Rimbaud down through Nietzsche to the surrealists, to Picasso, Braque, or Dufy in painting, to Husserl, Heidegger, or Jean Wahl in philosophy. Helpful as discussion of those connections may be, Stevens's poems, in the end, have to be taken, one by one, on their own, and read as best we can read them. Like all great cultural inventions or creations, they appear in their essential features more or less out of nowhere.

To this resistance to casual explanation may be added another form of discontinuity. Many features of Stevens's poetry pervade all of it from beginning to end. There is a thematic continuity, for example, the poet's abiding concern with the interactions of imagination and reality, or mind and world; and there is a recurrent focus, both in the poems themselves and in essays and adages, on the power of metaphor as a fundamental feature of poetic language. Critics have identified a repertoire of recurrent imagery: the color symbolism of blue for imagination, red for the power of reality, green for the luxuriant fecundity of nature. The conceptual formulations of Stevens's poetry are deliberately attached to the round of the seasons. The cycle of the seasons is followed in the trajectory of the poet's entire career, from the gaudy, springlike exuberance of *Harmonium* through *Transport to Summer* to *The Auroras of Autumn*. Stevens is one of the greatest of solar poets, and the motif of the sun, or of the diurnal and annual rotation of the planet in relation to the sun, pervades his poetry. The local verbal texture of his poetry is dependent on certain recurrent forms of locution, such as aphoristic phrases taking the form of an assertion that "A" is "B," or the presentation of a long series of phrases in apposition, each one a slight modification of the one before. An obvious characteristic of Stevens's poetry is the concoction of witty and enigmatic titles. Sometimes these remind the reader of snatches of common speech or of journalism. Sometimes they are like the titles of abstract paintings such as those of Paul Klee. Often they have only an indirect or puzzling relation to the poems themselves: "Tea at the Palaz of Hoon"; "The Virgin Carrying a Lantern"; "Some Friends from Pascagoula"; "A Dish of Peaches in Russia"; "Montrachet-le-Jardin"; "Large Red Man Reading." Throughout Stevens's poetry, finally, there is the persistence, even in the most abstract and rarefied of the poems, of the figure of speech called prosopopoeia or personification. This is the one figure that he cannot evade even at the farthest reaches of the imagination. An example is that "giant, on the horizon, glistening," in "A Primitive Like an Orb," which remains as the best name for the sun in its role as the sense-perceptible figure for the ultimate abstraction. The latter Stevens calls, in the same poem, "the essential poem at the centre of things."

In spite of these continuities, however, and in spite of all the help they give the reader in reading an unfamiliar poem by Stevens in the light of what he or she knows from the others, Stevens's poetry is full of surprises and discontinuities, both from poem to poem and within a given poem. The reader soon learns that it is impossible to predict just what is going to come next. What comes next often does not seem to follow logically or according to any other discernible form of continuity from what has come before. An extreme mental and emotional agility is therefore demanded of the reader of Stevens. Stevens formulated these features of his poetry and of poetry in general in several aphorisms in the "Adagia"; "Poetry must resist the intelligence almost successfully"; "A poem need not have a meaning and like most things in nature often does not have"; "The acquistitions of poetry are fortuitous; *trouvailles*. (Hence, its disorder)"; "Poetry must be irrational."

Sometimes this irrationality and this resistance to interpretation take the form of sentences that seem grammatical enough but do not quite make sense logically. A famous example is the last stanza of a very early poem from *Harmonium*, "The Snow Man." In this poem the wind blows or perhaps there is misery (the syntax makes it impossible to tell for sure), "For the listener, who listens in the snow/ And, nothing himself, beholds/ Nothing that is not there and the nothing that is." But sometimes the irrationality of Stevens's poetry takes the form of a savage linguistic violence that does succeed in resisting the intelligence almost successfully. The sound of words for the sound's sake, or for the sake of echoes among words by rhyme and alliteration, rather than the organization of words according to grammatical or logical articulation, takes precedence: "Chieftain Iffucan of Azcan in caftan/ Of tan with henna hackles, halt!" ("Bantams in Pine-Woods"); "O bright, O bright,/ The chick, the chidder-barn and grassy chives/ And great moon, cricket-impresario,/ And, hoy, the impopulous purple-plated past" ("Montrachet-le-Jardin"); "And she that in the syllable between life/ And death cries quickly, in a flash of voice,/ Keep you, keep you, I am gone, oh keep you as/ My memory, is the mother of us all" ("The Owl in the Sarcophagus").

Why does Stevens's poetry contain these various forms of irrationality, of resistance to the reason and to the interpreter's desire to dominate a poem by being able, in one way or another, to say what it *means?* Is it simply because poetry has more to do with emotion than with reason and that the language of emotion is irrational? Or is there some other reason? I shall attempt to reach an answer to these questions by deepening a bit a description of the essential formal and thematic features of Stevens's poetry.

Stevens wrote three sorts of poems. Many of his most famous poems are short lyrics, only a few lines long, a page or two at most, like "Anecdote of the Jar," "The Snow Man," "Bantams in Pine-Woods," and "The Emperor of Ice-Cream," all from *Harmonium;* but included among this group are many very late poems, such as "The River of Rivers in Connecticut," "Not Ideas about the Thing but the Thing Itself," "A Child Asleep in Its Own Life," and "Of Mere Being," all from the poet's last three years.

Then there are the famous long poems, including "The Comedian as the Letter C," "The Man with the Blue Guitar," "Esthétique du Mal," "Notes toward a Supreme Fiction," and "An Ordinary Evening in New Haven." Though the first of these has a somewhat obscure narrative order, for the most part they are ordered as a series of discrete sections that make up a continuous meditation: primarily a meditation about the life of the meditating mind itself and about the nature and function of poetry as one of the major powers of the mind. The mind is the only force that can defend us from the otherwise overwhelming force of reality—a violence from within, as he called it, to match the violence from without. In the "Adagia," that invaluable series of aphorisms in *Opus Posthumous*, he defines the imagination as "man's power over nature," and poetry as "a response to the daily necessity of getting the world right." The reader should remember, however, that for Stevens even the most potent poet never succeeds in getting it right once and for all. Hence the attempt to get it right, to find satisfaction for the mind, has to be begun anew each day. Stevens's long poems are the record not of a moment of insight, when things fall in place for an instant, as is the case with some of the short lyrics, but of a segment of that never-ending meditation in which the mind sways this way and that, trying one formulation after another in a never finally successful attempt to get it right. "They'll get it straight one day at the Sorbonne," writes Stevens at the very end of his most sustained poetic meditation about poetry, "Notes toward a Supreme Fiction," and then the world, "my green, my fluent mundo," "will have stopped revolving except in crystal." That crystallization, however, always remains in the future, and so the work of meditation continues.

There is, however, another characteristic form of Stevens's poetry, one that has perhaps not received as much attention as it should, namely, poems of medium length that carry a single concentrated trajectory of meditation from the poem's beginning to its conclusion, often through a highly focused sequence of sections that remain within the same constellation of themes and images. Such poems, in my view, are among Stevens's greatest, as well as among his most obscure and most difficult. This may explain the relative absence of commentary on them. Among such poems are "The Idea of Order at Key West," "Chocorua to Its Neighbor," "The Auroras of Autumn," "The Owl in the Sarcophagus," and "The Rock."

As many critics have noted, the continuity of Stevens's poetry, from the gaudy exuberance of the early poems in *Harmonium* to the more somber, bare, and apparently abstract meditations of such late poems as "An Ordinary Evening in New Haven," lies in its continuous focus on the interaction of mind and world, or, in Stevens's terms, "imagination" and "reality." "Poetry," says Stevens categorically, "is the statement of a relation between a man and the world." Between the two poles of a submission of the mind to the authority and substantiality of reality, on the one hand, and an assertion of the mind's power over nature, on the other hand, Stevens's poetry fluctuates, now affirming the dominion of one pole, now the other, never able finally to adjudicate the quarrel or the antagonism between them. A world of unadorned bare reality is no place for man, but, as he says in the "Adagia," "eventually an imaginary world is entirely without interest." The "Adagia," in this as in other ways immensely helpful as a way of orienting oneself in Stevens's poetry, records these fluctuations in the form of aphorisms that are in blank contradiction to one another: "There is nothing in the world greater than reality. In this predicament we have to accept reality itself as the only genius." Then two pages later: "Imagination is the only genius."

Why this contradiction? Why can Stevens not sooner or later or in one way or another adjudicate between the opposing claims of mind and world?— for example, through his claim that poetry is the "supreme fiction" that will take the place of religion as "a means of redemption": "The final belief is to believe in a fiction, which you know to be a fiction, there being nothing else." One answer to these questions lies in a third element in Stevens's poetic theory and practice, namely, a constant concern with "language as the material of poetry not its mere medium or instrument." Reality does not expose itself immediately to the mind or make itself available to the imagination. Language, especially the language of poetry, especially figured language, metaphor, is itself the material force that brings reality out of hiding. "Words are everything else in the world," presumably everything else besides imagination and reality. "Metaphor creates a new reality from which the original appears to be unreal," and therefore "the great poem is the disengaging of [a] reality." When Stevens ends "Parochial Theme" with the injunction: "Piece the world together, boys, but not with your hands," he presumably means that the putting together is done with words. It is a way, without doubt the grandest way, to do things with words. Stevens's poetry is a prolonged exploration, both in theoretical speculation within the poetry itself and in poetic practice, of the powers of language not so much to name reality as to uncover it.

That seems clear enough as an agenda for poetry. Why does it not succeed, once and for all, in the creation out of words of a supreme fiction within which all men and women can live together, as happy as "Danes in Denmark," as the poet puts it in "The Auroras of Autumn"? Why is it "We never arrive intellectually," though emotionally "we arrive constantly," for example, in poetry? Why must poetry always be merely "notes *toward* a supreme fiction," not the thing itself accomplished once and for all? The answer is the recognition of yet a fourth element, motif, or nonpresent presence in Stevens's poetry, the most difficult, elusive, and evasive of all.

In this recognition Stevens joins Williams, though from a different direction and within a distinct poetic climate or poetic universe.

I say "nonpresent presence" because this fourth element, motif, or force within Stevens's poetry is never present as such, neither to perception nor to abstract thinking. Nor was it a presence in the past that might be remembered. Nor is it a goal of thought that might ever be reached in the future and become present to the mind as an achieved possession, "the palm at the end of the mind." This "it" is neither a thing nor a thought nor a word nor a spiritual entity within this world or beyond it. This "it" is to all these as antimatter is to matter in modern physics. When any one of them is brought into contact with this "it," the "it" and the thing, thought, word, or spiritual being annihilate one another. It is for this reason, perhaps, that Stevens's poetry, both in theory and in actual practice, is a poetry of evanescence—brief glimpses of something that vanishes before it can be seen, caught, named, tamed, pinned down. Like that mother figure, matrix of the imagination in "The Owl in the Sarcophagus," what poetry reveals it reveals in the moment of its vanishing: "Keep you, keep you, I am gone." As Stevens says in the "Adagia": "Poetry is a pheasant disappearing in the brush."

It would be a mistake to think of this "it" as some metaphysical or religious dimension of Stevens's poetry, in any of the ordinary senses of those words. Nor is it a feature present within language, an element created by language or nameable within it. Though Stevens names the "it" by various abstractions and figures—"it," "thing," "mere being," the sun, the giant on the horizon, "nothing," "the essential poem at the center of things," and so on—"it" is essentially nameless. It can therefore be named only indirectly, in an always inadequate and evasive figure. Whenever the poet thinks he has caught it, for example in a poetry of literal naming, faithful to the barest of bare realities, it vanishes, leaving him with the astonishing recognition that "Reality is a vacuum." Elsewhere in the "Adagia" Stevens roundly asserts, "The real is only the base. But it is the base." Now it turns out that even reality, that apparently most solid and substantial base of all cultural activities, including the writing of poetry, is hollowed out by the fourth element, the "it."

The contrary movement away from reality toward affirmation of the independent power of the imagination to create supreme fictions ultimately encounters a similar emptying out: "Eventually an imaginary world is entirely without interest." This nameless "it," moreover, though it is not language, nevertheless enters into language as something that is infinitely distant, infinitely near to it, something that inserts itself, so to speak, between the words of a poem. This something twists words away from logical or dialectical consistency so that they do not quite make sense. As a result, the mind can never satisfy itself through poetry, but must always begin again with another poem: "Poetry is an effort of a dissatisfied man to find satisfaction through words."

This strange force or element is at work from one end of Stevens's poetry to the other. It is there in the formulation about "nothing that is not there and the nothing that is" in "The Snow Man." It is still the motivation for poetry in the last poem of all in *The Collected Poems*, "Not Ideas about the Thing but the Thing Itself," with its iterated "it" that is a scrawny bird's cry but also an inaugural glimpse of the not yet risen sun, itself a figure for "the thing itself." This fourth element, no doubt, is what is personified by the strange "he" in the "deep essay" of "Chocorua to Its Neighbor." Stevens's poetry requires the hypothesis of this fourth element or component, along with imagination, reality, and words, in order to be understood or accounted for, insofar as that can happen at all. Of this fourth element, some lines in "A Primitive Like an Orb" about "the essential poem at the center of things" give one of the most direct expressions. The lines are characteristically odd in their logical contradictions, in their strange diction and word use ("accelerando"?; "captives"?; "the being"?), and in their somewhat twisted grammar and syntax. This oddness, perhaps more than any conceptual formulation, indirectly manifests the torsion of the "it":

> It is and it
> Is not and, therefore, is. In the instant of speech,
> The breadth of an accelerando moves,
> Captives the being, widens—and was there.

J. Hillis Miller

Literary Criticism

"These last thirty years," T. S. Eliot wrote in 1956, "have been, I think, a brilliant period in literary criticism in both Britain and America. It may even come to seem, in retrospect, too brilliant. Who knows?"

This essay is a history of assumptions and practices rather than of persons of that brilliant period. Nevertheless I have concentrated on individual figures, partly because practices are individual, and partly because these figures seemed to me to afford the best shorthand for much that was diffuse or anonymous. They are not authors of discourses, as Michel Foucault felt Marx and Freud were—American critics are on the whole too ironic or too elusive for that—but neither are they solitary monuments, voices without echoes. They are styles of critical thought, sometimes quite separate, often overlapping. My emphasis, therefore, is on criticism as a performance, a mode of writing in which ideas are entangled but not simply purveyed. Theory is involved in criticism, but not on theory's terms.

Criticism is as inevitable as breathing, Eliot thought; as universal as walking, R. P. Blackmur said. It occurs in many forms and arenas: in conversation; in classrooms and conferences; in newspapers, magazines, journals, books; in parodies and jokes; in sustained works of art. It helps to remember that criticism is an activity, not a genre; that criticism "by discussion" (which extended, Ezra Pound said, from "mere yatter" to the formulation of general principles) is a branch and not the whole proliferating tree; that imitation and translation (into other languages and media) are modes of critical commentary; and that very good criticism may be done, as Pound argued, not only by "the creative writer or artist who does the next job," but by that job itself.

The visible history of this period shows disagreements aplenty, about individual authors and movements, about the autonomy or usefulness of literature itself. But they rest on the shared ground of high art. Literature was rescued from the burden of expressed morality, then from that of ideas, then from all immediate connection with politics or society. When W. H. Auden wrote, in 1939, that "poetry makes nothing happen," he was articulating a view that had been collecting adherents for some fifty years. It was not the cry of art for art's sake, only a rueful admission of art's indirectness. It *makes* nothing happen. Even those who wanted to argue that art was essentially concerned with morality, ideas, or society usually found themselves conceding the difference of literary discourse from other discourses. The invisible history, the one we guess at, weave out of hindsight, seems to settle on the fact of form, the shape or the shaping of the work. The implicit signpost says, not as John Crowe Ransom thought, that there is no road through to action, but that the road is winding, and that short cuts are a way of getting lost.

In 1908 H. L. Mencken published *The Philosophy of Friedrich Nietzsche;* in 1910 George Santayana published *Three Philosophical Poets: Lucretius, Dante and Goethe.* The philosophical tilt, the dangerous or lofty names, were symptoms of a desire, also shared by other scholars and critics, to raise standards and disturb complacencies. A little earlier, in 1900, Santayana had deplored the "general moral crisis and imaginative degeneration" of the age. "The imagination of our time," he wrote, "has relapsed into barbarism," has cultivated temperaments which claimed "that life is an adventure, not a discipline; that the exercise of energy is the absolute good, irrespective of motives or of consequences." Santayana's exemplary culprits were Whitman and Browning. They espoused irrationality and thought passions were their own excuse. They were indifferent to perfection and couldn't see life whole. Santayana sounds a little like Matthew Arnold, but his writing is both more graceful and less urgent, his sternness a retreat to the high ground rather than a call to cultural action.

He was also capable of sympathy for what he condemned, and later seems to have felt that high ambitions were as much a way of losing life as of finding it. He is the graph of a historical shift. The new century begins (as the old one ended) with grand and ideal measurements for a disappointing world. By mid-century, what Ransom called the world's body seemed in danger of disappearing into the schemes we had designed for it. The world was still a problem, but a greater problem was what Ludwig Wittgenstein had diagnosed as our contempt for the particular case. A beginning of a return to wayward cases is memorably registered in Santayana's suggestion, in an essay of 1921, that Dickens did not exaggerate:

The world is a perpetual caricature of itself . . . there *are* such people; we are such people ourselves in our true moments. . . . The most grotesque creatures of Dickens . . . arise because nature generates them, like toadstools; they exist because they can't help it, as we all do.

Santayana does exaggerate; and he underestimates Dickens's art. But his sense of the undignified truth that comedy is after is impressive. In 1936 he saw Shakespeare, whom he had earlier thought insufficiently philosophic, as the most human of writers, because his characters act out our weakness and misery:

The existence that just now seemed merely vain, now seems also tempestuous and bitter. And the rhythms help; the verse struts and bangs, holds our attention suspended, obliges our thoughts to become rhetorical. . . . We should hardly have found courage in ourselves for so much passion and theatricality.

It is hard to think of a critical style further removed from Santayana's than the caustic, knockabout prose of H. L. Mencken, a "man of ruthless mind," as Joseph Conrad called him, and the most powerful and feared critic of a whole generation. The Nietzsche that Mencken admired was an apostle of the very energy Santayana decried, and Mencken himself was attracted to the idea that art was "wholly a magnificent adventure." But Mencken's feeling for what he called the eternal farce of life was not unlike Santayana's response to comedy, and Mencken too took a high line, although it involved a demand not so much for aesthetic order and reason as for practical wit and intelligence. He never suffered fools gladly and often refused to suffer them at all. He was a champion of Theodore Dreiser and the maligned school of naturalism, and an ardent reader of Conrad, in whom he characteristically saw a bleak humor, "a wild dance in a dissecting-room," where "the mutilated dead rise up and jig." He defended Conrad's style in terms that recall his own masterpiece, a three-volume study of the American language (1919), which Eliot described as a philologist's picnic. "No Oxford mincing is in him. If he cannot find his phrase above the salt, he seeks it below. His English, in a word, is innocent."

Mencken's style is not innocent, but mischievous. It is too erratic and casual to wear very well, but it was a liberation for writers like Robert Benchley, James Thurber, and S. J. Perelman, an invitation to linguistic risk rather than decorum. Mencken himself is perhaps best seen as a showman in prose rather than a man of theory or even principle. His essay "Being an American" offers reasons for staying in "this Eden of clowns" which are so withering that the exile of James and Pound and Eliot begins to look like the expression of deep patriotism. Yet we need to note both the love for America that hides in his blasting of it and the scorn for mankind that creeps back to complicate his love. It is an intricate and amusing performance in which the writer mocks himself as well as others. On his pages, words like *sniveling, poltroonish,* and *serfs* tug us toward the territory of W. C. Fields rather than that of a seriously wrathful sage.

Van Wyck Brooks was not a sage but a student. "I conducted my education in public," he wrote, but he educated America too, particularly in *The Ordeal of Mark Twain* (1920) and *The Pilgrimage of Henry James* (1925). He saw Europe as a "paradise of culture," bathed in a "mellowed splendor" that America scarcely knew that it lacked. America was the home of illustrious failures, writers devoured by their demons or a hostile world. Brooks situated his exemplary figures in their time and place, and his borrowing from psychoanalysis was lively and pioneering as well as clumsy. His great theme, as F. W. Dupee said, was "the difficulty of realizing oneself, not only as an artist in America, but as an American artist." In Brooks American criticism did not so much come of age as become self-consciously American.

In 1925 Edmund Wilson thought it was "becoming a commonplace to say of Mr. Van Wyck Brooks that he is really a social historian rather than a literary critic"—an observation that points to a tilt which was beginning to appear in the study of American literature. V. L. Parrington's *Main Currents in American Thought* (1927–30) traces a "political, economic, and social development, rather than the narrower belletristic," and although later work has often been subtler and more sophisticated than Parrington's, the criticism of American literature still tends to be a criticism of culture, part of a conversation about the national identity. The alternative is not pure literature but other literatures and cultures, and it is possible to combine the two approaches. In his remarkable *American Renaissance* (1941), F. O. Matthiessen expressed debts to Brooks and Parrington but also to Coleridge and Eliot, while showing too that cultural questions could be explored through close reading of major authors.

But American criticism in this century, as the work of Mencken and Santayana suggests, has not felt at all obliged to stay at home. Americans, once they had stopped avoiding or courting Europe, found themselves blessed with a sudden lightness or freedom of cultural choice. To be an American, in one sense, was to feel that one had the run of an infinite imaginary museum, without being daunted by the prospect. Greece and Rome, for example, even in translation, were closer to Americans than they had been to any European since the seventeenth century. According to Edmund Wilson, the most important things he got from his Princeton teacher were Flaubert and Dante. The American tradition in modern literature, to adapt an argument from Jorge Luis Borges, is not an allegiance to native scenes and customs but an uncoerced way of looking at a visitable world, America and Europe and Russia and the East. This freedom exacts a price, of course; and sometimes it is little more than a dream of freedom. But what Henry James called the complex fate of being an American is neither eluded nor betrayed by travel. In these terms the exiled, Anglican Eliot is as American as the stay-at-home Mencken.

James's prefaces to the New York Edition of his works appeared from 1907 to 1909, but achieved their most important effect rather later, thanks in large part to R. P. Blackmur's influential presentation of them in *The Art of the Novel* (1934). James had been writing criticism from the beginning of his literary career, but his early sarcasms (about Dickens, Whitman, and others) had given way to an intricate and smiling irony. Emerson, he said, "has not a grain of current contempt; one feels, at times, that he has not enough." "We have the impression . . . that life had never bribed him to look at anything but the soul." In 1884 James thought he detected an awakening of interest in the art of fiction in England and America, and recommended alertness to the critic, discipline and invention to the novelist. The latter was to "catch the color of life itself," "the very note and trick, the strange irregular rhythm of life"—a broad enough invitation. Yet he also had to select and arrange his catch, the life in his work being an "illusion," a "correspondence," not a raw slice. This is the chief tenet of James's prefaces, which were, he said, "a sort of plea for Criticism, for Discrimination, for Appreciation . . . as against the so almost universal Anglo-Saxon absence of these things."

James has much to say about technique, about the disposition of character and plot and scene in fiction, and about the circumstances, usually agreeable, in which he wrote or conceived his books. But he also makes important theoretical distinctions, for example between "the romantic" and "the real." The simplicity of the logic should not mislead us as to the subtlety and flexibility of the concepts.

The real represents to my perception the things we cannot possibly *not* know, sooner or later, in one way or another. . . . The romantic stands, on the other hand, for the things that, with all the facilities in the world, all the wealth and all the courage and all the wit and all the adventure, we never *can* directly know; the things that can reach us only through the beautiful circuit and subterfuge of our thought and our desire.

The real for James is a social, inhabited space, a world of others, where we are hampered but also tested. "Experience, as I see it, is our apprehension and our measure of what happens to us as social creatures."

F. R. Leavis suggested that the prefaces were overrated, requiring a greater effort of decipherment than they were worth, and likely to produce only a deadening academicism in critics. It is true that James's critical followers have often caught only the fussier side of his recommendations, but he was not the apostle of pure form he is often taken to be. He respected Zola, had much sympathy with the aims of Bennett and Wells, their "nearer view of common things," their bid for "the air and the very smell of packed actuality." He was an opponent of formlessness, and in this role quite unable to find any form at all in Tolstoy. Yet form for James was not an abstraction, a hollow beauty or decorum, but a design, a meaning, an effect of composition on the color of life. This poise, this difficult double loyalty to lived experience and shaped art, or in slightly altered terms, to "what we are to know and that prodigy of our knowing," is James's real legacy to criticism. His irony permitted him to tell the whole story, to glance at alternatives temporarily hidden by phrases leaning too hard in one direction. His fund of lively similes kept him from dogma, and above all he had the great gift of knowing when to seek precision and when to let it go. His conception of criticism as "the very education of our imaginative life," the reflection of a mind "reaching out for the reasons of its interest," still serves to answer those critics who demand only fierce judgments or starved objectivity, or excursions into the never less than infinite spaces of theory.

In a 1907 essay on *The Tempest*, James curiously raises the question of the poet's impersonality, later propounded by Eliot. What we find in Shakespeare's plays, James says, is not a person but "the artist, the monster and magician." "The man everywhere . . . is. . . . imprisoned in the artist." There is a "complete rupture . . . between the Poet and the Man." James borrows from a contemporary English critic what is in effect Eliot's argument—leave the man alone, concentrate on the poet, and there will be no problem—but only to reverse its terms. "This view is admirable," James says, "if you can get your mind to consent to it." Shakespeare's anonymity, in other words, is safe enough and needs accepting with good grace, but it is not a critical ideal. It is critically soothing at times, but at others "its power to torment us intellectually seems scarcely to be borne." What James is after is not gossip, or even facts, but a sense of a human creature, a set of motives, a story, a feeling for "the effect on him of being *able* to write *Lear* and *Othello*." This is just the line Stephen Dedalus pursues in *Ulysses* with his theory of *Hamlet*, and it is just what Eliot, and after him the New

Critics, thought poetry should use and then banish, dissolve in the chemistry of the poem itself.

"I am not a systematic thinker," Eliot wrote in a letter, "if indeed I am a thinker at all. I depend upon intuitions and perceptions." He later spoke publicly of the "truly embarrassing success in the world" of "a few notorious phrases," and he retained a healthy suspicion of abstractions, ideas cut loose from context and argument and feeling, as well as a ready responsiveness to time and place and personal pressure. But the notorious phrases matter too much to be whisked away into modesty, partly because of their considerable effect, and partly because of their continuing value, if we know how to attend to them.

Eliot's doctrine of the impersonality of the poet had several sources: Santayana, Rémy de Gourmont, Eliot's Harvard teacher Irving Babbitt. Santayana spoke of "the lamentable accidents" of an artist's "personality and opinions." Gourmont saw the moral life itself as a divestment or stripping down: "The aim of the proper activity of man is to cleanse the personality." Babbitt cultivated the mode of resonant generalization that Eliot and others were to take up, with and without irony, a habit that accounts for the pockets of emptiness found in even the best American critics. In Babbitt's view, loftily expressed in *Rousseau and Romanticism* (1919), modern philosophy was "bankrupt, not merely from Kant, but from Descartes." He berated what he called the romantic wherever he caught it ("A thing is romantic when it is strange, unexpected, intense, superlative, extreme, unique"). Like Leavis, he favored metaphors of maturity: "The person who is as much taken by Shelley at forty as he was at twenty has, one may surmise, failed to grow up." After such knowledge, there is a delicate, unintended comedy in Babbitt's saying that "to be a good humanist is merely to be moderate and sensible and decent." The prescription seems hopelessly tame, and even at that too much for some. Humanism, as defined by Babbitt and Paul Elmer More, another strenuously backward-looking critic, made a great flutter in American intellectual life in the 1920s, and then was heard of no more.

Eliot took up Babbitt's battle against the romantic, championing order against indulgence, but there is a sense in which this battle though important, was itself romantic, fought out on the terrains of dream. "The progress of an artist," Eliot said in "Tradition and the Individual Talent" (1919), "is a continual self-sacrifice, a continual extinction of personality." We note, as in Gourmont, the ethical stress, the life given rather than the work gained. The great artist-martyrs of Flaubert's letters and James's fiction hover here, and all those writers who wrote *instead* of living—a contrast Dickens, say, would not have understood. "The more perfect the artist," Eliot continues, "the more completely separate in him will be the man who suffers and the mind which creates." The phrase *completely separate* holds the attention, converts a truism (a work of art is not simple self-expression, a cry of pain or pleasure) into an extravagance (the suffering person evaporates). "The difference between art and the event is always absolute," Eliot emphatically says, expressing a need rather than anything observable in the world, which suggests that the difference is relative and unreliable.

An even more notorious phrase, the "objective correlative," occurs in "Hamlet and His Problems" (1919). "*Hamlet*, like the sonnets, is full of some stuff that the writer could not drag to light, contemplate, or manipulate into art." It offers only the "buffoonery" of an inexpressible emotion, and is thus unlike *Othello, Coriolanus, Antony and Cleopatra*, and *Macbeth*, which are "intelligible, self-complete, in the sunlight." This is powerful criticism, irreverent, clear-eyed, and responsive to the perceptible qualities of a troubling play. It forces us, I think, either to accept Eliot's view or to find a better one. We may want to see, for example, how deep and disheveled Shakespeare's art is here, and to question our assumptions about harmony and order and sunlight in art. Eliot's theory is another thing.

The only way of expressing emotion in the form of art is by finding an "objective correlative"; in other words, a set of objects, a situation, a chain of events which shall be the formula of that *particular* emotion; such that when the external facts, which must terminate in sensory experience, are given, the emotion is immediately evoked. . . . The artistic "inevitability" lies in this complete adequacy of the external to the emotion.

The concept is philosophically puzzling, and perhaps circular. We may wonder, too, whether broad words like *facts* and *emotion* and *external* will do anything like the technical work Eliot asks of them. His tone is a difficulty, since he seems so sure of himself, the desperation well hidden away in algebra. This tone, along with Eliot's reputation as a poet, accounts in part for the great influence of such pronouncements. But only in part. Eliot was projecting his version of the self-suppressing writer Thomas Mann had dreamed of in *Death in Venice*, a major modern legend, a man for a dry and frightened season. In some ways Eliot *was* Aschenbach, "the poet-spokesman of all those who labour at the edge of exhaustion," the author who rejects what he thinks of as "flabby humanitarianism" and "renounces sympathy with the abyss." The fact that Eliot adapted aspects of his thought from Nietzsche (there are plenty of other candidates: Allston, Coleridge, Bosanquet, Husserl, Santayana, Pound, and Whitman all use phrases very close to Eliot's) confirms this European connection. Nietzsche, writing of

Hamlet, saw what Eliot saw, except that he diagnosed it as a bottomless, despairing wisdom, a truth beneath the words of the text, rather than an artistic failure.

Eliot's objective correlative may be said, then, to gather many modern preoccupations, too many for more than a rather helpless listing: a claim for the autonomy of the work of art; an exaltation of discipline, which is not without its dubious political echoes; a sense of the pressure of the physical sciences and the new social sciences, like anthropology, psychology, and linguistics, on human understanding; an actual fear of emotion, bred who knows where or how; a desire to salvage something from time seen as an agent of sheer destruction, a futile succession that must be frozen into meaning. In short, it was another name for form, an antidote to the messiness of personal and public history.

Eliot wanted to restore mind to a culture of emotion, to balance thought and feeling, and so invented a tale that met his need. For the Elizabethans and Jacobeans, he said, "intellect was immediately at the tips of the senses." "A thought to Donne was an experience; it modified his sensibility." Then things fell apart. "In the seventeenth century a dissociation of sensibility set in, from which we have never recovered." "Tennyson and Browning are poets, and they think; but they do not feel their thought as immediately as the odour of a rose." It is hard to believe literally in a dissociation that just sets in, like frost or a long winter, or to see how feeling a thought would leave much room for thinking. But flimsy history and shaky logic sometimes make strong myth—its mythical status being underlined by the fact that Eliot was inclined to shift the date of the great dissociation, placing it mostly after Donne but sometimes between Shakespeare and Donne and sometimes even before Shakespeare. Whatever we make of the myth, it enabled a startling recovery of wit for literature, and a new respect for the intellect, both of the poet and of the reader. Without it, not only the New Criticism but much modern poetry is unthinkable.

"Make it new," Ezra Pound repeatedly urged, although the new was quite often a piece of the old he had just discovered. He sought out poems that contained "an invention, a definite contribution to the art of verbal expression," and he insisted, to very good effect, that poetry had to be at least as well written as prose. "His true Penelope was Flaubert," he wrote in *Hugh Selwyn Mauberley*, aiming to bury rather than praise himself. He knew that Flaubert was a harsh and unlikely muse for a poet, but he expected poets to get the lesson and the irony.

Pound and Eliot were, as René Wellek says, "the central figures in the shift of taste and change of theory in this century"; and Eliot paid hand-some tribute to Pound's energetic influence. Pound himself called his activ-ity a "pawing over the ancients and semi-ancients." He celebrated contem-poraries where he saw cause, spotting the talent of Robert Frost and Marianne Moore, for example; and he raided writers of the past, in the engaging belief that "people were much the same" in the twelfth century as in the twentieth ("Men were pressed for money. There was unspeakable boredom in the castles"). Pound cannot literally have believed this, since he knew that different conditions create different habits, but the past remained very immediate to him: not an ideal order or a tradition but *another*, displaced present, containing Provence, the work of Dante and Cavalcanti, some me-dieval English writing. "Have I dug him up again?" Pound asks in a note to a poem about a Provençal poet and warrior. He expects a positive an-swer. Either the past deserves to be buried or we are not digging hard enough. Similarly Pound's view of the impersonality of the poet has a char-acteristically brisk and practical coloring: the artist "may, apart from his art, be any kind of imbecile you like." The poet who strenuously disappears in Eliot's theory is simply sacked in Pound's.

Pound's criticism, even more than Eliot's, brings us close to the work-shop, makes clear those aspects of writing that we are apt to mystify. The only way of talking sense about literature, he says, is with *specimens* in hand: "e.g. particular works, passages of literature." "I believe in technique as the test of a man's sincerity"—a radical creed if we take it seriously. He is fond—too fond, no doubt—of medical analogies: language is to be kept clean like a bandage; we need an "antiseptic intolerance" for inaccuracy; abstrac-tion is a disease that has "spread like tuberculosis." His enemy is what he calls "slither" in writing. He wants a poetry "like granite"; beauty rather than sentimentalizing about beauty; a ban on "rhetorical din" and "painted adjectives."

Pound's influence on and help of other writers has been well docu-mented. He had, Allen Tate said, "done more than any other man to re-generate the language, if not the imaginative forms, of English verse." His criticism, *pace* Eliot, seems too ragged and piecemeal to possess major au-thority, but it does contain crucial hints: pleas for close reading, for atten-tion to craft and form, and above all for an end to the domination of the English perspective. "Anything that happens to mind in England," he breez-ily says, "has usually happened somewhere else." And sometimes it doesn't even happen in England.

All the developments in English verse since 1910 are due almost wholly to Ameri-cans. In fact, there is no longer any reason to call it English verse, and there is no present reason to think of England at all.

This was further than most American loyalists in literature were prepared to go. The year after Pound wrote these words (1927–28), Virginia Woolf, Edmund Wilson, and others were still arguing about whether the American language was a language.

The New Criticism was announced in a lecture of 1910 and in the title of an anthology of 1930, but both calls proved premature. By 1941, when John Crowe Ransom published a book called *The New Criticism*, a study of the work of Eliot, I. A. Richards, William Empson, Yvor Winters, and others, the time was right, and the label stuck. It is not a label that says a lot, and it lumps together a range of different practices. But the movement was real enough, and the family resemblances can hardly be denied. It seems to have required for its establishment and its fueling at least three conditions that were previously lacking: a body of literature, namely the works we call modernist, crying out for a criticism to match it and comment on it; a disenchantment with the snares and upsets of history, which made the "poem itself" an attractive haven, a paradise of poise and purity; the shift of criticism from journalism and publishing and private patronage to the university. The man of letters, with one or two notable exceptions, became the professor. Did this mean, as Eliot thought, that criticism reached "a more limited though not necessarily a smaller public"? Criticism in the classroom was often inventive, and it reached a lively public limited only by its youth. But two shifts were clearly under way. As the common reader became less literary, the academic reader became more technical. Criticism itself felt harassed by the proliferation of specialized knowledge, worried by all it saw it didn't know. The exemplary, contrasting figure was Edmund Wilson, who, though not a professor, diligently learned what he didn't know. He also, almost single-handedly, kept reviewing and criticism from falling apart, as they constantly threatened to do. In the universities, authors and periods became "fields" surrounded by very high fences.

The great virtue of the New Criticism was that it knew what criticism was and was not. It was not history or scholarship, or gossip about authors and works. It was not cultural commentary, it was not paraphrase. It was an attention to the text, to what Blackmur called "the words and the motions of the words," by which he meant "all the technical devices of literature." The critic needs to lean on the historian, Cleanth Brooks says, and may even be a historian when he wears another hat. But the functions are different. A poem is "not a statement" but a dramatization of an attitude, and the critic's job is to evoke the attitude, to picture its often complicated contents.

In its humdrum forms the New Criticism produced platitudinous studies of image-patterns and the like; it was more interested in imagery than in syntax and in poems than in novels. But even so it was preferable to mere gossip. More seriously, the movement so privileged irony, balance, paradox, and the organic unity of the individual work that it became an evasion of the nightmares and disorders of art. As Hillis Miller says, the New Criticism assumed not only that every detail counts but that it counts toward harmony, an assumption that "may become a temptation to leave out what does not fit, to see it as insignificant or as a flaw."

Structuralism in America was in one sense another formalism, bringing a vocabulary of codes and rules borrowed from linguistics and paying more attention to narrative. But poststructuralism and deconstruction questioned the deeper premises of earlier work by seeking out what Henry James called the bewilderment of a text, or the particular interests concealed in conspiracies of order. Psychoanalytic criticism, which was slow to shift out of a cumbersomely biographical mode, also came to focus on gaps or discords in a text, clues to unresolved conflicts in a character or the culture. We meet again Eliot's Hamlet, the fatherless prince who cannot externalize his ills; and Nietzsche's Hamlet, the philosopher who has looked into the abyss and seen that it doesn't end.

If many of the ingredients of the New Criticism lay to hand in the writings of James and Pound and especially Eliot, a more immediate impulse was the work of I. A. Richards, whose *Principles of Literary Criticism* (1925), Eliot thought, altered not only the course of criticism but the meaning of the term. It became a matter, Allen Tate said, of reading poetry "with all the brains one had and with one's arms and legs, as well as what may be inside the rib cage." Richards believed that the best of us read carelessly, hampered by prejudices and by more ignorance than we admit to. But he didn't think the case hopeless. "The lesson of all criticism," he said in *Practical Criticism* (1929), "is that we have nothing to rely upon in making choices but ourselves. The lesson of good poetry seems to be that, when we have understood it, in the degree in which we can order ourselves, we need nothing more." The New Criticism begins and ends in the close reading Richards showed to be so indispensable. In *Seven Types of Ambiguity* (1930), William Empson, Richards's pupil at Cambridge, provided an acrobatic unraveling of textual meanings so rich and dense that it made people feel that what they had been calling reading was a mere turning of the pages.

When John Crowe Ransom named the movement ("I think it is time to identify a powerful intellectual movement that deserves to be called a new criticism"), he also said that what was needed was "an ontological critic." A poem is nothing short of a desperate ontological or metaphysical manouevre. . . . The poet perpetuates in his poem an order of existence which in actual life is constantly crumbling beneath his touch. . . . The poet wishes to defend his object's existence against its enemies, and the critic wishes to know what he is doing, and how.

For this reason, he said, poets are "prodigious materialists." Poetry "has no great interest in improving or idealizing the world, which does well enough. It only wants to realize the world, to see it better." Yet surely Ransom's was a rather ghostly materialism. The world realized in the poem is contemplated rather than lived in; it offers what Schopenhauer called "knowledge without desire." It is a crumbling reality pictured as not crumbling; not a fantasy but a memory, a form of lateness. "The tense of poetry is the past—more accurately, it is the pluperfect."

Ransom, like other critics of his generation, was interested in technique. How many readers, he wonders, spot the ten unrhymed lines in *Lycidas*? His critical writing is graceful, thoughtful, often passionate, although his theories are cramped by just the insufficiency of philosophical equipment he finds in Eliot. He divides a poem into its "paraphrasable core" and its "living local details"—"a loose logical structure with a good deal of local texture"—in which the texture represents the irreplaceable, poetic elements that cannot be reduced to prose or made to serve practical purposes. The weakness here is surely the simple binary model, with its mutually exclusive terms. What if the logic itself has poetic life? What if the details are paraphrasable, or decay into mere frills? What if the two sets cannot usefully be told apart at all?

Two years before Ransom published *The New Criticism*, the movement had found a particularly elegant advocate in Cleanth Brooks, who argued, in *Modern Poetry and the Tradition* (1939), that "a critical revolution of the order of the Romantic Revolt" was in progress, or had just taken place. Modern poetry demanded not only appreciation in its own terms but a "radical revision of the existing conception of poetry." Eliot's work had brought in its wake a new appetite for Donne and Marvell, an elevation of Keats over all the other Romantics, and a much diminished enthusiasm for Arnold's "magnificent monotone." For Brooks, irony and ambiguity became a poem's defense against a skeptical age, a form of first strike against accusations of sentimentality. He admired works that allow for conflicting possibilities, saw a vulnerability in those that "ignore the complexity of experience." Brooks's criticism was stylish rather than forceful, but he read precisely and sensitively throughout a distinguished academic career, and unlike many of his contemporaries, turned his critical attention to prose as well as poetry.

Yvor Winters figures prominently in Ransom's book, and shares quite a bit of ground with the New Critics. But he was too much of a maverick to be part of even a loosely linked movement. His besetting word was *reason*, which he clung to against what seemed to him constantly worsening odds. He demanded a lot but didn't hope for much, since "life is painful if one expects more than two or three men in a century to behave as rational animals." His chief works are *Primitivism and Decadence* (1937), *Maule's Curse* (1938), and *The Anatomy of Nonsense* (1943). He was, Blackmur said, "an Irving Babbitt who *really* knows poetry"; and his severity of judgment was often accompanied by a great delicacy of comprehension. He saw that Donne's "bony step" was quite different from the "light pausing and shifting of Sidney"; that Wallace Stevens parodies the "slight affectation of elegance" of his own style, "or perhaps it were more accurate to say that this affectation itself is a parody, however slight, of the purity of his style in its best moments." But the preferred Winters accent is scathing. Eliot and Ransom "think as badly as possible"; William Carlos Williams is "wholly incapable of coherent thought"; Pound is "a sensibility without a mind, or with as little mind as is well possible." In place of Eliot's objective correlative for an emotion Winters wanted a grasp of the emotion's ground, its motive. "The task of the poet is to adjust feeling to motive precisely." This is not to say that Winters seeks a paraphrasable argument, or a sense detachable from the form of a poem; rather an understanding that governs the whole work, form and content, "persisting even into the sound of the least important syllable." He calls this, perhaps strangely, a judgment: "a work of art, like each detail comprising it, is by definition a judgment." *The Waste Land* fails in this respect because Eliot surrenders to a morbid mood that Baudelaire, for example, was able to master. "Eliot suffers from the delusion that he is judging it when he is merely exhibiting it." But such judgment is not classification or preaching: "it is a full and definitive account of a human experience."

There is much to be said for this insistence on the intelligible in art, and Winters's view is clearly more subtle, more attentive to the currents and contours of particular works, than he sometimes made it sound. Nevertheless, clarity can be constricting. If literature is more than the display of confused feelings, it is also more than rational knowledge. *The Waste Land*, we might say, neither judges nor exhibits a malaise; it explores it, tests it, visits its hiding places, and hints at its etiology. This may be what Winters means by judging, but it is more than the word, unaided, will say, and his own unexamined use of words like *reason* and *thought* leaves much of his criticism stranded in abstraction.

Winters thought there was "nearly nothing" in the thought of Allen Tate and R. P. Blackmur that was not to be found in Eliot and Ransom. This may be true, or nearly true, if we take thought to mean named doctrine or principle. But if it is an activity, the signature of a mind, then Tate and Blackmur are quite different from each other, and from anyone else. With James and Pound and Eliot and Kenneth Burke, they seem now the most durable critics of the period, the ones whose voices speak most clearly to us as continuing contemporaries. Tate and Blackmur are the major New Critics, but in looking at them, we must finally let go of the label, which threatens to hide their particularities.

Tate does sound like Eliot at times, and even like Winters: "the perfectly realized poem has no overflow of unrealized action." Poetry is "the art of apprehending and concentrating our experience in the mysterious limitations of form." But Winters would not have written *mysterious*, and Eliot was less eager for experience. Poetry, Tate also wrote, is "ideas tested by experience," and one of the great virtues of Tate's criticism, collected in *Reactionary Essays* (1936), *Reason in Madness* (1941), and other books, is that it places the perceiving, suffering, fallible human creature at the center of its concern. In "The Hovering Fly," an essay of 1943 that Denis Donoghue calls "one of the grand occasions of modern criticism," Tate asks us to remember the haunting scene near the end of *The Idiot* where a fly buzzes over a corpse and settles on a pillow. We cannot, Tate says, imagine this scene without its human figures, Roghozin and Prince Myshkin, we cannot contemplate the room emptied of everything except death and the fly, for this would be to "imagine ourselves out of our humanity":

to imagine the scene is to be there, and to be there, before the sheeted bed, is to have our interests powerfully affected. The fiction that we are neither here nor there, but are only spectators . . . is the great modern heresy.

Tate also speaks of "a deep illness of the modern mind," and of "the ingenious failure of our time." We have failed, he thinks, to stand up for values, to name and define "our standard of human nature and the good society." We have settled for what he calls, in a spectacular phrase, "the facile optimism of decay."

The heresy is to believe that an impersonal, inhuman perspective is possible or desirable for humans. For the critic, Tate says, "the total view is no view at all," and "even if (which is impossible) he sees everything, he has got to see it from somewhere." Tate's quarrel with literary scholarship, wittily conducted in the essay "Miss Emily and the Bibliographer" (1940), is that it fails to attend to actual works, to the "concrete form of the play, the poem, the novel," whether past or present, and that it won't judge. Tate is echoing Pound's complaint about "the grand abnegation." Won't history judge? "If we wait for history to judge," Tate replies, "there will be no judgment; for if we are not history then history is nobody." We have made a world, he thinks, and not only a literary world, in which we all act our sad role in "the plotless drama of withdrawal."

What modern literature has taught us is not merely that the man of letters has not participated fully in the action of society; it has taught us that nobody else has either. It is a fearful lesson.

It is easy to see how reactionary these ideas could look and were in the liberal times of Roosevelt and after, and it is important to note the anarchy and nostalgia that can creep into them. The relativity of human perspectives seems to have led Tate to a Catholic God who possesses precisely the total view we lack. Tate distinguished artfully between prejudice and dogma—dogma being merely "coherent thought in pursuit of principle"—but this is surely disingenuous. The trouble with dogma is that it has *found* its principle, and has no intention of looking any further.

And yet the force and eloquence of these arguments is considerable, whatever we feel about Tate's prescriptions and preferences. Like Ransom, he was a Southerner, and Ransom later thought the Agrarian group, to which both belonged, had lost the war against modernity before it had even started. "Historically, we were behind the times. But we were right in thinking that the times were bad." Or they were right in thinking that no times are so good that they have no need of honorable opponents. Tate fought for immediate values, Blackmur said, "with the tenacity and rage that usually go with lost causes"; and his lost cause was not the Old South but "the dignity of man." Literary criticism, Tate himself argued, is always in an "intolerable position," and this is just where it should be, "perpetually necessary . . . perpetually impossible." The pathos and the paradox may be a touch overdone, but the energy of the idea, along with the unfailing courtesy and grace of Tate's style, guarantees a vivid attention to particular texts and writers. "I often think of my poems," Tate said, "as commentaries on those human situations from which there is no escape." We may think of his criticism as a meditation on the reasons that remain for wanting to escape all the same. Common sense is "a good thing to have," Tate remarked, "but not good enough if it is all we have." Like James and Eliot, Tate held in his mind a "good society" that was not a dream or a memory but a summons, a demand made of the flagging historical world; an American refusal to abide by the merely available.

"There is a strength to his language," Blackmur said of Tate, "superior to any ideas that may be detached from it." He is describing what I have called criticism as performance, and the remark is also true of his own language, although we may wish to shift the emphasis a little. Blackmur's style is strong enough, but it is chiefly subtle, full of shades, an instrument not so much for arguing as for catching and displaying complicated movements of diction and meaning. Later in his career, in the 1950s and early 1960s, this style became very mannered, a sort of gloating on the arcane, but even then it clearly grew out of Blackmur's pursuit of textual qualities that he felt we could never directly name.

In *The Double Agent* (1935) and *The Expense of Greatness* (1940), and later in *Language as Gesture* (1952) and *The Lion and the Honeycomb* (1955), Blackmur sought to respond to what he called "the very tone of experience"—the experience that a poem or novel orders and evokes, and the experience of the poem or novel itself. "Poetry is . . . a special and fresh saying, and cannot for its life be said otherwise." This is to announce (in 1935) what Cleanth Brooks later denounced as the heresy of paraphrase, but Blackmur is not suggesting that paraphrase is heretical, only that it needs to be recognized for what it is: an abstraction, a form of fable. "What we make is a fiction to school the urgency of reading; no more." Critics "simply . . . set up clues." Blackmur's own criticism is alert, precise, and provisional, endlessly mindful of the gaps between knowledge and feeling, and between feeling and words. When he comments on the temptation of sociological and biographical critics to take the poet "as a fatal event in cultural history," he is not denying event or history, he is pointing to the unwary logical leap, the determinism that doesn't know itself. Similarly when a writer pretends to measure life directly, without the mediation of achieved form, the result, Blackmur says, is "a substitute for something that never was— like a tin soldier, or Peter Pan."

But Blackmur had great faith not only in works of literature as unique arrangements of words but in words themselves as bearers of historical reality. Wallace Stevens makes us "aware of how much is *already* condensed in a word," and Hart Crane has a "gift for the hearts of words."

An author should remember, with the Indians, that the reality of a word is anterior to, and greater than, his use of it can ever be; that there is a perfection to the feelings in words to which his mind cannot hope to attain.

So that if language fails us radically, as Blackmur elsewhere says it does, the fault is in us, not in the words. There is a flavor of mysticism here, and an approach to the distinction, so dear to structuralism, between *langue* and *parole*—the former being the great fund of available language, the latter the use any one speaker makes of the treasure. "It is language which happens through the speaker," Donald Davie says, commenting on a phrase of Mallarmé, "not the speaker who expresses himself through language." Davie thinks that this is what Eliot meant, but did not say, with his doctrine of impersonality. It may be that this sense of what words will do, or would do if we loved or trusted them enough, accounts for Blackmur's inclination to linger over strange or difficult terms, to make fetishes of them: he is saying his prayers to the language gods. Certainly it is this attitude to language that permits him to use religious metaphors with peculiar secular force. "We see what the words mean," he says of a lyrical passage in Eliot's *Burnt Norton:* "what is incarnated in them—though it is a partial incarnation: partial ecstasy and partial horror, and it may be we do not grasp what is not incarnated."

Much of Blackmur's close critical attention went to poets: Marianne Moore, E. E. Cummings, Stevens, Emily Dickinson, Eliot, Pound, Yeats. His approach, he said, was "technical in the widest sense." But he also wrote eloquently about Henry James, and left a long (unfinished) book on Henry Adams. He was an orthodox New Critic in his insistence on form. "Poetry is life at the remove of form and meaning; not life lived but life framed and identified"; it is a "means of putting a tolerable order upon the emotions." But these remarks need setting alongside others that clearly separate Blackmur from Eliot, Winters, and Tate. Blackmur insists, for example, on "the intolerableness of even the most necessary order," and defines "sound orders" as "those which invite as well as withstand disorder." Art *is* order for Blackmur, as it was for James; there is no virtue in randomly reported experience, or in "the merely self-expressed, or the merely argued." But for Blackmur it is disorder (or an unknown order, an order that is not ours) that calls the tune. Disorder is the truth our invented orders help us to bear. "Wholeness, preconceived, is a prison into which the mind is not compelled to thrust itself." Wholeness, like the perfection of feelings in words, is an absent target, a measure of our incompleteness, not a paradise we can scale or enter. A difficult failure, Blackmur suggests, is infinitely preferable to a deluded success.

As it is a condition of life to die, it is a condition of thought, in the end, to fail. Death is the expense of life and failure is the expense of greatness.

As with Tate, we may feel that the dark pathos is too eagerly courted. But we can also see Blackmur as defining thought rather than celebrating failure, in a light that makes Winters's rigors look lenient.

The real influence of the New Criticism was considerable, its imagined influence almost infinite. In 1958, Philip Rahv wishfully reported that it was "virtually done for." Yet it has since been attacked with regularity that justifies F. W. Dupee's fine phrase "an immortal scapegoat." Not only in the universities and schools but also in the general culture it was kept going at least as much by its enemies as by its friends. What was being opposed?

On one flank the New Criticism was felt, by a group of Chicago critics whose most eloquent spokesman was R. S. Crane, to be insufficiently formalist. Its interest was too "semantic," a pursuit of tone or meaning that excluded "all except the most general kind of formal distinctions." More recently Wellek has also suggested that the New Critics paid very little attention to formal devices, and worked largely through "psychological" concepts like attitude and tension and irony. These precisions are useful. Form was perhaps after all a moral term for the New Critics, and in this sense they reach back to Henry James and even join hands with Roland Barthes. But it is the term we need. To "reject the distinction of form and content" (Wellek) is to be, precisely, one kind of formalist. The Chicago variety took us back to Aristotle for rules and models and was in theory pluralist in its leanings. Crane saw criticism not as a discipline but as a collection of "frameworks" or "languages," the crucial issue being what a critic "thinks *with*" rather than "thinks *about*." Crane and his colleagues certainly helped to clarify fundamental issues of literary history and criticism, but in practice what they called formal principles were very general, and tended to leave little space for other perspectives.

But the major quarrel with the New Criticism, and perhaps the major quarrel of the period, concerned history. The New Critics, Lionel Trilling said, "forgot" the historicity of the literary work. They were themselves caught up in history, like everyone else, offered historical judgments, but made "the historical sense irrelevant to their aesthetic." At this distance they seem to be remembering history all too hard, energetically closing the door against its foot. It was not their ignoring of history that other critics resented but their claim for art's freedom from history's claws; this seemed undesirable to many, and just untrue to others. Critics of all persuasions agreed that literature is not life, but then felt differently about the difference. The opponents of the New Criticism wanted to close the gap rather than consecrate it, and they had another, forward-looking, Marxist or liberal history in mind.

It is a distortion to speak of the adversaries of the New Criticism as if they were a rival school. The New Criticism was not as central as that, except as a myth, and there was no united opposition. But there was an insistence, in varied voices, on historical engagement, and hindsight can piece together a counter-myth. It will simplify things (but not, I hope, falsify them) if we take the counter-myth to be answering Eliot's doctrine of the artist's separation from his suffering.

The hero of Edmund Wilson's novel *I Thought of Daisy* (1929) wishes to bring together in his life "the self that experiences and the self that writes." The formulation suggests a man starting where Eliot wants to end and heading in the other direction. Wilson's criticism very much follows this project. On the one hand, he is sometimes bland and reductive, not so much because he keeps guessing at the secret lives of writers as because the terms of the guesses are so clumsy. Dickens, once we have made proper allowance for English restraint, "seems almost as unstable as Dostoyevsky." The comparison is not farfetched, but the adjective is peculiarly unhelpful. Scrooge, if we could track him home after the jolly ending of *A Christmas Carol*, would "unquestionably . . . relapse . . . into moroseness, vindictiveness, suspicion . . . reveal himself as the victim of a manic-depressive cycle." Warner Berthoff identifies Wilson's chief fault as *knowingness*, a feeling that he can explain anything, and certainly the criticism seems thinnest when it talks briskly and sensibly about mysteries. "The psychological situation seems plain," he says of Yeats and *A Vision*. It hasn't seemed at all plain to anyone else.

On the other hand, Wilson can grasp and register difficult concepts without reducing them at all, and his writing can be precise and eloquent. He notes, in *The Waste Land*, Eliot's "shy sympathy with the common life"; sees that Joyce's stylistic bravura involves "a curious shrinking solicitude to conceal from the reader his real subjects"; hears the "clear and luminous music" that James gets "out of chords very queerly combined." Flaubert's *Education sentimentale*, Wilson says

is the tragedy of nobody in particular, but of the poor human race itself reduced to such ineptitude, such cowardice, such commonness, such weak irresolution.

This admirably answers James's strictures on Flaubert for his attachment to "inferior" or "abject human specimens" as his heroes. There is a tragedy of ordinariness in Flaubert, an alarming sense of mediocrity as fate. Wilson is funny, too. "Proust's heart breaks at the Ritz," he says, and a parody written in 1938 signals both the virtues of Wilson's plain prose and the distance American literary journalism had come in quite a short time:

With how sure an expectation of solace, amid the turmoil and perplexities of our time, do I turn, when the fires of evening are lit, to my silent companions in the library! Here the din of the city dies away.

"There are few things I enjoy so much as talking to people about books which I have read but they haven't." There is truth in this remark of Wilson's, but there is also self-satire. What Wilson mainly wanted, as he said elsewhere, was to persuade people to read books that were new to them. He was indefatigable in his homework, and patiently evoked and described all the books he discussed—a job as important for the critic, he thought, as the establishing of his characters is for a novelist. In his dedication to *Axel's Castle* (1931), he seems to muddle history and criticism ("what literary criticism ought to be—a history of men's ideas and imaginings in the setting of the conditions which have shaped them"). But at his best he argued that the two are not seriously separable. It is characteristic that what is commonly regarded as his best book, *To the Finland Station* (1940), should be subtitled "A study in the writing and acting of history," and should reconstruct revolutionary socialism as if it were a heroic, Balzacian novel. Wilson was a journalist in the most honored sense: he had all the virtues of the trade, and only a few of its flaws.

Wilson, along with Kenneth Burke and Lionel Trilling, was the chief articulator of what I have called the counter-myth to Eliot's. Far from being separate, art and suffering are tightly twinned, as in Sophocles' *Philoctetes*, memorably discussed in Wilson's *The Wound and the Bow* (1941). The great Greek archer has the bow and the skill that will win Troy; but he also has a festering wound that causes the Greeks to leave him to his pain and anger on Lemnos. The "fundamental idea," Wilson says, is of "superior strength as inseparable from disability": "genius and disease, like strength and mutilation, may be inextricably bound up together." The very art of Sophocles, Wilson suggests, has all the balance and order that are so much admired, "but these qualities only count because they master so much savagery and madness." The movement of thought here is dialectical, as in Nietzsche's *Birth of Tragedy* ("what suffering must this race have endured in order to achieve such beauty"), or in Freud, or in Marx.

It was Freud's career and vision of man, rather than the details of the psychoanalytic method, that mainly fired the critical imagination in this period. What Freud called the economy of the mind brings together the wound and the bow in a relation that is intimate but not simply causal. Kenneth Burke's image for this relation is a burden and its bearer: "nothing more deeply engrosses a man than his *burdens*, including those of a physical nature, such as disease," and the poet's burdens are "symbolic of his style, and his style symbolic of his burdens." Burke is thinking of Mann and *The Magic Mountain*, but we may think again of Aschenbach, whose discipline was itself the measure of all it had to hold at bay, and whose lapse could only end in dissolution. "What more fitting place to create one's church," Burke exclaims, in connection with the murky materials of Freud's profession, "than above a sewer! One might even say that sewers are what churches are for." For Lionel Trilling, Freud is the master of a "grim poetry" and a "tragic realism"; a teacher of heroic accommodations with defeat. Trilling's view is more nuanced than Wilson's or Burke's; indeed, he explicitly denies that the wound or the burden creates the artist. But Burke and Wilson do not quite say that it does, and Trilling's position belongs to the same dialectical family. To say that "we are ill in the service of health" is to change the emphasis but to keep the connection.

It is important to see that this myth is both older and newer than Eliot's: older because it is a version of the *poète maudit* and the romantic worship of distress—precisely the line of thought Eliot's myth was designed to combat; newer because it is more flexible, less exclusive, recognizes differences but puts together what Eliot set asunder. Suffering is acknowledged and made to work, rather than exiled or canceled. The artist, in Trilling's remarkable phrase, has the "power to shape the material of pain." This is quite different from the killing of pain, and a richer image of art.

Criticism may be interested in the shaping or the shape or both. In two out of the three cases, history returns, either as "an inextricable tangle of culture and biology" (Trilling) or as the economic conditions Burke and Wilson tried on and off to remember. Burke argued, for example, that the appeal of *Mein Kampf* for the Germans was that it offered "a noneconomic interpretation of a phenomenon economically engendered"; and Wilson thought that Americans in the 1920s were "making themselves neurotic in the attempt to introduce idealism" into an economic system dependent on cutthroat competition.

Marxism in America produced some well-intentioned and dogmatic criticism but no Georg Lukács or Walter Benjamin, or even collective approximations to them, and its lasting effect was obliquely achieved in writers who learned their materialist lessons and went their way. Burke was not only "a pastoral sort of Marxist," as Marius Bewley sharply said; he was also capable of regarding the class struggle as a myth. His insistence that it was *real* myth did not reassure his comrades at the American Writers' Congress in 1935. Philip Rahv, a founder and editor of the *Partisan Review*, more closely resembled a European Marxist, and his lucid and reflective criticism has considerable staying power. But he seems to stand mainly for shrewd sense and an awareness of context—we should realize, he reminds us, that "the greater part of the criticism of consequence . . . is shot through and through with ideological motives and postulations that remain for the most part unanalyzed and unacknowledged"—and is heir to the liberal literary taste of Marx rather than that of modern Marxism. He defends the

Eliot of *Murder in the Cathedral*, and writes very forcefully about Dostoev-sky. Wilson was moved by the moral courage he found in Marxism, and by its conscience, but he did not take on any of its theoretical equipment. Trilling was in some ways as loyal to Marxism as Rahv was, but it was the loyalty of an opposition, a continuing debate with an error felt to be close to the truth.

Kenneth Burke is perhaps best described as, in his own words, "a student of strategies." "Critical and imaginative works," he says, "are answers to questions posed by the situation in which they arose." He insists repeatedly on context, and urges that "if there is any slogan that should reign among critical precepts, it is that 'circumstances alter cases.' " Another, less pedes-trian slogan is "When in Rome, do as the Greeks"; and Burke's critical writings, notably in *Counter-Statement* (1931) and *The Philosophy of Literary Form* (1941), offer plenty of shifting strategies for dealing with strategies. "All questions," as he sees them, "are leading questions. . . . Every ques-tion selects a field of battle." We are caught in contexts we define and in others that are defined for us. Burke's prose is "generous to its reader," Benjamin De Mott says. "It tells him he has an active mind, is agile and quick, relishes complication, is scornful of emotional posturing and human enough to enjoy being silly now and then." Maybe there aren't enough such readers. Certainly Burke is less an influence on critical thought than he is someone who might have been, perhaps ought to have been an influence. Burke's useful sense of ideology, for example, is still not current in Amer-ica, and when it is available at all, seems to have been imported from France: "An ideology is an aggregate of beliefs sufficiently at odds with one another to justify opposite kinds of conduct." Much of Claude Lévi-Strauss's theory of myth lies here, some twenty-four years early. Burke is rare among mod-ern critics too in suggesting that we might make our home in anxiety rather than seeking to transcend or dispel it. The lesson of Mann and Gide, he argues, could be that we should accept our "social wilderness without an-guish," and regard "technical apprehension" as a challenging norm.

Still, there are difficulties in Burke's writing. It is plain enough, even breezy, but often shows a reckless disregard for the meanings of words—always a risky course for a writer. "Situation," Burke says, "is but another word for motive," making us wonder why the language bothered to develop the two words at all. "We have made these terms synonymous: form, psy-chology, and eloquence." "Form in literature is an arousing and fulfilment of desires"; "form would be the psychology of the audience." Burke calls his criticism "sociological" because it identifies strategies to be found not only in literature but in other social acts—in a dirty joke (Burke's example) as well as in a great sermon or a tragedy. Its effect is that it "breaks down the barriers erected about literature as a specialized pursuit." Burke was often rebuked for this, and pretended to repent, or at least to "wince." But as the piling up of impossible synonyms suggests, he was not much interested in differences, only in schemes of similarity. At times his zeal for the grand view seems positively heartless. "I should want to treat even suicide in real life as but the act of rebirth reduced to its simplest and most restricted form." That *but* is horribly revealing. The great menace to dictatorships, Burke says, is that "they deprive themselves of competitive collaboration." Can we wait for them to understand this, and what if they get just enough collaboration to keep them going?

The great attraction of Burke's criticism and theory is that they keep moving and will look anywhere. He has thrown away more good ideas than most people ever find. Even his "systematic" remarks, anathema in principle to so many American pragmatists, turn out to be quirky, full of wriggling, individual life. Here, for instance, is Burke's list of supposedly "universal experiences." They may *be* universal, but the list is far from standard, or homogenous: "mockery, despair, grimness, *sang-froid*, wonder, lamentation, melancholy, hatred, hopefulness, bashfulness, relief, boredom, dislike."

Much of Lionel Trilling's work and most of his reputation belong to the 1950s and 1960s, but he published books on Matthew Arnold and E. M. Forster in 1939 and 1944, and wrote some very substantial criticism in the early 1940s. *The Liberal Imagination* appeared in 1950. As this title and those English names suggest, he sought a discourse that was neither Marxist nor conservative. He was interested in what he called the politics of culture, but felt that liberalism needed to be reawakened rather than dutifully pursued.

The job of criticism would seem to be . . . to recall liberalism to its first essential imagination of variousness and possibility, which implies the awareness of complexity and difficulty.

"The world," Trilling said in those dark accents that spoke for so many in this period, "is a complex and unexpected and terrible place."

It has been suggested that Trilling was "more than a critic," but perhaps it is more accurate to say that he gave the word *criticism* a peculiar range and dignity and force. "We fulfill ourselves by choosing what is painful and difficult and necessary," he wrote. We learn to live in "the moral world of difficulty and pain," and criticism is a name for doing this responsibly and intelligently. But Trilling was also a passionate and troubled reader of the great illiberal modernists, and much of his career can be understood as a dialogue, often anxious, between the books that formed him and the values that he held to be needed. There was a resistance to literature in his work, which yet managed to respect literature's integrity, and deftly kept urgent ideas from slipping away into abstraction. *"Hamlet,"* Trilling wrote, "is not merely the product of Shakespeare's thought, it is the very instrument of his thought, and if meaning is intention, Shakespeare did not intend . . . anything less than *Hamlet."*

Trilling sees shadows too as part of reality ("one would not want a world without shadows, it would not even be a 'real' world"), and the mind as both a privilege and a strain—a strain that Americans often seem anxious to be rid of. "With us," Trilling says, "it is always a little too late for mind, yet never too late for honest stupidity." Sherwood Anderson saw mind as "a sort of malice." Some of Trilling's campaigns on behalf of mind were grandiose and half-empty, and his stock of cherished touchstones was small: *Rameau's Nephew*, Wordsworth, Jane Austen, Arnold, a few others. But he knew that a celebration of hard reality ("Reality, as conceived by us, is whatever is external and hard, gross, unpleasant") is a form of capitulation to power, and that only a belief in the mind offers any chance of freedom, of drawing relatively unforced breath in what Trilling called the haunted air. When he later spoke of the mind at the end of its tether, he was speaking in a desperate and honorable cause.

Lecturing at Princeton in 1942, Wallace Stevens evoked "the pressure of reality" on the diffident imagination. He was thinking of the war, and more generally of "life in a state of violence," and of the disappointments of an incoherent age.

All the great things have been denied and we live in an intricacy of new and local mythologies, political, economic, poetic. . . . Little of what we have believed has been true. Only the prophecies are true. The present is an opportunity to repent.

But the imagination, in good or bad times, does not escape reality. It adheres to it, in Stevens's image, but it rejects its bullying, it takes reality with it into its kingdom of metamorphosis. Stevens said these remarks were not criticism, and perhaps his best criticism is in his poetry, but they seem to me to express with great delicacy the multiple ambitions of criticism in this period: to celebrate form and see its context; to elude and to confront the world; to dissent without entire dissaffection. This all seems very close to what Roland Barthes means when he speaks of seeing the literary work as both a sign of history and a resistance to history. The relations of reality and the imagination vary from age to age, Stevens says. Criticism champions and charts particular variations, and only fails when it loses sight of both members. "There can be work," Stevens suggests, "in which neither the imagination nor reality is present"; and there can be criticism in which the absence isn't noticed or doesn't matter.

Was the criticism of the period too brilliant? It was too dark in some ways, insufficiently attuned to comedy and the modesty of prose, to what we might call the grace of accidents and jokes. It had plenty of feel for literature's high calling; less for its low liveliness. Its irony was austere, stretched between grave conflicts and contradictions, and its recurring words were *defeat, impossibility, tragedy, waste, failure.* But it was a criticism appropriate to an age of great literary achievement and much moral uncertainty, in which America entered two world wars and a depression and altered its relation to ongoing history.

Was the criticism too brilliant in Eliot's sense, which I take to imply that it was too preoccupied with its own cleverness, lacking heart, unable to see the sacred wood for the tempting trees? Occasionally it seemed so: so many gifted critics, so much confidence and presumed wisdom, so much talk about talk. But time sifts all claims to authority, and what is left now seems to be not confidence but nervous intelligence; not wisdom, but patience, and a trust in literature as a mode of understanding. The mind, in James's phrase, reached out for the reasons of its interest, and found good reasons.

Michael Wood

Part Five

1945 to the Present

I. The Postwar Era

Culture, Power, and Society

Most of the political and social history of postwar America takes place in the context of two overwhelming developments: the international leadership of America in terms of global strategy and economic development for the Western nations, and the gradual but seemingly inevitable growth of a postindustrial society. We could perhaps take another step and assert that the first of these developments determined the political shape of America while the second determined its social structure. But this tendency to separate the social from the political is itself perhaps the third most important development in postwar history. The traditions of Western political discourse, long dominated by a rich set of transcendent ideals and relying on a Greek notion of the *polis* as a place where the good life might flourish, were increasingly challenged by a sociology that prized empirical and technocratic measures of value. Some people have referred to this as the "retreat from the political," that is, the dismissal or devaluation of what were once considered specifically political issues in favor of more narrow economic and managerial concerns. Still others have seen in this separation of politics and social concerns the basis for the claim that "everything is political," since there can be no specifically political vocabulary or agenda that is not eventually usurped by, or reduced to, questions of social engineering. This condition, the impoverishment of the political imagination, has had large consequences in our cultural life, not the least of which is a distrust and misunderstanding of, and lack of interest in, the real nature of political power. The social and political ideology of much of postwar American literature must be seen in this context.

One of the immediate consequences of such a context is that it is difficult to separate clearly the cultural and political interrelationships that make up our national life. Unlike their counterparts in France, for example, writers in America are extremely skittish about political labels, and even those who are drawn most forcibly to political and social questions seldom announce their party affiliations or accept even the most general political classification with equanimity. But there are nevertheless political aspects to American literature. Some writers attempt to represent the political imagination in the largest terms. Robert Lowell meditated at length on the course of empire, and Charles Olson could write that "Polis is eyes," meaning that the realms of the phenomenological and the political were identical. Novelists such as E. L. Doctorow and Jack Kerouac strained against the traditions of the realist novel in shaping satirical and lyric narratives that revealed great political contradictions in American society. These four writers had little in common, and any attempt to arrive at a composite view of American political vision through their writings would only illustrate our national heterogeneity. It remains, for example, fruitless to use European notions of "left" or "right" in placing these four figures along a political spectrum. But even these writers might separate their social observations from political theorizing, because the role of "political seer" would probably make them feel uncomfortable. If the poets and novelists who most directly addressed political and social issues shy away from explicit, large-scale political utterances, it is even more the case that the average American author treats politics as either taboo or reserved for cranks and visionaries. In this, our writers reflect trends in political thought since the middle of the nineteenth century.

Of course, the experience of totalitarianism in this century only added to the reluctance to formulate authoritative political pronouncements. Furthermore, the overwhelming dominance in the works of high modernism of an ironic view of life, combined with an emphasis on formalism that praised the "purely" literary over the "committed" or "engaged" artistic stance, served to sharpen this split between the cultural and the political realms in American literature. But other events, such as the revelations about CIA involvement in policy making, especially its infiltration of cultural committees in the postwar years, the war in Vietnam, and the oil embargo of 1976, served to diminish the split. Combined with these international events there were several domestic developments of consequence, though they are harder to date precisely. We could mention, however, the increased strain put on the ideals of an open and pluralistic society by such issues as abortion and employment quotas for minorities, all part of the increased questioning of the welfare state and its tendency to submerge its liberal goals in forms of bureaucratic rationalization. American writers address these issues, though often in tangential ways and they frequently do so with the values of populism, democratic liberalism, and social tolerance. Speaking in the largest terms, most of our writers have continued to operate in a context determined by the nineteenth-century liberal tradition epitomized by Emerson, but such a tradition may be close to exhaustion, as Irving Howe and others have suggested. If this tradition is exhausted, it may be because subtle but extensive changes in social structure and psychology, brought about by developments in a postindustrial, postcapitalist order, have outstripped the consensual models of political order on which liberalism is based. But whether liberalism has failed, or become outdated, or was never sufficiently put into practice is itself a political question of a most complex sort. Just as complex is the question of how liberalism contributed to the separation of political and social questions.

The separation of the social from the political often takes the form of assigning to each its proper concerns. On the one hand, politics often tends to be dominated by foreign policy: the Cold War, detente, Vietnam, Central America. Society, on the other hand, is concerned with wage structures, family patterns, urban migration, professionalism. Clearly the challenge is to see that these two separate orders, the political and the social, are interrelated. Many politicians and public spokesmen repeat the clichés about how the strongest force in America's foreign policy is the strength and diversity of American society (often imaged forth as the strength of the American dollar). This is less a form of analytic interrelatedness than it is a crude form of chauvinism. But American writers, especially those most noticeably affected by the Vietnam War, came increasingly to see that such an interrelatedness might well be the clue to the destiny of the country in this historical epoch, the so-called American Century. From the agonized political and social theorizing of Norman Mailer in such novels as *An American Dream* (1965) and *Why Are We in Vietnam?* (1967) to the black comedy focused on rationalized bureaucracy and blind nationalism in Joseph Heller's *Catch-22* (1961), to the special forms of the black experience in Ishmael Reed, to the scorching attack on sexism in Adrienne Rich, many of the concerns of our leading writers of this period were focused on such interrelatedness.

Obviously not every writer of note was preoccupied with American global hegemony or the new social mores in the same way or to the same extent. But from the Eisenhower years on to Kennedy's presidency, the Vietnam War, the "me" decade of the seventies, and the widespread dominance of what is loosely called Reaganism, the curve of political and social consciousness was varied and dramatic. One could almost say that one of the main themes of literature in this period was just how much social and political consciousness would count as enough. The period began with the ascendancy of New Criticism in the universities, a methodology that militated against the use of biographical and historical material in analyzing and evaluating literature, lest the disinterested artistic vision become contaminated by "extraliterary" concerns. Much of what followed was either a refinement of New Critical principles, even if it took the form of an apparent contextualizing of cultural myth as in Northrop Frye, or a sharp reaction against them, as in the reinvigorated Marxist criticism of the late 1970s. Some people argue that writers pay little attention to, and are hence scarcely affected by, the reigning critical theories. But another concern that came to the fore in the postwar period was the question of how reading habits, themselves the result of historical periods and styles, must invariably have their impact on the total "production" of the literary text. Such an argument depended upon the growing political consciousness of American writers, since it opened up the literary work to forces that shaped the audience's expectations, expectations that had in their turn been formed by the "transpersonal" forces of political and social structures. Put very simply, what had been an easy assumption in the 1950s, that the artist worked in a realm and with truths that existed beyond any specific political and social moments, became for the 1960s a matter of great dispute, and for the 1970s and beyond a matter of lingering and unresolved doubt and concern.

Of course politics includes more than foreign policy, for not only are there the complex and intriguing issues of national political life but there are even the relatively mundane (but still pressing) issues of cultural politics. Here the period was dominated not only by the larger international issues, most notably those involved with the Cold War and the third world, but also by such heated topics as the use of cultural resources, the government support of the arts, the influence of such institutions as the media and the universities on the actual workaday situations of writers, and so forth. On the one hand, the growing support of the arts by such agencies as the National Endowment for the Arts, and similar agencies on the state and local levels, can be viewed as both cause and effect for the increased political and social consciousness of many American writers. On the other hand, many would see such forms of state support as providing a cushion for a semiofficial form of art. In either case, questions about such support took the form of in-fighting and control of the nominating and judging panels for such agencies, though such issues often had as their background various and distinct ways of conceiving the relation of the artist to his or her social milieu.

One striking example of political awareness can readily be found in the feminist movement that grew so vigorously after 1970 or so. Many feminists were concerned to establish their own publishing outlets, to see that the universities responded with courses in women's studies and that awards and grants were no longer given disproportionately to male writers. In fact, it is safe to say that one of the chief sources of organizational energies, not to say ideological refinement, in the feminist movement came from an extensive (and intensive) use of the printed word by women from a wide array of social and political positions. These positions ranged from traditional liberal calls for civil rights legislation to polemical demands for a radical separatism based on gender, and were expressed in both academic forums and mass audience journals such as *Ms.* magazine. While it has been one of the clichés of the post-Gutenberg era that print culture was dead or dying, one must also realize how the use of the publishing and academic sectors by such politically motivated groups as the feminists not only attests to the continued power of the written word but in fact serves to enhance that power. Whether or not such enhanced power can be used in turn to leaven the political discourse of the entire population is another matter. Politics in America continues to be involved with the struggle of special interest groups, and this has often led to a narrowing not only of the range of specifically political vocabularies but of the artistic spectrum as well. But with the emergence of notable writers who are outspokenly feminists, blacks, gays, immigrants, and other "minority" members, literature in America continually reawakens the myths of the melting pot, upward mobility, and a free and enlightened republic. Such reawakened myths, to be sure, are often entangled with a charged and even violent expression of dissatisfaction at their betrayal or deferral, but seen from a distance these myths are the true genius of our literature.

We must, however, be careful to guard against the sort of optimism that has often characterized descriptions of American society in the past, and that has led to bland statements about consensus when in fact deep and serious social divisions and problems persist. The whole complex question of nationalistic optimism has affected our writers, from Walt Whitman and Margaret Fuller down through Hart Crane and such contemporary figures as Saul Bellow, Allen Ginsberg, Susan Sontag, Amiri Baraka, and Sam Shepard. The argument over optimism is related to the problem mentioned earlier, namely, the question of how much social and political consciousness will count as enough. Many people of a conservative persuasion feel that our writers have often abused their status and privilege by repeatedly mouthing a cant version of pessimistic liberal guilt, specifically adapted to a postimperialist America. Such a position has received increased attention as such writers as Norman Podhoretz, Joseph Epstein, and Hilton Kramer have erected a series of arguments increasingly known as "neoconservatism." This neoconservatism is fundamentally a defense of laissez-faire capitalism combined with an attack on the welfare liberalism of the postwar era, and its chief positions are a call for the reduction of the budget for social services and an end to governmental "interference," with a concurrent increase in military power to protect against Soviet expansionism. In response, liberal and radical writers have often charged that the anticommunist rhetoric of neoconservative writers acts, wittingly or unwittingly, to mask the hegemonic or even expansionist aims of American foreign policy by portraying Soviet Russia as the sole source of evil in the world. When this anticommunism shows a positive and optimistic face, liberals instinctively recall the Babbittry and "ugly American" stance of earlier decades. The bland academic response to this pair of opposed characterizations is to say that they both contain a portion of the truth but that each so distorts its opponent for ideological reasons that little is to be gained from continuing any attempt at dialogue. Instead, one had best retreat (or advance) to a position of antipolitical or suprapolitical disinterestedness. Perhaps one of the chief characteristics of our postwar literature, viewed in its social and political contexts, is that such a bland academic response seems less and less insightful or even serviceable. It remains to be seen whether the heightened consciousness of American writers can allow them to avoid the stale and exhausted terms of political discussion of the 1930s, and instead achieve an intelligent, sophisticated political dialogue that addresses a broad range of issues as effectively as certain interest groups have outlined their grievances and hopes. One chance for success in this area is measured by how realistically and convincingly our writers can address and illumine the questions of power.

Whatever counts as important in the social and political background of post–World War II literature might best be discussed under the heading of power. From the hackneyed cry of "Power to the people!" to questions about the realignment of traditional New Deal forces in the Democratic party as a result of its loss of power in the era of Reaganism, questions and claims about power have been persistent and ubiquitous. Instead of a politics of interests, or a social fabric woven from a consensus about value, more and more people have discussed issues in terms of power. There were at least three important books of sociology published in the early 1950s that dealt with this sense of power. David Riesman's *The Lonely Crowd* (1953), William H. Whyte's *The Organization Man* (1955), and C. Wright Mills's *The Power Elite* (1956) all seem to be about very different social types, but all share the assumption that social definition always revolves around social power. To generalize, these books all presented pictures of new social types and classes who had developed distinctive forms of social stratification but who had very different relationships to political power.

Here is a passage from Mills's *Power Elite* that speaks very clearly about the relationship between stratification and power:

There has developed on the middle levels of power a semi-organized stalemate, and . . . on the bottom level there has come into being a mass-like society which has little resemblance to the image of a society in which voluntary associations and classic publics hold the keys to power. The top of the American system of power is much more unified and much more powerful, the bottom is much more fragmented, and in truth, impotent, than is generally supposed by those who are distracted by the middling units of power which neither express such will as exists at the bottom nor determine decisions at the top.

The ideas of a classic public and voluntary association are powerful ones that are reinstalled in every generation of Americans whose schooling goes beyond the elementary levels. This set of social ideas (and ideals) often mitigates against any thoroughgoing understanding of the power relationships in American society. Yet often people have a direct experience of the sort of stalemate that Mills describes, and some even develop an understanding of the unified power at the top of society. But for a great many Americans, this stalemate and this unification of power at the top create an overriding sense of American society as a place of mystification and mismanagement. The dominant mystifying belief still remains that of upward mobility, in economic if not in status terms, while the mismanagement is viewed as endemic to bigness and bureaucracy.

A somewhat more benign view of things is offered by sociologists such as Riesman, who advanced a notion called the "veto effect." Here is how that is described by Mills's biographer, Irving Horowitz:

David Riesman's notion of veto effect was a theory of power which differed from a power-elite approach by viewing influential groups as interest elements whose power is limited by either psychologically felt or socially imposed limitations to power concentration. Like energy, power can run down (something Mills failed to note); hence the relationships of powerful groups are diffuse, distant, and limited. To see that a group has power is not the same as predicting accurately how and to what ends such power would be employed.

Riesman's formulation is, I think, the one that prevails in the mass media, for it postulates an American society that is consonant with such notions as the "melting pot," the "open society," and other such pluralistic schemes. Such a formulation would also allow a believer to tolerate mismanagement as part of the "natural" cost of a complex society in which competing interest groups must share legitimacy and hence power. The notion also allows for the unpredictability entailed in such a heterogeneous mixture; more important, perhaps, is the fact that such a notion displaces any questions about the ultimate containing power of such a society. This displacement allows each interest group to stand in for the whole body politic in a sense, for each group is not only legitimated on its own terms, but it stands equally with and for any other such group as the indispensable source of strength in the republic. In effect, this displacement of the question of containment produces its own myth, that of strength in diversity, or *e pluribus unum*.

We could force the issue somewhat and declare a sort of cross-symmetry in these two views of American society. Mills's power elite, which is negative and pessimistic, nevertheless allows a belief in a positive myth of upward mobility, while Riesman's veto effect, which is highly pragmatic and optimistic, needs the idealism of *e pluribus unum* to function effectively. Both of these myths of social cohesion, that of upward mobility and that of strength in diversity, merge in a parodic form in the structure and mores discussed in Whyte's *Organization Man*. Here the conditions of postindustrial society find a kind of fulfillment in a social structure that glorifies the values of what Max Horkheimer called "instrumental reason," that trust in means instead of ends, in which manner triumphs over matter, form over substance. This social type, the organization man, is depicted directly in such works as Joseph Heller's *Something Happened* (1974), but its force is felt as a negative model in such diverse examples as the escapist machismo of Saul Bellow's *Henderson the Rain King* (1959), the frustrated romantic ideals of the sensitive anti-hero in the works of writers like J. D. Salinger and John Berryman, and the fascination with paranoid versions of an overstructured reality in the novels of Thomas Pynchon. The negative model also has great force for a large number of less critically regarded writers such as Tom Robbins, Richard Brautigan, and Joan Didion. By its persistence in works of both "high-art" pretensions and popular appeal, such a model, considered in its positive and negative versions, might well be taken as the key social question of postwar American literature. In its simplest form this question might be put in this way: "How can anyone personally maintain our society's most elevated ideals—those of freedom and autonomy—while not succumbing to our most persistent social structures, which are increasingly based on conformity and submission to a rationalized authority?"

In a provocative study of American postwar fiction, Richard Ohmann has formulated a master plot, what he calls *"the* story" of this period, in which "social contradictions were easily displaced into images of personal illness." This story concerns an individual who imagines himself or herself as sick, struck by an emotional malaise when society, with its demands for conformity, "comes back at the individual as a hostile force, threatening to diminish or annihilate one's 'real' self." This malaise often takes the form of the character's desire to cling to childhood, but there is another key transformation in the story. As Ohmann puts it: "The person hanging onto childhood as the only defense against capitalist and patriarchal social relations is most often a man or woman already implanted in an adult role but only masquerading as a productive and well-adjusted member of society. In other words, the rite of passage marked by illness and movement towards recovery may be, and usually is, an adult crisis." Easily recognized adolescent social misfits, in a long tradition stretching from Huck Finn to Holden Caulfield, were now depicted as grown men and women, but the problems, in novels as various as *One Flew Over the Cockoo's Nest, An American Dream, Portnoy's Complaint, The Bell Jar,* and *Herzog,* remained the same.

An adolescent sensibility cloaked in an adult role thus allowed the postwar novelist a way to mediate the powerlessness of individuals in a mass, postindustrial society with the continuing belief in the power of the single, sensitive personality. Many novels mentioned here end with their main characters no nearer emotional or social health than when they began, but they have buried within them a vision of social and personal wholeness that is set against the suffocating social fabric that chokes their characters' longing for a better life. These novels posit imagination not as the highest power but as the *only* power, that is, the only power that can have commerce with sensitivity. Other forms of power—economic, managerial, institutional— are felt to be distortions of true control in the service of ends that the agents of power seldom truly understand. These novels recognize the many shapes of "instrumental reason," but by focusing on the negative models of it, by portraying chiefly its victims rather than its practictioners, they turn the organization man into a caricature of a social type rather than the dominant model of our society. Again, questions of pessimism and optimism resurface: is the adolescent psyche of the prototypical character in American literature a way of burying and yet preserving our self-image, or merely a way of avoiding the unpleasant truths about the direction of our social development since 1945? One thing seems certain, however: the organization man never confronts the childlike hero on common grounds, for whatever real contact they might experience in social reality, in fiction they exist in two different realms. This is another way of saying that our writers cannot conceive of power passing between them.

In the modern era the way writers most often tried to maneuver from the realm of the imagination to that of social reality was to reach a wide audience of readers. The tremendous spread of literacy that made such an attempt feasible was energetic, in the form not only of novels or poems but also of essays and all the ragged forms of nonfictional prose published by magazines. In the nineteenth and early twentieth centuries literary influence and social power in this country were conjoined in such publications as *The Nation, The Dial, Atlantic Monthly,* and *The Saturday Evening Post.* Since 1945 the major journals that purveyed the triumph of modernist culture, and that were able to present both critical and creative writing of a high order, journals such as *Partisan Review* and *Kenyon Review,* have lost not only their vigor but their audiences. In part this loss is accountable by sociologically determined reasons such as the virtual hegemony of television as the medium of greatest cultural power. But contributing to this shift away from the once powerful literary quarterlies has been the development of a style of writing called by the loosely defined term the "new journalism." The writers mainly active in developing this new genre, people such as Gay Talese, Tom Wolfe, Joan Didion, and others, are often polished to the point of glibness, and they address their audience in part by mimicking attitudes and devices drawn from the other media, even the electronic ones. "New journalism" borrowed from narrative traditions such as the novel and short story and has often been cited as the advance guard of the breakdown or merging of the traditional literary genres; it has also been seen as yet another chapter in that long-running soap opera called "the death of the novel." The successful ascendancy of the genre was marked when several established novelists, chief among them Norman Mailer, began to offer their versions of this new approach to conveying information, opinions, and cultural attitudes. One way to see this phenomenon is to consider it the updated version of the old-fashioned belletristic essay, a sometimes fussy, always genteel form adapted ironically to the abrasions and disruptions of contemporaneity. In fact, these writers were relying on a sense of irony that often verged on cynicism. Occasionally a writer would argue for the aesthetic importance of the new form, but such claims were usually examples of egregious self-promotion, as with Truman Capote's *In Cold Blood*

(1966), or uniquely skilled exceptions built on no particular rule, such as Mailer's *Armies of the Night* (1968).

But a contrary view is possible. This would see the old-fashioned literary essay, and the literary critic who produced it, as always having been enchanted with the possibility of speaking about things other than literature— or speaking about anything and everything while pretending chiefly to discuss literary matters. This form of essay writing, less glib than the "new journalism" but equally concerned with contemporary issues, is still very actively pursued today. Here the distant precursors are people like Matthew Arnold who developed a sophisticated tradition of cultural criticism. But in the postwar era even people most clearly in this tradition, such as Lionel Trilling, could no longer draw definite boundaries between literature and other forms of cultural "writing." Freud and Nietzsche had long before blurred the lines between the artistic imagination and the more engrossing forms of cultural exploration and self-examination. So when writers such as Susan Sontag, Renata Adler, Elizabeth Hardwick, Edward Said, or Stanley Cavell write about authors or books or movies, their main focus is not a narrow aesthetic one. Rather, their approach to aesthetic matters has percolated into every part of their consciousness, and they are as likely to "read" an event, a public personality, or a popular art form as they are a lyric poem or novel. For such writers one of the chief forms of displaying and extending their persuasive powers is the magazine article. But the spectrum of magazines that was willing to publish and encourage such writing was a constantly changing one.

In few other places is the pluralism, the diffuse power of our literary and cultural life, so apparent as in the constantly shifting fortunes of our magazines and journals. This can be shown in part by the complete lack of consensus about which, if any, of these magazines would be considered indispensable for intelligent readers from a wide spectrum of professions and backgrounds. Some might argue strenuously for the *New York Review of Books*, for example, but just as many would respond by pointing to that journal's virtually ignoring all but the most select views of contemporary poetry, its generally unchallenging view of fiction, and its hostility to such developments in critical thought as deconstruction. Journals like *Salmagundi* and *Raritan* feature a strong and consistent battery of writers whose interests and skills are broad and deep, but they seldom have a circulation that exceeds a few thousand. Such journals are also constantly fighting a predilection to academicize thoroughly their interests and their language. Those journals that are limited by an academicized language—*Representations* and *Telos* come to mind—are usually in thrall to a particular academic discipline, such as art history in the case of *Representations* or sociology in the case of *Telos*.

Often this limitation is the result of the circumstances surrounding the founding of the journal, and editors trying to make their efforts more broadly interesting and culturally literate are waging a difficult struggle. This is due, of course, to the fact that there are few intellectuals in American life outside the university. Those places where society has traditionally harbored or encouraged intellectuals, such as law, medicine, or public administration, have in America (as in many other countries) become areas that more resemble trades than professions. Outside the special jargon of their disciplines, intelligent people in America find it difficult to speak a language that will answer to the complexity of our social and political order. The domination and consequent pollution of language and political thought by the mass media is not only an Orwellian fantasy come true, it is a striking measure of the way we have organized the expression of intellect and the conduct of culture. Other journals that boast of a larger circulation, such as the *American Poetry Review*, which has claimed a readership of 40,000, often justify the common fear that a large readership is a sign of misused talents. Many readers point out that *The New Yorker*, despite its obvious catering to an audience built on acquisitive values, publishes literate and readable essays and excerpts from books by writers as talented as John McPhee, Jane Kramer, and Pauline Kael. But many find the poetry there is often as predictably overrefined as that of the *American Poetry Review* is trite. Literature, alas, is still something generally cordoned off from the daily awareness of a large portion of the intelligent citizenry, let alone the intelligentsia.

Magazines and journals have seldom been convenient markers of power in America because they often reflect diversity and changeableness. Even that proud publisher of Joyce, Mann, and Eliot, *The Dial*, by the time of its demise in 1929, struggled to maintain circulation, and each issue was literally surrounded by rather garish advertising sections that looked quite different from the well laid out pages most American academics call to mind when the journal's title is mentioned. While some of the journal's difficulties could be ascribed to its championing literature that would never win a mass audience, some writers such as Ezra Pound and William Carlos Williams thought it had become much too tame and closed to experimentalism. But for putting new ideas into circulation and earning a general consensus of high regard among intellectuals and writers, few postwar journals could compare with *The Dial* of the 1920s or the *Partisan Review* of the 1930s. The real question might be, is there any journal that even aspires to such power? During the Reagan administration *The New Criterion* and *Commentary* have

become influential to the extent they have espoused ideas and values associated with neoconservatism, but they have frequently seemed mired in
sour polemics and, despite their avowals of energy, they have discovered
few if any writers who appeal beyond a restricted range of taste and political affiliation. It is unlikely that their influence will last long beyond the
tenure of the Reagan administration; at the very least, unforseeable developments in partisan politics will generate considerable pressure on their
editorial policies.

A more complex and irresolvable question is just how a magazine reflects
social and political ideology. Does it do so by having frequent editorial
positions that may or may not be in concert with the pluralistic stances of
its several contributors? In 1985 *The New Republic* adopted a conservative,
pro-Reagan stance on the question of military aid to the rebel forces in
Nicaragua only to have many of its contributors and regular staff writers
respond with a sharply opposed position paper in the next issue. This can
be seen as American diversity of opinion in active operation, or as an intellectual and political muddle. One narrow, perhaps cynical, view would ask
whether, say, the movie reviewer of such a journal has any real stake in the
editorial stance of those who control the "hard news" contents. Cannot cultural criticism—often symbolically placed in the back pages of journals—
operate more or less unhampered by questions of political and social policy,
since most people involved in what has come to be known as the culture
industry have limited impact on such questions? But increasingly intellectuals and writers have insisted on the unreality of claims that culture or
even the social sciences can conduct themselves in a politically innocent,
value-free way, or that our political allegiances and our cultural tastes are
distinct. This insistence has often eventually produced what some think of
as a contorted notion, namely, that adopting an apolitical attitude is itself
fraught with political value and even consequences. But writers interested
in a magazine format often desire the broadest possible audience, not one
restricted to the "correct" political position, and so they resent any suggestion that what they write has an inescapably political attitude.

What makes many of the practitioners of the "new journalism" attractive
to literate readers is that they convey an impression that they are free of
such benighted habits as political prejudice and ideological conformity. The
cost of such an impression is that these writers often have to resort to irony
and detachment as their controlling idiom; idealism of any sort is likely to
"place" the writer in some political camp. Another way of avoiding such
political labels is to write on subjects that have no easy or as yet defined
political position attached to them. A good example here would be Gay

Talese's essay entitled "Frank Sinatra Has a Cold." Ostensibly the writer presents a phenomenon that nearly everyone is interested in—the daily life of a celebrity—and that readily lends itself to a display of sophistication; the presentation can be polished and detailed without seeming to take any overt stance or judgment about its subject's real political or social value. Tom Wolfe has made an entire career on the basis of such writing, even though his personal political orientation as a neoconservative gadfly became clearer with each article or book. This sort of writing thrives in a society where power is diffuse, and where pluralism and a certain amount of political cynicism are the order of the day. (Raymond Williams, the English critic, says that cynicism is opposition that refuses to surrender its privileges.) Much of postwar culture in America has been in some way involved with avoiding the kind of political enthusiasm that all too often gets labeled as extremism. What is here called avoidance can, of course, be redrawn as a virtue, the virtue of tolerance and respect for personal differences. Contrariwise, what is sometimes applauded as the diffusion of power can be seen as the concealment of the sustaining structures of power. The magazine article has about it the aura of contemporaneity, and as such it appears to be uncovering the secrets of "the way we live now." But this genre may be a chief instance of how even the most scrupulous and talented writing can sometimes merely exemplify the culture an author thinks he or she is exposing.

Some of these paradoxes apply as well to a magazine's editorial stance. Many magazines achieve a style and hence capture an audience by a distinctive "feel" that may foster a vague political or social sensibility. But to define a position too sharply is to risk losing any chance to widen one's audience. One is haunted by Harold Rosenberg's phrase "the herd of independent minds." While many intellectuals and writers think of themselves as shrewd and free of ordinary political illusions, they have interests rooted in their economic identities and class affiliations. Likewise, magazines have a social character, a look as well as a feel that lets their readers enjoy a sense of belonging not simply to an audience but something like a community. In this sense magazines cannot escape being in some way consumer items, part of the modern, "postcapitalist" economic order where one's habits of consumption are as much an indicator of one's social identity as heredity or occupation. Creating the "image" of a magazine may be an unavoidable consequence of wanting to have an editorial policy in the first place, or at least of wanting to have such a policy cast in an appropriate "format." At its most crass, or its most intriguing, level, the problem is one that confronts all products of the mind in America. William Carlos Williams once said that "the pure products of America go crazy," by which he meant that the presumed stability of the indigenous or authentic is always at the mercy of the encompassing energies of the commercial and the mercenary. Whether the mind can display its integrity without succumbing to market forces is the sort of risky question that magazine and journal writing explores, though often without full self-awareness of how nettlesome the paradoxes of representation can be.

When we consider questions of power as they are represented in literature we must first have some notion of how power represents itself in the actual social and political realms. Here many of our writers tend to project back from their artistic experience onto the "body politic." One striking example of this might be Sylvia Plath's use of authoritarian, even totalitarian, models of government in her poetry to express her sense of a paradoxically blocked psychological experience, which is felt as both overwhelmingly powerful and yet ineluctably attractive. Whether her actual father had a "Mein Kampf" look or not does not affect the value of the poetry, we are told; but, at the same time, are we to ask whether we should imagine fascism as a twisted form of the family romance, or some Electra complex writ large? Many scholarly and popular versions of the psychology of fascism utilize notions of paternalism and the family-centered models of socialization, and the tendency of many "confessional poets" such as Plath is to take the psychological realm as the key to all of reality. When this happens often enough, and without any critical response, writers tend to abandon the other useful representations of power, most notably the historical and philosophical. It becomes increasingly difficult in such a situation to have any sense how "thought" itself might address power. Karl Shapiro said in *The Bourgeois Poet* (1964), speaking about the boardroom of a corporation, "There the power lies and is sexless." Power, in other words, can be imagined only as a nonhuman form. Robert Lowell, in 1967, could picture President Lyndon Johnson, then prosecuting a futile war in southeast Asia, as "free to chaff/ his own thoughts with his bear-cuffed staff,/ swimming nude, unbuttoned, sick/ of his own ghost-written rhetoric!" This tends to make the scene of the war an extension of Johnson's psyche, hemmed in by systems and conventions, taking delight in a sort of juvenile desublimation. This is not to say that the exercise of power, even on a global scale, cannot or should not be explained in part by resorting to a psychological vocabulary. But increasingly in postwar America this vocabulary has tended to drive out all others, at least as far as many of our poets and novelists are concerned. What results is a powerful body of political feeling and social sentiment, but very little thought about how and why we have ended up with the sort of society we have.

Some of this is the legacy of certain figures, such as Wilhelm Reich, as well as the pervasive presence of psychological notions in our daily life. In consequence, many of the more traditional frameworks used to discuss political and social reality seem outdated or uninformed. To this we may add very real social changes, such as those described by Richard Sennett in *The Fall of Public Man* (1977) and Christopher Lasch in *The Culture of Narcissism* (1978), that work against any genuine sense of citizenship or civic duty, or at least that work against such notions being ready-at-hand to criticize or explain the nature of our national life. Many people have remarked on the rather stunning depletion of the political vocabulary in America in the last two or three generations, and artists have generally reacted to this with something like an exhausted cynicism. If it be granted that our political life is essentially a sort of debased, media-dominated Machiavellian dance of "image-making," then it is hard to see how any literary representation can manage to outmaneuver what has turned into an unreal spectacle. One might imagine that satire or farce would thrive if such debasement were indeed the order of the day, but reality becomes increasingly harder to mock if the average observer assumes the "official" version of reality is inherently false and self-serving. If what started in history as tragedy, as Marx suggested, is repeated as farce, then the farcical becomes, by frequent repetition, standardized in the media and so-called common-sense reality, despite its being unwittingly self-satirizing. Attempts at farce, such as Philip Roth's *Our Gang* (1971) and Robert Coover's *The Public Burning* (1976), have been largely read as valiant but failed attempts to hold political figures such as Richard Nixon to some rational standard of ethical behavior. From the benevolent paternalism that was one of the hallmarks of the Eisenhower years, to the good-natured avuncularism of Ronald Reagan, American political life has seen "thought" increasingly at odds with power, or rather, not so much at odds, but existing in a totally separate realm of discourse.

One result of this condition of an impoverished political vocabulary is the diffusion of the representations of power. What might be seen as a positive political development, namely, the widespread distribution of the power to control one's political destiny, can instead be felt as the atomization of political life. More and more people are reluctant to identify the repositories of power, beyond the vague and impersonal references to "them" or, as the occasion of a single-issue crisis arises, to "the oil companies" or the "military-industrial complex," or "big money." As Hannah Arendt said in *On Violence* (1970), when discussing the bureaucratized and rationalized form of modern government, what we often have is "rule by nobody." Such an understanding of the national life is bound to be reflected in literature in at least three ways: (1) writers will abandon all political thought as hopeless self-deception, the result of unresolved psychic tensions; (2) they will turn to conspiracy theories; (3) they will readjust their political scale to local or closely defined issues. One of these three options—call them the apolitical, the paranoid, and the separatist positions—can be seen at work in many of our writers today, even those with clearly held and voiced political beliefs. The one thing that unites the three is that they all abandon any hope of expressing a truly coherent national spirit that might serve to provoke a period of widespread and effective belief in the dignity of the political life. This abandoned hope is felt most sharply against the persistent notion that some writers—Victor Hugo, say, or Walt Whitman—have in the past expressed a national spirit, even if we suspect that its true coherence is often the product of latter-day desires on the part of readers and critics with their own nationalistic dreams.

This might be the place to say something about an especially important social and political issue of postwar America: ethnicity. Here is a topic that lies right along the fault line between the optimistic and pessimistic views of American diversity and the theme of shared power. On the one hand, ethnicity proclaims the virtue of difference and makes of such a "status group" something like the high-water mark of social identity. Some sociologists even argue that such a status group identification as is allowed by membership in an ethnic group replaces older and less useful notions of a class structure or economic stratification. Ethnic identity recalls the organic ideal of a society based on true feeling, far removed from the cash nexus and the depersonalized existence of the market system. On the other hand, some critics take a less sanguine view; they see the persistence and revival of ethnic politics as the sign of a failure in the American system, a failure to achieve the sort of truly egalitarian society it promises. This tension has its analogous force-field in the literature of ethnicity, for the more accurately the writer is able to present the picture of ethnic life the less likely is his or her work to join in the "mainstream" of popular literature. Instead what we often get is the overnight sensation of the ethnic writer who is lauded by academic critics but then quickly forgotten: one thinks of such writers as Maxine Hong Kingston. However, there are other larger talents who nevertheless face the prospect of their art being seen only as a sort of leavening for more established authors, or, possibly worse, of merely serving the interests of a social voyeurism: here one thinks of Issac Bashevis Singer, whose work escapes such a narrow response but is always threatened with it. In addition, there are the many writers from other traditions and cultures who have immigrated to America—one thinks first of Vladimir Nabokov, Czeslaw Milosz, and Joseph Brodsky—and contributed in important ways to our cultural life. Here there is a mordant paradox, for the very presence of such writers contributes to the notion of America as an open society, and yet they often bring a historical understanding and an international perspective that frequently show us how parochial our national concerns can be. Unless there is careful and informed criticism, and a generous and politically informed response on the part of the general reader, ethnic identity in works of literature often ends by being either a badge of momentary distinction or a sign of eventual assimilation.

For one of the leading sociologists of the postwar era, Daniel Bell, the new postindustrial society has one key, "axial" principle, and that is "the centrality and codification of theoretical knowledge." This centrality of knowledge makes for a form of authority that is largely elitist and meritocratic, and because it is knowledge and not, say, property that is centralized it becomes harder and harder to avoid recourse to certain theories of mystification when discussing our society and its culture. In a sense these theories of mystification might be seen as an extension of the notions of Thorstein Veblen, who claimed to see a contradiction in American society between a price structure that encourages competition and a social order that leaves little genuine room for the old markers of class distinctions, thus producing the phenomenon of "conspicuous consumption" by which people define themselves only by the esteem they can wrest from others in terms of desirably wasteful expenditures. Veblen's "leisure class" was above all a "knowing" class, not, to be sure, a class possessed of great theoretical knowledge, but one that consistently set the standards for the possession and exercise of power. If we can rather too generally, for the moment, blur the distinctions between Veblen's "leisure class" and Bell's "technocratic elite," we can begin to see how the notion of inflation might be taken as central to postwar American culture. (Charles Newman has discussed inflation, both as a real economic phenomenon and as an explanatory metaphor, in his intriguing study, *The Postmodern Aura* [1985].) In inflation we can see many of our cultural dilemmas in another form. Inflation, in the classic definition, is a condition that results from too much money chasing too few goods. Recession, on the other hand, is caused when there are too many goods, but too little money.

But what is the condition called when there are too many goods and too much money? Stagflation. Stagflation is the postmodern version of inflation, a condition in which prices continue to rise (and values, therefore, continue to fall), but at the same time goods tend to proliferate beyond any rational measure of need. Many critics have used the outlines of such a situation to characterize our cultural moment. More and more we hear the complaint that there are too many novels, too much poetry, too many plays written, and yet all the poor work that is being published is only lowering the taste of the audience. (One is reminded of Woody Allen's favorite joke about the woman who complains, "The food at this resort is so bad"; "Yes," agrees one of her friends, "and besides, the portions are so small.") The conjunction of overproduction and overconsumption creates a cultural as well as an economic scandal, but those who "know" tell us that such a condition is inevitable if we are to maintain personal liberties and a free market system. To object to more and more art, or to object to the blurring of standards, or to object to the trivialization and marginalization of culture even as it is increasingly turned into a commodity is often to be labeled as one of the unknowing. Our social and political faith in diversity, growth, and satisfaction at the right price has a more or less direct set of literary consequences. The pessimistic evaluation of the "culture industry" by such European thinkers as Theodor Adorno might be difficult to countermand, yet it is hard to believe such pessimism ever prevented a single writer from pursuing his or her own dream of success.

However, if everything in our cultural life is subject to inflation or stag-flation, perhaps even pessimism has become too available a commodity. Not all of postwar culture is bleak about its own self-image; indeed, there were even periods of real enthusiasm in the arts in the postwar era. Many contemporary poets, for example, were beginning to celebrate a new era in the art in the late 1960s and early 1970s. There seemed to be a great many talented poets writing in new and different styles, content and even pleased to let one another add to the general flourishing. This era of good feeling came after the breakup of the dominance of "academic poetry" that had held sway immediately after World War II, and after a period of some internecine strife as well. Many American poets, if not comfortably well-off, were at least situated in a host of universities and creative writing programs. But then a feeling spread that perhaps these programs had become too institutionalized; this feeling coincided with a sharp decrease in university budgets, and a whole new generation of young poets were less secure in their employment situations. Social and political factors seemed to be holding sway uncomfortably. A mistrust of settled patterns, both life patterns and writing patterns, began to spread. One could see this mistrust exemplified in the background of a new movement of young poets who call themselves the "Language poets." These poets are simultaneously very academic in some of their concerns—for example, their preoccupation with the latest developments in linguistic theory—and in their frequently abstruse styles, and yet their work often contains distinct rumblings of social discontent, sometimes informed by a knowledge of Marxist theory. Indeed, their style is least abstruse when they are often striving to render justice to the complexity of "ordinary" reality and address common political and social issues. These rumblings can be seen as merely continuing the modernist mix of an anticultural stance with a severe and forbidding sense of style; however, they can also be seen as expressing the attitudes of a generation whose education far outstripped its social standing. Poets share the plight of many a Ph.D. in the humanities, and even in the sciences, who are forced to work at low-skilled, underpaid jobs, making up a new social class, the "underemployed." Plainly impatient with the conduct of poetry as it is generally practiced, these poets often seem on the verge of writing a manifesto, and yet at the same time appear trapped in an outworn formalism that all too often contains a large element of ennui. As a case study of the social reality that acts as both a context and a set of concerns for artists, the background of the Language poets might seem inconclusive or indistinct. Yet, as some critics have said of modernism generally, a spirit of continual disaffection with culture reasserts itself in our postwar poetry, from the Beats and the Black Mountain school to the deep image poets and on to the Language poets, just to name the more obvious examples from this era. That disaffection is often shaped in some measure by the poet's "workaday" situation, however much other purely aesthetic factors might contribute.

One way to imagine the change in our society from the immediate postwar period to the 1980s is to focus on the two consumer items that represent the beginning and end of the last half of the American century: the automobile and the computer. The automobile, on the one hand, represented the dominance of American industrial might: both capital- and labor-intensive, consuming vast resources, universally desired, constantly "updated," financed with extended credit, the automobile was the dream object of capitalism at its height. In cultural terms it represented our paradoxes nicely, for it stood for personal mobility and for urban congestion; it supported a status system all could be measured by, while it held out the hope of personal distinctiveness. The computer, on the other hand, nicely represented postindustrial society. Its operation was noiseless and pollution free, and it both centralized knowledge and dispersed it (albeit in fixed forms); furthermore, it held out the hope of a universal adaptability, a way of mastering all operational difficulties by a tireless and errorless application of method. Currently its cultural ramifications are not completely clear. No one has yet done for the computer what Jack Kerouac did for the automobile in *On the Road* (1957). But many people realized, perhaps dimly and only for a short while, that the oil embargo of 1976 might spell the end of the American automobile, at least in its most extravagant guises. The so-called computer revolution of the 1980s has forced a less dramatic realization on the American consumer: the availability of leisure time can be viewed in terms of the same sort of commodification as was work time at the beginning of the industrial revolution. Now with many standard chores in and out of the home potentially subject to "programming," businessmen and economic planners will more and more ask what possible use can be made of all our spare hours. Though few people have suggested they might be spent reading books, still this new social order will have a definite, if unpredictable, impact on our culture.

In some ways this impact is already being felt. In painting and music especially, the 1960s and 1970s saw a growing obsession with the recycling of styles. Instead of being a definite historical or psychological marker, style has itself become a commodity, used, as often as not, simply to stimulate more demand, to ensure the reawakening of acquisitive desires. In literature this situation has taken several forms, most noticeably the use by "metafictionists" and even some popular writers of the apparently arbitrary choice of style as a theme or a structural principle in its own right. Novelists like John Gardner, John Irving, and Joyce Carol Oates and "metafictionists" such as Donald Barthelme and John Barth have simultaneously put a premium on style and treated it playfully. While this, too, can be seen as merely the working out of the last vestiges of modernism, it can also be understood as the end of the belief in style as an autonomous aesthetic principle. Now style is to be treated more like fashion or mere stylishness, something to be taken up randomly, whimsically, more as entertainment than as testament. The modernist belief in the transforming power of style has been translated into the availability of style as a consumerist diversion. This may be the main legacy of postindustrial culture.

Both modernism and postmodernism have left unanswered the question of how art can—or, some would say, even whether it should—take as its objective the direct focusing of the power of the imagination on social and political forces. Postwar literature has generated certain consequences by leaving this question unanswered, and these consequences, seen and unforeseen, are themselves in part political. Perhaps the most important part of postwar ideology as it affects literature is the growing awareness of how political and social issues have an unavoidable impact on cultural acts (and vice versa). What remains to be seen is how such impact and such awareness can best be represented, not only in intellectual terms but in artistic ones as well. When one form of power—the political, say—confronts another form of power—that of the imagination, say—all one can predict is that there will be transformations. In which direction, to what extent, and to what purpose such transformations will occur is often beyond the power of political forces to control, and sometimes beyond the power of the imagination to envision accurately. What does seem to be a constant is the idea that literature is at its fullest when it dares to address whatever is "beyond"—beyond the current fashion, the safe belief, the established style. If this is so, then obviously literature will continue to be a place where we can see and feel not only the changes that take place when imagination addresses power but the limits of those changes, and the forces that keep those limits in place.

Charles Molesworth

The New Philosophy

Philosophy as science, as serious, rigorous, indeed apodictically rigorous science—
the dream is over.

—Edmund Husserl

The idea that philosophy is a rigorous science—apodictically rigorous in the sense of being founded on something other than opinion or uncontested talk—is rooted in the ancient belief that philosophy is something different from poetry, whose foundations are entirely inside of language. For philosophy, the worst thing that could happen would be for it to fall into the hands of people who cannot tell the difference between philosophy and poetry, or between statements grounded upon unshakable foundations and those that are just "in the air," circulating like songs, stories, sayings, and memories of the intoxicating presence of human beings. The dissipation of scientific philosophy (as if it were a dream) is simply a sign that the worst has happened. Another sign would be the appearance in a history of literature of an essay on the history of philosophy. This would mean, to borrow Richard Rorty's expression, that philosophy is not a science but "a kind of writing," and that, like literature (and, for all of that, like the law or the Scriptures) it is made up of texts that come down to us from the past. A corollary of this textualizing of philosophy would be an alteration in our sense of what counts as literature. It would mean that literature could no longer be figured purely in terms of the aesthetic categories that come down to us from the nineteenth century but could now be opened up to include whatever is written, including philosophy. And this would mean that the literary study of philosophy would not simply be a study of its aesthetic features—a study of the treatise, the dialogue, the remark, or the densely woven essay; it would also be a study of its history.

Yet such a study is a perilous business because there is no noncontroversial way of determining what is to count as philosophy. Perhaps the simplest way to begin is by thinking of philosophy in terms of its school curriculum: logic, epistemology, metaphysics, and, at a lower level, ethics, aesthetics, history, and (lower still) politics. Logic, epistemology, and so on (but particularly logic and epistemology) make up a course of training that one has to go through to become a philosopher. A corollary of this program would be that the traditional texts of philosophy—for example, Immanuel Kant's *Critique of Pure Reason* (1781; 1787) or Alfred Tarski's "The Concept of Truth in Formalized Languages" (1933)—set an agenda of specifically philosophical problems, such as how knowledge is possible or what conditions must be met for a sentence to be true. One could then divide philosophers (or philosophy) into traditions, movements, doctrines, or styles of philosophizing—Anglo-American philosophy, Continental philosophy, logical empiricism, various phenomenologies, ordinary language philosophy, deconstruction, and so on to no determinate end. One could then study philosophy by following the historical distribution of its traditions across the map of Western civilization since the seventeenth century, when philosophy began the process of secularization, professionalization, and critical self-reflection that continues to this day. It appears that a regulating theme of this process is that philosophy is the kind of thinking that is concerned with what we know. Philosophy is about what we are justified in saying. Philosophy is about how we connect up with reality. It is about how we make sense of things. It aims at emancipation from illusion, or from mistaken or just plain empty notions of how things are.

For example, here is a basic schoolroom question: Is the world we know already made or is it of our own construction? On this question people divide into followers of Aristotle and followers of Kant, or into those who take what lies before us as it is given, or as it appears, and those who question whether anything just lies before us in the way we experience it. The basic idea of Kantian idealism, for example, is that our experience of the world is conceptual as well as empirical. Empirically, experience reduces simply to a chaos of undifferentiated sensations. If this is so, however, how is it that the world nevertheless appears intelligible to us, that is, how is it that we experience it as a world of objects extended in time and space and behaving more or less predictably according to the laws of physical science? What is the source of this intelligibility? Or, in Kant's own idiom, how is scientific knowledge (knowledge that is objective and logically valid) possible? An answer to this question cannot be derived from experience itself. It must be given *a priori* by determining the laws of cognition as such. One must, in effect, give an account of how the mind works. In the *Critique of Pure Reason* this becomes an account of the mental structures by which reality is constituted for us as an objective and therefore knowable entity. The word "constitute" here simply means to establish something as a determinate object. This is what the mind does in experience. The mind objectifies a world for itself by synthesizing the chaos of sensation according to the forms of time and space and the categories of substance, causality, and so on. Technically, what this means is that we are able, by means of transcendental idealism, to hold the position of empirical realism. Most people who call themselves realists turn out to be Kantians rather than Aristotelians.

In this century a more elaborate version of Kant's constructionalism has been provided by Ernst Cassirer in his *Philosophy of Symbolic Forms* (1923–29). Cassirer recognized that Kant had construed the foundations of intelligibility too narrowly. "Not only science," Cassirer says, "but language, myth, art and religion as well provide the building stones from which the world of 'reality' is constructed for us, as well as that of the human spirit, in sum the World-of-the-I. Like scientific cognition, they are not simple *structures* which we can insert into a given world, we must understand them as *functions* by means of which a particular form is given to reality and in each of which specific distinctions are effected." Or, in other words, the mind cannot be characterized purely in terms of scientific reason. The intelligibility of human culture as such, not just the intelligibility of science, requires that we postulate, Cassirer says, "a basic function of signification" as the foundation of all human activity. What is important to understand, however, is that this function is formative rather than mimetic: signification is a process of world-making. "Myth and art, language and science, are in this sense configurations *towards* being: they are not simple copies of an existing reality but represent the main directions of the spiritual movement, of the ideal process by which reality is constituted for us as one and many— as a diversity of forms which are ultimately held together by a unity of meaning." It is true, Cassirer says, that we find ourselves therefore "in a world of 'images'—but these are not images which reproduce a self-subsistent world of 'things'; they are image-worlds whose principle and origin are to be sought in an autonomous creation of the spirit. Through them alone we see what we call 'reality,' and in them alone we possess it: for the highest objective truth that is accessible to the spirit is ultimately the form of its own activity." What is outside the activity of the spirit simply cannot be thought, but for Cassirer this is not so much a problem as it is "a fallacy in formulation, an intellectual phantasm. The true concept of reality cannot be squeezed into the form of mere abstract being; it opens out into the diversity and richness of the forms of spiritual life—but of a spiritual life which bears the stamp of inner necessity and hence of objectivity." The task of philosophy, as Cassirer understands it, is not to find a way outside the forms of signification. "If all culture is manifested in the creation of specific image-worlds, of specific symbolic forms, the aim of philosophy is not to go behind all these creations but rather to understand and elucidate their basic formative principle." The question of questions for philosophy is not whether these "image-worlds" of human culture are true; the question is rather the formal one of how they are made. This is the question that *The Philosophy of Symbolic Forms* tries to answer with its studies of the formative principles of language, myth, and science.

As it happens, this is also the regulating question of structuralist thinking. Essentially, structuralism is Kantian idealism with a displaced theory of reason, mind, or subjectivity. It is idealism inscribed not in the language of German philosophy of the spirit but in the language of semiotics or the theory of signs. Thus whereas the German tradition thinks in terms of the relation of mind and world, the structuralist tradition thinks in terms of signifier and signified and again in terms of signifier and the system in which it operates. In both traditions, however, the relationship in question does not reduce to a copy-theory of intelligibility or a mimetic theory of representation or signification; rather, intelligibility is a process of differentiation within a region of discrete elements. In the German tradition these elements are empirical (the so-called data of sensation); in structuralism they are linguistic or, more accurately, semiotic, that is, elements within a system of differential relations. Intelligibility (that is, signification) is a product of relationships among signifiers and does not depend on anything outside the system, just as, in idealism, the world is said to be phenomenal in character and does not require to be grounded in a noumenon or Thing-in-itself. This allows the structuralists to speak not only of the construction of the world but also of the construction of the logical subject, the "I" of subjectivity. This last has been a particularly fruitful theme in Freudian and Marxist inflections of structuralism, that is, in the work of Jacques Lacan and Louis Althusser. Here a theory of the unconscious, which is certainly the most powerful of the implications of Kantian idealism, is brought into the foreground. To learn a language, for example, is to enter into a system of constraints, a symbolic order that structures both self and world, constituting them as what they are in consciousness. In this event, however, it is no longer accurate to speak of consciousness itself as constitutive or productive. On the contrary, it is the unconscious that is now to be described as a signifying system (that is, as a chain, place, or play of signifiers), or, at a higher level, as an ideological system, that is, a structure of images, myths, ideas, beliefs, values, and works whose modes of production are no longer spiritual and transcendental in Cassirer's sense but are embedded in the social forces of labor and technology.

At this point, however, the intelligibility of the notion of intelligibility itself begins to weaken. For example, it is by no means clear that a structuralist's account of the logic of signification will always remain consistent with the norms of inferential and differential reasoning. Indeed, the linguistic turn that structuralism gives to Kantian idealism is basically a turn away from logic toward rhetoric, that is, away from a concern for the logical form of knowledge or of statements about the world toward the problem of figuration. This turn is quite visible in Roman Jakobson's reduction of signification to the metaphoric and metonymic poles of mental or linguistic functioning. The historical point would be to see in this rhetorical bias a turn away from the tradition of Kant and Cassirer—the tradition of transcendental reason—toward the renegade tradition of Friedrich Nietzsche, where reason is radically historicized. For many this is just a turn away from philosophy itself. Nietzsche, after all, was not a philosophy professor but a classical philologist who did not find it contradictory to hold, as he did, that figuration or metaphor is the whole basis of intelligibility. Reason, language, the whole business of making sense of things—these are, according to the Nietzschean motto, "figurative all the way down." In a famous fragment from 1883–88 collected in *The Will to Power*, Nietzsche writes:

> Against positivism, which halts at phenomena—"There are only *facts*"—I would say: No, facts is precisely what there is not, only interpretations. We cannot establish any fact "in itself": perhaps it is folly to want to do such a thing.
>
> "Everything is subjective," you say; but even this is interpretation. The "subject" is not something given, it is something added and invented and projected behind what there is.—Finally, is it necessary to posit an interpreter behind the interpretation? Even this is invention, hypothesis.
>
> In so far as the word "knowledge" has any meaning, the world is knowable; but it is *interpretable* otherwise, it has not meaning behind it, but countless meanings.—"Perspectivism."
>
> It is our needs that interpret the world; our drives and their For and Against. Every drive is a kind of lust to rule; each one has its perspective that it would like to compel all the other drives to accept as a norm.

If there is a threshold between philosophy as a rigorous science and postscientific philosophy, or between structuralist and poststructuralist thinking, it is just this Nietzschean idea that there are no transcendental standpoints, that reason is finite and historical, that consciousness is internal to the languages it uses to frame its representations of things. In recent years this idea has taken the form of a radical questioning of the institutions of knowledge, as in the later writings of Martin Heidegger with respect to philosophy, and in the work of Michel Foucault with respect to the human sciences. Hence also the deconstructive philosophy of Jacques Derrida and Paul de Man, who argue that language is not a logical system for constructing descriptions of an independent reality but a historicized totality of texts— call them philosophy, science, literature, law, religion, literary criticism— within which what gets counted as reality is in a state of constant, interminable, aporetic redescription. Whatever in nature or in culture we place before ourselves as an object of knowledge is always interpretable otherwise.

A similar Nietzschean turn occurred within the tradition of logical empiricism that forms the backbone of Anglo-American philosophy, with its notion of conceptual frameworks. This notion is a basic corollary of an empiricist theory of language, where words have meaning, according to W. V. O. Quine, "only as their use in sentences is conditioned to sensory stimuli." For Quine, however, language is holistic as well as empirical. It is a "fabric" of interwoven sentences, that is, a vast verbal structure held together by inferential reasoning. Another term for this vast structure is "theory," but it is more commonly known as a "conceptual scheme." A conceptual scheme is a way of organizing experience into a coherent picture of the world. It includes, Quine says, "all sciences and indeed everything we say about the world." However, the truth or falsity of what is said will, in practice, be determined by how congruously a statement fits into the total framework rather than by any single empirical test. This is what Quine means by "the underdetermination of theory": more gets said about the world, and gets counted as true, than can be accounted for empirically. What we call "things," for example, are not the objects we say we encounter in experience but only "posits" called for by the particular conceptual scheme we happen to inhabit—call it the scheme of objectifying rationality. In a famous essay, "Two Dogmas of Empiricism" (1951), Quine has this to say about objects:

As an empiricist I continue to think of the conceptual scheme of science as a tool, ultimately, for predicting future experience in the light of past experience. Physical objects are conceptually imported into the situation as convenient intermediaries— not by definition in terms of experience, but simply as irreducible posits comparable, epistemologically, to the gods of Homer. For my part I do, qua lay physicist, believe in physical objects and not in Homer's gods; and I consider it a scientific error to believe otherwise. But in point of epistemological footing the physical objects and the gods differ only in degree and not in kind. Both sorts of entities enter our conception only as cultural posits. The myth of physical objects is epistemologically superior to most in that it has proved more efficacious than other myths as a device for working a manageable structure into the flux of experience.

"Physical objects are conceptually imported into the situation as convenient intermediaries": that is, they belong to the *logical* construction of the world. Or, in other words, what we have here is a sort of relativized and pragmatic Kantianism in which logical empiricism has replaced the German idealist account of mental functioning, with (materially, at least) no change in results. I say "relativized and pragmatic" because the upshot of Quine's argument is that a diversity of conceptual frameworks can be raised on the same empirical base, in which case the same experience could in principle confirm rival theories. The point is that between a Homeric universe and the universe pictured for us in modern physics, or between myth and science, there is little to choose in terms of how each connects up with reality: each is a reasonably self-consistent way of organizing experience, and, as Cassirer and the structuralists would say, the right question to ask about it is not whether it is true or false but how it is made, how it works, or how it is done. Questions of truth and meaning are internal to questions of structure. In *Ways of Worldmaking* (1978), Nelson Goodman puts the structuralist's question from the side of Anglo-American philosophy, calling it "analytic constructionalism."

Call it what you will, however, constructionalism ends up implying a plurality of criteria of rationality without telling you how to choose among them, that is, how to make your choice rational rather than arbitrary, interest-based, ethnocentric, emotive, or in any of a variety of ways historically contingent; and this makes the idea of a plurality of criteria of rationality itself sound a little self-contradictory, the more so if by reason you mean analytic and objectifying rationality, or the norms of inferential and differential reasoning. Cassirer's idea was that the same rationality—the formative power of the spirit—exhibits itself differently, but on a rising scale, in language, myth, and science, with science able to study language and myth because of its superior position on the scale. What saves science, or authorizes it, is the idea of "same rationality," or rationality as such, however differently exhibited. For Cassirer, the historicality of reason—the different ways it builds a world for man—turns out to be Hegelian, that is, it means absolute reason coming to terms with itself, or becoming more like itself (more scientific) over time. But what this means is that you do not choose among criteria of rationality—you do not choose to be mythic or scientific—rather history chooses for you. And so you have got to believe, as Hegel and Cassirer did, that history is in your favor.

The difficulty in determining reasons for such a belief has had important consequences in the social sciences, particularly in anthropology, where the problem has been to combat primitivism, or the idea ᵻhat history is in favor of the anthropologists as against those whom they study. The structural anthropology of Claude Lévi-Strauss, for example, tries to produce a sort of non-Hegelian philosophy of symbolic forms by distributing the logic of myth and the logic of science along a common axis of differential signification. However, the hard question is this: How do you study conceptual schemes (or cultures) whose criteria of rationality, or principles of construction, are different from your own, particularly when this difference cannot be adjudicated by an appeal to transcendental reason, philosophy of history, or a common axis of mental or linguistic functioning? Peter Winch has tried to follow out this question from the standpoint of Ludwig Wittgenstein's later reflections on the social nature of rationality, where rationality means something like rule-governed behavior. In "Understanding a Primitive Society" (1964), for example, Winch asks, "What is it for us to see the *point* of the rules and conventions followed in an alien form of life?"— where alien means rites of magic plainly offensive to basic rules of logic. Now what is interesting about this question is the way it is loaded, because asking about the *point* of rules and conventions is different from asking about their formal intelligibility, or how they work. It is as if Winch were turning structuralism into hermeneutics, where the idea that one can understand an alien form of life only by entering into it and living through it replaces the idea that knowledge means objectification and analysis. It was on this idea of understanding or *verstehen* that Wilhelm Dilthey tried to determine the validity of the human sciences. The point here would be that a conceptual scheme can only be understood from the inside out, not from the outside in, or by way of participation rather than by way of structural analysis. However, understanding alien forms of life would thus confront serious obstacles, because it is by no means clear that one can simply cross a threshold from one scheme to another. This is another way of putting the problem of historicality or the finitude of reason, and it is why understanding alien conceptual schemes—and perhaps understanding as such—always requires a liberal application of the principle of charity. This principle holds that for understanding to be possible we must always assume that what someone is saying is true, even when we are not sure *what* that someone is saying. Charity is what replaces belief in the universal distribution of reason or common axes of rationality. It is what compels Winch to posit as basic to the study of alien cultures what he calls "limiting notions"—notions of birth, death, and sexuality—which are, he says, "inescapably involved in the life of all known human societies in a way which gives us a clue where to look, if we are puzzled about the point of an alien system of institutions." This simply means that if we want to understand other people we have to assume that they are sufficiently like us for agreement between us to be possible, or at least for us to learn something from them concerning matters of importance to us; only we cannot be sure that what matters to us does also in fact matter to them. We are not in a position to say what matters to them or not, unless we can say it, as one of them, in their language; or, in other words, we are not in a position to determine either common interests *or* differences, which is why the doctrine of charity is not an option but our only recourse.

This gets us back to the idea that we are not in any position to get a good look at conceptual schemes, and so we cannot be sure there are such things. This is the argument of Donald Davidson's essay "On the Very Idea of a Conceptual Scheme" (1974). It is all very well to talk about conceptual relativism, Davidson says, but it is a different thing to make sense of it. The idea of "differing points of view" makes a kind of sense, "but only if there is a common co-ordinate system [a common axis] on which to plot them," that is, a nonideological place where knowledge of the kind Kant wanted, science rather than hermeneutics, is possible. "We may accept the doctrine," Davidson says, "that associates having a language with having a conceptual scheme," but the problem is that "speaking a language is not a trait anyone can lose while retaining the power of thought. So there is no chance that someone can take up a vantage point for comparing conceptual schemes by temporarily shedding his own." And if we follow out Davidson's argument, which is that the "dualism of scheme and content, of organizing system and something wanting to be organized, cannot be made intelligible and defensible," we come to this: namely, that we have in our current intellectual situation a terrific surplus of conceptual-scheme theories—idealist theories of symbolic forms, structuralist systems of formal constraint, analytic conceptual holism, prison-house theories of language, ideology, and metaphysics, Nietzschean perspectivism, internalist realism, theories of archives, paradigms, language games, communicative communities, interpretive communities, intersubjective communities, what-you-will: in short, a plenitude of structuralisms, and no determinate reason for holding any one of them.

However, this poverty of reasons may not matter. As Nelson Goodman says, "With false hope of firm foundation gone, with the world displaced by worlds that are but versions, with substance dissolved into function, and with the given acknowledged as taken, we face the question of how worlds are made, tested, and known"—which is just to say that, with firm foundation gone, we should go on being the structuralists we have always been, holding with the tradition of analytic and objectifying rationality as if this were still the nonideological place we thought it was when we first began to put the Kantian question of "how worlds are made, tested, and known." It is as if awareness of the finitude of reason did not diminish the sheer technical power of analysis. This is in fact the conclusion reached by Jonathan Culler in *Structuralist Poetics* (1975) and again in *On Deconstruction: Theory and Criticism after Structuralism* (1983): namely, there is no *after* after structuralism—no *post*-structuralist thinking that thinking could get into, only *pre*-structuralism. We are at what Martin Heidegger called "the end of philosophy," which does not mean that philosophy now stops but only that it has now turned out to be what we wanted it to be: "the operational and model character of representational-calculative thinking," which is Heidegger's description of analytical and objectifying reason, or structuralism for short—the thinking that is proper to philosophy has now reached its fulfillment. Reason can only now begin reproducing itself technologically in the form of formalized languages and programs of artificial intelligence. Hegel, in other words, was right: there is a point at which we cannot get more rational than we are, and here we are. What this means historically is that thinking could not now become anything that philosophy has not already abandoned along its way as not being proper to itself: that is, thinking could now only become regressive—pre-critical, pre-Kantian, pre-structuralist, disenlightened, Aristotelian, mystified, or merely poetic. For philosophy to become anything new one would have to imagine philosophers bereft of deductive arguments; or perhaps one would have to imagine the history of philosophy starting all over again like one of Northrop Frye's great recorsos that recuperates the journey of mankind from myth to irony.

So the phrase "finitude of reason" has a double meaning; it is one that opens up a region in which we can bring together a number of disparate intellectual phenomena. I have already mentioned deconstruction, with its special feeling for systematic bondage or the double bind, but the historical point to be made about deconstruction would stress its avant-garde relationship to the philosophical tradition. Deconstruction is a sort of ad hoc negative questioning that tries, in the spirit of Nietzsche, to shake philosophy loose from the dogmatism of thinking only in terms of what is proper to itself; but deconstruction is philosophy all the same. Its playfulness is rigorously analytical, not regressive. A related phenomenon would be what Jean-François Lyotard calls the decline in the credibility of narratives that seek to legitimate the claims of analytical and emancipatory reason—Descartes's *Discourse on Method* (1637) would be one such narrative, and another would be Marx's contribution to the *Critique of Political Economy* (1859). But the decline in the credibility of such metanarratives has combined with a dramatic increase in their desirability. Constructionalism makes it impossible to determine a nonideological place where the unmasking of false objectivity can go on; speaking a language is not a trait anyone can lose while retaining the power of critique. But this only intensifies the problem of authority vis-à-vis the conflict of interpretations, for what awareness of finitude seems to entail is a heightened sensitivity to the unequal circulation of power in any system. This was Nietzsche's insight: the poverty of reasons magnifies the problem of power. The paradox of reason is that it cannot justify itself rationally but only instrumentally.

Indeed, it appears that the awareness of the plurality of constructions and the corresponding inaccessibility of any nonideological place has shifted the center of philosophical gravity away from the pole of logic and epistemology toward ethics, aesthetics, history, and politics, that is, away from school philosophy and all of its argumentative brilliance toward what used to be called the human sciences, where dialogue replaces method, or where an improvisatory give-and-take among human beings replaces the relationship between mind and world, subject and object, signifier and system, or rule and behavior. Conservatives like Alasdair MacIntyre are ambiguous about this shift, because on the one hand it seems to open a way back from Kant to Aristotle, but on the other hand it looks just like more of the decay of reason that produced such things as conceptual relativism and emotivism in moral philosophy, where all judgments reduce to feeling or preference and can only be adjudicated by some form of manipulative or bureaucratic reason (that is, by coercion). For liberals like Richard Rorty, this shift means that we should stop feeling guilty about our "ethnocentrism," that is (among other things), our tradition of analytical reason, which has, after all, made us what we are, even if we cannot quite justify what we are. We cannot help analyzing things and making rigorous arguments as if these were the only rational things to do; but we ought to stop imagining, Rorty says, that this sort of rationality links us up with reality in a way that makes logicians more objective than poets. Instead of trying to determine who is objective and who is given to "mere talk," we ought to pay attention to history, or to that which has made us what we are, with the proviso that no one's history is Hegel's history of reason.

This so-called shift from logic to politics is only a convenient way of summarizing what all of this comes to, which is a widespread recognition, in our current intellectual situation, of the priority of practice over theory, or what Marxists like E. P. Thompson call "the poverty of theory," which turns out to be not much different from what Quine called "the underdetermination of theory," or what I have called the "poverty of reasons." Remember how cheerfully Quine accepted the equal intelligibility of Homeric gods and the laws of physics, saying only that, "qua lay physicist," he found it more workable, and to that extent more reasonable, to believe in the latter. Only within physics can a physicist practice physics, but what this means is that practice is no longer reducible to concepts of method and technique, or to what Karl-Otto Apel calls "methodological solipsism," which is the idea that "one person, alone, could at least in principle practice science." Rather, the practice of science is different from the logic of it; it presupposes social conventions mediated not by "the scientific rationality of operation on objects . . . but rather the pre- and meta-scientific rationality of intersubjective discourse mediated by explication of concepts and interpretation of intentions." Or, in other words, science presupposes hermeneutics, or the understanding of other people.

So when Nelson Goodman says that, with firm foundation gone, we should go ahead and practice "analytical constructionalism" anyway, taking this as our Archimedean point for asking "how worlds are made, tested, and known," he is smiling Quine's smile. Rorty would say that this smile is what accepting one's ethnocentricity produces, namely, a feeling of solidarity to replace the Cartesian-Kantian feeling of mathematical certainty. Quine, Goodman, and Rorty are squarely within the tradition of American pragmatism, which teaches us, in effect, how to live, and also how to practice science, without Kantian foundations. It was William James who proposed the notion of a plural universe as against the rationalist claims of Kantian idealism that the only world worth having is the one that answers to the laws of physical science. James never concealed his preference for the universe of the scientists, but he understood that we do not live *just* in this world. Our world of everyday is not reducible to a single, justifiable account of it; we have to keep it loose in order to get on with one another, that is, we have to learn to speak of a plurality of worlds, each one able to be kept reasonably consistent with experience by a regular adjustment in what we say about it. There is no saying anything once for all. Theory always has to be revised in the light of new experience, and philosophy ought to think of itself as keeping us equal to this revisionary task—instead of trying to close us up in final determinations of reality or so-called logical constructions of the world. The only revision that would now have to be made in James's notion of a revisable universe is that, as Davidson says, since we cannot discriminate between scheme and content, or between experience and the language we use to make sense of it, there is no longer much sense to be made of the concept of experience. Davidson calls this getting rid of the third and last dogma of empiricism, meaning that it is no longer clear "that there is anything left to call empiricism." James would have understood this point very well. It is not our solitary experience of the world that requires us to live with our ideas under correction, rather it is the people whose company we keep.

Another way to put this would be to say that we connect up with the world by way of ordinary rather than philosophical language, or by way of people rather than things. This was the insight of J. L. Austin and of the Wittgenstein of *Philosophical Investigations* (1953). In our time, however, no philosopher has followed out this insight with greater intensity than Stanley Cavell, particularly in a series of writings that confound the distinction between philosophy and literature—"The Avoidance of Love: A Reading of *King Lear*" (1969), *The Senses of Walden* (1972), "Thinking of Emerson" (1978), and *The Claim of Reason: Wittgenstein, Skepticism, Morality, and Tragedy* (1979). Cavell takes up the opposition of the ordinary and the philosophical by returning to Emerson and Thoreau as inaugurators of the American philosophical tradition. In *The Senses of Walden*, Cavell asks, "Why has America never expressed itself philosophically?" The fact of the matter is that it has, and without our knowing it, because Emerson and Thoreau understood, as Austin and Wittgenstein would later understand, "that there are more ways of making a habitable world . . . than Kant's twelve concepts of the understanding would accommodate." The key word here is "habitable." The problem with school philosophers, who brush Emerson and Thoreau aside with a weary gesture, is that they always picture themselves as outsiders to the world, spectators rather than inhabitants, conceptual schemers wondering how knowledge is possible or how words hook onto the world. This is not how Emerson and Thoreau pictured themselves. We should think twice before calling them transcendentalists. Cavell, at any rate, calls them "philosophers of direction, orienters, tirelessly prompting us to be on our way, endlessly asking us where we stand, what it is we face." These are not epistemological questions. The mode of Emerson and Thoreau was not that of transcendence and representation. They understood what Cavell, in *The Claim of Reason*, calls "the moral of skepticism, namely, that the human creature's basis in the world as a whole, its relation to the world as such, is not that of knowing, anyway not what we think of as knowing."

This moral is Cavell's way of bringing the Kantian tradition, or philosophy, back to earth, resettling it among human beings, making it ordinary.

Kant set out to refute the skepticism of Hume by redescribing human understanding as "the author of the experience in which its objects are found."
Here is where the myth of worldmaking gets its start. Cavell appropriates
this Kantian task, only his way of answering skepticism is not to refute it
but to see, Thoreau-like, where it leads. The crucial Cavellian point is that
the world is made up of other people, not Kantian objects, and others are
not the products of our construction—it is in their nature to remain, Des-
demona-like, outside our capacity to know, or Cordelia-like, resistant to our
worldmaking. As Emmanuel Levinas says in *Totality and Infinity* (1961),
knowledge is not a relation to the other but the destruction of it; it is "the
reduction of the other to the same." It is a refusal of otherness. The other,
however, is for its part just what refuses to be contained within the conceptual structures that we build up in order to make sense of things. This is
what the otherness of the other means. Otherness defines our finitude or
historicality; it inscribes, as if on the other side of Kant, the limits of reason. We cannot know (cannot be certain of the existence of) other minds,
cannot experience another's pain or existence, cannot bring the other under
conceptual control in order to remove her strangeness. Here is the "poverty
of reasons" in its most practical and compelling form. Cavell says, "A statue,
a stone, is something whose existence is fundamentally open to ocular proof.
A human being is not."

So with respect to others we are reduced to skepticism. In Cavell's language, with others (with the world) we must "live our skepticism." This
means learning to forgo knowledge of the other; it means learning that our
relation to the other, or to the world, is deeper than knowing. What Cor-
delia asks of Lear is not his certain knowledge but his acceptance of her
existence (her otherness, her difference). Cavell calls this acceptance "acknowledgment." Acknowledgment is knowledge as moral praxis rather than
as self-certainty as to reality. Its opposite is not error or illusion or ideology
but willful blindness and delusion—delusion above all with respect to Godlike reason that knows only worlds of its own making and can accept nothing else as real. Think of Othello as a figure of reason caught up in an
epistemological crisis, or tragedy. The link between tragedy and skepticism
for Cavell lies in the exposure of reason to its own blindness—to the short-
fall of its power or sovereignty. Cavell speaks paradoxically of "the truth of
skepticism." Shakespearean tragedy, as Cavell reads it, is the working-out
of this paradox. So tragic knowledge is always of limits, not of objects, and
what limits require is acknowledgment or acceptance, not objectification.
So also with the strangeness, or existence, of the world.

Cavell's philosophical investigations may seem to range great distances from normal philosophy, especially in his works on film, *The World Viewed: Reflections on the Ontology of Film* (1971) and *Pursuits of Happiness: The Hollywood Comedy of Remarriage* (1981), but they are central to the intellectual culture shaped by such texts as Michel Foucault's *Madness and Civilization* (1961), John Ashbery's "Self-Portrait in a Convex Mirror" (1969), T. W. Adorno's *Aesthetic Theory* (1970), and Jacques Derrida's *Glas* (1974). In the culture defined by these texts the question of the other is dominant in the way the problem of language was dominant for the Kantian culture of structuralism, analytic philosophy, semiotics, and instrumental reasoning. It is no accident that this culture of otherness has seen the development of feminist theory and the resurgence of psychoanalysis and radical politics, all three of which come together dramatically in the recent (postsemiotic) work of Julia Kristeva—for example, in *About Chinese Women* (1974), "A New Type of Intellectual: The Dissident" (1977), and "Psychoanalysis and the Polis" (1981). Here what was marginal is now central. In this state of affairs, it is no longer possible to speak either of the end of philosophy or of its new beginning. Better to say that the turn from knowledge to praxis means a turn toward the otherness of thinking itself, where philosophy is no longer containable within the forms it had constructed to secure itself against what is alien to it. Or say that what is new in philosophy is that nothing is any longer alien to it.

Gerald L. Bruns

Literature as Radical Statement

Finality is not the language of politics.
—Benjamin Disraeli (1859)

In the 1930s, the literature of radical statement was inseparable from Marxism and socialism, a set of conflicting ideas. Marxism itself had promised a comprehensive theory about history and revolutionary change; communism, a comprehensive set of political principles on which to act; the Soviet Union, a state that would embody these principles; Joseph Stalin, heroic leadership of that state. Dramatizing these promises, radical literature would practice "socialist realism" and show the working class in its struggle for liberation and fulfillment.

After World War II, American writers reacted against such beliefs in at least four ways. First, many deserted their old cause, in part because of the recognition of the real horrors of the Soviet state and a renewed patriotism. Their disenchantment often began in 1939; disappeared during World War II; loomed again after 1945. In 1949, a collection of essays, *The God That Failed*, revealed the deconversion experiences of several European and American writers. Simultaneously, two novels by the skeptical English writer George Orwell, *Animal Farm* (1946) and *1984* (1949), were read as fables against a totalitarian Left. The 1970s and 1980s repeated the process of disenchantment, taking as their text the American edition, in 1973, of *The Gulag Archipelago* by Aleksandr I. Solzhenitsyn, a Russian now living in exile in America. Inexorably, *The Gulag Archipelago* anathematized the Soviet system. Solzhenitsyn, like some Eastern European writers, insisted that people admit how brutal Communist states could be. Supplementing his disclosures was the evidence of Soviet anti-Semitism, of the travails of the Solidarity Movement in Poland, and of violations of civil liberties and freedom in Cuba. Symbolically, in the early 1980s, the experimental writer and radical critic Susan Sontag began to decry the "appalling" conditions for people of conscience under communism.

Second, other writers moved beyond disenchantment into a rigid anti-communism and pro-Americanism. The literary codification of this movement was *Witness* (1952), an autobiography by Whittaker Chambers. A lapsed Communist, Chambers had testified before a congressional committee, with the support of Richard M. Nixon, about Communist influence in the United States. *Witness* dramatizes an apocalyptic struggle between freedom, which God supports, and communism, which the Devil supports but which nevertheless seems to be winning. In the 1970s, the conservative writer and editor William F. Buckley, Jr., a friend of Chambers, began to graft such an ideology to a popular genre, a series of spy stories. Buckley's hero is Blackwood Oakes, Yale '51, a debonair CIA agent. Blackie's lover is a Jane Austen scholar. His principles (God, country, freedom) are as clear as are his enemies (the vicious rulers of the USSR, their clients, and liberal dupes). This strain of literary radicalism was part of a larger movement: the emergence of the "Radical Right," an amalgam of social conservatism, arch-patriotism, and a Christian fundamentalism that declared its primary allegiance to a single book, the Holy Bible.

Third, some writers transmogrified a stock hero of the 1930s: the proletarian white male, the industrial worker. This figure almost disappeared from literature, often becoming an anti-hero instead: a crude, paunchy man who beat up people of whom he disapproved. However, because of their own lives, and because of their sympathy for the powerless, women writers countered this trend by being among the most responsive observers of working-class life for both men and women, but especially for women. In 1962, Tillie Olsen published her poignant collection of stories about working-class families, *Tell Me a Riddle*. In 1973, in *Small Changes*, Marge Piercy, among the most political of contemporary writers, explored the transformations of Beth, the child of a Syracuse, New York, factory family.

Fourth, even the most socially concerned writers tended to separate art from all politics, radical or not. In 1949, in his essay "Everybody's Protest Novel," the black writer James Baldwin offered the maxim that writers are not Congressmen; instead, the "power or revelation . . . is the business of the novelist, this journey towards a more vast reality." Poets might be the unacknowledged legislators of the world, but poetry was to be neither rhetoric nor polemic. In his collection of poems entitled *Decompressions* (1978), Philip Whalen thought only a "complete political revolution" could end America's evil economic system, its war machine, the conspiracy between government and industry, and pollution. Whalen regretted his earlier "topical political poems." Produced out of a belief in the "poet's duty to speak out in behalf of the oppressed masses bleeding under tyrannical heels," they now seemed like "oatmeal."

The belief in the freedom of the writer and of art was compatible with a down-home American cultural formula: giving credence to the clear waters of the individual. Like the artist, the soul is to select its own society. So choosing, it can flee from ordinary domestic and communal orders, which often punish the soul's transgressions. It seeks solitude and salvation, a beatitude and bliss, a myth and magic; for some, these things exist most preciously with a few boon companions or in nature. The soul is contemptuous of ideology, that shared set of perceptions and interpretations of the world. The soul's politics can lead to anarchism. In his *Collected Poems* (1973), Paul Goodman confesses:

My anarchy as I grow old
is, Let me alone with my habits
I learned when I was poor
—nor did they ever work.
I like to have a flag,
I too, and hold it up.
I really don't expect
anybody to salute.

Although such cultural individualism can be sloppily self-involved, it tends to sympathize with the powerless, to find the underdog more virtuous than the top dog. In many texts, such sentiments modulate into a preference for the lonely, alienated, and misunderstood; for the "rebels without a cause" over the gregarious, bouncy, and secure. Because these attitudes subvert authority, they open up cultural spaces for radical protest.

However, few reactions, even the most acid, can wholly neutralize the past. Two figures from the older radicalism haunt contemporary literature, especially that of the urban East: Ethel and Julius Rosenberg. Both born during World War I, they were found guilty, in 1951, of transmitting atomic secrets to the Soviet Union during World War II. Despite appeals for clemency, they died in the electric chair on July 19, 1953. For several imaginative writers, for example, Robert Coover in *The Public Burning* (1967) and E. L. Doctorow in *The Book of Daniel* (1971), the Rosenbergs are a symbol of America. Moreover, socialist, Marxist, and post-Marxist thought still influences contemporary American thinking and writing. In 1971, to give an obvious example, Angela Y. Davis edited a collection of writings by and about prisoners, including herself. The book announces that the "entire apparatus of the *bourgeois democratic* state . . . is disintegrating." Flailing, the state will move against the most radical, the politically conscious elements of the working class, those in black, Puerto Rican, and Chicano communities.

A conventional account of contemporary American culture professes that literature as radical statement did not exist in the 1940s and 1950s. Then, in the 1960s, revolutionary texts exploded, to falter into ashy murmurs and obsolete mumbles in the 1970s and 1980s. The myth is partly true. The fiery writing of the 1960s did cry out for revolution, not reform. It did warn of catastrophe, not cajole for gradual change. In the 1960s, too, some critics and writers took on the task of reconciling the apparently autonomous claims of art and the collective demands of radical politics. In his 1967 paper, "Art in the One-Dimensional Society," Herbert Marcuse, the philosopher indebted to both Marx and Freud, suggested that art (music, literature, painting, sculpture) is liberating in and of itself. It negates, denies, refuses the established order. Then, through "beautiful and pleasurable Form," art gives an image of a new society in which that society itself will be a work of art. Later, in 1981, at a symposium on the writer and human rights, the poet Carolyn Forché said that art was at once "art," which says nothing about the world, and "interpretation," which does.

However, the myth is only partly true. For some writers in the late 1940s and the 1950s prepared the ground, not only for the radical right, but for the other opposing literatures of the 1960s. Addressing both public and private life, the subjects of these other radical literatures included race and ethnicity; sex, sexuality, and gender; war, political violence and economic exploitation; and the destruction of nature. In turn, these statements altered culture in the United States in the 1970s and 1980s.

After 1945, blacks were America's most formidable voices of protest. During the 1960s, three other racial groups forcefully claimed literary space: the Native American (or American Indian), with many tribal loyalties; the Hispanic, Puerto Rican, and Mexican American (Chicano/Chicana); and the Asian American, including people of Chinese, Filipino, Japanese, Korean, and Polynesian descent. Each group has its own past and present set of wrongs. Native Americans had suffered from the destruction of traditional cultures, which many called the breaking and scattering of a nation's hoop; Chicano/Chicanas, "La Raza," from Western conquest and colonization; Japanese Americans, from World War II internment camps.

About 1970, women within these racial and ethnic groups began to write, openly and systematically, about their "double jeopardy," that is, the experience of being a woman as well as a member of a "minority." The anthology *The Third Woman: Minority Women Writers of the United States* (1980) helped to record their achievements. These women were exploring what their situation might be; what destructive social and psychological forces they had to confront and surmount; what triumphs they might be able to celebrate; what "freedom" might mean for them. In one of the first of such endeavors, Toni Cade Bambara wrote, in the "Preface" of her anthology *The Black Woman* (1970): "We are involved in a struggle for liberation . . . from . . . racism . . . corporate society . . . 'mainstream' culture. What characterizes the current movement of the 60s is a turning away from the larger society and a turning toward each other." Such women of color were also to claim a legacy: their own history, their own communal, familial, and linguistic memories, including those of strong women. The emerging past included a new literary history that mapped overlapping generations. Among the black women writers were Ntozake Shange and Alice Walker; June Jordan and Toni Morrison; Lorraine Hansberry, the author of *A Raisin in the Sun* (1959), the first play by a black woman produced on Broadway, and Maya Angelou; Gwendolyn Brooks and Margaret Walker; Zora Neale Hurston.

Writing of both race and gender, women of color were to reject, adapt, and help to create the insights and images of the New Feminism that began in the 1960s. Like the black movement, feminism had a political legacy from the nineteenth century. Unlike the black movement, it had been subdued immediately after World War II. Then, in 1963, four texts quickened what had seemed dead: *American Women*, a report from the President's Commission on the Status of Women; *The Feminine Mystique* by Betty Friedan, a vigorous polemic about a "problem that had no name," women's inferior position; *The Bell Jar* by Sylvia Plath, a novel about a middle-class young woman haunted by both ambition and suicidal depression, which preceded Plath's posthumous book of poetry, *Ariel* (1965); and, finally, *The Group* by Mary McCarthy, a novel about nine Vassar classmates in the 1930s.

The New Feminist literature reflected the confluence of strong historical forces: the number of women, of all races and classes, in the public labor force; the number of women, of all races and classes, with some education; new forms of control of reproduction; changing patterns of marriage and divorce; women's response to other liberation movements. The New Feminism nurtured scores of valuable writers. The poetry and prose of Adrienne Rich consistently defines its major themes: the analysis of male power over women; the rejection of that power; the deconstruction of dominant images of women; the need for women to construct their own experience, history, and identity; and the tension between two possible futures. In one, the differences between the sexes have disappeared; we are androgynous. In the other, women celebrate female difference, their own "common language."

In the 1970s, Rich explored lesbianism as well, a theme that *The Group* had helped to publicize, for McCarthy's heroine, Lakey, is a glamorous, cultivated, antifascist lesbian. McCarthy was daring, for in 1963 homosexuality was considered sinful, sick, or criminal, illegal in every state except Illinois. However, during the late 1940s and 1950s, homosexuals both attracted some liberal sympathy and created the rudiments of protest organizations. In 1948, Gore Vidal published his striking novel *The City and the Pillar*. Its hero, a "nice," good-looking young man, is a homosexual. In a crime of passion, he murders the man with whom he first had gay sex, but who now rebuffs him. Vidal predicted one concern of contemporary homosexual literature: sexual stigmas and the damage they breed. In 1955, in San Francisco, Allen Ginsberg, indebted to William Blake and Walt Whitman, first read his poem "Howl." Like William Burroughs, Ginsberg was central to the "Beats," a 1950s sensibility that rebelled against United States conformity and repression. "Howl" projected America as Moloch, the god in the Old Testament who demands the sacrifices of children. Ginsberg denounced "Robot apartments! Invisible suburbs! skeleton treasuries! blind capitals! demonic industries! . . . granite cocks! monstrous bombs!" Yet, the poet calls as well for holiness. In so doing, Ginsberg predicted another element of homosexual literature: sexual happiness. Eighteen years later, *Rubyfruit Jungle* by Rita May Brown as openly rejoiced in lesbian sexuality. Sexual curses became sexual blessings.

Although some feminists advocated lesbianism more vigorously than others, the impieties of the feminist queries about heterosexuality were compatible with gay and lesbian writing. Not all gay and lesbian literature was politically radical. Not all argued for the destruction of capitalism or the transformation of the state. However, it was culturally radical and emancipatory. Even its less explicitly ideological texts, the poems of Frank O'Hara or the novels of Edmund White, spoke openly of once "closeted," guilty sexual secrets.

Many feminist, gay, and lesbian writers argued that the machine tools that manufactured American masculinity, those "granite cocks," were dangerous. They mass-produced rigid, repressive, repressed heterosexual men who were incapable of love and charity, but who were capable of abusing and killing Asian peasants, "uppity" blacks, and their own wives. Such an analysis extended and deepened that of antinuclear and pacifist groups who feared state violence in the nuclear age. Weighing upon them all was a catastrophic mutation in human history: the origin of atomic warfare, which began in July 1945 when the United States tested the first atomic bomb.

During much of the 1960s, radical literature about atomic war and peace focused on three other, related wars. The first was the war abroad, in Vietnam, particularly after 1965 when American troop strength increased from 23,000 to 184,000. Writers like Rich, Sontag, McCarthy, Denise Levertov, Grace Paley, Robert Bly, and Galway Kinnell used literature to argue passionately against the United States presence in Vietnam. In the 1980s, radical literature against a war abroad was to expose American force in Central America. The second war was at home, against racism. One's label for ghetto "disturbances" revealed one's politics. Were they "riots" or "rebellions"? (A riot, said Martin Luther King, Jr., is the language of the uneducated.) A third war at home, less vicious, less tough, was the struggle on university and college campuses about the wars abroad and at home.

This third war was inseparable from the "youth movement." Indebted to Rousseauean theories of the innocence of children, until society corrupts them; to some Victorian theories of the purity of a child's point of view; and to twentieth-century theories of progressive educational reform, the movement legitimately demanded greater freedom, sexual self-determination, and respect for the young. At its least attractive, it denied the possible virtues of discretion, restraint, deferred gratification, and maturity. The *Bildungsroman* became, not the narrative of adjustment to society, but a narrative of the right to, and rightness of, the rejection of both adjustment and society. Some of the wilder elements of the youth movement—distrust of structure and rationality, trust of sexuality, a preference for musical over literary texts, a delight in costumes and performances, drug use—were antecedents of Punk sensibility and writing in the 1970s and 1980s.

A related form of protest, the ecology movement, spoke of the destruction of nature, of the biological and physical world. At once pastoral and bleak in mood, ecological literature is the most elegaic of radical writing. One society can replace another; we have but one earth. In the late 1950s, the poet Gary Snyder, a student of Eastern religions, began to call for a "gentle stewardship" of nature, for a more sensitive awareness of our place in the "ecosystem." Then, in 1962, Rachel Carson published *Silent Spring*, which was to shape public consciousness about ecology as vividly as *The Feminine Mystique* was to do a year later about women and gender. Carson documented a lethal assault on the biosphere through fallout from atomic testing, radiation, pesticides, insecticides, and other possible carcinogens. She saw a quiet, sterile America. "No witchcraft, no enemy action had silenced the rebirth of new life in this stricken world. The people had done it themselves."

In the late 1960s and 1970s, a major strand of radical feminism fused ecological and feminist thinking through its revision of a traditional association of nature and women. Such writing promised that nature would survive if women were to liberate and empower themselves. In 1978, two philosophical prose poems dramatized that promise. In *Gyn/Ecology*, the theologian Mary Daly, remembering Rachel Carson, called for women to journey toward a new "Spring" of being. In *Woman and Nature: The Roaring Inside Her*, the poet and essayist Susan Griffin embodied the premises of ecofeminism. Contrasting two languages, the "male" and the "female," "he" and she," Griffin anatomized an impersonal, abstract, rational masculinity that controls and mutilates both nature and the women who represent it. She called for a nurturing femaleness to speak, chant, and sing so that all people might live.

Brought into existence because of a nonnegotiable conflict with the dominant culture, the literatures of radical statement often opposed each other. A common capacity for saying "no" need not entail a common capacity for saying "yes." For each of us dwells in more than one community. As citizens of one, we may be victims; as citizens of another, may victimize. The writings of women of color pungently dramatize such a tension. Like white women, they are women, but white women can rule over blacks of both sexes. In 1970, the black feminist lesbian writer Audre Lorde sharply and influentially evoked such a dilemma. The narrator of her poem "Who Said It Was Simple" watches white women sitting at a lunch counter before a political march and discussing "problematic girls," their black maids. Lorde finishes:

> But I who am bound by my mirror
> as well as my bed
> see causes in color
> as well as sex
>
> and sit here wondering
> which me will survive
> all these liberations.

Ironically, male chauvinism within radical movements helped to generate feminist consciousness. The more militant the movement, the more it tended to genderize political activity and language. Political, cultural, and sexual leadership was masculine; political, cultural, and sexual support feminine. Rhetorically, radical language often reconstituted a traditional binary pattern of associating women *either* with the erotically desirable, the erotically awesome, deserving of praise, *or* with the morally contemptible, the morally awful, deserving of rape. One poem, "In Cuba," begins: "The Cuban night is a Negress . . . and I aslumber in her womb." It ends: "I bear my America where I go . . . like a pale cruel hawk-nailed wife." More romantic, mythic, and/or ecological writers delighted in archetypal images of Woman as the Great Mother/Lover/Goddess/Earth Figure—nothing less, nothing more.

Nor is any radical group smoothly ideological, any body of literature serenely consistent. The more broadly based a movement becomes, as the civil rights and antiwar and women's movements were to become, the more that movement will separate out into radical, mainstream, and conservative positions. The more honest the literature, the more it will reveal gaping theoretical, emotional, and strategic fissures, at any given moment or over time. One divisive question has been the political and social end of action. Is the aim to become separate from the dominant society, or is it to integrate the movement within that society? Should a movement bleed and sweat for civil rights within a nation, or should it seek an independent nation (at least culturally) that would inspire its own pledges of allegiance? Is difference ultimately a source of survival and celebration or a source of inferiority and grief? In 1944, in a prophetic essay, "The Homosexual in Society," the poet Robert Duncan asked homosexuals to stop proclaiming a sense of difference that had two bad causes: society's insistence that homosexuals were different and lesser; the homosexuals' compensatory response, that they were different and better. Look to the "Negroes," Duncan suggested, and their struggle for freedom in a hostile society for a model of behavior.

In the 1960s, blacks asked each other if they wished to end segregation and live within an integrated society, or if they wished to create a black nation, organized around the principles of black power and cultural nationalism. In the late 1960s and 1970s, feminists asked each other if they wanted a "human culture," organized around the absence of gender differences (the liberal answer), or a separate women's culture, focused on the potential of the relationships of mother/daughter, sisters, and lovers (the radical answer). In 1972, in "The Phenomenology of Anger," Adrienne Rich hoped for "a world/ of women and men gaily/ in collusion with green leaves." However, in 1977, in another poem, "Natural Resources," she imagined an alternative community of women. Later still she was to present a third possibility: a society and culture that reflected many differences among people—multiple, crisscrossing, cross-fertilizing identities, of which gender was only one source.

Another quarrel has been about the object of revolutionary action. Is it, as it traditionally had been, the public world of political and economic structures? Or is it conscousness, behavior? Or, critically, everything? A total revolution? In 1971, Todd Gitlin edited a volume of poetry from "The Movement." Dedicated to "all prisoners," the book was entitled *Campfires of the Resistance*. The words evoke that dream of a rural idyll that grounds so much American radicalism, images of the nineteenth-century Civil War, and the street fires of urban riots/rebellions. The poems, Gitlin wrote, are about both the "political universe" (the war in Vietnam, the American empire, racism, universities, capitalism, the subjugation of women) *and* "love and death and choice and pain." For his poets are both "public and private." They blur the lines between self and society.

If there is to be revolution, is it to be violent? This question haunts one of the most sensitive novels about radical politics: Alice Walker's *Meridian* (1976). America has had an old marriage with violence. It fought in Korea from 1950 to 1953; in Vietnam from 1961 to 1973, a war that was to generate its own chaotic, convulsive literature. The American internal security apparatus and police were well-armored. Murders and assassinations scarred the 1960s: those of John F. Kennedy, Medgar Evers, and little black children in a Birmingham church in 1963; of three civil rights workers in Mississippi (James Chaney, Andrew Goodman, Michael Schwerner) in 1964; of Malcolm X in 1965; of Martin Luther King, Jr., and Robert F. Kennedy in 1968.

How, then, to respond? Survivors could lament the victims and elevate them to heroic martyrdom. Survivors could also match violence with nonviolence. King defended "nonviolent direct action." In public letters and essays, sermons and speeches, he translated the theories of Gandhi for America. In his "Letter from a Birmingham Jail," of April 1963, he notes that "freedom is never voluntarily given by the oppressor." Yet, he proudly asserts, both God's will and America's national heritage support his nonviolent civil disobedience. The civil rights movement is not revolutionary. On the contrary, it fulfills, it realizes, America's moral promise. In the speech "I Have a Dream," which he gave at a great march on Washington in August 1963, King called for "dignity and discipline," for a confrontation of "physical force with soul force." The memoirs of civil rights workers, like those of Anne Moody, *Coming of Age in Mississippi* (1968), revealed what immense endurance soul force demanded. Later, Gary Snyder, in *Plain*

Talk, listing practical steps a radical might take, warned that bloody force would not work.

Congress passed a civil rights bill in 1964, a voting rights bill in 1965. Yet, in part because of the Vietnam War, in part because of the poverty amidst American affluence, radicalism became more militant, black radicalism more separatist. Defined as self-defense, and as the only means left for revolutionary change, political violence became more accepted. Political rhetoric shifted from persuasive strategies to threats, from promises of the apotheosis of the American dream to promises of revenge and punishment. America was no longer a land capable of change, but Amerika, a decadent and unyielding Babylon. Clarence Major, the editor of a striking volume, *The New Black Poetry* (1969), praised the poems for showing reality; for working for liberation; for celebrating "Black radiance"; and for being "death cries to the pimp *par excellence* of the recent capitalist stages of the world, testimonies against the brutal psychological engravings of his base self-profit oriented psychology, his sham stance."

Adapting the aesthetics of radicalism before World War II, such beliefs saw literature, if literature was to exist, as a weapon for a vanguard. Arts and letters were inseparable from a community's struggle. The artist, the writer, was to bear visions, strength, and beauty to, and from, the masses. Direct, potentially a visceral arena of representative actions and inspiriting images, the theater was an obvious medium through which the engaged writer might communicate to his or her community; through which that community might enact and reaffirm its myths, rituals, history, and experience. In 1965, for example, Luís Valdez became the director of the bilingual El Teatro Campesino, which was "to teach and organize Chicano farm workers." Significantly, the theater had its beginnings in a "shack" in Delano, California, that also served as the headquarters for César Chávez's farm workers' union.

Political and cultural intensities changed individual writers. Before the 1960s, the fiction and poetry of Gwendolyn Brooks had balanced "mainstream" Western influences and black culture; a shrewd, acerbic anatomy of white behavior and explorations of black experience, symbolized by an urban community, "Bronzeville." Then, in 1967, she attended the Second Black Writers' Conference at Fisk University with more overtly radical, new black writers. In her 1972 autobiography, *Report from Part One*, she writes of a "new note that would become a scream, an intensifying fury" in black culture. Her own poetry became harder, tighter, angrier; her molten irony, iron.

The career of LeRoi Jones is more turbulent. In the 1950s, Jones traveled within radical, literary, largely white bohemian circles. In 1960, in the essay "cuba libre," he tells of his return from a trip to the revolutionary Cuba of Fidel Castro. He affirms that art is an autonomous activity that should have nothing to do with politics. However, in the 1960s, Jones renamed himself Imamu Amiri Baraka. His 1964 play, *Dutchman*, consists of two characters in a subway: Clay, a young black man, a reader; and Lula, a white woman, who seduces, enrages, and murders him. After his allegory of the homicidal rule of the whites, Baraka initiated an extended series of changes. He moved toward black nationalism, calling for a "Revolutionary Theater" to prepare blacks for an approaching Armageddon; toward Islamic religion; and then, toward a form of Marxist-Leninism.

Yet, movements are not monoliths. In 1969, the culturally radical black writer Ishmael Reed mocked stern versions of such beliefs. *Yellow Back Radio Broke Down* is a postmodernist fiction about a Dionysiac black cowboy, the Loop Garoo Kid. Arguing with Bo Shmo, a "neo-social realist" con artist, the Kid asks:

"What's your beef with me Bo Shmo, what if I write circuses? No one says a novel has to be one thing. It can be anything it wants to be, a vaudeville show, the six o'clock news, the mumblings of wild men saddled by demons."

The villainous Bo responds:

"All art must be for the end of liberating the masses. A landscape is only good when it shows the oppressor hanging from a tree."

However, the Kid, and his green horse, win out.

The literature of radical statement has transformed many existing genres. Especially in urban and campus settings, graffiti were an anonymous source of slogans, aphorisms, epigraphs, epitaphs, and cries of protest. Indeed, *The Women's Room* (1977) by Marilyn French, one of the most powerful of the realistic feminist novels, opens in a women's bathroom at Harvard University in 1968. Blunt scrawls, "KILL ALL FASCIST PIGS!" turn a toilet booth into a book. In the 1960s, the underground press vividly, often raucously, conveyed radical analyses, news, emotions, and styles. One history, *Uncovering the Sixties*, estimates that twenty or so alternative papers existed in 1967. Two years later, perhaps 500 were in print. Inevitably they provoked reactions from law enforcement officials and the Far Right. In the late 1960s, in an apocalyptic touch characteristic of the decade, the FBI set up a fake rag, the *Armageddon*, to discredit the genre.

More conventional genres also assumed an organic relationship between writing and an unmediated life, between texts and context, representations and reality, expressions and experience. Serious movements cannot rage at cutout dragons. The poetry of Muriel Rukeyser engages the major political struggles of her century. In "Poem Out of Childhood," she writes of her search for the "affirmative clap of truth." The belief in the writer as the teller of truths, as well as of tales, permits the writer to serve as a witness, as a compassionate, impassioned observer of a corrupt, cruel world. In *Relearning the Alphabet* (1970), a significant example, Denise Levertov mourns the wars abroad, the wars at home, and an American public that hides from war in picnics, TV, and the hustle for money.

What life, then, should the writer witness? High or low? Extraordinary or ordinary? Like the poetry of Walt Whitman in the nineteenth century, literature as radical statement in the twentieth century preferred the ordinary. "The vitality of literature," wrote the editors of *Aiieeeee!* (1974), the first anthology of radical Asian American texts, "stems from its ability to codify and legitimize ordinary experience in terms of that experience and to celebrate life as it is lived." The lesbian feminist poet Judy Grahn tells of the "common woman," common as rattlesnakes, common as nails. Search, Alice Walker urges, for our mothers' gardens.

If literature was to codify, legitimize, and celebrate life as it is lived, literature was to be authentic. Persistently, the radical analysis of culture attacked the presumption that one group can name another, that one group can speak for another: the powerful for the powerless; professors for students; middle class for working class; straight for gay or lesbian; white for black; men for women; Anglos for Chicanos and Chicanas. Such convictions helped to ignite a bitter, famous argument in the 1960s. In 1967, the white novelist William Styron published, to much applause, *The Confessions of Nat Turner*. Turner, a preacher who had led a slave rebellion in 1831, was an exemplary figure in black history. In 1968, ten black intellectuals and writers responded in *William Styron's Nat Turner*. No one suggested that anyone censor Styron. Nevertheless, as blacks argued, Styron had appropriated a black voice, and, in so doing, had cut demeaning stereotypes even more deeply.

Writing about the past authentically demanded revisionary histories by and about women, minority groups, and the working class. History was to include the perspectives of victims as well as victors, the illiterate as well as the literate, the everyday as well as the exceptional. Inseparable from that fresh scholarship about the past were new approaches to literature itself, many of which were collected in 1973 in *The Politics of Literature: Dissenting Essays on the Teaching of English*. Attempting to "define different cultural ends for literature and for learning," the editors expressed their debt to black culture; asked critics to recognize the influence of ideology; and published essays about the literary profession, pedagogy, nonstandard English, working-class poems, slave narratives, and feminist criticism. In the 1970s, feminist criticism was to develop into an international school that analyzed four subjects: what men had written about women; what women, in all their variety, themselves had written, a history that Sandra M. Gilbert and Susan Gubar outlined in *The Norton Anthology of Literature by Women* (1985); the ways in which culture creates and uses gender, those differences between "masculine" and "feminine"; and, finally, the relationship of culture to feminism itself.

For literature as radical statement, writing about the present authentically often meant flooding a text with a community's speech: its oral traditions, litanies, rituals, and music. If a writer had a vibrant spoken language, why should he or she bear, or bear with, the standards of written English alone? Writing about the present authentically also meant adapting literary forms that had traditionally bottled up "experience": lyric poems; realistic stories and novels; biographies and autobiographies. In 1978, the radical feminist writer Alix Kates Shulman parodied the common impulse toward the "I" in the half-mocking "autobiography" of a radical feminist, *Burning Questions*.

First-person narrative followed at least three patterns. One was an introspective account of being a cultural radical. In the 1970s, Kate Millett, the author of *Sexual Politics* (1970), a major work of feminist theory, began to publish a series of self-portraits, at once cinematic and meditative, about love and sexuality, avant-garde art and radical politics, fame and loneliness. Like other autobiographies by contemporary women, hers deliberately pushed back the boundaries of permissible "women's speech."

The second pattern was characteristic of many repressive societies: the prison letter, written in a jail cell. In 1970, the letters of George Jackson were published as *Soledad Brother* one year before his murder in prison. Calling for resistance, for "Power to the People," Jackson became a martyr whose death showed the need for resistance; for power to the people, not to "legal" authorities.

The third pattern was the exemplary autobiography, the self-presentation of the charismatic leader who had, almost miraculously, survived and triumphed. Among the most influential of such works was *The Autobiography of Malcolm X* (1964). Born Malcolm Little in 1925, the son of a Baptist minister, Malcolm X became a hustler, "uneducated, unskilled at anything honorable." Jailed, he became a Black Muslim; later, the year before his assassination, he was to found the Organization of Afro-American Unity and to advocate black nationalism and power.

The Autobiography was also a prophetic jeremiad. The prophet warns a country of its sins and of a struggle between good and evil too vast for ordinary politics. He (or she) promises an apocalyptic end to history if sinners will not change. Addressing contemporary America, the prophet announces that if it cannot cease to kill, it must die. In 1962, writing about the war at home in *The Fire Next Time*, James Baldwin called on whites and blacks to "end the racial nightmare . . . achieve our country, and change the history of the world." If we did not, he cried out in biblical language, we would suffer immeasurably. "No more water, the fire next time." In 1968, writing about the war in Vietnam, Norman Mailer, in *Armies of the Night*, presented an account of an October 1967 antiwar march on the Pentagon, a bloody event that many literary notables, among them Mailer, had joined. Representing nearly every radical constituency, the marchers confronted the force of the state. Mailer projects an American in grave crisis, so torn between "the old frontier" and the "new ranch home" that it must exorcise its pain in violence abroad. He ends with an apocalyptic vision of a woman in labor. For Mailer, she is pregnant with the American future, but the conflicts of history are too difficult, his prophetic sight too short, to see if she will deliver damnation or salvation.

The wish to send urgent signals and to tell previously untold stories pushes the literature of radical statement toward accessibility. Writers want to touch readers. In turn, because they wish to belong to a community with the writer, readers ask for a readable script. However, because eschatology tests the rules of realism, prophets and Jeremiahs often flout convention. William Burroughs is among the most audacious to do so. Fragmented in form, hyperbolic, lyrical, and savagely ironic in tone, his autobiographical fantasy, *Naked Lunch* (1959), is set in the domains of the lawless (junky, homosexual, criminal) and in an interplanetary battlefield. One struggle, on earth and in space, is between the Factualists, who see reality as it is, and forces that seek total control, for its sake and for their malicious ends.

The quest for authenticity is arduous, for it can neither be put on, like clothing, nor turned on, like a television set. Authenticity demands not only knowing the actual but stripping away the old myths and lies that have wrapped themselves around consciousness, as if they were infected skin. Much of the literature of radical statement is a psychological narrative of the discovery that one's past identity was imposed, a mask, a stereotype, a burden. "I am," shouts Tam Lum, in Frank Chin's play *The Chickencoop*

Chinaman (1972), "the natural born ragmouth speaking the motherless bloody tongue." This discovery of being psychologically duped leads to another: that of the pressure of politics on psychology, of public forces on private identity.

The effects of the leap from "false" to "true" consciousness are alienation from, and an angry opposition to, one's old identity and to the orders that established it. Agonistic, antagonistic, the writer's vocabulary then protestingly names the painful injustices that the powerful have practiced: bias, discrimination, repression, exploitation, oppression, torture, death. N. Scott Momaday's novel *House Made of Dawn* (1968) is the story of Abel, a young Indian, whom the Cain of modern America destroys. If the marginal and the powerless are to survive, they must escape from the powerful, commonly figured as viruses or as cancer. Another pervasive metaphor in the literature of radical statement is that of flying; of free, freeing motion away from the cages that would trap mind and body.

Flight, if necessary, is insufficient. Literature as radical statement, unlike that of exile, encourages further action. In her poem "Käthe Kollwitz," Muriel Rukeyser admires

> a look as of music
> the revolutionary look
> that says I am in the world
> to change the world

Texts then explicitly galvanize one of two audiences: the powerful into changing their ways, or the powerless into lashing out against the powerful and discovering their own strength. Such a progressive narrative, which starts in resistance and rebellion, can end in reform or revolution. A metaphor, in the texts of known and unknown writers alike, was that of fire, of flames that would consume and purge the citadels of power, that would light up outrage. In 1970, for example, Robin Morgan published "Goodbye to All That," a crackling polemic against America and chauvinistic revolutionaries: "Goodbye, goodbye forever, counterfeit Left, counterleft, male-dominated cracked-glass-mirror reflection of the Amerikan Nightmare. Women are the real Left. We are rising . . . in our unclean bodies; bright glowing mad in our inferior brains."

Morgan's sarcastic language, her "unclean bodies" and "inferior brains," reflects a reversal of values that the rebellious narrative often insists upon. The ugly is now beautiful; the feared is now desired; the helpless are now in charge. "I am Black," Audre Lorde says in "Coal" (1962), "because I come from the earth's inside/ now take my word for jewel in the open light." However, contemporary literature not only sees jewels in the coal. It also imagines a new world that treasures freedom, justice, and pleasure, Blake's lineaments of gratified desire. Frequently, this new world, spiritually graceful, harmonizes the secular and the sacred. It redeems history. Texts that project desire as well as disgust, dream as well as nightmare, are fantasies; reenactments of ancient rituals; science fiction, like the novels of Ursula LeGuin or Joanna Russ; and utopias.

Post–World War II utopias begin with *Walden II* (1948), which B. F. Skinner, a behavioral psychologist, constructed. Applying the principles of positive reinforcement to child-rearing and of mass production to a domestic economy, Walden II is a harmonious, peace-loving community. It takes a third way between the centralized planning of communism and the "tyranny of the majority" of Western democracy. However, the romantics of the 1950s and the Movement radicals of the 1960s were to rebel against the managed spirit of a Walden II. In Piercy's utopian *Woman on the Edge of Time* (1976) for example, a poor battered Chicana, Connie, time-travels to Mattapoisett, a society of A.D. 2137. Like Walden II, Mattapoisett balances technology and nature, liberty and responsibility, happiness and self-control. Far more imaginatively than Walden II, however, Mattapoisett has abolished sexual and racial classifications. At peace, it has achieved a revolution of consciousness and culture, of social and economic structures. Dragons have become dragonflies.

Disraeli's quip, "Finality is not the language of politics," suggests that bills and deals, positions and impositions, treaties and entreaties, are always open to negotiation. Therefore, we can never bring the language of politics to closure or cloture. In the late twentieth century, a literary theory would interpret Disraeli's quip in another way. It would say that language can never be perfectly referential; language can never transparently represent values, agendas, needs, and strategies. Finality is not the language of politics, because we can never trust language to be final about anything. But, by definition, the literature of radical statement does want to assist in the birth of a different and better world.

Catharine R. Stimpson

II. Forms and Genres

Poetry

In his 1958 essay "The Present State of Poetry," Delmore Schwartz remarked that "what was once a battlefield has become a peaceful public park on a pleasant summer Sunday afternoon." With his image of a pleasant, timeless, cultivated space that has walled off sordid urban realities and disturbing psychic energies, Schwartz aptly characterizes the diminished "present" of American poetry in the late 1950s. By that time the once provocative and disruptive principles of modernism were assumed as the comfortable starting point for young poets and critics; these principles—no longer scandalous, no longer *modern*—generated a poetry that was more genteel than passionate and more civil than insurrectionary. Modernism had been gentrified.

The literary urban renewal project that had transformed the polemical battleground of the twenties into the peaceful public park of the fifties had, in many respects, been supported by the modernists themselves. By 1958 the poets "H. D." (Hilda Doolittle), T. S. Eliot, Marianne Moore, Ezra Pound, Wallace Stevens, and William Carlos Williams were still alive and already canonical; they were iconoclasts who themselves had become the living icons of twentieth-century poetry. Moreover, they were all now at least seventy and were understandably more concerned with preserving their work, summing up their careers, and consolidating their revolutionary gains than in stirring up challenges to an authority that was now their own. Living, revered, rebellious, conservative, they were intimidating presences for a young writer to have looking over his or her shoulder.

The modernist canon of 1958 was not a gregarious company of equals but a hierarchical structure, with T. S. Eliot rising, during the ten years following World War II, to a position of almost papal power and eminence. His authority, as both poet and literary theorist, might be accepted or it might be resisted, but it was ubiquitous and mostly it was accepted. Delmore Schwartz described Eliot as the "literary dictator" of the period. Eliot had gained his ascendancy through his innovative poetry and his polemical essays; his later years, however, were devoted to softening the edges of his earlier positions and cautioning young writers against the dangers of innovation. "We cannot, in literature, any more than in the rest of life, live in a perpetual state of revolution," Eliot warned in a 1947 lecture, adding that poetry should "refine" rather than keep "up to date with the spoken language." He was really warning against *any* revolution—by stressing poetry's role in civilizing popular linguistic energies. From this point of view, High Culture works as a defense against popular culture, and the realm of the aesthetic, like an urban park, becomes a sanctuary from what Eliot himself once called "the immense panorama of futility and anarchy which is contemporary history."

In postwar America, the reception of modernism in general and of T. S. Eliot in particular had been crucially shaped by the New Criticism. John Crowe Ransom, in "Poetry: A Note to Ontology" (1938), and Allen Tate, in "Tension in Poetry" (1938), articulated the movement's theoretical foundations. Like most defenses of literature since 1800, theirs began from a division between prose (or science), which is rational, abstract, and manipulative, and poetry (or art), which blended thinking and feeling in a seamless whole. A poem was thus a "well-wrought urn" (Cleanth Brooks's phrase) or a "verbal icon" (W. K. Wimsatt's), a self-enclosed space that transcended personal, social, political biases and affirmed imaginative activity as disinterested. The theory privileged the brief, intense, ironically self-conscious lyric; it excluded the discursive, narrative, spontaneous, passionate, committed—in short, vast stretches of human and literary experience. Nevertheless, by the mid-1950s Eliot and the New Criticism had established a literary hegemony, providing the standards adopted by most of the editors, teachers, readers, critics, and writers of American poetry.

Many of the strollers in Delmore Schwartz's peaceful public park were members of a middle generation of twentieth-century American poets: John Berryman, Randall Jarrell, Robert Lowell, Theodore Roethke, Karl Shapiro, and Schwartz himself. Born between 1900 and 1920, these poets grew up with and on modernism, enthusiastically absorbing its newest works, and when they themselves began to write they did not have to struggle to create an audience, as the modernists did; they had an audience already prepared for them by the modernists. Some of these poets—Berryman, Jarrell, and Lowell—early achieved not just recognition but literary fame. But their advantages carried limitations. Where, after all, was *their* Revolution of the Word? The modernists proved to be very powerful fathers who inspired, and defeated, rivalrous ambitions. As John Berryman complained in "Two Organs": "I didn't want my next poem to be *exactly* like Yeats/ or exactly like Auden/ since in that case where the hell was *I?*/ but what instead *did* I want it to sound like?" By the mid-1950s these poets had not invented any alternative to the modernist hegemony; the few poets of this generation who had done so—Elizabeth Bishop, Charles Olson, George Oppen, Muriel Rukeyser, Louis Zukofsky—were viewed as marginal figures. The middle generation's apparent failure to separate from a now almost fifty-year-old modernism made it—particularly from the perspective of the still younger poets beginning their careers in the 1950s—part of the period's malaise.

Modernist poets, however ambivalently, had criticized bourgeois culture; by mid-century, however, their successors had renounced not just the literary ambitions but the social dissidence of modernism. In his "The Present State of Poetry," Delmore Schwartz, asserting that "America, not Europe, is now the sanctuary of culture," concluded that "to criticize the actuality upon which all hope depends"—that is, America—"thus becomes a criticism of hope itself." His statement suggests how Cold War politics created the social conformity, intellectual diffidence, and consensus politics of the fifties. "Domesticity, religiosity, respectability, security through compliance with the system" (in the words of Douglas T. Miller and Marion Nowak's *The Fifties* [1977]) were the bourgeois essence of Schwartz's "sanctuary of culture." In New Critical theory, poetry created a realm separate from and transcendent of history; but in fact this very theory reflected the predominant social wish to withdraw from history—one reason the theory achieved such wide acceptance.

American poetry had become at once dissociated from, and all too comfortably part of, its present. The complacency, and its attendant crisis, were most evident in the early work of the writers—James Merrill, W. S. Merwin, Adrienne Rich, Peter Viereck, Richard Wilbur—who constituted a third generation of twentieth-century American poets. Born between 1920 and 1940, this generation grew up with the poetic revolution of 1910 a legendary event of the distant past, and when its members began to write they heard some very heavy footsteps behind them: modernism seemed pretty much played out, yet its achievements had the monumental status of a literary Mount Rushmore, while the middle generation only offered a model of how *not* to deal with imposing predecessors. At first, the third generation responded with a gentle swerve to the literary right; they stayed within New Critical decorums but built a poetic program out of the gradual return of accentual meters and predetermined forms that had been going on since the early 1930s. Called the "New Formalists," they imagined themselves completing the modernist revolution when their return to tradition actually undermined modernism.

Intimidating literary grandfathers, disappointing fathers, economic prosperity, and social and political conservatism combined to create the bland literary hegemony of the fifties. In literature, as in practically all spheres of American life, the basic procedures had already been invented. Theories, alternative ways of understanding present practices and imagining new future ones, were not just unnecessary but positively harmful. What was needed were skillful but deferential practitioners—new formalists, new critics, literary bureaucrats who could be relied upon to keep providing new answers to old questions. Yet, despite its extensive rule, this hegemony was an inherently vulnerable one. Modernism, its energetic core lost, had been revised into a hollow shell that could be attacked as merely overbearing; and the art-as-sanctuary consensus of the fifties required exclusion of too many pressing social realities and repression of too many enlivening mental activities. All during the decade murmurs of uneasiness with these restrictions could be heard even from some of those—such as Randall Jarrell and Robert Lowell—who had most benefited from them. But with the 1957 publication of the anthology *New Poets of England and America*, the amiable "slightness" of the young generation became clear, even to many of its members and supporters.

The poetic establishment, centered in such New Critical strongholds as the *Kenyon Review* and *Sewanee Review*, could refuse recognition or even publication, but it could hardly suppress disruptive activity. Beginning with Charles Olson's influential "Projective Verse" manifesto (1950), the fifties were rich in underground work, producing alternative theories, styles, poetic communities, journals, presses. Along the borders of Delmore Schwartz's peaceful public park, dissidents formed into loose clusters: the beats, the confessionals, the Black Mountain, deep image, and New York poets. Often warring among themselves, these groups were united in their sometimes strident rejection of the ruling authorities. With the publication of the anthology *The New American Poetry* (1960) by Donald M. Allen, the avantgarde became visible and American poetry once again became a battleground.

In the late 1950s and early 1960s, then, American poetry experienced a new eruption of innovative energy in which both the younger writers and some of the middle generation—notably John Berryman, Robert Lowell, and Charles Olson—participated. The new guard was not cheered as a liberating army, however; and in the ensuing battle the opposition was simplified, by both sides, into an opposition between "cooked" and "raw," "academic" and "bohemian," "civilized" and "barbarian." Poetic measure became the most charged issue. The accentual meters and predetermined forms advocated by New Critics and the Formalists were now derided as anachronistic and "closed," while "open," free verse methods were advanced with a salvationist fervor. Yet the debate over measure was the place where a more basic disagreement about poetic form was joined; the dissenting poets, accused of resisting all form, urged a different *kind* of form. As diverse as they were in style and voice, many of these poets shared a desire to find more elastic forms that could stretch to include the areas of personal and social experience ignored by official work.

Specifically, these poets sought to break open the enclosed space of the autotelic poem and to reconceive form as temporal, as process. Creation now becomes an act not of containment but of discovery, with form evolved *in* the process of composition. Robert Creeley says that his poetry is "a way of finding things, a way of looking for things, a way of gaining recognition of them as they occur in writing"; Adrienne Rich testifies that "the poem itself engenders new sensations, new awareness in me as it progresses"; and John Ashbery compares beginning a poem to "a door that suddenly pops open and leads into an unknown space." From these assumptions poetry becomes more spontaneous and unpredictable, more concrete and immediate, and it once again establishes an energizing connection with the unknown, shifting space of the present.

To maintain this connection the poet must constantly resist any yearning for rest, for synthesis, for completion. "I see narrow orders, limited tightness, but will/ not run to that easy victory," A. R. Ammons writes in "Corsons Inlet"; rather "I will try/ to fasten into order enlarging grasps of disorder, widening scope, but enjoying freedom that/ Scope eludes my grasp, that there is no finality of vision,/ that I have perceived nothing completely,/ that tomorrow a new walk is a new walk." In this new poetic, emphasis moves from the easy victories of a tight overall unity to the enlarging grasps of ongoing process, moments of provisional order, parts that stubbornly refuse to be absorbed into larger wholes. "Each part is a thing in itself," Robert Duncan urges, "the junctures not binding but freeing the elements of configuration." The work is not owned by the poet as if it were a piece of private property; the writing instead is "multiphasic," in Duncan's word, "polyphonic," in John Ashbery's—an ungovernable event that happens *to* the poet. As Robert Creeley stresses, "I'm *given* to write poems." Hence, while the lyric remains the norm after 1960, its form has been reconceived; and many poets resist the lyric's propensity to transform temporal flux into crystalline form by writing lyric sequences that dramatize the shifts, gaps, interruptions, leaps, digressions of imaginative activity in time. In works such as Robert Duncan's "Passages" (1968–) and Charles Olson's *The Maximus Poems* (1960–68), resolution, briefly achieved at the close of each part, immediately dissolves back into a temporal flow the poet cannot fully master.

The theoretical shift around 1960 was both based upon and led to a major canon revision of the canon. T. S. Eliot and the New Critics were disestablished, but they were not usurped: no poet or group of poets has since achieved their dominance. Authority in American poetry has been dispersed, permitting a plurality of theories and styles. At the feverish moment of insurrection, many of the young poets, equating the hegemony of the fifties with "literature" itself, claimed an absolute break with the literary tradition; in reality they established creative links with canonically marginal writers who offered stimulating new possibilities. This account of the new poetic will have already suggested its broad relation to romantic organicism; in particular, William Blake and Walt Whitman, romantic visionaries lacking in New Critical ironic self-consciousness, were elevated from minor to major status. Marginal modern poets—Ezra Pound, Wallace Stevens, and William Carlos Williams—became liberating models and central figures, while then-marginal literary movements, such as French surrealism and its Latin American variants, were freshly explored.

Oppositional forces had been developing throughout the 1950s, but they first became publicly visible through the beat poets, the most outrageously provocative of the new vanguard. The beginning of their movement can be dated to a poetry reading held at the Six Gallery in San Francisco in the fall of 1955. Kenneth Rexroth, mentor of young West Coast poets for many years, was master of ceremonies and the readers were Allen Ginsberg, Philip Lamantia, Michael McClure, Gary Snyder, Lew Welsh, and Philip Whalen, with Neal Cassady, Lawrence Ferlinghetti, and Jack Kerouac in the audience. Except for Gregory Corso and William Everson, all the principal beat poets were in attendance, with Allen Ginsberg's reading of his recently completed "Howl" the evening's dramatic high point.

Yet "Howl" was not the spontaneous expression of an angry *young* man; Ginsberg was thirty when he wrote the poem, and *Howl and Other Poems* (1956) was the first book Ginsberg published but the third he had written. Pressing familial problems inhibited his development, but his slow growth was prototypical for many of his generation of poets and their difficult search for alternatives to the presiding orthodoxy. Ginsberg's visionary consciousness marked him as a literary outsider from the start. His earliest poems, later published in *Gates of Wrath* (1972), had packed mystical experiences into tight, rhymed, metrical stanzas—with stilted results. Ginsberg's second collection—*Empty Mirror* (1961)—renounced the eternal for the material world and substituted William Carlos Williams's breath-spaced lines for traditional versification—this time with flat results. But in "Howl" Ginsberg linked the transcendent with the material, mystical ecstasy with urban torment, in long surging Whitmanesque lines. His poem had the impact of an angry, impassioned breaking with constraints, and many of the beginning poets who read it felt that Ginsberg had given voice to—and thus opened up—areas hidden or denied by the decorum of accepted work.

To be "beat" is to be beaten, defeated; to be "beat" is to be beatific, holy. "Howl" describes a painful immersion in modern urban life that tortures the sufferer into transcendent vision; it turns defeat into sacred experience. "Poetry makes nothing happen," W. H. Auden had written in "In Memory of W. B. Yeats" (1940); much of the wearied poetry of the fifties had assumed that poetry not only couldn't but shouldn't make anything happen but itself. Part II of "Howl" tries to exorcise "Moloch," youth-devouring god of social repression and mechanical consciousness; Part I angrily laments the bums, criminals, madmen, dissidents hounded by Moloch. Ginsberg returned the Whitmanesque conception of poet as prophet to American poetry, and because he was so much more embattled than the equable Whitman had been a hundred years before, Ginsberg was an *angry* social prophet, his poem an act of social protest.

Against a persecutorial social system and the literary ideals of impersonality and scrupulous craftsmanship, Ginsberg proclaimed naked self-expression and spontaneous composition. Influenced by Jack Kerouac's "Essentials of Spontaneous Prose" (1957), Ginsberg wanted to make writing an unmediated expression of his person, his emotions while writing, and he claimed, for instance, to have written Part II of "Howl" "nearly intact" while high on peyote. Drugs, madness, extreme experiences of all kinds were sought to dislocate ordinary into visionary consciousness. Jazz was invoked as a model for poetic improvisation. The beat rebellion appropriately began with a poetry reading, for as a poetics of presence, Ginsberg's theory stressed the poem as an *oral* event, drawing on the very popular speech that Eliot warned against. "Howl" crossed rhapsodic utterances with street talk; the poem also included tones—rhapsodic, angry, zany—then judged beyond the boundaries of literary expression.

The beat poets boldly combined the mystical, the political, *and* the physiological. Sexual desire and bodily experience generally had been assigned a place outside the perimeters of Delmore Schwartz's public park—one reason it was so peaceful. The beat poets attempted a resurrection of the body for American poetry. Sexuality, sometimes "deviant" homosexuality, was treated with a defiant frankness. The poem itself, its lines measured by the lengths of the composing poet's breaths, incarnates the bodily presence of the poet. In "Howl" the body is stripped bare and exposed to painful experiences that eventually flail it into vision; in poets such as William Everson, Michael McClure, and Gary Snyder, exploration of the body becomes part of a primitivism or a nature mysticism.

In both his life and his writing, the style of Gary Snyder, for example, strikingly differs from that of Ginsberg. As a young man Snyder studied Oriental languages, worked as a logger and fire lookout, hiked the California wilderness, and eventually spent nine years studying in Japanese Zen monasteries. Ginsberg is a bristling urban messiah; Snyder is a solitary rural contemplative. Ginsberg is frenzied, self-exposing, outrageous, tender; Snyder is disciplined, withdrawn, patient, meditative. In "Howl" Ginsberg writes in long, packed, fast-moving lines that crackle with sudden associative leaps; in *Riprap* (1959) and *Myths and Texts* (1960) Snyder writes in short, spare, slow-moving lines that carefully space off detailed natural observations. If Ginsberg crosses Walt Whitman with Antonin Artaud, Snyder crosses Ezra Pound with Henry David Thoreau.

Snyder's process of stripping away the ego is a formal, disciplined, and even traditional one and his end is a state of stillness and composure, not Ginsberg's half-painful, half-ecstatic self-apotheosis. But both poets seek mystical illumination; both adopt religious perspectives that have strong political implications; and both repudiate the conception of the poet as man of letters. Ginsberg said that he was only able to start "Howl" by imagining that he was writing not a poem but something more intimate, like a letter to a close friend. Snyder likewise holds that "poetry is not writing or books" but something more basically human, even preliterate. Ginsberg's poet is a biblical prophet; Snyder's is a tribal shaman, participant in an ancient oral tradition that draws on "the breath, the voice, and trance." The beat poets were the most stridently antiliterary of the young poets, but as the very different cases of Ginsberg and Snyder show, they derided the literary because they expected not less but more from literature.

Like the beat poets, the confessional poets repudiated the orthodoxies of the 1950s. But if the beats mounted revolutionary barricades in the streets, the confessionals, including such New Critical protégés as John Berryman and Robert Lowell, conducted something more like a palace coup. Less socially and ideologically close than the beats, the confessional poets were unified in defining the creative act as a painful self-exposure, a direct expression of urgent emotion aroused by personal, often extreme, experiences. Robert Lowell is often credited with founding the movement with his autobiographical *Life Studies* (1959); but Allen Ginsberg's "naked poetics" and confessional tone in "Howl" anticipated it, John Berryman had begun his *Dream Songs* (1964–69) as early as 1955, W. D. Snodgrass published parts of *Heart's Needle* (1959) in 1957, and Anne Sexton had written most of *To Bedlam and Part Way Back* (1960) before she became Lowell's student in 1958. Sylvia Plath, influenced by both Lowell and Sexton, arrived somewhat later, with her posthumous *Ariel* (1965). Lacking a leader, a geographical center, or a ringing manifesto, the confessional movement was less the result of a shared program for poetry than the result of independent writers working along similar lines at more or less the same time.

What these poets did share was their rejection of the New Critical doctrine of the poem as mask. In "The Love Song of J. Alfred Prufrock," T. S. Eliot had presented a dramatic character, one who longs to discard his social mask and bare his "true" self, but cannot. In "Lady Lazarus" (1965), Sylvia Plath, drawing directly on her own experience of attempted suicide and feelings of bitter rage, reviles the doctors who re-create her social identity ("a smiling woman"); she ends by releasing her soaring, fiery, vengeful—"true"—self. In Plath, distance between poet and poem, poem and reader—aesthetic distance—breaks down. Writing, as she sardonically comments in "Lady Lazarus," is "the big strip tease"; "I hold back nothing," says Anne Sexton. Rather than expressing ironies that cancel each other out, confessional poets advocate a brutally frank self-exposure.

In fact, self-inflicted violence is not just a frequent subject but the very way to creativity for many of these poets. For Sylvia Plath, "the blood jet is poetry"; the *Dream Songs* is "Henry's pelt . . . put on sundry walls" (Berryman quotes Gottfried Benn: "We are using our own skins for wallpaper and we cannot win"); Sexton, paraphrasing Franz Kafka, says that "a poem should serve as the axe for the frozen sea within us," and she thinks of Christ as the archetype for this mode because he "performed the greatest act of confession, and I mean with his body." In "Howl," Ginsberg similarly imagines his poem as "butchered" out of his body. From this point of view a poem is no verbal icon but more like a piece of flesh torn from the poet's body—to be judged not for its exquisite beauty but for its authenticity.

Speaking of the effect of Robert Lowell and Anne Sexton on her own work, Sylvia Plath was "excited," she said, by their "intense breakthrough into very serious, very personal, emotional experience which I feel has been partly taboo." The confessional poets, however, were reacting not just against the idea of the poem as mask but also against wider social and literary taboos of the 1950s. In the first poetry workshop she attended, Anne Sexton was told by the instructor that her poems about the madhouse were not "a fit subject for poetry"; but she insisted on "this inward look that society scorns" and she refused to tame or beautify what she saw. The confessional poets thus explored psychic and physical experiences—madness, suicide, incest, hatred, drugs, surgery, masturbation, menstruation—that were repressed by the reigning poetic decorum. Sexton in particular treated female physicality with a directness that was strikingly new. One measure of what had become of the modernist revolution may be suggested through the differing responses of T. S. Eliot and Allen Tate to Robert Lowell's *Life Studies:* Eliot praised the poems and had his company Faber and Faber publish them; Tate said that they were too "intimate" to have any "public or literary interest" and recommended that Lowell not publish them.

Tate also lamented Lowell's failure to push toward a "symbolic order" and his use of "free verse." But Lowell now felt the symbolism of his earlier work—*Lord Weary's Castle* (1946) and *The Mills of the Kavanaughs* (1951)—to be emotionally self-protective. *Life Studies* had begun in tight forms, "Commander Lowell," for instance, having originally been written in "perfectly strict four-foot couplets." But "that regularity just seemed to ruin the honesty of sentiment, and became rhetorical; it said, 'I'm a poem.' " Ginsberg started by deciding not to write a poem; Lowell began by writing a poem that sounded too much like a poem. Both ended by transgressing the boundaries of what was then acceptable as literary; and both—along with other of the beat and confessional poets—did so by adopting open forms.

For these writers, opening the self entailed opening literary form. In an extreme statement of her artistic credo, Anne Sexton urged, "take out rules and leave the instant." The poems of Sylvia Plath's *The Colossus* (1960), with their "intricate rhyming and metrical schemes," were "composed very slowly, consulting her Thesaurus and Dictionary for almost every word," while the *Ariel* poems were, according to Plath's husband, Ted Hughes, "written at great speed, as she might take dictation, where she ignores metre and rhyme for rhythm and momentum." Rapid, improvisatory composition short-circuited the social and literary censors and permitted access to the unconscious; confessional poems are thus acts of self-discovery in which the poets end up by revealing what they have hitherto managed to conceal even from themselves. It is particularly disastrous for such a writer to be or even appear to be derivative or literary; form must remain hidden, "natural." More concerned with emotional directness than with formal violence and not locked into rigid theoretical positions, the confessional poets were free to remain flexible in the battle over set forms. W. D. Snodgrass's "Heart's Needle" was written in syllabics; Anne Sexton and Robert Lowell oscillated between "closed" and "open" forms throughout their careers; John Berryman's individual dream songs are written in intricately metered and rhymed eighteen-line sections, while Robert Lowell's *Notebook* (1969–73) is composed of sonnets—though both Berryman and Lowell use these regular "parts" to evolve long, open-ended autobiographical wholes.

In their immediate historical context, the confessional poets were risk-taking innovators. But they were not—like Allen Ginsberg or Charles Olson—promethean in their attitudes toward literary form; nor did they delude themselves into adopting extreme "anti-art" postures. Robert Lowell wanted his poems to have "the virtue of a photograph but all the finish of art" and Sylvia Plath thought of her poems not "as a cry from the heart" but as attempts to "control and manipulate experience." Like other autobiographical writers, confessional poets selected, organized, and even fabricated material from their lives, in part for aesthetic reasons. Anne Sexton freely admitted she sometimes invented "facts" in her poems; so did Robert Lowell, who added that "the reader was to believe he was getting the *real* Robert Lowell." Confessional poems—Sylvia Plath's "Daddy" (1965), for example—often sound like the upwelling of a compelled feeling; their intimacy about painful experiences often makes the reader feel that to introduce aesthetic criteria would be cruelly trivializing. Yet these very responses, as Lowell suggests, testify to the power of the poet's art. If the confessional poets sought to break down the distinction between art and life, they also knew that such immediacy was itself the creation of a persuasive artistic illusion.

Unlike the beats, the confessional poets had a wide and deep impact on contemporary poetry—by creating an atmosphere of permission for the use of intense personal emotion and autobiographical subjects. Many of the poets they affected held assumptions quite different from the confessionals. In his *First Poems* (1951) and *The Country of a Thousand Years of Peace* (1959), James Merrill, for instance, created a frigid, ornate style. Merrill has remained a writer who is more engaged with poetic artifice than with the desire to bare his inmost secrets. For the confessional poet, manners are a social mask to be stripped away; for Merrill they are "the touch of nature, an artifice in the very blood stream." Still, autobiographical content infused his *Water Street* (1962) and *Nights and Days* (1966) with an emotional substance his early work lacked. Women poets in particular were stimulated by the confessional breakthrough. The notion of the poem as mask implicitly defined the imagination as transcendent of personality, history, race, gender; but while affirming creative activity as disinterested, the doctrine actually institutionalized fairly narrow ideas of personality, history, race, and gender. For women poets to adopt a mask, especially one of male invention, was self-alienating. In the modest, neatly crafted poems of *A Change of World* (1951) and *The Diamond Cutters* (1955), Adrienne Rich established herself as a solid, deferential citizen in the predominantly male crowd strolling through Delmore Schwartz's public park. In the title poem of *Snapshots of a Daughter-in-Law* (1963) she began to explore and assert her consciousness as a woman, but only through the creation of a series of female poetic personae. But in *Necessities of Life* (1966), *Leaflets* (1969), and *The Will to Change* (1971), Rich drew directly on her own experience to evolve an alternative to what she experienced as patriarchal language. Muriel Rukeyser was speaking for many contemporary women poets when she declared in "Orpheus" (1971), "No more masks! No more mythologies!"

In "Fever 103°" (1965), Sylvia Plath represents herself as a "pure acetylene/ Virgin" whose anger in the end consumes only herself; in "The Phenomenology of Anger" (1973), Adrienne Rich writes of "white acetylene/ ripples from my body/ effortlessly released/ perfectly trained on the true enemy." Adrienne Rich's revision of Sylvia Plath's metaphor replaces private self-destructiveness with an angry vision of social transformation; Rich replaces a confessional with a political poetry. Confessional poets assumed the social self to be alien and dead, and so they sought release of a core self hidden beneath numbing social conventions. For them, all that is knowable and all that is worth communicating is the private self. According to Anne Sexton, "poems of the inner life can reach the inner lives of readers in a way that anti-war poems can never stop a war"; W. D. Snodgrass believes that "family trouble, troubles in your love-life, has caused people a hundred times more real agony than all the wars, famines, oppressions and the other stuff that gets in the history books." The point is not whether Sexton and Snodgrass are right or wrong, but that they sever the private from the public, the aesthetic from the historical. When the confessional poets do deal with history, they do so by making historical events metaphors for personal crises, as in Sylvia Plath's use of the holocaust.

Both the beats and the confessional poets reacted against many of the poetic premises of the 1950s; by doing so they let basic human feelings and experiences back into American poetry. Yet neither group was able to think its way entirely out of its historical context. Like many of their contemporaries, both groups remained dependent upon the New Critical aesthetic as a kind of energizing antagonist. More important, they both rejected spatial-ized ideas of form and the definition of the imagination as transcendent that justified those ideas. Yet neither group was comfortable in secular time, in history. The propensity of the confessionals was to withdraw into the private self; the propensity of the beats was to withdraw into religious vision. Both approaches proved generative for American poetry, but they also made their adherents complicit in the 1950s flight from history.

The confessional poets probed psychic wounds and sought emotional catharsis; the Black Mountain poets proposed a physiology of consciousness as the basis for a formal revolution. Not just reacting to the social conformity and literary timidity of the fifties, the Black Mountain group envisioned nothing less than a refounding of Western thought and writing. Ambitious, combative, often prophetic, the Black Mountain group was socially and theoretically closely knit, with Charles Olson as its dynamic center and chief inventor. Black Mountain was a small experimental college in western North Carolina; between 1951 and 1957 Olson was its rector, Robert Creeley and Robert Duncan taught there, and Edward Dorn, Robert Kelly, and Gilbert Sorrentino were among their students. Paul Blackburn, Larry Eigner, and Denise Levertov, though never at the college, were allied with the movement. Robert Creeley edited the *Black Mountain Review;* since publishing in such New Critical journals as the *Kenyon Review* was, in his words, "too much like being 'tapped' for a fraternity," he wanted "a magazine absolutely specific to one's own commitments and possibilities." *Black Mountain Review* became an important outlet for avant-garde writing in the fifties, devoting one issue, for example, to the beat writers.

At a Brandeis poetry reading Charles Olson "got so damned offended" with his audience that he yelled, "You people are so literate I don't want to read to you anymore." Allen Ginsberg and Robert Lowell reinvigorated American poetry by refusing to write what sounded too much like a poem, but Olson is not just impatient with the current definition of literariness, he is impatient with the very structures of literacy itself—syntax; logical categories—which alienate Western man from his messy but fecund physical origins. Olson often quoted Heraclitus's dictum that "man is estranged from that which is most familiar." What is (or should be) most familiar is physical immediacy, a field of constantly changing energies, from which we are estranged when we break it down into discrete, logical categories. For Olson, an avid admirer of the process philosophy of Alfred North Whitehead, reality *is* process—fluid, continuous, multilayered—and the poet's job is to find "a way that bears *in*" to reality "instead of away."

Robert Creeley and Robert Duncan experience this energy as a force in language as much as in physical reality. In *The Truth and Life of Myth* (1968),

Duncan, for example, writes: "Speaking of a thing I call upon its name, and the Name takes over from me the story I would tell." But wherever the energy is located, the danger, for all of these poets, lies in containing it, in imposing what Olson calls "the too strong grasping of it." In social terms this point of view produces a critique not just of modern industrialism, capitalism, and imperialism but of the abstract will itself, Western man's quest for domination. In literary terms, the perspective generates a critique of the idea of art as mastery, particularly of the use of predetermined or "closed" forms and of what Olson dismissed, in his famous essay "Projective Verse," as "the lyrical interference of the individual as ego." In both social and literary cases, man attempts to step outside the instant, to detach himself from its energies in order to control them, and only ends up by severing himself and his language from their sources of life and power.

The Black Mountain poetic also offers a critique of the Western tradition of art as mimesis. In "Human Universe" (1965), Charles Olson distinguishes "between language as the act of the instant and language as the act of thought about the instant"; as "the act of the instant" poetic language is not descriptive or mimetic, not referential and outside, but *is* reality and thus possesses an ontological fullness. As Denise Levertov puts it, a poem is "not reference but pheonomenon." The "open" poetics that Charles Olson propounded in "Projective Verse" thus urges a repositioning of the self, and the poem, inside the instant, in a relation that does not tame its energies or violate its particulars. The poetic self becomes a "participant in the larger force," in Charles Olson's words, or it enters a "world of thought and feeling in which we may participate but not dominate, where we are used by things even as we use them," in Robert Duncan's. In Olson's version of the naked poetics found in both beat and confessional writers, the projective poet remains exposed, open to the multiple, unknown forces of the moment. When he began to write, Robert Creeley recalls, "I wanted the categories prior to the content which might in any sense inform them," as if he were afraid of contents not already under his control. But Creeley came to see—with the acknowledged help of "Projective Verse"—that composition was really "the attempt to find the intimate form of what's being stated as it's being stated"—what Olson calls an *"act* of the instant."

The practical thrust of Olson's theories was to open American poetry to a wide variety of speculative, emotional, and physical experiences dismissed as marginal or dangerous by the presiding literary powers. According to Robert Creeley, Olson created a possibility "in which the mind may make evident its resources apart from the limits of intention and purpose"; Robert Duncan declares that "I evolve the form of a poem by an insistent attention to what happens in inattentions." Inattentions were not what, say, Allen Tate was heeding in his poems. Crucial to the poet's openness was his or her tolerance for interruptions, digressions, associative leaps, unforeseen puns, etymological leads—for those unexpected moments when the poem speaks back to its creator. So committed is Robert Duncan to recording the shifting energies of the moments that, as a matter of policy, he refuses to revise; in Olson's poems a parenthesis will open but never close—because there is no main direction to return to. The aesthetic of the New Criticism, Duncan writes, "removes the reasonable thing from its swarming background of unreason"—precisely the area Duncan lets swarm into the foreground of his own creations.

If a poem is an "act of the instant," it is a physical act, and one of Olson's most important contributions was his return of the human body to American poetry. He refused to separate the imagination from its bodily origins, one reason for his suspicion of logic and literacy. Both beat and confessional poets had placed a new emphasis on physical experience, but they stressed physical pain and made it the subject of their poetry; Olson made artistic creation a physiological process. In "Projective Verse" he conceived of the verse line as a measure not of stressed and unstressed syllables but of the breathings of the poet as he writes, incarnating his bodily rhythms in the movements of the poem.

Yet even such a "high energy-construct," in Olson's phrase, cannot make physical immediacy fully present. Any articulation, no matter how generously it permits material from the edges of consciousness to swarm into the poem, no matter how "heraclitean" its form, still must throw limits around the limitless. Robert Duncan is perhaps the Black Mountain poet most conscious of this problem, and so he seeks a "design/ constantly in reconstruction./ Destroyed./ Reformd." In many poets of this group there is a consequent tendency to move away from the self-contained lyric to the open-ended lyric sequences: Duncan's "The Structure of Rime" (1960) and "Passages," Olson's *The Maximus Poems*, or a book like Creeley's *Pieces* (1969). In these works the individual poem momentarily creates a *whole*, which then folds back into the larger field, in which it functions as a *part*.

For all his contempt for literateurs and for all the muscular vigor of his own poetry, Charles Olson was not only a literate but a downright bookish man, whose theories are fairly derivative. Often he made no secret of his literary origins, unabashedly citing Pound and Williams as his predecessors; Olson's open poetics also derived from the romantic concept of the poet as medium, familiar to him from his readings of Emerson and Whitman. Yet Olson's sources were all marginal figures in American poetry in 1950 and one of Olson's accomplishments was to initiate the canonical shift that granted these writers major status; the Black Mountain reevaluation of Pound and Williams in the first generation, Oppen and Zukofsky in the second, made available for contemporary poetry a modernism that was a generative alternative to the heterodoxy of Eliot and the New Critics. Moreover, Olson emphasized that his theory was for "use," and however original it may or may not have been, his "Projective Verse" was certainly seminal.

The deep image or surrealist poets repudiated what they perceived as the sterile excitement of the beats, the psychological sensationalism of the confessionals, and the Black Mountain fetishizing of technique. Less socially and even less intellectually close than rival contemporary groups, they did share their generation's disaffiliation with Eliotic modernism, and in Robert Bly they had a poet, editor, and theoretician whose polemics created an opening for such poets as Galway Kinnell, W. S. Merwin, Louis Simpson, and James Wright. Characterizing Anglo-American modernism as "A Wrong Turning," Bly was not, like Olson, interested in aligning himself with its neglected masters; instead he went outside its (to him) provincial limits to recover "the modern poetry of the deep images of the unconscious," which he located mainly in Spanish and Latin American surrealist poetry, especially that of Federico García Lorca, Pablo Neruda, and César Vallejo.

Like many of the theorists he vehemently opposed, Bly begins by separating the public from the private, the social from the interior. The public is the realm of industrial capitalism, the imperial will, abstract reason; it is the "dead world." This social critique resembles those of both Ginsberg and Olson, but whereas Olson sought to renew Western consciousness and writing by eliminating the "lyrical interference" of the emotional subject and Ginsberg sought to release a "howl" of social protest by a painful surrender to urban pressures, Bly proposes "deep inwardness" in a hushed rural solitude; this is his "live world." In Bly's *Silence in the Snowy Fields* (1962) and Wright's *The Branch Will Not Break* (1963) the poet thus withdraws into himself not, as the confessional poets did, to explore the history of the private psyche but to enact a spiritual journey toward self-transcendence. In this respect, Bly and Wright do importantly derive from one second-generation modern American poet, Theodore Roethke.

In an essay on Wright, Bly complained that in the 1950s poetry was understood in America as "a climb over a wall into an enclosure," into, say, a peaceful public park. The beats responded by deciding to batter down the walls; the deep image poets responded by searching the grounds for caves, hidden spaces in which some ancient primitive life might persist.

The cave recurs in the poetry of Bly and Wright as an image of the unconscious, a source of mysterious spiritual and instinctual energies, the sacred ground of the imagination. For deep image poets, as Bly says of García Lorca, "writing a poem" involves "a climb from [the poet's] own world into a wilder world." What results is a poetry, in two of Bly's key terms, of "leaping" and "images."

Deep image poetry, according to Bly, differs basically from imagism, which, he contends, "was largely 'Picturism' "; the distinction between a picture and an image is that the latter "cannot be drawn from or inserted back into the real world." Imagism is mimetic; Bly's theory is antimimetic; his image "is an animal native to the imagination." Mimesis enacts a submission to the dead public world and Bly denounces the moderns for placing "more trust in the objective, outer world than in the inner world." Creation is not a reflecting but a leaping about the psyche, producing startling associations, metaphoric transformations "in which the image is released from imprisonment among the objects." When Wright, for example, speaks of "the hallway/ Of a dark leaf" or "the cathedral/ Of the wind," he is not creating visual images but making an imaginative leap—from "hallway" to "leaf," from "cathedral" to "wind." The deep image *is* the leap, intuitive, trusting of the unconscious, an *animal* native to the live world of the imagination.

Deep image poets, however, do not turn inward merely to withdraw into the private self; to do that would be to substitute the walls of the cave for the walls of the park. In fact, the image of the cave often metamorphizes into the tunnel or hallway, a dark, open-ended passageway. These poets conceive of the unconscious less in Freudian than in Jungian terms, as a passage to collective and thus shared images and feelings. Their journey inward is also a journey beyond the self and toward connection, a descent into both the body and the natural world. "If you could keep going deeper and deeper, you'd finally not be a person," says Kinnell, "you'd be an animal; and if you kept going deeper and deeper, you'd be a blade of grass or ultimately perhaps a stone." For Bly, the poet "senses the interdependence of all things alive, and longs to bring them inside the work of art." The spirit is physicalized; the physical is spiritualized, as in Bly's title *The Light Around the Body* (1967); the poem itself becomes a mystical body: "the substance of the man who wrote the poem reaches far out into the darkness and the poem is his whole body, seeing with his ears and his fingers and his hair."

Moreover, like the beats, the deep image poets were visionaries with a politics in view. Bly, who attacked the absence of revolutionary politics in the poetry of the 1950s, did not want to exchange New Critical aestheticism for a mystical hermeticism. During the late 1960s, Ginsberg, Duncan, Levertov, Lowell, Rich—among many others—confronted political issues such as the war in Vietnam and the destruction of the natural environment in their poetry. Deep image poets, whose surrealist models were often political, were among the most active. Bly founded "American Writers Against the Vietnam War" (1966) and contributed the money from his National Book Award prize to a draft resistance group (1968). He passionately denounced the war in "The Teeth Mother Naked At Last" (1970); Wright viewed its demonic force with a visionary irony in "A Mad Fight Song for William S. Carpenter, 1966"; Kinnell condemned it with bitter sarcasm in "The Dead Shall Be Raised Incorruptible" (1971); and Merwin's chilled, spare language evoked a postapocalyptic desolation in poems such as "The Asians Dying" in *The Lice* (1967). All of these poets are political not in spite of but because of their inwardness; the unconscious becomes a ground for ethical values, which are then used to assess historical realities.

Yet what these poets see when they gaze into the unconscious depths is by no means identical. Where Bly and Wright find original unity, Kinnell and Merwin, for example, find division and violation—original strife. Kinnell darkly urges "breaking to a sacred, bloodier speech," and in such poems as "The Porcupine" and "The Bear" from *Body Rags* (1968), cosmic vision is achieved through a torturous process of self-extinction, a violent fusion with animal life in which the poet is at once victim and victimizer. Like Kinnell, W. S. Merwin frequently imagines mystical union as a oneness with animals, but rather than of a passionate, bloody merging, he writes coolly of our necessary alienation from the silent being of natural creatures. Merwin, too, exposes social violence toward wildlife but he implicates language, its violent desire to possess the other, in this process. Poetry does not, as it does for Bly and Wright, offer a redeeming language that heals the poet (and society) by making a lost world present. In *The Moving Target* (1963), *The Lice*, and *The Carrier of Ladders* (1970), Merwin's impersonal voice, pared-down language, and Orphic brevity move the lyric poem to the very edge of silence. Even so, the poet is still left separate, alien; his muse is "Division, mother of Pain."

Around 1960 Bly, Ginsberg, and Olson were key liberators of American poetry. Not just by the example of their work but also by their provocative reviews, essays, manifestos, they stimulated their contemporaries by dismantling accepted models and by posing fresh alternatives. Even for those poets not persuaded by their specific programs, they helped create an enlivening atmosphere of risk-taking. Yet the very energy and seriousness of their response created a problem for these innovators. The literary battles of the time—"academic" versus "experimental" or "closed" versus "open" verse—were fierce enough to generate positions, on both sides, that were rigid and simplified and so left little chance for complexity, self-doubt, or change. In this way, the advance guard could (and by the late sixties did) find itself marching rapidly in place or launching charges against walls that had long since collapsed. Moreover, Bly, Ginsberg, and Olson were all caught in the tricky dilemma of producing a theory of immediacy or an ideology of openness; they were all antitheoretical theorists who formulate in advance what, in theory, must be left to the spontaneities of the unmediated moment.

The poets of the New York school, the most self-conscious and the least programmatic of their generation, were also the least susceptible to this kind of ironic critique, mainly because they were continually supplying it themselves. The group, including John Ashbery, Barbara Guest, Kenneth Koch, Frank O'Hara, and James Schuyler, shared their contemporaries' refusal of New Critical social and linguistic decorum. Ashbery recalls that when he began to write in the late 1940s, "there was in fact almost no experimental poetry being written in this country." The solution of the New York poets, however, was not to commit themselves to an alternative position but to question commitment itself. "To move is to love," O'Hara wrote, rejecting the ordinary sense of love as commitment and endorsing instead mobility, instability, change. Thus uncommitted, the New York poets, especially Ashbery and O'Hara, produced some of the most boldly experimental poetry written in this country in the fifties and sixties.

Williams and Whitman were important to O'Hara, as was Wallace Stevens to the young Ashbery, but the main literary antecedents for these writers lie in French dadaism and surrealism, the source of such radically disjunctive works as O'Hara's "Easter" (1952) and "Second Avenue" (1953) and Ashbery's *The Tennis Court Oath* (1962). But Ashbery is speaking for many in the New York school when he says, "I have perhaps been more influenced by modern painting and music than by poetry." Ashbery, like O'Hara, was affected "by the music of John Cage in which there are long periods of silence and where the noises of the environment will be picked up and perhaps replayed at some point"; Cage's admission of chance elements into musical composition took surrealist proposals about automatic writing one step further—as did the abstract expressionist painters, the crucial models for the New York poets in the early 1950s.

O'Hara and Ashbery are both poets with an acute knowledge of and interest in painting. Both wrote many poems about specific paintings; O'Hara was a curator at the Museum of Modern Art, a prolific art critic, and a collaborator on poem-painting projects with such artists as Norman Bluhm and Larry Rivers, while Ashbery has written extensively on art for the Paris *Herald Tribune*, *Art News*, *New York* magazine, and *Newsweek*. When Ashbery and O'Hara began writing, timidity and decadence in American poetry coincided with the heroic age of American painting—the abstract expressionists. For the New York poets, as for some of the Black Mountain writers, these painters were inspiring models of risk-taking, bravely declaring that "only the unacceptable is acceptable." The poets did not so much derive specific techniques or subject matters from the painters as they adopted a "concept of the poem as the chronicle of the creative act that produces it," the ambition, as O'Hara put it, "to be the work yourself."

Without commitment to any stable ideological center, Ashbery and O'Hara were freed to write many different kinds of poems and differed markedly from each other. O'Hara's poems are often speedy, literalistic, transparent, as in his transcriptions of the random events of a New York lunch hour; Ashbery's work is generally more inward, ruminative, opaque, constantly circling around a literal occasion it can neither enter nor leave behind. Yet both poets begin with the premise that "every moment has a validity." O'Hara passes through the moment very rapidly, Ashbery circles around it very slowly, but both reach toward an immediacy that they cannot fully grasp. "After all/ who does own any thing?" O'Hara asks in "The Three-Penny Opera" (1950); Ashbery, similarly emphasizing the slipperiness of experience, says life is a "permanent unraveling," "a unity constantly separating." Unlike Olson, who claims to be at one with the moment, O'Hara and Ashbery can neither surrender to nor master the moment—a condition that pushes them on to the next moment and its utterance. In Ashbery's words, they thus "draw attention to the continuing nature of poetry, which has to come into being, pass from being, in order to return to a further state of being." What O'Hara and Ashbery love is plurality and movement, and of all their generation they are the most engaged with process, ongoingness, temporality.

Skeptical of rest, finality, or the comforts of a fixed position, the New York poets were not generally producers of literary manifestos—the major exception being O'Hara's "Personism: A Manifesto" (1959). This essay does resemble many of the polemical outbursts of the late fifties and early sixties in its desire to break down the boundaries between literature and life. O'Hara airily dismisses craft: "I don't even like rhythm, assonance, all that stuff." Nor, like Bly and Olson, does he much admire abstract thinking: "Pain always produces logic, which is very bad for you." His own literary movement began when O'Hara, having just written a love poem, realized "that if I wanted to I could use the telephone instead of writing the poem," as if a poem were no different from a phone call. Personism, opposed to modernist "personal removal by the poet," now places the poem "at last between two persons instead of two pages." Yet O'Hara contradicts and parodies his position as much as he asserts it. Craft is just a matter of "common sense: if you're going to buy a pair of pants you want them to be tight enough so everyone will want to go to bed with you." His own ideas are sometimes "the most lofty ideas of anyone writing today," and personism, while against impersonality, "does not have to do with personality or intimacy"; it is "all art," as if a poem *were* different from a phone call. O'Hara's commitment to personism is qualified by his flip tone, his precise dating of the start of the movement ("it was founded by me after lunch with LeRoi Jones on August 27, 1959") and his advancement of it in the form of a letter; by fixing both the origin and the formulation of personism in time O'Hara disengages himself by implying that at other times he may think differently. "Personism" mocks the grandiosity and inflexibility of the manifestos of the 1950s; the essay provides not a solution for readers troubled by O'Hara's poems but yet another instance of their elusive contradictoriness. After all, not even O'Hara could own O'Hara.

John Ashbery has spoken of each generation's "desire to destroy or negate all previous writings in order to give things their true names and at the same time to build a wall around an impossibly large area." By mid-century, American poetry had lost this destructive-creative energy; reacting against modernism's experimental boldness and reflecting the timidity of their own historical era, our poets had withdrawn to a small, comfortable area, in which they remained on congenial terms with their predecessors, their audience, their critics, their society, and their all-too-predictable means. In the late 1950s and early 1960s, however, many young poets, negating the accomplishments of their immediate predecessors and stretching poetic language toward the impossibly fluid and complex space of the present, made American poetry once again become critical, passionate, innovative— alive. Their disruptive energies, the broad range of theories and styles they initiated, continue to vitalize American poetry today.

What about the poetry of the last fifteen years? Mapping this field is like trying to diagram the movements of a mobile to which new parts are constantly being added. Yet certain features of the terrain are clear. Programmatic innovation has generally been absent; no anthology has asserted the revolutionary presence of a *New American Poetry* the way Donald Allen's did in 1960. At the same time, no central authority—either of person or of mode—has established itself, as T. S. Eliot and the New Criticism did in the 1950s. First confessionalism, then deep image surrealism predominated in the 1970s, but both are now viewed with deep skepticism. More recently, the short, autobiographical lyric—its imagery drawn from natural or domestic life—has established a mainstream, with the dissidence of the "language poets" (treated in Henry Sayre's chapter in this volume) on the left bank and, on the right, a New New Formalism attracting much attention if not all that many adherents. But in the 1980s poetic authority remains dispersed along either ideological lines (feminist, gay, ethnic) or geographical lines (New York school, Iowa City surrealism). Communities—not *a* community—mark the pluralistic scene of contemporary poetry in the United States.

James E. B. Breslin

Twentieth-Century Drama

"I will not think, to think is torment—Ha!" (*The Prince of Parthia* by Thomas Godfrey, 1767)

"Thoughts . . . damn pests! . . . . mosquitoes of the soul." (*Strange Interlude* by Eugene O'Neill, 1928)

"Think in stitches." (*Paiseau* by Gertrude Stein, 1928)

"How can you know this thought? In me." (*A Lie of the Mind* by Sam Shepard, 1986)

Given the chokehold on drama of a misnamed *Broad*way, given the lure of Hollywood, and given the power of some small-minded reviewers in the daily press, it is a virtual miracle that American drama merits admission to a history of American *literature*. In our time, when the Communications Revolution has displaced the Industrial Revolution, the public at large is less and less responsive to the serious performance for which dramatic literature was written. It can nevertheless be read pleasurably and even intelligently by those who have never seen a live performance—as I can testify, after decades of teaching dramatic literature. A narrative history of that literature is taught in classrooms throughout the United States, and it is summarized in surveys that reach more readers than the plays themselves.

That narrative begins with Eugene O'Neill, generally acclaimed as America's greatest dramatist. He stumbled, however, through several styles and subjects in his resolution to create tragedy on the modern stage. Son of James O'Neill, a famous actor who made a small fortune as a matinee idol in *The Count of Monte Cristo*, O'Neill began by writing melodramas. In 1912, at age twenty-four, having survived a suicide attempt and tuberculosis, O'Neill determined to become a playwright, and he spent the next three decades in dedication to that mission. After variants on melodrama, he steered into realistic sea plays, then toward expressionist agons, and finally to sprawling realistic plays with an epic dimension. O'Neill was haunted by death, but he gave dramatic life to America's history and geography, men and women, poets and stutterers, illusion and disillusion. Earnest of

purpose and contemptuous of facility, O'Neill shaped his thought and torment into forty-nine (published) plays, destroying others that illness prevented him from completing.

O'Neill's early melodramas have survived by accident, and they provide
instructive contrast with *Bound East for Cardiff*, the first of his "S.S. Glen-
cairn" plays. Astonishing is young O'Neill's graduation from imitative crises
to experiential authenticity, from stilted dialogue to salty colloquialism, from
exotic settings to a minutely observed ship, from climactic violence to endless drifting, for O'Neill already translated his own seagoing adventures
into a long day's dramatic journey into night.

Beyond the Horizon, a three-act tragedy now rarely performed, brought
O'Neill beyond the horizon of the Provincetown Playhouse to New York
mainstream theater. Having found his sea legs in realism, O'Neill reached
out toward expressionism. Between 1920 and 1924 he tried to create—in
his words—"original rhythms of beauty, where beauty apparently isn't."
The Emperor Jones, *The Hairy Ape*, *All God's Chillun Got Wings*, and *Desire
Under the Elms* are daring forays into race relations, class conflict, sexual
bondage, and American tragedy on the Greek model. *Desire* is often revived, in part because the plot is an Americanization of the Phaedra-Hip-
polytus-Theseus myth and in part because the indoor-outdoor setting permits visualization of the private-public resonances of that plot. Although
marred by turgid dialogue and abuse of repetition, *Desire* nevertheless achieves
moments of passionate intensity that predict O'Neill's wholly functional
final tragedies.

Ever productive though he was, O'Neill only gradually worked up to
that summit. From the mid-1920s to the mid-1930s he cast about for non-
realistic forms to contain his tragic vision. *Marco Millions* (1923) stages a
picaresque and satirized Babbitt. In that same year, masks theatricalize an
Apollonian-Dionysian conflict in *The Great God Brown*. Shortly afterward
O'Neill wrote his most ambitious play, *Lazarus Laughed*, which draws upon
the Bible, Greek choruses, Elizabethan tirades, expressionist masks, populous crowd scenes, and orchestrated laughter that is intended to damn materialism. Reverting to the American twentieth century for *Strange Interlude*
(1927), O'Neill in his "woman play" resurrects the stage aside to reveal
repressed desires. *Mourning Becomes Electra* (1931) transplants the *Oresteia* to
the American Civil War.

In 1932, at age forty-four, O'Neill conceived the idea of a cycle of plays
about several generations of an American family—"A Tale of Possessors
Self-Dispossessed." By 1941 he noted in his Work Diary: "Idea was first 5
plays, then 7, then 8, then 9, now 11!—will never live to do it—but what

price anything but a dream these days!" His prediction was accurate. Ill and unable to write, O'Neill salvaged only *A Touch of the Poet* from that cycle, but *More Stately Mansions* was rescued after his death.

Ironically, O'Neill's extra-cycle plays are his greatest achievements—*The Iceman Cometh* (written 1939; published 1946), *Long Day's Journey into Night* (1940), and *Hughie* (1941, intended for another cycle, "By Way of Obit"). The two long plays are similar in their return to surface realism, their concentration and specificity of place and time (the year 1912), their tender comedy that intensifies the tragic drive, their memorable characters that attain without strain to a mythic dimension. No one today seriously questions O'Neill's preeminence, as set forth in the traditional narrative of American drama.

Yet O'Neill lives in contradictions. The sheer bulk of his output precipitates to about a dozen plays that continue to invite professional production. O'Neill did not live to see the work of his most faithful director, Jose Quintero, or his most dedicated actor, Jason Robards. His stubborn experimentation was subdued to rest in realism. His obsession with tragedy has been eroded by productions that stress comedy, stasis, or existential irony. The tragic fate that O'Neill pursued theatrically through play after play crystallizes in palpable moments of stage grace, and the whole of his achievement is an accumulation more telling than any of its parts.

Emerging from O'Neill's dark shadow, the narrative of American dramatic literature pinpoints lesser American dramatists of the interwar years, who may be grouped as social satirists (Philip Barry, S. N. Behrman, Rachel Crothers, George Kelly, Robert Sherwood); social realists (Lillian Hellman, Sidney Howard, Sidney Kingsley, Clifford Odets); occasional experimenters (Maxwell Anderson in verse plays, Elmer Rice in his few expressionist plays, William Saroyan in atmospheric fables, Thornton Wilder in metatheatrical plays). During World War II Broadway turned irreversibly right into escape—the modern musical and the frivolous comedy—while O'Neill languished ill, unappreciated, and all but forgotten.

Before the production of O'Neill's last tragedies, two playwrights moved haltingly into that genre. Tennessee Williams shaped his dramas by lurid violence, whereas Arthur Miller staged ethical imperatives. Each remained faithful to his own idiom, which the British critic Kenneth Tynan summarized pithily: "Miller's plays are hard, 'patrist,' athletic, concerned mostly with men. Williams's are soft, 'matrist,' sickly, concerned mostly with women." Moreover, Miller sees himself as a responsible realist whereas Williams is a lyrical romantic.

Born four years before Miller, Williams was steeped in Southern Episcopalian tradition. While still in his teens, Williams published verse, fiction, and plays—a generic diversity that lasted through his life. During the 1930s he was an unenthusiastic student at several universities and an enthusiastic playwright for a little-theater group in St. Louis. In 1939, falsifying his age, he won a Group Theater award for a series of short plays, acquired Audrey Wood as his agent, and took the name Tennessee. After 1945 when *The Glass Menagerie* opened on Broadway (to unexpected acclaim), Williams produced some thirty-five plays of uneven quality, as well as verse, fiction, essays, and a pointless autobiography. When he died in a New York hotel in 1983, that city seemed surprised to find him there.

Williams was aware: "My longer plays emerge out of earlier one-acters or short stories I may have written years before. I work over them again and again." Thus the Boston failure *Battle of Angels* (1940) became *Orpheus Descending* (1957); *Summer and Smoke* (1948) changed into *Eccentricities of a Nightingale* (1975); *The Seven Descents of Myrtle* (1964) took only four years to appear as *Kingdom of Earth*. And *Out Cry* preoccupied Williams for a decade. Critics disagree as to whether the later versions are improvements.

But there is no disagreement that *The Glass Menagerie* outshines the short story, earlier dramatizations, and movie scenario that preceded the play we know. (Most of us know a frequently anthologized version that is less vivid than the so-called acting version.) Brilliantly acted, *Menagerie* seduced both Chicago and New York with a new lyricism on the American stage, differently melodic for each of the memorable characters—the moviegoing narrator Tom (who bears Williams's actual name), his frail sister Laura with her delicate zoo of glass figurines, her gentleman caller who was not calling on her, and the imperious, irritating, impractical, and courageous mother.

With *A Streetcar Named Desire* Williams brought sex, the South, and violence to Broadway in 1947, and that triad was thereafter assumed as his signature. Williams was hailed as a dynamic creator of actors' vehicles and simultaneously as a Chekhovian elegist of the Old South. Mothlike Blanche DuBois and poker-playing Stanley Kowalski instantly commanded imposing positions in the American dramatic pantheon. *Streetcar* is a perfect amalgam of plot, character, thought, diction, spectacle—that Aristotelian residue—but it is a twentieth-century drama in its dependence on atmosphere, lighting, inside-outside set, and telling properties that resonate symbolically—meat, cards, clothes, light bulb, and straitjacket.

The traditional narrative of American drama accords no other Williams play such high value. *Summer and Smoke* (1948) is belittled as a body-versus-mind allegory. *The Rose Tattoo* (1950), a venture into festive farce, is too prodigal of symbolic roses. *Cat on a Hot Tin Roof* (1954), again offering sultry sex in the South, dilutes violence with humor, and the director Elia Kazan prevailed upon Williams to dilute the ambivalence of his ending, but the playwright slyly published both versions. Violence returns with a vengeance in *Suddenly Last Summer* (1958), with its threat of lobotomy and its climactic revelation of cannibalism; in the shock reaction to the subject, there was little praise for Williams's deft tapestry of *absence*, as two women evoke the dead poet who has exploited them. In this harrowing drama, as in *The Night of the Iguana* (1961), Williams reaches out beyond the South to cruelty at large, and he offers touching moments of communion as the only defense.

Suffering from illness, opiates, and the death of his lover, Williams has called the 1960s his Stoned Age, and though he wrote indomitably on, the conventional narrative ignores his daring forays outside of realism. As early as 1953 his *Camino Real* failed on a Broadway that was cold to a quest play centered on Kilroy, the mythical all-American naïve romantic. Other experiments received short shrift—the patently symbolic *Milk Train Doesn't Stop Here Anymore* (1963), the two short plays constituting *Slapstick Tragedy* (1966), the fragmented phrases of *In the Bar of a Tokyo Hotel* (1969), a prelude to the plays of the 1970s, focused on artists.

The conventional narrative ignores *Vieux Carré* (1977), which recalls Williams's early plays in its quasi-realistic staging of sex and violence in the South. As in *The Glass Menagerie* a narrator is both in and outside of the action, set during the 1930s in a tawdry rooming house inhabited by artists in various stages of want. And criticism has yet to explore the 1977 version of *Out Cry* that economically enfolds the South, sex, violence, and art into a brother-sister tale of incest and madness. The familiar Williams triad announces its own theatricality in a drama that cries out for human warmth in a cold theater.

It is fitting that Williams's last major play, *Clothes for a Summer Hotel* (1980), should be subtitled "a ghost play." Williams resurrects Scott and Zelda Fitzgerald, Ernest Hemingway, and their entourage as ghosts who can look back in compassion at passionate lives misspent for art. They see themselves as instruments to fill demanding blank pages. Having fulfilled that same demand from adolescence on, Williams dramatized it in these three strikingly dissimilar late works for which he garnered no prizes and little praise.

Of the three giants of twentieth-century American drama, Arthur Miller alone goes gracefully into his golden years. And although the traditional narrative grants him equality with, if not superiority to, Williams, he has published less than twenty plays (in my view not only fewer, but lesser plays), as well as a novel, some short stories, some travel books, and a volume of essays about the theater—mainly his own. In that volume he writes: "I don't see how you can write anything decent without using the question of right and wrong as the basis."

This eminently decent man was born in 1915, one of the two sons of a prosperous Jewish clothing manufacturer who was ruined by the crash of 1929. Moved to Brooklyn and a series of thankless jobs, Miller was impelled to become a writer after he read *The Brothers Karamazov*. Enrolling in journalism at the University of Michigan, he won a Hopwood Award in Drama for his first play. He wrote about a dozen (unpublished) plays before his first Broadway production in 1944—*The Man Who Had All the Luck*. It closed after four performances, but his next offering, *All My Sons* (1947), ran for a prosperous year, shrewdly enfolding topicality into the dependable form of the well-made play. In retrospect, one can see the aptness of the title (not "All My Children"), since several Miller dramas will pivot on father-son relations.

In 1949 Miller opened his American classic, *Death of a Salesman*. In spite of a few adverse cranks, the drama was instantly hailed as an American myth and a contemporary tragedy. Rooted in a realistic family, *Salesman* stages the memories, aspirations, and hallucinations of a middle-aged failure. Like O'Neill's *Desire* and Williams's *Streetcar*, the indoor-outdoor set encourages intimacy with the characters, even while it imposes a wider social resonance. Willy Loman's father sold the flutes he made in a pastoral America, but Willy's "making" is unappreciated as he tries to sell himself in a dehumanized country. Throughout Miller's dialogue the verbs "make" and "sell" are implicitly opposed, while his intricate lighting juxtaposes dreams and facts, future and past, a moldering house and a mechanized civilization. *Death of a Salesman* encapsulated the drift of a nation at mid-century, and it has acquired a deep patina with the decades.

Miller's next play, the 1953 *Crucible*, is often called his McCarthyism allegory, but long after the demise of the House Un-American Activities Committee and Joseph McCarthy, it remains Miller's most frequently performed play. Fact imitated fiction when Miller himself was indicted, like his protagonist John Proctor, by self-righteous accusers. And like his protagonist before him, Miller behaved with honor and dignity (unlike certain colleagues). It was therefore disappointing when he recently censored use of this play by New York's Wooster Group, since he evidently did not understand that parody can be homage.

After *The Crucible* a 1955 double bill nods to his predecessors, O'Neill and Williams. Like several plays of the latter, *A View from the Bridge* blends violence and lyricism in its single act focused on a lovers' triangle, but the action is distanced through the memory of a narrator. Drawing more directly on Miller's own experience during the Depression, *A Memory of Two Mondays* shows the erosive effect of dulling work in an automobile-parts warehouse; as in O'Neill's sea plays, an embelmatic humanity is suggested by different dialects.

After a cool reception of the double bill on Broadway, Miller abandoned the stage for nearly a decade, returning with *After the Fall* (1964). Produced only two years after the death of Marilyn Monroe, the play was criticized as biography rather than an effort to revive the technique of *Salesman*, blending past and present, memory and anticipation. However, a concentration camp tower replaces the little home in Brooklyn, and private inadequacies are stubbornly thumped for public resonance, which is in turn implicitly associated with the biblical fall—too weighty a burden for a frail inward-looking protagonist. (The Bible is not Miller's happiest source, as evidenced in *The Creation of the World and Other Business* [1972], subsequently revised as the musical *Up from Paradise*.) More limited in ambition, *Incident at Vichy* (1965) attempts to dramatize the ethical response of a number of (mainly Jewish) individuals rounded up by the Nazis in France.

In 1968, the year of widespread student unrest, Miller returned to Broadway with *The Price*, a realistic drama setting forth his old themes—individual responsibility, contrasting brothers, mutually uncomprehending generations. A new humility relieves the play of mythic strain, and a new flair for the comic creates one of his most serious characters, eighty-nine-year-old Solomon Gregory Solomon, dealer in used furniture that proves to be more metaphysical than physical.

Although the traditional narrative of Miller's drama tends to end with the elegiac *Price*, Miller the playwright blossomed forth again in his sixties. *The Archbishop's Ceiling* (1977) is a new departure for Miller, not only because of its East European setting, but because the possibility of hidden electronic devices transforms the four characters—three East Europeans and one American—into actors for the benefit of their unseen audience. *Playing for Time*, a television play of 1980, probes the morality of a woman's orchestra in a concentration camp, playing for their lives while other women go to their deaths. *The American Clock* (1980, inspired by Studs Terkel's *Hard Times*) returns to Miller's home terrain in a mosaic of the Depression's effect on a single family, set within the country at large. More evanescent are two two-handers paired as *Two-Way Mirror* (1983), where reflections on reflection grow into stage reality. Another two short plays carry the title *Danger: Memory* (1985), the first one elegiac about the past and the second leading

to self-confrontation. Miller admirers see in these late plays a moving ambivalence about the nature of reality and responsibility, which seemed such
stable ground in his best-known works.

Viewed retrospectively, the corpus of Williams and Miller is not predicted by their masterpieces *A Streetcar Named Desire* and *Death of a Salesman*.
The final words of Blanche DuBois—"Whoever you are—I have always
depended on the kindness of strangers"—and Charley's requiem for Willy
Loman—"Nobody dast blame this man. A salesman is got to dream, boy"—
belie the subsequent plays of their respective creators. Williams's lyrical
victims are betrayed by unkind strangers, and Miller's dramas tend to dismantle dreams, even while admiring the dreamer.

The traditional narrative of American drama often ends with Edward
Albee, who, like his predecessors Williams and Miller, is celebrated mainly
for his early plays. Over the span of a quarter century he has published
some dozen plays. Born in 1928 in Washington, D.C., he was adopted by
the movie magnate Reed Albee. A rebellious child, he was expelled from
various schools but began writing while still in his teens. He has himself
announced the imperatives of the dramatist: "first, to make some statement
about the condition of 'man' . . . and, second, to make some statement
about the nature of the art form with which he is working. In both instances he must attempt change." Albee has accomplished the second,
sometimes at the expense of the first.

Albee has fostered the legend that his first play, written as he approached
his thirtieth birthday, was *The Zoo Story*, but he actually wrote plays for a
decade earlier. Considered difficult in its day, *The Zoo Story* can now be
seen to predict Albee's subsequent work—the obliquity of its expression,
its theme of emotional commitment, its shifting linguistic rhythms, its dynamic colloquial lexicon. The protagonist Jerry, like his creator, is appalled
at the humdrum quality of modern America, and he sacrifices his own life
to arouse Peter emotionally. Conversely, *The Death of Bessie Smith* (1960)
implicitly condemns the emotional torpor of the South in the 1930s, with
no hand held out to help the dying singer. *The American Dream* (1960), like
The Sandbox (1959), is a devastating satire on the degradation of that dream;
Mommy and a henpecked Daddy are boxed into consumerism and social
clichés, whereas Grandma still retains the old American frontier spirit. Into
their midst arrives a handsome Young Man, whom Grandma dubs the
American Dream, and he will "do almost anything for money."

The toast of Off-Broadway, Albee insisted on bringing his next play to
Broadway, and he reaped rich rewards for *Who's Afraid of Virginia Woolf?*
(1962). Like *Long Day's Journey into Night* in its drinking foursome, Albee's

drama is a refutation of *The Iceman Cometh*, for dawn breaks on the death of illusion. With his sharp verbal scalpel, Albee dissects two marriages to cut away the lies on which they are based. Since the main couple is named George and Martha (even as our first president and his lady), the drama implies that illusion is not merely an individual problem but a national malady. George defends Western civilization against its sex-oriented, success-oriented assailants—"I will not give up Berlin"—and his weapon is the most excoriating invective ever heard on the American stage.

In Albee's subsequent plays his characters pale into their stylized phrases. *Tiny Alice* (1964) tries to dramatize the secular martyrdom of Brother Julian, but his intractable monologues dispose an audience toward his witty if cruel antagonists. *A Delicate Balance* (1966) suspends a family in the comfortable equilibrium that they prefer to the risk of harboring friends haunted by a mysterious horror. Driving further into unexplored terrain, Albee was forced away from Broadway for his double bill *Box* and *Quotations from Chairman Mao Tse-Tung* (1968), which weave elegiac patterns while defying the Western dramatic tradition of *interaction* among characters. *All Over* (1971) puns on the ubiquity of death, as a family is screened from its dying progenitor. *Seascape* (1975) turns maudlin when a middle-aged couple gives lessons in feeling to a couple of quite human lizards. *The Lady from Dubuque* (1980) dwells in Albee's more habitual horror, when a group of friends, incapable of facing the dying young woman in their midst, surrender her to a mysterious couple—a dark man and the titular lady from Dubuque. In all these plays Albee shows his deft hand with linguistic patterns, but characters have been displaced by wraiths. Respecting Albee's refusal to repeat verbal forms, we can only look back nostalgically at the fun, games, and even *Walpurgisnacht* of *Virginia Woolf*.

After Albee, a narrative of American drama might skim over the performance craze of the 1960s, the extravagant musicals of the 1970s, and the dispersed regionalism of the 1980s. More intrepid narrators mention that the 1960s saw an explosion of writing as well as performing energy—off Broadway both literally and figuratively, that is, sexually, racially, generationally. Most narratives ignore Neil Simon, America's most successful playwright, measured in dollars. Although Sam Shepard has written plays through these three decades, he enters the narrative only after becoming a film star.

The narrative may be bent to suit the inclinations of the particular critic; for example, shrinking stage space (Christopher Bigsby), avatars of the Gothic (Herbert Blau), heritage of Chekhov (John Styan). Or the narrative may be revised when a new production inspires reexploration of old territory. For example, Keith Hack's staging of *Strange Interlude* urges an ironic view of O'Neill's famous asides. Far funnier than the tame *Ah, Wilderness!* (1933), O'Neill's "woman play" emerges as witty as a cubist painting that confronts us with features usually observed in sequence. In the long but lively drama, life's interlude is not so much strange as seriocomic because the characters are myopic, often wrong, and finally forgetful spectators of their own behavior—like us all.

O'Neill's "woman play" has not sparked feminist admiration, and blacks tend to be scornful of *The Emperor Jones* and *All God's Chillun Got Wings*, written at the very time of the Harlem Renaissance, which could muster no funding for black theater outside of patronizing white structures. Among attempts at black drama in the first half of the century, only Langston Hughes persisted in writing plays, adaptations, musicals—largely unpublished and unproduced. In contrast, women were offered roles from the inception of the Provincetown Players, and Susan Glaspell's plays are today being favorably compared to O'Neill's early work for that company. Although Glaspell did not experiment as boldly as O'Neill, she too dramatized the psychopathology of modern American experience. As a woman, she portrayed female bonding, as in *Trifles* (1916) or *The Outside* (1917). Her *Verge* (1921) preceded *Strange Interlude* as a woman play, in which the protagonist is also loved by three very different men, representing three different ways of life. Glaspell's Claire Archer achieves stature apart from the men in her life, as O'Neill's women never do.

Still another woman play was a *cause célèbre* at its 1928 premiere. E. E. Cummings's *him* was favorably reviewed on publication in 1927, but *theater* reviewers trounced the performance with every adjective from "crass" to "pretentious," before the play was neglected during the socially conscious 1930s. Since World War II *him* is again acquiring admirers, but not among theater professionals, who are wary of its three long acts involving over a hundred characters and a dozen styles. Despite its masculine title, *him* is a woman play by virtue of the backdrop "on which is painted a DOCTOR anaesthetizing a WOMAN," so that the whole exuberant drama becomes the drug-induced phantasmagoria of the woman (named Me) while giving birth to a baby. Self-indulgently prolix though it is, *him* nevertheless sports elements that appeal to recent theater artists—discontinuous plot, surrealistic characters, a view of the stage as a space rather than a setting for events in time, metadramatic commentary within the dialogue, and a panoply of popular genres in many dialects.

Gertrude Stein's plays were rediscovered in the performance-oriented antiverbal 1960s. Viewing drama as a moment-by-moment participation of the audience, Stein inaugurated techniques that undermined the very foundations of drama. For her, as for Antonin Artaud and Cummings, theater was space to be filled. She dispensed with action and character designation; her scenic directions are indistinguishable from her dialogue; metadramatic commentary is embedded in the verbal texture of many of her plays. Only in the work of her last decade does she allow herself the semblance of a plot, but it is her earlier immediacy that delighted the exponents of happenings, who were jubilant when the 1964 production of her "meaningless" *What Happened* won an Obie award (Obie = Off-Broadway). Stein was welcomed as a performance playwright.

In the main, however, there has been little revisionism of American drama of the first half of the century. Rather, it was the very tradition of dramatic performance that was questioned in the 1960s, that is, that actors play characters for passive spectators. Rebellious performers moved out of conventional structures into lofts, stores, cellars, cafés, churches, subways, streets. Scripts were scrapped in favor of improvisations and happenings. The inward probe of the feeling Method and the expressive urge of action painting coalesced in happenings, where language was cramped. Adventurous theater of the 1960s mistrusted a language debased by the media, but words came bouncing back to the theater when modern dance and, later, performance art included dialogue.

A contemporary Rip Van Winkle would register bewilderment if he happened to have a taste for American drama. Although most drama has moved back into the theater—and, indeed, mainstream drama never left—there are no taboo subjects and no ineluctable forms. Actors may play characters, be counters in a structure, or express what they fancy as themselves. They may play nude on bare boards, or they may be elaborately painted and costumed on intricately movable stages. They may cleave to the director's blocking and the playwright's every word, or they may improvise freely at each performance. They may pretend that there are no spectators, or they may invite the participation of the audience. But little of this theater variety has found its way into dramatic literature, which is absorbed through print as well as the stage.

If Rip Van Winkle were a reader rather than a theatergoer, he might chuckle at a punning extension of his name: contemporary reviewers rip last season's plays out of their consciousness, contemporary anthologies are ripped out of print soon after publication, contemporary dramatists rip themselves away from a thankless genre. R. I. P. indeed! If Rip had fallen asleep during the melting-pot era of American culture, he might be struck by today's militant deviation from a WASP norm. As the playwright David

Henry Hwang wrote: "American theater is beginning to discover Americans. Black theater, women's theater, gay theater, Asian American theater, Hispanic theater." He might have added politically committed theater. Dramatists who affiliate with these groups benefit from specially receptive audiences, yet many of these dramatists desire wider exposure. A minor critical problem arises as to how to assign playwrights to a group—by birth or allegiance, or both?

The problem arises for women playwrights. Choosing to group dramatists by the orientation of their work, I insist that women playwrights are not necessarily feminists; for example, Beth Henley, Tina Howe, Marsha Norman, and Adele Shank might be more accurately classed as family playwrights. Few feminists have published a body of plays, but Megan Terry is an exception. Beginning to write in the 1950s in her native Seattle, she shows compassion for society's rejects—especially women. In the Open Theater off Broadway during the 1960s, she grew adept at "transformation" technique, which requires the actor instantly to transform sex, age, class, or temperament, and even to portray an object. Her short transformation plays culminated in *Viet Rock* (1966). Perhaps these transformations helped Terry break down sexual stereotypes and create her first sustained "woman play," *Approaching Simone* (1970). Tracing the life of Simone Weil from childhood to sainthood, Terry compensates for flat dialogue with inventive images. In 1971 Terry moved to the Omaha Magic Theater, for which most of her subsequent work was written—the female generational bonding of *Hothouse* (1974), the female prisoner bonding of *Babes in the Bighouse* (1974), the sexism of our language in *American Kings English for Queens* (1978). Incorporating music, dance, mime, as well as tranformations, Terry has published over two dozen plays (of some sixty). No other feminist dramatist has published as much, but there are so many active women playwrights that even the *New York Times* and the Pulitzer Prize Committee acknowledge them.

They have not, however, acknowledged another seasoned dramatist who worked with the Open Theater—Maria Irene Fornès. Her early short plays are not as calculatedly transformational as Terry's, but her characters tend to be mercurial, acting and reacting in defiance of logic and psychology. Busy and good-humored, these light plays scarcely predict the serious depth of *Fefu and Her Friends* (1977). Feminist in sensibility, the play transports an audience through five rooms of a New England country house, to witness scenes between Fefu and her seven women friends. A basic conflict arises between Fefu's independent stance and paralyzed Julia's submissive portrait of women, but the intimacy of the staging engenders a feeling of feminine friendship that is abruptly disturbed by the violent ending. Other all-women plays—Clare Boothe Luce's *The Women* (1936) and Wendy Wasserstein's *Uncommon Women* (1977)—disagree radically on women's place in society, but both plays are aesthetically conservative, whereas Fornès's subtlety challenges prevailing female stereotypes.

It is possible to argue that the very existence of a tough, nonconformist woman playwright challenges stereotyped sex roles, and this has indeed been argued for Rochelle Owens. Her strident plays energized the performative mood of the 1960s—especially *Futz* (1959, revised 1968) with its sympathetic portrait of sodomy, and *Beclch* (1966) with its sadomasochism ablaze in imagery. When Owens turned to fantastic history in *The Karl Marx Play* (1973) and *Emma Instigated Me* (1975), the outrageous animality made for unintentional comedy, and her subsequent plays have received little attention.

Politically radical playwrights differ markedly from their predecessors in the 1930s by flaunting their comic gifts. Clifford Odets's *Waiting for Lefty* (1935) uses five serious flashbacks to punctuate its strike plea; moving backwards in time, Joan Holden's *Steeltown* (1982) juxtaposes present union complacency against postwar labor ebullience. The Depression gave dramatic immediacy to the hackneyed situations of *Lefty;* Reaganomics is the background for the contemporary play that delivers its union critique with songs, jokes, and the acrobatic acting of the San Francisco Mime Troupe. Not only does Holden's second act flash back forty years in time, but it shifts sharply in comic style. Act I is a farce of contemporary consumption, whereas Act II is a romantic musical comedy of hopeful dreams. In retrospect, farce is unveiled as nightmare.

During two decades of playwriting for the San Francisco Mime Troupe (always using words, and a collective since 1970), Holden has patterned her highly political plays on commedia dell'arte, melodrama, soap opera, musical comedy, and comic strip. Most often performed by other groups is her *Independent Female* (1970), which ends happily on the *separation* of the young lovers, for the handsome young hero is sexist and the beautiful young heroine decides to be an independent female. In recent plays Holden blends burlesque with more realistic depiction of working-class characters, in their strength *and* weakness. But the comic-strip Superman inspires Factwino, perhaps her most popular character, who has appeared in three plays to date. Written for a multiracial collective, Holden's dramas champion ethnic minorities. Her Factwino is black, speaking the dialect of black street smarts;

his friend Buddy is Mexican American, colorful in his dialect. Ethnic expression is, however, subordinated to the large political purpose of the particular play.

In contrast, the active Asian American, black, and Chicano theater movements focus on the experience of their respective constituencies. Many of their playwrights address themselves only to their own communities, but several have crossed the frontier into mainstream minority theater, that seeming contradiction encouraged by several subsidies. Asian American theater, harboring different national cultures, has been slow to see print. Plays of the immigrant experience, such as those of Frank Chin and David Henry Hwang, seem vaguely familiar because there has been so much literature on this subject—for other national groups. Both playwrights are young and inventive, so that we may hope for new forms of expression as they ponder their heritage in an increasingly un-Caucasian country.

Although there are well over a hundred Chicano theater companies, playing in Spanish and English, only one Chicano playwright has a national reputation—Luís Valdez. Introduced to theater by the San Francisco Mime Troupe's performance, Valdez was for a time a member of that company, but in 1965 he founded El Teatro Campesino, for which he wrote politically motivated short plays or *actos*. Gradually, however, the company grew more concerned with aesthetic polish, and in 1971 it published a volume of nine *actos*, with only three based on the issue of farm labor. The longest one, for example, *No Saco Nada de la Escuela* (I Don't Get Anything Out of School [1969]), follows black, Chicano, and white students through their schooling, to reveal that Anglo education does not prepare the others for the realities of their respective worlds. Similarly the Vietnam War *actos* show the folly of Chicano soldiers fighting for an Anglo-dominated government. More recently, Valdez has written *mitos*, which are less political in purpose, and which introduce fantastic and surreal elements of an Azatlan cultural heritage. Seemingly uninterested in readers, Valdez has made no attempt to publish his most sustained works. Like several mainstream playwrights, he is turning from the stage to film because "movies are the poor people's theater."

Black playwrights might have gone to Hollywood, had any welcoming hand been extended to greet them. In spite of mammoth obstacles in most theaters, however, three black playwrights have produced a body of plays that enrich American drama—Amiri Baraka, Ed Bullins, and Adrienne Kennedy. Baraka, born LeRoi Jones in a middle-class family, has several times changed his political stance, and his plays reflect those changes. Werner Sollors offers the following chronology: 1958–61—Bohemian period, with an expressive aesthetic (in verse, fiction, and drama); 1960–65—New Left period, with a mimetic aesthetic (although his plays are not realistic); 1964–74—Kawaida period, with a pragmatic aesthetic (intending his drama for the black community); since 1974—Marxist-Leninist-Maoist period, with a pragmatic aesthetic (and few plays published). In 1964, not yet thirty years old, Baraka had four plays running Off-Broadway—*The Baptism, The Toilet, Dutchman,* and *The Slave.* Obscene, blasphemous, and iconoclastic, these plays gained him notoriety in the white press, and to this day he retains marked influence on educated young blacks. His most recent writing recalls the agitprop plays of the 1920s, except that the leading characters are black.

The same age as Baraka, Ed Bullins was born into a very different kind of black family, whose males were criminals, and Bullins draws upon his own background. Like Baraka, Bullins read omnivorously, and like him exploded into verse, essays, and fiction, but "I turned to writing plays because I found that the people I was interested in writing about or writing to—my people—didn't read much fiction, essays, or poetry." Bullins has since found that they don't read much drama either, but he persists in writing plays—of uneven quality. *Clara's Ole Man* (1965), one of his strongest dramas, is one of his earliest. At once funny and brutal, it stages the visit to eighteen-year-old Clara by Jack of the Ivy League suit and diction, "when her ole man would be at work." The drama juxtaposes Jack with tough slum blacks, particularly Big Girl, who proves to be Clara's "ole man." Shortly after completing that play, Bullins announced his intention of producing a cycle of twenty plays about Afro-Americans between 1900 and 1999, but he has written plays both within and outside the cycle. Most Bullins plays are set in urban slums, where drink, drugs, theft, gambling, and prostitution are routine activities. Not didactic, Bullins nevertheless depicts the pointless monotony of such existence, but he also depicts the tough humor and the sheer durability of the characters, against all odds.

Baraka and Bullins, in their different idioms, have dramatized black *male* consciousness, whereas Adrienne Kennedy's lyrical plays are rooted in her own female *un*conscious: "I see my writing as being an outlet for inner, psychological confusion and questions stemming from childhood. . . . You try to struggle with the material that is lodged in your unconscious, and try to bring it to the conscious level." Her plays stage the seductions of white culture for the sensitive black artist. *Funnyhouse of a Negro* (1962) is both setting and symbol of where Negro Sarah lives, torn as she is between the white and black strands of her heritage. Born of a light mother and a dark father, she finds avatars of herself in white Queen Victoria and the

Duchess of Hapsburg, as well as in a colored Jesus and Patrice Lumumba. With finely etched images and incantatory repetitions, these alternative selves of Sarah shift kaleidoscopically within the distorting white funnyhouse. The play circles back to its beginning, with a rope around the neck of black-clad Sarah; it is at once shocking and inevitable that the play ends with her suicide by hanging.

Kennedy's other plays of the 1960s use animal imagery to stage both the black condition and the dark of the unconscious. Expressionist in their presentational subjectivity, surrealistic in their dreamglide and imagery, Kennedy's plays penetrate racial America and the feminine imagination. Although Kennedy wrote more realistic plays during the 1970s, she has returned to her earlier unique mode in *A Movie Star Has to Star in Black and White* (1976).

If American theater is, as David Henry Hwang announced, beginning to discover Americans, it seeks particularly *theatrical* Americans, and after centuries of relegation to the closet, gay America burst out in full color in the second half of the century, first in Off-Off-Broadway of the 1960s, but even entering the mainstream in a vehicle like Harvey Fierstein's *Torch Song Trilogy* (1978). A recent directory lists "some 400 plays relevant to lesbians and gay men," with the greater number in the second category. Sometimes called Queer Theater, these plays have been published even more erratically than those of other contemporary playwrights, although this situation may change with the establishment of several gay presses.

The effervescent originators of New York's gay drama—Ronald Tavel, Charles Ludlam, and Kenneth Bernard—prefer the adjective "ridiculous." Tavel took to the stage almost accidentally, when his film script *Shower* (1965) was rejected by Andy Warhol but accepted as a play by director John Vaccaro. His style is already evident—disjointed episodes of a skeletal plot, characters of uncertain identity, extravagant sets and props, affection for popular genres, obscene wordplay, sexual ambiguity, metadramatic winks to the audience. Relying on these techniques, Tavel quickly produced a series of short plays of which the liveliest is *The Life of Lady Godiva* (1965). With *Gorilla Queen* (1967) Tavel claims that he became an Aristotelian dramatist, but the "later" plays differ from the earlier group mainly in increased length and philosophic pretension. An exception to his usual style is *Boy on the Straight-Back Chair* (1969), a tense and economical dramatization of "our town's dirty laundry," based on actual heterosexual "pleasure" killers. Decidedly not focused on the problematic position of gay people in straight America, most of Tavel's plays are literally gay, romping around sexual role-playing.

The same statement might sum up the plays of Charles Ludlam, who is, however, more firmly grounded on parody. Thus, *Big Hotel* (1967) bounces over the movie *Grand Hotel; When Queens Collide* (1968) over Marlowe's *Tamburlaine; Corn* (1972) over the Hatfield-McCoy feud; a self-evident *Camille* (1973), *Der Ring* (1977), and *The Elephant Woman* (1979) parody the originals. Like Tavel, Ludlam also thrives on extravagant costuming and sexual puns, but he nevertheless manages to create consistent characters, in a rather mellow, old-fashioned manner.

Of the three playwrights of the Ridiculous, it is Kenneth Bernard who is most serious and least known. His dramas are unsparingly cruel in both the mundane and the Artaudian sense of the word. In several plays Bernard creates a sexually ambiguous shaman/master of ceremonies who presides at victimization for entertainment—Alec in *The Moke-Eater* (1968), Bubi in *Night Club* (1970), the titular character of *The Magic Show of Dr. Ma-Gico* (1973). Through this device, Bernard makes accomplices of his audience, especially in more recent unpublished plays that deliberately decimate plots and personalities. In Bernard's dramas desire is a universal malady, which is not slaked even in death. Bernard is still too disturbing for most audiences, while *Torch Song Trilogy* woos them with its savory recipe of gay sentimentalities, the titilation of an urbane subculture, and a liberal spice of one-liners.

Other dramatists survive on and off Broadway, without belonging to any of the groups I have surveyed. Many of their works center on the American family and are usually set in a middle-class home that proves to be a jail for the sensitive protagonist. Lanford Wilson may encumber his St. Louis Talley's with homosexuals and Jews—in *Fifth of July* (1978) and *Talley's Folly* (1979) respectively. David Rabe may charge his Nelson family with murderous callousness toward their Vietnam veteran son—*Sticks and Bones* (1971). John Guare may depict Catholics straining comically against their faith— *The House of Blue Leaves* (1970). But the minute we see a living room in the scenic directions—whether in Texas, St. Louis, Queens, or California—we are primed for an exposition, an action rising remorselessly to climax, and an inevitable resolution (less resolved in recent years) in the pattern designed by Ibsen a century ago.

I have isolated these well-known and usually well-made plays from an author's corpus, but I have chosen the playwrights with some respect, for they have shown serious fidelity to drama in spite of competing media. Arthur Kopit belongs among them. After early acclaim for a burlesque *Oh Dad, Poor Dad, Mamma's Hung You in the Closet and I'm Feelin' So Sad* (1960) he has ranged through several styles: realistic and surrealistic one-acts, a metatheatrical view of history in *Indians* (1968), an examination of language learning in *Wings* (1978), and a Pirandellian play on nuclear holocaust in *End of the World* (1984). More prolific (perhaps because of his relationship with New York's Circle Repertory Company), Lanford Wilson writes as the champion of urban dregs and misfits in such plays as *Balm in Gilead* (1965) and *The Hot l Baltimore* (1973), but he can also anatomize a town in *The Rimers of Eldritch* (1966) or *The Mound Builders* (1974). In his *Angels Fall* (1984) Wilson obliquely and realistically treats two Kopit subjects—the exploitation of American Indians and the peril of American nuclear weapons.

David Rabe, a Vietnam War veteran, seems locked into two main subjects—the American army during the Vietnam War and the sexual exploitation of women. After castigating both the army and civilians in his war trilogy, Rabe attacks a macho mercantilism in *In the Boom Boom Room* (1974) and *Hurlyburly* (1984). Rabe tends to lunge at his targets, but Guare cuts with a razor wit. Anti-Vietnam War plays, Rabe's *Basic Training of Pavlo Hummel* (1971) parallels Guare's *Muzeeka* (1967), both now as distant as the plays of World War II. Closer to his experience, Guare satirized the Me generation—especially the Me artist—in *The House of Blue Leaves* (1970), *Rich and Famous* (1976), and *Marco Polo Sings a Solo* (1977). Guare's penchant for farce is so irrepressible that the edge of his satire dulls, but, disciplining his extravagant invention, he dramatized the inner torment of three spirited neurotics in *Bosoms and Neglect* (1979), and his most recent work (aside from film) is focused on a series of plays on utopia-seekers in post–Civil War America.

The problem with a swift survey is the space usurped by mere titles trailing an inadequate descriptive phrase, but, having flown over the broad terrain, I linger now on the most thoughtful drama of the second half of the century, and I insist on the word "thoughtful." However, the thought is embedded in the drama, and cannot be reductively paraphrased—even when I feel compelled to try. For the experienced theatergoer, such thought is palpable, springing forth from the page, but other readers may have to work harder to pierce to the thought behind the print.

Two active playwrights—Sam Shepard and David Mamet—might well object to this approach to their work, since they are mainly admired for the music rather than the meaning of their language, but I maintain that the music is part of the meaning. Both were born in the 1940s, both were produced in their early twenties; celebrated before the age of thirty, both nevertheless refuse to bend to Broadway taste. They have forged the most distinctive idiolects in white American drama, but whereas Mamet's usually brief plays resemble one another through a series of two-character confrontations, some fifty plays of Shepard may be classified in three convenient groups.

Born at a Midwestern army base in 1943, moving from base to base as he was growing up, briefly touring the United States as an actor in 1962, arriving in New York City in 1963, living in London between 1971 and 1974, Shepard had various landscapes at his disposal. Bored at school, absorbed in jazz, an enthusiast of sports, he thinks in terms of popular rather than erudite myths. In Greenwich Village of the 1960s he tried his hand at song lyrics, brief vignettes, and short plays. Three Obie awards in swift succession fixed his genre. His early short plays may change locale—indoors, outdoors, home, or hotel—but the time is always now. In form, associative monologues or "riffs" are glued on to disjunctive exchanges. From *The Rock Garden* (1964) to *The Unseen Hand* (1969) his collages seemed to shy away from themes, only hinting at his future concerns—father-son relationships, the artist in a commercial society, the magnetism of wide-open spaces, the rebellion against authority.

A second group of plays starts with *La Turista* (1967), although Shepard continued to write residual collages. Blending popular and fantastic elements, Shepard gives more attention to plot and even elementary character development. In *La Turista*, a drama of sickness and spurious cures, Shepard draws upon film and advertisements, as he spurns exposition and resolution. In *Operation Sidewinder* (1970), a play commissioned by New York's Lincoln Center, he attempts to blend black talk, science fiction, military lingo, the argot of movie Indians, to bring about a grand finale of costumed dances, billowing breezes, and colored lights. *Mad Dog Blues* (1971) ends in comparable revels after a plot patterned on the movie *Treasure of the Sierra Madre*. All his characters are remarkably articulate in this period of devalued language, sometimes dueling with verbal riffs.

. Straddling the first and second Shepard groups are several plays about artists (never writers)—*Melodrama Play* (1967), *Mad Dog Blues* (1971), *Cowboy Mouth* (1971), *Tooth of Crime* (1973), *Angel City* (1976), and *Suicide in B Flat* (1976)—all thriving on various forms of fantasy. And yet he had already confessed in 1974: "I'd like to try a whole different way of writing now, which is very stark and not so flashy and not full of a lot of mythic figures and everything, and try to scrape it down to the bone as much as possible."

The effort resulted in five family plays of a third group, although Shepard himself has designated only the first three as a "family trilogy." *Curse of the Starving Class* (1976) dramatizes a disintegrating family on a Western avocado farm that falls prey to human predators. *Buried Child* (1978) unearths a literal skeleton buried on a Midwestern farm gone to seed, along with the

family potential. *True West* (1980) pits two brothers against one another—
Ivy League Austin and ne'er-do-well Lee in a competition to compose a
movie scenario about the true West. In this trilogy, as in O'Neill's *Mourning
Becomes Electra*, the playwright dramatizes a tragic America, wasteful of its
heritage and mired in acquisition, but Shepard does so in vividly imaged,
colloquial language.

Fool for Love (1983) and *A Lie of the Mind* (1986) penetrate more intensely
into man-woman relationships—the ecstasy, the cruelty, and the difficulty
of durability. The first of these (not improved by Shepard's own appearance in the movie version) portrays the stormy reunion of lovers, who are
also half-brother and -sister. Outside the realistic frame, their father is witness to their fabulations and recriminations. Finally, the son imitates the
father in his infidelity, but for the first time Shepard focuses dramatically
not on the father-son tension but on the pain of the woman.

Women dominate *A Lie of the Mind*, even though one is brain-damaged
and her mother somewhat feebleminded. They alone articulate the succor-
ing force of love. In his most intricate and populated drama (eight characters) Shepard juxtaposes two families, one shakily perched in California and
the other rooted in Montana, alternating the scenes between them. Some
two decades after the maladies and attempted cures of *La Turista*, Shepard
stages a slow recovery after murderous violence. A husband, having beaten
his actress wife nearly to death, is distraught with contrition. As her family
ineptly nurses her, his family attempts to aid him, and Shepard achieves
uncanny resonance from the virtually monosyllabic utterances of these earnest but ineffectual families. Finally, the play promises a new life in the
union of the injured woman and her husband's brother, in a search for the
Irish home of the California family, and in the ritual folding of the American flag by the Montana parents. The brilliance of the dramatization lies in
the simultaneity of the presentation, so that actions reflect across the divided stage. Thus, when the California mother sets fire to the house poi-
soned by the past, the Montana mother closes the play: "Looks like a fire
in the snow. How could that be?"

Unlike the range and rhythms of Shepard's plays is David Mamet's urban
economy. Born and brought up in Chicago, Mamet worked with the Second City group while still in his teens. He acquired further theater experience at Godard College and New York's Neighborhood Playhouse. Still
dabbling in theater, he had a series of odd and dull jobs, returning to Chicago in 1972. When *Sexual Perversity in Chicago* (1974) won that city's best-
play award, he decided that playwriting was his proper niche in the theater,
although he has continued to teach and direct.

From Mamet's earliest sketches to *Glengarry Glen Ross* (1984) he accumulates two-character scenes in which the words seem to reel in their own momentum—tripping over each other, repeating each other, sometimes hesitating and stumbling, often punctuated with casual obscenities, gnawing at decorum, and enunciating a half-baked philosophy. The words ooze out of little people under stress, and Mamet's contractions, ellipses, and tautologies impose a similarity on most of the speakers, whose milieu nevertheless differentiates them. (For an American playwright Mamet is surprisingly uninterested in the family, but like the major American playwrights he dramatizes men far more searchingly than women.)

Duck Variations (1971) announces the theme and method of a duet by two old men on a park bench. Other two-character plays dramatize the difficulties in a weekend affair, in a father's reunion with his adult daughter, in the juxtaposition of a rising young actor and his aging colleague. But two-character scenes build multi-character plays as well: *Sexual Perversity in Chicago* involves four young people in thirty-four variations on the theme of sex; *American Buffalo* (1975) shows three petty criminals planning a theft. Mamet is perhaps most ambitious in *The Water Engine* (1977), which presents a play within a 1930s radio play in order to indict the American business ethic. More obliquely critical of capitalism are *Lakeboat* (1981) and *Glengarry Glen Ross*, set in the world of real-estate speculation. In contrast, *Edmond* (1983) traces the disintegration of the titular character through a series of duologues. Around the limited articulations of his characters, straining toward ideals they can hardly imagine, Mamet weaves a tapestry in which the warp is compassion for the individual and the woof condemnation of a mercantile society—not unlike the young Arthur Miller in theme, but wholly new in rhythm.

The second half of twentieth-century American drama displays an unprecedented number of accomplished playwrights but relatively few memorable plays. Some remain in the memory, however, and I close by recalling their presence. Jack Gelber and Jean-Claude van Itallie were among the first dramtists to turn their backs on Broadway, and like so many others they are best known for early plays. Gelber's *Connection* (1957) is in some ways an old-fashioned play, like its cousin across the ocean, John Osborne's *Look Back in Anger* (1956), but it still speaks to young people looking for metaphoric connections. Historically, *The Connection* in a Living Theater production sparked the Off-Off-Broadway movement, with its disaffiliation, audience participation, racial mixture, drug tolerance, and intolerance of authority. Although the play has sentimental elements—good guys versus bad guys, suspense, happy ending—its text still projects the feeling of a dreamlike state. Within the Pirandellian frame of a movie about dope addicts, jazz riffs punctuate desultory conversations and disjunctive monologues that marry the realistic to the symbolic as performed by the aptly named *Living* Theater.

New York's Open Theater was at first an offshoot of the Living Theater, but its center was always actor growth. Jean-Claude van Itallie was the playwright most capable of scripting its actors' exercises, but it is his trilogy *America Hurrah* that chillingly caricatures aspects of American culture. *Motel* (1962), one of the plays of the trilogy, is performed by three actors wearing platform shoes and doll-masks three times the size of a human head. The Motel-Keeper doll is the first one on stage, replete with hair-curlers, mirror eyeglasses, and a nondescript gray dress; she immediately erupts into a stream of monologue, which is heard on voice-over. After a flash of headlights into the audience, the Man and the Woman—garish and silent dolls—enter the "anonymously modern" motel room. During the play, stage lights and voice grow continuously harsher. As folksy platitudes drone away on voice-over, violence invades the room. After the couple undress, they systematically and maniacally dismantle everything in sight, while the voice drawls imperturbably on. As rock music blares on television, and the voice-over recites comforting incongruities, the doll-couple scrawl obscenities on the walls, writhe in mock-copulation, smash what is left in the room, and tear the arms off the Motel-Keeper doll. Sirens and rock music drown out the voice, and headlights again blind the audience. The couple behead the Motel-Keeper, then walk indifferently and separately down the theater aisle and out of sight. By its counterpoint of platitudes and rampancy, *Motel* inscribes us in an American automobile association of mass-produced mediocrity, meaningless homilies, and gratuitous trashing.

Another intense and violent drama is Baraka's *Dutchman* (1964). Scantily dressed, munching an apple, white Lula takes a vacant subway seat next to well-dressed black Clay. First flirting, Lula abruptly lashes out at Clay: "I bet you never once thought you were a black nigger." In spite of her insults, however, Clay keeps cool, and by the second scene she is teasing him sexually. When she rises to dance in the now crowded subway car, when she jeers racially and sexually at his passivity, he slaps her "as hard as he can, across the mouth" and gives voice to murderous rage. The burden of his tirade is that blacks are forever unknowable to whites, and that precisely when the black man appears to be integrated into white society he will be most deadly. And yet, Clay does not kill Lula but reaches for his books to leave the subway, at which point Lula stabs him to death. On her orders, the subway passengers throw Clay's body out of the car. Another young black man enters and sits near Lula; they exchange looks.

At one level the play is realistic—familiar setting, plausible characters, understandable violence. But the language rises above and beyond realism. The play's title in a single word conveys a hereditary curse. The names of the characters suggest that black humanity is clay in the hands of the diabolic apple-munching temptress Lilith. But these are merely pointers to the mercurial journey "in the flying underbelly of the city." Urbane banter, timid probing, rapier insults, bullet interruptions accumulate into Clay's eloquent tirade—his unwitting swan song in American society. At once actual and archetypical, *Dutchman* sails closer home than the legendary Cape of Good Hope.

It is possible that all three of these plays that were performed Off-Broadway in the 1960s nourished Sam Shepard's *Tooth of Crime*, written in England in 1972. Like Gelber's *Connection*, Shepard's drama is dependent on music. Like van Itallie's *Motel*, it invents an idiom for larger-than-life figures. Like Baraka's *Dutchman*, it dramatizes a duel to the death. Like no other playwright, Shepard fuses the lexicons of rock, cowboys, crime, and sports into the dangerous weapons of his duelists—the reigning Hoss and the challenger Crow. A starkly simple set—a silver-studded, high-backed throne—supports Shepard's cosmic endgame.

The Tooth of Crime opens close to its crisis: Hoss needs a kill in "the game." He consults his Star-Man, who discourages him. He consults Galactic Jack, who offers shaky assurance. He consults his chauffeur Cheyenne, who demurs against violating "the code." Hoss is tempted by an alliance with Little Willard in the East, only to learn of his suicide. Doc's injection does not tranquilize Hoss, who reveals his full dread to his mistress-servant-tutor Becky. Alone on stage, Hoss bifurcates into a dialogue with his father: "They're all countin' on me. The bookies, the agents, the Keepers. I'm a fucking industry." Once Hoss accepts his father's reply—"You're just a man, Hoss. Just a man"—he can accept the challenge of Crow.

Their duel fills the second act of the drama, adjudicated by a Referee. In Round 1 Crow attacks Hoss with a capsule biography of a coward, and Ref awards the round to Crow. In Round 2 Hoss accuses Crow of denying his musical origins in the blues of black people, and Ref declares it a draw. In Round 3 Crow ridicules Hoss's outdated music and accuses him of stealing styles. The Ref calls it a T.K.O., so an infuriated Hoss shoots him. Having thus violated the code, Hoss automatically becomes a Gypsy, needing lessons in survival from Crow. In defeat, however, Hoss cannot learn to talk, walk, and sing as a Gypsy. He shoots himself, and the reign of Crow begins. His trail to the throne is strewn with the paradoxically lively language of a decaying culture.

In Mamet's *American Buffalo* that language is in a more advanced state of decay: the lexicon has shrunk, the obscenities are tautologies, and pleonasms are rife. But then we are privy, not to an agon of stars, but to the ponderous articulations of three petty criminals—Don, the owner of a junkshop; Bob, his young "gopher"; and Teach, his friend and would-be business associate. The frail plot is strung on the intended theft of a buffalo nickel from a customer who has bought it from Don, but the play's vigor resides in the foul-mouthed ethical imperatives that circle around shifting notions of business and friendship—finally indistinguishable. Mamet is evidently under the impression that his petty crooks are a synecdoche for American capitalism, but they are too ineffectual, affectionate, and unconsciously funny for that.

Adrienne Kennedy's title *A Movie Star Has to Star in Black and White* sounds like a covert plea for films of relevance to blacks as well as whites, but the play itself is a complex interweaving of black sorrows and selected scenes from three white movies. The thirty-three-year-old black protagonist Clara reflects on the accusation of her husband: "He thinks sometimes . . . to me my life is one of my black and white movies that I love so . . . with me playing a bit part." Although Clara is Kennedy's protagonist—and not a bit player—many of her words are spoken by the heroines of black-and-white movies. Clara's divorced parents are juxtaposed against the shipboard scene of *Now Voyager*, when Bette Davis and Paul Henreid fell in love. The quarrel of Clara's divorced parents at the hospital bedside of her comatose brother is juxtaposed against the wedding scene of *Viva Zapata*. A pregnant Clara's own divorce is paralleled by the scene from *A Place in the Sun* when Montgomery Clift stonily watches the drowning of a pregnant Shelley Winters. Although Clara speaks intermittently during the course of the play, it is only in the final scene in her own room that she emerges as a dramatist. With remarkable economy, Kennedy encompasses black history, family grief, feminine independence, and artistic integrity in this enfolding of film scenes into her drama.

And I conclude with a text by a playwright I have not yet mentioned— Lee Breuer. Better known as a director than as a dramatist, Breuer has published *Animations* (1979), a trilogy of plays as performed by the Mabou Mines theater group. *Sui generis*, Breuer is more literary than most visual artists, more visual than most writers, and more musical and technological than both. The printed text of *Hajj* (1983) divides almost equally between highly complex scenic directions and the single performer's monologue printed in block capital letters and punctuated only by periods, in Breuer's usual fashion. Back to us, the performer is seen through an architecture of mirrors. Closed-circuit television monitors her present associations, and taped sequences superimpose many images of her past. We slowly absorb her many textures as we hear her speak numbers, fractured quotations, puns, references to an Alex, a companion on a mysterious journey into a desolate unknown. The performer is actress, whore, child, adult, dervish, old man. In the final part of the performance, we hear of Alexander Lujak, who shot himself at age seventy-one, before his daughter could repay the sum she owed him—a symbolic and literal debt. In a final retrospect the daughter becomes her father: "WE'LL NEVER SORT EACH OTHER'S ATOMS OUT." Even in black-and-white print, we are sensitized to these myriad impressions of life's journey.

In theater of the second half of the century performances have sometimes emerged from fiction and documents. If, conversely, we are now offered performances to read, we never *will* sort each other's atoms out. And that, it seems to me, is all to the living good.

Ruby Cohn

Neorealist Fiction

The novelist, in his ideal character, is the artist who is consumed by the desire to know how things really are, who has entered into an elaborate romance with actuality. He is the artist of the conditioned, of the impingement of things upon spirit and of spirit upon things, and the success of his enterprise depends as much upon his awareness of things as upon his awareness of spirit.

Lionel Trilling, in *A Gathering of Fugitives* (1956)

Even now, the writers of many other countries begin to stand to their own past in a relation as uneasy as our own; and in our novel they find raised nakedly at last the question that underlay the experimentation of the 'twenties, the "social consciousness" of the 'thirties, the search for formal security of the 'forties: "Can the lonely individual, unsustained by tradition in an atomized society, achieve a poetry adult and complicated enough to be the consciousness of its age?" To have posed that question for the world is the achievement of the American novel at the moment.

Leslie Fiedler, in *An End to Innocence* (1955)

"The empire of signs is prose," wrote Jean-Paul Sartre in his philosophical and critical study *What Is Literature?* (1947), probably the most influential and compelling statement we have of the immediate postwar mood in literature. Sartre's book was, among other things, a celebration of prose as a literary medium, and it spoke to the belief that the crisis of signification that had been so marked a feature of modern and modernist writing was redeemable. "The war of 1914 precipitated a crisis of language," Sartre observed; "I would say that the war of 1940 has revalorized it." Half a century of modernism had challenged the tradition of literary realism and spoken of a crisis of the word. But in the wake of war, signs signified again, and through the path of purpose and commitment prose could reauthenticate itself, recover its denotative and representational functions.

The move toward the recovery of realism that marked Sartre's writing was, like his assertion of a potential recovery of humanism, tentative. But it expressed an attitude—one of revolt both against the obscurities of literary modernism and against the more naïve political commitments of the 1930s—that affected the fortunes of the novel internationally in the years after World War II. The most obvious examples were in those European countries that had faced the war directly, seen their political systems collapse, their cities destroyed, their countries occupied and perhaps defeated. In a France tainted by the Occupation and the history of intellectual collaboration, Sartre himself, along with Albert Camus, pointed the novel toward an existentialist realism. In a Germany where not only wartime defeat but the burning of books and the pressure of party propaganda had silenced literary honesty, the writers who gathered in 1947 to form Gruppe 47 saw as their essential task the cleansing of the world and the revealing of the fact. In an Italy that had likewise suffered defeat, the dominant postwar tendency was a new neorealism that responded both to the political distortions of wartime and the poverty and social disorder that followed it. In a Britain that, though victorious, had experienced terrible bombings and a steady fear of totalitarianism, and was now undergoing a major social change toward the welfare state just at the same time that it was beginning to lose its world-role, the need to record and express a new historical situation from a new social and political standpoint was strongly felt by literary intellectuals. And it was the note of authenticity sounded by George Orwell—who throughout the war had been warning of the threatened collapse of the liberal-realist novel and its replacement by a new form of totalitarian writing that was "scarcely imaginable"—that led the way in the discovery of a new voice for a new generation.

In the more convenient histories of literature it often seems that the literary and artistic history of the twentieth century can be written in two large strokes: there was modernism, and then in due time there was postmodernism. It is a history that misleads and abbreviates, for throughout the century there has been, in the line of the novel, a sustaining and powerful history of realism, along with a sequence of persistent and various disputes with its veracity, its philosophical possibility, its relevance. Virtually no work that asserts itself as antithetical to realism does not contain it as a primary constituent, and most of the major movements that have been regarded as essentially antirealist have argued that they are in effect a *form* of realism—as, for example, Alain Robbe-Grillet has argued with regard to the *nouveau roman*. If the fictionalist and nominalist emphasis that has persisted through fiction from the second half of the nineteenth century—as Roland Barthes has suggested, the rise of the quarrel with realistic representation in literature in fact begins *within* the movement that called itself realism—had made innocent representation problematical in the modern novel, that has not prevented our modern novelists from claiming the rights of verisimilitude, reportorial representation, and mimesis when the occasion arises. If we live in an age of what Robert Alter calls "the self-aware novel," which is "a consistent effort to convey to us a sense of the fictional world as an authorial construct set up against a background of literary tradition and convention," we also live in a time when the oppressive power of history and the obligation of the writer to attend to the realities of political power and force, human outrage and human terror, and the pressures that assault the imagination in the interest of their own larger fictions have never been greater. "The contemporary writer who is acutely in touch with the life of which he is a part is forced to start from scratch," Ronald Sukenick tells us in his aptly named *The Death of the Novel and Other Stories* (1969). "Reality doesn't exist, personality doesn't exist. . . ," and yet the task depends on the acknowledgment that there is a life of which we are a part. Like most modern empires, Sartre's empire of signs has been in much disarray, and the crisis of signification he hoped to overcome through the commitment to reality and society he saw engrained in prose has been widely questioned. And just as the dispute with Sartre has been central to the evolution of those areas of philosophical and linguistic theory we call structuralism and deconstruction, so the fate and future of the empire of signs has been crucial to the recent history of fictional prose. Yet in complex modern literary conceptions, like that of "magical realism," we see the insistent pressure of the realist case within the fictionalist anxiety, and we could well say that it is out of this tension that much of the history of the recent novel has been made.

In this history, the revival of realism that came in the postwar years was no minor event, but rather part of the attempt of many of the most significant figures of a generation successor to modernism to articulate the purpose and direction of the novel form in an era that followed on, not only from modernism itself, but also from the holocaust, the coming of the nuclear age, the global political conflict developing between totalitarianism and liberalism, or communism and capitalism; and it came out of the new need felt among many writers to function authoritatively as intellectuals in an era where intellectual life had recently been repressed and was still threatened. The multiple heritages of realism—a term that means many things—had in no way died in twentieth-century Western fiction, for all the images of artifice and counterfeit, of self-conscious fictionality and parodic enterprise that had marked the development of modernism. In the United States there was a powerful tradition of naturalism that reached back to the late nineteenth century, when that movement from Europe became firmly rooted in what Alfred Kazin, in an important book of 1941 on American fictional realism, called "native grounds." The intellectual revival of ideas of realism in the later 1940s and 1950s had, indeed, a strong critical foundation. Erich Auerbach's remarkable book *Mimesis: The Representation of Reality in Western Literature*, written, as a note tells us, in Istanbul between May 1942 and April 1945, then published in Berne in 1946 and in the United States in 1953, was an extraordinary study of the representational, the instinct toward the motif of the real, in literary art. In Britain, F. R. Leavis's study *The Great Tradition* (1948) argued that the central lineage in the tradition of the English novel was that of social and moral realism. In the United States Lionel Trilling's influential collection of essays *The Liberal Imagination* (1950) expressed a similar mood.

Trilling's book represented a revolt against the ideological certainties of the 1930s, and he saw the postwar need as being for what he called a sense of "variousness and possibility." For this he looked to literature and especially the novel, the form that, invested with the spirit of realism, saw in the social world the multiplicity and variety, the contradiction and hypocrisy, the complexity of the experiental and the real that lay beyond system and ideology. "The novel, then, is a perpetual quest for reality," he wrote in a key essay, "Manners, Morals, and the Novel," "the field of its research being always the social world, the material of its analysis being always manners as the indication of the direction of man's soul." But, he also added, "the novel as I have described it has never really established itself in America." In saying this Trilling was expressing another familiar critical assumption of the time that was to be more fully asserted a little later in two other notable studies, Richard Chase's *The American Novel and Its Tradition* (1957) and Leslie Fiedler's *Love and Death in the American Novel* (1960), both of which argued the case for a distinctive American fictional tradition, suggesting that because of its lack of established manners and the mythical basis of its history America had developed a countertradition of fiction, characterized by a commitment to "romance" and the "gothic." Today this emphasis is likely to seem overstated, if only because it takes too literally the claim that the dominant European tradition in fiction had been a realistic one, and underestimates the powerful impact that realism and naturalism had had in the American tradition.

Nonetheless the mythic and romantic impulse of American fiction, even during the period of naturalism, does seem to distinguish it from a good part of European fiction, long attentive as it had been to what Trilling called "the hum and buzz of culture" and above all to the detailed processes of history. Historical process has played a far more powerful part in American fiction than many of its critics have acknowledged, as indeed Philip Rahv pointed out in an essay, "The Myth and the Powerhouse," published in *Partisan Review* in 1953, where he noted the fashionable prevalence of myth-criticism and a critical taste for detaching literature from history, Stephen Dedalus's "nightmare from which I am trying to awake." Like Trilling, who published in the same magazine, Rahv was calling American writers to a social and cultural concern and to a recognition of the Nietzschean "sixth sense," an awareness of history and historicism, of power and process. And indeed, supported by such arguments, by the emphasis of Sartre, and by the pressure of recent historical events, American writers of what Sartre called the "third generation" of the century seemed to be drawn toward a more profound historical attention. When R. W. B. Lewis looked round for the novelists of the immediate postwar generation in America, this was precisely what he noted: "It is as though these novelists, and the characters they create, have been shaken loose by the amount and the violence of the history America has passed through (America, it must be remembered, has until late been unaccustomed to history)."

The climate of recovered realism that passed through Western fiction in the years immediately after the war thus had its impact in the United States too. For there was a "third generation" of writers appearing, and growing in numbers and in quality as the 1940s turned into the 1950s. By this time one of the most powerful and remarkable of generations in the modern American novel was coming toward the end of its production. F. Scott Fitzgerald and Nathanael West died within a few days of each other in 1940, Sherwood Anderson died in 1941, Gertrude Stein in 1945. Hemingway, Faulkner, Dos Passos, and Steinbeck continued to write, and indeed three of these won Nobel Prizes in the postwar years. But their work, which in the 1920s and 1930s had transformed the modern conception of the novel, did not have the same impact in the postwar mood. Faulkner's late trilogy *The Hamlet* (1941), *The Town* (1957), and *The Mansion* (1959) was an important addition to the Yoknapatawpha sequence, but his late ambitious work about World War I, *A Fable* (1954), was an impressive failure. Hemingway's later work showed his modern manner hardening into a kind of carapace, and *The Old Man and the Sea* (1952) was a sentimental myth. Dos Passos could not repeat the triumph of *U.S.A.* with *Mid-Century* (1961), nor Steinbeck that of *The Grapes of Wrath* in his later novels. The achievement of these writers was remarkable; they had explored the essential passages of the earlier part of the century—from country to city, mythic pastoral to modern irony, national self-preoccupation to a larger awareness of international processes. They had drawn the potential of naturalism onward toward a modernism that seemed comfortably appropriate to twentieth-century American experience, and had constructed a modern, experimental tradition of American fiction. But their writing seemed to some degree detached from the new postwar world, with its sense of historical disaster, of changed destiny, of nuclear threat, accumulating mass society, growing materialism, and technological transformation.

The kind of fiction the postwar world called for was a matter of substantial discussion in the late 1940s and the 1950s. There were critics who compared the situation with that after World War I, when the "lost generation" of novelists established a new experimental era, and found themselves disappointed. John Aldridge in *After the Lost Generation* (1951), Malcolm Cowley in *The Literary Situation* (1954), considered that the great flowering of modern fiction was now over, and that the new American novel, like postwar American life, was gray, conventional, and conformist, lacking an avant-garde energy and an intellectual excitement. The notion that the world of material reward and of an urbanized and suburbanized new social order was dulling the instincts of art and generating an age of dull conformity was pursued both by the sociologists who analyzed the new era of American life in books like David Riesman's *The Lonely Crowd* (1953) and William H. Whyte's *The Organization Man* (1955), and in literary criticism. "Let us assume for a moment that we have reached the end of one of those recurrent periods of cultural unrest, innovation and excitement we call 'modern,' " wrote Irving Howe in an essay of 1959 notable not only for its argument but also for its use of a significant word, "postmodern." Howe argued, in "Mass Society and Post-Modern Fiction," that the age of the avant-garde and of radical modernity was itself at an end. And, using the term "postmodern" in a sense significantly different from that which was to develop later, he wrote of "postmodern fiction" as the fiction of modern mass-society, "a relatively comfortable, half-welfare and half-garrison society in which the population grows passive, indifferent and atomized." This was a situation inhibiting to the arts, which could only convey "the hovering sickness of soul, the despairing contentment, the prosperous malaise" of the postwar American spirit in a new time when the old anxieties of the age of the Great Depression were over, but the depressions of the age of anxiety had begun. Encouraged by the global threat from without and the new cohesion within, Americans indeed seemed to have entered an age of corporatism and conformity that required no avant-garde, expected no bohemia, sought the support of its intellectuals, and suspected many of their functions. For Howe it was modernism that had faced reality and historical responsibility. The new novel developing among the important writers of the postwar generation—Saul Bellow, J. D. Salinger, Bernard Malamud, Norman Mailer, Herbert Gold, Nelson Algren, Wright Morris—was the disoriented fiction of such a society, and, said Howe, it was in "their distance from fixed social categories and their concern with the metaphysical implications of this distance" that such writers "constitute what I would call 'post-modern' fiction."

Howe's obvious difficulty of defining the character of what evidently was a new mood in American fiction was to be shared by most of the critical commentators, and that fact is all too evident now if we look back over studies of the time that attempted to define the main trends that now developed. What was the direction of the new American novel in the age of consumerism and conformity, mass and modernity, suburbia and superpower? For Edmund Fuller, in his study *Man in Modern Fiction* (1958), the predominant image was one of alienation, philosophical and social, of dissolving images of the individual in a mass age, so that he was portrayed as "an ironic biological accident, inadequate, aimless, meaningless. . . . His uniqueness as a person is denied or suppressed. He inhabits a hostile universe." For Ihab Hassan, in *Radical Innocence* (1961), the main spirit at work was one of radical recovery, as the postwar writing generated a new image of the hero, "extreme, impulsive, anarchic, troubled with vision," an aboriginal self who refuses to accept the immitigable rule of reality. For Marcus Klein, in *After Alienation* (1964), the image of the alienated self that had dominated the darker aspects of modernism was in fact amended in postwar American fiction, and its general spirit was that of the desire to transcend alienation and reach a new accommodation, in forms cautious and oblique, comic and often absurd. For Nathan A. Scott, examining three of the major figures who seemed central to the temper of the time, Norman Mailer, Saul Bellow, and Lionel Trilling, in *Three American Moralists* (1973), the age both of *kulturkampf* and prudence that came after the war brought a new moral emphasis to fiction, a hunger to overcome despair and brutality through applying moral energy to culture.

Such critical differences of emphasis are entirely understandable, given the enormous variety of the new writers who were now emerging in the United States, the lack of a certain tradition or tendency, and the very degree of tension and contradiction that was to be embodied in the fiction that came from the American "third generation." Most of these studies recognize a general literary temper that has been shaped and forged by the transformations of the modern psyche brought about by World War II, when the impact of the Jewish holocaust and the dropping of the atomic bomb on Japan at the war's end, this to be followed by a new geopolitical map in which the United States and the Soviet Union faced each other as hostile and antithetical superpowers, changed moral, intellectual, political, and historical consciousness. They acknowledge the massive impact of the existentialist revolution in thought that radiated out of Paris in the postwar years, with its burden of anxiety, its consciousness of modern nihilism, its hunger for moral recovery. They see the decline both of the experimental joy that had fun through the modernism of the early century, and of the political and ideological certainties that had given a sense of urgency and commitment to the more realistic writing of the 1930s. They acknowledge the dominant spirit of what came to be called the "new liberalism," that view of the world that could itself be called "realistic," a view invested with the tragic awareness both of political and historical skepticism and the desire for transcendent certainties, with the sense of history as stain and taint and with the need for a skeptical recovery. This, of course, was the spirit expressed in Arthur M. Schlesinger's influential book *The Vital Center* (1949), where he said:

Today, finally and tardily, the skeptical insights are in process of restoration to the liberal mind. The psychology of Freud has renewed the intellectual's belief in the dark, slumbering forces of the will. The theology of Barth and Niebuhr has given a new power to old and chastening truths of Christianity. More than anything else, the rise of Hitler and Stalin has revealed in terms no one can deny the awful reality of human impulses toward aggrandizement and destruction.

If, as Irving Howe commented, "moral musings" rather than political and historical certainties seemed to be the order of the day in intellectual life and in what Lionel Trilling saw as its strongest ally, the novel, then we can see that there is indeed a connection between ideas of fictional realism and the "new liberalism." That, of course, was what Trilling looked to in his criticism, which used as its habitual model of the writer what he called "the opposing self," the self that is romantically at odds with culture yet, acknowledging a larger humanism, is forced to compromise with it. As he said in an essay on Freud, it was Freud who put the essential modern question—"whether or not we want to *accept* civilization, . . . with all its contradictions." He also suggested that Freud put the essential answer: "We do well to accept it, though we also do well to cast a cold eye on the fate that makes it our better part to accept it."

That "cold eye" seemed to have much to do with the spirit of postwar fiction, in the United States and throughout much of the West. For Trilling literature spoke to the double sense of life, in an age beyond utopia, ideology, and political certainty. Above all it was the novel that was the key form of the necessary imagination, its power lying in its "moral realism," its sense of life as lived in complexity, contingency, and actuality. Hence the American fiction of the period from the end of the war and into the early 1960s was notably marked by its sense of distinctive historical tensions, in which the contrary claims of opposition and engagement, alienation and accommodation, an isolated self and a massed social system, a comically absurd individual struggling to make existential sense of an anarchic and terrible process of history, combine and recombine. The pressure of history, the sense of necessity, the hunger both to differentiate and reunite the self and the society, allow for a strong apprehension of reality in such fiction. Yet the spirit of realism was not quite that of the historical tradition. It was not the normative realism of the middle of the nineteenth century, where in a dense and historical social world individual purposes are amended toward the Whiggish promise of society and history. It was not the realism of manners and social institutions that, as Henry James argued, gave "solidity of specification" to aesthetic and moral apprehension. It was not the deterministic, necessitarian realism that is called naturalism, and has indeed played a large part in the American fictional tradition, from Crane and Norris to Dreiser and Steinbeck. It was not the reportorial muckraking realism of Jack London or Upton Sinclair, working like journalists to be there and discover the hard fact of American life. It was not the urgent and often ideologically committed political realism of some writers of the 1930s, from Michael Gold to James Farrell.

Realism is indeed a term that is constantly rearguing itself into existence, and Sartre's "empire of signs" was forged from the preoccupations of an age, one in which the endeavor was made to draw humanist conclusions from potentially totalitarian situations, moral assessment for a world of Cold War ideology, what was now called "the tragic sense of life" from a time that seemed to assert optimism in every advertising slogan and joy in every bottle of Pepsi. It was a realism that, as Philip Roth said in a famous essay of 1961, "Writing American Fiction," attempted to deal with and make credible an American reality that "stupefies, . . . sickens, . . . infuriates, and finally . . . is a kind of embarrassment to one's own meagre imagination. The actuality is continually outdoing our talents." It was also a realism that, as Saul Bellow complained in his essay "Some Notes on Recent American Fiction" (1963), expressed "the pressure of a vast public life, which may dwarf [the writer] as an individual while permitting him to be a giant in hatred or fantasy." Hence the novel is deprived of the dense private life once thought essential to it, and the liberal equation of realistic fiction becomes almost impossible to realize. In *Herzog* (1964) Bellow mocks the "reality-instructors" who seek to impose this as truth, while himself representing the psychic crisis of a modern historical individual who does seriously attempt, morally and intellectually, to assess his own time. It was little wonder that critics could read this realistic spirit both as negative and affirmative, consider it both as representation and apocalyptic imagining, and see it, as in fact we see most novels, as both realistic and fictive.

The American novel that developed after 1945 was in many ways different from the work of its immediate predecessors, not least in its break away from the large mythic landscapes and the pastoralizing tendencies that had had so much power even in the novel of American modernism. If we want origins for it, we are likely to go back to the immigrant, ethnic, and regional traditions that had been developing behind the dominant work of Hemingway, Faulkner, Fitzgerald, or Dos Passos, the tradition of Jewish-American fiction that had grown through Abraham Cahan, Michael Gold, and Henry Roth, for example, the tradition of black fiction that had developed through Paul Laurence Dunbar and Richard Wright, or the tradition of Southern fiction that had grown with Ellen Glasgow, William Faulkner, Robert Penn Warren, and the Southern Agrarians. We are likely to observe the way the tradition of urban realism and naturalism had quarreled with the pastoral version of America in writers like Dreiser and Farrell, and the way the tradition of urban international modernism had been sustained in such metropolitan and political venues as *Partisan Review*, out of which a significant number of the new writers came. But we are also likely to note how strongly oriented the newer writers were to literary developments in Europe, for the tendency of realism, particularly a realism with strongly existentialist and absurdist overtones, was a Western phenomenon in the late wartime and postwar years. As in contemporary European writing, what was being called realism was asserted less as a politics than a morality, less as a report than a contemporary vision. It was the voice of a humanism desperately seeking to recover itself after an era of totalitarianism, of a concern with a historical situation struggling to establish itself after an era of myth.

In many ways the fiction written in America in the postwar years was a fiction far more "alienated" than that being written in Europe, certainly in Britain, but even in France, where the absurdist vision was far more philosophical than social. If humanism, moralism, and an attendant realism seemed everywhere returning to the spirit of fiction, then American fiction seemed especially preoccupied with human existence fighting for its selfhood in an era of modern mass and power, and for its attempt to distill some form of connectedness and civility from the pressures of ideology, historicism, and the sense of human victimization in a time tainted by totalitarian pressures and forces. The international impact of American fiction had much to do with this vision, as Saul Bellow was ironically to observe. He noted, in the essay "Some Recent Notes on American Fiction," that where the sense of the defeated Self was strong in European writing also, this was as a result of new philosophical, physiological, and psychological theories. "American writers, when they are moved by a similar spirit to reject and despise the Self, are seldom encumbered by such intellectual baggage, and this fact pleases their European contemporaries, who find in them a natural, that is, a brutal or violent acceptance of the new universal truth by minds free from intellectual preconceptions," he added, suggesting the need to struggle against the new intellectual preconception. But the impact of the contemporary European tradition seems everywhere present in Bellow's own work, as in that of many of his immediate contemporaries. It was, essentially, the tradition of historical modernism, that aspect of modernist writing that had confronted the anguish of modern history, and of which writers like Dostoevsky, Conrad, Musil, Kafka, Sartre, and Camus were exemplary cases.

There is good reason for taking Bellow's own first novel, *Dangling Man* (1944), as a major starting place for the new mood. The story of an aimless man awaiting his wartime induction into the American army, in an urban, hostile Chicago in the winter of 1942, it evidently owes much to Sartre's prewar novel *La Nausée* as well as to the tradition of modernism going back to Dostoevsky. Joseph, the central character, is a modern underground man, a diary-keeper experiencing inner withdrawal and disintegration as his familiar world breaks down, as old political orientations and commitments collapse, and as the real life outside empties of significance. His dreadful freedom is finally canceled at the end of the book in an ending of great ambiguity; his army papers come and, crying "Long live regimentation!,", he enters the army in a complex compromise of existentialism and force that might, indeed, be called a kind of moral realism. It is the realism that Norman Mailer fails to consent to in *The Naked and the Dead* (1948), a novel that is in part devoted to a naturalist version of wartime experience on service in the Pacific, but also to the accumulating totalitarianism of the military machine and the defeat of liberal opposition to it. The army machine becomes an image of the future, and Mailer himself looks toward existentialist solutions, both in this book and, far more systematically, in the novels that were to follow as he explored postwar American culture, politics, and sexuality. "He asked himself a question I still would like answered, namely, 'How should a good man lie; what ought he to do?,' " Bellow's Joseph asks himself, and we can see that need to discover the human measure in a harsh and victimizing world growing as a key theme in Bellow's work. His next novel was called, indeed, *The Victim* (1947), and it explores in a hot, naturalistic New York in which everyone is in Darwinian competition the complex path toward a sense of human responsibility that the Jewish Asa Leventhal discovers links him to a Gentile oppressor, Albee, who comes to appear a victim like himself. Bellow does retrieve from a deterministic and necessitarian world a humanistic moral bond, and thereafter his fiction enlarges in scope and flamboyance. Yet through to the present its themes remain; the massing of cities, the apocalyptic dreams that run through culture, the vain material and spiritual hungers of the artificial self, the growth of the "it" and the pressure on the "we." The ethical and metaphysical texture of Bellow's writing habitually takes it beyond any conventional account of realism, and its intellectual heritage is vast, relating its vision to the tradition of Western thought through the romantic and the modernist revolutions. Bellow's humanistic questions, which have grown ever more transcendental, still show all the pressure of the age. And if he has chosen to assert his resistance to the fictional tradition of the *nouveau roman* and insist that the novel is a hovel in which the human spirit takes shelter, this is surely not in the interests of defending a naïve or a reportorial realism.

Bellow's central role in the postwar American novel, confirmed in his well-deserved Nobel Prize, evidently owes much to a double heritage that related a strong body of modernist concerns (he evokes many of these in the early part of *Humboldt's Gift* [1975]) with a tradition of Jewish humanist responsibility. He shared this with many other writers of his time, including Lionel Trilling himself, who, in some telling phrases in his late book *Sincerity and Authenticity* (1972), wrote of the dangers of the mind that neglects the celebration of the real, that avoids "the inconvenience of undertaking to intercede, of being a sacrifice, of reasoning with rabbis, of making sermons, of having disciples, of going to weddings and to funerals, of beginning something and at a certain point remarking that it is finished." Bellow is a novelist of those intercessions, those debates with rabbis, those weddings and funerals, and that urgent postwar sense of being a survivor of the holocaust and a necessary witness in the modern world; and this he shared with a good many contemporaries, including fellow Jewish writers like Trilling, Bernard Malamud, and Philip Roth, for whom those rabbis were also real. Trilling published his own novel, *The Middle of the Journey* (1947), a book that lacks Bellow's panache but seriously tackles the intellectual inheritance from the 1930s and the nature of moral realism. Concerned with the attraction of communism for American intellectuals in the 1930s and 1940s, and hence, as he said later, "committed to history," it tackles political life from the point of view of the moral imperatives that might lead us into it. When its central character, John Laskell, reaches the middle of his life's journey he finds himself in the dark wood of serious illness. Afterward his friends seek to lead him back into the great abstract ideas of the world, History, Faith, Communism, Capitalism, history as process and politics as necessity. Laskell realizes that they ignore the moral contemplation of being, the mortal fact of death, the personal nature of pain, the specificities of suffering. And, in an ending of exemplary moral realism, Laskell finds himself somewhere in the middle of things, this side of apocalyptic history, and he comes to the liberal pluralism that accepts the complexity of life, the intractibility of experience, the bulky shapelessness of reality. It is a fable *of* realism, told through the means of realism, an expression of the ambiguity of human nature in the age after Auschwitz, a celebration of the liberal imagination of and in the novel.

Yet this is in part why Trilling's book seems—like some other very important postwar novels, from the work of, say, John Cheever and John Updike to that of Mary McCarthy or Alison Lurie—to recover realism's classic tradition, rather than develop a new one. In fact, the convention has proved remarkably various, even within the careers of individual writers themselves. We can read in many of these writers a tense motion toward contingency and civility; in the early fictions of John Updike, that expert, mannered recorder of the containments of the 1950s and then of the emotional explosions of the 1960s, the great explorer of the world not of weddings and funerals but marriages and divorces; in the vivid personal force of J. D. Salinger's *The Catcher in the Rye* (1951), where the vernacular realism of Holden Caulfield, that modern Huck Finn, undermines hypocrisy, venality, and squalor through a plainspoken language of innocence; in the Jewish-American fiction of Bernard Malamud, which moved from the mythic underpinning of *The Natural* (1952) to the moral realism of *The Assistant* (1957). Yet realism often seems a ritual of redemptive form laid over chaos, and many of these writers have claimed the right to a freedom from it. John Cheever, a writer who seemed firmly anchored in the *New Yorker* school of the fiction of reported manners, wrote in later life the extraordinary, fantastic *Falconer* (1977). Mary McCarthy's fiction, in some ways associated, like much good modern American writing, with the same school, has a reportorial instinct but a very cold eye, an instinct for complex ironies. Updike, often seen as the most realistic of all the remarkable new novelists who emerged in the generation just after the war, claimed the mythic freedoms of *The Centaur* (1963) and the imaginative, imaginary scope of *The*

Coup (1979). Indeed, his remarkable stylistic precision has always been seeded with painterly aesthetic effects, and his realism can be said at the most to have the quality he identifies in his writer-hero Henry Bech, a concern with "a tightness perhaps equivalent to the terribly tight knit of reality." J. D. Salinger's fiction after *The Catcher in the Rye* came more and more to assert the fictionality present in it, rendering fragile and mysterious the things of the real to the point where they and the writing itself tailed off altogether. Even the works of the "New Journalists," such as Tom Wolfe and John McPhee, often cross this borderline.

What has come to be thought of as the climate of a new realism hence included much. There was a revival of the naturalist novel as an instrument for dealing with the recent horrors of wartime and the postwar pressures of the modern urban jungle, in books that ranged from Willard Motley's *Knock on Any Door* (1947) to Mailer's *The Naked and the Dead* (1948), Nelson Algren's *The Man with the Golden Arm* (1949) to James Jones's *From Here to Eternity* (1951). There was the revival of the Jewish-American novel, the black novel, the immigrant novel, though their move to center-stage suggested a deep disquiet hidden in contemporary American life, and in them the sense of existential crisis, an awareness of absurdity and nihilism, made them realism of a new kind. Richard Wright's black novel *The Outsider* (1950) signaled this with an existentialist title, as did Ralph Ellison's *Invisible Man* (1952), with its bleak and disturbing message of being written out of culture, and its Dostoevskian overtones: "Who knows but that, on the lower frequencies, I speak for you?" The tradition passed on to James Baldwin and the black novel of the later 1950s, which speaks as much to the sense of human exile and displacement as it does to the world of historical and social facts. Indeed, only rarely was this new neorealism a way of domesticating and familiarizing the world, as was so often the case in nineteenth-century realistic fiction; rather it was a search for a vision that could relate an oppressed response to society and history to an awareness of individual loneliness, moral and transcendental hunger, and which in its quest for the reality of moral and existential existence often reached extremity or despair.

Similar disturbances were apparent in the strong tradition of Southern fiction that developed at the same time, mixing the lineage of the gothic and the grotesque with a strong sense of evil and human pain. Books like Carson McCuller's *The Heart Is a Lonely Hunter* (1940) and *The Member of the Wedding* (1946), Eudora Welty's *A Curtain of Green* (1941) and *Delta Wedding* (1946), Truman Capote's *Other Voices, Other Rooms* (1948), Flannery O'Connor's *Wise Blood* (1952), and Walker Percy's *The Moviegoer* (1961): these novels and others, often of displacement, human disablement, and distorted innocence, not only explored the postwar South but were touched with that "tragic sense of life" that indeed marked much of the fiction of the time. Many are finely and graciously written, and they constitute an important tradition, but it is one where in regional, small-town, or often rural settings the disquiet of American culture is expressed as strongly as in the metropolitan and urban fiction that largely dominated in the period. Like the urban novels, they went beyond the sense of rural innocence and pastoral promise that had once been strong in American writing, and that belonged in the postwar world of what J. D. Salinger called "love and squalor." A sense of the extremity of reality marks most of the American fiction of the postwar world, and it is not surprising that the tradition of realism came increasingly to question itself, and to be questioned. The fantastic and gothic, the absurdist and the self-consciously fictive, those elements that came to be viewed as the constituents of the writing we today identify as "postmodern" were already there in the fiction of the 1940s and the 1950s. John Hawkes had published his first hyper-Gothic novel, *The Cannibal*, as early as 1949. William Gaddis produced his large novel of art as counterfeiting, *The Recognitions*, in 1955, the same year that Vladimir Nabokov published, in Paris, his crucial novel *Lolita*. Jack Kerouac's "Beat" novel *On the Road* came out in 1957, the year of Norman Mailer's essay "The White Negro," celebrating the existentialist "hipster"; William S. Burroughs's *The Naked Lunch*, with its cut-up, fold-in method, appeared, also in Paris, in 1959. Out of the apparently realistic conventions of the 1940s and 1950s a new emphasis, a new spirit of absurdism, black humor, and hyper-fictionality, was emerging.

"Men have learned to live with a black burden, a huge aching hump: the supposition that 'reality' may only be a dream," wrote Nabokov, in his novel *The Real Life of Sebastian Knight*, as early as 1941. "How much more dreadful it would be if the very awareness of your being aware of reality's dream-like nature were also a dream, a built-in hallucination." Nabokov, like Beckett and Borges, was born in the world of modernism and its anti-realist skepticism, and he was, like the other two writers, to translate this into the American fiction of the 1960s, which reasserts as well as disputes with many of the presumptions of earlier modernism. Indeed, the postmodernism that is often identified as peculiarly American owes much to the founding influence of these three writers born outside it; but they exercised a peculiar and distinctive impact there, bringing home to its always disputed tradition of the novel that sense of pervasive skepticism, of sharpened absurdity and narcissistic self-awareness that has led us to see the novel as the testing ground of language's power of nomination. The new sense of fictionality that dominated the 1960s and helped change the direction of the novel did not avoid history; indeed it implicated it, both in its form as historiography and in any claim we might make for it to transcend language or fictionality, disputing the entire area of reportage—so that Norman Mailer could appropriately subtitle his novel/non-novel *The Armies of the Night*, in 1968, "History as a Novel, The Novel as History," compounding the paradox of all forms of literary referentiality.

So, like criticism and philosophy at the time, the novel found itself amidst the failing empire of signs, bearing its burden of slippage, its lexical crisis, its sense of the displaced relation between the sign and what it sought to signify. For a period this seemed to mark the virtual end of serious literary realism, though throughout the "postmodern" phase the tension between realism and the metafictional paradox remained: and not only between the postmodern novel and more conventional forms, but *within* the metatexts themselves—in Barth, in Vonnegut, in Pynchon, in Hawkes, in Coover. If realism grew more skeptical, if its philosophical support in existentialism faded in the era of structuralism and deconstruction, if the tradition of the *lisible* gave way to the rising tradition of the *scriptible*, it still held onto a claim, the claim that fiction possesses to intensify and extend the sense of life as we live it, the claim that it also possesses to intervene in society and history. And indeed, from the 1970s onward, a new neorealism, minimalized and self-examining, has grown up again, in the very various work of writers like Walter Abish, Raymond Carver, Joyce Carol Oates, Toni Morrison, Robert Stone, Richard Ford, and more. If there has been, for our postwar generations, warfare in the Empire of Signs, there is also every sign, as we survey contemporary fiction both in the United States and elsewhere, that the Empire can indeed strike back.

Malcolm Bradbury

Self-Reflexive Fiction

Writing about self-reflexive fiction in the mid-1980s, one could say, with a sigh of relief, at last "we got rid of it," we have come to the end of this troublesome, irritating, exasperating form of narrative. But if self-reflexive fiction is finished, if we are finished with its gimmicks, its playfulness, its narcissism, nonetheless one should ask: What have we learned from it? In what sense has self-reflexiveness made the writing of fiction more interesting and perhaps even more potent? To what extent have the interrogations of self-reflexivity liberated the novel from certain obsolete conventions? And furthermore, to what extent has self-reflexiveness now been incorporated into the fiction of the 1980s, and as such been rendered acceptable and even marketable?

While self-reflexive fiction was playing its tricks during the past two decades, insisting on drawing the reader into the confidence that the text was the only reality (not a mirror-image, but an image of itself), most critics were quick to point out that there was nothing new in that, that it had all been done before, and inevitably sent the self-reflexive fictioneer (tail between his legs) back to *Tristram Shandy* or other such "preposterous" novels of the eighteenth century that had used and abused self-reflexive and self-conscious techniques, to good or bad purpose. And surely the history of the novel would be incomplete and incomprehensible without such novels as *Tristram Shandy* or Denis Diderot's *Jacques le Fataliste*, to mention only two of these so-called preposterous novels.

Certainly self-reflexiveness and self-consciousness are not new in the novel. They are not inventions of the 1960s and 1970s. In fact, all works of fiction are ultimately about themselves, about their process of coming into being and maintaining existence. That much any careful reader of fiction knows. Whether self-reflecting or simply reflecting, a work of fiction continually turns back on itself and draws the reader into itself as a text, as an ongoing narration, and before the reader knows what is happening, the text is telling him about itself. That is the fundamental truth of all fiction: it is always *implicitly* reflexive. The self-reflexive text, however, is one that *explicitly* concerns itself with the process of narration, with writing, with composition.

"In this matter of writing," Herman Melville states at the beginning of Chapter IV of *Billy Budd,* "resolve as one may to keep to the main road, some bypaths have an enticement not readily to be withstood. I am going to err into such a bypath. If the reader will keep me company I shall be glad. At least we can promise ourselves that pleasure which is wickedly said to be in sinning, for a literary sin the divergence will be."

At various moments in the history of literature, the novel commits "the sin of divergence" whenever it needs to reaffirm its course; consequently self-reflexiveness becomes more explicit, more overt, and of course less subtle when the novel tries to extricate itself from an exhausted context in order to establish itself into a new context. But whatever it does, narration is always fascinated by the telling of the tale. This begins with Cervantes's *Don Quixote,* it is present in the great work of Rabelais, *Gargantua and Pantagruel,* and it reaches its most explicit form in Laurence Sterne's *Tristram Shandy* where the author-narrator (or rather the text itself) addresses the reader directly: "You must have a little patience. I have undertaken, you see, to write not only my life, but my opinions also."

This is explicit self-consciousness, and not all readers are willing to be "patient" while the author expresses his "opinions" or digresses away from the story. Impatient readers who want their fiction straight, without the author meddling with it, are quick to scream in frustration: skip the jazz and get on with the tale!

If *Tristram Shandy* were an exception, an anomaly in the history of the novel, one would be tempted to ignore it, to skip it altogether, and get on with the tale. But along the way (from Cervantes to John Barth and beyond), one finds so many such splendid anomalies that one begins to wonder if in fact what is known as the tale, the conventional realistic tale, is not itself the anomaly. However, as it progresses in time toward the modern novel and gradually rejects realism, self-reflexiveness undergoes degrees of sophistication. From *Tristram Shandy* to *Jacques le Fataliste,* though the two are almost contemporaneous, there is already a marked difference in the use of self-reflexiveness that affects the degree of realistic illusion. Though Sterne disrupts chronology with digressions and opinions, he anchors events firmly in time and place. His characters may be odd, but they are nonetheless saddled with everything necessary to make the reader believe in their actual existence. Diderot creates a space never before seen in the landscape of the novel: a timeless stage without scenery (not unlike that of the plays and novels of Samuel Beckett) where his characters function more as voices than as full-fledged personalities. And yet, I know of no opening of a novel more fascinating, more engaging, and more self-reflexive than that of *Jacques le Fataliste:*

How did they meet? By chance, like everyone else. What were their names? What do you care? Where were they coming from? The nearest place. Where were they going? Does one really know where one is going? What were they saying? The master said nothing, and Jacques was saying that his captain was saying that everything that happens to us here on earth, good or bad, is written above. [my translation]

It is certainly the playful self-reflexiveness of *Jacques le Fataliste* that makes of this novel the great fun book that it is, and this because Diderot not only meddles with the text but also offers the reader the possibility of participating in the fiction: "No, no. Of all the different abodes possible, which I have just enumerated, choose the one most appropriate to the present situation." Or even better, the author seduces the reader into the interplay of self-reflexiveness while pretending to be annoyed by the reader's impatience:

Where?—Where? Reader, you are of a rather cumbersome curiosity! By the Devil what does it matter? Even if I were to tell you that it was in Pontoise or in Saint-Germain, or in Notre-Dame de Lorette or Saint-Jacques de Compostelle, would you be better off? If you insist, I will tell you that they were going toward—yes, why not?—toward an immense castle, on the frontispiece of which was written: I belong to no one and I belong to everyone. You were here already before entering, and you will be here after departing.

Clearly, Diderot, like Sterne and numerous other great novelists after him, understood that the novel is very much like the inscription on the frontispiece of the imaginary castle he invents on the spot: the novel belongs to no one and it belongs to everyone. We (as readers) were here before entering it and we will still be here after departing from it. This suggests that the process of reading a novel can be measured by the reader's willingness to engage—or let himself be engaged by—the self-reflexiveness of the text. In this respect, the reader can be fascinated either by the tale only (which sends him back to his own reality) or by the telling of the tale (which keeps him inside the fiction).

One could go on quoting endlessly passages from great novels of the past that are self-reflexive either implicitly or explicitly, for quite clearly most works of fiction are self-reflexive or self-conscious, but in various degrees. What is not clear, however—and critics have often confused the terms—is the difference between self-reflexiveness and self-consciousness in a work of fiction. It seems essential at this point to try and clarify this question.

Self-consciousness, often irritating to the reader, establishes a conniving relation between author and reader, and is played above the text. As such it deals with the reading process. One could say that it is a public act that draws the reader into the privacy of the text, and therefore functions as a window that opens from the outside into the text.

Self-reflexiveness, normally fascinating to the reader, establishes a relation between author and text, and therefore relates to the writing process. It is a private act but one that makes itself public since it allows the reader to witness the interplay between author and creation. As such it functions like a mirror inside the text. Of course, self-consciousness and self-reflexiveness often intersect within the same novel and are not always distinguishable, for they both use the same tools—parody, irony, digression, playfulness—to demystify the illusionary aspect of the story.

The crucial difference between the kind of explicit self-reflexiveness one finds in the eighteenth-century novel, and that at work in the novel (the new novel) written in America during the 1960s and 1970s, is that the former reflected upon itself, unveiled its secrets, questioned its possibilities in order to establish itself as a genre, as a respected genre, at a time when the novel was considered frivolous and even immoral, whereas the latter used similar techniques to extricate itself from the postures and impostures of realism and naturalism. In the first case it was a question of establishing a continuity for the novel, in the other it was a matter of creating a rupture in order to revive an "exhausted" genre—a genre that could no longer accommodate and express the extravagant notions of time and space of modern reality.

The publication in 1959 of *Naked Lunch* by William Burroughs marks the beginning of the new self-reflexive novel in America. Burroughs writes in *Naked Lunch:* "The world cannot be expressed, it can perhaps be indicated by mosaics of juxtaposition, like objects abandoned in a hotel room, defined by negatives and absence." And certainly, "negatives and absence" are the terms that best define the fiction written by the prominent new writers of the 1960s. William Burroughs, Flannery O'Connor, John Hawkes, Kurt Vonnegut, Jr., John Barth, Richard Brautigan, Thomas Pynchon, Ishmael Reed, Jerzy Kosinski, William Gass, Robert Coover, Donald Barthelme, and others form the first group, the first wave of self-reflexive (sometimes called postmodern) fictioneers who deliberately opposed the literary tendencies of what was then known as modernism. Already in the late 1950s these writers began to challenge the terms that define modernist fiction—that is to say, the element of description and representation of social reality and its language, and the formalism (stream of consciousness, interior monologue, psychological depth, syncopated syntax) associated with the inscribing of the subject into a fictional text. However, it cannot be said that these writers formed a unified movement for which a coherent theory could be formulated. On the contrary, the new fiction was characterized by a multiplicity of individual voices that were defying critical ordering and rational interpretation (often to the despair of the critics).

In fact, it can be said of the new fiction that it presented itself as a *mess*, and that therefore disorder, deliberate chaos, fragmentation, dislocation were its most striking aspects. But in this multiplicity of voices that echoed one another across the devastated landscape of fiction, there was a complicity of purpose that Jerome Klinkowitz loosely classified under the terms of *literary disruptions* (the title of his 1975 seminal study of what he called "Postcontemporary Fiction").

It is true that this new fiction created a disruptive complicity as it undermined the modernist tradition and rejected its mimetic function. While reflecting upon itself, upon its own means and possibilities, the new novel offered itself as a collection of fragments, as a puzzling catalogue of lists, as a montage or collage of disparate elements. This tendency toward bringing together the incongruous and even the incompatible opposed the type of fiction based on metaphoric and symbolic representation of reality. Consequently the new novel was viewed, by most critics, as being caught between paranoia and schizophrenia, as though hesitating between conjunction and disjunction, and thus unable to render itself coherent and logical, unable to probe below the surface. What was not clearly understood, however, is that this so-called fiction of surfaces deliberately refused to fall into the old psychological trap of modernism.

If the traditional novel continued to describe and explain reality in an effort to give that reality a certain moral and even spiritual order, based on the obsolete formulas of realism and naturalism, the new fiction (created on the margin of the literary establishment) sought to show the form rather than the content of American reality. It tried to render concrete and even visual in its language, in its syntax, in its typography and topology, the disorder, the chaos, the violence, the incongruity, but also the energy and vitality, of American reality. In this sense, the new fiction was closer to the truth of America than the old ponderous and realistic novel of the 1950s.

To achieve its aims, the new fiction brought together fragments of that reality, remnants, detritus, or what Donald Barthelme calls "the American dreck," and what Gilbert Sorrentino defines as "the imaginative qualities of actual things" (which happens to be the title of one of his more self-reflexive novels).

Whereas modernist literature manipulated ancient myths and stable symbols, the new fiction confronted and exploded contemporary myths and clichés. In this sense there was a rupture with the modernist tradition. But beyond this literary or formalistic rupture, which critics have been discussing and analyzing for quite some time now, there is another form of rupture relevant to the understanding of the self-reflexive novel that has become visible, and that is the rupture that occurred during the 1960s between the official discourse and the subject. By official discourse I mean that of the State, that of the Establishment, and by subject I mean the individual who receives the official discourse whether it is political, economic, social, or cultural.

The first signs of this rupture appeared around 1960, and corresponded to some degree to the emergence of the new fiction. From the end of World War II to the election of John F. Kennedy (in 1960) there was in America a kind of unequivocal relation between individual desires and the mechanism through which the State expressed itself. By State it must be understood that I mean not only the government but all the institutions that make America, including of course the university as well as the publishing industry.

The 1950s, on the surface at any rate, were a period of social and economic optimism. The American economy was booming as a follow-up to the war, resulting in a great demand for a better standard of living (that is to say a great demand for objects: cars, televisions, washing machines, houses, etc.—many of these quickly becoming status symbols). At the same time America was asserting its position of strength throughout the world, making its political but also its cultural impact felt. The key term in public life was the achievement of *success*. The 1950s, in other words, were a period of *valorization* and *symbolization* of the American way of life and the American reality. However, underlying this economic and spiritual boom was a sense of absurdity to the whole undertaking—a sense of the absurd left over from existentialism, which had come to America from across the Atlantic and was now reflected in such wartime and postwar novels as Saul Bellow's *Dangling Man* (1944), John Hawkes's *The Cannibal* (1949), and even in John Barth's early novels, *The Floating Opera* (1956) and *The End of the Road* (1958).

The American writers of the 1950s were known as "the Silent Generation," not because they had nothing to say, or said nothing, but rather because they, to a great extent, expressed in their work a silent agreement with the official moral, political, and social attitudes of the State. Yet, in most of the novels published during that decade (one thinks of the novels of Saul Bellow, Norman Mailer, J. D. Salinger, Bernard Malamud, William Styron, Herman Wouk, and many others), a sense of the absurd permeated the texts though it never really surfaced. It was only with *Catch-22* by Joseph Heller, published in 1961, that the absurdity of World War II exploded into the open in a self-reflexive manner. In general, however, the fiction of the 1950s (except for the stir created by the Beat Generation, perhaps more over personalities than literary works) offered a somewhat optimistic and moralistic resolution to contemporary problems.

By the time President Kennedy took office, America was ready to receive the kind of electrifying and electronic image he projected through the mass media and that quickly lodged itself in the American consciousness. And it is that image, that sublimated image, especially when it appeared on television, that structured the subject (the American people). The message and the image that Kennedy presented offered themselves as the defenders of a rational discourse that had finally triumphed over the irrational discourse that had led to Nazi and Fascist politics, and that was then openly shaping Communist ideology and action in Budapest in 1956, in Cuba in 1962, and in other parts of the world. In other words, the official image and message of the 1950s and early 1960s seemed good, honest, truthful, and tough when necessary. Thus when Kennedy smiled that meant that he was happy, and America was happy. When he spoke in a grave tone of voice and announced that the country could be destroyed in an atomic blast coming from Cuba, the entire nation changed mood. There existed then an element of mutual trust between the official discourse and the subject, just as there existed an element of trust on the part of the readers for the fiction written at that time. That discourse presented itself as a personal friend, and so did, in fact, much of the fiction written immediately after World War II—a fiction of easy moral and social resolutions, as for instance Herman Wouk's *Marjorie Morningstar* or Norman Mailer's *The Deer Park*, both published in 1955 with great popular success. This is why the assassination of John F. Kennedy (public and televised as it were) had such a traumatic impact on the American consciousness.

Suddenly things were not as good as they appeared. Suddenly the American people were doubting the very reality of the events they were witnessing, especially on television. It took certain blunders of the Johnson administration, and subsequently the manipulations and lies of the Nixon administration, and of course the Vietnam War, and the Watergate debacle to awaken America from its mass-media state of illusion and optimism. Suddenly there was a general distrust of the official discourse whether spoken, written, or televised as images. For indeed, if the content of history can be manipulated by the mass media, if television and newspapers can falsify or justify historical facts, then the unequivocal relation between the real and the imaginary disappears. The clear line that separates fact from fiction is blurred. Consequently, history must be reviewd, reexamined, especially recent historical events as presented, or rather as RE-presented to us by the mass media and by fiction.

By the end of the Watergate crisis, all the official versions dealing with the Cold War, the McCarthy era, the Korean War (which was never officially designated a war), CIA activities in various parts of the world, the Vietnam War of course, and so on are being mistrusted, questioned, and challenged not only in political writing, not only in the New Journalism that emerges as a new mode of writing in the 1960s as a result of the blurring of fact and fiction, but also in the novel as it establishes a new relation with reality and with history, a relation based on doubt.

The self-reflexive novel that takes shape during the 1960s in a way fills the linguistic gap created by the disarticulation of the official discourse in its relation with the individual. It places into the open, in order to challenge it, the question of representation in fiction, especially now that the line between the real and the imaginary has been erased.

In a world where the referential element itself is denounced as a mere electronic image, the old question of historical truth and credibility, but also the question of the stability of the real, as well as the psychic depth of the subject, are no longer valid. These are now impossible questions to ask. When the historical discourse is falsified as a language, all referential coherence becomes irrelevant and even laughable. It is this idea that sets off the first wave of self-reflexiveness (between 1960 and 1968) in the American novel when it begins to question but also to mock and parody the official discourse, and even more so the historical discourse of America.

Though the syntax remains normative, discursive, and even linear, and the narrative metonymic, nonetheless these novels are audacious in terms of their subject matter, and of what can be called their *irrealism*. Most of them continue to perform on the principle that storytelling cannot be totally eliminated, but the narrative becomes fragmented, discontinuous, and ironic, as if it had lost control in relation to the electronic mirror where life (and death in many cases) is decided by technological absurdity. This produced what became known as *black humor*.

As presented in these novels, history and the subject are two faces of an immense farce, a collective farce, and the text simply shows the absurd relation between the two. In the novel of the 1960s, where official history is mixed with the picaresque and burlesque adventures of the individual, where the characters have no other substance than their fictitious personalities since they now exist as verbal beings, the author denounces the symbolic strata that shape history and the individual. Most of these novels propose nothing, they only illustrate the fact that reality is but a fraudulent verbal network, for to replace one reality with another is a senseless undertaking, because one merely substitutes one symbolic system for another—one set of illusions for another. Therefore, all periods of American history are now being remade, replayed ironically, as well as self-reflexively in these parody-novels that often use the mass media as a backdrop, as for instance in the early fiction of Kurt Vonnegut, Jr., Robert Coover, Donald Barthelme, and Richard Brautigan.

The Sotweed Factor (1960) by John Barth retells the history of the colonial period in an inverted direction: no longer the traditional picaresque and burlesque adventures of the European who comes to the New World to seek his fortune, but the American who returns to the Old World to retrace his confused origin and unmake his fortune, and in the process demystifies American history and its language. *A Confederate General from Big Sur* (1964) by Richard Brautigan neutralizes the Civil War, and thus negates its dramatic and traumatic impact in order to expose its absurdity. Robert Coover in *The Origin of the Brunists* (1965) makes a mockery of religious cults in America by using a complex plot founded upon a prior mythic and historical source that eventually releases an antiformal revelation; by abusing a familiar form, Coover undercuts the hold that the content of this form has on people. Ishmael Reed in *The Free-Lance Pallbearers* (1967), but especially in *Mumbo Jumbo* (1972) and *Fight to Canada* (1976), retells in satirical terms the history of slavery in America; it is as though the old classic, *Uncle Tom's Cabin*, is being reshuffled and presented from a reversed point of view. However, it is particularly World War II and the Cold War, the events that shaped the very life of this generation of writers, that become the main targets of their parody-novels.

Most novels written during the 1950s glorified World War II as a good war, a necessary war, and even as a great adventure, in spite of its tragic aspects. One thinks, for instance, of such novels as *From Here to Eternity* (James Jones), *The Young Lions* (Irwin Shaw), *The Naked and the Dead* (Norman Mailer), *The Caine Mutiny* (Herman Wouk), and so many other war-inspired novels. This type of fiction is now being demystified and undercut by the parody and irony of the new novel. *Catch-22* is, of course, the most striking example, but such novels as *V* (1963) by Thomas Pynchon, *Mother Night* (1961) and especially *Slaughterhouse Five* (1968) by Kurt Vonnegut, Jr., *The Painted Bird* (1965) by Jerzy Kosinski, and *Giles Goat-Boy* (1966) by John Barth also mock recent American history to the point of reducing it to an absurd farce.

What these novels are doing is questioning the official versions of historical events. In most cases, the protagonists seem to be searching for a missing coherence in their lives and in their actions. Most of these authors are intent on revising their position and their views in relation to the events that they themselves helped shape, and they do so self-reflexively in the dual role of narrator and protagonist of their own fiction. Often they cannot decide (as the grandiose disembodied figure of Samuel Beckett's *The Unnamable*—a model of many novels of the 1960s—states of himself) whether they are "the teller or the told."

In *Slaughterhouse Five*, the author himself (under his own name, Kurt Vonnegut) as the narrator-protagonist of the story returns to the place where he participated in the war (in this case Dresden), but not to remember how it was, not to relive what he did, not to experience again the feeling of the great adventure, but to rethink, revise his vision of that tragic and absurd moment. In other words, Kurt Vonnegut does not simply write a novel to remember for us "how it was in the war," he does not offer to the reader memories or souvenirs of the war, but instead confronts and even implicates that reader with self-reflexive visions and revisions of the events in which the author participated, thus denouncing in the process the absurdity of these events as well as the vehicle through which they were related.

The fundamental rule of these self-reflexive narratives is the absurd and the arbitrary. The fictional machine seems to turn in a void, but not without cringing irony and black humor. At the end of these intricate stories there is no real message, no order, no easy resolution, no pseudomoral statement, only a text that offers itself as a kind of nonsense delirium that, to a great extent, reflects the nonsense of historical events and the delirium of the language recounting these events.

Though the same ironic mood is maintained in much of the fiction written after 1968 through the 1970s, suddenly a more experimental and innovative form of writing appears. The language of fiction again undergoes radical changes: the syntax is pulverized, in some cases reaching into visual concreteness on the pages, as in such works as Steve Katz's *The Exagggerations of Peter Prince* (with three *g*'s—1968), Madeline Gins's *Word Rain* (1969), or William Gass's *Willie Master's Lonesome Wife* (1971). The language of fiction now takes on the form of what Ihab Hassan has called (in reference to my own novel *Double or Nothing* [1971]) "visual self-reflexive exuberance . . . and typographical laughter" as the book itself becomes a performance where the narrative constantly deviates from linear movement and sequential logic into a spiraling mode of digressions, or what has been called "the leap-frog technique."

In some of these novels, such as *Gravity's Rainbow* (1973) by Thomas Pynchon, or *The Public Burning* (1977) by Robert Coover, the subject remains a parody of World War II or the Cold War: Pynchon gives a gigantic and grotesquely confused, deliberately confused picture of the war in England, while Coover recounts in his own mocking and carnivalesque manner the story of the Rosenbergs with Richard Nixon as the central, pathetic, and comic figure. However, in these novels, and others that appear after 1968, the element of parody is gradually replaced by pure irony and explicit self-reflexiveness, which release new energies into the language of fiction. Moreover, the blasphemous humor and the playfulness of these novels displace not only the somber black humor of the early postmodern novels but especially the seriousness of the intellectual and often moralistic novels of the 1950s, in particular that of the Jewish novel and that of the Southern novel.

The heavy morality of the Jewish novel (which took shape during the 1950s), whose psychologically insecure hero carried on his shoulder the entire burden of truth (the traumatic truth learned during the war) and of guilt, is now exploded in the late 1960s. The typical Jewish novel of Saul Bellow, Bernard Malamud, Isaac Bashevis Singer, Herbert Gold, and to some extent Norman Mailer, which imposed on its characters, and its readers too, a gloomy sense of responsibility and culpability, is demystified by such novels as Philip Roth's *Portnoy's Complaint* (1969), or in a much more experimental and playful manner, by Ronald Sukenick in his novel *Up* (1968), by Jonathan Baumbach in *Reruns* (1974), or in my own novel *Take It or Leave It* (1976).

The Jewish novel, and similarly the Southern novel—those literary discourses of moral responsibility and of silent agreement with the official discourse of the State—seem as hollow today as the historical discourse out of which they took shape. These novels are transformed in the late 1960s and in the 1970s by the use of humor and irony, but above all by the introduction of explicit sexuality into the text whereby the protagonists become (as in the case of Portnoy) outrageous libidinal figures who mock by their actions and their language the social, ethnic, regional, and moral tradition within which they function. (The same is also true of the black novel. Ralph

Ellison's *Invisible Man* [1952] and James Baldwin's *Another Country* [1962], which remain powerful novels, are nonetheless radically transformed in the fiction of Ishmael Reed and Clarence Major, two of the more experimental and self-reflexive black novelists of the last two decades.)

As for the great mythic dramas of the South, so beautifully orchestrated by William Faulkner, and perpetuated in a similar vein by William Styron in *Lie Down in Darkness* (1951), or Walker Percy in *The Moviegoer* (1962), these are now reduced to a kind of comic-strip fiction in Richard Brautigan's work and especially in the stories of Flannery O'Connor. The Civil War, that great historical discourse so typically American, which persisted to shape Southern fiction and produced somber, serious characters who existed within sophisticated dramatic situations, such as those created by Faulkner, the Civil War is no longer the traumatic event that cornered its subject into an eternal Oedipus complex and an incestuous social and familial existence. In Flannery O'Connor's fiction, the Civil War is barely a memory in the minds of middle-class people who are shaped by the clichés of the language. Though still writing within the formulas of modernism, in such fine books as *A Good Man Is Hard to Find* (1955) and *The Violent Bear It Away* (1960), Flannery O'Connor announces the principles of self-reflexive fiction in her fragmented narratives, and her subtle use of clichés, but especially in the way she reduces the seriousness of the Southern novel to a mocking casualness. For it is certainly fragmented narrative, the use, or rather the abuse of clichés, and the burlesque enunciation of social and historical events that best characterize the new fiction written in America during the 1970s, as if it were now functioning on the brink of constant disaster.

The work of Donald Barthelme, especially in his shorter stories, typifies this kind of fiction, which gives a sense that one must accept the limits of language and its trashy condition. Thus it is in the way language disarticulates itself, and in the way the text reflects upon itself in the fiction of the 1970s, whereby self-reflexiveness makes it impossible for a traditional story to be told, that the second wave of postmodern writers become more radical and innovative.

If William Burroughs's *Naked Lunch*, as early as 1959, implied the initial rupture between the individual and the structuring discourse of the State, his trilogy—*The Soft Machine* (1961), *The Ticket That Exploded* (1962), and *Nova Express* (1964)—went further than most of the early postmodern texts in proposing a radical linguistic experience instead of a linear satire of history. For Burroughs, the text itself is never innocent, and therefore a friendly, accommodating relationship between author and reader, between the writing subject and the reading subject, is not to be sought. The literary discourse and the words that make that discourse are biological enemies, for these are the fundamental elements of representation of a human being and of his place in history. What William Burroughs denounces in his novels is the political processus as it is described, as it is reported in language, either in public speeches (by politicians) or in the news media.

The historical and political parody-novels of the early 1960s (those of Barth, Pynchon, Reed, Heller, etc.) described a world where imaginary beings wandered aimlessly in a baroque landscape, and where narrative possibilities were infinite. What these authors were suggesting in their fiction is that the central machine, the giant computer ("The mighty WES-CAC," of John Barth's *Giles Goat-Boy*) that controls the relation between images and desire, between the real and the imaginary, was now in a perpetual state of disorder and disarray. But there were no real political implications in the work of these writers, unless parody as such can be viewed as a political gesture.

The political nature of William Burroughs's fiction goes beyond mere satire or parody because he is not satisfied simply to mock the world, or to show the absurdity of the world for the sake of intelligence or the sake of art. He wants to denounce the very mechanism that creates evil and injustice in the world. Since evil is deeply rooted in human flesh and in human desire, and reveals itself in language, the controlling machine perpetuates what Burroughs calls "the virus-word," which produces the identification of desire through linguistic fixation.

Though using more radical and even more reductive techniques, the new fiction writers who emerge after 1968 work in the same direction as William Burroughs. Their work may not be as political as his, but nonetheless it is subversive, for these writers are less interested in parodying the world or mocking history than in transforming the language through which the world and history are represented. Rather than reducing history and the individual who performs in history to a kind of absurd comic strip, as the early postmodernists did, the second wave of writers use experimental forms to disarticulate language from the inside. They achieve this especially through self-reflexiveness that liberates the text from illusionism and even from fictionality. Some of the novels written in the 1970s read more like "critifiction" than pure fiction, that is to say, a kind of narrative that contains its own theory and even its own criticism.

I have already mentioned Ronald Sukenick, whose first novel, *Up* (1968), announced this new trend. In 1970, Sukenick published a brilliant collection of stories appropriately entitled *The Death of the Novel and Other Stories*, followed by the novel *Out* (1973), then in 1976 another novel curiously entitled *98.6*, and in 1980, *Long Talking Bad Conditions Blues*. Sukenick's work exemplifies the way language and narrative structures are exploded in the fiction of the 1970s. He constructs his fiction on the principle of a fundamental and sustained opposition: the construction of a fictional illusion and the laying bare of that illusion. In other words, he creates a fiction and simultaneously makes a statement about the creation of that fiction. The two processes are held together in a formal tension that breaks down the distinction between fiction and criticism, between imagination and reflection, and as a result the concepts of creation and interpretation merge into a new type of discourse. To achieve this, Ronald Sukenick (the author) is always present in his fiction (usually under his own name) but as a fictional/mythical figure: an author-narrator-critic-protagonist.

Walter Abish, Steve Katz, George Chambers, Gilbert Sorrentino, Madeline Gins, Kenneth Gangemi, Clarence Major (and I suppose I should place my name among these) are writers of the 1970s who work in the same vein as Ronald Sukenick. What differentiates this group from the early postmodernists is a more daring, a more radical use of language, but also a total rejection of traditional forms of narration, and especially of mimetic realism and mimetic pretension. One could say that the new fiction of the 1970s evolved from a manipulation of language as a trap in its relation to reality and history to the conceptualization of a new type of text that constantly draws attention to its own medium, its own process of fiction-making.

As of 1968, fiction offers texts that are analogous to language, that reflect upon their own movement, and that function beyond social reality and subjectivity, or rather function between social reality and subjectivity in order to undermine the illusory relationship between the two. It is no longer a question of representing or explaining or even justifying American reality, but a question of denouncing the very vehicle that expressed and represented that reality: discursive language and the traditional form of the novel. In other words, the new fiction writers confront their own writing, place themselves in front or inside their own texts in order to question the very act of using language and of writing fiction, even at the risk of alienating the reader.

The spirals of self-reflexiveness have often been accused of being unhealthy both for the writer and for the reader. In a world where daily reality offers fantasies and phantasms that go beyond those the writer can invent, certain critics have deplored the fact that writers abandon realism, desert the facts of history, and mock the idea of credibility in order to indulge in narcissistic games that prevent the reader from identifying with the characters of the fiction. Self-reflexive writers have been attacked for turning their backs on social consciousness and human commitment, for refusing to explain reality, for refusing to pretend any longer that reality is equivalent to truth, and therefore failing to render reality coherent and rational. Of course such arguments fail to understand that perhaps there are deeper reasons—reasons of psychological and even political order—that force the new writers to abandon the tradition of realism. Such arguments fail to recognize that the techniques of parody, irony, introspection, and self-reflexiveness directly challenge the oppressive forces of social and literary authorities.

Confronting the fiasco of recent historical events, the new novelists— "chaos-drunk writers," as they have been called—offer a new idea of history: since civilization has become fraudulent, since it has turned into an enormous lie, it is important to examine its deceptions, its ruins, its clichés— the mess of civilization and culture. But above all it is important to examine and denounce the language that continues to perpetuate lies and illusions. Therefore, for the self-reflexive writers who see culture, or rather the discourse produced by culture, as a mystification, it becomes crucial to empty language of its symbolic power. It is in this sense that the new fiction writers are involved in an act of *disruptive complicity* as they confront the mess of reality, or what I have called elsewhere "the unreality of reality."

Of course the game is never innocent, the farce never totally gratuitous. Everything happens in the new fiction as if the world suddenly confronted the dilemma of having to choose between renouncing the rationality of language or renouncing individual desires. The new novelists of the 1970s abandon the search for stable points of reference in reality and in history, abandon also the purely formalistic temptation that dominated literature before World War II and that ultimately led to James Joyce's *Finnegans Wake*, certainly the greatest unreadable linguistic tour de force ever written. Instead the new writers have chosen the play of irrationality, the free play of language over discursive coherence and formalistic unity. Gradually then the stable syntax and the readable irony of the early parody-novels of the 1960s, are distintegrated into a form of deliberate unreadability not unlike that of *Finnegans Wake*, not simply for aesthetic reasons, however, but for subversive reasons.

Such works as George Chambers's *The Bonnyclabber* (1972), Walter Abish's *Alphabetical Africa* (1974), Gilbert Sorrentino's *Mulligan Stew* (1979), Ronald Sukenick's *Long Talking Bad Conditions Blues*, Clarence Major's *Emergency Exit* (1979), and my own novel *The Voice in the Closet* (1979) are books that, on first reading, may be declared unreadable and exasperating because of their outrageous self-reflexivity, yet that so-called unreadability raises serious questions about the role of fiction today. Basically it exposes the fixation of desires in language. By rendering language seemingly irrational, illogical, incoherent, and even meaningless—as in much of Samuel Beckett's recent fiction, which remains the ultimate model for most serious fiction written in America during the 1960s and 1970s—these works of fiction negate the symbolic power of language while proposing at the same time a purification of that language that will perhaps prevent it from structuring or even enslaving the individual into a sociohistorical scenario prepared in advance and replayed by the official discourse on television, in the mass media, and in the political arena.

"The world cannot be expressed, it can perhaps be indicated by mosaics of juxtaposition, like objects abandoned in a hotel room, defined by negatives and absence." It is worth quoting again this passage from *Naked Lunch*. In many ways, the American novel of the last two decades seems to have asserted the truth of this statement. For indeed by rendering language irrational, and even unreadable, the new fiction writers have also neutralized the fiasco of reality and the imposture of history. By confronting the unreality of reality, they have come closer to the truth of the world today, just as Laurence Sterne and Denis Diderot did in their own time.

Raymond Federman

III. The Present

The Fictions of the Present

The sky above the port was the color of television, tuned to a dead channel.
  —The opening line to William Gibson's *Neuromancer* (1984)

The world inhabited by American writers in the mid-1980s is very different from the world of the 1960s that produced the flamboyant formal innovations and central thematic preoccupations associated with postmodernism. And while certain recent trends in our fiction can be seen as extensions of the characteristic features of postmodernism (for instance, the interminglings of fabulism and realism, poetry and prose, criticism and fiction) or as reactions against these features (as with the rise to prominence of the so-called new realist or minimalist fiction), the most significant new directions are emerging naturally as responses to the new "style" and "content" of life today. A number of critics, noting that one key change between the 1980s and the 1960s is our culture's increasingly conservative and repressive attitudes toward politics and life-styles in general, have been quick to link the literary aesthetics of our age with the authoritarian, reactionary, anti-intellectual political climate of the 1980s. Thus Joe David Bellamy, echoing the sentiments shared by nearly all of the critics who contributed essays to a special "minimalist fiction" issue of the *Mississippi Review*, suggests that American literature is currently enduring "a downpour of literary Republicanism" (1985).

The actual current state of American fiction is, however, hardly reducible to this simplistic association. While there is some indication that fictional aesthetics in the United States became generally more conservative during the late 1970s and early 1980s, reports of "the death of experimentalism" have been greatly exaggerated. Our best authors have certainly *not* aligned their fiction with the reactionary societal forces around them, nor have they thrown up their collective hands in despair, retreated to their ranch-style homes, and churned out more realistic chronicles extolling the virtues of the American Way of Life on their new word-processors. The oft-repeated analogy between the 1980s and the 1950s, though misleading in many particulars, has useful applications for fiction. Many of the most significant writers of the 1950s (John Hawkes, Flannery O'Connor, William Burroughs, Philip K. Dick, John Barth, Vladimir Nabokov, Theodore Sturgeon, Jack Kerouac, Bernard Malamud) reacted to America's current *zeitgeist* by writing startlingly unconventional fiction expressing a deeply felt alienation from societal norms—and from the contexts (personal, political, economic, literary, etc.) that had trivialized language's power, multiplicity, and sensuality.

Similarly, a listing of some of the most significant new directions in recent American fiction indicates that our best writing continues to evolve in opposition to our culture's reigning ideologies and its ongoing exploitation of people and language. These new directions include: the emergence of science fiction (and its various hybrid forms) as a major literary genre that has produced a body of work probably unrivaled in stylistic versatility and thematic relevance; a more general interaction among literary genres, including critical theory and literature; the vitality and diversity of forms, voices, and myths developed by women writers and by authors from other marginalized groups (blacks, Native Americans, gays, Chicanos, etc.); the exploration of various new powerfully resonant metaphors and systems of thought, drawn from science, computers, linguistics, pop culture, economics, and many other contemporary sources; the recent flowering of the American short story, in particular the terse, cool-surfaced minimalist (or new realist) fiction. Such new directions indicate that during the past decade fiction has assimilated the most useful features of postmodern experimentalism (including its redefinition of "realism") and discarded the aspects that had proved to be mere gimmickry or readily exhausted. Thus, the frequently heard criticism that contemporary American fiction is unambitious and reactionary in spirit has validity only when comparing the relative achievements of recent fiction with the remarkable corpus of postmodern works that appeared in the 1960s. Indeed, on the whole, contemporary fiction has continued to undergo a healthy mutation while producing new forms and lingos suitable for conveying a vivid and varied sense about what is most distinctive regarding the shape, texture, and "feel" of contemporary life.

Precisely because the feel of life today *is* distinctive, contemporary authors are naturally creating works with a distinctly different "feel" from that of the willfully disruptive, ironic, playfully experimental works of the 1960s. The central figures of the postmodernist movement of the sixties in the United States (Thomas Pynchon, Robert Coover, John Barth, William

Gass, Donald Barthelme, Ronald Sukenick, Susan Sontag, Raymond Federman, Kurt Vonnegut, and so on) hardly shared a unified aesthetic sensibility; but they did share a common sense that a crisis was at hand, for our society and for literature, and that *all* forms of dogma, convention, and covert ideology—whether handed down by LBJ or Henry James—needed to be reexamined, exposed as artifices, and replaced if necessary by fresher systems more suitable to the times. The self-reflexiveness, flaunting of artifice, and defiance of established conventions so evident in the fiction of that period mirrored a similar process of self-evaluation occurring in the society at large over a broad range of social, political, sexual, and cultural issues. Such a process was profoundly troubling to a nation whose assurances about its national identity and value systems were already being shaken by political assassinations, the Vietnam War, the Watergate scandal, and a general loss of power, influence, and prestige abroad. Signaled by the election of Ronald Reagan in 1980, the American public's renewed faith in the old-fashioned, simplistic answers and assurances of militarism, patriotism, consumerism, and religion was a predictable outcome of this widespread national sense of bewilderment and uncertainty.

In a very general way, American writers during the late 1970s and 1980s can be said to have shared with the public at large the conviction that a retreat was needed from what were perceived as the "excesses" of postmodernism (such "retreats," of course, inevitably signal more complex movements in the avant-garde). This shift in aesthetic orientation could be seen in several ways: although highly experimental works continued to be published, both by established postmodernist figures (John Barth's *Letters* [1979], Gilbert Sorrentino's *Mulligan Stew* [1979], Don DeLillo's *The Names* [1982], Robert Coover's *Gerald's Party* [1986], Joseph McElroy's *Women and Men* [1987]) and by authors publishing with smaller presses such as the Fiction Collective, Sun & Moon Press, and McPherson Publishing Co., there was less evidence of experimentalism per se to be found in the fiction of this period; realistic forms came back into favor among many of the best emerging writers (Frederick Barthelme, Tobias Wolff, Bobbie Ann Mason, Raymond Carver, Ann Beattie, Richard Ford, Mary Robison, Alice Adams, Jay McInerney, Alice Walker)—though, significantly, old-fashioned realism was increasingly combined with fabulism by such major new talents as Max Apple, David Carkeet, Steve Dixon, T. C. Boyle, William Kennedy, Tim O'Brien, Russell Hoban, Toni Morrison, Ted Mooney and Rachel Ingalls; and the postmodernist emphasis on subjectivity, metafiction, and hermeticism diminished somewhat as writers refocused their gaze on the daily world outside the page. Crucially, however, that "daily world" was frequently portrayed as an ambiguous construct in constant flux, a mass of information, words, and images whose "meaning" was deferred, whose very "reality" was suspect, unknowable. In short, this daily world was a shifting, fabulous entity greatly resembling the poststructuralist text, a world whose depiction required a definition of "realism" flexible enough to accommodate the claims to "realistic aims" made by writers as different as Robert Coover, Raymond Carver, Larry McMurtry, Joyce Carol Oates, Walter Abish, Toni Morrison, William Gibson, Max Apple, and Leslie Silko.

"Realism," of course, had never been so rigid, naïve, and monolithic a notion as postmodernist apologists had implied. During the 1970s the various impassioned debates about "The Death of the Novel," "Moral versus Immoral Fiction," "The Literature of Exhaustion," "Self-reflexive versus Mimetic Fiction" gradually lost their energy, but these discussions had established widespread acceptance of the view that "realism" encompasses many different stylistic approaches and that even seemingly anti (or non) realistic fictional methods express a vision of external reality. Thus Walter Abish's *How German Is It* (1980), with its sharply etched descriptions of contemporary Germany, was a "realistic depiction" not of Germany (which Abish had never visited) but of the Germany existing in the American public's imagination. William Gibson's futuristic "cyberpunk" novel, *Neuromancer* (1984), describes a punked-out, high-tech world of cyber realities, tribal jungles operating on society's marginalized fringes, and dizzying labyrinths of images reflecting human desires that are endlessly replicated in mirrors and computers; yet for all its exoticism, *Neuromancer* offers a compelling vision of the way technology has *already affected* our lives. For a native American writer such as Leslie Silko, however, the effects of technology may be less relevant to the realism of her life than the tribal myths, stories, photographs, and personal histories she grew up with—aspects incorporated in her book *Storyteller* (1980) so that their contradictory and complementary elements are allowed to interact and slowly coalesce into a unified portrait.

By contrast, Frederick Barthelme's *Moon Deluxe* (1983) and *Second Marriage* (1984) present a milieu whose distinctly "contemporary" blend of banality and the fantastic requires yet another style to capture its essence. Barthelme's world is the tacky underbelly inhabited by America's lower-middle class; it is a territory roughly equivalent to the sleazed-out Los Angeles of Raymond Chandler—a world of neon jungles, fast-food joints, shopping malls, and of condominium life, with its illusions of community and its anonymous poolside chitchat about business and failed marriages. Barthelme, like most of the other writers associated with minimalism (Ann

Beattie, Tobias Wolff, Mary Robison, and Raymond Carver), deals with basically inarticulate people who typically feel adrift and bewildered by what is happening in their lives; he signals the sources of their unhappiness not by psychological introspection or analysis but via a careful selection of revealing surface details. This dispassionate presentation of details serves a symbolic function—so that a burning cigarette, an empty beer bottle, or a large hole dug in the backyard becomes an emotionally resonant signifier— and his oblique angle of perspective often imbues his scenes with a hint of mystery. Although minimalist methods have been attacked as a cop-out or a disguise for irony, minimalism's terse, rigidly controlled manner of exposition—which has much in common with the highly stylized, meticulously sculpted approach of Hemingway and Chekhov—allows for the economical construction of scenes of great vividness and emotional depth without requiring an intrusive (and inappropriate) overlay of analysis. And as is obvious in the works of such authors as Frederick Barthelme, Ann Beattie, or Raymond Carver (whose *What We Talk About When We Talk About Love* [1981] is minimalism's masterpiece thus far), this emphasis on slight plots, the elliptical development of dramatic conflicts (whose resolution is usually ambiguous), and the meticulous re-creation of quirky local speech patterns—while aspects of a realist aesthetic—are also formal features of a nontraditional style providing an appropriate entryway into the "realism" it seeks to examine. It may perhaps be true, as detractors of minimalist fictions maintain, that some of the appeal of this fiction lies in the reading public's ever-dwindling attention span and its preference for simplistic, nonintellectual writing; but as John Barth noted in "A Few Words About Minimalism" (1986), minimalist principles underlie "the most impressive phenomenon on the current (North American, especially the United States) literary scene (the gringo equivalent of *el boom* in the Latin American novel): the new flowering of the (North American) short story." (It should be emphasized that there is a clear difference between the minimalism practiced by Carver or Barthelme and the truly radical minimalism—analogous to that devised by musicians and painters in the 1960s—of someone like Richard Kostelanetz, who since 1970 has produced a number of highly original fictions in the forms of lines, numbers, one- two- and-three-word sequences, and other severely attenuated elements.)

Barthelme's fiction, then, demonstrates the way formal principles evolve to deal with the content of newly emerging (and hence previously unexamined) life-styles of contemporary Americans. And life-styles in the United States are rapidly changing. The conservative political and social attitudes that have predominated in the United States since the late 1970s have tended to obscure the fact that the daily rhythms and textures of American life in the 1980s have been undergoing a "revolution" no less profound in its implications than what took place in the 1960s. To a great extent this revolution has resulted from the enormous changes technology has introduced into our lives in the past twenty years. It is a revolution involving information exchange, the saturation of our culture with media-produced images and words, humans interfacing with machines, the ever-increasing efficiency with which our economic system reduces all aspects of our lives into abstractions it can analyze and manipulate for its own benefit. Some of the immediate results of this revolution are easy to observe: suddenly computer terminals and versatellers are everywhere, and so are satellite dishes, economy cars, more television channels, de-tox centers, answering machines, VCR's, compact discs, xerox machines, the whine of car alarms. One morning there is a modest home next door that is replaced the next afternoon by a bustling apartment building that is transformed into a condominium by nightfall; suburbs boom and bust, inner city ghettos with mean streets become Yuppie havens serviced by interstate freeways. Other equally crucial changes are as yet only dimly perceived by most Americans. These developments include the rapid strides being made in medicine (organ transplants, artificial insemination, surgery methods, etc.) and in weaponry and surveillance equipment; the massive accumulation of toxic waste materials (one of several potentially disastrous ecological problems); and research whose long-term impact on our lives is bound to be far-reaching.

Of course, scientific research and technological progress have had a significant impact on our daily lives for at least two hundred years; and concurrently writers—chiefly science fiction writers—have been speculating on what form this impact is taking and where it is likely to lead. What has changed during this period is chiefly the extent to which contemporary life is affected by these factors (which creates an urgency for fiction capable of dealing with science and technology) and the growing complexity and specialization within the fields (which makes it increasingly difficult for nonspecialists to write fiction about them). Ironically it has only been during the past twenty years that truly major literary talents have been drawn to science fiction in the country that produced the atom bomb and landed on the moon. The growth and maturity of science fiction in the United States was signaled in the 1960s and early 1970s both by the appropriation of science fiction forms by "mainstream" writers such as Vladimir Nabokov (*Ada* [1969]), Marge Piercy (*Woman on the Edge of Time* [1976]), Kurt Vonnegut (*Slaughterhouse Five* [1968]), John Barth (*Giles Goat-Boy* [1966]), and Thomas Berger (*Regiment of Women* [1973]), and by the emergence of a "New

Wave" of young, talented science fiction authors. These New Wave authors—including Harlan Ellison, Samuel Delany, Roger Zelazny, Gene Wolfe, J. G. Ballard, Joanna Russ, Tom Disch, and Ursula LeGuin—were equally at home with literature and with science, and like their postmodern "mainstream" counterparts they were anxious to develop experimental forms suitable for expressing their themes. Although some of these experiments were awkward failures, the example of these ambitious attempts to create a genuinely literate science fiction—combined with the appearance of various uncategorizable fictions by such writers as J. L. Borges, Stanislaw Lem, William Burroughs, Philip K. Dick, and Italo Calvino—laid the groundwork for the remarkable science fiction that has appeared in the United States since the mid-1970s.

In examining the achievement of recent science fiction, what is certain to strike one is the ability of science fiction to incorporate such a wide range of stylistic influences and thematic concerns. Thus recent works by Samuel Delany (*Triton* [1976], *Stars in My Pocket Like Grains of Sand* [1984], and his *Neveryon* series) have been shaped as much by Borges and poststructuralist criticism as by the science fiction pulps; William Burroughs, Dashiell Hammett and Thomas Pynchon all significantly affected the creation of William Gibson's *Neuromancer* (as did Delany and Alfred Bester); the influence of the Latin American magical realists is evident in Steve Erickson's haunting, surreal depictions of Los Angeles (in *Station to Station* [1985] and *Rubicon Beach* [1986]); and Ursula LeGuin's fiction draws upon sources as varied as Dostoevsky, Borges, Philip K. Dick, and numerous anthropologists, linguists, and political thinkers. Influences, of course, tend to travel in both directions, and this is evident in the effect science fiction has had on works by writers not usually associated with the genre, such as Raymond Federman's *The Twofold Vibration* (1982), John Calvin Batchelor's *The Birth of the People's Republic of Antarctica* (1983), Ted Mooney's *Easy Travel to Other Planets* (1981), Margaret Atwood's *A Handmaid's Tale* (1986), Joseph McElroy's *Plus* (1977), and Don DeLillo's *White Noise* (1984). Yet despite the production of what is arguably the most significant body of work in contemporary fiction, the accomplishments of science fiction have continued to remain relatively overlooked by the literary establishment in the United States, this despite the fact that science fiction is now regularly taught in our universities and has established its own literary journals (most notably, *Science Fiction Studies*) and a scholarly society (the Science Fiction Research Association). The suspicion with which science fiction is often viewed results partly from the fact that it emerged in the United States from the pulp magazines. This literary ghetto, to which all American science fiction authors were consigned up until the 1950s, produced a lot of campy schlock, a few writers who combined scientific knowledge with some literary skills (Isaac Asimov, Robert Heinlein, Jack Williamson, among others), but only an occasional author possessing a first-rate literary imagination (such as Theodore Sturgeon, Alfred Bester, and—a marginal case—Ray Bradbury). Significantly, science fiction has never been relegated to a secondary status in Europe, where the visionary science fiction of H. G. Wells, Eugene Zamiatin, Olaf Stapledon, Karel Čapek, Aldous Huxley, George Orwell, Stanislaw Lem, and Italo Calvino has long been recognized as "serious" literature. Undoubtedly, the postmodernist collapsing of literary categories and the broader acceptance of nonmimetic forms have contributed to the growing importance of science fiction. More to the point, however, is technology's transformation of our world into what seems eerily similar to a science fiction novel.

Meanwhile, equally profound changes in our social and political lives compound this sense of newness. Since the 1960s the American public has drastically altered its attitudes toward sexuality (including sexual identity), violence, the use of drugs and alcohol, religion, law-and-order issues. We have had a massive influx of Vietnamese, Cambodian, and (in particular) Mexican immigrants into our society while our "native" population has migrated in droves to the Southwest and Sun Belt regions; the civil rights movement in the 1960s and the feminist and gay rights movements of the 1970s not only created fundamental changes in the way the people involved in these movements live (including where they live and what kinds of jobs they hold) but produced newer (usually more diffused) forms of racism and oppression, as well. Such societal changes have necessarily had a very direct and often far-reaching impact on the lives of millions of Americans.

Many of the most obvious changes can be dealt with in fiction relatively easily merely by inserting the new content into familiar narrative structures. This approach, of course, is the one favored by most popular novelists writing about contemporary life (and by most "serious" writers, as well). Thus, if you want to portray the emptiness of life-in-the-fast-lane, as Bret Ellis does in his best-selling *Less Than Zero* (1985) or as Jay McInerney does in *Bright Lights, Big City* (1984), you set the novel in a decadent environment (Los Angeles in Ellis's novel, New York in McInerney's), add the appropriate topical references to cocaine, casual sex, MTV, Reagan and Quaddafi, and Jordache jeans, and go about your business. Such novels can be largely trivial (as with *Less Than Zero*) or genuinely moving and amusing (as with *Bright Lights*), but in both cases the sense of "newness" is a function of decorative details being used as a backdrop to what is otherwise a fairly traditional narrative.

By contrast, novels such as Ted Mooney's *Easy Travel to Other Planets* (1981), Don DeLillo's *White Noise* (1984), Donald Barthelme's *Paradise* (1986), and Ann Beattie's *Love Always* (1985) not only describe the physical changes in our environment but attempt to invent a style suitable for suggesting the way these physical changes produce alterations in what we value, what disturbs (or satisfies) us, even in the basic temporal and spatial ways we relate to the world around us. The experimental stylistic features of Mooney's haunting and strangely moving novel are especially successful in rendering a palpable sense of what it feels like to be alive in America *today*. This sense principally involves life's *strangeness*, its sense of dislocation, its ability to overstimulate us, the fears and anxieties it instills within us (often without our being aware of it), its frightening power to separate us from each other, its distortion of our erotic impulses. Like more traditional works, *Easy Travel* conveys some of these features via a careful selection of instantly recognizable details. But Mooney's world, for all its surface realism, is not quite our own—at least not literally. It is a world in which people suffer from a disease called " information sickness," the symptoms of which can be relieved by assuming "the memory elimination posture." It is a world where ice cubes fall from the skies, where a mysterious "new emotion" is emerging (so is telepathy), where wealthy nations are about to go to war over Antarctica. Like the equally unsettling Americas presented in such other quasi–science fiction novels as Don DeLillo's *White Noise*, Steve Erickson's *Days Between Stations*, and Rachel Ingalls's *Mrs. Caliban* (1981), Mooney's "now" is composed of familiar elements pushed just far enough to highlight their true fabulousness.

The strangeness of Mooney's world, however, derives as much from its manner of presentation as from what it contains. The linear flow of narrative, for example, is constantly interrupted by rapid cinematic cuts between scenes and even within individual paragraphs, which often contain wildly disparate elements presented in a simultaneous, collagelike fashion. The effect of such a presentation is to re-create the sense, increasingly common to many Americans, of being inundated by conflicting stimuli at once. Such pressures on our physical senses (and on our intellects and emotions, which must "make sense" of this jumble of sensations) generate within us the vague but persistent feelings of nervousness, anxiety, and sadness so characteristic of the modern age—with the feeling of *over*stimulation being intimately related to the sense of dislocation, of having no sense of personal stability, direction, or purpose. And within such a context, the drive for secure personal relationships and erotic outlets becomes especially essential for individuals who otherwise are confronted constantly by change, loss, and confusion. Lost and alone, they remain biologically driven to seek out sexual unions and psychologically driven to find the security of a permanent personal relationship. But everything else in contemporary life—its frantic pace, its casual sexual mores, the loss of religious assurances, the sensory overstimulation, the debasement of language into deceptive slogans and empty abstractions that actively inhibit human communication—conspires to separate us from each other and makes it impossible to find anything that is permanent and reliable. Mooney's unconventional style and content (his central plot involves a love affair between a woman and a dolphin) are aspects of a vision very much embedded in the "real world" around us.

Such flexible but nontraditional notions of "realism" are also readily apparent in the work of American women writers, who have produced an extraordinarily rich and diversified body of writing since 1975. The energy and vitality of women's fiction derives in part from the feminist movement of the late 1960s, which not only opened up what could be publicly said about women but also encouraged all women to investigate new ways of thinking about what the "realism" of female experience actually involved. The feminist movement, like the gay lib and civil rights movements, created for its members a new sense of self-respect and a feeling of community; and it fostered a deeper understanding of the sources of oppression and the distorting effects that oppression has on its victims. Predictably, the first wave of feminist fiction dealt primarily with the "content" of feminist insights within fairly traditional structures. Thus the early-to-mid 1970s saw a proliferation of feminist novels presenting women's sexuality, victimization, and daily lives more openly and sympathetically than ever before, but the *form* of these presentations was usually conventional (in this regard, one thinks of Erica Jong's *Fear of Flying* [1973] and *Flying* [1974], Judith Rossner's *Looking for Mr. Goodbar* [1975], Alix Kates Shulman's *Memoirs of an Ex-Prom Queen* [1973], Lisa Alther's *Kinflicks* [1976], and Marilyn French's *The Women's Room* [1977]). These novels succeeded in publicizing (and in some cases, sensationalizing) certain aspects of women's lives that had tended to be hidden from view (women's sexuality, for example); but it quickly became obvious to a number of important female authors that the basic assumpions and conventions underlying realistic fiction—its reliance on reason and causality, its central myths, its requirements for a dramatic action in which conflicts could be resolved, its implications about what constituted "heroism" and "significant" action—were inherently male-defined and hence in many ways inadequate to convey the most salient features of women's lives. As a result, since the mid-1970s many of the most significant fictional constructions and deconstructions of the female self have experimental underpinnings. Examples of these unconventional approaches would include the surreal, poetic intensity of Marianne Hauser's *The Talking Room* (1975), Toni Morrison's *The Bluest Eye* (1970), Marilynne Robinson's *Housekeeping* (1981), and Jayne Anne Phillips's *Black Tickets* (1979); the combining of myth, fiction, and autobiography found in Maxine Hong Kingston's *The Woman Warrior* (1976) and *China Men* (1980), Rhoda Lerman's *Call Me Ishtar* (1973), Audre Lorde's *Zami: A New Spelling of My Name* (1982), and Louise Erdrich's *Love Medicine* (1984); the metafictional methods, which have the effect of questioning male-dominant fictions and discourses, found in Erica Jong's *Fanny* (1980), Joanna Russ's *The Female Man* (1975), Ntozake's Shange's *Sassafrass, Cypress & Indigo* (1982), and Lyn Hejinian's *My Life* (1980); the turn toward popular genres to find plots and myths more appropriate to female life than those of conventional realism, such as Anne Rice's use of the vampire mythos in *Interview with the Vampire* (1977) and *Vampire Lestat* (1985), Rachel Ingalls's employment of horror movies in *Mrs. Caliban*, the gothic subtexts (long popular with women writers) used by Joyce Carol Oates in *Bellefleur* (1980), Margaret Atwood in *Lady Oracle* (1976), and Gail Godwin in *Violet Clay* (1980), or the mystery premises found in Diane Johnson's *The Shadow Knows* (1974), and Kathy Acker's appropriation of pornographic clichés (among many other forms of discourse) in her various "punk" novels.

However, the most significant popular genre employed by feminist writers is science fiction, which women writers tend to use for different purposes than their male counterparts. Drawn to science fiction by its open-ended formal features and by its ability to invent contexts suitable for exploration and innovation, women writers have found the genre to be an ideal territory to examine the full implications of feminist theory and of alternative approaches to sexual roles. Among the major works produced in this area are the feminist utopian novels of Marge Piercy *(Woman on the Edge of Time)* and Sally Gearhart *(The Wanderground* [1978]), Margaret Atwood's wonderfully savage and poetic dystopia *(A Handmaid's Tale)*, Ursula LeGuin's investigations into political and cultural anthropological science fiction (notably, *The Left-Hand of Darkness* [1969], *The Dispossessed* [1974], and *Always Coming Home* [1984]), and Joanna Russ's explicitly feminist, highly experimental novels *(The Female Man* and *The Two of Them* [1978]).

An analogous stylistic diversity characterizes serious writing by gay men and women, blacks, Native Americans, Mexican Americans, Oriental

Americans, and other marginalized members of our society. Sharing with their female counterparts the recognition that the essence of their identities and experiences is not reducible to empirical biases of most realistic fiction, many of the most successful novelists of ethnic backgrounds draw on the non-Western, nonempirical traditions of their native cultures—magic, music, legends, and customs—to present a world view more in keeping with their experience. These sorts of "organic," nonstereotyped approaches are evident in the recent works of Native American authors such as N. Scott Momaday (*House Made of Dawn* [1968] and *The Way to Rainy Mountain* [1969], Gerald Vizenor (*Darkness in Saint Louis Bearheart* [1978]), Leslie Silko, Louise Erdrich (*Love Medicine* [1984] and *The Beet Queen* [1985]), and James Welch (*Winter in the Blood* [1974] and *The Death of Jim Loney* [1979]), as well as in dozens of equally notable novels by writers with non-European roots. In attempting to create more honest, nonstereotyped presentations of their experience, these authors have had to resist the formulaic approaches favored by the publishing industry, which has its own opinions about what constitutes the "proper" form and content of minority fiction. The difficulty in combating these pre-set expectations is evident in the struggle of gay authors to publish anything other than relatively predictable novels about gay life (among the writers who have successfully developed openly gay themes in experimental forms are Kate Millet, Joanna Russ, Bertha Harris, Coleman Dowell, Edmund White, and Terry Andrews). But the most dramatic evidence of this newly won freedom of minority writers to transcend the pigeonholing of publishers and readers can be seen in the recent fiction of black authors such as Ishmael Reed, Toni Morrison, Nathaniel Mackey, Clarence Major, Toni Cade Bambara, Octavia Butler, and Samuel Delany, who present black experiences though a startling variety of fresh perspectives.

Reed, of course, has long been a spokesman for the need of black fiction to break from the pseudoautobiographical forms used by most black authors; borrowing from black poetry, myth, and ritual, Reed has created a black aesthetic founded on such primitive, uniquely black elements as voodoo, hoodoo, jazz, and the myth of Osiris. His recent novels—*The Terrible Twos* (1982) and his controversial *Reckless Eyeballing* (1986)—while downplaying the hoodoo aesthetic of his earlier works, combine farce, allegory, and parody to present a devastating (but often hilarious) look at racism, the battle of the sexes (*Eyeballing* was denounced by many feminists), the marketplace's co-option of black culture, and any other target within his troubling satiric vision. Toni Morrison's *Song of Solomon*, with its earthy, poetic language, its blend of fantasy and realism, and its striking use of folklore and myth (notably, the flying metaphor whose roots trace back to slave narratives), is even more successful than Alice Walker's *The Color Purple* (1982) in creating a form and voice capable of rendering the contradictory nuances of black life in America. Less celebrated than Morrison or Walker, Toni Cade Bambara is just as powerful a writer (indeed, her poetic rendering of black dialect is unmatched). Best known for her story collections, *Gorilla, My Love* (1972) and *The Sea Birds Are Singing* (1977), Bambara convincingly creates an idiosyncratic assortment of black people in her novel *The Salt Eaters* (1980)—welfare mothers, political organizers, primordial mud mothers, singers, faith healers, ex-pimps—and juxtaposes the values and beliefs of the Old and New South with revealing results. Butler and Delany are science fiction authors of considerable verbal and formal originality whose works explore racial issues as part of a larger critique of social forms. Butler, while operating more frequently within familiar science fiction conventions than Delany, has nevertheless presented striking projections of feminist theory, sexual and racial oppression, and civilization's capacity to dehumanize people in its rush toward progress. As has already been indicated, Delany is quite simply one of contemporary fiction's boldest innovators. His early novels, such as *The Einstein Intersection* (1967), *Babel-17* (1966), and *Nova* (1968), were metafictional excursions into new cultures, languages, myths, and social milieus; thematically they shared a great deal with self-reflexive texts appearing at the same time in mainstream fiction. However, since the appearance of his massive, unclassifiable, phantasmagoric novel *Dhalgren* in 1975, Delany's fiction has become increasingly dense and prismatic. In essence Delany employs science fiction conventions and metaphors as multilayered vehicles exploring not only racial issues but also sexuality, the effects of language on perception and identity, and the way artists generate beauty and meaning in a random, ambiguous cosmos governed by the second law of thermodynamics—and the similarity of the whole artistic process to crime. In the rigor of his methods, his formal ingenuity, and his ability to invent otherworldly cultures that investigate the contours of our own societal givens, Delany's fiction illustrates the variety of avenues (many of them previously untraveled or marked "Do Not Pass") now open to black authors.

In many respects, the open-ended view of "meaning" and textuality evident in so much contemporary fiction parallels the assumptions underlying the critical investigations being conducted by such major poststructuralist and feminist critics as Roland Barthes, Tzvetan Todorov, Jacques Derrida, Michel Foucault, Paul de Man, Ihab Hassan, Julia Kristeva, and Helene Cixous. Though formulated in different ways, the chief tenets of this criticism had much the same thrust as the aesthetic principles underlying post-modernist fiction. For both fiction writers and critics, the main emphases often involved: the artificiality and self-referentiality of the symbol-making process; the "deferred" meaning of all texts (and hence the absence of any "objective" or final meaning); the importance of authorial play (or *jouissance*) in allowing language to engage with the ambiguous, endlessly transforming reality around us; the differences between "healthy signs" (which display their artifice openly) and "unhealthy" ones (which fraudulently attempt to pass themselves off as natural or objective). In short, critics and fiction writers found more and more common ground. As Harold Bloom put it in *The Anxiety of Influence* (1973), "There are no interpretations, but only misinterpretations, and so all criticism is prose poetry."

The line between fiction and nonfiction, novel and autobiography, literature and literary criticism, had already become permeable in the 1960s when works such as Vladimir Nabokov's *Pale Fire* (1962), Norman Mailer's *The Armies of the Night* (1968), Truman Capote's *In Cold Blood* (1966), Hunter Thompson's *Fear and Loathing* series, Kurt Vonnegut's *Slaughterhouse Five*, Ronald Sukenick's *Up* (1968), and Steven Millhauser's *Edwin Mullhouse* (1972) began to hasten the collapse of genre categories. This "collapse" had the effect of engendering all sorts of strange, undefinable texts. Barthes's *S/Z* (English translation, 1977) and *Barthes by Barthes* (1977), William Gass's *Willie Masters' Lonesome Wife* (1971) and *The World Within the Word* (1978), Michelle Cliff's *Claiming an Identity They Taught Me to Despise* (1980), Ihab Hassan's *Paracriticisms* (1975) and *The Right Promethean Fire* (1980), and Harold Bloom's *The Anxiety of Influence* (1973) are part literary criticism, part prose poetry, part personal memoir and philosophical musing. Susan Griffin's *Word and Nature* (1978) is a poetic essay that reads like a *nouveau roman*, while John Ashbery's *Three Poems* (1972) and Lyn Hejinian's *My Life* (1980) are lengthy prose poems that read like reflexive novels; Guy Davenport's *Tatlin!* (1974) and *Da Vinci's Bicycle* (1979) are assemblages of factual materials; Maxine Hong Kingston's *The Woman Warrior* and *China Men* and Kathy Acker's *Blood and Guts in High School* (1981) and *Great Expectations* (1983) all combine fiction, myth, autobiography (and, in Acker's case, pornography, drawings, literary criticism, and dozens of unacknowledged plagiarized texts) as a means to write about the self.

Creating texts that refuse to privilege one form of discourse over another—that in fact openly acknowledge the problematics of the text, textuality, objectivity, ideology, meaning, and representation—has important social and political implications; and these implications have been recognized by a number of recent authors to redefine the nature of politically "engaged" writing. Traditionalists naturally continue to insist that political issues find their best expression in straightforward, realistic formulas, with clearly defined problems presented by means of dramatic oppositions that are then resolved with dramatic (and didactic) effect. Certainly the most popular novelistic treatments of political themes remain traditional in approach, as is evident by the ongoing mass-market appeal of trashy Capitol Hill potboilers and espionage thrillers—and of works of a considerably higher literary merit such as Alice Walker's *The Color Purple*, Richard Price's *Ladies Man* (1978), Joyce Carol Oates's *Angel of Light* (1981) and John Irving's *The World According to Garp* (1978) and *The Cider House Rules* (1985). But a close look at the best political works in recent years suggests that many writers interested in presenting political issues have concluded that social realist approaches are unduly limiting and simplistic (this view was undoubtedly reinforced by the brilliant examples of politics-cum-experimentalism in the works of Latin American authors such as Gabriel García Márquez, Mario Vargas Llosa, Julio Cortázar, Carlos Fuentes, and Manuel Puig, whose translations were widely available by the 1970s). Since the mid-1970s an impressive variety of innovative political fiction has been published by such writers as: Robert Coover (*The Public Burning* [1977]), Walter Abish (*Alphabetical Africa* [1974] and *How German Is It* [1980]), Kathy Acker (*Blood and Guts in High School*), Raymond Federman (*The Twofold Vibration*), Harold Jaffe (*Mourning Crazy Horse* [1982] and *Beasts* [1986]), Toni Morrison (*Song of Solomon*), Don DeLillo (*The Names* and *White Noise*), Joanna Russ (*The Female Man*), Ursula LeGuin (*The Dispossed* and *Always Coming Home*), the prose experimenters grouped together as "Language-centered Writers" (Ron Silliman, Bruce Andrews, Charles Bernstein, Bob Perelman, Lyn Hejinian), John Calvin Batchelor (*The Birth of the People's Republic of Antarctica*), John Barth (*Letters* [1979] and *Sabbatical* [1982]), and Ishmael Reed (*Flight to Canada* [1976], *The Terrible Twos*, and *Reckless Eyeballing*). Interestingly enough, a number of nontraditional novels with political themes became commercial successes (examples would include E. L. Doctorow's *Ragtime* [1974], Joyce Carol Oates's *Bellefleur*, Tom Robbins's *Still Life with Woodpecker* [1980]), Gore Vidal's *Burr* [1973], John Irving's *The World According to Garp* and *The Cider House Rules*, and Samuel Delany's *Dhalgren*), but even the popular novels used various postmodernist devices (metafictional asides, mixing the fabulous with the real, the use of actual historical events and figures) to emphasize the way historical and political perspectives are the product of the imagination generally and of language in particular—and to show how power is exerted over people and things through the invention of fictions that are then imposed on others.

Significantly, however, it has been the use of much more radical formal effects to reinforce political themes that has been the most intriguing feature of recent engaged writing. As Barthes and Derrida—probably the two most influential postmodern critics—have demonstrated, there is no fundamental opposition between a fiction that emphasizes its unnaturalness, its arbitrariness, that reveals (and revels) in its *differances*, and one that deals with history, politics, and social issues in a significant fashion; and authors such as Harold Jaffe, Kathy Acker, Walter Abish, Raymond Federman, Robert Coover, Richard Kostelanetz, Don DeLillo, Joanna Russ, Ron Silliman, June Arnold, and Samuel Delany share a common interest in creating fictions that offer exemplars of freely created fictions opposing publicly accepted ones. Rather than using character and action in the service of presenting a conflict that can be conveniently resolved, these authors tend to eschew traditional plot structures in favor of arbitrary or deliberately disjointed, oblique methods of presentation. On the one hand, texts such as Walter Abish's *Alphabetical Africa*, Federman's *The Voice in the Closet* (1979), Coover's *Spanking the Maid* (1981), or Silliman's *Ketjak* (1978) at first glance may seem almost apolitical exercises in formal ingenuity, as their creators manipulate words, sentences, and metaphors into verbal constructions whose unfolding relies on predetermined rules of transformation rather than on "progression" in the usual sense; on the other hand, in the case of works such as June Arnold's *Sister Gin* (1982), Kathy Acker's *Don Quixote* (1986), Walter Abish's *How German Is It*, Joanna Russ's *The Female Man*, Harold Jaffe's *Beasts*, and Samuel Delany's *Dhalgren*, it is larger structures of narrative that are manipulated, teasingly presented for our inspection, assembled and then demolished as plot elements dissolve or fail to cohere, characters divide, and other readerly expectations are mocked. Such formal methods necessarily create an ongoing metafictional critique of traditional fictional assumptions, but the focus also extends outward from a questioning of how literary conventions are formed to questions about how all ideologies and authorities are created. These authors are aware that the sources of oppression and marginalization today are often no longer a specific enemy—a racial bigot, an evil politician, a greedy oil company—but the larger, amorphous, less easily identifiable networks of words, images, and information through which people and objects are controlled and deceived. By subverting the usual ways in which words and other literary elements circulate in a text to produce an orderly flow of information—and by replacing them with new patterns—these authors only offer an analysis of how meanings are created and then imposed on situations. As with the other recent tendencies discussed here, this direction in our political fiction illustrates a dynamic interplay between changes in our literature and changes in our culture. If our political and economic systems have gained greater control over the production of the meanings that govern out lives, our best contemporary writers continue to demonstrate that people willing to exercise their imaginative and linguistic powers can still freely create the "text" of their own realities.

Larry McCaffery

The Avant-Garde and Experimental Writing

Since roughly the mid-1960s a new literary avant-garde has taken shape in the United States. Like the traditional modernist avant-gardes, this new avant-garde can be defined primarily in terms of its rejection of the dominant forms of literary discourse and culture, and its work can be characterized both by its spirit of experimentation and innovation and by its recognizably "anti-art" attitudes. But this new avant-garde does not oppose the same bourgeois culture against which the original modern avant-gardes aligned themselves. Rather, it opposes a contemporary culture that has absorbed and defused that complex array of forces and energies out of which the very idea of an avant-garde originally sprang. In short, the new avant-garde repudiates modernism itself. As Fredric Jameson has put it in an essay entitled "Postmodernism and Consumer Society" (1983): "Those formerly subversive and embattled styles—Abstract Expressionism; the great modernist poetry of Pound, Eliot or Wallace Stevens; the International Style (Le Corbusier, Frank Lloyd Wright, Mies); Stravinsky; Joyce, Proust and Mann—felt to be scandalous or shocking by our grandparents are, for the generation which arrives at the gate in the 1960s, felt to be the establishment and the enemy—dead, stifling, canonical, the reified monuments one has to destroy to do anything new."

Jameson has identified a number of the most significant features of the new avant-garde art: "The effacement in it of some key boundaries or separations, most notably the erosion of the older distinction between high culture and so-called mass or popular culture"; a tendency toward pastiche—that is, the imitation, as in parody, of a peculiar or unique style, but without parody's "satirical impulse, without laughter, without that still latent feeling that there exists something *normal* compared to which what is being imitated is rather comic"; the so-called death of the subject, or the end of the modernist cult of individualism and originality; and, finally, a breakdown of signification in which we experience the world—and language particularly—as "isolated, disconnected, discontinuous material . . . which fail[s] to link up into a coherent sequence." These are all useful ways to describe contemporary avant-garde art (and it will be useful to return to them) but they are part and parcel of a much more basic phenomenon— that is, the rejection by the avant-garde of formalist aesthetic thought.

Formalism is as various and complex as the modernist art that it has supported and inspired, but one of its most characteristic features is its insistence on the integrity of genre and medium. In the words of Clement Greenberg, perhaps the greatest of the formalist art critics (and, for many of the new avant-garde, the "enemy" incarnate):

> The essence of Modernism lies . . . in the use of the characteristic methods of a discipline to criticize the discipline itself—not in order to subvert it, but to entrench it more firmly in its area of competence. . . . What had to be exhibited was that which was unique and irreducible not only in art in general but also in each particular art. Each art had to determine, through the operations peculiar to itself, the effects peculiar and exclusive to itself. By doing this, each art would, to be sure, narrow its area of competence, but at the same time it would make its possession of this area all the more secure.
>
> It quickly emerged that the unique and proper area of competence of each art coincided with all that was unique to the nature of its medium. The task of self-criticism became to eliminate from the effects of each art any and every effect that might conceivably be borrowed from or by the medium of any other art. Thereby each art would be rendered "pure," and in its "purity" find the guarantee of its standards of quality as well as of its independence.

It is not, then, as Jameson claims, so much the boundary between the forms of high culture and those of mass or popular culture that the avant-garde seeks to efface—that is only a specialized instance (though one especially distasteful to the formalist critic) of a larger desire to dissolve the boundaries among and between the various arts and media as a whole. The avant-garde seeks to render impure again that which modernism "purified."

There is, as a result, simply no way to consider the contemporary avant-garde in purely "literary" terms. Not only do generic distinctions within the individual arts break down—most notably between poetry and prose in literature—but all of the arts themselves collide. Literature, painting, music, and dance intermingle and interpenetrate. The arts themselves draw upon and even nurture less "artistic" media—criticism, journalism, video, fashion, rock and roll. And all of these media are themselves inextricably linked by the avant-garde to the non- or extra-artistic phenomena of contemporary culture as a whole, especially to questions of history, economics, and politics.

The many connections between contemporary painting and poetry in the work of John Ashbery offer an interesting case in point. Ashbery has had a long, esteemed career as an art critic (and it is worth noting that other poets—among them David Antin, John Perreault, Carter Ratcliff, Peter Schjeldahl, and David Shapiro—can likewise be numbered among the better art critics of the day). It is hardly surprising, then, that Ashbery's most famous poem—perhaps the most famous poem of the 1970s—"Self-Portrait in a Convex Mirror," is not only based upon a painting by Parmigianino of the same name but appeared, soon after its original publication in *Poetry*, in a special issue of *Art in America* (1975) dedicated to the portrait. David Shapiro, in his book on Ashbery, has labeled such work "action poetry." The reference is to Harold Rosenberg's famous definition of the abstract expressionist painting of Jackson Pollock, Franz Kline, and Willem de Kooning: "At a certain moment the canvas began to appear to one American painter after another as an arena in which to act—rather than as a space in which to reproduce, redesign, analyze or 'express' an object, actual or imagined. What was to go on the canvas was not a picture but an event." "Self-Portrait in a Convex Mirror" is just such an event, the record of Ashbery's confrontation with the Parmigianino, not a re-creation in language of the painting but a kind of phenomenology of Ashbery's encounter with it. "I didn't go and look at a Jackson Pollock painting and decide to try to imitate this in poetry somehow," Ashbery told an interviewer in 1974, "but it's just the idea of being as close as possible to the original impulse to work, which somehow makes the poem, like the painting, a kind of history of its own coming into being."

There are many other segues between Ashbery's poetry and recent American art that help define the avant-garde direction of his work. He has, for instance, acknowledged ties to the junk collages of Robert Rauschenberg, the erased drawings of de Kooning and Larry Rivers (who incidentally painted a large portrait of Ashbery that included, as a backdrop, the typescript to "Pyrography" from the 1977 volume *Houseboat Days*), as well as to the flags, maps, and numbers of Jasper Johns. Like them all he disrupts the circuitry of meaning and reference, explodes it. "Self-Portrait" becomes a figure for the endless self-reflexivity of language and art—"The words are only speculation/ (From the Latin *speculum*, mirror)": as Parmigianino reflects upon himself reflected in a mirror, Ashbery reflects upon himself reflecting upon the Parmigianino, and the reader reflects upon what it means to reflect upon them all. It is, Ashbery writes, rather like "the game where/ A whispered phrase passed around the room/ Ends up as something completely different," not a question of meaninglessness so much as the polyvalance of meaning itself.

David Antin arrives at a comparable sense of indeterminacy in his work. And for Antin, as for Ashbery, the poem becomes "a kind of history of its own coming into being"—an event. Since early in the 1970s Antin has been "talking" his poems. He literally enters a room, sets up a tape recorder in front of himself, and starts to talk to the audience. (This emphasis upon "live" performance has resulted in his leading, along with Jerome Rothenberg, an informal but active "oral poetics" movement.) Though he begins with some notion about what he is going to say—the nominal "subject" of his remarks—the occasion itself dictates the flow and direction of these improvisations. Afterward, he transcribes his performances for publication, but these transcriptions are as untraditional as their original presentation. In order to create for the reader a sense of the "live" event, Antin dispenses with punctuation, capitalization, and that marker of the written text that we most readily take for granted, the justified margin, both right and left. But the most important feature of these "talk-pieces" (he calls them "pieces" as often as "poems") is their indeterminate generic status. They almost always begin in an essayistic, discursive mode and then gradually move into a more and more anecdotal, fictional, and eventually poetic discourse.

The occasion of a 1981 piece called "the value of the real thing," from the volume *tuning*, was the opening of an exhibition of impressionist paintings at the University of California at San Diego where Antin teaches art history and criticism (like Ashbery's "Self-Portrait," the piece first appeared in *Art in America*). The paintings had been donated to the university, and Antin had been asked to help the university community understand what it meant to own "real original old art." The piece begins more or less like any gallery talk and then moves into an anecdote about the time that Antin visited a lumberyard and one of the workers showed him a small landscape done around Camp Pendleton. The painting, Antin admits, is "very nice," but when asked if it is valuable, he is forced to say "no":

<pre>
                                        and he asked me
how come   and i thought how come   surely i was standing
   in front of an outcome of a particular painters impulses as they
      collided with the arbitrary materials of painting   the
arbitrary and conventional procedures   as he conceived them
      and there was nothing vulgar about this painting or
</pre>

incompetent   there was in fact remarkable refinement and
a very light touch   and all the competence he needed to do
what he wanted to do this little master of the lumberyard   it
    was certainly inventive   i had never seen a painting anywhere
      quite like this nor have you

This is followed by several other anecdotes that circle around the same questions—is it valuable and why?—as Antin moves back and forth between his own befuddlement about what makes art valuable and a consideration of the works in the exhibition. Finally he moves into a story about his grandmother and the difficulty he had as a child determining not only the value of the real thing but just what a "real" thing might be. There was a story about her, which Antin had often heard: as a little girl in Russia she had one day given the family's horses as much wine as they could drink, hitched them to a wagon, and raced them out of control through the village. He remembers worrying about whether the story was "real"—that is, "true"—until one day, during spring housecleaning, there was a giant crash in the basement of his grandmother's house where she kept her home-made wines:

      and when we turned the lights on my grandmother was lying
    beside an overturned wine barrel and pail under a ladder that
      she must have been standing on to wash the inside of the
  basement windows before it collapsed on her . . .
          and my little grandmother wiping the wine
  from her face with the cloth that shed been using to wash the
    windows turned her face toward my aunt and looked at her with
  this curious look   her head tilted to one side and one eyebrow
raised   and said nothing   and when i saw that look i was
certain she had driven those horses

This is how "the value of the real thing" ends, and we are no more certain at the end about what constitutes value in art than we were when we began. But we are aware of the parameters of the problem, its indeterminacy, especially the tension between private notions of value and truth and public ones (or, in other terms, the tension between use-value and exchange-value). Perhaps the oddest effect of Antin's piece—and this is generally true of all his writing—is that it is hard to say just how the final story informs the more discursive issues at hand. The connection can only be described as "poetic"—the expression of a vast network of parallelisms and metaphors—bridging the gap between the "properly" literary and broader philosophical and social concerns.

    Perhaps the most radical expression of such a poetics can be found in the writings of the so-called Language group. The work of such writers as Bruce

Andrews, Charles Bernstein, David Bromige, Clark Coolidge, Michael Davidson, Susan Howe, Douglas Messerli, Michael Palmer, Bob Perelman, Ron Silliman, and others resonates in various ways with both Ashbery's and Antin's. These lines, from Charles Bernstein's poem "Sprocket Damage," recall the aesthetic gist of Ashbery's "Self-Portrait":

> What happens opens up into what
> happens next time.

In an essay entitled "Semblance" (1981), Bernstein has described his own poetic practice in terms reminiscent of the competing voices of Ashbery's two-column "Litany": "In much of my own work: working at angles to the strong tidal pull of an expected sequence of a sentence—or by cutting off a sentence or a phrase midway and counting on the mind to complete where the poem goes off in another direction, giving two vectors at once—the anticipated projection underneath and the actual wording above." Like Antin, he insists on the unity of his discursive and poetic practices: "One of the things that has characterized my 'critical' work," he told an interviewer in 1982, "is the use of writing methods basic to the practice of my own 'poetry.' . . . To break the work down into two basic types seems to me not founded in actually reading the texts and tuning into the primary unity of them . . . [like saying] 'I like his drawing but not his color.' "

And yet reading Bernstein is not at all comparable to reading either Ashbery or Antin. His work eschews—purposefully—what he has called Ashbery's "fluid image generation" and "elegant transitions," and he does not violate the integrity of genre in Antin's manner, choosing instead to write what is recognizably either poem or essay. Here is a short poem by Bernstein, "Air Shaft," from his 1983 collection *Resistance*:

> Quick as a whip
> Wide as a gap
> Is wide. Somewhere
> Someone sears.
> Cachet in the hypochondriac
> Moonlight, sway in
> The censorious
> Goon flight.

In its peculiar way, this poem edges at sense, but simultaneously withdraws from it. The first line, for instance, is a sort of neologistic cliché—it *seems* to make sense, to be utterly recognizable, until one realizes that the phrase should "actually" be *smart as a whip*, or perhaps *quick as a wink*. The next phrase is, of course, a tautology that renders meaningless the idea of width (and, by extension, poetic measurement), and yet the enjambment—that "gap" in the text—does in fact determine measure. But the first truly disruptive word in the poem is "sears." Someone sears what? Here Bernstein cuts off the phrase, creating now another gap into which the reader more or less falls as the poet veers off in another direction, into a completely different level of diction, one marked by sensuous latinates, luxurious rhymes, and convoluted wordplay (as "cachet" and "sway" combine to make *sashay*), only to conclude, in a kind of terrorism of the word, with some vision of goons fleeing in the moonlight. The specifics remain as shadowy as the scene, as slippery as the poem's sense.

The first lines of an untitled poem near the end of *Resistance* help explain the ambiguous sense of meaning that "Air Shaft" evokes:

These [poems?] line out
a sense of gloss
or garbled
hope

What Bernstein's poetry is about, at base, is the *anxiety* we all share about the production of meaning, the promise of reference that somehow gets lost in the saying. It is not that he wishes to strip the word of reference; rather, he attempts to explore what he recognizes as "the multiple powers and scope of reference (denotative, connotative, associational)" generated by the word. The sort of active reading that such a poetry demands, as we fill in the suggestive gaps of the poem, violates the habits of passive consumption with which the average reader approaches the work of art. In the introduction to *The L=A=N=G=U=A=G=E Book*, a selection of work from *L=A=N=G=U=A=G=E* magazine that first appeared in 1978, Bernstein and his co-editor Bruce Andrews explain that in "conventional descriptive and narrative forms of writing" language becomes "transparent, leaving the picture of a physical world the reader can then consume as if it were a commodity." For the Language group, "poetry does not involve," in Bernstein's words, "turning language into a commodity for consumption; instead, it involves repossessing the sign through close attention to, and active participation [by the reader] in, its production." Such a project announces, simultaneously, the "death of the author." "It's a mistake," Bernstein has said, "to posit the self as the primary organizing feature of writing. As many others have pointed out, a poem exists in a matrix of social and historical relations [especially among them its relation to its reader who also exists in a matrix of social and historical relations] that are more significant to the formation of an individual text than any personal qualities of the life or voice of an author."

There are, nevertheless, undeniable formalist overtones in the work of the Language group generally and in Bernstein's work in particular. Susan Howe, whose own *Defenestration of Prague* is an important attempt to collapse the medieval into the contemporary (thereby asserting the irrelevance of the bulk of our literary development), asked Bernstein in an interview to confirm her feeling that the Language group shared with *Artforum* certain avant-garde aesthetic concerns. But Bernstein replied in terms very much like those of Clement Greenberg: "I think that specifically the kind of work that I'm most interested in deals with questions that have been dominant in other advanced arts in the century and have to do with what is customarily thought of as the modernist project in those other arts—that is, an exploration of the intrinsic qualities and possibilities of the medium in which the art takes place." What mitigates—even contradicts—this formalist direction is Bernstein's insistence on the reader's "production" of his meaning, together with his conviction that his medium is by no means "pure," that it is intrinsically ideological.

It is, of course, this tension between the more or less formalist impulses of the poetry of the Language group and the broader, more discursive intentions of their essays that has led many readers to see the latter as their most interesting and important work. But Bernstein's contention that there is a "primary unity" between his "critical" work and his poems is worth considering within the larger context of a new American writing in which the critical essay has emerged as a primary literary form. Without a doubt, the French "new criticism"—the writings, particularly, of Roland Barthes, Jacques Derrida, Julia Kristeva, Michel Foucault, and Jacques Lacan—with its emphasis on the polyvalence of the textual object and the critic's necessarily contingent relation to it, has contributed to this revitalization of the form. In an essay on Giotto in her book *Desire in Language*, Julia Kristeva has formulated her own relation to the object of her criticism in especially incisive terms:

A particular "sign" has already come into being. It has organized "something" into a painting with no hopelessly *separate* referent; or rather, the painting is its own reality. There is also an "I" speaking, any number of "I's" speaking differently before the "same" painting. The question, then, is to insert the signs of language into this already-produced reality-sign—the painting. . . . We must retrace the speaking threat, put back into words that from which words have withdrawn.

Such a consciousness of the transformative power of criticism, and the active response demanded of the critic as a result, argues for the essential continuity of the critical and creative acts. As Roland Barthes has put it, "Criticism is not at all a table of results or a body of judgments, it is essentially an activity, i.e., a series of intellectual acts profoundly committed to the historical and subjective existence (they are the same thing) of the man who performs them."

Of all American critics, perhaps the one who has most often and most systematically edged her theory away from the criterion of objectivity and into more subjective modes of expression has been Susan Sontag. "Against Interpretation," published in the early sixties, advocates a relation to art based on the immediacy of art's experience. "We must learn to *see* more, to *hear* more, to *feel* more," the essay concludes. "In place of a hermeneutics we need an erotics of art." Sontag discovered her erotics in many places. Her admiration for Antonin Artaud (whose life she sees as something of an exemplary performance) and for a post-Artaudian theater such as Peter Weiss's *Marat/Sade* (which she was quick to recognize as a performance about performance) underscores a consistent prejudice in her work toward defining art phenomenologically, art's essence existing for us only in its live experience. So, too, her preoccupation with film (what matters in film, she says, is "the pure, untranslatable, sensuous immediacy" of the image), her early attraction and commitment to Happenings, and her virtual adoration of Roland Barthes. In a eulogy for Barthes, published in the *New York Review of Books* in 1980, she describes not merely Barthes's powers as a writer but the ideal to which she herself aspires:

In *S/Z*, he reinvented a Balzac novella in the form of a doggedly ingenious textual gloss. There were the dazzling Borgesian appendices to *Sade, Fourier, Loyola*; the para-fictional pyrotechnics of the exchanges between text and photographs, between text and semi-obscured references in his autobiographical writings; the celebrations of illusion in his last book, on photography. . . . [His] most wonderful books— *Roland Barthes by Roland Barthes* and *A Lover's Discourse*—are themselves triumphs of modernist fiction in that tradition inaugurated by Rilke's *The Notebooks of Malte Laurids Brigge*, which crossbreeds fiction, essayistic speculation, and autobiography, in a linear-notebook rather than a linear-narrative form. . . . With his boundless capacity for self-referring, he enrolled the invention of sense in the search for pleasure. The two were identified: reading as *jouissance* (the French word for joy that also means coming); the pleasure of the text.

Sontag's interest in photography—her own book, *On Photography*, anticipated that of Barthes by four years—is based on the ephemeral quality of the image, the "illusion" of a captured reality that it claims to hold before the viewer as a presence. But Sontag recognizes that the photograph is actually "a pseudo-presence and a token of absence." Derrida labels such objects *traces*. By definition, a trace is always incomplete; it cannot possibly be encompassed in a determinate reading. And as a result it continually generates successive readers and readings—that is, it demands a critical involvement that is ongoing and dynamic.

Such a critical method finds frankly suspect more traditional claims for the objectivity of critical discourse, labeling them "idealist" or "nostalgic," since what they seek is a more or less determinable art object. Geoffrey Hartman, in the tellingly titled essay "The New Wilderness: Critics as Connoisseurs of Chaos," has called the new approach to art embodied in the work of writers like Sontag "creative criticism." For Hartman, the line between the "original" text and critical commentary is not only precarious but, in the best contemporary writing, virtually nonexistent, and the heretofore neatly defined territorial prerogatives of each kind of writing have opened into a new chaotic wilderness of expression. Consider, he says, the commentaries of

Jacques Derrida in *Glas* or Roland Barthes in *S/Z* (his study of Balzac), of Ihab Hassan's paracriticism or Maurice Blanchot's self-reflective critical narratives, or Heidegger's ruminations or Harold Bloom's "misreadings" or—to add novels that unfold a synthetic poem—Nabokov's *Pale Fire* and D. M. Thomas's *The White Hotel*. These works of scholarship, or fiction based on scholarship . . . are crossing the line and merging with the expressive force of interpretive commentary with the inspiring, sometimes disruptive, force of the work of art that is the object of the commentary. Whatever distinctions of value and character we wish to make between these writers, they all challenge T. S. Eliot's magisterial pronouncement that there can be no creative criticism.

Hartman's distinction (or rather collapse of distinctions) can be discovered in one form or another at work in the writing of most continental theorists today—and one has to call them "theorists," rather than "literary theorists," because their interests range across the borders of the various disciplines and into what Derrida has called "the margins of discourse." One contemporary French theorist, Jean-François Lyotard, has summarized the situation in these terms: "The difference between what I write and poetry and literature is that, in principle, what I write is not fiction. But I do wonder more and more: Is there a real difference between a theory and a fiction? After all, don't we have the right to present theoretical statements under the form of fictions, in the form of fictions? Not *under* the form, but *in* the form."

Such criticism is primarily antiformalist in its intentions. In a 1976 essay on the New York woman artist Jackie Ferrara, Robert Pincus-Witten put the matter this way: "Until late in the sixties, solemn formalism was assumed to be the only way one talked about art. The mandarin tone obtained as the signal characteristic of distinguished critical and historical discussion. Disinterestedness. I don't get it anymore—well, not exclusively. There's this other side of me, the other avenue—work perceived as significant must be invested with the value deriving from biography, the really lived, the idiosyncratic datum, the human. Biography as form; biography is form." Later in the same essay Pincus-Witten goes on to say that this biographical urge—or, as he himself calls it, this "formalist dysfunction"—is a result of the fact that in Ferrara's work he encountered an art for which formalist criticism had not yet developed a vocabulary, an art in this case conceived in the context of feminist activism and purposefully developing outside the mainstream of art and art appreciation.

In short, criticism most often asserts its creative side when it confronts art that is itself antiformalist. The minimalist work of sculptors like Donald Judd and Robert Morris managed successfully to baffle New York art critics for a long while because it seemed so obviously *formal*: the work of art literally became its shape. And confronted by this literalness, formalist criticism quickly found itself exhausted. This is about all Clement Greenberg could muster, for instance, on minimalist sculpture:

Everything is rigorously rectilinear or spherical. Development within the given piece is usually by repetition of the same modular shape, which may or may not be varied in size.. . . . Still, no matter how simple the object may be, there remain the relations and interrelations of surface, contour, and spatial interval. Minimal works are readable as art, as almost anything is today—including a door, a table, or a blank sheet of paper. . . . I find myself back in the realm of Good Design.

The impoverishment of Greenberg's response is revealed by the texts that the best minimalist works have generated. An exemplary body of such work is the essays of the earthwork sculptor Robert Smithson, two of the best of which, "A Tour of the Monuments of Passaic, New Jersey," and "Incidents of Mirror-Travel in the Yucatan," were published in *Artforum* in 1967 and 1968 respectively. Smithson's essays, as Lawrence Alloway has pointed out, follow "the preambulatory form of a guide book, including meditations on time and monuments," but theirs is a "fictionalized documentary" mode. The "Incidents of Mirror-Travel," for instance, records a series of nine separate "mirror displacements" in which twelve mirrors were located at different sites in the Yucatan landscape and subsequently photographed. This is the text accompanying the first displacement:

Somewhere between Uman and Muna is a charred site. The people in this region clear land by burning it out. On this field of ashes (called by the natives a "milpa") twelve mirrors were cantilevered into low mounds of red soil. Each mirror was twelve inches square, and supported from above and below by the scorched earth alone. The distribution of the squares followed the irregular contours of the ground, and they were placed in a random parallel direction. Bits of earth spilled onto the surfaces, thus sabotaging the perfect reflections of the sky. Dirt hung in the sultry sky. Bits of blazing cloud mixed with ashy mass. The displacement was *in* the ground, not *on* it. Burnt tree stumps spread around the mirrors and vanished into the arid jungles.

The mirrors here function not unlike the text: in re-presenting the sky in the context of the ashy ground they disrupt both sky and ground. They literally transform the site. Such a transformation is in fact embodied on the cover of Smithson's *Tourist Guide and Directory of Yucatan-Campeche:* on the top left-hand corner was printed " 'UY U TAN A KIN PECH' (listen how they talk)—EXCLAIMED THE MAYANS ON HEARING THE SPANISH LANGUAGE," and in the bottom left-hand corner " 'YUCATAN CAMPECHE'—REPEATED THE SPANIARDS WHEN THEY HEARD THESE WORDS." It is part and parcel of the place, this asymmetrical reflection in which what seems the same is actually very different, a repetition that inaugurates a system of differences in first the mirror displacements themselves, then the photographs of them, and, finally, the text that they generate. "If you visit the sites (a doubtful probability)," Smithson concludes, "you find nothing but memory-traces, for the mirror displacements were dismantled right after they were photographed. The mirrors are somewhere in New York. The reflected light has been erased. . . . Yucatan is elsewhere." The text is such a "memory-trace" itself, but, as Smithson says, "every artist owes his existence to such mirages."

Lucy Lippard's *Six Years: The Dematerialization of the Art Object 1966 to 1972* represents a different but equally interesting sort of creative criticism. As Lippard's title implies, her concern is with the conceptual and performance art works that in the last years of the sixties conceived of themselves as undermining both formalism's advocacy of the object and, more important, the commodity fetishism of the art market, which formalism served. On the most basic level, the book is merely an extended exercise in documentation, in the words of her extended subtitle: "a cross-reference book of information on some esthetic boundaries: consisting of a bibliography into which are inserted a fragmented text, art works, documents, interviews, and symposia, arranged chronologically and focussed on so-called conceptual or information or idea art with mention of such vaguely designated areas as minimal, anti-form, systems, earth, or process art, occurring now in the Americas, Europe, England, Australia, and Asia (with occasional political overtones)." This collage format—which Gregory Ulmer, in his essay "The Object of Post-Criticism," has defined as the dominant mode of creative criticism—turns out to possess surprising critical power. In the first place, chronology, though ostensibly a method of ordering experience, is actually experienced in *Six Years* as anything but orderly. "The form of the book," Lippard blithely asserts in the first paragraph of its preface, "reflects chaos." That is, the voluminous materials it includes are so diverse that rather than providing a unified history of the years 1966–72, the book instead tends to emphasize "timing, variety, fragmentation and interrelationships." Lippard concludes that one of the book's principal accomplishments is to force "the reader to make up his or her own mind when confronted with such a curious mass of information."

This emphasis on the reader—on forcing each reader to work individually—is finally what makes *Six Years* something larger than just a documentary anthology. Conceptual art always invites its eventual realization—and this sense of deferral, as much as anything, is the source of its excitement—so that any collage of conceptual pieces worth its salt is inevitably going to stir up performance aspirations in its audience. The intention is doubly clear when *Six Years* is seen as another, larger version of Lippard's other major critical work of the period, the "catalogue" to the show *557,087*, actually a small manila envelope containing 95 4 × 6 index cards in random order, including 64 cards contributed by 64 different conceptual artists, 20 text-cards by Lippard, a title page, a bibliography, and so forth, all designed to be reordered, rearranged, and variously shuffled by a "catalogue"-reading exhibition audience of potentially 557,087 people (the population of Seattle where the show took place), to make 557,087 different "works," or art experiences, out of the exhibition/catalogue itself.

Eventually what books like Lippard's force us to understand is that art exists in social—which is to say, political—situations. "I don't mean that art itself has to be seen in political terms," she says in *Six Years*, "or *look* political, but the way artists handle their art, where they make it, the chances they get to market it, how they are going to let it out, and to whom—it's all part of a life style and a political situation." The corollary to this, of course, is that the way *we* handle art, what *we* make of it, the chances *we* get to see it or read it, how it comes to us and why it comes to us particularly, are likewise all part of a particular political set of circumstances.

Kathy Acker's bizarre pastiche novels are among the avant-garde's most telling revelations of such a politics of reception. In *Great Expectations* she has constructed a narrative out of passages mined from the works of other authors—Dickens, as the title implies, Proust, Victoria Holt, and others—and combined these with a kind of untrustworthy autobiography, disarming addresses to both the hypothetical reader and actual contemporaries (such as Susan Sontag), and the story of one ambiguous youth variously named Pip and Rosa. The collage structure of the novel, in fact, is reminiscent of Lippard's *Six Years*. What distinguishes the two is Acker's sensitivity to the transformative power of the rhetorical situation itself. Her voice modulates between a fully blown nineteenth-century diction and an almost mindless punk vernacular as the novel explores the kinds of expectations language can generate. Most notably, it explores the role of gender distinctions—what it means to be named "Pip" instead of "Rosa"—in the social construction of the self.

Ron Silliman's pastiche of Claude Mauriac's *nouveau roman*, *La Marquise sortit a cinq heures*, the 600-word "Blue," which Bernstein included in "The Language Sampler" he put together for *The Paris Review* in 1982, is a shorter example of the same sort of thing. Mauriac's novel was inspired by a particular high modernist literary anecdote: Paul Valéry said one day to André Breton that, so far as he was concerned, he would never write a sentence like "The Marchioness went out at five o'clock," by which he meant to underscore the insignificance of all novelistic language. Mauriac wished to convey in the novel a sense of time in passage that Valéry, musing on eternal verities and azure spaces, would hardly have appreciated. The novel, therefore, takes place in a restricted physical and temporal space: it tells us fragments of the histories of everyone who lives on or passes through the Carrefour de Buci (the intersection of five streets on the Left Bank in Paris) from five to six o'clock one summer afternoon, including a scrap of conversation from an airplane flying overhead.

Mauriac's novel shares with Silliman's pastiche certain important concerns, especially the demands it makes upon the reader in helping to produce meaning and the sense of "presentness" such active participation inspires. But Silliman's piece is very different in its effect. It begins and ends with a more or less conventionally referential writing, a kind of high bourgeois realist prose that echoes Mauriac's own parody of the nineteenth-century French novel. But the direction of Silliman's "Blue" quickly shifts. Here are its opening paragraphs:

The Marchioness went out at five o'clock. The sky was blue yet tinged with pink over the white spires which broke up the east horizon. The smell of the afternoon's brief shower was still evident and small pools of water collected in the tilt of the gutters, leaves and tiny curling scraps of paper drifting in the miniature tides which nonetheless caught and reflected the swollen sun, giving the boulevard its jeweled expression.

Government was therefore an attitude. Dour, the camel pushed with his nose against the cyclone fence. The smell of damp eucalyptus is everything! You stare at your car before you get in.

From here we can see the sex. They are folding the flyers before stuffing them into envelopes. Badminton is nothing to be ashamed of. Grease and old tire marks streak the road. From here we can tell the sex.

"Blue," like Ashbery's "Self-Portrait" or Smithson's "Incidents of Mirror-Travel in the Yucatan," is a reflection upon a reflection (inspired by yet another short reflection—Valéry's, upon the difference between his poetics and the novel). Its reference is not "the world" but another text. Reality here is a series of shifting, dislocated images and disembodied voices—images of images and re-presentations of voices—as flat as Silliman's own "translation" of the symbolist's infinite "azure" into a mundane "blue." Everything about the piece—except the act of reading itself—implicates language in the debilitating mechanisms of consumption. The Marchioness's goal upon going out at five o'clock is a restaurant, and "Blue" ends as "the host, recognizing the Marchioness, invites her in." It is this same invitation to consume that Silliman both proffers and retracts. It is our *urge* to consume that "blue" underscores—and the pleasures involved in rejecting the invitation.

Laurie Anderson probably takes on the issues of commodity culture more thoroughly than any other single avant-garde artist. She is, in the first place, a "star"—her song "O Superman" was a number-one hit—and like Andy Warhol she is a kind of commodity in her own right, a Warner Brothers image consumed by the very rock-and-roll culture that, in an eminently punk gesture, she attacks. In yet another contradictory gesture (but again in the manner of a punk band like Devo), she has "decharacterized" herself, recycling her voice through electric filters so that it is alternatively inflectionless, mechanical, or hypocritical (but almost always male) and disguising herself in featureless, expressionless masks. Her musical orientation derives, most certainly, from the example of John Cage (whose vast interdisciplinary repertoire may be said to inform the work of every artist under discussion here), an orientation that is tempered by her training in art, both studio and history, and her early, relatively successful career as an art critic and writer. By the late 1970s she had begun to produce what has become known as her "electric cabaret," described by *New York Times* music critic John Rockwell as "a poetry reading writ very large indeed, with every aspect of the poetic concept amplified and counterpointed by aural and visual imagery." Her performances are a kind of pop pastiche meant to address every aspect of American culture—not least of all her own eminence—as the title to her two-night, four-part performance *United States* indicates. One of the work's most powerful images is Anderson before a tableau of oncoming traffic at night, her own eyes emblazoned by a pair of illuminated headlight goggles, reciting this:

You're driving and it's dark
and it's raining. . . .
You've been on this road before.
You can read the signs.
You can feel your way.
You can do this
in your sleep.

The American self here becomes its car. The automobile, as Roland Barthes noted in the early 1970s, is no longer an object of desire, a thing to be possessed, but something to *drive*, the embodiment of power, mastery, and control. But if this is the dream of the new professional-managerial class, Anderson undermines it by the monotony of her image.

Probably nothing helps promote the easy consumption of art more than the idea of generic integrity. As Silliman has put it in an essay outlining the centrality of "performance art" such as Anderson's to avant-garde aesthetics (he is not comfortable, even, with such new generic designations, preferring instead to call this new "polyart," in the title of his essay, "Art with No Name"), "such enclosures . . . prevent, rather than aid, the viewer from seeking work freshly and directly, without a set of preconceived 'aesthetic' notions." As we have noted, what Lucy Lippard termed "the dematerialization of art" in the late 1960s was an explicit attempt to free art from even its "enclosing" object status as a *work* of art—that is, to insist on art as a process, a working, rather than as a thing, a product to be consumed. Such a notion inevitably gave rise to the idea of art as a kind of performance (the "concept" in conceptual art acted out), and it also gave rise to a wide variety of documentary records of these performances—records, audiotapes, and videotapes, as well as texts—a kind of new "literature with no name."

Much of this new, nameless literature arises out of the music scene, especially out of the post-Cageian experimentation of such composers as Philip Glass, Steve Reich, and Robert Ashley. Glass's collaborations—most notably, with Robert Wilson on *Einstein on the Beach*—seek to establish themselves as precise examples of the kind of "polyart" of which Silliman speaks, muddying distinctions among and between media even as they begin to define a new sort of *gesamtkunstwerk*. What marks Glass's works is the sense of random or chance-generated texts, movements, and musical motifs that are juxtaposed to highly determined minimalist strategies—primarily both musical and verbal serial composition and visual geometric patterning of the stage space—in the performance itself. Such a relation between chance operations and abstract structural principles lies at the heart of Cageian aesthetics, but Cage's impact on avant-garde text is even more profound in terms of his sense that language is, in and of itself, sound. Considered as a body of sounds, language is freed not only of melody (song) but also of syntax and meaning. Steve Reich's *It's Gonna Rain* is the sort of work that results from such a conception of language. The piece is influenced by Cage's 1952 *Williams Mix*, one of the first electronic pieces composed in this country. Cage's work consists of various prerecorded sounds—"A (city sounds), B (country sounds), C (electric sounds), D (manually produced sounds, including the literature of music), E (wind-produced sounds, including songs) and F (small sounds requiring amplification to be heard with the others)." The sources of Reich's piece are somewhat less complex. "The voice belongs to a young black Pentacostal preacher who called himself Brother Walter," Reich explains on the record jacket to the work. "I recorded him along with the pigeons one Sunday afternoon in Union Square in downtown San Francisco. Later at home I started playing the tape loops of his voice and, by accident, discovered the process of letting two identical loops go gradually in and out of phase with each other." The result is a hypnotic aural web that bears certain relations to primitive chant, on the one hand, and mathematical series theory, on the other hand.

But perhaps the best example of this kind of composition, which Richard Kostelanetz has labeled "text-sound poetry," is by John Cage himself, the 1973 *Empty Words*. The work consists of four movements: (1) phrases, words, syllables, and letters (that is, sounds); (2) words, syllables, and letters; (3) syllables and letters; and finally (4) only letters. The fourth part is accompanied by a series of four projected images. Marjorie Perloff has described a performance of *Empty Words* in her book *The Poetics of Indeterminacy*:

While we see and don't see these images (they appear and disappear as slowly as possible and there are temporal intervals between projection), we are treated to a series of sounds that includes such types as: 1) guttural animal sounds, 2) exercises in the use of voiced and voiceless stops, 3) spirant series, 4) a "French" network exploiting sounds like "ce" and "ton," 5) sound units made up of the ending of one word and the beginning of another, 6) crescendos and diminuendos, 7) miniature chants. Throughout, we perceive approximations of musical intervals. No two "phrases" are the same yet there is a continuous patterning. At first, the stress is on decomposition, but toward the end of the performance sounds once again coalesce and begin to approximate syllables and words. . . . The auditor is gradually drawn into the performance; one wants to articulate one's own sounds, to create one's own phonemic patterning.

Post-Cageian experimental music has been marked by a return to melody, harmony, and tonality, and it has likewise insisted on the meaning of its linguistic utterances. But the new music has underscored, simultaneously, the purely aural dimensions of its texts. Robert Ashley, for instance, recognizes that his "operas," such as *Perfect Lives (Private Parts)* and *Atalanta*, in some sense reject Cage's deployment of the text as a "sonic object." For Cage, Ashley believes, the "use of words has always been drawn toward his involvement with abstract formulas," but Ashley, given his interest in opera, uses words to a different end, toward narration and the delineation of character. Still, for Cage, sound is primarily social, as Perloff's desire to create her own phonemic patterning of Cage's *Empty Words* makes clear, a means of engaging not only the accidental sounds of the event—from the audience's restlessness to ambient "street noise"—but also the participatory impulses of the audience itself. Ashley's operas are an exploration of music—and the musical text—as a form of social interaction. He relies not only upon the traditional resources of linguistic meaning and musical tonality but also upon the more abstract "sonic" effects introduced by Cage.

A second type of "literature with no name" has developed not out of the music scene but in the plastic arts, especially in its more conceptual and performance-oriented modes. An example of just such a literature is a "First Class Mail" piece done by the New York Graphic Workshop, an artist's collective, in 1967. It consists of a postcard with the following message printed on it:

THIS IS A MIRROR.
YOU ARE A WRITTEN
SENTENCE.

This implicates the audience not only in the text, requiring it to produce whatever "sentence" it thinks it "sees" (the artwork as both self-reflexive and self-creating), but also in a larger art historical discourse, as the audience reproduces itself after the fashion of the mirror-writing in Leonardo's secret notebooks. Another example is Shusaku Arakawa's *Untitled 1969*, a large 4-by-6-foot canvas with the words "I have decided to leave this canvas completely blank" stenciled into the middle of it. This statement is "true" only insofar as language is not painting, but Arakawa's gesture irrevocably implicates one genre in the other. His interest in the collision of the visual and the verbal culminated in 1979 with the publication of *The Mechanism of Meaning*, co-authored with poet Madeline Gins, a book that aligned him with the Language group. Bernstein and Susan B. Laufer have discussed Arakawa's work in an essay called "Meaning the Meaning":

For Arakawa, the act or experience of seeing is an act or experience of language. Language, in this view, cannot be thought of only as a verbal, word-bound system but is equally involved with the construction and mediation of visual seeing and of space. . . . In Arakawa's work the consistent use of superimposed written texts becomes a system for determining (constructing) visual space, at the same time defining a textual space (literally inside the paintings) and commenting on and critiquing the other spaces within the painting. The placement of writing, which forms internal captions, suggests that the canvas is to be seen as a page and, indeed, that all marks on these canvases are to be seen as inscription.

Repeatedly in *The Mechanism of Meaning* language challenges painting and vice versa. Thus, on one page entitled "The Ambiguous Zones of a Lemon," any number of different shapes, some looking like a lemon and some not, all variously colored, are labeled "actual lemon," "almost lemon," "reflection of a lemon," "photo of a lemon," "memory of lemon," "illusion of a lemon," "subject of a lemon," "dream of a lemon," "misapprehension of a lemon," and so on. The point, as another caption makes clear, is that, whether "statement or representation," zones of ambiguity "exist within . . . and across the conceptual distances which separate" the verbal and the visual, so that their differences in fact collapse.

Since the late 1960s there have been many instances of poets and visual artists moving into one another's "proper" areas of expertise. Predominantly, as in the hundreds of short videos produced by William Wegman between 1970 and 1978, language serves to challenge the authenticity of visual experience. In *Rage & Depression*, for instance, Wegman sits before the camera, a genial smile on his face, and tells this story:

I had these terrible fits of rage and depression all the time. I just got worse and worse and worse. Finally my parents had me committed. They tried all kinds of therapy. Finally they settled on shock. . . . I was just the meanest cuss you could imagine and when they put this cold, metal electrode, or whatever it was, to my chest, I started to giggle and then when they shocked me, it froze my face into this smile and even though I'm still incredibly depressed—everyone thinks I'm happy. I don't know what I'm going to do.

The immediacy of such video language is countered by the sense of language's physical weight and body in the work of conceptual artist Lawrence Weiner. A poet before he became an artist, he has directed much of his work toward measuring physical space in terms of language and vice versa. One of the inspirations for this line of inquiry was the example of the Great Barrens Eskimos whom he encountered while working on a series of pieces at the Arctic Circle that investigate the imaginative power of that hypothetical line in space. When an Eskimo is angry he walks out that anger in a straight line and plants an "anger stick" at the point where the anger subsides. Thus the intensity of his emotions can be physically measured. The word "anger" finds a plastic expression. In a short piece in *The L = A = N = G = U = A = G = E Book* Weiner takes an opposite, though related tack:

DARWIN IN *THE VOYAGE OF THE BEAGLE* INQUIRED OF A PATA-
GONIAN INDIAN
WHY THEY (THE INDIANS) DID NOT EAT THEIR DOGS IN TIME
OF FAMINE
INSTEAD OF EATING THEIR (THE INDIANS) OLD WOMEN
"Dogs kill otters, old women don't"
THEY REPLIED

Here language measures the "distance" between two physical places—our own and Patagonia—far more convincingly than any actual physical measurement could. John Baldessari's art is, like Arakawa's, more concerned with the experience of seeing as an act of language. His piece *The Pencil Story* (1972–73), for instance, consists of two pictures of the same pencil before and after sharpening. Written below them is this story: "I had this old pencil on the dashboard of my car for a long time. Every time I saw it, I felt uncomfortable since its point was so dull and dirty. I always intended to sharpen it and finally couldn't bear it any longer and did sharpen it. I'm not sure, but I think that has something to do with art." The elliptical effect of Baldessari's story—the uncertainty of the meanings it generates—is reminiscent of David Antin's disquieting narratives.

But by far the greatest impetus to this collapse of distinctions between genres and media has been the feminist movement. In her important assessment of the contribution of feminism to the art of the 1970s, "Sweeping Exchanges" (1981), Lucy Lippard has summed up the situation this way:

Feminism's greatest contribution to the future of art has probably been precisely its *lack* of contribution to modernism. Feminist methods and theories have instead offered a socially concerned alternative to the increasingly mechanical "evolution" of art about art. . . . The feminist insistence that the personal (and thereby art itself) is the political has, like a serious flood, interrupted the mainstream's flow, sending it off into hundreds of tributaries. . . . At its most provocative and instructive, feminism questions all the precepts of art as we know it. . . . The goal of feminism is *to change the character of art*. . . . One of the feminist goals is to reintegrate the aesthetic self and the social self and to make it possible for both to function without guilt or frustration. In the process, we have begun to see art as something subtly but significantly different from what it is in the dominant culture.

Often, of course, the dominant (masculine) culture is the object of attack. Barbara Kruger's large captioned photographs juxtapose images and text in order to undermine cultural stereotypes and clichés, declaring, for instance, across the face of a photograph of a woman in repose, "We won't play nature to your culture," thereby implicating the audience and the art world in the structure of a colonizing, sexist social order. Her text literally destroys the passivity of the image, and reveals the image to be a construct of "your culture." As Kruger herself puts it, "I see my work as a series of attempts to ruin certain representations, to displace the subject and to welcome a female spectator into the audience of men." Similarly, in a more or less exemplary moment from her *Aspects of the Liberal Dilemma*, Adrian Piper, herself a black, accompanies a picture of angry blacks surging down a staircase with an audiotape that asks, "What exactly is the esthetic *content* of this work?" Here Piper underscores the vast gap between a formalist reading of the image—the kind of aesthetic reading white, liberal audiences have been trained to see as the "authentic" approach to all representation—and one more cognizant of the social and political implications of the work. And Eleanor Antin has outlined the strategies of marginalization (sexist, racist, and classist) that pervade our culture, especially in the body of work surrounding her persona Eleanora Antinova, "the once celebrated but now retired Black Ballerina of Diaghilev's Ballet Russe"—a compendium of performances, videos, drawings, photographs, installations, and, above all, two alternative and competing narratives, Antinova's *Recollections of My Life with Diaghilev* and Antin's "autobiographical" pastiche, *Being Antinova*. Not only is the persona Antinova a sort of living example of high modernism's perverse ability to remove art from any meaningful social context, but as she rages against the collapse of her image over time—both in her aging and in her "disappearance" from "real" history—she embodies the fate of all women artists, all marginalized people, for that matter.

In contrast, Linda Montano's performance pieces, many of which are collected in her anthology/collage book, *Art in Everyday Life*, at least overtly possesses a much more private and introspective character. In an introductory essay—which appears, in a more or less overt attack on traditional systems of order, more than halfway through the book—Montano briefly describes the event that led to one of her most famous performances, and then goes on to describe the relation of her art to her life:

> On August 19, 1977 Mitchell Payne [whom she had married in 1971 and from whom she had separated in 1975] died very suddenly and tragically in Kansas City. I was shocked. I repeated the story of his death over and over on tape and found that I was able to mourn him in my work.
>
> Art has been generous and has allowed me to explore fears, exuberances, unconscious subject matter, fantasies and ideas.
>
> It is the place where I practice for life.

"Mitchell's Death," the performance piece that Montano created out of the tragedy of her husband's accidental shooting, is a sublimely powerful piece of writing. It is probably fair to say that it epitomizes—though the relations between the two are almost certainly coincidental—the direction that Lucy Lippard had outlined for herself a year earlier in her first consciously feminist collection of essays, *From the Center*. "The woman's movement changed my life in many ways," Lippard wrote in the introduction to that book, "not the least being my approach to criticism. It may not show . . . but from inside, from where I live, there is a new freedom to say how I feel and to respond to art on a far more personal level. I'm more willing to be confessional, vulnerable, autobiographical, even embarrassing." In a similar vein, "Mitchell's Death" represents the public presentation of what one recognizes, in hearing or reading the work, is a profoundly private space, so private (so taboo) that one feels a virtually voyeuristic relation to it. And yet, Montano's catharsis becomes one's own. Her ability to expose her private feelings in public space, and to share her grief with us in terms that humanize death—she doesn't ennoble it, she simply makes us acknowledge our common, human burden before it—makes us wonder why, as a society, we repress grief, marginalize death, and literally expunge them from "polite society." For Montano, death is a part of everyday life, just like art.

"The dilemma," as Lippard puts it at the beginning of *Get the Message?: A Decade of Art for Social Change* (1984), "is how to integrate art and politics," art and life. The way out of that dilemma, she also argues, is "to focus culturally not only on inward relationships but on the broader outward relationships that control them." In one way or another, this network of broader relationships—between one genre and another, between the various media themselves, between, finally, art and life—has become the focus of the new avant-garde as a whole. If most of this activity has, in recent years, happened outside the "canon," as a kind of extraliterary literature, it remains for literary studies to extend outward into the broader culture as forcefully as the broader culture—both the larger artworld and the culture at large—has been for some time utilizing the considerable resources of the word.

Henry M. Sayre

Notes on Contributors

Daniel Aaron is Victor S. Thomas Professor, Emeritus, Department of English and American Language and Literature, Harvard University, and president of the Library of America. His works include *Men of Good Hope*, *Writers on the Left*, and *The Unwritten War: American Writers and the Civil War*.

Quentin Anderson, author of *The American Henry James* and *The Imperial Self*, is Julian Clarence Levi Professor in the Humanities, Emeritus, of Columbia University and a Fellow of the New York Institute for the Humanities.

Houston A. Baker is Albert M. Greenfield Professor of Human Relations at the University of Pennsylvania. He is the author of *The Journey Back: Issues in Black Literature and Criticism*, *Blues, Ideology and Afro-American Literature: A Vernacular Theory*, and *Modernism and the Harlem Renaissance*.

Martha Banta is Professor of English at the University of California, Los Angeles. She has written many articles on Henry James and is editor of *New Essays on The American*. Her books include *Henry James and the Occult*, *Failure and Success in America*, and *Imaging American Women: Idea and Ideals in Cultural History*. She is also an editor of *The Harper American Literature*.

Nina Baym is Professor of English at the University of Illinois. She is the author of *The Shape of Hawthorne's Career*, *Women's Fiction: A Guide to Novels by and about Women in America, 1820–1870*, and *Novels, Readers, and Reviewers: Responses to Fiction in Antebellum America*.

Michael Davitt Bell is Professor of English at Williams College. He is the author of *Hawthorne and the Historical Romance of New England* and *The Development of American Romance: The Sacrifice of Relation*.

Sacvan Bercovitch is Carswell Professor of English and American Literature and Professor of Comparative Literature at Harvard University. His major works on American Puritanism include *The Puritan Origins of the American Self* and *The American Jeremiad*, and he is the editor of several important collections, from *Typology and Early American Literature* to *Reconstructing American Literary History*.

Warner Berthoff is Henry B. and Anne M. Cabot Professor of English and American Literature at Harvard University. Among his publications are *The Example of Melville*, *The Ferment of Realism: American Literature, 1884–1919*, and *A Literature Without Qualities: American Writing Since 1945*.

Malcolm Bradbury is Professor of American Studies at the University of East Anglia, England. He is the author of many books and monographs on modernism and postmodernism and is the co-editor of the *Penguin Companion to American Literature* and the volume on *Modernism* in the Pelican Guides series. Bradbury has also written many novels, including *The History Man* and *Cuttings*.

James E. B. Breslin is Professor of English at the University of California, Berkeley. He is the author of *William Carlos Williams, an American Artist* and *From Modern to Contemporary: American Poetry 1945–65*.

Richard H. Brodhead, Professor of English at Yale University, is the author of *Hawthorne, Melville, and the Novel* and *The School of Hawthorne*. He is the editor of *New Essays on Moby-Dick* and *Faulkner: New Perspectives*.

Gerald L. Bruns is William and Hazel White Professor of English at the University of Notre Dame. He is the author of *Modern Poetry and the Idea of Language* and *Inventions: Writing, Textuality, and Understanding in Literary History*.

Lawrence Buell is Professor of English at Oberlin College. He is the author of *Literary Transcendentalism: Style and Vision in the American Renaissance* and *New England Literary Culture: From Revolution through Renaissance*.

Sargent Bush, Jr., is Professor of English at the University of Wisconsin. He is the author of *The Writings of Thomas Hooker* and has compiled the definitive bibliography of Hooker and a detailed catalogue of *The Library of Emmanuel College, Cambridge, 1584–1637*. He has written articles on American authors from Edward Taylor to Mark Twain and Willa Cather.

Ruby Cohn is Professor of Comparative Drama at the University of California, Davis. Her books include *Back to Beckett, Just Play: Beckett's Theatre,* and *From Desire to Godot.* She is also the author of *Dialogue in American Drama: New American Dramatists 1960–80* and of many essays and reviews about modern and contemporary drama.

Michael J. Colacurcio is Professor of English at the University of California, Los Angeles. He is the author of *The Province of Piety: Moral History in Hawthorne's Early Tales* and editor of *New Essays on The Scarlet Letter.*

James M. Cox is Professor of English at Dartmouth College and author of *Mark Twain: The Fate of Humor.* He has also published essays on many American writers, among them Emerson, Hawthorne, Poe, James, Adams, Frost, and Faulkner.

Emory Elliott is Professor of English and Chair of the English Department at Princeton University. He is the author of *Power and the Pulpit in Puritan New England* and *Revolutionary Writers: Literature and Authority in the New Republic, 1725–1810,* as well as essays on a wide range of subjects in English and American literature and culture. He is also the editor of *Puritan Influences in American Literature* and is series editor of *The American Novel* (Cambridge University Press) and *Penn Studies in Contemporary American Fiction.*

Everett Emerson is Professor of English at the University of North Carolina and since 1969 has been editor of the journal *Early American Literature.* He has written or edited eight books, including ones on Captain John Smith, John Cotton, and Mark Twain and *Letters from New England, 1629–1638.*

Raymond Federman is Professor of English at the State University of New York, Buffalo. A bilingual (French and English) writer, he is the author of two volumes of poetry, three books of criticism on Samuel Beckett, and six novels, including *Double or Nothing, Take It or Leave It, The Voice in the Closet,* and *Smiles on Washington Square* (the winner of the American Book Award for 1986).

Philip Fisher is Professor of English at Harvard University. He has written essays on Theodore Dreiser and is the author of *Hard Facts: Setting and Form in the American Novel.*

Wayne Franklin is Professor of American Studies and English at the University of Iowa. Author of *Discoverers, Explorers, Settlers: The Diligent Writers of Early America* and *The New World of James Fenimore Cooper,* he has also published articles on Charles Brockden Brown, Washington Irving, and a variety of topics in American literature and culture.

Frederick Garber is Distinguished Professor of Comparative Literature at the State University of New York, Binghamton. He is the author of *Wordsworth and the Poetry of Encounter, Thoreau's Redemptive Imagination,* and *The Autonomy of the Self from Richardson to Huysmans.*

William L. Hedges is Professor of English at Goucher College. He is co-author-editor of *Land and Imagination: The Rural Dream in America* and has written exclusively on Irving, notably in *Washington Irving: An American Study, 1802–32.* His articles include treatments of John Woolman, Charles Brockden Brown, and Hawthorne, as well as, more broadly, the literature of the early republic.

Alan Heimert is Cabot Professor of American Literature at Harvard University. He is the author of *Religion and the American Mind: From the Great Awakening to the Revolution* and co-author, with Reinhold Niebuhr, of *A Nation So Conceived.* His contributions to early American studies include two important collections of which he is co-editor, *The Great Awakening* and *The Puritans in America.*

Claudia Johnson is Professor of English at the University of Alabama. She is the author of *The Productive Tension of Hawthorne's Art* and *American Actress: Perspective on the Nineteenth Century,* and has compiled, with Vernon E. Johnson, *Nineteenth-Century Theatrical Manners.*

Donald M. Kartiganer is Professor of English at the University of Washington. He is the author of *The Fragile Thread: The Meaning of Form in Faulkner's Novels* and co-editor of *Theories of American Literature.*

Elaine H. Kim is Associate Professor and Head of the Asian American Studies program at the University of California, Berkeley. She is the author of *Asian American Literature: An Introduction to the Writings and Their Social Context* and *With Silk Wings: Asian American Women at Work,* as well as a number of articles on literature, race, culture, and gender.

Barbara Kiefer Lewalski is Kenan Professor of English and of History and Literature at Harvard University. She has written extensively on seventeenth-century English literature, including books on *Paradise Lost* and *Paradise Regained* and on John Donne's "Anniversaries." A chapter on Edward Taylor concludes her study *Protestant Poetics and the Seventeenth-Century Religious Lyric,* which received the James Russell Lowell Prize in 1979.

A. Walton Litz, Holmes Professor of English Literature at Princeton University, has published numerous studies and editions of modern American writers. Among these are *Eliot in His Time* and *Ezra Pound and Dorothy Shakespear: Their Letters, 1909–1914* (edited with Omar Pound).

Jerome Loving is Professor of English at Texas A&M University. He is the author of *Walt Whitman's Champion: William Douglas O'Connor, Emerson, Whitman, and the American Muse,* and *Emily Dickinson: The Poet on the Second Story.*

Mason I. Lowance, Jr., is Professor of English at the University of Massachusetts and the author of *The Language of Canaan.* He has published widely on typology and nineteenth-century American writers, has written a study of Increase Mather, is an editor of the Yale edition of *The Works of Jonathan Edwards,* and has edited *Massachusetts Broadsides of the American Revolution.*

Larry McCaffery is Professor of English at San Diego State University. He is the author of *The Metafictional Muse: The Work of Robert Coover, Donald Barthelme, and William H. Gass* and co-editor of two collections of interviews, *Anything Can Happen: Interviews with Contemporary American Novelists* and *Alive and Writing: Interviews with American Authors of the 1980s.* He is editor of *Fiction International.*

Donald McQuade is Professor of English at the University of California, Berkeley. His works include *Popular Writing in America* and *Edsels, Luckies, and Frigidaires: Advertising the American Way.* He is also the general editor of *The Harper American Literature.*

John McWilliams is Professor of American Literature at Middlebury College. He is the author of *Political Justice in a Republic* and *Hawthorne, Melville and the American Character,* co-author of *Law and American Literature,* and has co-edited the Critical Heritage essays on James Fenimore Cooper. He has written articles on the historical and literary treatment of such subjects as Thomas Morton's Merry Mount, the American Revolution, and Indian removal.

Terence Martin is Distinguished Professor of English at Indiana University. He is the author of *The Instructed Vision: Scottish Common Sense Philosophy and the Origins of American Fiction* and *Nathaniel Hawthorne.*

Wendy Martin, Professor of English and American Studies at Claremont Graduate School, has published *An American Triptych: Anne Bradstreet, Emily Dickinson, and Adrienne Rich.* Author of many articles on women writers, she edits the journal *Women's Studies* and is editor of *New Essays on The Awakening*.

Robert Milder is Associate Professor of English at Washington University. He has published essays on Melville, Cooper, and other American writers and has written the section on Melville in *American Literary Scholarship*.

J. Hillis Miller is UCI Distinguished Professor of English and Comparative Literature at the University of California, Irvine. He is the author of numerous works on nineteenth- and twentieth-century literature and on literary theory, including *Poets of Reality: Six Twentieth Century Writers*.

David Minter is Professor of English at Emory University. His works include *The Interpreted Design as a Structural Principle in American Prose* and *William Faulkner: His Life and Work*. He is also an editor of *The Harper American Literature*.

Lee Clark Mitchell, Associate Professor of English and presently chairman of the American Studies Program at Princeton University, is author of *Witnesses to a Vanishing America*, several essays on the Western and on Henry James, and is editor of *New Essays on The Red Badge of Courage*.

Charles Molesworth is currently Chairman of the English Department at Queens College and Professor of English at the Graduate Center, City University of New York. He is the author of *The Fierce Embrace: A Study in Contemporary Poetry*, books on Donald Barthelme and Gary Snyder, and two volumes of poetry.

N. Scott Momaday is Professor of English at the University of Arizona. He is a poet, novelist, and painter. His novel *House Made of Dawn* won the Pulitzer Prize and was followed by *On the Way to Rainy Mountain* and *The Names: A Memoir*. He has written on Native American poetry, edited *The Complete Poems of Frederick Goddard Tuckerman*, and published several volumes of his own poetry, including *The Gourd Dancer*.

Cary Nelson is Professor of English and Criticism and Theory at the University of Illinois. He is the author of *The Incarnate Word: Literature as Verbal Space* and *Our Last First Poets: Vision and History in Contemporary American Poetry*, the editor of *Theory in the Classroom*, and the co-editor of *W. S. Merwin: Essays on the Poetry* and *Marxism and the Interpretation of Culture*.

Barbara Packer is Professor of English at the University of California, Los Angeles. She is the author of *Emerson's Fall: A New Interpretation of the Major Essays*.

Raymund A. Paredes is Professor of English and Associate Dean of the Graduate Division at the University of California, Los Angeles. He has written extensively on Mexican American literature.

Jay Parini is Associate Professor of English at Middlebury College. He is a poet, novelist, and critic; his most recent books are *The Patch Boys* (a novel) and *Town Life* (poems).

H. Daniel Peck is Professor of English at Vassar College. He is the author of *A World by Itself: The Pastoral Moment in Cooper's Fiction.*

Marjorie Perloff is Professor of English and Comparative Literature at Stanford University. She has written books on Yeats, Robert Lowell, and Frank O'Hara, as well as *The Poetics of Indeterminacy: Rimbaud to Cage, The Dance of the Intellect,* and *The Futurist Moment: Avant-Garde, Avant-Guerre, and the Language of Rupture.*

Thomas Philbrick, Professor Emeritus of the University of Pittsburgh, is both an editor of the State University of New York edition of the works of Cooper and the author of *James Fenimore Cooper and the Development of American Sea Fiction.* His other writings include a book on St. John de Crèvecoeur and articles on Melville and Jefferson.

Carolyn Porter is Professor of English at the University of California, Berkeley. She is the author of *Seeing and Being: The Plight of the Participant Observer in Emerson, James, Adams, and Faulkner.*

John Carlos Rowe, Professor of English at the University of California, Irvine, has written numerous articles on literary theory. His books include *The Theoretical Dimensions of Henry James, Through the Custom-House: Nineteenth-Century American Fiction and Modern Theory,* and *At Emerson's Tomb: The Politics of American Modernism.*

Louis D. Rubin, Jr., is University Distinguished Professor of English at the University of North Carolina at Chapel Hill and editorial director of Algonquin Books of Chapel Hill. He is author and editor of thirty-five books, many of them about the literature and history of the American South.

Jack Salzman, Director of the Center for American Cultural Studies at Columbia University, edits *Prospects: An Annual of American Cultural Studies.* He is editor of *The Cambridge Handbook of American Literature* and collections of the protest poetry and prose of the 1930s.

Henry M. Sayre is Associate Professor of Art History at Oregon State University. He is the author of *The Visual Text of William Carlos Williams* and of numerous essays on postmodern poetry, fiction, and artworks.

William J. Scheick is Professor of English at the University of Texas where he also edits *Texas Studies in Literature and Language*. He is the author of *The Will and the Word: The Poetry of Edward Taylor*, *The Slender Human Word: Emerson's Artistry in Prose*, *The Writings of Jonathan Edwards*, and *The Half-Blood: A Cultural Symbol in Nineteenth-Century American Fiction*. He has also edited collections of essays on Jonathan Edwards and Patrick White.

Neil Schmitz is Professor of English at the State University of New York, Buffalo. He is the author of *Of Huck and Alice: Humorous Writing in American Literature*.

John Seelye is Graduate Research Professor of American Literature at the University of Florida. He has written fiction and, in *The True Adventures of Huckleberry Finn*, fiction as criticism. His critical work on American literature includes a book on Melville, an illustrated "meditation" on *Mark Twain in the Movies*, and *Prophetic Waters: The River in Early American Life and Literature*.

Daniel B. Shea is Professor of English and American Literature at Washington University. He is the author of *Spiritual Autobiography in Early America* and of essays on Thomas Morton, Jonathan Edwards, B. F. Skinner, and Emerson and "the American Metamorphosis."

Elaine Showalter is Professor of English at Princeton University. Her books include *A Literature of Their Own: British Women Novelists from Brontë to Lessing*, *These Modern Women*, and *The Female Malady: Women, Madness and Culture*.

Kenneth Silverman, Professor of English at New York University, is the author of *The Life and Times of Cotton Mather*, for which he received the Pulitzer and Bancroft prizes. He has also edited a collection of Mather's letters and a selection of colonial American poetry, and has written a study of Timothy Dwight and *A Cultural History of the American Revolution*.

Lewis P. Simpson is Boyd Professor of English at Louisiana State University and editor of *The Southern Review*. His books include *The Man of Letters in New England and the South*, *The Dispossessed Garden: Pastoral and History in*

Southern Literature, and *The Brazen Face of History: Studies in the Literary Consciousness in America.*

Werner Sollors, Professor of American Literature and Language and of Afro-American Studies at Harvard University, has published *Amiri Baraka/LeRoi Jones* and *Beyond Ethnicity: Consent and Descent in American Culture.*

Haskell Springer is Professor of English at the University of Kansas. He is the editor of Washington Irving's *The Sketch Book of Geoffrey Crayon, Gent.* and, with Marlene Springer, of *Plains Woman: The Diary of Martha Farnsworth, 1882–1922.*

Wendy Steiner is Professor of English at the University of Pennsylvania. Her publications include *Exact Resemblance to Exact Resemblance: The Literary Portraiture of Gertrude Stein, The Colors of Rhetoric: Problems in the Relations Between Modern Literature and Painting*, and *Pictures of Romance: Form Against Context in Painting and Literature.*

Robert Stepto is Professor of English, American Studies, and Afro-American Studies at Yale University. He is the author of *From Behind the Veil: A Study of Afro-American Narrative* and numerous articles. He has co-edited *Chant of Saints: A Gathering of Afro-American Literature, Art, and Scholarship* and *Afro-American Literature: The Reconstruction of Instruction.*

Catharine R. Stimpson is Professor of English and Dean of the Graduate School at Rutgers University. Now the editor of a book series about women in culture and society for the University of Chicago Press, she was the founding editor of *Signs: Journal of Women in Culture and Society.* She is the author of a novel *(Class Notes)* and of monographs, essays, and reviews about education, modern culture and literature, and feminism.

Eric J. Sundquist, Professor of English at the University of California, Berkeley, is editor of *American Realism* and *New Essays on Uncle Tom's Cabin.* His books number *Faulkner: The House Divided* and *Home as Found: Authority and Genealogy in Nineteenth-Century American Literature.*

G. R. Thompson is Professor of English at Purdue University. He is the author of *Poe's Fiction: Romantic Irony in the Gothic Tales* and editor of *The Gothic Imagination: Essays in Dark Romanticism.*

Cecelia Tichi, Professor of English at Vanderbilt University, has published essays on the American Puritans and is author of *New World, New Earth:*

Environmental Reform in American Literature from the Puritans through Whitman and *Shifting Gears: Technology, Literature, Culture in Modernist America.*

Linda W. Wagner is Professor of English at Michigan State University. She has published widely on American literature, including the collection *Critical Essays on Sylvia Plath.*

Michael Wood is Professor of English at the University of Exeter. He is the author of *Stendhal, America in the Movies,* and many essays on literature and on film.

Thomas Wortham is Professor of English at the University of California, Los Angeles. He is the editor of *James Russell Lowell's The Biglow Papers, First Series* and co-editor of *Nineteenth-Century Literature.*

Ruth Bernard Yeazell, Professor of English at the University of California, Los Angeles, is author of *Language and Knowledge in the Late Novels of Henry James* and *The Death and Letters of Alice James.* She was formerly co-editor of the journal *Nineteenth-Century Literature* and is editor of *Sex, Politics, and Science in the Nineteenth-Century Novel.*

Index

Abbott, Lyman (1835–1922), 576

Abish, Walter (1931–), 1141, 1155, 1164, 1176; *Alphabetical Africa*, 1156, 1175-76; *How German Is It*, 1164, 1175-76

Abolitionism, 66, 212, 263, 283, 294, 304-5, 331, 346-47, 350-56, 358-59, 372-73, 408-11, 571

Abstract expressionism, 1180, 1098

Absurdism, 1135, 1140, 1148-51

Academic poetry, 1041

Acker, Kathy (1948-), 1171, 1176; *Blood and Guts in High School*, 1174-75; *Don Quixote*, 1176; *Great Expectations*, 1174, 1190-91

Acosta, Oscar Zeta (1936–): *The Autobiography of a Brown Buffalo*, 809; *The Revolt of the Cockroach People*, 809

Action poetry, 1180

Adams, Abigail (1744–1818), 195-96

Adams, Alice (1926–), 1163

Adams, Brooks (1848–1927): *America's Economic Supremacy*, 484; *The New Empire*, 484

Adams, Charles Follen (1842–1918): *Leedle Yawcob Strauss and Other Poems*, 578

Adams, Henry (1838–1918), 48, 363, 488, 491, 645-67, 707-8, 733, 772; *The Degradation of the Democratic Dogma*, 662-63; *Democracy*, 520, 647, 656-59; *The Education of Henry Adams*, 483, 645, 647, 650, 652, 656, 659-61, 663-67, 707, 856-57; *Essays in Anglo-Saxon Law*, 652; *Esther*, 647, 656-59; "The Gold Conspiracy," 651; "The Great Secession Winter of 1860-61," 649; historical works, 652-57, 662-64, 667; *The History of the United States in the Administrations of Jefferson and Madison*, 654-56, 761; *John Randolph*, 656-57; journalism, 649-50; "A Letter to American Teachers of History," 662; letters, 649; *The Life and Writings of Albert Gallatin*, 653-57; *The Life of George Cabot Lodge*, 666; *Memoirs of Arii Taimai E*, 661; *Memoirs of Maura Taaroa, Last Queen of Tahiti*, 661; *Mont-Saint-Michel and Chartres*, 640, 647, 652, 656, 663-64, 707; "Primitive Rights of Women," 652; *Principles of Geology*, 651; "The Rule of Phase Applied to History," 662-63; scientific writing, 651; "The Tendency of History," 662

Adams, John (1735–1826), 41, 142-43, 149, 153, 195-96; *A Dissertation on the Canon and Feudal Law*, 192-93

Adams, Léonie (1899–), 828, 830

Adams, Samuel (1722–1803), 193

Adams, Thomas (fl. 1612–53), 27

Adams, William (1650–85), 41

Addams, Jane (1860–1935), 522, 823; *Democracy and Social Ethics*, 494, 606

Adler, Mortimer J. (1902–), 731

Adler, Renata (1938–), 1033

Adolescent sensibility: post-World War II fiction, 1031

Adorno, Theodor (1903–69), 1041; *Aesthetic Theory*, 1059

Adventure stories, 173, 175, 177, 517

Advertising, 475-76, 552-53, 723

Advice books, 595-96

Aestheticism: debate over, in 1880s, 680

Africa, preoccupation with: post-World War I, 854

African Grove Theater, New York City, 334
African Methodist Episcopal Church Magazine, 581
Afro-Americans, *see* Blacks
Afterwit, Anthony, *see* Franklin, Benjamin
Agassiz, Louis (1807–73), 651
Agee, James (1909–55): *Let Us Now Praise Famous Men*, 755, 852, 866-67
Ager, Waldemar (1869–1941): *Paa veien til smeltepotten*, 587
Agohazushi, 580
Agrarian group, 853, 865, 935, 1008, 1135
Aiieeeee! (anthology), 1072
Aiken, Conrad (1889–1973), 752, 770; *Blue Voyage*, 858; *Great Circle*, 858; *King Coffin*, 858
Aiken, George L. (1830–76), 335
Ainslee's magazine, 477
Ainsworth, Henry (1571–1623?), 84
Albee, Edward (1928–), 1108-9; *All Over*, 1109; *The American Dream*, 1108; *Box*, 1109; *The Death of Bessie Smith*, 1108; *A Delicate Balance*, 1109; *The Lady from Dubuque*, 1109; *Quotations from Chairman Mao Tse-Tung*, 1109; *The Sandbox*, 1108; *Seascape*, 1109; *Tiny Alice*, 1109; *Who's Afraid of Virginia Woolf?* 1108-9; *The Zoo Story*, 1108
Alcott, Amos Bronson (1799–1888), 212, 215, 365, 372, 374-75, 454; *Conversations with Children on the Gospels*, 210, 371-72
Alcott, Louisa May (1832–88), 303-4, 592; *Little Women*, 301, 303-4, 561; *Work*, 494, 510
Aldrich, Thomas Bailey (1836–1907), 473, 478, 575; *The Stillwater Tragedy*, 520
Aldridge, Ira (1807–67), *The Black Doctor*, 334
Aldridge, John (1922–), 822; *After the Lost Generation*, 1131
Alexander, Michael (1941–), 971
Alger, Horatio, Jr. (1832–99), 556-58, 573, 583; *In a New World*, 557; *Ragged Dick; or, Street Life in New York*, 556-57; *Struggling Upward*, 557; "Writing Stories for Boys," 556
Algren, Nelson (1909–81), 1132; *The Man with the Golden Arm*, 1139
Alien and Sedition Acts, 179, 181
Alienation, 860-61, 1132, 1134-35
Allegory, 61, 250-51, 253, 261, 422-23, 440
Allen, Donald M. (1912–): *The New American Poetry*, 1082, 1099
Allen, Ethan (1738–89), 196; *A Narrative of*

Colonel Ethan Allen's Captivity, 152, 155, 197-98; *Reason the Only Oracle of Man*, 197
Allen, Frances N. S. (1865–?): *The Invaders*, 583
Allen, Gay Wilson (1903–), 459
Allen, Hervey (1889–1949): *Anthony Adverse*, 853
Allen, James (1632–1710), 41
Allen, James Lane (1849–1925): *The Bride of the Mistletoe*, 515; *The Choir Invisible*, 515; *The Reign of Law*, 515; *Summer in Arcady*, 515; "Two Principles in Recent American Fiction," 515
Allen, John (fl. 1764–88): *An Oration, upon the Beauties of Liberty*, 141
Allen, Paul (1775–1826): "Poem on the Happiness of America," 160
Allen, William Francis (1830–89): *Slave Songs of the United States*, 574
Alloway, Lawrence (1926–), 1188
Alsop, George (1638–post 1673): *A Character of the Province of Maryland*, 21, 89
Alsop, Richard (1761–1815): *The Charms of Fancy*, 158, 161
Alter, Robert (1935–), 1128
Alther, Lisa (1944–): *Kinflicks*, 1170
Althusser, Louis (1918–), 1048
Amadas, Philip (1550–1618), 19
Ambrose, Isaac (1604–64), 30
American Academy of Arts and Letters, 477-78, 747
American Agriculturalist, The, 351
American Civil Liberties Union, 721
American Economic Association, 489-90
American Guide Series, 752, 865
American identity, 40-44, 549-51
American Indians, *see* Native Americans
American Jewess, 577
American Magazine, 851, 934
American Mercury, The, 720-21, 741, 867
American Philosophical Society, 109
American Poetry Review, 1034
American Renaissance, 209, 221, 225, 381, 454
American Revolution, 139-55, 247-49, 268, 326-27, 566
American Tradition in Literature, The, 789-90
American Women (1963 report), 1064
American Writers Against the Vietnam War, 1096

American Writers' Congress, 749, 1014

Amerikán, 581

Ames, Fisher (1758–1808): *The Works of Fisher Ames*, 189

Ames, William (1576–1633): *The Marrow of Sacred Divinity*, 28, 58

Ammons, A. R. (Archie Randolph Ammons) (1926–): "Carsons Inlet," 1083

Amygism, 954

Analectic Magazine, 233, 238

Analytic constructionalism, 1051, 1056

Anaya, Rudolfo (1937–), 807-9; *Bless Me, Ultima*, 808-9

Anderson, Benedict, 568-70

Anderson, George K. (1901–): *This Generation*, 791

Anderson, Laurie (1947–), 1192; *United States*, 1192-93

Anderson, Margaret (1886–1973), 737, 852, 930

Anderson, Maxwell (1888–1959), 834, 1103

Anderson, Sherwood (1876–1941), 716, 720, 740, 744, 747, 773, 779, 851, 871, 893, 1017, 1130; *Dark Laughter*, 850, 854-55; *Many Marriages*, 861; *Mid-American Chants*, 917; *Poor White*, 860; *Winesburg, Ohio*, 776, 862-63

Andrewes, Lancelot (1555–1626), 27

Andrews, Bruce (1948–), 1175, 1183; *The L=A=N=G=U=A=G=E Book*, 1184

Andrews, Terry, 1172

Andrews, William L. (1946–), 793

Andros, Thomas (1759–1845): *The Old Jersey Captive*, 152

Angelou, Maya (1928–), 1064

Anglicanism, *see* Church of England

Anglo-African Magazine, 582

Anthropology, 853-54, 1052

Anti-hero, 1030, 1061

Anti-intellectualism, 120, 549

Antin, David (1932–), 1180-83; *tuning*, 1181; "the value of the real thing," 1181-82

Antin, Eleanor (1935–), 1198

Antin, Mary (1881–1949): *Promised Land*, 576-77; *They Who Knock at Our Gates*, 577

Antinomianism, 62-63, 122

Antislavery movement, *see* Abolitionism

Anvil, The, 921

Apel, Karl-Otto (1922–), 1056

Apple, Max (1941–), 1163-64

Appleton's, 587

Arakawa, Shusaku (1936–): *The Mechanism of Meaning*, 1195-96; *Untitled 1969*, 1195

Arbeiterzeitung, 581

Arcadia, myth of, 25-26

Arce, Julio (1870–1926), 802

Arena, 576

Arendt, Hannah (1906–75): *On Violence*, 1038

Arensberg, Walter Conrad (1878–1954), 916

Arizona Quarterly, 805

Armageddon, 1071

Arminianism, 117

Armory Show (International Exhibition of Modern Art, 1913), 719, 738-39, 845, 917

Arnold, June (1926–), 1176; *Sister Gin*, 1176

Arnold, Matthew (1822–88), 1033

Artforum, 1185, 1188

Art in America, 1180-81

Art magazines, 479

Ashbery, John (1927–), 1083, 1097-99, 1180-81, 1183; *Houseboat Days*, 1180; "Pyrography," 1180; "Self-Portrait in a Convex Mirror," 1059, 1180-81; *The Tennis Court Oath*, 1097; *Three Poems*, 1174

Ashbridge, Elizabeth (1713–55): *Some Account of the Fore-Part of the Life of Elizabeth Ashbridge . . . Wrote by Herself*, 68, 79-81

Ashley, Robert (1930–), 1193; *Atalanta*, 1195; *Perfect Lives (Private Parts)*, 1195

Asian American literature, 517, 811-21, 1063, 1072, 1114

Asimov, Isaac (1920–), 1168

Aspinwall, Thomas, 37

Asselineau, Roger (1915–), 453

Astor Place Riot (1849), 334

Atherton, Gertrude (1857–1948): *Patience Sparhawk and Her Times*, 595

Atlanta Constitution, 574, 586-87

Atlantic Monthly, 354, 472-74, 476, 574-77, 637, 672, 676, 851, 934; and William Dean Howells, 503, 505, 510, 516, 766

Atomic bomb, 757, 1066

Attaway, William (1912–), 866

Atwood, Margaret (1939–): *A Handmaid's Tale*, 1167, 1171; *Lady Oracle*, 1171

Auden, W. H. (Wystan Hugh Auden) (1907–73), 749, 994; "In Memory of W. B. Yeats," 1085

Auerbach, Erich (1892–1957): *Mimesis: The Representation of Reality in Western Literature*, 1129

Austin, John Langshaw (1911–60), 1057

Austin, Mary (1868–1934), 823

Autobiography, *see* Biography and autobiography

Automobile, 728-29, 1042-43

Avant-garde movements, 719-20, 738, 744, 847, 849, 1178-99

Babbitt, Irving (1865–1933), 496, 746, 999; *Rousseau and Romanticism*, 999

Backus, Isaac (1724–1806), 119, 123

Bacon, Francis (1561–1626): *New Atlantis*, 27

Bacone Indian University Instructor, 580

Bailey, Jacob (1731–1808), 166

Bailyn, Bernard (1922–), 147

Baker, Benjamin A. (1818–90), 333

Baker, Estelle: *The Rose Door*, 523

Baldessari, John (1931–): *The Pencil Story*, 1197

Baldwin, James (1924–), 1139; *Another Country*, 1153; "Everybody's Protest Novel," 1061; *The Fire Next Time*, 1074

Baldwin, Joseph Glover (1815–64), 266

Ballard, J. G. (James Graham Ballard) (1930–), 1167

Baltimore American, 571

Bambara, Toni Cade (1939–), 1172-73; *The Black Woman*, 1064; *Gorilla, My Love*, 1173; *The Salt Eaters*, 1173; *The Sea Birds Are Singing*, 1173

Bancroft, George (1800–1891), 357; *History of the United States*, 357

Bancroft, Hubert Howe (1832–1918): *History of California*, 517

Baraka, Imamu Amiri (LeRoi Jones) (1934–), 1027, 1070-71, 1099, 1114–15; *The Baptism*, 1115; "cuba libre," 1071; *Dutchman*, 1071, 1115, 1122-23; *The Slave*, 1115; *The Toilet*, 1115

Barker, Colin A. (Henry J. Thomas), 552

Barker, James Nelson (1784–1858): *She Would Be a Soldier; or, The Plains of Chippewa*, 329

Barlow, Joel (1754–1812), 156-58, 162-64, 166; "Advice to a Raven in Russia," 163; *Advice to the Privileged Orders in the Several States of Europe*, 192; *The Anarchiad*, 157, 165; *The Columbiad*, 161; "The Conspiracy of Kings," 163; "The Hasty Pudding," 156, 165; "The Prospect of Peace," 160; *The Vision of Columbus*, 156, 159, 161, 192

Barlowe, Arthur, 19

Barnes, Barnabe (1569?–1609), 28

Barnes, Djuna (1892–1982), 851; *Ladies' Almanack*, 859; *Nightwood*, 869

Barras, Charles M. (1820–93): *The Black Crook*, 336

Barry, Philip (1896–1949), 1103

Barth, John (1930–), 1043, 1141, 1143, 1145, 1154, 1162; *The End of the Road*, 1147; "A Few Words About Minimalism," 1165; *The Floating Opera*, 1147; *Giles Goat-Boy*, 1151, 1154, 1166; *Letters*, 1163, 1175; *Sabbatical*, 1175; *The Sotweed Factor*, 1150

Barthelme, Donald (1931–), 1043, 1145, 1147, 1150, 1153, 1163; *Paradise*, 1169

Barthelme, Frederick (1943–), 1163, 1165; *Moon Deluxe*, 1164; *Second Marriage*, 1164

Barthes, Roland (1915–80), 1017, 1127, 1173, 1176, 1185-86; *Barthes by Barthes*, 1174; *S/Z*, 1174

Bartol, Cyrus (1813–1900), 375; *Pictures of Europe*, 374; *Radical Problems*, 374

Bartram, William (1739–1823), 23; *The Travels of William Bartram*, 80; *Travels through North and South Carolina, Georgia, East & West Florida*, 190-91

Barzun, Jacques (1907–): *The Energies of Art*, 696

Batchelor, John Calvin (1948–): *The Birth of the People's Republic of Antarctica*, 1167, 1175

Bateman, Sidney Frances (1823–81), 332

Battle of Brooklyn, The, 150, 326

Baudelaire, Charles (1821–67), 956-57

Baumbach, Jonathan (1933–): *Reruns*, 1152

Baxter, Richard (1615–91): *Holy Commonwealth*, 27; *The Saints Everlasting Rest*, 30

Bayley, Lewis (d. 1631): *The Practice of Piety*, 56

Bay Psalm Book, 28, 83-84

Beach, Joseph Warren (1880–1957), 704

Beach, Rex (1877–1949): *The Iron Trail*, 593

Beach, Sylvia (1887–1962), 851

Beadle, Erastus (1821–94), 469-71, 551-55

Beadle's Dime Library, 555

Beadle's Dime Novel series, 555

Beadle's Half-Dime Library, 555

Beadle's New Dime Novels, 555

Beard, Charles A. (1874–1948), 482, 720

Beard, Mary R. (1876–1958), 482

Beattie, Ann (1947–), 1163, 1165; *Love Always*, 1169

Beat writers, 1042, 1065, 1082, 1084-86, 1090-94, 1140, 1148

Beaulieu, Gustave H., 580

Beckett, Samuel (1906–), 1140, 1157; *The Unnamable*, 1151

Beddoes, Thomas Lovell (1803–49): *Death's Jest-Book*, 950

Beecher, Catharine (1800–1878): *Treatise on Domestic Economy*, 347

Beecher, Henry Ward (1813–87), 551

Beecher, Lyman (1775–1863), 347

Behrman, S. N. (Samuel Nathaniel Behrman) (1893–1973), 1103

Bell, Daniel (1919–), 1040

Bell, Thomas (1903–61): *Out of This Furnace*, 726

Bellamy, Edward (1850–98), 489, 565; *Looking Backward*, 487-88, 507, 520

Bellamy, Joe David (1941–), 1161

Bellamy, Joseph (1719–90): *The Millennium*, 122; *True Religion Delineated*, 119

Bellow, Saul (1915–), 753, 1027, 1132, 1148, 1152; *Dangling Man*, 1136, 1147; *Henderson the Rain King*, 1030; *Herzog*, 1031, 1134; *Humboldt's Gift*, 1137; Nobel Prize, 1137; "Some Notes on Recent American Fiction," 1134, 1136; *The Victim*, 1137

Benchley, Robert (1889–1945), 995

Benevolent Empire, 331

Benezet, Anthony (1713–84), 66

Benn, Gottfried (1886–1956), 1087

Bennett, James Gordon (1795–1872), 351-53

Berger, Thomas (1924–): *Regiment of Women*, 1166

Bergson, Henri (1859–1941), 863, 874, 956

Berkman, Alexander (1870?–1936), 850

Bernal, Victor (1888–1915): *Las primicias*, 803

Bernard, Kenneth (1930–), 1116-17; *The Magic Show of Dr. Ma-Gico*, 1117; *The Moke-Eater*, 1117; *Night Club*, 1117

Bernard, Richard (1567?–1641): *The Faithfull Shepheard*, 58

Bernstein, Charles (1950–), 1175, 1183-85; "Air Shaft," 1183-84; *The L=A=N=G=U=A=G=E Book*, 1184, 1197; "The Language Sampler," 1191; "Meaning the Meaning," 1195–96; *Resistance*, 1183-84; "Semblance," 1183; "Sprocket Damage," 1183

Bernstein, Z., 581

Berryman, John (1914–72), 926, 957, 1030, 1080, 1082, 1086, 1089; *Dream Songs*, 1087; "Two Organs," 1081

Berssenbrugge, Mei Mei (1947–): *Random Possession*, 821

Berthoff, Warner (1925–), 181, 1012

Besant, Walter (1836–1901), 678

Bester, Alfred (1913–), 1167-68

Best-sellers, 469, 478, 487, 529, 566, 730, 840

Beverley, Robert (c. 1673–c.1722), 128-29, 133; *The History and Present State of Virginia*, 53, 55, 128

Bewley, Marius (1918–73), 1014

Bible, 24, 26-29, 32, 35; colonial writers, influence on, 67, 69-71, 83-84, 88-90, 95-97, 102; John Eliot, translation by, 61

Bierce, Ambrose (1842–1914?), 529, 532, 735; *Can Such Things Be?* 533; "An Occurrence at Owl Creek Bridge," 533; *Tales of Soldiers and Civilians*, 533

Big Business, 527; *see also* Corporate enterprise

Bigsby, Christopher (1941–), 1109

Bigsby, W. E., 854

Biography and autobiography, 31, 67-82, 105-6, 195-96, 752, 853, 1073-74; immigrant and ethnic writers, 573-76, 584-86, 811-14; *mexicano* narratives, 517; slave narratives, 349-50, 358-62

Bird, Robert Montgomery (1806-54): *Nick of the Woods*, 240-42

Birth of a Nation, The (film), 512, 583

Bishop, Elizabeth (1911–79), 926, 1081

Blackburn, Paul (1926–71), 1091

Black English, 863

Black humor, 1140, 1149-51

Black Mask, 867

Black Mountain poets, 1042, 1082, 1091-94, 1098

Black Mountain Review, 1091

Blackmur, R. P. (Richard Palmer Blackmur) (1904–65), 993, 1003, 1006-10; *The Art of the Novel*, 997; *The Double Agent*, 1009; *The Expense of Greatness*, 1009; *Language as Gesture*, 1009; *The Lion and the Honeycomb*, 1009

Blacks: (1865–1910) 479, 574-76, 583-86, (1910–45) 725-26, 733, 737, 785-99, 850, 855, 864, (post–World War II) 1061, 1063-64, 1066-75, 1135, 1139, 1172; Africa, preoccupation with, 854; avant-garde art, 1198; dialect literature, 863; drama, 334-35, 1110, 1114, 1122-24; Federal Writers' Project, 866; feminization of, 355-56; folk music, 574; folk tales, 574; newspapers and magazines, 571, 581-82, 585, 726, 852; novels of "passing," 860; poetry, 165-66, 915, 918-19, 927, 929, 931; realistic and regional fiction, 512-15; self-reflexive fiction, 1152-53; slave narratives, 68-69, 75, 78-79,

Blacks (*Continued*)
349-50, 358-62; women writers of the 1920s and 1930s, 835-41; *see also* Civil rights movement; Harlem Renaissance; Slavery; *and names of specific writers*

"Black Sox" scandal, 741

Black Writers' Conference, Second (1967), 1070

Blair, Emily Newell (1877–1951), 823

Blair, James (1655–1743), 59

Blake, William (1757–1827), 1084

Bland, Richard (1710–76): *Inquiry into the Rights of the British Colonies*, 140

Blast, 929, 973, 975

Blau, Herbert (1926–), 1109

Bleecker, Ann Eliza (1752–83): "On Reading Dryden's Virgil," 167; "Written in the Retreat from Burgoyne," 167

Blockheads, The, 149, 326

Blockheads, The; or, Fortunate Contractor, 150

Bloom, Harold (1930–): *The Anxiety of Influence*, 1174

Blues, 922, 928

Bly, Robert (1926–), 1066, 1094–97; *The Light Around the Body*, 1095; *Silence in the Snowy Field*, 1094; "The Teeth Mother Naked at Last," 1096

Boas, Franz (1858–1942), 865

Bodenheim, Maxwell (1893–1954), 858

Bogan, Louise (1897–1970), 822, 828-30; *Body of This Death*, 919; "Cassandra," 827, 919; *Dark Summer*, 919; "Medusa," 827

Bok, Edward (1863–1930), 476, 573, 586; *The Americanization of Edward Bok*, 573; *The Boy Who Followed Ben Franklin*, 574

Boker, George Henry (1823–90): *Francesca da Rimini*, 336

Bone, Robert (1924–), 864; *Down Home*, 793-95

Bontemps, Arna (1902–73), 866; *The Poetry of the Negro*, 792

Bookman, The, 848

Book-of-the-Month Club, 731

Boone, Daniel (1734–1820), 81

Boorstin, Daniel (1914–), 718

Borges, Jorge Luis (1899–1986), 1140, 1167

Börnstein, Heinrich (1805–92): *Die Geheimnisse von St. Louis*, 582

Boston Advertiser, 649

Boston Courier, 294, 320

Boston Daily Courier, 649

Boston Gazette and Country Journal, 193

Boston Guardian, 582

Boston Herald, 576

Boston Pilot, 586

Boston Quarterly Review, The, 366, 371

Boston Sunday Herald, 578

Boston Transcript, 576

Boucher, Jonathan (1738–1804): "On Civil Liberty, Passive Obedience, and Nonresistance," 142

Boucicault, Dion (1820–90): *Franklin*, 588; *The Octoroon*, 588; *Rip Van Winkle*, 336

Boudinot, Elias (c. 1803–1839), 580

Bourke-White, Margaret (1904–71): *You Have Seen Their Faces*, 866

Bourne, Randolph (1886–1918), 720, 732, 738-40; "The Puritan's Will to Power," 858

Bowen, Francis (1811–90), 215

Bowles, Samuel (1826–78), 612, 617, 625

Boyesen, Hjalmar Hjorth (1848–95), 573; "The American Novelist and His Public," 521; *The Mammon of Righteousness*, 520; *The Social Struggles*, 487, 521; *Tales from Two Hemispheres*, 585

Boyle, Kay (1902–): *Avalanche*, 871; *Primer for Combat*, 871

Boyle, T. C. (1948–), 1163

Boynton, Henry Walcott (1869–1947), 848

Brackenridge, Hugh Henry (1748–1816), 173-74, 197; *The Battle of Bunkers-Hill*, 150; *The Death of General Montgomery*, 150; *Modern Chivalry*, 173-75, 177, 198-200; *The Narrative of the Perils and Sufferings . . . of John Slover*, 152; "The Rising Glory of America," 160

Bradbury, Ray (1920–), 1168

Bradford, William (1590–1657), 25-26, 47, 55, 70; "Epitaphium Meum," 87; *Mourts Relation*, 21-22; *Of Plimmoth Plantation*, 22, 48-50, 71, 73, 768; poetry, 87

Bradley, Francis Herbert (1846–1924), 874

Bradstreet, Anne (c. 1612–1672), 29, 37, 90-91, 104; "The Author to Her Book," 91; autobiography, 92; "Contemplations," 91, 93-94; "Dialogue between Old England and New," 29; "The Four Elements," 90; "The Four Humors of Man," 90; "The Four Monarchies," 91; "The Four Seasons," 91; "Occasional Meditations," 30; *Quaternion*, 28-29; *Several Poems*, 91; *The Tenth Muse Lately Sprung Up in America*, 91-92; "To My Dear Children," 72; "Upon My Son Samuel His Goeing to England, Novem. 6,

1657," 92; "Upon the Burning of Our House, July 10th, 1666," 91-92

Brainerd, David (1718–47), 122

Brautigan, Richard (1935–84), 1030, 1145, 1150, 1153; *A Confederate General from Big Sur*, 1150

Brawley, Benjamin (1882–1939), 791

Bray, Thomas (1656–1730), 59

Breuer, Lee (1937–), 1124-25; *Animations*, 1124; *Hajj*, 1125

Briant, Lemuel (1722–54): *The Absurdity of Depreciating Moral Virtue*, 121

Briggs, Charles Frederick (1804–77), 351

Brinton, Daniel (1837–99): *Myths of the Americas*, 574

Broadway Journal, 275-76, 351

Brockway, Thomas (1745–1807), 166

Brodsky, Joseph (1940–), 1040

Bromfield, Louis (1896–1956), 849, 851

Bromige, David (1935–), 1183

Brook Farm, 212, 223, 365, 371-72, 416-17, 425, 427, 454

Brooks, Charles T. (1813–83), 376

Brooks, Cleanth (1906–), 865, 1003, 1005, 1009, 1080; *Modern Poetry and the Tradition*, 1005

Brooks, Gwendolyn (1917–), 790, 796-98, 926, 1064, 1070; "Gay Chaps at the Bar," 796; *Report from Part One*, 1070; "Sonnet Ballad," 797

Brooks, Van Wyck (1886–1963), 720, 732, 735, 738-40, 744, 755, 828; *America's Coming of Age*, 730, 738; *The Flowering of New England*, 730; *The Ordeal of Mark Twain*, 996; *The Pilgrimage of Henry James*, 996

Broom, 852, 928

Brougham, John (1810–80): *Metamora; or, The Last of the Pollywogs*, 333; *Po-ca-hon-tas*, 333, 336

Brown, Alice (1857–1948), 767, 771

Brown, Bob (Robert Carlton Brown) (1886–1959): *1450–1950*, 923-24

Brown, Charles Brockden (1771–1810), 168-69, 177-86, 190; *Alcuin*, 178; *Arthur Mervyn*, 179-82; *Clara Howard*, 184; *Edgar Huntly*, 184-86; *Jane Talbot*, 184; *Ormond*, 181-84; *Wieland*, 180-84, 223

Brown, Henry, 334

Brown, John (1800–1859), 355-56, 373, 408-9

Brown, Rita May (1944–): *Rubyfruit Jungle*, 1065

Brown, Slater (1896–), 849

Brown, Sterling A. (1901–), 786-87, 791, 795, 797-98, 838; *Collected Poems*, 919; *Negro Caravan*, 792; *Negro Poetry and Drama*, 792; "Scotty Has His Say," 919; "Sharecroppers," 792; *Southern Road*, 794, 919

Brown, William Hill (1765-93), 182; *The Power of Sympathy*, 169, 172, 177, 182

Brown, William Wells (1816?–84): *Clotel; or, The President's Daughter*, 334, 574, 583; *The Escape; or, A Leap to Freedom*, 334-35; *Experience; or, How to Give a Northern Man a Backbone*, 334-35; *Life at the South*, 335; *Miralda*, 335; *Narrative of William Wells Brown, a Fugitive Slave, Written by Himself*, 358

Brownson, Orestes Augustus (1803–76), 207, 212, 366, 369, 371, 374; *Charles Elwood; or, The Infidel Converted*, 377; "The Laboring Classes," 366; *New Views of Christianity, Society, and the Church*, 209, 371

Brulé, Etienne (c. 1592–1632), 22

Bryant, William Cullen (1794–1878), 156, 159, 214, 232, 239, 278-81, 286-88, 580; "Earth," 281; "The Flood of Years," 281; "A Forest Hymn," 214, 281; "Inscription for the Entrance to a Wood," 281; "Oh Mother of a Mighty Race," 281; *Selections from the American Poets*, 278; "Thanatopsis," 281; "To a Waterfowl," 281; "To the Fringed Gentian," 281; translations, 280

Buck, Pearl (1892–1973): *The Good Earth*, 840, 867

Buckley, William F., Jr. (1925–), 1061

Buell, Samuel (1716–98), 114

Buffalo Bill (William F. Cody) (1846–1917), 555, 566

Bulkeley, Peter (1583–1659), 61; *The Gospel-Covenant*, 60

Bullins, Ed (1935–): *Clara's Ole Man*, 1115

Bulosan, Carlos (1913–56), 817–18, 820; *America Is in the Heart*, 812-13

Buntline, Ned (E. Z. C. Judson) (1823–86), 554-55, 566; *The Mysteries and Miseries of New York*, 582

Bunyan, John (1628-88): *Grace Abounding to the Chief of Sinners*, 31, 68; *The Pilgrim's Progress*, 24, 32, 61

Burgoyne, John (1722–92): *The Blockade*, 149, 326

Burke, Fielding (Olive Tilford Dargan) (1869–1968), 864

Burke, Kenneth (1897–), 498, 1007, 1013-16;

Burke, Kenneth (*Continued*)
  Counter-Statement, 1015; *The Philosophy of Literary Form*, 1015
Burke, Thomas (c. 1747–1783), 166
Burlesques, 164, 273, 333-34
Burmese-American literature, 811*n*, 819, 821
Burnaby, Andrew (1734?–1812), 166
Burnett, Frances Hodgson (1849–1924): *Little Lord Fauntleroy*, 332
Burrard, Mr., *see* Byrd, William, II
Burroughs, Edgar Rice (1875–1950), 722
Burroughs, William (1914–), 1065, 1154, 1162, 1167; *Naked Lunch*, 1074, 1140, 1145, 1153, 1157; *Nova Express*, 1153; *The Soft Machine*, 1153; *The Ticket That Exploded*, 1153
Business fiction, 520, 522-23
Butler, Octavia (1947–), 1172-73
Byles, Mather (1707–88), 86, 107, 115; *Poems on Several Occasions*, 97
Byrd, William, II (1674–1744), 87, 130, 133; *History of the Dividing Line betwixt Virginia and North Carolina, Run in the Year of Our Lord 1728*, 54, 130; *London Diary*, 73; secret diaries, 67, 73-74; *The Secret History of the Line*, 54

Cabell, James Branch (1879–1958), 857, 863; *Jurgen: A Comedy of Justice*, 854-55; *The Line of Love*, 855
Cabeza de Vaca, Álvar Núñez (c. 1490–c. 1557): *Relación*, 17
Cable, George Washington (1844–1925), 473-74, 488, 512, 778; *The Creoles of New Orleans*, 515; "The Freedman's Case in Equity," 514; *The Grandissimes*, 473, 515; *The Negro Question*, 514; *Old Creole Days*, 515, 587; *The Silent South*, 514
Cabot, James Elliot (1821–1903), 398
Cade, Toni, *see* Bambara, Toni Cade
Cage, John (1912–), 1097, 1192-95; *Empty Words*, 1194-95
Cahan, Abraham (1860–1951), 504, 529, 573, 581; "The Chasm," 585; *The Imported Bridegroom, and Other Stories of the New York Ghetto*, 479, 521; "Realism," 520; *The Rise of David Levinsky*, 520-21, 577, 726; *Yekl, a Tale of the New York Ghetto*, 521, 586
Cain, James M. (1892–1977): *The Postman Always Rings Twice*, 867
Cajuns, 514
Calamy, Edmund (1600–1666), 30

Caldwell, Erskine (1903–87), 747, 753; *Tobacco Road*, 864; *You Have Seen Their Faces*, 866
Caldwell, Patricia: *The Puritan Conversion Narrative*, 71
Calhoun, John C. (1782–1850), 350-51
Calloway Tomahawk, 580
Calvino, Italo (1923–), 1167
Cambridge Platonists, 210
Camerarius, Joachim (1534–98): *Centuries*, 26
Camera Work, 917
Camus, Albert (1913–60), 1127; *L'Etranger*, 867
Canby, Henry Seidel (1878–1961), 461, 732; *The Age of Confidence*, 551, 554-55
Capote, Truman (1924–84): *In Cold Blood*, 1032, 1174
Carkeet, David (1946–), 1163
Carlyle, Thomas (1795–1881), 68, 370, 384, 396
Carnegie, Andrew (1835–1919): "The Gospel of Wealth," 528
Carson, Rachel (1907–64): *Silent Spring*, 1066-67
Carter, Landon (1710–78), 74, 131
Carter, Robert (1663–1732), 128
Cartier, Jacques (1491–1557), 17-18
Caruthers, William Alexander (1802–46), 267; *The Cavaliers of Virginia*, 268; *The Kentuckian in New York*, 268; *The Knights of the Golden Horse-Shoe*, 268
Carver, Raymond (1938–), 1141, 1163-65; *What We Talk About When We Talk About Love*, 1165
Cary, Alice (1820–71), 299; *Clovernook*, 299
Cary, Phoebe (1824–71), 299
Cassady, Neal (1926–68), 1084
Cassirer, Ernst (1874–1945), 1051; *Philosophy of Symbolic Forms*, 1047-48
Cather, Willa Sibert (1873–1947), 573, 589, 591-92, 597, 602, 605-6, 773, 775, 823, 825, 846, 857, 868; "Coming, Aphrodite!" 857; *Death Comes for the Archbishop*, 853; *A Lost Lady*, 881; *My Ántonia*, 508, 605, 853, 857; *O Pioneers!* 597, 605, 853; *The Professor's House*, 857, 861; *Shadows on the Rock*, 853; *The Song of the Lark*, 519, 605
Cavell, Stanley (1926–), 1033, 1057-59; "The Avoidance of Love: A Reading of *King Lear*," 1057; *The Claim of Reason*, 1057; *Pursuits of Happiness*, 1059; *The Senses of Walden*, 1057; *The World Viewed*, 1059

Cavendish, Harry (Charles Jacobs Peterson) (1819–87), 552

Cayton, Horace (1903–70), 787

Centennial Exposition (1876), 527

Century, The, 472-75, 586, 934

Cervantes, Lorna Dee (1954–): *Emplumada,* 809

Cervantes, Miguel de (1547–1616): *Don Quixote,* 1143

Cha, Theresa Hak Kyung: *Dictee,* 816

Chacón, Eusebio (1869–1948): *El hijo de la tempestad,* 801; *Trans de la tormenta la calma,* 801

Chacón, Felipe Maximiliano (1873–?): *Obras,* 803

Chaderton, Laurence (c. 1537–1640), 58

Challenge, 865

Chambers, George, 1155; *The Bonnyclabber,* 1156

Chambers, Whittaker (1901–61), 832; *Witness,* 1061

Champlain, Samuel de (c. 1567–1635), 22

Chan, Jeffery Paul, 818-19; "Jackrabbit," 819

Chandler, Raymond (1888–1959), 867

Chandler, Thomas (1726-90): *A Friendly Address,* 141-42

Channing, Edward Tyrell (1790–1856): "On Models in Literature," 189-91

Channing, William Ellery (1780–1842), 216, 367, 373; "The Evidence of Revealed Religions," 211; "Likeness to God," 209; *Moral Argument against Calvinism,* 122

Channing, William Ellery, II (1818–1901), 213, 375-76; *Near Home,* 376; *Poems,* 376; *Poems: Second Series,* 376; *Thoreau: The Poet-Naturalist,* 375-76; *The Wanderer,* 376

Channing, William Henry (1810–84), 218, 355, 367, 371; *Memoirs of Margaret Fuller Ossoli,* 372

Chap-Book, The, 479-81

Chaplin, Charlie (Charles Spencer Chaplin) (1889–1977), 560, 719, 727

Chapman, John Gadsby (1808–89), 312-13

Chapman, John Jay (1862–1933), 486, 731; *Causes and Consequences,* 484

Chappell, William (1582–1649): *The Preacher (Methodus Concionandi),* 58, 60

Chase, Richard (1914–62): *The American Novel and Its Tradition,* 424, 1129

Chase, Salmon P. (1808–73), 356

Chauncy, Charles (1592–1672): *Gods Mercie, Showed to His People,* 58

Chauncy, Charles (1705–87), 113, 116, 119, 123, 125-26; *Enthusiasm Describ'd and Caution'd Against,* 121; *Seasonable Thoughts on the State of Religion in New-England,* 118

Chautauqua movement, 490

Chautauquan, 576

Chávez, Angélico (1910–): *Eleven Lady-Lyrics and Other Poems,* 803; *New Mexico Triptych,* 803

Chávez, César (1927–), 802, 806

Cheever, John (1912–82), 752, 1138; *Falconer,* 1138

Cherokee Advocate, 580

Cherokee Phoenix (later *Cherokee Phoenix, and Indians' Advocate*), 580

Chesebro', Caroline (1825–73): *The Children of Light,* 303; *Getting Along,* 303; *Isa,* 303

Chesnut, Mary Boykin (1823–86): *Diary from Dixie,* 574

Chesnutt, Charles W. (1858–1932), 479-80, 504, 574; "Baxter's Procrustes," 575; *The Colonel's Dream,* 575; *The Conjure Woman,* 513-14, 575; *Frederick Douglass,* 575; "The Goophered Grapevine," 574-75; "Her Virginia Mammy," 587; *The House Behind the Cedars,* 513, 575; *The Marrow of Tradition,* 513, 575; "A Matter of Principle," 575; "Uncle Peter's House," 574; *The Wife of His Youth and Other Stories of the Color Line,* 575

Chicago, Illinois, 735; in realistic and regional fiction, 518-19, 522

Chicago Journal, 587

Chicago Svornost, 581

Chicano literature, *see* Mexican American literature

Child, Lydia Maria (1802–80), 232, 294–95; *An Appeal in Favor of That Class of Americans Called Africans,* 294; *The First Settlers of New England,* 580; *Hobomok,* 294; *Letters from New York,* 294; *Philothea: A Romance,* 294, 377; *The Rebels,* 294

Child labor, 932

Children's literature: and Horatio Alger, 556-58; Elsie Dinsmore stories, 560-62; Frank Merriwell stories, 558-59; and Nathaniel Hawthorne, 416-17; and Mark Twain, 635, 638; women writers, 303

Chilton, Thomas: *A Narrative of the Life of David Crockett,* 309, 312-13

Chin, Frank (1940–), 818-19, 1114; *The Chickencoop Chinaman,* 819, 1074-75

Chinese American literature, 811n, 812-13, 815-20

Chivers, Thomas Holley (1809-58), 265; *The Eonchs of Ruby*, 265; *The Lost Pleiad*, 265

Choctaw News, 580

Choctaw Telegraph, 580

Chopin, Kate O'Flaherty (1851-1904), 589, 596-98, 604, 768; *The Awakening*, 479-80, 514, 577, 590-92, 595, 597, 601-2; *Bayou Folk*, 514, 597; "The Storm," 591

Chotek, Hugo: "Z Dob Utrpeni," 581

Chouart, Médart (1618-96?), 22

Christian Examiner, The, 215, 369

Christian Recorder, 582

Chu, Louis (1915-): *Eat a Bowl of Tea*, 815, 818

Church, Benjamin, II (1734-76), 166-67; "The Choice," 166; "The Times," 166

Churchill, Winston (1871-1947): *The Crisis*, 566; *The Dwelling Place of Light*, 520; *A Modern Chronicle*, 523; *Richard Carvel*, 566

Church of England, 117-18

Ciambelli, Bernardino, 582-83

Cincinnati Commercial, 587

Cincinnati Deutscher Franklin, 582

Cincinnati Republikaner, 582

Cisneros, Sandra: *The House on Mango Street*, 809

Civil rights movement (1960s), 1066, 1068-70, 1168

Civil War, American, 482-83, 511, 550, 567, 650, 700, 717, 762-64, 777, 779, 1153

Civil War, English, 24, 26, 28-29

Civil War, Spanish, *see* Spanish Civil War

Cixous, Helene (1937-), 1173

Clark, William: *An Account of Colonel Crockett's Tour to the North and Down East*, 309, 312

Clark, William (1770-1838): *The Original Journals of the Lewis and Clark Expedition*, 201-2

Clarke, James Freeman (1810-88), 355, 367-68, 371; *Autobiography*, 212; *Memoirs of Margaret Fuller Ossoli*, 372

Clarke, John (1609-76), 62

Class conflict: in realistic fiction, 505, 516

Clemens, Samuel Langhorne, *see* Twain, Mark

Cliff, Michelle (1946-): *Claiming an Identity They Taught Me to Despise*, 1174

Cliffton, William (1772-99), 166

Coady, Robert, 852

Cobbett, Thomas (1608-85), 62

Cody, William F., *see* Buffalo Bill

Cognitive revolution, nineteenth century, 489-90

Cohen, John Michael (1903-): *The Four Voyages of Christopher Columbus*, 16

Colacurcio, Michael (1936-): *The Province of Piety*, 420

Colden, Cadwallader (1688-1776): *The History of the Five Indian Nations*, 53

Cold War, 1081, 1152

Cole, Bob (1863-1911), 586; *A Trip to Coontown*, 335

Coleridge, Samuel Taylor (1772-1834), 210, 369-70, 394-95, 938: *Aids to Reflection*, 370

Collier's Weekly, 718, 731, 851, 934

Colloquial writing, Southern, 308-9

Colonial period: biography and autobiography, 67-82; drama, 325-26; Great Awakening, 113-26; history and chronicle, 47-55; poetry, 83-97; Puritans, 33-44; satire, 86-87; sermons and theological writings, 56-66; Southern writings, 127-35

Colored American Magazine, 582

Colum, Padraic (1881-1972), 737

Columbus, Christopher (1451-1506), 16, 33, 35

Comic strips, 572-73

Commentary, 1034

Commercial Advertiser, 569, 573, 581

Common people: in realistic fiction, 504

Commons, John R. (1862-1945), 489

Communications revolution, 750

Communism, 746-51, 754-55, 830, 832-33, 835, 850, 867, 1060-61

Communitarian experiments, 27, 371; *see also* Brook Farm; Fruitlands

Compton, Francis Snow, *see* Adams, Henry

Comstock, Anthony (1844-1915), 736-37; *Traps for the Young*, 558

Comstock Society, 854, 858

Comte, Auguste (1798-1857), 526

Conceptual art, 1189-90

Conceptual-scheme theories, 1050-53, 1055

Concord School of Philosophy, 365, 378

Confessional poets, 961, 1037, 1082, 1086-94, 1100

Connecticut Wits, the, 157, 163

Conrad, Joseph (1857-1924), 995; *Heart of Darkness*, 643, 964

Conservationists, *see* Ecology movement

Conspicuous consumption, 716, 1040

Constitution of the United States, 27, 146, 194

Constructionalism, 1047, 1051, 1055-56

Consumer society, 523, 527, 715-18, 723, 1040

Contact, 928, 973

Contempo, 929

Convention of the Friends of Universal Reform (1840), 213

Cook (Cooke), Ebenezer (fl. 1702–32): *The Maryland Muse*, 87; *The Sot-Weed Factor*, 87; *Sotweed Redivivus*, 87

Cook, George Cram (1873–1924), 737

Cook, Marion (1869–1944): *Clorindy, the Origin of the Cake Walk*, 335

Cooke, John Esten (1830–86), 778; *Henry St. John, Gentleman*, 267; *The Virginia Comedians*, 267

Cooke, Philip Pendleton (1816–50), 267

Cooley, Charles Horton (1864–1929): *Human Nature and the Social Order*, 496

Coolidge, Clark (1939–), 1183

Cooper, James Fenimore (1789–1851), 155, 189, 222, 232, 239-61, 468, 635, 769; *Afloat and Ashore*, 254; *The American Democrat*, 222, 254; *The Bravo*, 252; *The Chainbearer*, 255; *The Crater*, 249-51; *The Deerslayer*, 257, 259-60; *Gleanings in Europe*, 253; *The Headsman*, 252; *The Heidenmauer*, 252; history of U.S. Navy, 261; *Home as Found*, 253-54; *Homeward Bound*, 253; *Jack Tier*, 251; *The Last of the Mohicans*, 241-43, 250, 256-58; Leatherstocking tales, 245, 256-60, 566; *Letter to His Countrymen*, 253; *Lionel Lincoln*, 248-49; Littlepage trilogy, 255-56; *Mercedes of Castile*, 261; *Miles Wallingford*, 254; *The Monikins*, 253; *Notions of the Americans*, 222, 252, 254, 306; *The Oak Openings*, 251-52, 258; *The Pathfinder*, 257-60; *The Pilot*, 248; *The Pioneers*, 238, 243-45, 247-48, 251, 256-57, 260; *The Prairie*, 243, 252, 256-57; *Precaution*, 243, 247; *The Red Rover*, 248; *The Redskins*, 256; *Satanstoe*, 222-23, 255; *The Sea Lions*, 251; *Sketches of Switzerland*, 253; *The Spy*, 243, 247-48; *The Two Admirals*, 251; *The Water Witch*, 248; *The Ways of the Hour*, 255-56; *The Wept of Wish-ton-Wish*, 249-50; *Wing-and-Wing*, 258; *Wyandotté*, 249-50

Coover, Robert (1932–), 1141, 1145, 1150, 1162, 1164, 1176; *Gerald's Party*, 1163; *The Origin of the Brunists*, 1150; *The Public Burning*, 1038, 1062, 1152, 1175; *Spanking the Maid*, 1176

Copway, George (1818–c. 1863): *The Traditional History and Characteristic Sketches of the Ojibway Nation*, 574

Copway's American Indian, 580

Corporate enterprise, 484, 517, 716-18, 721-24, 728

Correo Atlantico, El, 579

Corrido, 801-3

Corso, Gregory (1930–), 1084

Cortés, Hernán (1485–1547), 17

"Corwalliad, The, an Heroi-comic Poem," 197

Cosmopolitan, 475-76, 573

Costumbrismo movement, 807-8

Cotton, John (1584–1652), 37, 39, 58, 60-61, 71; *The Bloudy Tenent, Washed and Made White in the Bloud of the Lamb*, 63; *Briefe Exposition on the Whole Book of Canticles*, 65; "God's Promise to His Plantations," 59; *The Keyes of the Kingdom of Heaven*, 63; *Treatise of the Covenant of Grace*, 60; *The Way of Life*, 60; *The Way of the Churches of Christ in New-England*, 63

Courbet, Gustave (1819–77), 502

Courier & Enquirer, 352

Cowboy stories, 517, 566

Cowie, Alexander (1896–): *The Rise of the American Novel*, 175

Cowley, Malcolm (1898–), 740, 747, 849, 885; *Exile's Return*, 864; *The Literary Situation*, 1131; *The Portable Faulkner*, 905

Cox, James M. (1925–), 942

Cozzens, James Gould (1903–78), 770

Craddock, Charles Egbert, *see* Murfree, Mary Noailles

Craft, William: *Running a Thousand Miles for Freedom; or, The Escape of William and Ellen Craft from Slavery*, 358, 362

Cranch, Christopher Pearse (1813–92), 371, 376-77; "Enosis," 376; "Veils," 376

Crane, Hart (1899–1932), 720, 744, 1009, 1027; *The Bridge*, 853, 924

Crane, Ronald Salmon (1886–1967), 1011

Crane, Stephen (1871–1900), 477, 502, 504, 519, 525, 529, 534-37, 545, 570, 868; "The Blue Hotel," 516, 535-36; "The Bride Comes to Yellow Sky," 516, 536; *Maggie: A Girl of the Streets*, 502, 521, 523, 535-36; "The Open Boat," 535-36; *The Red Badge of Courage*, 511, 535-36; *Wounds in the Rain*, 588

Crawford, Charles (1752–c. 1815), 166

Creative criticism, 1187, 1189

Creeley, Robert (1926–), 448, 1083, 1091-92; *Pieces*, 1093

Crèvecoeur, Michel Guillaume Jean de (J. Hector St. John) (1735–1813), 549-50; "Landscapes," 150-51; *Letters from an American Farmer*, 68, 151, 177, 187-88

Crime stories, *see* Detective stories

Crisis, The, 733, 799, 836, 919, 929

Criterion, The, 963

Criticism, 735, 993-1018, 1033, 1072-73, 1126-36, 1173-74, 1176; Afro-American, 791; antifeminism of 1920s, 856; of T. S. Eliot, 958-59, 961, 965; feminist, 169, 1073; French "new criticism," 1185; Freud's influence on, 858; of William Dean Howells, 504; of Henry James, 672, 677-78; Marxist, 832; of Edgar Allan Poe, 274-77; of Ezra Pound, 952-54; of William Carlos Williams, 975; of Edmund Wilson, 745; *see also* New Criticism

Crockett, David (Davy Crockett) (1786–1836), 266, 309-14, 318-19, 336

Croly, Herbert (1869–1930), 737; *The Promise of American Life*, 494-95

Cromwell, Oliver (1599–1658), 36

Crosby, Harry (1898–1929), 849, 924

Crothers, Rachel (1878–1958), 1103

Cullen, Countee (1903–46), 787, 789-90, 794, 798; *The Black Christ*, 919; *Caroling Dusk*, 919; *Color*, 919; *One Way to Heaven*, 861-62

Culler, Jonathan (1944–): *On Deconstruction*, 1054; *Structuralist Poetics*, 1054

Culture industry, 1041

Cummings, E. E. (Edward Estlin Cummings) (1894–1962), 566, 719-20, 740, 743-44, 770, 849, 919-20, 925; *&*, 920; *The Enormous Room*, 849; *XLI*, 920; *him*, 1110; *Tulips and Chimneys*, 920

Cummins, Maria Susanna (1827–66): *The Lamplighter*, 301, 469; *Mabel Vaughan*, 301

Curtis, Cyrus (1850–1933), 573

Custis, George Washington Parke (1781–1857): *Pocahontas; or, The Settlers of Virginia*, 330

Cutter, John, 83

Czech-language newspapers and periodicals, 579-81

Dadaism, 696, 915-16, 918, 927, 1097

Daily Worker, 835

Daly, Augustin (1838–99): *Under the Gaslight*, 336

Daly, Mary (1928–): *Gyn/Ecology*, 1067

Dana, Charles Anderson (1819–97), 572

Dana, Richard Henry, Sr. (1787–1879), 234, 239, 279

Dana, Richard Henry, Jr. (1815–82), 239; *Two Years Before the Mast*, 362

"Dance, The" (ballad), 197

Danforth, Samuel (1626–74), 40, 89; *Brief Recognition of New England's Errand into the Wilderness*, 41, 64

Darby, William: *Ye Bare and Ye Cubb*, 325-26

Dargan, Olive Tilford, *see* Burke, Fielding

Darwin, Charles (1809–82), 528; *The Descent of Man*, 486; *The Origin of Species*, 486

Davenport, Guy (1927–): *Da Vinci's Bicycle*, 1174; *Tatlin!*, 1174

Davenport, James (1716–57): *Confessions and Retractions*, 117

Davenport, John (1597–1670), 61; *Answer of the Elders . . . unto Nine Positions*, 63

Davidman, Joy (1915–60), 922; "Letter to a Comrade," 922

Davidson, Cathy (1949–), 169

Davidson, Donald (1893–1968), 742, 923; "Lee in the Mountains," 923

Davidson, Donald (1917–), 1056-57; "On the Very Idea of a Conceptual Scheme," 1053

Davidson, Michael (1944–), 1183

Davie, Donald (1922–), 1010

Davies, Samuel (1723–61), 118; *Diary of a Journey to England and Scotland*, 74; *Miscellaneous Poems, Chiefly on Divine Subjects*, 90, 120

Davis, Angela Y. (1944–), 1062

Davis, Arthur P. (1904–), 786

Davis, Noah (1804–?), 358, 361

Davis, Owen (1874–1956), 336

Davis, Rebecca Harding (1831–1910): *Life in the Iron Mills*, 472, 510, 534; *Margret Howth*, 510

Davis, Richard Beale (1907–), 67

Davis, Richard Harding (1864–1916): "The Deserter," 848; *Soldiers of Fortune*, 517

Davy Crockett's Almanack of Wild Sports of the West, and Life in the Backwoods, 309

Declaration of Independence, 347-48

Deconstruction, 1004, 1050, 1054, 1128, 1141

Deep image poets, 1042, 1082, 1094-96, 1100

De Forest, John William (1826–1906), 484, 504, 511; *Honest John Vane*, 511; *Kate Beaumont*, 511; *Miss Ravenel's Conversion from Secession to Loyalty*, 511; *A Volunteer's Adventures*, 511

Deland, Margaret (1857–1945), 594–95; *The Awakening of Helena Ritchie*, 594; *The Iron Woman*, 594

Delany, Martin Robinson (1812–85), 582; *Blake; or, The Huts of America*, 582; *The Condition, Elevation, Emigration, and Destiny of the Colored People of the United States*, 582

Delany, Samuel (1942–), 1167, 1172–73, 1176; *Babel-17*, 1173; *Dhalgren*, 1173, 1175–76; *The Einstein Intersection*, 1173; *Neveryon*, 1167; *Nova*, 1173; *Stars in My Pocket Like Grains of Sand*, 1167; *Triton*, 1167

DeLillo, Don (1936–), 1176; *The Names*, 1163, 1175; *White Noise*, 1167, 1169, 1175

Delineator, The, 477

Dell, Floyd (1887–1969), 720-21, 731, 845, 858, 865

de Man, Paul (1919–83), 889, 1050, 1173

Democraten, 587

Democratic Review, 279

Demorest's, 477

De Mott, Benjamin (1924–), 1015

Denison, Mary A. (1826–1911), 552

Depression, the, *see* Great Depression

Derrida, Jacques (1930–), 1050, 1173, 1176, 1185-87; *Glas*, 1059

Descartes, René (1596–1650): *Discourse on Method*, 1055

Detective stories, 184, 555-56, 858, 867-68

Determinism, 525-27; *see also* Naturalism; Pessimistic determinism

De Voto, Bernard (1897–1955): *The Journals of Lewis and Clark*, 202

Dew, Thomas R. (1802–46), 350

Dewey, John (1859–1952), 373, 491-92, 720, 729, 874; *Democracy and Education*, 491-92; "Intelligence and Morals," 492; *The School and Society*, 492

DeWitt's Ten Cent Romance, 555

Dial, The, 207, 213-14, 218, 296, 366, 371, 376, 400, 402, 454; revived magazine, 387, 720, 744-45, 799, 852, 864, 1034

Dialect literature, 516, 586-87, 863; blacks, 795, 839, 854, 919, 927; Southerners, 778

Diaries and journals: colonial period, 31, 67, 72-75

Dick, Philip K. (1928–), 1162, 1167

Dickens, Charles (1812–70), 635-36; *Martin Chuzzlewit*, 636

Dickinson, Emily (1830–86), 61, 298, 375, 468, 497, 609-26, 709, 714, 769, 826; "Master" letters, 612-13

Dickinson, John (1732–1808): *Letters from a Farmer in Pennsylvania*, 140-41; *The Letters of Fabius*, 146

Dickinson, Jonathan (1688–1747): *A Display of God's Special Grace*, 120

Didactic fiction, 169-70, 184

Diderot, Denis (1713–84): *Jacques la Fataliste*, 1142-44

Didion, Joan (1934–), 1030, 1032

Dilthey, Wilhelm (1833–1911), 1052

Dime novels, 295, 469, 516, 551-58, 565-66

Dirks, Rudolph (1877–1968): "The Katzenjammer Kids," 573

Disch, Tom (1940–), 1167

Discovery and exploration, literature of, 16-23

Dixon, Steve (1936–), 1163

Dixon, Thomas (1864–1946): *The Clansman*, 512, 583; *The Leopard's Spots*, 512, 583

Doctorow, E. L. (Edgar Lawrence Doctorow) (1931–), 1024; *The Book of Daniel*, 1062; *Ragtime*, 1175

Documentary works, 859, 866, 868

Dod, John (c. 1549–1645), 58

Dodge, Mabel (1879–1962), 736-38

Dogood, Silence, *see* Franklin, Benjamin

Domestic novel, 562-65

Donne, John (1572–1631), 28, 30; "Anatomie of the World," 26; *Devotions upon Emergent Occasions*, 30

Donnelly, Ignatius (1831–1901): *Caesar's Column*, 507, 520

Donoghue, Denis (1928–), 1007

Doolittle, Hilda ("H. D.") (1886–1961), 708, 716, 719, 825, 828, 840, 917, 950, 953, 1079; *Collected Poems 1912–1944*, 928; "Dread," 917; "Eurydice," 827; *Tribute to the Angels*, 925; *The Walls Do Not Fall*, 925

Dorn, Edward (1929–), 1091

Dos Passos, John (1896–1970), 545, 716, 720, 740, 743, 745-56, 749-50, 755, 770, 849-52; *Manhattan Transfer*, 852, 856, 858-60; *Mid-Century*, 1130; *One Man's Initiation . . . 1917*, 849; *Three Soldiers*, 849; *U.S.A.*, 495, 741, 746, 753, 862

Douglas, Amanda (1831–1916): *Hope Mills*, 510

Douglas, Lloyd C. (1877–1951): *Magnificent Obsession*, 730

Douglass, Frederick (1817–95), 570-71, 581-82; autobiography, 78, 358-61, 571, 574; *My Bondage and My Freedom*, 571

Dowell, Coleman (1925–85), 1172

Downer, Silas (1729–85), 193

Drake, Joseph Rodman (1795–1820), 276

Drake, St. Clair (1911–), 787

Drama, 149-50, 324-41, 588, 1101-25; Asian American, 816-17, 819; Mexican American, 802, 806; radical theater, 1070-71, 1074

Dreiser, Theodore (1871–1945), 477, 502, 522-23, 525, 529, 534, 542-45, 570, 716, 720, 736-37, 740, 747, 773, 865, 868, 871, 995; *An American Tragedy*, 493, 543-44, 557; *The Financier*, 520, 544, 846; *Jennie Gerhardt*, 523, 543-44; *Sister Carrie*, 477, 480, 504, 519, 523, 543-44, 550, 557, 571, 774; *The Stoic*, 544; *The Titan*, 544, 846

Dring, Thomas (1758–1825): *Recollections of the Jersey Prison-Ship*, 152

Du Bartas, Guillaume Salluste (1544–90), 28-29; *Les Semaines*, 28-29; *Uranie*, 28

Du Bois, W. E. B. (William Edward Burghardt Du Bois) (1868–1963), 733, 787, 793; "A Litany at Atlanta," 794; *The Philadelphia Negro*, 584; *The Quest of the Silver Fleece*, 513, 584; *The Souls of Black Folk*, 494, 584-85, 795

Duke, William (1757–1840), 166

Dulany, Daniel (1722–97): *Considerations on the Propriety of Imposing Taxes in the British Colonies*, 140

Dunbar, Paul Laurence (1872–1906), 786-87, 790, 794-95, 797-98; "Circumstances Alter Cases," 586; *Clorindy, the Origin of the Cake Walk*, 335; *Folks from Dixie*, 513; *Lyrics of Lowly Life*, 583; "One Man's Fortune," 583; *Poems of the Cabin and the Field*, 583; *The Sport of the Gods*, 513; *The Strength of Gideon*, 583; "We Wear the Mask," 586; "When Malindy Sings," 586

Duncan, Robert (1919–), 1083, 1091-93; "The Homosexual in Society," 1068; "Passages," 1084, 1093; "The Structure of Rime," 1093; *The Truth and Life of Myth*, 1091-92

Dunlap, William (1766–1839), 179, 181; *André*, 326-27; *The Father*, 326

Dunne, Finley Peter (1867–1936): Mr. Dooley sketches, 587, 589, 591-93

Dunster, Henry (1609–59), 83

Dupee, Frederick W. (1904–79), 996, 1011

Durfee, Job (1790–1847): *The Panidea*, 376

Dutch literature: New Netherland, 22

Dwight, John Sullivan (1813–93), 376-77

Dwight, Timothy (1752–1817), 111, 156-58, 163-64, 166; "America; or, A Poem on the Settlement of the British Colonies," 160; *The Anarchiad*, 157, 165; "Columbia, Columbia, to Glory Arise," 161; *The Conquest of Canaan*, 161-62; *Greenfield Hill*, 156, 158, 161, 187; "The Triumph of Infidelity," 162

Dwight's Journal of Music, 376

Dynamo, 921

Eastman, Charles Alexander (1858–1939): *An Indian Boyhood*, 585; *The Soul of the Indian*, 585

Eastman, Mary (1818–80): *Aunt Phillis's Cabin*, 583

Eastman, Max (1883–1969), 721, 732, 737, 740, 931; *Venture*, 726

Easton, William (1861–?): *Dessalines, a Dramatic Tale; a Single Chapter from Haiti's History*, 335

Eaton, Edith Maud (Sui Sin Far): *Mrs. Spring Fragrance*, 517

Ebony, 726

Ecology movement, 722, 1066-67

Edel, Leon (1907–), 683

Edenic places, 26-27, 35

Edison, Thomas (1847–1931): "The Woman of the Future," 723

Education, 24, 471-72, 491, 726; and transcendentalists, 372; university system, development of, 489-92; women's colleges, 824

Edwards, Jonathan (1703–58), 113-20, 122-26, 212; *Concerning the End for Which God Created the World*, 118, 124; *The Distinguishing Marks of a Work of the Spirit*, 122; *A Faithful Narrative of the Surprising Work of God*, 76; *Farewell Sermon*, 118; *Freedom of the Will*, 118; *The Great Christian Doctrine of Original Sin*, 118; *The History of the Work of Redemption*, 122; *An Humble Attempt to Promote Explicit Agreement and Visible Union of God's People*, 122, 125-26; *Images or Shadows of Divine Things*, 26, 125; *Justification by Faith Alone*, 116, 124; *Life of David Brainerd*, 76, 118; *The Nature of True Virtue*, 118, 125; *Personal Narrative*, 68, 75-76; *Sinners in the Hand of an Angry God*, 113, 117; *Some Thoughts Concerning the Present Revival of Religion in New England*, 118, 122; *Treatise Concerning Religious Affections*, 118, 122, 124; *Treatise on Grace*, 125

Eggleston, Edward (1837–1902), 529, 534, 773;

The Circuit Rider, 518; *The End of the World*, 518; *The Faith Doctor*, 487; *The Hoosier Schoolmaster*, 518, 768; *Roxy*, 518

Eigner, Larry (1927–), 1091

Elegy: in colonial period, 84-86

Eliot, John (1604–90), 37, 57, 61, 83; Bible, translation of, 61; *The Christian Commonwealth*, 27; *Indian Grammar Begun*, 61; *Indian Primer*, 61

Eliot, Samuel (1798–1862): *The Life of Josiah Henson, Formerly a Slave, . . . as Narrated by Himself to Samuel Eliot*, 358

Eliot, T. S. (Thomas Stearns Eliot) (1888–1965), 61, 493, 498, 716, 719-20, 740, 744, 749, 757, 770, 773, 775-76, 826, 847, 874, 882, 913, 930, 947-49, 955-68, 1079-80, 1084; *After Strange Gods*, 965; *Ariel*, 964; *Ash-Wednesday*, 964; "The *Boston Evening Transcript*," 958; "Burbank with a Baedeker: Bleistein with a Cigar," 960; *Burnt Norton*, 963, 966-67, 1010; *The Cocktail Party*, 968; *The Confidential Clerk*, 968; "A Cooking Egg," 960; "Cousin Nancy," 958; "The Death of St. Narcissus," 962; *The Dry Salvages*, 967; *East Coker*, 947, 966-67; *The Elder Statesman*, 968; *The Family Reunion*, 965–66; "La Figlia Che Piange," 957; *For Lancelot Andrewes*, 964; *Four Quartets*, 908, 925, 947, 949, 963, 965-68, "Gerontion," 960-61, 964; "Hamlet and His Problems," 1000; "The Hollow Men," 933, 964; *Homage to John Dryden*, 958; "Journey of the Magi," 964; literary criticism, 958-59, 961, 965, 993, 995, 998-1008, 1010, 1014, 1018; *Little Gidding*, 967; "The Love Song of J. Alfred Prufrock," 933, 956-57, 1087; Robert Lowell, response to, 1088; modernism, 698, 708, 710, 712-13; *Murder in the Cathedral*, 1015; "New Hampshire," 966; Nobel Prize, 949; plays, 966, 968; *Poems*, 959-60, 962; "Portrait of a Lady," 957; *Prufrock and Other Observations*, 957-58; religion, 930, 964; *The Sacred Wood*, 958; "Spleen," 957; "Sweeney among the Nightingales," 960; "Tradition and the Individual Talent," 952, 959, 999; *The Use of Poetry and the Use of Criticism*, 965; "Virginia," 966; *The Waste Land*, 712, 741, 745, 849, 853, 862, 869, 915, 918, 933-34, 956, 960-63, 966-67, 974, 1006, 1012

Elliott, Lawrence (1924–): *Journey to Washington*, 814

Ellis, Bret (1964–): *Less Than Zero*, 1168

Ellis, Edward S. (1840–1916): *Seth Jones*, 552-54

Ellis, Thomas, 18

Ellison, Harlan (1934–), 1167

Ellison, Ralph (1914–), 514, 752, 838, 866; *Invisible Man*, 1139, 1153

Ely, Richard T. (1854–1943), 489; *Social Aspects of Christianity*, 490

Emancipator, 350

Emblematic poetry, 94

Embree, Elihu (1782–1820), 350

Emerson, Ralph Waldo (1803–82), 42, 68, 190, 207-26, 279, 283, 296, 349, 381-98, 549, 768, 770-71, 997, 1057; "The American Scholar," 213, 386, 390, 399; "The Authority of Jesus," 211; "Bacchus," 394-95; "Character," 392; "Circles," 388-89; *The Conduct of Life*, 397; "Divinity School Address," 210, 216, 368, 386-87; *English Traits*, 384, 396; *Essays: First Series*, 216, 387-89; *Essays: Second Series*, 390-92; "Experience," 216, 369, 391; "Fate," 216, 397, 454; "Hamatreya," 395; "Historic Notes on Life and Letters in New England," 371, 377, 485; "Illusions," 397; "Intellect," 369; journals, 382-83, 389; lectures and sermons, 383-87, 392-93, 397, 633-34; *Letters and Social Aims*, 390, 398; literary influences, 394-95; *May-Day and Other Pieces*, 375, 398; *Memoirs of Margaret Fuller Ossoli*, 372; "Merlin," 394-95; "Miracles," 211; modernism, anticipation of, 696-97, 699-708, 711-14; *Natural History of Intellect*, 369; "Natural Science," 216; *Nature*, 209, 215-16, 369, 371, 385, 390, 400, 427, 496-97, 718; "Nature and the Powers of the Poet," 450, 454; "The New England Reformers," 213, 377, 392; "Nominalist and Realist," 382, 392; "Ode," 218; "The Over-Soul," 388; "The Park," 394; *Parnassus*, 460; *Poems*, 375, 393-95; "The Poet," 214, 390-91; poetry, 393-95, 398; "Poetry and Imagination," 390; "Power," 397; radicals, influence on, 738; religious beliefs, 384, 386-87, 397; *Representative Men* (book), 393; "Representative Men" (lectures), 392-93; "Saadi," 395; "Self-Reliance," 369, 383, 388, 390, 454; "The Skeptic," 216; "The Snow-Storm," 395; *Society and Solitude*, 398; "Spiritual Laws," 388; style, 389; "Summer," 216; transcendentalism, 364-78; "The Transcendentalist," 207-8, 210, 585; "Uriel," 395; "Worship,"

Emerson, Ralph Waldo (*Continued*)
397; and Walt Whitman, 450-56, 460;
"Woman," 653; women, view of, 701
Emotivism, 1055
Empiricism, 212, 367-68, 370, 1046-48, 1050
Empson, William (1906-84): *Seven Types of Ambiguity*, 1004
English, Mary (1652?-1694), 93
English literature, 24-32; discovery and exploration, accounts of, 18-22
Enlightenment, 103, 107, 180, 182-84; and Henry Adams, 646-50, 654, 657, 660-61, 665, 667
Ensei, 579
Environmentalists, *see* Ecology movement
Epistolary fiction, 172, 176-77, 182, 185
Epstein, Joseph (1917-), 1028
Equiano, Olaudah (c. 1745-c. 1801): *The Interesting Narrative of the Life of Olaudah Equiano, or Gustavus Vassa, the African, Written by Himself*, 78-81
Erdrich, Louise (1954-): *The Beet Queen*, 15, 1172; *Love Medicine*, 15, 1171-72
Erickson, Steve: *Days Between Stations*, 1169; *Rubicon Beach*, 1167; *Station to Station*, 1167
Espinosa, Aurelio M. (1880-1958), 803
Esquire, 884
Essays, 731, 1033; Language group, 1185; transcendentalists, 364, 374-75
Ethnic groups, 582-88, 726, 751, 1039-40, 1135, 1171-72; drama of 1970s, 1113-14; journalism, newspapers, and magazines, 569-72, 578-82, 585-88; socially concerned writers, 1063-64; stereotypes, 578; *see also specific ethnic groups*
Ethnocentrism, 1055-56
Eufaula Indian Journal, 580
Evangelical religion, 346-47
Evans, Nathaniel (1742-67), 166
Evans, Walker (1903-75): *Let Us Now Praise Famous Men*, 755, 866-67
Everson, William (1912-), 1084, 1086
Existentialism, 868, 1133, 1135, 1141, 1147
Expatriates, 719, 743-44, 822, 845, 851-52, 869
Experimentation, *see* Avant-garde movements
Expressionism, 695-96, 719, 873, 1102-3, 1116

Fabulism, 1163
Falkner, William Clark (1825-89), 890, 894; *The White Rose of Memphis*, 588
Fanning, Nathaniel (1755-1805): *Narrative of the Adventures of an American Navy Officer*, 154-55
Fantasy, 928
Farm workers movement, 1070
Farquharson, Martha, *see* Finley, Martha
Farrell, James T. (1904-79), 545, 871
Fascism, 748-49, 751, 756, 969, 1037
Fast, Howard (1914-), 853
Faulkner, William (1897-1962), 134-35, 319, 323, 345, 498, 511, 514, 545, 740, 753, 779-83, 849, 851, 859, 863-64, 887-909, 1153; *Absalom, Absalom!* 134, 307-8, 315, 493, 752, 754, 887-88, 899-903, 905; *As I Lay Dying*, 754, 888, 898-99, 906; "Barn Burning," 904; "The Bear," 245; "Dry September," 894, 904; *A Fable*, 909, 1130; *Father Abraham*, 893-95, 906; film scripts, 904; *Flags in the Dust*, 893-95, 905; *Go Down, Moses*, 134, 574, 907-8; *Green Bough*, 892; *The Hamlet*, 134, 895, 905-6, 908, 1130; income of, 905; *Intruder in the Dust*, 905-6, 908; *Light in August*, 754, 864, 888, 894, 899-900; *The Mansion*, 906, 909, 1130; *The Marble Faun*, 892; mental flow, imitation of, 862; modernism, 697, 714; *Mosquitoes*, 893; Nobel Prize, 905; poetry, 892-93; *The Portable Faulkner*, 905; "Red Leaves," 904; *The Reivers*, 905, 908; *Requiem for a Nun*, 908; "A Rose for Emily," 904; *Sanctuary*, 894; *Sartoris*, 893; short stories, 904; *Soldiers' Pay*, 893; *The Sound and the Fury*, 311, 777, 780, 856, 858, 888, 896-97, 905; "That Evening Sun," 904; *The Town*, 906, 1130; "Uncle Willy," 894; *The Wild Palms*, 906
Fauset, Jessie Redmon (1885-1961), 798, 836-37; *Plum Bun*, 847, 860; *There Is Confusion*, 836
Fay, Theodore S. (1807-98): *Norman Leslie*, 276
Fearing, Kenneth (1902-61), 921
Federal Art Project, 753
Federal Writers' Project (FWP), 752-53, 865-67
Federman, Raymond (1928-), 1163, 1176; *Double or Nothing*, 1152; *Take It or Leave It*, 1152; *The Twofold Vibration*, 1167, 1175; *The Voice in the Closet*, 1156, 1176
Feminism, *see* Women's movement
Fenollosa, Ernest (1853-1908), 954-55
Fergusson, Elizabeth (1737-1801), 166
Ferlinghetti, Lawrence (1920-), 1084

Fern, Fanny (Sara Payson Willis Parton) (1811–72), 292, 623; *Ruth Hall*, 290

Fiedler, Leslie (1917–), 184; *An End to Innocence*, 1126; *Love and Death in the American Novel*, 169, 1129

Fields, James T. (1817–81), 417, 470

Fierstein, Harvey (1954–): *Torch Song Trilogy*, 1116-17

Filipino-American literature, 811*n*, 813, 816-18, 820

Films, *see* Motion pictures

Filson, John (1747?–1788): *The Discovery, Settlement, and Present State of Kentucke*, 81

Finley, Martha (Martha Farquharson) (1828–1909): Elsie Dinsmore stories, 560-62; Mildred Keith stories, 561

Finley, Samuel (1715–66), 117; *Christ Triumphing and Satan Raging*, 120

Finney, Charles Grandison (1792–1875), 346

Firbank, Ronald (1886–1926): *Prancing Nigger*, 788

Fire (black periodical), 852

Fire! (1926 periodical), 928

Fireside Poets (Schoolroom Poets), 213, 279-88, 356, 769

Firkins, Oscar W. (1864–1932), 389

Fisher, Dorothy Canfield (1879–1958): *The Home-Maker*, 725

Fitch, Clyde (1865–1909), 339-40; *The City*, 340

Fitch, Elijah (1746–88), 166

Fitzgerald, F. Scott (1896–1940), 21, 498, 716, 719, 721, 773-74, 825, 847, 851-52, 857, 859, 871, 873, 878, 880-86, 1130; *All the Sad Young Men*, 883; *The Beautiful and Damned*, 850, 881; "The Crack-Up," 884; *The Crack-Up*, 884; *Flappers and Philosophers*, 881; *The Great Gatsby*, 493, 602, 741, 856, 862, 881-83, 885; income, 883; *The Last Tycoon*, 884; *Tales of the Jazz Age*, 881; *Taps at Reveille*, 883; *Tender Is the Night*, 856, 858-59, 863, 883-84; *This Side of Paradise*, 730, 881; *The Vegetable*, 881

Fitzgerald, Zelda Sayre (1900–1948), 881; *Save Me the Waltz*, 859, 883

Fitzhugh, George (1806–81), 134; *Cannibals All!* 350; *A Sociology for the South*, 350

Fitzhugh, William (c. 1651–1701), 128

Flappers, 824, 856

Flaubert, Gustave (1821–80), 502, 504, 846-47, 1012

Fletcher, John Gould (1886–1950), 917, 930

Florio, John (1553?–1625), 17-18

Folklore, 574, 853-54; heroes, 721; in Mexican American literature, 803; in regional fiction, 513-14

Folk music, black, 574

Forbes, Esther (1891–1967), 853

Forché, Carolyn (1950–), 1063

Ford, Charles Henri (1913–), 922

Ford, Ford Madox (1873–1939), 874, 930, 952

Ford, Richard (1944–), 1141, 1163

Foreign-language press, 579-82

Forerunner, 929

Formalism, 739, 756, 1024, 1083; in post–World War II poetry, 1042; rejection of, 1179

Fornès, Maria Irene (1930–), 1112; *Fefu and Her Friends*, 1112

Forrest, Edwin (1806–72), 329-30, 334

Fortune, T. Thomas (1856–1928), 582

Fortune, 730, 756

Forum Magazine, 490, 576

Forverts, see *Jewish Daily Forward*

Foster, Hannah (1759–1840): *The Coquette*, 172, 184

Foucault, Michel (1926–84), 993, 1050, 1173, 1185; *Madness and Civilization*, 1059

Foxe, John (1516–87): *Book of Martyrs*, 24, 31-32

Frank, Waldo (1889–1967), 858, 865; *Holiday*, 788, 854; *Our America*, 858

Franklin, Benjamin (1706–90), 101, 106-12, 115, 211, 549, 573, 772; "Articles of Belief and Acts of Religion," 107; *Autobiography*, 68, 80-81, 108, 110-11, 570; "Dissertation on Liberty and Necessity, Pleasure and Pain," 107; "An Edict by the King of Prussia," 151; *Experiments and Observations on Electricity, Made at Philadelphia*, 109; "Observations Concerning the Increase of Mankind," 111; *Poor Richard*, 108; "The Sale of the Hessians," 151; *The Way to Wealth*, 110

Franklin Press, 570

Frederic, Harold (1856–98), 529, 534; *The Damnation of Theron Ware*, 487, 522; *Gloria Mundi*, 521; *The Lawton Girl*, 521; *The Market-Place*, 521; *Seth's Brother's Wife*, 521

Frederick Douglass's Paper, 571

Freedom's Journal, 581

Freeman, Joseph (1897–1965), 835, 845

Freeman, Mary Eleanor Wilkins (1852–1930), 474, 509, 590-91, 595-97, 599-600, 603, 767; "Christmas Jenny," 599; "A Church Mouse," 599; *A Humble Romance*, 509, 597; *A New England Nun*, 509, 597, 599; *Pembroke*, 509; *The Portion of Labor*, 510; "The Revolt of 'Mother,' "599; "Sister Liddy," 599; "The Village Singer," 599

Freeman, The, 744-45

Freeman's Journal, 152

Free verse, 873

Frelinghuysen, Theodorus (1691–c. 1748), 116

French, James Strange (1807–86): *Sketches and Eccentricities of Colonel David Crockett of West Tennessee*, 309, 312-13

French, Marilyn (1929–): *The Women's Room*, 1071, 1170

French-Canadian immigrants, 585

French-language periodicals, 579

French literature: discovery and exploration, accounts of, 22-23; "new criticism," 1185; realism in, 502

Freneau, Philip (1752–1832), 123, 156-57, 162-64, 166, 190; "American Independent," 148; "The Argonaut," 163; "The Beauties of Santa Cruz," 158, 163; *The British Prison-Ship*, 149; "The Hurricane," 163; "The Indian Burying Ground," 163; *Letters on Various Interesting and Important Subjects*, 198; "The Millennium: To a Ranting Field Orator," 163; "On Observing a Large Red-streak Apple," 163; "On the Fall of General Earl Cornwallis," 148; "A Picture of the Times," 163; "The Power of Fancy," 158; "Reflections . . . on the Gradual Progress of Nations from Democratic States to Despotic Empires," 163; *The Rising Empire*, 161; "The Rising Glory of America," 160; "To an Author," 163; "To the Memory of the Brave Americans," 149; "A Warning to America," 163; "The Wild Honeysuckle," 163; "Written at Port Royal," 163

Freud, Sigmund (1856–1939), 491, 858-59, 934, 1013-14, 1033, 1133

Freytag-Loringhoven, Else von (1874–1927), 915, 930

Friedan, Betty (1921–): *The Feminine Mystique*, 1064

Friedman, Isaac K. (1870–1931): *By Bread Alone*, 520

Frobisher, Sir Martin (1535?–1594), 18

Frontier, the, in fiction, 177, 184-85, 265, 516,

519; and Robert Montgomery Bird, 240-42; and James Fenimore Cooper, 222, 240-45, 249-51, 256-60; and William Gilmore Simms, 240, 242-43

Frost, Robert (1874–1963), 498, 708, 714, 720, 740, 770-72, 913, 917-18, 937-46, 952, 968, 1002; "Acquainted with the Night," 944; "The Bear," 942; "Birches," 942, 945; "Bond and Free," 942; *A Boy's Will*, 771, 917, 937-38, 940; "The Death of the Hired Man," 942; "Desert Places," 944; "Design," 943-44; "Directive," 943, 945-46; *A Further Range*, 754; "Gathering Leaves," 945; "The Grindstone," 945; "The Hill Wife," 942-43; "Home Burial," 942-43; "In Hardwood Groves," 918; "In White," 943; "Mending Wall," 945; "The Most of It," 943; *Mountain Interval*, 942; "Mowing," 941, 943, 945; *North of Boston*, 771, 917, 937, 940, 942; "An Old Man's Winter Night," 942; "Out, Out—," 942-43; "The Oven Bird," 280; "Putting in the Seed," 942, 945; "The Rabbit-Hunter," 918; "The Road Not Taken," 944-45; "The Silken Tent," 943; "Spring Pools," 944; "Stopping by Woods on a Snowy Evening," 942; "Storm Fear," 939-40; "The Subverted Flower," 943; "Take Something Like a Star," 943; "Two Look at Two," 945; *West-running Brook*, 943; "The Wood-Pile," 941-42

Fruitlands, 212, 371

Frye, Northrop (1912–), 1026, 1054

Fugitive, The, 742, 923, 930

Fugitives, *see* Agrarian group

Fugitives: An Anthology of Verse, 935

Fugitive Slave Act, 396, 408, 451-52

Fuller, Edmund (1914–): *Man in Modern Fiction*, 1132

Fuller, Edward (1860–1938): *The Complaining Millions of Men*, 583

Fuller, Henry Blake (1857–1929): *The Cliff-Dwellers*, 522; "Howells or James?" 522; *With the Procession*, 522

Fuller, Margaret (1810–50), 207, 213, 295-96, 1027; *At Home and Abroad*, 572; "Great Lawsuit," 212; *Life Without and Life Within*, 374; *Papers on Literature and Art*, 374; *Summer on the Lakes*, 374; transcendentalism, 366, 371-72, 374-75; *Woman in the Nineteenth Century*, 212, 296, 356, 372, 374

Fuller, Thomas (1608–61): *The Holy State; the Profane State*, 31

Funeral elegies, 85-86

Furness, William Henry (1802–96): *Remarks on the Four Gospels*, 367, 371

Fussell, Edwin (1922–), 184

Futurism, 696, 917

FWP, *see* Federal Writers' Project

Gaddis, William (1922–): *The Recognitions*, 1140

Gale, Zona (1874–1938): *Preface to a Life*, 861

Gallatin, Albert (1761–1849), 653-54, 657

Gangemi, Kenneth (1937–), 1155

García Lorca, Federico (1898–1936), 1094–95

Gardner, John (1933–82), 1043

Garland, Hamlin (1860–1940), 337, 489, 502, 504, 510, 518-19, 522, 534, 768; *The Book of the American Indian*, 519; *Boy Life on the Prairie*, 519; "A Branch Road," 519; *The Captain of the Gray-Horse Troop*, 519; *Crumbling Idols*, 518; "A Daughter of the Middle Border," 519; *The Eagle's Heart*, 519; *Jason Edwards*, 519; "Local Color in Fiction," 516; "Lucretia Burns," 519; *Main-Travelled Roads*, 508, 519; *The Moccasin Ranch*, 519; *Money Magic*, 519; *Prairie Folks*, 519; *Rose of Dutcher's Coolly*, 519; *A Son of the Middle Border*, 474, 519; *A Spoil of Office*, 519; "Up the Coulee," 519

Garrison, William Lloyd (1805–79), 331, 347, 350-53, 359, 571; *Thoughts on African Colonization*, 350

Garvey, Marcus (1887–1940), 854

Gass, William (1924–), 1145, 1163; *Willie Master's Lonesome Wife*, 1151, 1174; *The World Within the Word*, 1174

Gautier, Théophile (1811–72), 959

Gearhart, Sally: *The Wanderground*, 1171

Geheimnisse von Philadelphia, 582

Gelber, Jack (1932–), 1121; *The Connection*, 1121-23

Gellhorn, Martha (1908–), 756, 831

General Magazine, 570

Genteel tradition, 734-37, 934, 936

Geopolitical division: early American fiction, 174-75, 179, 184

Geopolitical expansion, 345-46

George, Henry (1839–97), 489, 527; *Progress and Poverty*, 487-88

Georgian poets, 938, 942

Geringer, August, 580

German-language newspapers and magazines, 572, 579, 582

Ghetto life: in realistic fiction, 520-21

Gibson, Donald (1933–): *Modern Black Poets*, 792

Gibson, William (1948–), 1164; *Neuromancer*, 1161, 1164, 1167

Gilbert, Humfry (1539?–1583), 18-19

Gilbert, Sandra (1936–), 840; *The Norton Anthology of Literature by Women*, 1073

Gilded Age, 472, 484, 527, 651, 717, 734

Gilder, Richard Watson (1844–1909), 473, 768

Gillespie, Abraham Lincoln (1895–1950): "Textighter Eye-Ploy or Hothouse Bromidick?" 916

Gilman, Charlotte Perkins (1860–1935), 523, 589, 591-92, 602-3, 929; "The Cottagette," 603; *Herland*, 603; "If I Were a Man," 603; "When I Was a Witch," 603; *Women and Economics*, 724; "The Yellow Wallpaper," 596, 598

Gins, Madeline (1941–), 1155; *The Mechanism of Meaning*, 1195–96; *Word Rain*, 1151

Ginsberg, Allen (1926–), 1027, 1084–86, 1088–89, 1091, 1094, 1096–97; *Empty Mirror*, 1085; *Gates of Wrath*, 1085; "Howl," 1065, 1084-87; *Howl and Other Poems*, 1084

Gitlin, Todd (1943–): *Campfires of the Resistance*, 1069

Glasgow, Ellen (1874–1945), 589, 591-92, 597-98, 602-4, 753, 781, 846, 857, 871; *Barren Ground*, 515, 603-4; *The Battle-Ground*, 515; *The Builders*, 603, 848; *The Deliverance*, 515; *Life and Gabriella*, 603; *Phases of an Inferior Planet*, 593; *The Romantic Comedians*, 603; *They Stooped to Folly*, 603; *Vein of Iron*, 515; *Virginia*, 591, 596-97, 603; *The Voice of the People*, 516

Glaspell, Susan (1882–1948), 1110; *The Outside*, 1110; *Trifles*, 1110; *Verge*, 1110

Glass, Philip (1937–), 1193; *Einstein on the Beach*, 1193

Godey's Lady's Book, 292, 351

Godfrey, Thomas (1736–63), 166; *The Prince of Parthia*, 326, 328

God That Failed, The, 1060

Godwin, Gail (1937–): *Violet Clay*, 1171

Godwin, William (1756–1836), 176, 180-81, 183, 185

Goethe, Johann Wolfgang von (1749–1832), 394–95

Gold, Herbert (1924–), 1132, 1152

Gold, Michael (1893–1967), 721, 745-46, 865, 921, 931; "Go Left, Young Writers," 831

Golden Gate Daily, 579

Goldman, Emma (1869–1940), 850, 930; *Anarchism and Other Essays*, 721; *Living My Life*, 865

Goldman, Eric (1915–), 845

Gold rush, 627-28

Gonnaud, Maurice, 391

Goodman, Nelson (1906–), 1053, 1056; *Ways of Worldmaking*, 1051

Goodman, Paul (1911–72): *Collected Poems*, 1062

Goodrich, Samuel G. (1793–1860), 414

Gookin, Daniel (1612–87): *An Historical Account of the Doings and Sufferings of the Christian Indians*, 61; *Historical Collection of the Indians in New England*, 61

Gordon, William (1728–1807): *The History of the Rise, Progress, and Establishment of the Independence of the United States of America*, 195

Gorton, Samuel (c. 1592–1677), 62

Gothic fiction, 168, 178, 182, 184-86, 1139-40; and Edgar Allan Poe, 270, 272-73

Gourmont, Rémy de (1858–1915), 999

Graham's Magazine, 276, 295, 419

Grahn, Judy (1940–), 1072

Grant, Robert (1852–1940): *Unleavened Bread*, 523

Grant, Ulysses S. (1822–85): memoirs, 628

Graydon, Alexander (1752–1818): *Memoirs of a Life*, 153-55

Great American novel, the: De Forest essay, 511

Great Awakening, 76, 86, 114-26

Great Books of the Western World, 731

Great Depression, 717, 722, 726, 746-57, 750-55, 777, 780, 830, 867-68, 933; documentary works, 866-67

Greeley, Horace (1811–72), 296, 366, 572

Green, Joseph (1706–80), 86

Green, Julian (1900–), 849

Greenberg, Clement (1909–), 1179, 1188

Grey, Zane (1872–1939): *The Light of Western Stars*, 566; *Riders of the Purple Sage*, 566

Griffin, Susan (1943–): *Woman and Nature: The Roaring Inside Her*, 1067; *Word and Nature*, 1174

Grimké, Angelina (1805–79), 347

Grimké, Sarah (1792–1873), 347

Griswold, Rufus Wilmot (1815–57): *The Poets and Poetry of America*, 278-79

Grotesque: and Edgar Allan Poe, 270, 273

Gruppe 47 (German writers), 1127

Guare, John (1938–): *Bosoms and Neglect*, 1118; *The House of Blue Leaves*, 1117-18; *Marco Polo Sings a Solo*, 1118; *Muzeeka*, 1118; *Rich and Famous*, 1118

Gubar, Susan (1944–), 840; *The Norton Anthology of Literature by Women*, 1073

Guest, Barbara (1920–), 1097

Guillen, Claudio (1924–), 797

Hagedorn, Jessica Tarahata (1949–): "The Blossoming of Bongbong," 820; "Song for My Father," 820

Hagiography, 31, 71, 80-81

Hakluyt, Richard (1552?–1616), 19-20; *Discourse of Western Planting*, 20; *Principall Navigations, Voyages, Traffiques, and Discoveries of the English Nation*, 18-20, 25

Hale, Edward Everett (1822–1909), 219

Hale, Marie Louise Gibson, *see* Rutledge, Marice

Hale, Sarah Josepha (1788–1879), 292, 562

Half-dime novels, 555, 558, 566

Halfway Covenant, 101

Hall, Christopher, 18

Hall, G. Stanley (1844–1924), 492

Hall, Joseph (1574–1656): *Arte of Divine Meditation*, 30; *Occasionall Meditations*, 30

Halleck, Fitz-Greene (1790–1867), 232, 276, 279

Halper, Albert (1904–84), 864

Hamilton, Dr. Alexander (1712–56): *Itinerarium*, 129

Hamilton, Alexander (1755–1804): *The Farmer Refuted*, 142; *The Federalist*, 146-47, 194-95; *A Full Vindication of the Measures of Congress*, 142

Hamilton, Thomas (1789–1842): *Men and Manners in America*, 351

Hamilton, Thomas (editor), 582

Hammett, Dashiell (1894–1961), 849, 859-60, 867, 1167; *The Maltese Falcon*, 856-58, 861-62; *Red Harvest*, 864

Hammon, Briton (fl. 1747–60): *A Narrative of the Uncommon Sufferings, and Surprizing Deliverance of Briton Hammon, a Negro Man . . .*, 69, 78

Hammon, Jupiter (c. 1720–c. 1820): "An Evening Thought. Salvation by Christ," 165; "The Kind Master and the Dutiful Servant," 165-66

Hammond, James Henry (1807–64), 350

Hammond, John (fl. 1635–56): *Leah and Rachel*, 21

Hansberry, Lorraine (1930–65): *A Raisin in the Sun*, 1064

Hapgood, Hutchins (1869–1944): *Children of the Ghetto*, 583; *The Spirit of the Ghetto*, 581; *Types from City Streets*, 584

Happenings, 737, 1111, 1186

Harbinger, The, 371, 374

Hardwick, Elizabeth (1916–), 1033

Hardy, Thomas (1840–1928), 504, 698

Harjo, Joy (1951–), 15

Harland, Henry (Sidney Luska) (1861–1905): *As It Was Written: A Jewish Musician's Story*, 586; *Mrs. Peixada*, 586; *The Yoke of the Thorah*, 586

Harland, Marion (Mary Virginia Terhune) (1830–1922), 302; *Eve's Daughters; or, Common Sense for Maid, Wife, and Mother*, 596

Harlem (magazine), 582

Harlem Renaissance, 726, 737, 786, 788, 793–95, 854–55, 933; dialect literature, 863; poetry, 918–19, 927; women writers, 835–40

Harper, Frances Ellen Watkins (1825–1911): "Eliza Harris," 583; "Eva's Farewell," 583; *Iola Leroy; or, Shadows Uplifted*, 584; *Sketches of Southern Life*, 583; "The Two Offers," 582

Harper's, 438, 472, 473–75, 511, 576, 586, 851, 934; and William Dean Howells, 503–5

Harper's Weekly, 572

Harrigan, Edward (1845–1911), 336

Harrington, James (1611–77): *Oceana*, 27

Harriot, Thomas (1560–1621): *A Brief and True Report . . . of Virginia*, 19

Harris, Bertha (1937–), 1172

Harris, George Washington (1814–69): *Sut Lovingood's Yarns*, 310, 320–23

Harris, Joel Chandler (1848–1908), 512, 573–74, 768; *Free Joe and Other Georgian Sketches*, 514; *Gabriel Tolliver*, 514; Uncle Remus stories, 513–14, 574, 586

Harris, William Torrey (1835–1909), 378

Hart, William (1713–84): *The Nature of Regeneration*, 121

Harte, Bret (1836–1902), 239, 510, 516, 636; "The Luck of Roaring Camp," 516; "The Outcasts of Poker Flat," 516

Hartley, Marsden (1877–1943), 930; *Twenty-Five Poems*, 916

Hartman, Geoffrey (1929–): "The New Wilderness: Critics as Connoisseurs of Chaos," 1187

Harvard Advocate, 982

Harvard University, 770

Harvey, George (1864–1928), 478

Hassan, Ihab (1925–), 1152, 1173; *Paracriticisms*, 1174; *Radical Innocence*, 1132; *The Right Promethean Fire*, 1174

Hatton, Anne Kemble: *Tammany*, 329

Hauser, Marianne (1910–): *The Talking Room*, 1171

Hawkes, John (1925–), 1141, 1145, 1162; *The Cannibal*, 1140, 1147

Hawthorne, Nathaniel (1804–64), 61, 181, 208–9, 211–12, 214, 220–23, 225–26, 239, 306, 413–28, 482, 502, 549, 697, 768; "The Artist of the Beautiful," 214, 224, 423; *Biographical Stories for Children*, 416; "The Birth-mark," 214, 224, 423, 428; *The Blithedale Romance*, 225, 371, 417, 424–28; "The Celestial Rail-road," 224, 427; "Chiefly About War Matters," 354; "The Christmas Banquet," 224; "The Custom-House," 416, 419, 424–26; *Dr. Grimshawe's Secret*, 418; *The Dolliver Romance*, 418; "Earth's Holocaust," 224; "Endicott and the Red Cross," 421; *Famous Old People*, 416; *Fanshawe*, 414; "The Gentle Boy," 421; *Grandfather's Chair*, 416; "The Gray Champion," 420–21; "The Great Carbuncle," 419; "The Hall of Fantasy," 224; *The House of the Seven Gables*, 225, 417, 424, 427; *The Liberty Tree*, 416; "Main Street," 420–21; *The Marble Faun*, 225–26, 424, 427–28; "The Maypole of Merrymount," 49–50; and Herman Melville, 433–34, 437, 443; "The Minister's Black Veil," 426; *Mosses from an Old Manse*, 223, 416, 419, 427; "My Kinsman, Major Molineux," 419, 421; "The Old Manse," 208, 223, 427; *Our Old Home*, 418; Franklin Pierce, biography of, 417; radical writers, influence on, 738; "Rappaccini's Daughter," 208, 224, 378, 423; "A Rill from the Town-Pump," 419; "Roger Malvin's Burial," 419, 421, 449; *The Scarlet Letter*, 39, 225, 414, 416–22, 424–27; *Septimius Felton; or, The Elixir of Life*, 418; *The Snow-Image, and Other Twice-told Tales*, 417, 419–20, 425–26; *Tanglewood Tales for Girls and Boys*, 417; "Three American Romances," 223; transcendentalism, 364; *True Stories from History and Biography*, 417; *Twice-told Tales*, 223, 413–19, 428, 468, 768;

Hawthorne, Nathaniel (*Continued*)
  women writers, opinion of, 290, 354; *A
  Wonder-Book for Girls and Boys*, 417; "Young
  Goodman Brown," 419-23, 426
Hay, John (1838–1905): *The Breadwinners*, 520
Hayden, Robert (1913–80), 926; "Middle
  Passage," 797
Hayes, Edward (c. 1550–c. 1613), 18-19
Hayne, Paul Hamilton (1830–86), 264-65
"H. D.," *see* Doolittle, Hilda
Heap, Jane (d. 1964), 852
Hearn, Lafcadio (1850–1904), 587; *Chita*, 514
Hearst, William Randolph (1863–1951), 573,
  633
Heavenly Meditation, 30
Hecht, Ben (1894–1964), 858
Heckewelder, John (1743–1823), 241
Hedge, Frederic Henry (1805–90), 207, 213,
  366, 369-70
Hegel, Georg Wilhelm Friedrich (1770–1831),
  646
Heidegger, Martin (1889–1976), 1050, 1054
Heinlein, Robert (1907–), 1168
Hejinian, Lyn (1941–), 1175; *My Life*, 1171,
  1174
Held, John, Jr. (1889–1958), 856
Heller, Joseph (1923–), 756, 1154; *Catch-22*,
  1025, 1148, 1151; *Something Happened*, 1030
Hellman, Lillian (1905–84), 824, 864, 1103
Helper, Hinton Rowan (1829–1909), 350
Hemingway, Ernest (1899–1961), 498, 509,
  545, 570, 716, 719, 739-40, 743-45, 749,
  755, 773, 779-80, 847, 849, 851-52, 857,
  872-78, 882-86, 968; *Across the River and into
  the Trees*, 885; "Cat in the Rain," 876; *Death
  in the Afternoon*, 850, 863, 883; "The End
  of Something," 876; *A Farewell to Arms*, 877,
  883; *The Fifth Column*, 884; *For Whom the
  Bell Tolls*, 884; *The Garden of Eden*, 885; *Green
  Hills of Africa*, 883; *in our time*, 876; *In Our
  Time*, 776-77, 850, 862, 874, 876; *Islands in
  the Stream*, 885; *Men Without Women*, 877,
  883; modernism, 698; *A Moveable Feast*, 825;
  Nobel Prize, 885; *The Old Man and the Sea*,
  885, 1130; "Soldier's Home," 557, 876; *The
  Sun Also Rises*, 850, 858, 861, 876-77; *Three
  Stories and Ten Poems*, 876; *To Have and Have
  Not*, 884; *Winner Take Nothing*, 754, 883
Henderson, Alice Corbin (1881–1949), 732
Henley, Beth (1952–), 1112
Hennepin, Louis (1640–1701?): *Description de
  la Louisiane*, 23

Henry, O., *see* O. Henry
Henry, Patrick (1736–99), 131, 196
Henson, Josiah (1789–1883), 358
Hentz, Caroline Lee (1800–1856), 469; *Ernest
  Linwood*, 302; *Linda*, 302; *The Planter's
  Northern Bride*, 302
Herbert, George (1593–1633), 25, 28; *Church-
  Militant*, 31; "Jordan" poems, 28; *The Tem-
  ple*, 25, 31
Herbst, Josephine (1897–1969), 831, 834, 865;
  Pity Is Not Enough, 726
Hergesheimer, Joseph (1880–1954): "The
  Feminine Nuisance in American Litera-
  ture," 825
Hermeneutics, 1052, 1056
Herne, James A. (1839–1901), 337; *Margaret
  Fleming*, 337-38; *Shore Acres*, 329, 338-39
Herrick, Robert (1868–1938), 502, 504, 522-
  23, 825; "The Background of the American
  Novel," 522; *The Common Lot*, 522; *The
  Memoirs of an American Citizen*, 520, 522;
  Waste, 855; *The Web of Life*, 522
Herring, Fanny (1832–1906), 332
Herrmann, John (1900–1959), 834
Hewlett, James (?–1840s), 334
Heyward, DuBose (1885–1940): *Mamba's
  Daughters*, 854; *Porgy*, 854
Higginson, John (1616–1708), 41
Higginson, Thomas Wentworth (1823–1911),
  355, 376; and Emily Dickinson, 613-14, 617,
  620; "Negro Spirituals," 574; "Ought
  Women to Learn the Alphabet?" 472
Hildersam, Arthur (1563–1632), 30
Hill, Joe (Joseph Hillstrom) (1879–1915),
  914
Hillyer, Robert (1895–1961), 849
Hinojosa-Smith, Rolando (1929–), 807-10;
  Estampas del valle y otras obras, 808; *Genera-
  ciones y semblanzas*, 808
Historical consciousness, post–World War II,
  1129-30, 1133-34, 1141; self-reflexive fic-
  tion, 1149-56
Historical fiction, 222-23, 225, 516, 529, 566,
  853; Southern writers, 266-68
History and chronicle, 195, 357-58, 853; Asian
  Americans, 817; colonial period, 47-55, 69-
  70; discovery and exploration, 16-23; radi-
  cal writers, 1072
Hoban, Russell (1925–), 1163
Hoffman, Frederick J. (1909–67): *The 20's*, 788
Hogan, Linda (1947–): "Bees in Transit:
  Osage County," 14

Holden, Joan, 1113; *Independent Female*, 1113; *Steeltown*, 1113

Holland, Laurence (1920–80), 705

Holmes, Mary Jane (1825–1907), 469; *The English Orphans*, 302; *Tempest and Sunshine*, 302

Holmes, Oliver Wendell (1809–94), 279-80, 282-83, 286-88, 470, 472, 768; *Breakfast Table* books, 283; "The Chambered Nautilus," 283; *Elsie Venner*, 283; "The Last Leaf," 283; "The Limitations," 283; "My Aunt," 283

Holt, Hamilton (1872–1951), 584

Holy Community, Puritan concept of, 27

Homestead Act, 161

Homosexuality, 1065, 1068; experimental fiction, 1172; gay drama, 1116-17; gay rights movement, 1168

Hongo, Garrett Kaoru (1951–), 816

Hook, Sidney (1902–), 747

Hooker, Samuel (1635–97), 65

Hooker, Thomas (1586–1647), 37, 56-58, 61; *The Application of Redemption*, 58, 60; *The Churches Deliverances*, 64; *The Danger of Desertion*, 64; "The Faithful Covenanter," 59-60; *The Poor Doubting Christian*, 56; *The Soules Exaltation*, 60; *The Soules Humiliation*, 60; *The Soules Implantation*, 60; *The Soules Preparation*, 60; *The Soules Vocation*, 60; *A Survey of the Summe of Church Discipline*, 63

Hooper, Ellen Sturgis (1815–41), 376

Hooper, Johnson Jones (1815–62), 266; *Some Adventures of Captain Simon Suggs, Late of the Tallapoosa Volunteers*, 310, 316, 318

Hopkins, Gerard Manley (1844–89), 939

Hopkins, Lemuel (1750–1801), 165

Hopkins, Pauline (1859–1930): *Contending Forces*, 513; "Winona: A Tale of Negro Life in the South and Southwest," 582

Hopkinson, Francis (1737–91), 163; "The Battle of the Kegs," 149, 165, 197; *A Pretty Story*, 151; "Some Thoughts on Diseases of the Mind," 199

Horkheimer, Max (1895–1973), 1030

Horowitz, Irving (1929–), 1029

Hosokawa, William K. (1915–): *The Two Worlds of Jim Yoshida*, 814

Hound and Horn, 928

Houston, Jeanne Wakatsuki (1934–), and James D. Houston (1933–): *Farewell to Manzanar*, 814, 817

Howard, Bronson (1842–1908): *Shenandoah*, 339

Howard, Sidney (1891–1939), 849, 1103

Howe, Edgar Watson (1853–1937), 529, 534; *The Anthology of Another Town*, 518; *A Man Story*, 518; *Plain People*, 518; *The Story of a Country Town*, 518

Howe, Irving (1920–), 886, 1025, 1133; "Mass Society and Post-Modern Fiction," 1131-32

Howe, Julia Ward (1819–1910), 487

Howe, Susan (1937–), 1183; *Defenestration of Prague*, 1185

Howe, Tina, 1112

Howells, William Dean (1837–1920), 222, 225, 337-38, 340, 472-73, 476, 478, 482, 512, 529-30, 735, 769; *Annie Kilburn*, 507, 594; "Are We a Plutocracy?" 507; *A Boy's Town*, 505; *A Chance Acquaintance*, 506; and Charles W. Chesnutt, 575; *Criticism and Fiction*, 504; "Equality as the Basis of Good Society," 507; *A Fearful Responsibility*, 506; *A Foregone Conclusion*, 505; and Robert Frost, 772; *A Hazard of New Fortunes*, 505-8, 532; "Henrik Ibsen," 504; "Henry James, Jr.," 504; *Imaginary Interviews*, 588; *An Imperative Duty*, 508; *Italian Journey*, 505; and Henry James, 676; *The Lady of the Aroostook*, 505; *The Landlord at Lion's Head*, 508; *The Leatherwood God*, 508; Abraham Lincoln, biography of, 505; *Literary Friends and Acquaintance*, 470, 505, 763-64; "The Man of Letters as a Man of Business," 507; "Mark Twain: An Inquiry," 504; *The Minister's Charge*, 487, 507; *A Modern Instance*, 476, 490, 506-7, 532; "My First Visit to New England," 470-71, 475; *My Mark Twain*, 506; *The Quality of Mercy*, 520; realism, 502-9, 511, 519, 521, 532, 766-67; regionalism, 766-68; *The Rise of Silas Lapham*, 474, 490, 506, 530-31; *The Son of Royal Langbrith*, 508; *Suburban Sketches*, 506; *Their Wedding Journey*, 506; *A Traveler from Altruria*, 485, 507; and Mark Twain, 632; *The Vacation of the Kelwyns*, 488; *Venetian Life*, 505; war, effect of, on literature, 849; *The World of Chance*, 507; *Years of My Youth*, 505

Hubbard, William (c. 1621–1704): *Narrative of the Troubles with the Indians*, 51

Hughes, Langston (1902–67), 726, 737, 747, 787, 789-90, 792, 794-95, 797-98, 836, 915, 919, 927; "Christ in Alabama," 929; *Fine Clothes to the Jew*, 919, 927; *A New Song*, 931; *Not Without Laughter*, 794; plays, 1110; *The Poetry of the Negro*, 792; *Selected Poems*,

Hughes, Langston (*Continued*)
  928; "Seven Moments of Love: An Un-
  Sonnet Sequence in Blues," 797; *The Weary
  Blues*, 788, 919
Hughes, Ted (1930–), 1088
Huit, Ephraim (fl. 1611–44), 37
Humanism, 999, 1135, 1137
Humanism and America, 746
Humanitarianism, 486
Hume, David (1711–76), 211
Humor, 165, 197; plays, 328; regional, 306-
  23; Southern writers, 265-66, 308-23, 778,
  782-83
Humphreys, David (1752–1818), 156-57, 162;
  The Anarchiad, 157, 165; "A Poem Ad-
  dressed to the Armies of the United States
  of America," 159; "A Poem on the Death
  of General Washington," 162; "Poem on the
  Future Glory of America," 162; "A Poem
  on the Happiness of America," 160
Huneker, James Gibbons (1860–1921), 735-
  36
Hunter, Robert (d. 1734): *Androboros*, 326, 328
Hurston, Zora Neale (1901–60), 716, 787, 792,
  794-95, 797-98, 838-41, 853, 868, 916, 1064;
  "How It Feels to Be Colored Me," 838;
  Moses: Man of the Mountain, 838; *Mules and
  Men*, 797, 838; "Sweat," 868; *Their Eyes Were
  Watching God*, 838-39, 841, 868
Hutchins, Robert M. (1899-1977), 731
Hutchinson, Anne (c. 1591–1643), 37, 62
Hutchinson, Thomas (1711–80): *History of the
  Colony*, 53
Hwang, David Henry, 1112, 1114, 1116;
  Broken Promises, 816; *The Dance and the Rail-
  road*, 817; *FOB*, 819

Ibsen, Henrik (1828–1906), 504, 523
Idealism, 181-82, 207-26, 369-70, 373, 1046-
  49, 1053, 1056
I'll Take My Stand, 743, 935
Illuminati, 181, 183
Imagism, 719, 828, 845, 863, 874, 917-18, 920,
  953-55, 958, 1095
Imlay, Gilbert (c. 1754–1828), 176, 181-85;
  The Emigrants, 175-78; *Topographical De-
  scription of the Western Territory of North
  America*, 176-77
Immigration, 501-3, 512, 517, 569, 737, 1040,
  1135, 1168; anti-immigrationists, 751; eth-
  nic and national communities, 569; ethnic
  writers, 584, 726; journalism, contribu-
tions of immigrants to, 571-73, 579-82; re-
  alistic fiction, 520-21; *see also specific ethnic
  groups*
Impressionism, 873-74
Inada, Lawson (1938–): *Before the War*, 817
Incorporation of American life, 483, 569
Indentured servants, 68, 79-80
Independent, The, 584, 730
Indian Journal, 580
Indians, American, *see* Native Americans
Industrialization, 345-46, 501, 517, 527, 695,
  716-19, 932; alienation and, 860; in realistic
  fiction, 507, 510, 520
Industrial Workers of the World (I.W.W.), 914
Inflation, post–World War II, 1040-41
Ingalls, Rachel, 1163; *Mrs. Caliban*, 1169, 1171
Ingraham, Prentiss (1843–1904), 470
Inouye, Daniel (1924–): *Journey to Washing-
  ton*, 814
Inspirational novels, 529
Instrumental reason, 1030-31
International Literature, 928
International Workers Order, 931
Inventions, 723-24, 860
Iowa City surrealism, 1100
Irish-American literature, 583-84, 588
Irvine, Alexander (1863–?): *From the Bottom
  Up: The Story of Alexander Irvine*, 584
Irving, John (1942–), 1043; *The Cider House
  Rules*, 1175; *The World According to Garp*,
  1175
Irving, Washington (1783–1859), 179, 200,
  229-39, 267, 281, 306, 550, 580; *The Ad-
  ventures of Captain Bonneville*, 238; *The Al-
  hambra*, 236-37; *Astoria*, 238; *Bracebridge Hall*,
  236; *The Conquest of Granada*, 237; *A History
  of New York*, 201, 231-33, 235-37; "The
  Legend of Sleepy Hollow," 221, 235, 239;
  Legends of the Conquest of Spain, 237; *The Life
  and Voyages of Christopher Columbus*, 237; *The
  Life of George Washington*, 238-39; *Mahomet
  and His Successors*, 238; "Rip Van Winkle,"
  221, 235-36, 336; *Salmagundi; or, The Whim-
  Whams and Opinions of Launcelot Langstaff,
  Esq., and Others*, 231; *The Sketch Book of
  Geoffrey Crayon, Gent.*, 221, 233-36, 238, 768-
  69; *Tales of a Traveller*, 236-37; *A Tour of the
  Prairies*, 238; *Voyages of the Companions of
  Columbus*, 237
*Island: Poetry and History of Chinese Immigrants
  on Angel Island*, 817
Italian-American literature, 582-83, 587

Italian-language periodicals, 579

Ives, Charles (1874-1954), 492

I.W.W., *see* Industrial Workers of the World

Jackson, Andrew (1767–1845), 631-32

Jackson, George (1941–): *Soledad Brother*, 1073

Jackson, Helen Hunt (1830–85), 579, 622-23; *Ramona*, 516

Jacksonville Daily American, 585

Jacobin/Anti-Jacobin fiction, 169, 176, 178, 180-83, 185

Jacobs, Harriet (1818–96): *Linda: Incidents in the Life of a Slave Girl, Written by Herself*, 358, 361-62

Jaffe, Harold (1940–), 1176; *Beasts*, 1175–76; *Mourning Crazy Horse*, 1175

Jakobson, Roman (1896–1982), 1049

James, Alice (1848–92), 589-90, 602-3, 671

James, Henry (1811–82), 382, 669-71, 704

James, Henry (1843–1916), 225-26, 337, 473-74, 478, 482, 497, 504, 523, 529, 668-69, 735, 769, 847-48, 963; *The Ambassadors*, 669, 675, 681, 685-86; *The American*, 473, 669, 674-76, 681, 686, 773; *The American Scene*, 588, 688, 703; "Artist Tales," 680;" The Art of Fiction," 676, 678; *The Aspern Papers*, 473; *The Awkward Age*, 682-84; "The Beast in the Jungle," 706; *The Bostonians*, 474, 476, 678-79; "Daisy Miller," 675; dramas, 681; England, settlement in, 673; *The Europeans*, 488, 675; *French Poets and Novelists*, 677; "The Future of the Novel," 684; *The Golden Bowl*, 669, 683, 685, 687-88, 706-7; *Guy Domville*, 681; *Hawthorne*, 226, 673; and William Dean Howells, 506, 766; "In the Cage," 683; "The Jolly Corner," 706, 965; "The Lesson of the Master," 680; literary criticism, 672, 677-78, 997-98, 1004, 1007-8, 1010, 1012, 1018; memoirs, 668, 670-71; *The Middle Years*, 688; modernism, 696, 702-8; New York Edition, 688-89; Notebooks, 682; *Notes of a Son and Brother*, 670-71, 688; "The Passionate Pilgrim," 673; point of view, use of, 704-6; *The Portrait of a Lady*, 473, 488, 531, 593-94, 674, 676-77, 683, 687; *The Princess Casamassima*, 678-80; "The Real Thing," 680; *Roderick Hudson*, 672-73, 680; *The Sacred Fount*, 684-85; *A Small Boy and Others*, 670, 688; Southern themes in fiction of, 512; *The Spoils of Poynton*, 473, 532, 682; *The Tragic Muse*, 679-81; *The Turn of the Screw*, 522, 683-85; *Washing-ton Square*, 488, 675-76; *Watch and Ward*, 672; *What Maisie Knew*, 479, 532, 682-83, 685; *The Wings of the Dove*, 531-32, 670, 681, 685-87, 706

James, Jesse (1847–82), 556

James, William (1842–1910), 373, 492, 496-98, 549, 670-71, 718, 874, 878, 1056-57; "Does 'Consciousness' Exist?" 497; "On a Certain Blindness in Human Beings," 497; *The Principles of Psychology*, 497, 880; "The Sentiment of Rationality," 497; and Gertrude Stein, 606; *The Varieties of Religious Experience*, 497, 670

Jameson, Fredric (1934–): "Postmodernism and Consumer Society," 1178-79

Janson, Kristofer (1841–1917): *Bag gardinet*, 584

Japanese American literature, 811n, 813-18, 820

Japanese-American News, 580

Japanese-language periodicals, 579-80

Japan Herald, 580

Japan News, 580

Jarrell, Randall (1914–65), 1080, 1082; "To the Laodiceans," 938

Jay, John (1745–1829): *Address to the People of the State of New York*, 146; *The Federalist*, 146-47, 194-95

Jazz Age, 590, 721, 741, 824, 854-55, 881, 883, 933

Jazz music, 514, 854

Jeffers, Robinson (1887–1962), 933

Jefferson, Joseph (1829–1905), 336

Jefferson, Thomas (1743–1826), 127-28, 130-35, 146-47, 195, 200-2, 233, 653-55, 761; autobiography, 81; Declaration of Independence, 144-45; *Notes on the State of Virginia*, 81, 131-33, 145; *A Summary View of the Rights of British America*, 144, 193

Jet, 726

Jewett, Sarah Orne (1849–1909), 473-74, 488, 502, 504, 509, 573, 590, 595, 597-98, 600, 767, 823; *A Country Doctor*, 590-91, 600; *The Country of the Pointed Firs*, 474, 508, 600, 604; *Deephaven*, 509; "The Dunnet Shepherdess," 509

Jewish-American literature, 479, 521, 576-77, 584, 1135, 1137-39; self-reflexive fiction, 1152; Yiddish-language press, 581

Jewish Daily Forward, 479, 520, 560, 581

Jiji, 579

Jim Crow, 309-10, 335

John Reed Clubs, 748, 831
Johns Hopkins University, 491-92
Johnson, Diane (1934–): *The Shadow Knows*, 1171
Johnson, Edward (1598–1672), 37; *A History of New-England*, 50-51
Johnson, Georgia Douglas (1886–1966), 798
Johnson, James Weldon (1871–1938), 737, 787, 794-95, 797-98; *Along This Way*, 586; *The Autobiography of an Ex-Coloured Man*, 521, 585, 847; *The Book of American Negro Poetry*, 792, 918-19; *God's Trombones*, 797, 919; "Lift Every Voice and Sing," 585; "Under the Bamboo Tree," 586
Johnson, Rosamond (1873–1954), 586
Johnson, Samuel (1696–1772), 113, 117-18, 125-26, 378; *Elementa Philosophica*, 119; "Raphael; or, The Genius of English America: A Rhapsody," 125-26; *Three Letters to Dissenters*, 117
Johnson, Thomas, 622
Johnston, John, 166
Johnston, Mary (1870–1936): *To Have and to Hold*, 595
Jolas, Eugene (1894–1952), 924; "Firedeath," 924
Jolliet, Louis (1645–1700), 22
Jones, Hugh (c. 1670–1760): *The Present State of Virginia*, 129
Jones, James (1921–77), 756; *From Here to Eternity*, 1139, 1150
Jones, LeRoi, *see* Baraka, Imamu Amiri
Jong, Erica (1942–): *Fanny*, 1171; *Fear of Flying*, 1170; *Flying*, 1170
Jonson, Ben (1572–1637): "To Penshurst," 26
Jordan, June (1936–), 1064
Josselyn, John (fl. 1638–75): *New England's Rarities*, 21
Journalism, 199-200, 351-53, 529, 570-74, 578-82, 585, 587-88, 735-36; ethnic groups, 570-72, 578-82, 585-88; in Great Depression, 751; muckraking, 577-78; penny press, 469; transcendentalists, 371; underground press, 1071; women writers, 832; World War II, 756; *see also* New journalism; Newspapers
Journals, *see* Magazines
Journals, personal, *see* Diaries and journals
Joutel, Henri (c. 1645–post 1723): *Journal*, 23
Joyce, James (1882–1941), 847, 863, 870, 968, 1012; *Finnegans Wake*, 1156; *Ulysses*, 698, 744-45, 930, 959, 961, 998

Judd, Sylvester (1813–53): *Margaret: A Tale of the Real and Ideal*, 377
Judson, E. Z. C., *see* Buntline, Ned

Kael, Pauline (1919–), 1034
Kafka, Franz (1883–1924), 1087
Kang, Younghill (1903–72): *East Goes West*, 812
Kansas City Star, 875
Kant, Immanuel (1724–1804), 364, 369-70, 385, 646, 1057-58; *Critique of Pure Reason*, 1046-47
Katz, Steve (1935–), 1155; *The Exagggerations of Peter Prince*, 1151
Kauffman, Reginald (1877–1959): *The House of Bondage*, 523
Kazin, Alfred (1915–), 396, 865, 1129; *On Native Grounds*, 787
Keayne, Robert (1595–1656): *Apologia*, 72
Keene, Laura (c. 1826–1873), 332
Keese, John (1805–56): *The Poets of America: Illustrated by One of Her Painters*, 278
Keith, George (c. 1638–1716), 59
Kelly, Myra (1875–1910): *Little Citizens: The Humors of School Life*, 583
Kelly, Robert (1935–), 1091
Kennedy, Adrienne (1931–), 1114-16; *Funnyhouse of a Negro*, 1115; *A Movie Star Has to Star in Black and White*, 1116, 1124
Kennedy, John Fitzgerald (1917–63), 1147-48
Kennedy, John Pendleton (1795–1870), 222, 267; *Horse-Shoe Robinson*, 267; *Red-Book*, 267; *Rob of the Bowl*, 267; *Swallow Barn*, 267
Kennedy, William (1928–), 1163
Kenner, Hugh (1923–), 828
Kenyon Review, 1032, 1082, 1091
Kerouac, Jack (1922–69), 1024, 1084, 1162; "Essentials of Spontaneous Prose," 1085; *On the Road*, 1043, 1140
Kessler-Harris, Alice, 831
Kettell, Samuel (1800–1855): *Specimens of American Poetry*, 264, 278
Key, Francis Scott (1779–1843): "The Star Spangled Banner," 161
Kim, Kichung: "A Homecoming," 821
King, Edward (1848–96): *The Gentle Savage*, 587; *Joseph Zalmonah*, 520
King, Grace (1852–1932), 768; *Balcony Stories*, 514
King, Martin Luther, Jr. (1929–68), 1066,

1069; "I Have a Dream," 1069; "Letters from a Birmingham Jail," 1069

King, Richard H. (1942–), 891

King Shotaway, 334

Kingsley, Sidney (1906–), 1103

Kingston, Maxine Hong (1940–), 816, 1039, 1171; *China Men*, 1171, 1174; *The Woman Warrior*, 812, 1171, 1174

Kinnell, Galway (1927–), 1066, 1094-96; "The Bear," 1096; *Body Rags*, 1096; "The Dead Shall Be Raised Incorruptible," 1096; "The Porcupine," 1096

Kirkland, Caroline (1801–64), 623; *A New Home, Who'll Follow?* 299

Kirkland, Joseph (1830–94), 522, 534; *The McVeys*, 518; *Zury*, 518

Klauprecht, Emil, 582; *Cincinnati; oder, Geheimnisse des Westens*, 582

Klein, Marcus (1928–): *After Alienation*, 1132

Klinkowitz, Jerome (1943–): "Postcontemporary Fiction," 1146

Knickerbocker Magazine, 232, 419

Knickerbocker School, 232

Knight, Sarah Kemble (1666–1727), 86; *The Journal of Madame Knight*, 80

Knopf, Alfred A. (1892–1984), 741

Koch, Kenneth (1925–), 1097

Kogawa, Joy (1935–): *Obasan*, 817

Kolkin, Nils: *Winona*, 587

Kolodny, Annette (1941–), 177

Kopit, Arthur (1937–): *End of the World*, 1118; *Indians*, 1118; *Oh Dad, Poor Dad, Mama's Hung You in the Closet and I'm Feelin' So Sad*, 1117; *Wings*, 1118

Korean American literature, 811*n*, 812, 816, 821

Korizek, Frantisek, 580

Kosinski, Jerzy (1933–), 1145; *The Painted Bird*, 1151

Kosmos, 928

Kostelanetz, Richard (1940–), 1165, 1176, 1194

Kramer, Hilton (1928–), 1028

Kramer, Jane (1938–), 1034

Kreymborg, Alfred (1883–1966), 737

Kristeva, Julia (1941–), 1173, 1185; *About Chinese Women*, 1059; *Desire in Language*, 1185; "A New Type of Intellectual: The Dissident," 1059; "Psychoanalysis and the Polis," 1059

Kruger, Barbara (1945–), 1197-98

Krutch, Joseph Wood (1893–1970), 721, 732

Ku Klux Klan, 512-13, 721, 933

Kuttner, Alfred (1886–?), 856

Labor issues, 932-33; in fiction, 507, 510, 520, 522, 533-34

Laborsaving devices, 723-24, 860

Lacan, Jacques (1901–81), 1048, 1185

Ladd, Joseph Brown (1764–86), 165; "Prospect of America," 160

Ladies' Companion, The, 295, 551

Ladies' Home Journal, 475-76, 573, 586, 851

Ladies' Magazine, The, 552

Ladies' World, The, 552

La Flesche, Francis (1857–1932): *The Middle Five: Indian Schoolboys of the Omaha Tribe*, 584

LaFollette, Suzanne (1894?–1983), 865

Laforgue, Jules (1860–87), 956-57

Lamantia, Philip (1927–), 1084

LaMotte, Ellen N. (1873–1961): *The Backwash of War*, 849

Landscape poetry, 966; British, 160-61

Landscape writing, Western, 516-17

Lane, Charles (1800–1870), 372

Lane, Lunsford (1803–?): *The Narrative of Lunsford Lane*, 358-60, 362

Lange, Dorothea (1895–1965): *An American Exodus*, 866

Langer, Elinor (1939–), 830

Language, 762; experiments with, in 1920s prose, 862-64; manipulation of, in self-reflexive fiction, 1154-57

Language-centered Writers, 1175

Language group, 1042, 1182-85, 1195

L=A=N=G=U=A=G=E magazine, 1184

Larcom, Lucy (1824–93): *A New England Girlhood*, 562

Lardner, Ring (1885–1933), 773, 775, 863; "Haircut," 782-83, 859

Larsen, Nella (1893–1963), 798, 837-38; *Passing*, 837, 860; *Quicksand*, 837-38, 858

La Salle, René Robert Cavelier, sieur de (1643–87), 22-23

Lasch, Christopher (1932–): *The Culture of Narcissism*, 1038

Latin Quarterly, The, 921

Lau, Alan Chong: *Songs for Jadina*, 821

Laufer, Susan B.: "Meaning the Meaning," 1195-96

Lauter, Paul (1932–), 825, 831

Lawrence, D. H. (David Herbert Lawrence) (1885–1930), 244, 260, 387-88, 832, 945; *Studies in Classic American Literature,* 709

Lawson, John (d. 1711): *A New Voyage to Carolina,* 21, 53

Lawson, John Howard (1895–1977), 849

Leacock, John (1729–1802): *The Fall of British Tyranny,* 150, 326-27

League of American Writers, 748

League of Youth, 739-40

Leavis, Frank Raymond (1895–1978), 998-99; *The Great Tradition,* 1129

Lee, Charles (1731–82): *Strictures on a Pamphlet,* 141

Lee, Chauncey (1763–1842), 166

Lee, Chin Yang (1917–): *Flower Drum Song,* 815

Lee, Richard Henry (1732-94), 131; *Letters from the Federal Farmer,* 146

Lee Yan Phou: *When I Was a Boy in China,* 812

Legaré, James Mathewes (1823–59): *Orta-Undis,* 265

LeGuin, Ursula (1929–), 1076, 1167; *Always Coming Home,* 1171, 1175; *The Dispossessed,* 1171, 1175; *The Left-Hand of Darkness,* 1171

Lem, Stanislaw (1921–), 1167

Lemay, J. A. Leo (1935–), 196

Leonard, Daniel (1740–1829), 142

Lerman, Rhoda (1936–): *Call Me Ishtar,* 1171

LeSueur, Meridel (1900–), 831-33; "Annunciation," 833; *The Girl,* 833; "Persephone," 833; "Wind," 833; "Women Are Hungry," 832

Letters from Virginia, 266

Levertov, Denise (1923–), 926, 1066, 1091-92; *Relearning the Alphabet,* 1072

Levin, David (1924–): *History as Romantic Art,* 357

Levinas, Emmanuel: *Totality and Infinity,* 1058

Lévi-Strauss, Claude (1908–), 1052

Lewis, Henry Clay (1825–50), 266, 316-17; "The Indefatigible Bear Hunter," 310, 317-18

Lewis, Meriwether (1774–1809): *The Original Journals of the Lewis and Clark Expedition,* 201-2

Lewis, R. W. B. (1917–), 1130

Lewis, Richard (1699?–1733?): "Food for Criticks," 90; "Journey from Patapsco in Maryland to Annapolis," 90

Lewis, Sinclair (1885–1951), 498, 716, 740, 743, 751, 773-75, 856; *Babbitt,* 861; *Elmer Gantry,* 508, 741, 861; *Main Street,* 518, 855; *The Man Who Knew Coolidge,* 863; Nobel Prize, 746-47, 864

Lewis, Wyndham (1882–1957), 929-30, 968

Lewisohn, Ludwig (1882–1955), 735

Liberator, The (Garrison's paper), 331, 350-52, 571

Liberator, The (founded 1918), 721, 745, 921, 928

Liberty Tree, 193

Lieber, Francis (1800–1872), 350, 356, 488

Life magazine, 725, 730, 756

Life Stories of Undistinguished Americans as Told by Themselves, The, 584

Lincoln, Abraham (1809–65), 346-48, 631, 763, 767; Gettysburg Address, 348; second inaugural address, 348

Lindsay, Vachel (1879–1931), 827, 915-16; *The Art of the Moving Picture,* 727; *The Congo and Other Poems,* 917; *General William Booth Enters into Heaven and Other Poems,* 917

Linn, John Blair (1777–1804), 179; "The Blessings of America," 160

Lin Yutang (1895–1976): *Chinatown Family,* 815; *My Country and My People,* 812

Lippard, George (1822–54): *The Quaker City; or, The Monks of Monk Hall,* 582

Lippard, Lucy (1937–): *557,087* "catalogue," 1190; *From the Center,* 1199; *Get the Message? A Decade of Art for Social Change,* 1199; *Six Years: The Dematerialization of the Art Object 1966–1972,* 1189-91, 1193; "Sweeping Exchanges," 1197

Lippmann, Walter (1889–1974), 493, 717, 720, 731, 737

Literary criticism, *see* Criticism

Literary History of the United States, 461, 828

Literary World, 420

Little magazines, 481, 731-32, 737, 744, 799, 851-52, 928

Little Red Song Book, 914

Little renaissance (1910–20), 734, 739

Little Review, The, 737, 744, 852, 864, 930

Living Age, The, 584

Livingston, William (1723–90), 115; *Philosophic Solitude,* 90

Living Theater, 1121-22

Lloyd, Henry Demarest (1847–1903), 489; *Wealth Against Commonwealth,* 487-88

Local color, 503, 508-9, 597, 767-68; *see also* Regionalism

Locke, Alain (1886–1954), 791, 795; *The New Negro*, 792, 795, 835, 919

Locke, John (1632–1704), 123, 125, 367-70; *Essay Concerning Human Understanding*, 121

Locomotive, Die, 572

Lodge, George Cabot (1873–1909), 666; *Cain*, 666; *Herakles*, 666

Logan, Olive (1839–1909), 332

Loggins, Vernon (1893–1968), 791

Logical empiricism, 1050–51

London, Jack (1876–1916), 525, 534, 540-42, 545, 716, 735, 845; *The Call of the Wild*, 540-41, 722; income, 851; *The Iron Heel*, 542; *The Little Lady of the Big House*, 594; *Martin Eden*, 541, 847; *The People of the Abyss*, 542; *The Sea Wolf*, 541; "To Build a Fire," 540; *The Valley of the Moon*, 583; *White Fang*, 540-41

Long, Huey (1893–1935), 751

Longfellow, Henry Wadsworth (1807–82), 211, 213, 239, 279-80, 282, 286-88, 297, 768; "The Building of the Ship," 282; "The Courtship of Miles Standish," 282; "The Cross of Snow," 282; "The Day Is Done," 284; *Divine Comedy*, translation of, 282; "Evangeline," 282; "Excelsior," 282; and Nathaniel Hawthorne, 414-15, 418-19; "The Jewish Cemetery at Newport," 282; "My Lost Youth," 282; "Paul Revere's Ride," 282; "The Psalm of Life," 282; "The Song of Hiawatha," 282; *Tales of a Wayside Inn*, 285; "The Tide Rises, the Tide Falls," 282; "The Village Blacksmith," 282

Long Islander, 450

Longstreet, Augustus Baldwin (1790–1870): *Georgia Scenes*, 266, 310, 315-16, 321

Look magazine, 725, 813

Lorde, Audre (1934–): "Coal," 1075; "Who Said It Was Simple," 1067; *Zami: A New Spelling of My Name*, 1171

Lorentz, Pare (1905–), 859

Lorimer, George Horace (1867-1937), 574

Losada y Plisé, Elias de, 579

Lost generation, 719, 740, 743, 822, 850, 881, 1131

Lovejoy, Elijah P. (1802–37), 346

Low, Samuel (1765–1819?): "Peace," 160

Low comedies, in nineteenth century, 328

Lowe, Pardee: *Father and Glorious Descendant*, 813

Lowell, Amy (1874–1925), 719-20, 826, 917, 920, 928, 930, 954; *Con Grande's Castle*, 920;

East Wind, 920; "The Sisters," 826; "Twenty-four Hokku on a Modern Theme," 920-21; "The Weather-Cock Points South," 920

Lowell, James Russell (1819–91), 279-80, 283-84, 287-88, 356, 398, 470, 472, 766, 768; *The Biglow Papers*, 283-84, 310, 320-21; "Commemoration Day Ode," 287; "The Courtin'," 285; *A Fable for Critics*, 269; "On the Capture of Fugitive Slaves near Washington," 283; "The Present Crisis," 283; *Under the Willows*, 283

Lowell, Robert (1917–77), 770, 926, 1024, 1037, 1080, 1082, 1086-89, 1091; "Commander Lowell," 1088; *Life Studies*, 1087-88; *Lord Weary's Castle*, 1088; *The Mills of the Kavanaughs*, 1088; *Notebook*, 1089

Lowenfels, Walter (1897–1976), 916

Löwith, Karl (1897–1973), 907

"Lowly, the," literature about, 583-84

Loy, Mina (1882–1966), 916; "Anglo-Mongrels and the Rose," 928; "Aphorisms on Futurism," 917; *Last Lunar Baedeker*, 928

Luce, Clare Boothe (1903–): *The Women*, 1113

Luce, Henry R. (1898–1967), 756

Lucette-Ryley, Madeline, 332

Ludlum, Charles (1943–87), 1116; *Big Hotel*, 1117; *Camille*, 1117; *Corn*, 1117; *The Elephant Woman*, 1117; *Der Ring*, 1117; *When Queens Collide*, 1117

Luhan, Mabel Dodge, *see* Dodge, Mabel

Lum, Wing Tek: "A Picture of My Mother's Family," 817

Lurie, Alison (1926–), 1138

Luska, Sidney, *see* Harland, Henry

Luther, Martin (1483–1546), 36

Lynd, Helen Merrell (1892–1982): *Middletown*, 729

Lynd, Robert Staughton (1892–1970): *Middletown*, 729

Lynen, John F. (1924–): *The Pastoral Art of Robert Frost*, 940

Lynn, Kenneth (1923–): *Mark Twain and Southwestern Humor*, 315-16

Lyon, Richard (fl. 1620–51), 83

Lyotard, Jean-François (1924–), 1054, 1187

Lyricism, in fiction, 873

Lyric poetry: and transcendentalists, 375-76

McAlmon, Robert (1896–1956), 851, 876

McCarthy, Mary (1912–), 831, 1066, 1138; *The Group*, 1064-65

McClure, Michael (1932–), 1084, 1086
McClure, Samuel Sidney (1857–1949), 573; *My Autobiography*, 573
McClure's Magazine, 475, 521, 573, 577-78
McCullers, Carson (1917–67): *The Heart Is a Lonely Hunter*, 1139; *The Member of the Wedding*, 1139
Macdonald, Dwight (1906–82), 756
McElroy, Joseph (1930–): *Plus*, 1167; *Women and Men*, 1163
Macgreedy (burlesque), 334
Machann, Clinton, 580
McInerney, Jay (1955–), 1163; *Bright Lights, Big City*, 1168
MacIntyre, Alasdair (1929–), 1055
McKay, Claude (1890–1948), 737, 794-96, 798, 836; *Harlem Shadows*, 918, 931; "White Houses," 796
MacKaye, Steele (1842–94): *Hazel Kirke*, 337
Mackey, Nathaniel, 1172
MacLeish, Archibald (1892–1982), 749, 752, 866; "The Irresponsibles," 755-56
McLuhan, Marshall (1911–80), 34
McMurtry, Larry (1936–), 1164
McPhee, John (1931–), 1034, 1139
McPherson, Aimee Semple (1890–1944), 741
Macready, William Charles (1793–1873), 334
Macy, John (1877–1932): *The Spirit of American Literature*, 730
Madison, James (1751–1836), 131, 655; *The Federalist*, 146-47, 194-95, 699
Magazines: (early republic) 189-200, (1810–65) 351, 468, (1865–1910), 471-77, 479, 569-70, 573-82, 586-88, (1910–45) 720-21, 730-31, 737, 739, 744-46, 748, 851, 865, 921, 928-31, (post–World War II) 1032-37; ethnic groups, 569, 579-82, 726, 799; transcendentalists, 371; women writers and editors, 292-93, 295; *see also* names of specific magazines
Magical realism, 1128, 1167
Magon, Ricardo Flores (1873–1922), 802
Mailer, Norman (1923–), 545, 756, 770, 1132, 1148, 1152; *An American Dream*, 1025, 1031; *Armies of the Night*, 1033, 1074, 1141, 1174; *The Deer Park*, 1148; *The Naked and the Dead*, 1136, 1139, 1150; and new journalism, 1032; "The White Negro," 1140; *Why Are We in Vietnam?* 1025
Major, Clarence (1936–), 1153, 1155, 1172; *Emergency Exit*, 1156; *The New Black Poetry*, 1070

Major American Writers, 840
Makemie, Francis (c. 1658–1708), 59
Malamud, Bernard (1914–86), 1132, 1137, 1148, 1152, 1162; *The Assistant*, 1138; *The Natural*, 1138
Malcolm X (Malcolm Little) (1925–1965): *The Autobiography of Malcolm X*, 1073-74
Mamet, David (1947–), 1118, 1120-21; *American Buffalo*, 1121, 1124; *Duck Variations*, 1121; *Edmond*, 1121; *Glengarry Glen Ross*, 1121; *Lakeboat*, 1121; *Sexual Perversity in Chicago*, 1120-21; *The Water Engine*, 1121
Manifest Destiny, 160-61, 503, 517
Mann, Thomas (1875–1955), 698; *Death in Venice*, 1000; *The Magic Mountain*, 1013
Mansfield, Katherine (1888–1923), 834
Marcuse, Herbert (1898–1979): "Art in One-Dimensional Society," 1063
Marketing of books, 469; subscription sales, 633
Markham, Edwin (1852–1940), 931
Markland, John (fl. 1723–34), 129
Marquette, Jacques (1637–75): *Journal*, 22
Marrant, John (1755–981): *A Narrative of the Lord's Wonderful Dealings with John Marrant, a Black Now Going to Preach the Gospel in Nova Scotia, Born in New York, in North America*, 78
Marsh, Edward (1872–1953): *Georgian Anthology*, 938
Marsh, James (1794–1842): "Preliminary Essay," 210; transcendentalism, 370
Marshall, John (1755–1835): *The Life of George Washington*, 195
Martin, Alexander (1740–1807): "America," 160
Martin, Joseph Plumb (1760–1850): *A Narrative of the Adventures, Dangers and Sufferings of a Revolutionary Soldier*, 154-55
Marvell, Andrew (1621–78): "Bermudas," 26-27; "Upon Appleton House," 26
Marx, Karl (1818–83), 572, 700; *Critique of Political Economy*, 1055
Marx, Leo (1919–), 346
Marxism, 746, 748, 865, 921, 1056, 1060, 1062; literary criticism, 1014-15, 1026; *see also* Communism
Mason, Bobbie Ann (1940–), 1163
Mason, George (1725–92), 131
Masque of Poets, The, 623
Massachusettensis, *see* Leonard, Daniel
Massachusetts Quarterly Review, The, 371

Mass culture and society, 352, 469-70, 1131-32, 1134

Masses, The, 720-21, 737, 739-40, 746, 830, 918, 921, 929, 931

Mass markets, 478-79, 730

Mass media, 1149; dime novels, 554; magazines, 475-77

Mass production, 718-19, 722-23, 860

Masters, Edgar Lee (1868–1950), 489, 931; *Spoon River Anthology*, 917

Mather, Cotton (1663–1728), 31, 33-34, 39, 47, 55, 66, 73, 101-12; *Angel of Bethesda*, 104; "Biblia Americana," 102; *Bonifacius (Essays to Do Good)*, 103, 108; *The Christian Philosopher*, 103-4; "Curiosa Americana," 104; *Diary*, 75; *Lex Mercatoria*, 105; *Magnalia Christi Americana*, 31-32, 34, 42-43, 51-52, 68-72, 104-6; *Malachi*, 103; *Manuductio ad Ministerium*, 58; *Memorable Providences*, 102; *Parentator*, 71; *Paterna*, 75, 102; *Psalterium Americanum*, 102; *Ratio Disciplinae*, 102-3; *Right Thoughts in Sad Hours*, 94; *Theopolis Americana*, 105; *The Wonders of the Invisible World*, 102

Mather, Increase (1639–1723), 41, 57; *Autobiography*, 71; *Brief History of the Warr with the Indians*, 51; *The Day of Trouble Is Near*, 65; *A Discourse Concerning the Danger of Apostacy*, 64; *An Essay for the Recording of Illustrious Providences*, 65-66; *The Life and Death of That Reverend Man of God, Mr. Richard Mather*, 71; *A Relation of the Troubles Which Have Hapned in New-England, by Reason of the Indians There*, 51, 76

Mather, Richard (1596–1669), 37, 57, 61, 83-84; *Church-Government and Church-Covenant Discussed*, 63

Mather, Samuel (1706–85), 107

Matson, Morris: *Paul Ulric*, 276

Matthews, Brander (1852–1929): *Vignettes of Manhattan*, 588

Matthiessen, Francis Otto (1902–50), 121, 732, 865; *American Renaissance*, 996; "Henry Adams: The Real Education," 655

Mauriac, Claude (1914–): *La Marquise sortir a cinq heures*, 1191

Mayhew, Jonathan (1720–66), 122-23

Mead, George Herbert (1863–1931), 489

Mede, Joseph (1586–1638), 65

Medina, Louise (1795–1838), 332

Meditational poetry, 93-97

Meditation manuals, 29-30

Melendy, Mary R. (1841–?): *The Perfect Woman . . . A Complete Medical Guide for Women*, 595

Melville, Herman (1819–91), 41, 181, 223, 230, 239, 261, 341, 429-47, 502, 549, 769; "Bartleby, the Scrivener," 439; *Battle-Pieces and Aspects of the War*, 429, 442-43; "Benito Cereno," 439; *Billy Budd, Sailor*, 225, 429, 446-47, 1143; "Billy in the Darbies," 446; "Bridegroom Dick," 445; *Clarel: A Poem and a Pilgrimage*, 429, 441, 443-45; "Cock-a-Doodle-Doo!" 439; *The Confidence-Man: His Masquerade*, 224, 429, 440-41, 588; "The Encantadas," 439; "Fruit of Travel Long Ago," 442; and Nathaniel Hawthorne, 413, 417, 428; "Hawthorne and His Mosses," 413, 420, 434; "I and My Chimney," 439; *Israel Potter: His Fifty Years of Exile*, 155, 438-39; "Jack Roy," 445; *John Marr and Other Sailors*, 445-46; lectures, 441; *Mardi: And a Voyage Thither*, 224, 431-32, 446; *Moby-Dick; or, The Whale*, 32, 173, 186, 362, 413, 429, 434-36, 702; modernism, anticipation of, 698, 702, 704; *Omoo: A Narrative of Adventures in the South Seas*, 431; "The Paradise of Bachelors and the Tartarus of Maids," 439; *Pierre; or, The Ambiguities*, 224, 429, 431, 436-38, 445; poetry, 442-46; *Redburn: His First Voyage*, 432-33; "Sea Pieces," 445; "Statues of Rome," 441; *Timoleon*, 442, 445; *Typee: A Peep at Polynesian Life*, 224, 362, 429-31, 440; *Weeds and Wildings Chiefly: With a Rose or Two*, 442, 445-46; *White-Jacket; or, The World in a Man-of-War*, 432-34, 446

Mencken, H. L. (Henry Louis Mencken) (1880–1956), 720-21, 731, 736-37, 739-43, 750-51, 854-55, 867; *The American Language*, 995; "Being an American," 995; literary criticism, 995-96; *The Philosophy of Friedrich Nietzsche*, 994; *Prejudices*, 742; "Puritanism as a Literary Force," 858; "The Sahara of the Bozarts," 742

Menorah Journal, 834, 859

Meredith, George (1828–1909): "Lucifer in Starlight," 958

Mergenthaler, Ottmar (1854–99), 571

Merington, Marguerite (1860–1951), 332

Merrill, James (1926–), 1081; *The Country of a Thousand Years of Peace*, 1089; *First Poems*, 1089; *Nights and Days*, 1089; *Water Street*, 1089

Merwin, W. S. (William Stanley Merwin) (1927–), 1081, 1094, 1096; "The Asians Dying," 1096; *The Carrier of Ladders*, 1096; *The Lice*, 1096; *The Moving Target*, 1096

Messenger, The, 852

Messerli, Douglas (1947–), 1183

Metafiction, 1043, 1163

Metaphysical poetry, 95

Mexican American farm workers, 1070

Mexican American literature, 800-10, 1063; autobiographical narratives, 517; drama, 1114

Middle class, 735, 773-76; and realism; 504

Midwest, 518-20, 761-62, 768, 772-76, 855

Migration, 501; *see also* Westward movement

Millay, Edna St. Vincent (1892–1950), 745, 825, 829-30, 840, 922; "An Ancient Gesture," 827; *Fatal Interview*, 829; *A Few Figs from Thistles*, 829; "First Fig," 829; "Menses," 829; "Renascence," 829

Millennialism, 487

Miller, Arthur (1915–), 1103, 1105-8; *After the Fall*, 1107; *All My Sons*, 1106; *The American Clock*, 1107; *The Archbishop's Ceiling*, 1107; *The Creation of the World and Other Business*, 1107; *The Crucible*, 1106; *Danger: Memory*, 1107; *Death of a Salesman*, 1106, 1108; *Incident at Vichy*, 1107; *The Man Who Had All the Luck*, 1106; *A Memory of Two Mondays*, 1107; *Playing for Time*, 1107; *The Price*, 1107; *Two-Way Mirror*, 1107; *Up from Paradise*, 1107; *A View from the Bridge*, 1106

Miller, Douglas T. (1937–): *The Fifties*, 1081

Miller, Henry (1891–1980), 847, 851, 868; *Black Spring*, 870-71; "The Third or Fourth Day of Spring," 859, 870; *Tropic of Cancer*, 869-71; "Walking Up and Down in China," 848

Miller, J. Hillis (1928–), 1004

Miller, James E., Jr. (1920–), 458

Miller, Joaquin (1841?–1913), 517

Miller, Perry (1905-63), 37, 118, 225; *Jonathan Edwards*, 114; *The Transcendentalists*, 210

Miller, Samuel (1769–1850): *A Brief Retrospect for the Eighteenth Century*, 188

Millett, Fred B. (1890–1976), 860

Millett, Kate (1934–), 1073, 1172; *Sexual Politics*, 1073

Millhauser, Steven (1943–): *Edwin Mullhouse*, 1174

Mills, C. Wright (1916-62): *The Power Elite*, 1029-30

Milosz, Czeslaw (1911–), 1040

Milton, John (1608-74), 29; *Comus*, 26; *Paradise Lost*, 24, 26, 29, 32, 160, 939; *Prolusions*, 24; *Reason of Church Government*, 28

Minimalist (new realist) fiction, 1161-62, 1164-65

Minimalist sculpture, 1188

Minorities, *see* Ethnic groups

Minstrel shows, 334-35, 725

Miracles Controversy, 210, 216, 368, 371

Mirikitani, Janice, 816; "Japs," 820

Mirror of Liberty, 581

Mississippi Review, 1161

Mitchel, Jonathan (1624–68), 65

Mitchell, Margaret (1900–1949), 319; *Gone with the Wind*, 752, 840, 853, 867

Mitsui, James (1940–): *Crossing the Phantom River*, 821

Miyakawa, Edward: *Tule Lake*, 817

Mock epics, 164-65, 197

Modern art, 696; Armory Show, 719, 738-39

Modernism, 695-714, 719, 846-47, 873-75, 877, 884-86, 892, 908, 1024, 1042-43; and Henry Adams, 647, 664, 667; dilemma of, 897; fiction, 1126-27, 1131, 1135-37; key elements of, 926; little magazines, 851; New Criticism, 1003; poetry, 853, 913, 915-36, 1079-82, 1094; "primitive" models, 854; regional writers, 773, 775-77, 781; rejection of, 1146-47; and Gertrude Stein, 606; women writers, 827-28, 834, 839

Modern Negro Renaissance, *see* Harlem Renaissance

Modern Quarterly, The, 928

Modern Times (film), 719

Moers, Ellen (1928–79), 542

Momaday, N. Scott (1934–): *House Made of Dawn*, 1075, 1172; *The Way to Rainy Mountain*, 1172

"Monkey Trial" (1925), 742

Monroe, Harriet (1860–1936), 717, 731, 737, 917

Monroe Doctrine, 160

Montage, literary, 862

Montano, Linda (1942–): *Art in Everyday Life*, 1198; "Mitchell's Death," 1198-99

Monthly Review, 928

Montoya, José (1932–), 807

Moody, Anne (1940–): *Coming of Age in Mississippi*, 1069

Moody, William Vaughn (1869–1910), 931;

The Great Divide, 339; "An Ode in Time of Hesitation," 932

Mooney, Ted (1951–), 1163; *Easy Travel to Other Planets*, 1167, 1169-70

Moore, Marianne (1887–1972), 498, 626, 720, 744, 828, 840, 852, 1002, 1079; *Observations*, 918; *Poems*, 918

Morada, 921

Moraga, Cherrie: *Loving in the War Years*, 809

Moral complicity, Howells's theory of, 507

Moral realism, 1129, 1133, 1138

More, Paul Elmer (1864–1937), 720, 732, 746-47, 999

More, Thomas (1478–1535): *Utopia*, 19, 27

Morgan, Edmund (1916–): *American Slavery, American Freedom: The Ordeal of Colonial Virginia*, 130

Morgan, Joseph (1671–1749), 42; *The History of the Kingdom of Basaruah*, 61, 116

Morgan, Lewis Henry (1818–81), 580

Morgan, Robin (1941–): "Goodbye to All That," 1075

Mori, Toshio (1910–), 818; *The Chauvinist and Other Stories*, 814

Morris, Wright (1910–), 1132

Morrison, Toni (1931–), 1064, 1141, 1163-64, 1172; *The Bluest Eye*, 1171; *Song of Solomon*, 1172, 1175

Morse, Jedidiah (1761–1826), 181, 183

Morton, Martha (1865–1925), 332-33

Morton, Nathaniel (1613–86): *New Englands Memoriall*, 85

Morton, Sarah (1759–1846), 166

Morton, Thomas (1590?–1647), 25; *New English Canaan*, 26, 49, 86

Motion pictures, 567, 726-27, 750, 753, 859-60, 1186

Motley, John Lothrop (1814–77), 357; *The Rise of the Dutch Republic*, 357

Motley, Willard (1912–65), 866; *Knock on Any Door*, 1139

Mott, Frank Luther (1886–1964), 351

Mourning Dove (Hum-Ishu-Ma) (1888–1936): *Cogewea the Half-Blood: A Depiction of the Great Montana Cattle Range*, 853

Mowatt, Anna Cora (1819–70): *Armand, the Child of the People*, 332; *Fashion; or, Life in New York*, 331-32

Ms. magazine, 1027

Muckraking, 502, 523, 533, 573, 577-78

Muir, John (1838–1914), 517, 722

Mulford, Clarence (1883–1956): Hopalong Cassidy stories, 566

Mumford, Lewis (1895–), 720, 731, 755: *The Culture of Cities*, 717; *The Golden Day*, 730; *Technics and Civilization*, 717

Munford, Robert (1730?–1784), 131; *The Patriots*, 150

Munford, William (1775–1825), 166

Munro, George (1825–96), 555

Munro, Norman, 555

Munro's Ten Cent Novels, 555

Munsey's Magazine, 475, 573

Murayama, Milton, 816; *All I Asking For Is My Body*, 815

Murdoch, Frank (1843–72): *Davy Crockett; or, Be Sure You're Right, Then Go Ahead*, 336-37

Murdock, Kenneth (1895–1975), 115

Murfree, Mary Noailles (Charles Egbert Craddock) (1850–1922), 512, 768; "The Dancin' Party at Harrison's Cave," 510; *In the "Stranger People's" Country*, 510; *In the Tennessee Mountains*, 510; *The Prophet of the Great Smoky Mountains*, 474, 510

Murray, Albert (1916–), 787

Murray, Judith (1751–1820), 166

Music: avant-garde, 1192–95; and blacks, 574, 585-86, 726; and John Cage, 1097; jazz, 854; popular songs, 567

Myrdal, Gunnar (1898–1987), 581

Mystery (later *Christian Recorder*), 582

Mystery stories, *see* Detective stories

Mythology, American, 191-202, 222, 263, 309-10; and James Fenimore Cooper, 260-61; and Henry Wadsworth Longfellow, 282

Nabokov, Vladimir (1899–1977), 1040, 1162; *Ada*, 1166; *Lolita*, 1140; *Pale Fire*, 1174; *The Real Life of Sebastian Knight*, 1140

Narodni noviny, 580

Nashville Union & American, 321

Nathan, George Jean (1882–1958), 721, 731, 736, 741, 867

"Nathan Hale" (ballad), 149

Nathan Todd; or, The Fate of the Sioux Captive, 76

Nation, The, 490, 505, 672, 720

National Anti-Slavery Standard, 294

National Committee for the Defense of Political Prisoners (NCDPP), 864-65

National Endowment for the Arts, 1026

National Era, 583

National Institute of Arts and Letters, 477

Nationalism: early republic, 187-202

Nationalization of American life and culture, 483

National Reformer, 581

Native Americans, 5-15, 357, 574-76, 585, 853, 1063, 1075, 1172; in American drama, 326-30, 333; and Bible translation, 61; captivity narratives, 68-69, 76-78, 152; in colonial histories and chronicles, 47-49, 51-54, 61; in early republic writings, 201-2; newspapers and periodicals, 580; in nineteenth-century fiction, 240-43, 245, 249-50, 252, 257-58, 516; in popular fiction, 552-54, 563; suppression of, 932

Naturalism, 337, 525-45, 848, 852, 855, 858, 868, 872, 995, 1128-30, 1135-37, 1139; realism compared with, 530-31, 545

Nature: in colonial poetry, 89-90, 93; in Midwestern regional works, 774-75

Nature restored, myth of America as, 26-27

Nautical novels: and James Fenimore Cooper, 248, 251, 254, 258, 261

NCDPP, *see* National Committee for the Defense of Political Prisoners

Negroes, *see* Blacks

Neie Tseit, Die, 581

Neihardt, John G. (1881–1973): *Black Elk Speaks*, 14

Neoconservatism, 1028, 1035-36

Neorealism, 1126-41

Neruda, Pablo (1904–73), 1094

New Canaan, Puritan's concept of America as, 38

New Challenge, The, 865

Newcomb, Charles King (1820–94), 376

New Criterion, The, 1034

New Criticism, 413, 757, 865, 935, 998-99, 1001, 1003-11, 1026, 1080-84, 1086-87, 1090, 1093

"New criticism," French, 1185

New Deal, 749-50, 752-54

New England, 761-72; colonial biography and autobiography, 67-76, 80; colonial histories and chronicles, 47-53; colonial poetry, 83-97; colonial sermons and theological writings, 56-66; English literary tradition in colonial period, 27-32; exploration and colonization, accounts of, 21-22; Great Awakening, 114-15, 117-26; local colorists, 508-10; national mythology, evolution of, 192; Puritans, 33-34, 38-44; transcendentalism, 364-78

New England Courant, 109

New Feminism, 1064-65

New Formalists, 1082

New Humanism, 746-47

New Il-Han: *When I Was a Boy in Korea*, 812

New journalism, 1032, 1035, 1139, 1149

New liberalism, 133

Newman, Charles (1938–): *The Postmodern Aura*, 1040

New Masses, The, 746, 748, 799, 831, 865, 921

New Negro Renaissance, *see* Harlem Renaissance

New Netherland, 22

New New Formalism, 1100

New Orleans Picayune, 587

New Orleans Times-Democrat, 577

New Orleans writers, 514-15

New Poets of England and America, 1082

New realism, *see* Minimalist fiction

New Republic, The, 717, 720, 737, 745-46, 1035

Newspapers, 351-53, 569-74, 576-82, 585, 587; Spanish-language, 801-2; underground press, 1071

New Wave fiction, 1167

New-woman writers, 589-606

New World, 450, 580

New York Age, 582, 585

New York Aurora, 450-51

New York Belletristiches Journal, 582

New York City, 735, 769-70, 932; theater, 333-34

New Yorker, The, 863, 1034, 1138

New York Evening Post, 280, 572-73

New York Graphic Workshop: "First Class Mail," 1195

New York Herald, 351-52

New York Journal, 573

New York Ledger, 292-93, 301

New York Mail & Express, 574

New York Mirror, 276

New York poets, 1082, 1097-1100

New York Recorder, 582

New York Review of Books, 1033, 1186

New York Sun, 351, 572

New York Sun and Press, 581

New York Times, 650

New York Tribune, 296, 298, 366, 572-73

New York World, 569, 572, 576, 581

Niebuhr, H. Richard (1894–1962): *The Kingdom of God in America*, 114

Niebuhr, Reinhold (1892–1971), 720, 732, 756-57

Niedecker, Lorine (1903–70), 925

Nietzsche, Friedrich Wilhelm (1844–1900), 995, 1000, 1004, 1033, 1049, 1055; *The Birth of Tragedy*, 1013; *The Will to Power*, 1049

Niggli, Josephina (1910–83): *Mexican Village*, 804

Nin, Anaïs (1903–77), 851, 869; *Diary*, 859

Nineteenth Century, 579

Nock, Albert Jay (1873–1945), 744

Noland, Charles F. M. (1810?–1858), 316

Nonfiction novel, 832

Nordhoff, Charles Bernard (1887–1947), 849

Norman, Marsha (1947–), 1112

Norris, Frank (1870–1902), 477, 502, 504, 525, 529–30, 534, 537–40, 545, 716, 735, 868; *Blix*, 537; "The Epic of the Wheat," 537; *McTeague*, 517, 537–38; *A Man's Woman*, 537; *Moran of the Lady Letty*, 537–38; *The Octopus*, 517, 537–39, 726, 848; *The Pit*, 537, 539; *Vandover and the Brute*, 537–38

North American, 580

North American Review, The, 189–90, 279, 415, 651-52, 672

Northeast, 762

North Star, 571, 582

Northwest Territory, 761-62

Norton, Andrews (1786–1853), 387; *Genuineness of the Gospels*, 211

Norton, Charles Eliot (1827–1908), 354, 356, 471, 478

Norton, John (1606–63), 37, 61-62; *Responsio ad totam quaestionum syllogen*, 63

Norton Anthology of American Literature, The, 789-90

Norton Anthology of Modern Poetry, The, 926

Norwegian-American literature, 584, 587

Norwegian-language newspapers, 587

Nostalgia, 488-89; and Southern writers, 512-13

Novanglus, *see* Adams, John

Novels, 168-86, 222-25, 846-50, 853-64, 867-72, 1030-31, 1043; Asian American, 816, 819; avant-garde, 1190-91; black writers, 575, 582-83, 585, 836-39; ethnic and minority writers, 575-77, 582-88; Jewish-American, 577, 586; mass audience for, 469-70; Mexican American, 801, 805, 808-9; modernist, 698, 702, 704-7; Native American, 575-76; naturalism, 525-45; neorealism, 1127-41; popular novels, 551-67; radical literature, 1060-61, 1064-65, 1069, 1071-72, 1075-76; realism and regionalism, 501-24, 765, 773-75, 779-81; self-reflexive, 1142-57; transcendentalist, 377; women authors, 293, 295, 299-305, 589-606, 833-39

Novels of ideas (novels of purpose), 169, 175, 181, 185

Nowak, Marion (1948–): *The Fifties*, 1081

Noyes, Nicholas (1647–1717), 42

Oakes, Urian (c. 1631–1681), 41, 65; *An Elegie upon . . . Thomas Shepard*, 85

Oates, Joyce Carol (1938–), 1043, 1141, 1164; *Angel of Light*, 1175; *Bellefleur*, 1171, 1175

Objectivism, 924-25, 978

"*Objectivists*" *Anthology, An*, 924

O'Brien, Tim (1946–), 1163

O'Connor, Flannery (1925–64), 781, 783, 1145, 1153, 1162; "The Displaced Person," 783; *A Good Man Is Hard to Find*, 1153; *The Violent Bear It Away*, 1153; *Wise Blood*, 1139

O'Connor, William Douglas (1832–89), 457-58

Odell, George C. D. (1866–1949): *Annals of the New York Stage*, 333-34

Odell, Jonathan (1737–1818), 148, 166, 199; *The American Times*, 149; *The Congratulation*, 149

Odets, Clifford (1906–63), 1103; *Waiting for Lefty*, 726, 1113

Odiorne, Thomas (1769–1851), 166

O'Gorman, Edmundo (1906–), 16

O'Hara, Frank (1926–66), 1065, 1097-99; "Easter," 1097; "Personism: A Manifesto," 1098-99; "Second Avenue," 1097; "The Three-Penny Opera," 1098

O'Hara, John (1905–70): *Butterfield 8*, 741

O. Henry (William Sydney Porter) (1862–1910): *The Four Million*, 583

Ohmann, Richard (1931–), 1031

Okada, John: *No-No Boy*, 814, 818

Okimoto, Daniel (1942–): *American in Disguise*, 814

Old Cap Collier Library, 555

Old Sleuth Library, 555

Old Southwest, 761-62; humor, 265-66, 778

Oldstyle, Jonathan, *see* Irving, Washington

Olmsted, Frederick Law (1822–1903), 320; *The Cotton Kingdom*, 362-63; *Journey in the Back Country*, 362; *Journey in the Seaboard Slave States*, 362; *Journey Through Texas*, 362

Olsen, Tillie (1913–), 831, 833-34; *Silences*, 833; *Tell Me a Riddle*, 833, 1061; *Yonnondio*, 833

Olson, Charles (1910–70), 770, 1024, 1081-82, 1089, 1091-94, 1096-98; "Human Universe," 1092; *The Maximus Poems*, 1084, 1093; "Projective Verse," 1082, 1092-94

Omaha Magic Theater, 1112

O'Neill, Eugene (1888–1953), 740, 1101-3; *Ah Wilderness!* 1110; *All God's Chillun Got Wings*, 1102, 1110; *Beyond the Horizon*, 1102; *Bound East for Cardiff*, 1102; *Desire Under the Elms*, 1102; *The Emperor Jones*, 1102, 1110; *The Great God Brown*, 1102; *The Hairy Ape*, 1102; *Hughie*, 1103; *The Iceman Cometh*, 1103; *Lazarus Laughed*, 1102; *Long Day's Journey into Night*, 1103; *Marco Millions*, 1102; *More Stately Mansions*, 1103; *Mourning Becomes Electra*, 1102, 1120; *Strange Interlude*, 1102, 1110; *A Touch of the Poet*, 1103

Open Theater, New York, 1112, 1122

Oppen, George (1908–84), 925, 1081

Oppenheim, James (1882–1932): *Dr. Rast*, 583; *The Nine-Tenths*, 583

Opportunity, 799, 919, 929

Opposing self, Lionel Trilling's notion of, 1133

Optimism, nationalistic, 1027-28, 1030-31

Oral forms of literature: Mexican American, 801-3; Native American, 6-7

Oral poetics movement, 1181

Organization man, the, 722

Ortiz, Simon (1941–), 15

Orwell, George (Eric Arthur Blair) (1903–50), 1127; *Animal Farm*, 1060; *1984*, 1060

Osborne, John (1929–): *Look Back in Anger*, 1121

Osgood, Frances (1811–50), 297-99; "A Flight of Fancy," 299

Otero Warren, Nina: *Old Spain in Our Southwest*, 803

Others, 737, 928, 973

Otis, Harrison Gray (1765–1848), 353

Otis, James (1725–83): *The Rights of the British Colonies*, 140; *A Vindication of the British Colonies*, 140

Ottley, Roi (1906–60), 866

Outcault, Richard Felton (1863–1928): "Origin of a New Species, or the Evolution of the Crocodile Explained," 572; "The Yellow Kid" ("Down Hogan's Alley"), 572

Outlook, 576

Overland Monthly, 516

Owens, Rochelle (1936–): *Belch*, 1113; *Emma Instigated Me*, 1113; *Futz*, 1113; *Karl Marx Play*, 1113

Page, Thomas Nelson (1853–1922), 319, 768, 778; *In Ole Virginia*, 514, 529, 586; "Marse Chan," 514; *The Negro*, 513; "No Haid Pawn," 514; *The Old South*, 513; *Red Rock*, 513

Pain, Philip (?–c. 1666), 93; *Daily Meditations*, 94

Paine, Thomas (1737–1809), 143-44; *The Age of Reason*, 144; *Common Sense*, 143-44, 193-94; *The Crisis*, 144; *The Rights of Man*, 144

Painting, 845, 917, 1098; Armory Show (1913), 738-39; avant-garde poetry, connection with, 1180-82; modernism, 695-96, 719

Paley, Grace (1922–), 1066

Paley, William (1743–1805): *A View of the Evidences of Christianity*, 211

Palmer, Michael (1943–), 1183

Palmer raids (1920), 721

Paris, France: post–World War I expatriates, 743-44, 851-52

Paris Review, The, 1191

Park, Robert (1864–1944), 579

Park, Ty: *Guilt Payment*, 821

Parker, Charlotte Blair (1868–1937): *Way Down East*, 332

Parker, Dorothy (1893–1967), 860, 863-64

Parker, Theodore (1810–60), 355-56, 366, 371-72, 374-75, 377, 386; *A Discourse of Matters Pertaining to Religions*, 368; *A Discourse of the Transient and Permanent in Christianity*, 368; "Sermon" (1846), 212

Parker, Thomas (1595–1677), 37

Parkman, Francis (1823–93), 189, 239, 356-57; *The Jesuits in North America in the Seventeenth Century*, 357; *Montcalm and Wolfe*, 357; *The Oregon Trail*, 362; *Pioneers of France in the New World*, 357

Parks, William (c. 1698–1750), 129

Parody: self-reflexive fiction, 1150-52, 1154, 1156

Parrington, Vernon Louis (1871–1929), 114, 732; *Main Currents in American Thought*, 996

Parsons, Jonathan (1705–76), 122

Partisan Review, 748, 756, 831, 835, 865, 921, 928, 1014, 1032, 1034, 1130, 1135

Parton, Sara Payson Willis, *see* Fern, Fanny

Pastiche, 1178, 1190-92, 1198

Pastor, Rose, 581

Pastoral poetry, 940

Patchen, Kenneth (1911–72), 921

Patten, Gilbert (Burt L. Standish) (1866–1945): Frank Merriwell stories, 558-59

Patten, Simon (1852–1922), 489

Paulding, James Kirke (1778–1860), 230; *The Diverting History of John Bull and Brother Jonathan*, 231; *The Dutchman's Fireside*, 232; life of George Washington, 232; *The Lion of the West*, 232, 309, 313; *Salmagundi; or, The Whim-Whams and Opinions of Launcelot Langstaff, Esq., and Others*, 231

Payne, John Howard (1791–1852), 232

Payne, Will (1865–1954): *The Money Captain*, 520

Peabody, Elizabeth (1804–94), 372, 376; *Record of a School*, 372

Peabody, Josephine Preston (1874–1922): *Harvest Moon*, 849

Peacham, Henry (1576?–1643?): *Minerva Britanna*, 26

Pead, Deuel (d. 1727), 59

Pearce, Roy Harvey (1919–), 457

Peck, Bradford: *The World a Department Store*, 520

Peirce, Charles Sanders (1839–1914), 492, 495–97; "The Fixation of Belief," 495; "How to Make Our Ideas Clear," 495

Peirce, Melusina Fay (1836–?): *Cooperative Housekeeping*, 472

Penn, William (1644–1718): *A Further Account of the Province of Pennsylvania*, 21

Pennsylvania Gazette, 199, 570, 574, 582

Penny press, 469

Percy, George (1580–c. 1632): *Discourse on the Plantation*, 20; *A Trewe Relacyon*, 21

Percy, Walker (1916–): *The Moviegoer*, 1139, 1153

Perelman, Bob (1947–), 1175, 1183

Perelman, S. J. (Sidney Joseph Perelman) (1904–79), 995

Performance art, 1189, 1192–93, 1198

Periodicals, *see* Magazines; Newspapers

Perkins, William (1558–1602), 29–30, 58, 123; *The Arte of Prophesying*, 28, 58; *Golden Chaine*, 28; *Of the Calling of the Ministerie*, 58

Perloff, Marjorie (1931–): *The Poetics of Indeterminacy*, 1194–95

Perreault, John (1937–), 1180

Personal narrative: Revolutionary period, 151–55

Personism, 1099

Pessimism, nationalistic: post–World War II, 1028, 1030–31

Pessimistic determinism, 536–37

Peterson, Charles Jacobs, *see* Cavendish, Harry

Peterson's Magazine, 295

Petter, Henri (1928–), 168

Phelps, Elizabeth (1815–52): *The Silent Partner*, 510

Philadelphia Ledger, 572

Philadelphische Zeitung, 582

Phillips, David Graham (1867–1911), 529, 532, 540; *The Deluge*, 523; *The Great God Success*, 523; *The Hungry Heart*, 523; *Susan Lennox: Her Fall and Rise*, 523, 533-34

Phillips, Jayne Anne (1952–): *Black Tickets*, 1171

Phillips, Wendell (1811–84), 356, 359

Philosophy, 491-98; in colonial period, 119; post–World War II, 1045-59; rational self-interest, 757; transcendentalists, 367-70, 373; *see also* Idealism; Pragmatism

Phips, Sir William (1651–95), 105-6

Photography, 750, 753, 755, 866, 1186

Physicotheologians, 103

Picaresque fiction, 173, 175

Pico, Pio (1801–94), 800

Pierce, Franklin (1804–69), 414, 416-18

Piercy, Marge (1936–): *Small Changes*, 1061; *Woman on the Edge of Time*, 1076, 1166, 1171

Pietists, 103

Pincus-Witten, Robert (1935–), 1187-88

Piper, Adrian: *Aspects of the Liberal Dilemma*, 1198

Plantation idylls, 266

Plath, Sylvia (1932–63), 1037, 1087, 1089; *Ariel*, 1064, 1087-88; *The Bell Jar*, 1031, 1064; *The Colossus*, 1088; "Daddy," 1089; "Fever 103°," 1090; "Lady Lazarus," 1087

Plays, *see* Drama

Plow That Broke the Plains, The (film), 859

Plutarch's Lives, 31, 67, 70

Podhoretz, Norman (1930–), 1028

Poe, Edgar Allan (1809–49), 214, 220, 226, 239, 262, 264-77, 279, 479-80, 570, 579, 588, 778; "Al Aaraaf," 214, 270; *Al Aaraaf, Tamerlane, and Minor Poems*, 270; "The Assignation," 273; "The Black Cat," 270; "Bon-Bon," 273; "The Cask of Amontillado," 272; "The City in the Sea," 270; "The Coliseum," 271; "A Descent into the Maelström," 270-73; "The Domain of Arnheim," 270; "Dream-Land," 271; "The Duc de L'Omelette," 273; "Eleven Tales of the Arabesque," 273; *Eureka*, 214, 269, 274, 378, 385; "Exordium to Critical Notices," 276-77; "The Fall of the House of Usher," 269,

Poe, Edgar Allan (*Continued*)
272-73, 778; and Nathaniel Hawthorne, 416, 419, 422, 768; "How to Write a Blackwood Article," 269; "Israfel," 271; "Letter to B——," 271; "Ligeia," 215, 269, 272-73; "Loss of Breath," 273; *Marginalia*, 271; "Metzengerstein," 269, 273; "MS. Found in a Bottle," 273; "The Murders in the Rue Morgue," 269-70; *The Narrative of Arthur Gordon Pym*, 269-70, 273-74; "The Philosophy of Composition," 271-72; *Poems, Second Edition*, 270-71; "The Poetic Principle," 214, 269, 271; "Power of Words," 271; radicals, influence on, 738; "The Rationale of Verse," 271; "The Raven," 265, 271-72; "Silence," 273; "The Sleeper," 270; "Sonnet to Science," 270; "A Tale of Jerusalem," 273; *Tales of the Folio Club*, 273; *Tales of the Grotesque and the Arabesque*, 273, 468; *Tamerlane and Other Poems*, 270-71; "To Helen," 215, 269-70; "Ulalume," 271; "The Valley of Unrest," 270
Poetry: Asian American, 816-17, 820-21; avant-garde, 1180-85, 1196; black writers, 586, 726, 790-97, 918-19, 927-29; collected works, 928; in colonial period, 83-97; in early republic, 156-67, 188-89, 191; Fireside Poets, 278-88; Mexican American, 801, 803, 807, 809-10; modernist, 707-8, 710-14, 775-76, 853, 913, 915-17, 926, 934-35; Native American, 8-10, 14-15; New England, 768-69; postmodernist, 916, 926; Revolutionary period, 148-49; social function of, 934, 936; Southern, 264-65; transcendentalist, 375-77; in twentieth century, 717, 729-30, 737, 846, 853, 913-36, 1037, 1041-42, 1061-62, 1064-65, 1067-70, 1072, 1075, 1079-1100; women writers, 296-99, 825-30, 840; *see also* Imagism
Poetry: A Magazine of Verse, 717, 720, 737, 799, 917, 924, 953, 984, 1180
Point of view, fictional technique of, 704-6
Poirier, Richard (1925-), 937, 941, 945
Pokagon, Simon (1830-99): *O-Gî-Mäw-Kwĕ Mit-I-Gwä-Kî (Queen of the Woods)*, 575-76; *Red Man's Greeting*, 575
Polish-language periodicals, 579
Political issues and themes: (colonial period) 106, (Revolutionary period) 139-47, (early republic) 191-92, (nineteenth century) 233, 252, 254, 261, (twentieth century) 721, 733-34, 746-50, 921-23, 930-31, 1023-30, 1035-

39, 1041-44, 1061-76, 1081, 1096, 1113-15, 1133, 1138, 1147-49, 1154, 1165, 1168, 1175-77; conservatism of 1980s, 1161-62; in realistic fiction, 504, 511, 519-20, 523; Southern, 777-78; women writers' involvement with, 830-33, 840
Political religion, 346-47
Politics of Literature, The: Dissenting Essays on the Teaching of English, 1072-73
Pollard, Percival (1869-1911), 735
Polyart, 1193
Poor of New York, The (play), 337
Pope, Alexander (1688-1744): "Windsor Forest," 160
Popular literature, 469, 551-67, 722
Popular magazines, in twentieth century, 730-31
Popular Science Monthly, 495
Populist movement, 489-90, 515, 517-19, 527, 918, 931
Porter, Katherine Anne (1890-1980), 740, 745, 781-83, 822, 834, 851; "The Circus," 782; "Flowering Judas," 853; "The Grave," 782; *Pale Horse, Pale Rider*, 871; *Ship of Fools*, 871
Porter, William Sydney, *see* O. Henry
Porter, William T. (1809-58): *Spirit of the Times: A Chronicle of the Turf, Agriculture, Field Sports, Literature and the Stage*, 316-17, 321
Portland Magazine, 295
Posey, Alexander Lawrence (1873-1908), 580
Post, The, 581
Postimpressionism, 917
Postindustrial society, 1023, 1025, 1030-31, 1040, 1042-43
Post-Marxist thought, 1062
Postmodernism, 870, 916, 926, 1043, 1131-32, 1140-41, 1161-63; self-reflexive fiction, 1142-57
Poststructuralism, 1004, 1173
Potter, David (1910-71), 724
Potter, Israel R. (1744-1826?): *Life and Remarkable Adventures of Israel R. Potter*, 155
Pound, Ezra (1885-1972), 498, 716, 719, 736-37, 739-40, 744, 775-76, 826, 845-46, 848-49, 874, 876, 884, 913, 916-17, 930, 935-36, 947-56, 958-63, 965-66, 968-71, 1079, 1084; *A Lume Spento*, 947, 950; arrest and detention, 969-70; *The Cantos*, 711, 853, 925, 935, 968-71; *Canzoni*, 952; *Cathay*, 955; *A Draft of 16 Cantos*, 968; *A Draft of Thirty Cantos*, 969; *Drafts and Fragments*, 970; "Ezra

Pound Speaking": Radio Speeches of World War II, 935; *The Fifth Decad of Cantos*, 969; *Homage to Sextus Propertius*, 960; *Hugh Selwyn Mauberley*, 959, 961, 968, 1001; "I Gather the Limbs of Osiris," 952-53; *Des Imagistes*, 954; "In a Station of the Metro," 954, 958; *Indiscretions*, 949; "In Durance," 950; *Jefferson and/or Mussolini*, 969; literary criticism, 952-54, 993, 1001-4, 1006-8; *Lustra*, 954, 958, 960; modernism, 696, 708, 710-12; musical theory and compositions, 953; "Near Perigord," 960; *Patria Mia*, 738, 949; *Personae* (1909), 951; *Personae: The Collected Poems* (1926), 951; *The Pisan Cantos*, 947, 950, 970; politics, 930; "Portrait d'une Femme," 953; "Provincia Deserta," 960; *A Quinzaine for This Yule*, 950; "The Return," 953; "Revolt, against the Crepuscular Spirit in Modern Poetry," 951; *Ripostes*, 953; *Rock-Drill*, 970; "The Seafarer," 952; *Selected Poems*, 955, 968; *The Spirit of Romance*, 952; *Three Cantos*, 960; *Thrones*, 970; translations, 952-53, 955, 960; "The Tree," 951; "Villonaud for This Yule," 951

Powell, John Wesley (1834–1902), 517

Pragmaticism, 496

Pragmatism, 373, 492, 496, 549, 654, 1056

Presbyterianism, 119-21

Prescott, William Hickling (1796–1859), 239, 357; *The History of Ferdinand and Isabella*, 357

Present, The, 371

President's Commission on the Status of Women, 1064

Preston, John (1587–1628), 57-58; *A Patterne of Wholesome Words*, 58

Price, Richard (1949–): *Ladies Man*, 1175

Prime, Benjamin (1733–91), 166; "Columbia's Glory," 160

"Primitive" cultural sources: in 1920s, 854

Prince, Thomas (1687–1758): *Chronological History of New England in the Form of Annuals*, 52-53

Prison letters, 1073

Pritchard, William H. (1932–), 937, 939

Professionalization of American life, 483

Progressive movement, 490, 493-94, 503, 523

Proletarian literature, 726, 748-49, 832-33, 840

Prospect poem, 160-63

Protestantism, 24-36; *see also specific denominations*

Proust, Marcel (1871–1922), 698

Provincetown Players, 737

Psychoanalytic criticism, 1004, 1013

Psychological vocabulary: post–World War II writers, 1037-38

Publishing industry, 289-90, 468, 478-79, 729, 874; popular fiction, 555; subscription selling, 633

Publius (pseudonym), 147, 195

Pulitzer, Joseph (1847–1911), 572, 633

Pulp magazines, 851

Pulver, Mary Brecht: "The Path of Glory," 848

Purchas, Samuel (1575?–1626): *Hakluytus Posthumus; or, Purchas His Pilgrimes*, 20

Puritanism, 24, 26-29, 31, 33-44, 101-12, 325; biography and autobiography, 67-76, 80; James Fenimore Cooper, Puritans in fiction of, 249; Emily Dickinson, influenced by, 623-24; funeral elegies, 85-86; nationalism, 192; poetry, 83-97; Psalms translations, 83-84; sermons and theological works, 56-66; spiritual diaries, 31; twentieth-century revolt against, 736-37

Putnam's Monthly, 219, 438

Pyle, Ernie (1900–1945), 756

Pynchon, Thomas (1937–), 1030, 1141, 1145, 1154, 1162, 1167; *Gravity's Rainbow*, 1152; *Mother Night*, 1151

Pynchon, William (c. 1590–1662), 62

Quakers, 75, 325

Quine, Willard Van Orman (1908–), 1050, 1056; "Two Dogmas of Empiricism," 1050-51

Quinto Sol Publications, 806-9

Rabe, David (1940–), 1118; *The Basic Training of Pavlo Hummel*, 1118; *Hurlyburly*, 1118; *In the Boom Boom Room*, 1118; *Sticks and Bones*, 1117

Rabelais, François (c. 1490–1553): *Gargantua and Pantagruel*, 1143

Racism, 355, 751, 814, 1066; in realistic and regional fiction, 512-13, 515

Radical literature: post–World War I, 721, 726, 740-55, 1113; post–World War II, 1028, 1060-76, 1113

Radical Right, 1061, 1063

Radio, 725-26, 728, 750

Radisson, Pierre Esprit (c. 1640–1710): *Voyages*, 22

Rahv, Philip (1908–73), 835, 1010, 1014; "The Myth and the Powerhouse," 1130

Raleigh, Sir Walter (1554?–1618), 19, 25

Ramsay, David (1749–1815): *The History of the American Revolution*, 195

Ramusio, Giovanni Battista (1485–1557), 17

Rand, Ayn (1905-82): *The Fountainhead*, 757

Ransom, John Crowe (1888–1974), 742, 865, 923, 935; "The Cloak Model," 923; "The Equilibrists," 923; *God Without Thunder*, 853; "The Innocent Doves," 923; literary criticism, 994, 1003-6, 1008; "The Manliness of Men," 923; *The New Criticism*, 1003; "The Poet as Woman," 826; "Poetry: A Note to Ontology," 1080; *Selected Poems*, 923

Raritan, 1033

Ratcliff, Carter (1941–), 1180

Rational self-interest, theory of, 757

Read, Opie (1852–1939): *My Young Master*, 515

Reader's Digest, 731

Reading habits: in twentieth century, 729-31, 1026

Realism, 473-74, 482, 501-8, 520-24, 764, 766-68, 774, 1163-64; definitions and theories of, 502; determinism in realist ficiton, 532; drama, 337-38, 1102-3; fusion of symbolism and, 893; naturalism compared with, 530-31, 545; in philosophy, 1047; regionalism compared with, 503; romance-realism dialectic, in novels of alienation, 861-62; *see also* Neorealism

Rebel Poet, The, 921, 928

Reconstruction period, 483-84, 510-14

Redding, J. Saunders (1906–): *To Make a Poet Black*, 794-95

Red Scare (1919–20), 721, 742, 850

Reed, Ishmael (1938–), 1025, 1145, 1153-54, 1172; *Flight to Canada*, 1150, 1175; *The Free-Lance Pallbearers*, 1150; *Mumbo Jumbo*, 1150; *Reckless Eyeballing*, 1172, 1175; *The Terrible Twos*, 1172, 1175; *Yellow Back Radio Broke Down*, 1071

Reed, John (1887–1920), 493, 720, 738, 845; *Ten Days That Shook the World*, 748, 850

Reed, Sampson (1800–1880), *Observations on the Growth of the Mind*, 209

Reformation, 24, 33, 36

Reform movements, 734, (1810–65) 212-13, 347, 371-73, (1865–1910) 487-88, 490, 527, (1919-45) 721, 726, 747; *see also* Abolitionism; Civil rights movement; Women's movement

Regeneracion, 802

Regionalism, 474, 501-3, 508-20, 524, 761-63, 1135; humor, 306-23; poetry, 918; realism

compared with, 503; women writers, 597-98

Reich, Steve (1936–), 1193; *It's Gonna Rain*, 1194

Reich, Wilhelm (1897–1957), 1038

Reid, James (fl. 1768): *The Religion of the Bible and the Religion of King William County Compared*, 129

Reid, Mayne (1818–83): *The Quadroon*, 588

Reinstitutionalization of American life, 483

Religion, 24-32, (1810–65) 209-13, 216-17, 346-47, (1865-1910) 486-87, 528; transcendentalism, 368-69, 373; *see also* Great Awakening; Protestantism; Puritanism; Reformation; Roman Catholic Church

Remarque, Erich Maria (1898–1970); *All Quiet on the Western Front*, 730

Representations, 1033-34

Review of Reviews, 576

Revista Ilustrada de Nueva York, La, 579

Revolution, American, *see* American Revolution

Rexroth, Kenneth (1905–82), 1084

Reznikoff, Charles (1894–1976), 917

Ribaut, Jean (c. 1520–1565): *The Whole and True Discovery of Terra Florida*, 18

Rice, Anne (1941–): *Interview with the Vampire*, 1171; *Vampire Lestat*, 1171

Rice, Elmer (1892–1967), 1103

Rice, Thomas D. "Daddy" (1808–60), 335

Rich, Adrienne (1929–), 1025, 1064-66, 1081, 1083; *A Change of World*, 1090; *The Diamond Cutters*, 1090; *Leaflets*, 1090; "Natural Resources," 1068; *Necessities of Life*, 1090; "The Phenomenology of Anger," 1068, 1090; *Snapshots of a Daughter-in-Law*, 1090; *The Will to Change*, 1090

Richards, George (c. 1760–1814), 166

Richards, I. A. (Ivor Armstrong Richards) (1893–1979): *Practical Criticism*, 1004; *Principles of Literary Criticism*, 1004

Richardson, Samuel (1689–1761); *Clarissa Harlowe*, 169

Ridge, Lola (1871–1941): *The Ghetto and Other Poems*, 918; *Red Flag*, 921

Ridiculous, playwrights of the, 1116-17

Riding, Laura (1901–), 925, 927; "Hulme, the New Barbarism, and Gertrude Stein," 854; "The Tiger," 925; "The Why of the Wind," 925

Riedesel, Friederike Charlotte Luise, Baroness von (1746–1808): *Journal*, 153-54

Riesman, David (1909–): *The Lonely Crowd*, 1029-30, 1131

Riis, Jacob (1849–1914), 573; *How the Other Half Lives*, 502, 560, 573; *The Making of an American*, 573; *Out of Mulberry Street: Stories of Tenement Life in New York*, 583

Riley, James Whitcomb (1849–1916), 773

Ripley, George (1802–80), 211-12, 216, 365-66, 369-71; *Discourses on the Philosophy of Religion*, 209, 369, 371; *Specimens of Foreign Standard Literature*, 369

Rising glory poem, 160-63

Risorgimento, Ezra Pound's notion of, 736, 846, 848, 864

River, The (film), 859

Rivera, Tomás (1935–84), 807-9

Rives, Amélie (1863–1945): *The Quick and the Dead?* 515

Roaring Twenties, 741, 854

Robbe-Grillet, Alain (1922–), 1127

Robbins, Tom (1936–), 1030; *Still Life with Woodpecker*, 1175

Roberts, Kenneth (1885–1957), 853

Robins, Elizabeth (1862–1952): *Ancilla's Share*, 857

Robinson, Edwin Arlington (1869–1935), 771, 917, 933

Robinson, Marilynne (1944–): *Housekeeping*, 1171

Robison, Mary (1949?–), 1163, 1165

Robles, Al, 817, 820

Rodriguez, Richard (1944–): *Hunger of Memory*, 809

Roethke, Theodore (1908–63), 626, 826, 829, 926, 1080, 1094

Rogers, John (c. 1572–1636), 58

Rogers, Robert (1731–95): *Ponteach*, 326-28

Rogue, 928

Rollins, Alice (1847–97): *Uncle Tom's Tenement*, 583

Rölvaag, O. E. (Ole Edvart Rölvaag) (1876–1931): *Giants in the Earth*, 726

Roman Catholic Church, 35-36

Romantic histories: and Washington Irving, 229, 239

Romanticism, 178, 182, 225, 426-28; and Henry Adams, 646-47, 649; and T. S. Eliot, 961-62; and Nathaniel Hawthorne, 424-25; Mexican American literature, 803-4; poetry, 915; romance-realism dialectic, in novels of alienation, 861-62; twentieth-century drama, 1103; women writers, 595

Roosevelt, Franklin Delano (1882–1945), 733, 750-51, 753, 755, 757

Roosevelt, Theodore (1858–1919), 631-32, 635, 733, 845; *The Strenuous Life*, 517; *The Winning of the West*, 517

Rorty, Richard (1931–), 1045, 1055-56

Rosenberg, Harold (1906–78), 770, 1036, 1180

Rosenberg spy case, 1062, 1152

Rosenfeld, Morris (1862–1923): *Songs of Labor and Other Poems*, 583

Ross, Edward Alsworth (1866–1951), 490

Ross, William P. (1820–91), 580

Rosskam, Edwin (1903–85): *12 Million Black Voices*, 866

Rossner, Judith (1935–): *Looking for Mr. Goodbar*, 1170

Roth, Henry (1906–), 754; *Call It Sleep*, 726, 755

Roth, Philip (1933–), 1137; *Our Gang*, 1038; *Portnoy's Complaint*, 1031, 1152; "Writing American Fiction," 1134

Rothenberg, Jerome (1931–), 1181

Rourke, Constance (1885–1941): *American Humor*, 309-10, 709

Rowlandson, Mary (c. 1635–c. 1678), 68; *The Soveraignty and Goodness of God . . .* , 76-78

Rowson, Susanna (c. 1762–1824), 166, 170, 184, 332; *Charlotte Temple*, 170-72, 175, 177-78, 186

Royce, Josiah (1855–1916), 494-96; *The World and the Individual*, 495

Ruffin, William, 54

Rugeley, Rowland (c. 1735–1776): *The Story of Aeneas and Dido Burlesqued*, 165

Rukeyser, Muriel (1913–80), 922, 1081; "Käthe Kollwitz," 1075; "Orpheus," 1090; "Poem Out of Childhood," 1072; *Theory of Flight*, 922

Rural themes: in realistic and regional fiction, 518-19, 534

Ruskin, John (1819–1900): *Stones of Venice*, 640

Russ, Joanna (1937–), 1076, 1167, 1172, 1176; *The Female Man*, 1171, 1175-76; *The Two of Them*, 1171

Russell, Dora (1894–1986): *Hypatia*, 857

Rutledge, Marice (Marie Louise Gibson Hale) (1886–?): *Children of Fate*, 849

Ryer, George: *The Old Homestead*, 337, 339

Sacco and Vanzetti case, 721, 745-46, 750, 850

Saffin, John (c. 1626–1710): *Brief and Candid Answer to . . . The Selling of Joseph*, 66

Said, Edward (1935–), 1033

St. Louis Post-Dispatch, 577

St. Louis Westliche Post, 572
Salinas, Omar (1937–): *Darkness Under the Trees/
Walking Behind the Spanish,* 809-10
Salinger, J. D. (Jerome David Salinger)
(1919–), 1030, 1132, 1139-40, 1148; *The
Catcher in the Rye,* 1138
Salmagundi (periodical, 1807–8), 200
Salmagundi (periodical, twentieth century),
1033
Saltus, Edgar (1855–1921), 735
Sanborn, Franklin Benjamin (1831–1917), 376
Sanborn, Pitts (1878–1941), 984
Sandburg, Carl (1878-1967), 751, 915-16, 930-
31; *Chicago Poems,* 917; *The People, Yes,* 752
Sandys, George (1578–1644), 25, 84
San Francisco, 735, 1084
San Francisco Mime Troupe, 1113-14
Santayana, George (1863–1952), 734, 739, 741;
Character and Opinion in the United States, 493;
"The Genteel Tradition in American Phi-
losophy," 494; literary criticism, 994-96,
999; *Reason in Society,* 493-94; *Three Philo-
sophical Poets: Lucretius, Dante and Goethe,* 994
Santos, Bienvenido N. (1911–), 817-18; *The
Day the Dancers Came,* 818; *Scent of Apples,*
818; *You Lovely People,* 816, 818
Saroyan, William (1908–81), 1103
Sartre, Jean-Paul (1905–80), 1127-28, 1130,
1134; *La Nausée,* 1136; *What Is Literature?*
1126
Satire, 86-87, 148-49, 174-75, 199-200, 721;
drama, 331, 1103; and Sinclair Lewis, 774;
and James Russell Lowell, 283-84; and
H. L. Mencken, 742-43
Saturday Evening Post, 574, 731, 848, 851, 934
Schjeldahl, Peter (1942–), 1180
Schlesinger, Arthur M., Jr. (1917–): *The Vital
Center,* 1133
Schoolcraft, Henry R. (1793–1864), 580
Schoolroom Poets, *see* Fireside Poets
Schumpeter, Joseph (1883–1950), 520
Schurz, Carl (1829–1906), 572; *Reminiscences,*
572; "True Americanism," 572
Schuyler, James (1923–), 1097
Schwartz, Delmore (1913–66), 1080; "The
Present State of Poetry," 1079, 1081
Science and technology, 103-4, 109, 528, 1166;
and Henry Adams, 651
Science fiction, 1076, 1162, 1166-68, 1171,
1173
Science Fiction Research Association, 1167
Science Fiction Studies, 1167

Scientific management, 730
Scopes trial (1925), 742
Scott, Nathan A. (1925–): *Three American
Moralists,* 1132
Scott, Sir Walter (1771–1832), 267, 306, 635-
36
Scottow, Joshua (1618–98), 42
Scottsboro case, 747, 929
Screen Writers' Guild, 835
Scribner's Magazine, 586-87, 851
Scribner's Monthly, 460, 472; see also *Century
Magazine*
Scudder, Horace (1838–1902), 471
Scudder, Vida (1861–1954), 824
Seabrook, William (1886–1945), 849
Seabury, Samuel (1729–96), 142
Searson, John, 166
Secession, 852
Second Black Renaissance, 793
Second Great Awakening, 114, 346-47, 369
Sectionalism, 266, 349-63, 763
Sedgwick, Catharine Maria (1789–1867), 222,
293-94; *Clarence,* 293; *Hope Leslie,* 293; *The
Linwoods,* 293; *Married or Single?* 293-94; *A
New England Tale,* 293; *Redwood,* 293
Seelye, John (1931–), 784
Séjour, Victor (1817–74), 334
Self-analysis: in Protestant poetics, 29-30
Self-conscious fiction, 1142-43, 1145
Self-identity, redefinitions of (1910–45), 716-
18, 721-22
Self-reflexive fiction, 1142-57, 1163; self-con-
sciousness compared with, 1145
Semiotics, 1048
Seneca Falls convention (1848), 349
Senior, Nassau W. (1790–1864): *Essays on Fic-
tion,* 671
Sennett, Richard (1943–): *The Fall of Public
Man,* 1038
Sentimental fiction: early American period,
170-73, 175, 184, 186; slave novels, 360-61
Separatists (Puritan group), 36
Sermons and theological writings, 37, 56-66,
113-16, 118-25, 194; English, 27-29
Settle, Dionise, 18
Settlement novels: and James Fenimore
Cooper, 249-51, 256
Seven Arts, The, 720, 737, 739, 744-45, 851
Sewall, Jonathan (1728–96): *The Americans
Roused, in a Cure for the Spleen,* 326; *A Cure
for the Spleen,* 150
Sewall, Samuel (1652–1730), 31, 90; *Diary,*

73; *Phaenomena quaedam Apocalyptica; or, A Description of the New Heavens as It Makes to Those Who Stand Upon the New Earth*, 42, 66; *The Selling of Joseph*, 66

Sewanee Review, 1082

Sexton, Anne (1928–74), 1087-90; *To Bedlam and Part Way Back*, 1087

Sexual themes, 857-58, 871, 1065, 1068; in beat poetry, 1086; in gay drama, 1116-17; in naturalistic fiction, 538; in realistic and regional fiction, 504, 506, 514-15, 519, 522-23; in self-reflexive fiction, 1152; women writers, 591, 597, 604-5, 832-33, 835, 837-40

Shaftesbury, Anthony Ashley Cooper, 3d earl of (1671–1713): *Characteristiks of Men, Manners, Opinions, Times*, 74

Shakespeare, William (1564–1616), 24, 998, 1000, 1017, 1058; *Macbeth*, 943; *The Tempest*, 21, 25-26

Shakespeare and Company, 851

Shange, Ntozake (1948–), 1064; *Sassafrass, Cypress & Indigo*, 1171

Shank, Adele, 1112

Shapiro, David (1947–), 1180

Shapiro, Karl (1913–), 1080; *The Bourgeois Poet*, 1037

Shaw, George Bernard (1856–1950), 738

Shaw, Irwin (1913–84): *The Young Lions*, 1150

Shea, Daniel (1936–): *Spiritual Autobiography in Early America*, 72

Sheldon, Charles (1857–1946): *In His Steps*, 529

Shepard, Sam (1942–), 1027, 1109, 1118-20; *Angel City*, 1119; *Buried Child*, 1119; *Cowboy Mouth*, 1119; *Curse of the Starving Class*, 1119; *Fool for Love*, 1120; *The Lie of the Mind*, 1120; *Mad Dog Blues*, 1119; *Melodrama Play*, 1119; *Operation Sidewinder*, 1119; *The Rock Garden*, 1119; *Suicide in B Flat*, 1119; *Tooth of Crime*, 1123-24; *True West*, 1120; *La Turista*, 1119; *The Unseen Hand*, 1119

Shepard, Thomas (1605–49), 31, 37, 61, 71; *Autobiography*, 68, 74; *The Sincere Convert*, 56, 60; *The Sound Believer*, 60; *Wine for Gospel Wantons*, 64

Shepard, Thomas, Jr. (1635–77), 65

Sheridan, Richard (1751–1816): *The School for Scandal*, 328

Sherwood, Robert (1896–1955), 1103

Shipp, Jesse A. (1869–1934): *Senegamian Carnival*, 335

Short stories, 851, 869, 1165; Asian American, 815-16, 819; Mexican American, 804-5, 807-8; minimalist fiction, 1162; regional, 776-77, 781-82; women writers of 1930s, 833

Shulman, Alix Kates (1932–): *Burning Questions*, 1073; *Memoirs of an Ex-Prom Queen*, 1170

Sibbes, Richard (1577–1635), 27, 30, 58

Sidney, Sir Philip (1554–86), 29; *Arcadia*, 25; *Defense of Poesy*, 28

Sienkiewicz, Henryk (1846–1916): *Quo Vadis?* 635

Sierra Club, 722

Sigourney, Lydia Huntley (1791–1865), 297-98, 550, 623

Silent Generation, 1147-48

Silko, Leslie (1948–), 1164, 1172; *Ceremony*, 15; *Storyteller*, 1164

Silliman, Ron (1946–), 1175-76, 1183, 1193; "Art with No Name," 1193; "Blue," 1191-92; *Ketjak*, 1176

Simms, William Gilmore (1806–70), 134, 222, 240, 242, 264, 268, 580, 777; *The Cassique of Kiawah*, 242; *Guy Rivers*, 243, 368; *Martin Faber*, 268; *The Partisan*, 268; *The Yemassee*, 242-43, 268

Simon, Neil (1927–), 1109

Simpson, Lewis (1916–), 779

Simpson, Louis (1923–), 1094

Sinclair, Upton (1878–1968), 477, 522, 532, 540, 845; *Boston*, 850; *The Jungle*, 522, 533, 560, 726, 932; *Oil*, 741

Singer, Isaac Bashevis (1904–), 1039, 1152

Single, Celia, *see* Franklin, Benjamin

Single-play combinations, 336

Sketches of Eighteenth-Century America, 151

Skinner, B. F. (Burrhus Frederic Skinner) (1904–): *Walden II*, 1076

Slave narratives, 68-69, 75, 78-79, 349-50, 358-62

Slave novels, 360-61

Slavery, 127, 130-35, 140, 145, 187, 194, 213, 314, 345; defense of, 263, 266-67, 269, 350, 352; as economic institution, 360-61; *see also* Abolitionism; Slave narratives; Slave novels

Slesinger, Tess (1905–45), 834-35; "Miss Flinders," 835; *The Unpossessed*, 834-35, 859

Slover, John (fl. 1773–82), 152

Slowan Amerikansky, 580

Small, Albion (1854–1926), 489

Smart Set, The, 720, 736, 741

Smith, Elizabeth Oakes (1806–93), 297-98; "The Sinless Child," 298; *Woman and Her Needs*, 298

Smith, John (1580–1631), 21, 25, 47-48; *Description of New England*, 48; *The Generall Historie of Virginia, New-England, and the Summer Isles*, 21, 47; *A Map of Virginia*, 21, 47-48; *A True Relation*, 21

Smith, Josiah (1704–81), 115

Smith, Richard Penn (1799–1854): *Col. Crockett's Exploits and Adventures in Texas*, 309, 312

Smith, Seba (1792–1868), 314

Smith, Venture (1729?–1805): *A Narrative of the Life and Adventures of Venture, a Native of Africa*, 78

Smith, William Henry (1806–72): *The Drunkard; or, The Fallen Saved*, 331, 335

Smithson, Robert (1938–73): "Incidents of Mirror-Travel in the Yucatan," 1188-89; *Tourist Guide and Directory of Yucatan-Campeche*, 1189; "A Tour of the Monuments of Passaic, New Jersey," 1188

Snodgrass, W. D. (William DeWitt Snodgrass) (1926–), 1090; "Heart's Needle," 1089; *Heart's Needle*, 1087

Snowden, Richard (fl. 1794), 164

Snyder, Gary (1930–), 1066, 1084, 1086; *Myths and Texts*, 1086; *Plain Talk*, 1069-70; *Riprap*, 1086

Social Darwinism, 486, 528, 537, 539

Social Gospel movement, 373, 490, 507

Socialism, 488, 520, 738, 1062

Social issues and themes, (1810–65) 212, (1865–1910) 507, (1910–45) 864, 921-22, 925-27, 929-33, (post–World War II) 1023-31, 1035-44, 1061-76, 1131-32, 1134, 1147-48, 1165-66, 1168; *see also* Great Depression; Racism; Radical literature; Reform movements; Slavery

Socialist Realism, 867, 1060

Social realism, 1103, 1129

Society comedies: in nineteenth century, 328

Soil, The, 852

Sollors, Werner (1943–), 1114

Solow, Herbert (1903–64), 834

Solzhenitsyn, Aleksandr I. (1918–): *The Gulag Archipelago*, 1060

Sone, Monica (1919–): *Nisei Daughter*, 813-14

Song, Cathy (1955–): *Picture Bride*, 821

Songs, popular, 196-97, 914-15

Sontag, Susan (1933–), 1027, 1033, 1061, 1066, 1163, 1186-87; "Against Interpretation," 1186; *On Photography*, 1186

Sorrentino, Gilbert (1929–), 1091, 1147, 1155; *Mulligan Stew*, 1156, 1163

Soto, Gary (1952–), 809-10; *Black Hair*, 810

Sound of sense, Robert Frost's concept of, 939

South, 761-63, 768, 777-84, (colonial period) 59, 67, 73-74, 86-87, 90, 127-35, (early republic) 166, (antebellum period) 242, 262-77, 301-2, 345, 349-63, (1865–1910) 510-16, (twentieth century) 753, 1135, 1139-40; Agrarians (Fugitive group), 742, 853, 865, 923; humor, 308-23; self-reflexive fiction, 1152-53; speech, 307-8; theater, 325; *see also* Slavery

Southeast, 762

Southern Literary Messenger, 262-64, 267, 269, 274-76

Southern Review, The, 865

Southern Workman, 799

Southwest, 762; Mexican American literature, 800-10

Southworth, E. D. E. N. (Emma Dorothy Eliza Nevitte Southworth) (1819–99), 292, 301-2; *The Hidden Hand*, 301; *Ishmael; or, In the Depths*, 563; *Retribution*, 469; *Self-Made; or, Out of the Depths*, 563-64; *Self-Raised; or, From the Depths*, 563

Spanish-American War, 517

Spanish Civil War, 749

Spanish-language periodicals, 579

Spanish literature, 16-17; *see also* Mexican American literature

Spector, Herman (1895–1959), 921

Spencer, Herbert (1820–1903), 486, 490, 528; *First Principles*, 486

Spender, Stephen (1909–), 698

Spengemann, William (1932–), 173

Spenser, Edmund (c. 1552–1599): *The Faerie Queene*, 24-25

Spiller, Robert (1896–): *Literary History of the United States*, 786-87

Spirit of the Age, The, 371

Spofford, Harriet Prescott (1835–1921): "Circumstance," 563-64

Sprague, Charles (1791–1875), 279

Springfield Republican, 622

Spy stories, 1061

Stagflation, post–World War II, 1040-41

Standish, Burt L., *see* Patten, Gilbert

Stansbury, Joseph (1740–1809), 166

Stead, William Thomas (1849–1912): *If Christ Came to Chicago!* 529

Stearns, Harold (1891–1943): *Civilization in the United States: An Inquiry by Thirty Americans*, 741, 856

Stedman, Edmund Clarence (1833–1908), 460, 473, 478, 768

Steere, Richard (1643–1721): "Earth's Felicities, Heaven's Allowance," 90; "Sea-Storm nigh the Coast," 90

Steffens, Lincoln (1866–1936), 578, 581, 747, 865, 929

Stein, Gertrude (1874–1946), 482, 498, 588-89, 591, 599, 602, 606, 719, 739-40, 743, 770, 773, 775-76, 822, 825, 840, 847, 850-51, 863, 869, 871, 873-74, 878-81, 884-86, 917, 1130; *Autobiography of Alice B. Toklas*, 848, 851, 880; *Bee Time Vine and Other Pieces*, 926; *Brewsie and Willie*, 880; *Counting Her Dresses. A Play*, 880; *Everybody's Autobiography*, 880; *Four Saints in Three Acts: An Opera to Be Sung*, 880; "The Gentle Lena," 879; *The Geographical History of America*, 880; *G. M. P. (Matisse, Picasso, and Gertrude Stein)*, 880; "The Good Anna," 879; *Ida: A Novel*, 880; *Lectures in America*, 880; *Lifting Belly*, 879, 926; literary portraits, 862; *A Long Gay Book*, 880; *Lucy Church Amiably*, 879-80; *The Making of Americans*, 775, 878, 880; *Many, Many Women*, 880; "Matisse," 879; "Melanctha," 857, 879; *Mrs. Reynolds: A Novel*, 880; modernism, 696, 708; *The Mother of Us All*, 880; *Narration*, 880; *Patriarchal Poetry*, 880, 926-27; *Picasso*, 880; *A Play of Pounds*, 880; plays, 1110-11; poetry, 926; *Stanzas in Meditation and Other Poems*, 926; *Tender Buttons*, 606, 879, 880, 917; *They Must. Be Wedded. To Their Wife, A Play*, 880; *Things As They Are* or *Q.E.D.*, 846, 880; *Three Lives*, 583, 846, 878-80; *Two: Gertrude Stein and Her Brother*, 880; *Wars I Have Seen*, 880; *What Are Masterpieces and Why Are There So Few of Them*, 880; *What Happened*, 1111

Steinbeck, John (1902-68), 545, 1130; *The Grapes of Wrath*, 726, 753-54, 859, 864, 868; *In Dubious Battle*, 868; *Of Mice and Men*, 864; *Tortilla Flat*, 805

Stephens, Ann Sophia (1813–86), 295, 552; *Fashion and Famine*, 295, 552; *Malaeska: The Indian Wife of the White Hunter*, 295, 551-52, 554; *The Old Homestead*, 295, 552

Sterne, Laurence (1713–68): *Tristram Shandy*, 1142-43

Sternhold-Hopkins psalter, 83

Stevens, Holly (1924–), 983-84, 986

Stevens, Wallace (1879–1955), 493, 498, 626, 740, 749, 770, 913, 930, 948, 954, 972, 981-92, 1006, 1009, 1017-18, 1079, 1084; "Adagia," 987, 989-91; "Anecdote of the Jar," 988; "Angels Surrounded by Paysans," 985; "The Auroras of Autumn," 989-90; *The Auroras of Autumn*, 985, 987; "Bantams in Pine-Woods," 988; "A Child Asleep in Its Own Life," 988; "Chocorua to Its Neighbor," 981-82, 986, 989, 992; *Collected Poems*, 985, 992; "The Comedian as the Letter C," 920, 985, 988; "A Dish of Peaches in Russia," 987; "The Emperor of Ice-Cream," 988; "Esthétique du Mal," 988; *Harmonium*, 920, 984-89; "The Idea of Order at Key West," 989; *Ideas of Order*, 754, 925, 985; journals, 983; "Large Red Man Reading," 987; *Letters*, 986; "The Man with the Blue Guitar," 988; *The Man with the Blue Guitar*, 754, 925, 985; "Montrachet-le-Jardin," 987-88; *The Necessary Angel: Essays on Reality and the Imagination*, 986; "Notes toward a Supreme Fiction," 981, 988-89; "Not Ideas about the Thing but the Thing Itself," 988, 992; "Nuances of a Theme by Williams," 972; "Of Mere Being," 988; *Opus Posthumous*, 986, 989; "An Ordinary Evening in New Haven," 988-89; "The Owl in the Sarcophagus," 986, 988-89, 991; *Owl's Clover*, 922; *The Palm at the End of the Mind*, 985-86; "Parochial Theme," 990; *Parts of a World*, 985; "A Primitive Like an Orb," 987, 992; "The River of Rivers in Connecticut," 988; "The Rock," 985, 989; "Sea Surface Full of Clouds," 920, 985; "The Snow Man," 986, 988, 992; "Some Friends from Pascagoula," 987; *Souvenirs and Prophecies: The Young Wallace Stevens*, 983, 986; "Sunday Morning," 920, 972, 984, 986; "Tea at the Palaz of Hoon," 987; "Thinking of a Relation Between the Images of Metaphors," 982; *Transport to Summer*, 985, 987; "The Virgin Carrying a Lantern," 987

Stevenson, Robert Louis (1850–94), 573

Steward, Austin (1794–1860): *Twenty-Two Years a Slave and Forty Years a Freeman*, 358-59

Stieglitz, Alfred (1864–1946), 719, 738, 917

Stith, William (1707–55): *The First Discovery and Settlement of Virginia*, 129

Stoddard, Elizabeth (1823–1902): *The Morgesons*, 302-3

Stoddard, Solomon (1643–1729), 65

Stone, B. H., 580

Stone, John Augustus (1800–1834): *Metamora; or, The Last of the Wampanoags*, 329-30

Stone, Robert (1937–), 1141

Stone and Kimball, 479, 481

Stoughton, William (1631–1701), 41; *New Englands True Interest*, 64-65

Stowe, Harriet Beecher (1811–96), 225, 304-5, 358, 488, 502, 579, 592, 636; *Dred: A Tale of the Great Dismal Swamp*, 305; *A Key to Uncle Tom's Cabin*, 512; *The Mayflower*, 765; *The May Flower*, 765; *The Minister's Wooing*, 305, 765; "A New England Sketch," 764; *Old Town Folks*, 305; *Pearl of Orr's Island*, 305; *Poganunc People*, 305; regionalism, 764-65, 768; *Uncle Tom's Cabin*, 170, 173, 186, 304-5, 310, 319-20, 331, 335, 347, 361, 510-11, 561, 583-85, 765

Strachey, William (1572–1621): "A True Reportory of the Wracke, and Redemption of Sir Thomas Gates," 20-21

Stream-of consciousness technique, 834, 873, 880

Street and Smith, 555, 559

Stribling, T. S. (Thomas Sigismund Stribling) (1881–1965), 753

Strindberg, August (1849–1912), 523

Strong, George Templeton (1820–75): *Diary*, 353-54, 356

Strong, Josiah (1847–1916): *The Twentieth Century City*, 501

Structuralism, 1004, 1009, 1048-49, 1051-54, 1128, 1141

Student and Schoolmate, 556

Sturgeon, Theodore (1918–85), 1162, 1168

Styan, John (1923–), 1109

Styles, recycling of: post–World War II, 1043

Styron, William (1925–), 1148; *The Confessions of Nat Turner*, 1072; *Lie Down in Darkness*, 1153

Suárez, Mario (1925–), 805

Success, 477

Sue, Eugène (1804–57): *Les Mystères de Paris*, 582

Suffragist, 931

Sui Sin Far, *see* Eaton, Edith Maud

Sukenick, Ronald (1932–), 1154-55, 1163; *The Death of the Novel and Other Stories*, 1128, 1154; *Long Talking Bad Conditions Blues*, 1155-56; *98.6*, 1155; *Out*, 1155; *Up*, 1152, 1154, 1174

Sullivan, James (1848–1938): *Tenement Tales of New York*, 583

Sullivan, Louis (1856–1924), 522, 719; "Kindergarten Chats," 492

Sumner, William Graham (1840–1910), 486, 489-90

Surrealism: in drama, 1116; in poetry, 915, 918, 922, 924, 1084, 1097

Surreal poets, *see* Deep image poets

Sutton, Christopher (1565?–1629), 30

Sylvester, Joshua (1563–1618): *The Divine Weekes and Workes*, 28

Symbolist movement, 892-93, 956

Symons, Arthur (1865–1945): *The Symbolist Movement in Literature*, 956-57

Syndicated journalism, 573

Tabios, Presco, 817

Tageblatt, 581

Taggard, Genevieve (1894–1948), 826, 834; "Everybody Alchemy," 922; *For Eager Lovers*, 830

Tahlequah Telephone, 580

Tailfer, Patrick (fl. 1741): *A True and Historical Narrative of the Colony of Georgia*, 53

Talese, Gay (1932–), 1032; "Frank Sinatra Has a Cold," 1036

Tall tales, Southern, 308-19, 322-23

Tanaka, Ronald (1944–): *Shino Suite*, 816

Tappan, Arthur (1786–1865), 347

Tappan, Caroline Sturgis (1819–88), 376

Tappan, Lewis (1788–1873), 347

Tarbell, Ida (1857–1944), 578

Tarkington, Booth (1869–1946): *The Magnificent Ambersons*, 518

Tarski, Alfred (1902–83): "The Concept of Truth in Formalized Languages," 1046

Tate, Allen (1899–1979), 742, 749, 865, 891, 923, 935, 1088; biographies, 853; "The Hovering Fly," 1007; literary criticism, 1002, 1004, 1007-8; "Miss Emily and the Bibliographer," 1007; "Ode to the Confederate Dead," 923; *Reactionary Essays*, 1007;

Reason in Madness, 1007; "A Southern Mode of the Imagination," 134; "Tension in Poetry," 1080

Tavel, Ronald (1941–), 1116; *Boy on the Straight-Back Chair*, 1116; *Gorilla Queen*, 1116; *The Life of Lady Godiva*, 1116; *Shower*, 1116

Taylor, Bayard (1825–78), 232

Taylor, Edward (c. 1644–1729), 26, 28, 30, 32, 65, 94-97, 104; *Christographia*, 65; *Gods Determinations Touching His Elect*, 88; *Preparatory Meditations*, 88, 95-97; "Spiritual Relation," 72; *Treatise Concerning the Lord's Supper*, 31

Taylor, Frederick W. (1856–1915), 730, 932

Taylor, Paul S. (1895–1984): *An American Exodus*, 866

Taylor, Thomas (1758–1835), 215

Taylor, William R. (1922–), 196

Teapot Dome affair, 741

Teasdale, Sara (1884–1933), 825, 827-28

Teatro Campesino, 806, 1070, 1114

Technology, *see* Science and technology

Telamaque, Eleanor Wong (1934): *It's Crazy to Stay Chinese in Minnesota*, 818-19

Telos, 1033-34

Temperance dramas, 331

Tennent, Gilbert (1703–64), 116-17; *The Dangers of an Unconverted Ministry*, 119-20

Tennyson, Alfred (1809–92), 948

Terhune, Mary Virginia, *see* Harland, Marion

Terkel, Studs (1912–): *Hard Times*, 1107

Terry, Lucy (1730–1821): "Bars Fight, August 28, 1746," 165

Terry, Megan (1932–), 1112; *American Kings English for Queens*, 1112; *Approaching Simone*, 1112; *Babes in the Bighouse*, 1112; *Hothouse*, 1112; *Viet Rock*, 1112

Textbooks: reform of 1880s, 471

Text-sound poetry, 1194

Thacher, James (1754–1844): *A Military Journal during the American Revolutionary War*, 153

Thayer, Scofield (1889–?), 744

Theater, *see* Drama

Theological writings, *see* Sermons and theological writings

Thibault, Anna-Marie: *Les Deux Testaments*, 585

Third Woman, The: Minority Women Writers of the United States, 1064

This Quarter, 744

Thomas, Edward (1878–1917), 938

Thomas, Henry J., *see* Barker, Colin A.

Thomas, William I. (1863–1947), 489

Thompson, Denman (1833–1911): *The Old Homestead*, 337, 339

Thompson, Edward Palmer (1924–), 1056

Thompson, Hunter (1939–): *Fear and Loathing*, 1174

Thompson, William Tappan (1812–82): 316

Thomson, James (1700–1748): *The Seasons*, 244

Thomson, John (c. 1690–1753): *The Government of the Church of Christ*, 121

Thoreau, Henry David (1817–62), 42, 190, 212-13, 218, 226, 296, 381, 399-412, 439, 454, 549-50, 762, 768, 770-71, 1057; abolitionism, 373; *Cape Cod*, 410; "Civil Disobedience," 405, 411; *Collected Poems*, 375; *Journal*, 401-2, 405; "The Landlord," 400; "Life Without Principle," 412; *The Maine Woods*, 409-10; modernism, anticipation of, 698-702, 704, 707-8, 713; "The Natural History of Massachusetts," 400-2; "A Plea for Captain John Brown," 408; radicals, influence on, 738; "Reform and the Reformation," 412; "Slavery in Massachusetts," 408; transcendentalism, 364-66, 372, 374-75, 377; *Walden*, 111, 218, 221, 223-25, 364, 403, 405-8, 410, 640, 702; "Walking," 407; "A Walk to Wachusett," 400-2; *A Week on the Concord and Merrimack Rivers*, 362, 402-5, 407-10, 468; "A Winter Walk," 400-1

Thorpe, Thomas Bangs (1815–78), 316; "The Big Bear of Arkansas," 310, 316-19, 574; *The Master's House*, 317

Thurber, James (1894–1961), 731, 995

Tichi, Cecelia (1942–), 67

Tilton, Theodore (1835–1907), 355

Time, 730, 756

Time management, 730

Timrod, Henry (1828–67), 265; "The Cotton Boll," 265; "Ethnogenesis," 265; "Ode Sung on the Occasion of Decorating of the Confederate Dead, at Magnolia Cemetery," 265; "The Unknown Dead," 265

Tip Top Weekly, 555

Tobenkin, Elias (1882–1963): *Witte Arrives*, 587

Tocqueville, Alexis de (1805–59), 226, 467, 491, 550, 569; *Democracy in America*, 485, 699

Todorov, Tzvetan (1939–), 1173

Token, The, 414

Tolson, Melvin (1900–1966), 790, 798

Tolstoy, Leo (1828–1910), 504

Tomahawk, 580

Tompkins, Jane (1940–), 169

Tompson, Benjamin (1642–1714), 86, 104; *New Englands Crisis*, 86, 88

Tonti, Henri de (1650–1704): *Mémoires*, 23

Toomer, Jean (1894–1967), 726, 737, 789, 794-95, 798; *Cane*, 788, 797, 863, 927

Toronto Star, 876

Torrey, Samuel (1632–1707), 41; "Upon the Death of Mr. William Thompson," 85-86

Tourgée, Albion (1838–1905), 511-14; *Bricks Without Straw*, 512; *A Fool's Errand*, 512, 584; *The Invisible Empire*, 512; *A Royal Gentleman*, 511; "The South as a Field for Fiction," 512; *'Toinette*, 511

Tousey, Frank, 555

Townsend, Edward (1855–1942): *A Daughter of the Tenements*, 583

Trachtenberg, Alan (1932–), 569

Traherne, Thomas (1637–74): *Centuries of Meditation*, 30

Transatlantic Review, The, 744

Transcendental Club, 207, 370-71

Transcendentalism, 207-26, 296, 364-78, 427, 453; social meaning of, 699-700

transition, 744, 852, 924

Traubel, Horace (1858–1919), 454; *With Walt Whitman in Camden*, 461

Travel literature, 80, 175, 177, 190-91, 362-63; American Guide Series, 752; and James Fenimore Cooper, 253, 261; and Mark Twain, 637-43

Tregaskis, Richard (1916–73), 756

Trend, The, 984

Tres Américas, Las, 579

Trilling, Lionel (1905–75), 757, 943-44, 1011, 1013-17, 1033, 1133; *A Gathering of Fugitives*, 1126; *The Liberal Imagination*, 1016, 1129; "Manners, Morals, and the Novel," 1129; *The Middle of the Journey*, 1137; modernism, 699; *Sincerity and Authenticity*, 1137

Trollope, Frances (1780–1863): *Domestic Manners of the Americans*, 314

Trotsky, Leon (1879–1940), 749, 871

Trotter, Monroe, 582

Trowbridge, John Townsend (1827–1916), 450

True Confessions, 851

Trumbull, John (1750–1831), 156-58, 164-65; *The Anarchiad*, 157, 165; "An Elegy on the Times," 161-62; *M'Fingal*, 148, 156, 161, 164, 198-99; *The Progress of Dulness*, 164, 166;

"Prospect of the Future Glory of America," 160-61

Tucker, George (1775–1861): *The Valley of Shenandoah*, 266; *A Voyage to the Moon*, 266

Tucker, Nathaniel (1750–1807), 164

Tucker, Nathaniel Beverley (1784–1851), 269; *George Balcombe*, 267; *The Partisan Leader: A Tale of the Future*, 267

Tucker, St. George (1752–1827), 131, 165, 264

Tuckerman, Frederick Goddard (1821–73), 288

Tudor, William (1779–1830), 189; *Life of James Otis of Massachusetts*, 195

Turell, Jane Colman (1708–35), 97

Turner, Frederick Jackson (1861–1932), 492, 516, 559, 722

Turner, Nat (1800–1831), 350, 355

Twain, Mark (Samuel Langhorne Clemens) (1835–1910), 134, 281, 319, 488, 502, 504, 511, 529, 570, 579, 588, 627-44, 733, 737, 778, 781; *Adventures of Huckleberry Finn*, 134, 308-9, 323, 474, 515, 530-31, 630, 635-41, 643, 769; *The Adventures of Tom Sawyer*, 628-30, 638-39, 644; *The American Claimant*, 485; "The Celebrated Jumping Frog of Calaveras County," 633, 636, 642; *A Connecticut Yankee in King Arthur's Court*, 531, 568, 578, 635, 638, 641, 643; Dickens compared with, 636; *Following the Equator*, 637; *The Gilded Age*, 484-85, 630-31; and William Dean Howells, 506, 766; *The Innocents Abroad*, 635-37, 640-42; lectures, 633-35; *Life on the Mississippi*, 314-15, 636-38, 640; "The Man That Corrupted Hadleyburg," 629, 639, 641-42; marketing of books, 633; "The Mysterious Stranger," 531, 639, 641; "Old Times on the Mississippi," 636-37, 639; "The £1,000,000 Bank Note," 628-29, 642; and Paige typesetter, 572, 628; *Personal Recollections of Joan of Arc*, 635, 638; *The Prince and the Pauper*, 635, 638-39; public persona, 632; *Pudd'nhead Wilson*, 134, 512-13, 515, 629; *Roughing It*, 628, 637-38, 640-41; "The $30,000 Bequest," 628; *A Tramp Abroad*, 637; travel works, 637-43

Tyler, Royall (1757–1826), 165, 173-74, 178; *The Algerine Captive*, 173, 175; *The Contrast*, 174-75, 177, 198, 328, 331, 340; "The Origin of Evil," 165

Tynan, Kenneth (1927–80), 1103

Ulmer, Gregory (1944–): "The Object of Post-Criticism," 1189
Uncovering the Sixties, 1071
Underground press, 1071
Unitarianism, 209-11, 365-71, 373-74, 383, 387
United States Magazine, 197
Universal Negro Improvement Association, 854
Unrest, 921
Updike, John (1932–), 1138; *The Centaur*, 1138; *The Coup*, 1139
Urban fiction, 502-3, 505-6, 521-22, 534, 1135
Urbanization, 501, 570, 716-17, 726
Utilitarianism, 654-55
Utopian literature, 27, 177, 487, 507, 520, 1076; feminist, 1171

Valdez, Luís (1940–), 806, 1070, 1114; *Corridos*, 802; *No Saco Nada de la Escuela*, 1114
Vallejo, César (1892–1938), 1094
Vallejo, Mariano (1808–90), 800; "Recuerdos historicos tocante a la alta California," 517
van der Donck, Adriaen (d. 1655): *Beschryvinge van Nieuw Nederlant*, 22; *Vertoogh van Nieu-Neder-land*, 22
Van Dinh, Tran (1923–): *Blue Dragon White Tiger*, 821
van Dyke, Henry (1852–1933), 735
van Itallie, Jean-Claude (1936–), 1121-22; *America Hurrah*, 1122; *Motel*, 1122-23
Vanity Fair, 745, 856, 863
Van Vechten, Carl (1880–1964): *Nigger Heaven*, 788, 854; *Parties*, 859
Vanzetti, Bartolomeo, *see* Sacco and Vanzetti case
Vaudeville, 725
Vaughan, Henry (1622–95), 26, 28, 30, 31
Veblen, Thorstein (1857–1929), 489, 492, 495, 523, 720, 1040; *Theory of the Leisure Class*, 520, 716
Ventura, Luigi Donato (1845–1912): *Peppino*, 587
Veritism, 518, 768
Verplanck, Gulian (1786–1870), 232
Very, Jones (1813–80), 213, 288, 375-76; *Essays and Poems*, 375
Veto effect, David Riesman's notion of, 1029-30
Victor, Metta Victoria (1831–86), 552
Vidal, Gore (1925–): *Burr*, 1175; *The City and the Pillar*, 1065
Videos, 1196

Viereck, Peter (1916–), 1081
Vietnamese-American literature, 811*n*, 821
Vietnam War, 1025, 1037, 1066, 1069-70, 1074, 1096, 1114, 1118, 1149
View, 922, 929
Villard, Oswald Garrison (1872–1949), 720
Villarreal, José Antonio (1924–): *Pocho*, 805-6
Virginia Gazette, 129
Vision poem, 160-63
Vizenor, Gerald (1934–): *Darkness in Saint Louis Bearheart*, 15, 1172
Vogue, 577, 863
Vonnegut, Kurt, Jr. (1922–), 1141, 1145, 1150, 1163; *Slaughterhouse Five*, 1151, 1166, 1174
Vorse, Mary Heaton (188?–1966), 831
Vorticism, 954-55

Wagner, Jean (1919–): *Black Poets of the United States*, 794
Walker, Alice (1944–), 841, 1064, 1072, 1163; *The Color Purple*, 1173, 1175; *Meridian*, 1069
Walker, Margaret (1915–), 797-98, 866, 1064; *For My People*, 925
Wallace, Lew (1827–1905): *Ben-Hur*, 336, 529, 635
Walton, Eda Lou (1896–): *This Generation*, 791
Walton, Izaak (1593–1683): *Life of John Donne*, 31
Ward, A. C. (1891–), 854-55, 860
Ward, Lester (1841–1913), 489
Ward, Nathaniel (c. 1578–1652): *The Simple Cobler of Aggawam in America*, 51, 63, 86
Warfel, Harry (1899–1971), 169
Warner, Charles Dudley (1829–1900), 473, 478; *The Gilded Age*, 484
Warner, Susan (1819–85), 301, 550, 529; *The Wide, Wide World*, 299-300, 469, 562-63
Warren, Joseph (1741–75): *An Oration Delivered March Sixth*, 141
Warren, Mercy Otis (1728–1814), 166; *The Adulateur*, 149, 326; *The Group*, 149, 326; *History of the Rise, Progress and Termination of the American Revolution*, 195; *The Motley Assembly*, 149
Warren, Robert Penn (1905–), 134, 288, 511, 743, 853, 865, 923, 935; *All the King's Men*, 868, 871; *At Heaven's Gate*, 871; *Brother to Dragons*, 135
Washington, Booker T. (1856–1915), 582; *Up From Slavery*, 576

Washington, George (1732–99), 81, 131, 326-27

Washington Post, 572

Washizu, Shakuma, 579

Wasserstein, Wendy (1950–): *Uncommon Women*, 1113

Watergate affair, 1149

Watson, J. S. (1894–), 744

Weaver, Raymond (1888–1948), 430

Webb, James Watson (1802–84), 352-53

Webster, Daniel (1782–1852), 346, 396

Webster, Noah (1758–1843), 189; *An Examination into the Leading Principles of the Federal Constitution*, 146

Weems, Mason (1759–1825), 81

We Gather Strength, 921

Wegman, William (1943–): *Rage & Depression*, 1196

Weiner, Lawrence (1940–), 1196-97

Welch, James (1940–): *The Death of Jim Loney*, 15, 1172; *Fool's Crow*, 15; *Winter in the Blood*, 15, 1172

Weld (Welde), Thomas (1595–1661), 62, 83

Wellek, René (1903–), 1001, 1011

Welles, Orson (1915–85), 728

Wells, H. G. (Herbert George Wells) (1866–1946): *Outline of History*, 730, 853; *The War of the Worlds*, 728

Welsh, Lew (1926–71), 1084

Welty, Eudora (1909–), 753, 781-83; *A Curtain of Green*, 869, 1139; *Delta Wedding*, 869, 1139; *The Golden Apples*, 782; "The Petrified Man," 782; "Powerhouse," 869; "Why I Live at the P.O.," 782; *The Wide Net*, 869

Wescott, Glenway (1901–87), 851; *Good-Bye Wisconsin*, 859

West, Dorothy, 836

West, Nathanael (1903–40), 716, 751, 754, 860, 871, 1130; *The Day of the Locust*, 859, 863; *Miss Lonelyhearts*, 855

West (Far West), 761-62, 784

Westchester Farmer, *see* Seabury, Samuel

Western Magazine, 764

Western Messenger, 367, 371

Western tradition, 516-20, 555-57, 566; and Washington Irving, 237-38; *see also* Frontier, the

Westward movement, 202, 345-46, 761-62

Whalen, Philip (1923–), .1084; *Decompression*, 1061

Wharton, Edith (1862–1937), 478, 523, 532, 589-90, 592, 602, 604-5, 825, 846-47, 851,

871; *The Age of Innocence*, 488, 598, 600-1, 604; "Beatrice Palmato," 605; *The Custom of the Country*, 523, 603-4; *Ethan Frome*, 509-10, 533, 597; *Fighting France*, 848; *The House of Mirth*, 523, 533, 604, 846-47, 857; and William Dean Howells, 506; *Madame de Treymes*, 596; *The Reef*, 598, 604; *Sanctuary*, 593; *Summer*, 510, 533, 597, 604

Wheatley, Phillis (1753?–1784), 79, 123, 165-66, 790; "Liberty and Peace," 160; "On Imagination," 158; "To His Excellency General Washington," 149

Wheeler, Edward L., 556

Wheelwright, John (c. 1592–1679), 62

Wheelwright, John (1897–1940), 921; "Paul and Virginia," 921-22; "Plantation Drouth," 922

Whitaker, Alexander (1585–1617?): *Good Newes from Virginia*, 59

White, E. B. (Elwyn Brooks White) (1899–1985), 731

White, Edmund (1940–), 1065, 1172

White, John (fl. 1577–1602), 19

White, Walter (1893–1955), 737; *Flight*, 860

Whitefield, George (1714–70), 115-18, 123; *The Nature and the Necessity of Our New Birth*, 116

Whitehead, Alfred North (1861–1947), 1091

Whiting, John (c. 1635–1689), 41

Whiting, Lillian (1859–1942): *The World Beautiful*, 595-96

Whitman, Sarah Helen (1803–78), 376

Whitman, Walt (1819–92), 218-21, 226, 288, 381-82, 448-62, 468, 502, 549, 570, 737, 769, 1027, 1084; "As a Strong Bird on Pinions Free," 459; "As I Ebb'd with the Ocean of Life," 456, 459, 472; "Beat! Beat! Drums!" 457; "Calamus," 455-56, 459; "Children of Adam," 455; "Crossing Brooklyn Ferry," 219, 460; *Democratic Vistas*, 459, 484; *Drum-Taps*, 458-59; *Franklin Evans; or, The Inebriate*, 449; "I Sing the Body Electric," 455; *Leaves of Grass*, 219, 364, 374, 448, 450-57, 459-62, 700; *Memoranda During the War*, 459; modernism, anticipation of, 699-702, 704, 707-8, 710, 712-13; "My Boys and Girls," 449; "Out of the Cradle Endlessly Rocking," 456-59; "Passage to India," 459-60; "Poets to Come," 448; "Prayer of Columbus," 460; "Proud Music of the Storm," 460; "Reuben's Last Wish," 449; *Sequel* (to *Drum Taps*), 458-59; "The Sleepers," 460; "So Long!" 462; "Song of Myself," 219-21, 223, 225, 448, 451-53, 459, 462; "Song of the Open Road," 362; *Specimen Days*, 459; "There Was a Child Went Forth," 219, 450; transcendentalism, 364, 374-75, 377; "When Lilacs Last in the Dooryard Bloom'd," 458-59; "A Word Out of the Sea," 457

Whitney, Geoffrey (1548?–1601?): *Choice of Emblems*, 26

Whittier, John Greenleaf (1807–92), 213, 239, 279-81, 286, 288, 356, 763, 768; "Abraham Davenport," 282; *Among the Hills*, 282; "Ichabod," 281; "Massachusetts to Virginia," 452; "Maud Muller," 282; "Proem," 286; "Skipper Ireson's Ride," 282; "Snow-Bound," 283, 285, 288

Whole Book of Psalms, The, see *Bay Psalm Book*

Whyte, William H. (1917–): *The Organization Man*, 1029-30, 1131

Wide Awake Library, 555

Wigglesworth, Michael (1631–1705), 31, 39, 71-72, 104; *The Day of Doom*, 29, 88-89; *God's Controversy with New England*, 29, 88; *Meat Out of the Eater*, 88

Wilbur, Richard (1921–), 215, 1081

Wilder, Thornton (1897–1975), 746, 851, 1103

Willard, Samuel (1640–1707): *The Child's Portion; or, The Unseen Glory*, 65; *A Compleat Body of Divinity*, 65; *The Duty of a People That Have Renewed Their Covenant*, 65; *The Only Sure Way to Prevent Threatned Calamity*, 65

Williams, John (1664–1729), 68; *The Redeemed Captive, Returning Unto Zion*, 76-78

Williams, Raymond (1921–), 1036

Williams, Roger (c. 1603–1683), 37; *The Bloody Tenent Yet More Bloody*, 63; *The Bloudy Tenent of Persecution, for Cause of Conscience*, 63; *A Key into the Language of America*, 61, 86, 94

Williams, Tennessee (Thomas Lanier Williams) (1911–83), 1103-5, 1108; *Battle of Angels*, 1104; *Camino Real*, 1105; *Cat on a Hot Tin Roof*, 1104; *Clothes for a Summer Hotel*, 1105; *Eccentricities of a Nightingale*, 1104; *The Glass Menagerie*, 1104; *In the Bar of a Tokyo Hotel*, 1105; *Kingdom of Earth*, 1104; *The Milk Train Doesn't Stop Here Anymore*, 1105; *The Night of the Iguana*, 1105; *Orpheus Descending*, 1104; *Out Cry*, 1104-5; *The Rose Tattoo*, 1104; *The Seven Descents of Myrtle*, 1104; *Slapstick Tragedy*, 1105; *A Streetcar Named Desire*, 1104, 1108; *Suddenly Last Summer*, 1105; *Summer and Smoke*, 1104; *Vieux Carré*, 1105

Williams, William Carlos (1883–1963), 21, 462, 498, 620, 626, 740, 744, 879, 913, 916, 925, 930, 948-50, 954, 972-81, 985, 1006, 1036-37, 1079, 1084; *Al Que Quiere!* 974; "Asphodel, That Greeny Flower," 980-81; *Autobiography*, 976, 980; "Between Walls," 973; *The Build-Up*, 975; *The Collected Earlier Poems*, 974; *The Collected Later Poems*, 974; "Danse Russe," 987; "Detail," 977; *The Farmers' Daughters*, 975; *The Great American Novel*, 882; *In the American Grain*, 709, 714, 852-53, 863, 976; *In the Money*, 975; *I Want to Write a Poem: The Autobiography of the Works of a Poet*, 976; *Kora in Hell*, 975; *Many Loves and Other Plays*, 975; modernism, 696, 708-10, 713-14; "On Measure—Statement for Cid Corman," 975; *Paterson*, 710, 853, 948, 974-75; *Pictures from Brueghel and Other Poems*, 974, 980; *Poems*, 973; "The Red Wheelbarrow," 973, 976; *Selected Essays*, 975; *Selected Letters*, 976; "Smell!" 978; "Spring and All," 973, 976; *Spring and All*, 927, 975-76; "Spring Strains," 977; *The Tempers*, 974; "This Is Just to Say," 978-79; "The Wanderer," 973; *White Mules*, 975; *Yes, Mrs. Williams: A Personal Record of My Mother*, 976

Williamson, Jack (1908–), 1168

William Styron's Nat Turner, 1072

Wilson, Augusta Evans (1835–1909), 302; *Beulah*, 564; *Inez: A Tale of the Alamo*, 302; *Macaria: or, The Altars of Sacrifice*, 302; *St. Elmo*, 302, 469, 564

Wilson, Edmund (1895–1972), 346, 720, 731-32, 745-47, 750, 756, 849, 866, 871, 884, 893; *Axel's Castle*, 1013; *I Thought of Daisy*, 856, 1012; literary criticism, 996, 1012-15; *Patriotic Gore*, 321; *To the Finland Station*, 865, 1013; *The Wound and the Bow*, 858, 1013

Wilson, Harriet (1808–c. 1870): *Our Nig; or, Sketches from the Life of a Free Black*, 361

Wilson, James (1742–98): *Considerations on the . . . Authority of the British Parliament*, 140

Wilson, John (c. 1591–1667), 62, 83

Wilson, Lanford (1937–): *Balm in Gilead*, 1118; *Fifth of July*, 1117; *The Hot l Baltimore*, 1118; *The Mound Builders*, 1118; *The Rimers of Eldritch*, 1118; *Talley's Folly*, 1117

Wilson, Robert (1944–): *Einstein on the Beach*, 1193

Wilson, Woodrow (1856–1924), 733-34, 756, 845, 850

Wimsatt, W. K. (1907–75), 1080

Winch, Peter (1926–): "Understanding a Primitive Society," 1052

Winchester, Elhanan (1751–97), 166

Winslow, Edward (1595–1655), 37, 62

Winters, Yvor (1900–1968), 1006-7; *The Anatomy of Nonsense*, 1006; *Maule's Curse*, 1006; *Primitivism and Decadence*, 1006

Winthrop, John (1588–1649), 31, 37, 39, 70-71, 73; journal, 31, 50; "A Modell of Christian Charity," 59

Wirt, William (1772–1834): *Letters of the British Spy*, 266; *Sketches of the Life and Character of Patrick Henry*, 196

Wister, Owen (1860–1938), 565, 567; *The Virginian*, 517, 566

Wither, George (1588–1667): *Preparation to the Psalter*, 28

Wittgenstein, Ludwig (1889–1951), 1052; *Philosophical Investigations*, 1057

Wolcott, Roger (1679–1767): "A Brief Account of the Agency of the Honourable John Winthrop," 97; *Poetical Meditations*, 97

Wolf, Emma (1865–?): *Other Things Being Equal*, 587

Wolfe, Gene (1931–), 1167

Wolfe, Thomas (1900–1938), 753, 779, 851, 863, 871; *Look Homeward, Angel*, 777; *Of Time and the River*, 868; *The Web and the Rock*, 868; *You Can't Go Home Again*, 868

Wolfe, Tom (Thomas Kennerly, Jr.) (1931–), 1032, 1036, 1139

Wolfert, Ira (1908–), 756

Wolff, Cynthia Griffin (1936–), 605

Wolff, Tobias (1945–), 1163, 1165

Wollstonecraft, Mary (1759–97), 175-78, 181, 183

Woman's Home Companion, 851

Women: antifeminism of 1920s, 855-57; changes in daily life of, 723; domestic ideology of nineteenth-century, 354-56; in early American fiction, 170; Emerson's view of, 701; and evangelical reform, 347; in realistic fiction, 523; in work force, 724-25, 831

Women's movement, 294, 349, 823-24, 1027, 1168, 1170; and Henry Adams, 652; avant-garde art, 1197-99; and Margaret Fuller, 296, 372; New Feminism, 1064-65; poetry magazines, 931; transcendentalists, 372

Women's suffrage, 823

Women writers, 289-305, 469, 562-65, 822-41, 855, 857, 1162, 1170-76; Asian Americans, 812-21; avant-garde writers, 1185-86, 1189-99; black writers, 361, 798, 1172-73; confessional poets, 1089-90; dramatists, 326, 331-33, 1110, 1112-13, 1115; feminist critics, 169, 1073; feminist poetry, 927; Mexican Americans, 809; New Wave writers, 1167; new-women writers, 589-606; regional writers, 767-68, 781-83; socially concerned writers, 1061, 1063-73, 1075-76

Wong, Jade Snow (1922–): *Fifth Chinese Daughter*, 813-14

Wong, Shawn Hsu: *Homebase*, 819-20

Wood, William (fl. 1629-35): *New Englands Prospect*, 21, 89

Woodworth, Samuel (1785–1842): *The Forest Rose; or, American Farmers*, 329

Woolf, Virginia (1882–1941), 834, 962

Woolman, John (1720–72), 66, 73; *Journal of John Woolman*, 75, 81

Woolson, Constance Fenimore (1840–94), 474, 512

"Word of Congress, The," 199

Wordsworth, William (1770–1850), 394, 396, 938

Working class, 722-23; literature, 726, 1061; theater, 328, 333-34; women in work force, 724-25, 831

World's Columbian Exposition (1893), 516, 522, 527, 565-66, 575

World's Fair (1939), 715-16, 728, 732

World War I, 740, 848-50, 933, 968

World War II, 725-26, 755-57, 871, 969, 1127, 1132, 1150, 1152

Wouk, Herman (1915–), 1148; *The Caine Mutiny*, 1150; *Marjorie Morningstar*, 1148

Wright, Frank Lloyd (1869–1959), 719; *On Architecture*, 492

Wright, James (1927–80), 1094-96; *The Branch Will Not Break*, 1094; "A Mad Fight Song for William S. Carpenter, 1966," 1096

Wright, Richard (1908–60), 513, 752, 787, 789-91, 797-98, 835, 838, 851-52, 865; *Black Boy*, 726, 789, 869; "Child of the Dead and Forgotten Gods," 921; "I Am a Red Slogan," 921; "I Have Seen Black Hands," 921; *Native Son*, 726, 786, 789, 859, 867-68; *The Outsider*, 1139; *12 Million Black Voices*, 866; *Uncle Tom's Children*, 789; "We of the Street," 921

Wright, Willard Huntington (1888–1939), 720

Wylie, Elinor (1885–1928), 828, 840, 863; "Jewelled Bindings," 828; *Nets to Catch the Wind*, 828; "Velvet Shoes," 828

Yale Review, 825
Yale Series of Younger Poets, 922, 925
Yamamoto, Hisaye (1921–), 815, 818; *Seventeen Syllables*, 815
Yamauchi, Wakako (1924–): "The Boatmen on River Toneh," 819; "That Was All," 819
"Yankee Doodle," 149, 196
Yau, John (1950–): *Crossing Canal Street*, 821
Yeats, William Butler (1865–1939), 738, 948, 950-51, 953-54, 966, 968; "The Second Coming," 961
Yellow journalism, 529, 572
Yep, Laurence (1948–): *Dragonwings*, 817
Yerby, Frank (1916–), 866
Yezierska, Anzia (1885–1970), 863; *Bread Givers*, 726, 860; "The Fat of the Land,"

860; *Hungry Hearts*, 584, 860; *Red Ribbon on a White Horse*, 584; *Salome of the Tenements*, 860
Yiddish-language newspapers and periodicals, 581
Yone, Wendy Law: *The Coffin Tree*, 819, 821
Yoshida, Jim (1921–): *The Two Worlds of Jim Yoshida*, 814
Young America, The, 573
Youth movement (1960s), 1066

Zangwill, Israel (1864–1926): *The Melting-Pot*, 584
Zelazny, Roger (1937–), 1167
Zola, Emile (1840–1902), 504, 525
Zugsmith, Leane (1903–69), 864
Zukofsky, Louis (1904–78), 924, 1081; "A," 924-25